New Essay

Human Understanding

Together with an appendix

Gottfried Wilhelm Leibniz

Alpha Editions

This edition published in 2020

ISBN : 9789354040009

Design and Setting By
Alpha Editions
www.alphaedis.com
email - alphaedis@gmail.com

To my Mother and Sister

SOMETIME GONE WHERE WE SHALL KNOW AS WE ARE KNOWN

And to my Father

STILL WHERE WE SEE AS IN A MIRROR OBSCURELY

IN DEEPEST LOVE AND GRATITUDE

I DEDICATE THIS BOOK

CONTENTS

Book III.—Words.

Book IV.—Of Knowledge

APPENDIX

TRANSLATOR'S PREFACE

The work herewith given to the public consists of a translation of the entire fifth volume of Gerhardt's *Die philosophischen Schriften von G. W. Leibniz,* sub-entitled "Leibniz und Locke," consisting of an Introduction by Gerhardt, several short pieces on Locke's *Essay* and the *New Essays on Human Understanding;* and of an Appendix containing a translation of other short pieces of Leibnitz bearing on the subjects discussed in the *New Essays* or referred to therein. The Introduction on The Philosophy of Leibnitz by the translator suggested and urged by Professors Palmer and Royce of Harvard University, and for some time contemplated, is deferred, and reserved, if at all, for another time and occasion, owing to the size of the present volume, as well as for other good and sufficient reasons which it is not necessary here to mention.

The translation of Leibnitz's *Nouveaux Essais sur l'Entendement Humain* was first suggested by the following sentence of the late Professor George S. Morris, of the University of Michigan, in a note to his *Philosophy and Christianity,* page 292: "It suggests no favorable comment on the philosophic interest of the countrymen of Locke that the above-mentioned reply of Leibnitz to Locke has never (so far as I can ascertain) been translated into English." Four instalments, consisting of Book I. and Book II., chapters 1–11 inclusive, were published in as many numbers of the "Journal of Speculative Philosophy."[1] Professor Morris very kindly sent me a careful criticism of about one-third of the first instalment, with valuable suggestions regarding the further work of translation. His corrections and suggestions received careful con-

[1] Vol. 19, No. 3, July, 1885; Vol. 21, No. 3, July, 1887; Vol. 21, No. 4, October, 1887; Vol. 22, No. 2, April, 1888.

sideration and were embodied in subsequent revisions of the translation in preparing it for the present issue.

The portion of the *New Essays* thus published being favorably received by professors and students of philosophy in this country and in Europe, and being encouraged to go on and translate the entire piece, the work begun in 1885 was continued in leisure hours until in June, 1891, the translation was completed. Revision, annotation, and the labor of getting it through the press have occupied the greater part of my free time since then. The annotation, which was not a part of the original plan, but which was found to be desirable, if not even necessary, as the sheets began to appear in type, has been the chief cause of the delay in the appearance of the book, the labor involved therein proving far greater and unavoidably more protracted than was expected, the annotation also, as is frequent in such cases, growing with the progress of the book.

The text-basis of the translation is that of C. I. Gerhardt, in his *Die philosophischen Schriften von G. W. Leibniz*, 7 vols., Berlin, 1875–1890, except for the Dynamical Pieces in the Appendix, Nos. IV., V., the text-basis of which is C. I. Gerhardt's *Leibnizens mathematische Schriften*, Berlin and Halle, 1849–1863, and Appendix No. VII., for which both these editions are used; for Appendix No. IX., the text is that given by Guhrauer, *G. W. Freiherr v. Leibnitz. Eine Biographie*, Breslau, 1846. The other editions used in the comparison of the text and the preparation of the notes are: J. E. Erdmann, *Leibnitii Opera Philosophica*, Berlin, 1839–1840; M. A. Jacques, *Œuvres de Leibniz*, Paris, 1842; P. Janet, *Œuvres Philosophiques de Leibniz*, Paris, 1866; Dutens, *Leibnitii Opera Omnia*, Geneva, 1768; Foucher de Careil, *Lettres et Opuscules inédits de Leibniz*, Paris, 1854, *Nouvelles Lettres et Opuscules de Leibniz inédits*, Paris, 1857, and *Œuvres de Leibniz*, Paris, 1859 *sq.*, 2d ed., Paris, 1867 *sq.* R. E. Raspe, *Œuvres Philosophiques de feu Mr. Leibnitz*, Amsterdam and Leipzig, 1765, was received too late to be of service, but as his text is the original printed text of the *New Essays*, and has been used by all subsequent editors, it is not probable that any important variation of reading has been overlooked; and Raspe's text has no notes. Besides these editions of Leibnitz's Works, the German translations of the *Théodicée* and of the smaller philosophically important works entitled *Die kleineren philosophisch wichtigeren Schriften* by J. H. von Kirchmann, in his *Philosophische Bibliothek*, Berlin, 1879, and the English translation of his important philosophical opuscules by Professor George M. Duncan of Yale University, entitled *The Philosophical Works of Leibnitz*, New Haven, 1890, have been consulted. From the last-named work, so as to include in one book all of Leibnitz's discussions of Locke, it was at first intended to reprint in the Appendix all the pieces bearing upon the subject discussed in the *New Essays*, or especially referred to therein. It finally seemed best to both Professor Duncan and myself to change the plan and translate new material, rather than duplicate that already translated, so that with the exception of Appendix No. VI., Professor Duncan's translation of which was either forgotten or unnoticed till after mine was in type, nothing appears in both books save such portions of the *New Essays* as he has included, and the piece entitled *On Locke's Essay on Human Understanding*, 1696. This statement will explain the references in certain notes, for example, page 101, note 1, page 154, note 1 (*cf. infra*, pages 737 and 749 respectively), to certain pieces of Leibnitz in the Appendix, which references are corrected in the Additions and Corrections by being changed to the proper pages of Professor Duncan's book.

Of great value in the revision of the translation, and of the greatest service in the preparation of the notes, has been the German translation of the *Nouveaux Essais*, with notes, by Professor Carl Schaarschmidt of the University of Bonn. His material has been freely used, either by direct translation and quotation, or in substance, in the notes of the present edition, though always, so far as possible, only after verification and further independent study. His notes, I regret to say, contain many numerical errors, occasioned presumably by insufficient care and accuracy in proof-reading; otherwise they are, for the most part, accurate. The fact that Professor Schaarschmidt's book was not received till after a portion of mine was in type accounts in part for the appearance of so much of his note-material in the Additions and Corrections, rather than in its proper place in the foot-notes to the text.

Professor A. C. Frazer's splendid edition of *Locke's Essay*, Oxford, 1894, did not appear until after most of the *New Essays* were in type; and P. Coste, *Essai philosophique concernant l'Entendement humain — par M. Locke*, Amsterdam, 1742, 1 vol., 4to, 1774, 4 vols., 12mo, could not be obtained until all the *New Essays* and most of the Appendix were in type. Both of these works, therefore, could be used only in the supplementary notes in the Additions and Corrections.

With regard to the text itself, particularly of the *New Essays*, a few words may not be out of place. The variations are slight and chiefly verbal, and scarcely ever essentially modify the thought. They are ultimately due either to the manuscript of Leibnitz — which Erdmann (Preface, p. xxii) says is "written in such small characters often, and so full of corrections, that it is very difficult to read it" ("tam parvis sæpe literis conscriptum et correctionibus adeo abundans ut perdifficile lectu") — or to certain changes made for the purpose of improving the literary style of the author, and of thus making his work more acceptable to his French readers. The chief difference between the text as given by Gerhardt, who has compared his impression "with the original, so far as it is still extant," and that of the other editors consists in a transposition of the text in Book I., chap. I., a transposition which is fully indicated in the note at the point in the text of the translation where it occurs, and which is, I suppose, due to Gerhardt's fidelity to Leibnitz's original text. All the important textual variations are listed in the notes.

Gerhardt's text, having been compared with the original, seems the most trustworthy, and accordingly has been followed in this translation, excepting in a few instances mentioned in the notes, where it is manifestly erroneous from inaccurate proof-reading or other cause, and where the text of some other editor seemed more consistent or correct. Gerhardt has introduced into his text the brackets, [ ], in which, "in the original, Leibnitz has enclosed the words of Philalethes, who states the views of Locke," "perhaps as an indication that they are not his own;" and I have introduced them into the translation precisely as they stand in the text of Gerhardt, in order that the translation may conform to and represent as perfectly as possible Leibnitz's original text in its integrity. There seems to be, however, little regularity or consistency in the employment of these brackets, so far, at least, as I can discover upon comparison with Locke's treatise.

Besides the editions and translations already named, the various separate editions of single works of Leibnitz, as also the various discussions of his philosophy, theology, etc., and the monographs on different parts of the same, were occasionally consulted or referred to, so far as these were accessible or could be procured. Among the monographs, especial mention should be made of Professor John Dewey's most excellent *Leibniz's New Essays concerning the Human Understanding. A Critical Exposition,* 1888, in the series of German Philosophical Classics edited by Professor George S. Morris, and published by S. C. Griggs & Co., Chicago; and of the earlier monograph of G. Hartenstein, *Locke's Lehre von der menschlichen Erkenntniss in Vergleichung mit Leibniz's Kritik derselben,* Leipzig, 1861.

The translation has purposely been made close rather than free, a philosophical treatise seeming properly to require a closer adherence on the part of the translator to the author's form of thought and expression than a history, novel, or poem. Whatever view may be taken on this point, — and I frankly admit that at least two views are possible and that each method of translation has its advantages and its disadvantages, its perils and its successes,— the form and style of the *New Essays* make an elegant and forceful translation well-nigh impossible. Such a translation would necessitate the entire re-writing of Leibnitz's work, would, in fact, be a reproduction rather than a translation, a task I have not attempted nor felt it incumbent on me to attempt. My aim has been simply to represent as faithfully and as accurately as possible, and in as good English as its form and expression admitted, Leibnitz's exact thought. The style of Leibnitz in the *New Essays,* especially in the abbreviations or abstracts of Locke's *Essay* put into the mouth of Philalethes, is often abrupt and obscure and sometimes even ungrammatical (*cf.*, for example, *New Essays*, Book III., chap. II., § 18, page 392, lines 6 and 7, and the note thereto, *infra,* page 768 *ad fin.*). This condition of things is due partly to the form of the work, but chiefly to the method of its composition (*cf.* Gerhardt's introduction, *infra*, page 8, and notes, and the letters of Leibnitz cited by Raspe in his Preface, page 12, note 6, and which he says, "I found with the manuscript of the *New Essays*," and "give as I found them"). A work so written, in spite of more or less revision, could not possibly be a finished treatise or a work of literary art like the Dialogues of Plato, and the character of the work must of necessity be reflected in the translation.

The notes aim to give the desirable or necessary biographical and bibliographical information regarding the persons and books referred to in the course of the work, so far as such information could be obtained; references to other pieces of Leibnitz, and occasionally to other authors, where the same topic is discussed; and explanations of a few terms thought to be obscure and the explanations of which are not generally known or easily accessible. The notes do not pretend to be a commentary on the text. Except in a few cases, the reader or student has purposely been left to gain his knowledge of Leibnitz's views from Leibnitz himself. Extended commentary was impossible within the necessary limits of the volume, and accordingly was not included in the plan. The philosophical notes, therefore, confine themselves to a brief statement of Leibnitz's views and to brief criticism or indication of criticism. The aim was to bring Leibnitz's great work within the reach of English students and to render it more easily accessible, with such annotation, literary and other, as would make it more acceptable to the student.

All material taken from other authors has, so far as possible, been verified and made the subject of such independent study as the case seemed to demand. All references to authorities have been verified when possible, and very great pains have been taken to secure perfect accuracy in all references. The citations have uniformly been taken and the references made to the best editions, and usually to the latest, when these editions were accessible. Occasionally other works or editions are referred to because of their accessibility or for other evident reasons. For the convenience of those possessing different editions of Leibnitz's works, as well as for those who may have access to only one of them, reference is usually made, especially in the earlier notes, to all of the editions. Later this procedure seemed to encumber the notes with an unnecessary amount of numerical reference, and it was for the most part discontinued.

Attention is called to the Additions and Corrections as containing matter of importance, most of which was not obtained till after the portion of the book to which it refers was already in type, and which, therefore, could not be inserted in its proper place in the book, but had to be reserved to the end.

The Indexes are intentionally full and complete and have been made with great care by Rev. Robert Kerr Eccles, M.D. There is no adequate index to Leibnitz's works, and none whatever exclusively devoted to the *New Essays*. The references thereto in the meagre index in Raspe's edition of the Philosophical Works, not generally accessible, and in the general index, full as it is, in Erdmann's edition, are by no means sufficient. It is hoped that the Indexes here furnished may prove adequate for the works of Leibnitz included in this volume, and that thus a beginning at least of an adequate index to Leibnitz's complete works shall have been made.

In Appendix No. IV., *infra*, page 663, and No. V., *infra*, pages 674, 682, and 686, the numbering of the cuts is changed from that of the original text to conform to their proper numerical order in this book. The fact is here noted to prevent confusion in referring to the original.

I gratefully acknowledge my obligations and express my thanks to all who have aided me in my long and arduous work. Especially to President E. B. Andrews of Brown University, for aid in the note on the term "*quarto modo*," page 455, and for the verification of references; to Professor Albert G. Harkness of Brown University, for aid in locating some of the Latin quotations in the *New Essays;* to Professor J. F. Jameson of Brown University, for the note, page 757, explaining the term "Promoter," page 227; to Professor John M. Manly of Brown University, for information and aid in the notes to the *New Essays*, Book III., chap. 2, page 294, notes 2, 3, page 295, notes 2, 3; to Professor E. B. Delabarre of Brown University, for aid in the note to page 122, lines 1, 2, *infra*, pages 739–740; to Professor H. P. Manning of Brown University, for aid in the note on the "perles" of De Sluse, page 768; to Rev. R. H. Ferguson, for aid in the same note, and in the revision of a portion of the Appendix; to Mr. Frank E. Thompson, A.M., Head-master of the Rogers High School, Newport, R. I., for aid in connection with a part of the subject-matter of the Dynamical Pieces in the Appendix; to Professor Benjamin O. True of Rochester Theological Seminary, for information and verification of references in connection with the notes to the *New Essays*, Book IV., chap. 19, page 599, note 2, 601, note 1, 602, note 1; to Professor F. A. March of Lafayette University, for the location of the Latin poetical quotation on page 603; to Professor Carl Schaarschmidt of Bonn University, for consulting books inaccessible in this country, and for information kindly furnished by letter, and for his cordial interest in my work, as well as for the very valuable notes to his translation of the *New Essays*, without which mine never would have been written in their present form; to the various libraries whose resources have in one way or another been placed at my disposal, among which should be mentioned the Boston Public Library, the Boston Athenæum, the libraries of Andover Theological Seminary, Newton Theological Institution, Rochester Theological Seminary, Brown University, Harvard University, Yale University through Professor Duncan, the Library of the Surgeon General's Office, Washington, D.C., and the Redwood Library, Newport, R.I.; to the libraries particularly of Newton Theological Institution, Brown University, and Harvard University, for the long-continued loan of needed books; to Professor Charles R. Brown of Newton Theological Institution for information and the verification of references; to my friend and former pupil Mr. Alfred R. Wightman, of the Morgan Park Academy of the University of Chicago, for the verification of references and aid in the revision of a portion of the Appendix; to Mr. Thomas J. Kiernan of the Harvard University Library, for special favors in the consultation of the library, for the loan of books from the same, and for information cordially furnished by mail; to Benjamin Rand, Ph.D., of the Department of Philosophy at Harvard University, for frequent consultation of authorities, verification of references and information furnished; to my friend Mr. Richard Bliss, Librarian of the Redwood Library, without whose competent criticism and constant advice and aid, added to his comprehensive and accurate knowledge in many fields, and especially in bibliography, my notes would have been far less full and accurate than, I trust, they now are; and last but not least, to my wife for literary criticism in the revision of the translation and notes, and aid in the laborious task of proof-reading. Had I always accepted and adopted her criticism and that of Mr. Bliss, my work would doubtless rank higher as a piece of literature than is now possible.

My thanks are also due and most heartily tendered to my publishers, Messrs. Macmillan & Co., for their uniform courtesy and long-suffering patience in the repeated but unavoidable delays which have characterized the appearance of this book; and to J. S. Cushing & Co., of the Norwood Press, for the excellence of their work, and the pains they have taken to secure the greatest possible accuracy in the same, and for their uniform courtesy and long-suffering patience amid the vexatious delays unavoidably incident to the preparation of the notes and the correction of the proof.

In editing the work of a thinker and writer so comprehensive as Leibnitz, it is impossible to escape all errors of fact or judgment. I have done the best I could in the circumstances in which I have had to work, away from large libraries and from the advice and criticism of fellow-students in the same lines. Competent and truth-loving criticism, and the correction of any and all real errors will be thankfully received.

With one sentence from Leibnitz's letter to Coste, June 16, 1707, as significant of his character and illustrative of his spirit, more truth-loving than polemical, and as beautifully expressing the essence of true criticism, I close this Preface: "Mon but a esté plustost d'eclaircir les choses, que de refuter les sentimens d'autruy," which, being interpreted, is: "My purpose has been to throw light upon things rather than to refute the opinions of another."

ALFRED G. LANGLEY.

NEWPORT, R.I., April 11, 1896.

LEIBNITZ'S CRITIQUE OF LOCKE ON HUMAN UNDERSTANDING

GERHARDT'S INTRODUCTION TO HIS EDITION OF LEIBNITZ'S NOUVEAUX ESSAIS

[*From the German*]

In the first philosophical treatise, ***Meditationes de Cognitione, Veritate, et Ideis,***[1] which Leibnitz published in the year 1684, he had firmly laid the foundations of human knowledge; he declared adequate and at the same time intuitive knowledge as the most complete. At the end he adds: Quod ad controversiam attinet, utrum omnia videamus in Deo . . . an vero proprias ideas habeamus, sciendum est, etsi omnia in Deo videremus, necesse tamen esse ut habeamus et ideas proprias, id est non quasi icunculas quasdam, sed affectiones sive modificationes mentis nostræ, respondentes ad id ipsum quod in Deo perciperemus: utique enim aliis atque aliis cogitationibus subeuntibus aliqua in mente nostra mutatio fit; rerum vero actu a nobis non cogitatarum Ideæ sunt in mente nostra, ut figura Herculis in rudi marmore. The assumption of these ideas slumbering in the mind, these innate ideas (*angebornen Ideen; idées innées*), Leibnitz regards as necessary in order to understand the nature of the mind. (Habet anima in se perceptiones et appetitus, iisque natura ejus continetur, he writes to Bierling, Hanoveræ 12. Augusti 1711.[2] Et ut in corpore intelligimus ἀντιτυπίαν, et figuram generatim, etsi nesciamus, quæ sint figuræ corporum insensibilium: ita in anima intelligimus perceptionem et appetitum, etsi non cognoscamus distincte insensibilia ingredientia perceptionum confusarum, quibus insensibilia corporum exprimuntur.) He could therefore only prove the necessary truths, *i.e.*

[1] C. I. Gerhardt: *Die philosophischen Schriften von G. W. Leibniz.* Vol. 4, pp. 422–426. J. E. Erdmann: *G. G. Leibnitii Opera Philosophica*, pp. 78–81. Translated by George M. Duncan, *The Philosophical Works of Leibnitz*, pp. 27–32, New Haven: Tuttle, Morehouse, & Taylor, 1890. — Tr.

[2] The letter is found in Gerhardt's ed., Vol. 7, pp. 500–502. — Tr.

those which are known by demonstration, inasmuch as the senses indeed teach what happens, but not what necessarily happens. Such ideas innate to the mind are, according to Leibnitz, the conceptions of substance, identity, the true and the good.

The writing of the man who questioned and rejected these fundamental principles of the system of Leibnitz could not fail to lay claim to Leibnitz's entire attention. It was John Locke (born, 1632, at Wrington, near Bristol; died, 1704, at Oates, in the county of Essex, in the house of Sir Francis Masham, whose wife was a daughter of Cudworth), who in his celebrated work ("An Essay concerning Human Understanding"; in four books, London, 1690[1]) sought to discover also the origin, the certainty, and the extent of human knowledge, but who denied the existence of innate ideas and principles, and affirmed that the mind is originally like an unwritten tab (*tabula rasa*). In the first book of the work named, Locke seeks to set forth the view that there are no innate ideas, and therefore no innate principles and truths; that the understanding is by nature like an unwritten sheet of paper. The second book contains the proof whence the understanding gets its ideas. Since there are no innate concepts and principles, the origin of all ideas can be only in experience. Experience, however, has a double sphere, that of external and of internal perception: the first Locke calls Sensation; the second, Reflection. Sensation is the perception of external objects mediated through the senses; reflection, the perception of activities of the soul in relation to the ideas presented through the senses. Ideas are partly simple, partly complex. Simple ideas arise through the single senses, remoter ideas through more senses, as extension, form, motion, rest; through reflection alone, for

[1] This work was already completed in the year 1687; an abstract made by Locke himself appeared in the following year, 1688, translated into French in Leclerc's "Bibliothèque universelle," T. VIII., pp. 49–142. The contents of the work, after it was completely published in the year 1690, was communicated in much detail by Leclerc in the "Biblioth. Univers.," T. XVII., p. 399 *sq.* The new editions, which already in the shortest time followed each other in quick succession in the years 1694, 1697, 1699, 1705, prove what a mighty impression Locke's work made upon cultivated circles. 1700 appeared Coste's French translation of Locke's work: it was enriched by Locke himself with improvements and additions. Leibnitz followed this French translation in the composition of his *Nouveaux Essais*.

example, the idea of thought and will; through union of sensation and reflection, the ideas of power, existence, unity. The complex ideas are of three kinds: modes, substances, relations. The modes, *i.e.* the complex concepts, which contain nothing existing for itself, are either pure (simple modes), as space, time, or mixed (mixed modes), as thought, motion, power. By substances Locke understands those combinations of simple ideas or groups of ideas, which are conceived upon the hypothesis that they correspond to definite, actually existing things, so that the substance (*substratum*) presupposed for and in them is considered as the point of union for the rest of the constituent parts contained in the group of ideas. Of substance, man has no clear conception; it is, according to Locke, worthless. According to him this conception is not limited to single things, but he extends it also to the collective ideas of many things; thus an army, a herd of sheep, is just as much a substance as a single man or one sheep. Relations arise from the comparison of many things with one another, as the conceptions of cause and effect, time—and place—relations, identity and diversity.

Ideas and their combinations are apprehended in language; therefore Locke begins in the third book with an investigation upon language, in so far as our knowledge, although relating to things, is bound to words, and words are an indispensable middle-term between thoughts and things. The extent and the certainty of knowledge are on this account conditioned upon the constitution and significance of words. In the fourth book Locke pronounces the concluding judgment upon the extent and the different grades of certainty in human knowledge.[1]

Leibnitz's attention was already turned from his own work to that of the English philosopher by the above-mentioned edition published by Locke himself in the "Bibliothèque universelle." When later Locke's work reached his hands, he threw off, as was his custom while he skimmed through the book, some remarks;[2] they follow here under the superscription: "Sur

[1] For the foregoing are of value: Hartenstein, *Locke's Lehre von der menschlichen Erkenntniss in Vergleichung mit Leibniz's Kritik derselben*. Leipzig, 1861.—Ueberweg, *Grundriss der Geschichte der Philosophie*, 3 Theil. Berlin, 1880.

[2] They came into being after the year 1693, since mention is made in them of Locke's Tract upon Education: *Thoughts on Education*, London, 1693. They were first printed in *Some Familiar Letters between Mr. Locke and Several of his Friends*, London, 1708, pp. 196–205.

l'Essay de l'entendement humain de Monsieur Lock."[1] Leibnitz sent it in accord with his pleasant custom to Thomas Burnett, with whom he corresponded.[2] Through him they came to the knowledge of Locke, who, however, upon vain pretexts, declined every reply thereto.[3] When Leibnitz received among others the communication from Burnett (July 26, 1698), that Locke had so far expressed his opinion that he for his part did not sufficiently understand Leibnitz's remarks upon his book, he resolved upon a remodelling of the same. Two fragments of the year 1698 are thereupon at hand; they are printed here for the first time, under the superscription: "Echantillon[4] de Reflexions sur le I. Livre de l'Essay de l'Entendement de l'homme. — Echantillon de Reflexions sur le II. Livre." Leibnitz again sent them to Burnett; through whom Locke received them; but this attempt also on Leibnitz's side remained without result, as appears from Burnett's letter to Leibnitz October 23, 1700.

[1] On Locke's Essay on Human Understanding. See *infra*, pp. 13–19. — Tr.

[2] Leibnitz to Thomas Burnett, 7th–17th March, 1696: "I found, also, finally, a rough draught which I had had copied formerly, of some remarks I made when running through the excellent essay of Locke upon Human Understanding; I take the liberty of sending you a copy." — Leibnitz to Th. Burnett, 17th–27th July, 1697: "What I sent you of my reflections upon the important book of Locke is entirely at your disposal, and you can communicate it to whomever it seems good to you; and if it falls into his hands, or those of his friends, so much the better; for that will give him an opportunity to instruct us and to clear up the matter."

[3] Highly characteristic is that which Burnett communicated to Leibnitz upon the 23d of July, 1697: "I must tell you a joke of Locke's the other day, on this matter. We began to speak of the controversies of savants with those of this country. He said: 'It seems to me we live very peaceably as good neighbors of the gentlemen in Germany, for they do not know our books, and we do not read theirs, so that the tale (*la* [? *le* — Tr.] *conte*) (? *le compte*, the account) was well adjusted on each side.'" — On the other hand, we find a very dissenting judgment of Locke's upon Leibnitz and his remarks in his letter to Dr. Molyneux, of April 10, 1697: "I must confess to you that Mr. L——'s great name had raised in me an expectation which the sight of his paper did not answer, nor that discourse of his in the 'Acta Eruditorum,' which he quotes, and I have since read, and had just the same thoughts of it, when I read it, as I find you have. From whence I only draw this inference, That even great parts will not master any subject without great thinking, and even the largest minds have but narrow swallows." — Not less disparaging is Locke's judgment upon Leibnitz in the next letter to Molyneux, of May 3, 1697. — The correspondence between Locke and Molyneux is contained in the already quoted book: *Some Familiar Letters between Mr. Locke*, etc.

[4] Specimen of Reflections on Book I. of the *Essay on Human Understanding*. Specimen of Reflections on Book II. See *infra*, pp. 20–25. — Tr.

In the year 1700 appeared the French translation of Locke's work published by Pierre Coste;[1] it was prepared according to the fourth edition and contained accordingly the additions which Locke had made to the previous editions of his book. Leibnitz at once took occasion thereof to write a sketch for the "Monatliche Auszug[2] aus allerhand neu-herausgegebenen, nützlichen und artigen Büchern," for the year 1700 (September, pp. 611–636). This follows here under No. III.[3] together with the supplement of the following year, 1701.[4] In this sketch Leibnitz discusses two of the weightiest of Locke's additions, filling two separate chapters, viz.: chapter 33 of the second book, wherein Locke treats of the Association of Ideas, and then chapter 19 of the fourth book, in which he discourses of Enthusiasm.

Through the French translation Leibnitz first gained real access to Locke's work.[5] He recognized the importance of its contents in its fullest extent; at the same time the extremely large circulation and the universal recognition, which expressed itself through the editions following each other in rapid succession, must have made upon him a deep impression. Evidently for these reasons Leibnitz conceived the plan of

[1] Essai Philosophique concernant l'entendement humain, où l'on montre, quelle est l'entendue de nos Connoissances certaines et la maniere dont nous y parvenons, traduit de l'Anglais de Mr. Locke par Mr. Pierre Coste, sur la quatrieme edition, revue, corrigée et augmentée par l'Auteur. A Amsterd., 1700. 4. This first edition of Coste's translation was not accessible to me: I have been able to make use of the second: Essai Philosophique concernant, etc. Traduit de l'Anglois par M. Coste. Seconde edition, revue, corrigée, et augmentée de quelques Additions importantes de l'Auteur qui n'ont paru qu'après sa mort, et de quelques Remarques du Traducteur. A Amsterd., 1729. 4.

[2] *I.e.* "'Monatliche Auszug' (Monthly Abstract) of the various newly published, profitable, and pleasing books." — Tr.

[3] See *infra*, pp. 26–38. — Tr.

[4] This "Monatliche Auszug" appeared in three annual sets from 1700–1702. Guhrauer (*Leibnitz's deutsche Schriften*, 2ter Band) has tried to prove in a very complete excursus that Leibnitz was the real editor of this Journal. Certainly the sketch of Locke's work originated with him.

[5] Leibnitz to Thomas Burnett, 17th–27th July, 1696: "I could wish I had the same knowledge of the English language" (as of the French); "but, not having had the occasion for it, all I can do is to understand passably the books written in this language. And at the age at which I have arrived, I doubt if I could ever make myself better acquainted with it." — Leibnitz to Coste, of June 16, 1701: "I have followed your French version, because I thought it proper to write my remarks in French, since nowadays this kind of investigation is but little in fashion in the Latin Quarter."

answering Locke's work with a more extensive writing. It grew out of the often hastily-thrown-off remarks which he occasionally put on paper in the years following that of 1700, in which he was not permitted to undertake any continuous work.[1] In order to obliterate the traces of this method of work, Leibnitz considered it advisable, before he published it, to submit his book, as to composition and style, to the judgment of a native Frenchman. This revision was protracted until the year 1705, as appears from a writing which has no signature.[2] Another delay occurred by reason of the fact that Leibnitz in the following year, 1706, entered into correspondence with Pierre Coste, the translator of Locke's work; Coste told him (April 20, 1707) that the translation of Locke itself would be examined and furnished with important improvements; he would urgently advise him (Leibnitz) to put off the publication of his work until he obtained a knowledge of these changes of Locke. This further consideration, that he learned of the dissenting opinions of Locke in his correspondence with Molyneux, as also Locke's death, which had

[1] "I have made these remarks in the leisure hours when I was travelling or at Herrenhausen, where I could not apply myself to researches which required more care" (*besoin*[1] in sense of *soin?* — Tr.).[1]

[2] "The frequent diversions to which I have been exposed have prevented me from pushing forward my remarks. Besides, I have been obliged to divide my time between the reading of your work and the commissions with which I have been entrusted by the Count de Schwerin, of which I must give account to him. You will find few remarks upon this paper; but I have taken the liberty of changing in the work itself a very large number of places in reference to which I did not at all hesitate when I saw that I could do this without disarranging the rest of the writing. I have not touched what is properly called the style; but the confidence with which you have honored me obliges me to say to you here that it greatly needs amendment, and that you seem too much to have neglected it. You know, sir, to what excess our French people have carried their well- or ill-founded delicacy. Too long periods are distasteful; an And (Et) or some other word too often repeated in the same period offends them; unusual constructions embarrass them; a trifle, so to speak, shocks them. It is proper, however, to accommodate yourself to their taste if you wish to write in their language; and, in case you should decide to print your work, I believe you will do well to retouch it with a little more severity. I am certain that you will not be displeased at the freedom with which I speak to you, since it comes from a person devoted to your service." — Feb. 2, 1705.

[1] W. T. Harris, editor of the "Journal of Speculative Philosophy," suggests that perhaps the reading was *besogne* (work) — instead of *besoin*. So that the passage read, "researches which required more work (or labor)." — Tr.

already followed in the year 1704, altered Leibnitz's original plan.[1]

In order to obtain an easier entrance for his own ideas, and at the same time to make his reader familiar with those of Locke, Leibnitz had composed his work in the form of a dialogue. Two friends, Philalethes and Theophilus, converse together; the first states the views of Locke, the second joins thereto his own (Leibnitz's) remarks. This form of composition Leibnitz thought of abandoning. He writes to Thomas Burnett, May 26, 1706: "The death of Locke has taken away my desire to publish my remarks upon his works. I prefer now to publish my thoughts independently of those of another." On the other hand, he remarks, wellnigh it seems in the opposite sense, to the same, three years later, May 12, 1709: "My remarks upon the excellent work of Locke are almost finished; although we are not of the same opinion, I do not cease to value it and to find it valuable."

Leibnitz's work remained, in form at least, unfinished; a magnificent torso, and unpublished.[2] He turned to the compo-

[1] Leibnitz to Coste, June 16, 1707: "The great merit of Mr. Locke, and the general esteem which his work has with so much justice gained, united to some intercourse by letters which I have had the pleasure of having with my Lady Masham, caused me to employ some weeks in remarks upon this important work, in the hope of conferring upon them with Mr. Locke himself. But his death shocked me, and caused my reflections to be behindhand, although they are finished. My purpose has been to throw light upon things rather than to refute the opinions of another. I shall be delighted, however, sir, to receive the additions and corrections of this excellent man, in order to profit from them." — Leibnitz to Remond, March 14, 1714: "He (Hugony) has also seen my somewhat extended reflections upon Locke's work, which treats of Human Understanding. But I dislike to publish refutations of dead authors, although they might appear during their lifetime and be communicated to the authors themselves. Some minor remarks escaped me, I know not how, and were carried to England by a relative of the late Mr. Burnett, bishop of Salisbury. Locke having seen them, spoke of them slightingly in a letter to Molyneux, which may be found among some posthumous letters of Locke. I learned his opinion of them only from this impression. I am not astonished at it: we differed a little too much in principles, and the views I advanced seemed to him paradoxical. However, a friend more biassed in my favor and less so in favor of Locke informs me that those of my reflections there inserted appear to him the best of the collection. I do not adopt this view, not having examined the collection."

[2] Over the Preface, which certainly was composed after the completion of the entire work, Leibnitz has written as the title of the work: *Nouveaux Essais sur l'entendement par l'Auteur du systeme de l'Harmonie preestablie.* In the Preface itself he leaves out the word "humain." The superscription of the

sition of the "Theodicy." For the first time, fifty years after his death, it was sent to the press in "Œuvres Philosophiques latines et françoises de feu Mr. de Leibnitz. Tirées de ses manuscrits qui se conservent dans la bibliothèque Royale à Hanovre, et publiées par Mr. Rud. Eric. Raspe. Avec une Préface de Mr. Kaestner, Professeur en Mathématiques à Göttingen. A Amsterdam et à Leipzig, 1765." The present impression has been newly compared with the original, so far as it is still extant.[1] The corrections in reference to the style proposed by the native Frenchman are not taken into consideration, in order not to obliterate Leibnitz's style of expression; they relate, indeed, only to the first books.

In the preface to his work, in which Leibnitz has put together the points of difference between his system and that of Locke, he remarks in the first place that Locke's Essay upon Human Understanding is one of the most beautiful and valuable works of its time; that he has determined to make some remarks upon it, because he himself has considered the same subject for a long time, and deemed it a good opportunity to create a favorable entrance for his own ideas in this way. His own system differs, in truth, from Locke's considerably, in so far as Locke's is more closely related to Aristotle, his own, on the other hand, to Plato; Locke's is more universally comprehensible, his own more abstract. Meanwhile, by clothing his own remarks in the form of a dialogue between two persons, one of whom presents Locke's views, the other joins thereto his own, he hopes to avoid the dryness belonging to abstract remarks; at the same time the reader is spared the labor of comparing the passages from Locke's essay under discussion. — The first important point of difference, wherein Leibnitz distinguishes himself from Locke, is in the question whether the soul is in itself empty like a *tabula rasa*, as Aristotle had already maintained, and that it receives everything through sense-perceptions and experience, or whether

fourth book runs thus: *Nouveaux Essays sur l'entendement;* in the case of the three first books we find the superscription: *Nouveaux Essais sur l'entendement humaine.*

[1] In the original, Leibnitz has enclosed the words of Philalethes, who states the views of Locke, in [], perhaps as an indication that they are not his own. Raspe has omitted them. — GERHARDT'S NOTE. In this translation Gerhardt's use of [ ] has been strictly followed. — TR.

the soul originally has the principles of many conceptions and doctrines, as Leibnitz with Plato thinks. Hence arises another question, whether all truths depend upon experience, or whether there is still another principle. The senses are necessary for our actual knowledge, but they give us only examples, *i.e.* individual truths, which are not adequate for grounding the universal necessity of a truth. The necessary truths, which are found in pure mathematics, appear to rest upon other principles, whose proof depends not upon experience and the testimony of the senses, — a point to be well considered. Logic, metaphysics, ethics, are full of such truths, which can arise only from such principles as are called innate. It is nevertheless possible, continues Leibnitz, that my opponent is not wholly remote from my view. For after he has rejected innate ideas in the first book of his essay, he begins the second book with the statement that the ideas which have not their origin in sensation arise through reflection. What, however, is reflection but a regard for what is in us and born in us? Such are the ideas of being, unity, substance, etc. If, thinks Leibnitz, an understanding with his opponent might easily, perhaps, be re-established in reference to the above, yet it might create more difficulty in reference to the affirmation that the soul does not always think, just as bodies do not always have motion. To this Leibnitz opposes the statement that bodies are always in motion and that a substance cannot exist without activity; there are in the soul a multitude of impressions too small to be separately distinguished, but which, however, united produce an activity, although simply inarticulate, like the noise of the waves. These little perceptions are of greater significance than we think. By means of these insensible perceptions the pre-established harmony between the soul and the body is explained. In the same manner they are of great importance for Physics, for thereupon rests the law of continuity. These minute insensible perceptions are also the reason why there are not two perfectly similar souls or things of the same kind.

Another point of difference between Leibnitz and Locke is in reference to the conception of the nature of Matter. Locke considered the smallest particles of matter to be rigid bodies, and therefore assumed that space is empty, else were any motion impossible. Leibnitz, on the other hand, supposes space to be filled with a fluid matter which is divisible to infinity; he calls especial attention to the fact that Locke, who at first professed the gravitation theory of Newton constantly contested by Leibnitz, viz.: that bodies work upon each other from any distance whatever without touching, at a later period freed himself from this assumption of Newton.

In discussing the concepts of space, time, and number, Locke had remarked that only with these concepts may that of infinity be united. Leibnitz agrees with him in this, that there is neither an infinite space, nor an infinite time, nor an infinite number, that in general the infinite is not given in that which is put together out of parts. But the true infinite, Leibnitz adds, is in the Absolute, which is without parts. From this proceeds the concept of the finite through limitation.

In the beginning of the third book Locke had undertaken a discussion of language as the expression of the forms of knowledge. He had made thereby a distinction between nominal and real being. Leibnitz rejects this distinction as a perplexing innovation. Things, Leibnitz affirms, have only one essence, but different definitions of them, nominal and real definitions, are possible.

The contents of the fourth book, in which is treated the knowledge of the truth, gives Leibnitz no occasion to raise an important point of controversy. In reference to the axioms, whose indispensableness to scientific investigations Leibnitz affirms, Locke contests, the former enters into a more protracted explanation. In like manner he turns against Locke's notion that the use of Logic is rather unfruitful.

I

ON LOCKE'S ESSAY ON HUMAN UNDERSTANDING,[1] 1696

[*From the French*]

I FIND so many marks of unusual penetration in what Mr. Locke has given us on the Human Understanding and on Education, and I consider the matter so important, that I have thought I should not employ the time to no purpose which I should give to such profitable reading; so much the more as I have myself meditated deeply upon the subject of the foundations of our knowledge. This is my reason for putting upon this sheet some of the reflections which have occurred to me while reading his Essay on the Understanding.

Of all researches, there is none of greater importance, since it is the key to all others. The first book considers chiefly the principles said to be born with us. Mr. Locke does not admit them, any more than he admits innate ideas. He has doubtless had good reasons for opposing himself on this point to ordinary prejudices, for the name of ideas and principles is greatly abused. Common philosophers manufacture for themselves principles according to their fancy; and the Cartesians, who profess greater accuracy, do not cease to intrench themselves behind so-called ideas of extension, of matter, and of the soul, desiring to avoid thereby the necessity of proving what they advance, on the pretext that those who will meditate on these ideas will discover in them the same thing as they; that is to say, that those who will accustom themselves to their jargon and mode of thought will have the same prepossessions, which is very true.

My view, then, is that nothing should be taken as first principles but experiences and the axiom of identity or (what

[1] Erdmann, *Leibnitii Opera Philosophica*, pp. 136–139. — TR.

is the same thing) contradiction, which is primitive, since otherwise there would be no difference between truth and falsehood; and all investigation would cease at once, if to say yes or no were a matter of indifference. We cannot, then, prevent ourselves from assuming this principle as soon as we wish to reason. All other truths are demonstrable, and I value very highly the method of Euclid, who, without stopping at what would be supposed to be sufficiently proved by the so-called ideas, has demonstrated (for instance) that in a triangle one side is always less than the sum of the other two. Yet Euclid was right in taking some axioms for granted, not as if they were truly primitive and indemonstrable, but because he would have come to a standstill if he had wished to reach his conclusions only after an exact discussion of principles. Thus he judged it proper to content himself with having pushed the proofs up to this small number of propositions, so that it may be said that if they are true, all that he says is also true. He has left to others the task of demonstrating further these principles themselves, which besides are already justified by experience; but with this we are not satisfied in these matters. This is why Apollonius, Proclus, and others have taken the pains to demonstrate some of Euclid's axioms. Philosophers should imitate this method of procedure in order finally to attain some fixed principles, even though they be only provisional, after the way I have just mentioned.

As for ideas, I have given some explanation of them in a brief essay printed in the "Actes des Sçavans"[1] of Leipzig for November, 1684 (p. 537), which is entitled *Meditationes de Cognitione, Veritate, et Ideis;*[2] and I could have wished that Mr. Locke had seen and examined it; for I am one of the most docile of men, and nothing is better suited to advance our thought than the considerations and remarks of clever persons, when they are made with attention and sincerity. I shall only say here, that true or real ideas are those whose

[1] The "Acta Eruditorum," Lipsiae, 1682–1731. — Tr.

[2] Gerhardt, Vol. 4, pp. 422–426; Erdmann, pp. 78–81. Translated in part by Sir William Hamilton, *Lectures on Logic*, Lect. X., ¶ XXX., pp. 127–129, Amer. ed.; and complete by George M. Duncan, *The Philosophical Works of Leibnitz*, pp. 27–32, New Haven: Tuttle, Morehouse, & Taylor, 1890; also by Professor Thomas Spencer Baynes, in the Appendix to his edition of the Port Royal Logic. — Tr.

execution we are assured is possible; the others are doubtful, or (in case of proved impossibility) chimerical. Now the possibility of ideas is proved as much *a priori* by demonstrations, by making use of the possibility of other more simple ideas, as *a posteriori* by experience; for what exists cannot fail to be possible. But primitive ideas are those whose possibility is indemonstrable, and which are in truth nothing else than the attributes of God.

I do not find it absolutely essential for the beginning or for the practice of the art of thinking to decide the question whether there are ideas and truths born with us; whether they all come to us from without or from ourselves; we will reason correctly provided we observe what I have said above, and proceed in an orderly way and without prejudice. The question of the origin of our ideas and of our maxims is not preliminary in Philosophy, and we must have made great progress in order to solve it successfully. I think, however, that I can say that our ideas, even those of sensible things, come from within our own soul,[1] of which view you can the better judge by what I have published[2] upon the nature and connection of substances and what is called the union of the soul with the body. For I have found that these things had not been well understood. I am nowise in favor of Aristotle's *tabula rasa;* and there is something substantial in what Plato called *reminiscence.* There is even something more; for we not only have a reminiscence of all our past thoughts, but also a presentiment of all our future thoughts. It is true that this is confused, and fails to distinguish them, in much the same way as when I hear the noise of the sea I hear that of all the particular waves which make up the noise as a whole, though without discerning one wave from another. Thus it is true in a certain sense, as I have explained, that not only our ideas, but also our sensations, spring from within our own soul, and that the soul is more independent than is thought, although it is always true that nothing takes place in it which is not deter-

[1] The French is: "de nostre propre fonds." — Tr.

[2] In the "Journal des Savants," June, 1695. For the piece, *cf.* Gerhardt, Vol. 4, pp. 477 *sq.* (first sketch 470 *sq.*); and the portion of his introduction and notes referring to the same, Vol. 4, pp. 414–417; Erdmann, pp. 124–128; *cf.* also pp. 129–136. For the translation, Appendix, pp. . — Tr.

mined, and nothing is found in creatures that God does not continually create.

In Book II., which comes to the details of ideas, I admit that the reasons brought forward by Mr. Locke to prove that the soul sometimes exists without thinking of anything, do not appear to me convincing, unless he gives the name of thoughts to those perceptions only which are sufficiently noticeable to be distinguished and retained. I hold that the soul (and even the body) is never without action, and that the soul is never without some perception: even in dreamless sleep we have a confused and dull sensation of the place where we are; and of other things. But even if experience should not confirm the view, I believe that it may be demonstrated. It is much the same as we cannot prove absolutely by experience whether there is a vacuum in space, and whether there is rest in matter. Nevertheless, questions of this kind appear to me, as well as to Mr. Locke, to be decided demonstratively.

I admit the difference which he puts with much reason between matter and space; but as for the vacuum, many clever people have believed in it. Mr. Locke is of this number. I was nearly persuaded of it myself; but I gave it up long ago. And the incomparable Mr. Huygens, who was also for the vacuum and the atoms, began at last to reflect upon my reasons, as his letters can testify. The proof of the vacuum derived from motion, of which Mr. Locke makes use, assumes that body is originally hard, and that it is composed of a certain number of inflexible parts. For in this case it would be true, whatever finite number of atoms might be taken, that motion could not take place without a vacuum. But all the parts of matter are divisible and even pliable.

There are also some other things in this second book which arrest my attention: for example, when it is said (chap. 17) that infinity should be attributed only to space, time, and numbers. I believe, indeed, with Mr. Locke that, properly speaking, we may say that there is no space, time, nor number which is infinite, but that it is only true that however great[1] may be

[1] Gerhardt's text seems here, for some reason, to be defective. It reads thus: "Mais qu'il est seulement vray que pour grand que luy sans fin," etc. Erdmann's seems the more correct, and is therefore followed in the translation. It reads thus: "Mais qu'il est seulement vrai que pour grand que soit un espace, un tems, ou un nombre, il y en a toujours un autre plus grand que lui

a space, a time, or a number, there is always another greater than it without end; and that thus the true infinite is not found in a whole composed of parts. It is none the less, however, found elsewhere; namely, in the *absolute*, which is without parts, and which has influence over compound things, because they result from the limitation of the absolute. The *positive infinite*, then, being nothing else than the absolute, it may be said that there is in this sense a positive idea of the infinite, and that it is anterior to that of the finite. For the rest, in rejecting a composite infinite, we do not deny the demonstrations of the geometers *de Seriebus infinitis*, and particularly what the excellent Mr. Newton has given us, not to mention my own contributions to the subject.

As for what is said (chap. 30) *de ideis adæquatis*, it is allowable to give to the terms the signification which one finds pertinent. Yet without finding fault with Mr. Locke's meaning, I put degrees in ideas, according to which I call those *adequate* in which there is nothing more to explain, much the same as in numbers. Now all ideas of sense-qualities, as of light, color, heat, not being of this nature, I do not reckon them among the adequate. So it is not through themselves, nor *a priori*, but through experience, that we know their reality or possibility.

There are further many good things in Book III. in which he treats of words or terms. It is very true that everything cannot be defined, and that sense-qualities have no *nominal definition:* thus they may be called primitive in this sense; but they can none the less receive a *real definition.* I have shown the difference between these two kinds of definition in the meditation[1] cited above. The *nominal definition* explains the name by the marks of the thing; but the *real definition* makes known *a priori* the possibility of the thing defined. For the rest, I strongly commend Mr. Locke's doctrine of the demonstrability of moral truths.

The fourth or last book, which treats of the knowledge of truth, shows the use of what has just been said. I find in it, as well as in the preceding books, an infinite number of beauti-

sans fin." p. 138 a. *Cf.* also *Leibniz's New Essays concerning the Human Understanding.—A Critical Exposition*, by John Dewey, Ph.D. pp. 190. Chicago: S. C. Griggs & Co., 1888.—Tr.

[1] I.e. *Meditationes de Cognitione, Veritate, et Ideis.*—Tr.

ful reflections. To make suitable remarks upon them would be to make a book as large as the work itself. It seems to me that the axioms receive therein a little less consideration than they deserve. The apparent reason for this is that, excepting those of the mathematicians, we ordinarily find none which are important and solid: I have tried to remedy this defect. I do not despise identical propositions, and I have found that they are of great use even in analysis. It is very true that we know our own existence by an immediate intuition, and that of God by demonstration; and that a mass of matter, whose parts are without perception, cannot make a thinking whole. I do not despise the argument invented some centuries ago by Anselm, archbishop of Canterbury, which proves that the perfect being must exist; although I find that the argument lacks something, because it assumes that the perfect being is possible. For if this single point were proved in addition, the whole demonstration would be complete.

As for the knowledge of other things, it is very well said, that experience alone does not suffice for a sufficient advance in Physics. A penetrating mind will draw more conclusions from some quite ordinary experiences, than another could draw from the most choice; besides, there is an art of experimenting upon and, so to speak, questioning nature. Yet it is always true that we can make progress in the details of Physics only in proportion as we have experience.

Our author shares with many able men the opinion that the forms of logic are of little use. I should be quite of another opinion, and I have often found that the paralogisms, even of mathematics, are the faults of form. Mr. Huygens has made the same observation. Much might be said upon this point, and many excellent things are despised because the use of which they are capable is not made of them. We are inclined to despise what we have learned in the schools. It is true we learn there many useless things; but it is good to exercise the function *della Crusca*,[1] *i.e.* to separate the good from the bad.

[1] "*La Crusca*, a celebrated academy of Florence, founded in 1582, for the purpose of maintaining the purity of the Italian language, that is to say, of separating the bran (*crusca*) from the flour: hence the name." Duncan's note. *Philos. Works of Leibnitz*, p. 378.

Mr. Locke can do this as well as any one whatsoever; and in addition he gives us important thoughts of his own invention; his penetration and fairness appear everywhere.[1] He is not only an assayer, but he is also a transmuter by the increase of good metal he gives. Should he continue to present it to the public, we should be greatly indebted to him.

[1] Erdmann omits this clause. — Tr.

II

SPECIMEN OF THOUGHTS UPON THE FIRST BOOK OF THE ESSAY ON HUMAN UNDERSTANDING

[*From the French*]

In order to prove that there are no ideas born with us, the excellent author of the Essay on Human Understanding adduces experience, which shows us that we need external occasions in order to think of these ideas. I agree with him, but it does not seem to me that it follows that the occasions which cause us to see them, cause them to spring into being. And this experience cannot determine whether it is through immission of a species or by impression of outlines upon an empty tablet, or whether it is by the development of what is already in us that we perceive ourselves. It is not extraordinary that there be somewhat in our mind of which we are not always conscious. Reminiscence shows us that we often have difficulty in remembering what we know, and in seizing what is already in the enclosure and possession of our understanding. This proving to be the truth in acquired knowledge, nothing prevents its being also true in the case of that which is innate. And, indeed, there is still more difficulty in perceiving this last, since it has not yet been modified and detailed by experience, as is the acquired, of which often the circumstances remind us.

The author undertakes to show in particular that impossibility and identity, whole and part, etc., are not innate ideas. But I do not understand the force of the proofs he brings. I admit that it is difficult to make men perceive distinctly these metaphysical notions, for abstraction and thought cost them effort. But one may have in himself that which he has difficulty in distinguishing there. Something else, however, than the idea of identity is necessary to answer the question, which is here proposed, viz.: Whether Euphorbus and Pythagoras and the cock,[1] in which the soul of Pythagoras dwelt for some time, were always the same individual, and it does not at all follow that those who cannot solve this question have no idea of identity. What is clearer than the ideas of geometry? Yet there are some questions which we have not yet been able to decide. But that one which considers the identity of Pythagoras following the story of his metempsychosis is not one of the most impenetrable.

Regarding the idea of God, he brings forward examples of some nations who have had no such knowledge. M. Fabritius, a very distinguished theologian of the late Elector Palatine Charles Louis, has published the "L'Apologie du genre humain contre l'accusation de l'Atheisme," in which he replies to such passages as are here cited. But I do not enter into this discussion. Suppose there are men, and even peoples, who have never thought of God; we may say that this fact proves only that there has not been an occasion sufficient to awaken in them the idea of the supreme substance.

Before passing to the complex principles or primitive truths, I will say that I agree that the knowledge, or better, the actual consideration (*envisagement*), of ideas and truths is not innate, and that it is not necessary that we have distinctly known them in a former state of being, according to Plato's doctrine of reminiscence. But the *idea* being taken for the immediate internal object of a notion, or of what the logicians call an incomplex term, there is nothing to prevent its always being in us, for these objects can subsist when they are not perceived. Ideas and truths may, furthermore, be divided into primitive and derivative: the knowledge of the primitives does not need to be formed; they must be distinguished only; that of the derivative is formed by the understanding and by the reason upon occasion. However, we may say in one sense, that the internal objects of this knowledge, that is to say, the ideas and truths themselves, primitive as well as derivative, are all in us, since all the derivative ideas and all the truths deduced from them result from the relations of primitive ideas which are in us. But usage makes it customary to call innate

[1] *Cf.* Locke, *Philos. Works* (Bohn's ed.), Vol. 1, p. 181 *sq.*, and note. — Tr.

the truths to which credence is given as soon as they are heard, and the ideas whose reality (that is to say, the possibility of the thing which it represents) is of the number of these truths, and needs not to be proved by experience or by reason; there is then considerable ambiguity in this question, and it suffices at the last to recognize that there is an internal light born with us, which comprises all the intelligible ideas and all the necessary truths which are only a result of these ideas and need not experience in order to be proved.

To reduce, then, this discussion to something practical, I believe that the true end one should have is the determination of the grounds of truths and their origin. I admit that contingent truths, or truths of fact, come to us by observation and experience; but I hold that necessary derivative truths depend upon demonstration, *i.e.* upon definitions or ideas, united with the primitive truths. And the primitive truths (such as the principle of contradiction) do not come at all from the senses or from experience, and cannot be perfectly proved, but from the natural internal light, and this is what I mean in saying that they are innate. The geometers also have very well understood this. They could prove passably their propositions (at least, the most important of them) by experience, and I do not doubt that the ancient Egyptian and the Chinese had such an experimental geometry. But the true geometers, above all, the Greeks, have desired to show the force of reason, and the excellence of science, by showing that they can in these matters foresee everything, by the internal light in advance of experience. It must also be admitted that experience never assures us of a perfect universality, and still less of necessity. Some of the ancients laughed at Euclid because he proved what a fool even is not ignorant of (as they say), viz.: that in a triangle two sides together are greater than the third. But those who know what genuine analysis is, are much obliged to Euclid for his proof. And it is much that the Greeks, if less exact in other things, have been so much so in geometry. I attribute it to providence; and I believe without that we should hardly know what demonstration is. I also believe that it is principally in that respect that we are thus far superior to the Chinese.

But it is needful further to look a little at what our clever and celebrated author says in chapters 2 and 3, to sustain his point that there are no innate principles. He is opposed to the universal consent alleged in their favor, maintaining that many races doubt even this famous principle that two contradictories cannot be true or false at once, and that the greater part of the human race ignores it altogether. I admit that there are an infinite number of persons who have never made a statement of them. I have indeed seen authors who desired to refute them, apprehending them, without doubt, wrongly. But where shall we find one who does not avail himself of them in practical life, and who is not offended with a liar who contradicts him? Nevertheless, I do not ground myself wholly upon universal consent; and as for propositions which are approved as soon as they are proposed, I admit that it is not at all necessary for them to be primitive or proximate to them, for they may be very common facts. As for this statement which teaches us that one and one make two (which the author brings forward as an example), it is not an axiom, but a definition. And when he says that sweetness is a different thing from bitterness, he states only a fact of primitive experience, or of immediate perception. Or better, we have only to say that the perception of what is understood by the term sweetness is different from the perception of that which is understood by the term bitterness. I do not here distinguish at all the practical truths from the speculative; they are always the same. And as we can say that it is one of the most manifest truths, that a substance whose knowledge and power are infinite should be honored, we can say that it emanates at once from the light which is born with us, provided one can give his attention to it.

SPECIMEN OF THOUGHTS UPON THE SECOND BOOK

[*From the French*]

It is very true that our perceptions of ideas come either from the external senses or from the internal sense, which may be called reflection; but this reflection is not limited to the operations alone of the mind, as is stated (chap. 1, § 4); it reaches even to the mind itself, and it is in the consciousness of self that we perceive substance.

I admit that I am of the opinion of those who believe that the soul always thinks, although often its thoughts are too confused and too feeble for it to be able distinctly to remember them. I believe I have certain proofs of the continual activity of the soul, and I believe also that the body can never be without motion. The objections raised by the author (Book II., chap. 1, §§ 10 to 19) can be easily met by what I have just said or am about to say. They are based upon the experience of sleep, which is sometimes dreamless; and in fact there are some persons who do not know what it is to dream. However, it is not always safe to deny everything that is not perceived. It is much the same as when there are people who deny the corpuscles and insensible motions, and laugh at the particles because they cannot be proved. But some one will tell me that there are proofs which force us to admit them. I reply that there are in like manner proofs which compel us to admit perceptions which are not marked enough for us to remember them. Experience, furthermore, favors this view; for instance, those who have slept in a cold place notice that they have had while sleeping a confused and feeble sensation. I know a person who wakes up when the lamp which he always keeps lighted at night in his room goes out. But here is something more precise, and which shows that if we did not always have perceptions, we could never be waked up from sleep. Let a man who is sleeping be called by several persons at once, and let it be assumed that the voice of each by itself is not loud enough to awake him, but that the noise of all these voices together awakes him: let us take one of them; it is very necessary that he be touched by this voice in particular, for the parts are in the whole, and if each one by itself does nothing at all, the whole will do nothing, either. Yet he would have continued to sleep, if the voice had been a single one, and that, too, without remembering that he had been called. Thus there are some perceptions too feeble to be noticed, although they are always retained, but among an infinite number of other small perceptions which we have continually. For neither motions nor perceptions are ever lost;

both continue always, only becoming indistinguishable through composition with many others. One might reply to this reasoning, that each voice by itself effectively touches the body, but that a certain quantity of it is needed in order that the motion of the body may reach the soul. I reply, that the least impression reaches the entire body, and consequently to that part whose motions correspond to the actions of the soul. And accordingly no principle of limitation can be found, however necessary a certain quantity may be. I do not wish to insist upon the interest that the immortality of the soul has in this doctrine. For if the soul is passive, it is also without life, and it seems that it can be immortal only by grace and by miracle — a view which there is reason to disapprove. I admit, however, that our interest is not the measure of truth, and I do not wish to mix here theological reasons with those of philosophy.

III

[*From the German*]

Essai Philosophique concernant l'Entendement humain, où l'on montre, quelle est l'entendue de nos connoissances certaines et la maniere dont nous y parvenons, traduit de l'Anglois de Mr. Locke par Mr. Pierre Coste, sur la quatrieme edition, revue, corrigée et augmentée par l'Auteur. A Amsterd. 1700 in 4to.

Philosophischer Versuch, betreffend den Menschlichen Verstand, alwo gewiesen wird, wie weit sich unsre gewisse Erkändtnüssen erstrecken, und auf wass Weise wir darzu gelangen; ausz den Englischen übersetzet von Hrn. Peter Coste nach der vierten vom Autor selbst übersehenen, verbesserten und vermehrten Edition. 5. Alph. 12. Bog.

It[1] is unnecessary for us to give a complete abstract of this notable book, after the author himself has relieved us of this task, since in the year 1688 he prepared such an abstract for Mr. Clerc for insertion in his "Bibliothèque universelle,"[2] T. VIII., p. 49 *sqq.*, before he gave it to the press. In the year 1690 it appeared first in London in folio, and Mr. Clerc again published lengthy excerpts in the said "Bibliothèque universelle," T. XVII., p. 399. Soon afterwards a new English edition appeared, enlarged with many pieces, and in particular with an entire chapter[3] on Identity and Diversity, which he treats in an exceedingly clear and excellent manner.

In the second edition mentioned, Locke acknowledges that he erred in the first edition when he assumed, in accordance with the common view, that what brings the will to any change of action in the course of arbitrary actions is the assurance of a much greater good. For when he considered the matter more carefully, he found that a present *unrest* which consists in *desire* or is constantly accompanied by the same, places its limits upon the will. For the reasons for this view, see Book

[1] From the "Monatliche Auszug," Sept. 1700, pp. 611–636. — Tr.

[2] "Bibliothèque universelle et historique," Amsterdam, 1686–1693. — Tr.

[3] In the present edition this chapter is 27 in the second book. — Gerhardt's note.

II., chap. 21. He will gladly, however, be informed of a better view. Some time after, a third, and in the year 1699, a fourth, edition appeared, in which last edition Locke either further explained his previous thoughts by many additions or supported them by wholly new grounds. Peter Coste made his translation on the basis of this edition, and when Locke sent him his manuscript, had worked upon the same for more than two years. Locke himself considered this translation a good one and presented his thanks accordingly, so that consequently it must be the more welcome by a great deal to us.

To enumerate all the new additions would take too long; hence we will content ourselves with the mention of the two most important, which make two separate chapters, of which the first is Book II., chap. 33, and treats of the Association of Ideas.

Locke says there is almost no one who does not find something in the opinions, conclusions, and actions of other people which seems to him fantastic and extravagant, and is so in fact. Every one may have eyes keen-sighted enough to mark the least fault of this kind in the case of another, if only it may be distinguished from his own, and he himself may have sufficient understanding to condemn the same, although he also may have in his own opinions and his own conduct the greatest errors of which he might be aware, and of which, where not impossible, he may yet with difficulty be convinced.

This arises, he continues, not merely from self-love, although this passion has often a great part therein. For one daily sees such people lying sick with the same disease, who are otherwise skilful and whole enough to make nothing of their own merits.

This defect of reason is customarily ascribed to education and to the force of prejudice, and this, according to the common opinion, not without cause, but according to Locke's statement, this explanation reaches not to the root of the disease, and does not show completely its origin and peculiarity.

He himself explains it as follows: Some of our ideas [his own words] have among themselves an exact correspondence and connection. The obligation and highest perfection of our reason consists in the fact that it reveals such ideas and holds them together in the selfsame unity and correspondence as that which is grounded in their particular nature. There is besides this another bond of ideas which depends upon chance or custom, so that the ideas which naturally are wholly unrelated become so exactly united in the minds (*esprit*[1]) of some men, that they can with difficulty be separated from one another. They accompany one another constantly, and one can no sooner present itself to the understanding (*intellectui*) than the others or, indeed, more of them, so united are they, appear also, nor can they at all be separated from one another.

This association of ideas, which the mind makes in itself either voluntarily or by chance, is the sole source of the defect of which we now speak. And as this strong union of ideas is not originally caused by nature, it is for this reason wholly different in different persons, viz.: according to their different inclinations, education, and self-interests.

That there are such associations of ideas, which custom begets in the minds of most men, no one, according to Locke's statement, can doubt, who with much earnestness considers himself and other people. And to this cause can perhaps with convenience and reason be ascribed the greater part of those sympathies and antipathies which one finds among men, and which work as strongly and produce as regular effects, as if they were natural, which fact then makes them to be called so, although at first view they had no other origin than the chance connection of two ideas, which the strength of a first impression, or of an excessively great compliance, so firmly united, that they always thereafter remain together in the mind of the man, as though only a single idea. Locke, however, in no respect denies that there are wholly natural antipathies which depend upon our original constitution and are born with us. He believes, however, that with proper consideration man would recognize the most of those which have been regarded as natural, as in the beginning caused by impressions which were not heeded, whether they were suggested sufficiently early or through a ridiculous fancy. Locke notices incidentally the difference which may be made between natural and acquired antipathies, so that those who have children or who

[1] This word I have voluntarily retained here and for the most part in what follows, because it cannot be expressed quite clearly in German. — Leibnitz's note, Gerhardt, p. 27.

Perhaps we should retain the word "esprit" in English. — Tr.

must educate them, may see how much heed they should take of this principle, and with what care this disorderly union of ideas in the mind of the youth should be prevented.

He thereupon points out by some examples how such a union of ideas, which are not of themselves united, yet depend one upon another, is sufficient to impede our moral and natural action, yea more, our notions themselves.

The ideas of goblins or of spirits agree as little with darkness as with light; if, however, a foolish maid instils and awakens these different ideas in the mind of a child, as though they were connected with each other, the child during his entire life will perhaps not be able to separate them from each other; so that the darkness ever more will seem to him to be accompanied with these horrible ideas.

If any one has suffered a grievous wrong on account of another, he thinks very often of the persons and the deed, and while he thus strongly or for a long time thinks thereupon, he at the same time glues these two ideas together so firmly, that he makes them almost one, as it were, and never remembers the person but that the wrong received also enters his head. And while he can scarcely distinguish these two things, he has just as much aversion for the one as for the other. Thence it comes, Locke adds, that hatred arises from slight and worthless reasons, and quarrels are taken up and continued in the world.

One of Locke's friends was wholly cured of madness by a certain man through a very painful operation, for which service he acknowledged himself under great obligation to him throughout his life, as he was so circumstanced that he required from no one a greater service during his life. Reason or gratitude might suggest to him what they would, yet he could never bear the sight of this surgeon. For as the sight of him always brought again to mind the idea of the very great pain which he had been obliged to endure at his hands, he could not endure this idea, so violent were the impressions it produced in his mind.

Many children hold their books, which were the occasion hereto, accountable for most of the ill treatment they endured at school, and they unite these ideas so well that they regard a book with great disgust, and all their life study and books cannot win their love, because to them reading, which might otherwise have greatly delighted them, became a genuine torture.

An example notable for its singularity is the following which an eminent man, who assured him he had himself seen it, relates to Locke: A young man had learned to dance very prettily and perfectly. There chanced to stand, however, in the hall where he first learned, an old trunk, the idea of which combined so imperceptibly with his turns and steps in the dance, that although he could dance incomparably well in this hall, he could do this only when the old trunk was there; in other places, however, he could not dance at all, unless the old trunk itself or one like it stood in its accustomed place.

The *habitus intellectuales* which are contracted through such association of ideas, are, as Locke further informs us, just as strong and numerous, even though very little heeded. Supposing the ideas of being and matter were very strongly united, either by education or by an excessively great application to these two ideas, according as they are combined in the mind, what notions and reasonings would they not produce concerning different spirits? If a custom accepted from childhood up had united a form or figure with the idea of God, into what absurdities would such a thought in the contemplation of deity not plunge us? We shall no doubt find, Locke adds, that it is nothing else than similar ill-grounded and unnatural combinations of ideas, which break the path for the many conflicting sects in philosophy and religion; for it is not to be supposed that each member of those different sects is willingly deceived, and against his better knowledge and conscience rejects the truth demonstrated to him by clear evidence. It is indeed certain that sometimes interest assists greatly in this sort of thing, yet no one could affirm that it could captivate and lead astray whole societies, so that they all, none excepted, should affirm plain and deliberate falsehoods. For it must be that some at least do what others pretend to do, viz.: seek truth sincerely.

Therefore there must be something which blinds their understanding and hinders them from recognizing the falsehood of what they consider as pure and refined truth. If now we investigate accurately what takes reason prisoner and darkens the understanding of otherwise sincere people, we find that it is simply and solely some free ideas, which, properly speaking, really have no bond among themselves, but which, by education, custom, and uninterrupted action on their part, are so united in the mind that they can no more be separated and distinguished from one another than a single idea. Thence it comes, Locke continues, that often the crudest things are taken for worthy opinions, absurdities for demonstrations, and intolerable and absurd results for strong and fluent reasonings.

The other chapter we promised to present, treats of Enthusiasm, and is the 19th in the 4th book. Locke's thoughts thereupon are as follows:—

Whoever will earnestly seek for truth must first before all things acquire a love for it. Whoever does not love the truth, to him we must necessarily attribute the opposite. Hence we can rightly say, that among those who pretend to seek it, there are very few who really lŏve it. We may recognize a genuine seeker of the truth, since he does not assume for a statement any greater certainty than the proofs upon which he grounds it warrant. Whoever steps beyond this limit lays hold of the truth not out of love for it, but from another indirect purpose. For while the unquestionable clearness of a statement truly consists in the evidence for it (excepting those which are sufficiently clear of themselves), yet it is plain that so far as space is given to assent beyond the unquestionable clearness of a proposition, the remaining portion of the assurance is not drawn from love for the truth, but from another passion. For as it is impossible that love for the truth can bring any one to give to any proposition an assent greater than that certified by the truth itself, just so is it also impossible that any one out of love for the truth can assent to a statement in view of evidence of such a character that from it he cannot see whether the statement is true; which would be actually equivalent to the assumption that the proposition is a truth because possibly, or, indeed, probably, it seems not to accord with the truth.

Locke adds, it follows indisputably from this evil disposition of the mind, that men assume the authority to dictate their own opinions to others. For how should one who has imposed on his own belief, not be willing also to impose on the belief of others? How is it to be expected that one will use valid arguments and proofs in dealing with others, who is not accustomed to use them in dealing with himself, who does violence to his own powers, who tyrannizes over his own mind, and misuses the advantage which truth alone has, viz.: that it assents to nothing but what is indisputably true?

After Locke has laid this foundation, he proceeds to the investigation of Enthusiasm, to which some people ascribe as much power as to faith and reason, and would establish revelation without the aid of reason, whereby, however, they would at once destroy both reason and revelation, and without any reason erect in their place the fancies forged in their own brain, which they choose as the plumb-line of their opinions and conduct. Reason is nothing else than a natural revelation, whereby God bestows upon men that portion of truth which he has poured into the capacity of their natural powers. Revelation is natural reason, enlarged by a new set of discoveries flowing immediately from God, the ground (*raison*) of which is the truth by testimony and proof they offer that these discoveries actually come from God.[1] Whoever, therefore, destroys reason to make room for revelation, extinguishes both these lights at the same time. As, however, men find that an immediate revelation is a much easier means of strengthening their opinions and of directing their conduct than the labor of arranging all according to strict reasoning, which is usually irksome, prejudiced, and for the most part without successful progress; so it is not to be wondered at that they often pretend revelations and persuade themselves that God directs them in particular as regards their actions and opinions, and especially in those things which they cannot justify by the principles of reason. If their minds are once possessed with this thought, the most absurd opinions which are firmly impressed upon their fancy, must seem to be illuminations coming from the Spirit of God and having divine authority. Every extraordinary thing to which they are led by a strong impulse, they consider as certainly a divine call

[1] On this whole discussion, *cf.* an article by the translator entitled "Revelation, Inspiration and Authority," in "The Andover Review," April 1891. —Tr.

which they must follow, and as a command from on high in whose execution it is impossible to err.

This is, properly speaking, what is meant by Enthusiasm, which is not adjusted to reason nor to divine revelation, but springs forth only from the imagination of a heated and conceited spirit, and which, as soon as it has taken a little root, plays much more strongly upon the opinion and actions of men than reason or revelation separately or together.

Although now the extravagant actions and opinions, wherein enthusiasm has involved men, should spur them on to be more on their guard and to avoid the false *principia*, which lead astray both their belief and their conduct; yet through its love for the extraordinary, through its ease and illumined by its glory, and through its extraordinary paths to knowledge it has come to pass that the laziness, ignorance, and vanity of many are so tickled, and they are brought to such a point, that after they are captivated by such ways of an immediate revelation, of an illumination without search, of a certainty without proof and investigation, it is very difficult to bring them out of it again.

They are transported beyond reason, and reason in their case perishes. They see a light infused into their understanding and can no longer be deceived. This light visibly appears as the clearest sunbeam and requires no other proof than its own clearness. They feel, according to their statements, the hand of God moving them within; they feel the impulses of the Spirit, and cannot be mistaken in their feeling. Thus they persuade themselves that reason has nothing to do with what they see and feel in themselves. The things which they clearly experience are beyond all doubt, and need no proof; and so of all the rest of their strange talk. They are sure of these things because they are sure of them, and their opinions are correct because they are firmly fixed in their mind. For this is the upshot of their words when stripped of the metaphors of *hearing* and *feeling* in which they are clothed.

Locke investigates the ground of this inner light and feeling, upon which these people so firmly base themselves, and speaks thus: Is this seeing of the light a perception of the truth of a certain particular statement, or perhaps of this, that it is a revelation from God? Is this feeling a perception of an inclination, which comes from a fancy to do something, or from the spirit of God, which begets in it this inclination? These are two wholly different feelings, which must be carefully distinguished from one another if we would not deceive ourselves. I can perceive the truth of a proposition; but I cannot thereby know as yet whether it is an immediate revelation from God. I can perceive the truth of a proposition in Euclid without its being or my knowing that it is a revelation. I may also know that I did not attain this knowledge through natural means, thence may indeed conclude that it is revealed to me, but I cannot thereby yet know it is a revelation from God; because there may be minds which without a divine commission for this work arouse these ideas in me and set them in such order in my mind that I may perceive their connection. So that the knowledge of a proposition, which enters my head, I know not how, is thus not an evidence that it comes from God. Still less is a firm persuasion that this fancy is true, a certain evidence that it comes from God, or that it is true.

We may call such a fancy *sight* or *light*, yet it is nothing more than belief and confidence.[1] For if the proposition under discussion be one which they have imagined, but do not know to be true, it cannot be *seeing*, but *believing*. One may also give to such fancy any name he pleases. What I believe, I must put forth as true upon another's testimony, and must know certainly in the case that this testimony is given; for without this my belief would be groundless. I must see whether God reveals this to me, or whether I see nothing. Thus the issue is, that I know how I am to know that God reveals something to me, that this impression in my soul occurs through the Holy Spirit, and that consequently I am bound to follow it. If I do not know this, my confidence, great as it may be, is without the least foundation, and all the light with which I perceive myself illumined, is but enthusiasm. For whether the proposition supposed to be revealed, be evidently true in itself, or visibly probable, or whether it be difficult to vindicate it by the ordinary paths of knowledge, this must nevertheless before all things be clearly established and proved, that God has revealed this proposition, and that

[1] The German is "Credulität und Confidentz." — TR.

what I take as a revelation certainly comes of itself into my mind, and is no illusion, which some one else has thrust in or my own fancy has awakened. Until one has come this far, all confidence that this revelation comes from God is a mere conjecture, and all this light which dazzles one is nothing but an ignis fatuus, which will unceasingly lead us into this circle: *This is a revelation because I firmly believe it; and I believe it because it is a revelation.*

It follows from this that those who imagine that they have such revelations of this or that truth must be assured that it is God who has revealed it to them. For to say, as they generally do, that they know it by the light which it brings with it, which shines and flashes in their souls, and which they cannot resist, means only that it is a revelation because they believe it certainly is one; since all the light of which they speak is nothing but a strong imagination which is firmly fixed in their mind, and yet has not the least ground that it is a truth. For they must consider that to assume accepted grounds as reasonable and as a proof that it is a truth, is a necessary acknowledgment that they have no such (grounds).[1] Because, if they have such, they receive this truth no longer as a revelation, but as a truth established upon common grounds. And if they believe it to be true, because it is no revelation, and if they have no other reason to prove it a revelation than simply because they are completely persuaded of its truth, without any other ground and only on account of this fancy, then they believe it to be a revelation only because they strongly believe it to be a revelation. Who does not see that if we build upon such grounds, we make our own fancy the only rule of our opinions and conduct, and consequently subject ourselves to the strangest errors and vexations. For once for all the strength of our opinions is no proof of their correctness. Meanwhile men can approve an error as a truth, as may be seen in the case of those zealous people who maintain in the sharpest manner two propositions contrary to one another.

In reference to which Locke well says, that if the light,

[1] The text is: "Denn dieses müssen sie vor raisonable und von einigem Beweise halten, der da zeige, dass es eine Warheit sey, genommene Gründe annehmen, dass sie erkennen müssen, wie sie dergleichen nicht haben." — Tr.

which every one thinks he has in himself, and which in this case is nothing but the strength of his own opinion, be a proof that his thought comes from God, then we must conclude that all contrary opinions have the right to pass as divine inspirations; and God would be not only the father of light, but also of wholly opposite lights, which lead men in ways wholly contrary.

Therefore Locke concludes that he who does not wish to fall into a mass of disorderly delusions and errors must first test thoroughly this inner light which offers itself as a guide. God, he says, does not destroy the man when he makes a prophet. He leaves all his faculties in their natural condition, so that he may thereby judge whether the inspirations which he feels within have sprung from God or not. If God will have us acknowledge the truth of a proposition, he permits us to see this truth either through the ordinary paths of natural reason, or he makes us know that it is a truth which we must receive upon his authority, while he convinces us by certain marks which reason cannot reject that it comes from him. I will not, however, Locke adds, say by this, that we are to examine by reason whether a proposition thus revealed to us by God may be proved by natural principles, and if not we may reject it; but I will say, that we must consult reason and by its aid see whether it be a revelation from God or no. For if reason finds it to be a divine revelation, it declares for it as such from that hour on as well as for any other truth, and makes it one of its rules, so that it cannot be rejected.

If this inner light, or a proposition which presents itself in our mind as revealed, accords with the principles of reason or with the word of God which is an attested revelation, we have the warrant of reason for it, and may accept this light as true, and direct our faith and walk accordingly. If, however, this light has the witness or proof of neither of these rules, we cannot consider it as a revelation; nay more, as a truth. For if we at the same time believe it to be a revelation, that does not, however, make it so; it may, however, be shown by some other mark to be really a revelation. The old prophets, when they were to receive revelations from God, had other proof than the inner light which assured them that these revelations really came from God. They imagined not only that their imaginations came from God, but they had also external signs which convinced them that God was the author of their revelation. And if they were to convince others of the same, they received beforehand a special power to set forth the truth of the commission given them of Heaven with visible signs. Thus Moses saw a burning bush which was yet not consumed and heard a voice out of the bush. This was something more than an inner feeling of an impulse to free the children of Israel from the hands of Pharaoh. Yet, Moses did not believe that this was enough to warrant him in going into Egypt with God's commission; until God assured him by still another miracle, of the rod changed into a serpent, that such was his real will, and granted him the power to work precisely similar wonders in the sight of Pharaoh. Precisely similar was it in Gideon's case. These and other examples of the old prophets show sufficiently that they did not believe that an inner vision or their own imagination attested by no other affirmation a sufficient evidence that their imagination came from God; although the Scripture does not everywhere mention that they always asked for or received such proofs.

These few passages from the clever work of Locke, under the guidance of the accurate translator Coste, we have brought forward as specimens. Perhaps we shall have further opportunity to speak of it, when the Latin translation, with which some one[1] is now occupied in England, is published.

In the "Monatliche Auszug" of the year 1701 is found (pp. 73–75) the following addition to the foregoing sketch:—

What Locke says of the connection and accompaniment of ideas is not to be despised, and serves often to arouse the emotions; as for errors and false judgments, however, they spring from other contiguous and peculiar causes, viz.: that one assumes false principles, and imagines that he once had proof of them in his mind, within which now a lapse of memory occurs; and then from incorrect conclusions which he produces from these principles assumed as known, because he gives not the time and labor to investigate all in a formal and orderly way.

[1] Burridge of Dublin. The version appeared in 1701.—Tr.

Meanwhile it is true that the emotions greatly assist this credulity concerning principles and carelessness in false deduction; for one believes and easily draws the conclusion he would gladly have. It is besides noticeable in this book of Locke's, that in his last writings against the Rev. Lord Bishop Stillingfleet he has changed a large part of his opinions concerning the nature of the body contained in this *Tentamen* or Essay on Human Understanding; while in this *Tentamen* he held opinions, in common with modern philosophers, especially the followers of Descartes and Gassendi, that in the body nothing is to be met with but size, solidity or impenetrability, and motion or change; now, however, he begins to hold the opinion that there is something to be found therein not revealed through these qualities. He repudiates, besides, in this essay innate ideas and the natural light, but appears not to distinguish sufficiently the necessary truths arising from possibility, from those others whose ground must be assumed from the experience of realities, and thus must be drawn from without.

Thus he accepts the *tabula rasa* of Aristotle, rather than the implanted (ideas) of Plato. It is true that we do not come upon thoughts in these most abstract matters, without external sensations, but in the case of these necessary truths, such sensations serve more as a reminder than as a proof; which (proof) must come simply and solely from internal grounds, as those do not sufficiently understand who deal little in demonstration proper.

NEW ESSAYS ON THE UNDERSTANDING

BY THE AUTHOR OF THE SYSTEM OF PRE-ESTABLISHED HARMONY

PREFACE

The Essay on the Understanding, by a distinguished Englishman, being one of the most beautiful and esteemed works of this period, I have resolved to make some remarks upon it, because having sufficiently meditated for a long time upon the same subject and upon the greater part of the matters therein touched upon, I have thought that it would be a favorable opportunity to publish something under the title of "New Essays on the Understanding," and to procure a favorable reception to my thoughts, by putting them in so good company. I[1] have thought also that I could profit from the labor of another not only to lessen my own (since in fact it is less difficult to follow the thread of a good author than to work wholly independently), but further to add something to what he has given us, which is always easier than to start from the beginning; for I think I have cleared up some difficulties which he had left in their entirety. Thus his reputation is an advantage to me; having for the rest a disposition to render justice, and very far from wishing to diminish the esteem in which this work is held, I would increase it, if my approval carried any weight. It is true I often differ in my views (from

[1] Gerhardt's text reads as follows: "J'ai crû encor pouvoir profiter du travail d'autruy non seulement pour diminuer le mien (puisqu'en effect il y a moins de peine à suivre le til d'un bon auteur qu'à travailler à nouveaux frais en tout), mais encor pour adjouter quelque chose à ce qu'il nous a donné, ce qui est tousjours plus facile que de commencer; car je crois d'avoir levé quelques difficultés qu'il avoit laissées en leur entier. Ainsi sa reputation m'est avantaguese; estant d'ailleurs d'humeur à rendre justice et bien loin de vouloir diminuer l'estime qu'on a pour cet ouvrage, je l'accroistrois, si mon approbation estoit de quelque poids. Il est vray que jé suis souvent d'un autre avis, mais bien loin de disconvenir du merite des Ecrivains celebres, on leur rend temoignage, en faisant connoistre en quoy et pour quoy on s'eloigne de leur sentiment, quand on juge necessaire d'empecher que leur autorité ne prevaille à la raison en quelques points de consequence, outre qu'en satisfaisant à de si excellens hommes, on rend la verité plus recevable, et il faut supposer que c'est principalement pour elle qu'ils travaillent." — Tr.

him[1]), but very far from denying the merit of celebrated writers, we bear witness to it, by making known in what and why we differ from their views, when we judge it necessary to prevent their authority from prevailing over reason on some important points; besides, by satisfying such excellent men, we render the truth more acceptable, and it must be supposed that it is principally for truth that they labor.

In fact, although the author of the Essay says a thousand beautiful things which I commend, our systems are very different. His has more relation to Aristotle, mine to Plato, although we both differ in many things from the doctrine of these two ancient philosophers. He is more popular, and I am compelled sometimes to be a little more *acroamatic* and more abstract, which is not an advantage to me, especially when writing in a living language. I think, nevertheless, that by making two persons speak, one of whom sets forth the views drawn from the Essay of this author, and the other joins thereto my observations, the parallel will be more to the liking of the reader than wholly dry remarks, the reading of which would be interrupted at every moment by the necessity of recurring to his book in order to understand mine. It will nevertheless be well still to compare sometimes our writings, and not to judge of his views except by his own work, although I have ordinarily preserved its expressions. It is true that the constraint, which another's discourse, whose thread must be followed, gives in making remarks, has prevented me from thinking to secure the charms of which the dialogue is susceptible; but I hope the matter will make amends for the defects of the style.

Our differences are upon subjects[2] of some importance. The question is to know whether the soul in itself is entirely empty as the tablets upon which as yet nothing has been written (*tabula rasa*) according to Aristotle, and the author of the Essay, and whether all that is traced thereon comes solely from the senses and from experience; or whether the soul contains originally the principles of many ideas and doctrines which external objects merely call up on occasion, as I believe

[1] Erdmann and Jacques read: "que lui," which does not occur in Gerhardt's text. — Tr.

[2] Erdmann and Jacques read: "objects." — Tr.

with Plato, and even with the schoolmen, and with all those who interpret in this way the passage of St. Paul (Rom. 2: 15) where he states that the law of God is written in the heart. The Stoics call these principles[1] *prolepses, i.e.* fundamental assumptions, or what is taken for granted in advance. The Mathematicians call them *general notions* (κοιναὶ ἔννοιαι). Modern philosophers give them other beautiful names, and Julius Scaliger in particular named them *semina æternitatis,* also *zopyra, i.e.* living fires, luminous flashes, concealed within us, but which the encounter of the senses makes appear like the sparks which the blow makes spring from the steel. And the belief is not without reason, that these glitterings indicate something divine and eternal which appears especially in the necessary truths. Whence another question arises, whether all truths depend upon experience, *i.e.* upon induction and examples, or whether there are some which have still another foundation. For if some events can be foreseen prior to any proof which may have been made of them, it is manifest that we ourselves contribute something thereto. The senses, although necessary for all our actual knowledge, are not sufficient to give it all to us, since the senses never give us anything but examples, *i.e.* particular or individual truths. Now all the examples which confirm a general truth, whatever their number, do not suffice to establish the universal necessity of that same truth, for it does not follow that what has happened will happen in the same way. For example, the Greeks and the Romans, and all the other peoples of the earth known to the ancients, have always observed that before the lapse of twenty-four hours day changes into night, and night into day. But we would be deceived, if we believed that the same law holds good everywhere else; for since then, the contrary has been experienced in the region of Nova Zembla. And he would still be in error who believed that, in our climates at least, this is a necessary and eternal truth, which will always endure, since we must think that the earth, and the sun even, do not necessarily exist, and that there will perhaps be a time when this beautiful star, together with its whole system, will not longer exist, at least in its present form. Whence it appears

[1] For a very full nomenclature of these principles, see Hamilton's Reid, Note A., § V., Vol. II., pp. 755–770. 8th ed., Edinburgh and London, 1880. — Tr.

that necessary truths such as are found in pure mathematics, and particularly in arithmetic and in geometry, must have principles whose proof does not depend upon examples, nor consequently upon the testimony of the senses, although without the senses it would never have occurred to us to think of them. This distinction must be carefully made, and was so well understood by Euclid, that he often proved by the reason, what is sufficiently seen through experience and by sensible images. Logic also, together with metaphysics and ethics, one of which shapes theology and the other jurisprudence, both natural (sciences), are full of such truths, and consequently their proof can come only from internal principles which are called innate. It is true that we must not imagine that these eternal laws of the reason can be read in the soul as in an open book, as the prætor's edict is read upon his *album* without difficulty and research; but it is sufficient that they can be discovered in us by dint of attention, for which the senses furnish occasions, and successful experience serves to confirm reason, in much the same way as proofs in arithmetic serve for the better avoidance of error in calculating when the reasoning is long. Herein, also, human knowledge differs from that of the brutes: the brutes are purely empirics and only guide themselves by examples; for, so far as we can judge of them, they never attain to the formation of necessary propositions; while men are capable of demonstrative sciences. It is also for this reason that the faculty the brutes have for making *consecutions* is something inferior to the reason of man. The consecutions of the brutes are merely like those of simple empirics, who claim that what has sometimes happened will happen again in a case where something strikes them as similar, without being able to judge whether the same reasons hold good. This is why it is so easy for men to entrap the brutes, and so easy for simple empirics to make mistakes. This is why persons who have become skilful through age and experience are not exempt (from error) when they depend too much upon their past experience, as has happened to many in civil and military affairs; because they do not consider sufficiently that the world changes, and that men become more skilful by finding a thousand new dexterities, while the deer and hares of the present do not become more cunning than those of the past. The consecutions of the brutes are only a shadow of reasoning, *i.e.* are only connections of the imagination and passages from one image to another, because in a new juncture which appears similar to the preceding they expect anew that connection which they formerly met with, as if things were united in fact because their images are united in the memory. It is true that reason also counsels us to expect ordinarily to see that happen in the future which is conformed to a long past experience, but it is not on this account a necessary and infallible truth, and success may cease when least expected, when the reasons change which have sustained it. Therefore the wisest men do not so commit themselves to it as not to try to discover, if possible, something of the reason of this fact in order to judge when it is necessary to make exceptions. For reason is alone capable of establishing sure rules, and supplying what is wanting to those which were not such by inserting their exceptions; and of finding at length certain connections in the force of necessary consequences, which often furnish the means of foreseeing the result without the necessity of experiencing the sense-connections of images, to which the brutes are reduced, so that that which justifies the internal principles of necessary truths also distinguishes man from the brutes.

Perhaps our clever author will not wholly differ from my view. For after having employed the whole of his first book in rejecting innate intelligence, taken in a certain sense, he nevertheless, at the beginning of the second and in the sequel, admits that ideas, which do not originate in sensation, come from reflection. Now reflection is nothing else than attention to what is in us, and the senses do not give us what we already carry with us. That being so, can it be denied that there is much that is innate in our mind, since we are innate, so to speak, in ourselves? and that there is in us: being, unity, substance, duration, change, action, perception, pleasure, and a thousand other objects of our intellectual ideas? And these objects being immediate to our understanding and always present (although they cannot always be perceived by reason of our distractions and needs), what wonder that we say that these ideas with all depending upon them are innate in us? I have made use also of the comparison of a block of marble which has veins, rather than of a block of marble wholly even, or of blank tablets, *i.e.* of what is called among philosophers a *tabula rasa.* For if the soul resembled these blank tablets, truths would be in us as the figure of Hercules is in the marble, when the marble is wholly indifferent to the reception of this figure or some other. But if there were veins in the block which should indicate the figure of Hercules rather than other figures, this block would be more determined thereto, and Hercules would be in it as in some sense innate, although it would be needful to labor to discover these veins, to clear them by polishing, and by cutting away what prevents them from appearing. Thus it is that ideas and truths are for us innate, as inclinations, dispositions, habits, or natural potentialities, and not as actions; although these potentialities are always accompanied by some actions, often insensible, which correspond to them.

It seems that our clever author claims that there is nothing *virtual* in us, and indeed nothing of which we are not always actually conscious; but he cannot take this rigorously, otherwise his opinion would be too paradoxical; since, moreover, acquired habits and the stores of our memory are not always perceived and do not even always come to our aid at need, although we often easily recall them to the mind upon some slight occasion which makes us remember them, just as we need only the beginning of a song to remember it.[1] He limits his thesis also in other places, by saying that there is nothing in us of which we have not at least formerly been conscious. But besides the fact that no one can be assured by reason alone how far our past *apperceptions*, which we may have forgotten, may have gone, especially according to the Platonic doctrine of reminiscence which, wholly fabulous as it is, is in no respect incompatible at least in part with reason wholly pure: besides this, I say, why must we acquire all through the perception of external things, and nothing be unearthed in ourselves? Is our soul then by itself such a blank that besides the images borrowed from without, it is nothing? This is not an opinion (I am sure) that our judicious author could approve.

[1] Erdmann and Jacques read: "le commencement d'une chanson pour nous faire ressouvenir du reste," *i.e.* the beginning of a song to remind us of the rest. — Tr.

And where do we find tablets that have no variety in themselves? For we never see a plane perfectly even and uniform. Why, then, could we not furnish also ourselves with something of thought from our own depths if we should dig therein? Thus I am led to believe that at bottom his opinion upon this point is not different from mine, or rather from the common view, inasmuch as he recognizes two sources of our knowledge, the Senses and Reflection.

I do not know whether it will be so easy to harmonize him with us and with the Cartesians, when he maintains that the mind does not always think, and particularly that it is without perception when we sleep without dreaming; and he objects[1] that since bodies can exist without motion, souls can also exist without thought. But here I make a somewhat different reply than is customary, for I hold that naturally a substance cannot exist without action, and that there is indeed never a body without movement. Experience already favors me, and you have only to consult the book of the distinguished Mr. Boyle against absolute rest, to be convinced of it; but I believe reason favors it also, and this is one of the proofs I have for doing away with atoms.

Moreover, there are a thousand indications which make us think that there are at every moment an infinite number of *perceptions* in us, but without apperception and reflection, *i.e.* changes in the soul itself of which we are not conscious, because the impressions are either too slight and too great in number, or too even, so that they have nothing sufficiently distinguishing them from each other; but joined to others, they do not fail to produce their effect and to make themselves felt at least confusedly in the mass. Thus it is that habit makes us take no notice of the motion of a mill or a waterfall when we have lived quite near it for some time. It is not that the motion does not always strike our organs, and that something no longer enters into the soul corresponding thereto, in virtue of the harmony of the soul and the body, but these impressions which are in the soul and the body, being destitute of the attractions of novelty, are not strong enough to attract our attention and our memory, attached to objects more engrossing. For all attention requires memory,

[1] Erdmann and Jacques read: "Il dit que," *i.e.* He says that. —TR.

and often when we are not admonished, so to speak, and warned to take note of some of our own present perceptions, we allow them to pass without reflection, and even without being noticed; but if any one directs our attention to them immediately after, and makes us notice, for example, some noise which was just heard, we remember it, and are conscious of having had at the time some feeling of it. Thus there were perceptions of which we were not conscious at once, consciousness arising in this case only from the warning after some interval, however small it may be. And to judge still better of the minute perceptions which we cannot distinguish in the crowd, I am wont to make use of the example of the roar or noise of the sea which strikes one when on its shore. To understand this noise as it is made, it would be necessary to hear the parts which compose this whole, *i.e.* the noise of each wave, although each of these little noises makes itself known only in the confused collection of all the others, *i.e.* in the roar itself, and would not be noticed if the wave which makes it were alone. For it must be that we are affected a little by the motion of this wave, and that we have some perception of each one of these noises, small as they are; otherwise we would not have that of a hundred thousand waves, since a hundred thousand nothings cannot make something. One never sleeps so soundly as not to have some feeble and confused sensation, and one would never be awakened by the greatest noise in the world if he did not have some perception of its small beginning; just as one would never break a rope by the greatest effort in the world if it were not stretched and lengthened a little by smaller efforts, although the slight extension they produce is not apparent.

These minute perceptions are, then, of greater efficacy in their results than one supposes. They form I know not what, these tastes, these images of the sense-qualities, clear in the mass, but confused in the parts, these impressions which surrounding bodies make upon us, which involve the infinite, this connection which each being has with all the rest of the universe. We may even say that in consequence of these minute perceptions, the present is big with the future and laden with the past, that all things conspire (*σύμπνοια πάντα*, as Hippocrates said), and that in the least of substances eyes as penetrating as those of God could read the whole course of the things in the universe.

Quæ sint, quæ fuerint, quæ mox futura trahantur.[1]

These insensible perceptions indicate also and constitute the same individual who is characterized by the traces or expressions which they conserve of preceding states of this individual, in making the connection with his present state; and they can be known by a superior mind, even if this individual himself should not be aware of them, *i.e.* when there would no longer be in him the express recollection of them. But they (these perceptions, I say) furnish, indeed, the means of finding again this recollection at need by the periodic developments which may some day happen. It is for this reason that death can be only a sleep, and cannot, indeed, continue, the perceptions ceasing merely to be sufficiently distinguished, and being reduced in the animals to a state of confusion which suspends consciousness, but which cannot last always; not to speak[2] here of man, who must have in this regard great privileges in order to preserve his personality.

It is also by means of the insensible perceptions that this admirable pre-established harmony of the soul and the body, and indeed of all the monads or simple substances, is explained;[3] which supplies the place of the unmaintainable influence of one upon the others, and which in the judgment of the author of the most excellent of dictionaries exalts the grandeur of the divine perceptions beyond what has ever been conceived. After this I would add little if I should say that it is these minute perceptions which *determine* us in many junctures without being thought of, and which deceive the vulgar by the appearance of an *indifference of equilibrium*, as if we were entirely indifferent whether we turned (for example) to the right or to the left. It is not needful also that I notice here, as I have done in the book itself, that they cause that *uneasiness* which I show to consist in something which differs from pain only as the small from the great, and which, however, often constitutes our desire and even our

[1] Erdmann reads: *quæ* mox, etc.; Jacques: *quæ* mox *ventura* trahantur. Gerhardt's reading: "que" is evidently an error. — Tr.

[2] Erdmann and Jacques omit: "pour ne parler icy de l'homme qui doit avoir en cela des grands privileges pour garder sa personalité." — Tr.

[3] Erdmann and Jacques read "j'explique," I explain. — Tr.

pleasure by giving to it an exciting flavor. It is also[1] the insensible parts of our sensible perceptions, which produce a relation between the perceptions of colors, heat, and other sensible qualities, and between the motions in bodies which correspond to them; while the Cartesians together with our author, penetrating as he is, conceive the perceptions which we have of these qualities as arbitrary, *i.e.* as if God had given them to the soul according to his good pleasure, without any regard to any essential relation between these perceptions and their objects: a view which surprises me and which appears to me little worthy of the wisdom of the Author of things, who does nothing without harmony and without reason.

In a word, *the insensible perceptions* are as eminently useful in Pneumatology[2] as are the insensible corpuscles in Physics, and it is equally unreasonable to reject the one or the other under the pretext that they are out of reach of our senses. Nothing is accomplished all at once, and it is one of my great maxims, and one of the most verified, that *nature makes no leaps:* a maxim which I called the *Law of Continuity,* when I spoke of it in the first "Nouvelles de la République des Lettres,"[3] and the use of this law is very considerable in Physics. This law declares that we pass always from the small to the great, and the reverse, through the medium, in degree as in parts, and that motion never springs immediately from rest, nor is reduced thereto save by a smaller motion, as one never completes the survey of any line or length until he has completed a smaller line, although hitherto those who have set forth the laws of motion have not observed this law, believing that a body can receive in a moment a motion contrary to the preceding. And all this makes one indeed think that the

[1] Erdmann and Jacques read: "Ce sont les mêmes parties insensibles," etc., It is the same insensible parts, etc. — Tr.

[2] *I.e.* Psychology. *Cf.* Hamilton's Reid, 8th ed., Vol. I., p. 217 a, and note. — Tr.

[3] A literary journal published by Pierre Bayle at Amsterdam, 1684–1687; afterwards continued, at Bayle's request, by Basnage, under the title "Histoire de ouvrages des Savants," 1687–1709. Leibnitz published in this journal in July, 1698, his *Eclaircissement des difficultés que M. Bayle a trouvées dans le système nouveau de l'union de l'âme et du corps.* Gerhardt, Vol. 4, pp. 517–524; Erdmann, pp. 150–154; Jacques, Vol. 1, pp. 481–487. Translation, Appendix, pp. 706–712. — Tr.

noticeable perceptions also arise by degrees from those which are too minute to be observed. To think otherwise, is to have little knowledge of the immense subtilty of things which always and everywhere surrounds an actual infinite.

I have also noticed that in virtue of these insensible variations, two individual things cannot be perfectly alike, and that they must always differ more than *numero:* a fact which destroys the blank tablets of the soul, a soul without thought, a substance without action, a vacuum in space, atoms and even particles not actually divided in matter, absolute rest, entire uniformity in one portion of time, place, or matter, perfect globes of the second element, born of cubes perfect and original, and a thousand other fictions of philosophers which arise from their incomplete notions, and which the nature of things does not allow, and which our ignorance and the little attention we give to the insensible let pass, but which cannot be made tolerable unless they are limited to the abstractions of the mind which protests that it does not deny what it puts aside, and thinks should not enter into any present consideration. Otherwise if it were very well understood, viz.: that things of which we are not conscious are neither in the soul nor the body, we should be lacking in philosophy as in politics, in neglecting *τὸ μικρόν,* the insensible progressions, while an abstraction is not an error, provided we know what it is that we feign therein. Just as the mathematicians employ it when they speak of the perfect lines which they propose to us, of uniform motions and of other regulated effects, although *matter* (*i.e.* the medley of the effects of the surrounding infinite) always makes some exception. It is for the sake of distinguishing the considerations and of reducing so far as we may do so the effects to reasons, and of foreseeing some of their consequences, that we proceed thus. For the more we are careful to neglect no consideration that we can regulate, the more practice corresponds to theory. But it belongs only to the supreme Reason, whom nothing escapes, distinctly to comprehend all the infinite and to see all the reasons and all the consequences. All that we can do in regard to infinites is to know them confusedly, and to know at least distinctly that they are such; otherwise we judge very wrongly of the beauty and the grandeur of the universe; so also we could not have a sound Physics explaining the nature of bodies in general, and still less a proper Pneumatology comprising the knowledge of God, of souls, and of simple substances in general.

This knowledge of insensible perceptions serves also to explain why and how two souls, human or otherwise,[1] of one and the same species never come forth perfectly alike from the hands of the Creator and have always each its original relation to the points of view which it will have in the universe. But this it is which already follows from the remarks I have made about two individuals, viz.: that their *difference* is always *more than numerical.* There is, moreover, another point of importance, in respect to which I am obliged to deviate not only from the opinions of our author, but also from those of the majority of modern philosophers: I believe with the majority of the ancients that all genii,[2] all souls, all simple created substances, are always joined to a body, and that there are never souls entirely separated. I have *a priori* reasons for my view; but the doctrine will be found to have this advantage, that it resolves all the philosophical difficulties as to the condition of souls, their perpetual conservation, their immortality, and their operation. The difference between one of their states and another, never being and never having been other than that of more sensible to less sensible, of more perfect to less perfect, or the reverse, this doctrine renders their past or future state as explicable as that of the present. One feels sufficiently, however little reflection he makes, that this is rational, and that a leap from one state to another infinitely different could not be natural. I am astonished that by leaving the natural without reason, the schoolmen have been willing purposely to plunge themselves into very great difficulties, and to supply matter for apparent triumphs of the strong-minded, all of whose reasons fall at once by this explanation of things, in which there is no more difficulty in conceiving the conservation of souls (or rather, according to my view, of the animal) than there is in conceiving the change of the caterpillar into the butterfly, and the conservation of thought in sleep, to which Jesus Christ has divinely well compared death. I have already said also that sleep could not

[1] Erdmann reads: "ou deux choses," or two things. — TR.
[2] *I.e.* Angels and archangels. — TR.

last always, and it will last least or almost not at all in the case of rational souls who are always destined to preserve the personality which has been given them in the City of God, and consequently remembrance: and this in order to be more susceptible of chastisements and recompenses. And I add further that in general no derangement of the visible organs is capable of throwing things into entire confusion in the animal or of destroying all the organs and depriving the soul of all its organic body and of the ineffaceable remains of all preceding traces. But the ease with which the ancient doctrine of subtile bodies connected with the angels (which was confounded with the corporeality of the angels themselves) has been abandoned, and the introduction of pretended separate intelligences in creatures (to which those who make the heavens of Aristotle revolve have contributed much), and finally the poorly understood view into which we have fallen, that the souls of brutes could not be preserved without falling into metempsychosis, and [1] without conducting them from body to body, and the perplexity into which men have fallen by their ignorance of what to do with them, have caused us, in my opinion, to neglect the natural explanation of the conservation of the soul. This has done much harm to natural religion, and has caused many to believe that our immortality was only a miraculous grace of God, of which also our celebrated author speaks with some hesitation, as I shall presently remark. But it would be well had all those who are of this opinion spoken as wisely and in as good faith as he, for it is to be feared that many who speak of immortality as a grace do so only to keep up appearances, and resemble at bottom these Averroists and some bad Quietists who picture to themselves an absorption and the reunion of the soul with the ocean of divinity: a notion whose impossibility my system alone perhaps evinces.

It seems also that we differ further in regard to matter, in that the author thinks that a vacuum is necessary to motion, because he thinks that the minute parts of matter are rigid. And I admit that if matter were composed of such parts,

[1] Gerhardt's text is: "et sans les promener de corps en corps, et l'embarras où l'on a esté en ne sachant ce qu'on en devoit faire." Erdmann and Jacques omit the clause. —TR.

motion in a *plenum* would be impossible, as if a room were full of a quantity of little pebbles without there being the least empty space. But this supposition, for which there appears also to be no reason, is not admissible, although this learned author goes as far as to believe that rigidity or cohesion of the minute parts makes the essence of the body. It is necessary rather to conceive space as full of a matter originally fluid, susceptible of all the divisions, and even actually subject to divisions and subdivisions to infinity, but with this difference, however, that it is divisible and divided unequally in different parts on account of the motions which more or less concur there. This it is which causes matter to have everywhere a degree of rigidity as well as of fluidity, and no body to be hard or fluid in the highest degree, *i.e.* no atom to be found of an insurmountable hardness nor any mass entirely indifferent to division. The order, also, of nature, and particularly the law of continuity, destroy equally the one and the other.

I have also shown that *cohesion*, which by itself would not be the effect of impulse or of motion, would cause a *traction*, taken strictly. For if there were a body originally rigid, — for example, an Epicurean atom, — which should have a part projecting like a hook (since we can imagine atoms of all sorts of shapes), this hook pushed would draw with it the rest of this atom; *i.e.* the part which is not pushed, and which does not fall in the line of the impulsion. Our learned author, however, is for himself opposed to these philosophic tractions, such as were formerly attributed to the abhorrence of a vacuum, and he reduces them to *impulsions*, maintaining with the moderns that one part of matter works immediately upon another only by pushing it by contact, in which I think they are right, because otherwise there is nothing intelligible in the operation.

I must not, however, conceal the fact that I have noticed a sort of retraction by our excellent author on this subject, whose modest sincerity I cannot forbear praising in this respect as much as I have admired on other occasions his penetrating genius. It is in his reply to the second letter of the late Bishop of Worcester,[1] printed in 1699, p. 408, where,

[1] Edward Stillingfleet, 1635-1699: Bishop of Worcester, 1689-1699. — Tr.

in order to justify the view which he had maintained against this wise prelate, viz.: that matter might think, he says among other things: "*I admit that I said* (Essay on Understanding, Book II. chap. 8, § 11) *that body acts by impulse and not otherwise. This also was my view when I wrote it, and even now I cannot conceive its action in any other way. But since then I have been convinced by the judicious Mr. Newton's incomparable book that there is too much presumption in wishing to limit the power of God by our limited conceptions. The gravitation of matter towards matter in ways inconceivable to me, is not only a demonstration that God, when it seems to him good, can put into bodies powers and modes of acting which are beyond what can be derived from our idea of body or explained by what we know of matter; but it is furthermore an incontestable instance that he has really done so. I shall therefore take care to correct this passage in the next edition of my book.*"[1] I find that in the French version of this book, made undoubtedly from the latest editions, the matter has been put thus in this § 11: *It is evident*, at least so far as we can conceive it, *that it is by impulse and not otherwise that bodies act on each other; for it is impossible for us to understand how the body can act upon what it does not touch, which is the same as to imagine that it can act where it is not.*

I can only praise this modest piety of our celebrated author, who recognizes that God can do more than we can understand, and that thus there may be inconceivable mysteries in the articles of faith; but I should not wish to be obliged to recur to the miracle in the ordinary course of nature and to admit powers and operations absolutely inexplicable. Otherwise too much license will be given poor philosophers, under cover of what God can do, and by admitting these *centripetal virtues* or these *immediate attractions* from afar without being able to make them intelligible, I see nothing to hinder our Scholastics from saying that everything is done simply by their faculties and from maintaining their intentional species which proceed

[1] I have retranslated the passage from the French version, as given by Gerhardt. For the original, *cf.* Locke, *Philos. Works* (Bohn's ed.), Vol. II., p. 395. The entire letter is found in Locke's Works, Vol. I., pp. 578–774; this particular passage, p. 754. Edition of 4 vols., 4to. 7th ed., 1768. Printed for H. Woodfall, A. Millar, and others. — TR.

from objects even to us and find means of entering even into our souls. If that is so,

Omnia jam fient, fieri quæ posse negabam.

So that it seems to me that our author, quite judicious as he is, goes here a little too much from one extreme to the other. He makes a difficulty in regard to the operations of *souls* when the question is only of admitting what is not *sensible*, and behold he gives to *bodies* what is not even *intelligible;* granting them powers and actions which surpass in my view all that a created spirit can do and understand, since he grants them attraction, and that even at great distances without limiting them to any sphere of activity, and this in order to maintain a view which does not appear less inexplicable, viz.: the possibility of the thought of matter in the natural order.

The question which he discusses with the celebrated Prelate who attacked him, is, *whether matter can think*, and as it is an important point even for the present work, I cannot refrain from entering upon it a little and from taking note of their controversy. I will give the substance of their discussion upon this subject, and take the liberty of saying what I think of it. The late Bishop of Worcester, fearing (but in my opinion without good reason) lest our author's doctrine of ideas might be liable to certain abuses prejudicial to the Christian faith, undertook to examine some points in it in his "Vindication of the Doctrine of the Trinity";[1] and having rendered justice to this excellent writer, by recognizing that he thinks the existence of spirit as certain as that of body, although one of these substances is as little known as the other, he asks (p. 241 *sq.*) how reflection can assure us of the existence of spirit, if God can give to matter the power of thought according to the view of our author, Book IV., chap. 3, since thus the way of ideas which must serve to discern[2] what may suit the soul or the body, would become useless; while he had said in Book II. of the Essay on Understanding, chap. 23, §§ 15, 27, 28, that the operations of the soul furnish us the idea of mind and the

[1] Published in the autumn of 1696. *Cf.* Alexander Campbell Fraser, *Locke*, pp. 245–246 (Philosophical Classics), Edinburgh: Wm. Blackwood and Sons, 1890. — Tr.

[2] Gerhardt reads: "discerner"; Erdmann and Jacques: "discuter," to discuss, debate, argue. — Tr.

understanding, and the will renders this idea as intelligible to us as the nature of body is rendered intelligible to us by solidity and impulse. This is how our author replies in his first letter (p. 65 *sq.*): "*I believe I have proved that there is a spiritual substance in us, for we experience in ourselves thought. Now this action or this mode cannot be the object of the idea of a thing subsisting by itself, and consequently this mode needs a support, a subject, in which it may inhere, and the idea of this support forms what we call substance. . . .* For since the general idea of substance is everywhere the same, *it follows that the modification, which is called thought or power of thinking, being joined to it, there results a mind without the necessity of considering what other modification it has besides; i.e. whether it has solidity or not. And, on the other hand, the substance which has the modification called solidity will be matter, whether thought is joined to it or not. But if by a spiritual substance you mean an immaterial substance, I admit that I have not proved that there is one in us, and that it cannot be demonstrably proved on my principles. Although what I have said on the systems of matter* (Book IV., chap. 10, § 16) *in proving that God is immaterial, renders it in the highest degree probable, that the substance which thinks in us is immaterial. . . . However, I have shown* [the author adds, p. 68] *that the great ends of religion and of morals are assured by the immortality of the soul, without the need of supposing its immateriality.*"[1]

The learned Bishop in his reply to this letter, in order to make it evident that our author held another view, when he wrote the second book of the Essay, quotes, p. 51, this passage (taken from the same book, chap. 23, § 15), where it is said, *that by the simple ideas which we have deduced from the operations of our mind, we can form the complex idea of a mind. And that putting together the ideas of thought, of perception, of liberty, and of power to move our body, we have as clear a notion of immaterial substances as of material.* He quotes still other passages to show that the author opposes mind to body. And he says (p. 54) that the ends of religion and of morals are the better

[1] I have retranslated the passage from the French version as given by Gerhardt. For the original, *cf.* Locke, *Philos. Works* (Bohn's ed.), Vol. II., p. 387. The entire letter is found in Locke's Works, Vol. I., pp. 458–517; this particular passage, p. 477. Edition of 4 vols., 4to. 7th ed., 1768. Printed for H. Woodfall, A. Millar, and others. — Tr.

assured by proving that the soul is immortal by its nature, *i.e.* immaterial. He quotes also (p. 70) this passage, *that the ideas we have of particular and distinct kinds of substances are nothing else than different combinations of simple ideas;*[1] and that thus the author believed that the idea of thinking and of willing gave another substance different from that which the idea of solidity and of impulse gives, and that (§ 17) he remarks that these ideas constitute the body as opposed to mind.

The Bishop of Worcester might add that from the fact that the *general idea* of substance is in the body and in the mind, it does not follow that their *differences* are *modifications* of one and the same thing, as our author has just said in the part of his first letter which I have quoted. It is necessary carefully to distinguish between modifications and attributes. The faculties of having perception and of acting, extension, solidity, are attributes or perpetual and principal predicates; but thought, impetuosity, figures, movements, are modifications of these attributes. Furthermore, we must distinguish between *physical* (or, rather, real) *genus* and *logical* or ideal *genus.* Things which are of the same physical genus, or which are *homogeneous,* are of the same *matter,* so to speak, and may often be changed the one into the other by the change of modification, as circles and squares. But two *heterogeneous* things may have a common logical genus, and then their *differences* are not simple accidental modifications of one and the same subject, or of one and the same metaphysical or physical matter. Thus time and space are very heterogeneous things, and we should do wrong to imagine I know not what real common subject which had only the continuous quantity in general, and whose modifications should cause the rise of time and space.[2] Some one will perhaps laugh at these distinctions of the philosophers of two genera, the one merely logical, the other real; and of two matters, the one physical, viz.: that of bodies, the other metaphysical only or general; as if some one said that two parts of space are of one and the same matter, or that two hours are likewise among themselves of one and

[1] Locke, *Philos. Works* (Bohn's ed.), Vol. 1, p. 426, chap. 23. § 6. — Tr.

[2] Erdmann and Jacques add: "Cependant leur genre logique commun est la quantité continuë," *i.e.* Nevertheless their common logical genus is the continuous quantity. — Tr.

the same matter. Nevertheless, these distinctions are not distinctions of terms merely, but of things themselves, and seem to come in here very opportunely, where their confusion has given rise to a false conclusion. These two genera have a common notion, and that of the real genus is common to the two matters, so that their genealogy will be as follows: —

Genus	*Logical* merely, varied by simple *differences*.	
	Real, whose *differences* are *modifications*, i.e. *Matter*.	*Metaphysical* only, where there is homogeneity.
		Physical, where there is a solid homogeneous mass.

I have not seen the second letter of the author to the Bishop, and the reply which this prelate makes to it scarcely touches the point relating to the thinking of matter. But the reply of our author to this second answer returns to it. *God* (says he, nearly in these words, p. 397) *adds to the essence of matter the qualities and perfections which please him, simple movement in some parts, but in plants, vegetation, and in animals, sentiency. Those who agree up to this point, cry out as soon as we go a step farther, and say that God can give to matter thought, reason, will, as if this destroyed the essence of matter. But to prove it, they allege that thought or reason is not included in the essence of matter, a point of no consequence, since movement and life are not included therein either. They assert, also, that we cannot conceive of matter as thinking; but our conception is not the measure of God's power.*[1] After this he cites the example of the attraction of matter (p. 99, but especially p. 408), where he speaks of the gravitation of matter towards matter, attributed to Mr. Newton (in the terms which I have quoted above), admitting that we can never conceive the manner of it. This is in reality to return to the occult, or, what is more, inexplicable qualities. He adds (p. 401) that nothing is more calculated to favor the sceptics than to deny what we do not understand; and (p. 402) that we do not conceive even how the soul thinks. He will have it (p. 403) that, since the two sub-

[1] For the original, *cf.* Locke, *Philos. Works* (Bohn's ed.), Vol. 2, pp. 390, 391. The entire letter is found in Locke's Works, Vol. 1, pp. 578–774; this particular passage, pp. 749, 750. Edition of 4 vols., 4to. 7th ed., 1768. Printed for H. Woodfall, A. Miller, and others. — Tr.

stances, material and immaterial, are capable of being conceived in their naked essence without any activity, it depends upon God to give to each the power of thought. And he wishes to take advantage of the admission of his opponent, who had granted sentiency to the brutes, but who would not grant them any immaterial substance. He claims that liberty, consciousness (p. 408), and the power of abstract thought (p. 409) can be bestowed upon matter, not as matter, but as enriched by a divine power. Finally, he quotes (p. 434) the remark of a traveller as eminent and judicious as M. de la Loubère,[1] that the pagans of the East acknowledge the immortality of the soul without being able to comprehend its immateriality.

On all this I would remark, before coming to the explanation of my view, that it is certain that matter is as little capable of mechanically producing feeling, as of producing reason, as our author admits; that in truth I acknowledge that it is not permissible to deny what we do not understand, but I add that we are right in denying (at least in the natural order) what is absolutely neither intelligible nor explicable. I maintain, also, that substances (material or immaterial) cannot be conceived in their naked essence without any activity; that activity belongs to the essence of substance in general; that, finally, the conception of creatures is not the measure of God's power, but that their conceptivity, or power of conception, is the measure of nature's power; all this is in harmony with the natural order, being capable of being conceived or understood by some creature.

Those who understand my system will think that I cannot wholly agree with the one or the other of these two excellent authors, whose discussion, however, is very instructive. But to explain myself distinctly, it is necessary before all things to consider that the modifications which may belong naturally or without miracle to a subject must come to it from the limitations or variations of a real genus, or of a constant and absolute original nature. For it is thus that Philosophers dis-

[1] La Loubère, Simon de, 1642–1729. Sent by Louis XIV. in 1687 to Siam, to establish diplomatic and commercial relations between that kingdom and France. While there he collected a large amount of exact and interesting information concerning the country, its history, customs, religion, etc., which, on his return, he published in his *Du royaume de Siam*, Paris, 1691; English translation, London, 1693. — Tr.

tinguish the modes of an absolute being from that being itself; as it is known that size, figure, and movement are manifestly limitations and variations of corporeal nature. For it is clear how a limited extension gives figures, and that the change which is made in it is nothing but motion. And whenever we find any quality in a subject, we must believe that if we understood the nature of this subject and of this quality, we should conceive how this quality can result therefrom. Thus in the order of nature (miracles aside) it is not optional with God to give to substances indifferently such or such qualities, and he will never give to them any, save those which will be natural to them, *i.e.* which can be derived from their nature as explicable modifications. Thus it may be asserted that matter will not naturally possess the attraction mentioned above, and will not proceed of itself in a curved line, because it is impossible to conceive how this takes place there, *i.e.* to explain it mechanically, while that which is natural must be capable of becoming distinctly conceivable if we were admitted into the secrets of things. This distinction between what is natural and explicable and what is inexplicable and miraculous removes all the difficulties, and by rejecting it, we should maintain something worse than the occult qualities; and in so doing would renounce philosophy and reason, by opening retreats for ignorance and idleness, though a dead system, which admits not only that there are qualities which we do not understand, of which there are only too many, but also that there are some which the greatest mind, if God gave him every possible opening, could not comprehend, *i.e.* which would be either miraculous or without rhyme and reason; and also that God should work miracles ordinarily would be without rhyme and reason, so that this hypothesis would destroy equally our philosophy which seeks reasons, and the divine wisdom which furnishes them.

Now as to thought, it is certain, and the author admits it more than once, that it could not be an intelligible modification of nature or one which could be comprised therein and explained, *i.e.* that a being who feels and thinks is not a mechanism like a watch or a mill, so that we might conceive sizes, figures, and movements, whose mechanical conjunction might produce something thinking, and even feeling in a mass in which there was nothing of the kind, which would cease also in the same manner upon the derangement of this mechanism. It is not then a natural thing for matter to feel and think, and this can happen within it only in two ways, of which one will be that God should unite with it a substance to which thought is natural, and the other that God by a miracle should put thought therein. In this, then, I am wholly of the opinion of the Cartesians, except that I extend it even to the brutes, and that I believe they have sentiency and (properly speaking) immaterial souls, and are as imperishable as the atoms of Democritus or Gassendi, while the Cartesians, perplexed without reason by the souls of brutes, and not knowing what they are to do with them if they are preserved (for want of having thought of the conservation of the same animal reduced to miniature), have been compelled to refuse even sentiency to the animals against all appearances and contrary to the judgment of the human race. But if any one should say that God at least may add the faculty of thinking to the prepared mechanism, I should reply that if this were done, and if God added this faculty to matter without putting therein at the same time a substance which was the subject of inhesion of this same faculty (as I conceive it), *i.e.* without adding thereto an immaterial soul, it would be necessary that matter should be miraculously exalted in order to receive a power of which it is naturally incapable; as some scholastics[1] claim that God exalts fire even to the point of giving it the force to burn immediately spirits separated from matter, a thing which would be a miracle, pure and simple. And it is enough that it cannot be maintained that matter thinks without putting into it an imperishable soul, or a miracle, and that thus the immortality of our souls follows from what is natural, since their extinction can be maintained only by a miracle, whether by exalting matter or by annihilating the soul. For we know well that God's power can make our souls mortal, wholly immaterial (or immortal by nature alone) as they may be, since he can annihilate them.

Now this truth of the immateriality of the soul is undoubt-

[1] Erdmann and Jacques read: "Quelques scholastiques ont prétendu quelque chose d'approchant savoir," *i.e.* Some scholastics have claimed something like this: viz. — TR.

edly of importance. For it is infinitely more advantageous to religion and morality, especially in our times (when many people hardly respect revelation alone and miracles [1]), to show that souls are immortal by nature, — and that it would be a miracle if they were not, — than to maintain that our souls ought naturally to die, but that it is in virtue of a miraculous grace grounded in the promise of God alone that they do not die. Also for a long time it has been known that those who have desired to destroy natural religion and to reduce all to revealed religion, as if reason taught us nothing regarding it, have been looked upon with suspicion; and not always without reason. But our author does not belong to that number. He maintains the demonstration of the existence of God, and he attributes to the immateriality of the soul a *probability in the highest degree*, which could consequently pass for a *moral certainty*, so that I think that, having as much sincerity as penetration, he could easily accommodate himself to the doctrine which I have just set forth, and which is fundamental in every rational philosophy. For otherwise I do not see how one can prevent himself from falling back into the *fanatical philosophy*,[2] such as the "Philosophia Mosaica" of Fludd,[3] which saves all phenomena by attributing them to God immediately and by miracle; or into the *barbaric* philosophy like that of certain philosophers and physicians of the past, which still manifested the barbarity of their age, and which to-day is with reason despised, who saved appearances by forging purposely occult qualities or faculties which they imagined to be like little demons or goblins capable of producing without ceremony what is demanded, just as if watches marked the hours by a certain horodeictic faculty without needing wheels, or as if mills ground the grain by a fractive faculty without needing anything resembling millstones. As to the difficulty that many people have had in conceiving an immaterial substance, it will easily cease (at least in good part) if they will not demand substances separated from matter, as in fact I do not believe there ever are any naturally among creatures.

[1] Erdmann and Jacques omit this clause. — Tr.

[2] Erdmann and Jacques read: "la philosophie ou fanatique," *i.e.* philosophy or fanaticism. — Tr.

[3] Robert Fludd (1574–1637), an English physician and mystical philosopher. The *Philosophia Mosaica* was published at Gouda in 1638. — Tr.

NEW ESSAYS ON HUMAN UNDERSTANDING

Book I. — Innate Ideas

CHAPTER I[1]

ARE THERE INNATE PRINCIPLES IN THE MIND OF MAN?

Philalethes. Having recrossed the sea after finishing my business in England, I thought at once of paying you a visit, sir, in order to cultivate our former friendship, and to converse upon matters which lie close to our hearts, and upon which I believe I have acquired some new light during my long stay in London. When we were living formerly quite near each other at Amsterdam, we both took much pleasure in making researches into the principles and means of penetrating into the heart of things. Although our opinions often differed, this diversity increased our satisfaction, when, in our conference together, notwithstanding the contrariety which sometimes existed, there mingled nothing disagreeable. You were for Descartes[2] and for the opinions of the celebrated author[2] of "The Search after Truth," and I found the opinions of Gassendi,[2] cleared up by Bernier, easier and more natural. Now I feel myself greatly strengthened by the excellent work which an illustrious Englishman, with whom I have the honor of a particular acquaintance, has since published, and which has several times been reprinted in England, under the modest

[1] Book I. of Locke's Essay has four chapters, of which chap. 1 is introductory. Chap. 1 of Leibnitz corresponds to chap. 2 of Locke. — Tr.

[2] René Descartes, 1596–1650; Nicolas Malebranche, 1638–1715, his chief work, *De la Recherche de la Vérité*, 1674; Pierre Gassendi, 1592–1655, *Abrégé de la Philosophie de Gassendi*, 8 vols., 1678, 2d ed., 7 vols., 1684, by François Bernier. — Tr.

title of "An Essay concerning Human Understanding." And I am delighted that it has appeared lately in Latin and in French, in order that it may be more generally useful. I have greatly profited by the reading of this work, and indeed from the conversation of the author, with whom I have talked often in London, and sometimes at Oates, at the house of my Lady Masham,[1] worthy daughter of the celebrated Cudworth,[2] a great English philosopher and theologian, author of the Intellectual System, from whom she has inherited the spirit of meditation and the love for good learning, which appeared particularly in the friendship which she kept up with the author of the Essay. And, as he had been attacked by some clever Doctors, I took pleasure in reading also the defence which a very wise and very intelligent young lady made for him, besides those which he made for himself. This author writes in the spirit of the system of Gassendi, which is at bottom that of Democritus;[2] he is for the vacuum and for atoms; he believes that matter might think; that there are no innate ideas, that our mind is a *tabula rasa,* and that we do not always think; and he appears disposed to approve the most of the objections which Gassendi has made[3] to Descartes. He has enriched and strengthened this system by a thousand beautiful reflections; and I do not at all doubt that now our party will triumph boldly over its adversaries, the Peripatetics and the Cartesians. This is why, if you have not yet read this book, I invite you to do so, and if you have read it, I ask you to give me your opinion of it.

Theophilus. I rejoice to see you, on your return after a long absence, happy in the conclusion of your important business, full of health, steadfast in your friendship for me, and always transported with an ardor equal to the search for the most

[1] The correspondence between Leibnitz and Lady Masham is given in full by Gerhardt, Vol. 3, pp. 331 *sq.* — TR.

[2] Ralph Cudworth, 1617–1688, his principal work, *The True Intellectual System of the Universe,* London, 1678; Democritus, born probably about the middle of the fifth century B.C., as he says (Diog. L., IX., 41) he was "still young when Anaxagoras," 500–428 B.C., "was already old (νέος κατὰ πρεσβύτην Ἀναξαγόραν)." . . . "The year of his death is unknown," Zeller, *Outlines of the History of Greek Philosophy,* pp. 76, 77, New York: H. Holt & Co., 1886. — TR.

[3] In Vol. 3 of his *Opera,* of which two editions were published: by Montmort, 1655, 6 vols. folio, Lyons; by Averanius, 1727, also 6 vols. folio. — TR.

important truths. I no less have continued my meditations in the same spirit, and I believe I have profited as much as, and, not to flatter myself, perhaps more than yourself. Indeed, my need therein was greater than yours, for you were more advanced than I. You were more conversant with speculative philosophers, and I was more inclined towards ethics. But I have learned more and more how ethics receives strength from the solid principles of true philosophy; therefore I have lately studied these principles more diligently, and have begun meditations quite new. So that we shall have the means of giving ourselves a reciprocal pleasure of long duration in communicating the one to the other our solutions. But it is necessary for me to tell you, as a piece of news, that I am no longer a Cartesian, and that, nevertheless, I am farther removed than ever from your Gassendi, whose knowledge and merit I, for the rest, recognize. I have been impressed with a new system, of which I have read something in the "Journaux des Savans" of Paris, Leipzig, and Holland, and in the marvellous Dictionary of Bayle, article "Rorarius"[1]; and since then I believe I see a new aspect of the interior of things. This system appears to unite Plato[2] and Democritus, Aristotle[2] and Descartes, the scholastics with the moderns, theology and ethics with the reason. It seems to take the best from all sides, and then it goes much farther than any has yet gone. I find in it an intelligible explanation of the union of soul and body, of which I had before this despaired. I find the true principles of things in the Unities of Substance, which this system introduces, and in their harmony pre-established by the primitive Substance. I find therein a wonderful simplicity and uniformity, so that it may be said that this substance is everywhere and always the same thing, differing only in degrees of perfection. I see now what Plato meant when he assumed matter to be an existence imperfect and transitory; what Aristotle meant by his Entelechy; what that promise of another life is which Democritus himself made according to Pliny; how far the Sceptics were right in declaiming against the senses; how animals are in fact automata

[1] *Cf.* Gerhardt, Vol. 4, pp. 524–554, the article "Rorarius" with Leibnitz's remarks. — TR.

[2] Plato, 427–347 B.C.; Aristotle, 384–322 B.C. — TR.

according to Descartes, and how they have, nevertheless, souls and feeling according to the opinion of mankind; how it is necessary to explain rationally those who have lodged life and perception in all things, as Cardan,[1] Campanella,[1] and, better than they, the late Countess of Connaway, a Platonist, and our friend, the late M. François Mercure van Helmont[2] (although elsewhere bristling with unintelligible paradoxes), with his friend, the late Mr. Henry More.[2] How the laws of nature (a good part of which were unknown before this system) have their origin in principles superior to matter, and how, nevertheless, everything takes place mechanically in matter, in which respect the spiritualizing authors I just named have failed with their Archæi,[3] and even the Cartesians, in believ-

[1] Girolamo Cardano, 1501–1576; Tommaso Campanella, 1568–1639; *cf.* Erdmann, *Grundriss d. Gesch. d. Philos.*, 3d ed., Vol. 1, §§ 242, 246, Berlin: Wilhelm Hertz, 1878, and the English translation of the same, London: Swan Sonnenschein & Co., 1889; also the articles "Cardan" and "Campanella" in the *Encyclopædia Britannica*, 9th ed. — TR.

[2] Van Helmont, 1618–1698: Henry More, 1614–1687. — TR.

[3] *Archæus*, *i*. Modern Latin, from the Greek ἀρχαῖος, ἀρχή, that which is at the beginning, source, origin, a first principle. Littré defines the term thus: "Archée. Terme de physiologie ancienne. Principe immatérial différent de l'âme intelligent et qu'on supposait présider à tous les phénomènes de la vie matérielle." *I.e.* "A term of ancient physiology. An immaterial principle different from the intelligent soul, and which is supposed to preside over all the phenomena of the material life." *The Century Dictionary* gives the following exposition and illustration: "In the philosophy of Paracelsus and other spagyrics, mystics, and theosophists, a spirit or invisible man or animal of ethereal substance, the counterpart of the visible body, within which it resides, and to which it imparts life, strength, and the power of assimilating food. The word is said to have been used by Basil Valentine, a German chemist of the fifteenth century, to denote the solar heat as the source of the life of plants. Paracelsus uses it with the above meaning. It is frequent in the writings of Van Helmont, who explains it as a material pre-existence of the human or animal form *in posse*. He regards the archæus as a fluid, *i.e.* as a semi-material substance like air, and seems to consider it a chemical constituent of the blood. Paracelsus has particularly made use of the hypothesis of the archæus to explain the assimilation of food. This function of the archæus became prominent in medicine. Van Helmont calls it the doorkeeper of the stomach (*janitor stomachi*). There are further divarications of meaning. Also spelled Archeus."

"As for the many pretended intricacies in the instance of the efformation of Wasps out of the Carcase of a Horse, I say, the *Archei* that formed them are no parts of the Horse's Soul that is dead, but several distinct *Archei* that do as naturally joyn with the matter of his body, so putrified and prepared, as the Crowes come to eat his flesh." — Dr. H. MORE, *Antidote against Atheism*, app. xi.

Cf. Leibnitz: *Considérations sur le Principe de Vie et sur les Natures Plas-*

ing that immaterial substances altered if not the force, at least the direction or determination, of the motions of bodies, whereas the soul and the body retain perfectly each its own laws, according to the new system, and yet one obeys the other as much as is necessary. In fine, it is since I have meditated upon this system that I have found out how the souls of beasts and their sensations are in no sense prejudicial to the immortality of human souls, or, rather, how nothing is more suited to establish our natural immortality than to conceive that all souls are imperishable (*morte carent animæ*), without, however, the fear of metempsychoses, since not only the souls, but further, the animals endure and will endure living, feeling, acting; it is everywhere as here, and always and everywhere as with us, according to what I have already said to you, except that the conditions of animals are more or less perfect and developed, without there ever being a need of souls wholly separate, while we nevertheless have always spirits as pure as possible, notwithstanding our (physical) organs, which cannot disturb by any influence the laws of our (spiritual) spontaneity. I find the vacuum and atoms excluded in quite another way than by the sophism of the Cartesians, grounded in the pretended coincidence of the idea of body and extension. I see all things determined and adorned beyond anything hitherto conceived; matter everywhere organic, no sterile, neglected vacuum, nothing too uniform, everything varied, but with order; and, what passes imagination, the entire universe in epitome, but with a different aspect in each of its parts, and likewise in each of its unities of substance. Besides this new analysis of things, I have a better comprehension of that of notions or ideas, and of truths. I understand what a true, clear, distinct, adequate idea is, if I dare adopt this word. I understand what are primitive truths, and true axioms, the distinction between necessary truths and

tiques par l'Auteur de l'Harmonie Préétablie, published in the "Histoire des Ouvrages des Savans," May, 1705, Gerhardt, Vol. 6, pp. 539–546; Erdmann, pp. 429–432; translation, Duncan, *Philos. Works of Leibnitz*, pp. 163–169. See also Erdmann, *Grundriss d. Gesch. d. Philos.* 3d ed., Vol. 1, § 241, 7, Vol. 2, § 290, 12, or the English translation of the same. Slight additional information may be found in the *Encyclopædia Britannica*, 9th ed., under the article, "Medicine," in the part giving an account of Paracelsus and Van Helmont. — TR.

truths of fact, between the reasoning of men and the consecutions of animals, which are a shadow of the reasoning of men. In short, you will be surprised to hear all that I have to say to you, and, above all, to understand how much the knowledge of the grandeur and of the perfection of God is therein exalted. For I cannot conceal from you, from whom I have had nothing concealed, how I have been thrilled now with admiration and (if we may dare to make use of the term) with love for this sovereign source of things and of beauty, having found that what this system discovers surpasses everything one has hitherto conceived. You know that I had gone a little too far formerly, and that I began to lean toward the side of the Spinozists,[1] who allow God only infinite power, without recognizing either perfection or wisdom in his case, and regarding with contempt the search for final causes, derive everything from brute necessity. But these new lights have cured me of this; and since then I sometimes take the name of *Theophilus*. I have read the book of this celebrated Englishman of whom you have just spoken. I value it highly, and I have found in it some good things. But it seems to me necessary to go much farther, and necessary even to turn aside from his views, since he has adopted some which limit us more than is necessary, and lower a little not only the condition of man, but, besides, that of the universe.

Ph. You astonish me in fact with all the marvels which you have recited to me in a manner a little too favorable for an easy credence of them on my part. However, I will hope that there will be something solid among so many novelties with which you desire to regale me. In this case you will find me very docile. You know that it was always my disposition to surrender myself to reason, and that I sometimes took the name of *Philalethes*. This is why, if you please, we will now make use of these two names which are so congruous with our mental constitution and methods. There are means of proceeding to the trial, for — since you have read the book of the

[1] On the relation of Leibnitz to Spinoza, see *Leibniz u. Spinoza*. Ein Beitrag zur Entwicklungsgeschichte der Leibnizischen Philosophie. Von Prof. Dr. Ludwig Stein. Mit neunzehn Ineditis aus dem Nachlass von Leibniz. Berlin: G. Reimer, 1890. pp. xvii., 362. Also "Mind," No. 62, p. 298; No. 63, pp. 443 *sq.*, the latter an extended note on Stein's book by Prof. George Croom Robertson, the late editor of "Mind." — Tr.

celebrated Englishman, which gives me so much satisfaction and which treats a good part of the subjects of which you were just speaking, and above all, the analysis of our ideas and knowledge — it will be the shortest way to follow the thread of this work, and to see what you will have to say.

Th. I approve your proposition. Here is the book.

§ 1. *Ph.* [I have read this book so thoroughly that I have retained even its expressions, which I shall be careful to follow. Thus I shall not need to recur to the book, except at certain junctures where we shall judge it necessary. We shall speak first of the origin of ideas or notions (Book I.), then of the different kinds of ideas (Book II.), and of the words that serve to express them (Book III.), lastly of the knowledge and truths which therefrom result (Book IV.); and it is this last part which will occupy us the most. As for the origin of ideas, I believe, with this author and a multitude of clever persons, that there are no innate ideas nor innate principles.] And, in order to refute the error of those who admit them, it is sufficient to show, as it appears eventually, that there is no need of them, and that men can acquire all their knowledge without the aid of any innate impression.

Th. [You know, Philalethes, that I have been for a long time of another opinion; that I have always held, as I still hold, to the innate idea of God, which Descartes maintained, and as a consequence to the other innate ideas, which cannot come to us from the senses. Now, I go still farther in conformity to the new system, and I believe even that all the thoughts and acts of our soul come from its own depths, with no possibility of their being given to it by the senses, as you shall see in the sequel. But at present I will put this investigation aside, and, accommodating myself to the received expressions, since in fact they are good and tenable, and one can say in a certain sense that the external senses are in part causes of our thoughts, I shall consider how in my opinion one must say even in the common system (speaking of the action of bodies upon the soul, as the Copernicans speak with other men of the movement of the sun, and with cause), that there are some ideas and some principles which do not come to us from the senses, and which we find in ourselves without forming them, although the senses give us occasion to perceive them.

I imagine that your clever author has remarked that under the name of innate principles one often maintains his prejudices, and wishes to free himself from the trouble of discussion, and that this abuse doubtless has stirred up his zeal against this supposition. He desired, no doubt, to combat the indolence and the superficial manner of thinking of those who, under the specious pretext of innate ideas and of truths naturally engraved upon the mind, to which we readily give our consent, care nothing about investigating or considering the sources, the relations, and the certainty of this knowledge. In that I am entirely agreed with him, and I go even farther. I would that our analysis should not be limited, that definitions should be given of all the terms which are capable of definition, and that one should demonstrate, or give the means of demonstrating, all the axioms which are not primitive, without distinguishing the opinions which men have of them, and without caring whether they give their consent or not. There would be more profit in this than one thinks. But it seems that the author has been carried too far on the other side by his zeal, otherwise very praiseworthy. He has not sufficiently distinguished, in my opinion, the origin of the necessary truths, whose source is in the understanding, from that of the truths of fact drawn from the experience of the senses, and even from those confused perceptions which are in us. You see, then, that I do not agree with what you lay down as fact — that we can acquire all our knowledge without the need of innate impressions. And the sequel will show which of us is right.]

§ 2. *Ph.* We shall see it indeed. I grant you, my dear Theophilus, that there is no opinion more commonly received than that which establishes the existence of certain principles of truth in which men generally agree; this is why they are called *general notions*, κοιναὶ ἔννοιαι; whence it is inferred that these principles must be so many impressions which our minds receive with their existence. § 3. But though it were certain that there are some principles in which the entire human race is agreed, this universal consent would not prove that they are innate if one can show, as I believe he can, another way through which men have been able to reach this uniformity of opinion. § 4. But, what is much worse, this universal consent is nowhere found, not even with regard to these two celebrated *speculative principles* (for we shall speak about the *practical* ones later), that *whatever is, is;* and that *it is impossible for a thing to be and not to be at the same time.* For there is a large part of the human race to which these two propositions, which will pass doubtless for *necessary truths* and for axioms with you, are not even known.

Th. [I do not ground the certainty of innate principles upon universal consent, for I have already told you, Philalethes, that my opinion is that we ought to labor to be able to demonstrate all the axioms which are not primitive. I grant you also that a consent very general, but which is not universal, may come from a tradition diffused throughout the human race, as the practice of smoking tobacco has been received by nearly all nations in less than a century, although some islanders have been found who, not being acquainted with fire even, were unable to smoke. Thus some clever people, even among theologians, but of the party of Arminius,[1] have believed that the knowledge of the Deity came from a very ancient and very general tradition; and I believe indeed that instruction has confirmed and rectified this knowledge. It appears, however, that nature has contributed to its attainment without learning; the marvels of the universe have made us think of a superior power. A child born deaf and dumb has been seen to show veneration for the full moon, and nations have been found, who seemed not to have learned anything of other peoples, fearing invisible powers. I grant you, my dear Philalethes, that this is not yet the idea of God that we have and ask for; but this idea itself does not cease to be in the depths of our souls, without being put there, as we shall see, and the eternal laws of God are in part engraved thereon in a manner still more legible and by a species of instinct. But they are practical principles of which we shall also have occasion to speak. It must be admitted, however, that the inclination we have to recognize the idea of God is in human nature. And, even if the first instruction therein should be attributed to revelation, the readiness which men have always shown to receive this doctrine comes from the nature of their souls.[2] But we will

[1] James Arminius, 1560–1609, a distinguished Dutch theologian. — Tr.
[2] From this point on Gerhardt, whose edition, it will be remembered, is the

suppose that these ideas which are innate comprehend incompatible notions.

§ 19. *Ph.* Although you maintain that these particular and self-evident propositions, whose truth is recognized as soon as one hears them stated (as that green is not red), are received as consequences of these other more general propositions, which are regarded as so many innate principles, it seems that you do not at all consider that these particular propositions are received as indubitable truths by those who have no knowledge of these more general maxims.

Th. I have already replied to that above. We build on these general maxims as we build upon the majors, which are suppressed when we reason by enthymemes; for, although very often we do not think distinctly of what we do in reasoning any more than of what we do in walking and leaping, it is always true that the force of the conclusion consists in part in that which is suppressed and could not elsewhere arise, as you will find should you wish to prove it.

§ 20. *Ph.* But it seems that general and abstract ideas are more foreign to our mind [than notions and particular truths; consequently particular truths will be more natural to the mind than the principle of contradiction, of which you admit they are only the application].

Th. It is true that we commence sooner to perceive particu-

basis of the present translation, transposes the text as given by Erdmann and Jacques as follows: "Mais nous jugerons que ces idées qui sont innées, renferment des notions incompatibles," the first three words of which will be found in Erdmann, p. 207, b., about two-thirds down the page, Jacques, Vol. 1, p. 29, about two-thirds down, the remainder in Erdmann, p. 211, a., at the middle of the page, Jacques, p. 36, first third, just preceding § 19 in each case, whence the three texts go on in agreement until § 26, G., p. 72, E., p. 212, b., J., p. 39. Here the Gerhardt text has the following: "S'il y a des verités innées, ne faut il pas qu'il y ait dans la suite, que la doctrine externe ne fait qu'exciter icy ce que est en nous": taking up with the words "dans la suite," the text as given by E., p. 207, b., J., p. 29, where it previously left it, the three texts continuing again in agreement until the words "dès qu'on s'apperçoit," G., p. 79, last third, E., 211, a., at the middle, J., 36, first third, whence G. completes his sentence with the last three words of the first sentence of § 26, as given by E., 212, b., J., 39, from which point again the three texts substantially agree to the end of Chap. 1. It may be added that the texts of Erdmann, Jacques, and Janet follow the order of Locke's Essay. Why Gerhardt has transposed the text in his edition, I do not know, as he has not alluded to the matter. From his statement that "the present impression has been newly compared with the original, so far as it is still extant" (Introduction, p. 10), I presume that the transposition is due to his fidelity to this original. — TR.

lar truths when we commence with ideas more complex and gross; but that does not prevent the order of nature from commencing with the most simple, and the proof of the more particular truths from depending upon the more general, of which they are only examples. And when we wish to consider what is in us virtually and before all *apperception*, we are right in commencing with the most simple. For the general principles enter into our thoughts, of which they form the soul and the connection. They are as necessary thereto as the muscles and sinews are for walking, although we do not at all think of them. The mind leans upon these principles every moment, but it does not come so easily to distinguish them and to represent them distinctly and separately, because that demands great attention to its acts, and the majority of people, little accustomed to think, has little of it. Have not the Chinese like ourselves articulate sounds? and yet being attached to another manner of writing, they have not yet thought of making an alphabet of these sounds. Thus it is that one possesses many things without knowing it.

§ 21. *Ph.* If the mind acquiesces so promptly in certain truths, cannot that acquiescence come from the consideration itself of the nature of things, which does not allow it to judge of them otherwise, rather than from the consideration that these propositions are engraved by nature in the mind?

Th. Both are true. The nature of things and the nature of mind agree. And since you oppose the consideration of the thing to the apperception of that which is engraven in the mind, this objection itself shows, sir, that those whose side you take understand by *innate truths* only those which would be approved naturally as *by instinct*, and even without knowing it, unless confusedly. There are some of this nature, and we shall have occasion to speak of them. But what is called *natural light* supposes a distinct knowledge, and very often the consideration of the nature of things is nothing else than the knowledge of the nature of our mind, and of these innate ideas which we have no need to seek outside. Thus I call innate the truths which need only this consideration for their verification. I have already replied (§ 5) to the objection (§ 22) which claimed that when it is said that innate notions are implicitly in the mind, the statement must mean simply that it has the faculty of knowing them; for I have pointed out that besides this it has the faculty of finding them in itself, and the disposition to approve them when it thinks of them as it should.

§ 23. *Ph.* It seems, then, that you claim that those to whom these general maxims are proposed for the first time learn nothing which is entirely new to them. But it is clear that they learn first the names, then the truths, and even the ideas upon which these truths rest.

Th. The question here is not of names, which are in some sense arbitrary, while ideas and truths are natural. But, with respect to these ideas and truths, you attribute to us, sir, a doctrine which we have strongly repudiated; for I agree that we learn ideas and innate truths either in considering their source, or in verifying them through experience. Thus I do not make the supposition which you aver, as if, in the case of which you speak, we learned nothing new. And I cannot admit this proposition: *all that one learns is not innate.* The truths of numbers are in us, and we are not left to learn them, either by drawing them from their source when we learn them through demonstrative proof (which shows that they are innate), or by testing them in examples, as do ordinary arithmeticians, who, in default of a knowledge of the proofs, learn their rules only by tradition, and, at most, before teaching them, justify them by experience, which they continue as far as they think expedient. And sometimes even a very skilful mathematician, not knowing the source of another's discovery, is obliged to content himself with this method of induction in examining it; as did a celebrated writer at Paris, when I was there, who continued a tolerably long time the examination of my arithmetical tetragonism, comparing it with the numbers of Ludolphe,[1] believing he had found therein some error; and he had reason to doubt until some one communicated to him the demonstration, which for us dispenses with these tests, which could always continue without ever being perfectly certain. And it is this very thing, namely, the imperfection of inductions, which may yet be verified by instances of experience. For there are progressions in which one can go very

[1] John Job Ludolphe, 1649–1711: his *Tetragonometria Tabularia*, Frankfort, 1690. — TR.

far before noticing the changes and the laws that are found there.

Ph. But is it not possible that not only the terms or words which we use, but even the ideas, come to us from without?

Th. It would then be necessary that we should be ourselves outside of ourselves, for the intellectual or reflective ideas are derived from our mind; and I should much like to know how we could have the idea of being if we were not beings ourselves, and did not thus find being in ourselves.

Ph. But what do you say, sir, to this challenge of one of my friends? If any one, says he, can find a proposition whose ideas are innate, that he can name to me, he would do me a very great favor.

Th. I would name the propositions of arithmetic and geometry, which are all of this nature; and, as regards necessary truths, no others could be found.

§ 25. *Ph.* That will appear strange to most people. Can it be said that the most difficult and the most profound sciences are innate?

Th. Their actual knowledge is not, but much that may be called virtual knowledge is innate, as the figure traced by the veins of the marble is in the marble, before one discovers them in working.

Ph. But is it possible that children, while receiving notions that come to them from without, and giving them their consent, may have no knowledge of those which you suppose to be inborn with them, and to make, as it were, a part of their mind, in which they are, you say, imprinted in ineffaceable characters in order to serve as a foundation? If that were so, nature would have taken trouble for nothing, or, at least, she would have badly engraved their characters, since they cannot be perceived by the eyes which see very well other things.

Th. The apperception of that which is in us depends upon attention and order. Now, not only is it possible, but it is also proper, that children give more attention to the ideas of the senses, because the attention is regulated by the need. The outcome, however, shows in the sequel that nature has not uselessly given herself the trouble of impressing upon us innate knowledge, since without it there would be no means of attaining actual knowledge of the truths necessary in the demonstrative sciences, and the reasons of facts; and we should possess nothing above the beasts.

§ 26. *Ph.* If there are innate truths, does it not necessarily follow that the external doctrine only stirs up here what is in us? I conclude that a consent sufficiently general among men is an indication, and not a demonstration, of an innate principle; but that the exact and decisive proof of these principles consists in showing that their certitude comes only from what is in us. To reply further to what you say against the general approbation which is given to the two great speculative principles, which are, nevertheless, the best established, I may say to you that even if they were not known they would not cease to be innate, because they are recognized as soon as heard; but I will add further that at bottom everybody knows them, and makes use at every moment of the principle of contradiction (for example) without considering it distinctly; and there is no barbarian who, in an affair of any moment, is not offended by the conduct of a liar who contradicts himself. Thus, these maxims are employed without an express consideration of them. And in nearly the same way we have virtually in the mind the propositions suppressed in enthymemes, which are set aside not only externally, but further in our thought.

§ 5. *Ph.* [What you say of this virtual knowledge and of these internal suppressions surprises me]; for to say that there are truths imprinted upon the soul which it does not perceive is, it seems to me, a veritable contradiction.

Th. [If you are thus prejudiced, I am not astonished that you reject innate knowledge. But I am astonished that the thought has not occurred to you that we have an infinite amount of knowledge of which we are not always conscious, not even when we need it. It is for the memory to preserve this, and for the reminiscence to represent it to us, as it often, but not always, does at need. That is very well called remembrance (*subvenire*), for reminiscence needs some aid. And it must certainly be that in this multiplicity of our knowledge we are determined by something to renew one part rather than another, since it is impossible to think distinctly and at once of everything we know.]

Ph. In that I believe you are right; and this too general

affirmation, that we always perceive all the truths which are in our soul, escaped me without my having given it sufficient attention. But you will have a little more trouble in replying to what I am going to show you. That is, that if you can say of some particular proposition that it is innate, you could maintain by the same reasoning that all propositions which are reasonable, and which the mind could always regard as such, are already impressed upon the soul.

Th. I agree with you in regard to pure ideas, which I oppose to the phantoms of the senses, and in regard to necessary truths, or those of the reason, which I oppose to truths of fact. In this sense it must be said that all arithmetic and all geometry are innate, and are in us virtually, so that we can find them there if we consider attentively and set in order what we already have in the mind, without making use of any truth learned through experience or through the tradition of another, as Plato has shown in a dialogue[1] in which he introduces Socrates leading a child to abstract truths by questions alone without giving him any information. We can then make for ourselves these sciences in our study, and even with closed eyes, without learning through sight or even through touch the truths which we need; although it is true that we would not consider the ideas in question if we had never seen or touched anything. For through an admirable economy of nature we cannot have abstract thoughts which have no need whatever of anything sensible, when that would only be of such a character as are the forms of the letters and the sounds, although there is no necessary connection between such arbitrary characters and such thoughts. And if the sensible outlines were not requisite, the pre-established harmony between soul and body, of which I shall have occasion to speak more fully, would have no place. But that does not prevent the mind from taking necessary ideas from itself. You see also sometimes how it can go far without any aid, by a logic and arithmetic purely natural, as that Swedish youth who, in cultivating his own (mind), went so far as to make great calculations immediately in his head without having learned the common method of computation, or even to read and write, if I remember correctly what has been told me of him. It is

[1] *Meno*, 82 *sq.* — TR.

true that he cannot work out intricate problems, such as those which demand the extraction of roots. But that does not at all prevent him from being able still to draw them from its depths by some new turn of mind. Thus that proves only that there are degrees in the difficulty of perceiving what is in us. There are innate principles which are common and very easy to all; there are theorems which are discovered likewise at once, and which compose the natural sciences, which are more understood in one case than in another. Finally, in a larger sense, which it is well to employ in order to have notions more comprehensive and more determinate, all truths which can be drawn from primitive innate knowledge can still be called innate, because the mind can draw them from its own depths, although often it would not be an easy thing so to do. But, if any one gives another meaning to the terms, I do not wish to dispute about words.

Ph. [I have agreed with you that we can have in the soul what we do not perceive there, for we do not always remember at once all that we know, but it must be always what we have learned or have known in former times expressly. Thus] if we can say that a thing is in the soul, although the soul has not yet known it, this can only be because it has the capacity or faculty of knowing it.

Th. [Why could not this have still another cause, such as the soul's being able to have this thing within it without its being perceived? for since an acquired knowledge can be concealed therein by the memory, as you admit, why could not nature have also concealed therein some original knowledge? Must everything that is natural to a substance which knows itself be known by it actually at once? Cannot and must not this substance (such as our soul) have many properties and affections which it is impossible to consider all at once and all together? It was the opinion of the Platonists that all our knowledge was reminiscence, and that thus the truths which the soul has brought with the birth of the man, and which are called innate, must be the remains of an express anterior knowledge. But this opinion has no foundation; and it is easy to believe that the soul must already have innate knowledge in the precedent state (if there were any pre-existence), however remote it might be, entirely as here: it would then have to come also from another precedent state, or[1] it would be finally innate, or at least concreate; or else it would be needful to go to infinity and to make souls eternal, in which case this knowledge would be innate in fact, because it would never have commenced in the soul; and if any one claimed that each anterior state has had something from another more anterior, which it has not left to the succeeding, the reply will be made that it is manifest that certain evident truths must have been in all these states; and in whatever manner it may be taken, it is always clear in all states of the soul that necessary truths are innate, and are proved by what is within, it not being possible to establish them through experience, as we establish truths of fact. Why should it be necessary also that we could have no possession in the soul of which we had never made use? And is it the same thing to have a thing without using it as to have only the faculty of acquiring it? If that were so, we should never possess anything but the things which we enjoy; instead of which, we know that, besides the faculty and the object, some disposition in the faculty or in the object, or in both, is often necessary, that the faculty may exercise itself upon the object.]

Ph. Taking it in that way, we could say that there are truths written in the soul which the soul has, however, never known, and which, indeed, it will never know. This appears to me strange.

Th. [I see there no absurdity, although in that case you could not be assured that there are such truths. For things more exalted than those which we can know in this present course of life may be developed some time in our souls, when they are in another state.]

Ph. But suppose there are truths which could be imprinted upon the understanding without its perceiving them; I do not see how, in relation to their origin, they could differ from the truths which it is only capable of knowing.

Th. The mind is not only capable of knowing them, but further of finding them in itself; and, if it had only the simple capacity of receiving knowledge, or the passive power therefor, as indeterminate as that which the wax has for receiving figures and the blank tablet for receiving letters, it would not

[1] The reading of Gerhardt and Erdmann; Jacques has "où," where. — Tr.

be the source of necessary truths, as I have just shown that it is; for it is incontestable that the senses do not suffice to show their necessity, and that thus the mind has a disposition (active as well as passive) to draw them itself from its own depths; although the senses are necessary to give it the occasion and attention for this, and to carry it to some rather than to others. You see, then, sir, that these elsewhere very clever persons who are of another opinion appear not to have thought enough upon the consequences of the difference which there is between necessary or eternal truths and the truths of experience, as I have already observed, and as all our discussion shows. The original proof of the necessary truths comes from the understanding alone, and the other truths come from experience or from the observation of the senses. Our mind is capable of knowing both; but it is the source of the former, and, whatever number of particular experiences we may have of a universal truth, we could not be assured of it forever by induction without knowing its necessity through the reason.

Ph. But is it not true that if the words, *to be in the understanding*, involve something positive, they signify to be perceived and comprehended by the understanding?

Th. They signify to us wholly another thing. It is enough that what is in the understanding can be found there, and that the sources or original proofs of the truths which are in question are only in the understanding; the senses can hint at, justify, and confirm these truths, but cannot demonstrate their infallible and perpetual certainty.

§ 11. *Ph.* Nevertheless, all those who will take the trouble to reflect with a little attention upon the operations of the understanding will find that this consent, which the mind gives *without difficulty* to certain truths, depends upon the faculty of the human mind.

Th. Very well. But it is this particular relation of the human mind to these truths which renders the exercise of the faculty easy and natural in respect to them, and which causes them to be called innate. It is not, then, a naked faculty which consists in the mere possibility of understanding them; it is a disposition, an aptitude, a preformation, which determines our soul and which makes it possible for them to be derived from it. Just as there is the difference between the figures which are given to the stone or the marble indifferently, and between those which its veins already indicate, or are disposed to indicate, if the workman profits by them.

Ph. But is it not true that the truths are subsequent to the ideas of which they are born? Now, the ideas come from the senses.

Th. The intellectual ideas, which are the source of necessary truths, do not come from the senses; and you admit that there are some ideas which are due to the reflection of the mind upon itself. For the rest, it is true that the express knowledge of truths is subsequent (*tempore vel natura*) to the express knowledge of ideas; as the nature of truths depends upon the nature of ideas, before we expressly form one or the other, and the truths, into which enter ideas which come from the senses, depend upon the senses, at least in part. But the ideas which come from the senses are confused, and the truths which depend upon them are likewise confused, at least in part; while the intellectual ideas, and the truths dependent upon them, are distinct, and neither the one nor the other have their origin in the senses, although it may be true that we would never think of them without the senses.

Ph. But, in your view, numbers are intellectual ideas, and yet it is found that the difficulty therein depends upon the express formation of the ideas; for example, a man knows that 18 and 19 equal 37 with the same evidence that he knows that 1 and 2 equal 3; but a child does not know the first proposition so soon as the second, a condition arising from the fact that he has not formed the ideas as soon as the words.

Th. I can agree with you that often the difficulty in the express formation of truths depends upon that in the express formation of ideas. Yet I believe that in your example the question concerns the use of ideas already formed. For those who have learned to count as far as 10, and the method of passing farther on by a certain repetition of tens, understand without difficulty what are 18, 19, 37; viz., 1, 2, or 3 times 10 with 8, or 9, or 7; but, in order to draw from it that 18 plus 19 make 37, more attention is necessary than to know that 2 plus 1 are 3, which at bottom is only the definition of 3.

§ 18. *Ph.* Furnishing propositions in which you infallibly acquiesce as soon as you hear them is not a privilege attached to the numbers or to the ideas, which you call intellectual. You meet these in physics and in all the other sciences, and the senses even furnish them. For example, this proposition: *two bodies cannot be in the same place at the same time,* is a truth of which you are not otherwise convinced than of the following maxims: *It is impossible for a thing to be and not to be in the same time;* white is not red; *the square is not a circle;* yellowness is not sweetness.

Th. There is a difference between these propositions. The first, which declares the impenetrability of bodies, needs proof. All those who believe in true and strictly formed condensation and rarefaction, as the Peripatetics and the late Chevalier Digby,[1] reject it, in fact; without speaking of the Christians who believe, for the most part, that the contrary view — namely, the penetration of space — is possible to God. But the other propositions are *identical,* or very nearly so, and identical or immediate propositions do not admit of proof. Those who look upon the senses as furnishing them, as that one who says that yellowness is not sweetness, have not applied the general identical maxim to particular cases.

Ph. Every proposition composed of two different ideas, of which one is the denial of the other — for example, that the square is not a circle, that to be yellow is not to be sweet — will be as certainly received as indubitable, as soon as its terms are understood, as *this general maxim:* It is impossible for a thing to be and not to be in the same time.

Th. That is, the one (namely, the general maxim) is the principle, and the other (that is to say, the negation of one idea by another opposed to it) is its application.

Ph. It seems to me rather that the maxim depends upon this negation, which is its ground; and that it is, besides, much easier to understand that *what is the same thing is not different,* than the maxim which rejects the contradictions. Now, according to this statement, it will be necessary for you to admit as innate truths an infinite number of propositions of this kind which deny one idea by another without speaking

[1] Sir Kenelm Digby, 1603–1665, an eminent English physical philosopher, who lived for a time in France, where he enjoyed the friendship of Descartes and other learned men, and wrote his *Treatise on the Nature of Bodies* and other works. — Tr.

of other truths. Add to this, that a proposition cannot be innate unless the ideas of which it is composed are innate; it will be necessary to suppose that all the ideas which we have of colors, sounds, tastes, figures, etc., are innate.

Th. I do not well see how this: *what is the same thing is not different,* is the origin of the principle of contradiction, and easier; for it appears to me that you give yourself more freedom in advancing that A is not B than in saying that A is not non-A. And the reason that prevents A from being B is that B includes non-A. For the rest this proposition: *the sweet is not the bitter,* is not innate, according to the sense which we have given to the term innate truth. For the sensations of sweet and bitter come from the external senses. Thus it is a mixed conclusion (*hybrida conclusio*), where the axiom is applied to a sensible truth. But as regards this proposition: *the square is not a circle,* you can affirm that it is innate, for, in considering it, you make a subsumption or application of the principle of contradiction to what the understanding itself furnishes as soon as you are conscious of innate thoughts.

Th. Not at all, for the thoughts are acts, and the knowledge or the truths, in so far as they are within us, even when we do not think of them, are habitudes or dispositions; and we are well acquainted with things of which we think but little.

Ph. It is very difficult to conceive that a truth may be in the mind if the mind has never thought of that truth.

Th. It is as if some one said it is difficult to conceive that there are veins in the marble before we have discovered them. This objection seems also to approach a little too much the begging of the question.[1] All those who admit innate truths, without grounding them in the Platonic reminiscence, admit some of which they have not yet thought. Besides, this reasoning proves too much; for, if truths are thoughts, we shall be deprived not only of the truths of which we have never thought, but also of those of which we have thought, and of which we no longer actually think; and if truths are not thoughts, but habits and aptitudes, natural or acquired, nothing prevents there being in us some of which we have never thought, nor will ever think.

[1] *Petitio principii.* — TR.

§ 27. *Ph.* If general maxims were innate, they would appear more vividly in the mind of certain persons where, however, we see no trace of them; I may mention children, idiots, and savages,[1] for of all men these are they who have the mind less altered and corrupted by custom and by the impress of extraneous opinions.

Th. I believe we must reason here very differently. Innate maxims appear only through the attention which is given to them; but these persons have little of it, or have it for entirely different things. Their thoughts are mostly confined to the needs of the body; and it is reasonable that pure and detached thoughts be the reward of cares more noble. It is true that children and savages have the mind less altered by customs, but they also have it exalted by the teaching which gives attention. It would not be very just that the brightest lights should shine better in minds which less deserve them, and which are enveloped in thicker clouds. I would not then have one give too much honor to ignorance and barbarism when one is as learned and as clever as you are, Philalethes, as well as your excellent author; that would be lowering the gifts of God. Some one will say that the more ignorant we are, the more we approach the advantage of a block of marble or of a piece of wood, which are infallible and sinless. But, unfortunately, it is not by ignorance that we approach this advantage; and, as far as we are capable of knowledge, we sin in neglecting to acquire it, and we shall fail so much the more easily as we are less instructed.

CHAPTER II

NO INNATE PRACTICAL PRINCIPLES

§ 1. *Ph.* Ethics is a demonstrative science, and yet it has no innate principles. And, indeed, it would be very difficult to produce a rule of ethics of a nature to be settled by an assent as general and as prompt as this maxim: *Whatever is, is.*

[1] For an excellent exposition of the content of the term *savage*, *cf.* Andrew Lang, *Myth, Ritual, and Religion*, Vol. 1, p. 31, and note; also chap. 3, pp. 46 *sq.*, London: Longmans, Green, & Co., 1887. — Tr.

Th. It is absolutely impossible that there be truths of reason as evident as those which are *identical* or immediate. And, although you can truly say that ethics has principles which are not demonstrable, and that one of the first and most practical is, that we ought to pursue joy and avoid sorrow, it is needful to add that this is not a truth which is known purely by reason, since it is based upon internal experience, or upon confused knowledge, for we do not feel what joy or sadness is.

Ph. It is only through processes of reasoning, through language, and through some mental application, that you can be assured of practical truths.

Th. Though that were so, they would not be less innate. However, the maxim I just adduced appears of another nature; it is not known by the reason, but, so to speak, by an *instinct.* It is an innate principle, but it does not form a part of the natural light, for it is not known luminously. But this principle admitted, you can draw from it scientific consequences, and I commend most heartily what you just said of ethics as a demonstrative science. Let us note also that it teaches truths so evident that thieves, pirates, and bandits are forced to observe them among themselves.

§ 2. *Ph.* But bandits keep the rules of justice among themselves without considering them as innate principles.

Th. What matters it? Does the world concern itself about questions of theory?

Ph. They observe the maxims of justice only as convenient rules, the practice of which is absolutely necessary to the conservation of their society.

Th. [Very well. You could say nothing better in general in respect to all men. And thus it is that these laws are written in the soul, namely, as the consequences of our preservation and of our true welfare. Do you imagine that we suppose that truths are in the understanding as independent the one of the other as the edicts of the prætor were on his placard or *album?* I put aside here the *instinct* which prompts man to love man, of which I shall presently speak, for now I wish to speak only of truths in so far as they are known by *the reason.* I admit, also, that certain rules of justice cannot be demonstrated, in all their extent and perfection, without supposing the existence of God and the immortality of the soul, and these, where the instinct of humanity does not impel us, are written in the soul only as other derivative truths.] Those, however, who base justice only upon the necessities of this life and upon the need they have of it, rather than upon the pleasure they ought to take in it, which is the greatest when God is its ground, are liable to resemble a little the society of bandits.

Sit spes fallendi, miscebunt sacra profanis.[1]

§ 3. *Ph.* I agree with you that nature has put in all men the desire for happiness and a strong aversion to misery. These are *the truly innate practical principles,* and principles which, according to the purpose of every practical principle, have a continual influence upon all our actions. But they are inclinations of the soul toward the good, and not impressions[2] of some truth which is written in our understanding.

Th. [I am delighted, sir, to see that you admit in effect innate truths, as I shall presently say. This principle agrees sufficiently with that which I just indicated, which prompts us to seek joy and shun sorrow. For *felicity* is only a lasting joy. Our inclination, however, does not tend to felicity proper, but to joy — that is to say, to the present; it is the reason which prompts to future and enduring welfare. Now, the inclination, expressed by the understanding, passes into a *precept* or practical truth; and if the inclination is innate, the truth is innate also, there being nothing in the soul which may not be expressed in the understanding, but not always by a consideration actually distinct, as I have sufficiently shown. The *instincts* also are not always practical; there are some which contain theoretical truths, and such are the internal principles of the sciences and of reasoning, when, without recognizing the reason in them, we employ them by a natural instinct. And in this sense you cannot dispense with the recognition of innate principles, even though you might be willing to deny that derivative truths are *innate.* But this would be a question of name merely after the explanation I

[1] *Cf.* Hor. *Epist.*, 1, 16, 54. Horace has "miscebis." — TR.

[2] Erdmann and Jacques read, "des imperfections de quelque vérité." Gerhardt reads, "des impressions de quelque vérité." Locke has, "impressions of truth." Book I., chap. 3, § 3. Vol. 1, p. 158, line 5, Bohn's edition. — TR.

have given of what I call *innate*. And if any one desires to give this appellation only to the truths which are received at first by instinct, I shall not contest the point with him.]

Ph. That is well. But if there were in our soul certain characters imprinted there by nature, like so many principles of knowledge, we could only perceive them acting in us, as we feel the influence of the two principles which are constantly active in us — namely, the desire of happiness and the fear of misery.

Th. [There are principles of knowledge which influence us as constantly in our reasoning processes as these practical principles influence us in our volitions; for example, everybody employs the rules of deduction by a *natural logic* without being aware of it.

§ 4. *Ph.* The rules of Morality need to be proved; they are then not innate, like that rule which is the source of the virtues which concern society: *Do to another only what you would have him do to yourself.*

Th. You always make me the objection which I have already refuted. I agree with you that there are moral rules which are not *innate principles;* but that does not prevent them from being innate truths, for a derivative truth will be innate, supposing that we can draw it from our mind. But there are innate truths, which we find in us in two ways — by insight and by instinct. Those which I have just indicated, show by our ideas what natural insight accomplishes. But there are conclusions of *natural light* which are principles in relation to *instinct.* It is thus that we are prompted to acts of humanity, by instinct because it pleases us, and by reason because it is just. There are then in us truths of instinct, which are innate principles, which we feel and approve, although we have not the proof of them which we obtain, however, when we give a reason for this instinct. It is thus that we make use of the laws of deduction conformably to a confused knowledge, and as by instinct, but logicians show the reason of them, as mathematicians also give a reason for what they do without thinking in walking and leaping. As for the rule which states that we ought to do to others only what we would have them do to us, it needs not only proof, but also to be proclaimed. We should wish too much for ourselves if we could have our own way; shall we say then that we also owe too much to others?[1] You will tell me that the rule means only a just will. But thus this rule, very far from being adequate to serve as a measure, would itself need one. The true sense of the rule is, that the place of another is the true point of view for equitable judgment when we attempt it.]

§ 9. *Ph.* Bad acts are often committed without any remorse of conscience; for example, when cities are carried by storm, the soldiers commit, without scruple, the worst acts; some civilized nations have exposed their children, some Caribbees castrate theirs in order to fatten and eat them. Garcilasso de la Vega[2] reports that certain peoples of Peru took prisoners in order to make concubines of them, and supported the children up to the age of thirteen, after which they ate them, and treated in the same manner the mothers so soon as they no longer bore children. In the travels of Baumgarten[3] it is related that there was a Santon[4] in Egypt who passed for a holy man, *eo quod non fœminarum unquam esset ac puerorum, sed tantum asellarum concubitor atque mularum.*

Th. Moral science (over and above the instincts like that which makes us seek joy and shun sadness) is not otherwise innate than is arithmetic, for it depends likewise upon demonstrations which internal light furnishes. And as the demonstrations do not at once leap into sight, it is no great wonder, if men do not perceive always and at once all that they possess in themselves, and do not read quite readily the *characters of the natural law, which God, according to St. Paul,[5] has written in their minds.* As morality, however, is more important than arithmetic, God has given to man *instincts* which prompt

[1] This sentence is found in the texts of Erdmann and Gerhardt; it is wanting in that of Jacques. — Tr.

[2] Garcilasso de la Vega, 1540–1616, the son of an Inca princess, and a Spanish conqueror, a companion of Pizarro. His *Commentarios reales* was published in two parts, the first at Lisbon, 1609, giving an account of the native traditions, customs, and history previous to the Spanish conquest; the second under the separate title of *Historia General del Peru*, Cordova, 1617, treating of the Spanish conquest. The earlier and more important part of the work has been translated, with "learned and ingenious notes," by Clements R. Markham, and published in the collection of the Hakluyt Society, 2 vols., London: 1869, 1871. — Tr.

[3] Martin Baumgarten, 1473–1535, *Travels through Egypt, Arabia, etc.* In Churchill, O. and J. Col., Vol. 1, 1744. — Tr.

[4] Mahometan monk. — Tr.

[5] Rom. 2:15; *cf.* 1:19. — Tr.

at once and without reasoning to some portion of that which reason ordains; just as we walk in obedience to the laws of mechanics without thinking of these laws, and as we eat, not only because eating is necessary for us, but further and much more because it gives us pleasure. But these instincts do not prompt to action in an invincible way; the passions may resist them, prejudices may obscure them, and contrary customs alter them. Nevertheless, we agree most frequently with these instincts of conscience, and we follow them also when stronger impressions do not overcome them. The greatest and most healthy part of the human race bears them witness. The Orientals, the Greeks and Romans, the Bible and the Koran agree in respect to them; the Mahometan police are wont to punish the thing Baumgarten tells of, and it would be needful to be as brutalized as the American savage in order to approve their customs, full of a cruelty which surpasses even that of the beasts. Yet these same savages perceive clearly what justice is on other occasions;[1] and although there is no bad practice, perhaps, which may not be authorized in some respects and upon some occasions, there are few of them, however, which are not condemned very frequently and by the larger part of mankind. That which has not been attained without reason, and was not attained by reasoning alone, should be referred in part to the natural instincts. Custom, tradition, discipline, are mingled therein, but it is due to instinct (*le naturel*) that custom is turned more generally to the good side of these duties. In the same way,[2] the *tradition* of God's existence is due to *instinct* (*le naturel*). Now nature

[1] *Cf.* J. G. Schurman, *The Ethical Import of Darwinism*, pp. 256–260, New York: Charles Scribner's Sons, 1887. He states that "some gropings amid the general darkness incline me, at least tentatively, to the belief that, apart from the domestic virtues, there is no such great difference between the morals of Christians and the morals of savages" (p. 256). This statement is modified further on, pp. 258, 259, and finally takes the following form: "The fighting men, actual and potential, in every uncivilized community recognize the same rights, obligations, and duties toward one another as constitute the essence of civilized morality. You never find a man without a moral nature, a nature essentially like our own; but the objects he includes within the scope of its outgoings vary" (p. 259). For the real significance of such facts, *cf.* Ex-Pres. E. G. Robinson, of Brown University, *Principles and Practice of Morality*, p. 43, Boston: Silver, Burdett & Co., 1888. — TR.

[2] Gerhardt reads, "C'est comme *le naturel*," etc.; Erdmann and Jacques, "Le naturel," etc. — TR.

gives to man and also to most of the animals affectionate and tender feeling for those of their species. The tiger even *parcit cognatis masculis;*[1] whence comes this *bon mot* of a Roman jurisconsult, *Quia inter omnes homines natura cognationem constituit, unde hominum homini insidiari nefas esse.* Spiders form almost the only exception, and these eat one another to this extent that the female devours the male after having enjoyed him. Besides this general instinct of *society*, which may be called *philanthropy* in man, there are some more particular forms of it, as the affection between the male and the female, the love which father and mother bear toward the children, which the Greeks call στοργή,[2] and other similar inclinations which make this natural law, or this image of law rather, which, according to Roman jurisconsults, nature has taught the animals. But in man in particular there is found a certain regard for dignity, for propriety, which leads him to conceal the things which lower us, to be sparing of shame, to have repugnance for incests, to bury dead bodies, not to eat men at all, nor living animals. One is led further to be careful of his reputation, even beyond need, and of life; to be subject to remorse of conscience, and to feel these *laniatus et ictus*, these tortures and torments of which Tacitus, following Plato, speaks;[3] besides the fear of a future and of a supreme power which arises, moreover, naturally enough. There is reality in all that; but at bottom these natural impressions, whatever they may be, are only aids to the reason and indices of the plan of nature. Custom, education, tradition, reason, contribute much, but human nature ceases not to participate therein. It is true that without the reason these aids would not suffice to give a complete certitude to morals. Finally, will you deny that man is naturally led, for example, to withdraw from vile things, under a pretext that races are found who like to speak only of filth, that there are some, indeed, whose mode of life obliges them to handle excrements, and that there are people of Boutan, where those of the king pass as an aromatic? I think that you are of my opinion at bottom in regard to these natural instincts which tend toward what is right and decent;

[1] Juv. *Sat.*, 15, 159–160. — TR.

[2] The reading (*nom.* στοργή) of Erdmann and Jacques. Gerhardt's reading, ὀργὴν, is evidently an error. — TR.

[3] *Gorgias*, 524 E; *Ann.* 6, 6. — TR.

although you will say, perhaps, as you have said with regard to the instinct which prompts to joy and felicity, that these impressions are not innate truths. But I have already replied that every feeling is the perception of a truth, and that the natural feeling is the (perception) of an innate truth, but very often confused, as are the experiences of the external senses; thus you can distinguish the *innate truths* from the *natural light* (which contains only the distinctly knowable), as the genus must be distinguished from its species, since *the innate truths* comprehend both *the instincts* and the *natural light.*]

§ 11. *Ph.* A person who knew the natural limits of justice and injustice, and (who) would not cease confusing them with each other, could only be regarded as the declared enemy of the repose and the welfare of the society of which he is a member. But men confuse them every moment, consequently they do not know them.

Th. [That is taking things a little too theoretically. It happens every day that men act contrary to their knowledge in concealing these (limits) from themselves when they turn the mind elsewhere, in order to follow their passions; otherwise, we should not see people eating and drinking what they know must cause them sickness and even death. They would not neglect their business; they would not do what entire nations have done in certain respects. The future and reason rarely make so strong an impression as the present and the senses. That Italian knew this well, who, before being put to torture, proposed to have the gallows continually in sight during the torments in order to resist them, and they heard him say sometimes, "*Io ti vedo,*" which he explained afterward when he had escaped. Unless you firmly resolve to look upon the true good and the true evil with the purpose of following or shunning them, you find yourself carried away, and it happens, with regard to the most important needs of this life, as it happens with regard to paradise and hell in the case of those, indeed, who believe in them the most: —

> Cantantur hæc, laudantur hæc,
> Dicuntur, audiuntur.
> Scribuntur hæc, leguntur hæc,
> Et lecta negliguntur.]

Ph. Every principle which you suppose innate can only be known by each one as just and advantageous.

Th. [You always return to this supposition, which I have refuted so many times, that every innate truth is known always and by all.]

§ 12. *Ph.* But a public permission to violate the law proves that this law is not innate; for example, the law requiring the love and preservation of children was violated among the ancients when they permitted their exposure.

Th. [This violation supposed, it follows only that you have not well read these characters of nature written in our soul, but sometimes obscure enough by reason of our excesses, not to mention that, in order to have a perfectly clear perception of the necessity of duties, men must see the demonstration of them — a condition that is rarely fulfilled. If geometry were as much opposed to our passions and present interests as is ethics, we should contest it and violate it but little less, notwithstanding all the demonstrations of Euclid[1] and of Archimedes,[1] which you would call dreams and believe full of paralogisms; and Joseph Scaliger, Hobbes,[2] and others, who have written against Euclid and Archimedes, would not find themselves in such a small company as at present. It was only the passion for glory, which these authors believed they found in the quadrature of the circle and other difficult problems, which could

[1] Euclid, not to be confounded with Euclid of Megara, a pupil of Socrates, founder of the Megarian school, the fundamental principle of whose philosophy was the union of the Eleatic idea of *being* with the Socratic idea of the *good*. The date of neither his birth nor death is known. Proclus, the Neo-Platonist, 410–485 A.D., says that Euclid lived in the time of Ptolemy I., king of Egypt, who reigned from 323–285 B.C., and that he was younger than Plato's associates, but older than Eratosthenes, "276–2—196–2 B.C.," "the celebrated scholar whose chronological dates were adopted for the history of philosophy" (Zeller, *Outlines*, §§ 3, 66), and Archimedes, 287–212 B.C. Proclus preserves Euclid's reply to King Ptolemy, who asked him if there were no easier way to learn geometry than by studying his elements. "There is no royal road to geometry." — TR.

[2] Thomas Hobbes, 1588–1679. The statement of his geometrical principles in opposition to those of Euclid is found in the Appendix to the English translation of the *De Corpore*, which appeared about the middle of 1656, entitled *Six Lessons to the Professors of Mathematics, one of Geometry, the other of Astronomy, in the University of Oxford*, English Works, Vol. 7, pp. 181–356. For an account of the controversy in which these appeared, *cf.* George Croom Robertson, *Hobbes*, pp. 167–178 (Philosophical Classics). Edinburgh: William Blackwood & Sons, 1886. — TR.

blind to such a point persons of so great merit. And if others had the same interest, they would make use of it in much the same manner.]

Ph. Every duty carries the idea of law, and a law cannot be known or supposed without a *legislator* who has prescribed it, or without reward and without punishment.

Th. [There can be *natural rewards and penalties* without a legislator; intemperance, for example, is punished by disease. As this, however, does not injure all at first, I admit that there are few precepts to which you would necessarily be bound if there were not a God who leaves no crime without chastisement, no good act without reward.]

Ph. The ideas of a God and of a life to come must then also be innate.

Th. [I am agreed in the sense in which I have explained myself.]

Ph. But these ideas are so far from being written by nature in the minds of all men, that they even do not appear very clear and very distinct in the minds of many students, who also profess to examine things with some accuracy; so far are they from being known by every human being.

Th. You return again to the same proposition, which maintains that what is not known is not innate, which I have, however, refuted so many times. What is innate is not at first known clearly and distinctly as such; often much attention and method is necessary in order to its perception, the student-class do not always adduce it, still less every human being.

§ 13. *Ph.* But if men can be ignorant of or call in question that which is innate, it is in vain for you to speak to us of innate principles, and to claim to show us their necessity; very far from their being able to serve as our instructors in the truth and certitude of things, as is maintained, we shall find ourselves, with these principles, in the same state of uncertainty as if they were not in us.

Th. You cannot call in question all the innate principles. You were agreed in regard to identical propositions or the principle of contradiction, admitting that there are incontestable principles, although you would not then recognize them as innate; but it does not at all follow that everything which is innate and necessarily connected with these innate principles, is also at first indubitably evident.

Ph. No one that I know of has yet undertaken to give us an exact catalogue of these principles.

Th. But has any one hitherto given us a full and exact catalogue of the axioms of geometry?

§ 15. *Ph.* My Lord Herbert[1] has been pleased to point out some of these principles, which are: 1. There is a supreme God. 2. He ought to be served. 3. Virtue united with piety is the best worship. 4. Repentance for sin is necessary. 5. There are penalties and rewards after this life. I agree that these are evident truths and of such a nature that when well explained a reasonable person can scarcely avoid giving them his consent. But our friends say that they are very far from being so many innate impressions, and if these five propositions are common notions written in our souls by the finger of God, there are many others which we ought also to put into this class.

Th. I agree with you, sir, for I take all the *necessary truths* as innate, and I connect with them also the *instincts*. But, I agree with you, that these five propositions are not innate principles; for I hold that they can and ought to be proved.

§ 18. *Ph.* In the third proposition, that virtue is the worship most agreeable to God, it is not clear what is meant by *virtue.* If you understand it in the sense most commonly given to the term, I mean that which passes as praiseworthy according to the different opinions which prevail in different countries, this proposition is so far from being evident that it is not even true. If you call *virtue*[2] the acts which are conformed to the will of God, this will be almost *idem per idem,* and the proposition will teach us nothing of importance; for it would mean only that God is pleased with that which is conformed to his will. It is the same with the notion of *sin* in the fourth proposition.

[1] Lord Edward Herbert of Cherbury, 1581–1648. His *De Veritate*, Paris, 1624, has had considerable influence on English philosophical and religious thought, and is of some importance in the interpretation of the polemic of Locke's Essay. — Tr.

[2] For an excellent but brief statement and discussion of the main theories of virtue, *cf.* E. G. Robinson: *Principles and Practice of Morality*, pp. 140–180. — Tr.

Th. I do not remember to have remarked that virtue is commonly taken as something which depends upon opinion; at least, the philosophers do not make it that. It is true that the name of virtue depends upon the opinion of those who give it to different habits or actions, according as they deem them good or bad and use their reason; but all are sufficiently agreed as to the notion of virtue in general, although they differ in its application. According to Aristotle[1] and several others, *virtue* is a habit of restraining the passions by the reason, and still more, simply a habit of acting according to reason. And that cannot fail to be agreeable to him who is the supreme and final reason of things, to whom nothing is indifferent, and the acts of rational creatures less than all others.

§ 20. *Ph.* You are wont to say that the custom, the education, and the general opinions of those with whom you converse may obscure these principles of morality which you suppose innate. But if this reply is a good one, it annihilates the proof which you pretend to draw from universal consent. The reasoning of many men reduces to this: The principles which men of right reason admit are innate; we and those of our mind are men of right reason; consequently our principles are innate. A pleasant method of reasoning, which goes straight on to infallibility!

Th. For myself, I make use of universal consent, not as a principal proof, but as a confirmatory one; for innate truths taken as the *natural light* of reason bear their marks with them as does geometry, for they are wrapped up in the immediate principles which you yourselves admit as incontestable. But I grant that it is more difficult to distinguish the *instincts* and some other natural habits from custom, although it may very often be possible so to do. For the rest, it appears to me that people who have cultivated their minds have some ground for attributing the use of right reason to themselves rather than to the barbarians, since in subduing them almost as easily as they do animals they show sufficiently their supe-

[1] *Eth. Nic.* II. 6, *ad init.* *Cf.* Zeller: *Outlines of the Hist. of Greek Philos.*, § 61; and E. Wallace: *Outlines of the Philos. of Aristotle*, 3d ed., § 59, pp. 97–99. Cambridge: University Press, 1883. In connection with each section of his brief English statement and exposition, Wallace gives the Greek text of "the more important passages in Aristotle's writings," with references to the Berlin Academy edition of Aristotle. — TR.

riority. But if they cannot always succeed in this, it is because just like the animals they conceal themselves in the thick forests, where it is difficult to hunt them down and the game is not worth the candle. It is doubtless an advantage to have cultivated the mind, and if we may speak for barbarism as against culture, we shall also have the right to attack reason in favor of the animals, and to take seriously the witty sallies of M. Despreaux,[1] in one of his satires, where, in order to contest with man his prerogative over the animals, he asks, whether,

> The bear is afraid of the passer-by, or the passer-by of the bear;
> And if, by decree of the shepherds of Libya,
> The lions would vacate the parks of Numidia, etc.

We must, however, admit that there are some points in which the barbarians surpass us, especially as regards vigor of body; and as regards the soul even we may say that in certain respects their practical morality is better than ours, because they have not the avarice of hoarding nor the ambition of ruling. And we may even add that association with Christians has made them worse in many respects.[2] They have taught them drunkenness (when carrying them the water of life), swearing, blasphemy, and other vices, which were little known to them. There is with us more of good and of evil than with them: a bad European is worse than a savage — he refines upon evil.[3] Still, nothing should prevent men from uniting the advantages which nature gives to these peoples with those which reason gives us.

[1] Nicolas Boileau-Despreaux, 1636–1711. The passage quoted is from Sat. 8, 62–64. The text as given by all the editions I have been able to consult, twelve, ranging from 1716–1873, reads thus:

> "L'ours a peur du passant, ou le passant de l'ours;
> Et si, sur un édit des pâtres de Nubie,
> Les lions de Barca videraient la Lybie;" etc.

Lines 63 and 64 of the text, as given by Leibnitz, editions of Gerhardt and Erdmann, Jacques modernizing the spelling and correcting the misplacement of "de" and "des" in line 63, read thus:

> "Et si par un édit de pastres des Lybie
> Les Lions vuideroient les parcs de Numidie," etc.

It seems evident that Leibnitz misquoted the lines. — Tr.

[2] Compare J. G. Schurman: *The Ethical Import of Darwinism*, pp. 256–260 as above. — Tr.

[3] The French is: "il rafine sur le mal." — Tr.

Ph. But what reply do you make, sir, to this dilemma of one of my friends? I would be pleased, he says, to have the advocates of innate ideas tell me whether these principles can or cannot be effaced by education and custom. If they cannot be effaced we ought to find them in all men, and they should clearly appear in the mind of each particular man. If they can be altered by extraneous ideas, they ought to appear more distinctly and with more lustre the nearer they are to their source. I mean in children or illiterate people, upon whom extraneous opinions have made less impression. Let them take which side they please, they will clearly see, he says, that it is contradicted by indubitable facts and by continual experience.

Th. I am astonished that your clever friend has confounded *obscurity* with *effacement*, as some in your party confound *non-being* with *non-appearance*. Innate ideas and truths cannot be effaced, but they are obscured in all men (as they are now) by their inclination toward the needs of the body, and oftener still by the occurrence of bad customs. These characteristics of the internal light would always be shining in the understanding and would give fervor to the will, if the confused perceptions of sense did not engross our attention. It is the struggle of which Holy Scripture no less than ancient and modern philosophy speaks.

Ph. Thus, then, we find ourselves in darkness as thick and in uncertainty as great as if there were no such light.

Th. God forbid; we should have neither science nor law, nay, not even reason.

§ 21, 22, etc. *Ph.* I hope that you will at least admit the force of prejudice, which often causes that to pass as natural which has come from the bad instruction to which children have been exposed, and the bad customs which education and association have given them.

Th. I admit that the excellent author whom you follow says some very fine things upon that subject, and which have their value if they are taken as they should be; but I do not believe that they are opposed to the doctrine properly understood of nature or of innate truths. And I am confident that he will not extend his remarks too far; for I am equally persuaded that a great many opinions pass for truths which are only the effects of custom and of credulity, and that there are many such opinions, too, which certain philosophers would fain account for as matters of prejudice, which are, however, grounded in right reason and in nature. There is as much or more ground for defending ourselves from those who through ambition oftenest make pretensions to innovation, than for challenging ancient impressions. And after having meditated sufficiently upon ancient and modern thought, I have found that the majority of the received doctrines may bear a good sense. So that I wish that sensible men would seek to satisfy their ambition by occupying themselves rather in building and advancing than in retrograding and destroying. And I desire them to resemble the Romans who constructed beautiful public works, rather than that Vandal king[1] whom his mother charged to seek the destruction of these grand structures, since he could not hope for the glory of equalling them.

Ph. The aim of the clever class who have contended against innate truths has been to prevent men from handing round their prejudices and seeking to cover their idleness beneath this fair name.

Th. We are agreed upon this point, for, very far from approving that doubtful principles be received, I would, for myself, seek even the demonstration of the axioms of Euclid, as some ancients also have done. And when you ask the means of knowing and examining innate principles, I reply, following what I said above, that with the exception of the instincts whose reason is unknown, you must try to reduce them to first principles, that is to say, to axioms identical or immediate by means of definitions, which are nothing else than a distinct exposition of ideas. I do not doubt even but that your friends, who have hitherto been opposed to innate truths, would approve this method, which appears consonant with their principal aim.

[1] Chrocus, who with the Sueves and Alans is said to have passed over the Rhine near Mayence, and following the evil counsel of his mother, to have ravaged in the most frightful manner in Germany as in Gaul. The story is given in the Chronicle of Idatius, chap. 62. *Cf.* Bouquet, *Rerum Gall. et Franc. Scriptores*, Tom. 2, p. 464. — TR.

CHAPTER III

OTHER CONSIDERATIONS TOUCHING INNATE PRINCIPLES, BOTH SPECULATIVE AND PRACTICAL

§ 3. *Ph.* You wish to reduce truths to first principles, and I grant you that if there is any such principle, it is without gainsaying this; *it is impossible for a thing to be and not to be at the same time.* It appears, however, difficult to maintain its innate character, since you must be convinced at the same time that the ideas of impossibility and identity are innate.

Th. It is quite necessary that those who favor innate truths maintain and be convinced that these ideas are also innate, and I admit that I am of their opinion. The ideas of *being*, of *possibility* of *identity*, are so completely innate that they enter into all our thoughts and reasonings, and I regard them as essential to our mind; but I have already said that we do not always pay them particular attention and that we discern them only with time. I have said hitherto that we are, so to speak, innate unto ourselves, and since we are beings, the being we is innate; and the knowledge of being is wrapped up in that knowledge which we have of ourselves. There is something similar in the case of other general notions.

§ 4. *Ph.* If the idea of *identity* is natural, and *consequently* so evident and so present to the mind that we ought to recognize it from the cradle, I would be pleased to have a child of seven years, and even a man of seventy, tell me whether a man who is a creature consisting of body and soul, is the same (man) when his body is changed, and whether, metempsychosis supposed, Euphorbus would be the same as Pythagoras.

Th. I have stated sufficiently that what is natural to us is not known to us as such from the cradle; and even an idea may be known to us without our being able to decide at once all questions which can be formed thereupon. It is as if some one maintained that a child cannot have a knowledge of the square and its diagonal, because he will have difficulty in recognizing that the diagonal is incommensurable with the side of the square. As for the question itself, it appears to me demonstratively solved by the doctrine of Monads, which I have elsewhere[1] shown in its true light, and we shall speak more fully of this matter in the sequel.

[1] *Cf.* the Essay, without title, Gerhardt, 4, 427 *sq.*, written at the beginning of 1686, and referred to as "un petit discours de Metaphysique," in Leibnitz's letter, Feb. 1–11, 1686, to the Landgraf Ernst von Hessen-Rheinfels, G. 2, 11. This 'Discours,' regarded by Leibnitz as the beginning of his philosophy, contains a summary, centring about the idea of *the individual substance*, of all his previous philosophical speculation. He gained this idea, and with it a seemingly satisfactory solution of the principal philosophical problem, at the end of 1685 or the beginning of 1686. For this idea, still in process of development, possessing the elements of force and individuality, but lacking those of continuity and perceptive activity evolved between 1686 and 1697, Leibnitz, in 1697, when the idea possessed all the elements essential to its completeness in his system, appropriated the term "monad." This term he borrowed, not from Giordano Bruno, 1548–1600, who used it in a similar though not precisely the same sense, but from François Mercure Van Helmont, 1618–1699. So far as known, the term "monad" is first mentioned in the letter to Fardella, Sept. 3–13, 1696, first published by Foucher de Careil, *Nouv. lettr. et opusc. de Leibniz.* p. 328, Paris, 1857. The doctrine in substance till 1697, and thereafter in name, Leibnitz frequently set forth with increasing clearness and completeness in letters to his numerous correspondents, and in the "Acta Eruditorum" and the "Journal des Savans." Reference may be made, among others, to the following: Correspondence with Antoine Arnauld, 1612–1694, especially the letter dated Venice, Mar. 23, 1690, G. 2, 134; Erdmann, 107; Jacques, 1, 443; trans., Appendix, ; the two systematic elaborations of his system of the year 1695, the mathematical in the *Specimen dynamicum pro admirandis naturæ legibus*, etc., Gerhardt, *Leibniz. math. Schrift.*, 6, 234 *sq.*; the metaphysical in the *Systeme nouveau de la nature*, etc., G. 4, 477; E. 124; trans., Appendix, ; *De ipsa natura*, etc., 1698, espec. §§ 11, 12, G. 4, 504; E. 154; J. 1, 455 (in French); trans., Appendix, ; *Response* (*Replique*, Erdmann) *aux reflexions continues dans la seconde edition du Dictionnaire Critique de M. Bayle*, etc., 1702, G. 4, 554; E. 183; trans., Appendix, ; Letters to Rud. Christ. Wagner *De vi activa corporis*, June 4, 1710, G. 7, 528; E. 465; trans., Duncan, *Philos. Wks. of Leibnitz*, 190; to Bierling, Aug. 12, 1711, G. 7, 500; E. 677; *Principes de la nature*, etc., c. 1714, G. 6, 598; E. 714; trans., Duncan, 209; *La Monadologie*, 1714, G. 6, 607; E. 705; trans., Duncan, 218, F. H. Hedge, "Jour. Spec. Philos.," Vol. 1, p. 129; Letters to Des Bosses, G. 2, 285 *sq.*, *passim*, which present most penetrating discussions of Leibnitz's metaphysic and form the most ample commentary on the *Monadologie*; to De Volder, 1643–1709, G. 2, 139 *sq.*, *passim*, proving the intimate connection of Leibnitz's dynamic and metaphysic; to Bourguet, Dec. 1714, G. 3, 575; E. 720; to Remond (de Montmort, E. 724), Feb. 11, 1715, §§ 3, 4, G. 3, 635; to Dangicourt, Sept. 1716, Dutens, *Leibnit. opera omnia*, 3, 499; E. 745. Of the pieces cited the most important are: The Letter to Arnauld, Mar. 23, 1690, the *Systeme nouveau*, the *De ipsa natura*, the *Principes de la nature*, and the *Monadologie*. As Leibnitz was occupied, more or less as circumstances permitted, with the composition and revision of his 'New Essays,' from 1700, when Coste's translation of Locke's 'Essay' appeared, to 1709 and perhaps later (*vid. ante*, p. 9 and note), possibly even as late as 1714 or 1716, the relative date of composition of the several pieces here cited to that of the 'New Essays' can easily

§ 6. *Ph.* [I see very well that to you I should object in vain that the axiom which declares that *the whole is greater than its part* is not innate, under pretext that the ideas of whole and part are relative, dependent upon those of number and extension; since you would apparently maintain that there are ideas conditionally innate, and that those of number and extension are to such a degree innate.[1]]

Th. You are right, and indeed I rather believe that the idea of extension is posterior to that of whole and part.

§ 7. *Ph.* [What say you of the truth that God should be worshipped; is it innate?]

Th. I believe that the duty of worshipping God declares that on occasion you ought to show that you honor him beyond every other object, and that this is a necessary consequence of the idea of him and of his existence; which signifies with me that this truth is innate.

§ 8. *Ph.* But the atheists seem to prove by their example that the idea of God is not innate. And without speaking of those whom the ancients have mentioned, have not entire nations been discovered, who have no idea of God nor of the terms which denote God and the soul, as at the bay of Soldania, in Brazil, in the Caribbee Islands, in Paraguay?

Th. [The late Mr. Fabricius,[2] a celebrated theologian of Heidelberg, has made an apology for the human race in order

be approximated. On the whole subject, *cf.* L. Stein, *Leibniz u. Spinoza*, chap. 6, pp. 111–219, Berlin: G. Reimer, 1890, who traces the history of the rise of the monad-doctrine from 1680 till all the elements of the complete conception were present in 1697; E. Dillmann, *E. neue Darstg. d. Leibniz. Monadenlehre auf Grund d. Quellen*, Leipzig: O. R. Reisland, 1891, whose monograph is an elaborate discussion of the entire subject with references to or quotations from all the sources. — TR.

[1] The French text is: "puisque vous soutiendrés apparemment, qu'il y a des idées innées respectives, et que celles des nombres et de l'étendue sont innées aussi." — TR.

[2] John Lewis Fabricius, 1632–1697. Professor, first of Greek, then of Philosophy and Theology, at Heidelberg. In 1664 he received the title of "Conseiller ecclésiastique de l'electeur palatin." Some years after, when Heidelberg was burning, he saved the archives of the church and the university, carrying them first to Eberbach, then to Frankfort, where he died. The title of the work referred to in the text (*vid. ante*, p. 21 also, where the name is given Fabritius, in accord with his own signature in the letter of Feb. 16, 1673, to Spinoza, offering him the professorship of Philosophy at Heidelberg) is: *Apologia generis humani contra calumniam atheismi.* It appeared in 1662. His collected works, with a life, were published by J. H. Heidegger, Zurich, 1698, in 4to. — TR.

to clear it of the imputation of atheism. He was an author of great accuracy, and decidedly above much prejudice; I do not, however, pretend to enter into this discussion of facts. I grant that entire peoples have never thought of the supreme substance, nor of the nature of the soul. And I remember, that when you wished at my request, countenanced by the illustrious Mr. Witsen, to obtain for me in Holland a translation of the Lord's Prayer into the language of Barantola, you were stopped at this point: *hallowed be thy name,* because you could not make the Barantoli understand what *hallowed* meant. I remember also that in the creed made for the Hottentots you were obliged to express Holy Spirit by words of the country which signify a pleasant and agreeable wind.[1] This was not unreasonable, for our Greek and Latin words *πνεῦμα, anima, spiritus,* mean ordinarily only the air or wind we breathe, as one of the most subtile things which we know through the senses; and we begin through the senses to lead men little by little to what is beyond the senses. All this difficulty, however, which you find in attaining abstract knowledge effects nothing against innate knowledge. There are peoples who have no word corresponding to the word *being;* does any one doubt their knowledge of what being is, although they seldom think of it in the abstract? Besides I find what I have read in our excellent author on the idea of God (Essay on Understanding, Book I., chap. 3,[2] § 9) so beautiful and so to my liking that I cannot refrain from quoting it.[3] Here it is:

"Men can scarcely avoid having some kind of idea of things of which those with whom they converse often have occasion to speak under certain names, and if the thing is one which carries with it the idea of excellence, of grandeur, or of some extraordinary quality which interests in some point and which impresses itself upon the mind under the idea of an absolute and irresistible power which none can help fearing" (I add: and under the idea of a superlatively great goodness which none can help loving), "such an idea ought, according to all

[1] *Cf.* Book III., chap. 1, § 5, Th. (2).—TR.

[2] Chap. 4, in Locke's treatise, Bohn's ed.—TR.

[3] The French translation of Locke's original, is, in my judgment, clearer in form of statement and style than Locke himself. Hence I have retranslated the French into English. If any reader prefers Locke's original, he can easily find it in the *Philos. Works*, Bohn's ed., Vol. 1, p. 188.—TR.

appearances, to make the strongest impression and to spread farther than any other, especially if it is an idea which accords with the simplest insight of *reason*, and which flows *naturally* from every part of knowledge. Now such is the idea of God, for the brilliant marks of extraordinary wisdom and power appear so plainly in all the works of the creation, that every rational creature who will reflect thereupon cannot fail to discover the author of all these marvels; and the impression that the discovery of such a Being must naturally make upon the souls of all those who have once heard him spoken of is so great, and carries with it thoughts of so great weight and so adapted to spread themselves in the world, that it appears to me wholly strange that an entire nation of men can be found upon the earth so stupid as to have no idea of God. This, I say, seems to me as surprising as to think of men who should have no idea of numbers or of fire."

I would I might always be allowed to copy word for word a number of other excellent passages of our author, which we are obliged to pass by. I will only say here, that this author, in speaking of *the simplest lights of reason*, which agree with the idea of God, and of that which naturally proceeds from it, appears to differ but little from my view of innate truths; and, concerning this, that it appears to him as strange that there may be men without any idea of God, as it would be surprising to find men who had no idea of numbers or of fire, I will remark that the inhabitants of the Marian Islands, to which has been given the name of the Queen of Spain, who has protected missions there, had no knowledge of fire when they were discovered, as appears from the narrative which Rev. Father Gobien,[1] a French Jesuit, charged with the care of distant missions, has given to the public and sent to me.]

§ 16. *Ph.* If you are right in concluding that the idea of God is innate, from the fact that all enlightened races have had this idea, virtue ought also to be innate because enlightened races have always had a true idea of it.

Th. [Not virtue, but the idea of virtue, is innate, and perhaps you intend only that.]

[1] Charles le Gobien, 1653–1708. Professor of Philosophy at Tours; secretary and procurator of Chinese missionaries; wrote and published a number of works on these missions in China; his *Histoire des Isles Mariannes*, Paris, 1700, 12mo. — Tr.

Ph. It is as certain that there is a God, as it is certain that the opposite angles made by the intersection of two straight lines are equal. And there has never been a rational creature who applied himself sincerely to the examination of the truth of these two propositions who has failed to give them his consent. Nevertheless, it is beyond doubt that there are many men who, having never turned their thoughts in this direction, are ignorant equally of these two truths.

Th. [I admit it; but that does not prevent them from being *innate* — that is to say, does not prevent you from being able to find them in yourself.]

§ 18. *Ph.* It would be more advantageous to have an innate idea of *substance;* but it turns out that we do not have it, either innate or acquired, since we have it neither through sensation nor reflection.

Th. [I am of opinion that reflection suffices to discover the idea of substance within ourselves, who are substances. And this notion is one of the most important. But we shall speak of it, perhaps more fully, in the sequel of our conference.]

§ 20.[1] *Ph.* If there are innate ideas in the mind without the mind's being actually aware of their presence, they must at least be in the memory, whence they must be drawn by means of *reminiscence* — that is to say, be known, when memory recalls them, as so many perceptions which have been in the mind before, unless reminiscence can subsist without reminiscence. For this conviction, where it is an inwardly certain one, that a given idea has previously been in our mind, is properly what distinguishes reminiscence from every other kind of thinking.

Th. [In order that knowledge, ideas, or truths be in our mind, it is not necessary that we have ever actually thought of them; they are only natural habitudes; *i.e.* dispositions and aptitudes, active and passive, and more than a *tabula rasa.* It is true, however, that the Platonists believed that we have already actually thought of that which we recognize in ourselves; and to refute them it is insufficient to say that we do not at all remember it, for it is certain that an infinite number

[1] Gerhardt's reading. So also Locke, *Philos. Works*, Vol. 1, p. 197, Bohn's ed. — Tr.

of thoughts recur to us which we have forgotten that we had. It has happened that a man believed he had composed a new verse, which it turned out he read word for word a long time previous in some ancient poet. And often we have an extraordinary facility of conceiving certain things, because we formerly conceived them, without remembering them. It is possible that a child, having become blind, forgets ever having seen light and colors, as happened at the age of two and a half years from small-pox in the case of the celebrated Ulric Schoenberg, a native of Weide, in the Upper Palatinate, who died at Königsberg, in Prussia, in 1649, where he taught philosophy and mathematics to the admiration of every one. It may be that such a man has remaining effects of former impressions without remembering them. I believe that dreams often thus revive in us former thoughts. Julius Scaliger,[1] having celebrated in verse the illustrious men of Verona, a certain self-styled Brugnolus, a Bavarian by birth, but afterward established at Verona, appeared to him in a dream and complained that he had been forgotten. Julius Scaliger, not remembering to have heard him spoken of before, did not allow himself to make elegiac verses in his honor in consequence of this dream. At length, the son, Joseph Scaliger,[2] travelling in Italy, learned more particularly that there had been formerly at Verona a celebrated grammarian or learned critic of this name, who had contributed to the re-establishment of polite literature in Italy. This story is found in the poems of Scaliger the father, together with the elegy, and in the letters of the son. It is related also in the "Scaligerana,"[3] which are culled from the

[1] Julius Cæsar Scaliger, 1484–1558. His Latin verse appeared in successive volumes in 1533, 1534, 1539, 1546, 1574. His tastes were, however, philosophical and scientific rather than literary. His scientific works, in the form of commentaries, have only a historical interest. The *Exotericarum exercitationum liber*, Paris, 1557, 4to, a philosophical treatise on the *De Subtilitate*, 1552, of Cardan (*vid. ante*, p. 67, note 1), is the work which best makes known Scaliger as a philosopher. It was a popular text-book until the final fall of Aristotle's physics. — Tr.

[2] Joseph Justus Scaliger, 1540–1609, reputed the greatest scholar of modern times. He was the first to set forth and apply sound principles of textual criticism and emendation in his editions of some of the classical authors, and with him arose a new school of historical criticism. He reconstructed the lost Chronicle of Eusebius, a work of considerable importance in the study of ancient history. — Tr.

[3] Two collections of anecdotes concerning Joseph Scaliger, numbered accord-

conversations of Joseph Scaliger. It is very likely that Julius Scaliger had known something of Brugnol which he no longer remembered, and that the dream was partly the revival of a former idea, although he may not have had that *reminiscence*, properly so called, which makes us know that we have already had this same idea; at least, I see no necessity which obliges us to assert that there remains no trace of a perception when there is not enough of it to remind us that we have had it.]

§ 24. *Ph.* [I must admit that your reply is natural enough to the difficulties which we have framed against innate truths. Perhaps, also, our authors do not contest them in the sense in which you maintain them. Thus I return only to say to you, sir] that we have had some reason to fear that the view of innate truths serves as a pretext for laziness, for exempting ourselves from the trouble of research, and gives opportunity to masters and teachers to lay down as a *principle of principles* that principles must not be questioned.

Th. [I have already said that if it is the aim of your friends to advise the search for the proofs of the truths which they can receive, without distinguishing whether or not they are innate, we are entirely agreed; and the view of innate truths, of the manner in which I take them, should deter no one from such search, for, besides being well to seek the reason of *the instincts*, it is one of my great maxims that it is good to seek demonstrations of the *axioms* also, and I remember that at Paris, when the late Mr. Roberval,[1] already an old man, was

ing to their date of composition. The first was written in Latin by François Vertunien, a friend of Scaliger, who took notes of his conversations with Scaliger, especially of all criticisms or anecdotes worthy of preservation, and afterwards wrote them out. An advocate, François de Sigogne, bought the MS. long after the author's death, and published it at Saumer in 1669. The second was written in French and Latin by two youths named Vassan, who, when students at Leyden, habitually conversed after supper with Scaliger, then Professor of Belles Lettres there, and on their return to their rooms wrote out all they could remember of his conversation. Their MS. was finally published at La Haye, 1666, by Isaac Vossius. The edition of the *Scaligerana*, accounted the best, is that of 1740, 12mo. The story is told at length, and the Elegy of the elder Scaliger cited, in the Cologne ed. of the *Scaligerana*, 1695, pp. 69–71.—TR.

[1] Gilles Personne de Roberval, a French geometer, born 1602, at Roberval, a small village of Beauvais, died 1675 at Paris. He was Professor of Mathematics in the Royal College of France for many years. One of the conditions of the tenure of this chair was that its holder should propose mathematical questions for solution, and resign in favor of any one solving them better than himself.

laughed at because he wished to demonstrate those of Euclid after the example of Apollonius[1] and Proclus,[2] I illustrated the utility of this investigation. As for the principle of those who say that it is wholly unnecessary to argue against the one who denies principles, it has no authority whatever in regard to these principles which can admit neither doubt nor proof. It is true that, in order to avoid scandal and disturbance, regulations may be made regarding public disputations and some other lectures, in virtue of which the discussion of certain established truths may be prohibited. But this is rather a question of police than of philosophy.]

Roberval kept the chair till his death. He is best known for his original method for the construction of tangents. — TR.

[1] Apollonius of Perga, born probably about 250 B.C., died in the reign of Ptolemy Philopater, 222–205 B.C. Next to Archimedes, he was the most noted of the Greek geometers. His fame has been transmitted to modern times chiefly by his treatise on the Conic Sections, the best edition of which, and the only one containing the Greek text that has yet appeared, is: *Apollonii pergaei conicorum libri octo*, etc., ed. Halley: Oxford, 1710, folio. He was the first to show that all three of the conic sections can be cut from the same cone by changing the position of the intersecting plane. — TR.

[2] Proclus Diadochus, 410–485, "the great schoolman of Neo-Platonism," the doctrines of which received at his hands the final form in which they have come down to us. He came to Athens in his twentieth year, and remained there teaching and writing till his death. Among his writings now extant are a Treatise on the Sphere, Commentaries on Euclid, and on several of Plato's dialogues, and the wholly independent works Στοιχείωσις Θεολογική, or *Institutes of Theology*, and the six books εἰς τὴν Πλάτωνος Θεολογίαν, or *Platonic Theology*. His philosophical work is found for the most part in the Commentaries on Plato. For his mathematical work, *cf. In primum Euclidis Elementorum librum Commentarii*, ex recognitione G. Friedlein: Lipsiæ, 1873; also George Johnston Allman, *Greek Geometry from Thales to Euclid*, Dublin: University Press, 1889; and in "Hermathena," a series of papers on literature, science, and philosophy, by members of Trinity College, Dublin, Nos. 5, 7, 10–13, Dublin: 1878, 1881, 1884–1887. For his philosophy, *cf.* Zeller, *Die Philos. d. Griech.*, 3d ed., 1881, Vol. 3, pp. 774 *sq.*, and *Outlines*, § 101; Hegel, *Gesch. d. Philos.*, 2d ed., Vol. 3, pp. 61–79; Alfred William Benn, *The Greek Philosophers*, Vol. 2, pp. 358–360, London: Kegan Paul, Trench, & Co., 1882. The *Philosophical and Mathematical Commentaries on the First Book of Euclid's Elements*, etc., were translated by Thomas Taylor, London, 1792, 2 vols. in 1, 4to. — TR.

NEW ESSAYS ON HUMAN UNDERSTANDING

Book II. — Ideas

CHAPTER I

WHICH TREATS OF IDEAS IN GENERAL, AND EXAMINES BY THE WAY WHETHER THE MIND OF MAN ALWAYS THINKS

§ 1. *Ph.* Having examined the question of innate ideas, let us consider their nature and their differences. Is it not true that the *idea* is the object of thought?

Th. [I admit it, provided you add that it is an immediate internal object, and that this object is an expression of the nature or the qualities of things. If the idea were the *form* of thought, it would spring up and cease with the actual thought to which it corresponds; but being the *object* it may exist previous to and after the thoughts. External sensible objects are only *mediate* because they cannot act immediately upon the soul.[1] God alone is the *external immediate* object. We might say that the soul itself is its own immediate *internal* object; but it is this in so far as it contains ideas, or what corresponds to things. For the soul is a little world,[2] in which distinct ideas are a representation of God, and in which confused ideas are a representation of the universe.]

§ 2. *Ph.* We who suppose that at the beginning the soul is a *tabula rasa*, void of all characters and without an idea, ask how it comes to receive ideas, and by what means it acquires this

[1] *Cf.* Book IV., chaps. 9 and 11. The opposition here set up between mediate and immediate knowledge corresponds to Kant's *a posteriori* and *a priori* knowledge. — Tr.

[2] *Microcosm.* — Tr.

prodigious quantity of them? To that question the reply in a word is: From experience.

Th. [This *tabula rasa*, of which so much is said, is in my opinion only a fiction which nature does not admit, and which is based only upon the imperfect notions of philosophers, like the vacuum, atoms, and rest, absolute or relative, of two parts of a whole, or like the primary matter[1] which is conceived as without form. Uniform things and those which contain no variety are never anything but abstractions, like time, space, and the other entities of pure mathematics. There is no body whatever whose parts are at rest, and there is no substance whatever that has nothing by which to distinguish it from every other. Human souls differ, not only from other souls, but also among themselves, although the difference is not at all of the kind called specific. And, according to the proofs which I believe we have, every substantial thing, be it soul or body, has its own characteristic relation to every other; and the one must always differ from the other by *intrinsic connotations.* Not to mention the fact that those who speak so frequently of this *tabula rasa* after having taken away the ideas cannot say what remains, like the scholastic philosophers, who leave nothing in their primary matter.[1] You may perhaps reply that this *tabula rasa* of the philosophers means that the soul has by nature and originally only bare faculties. But faculties without some act, in a word the pure powers of the school, are also only fictions, which nature knows not, and which are obtained only by the process of abstraction. For where in the world will you ever find a faculty which shuts itself up in the power alone without performing any act? There is always a particular disposition to action, and to one action rather than to another. And besides the disposition there is a tendency to action, of which tendencies there is always an infinity in each subject at once; and these tendencies are never without some effect. Experience is necessary, I admit, in order that the soul be determined to such or such thoughts, and in order that it take notice of the ideas which are in us; but by what means can experience and the senses give ideas? Has the soul windows, does it resemble tablets, is it like wax? It is plain that all who so regard the

[1] *Materia Prima.*—TR.

soul, represent it as at bottom corporeal. You oppose to me this axiom received by the philosophers, *that there is nothing in the soul which does not come from the senses.* But you must except the soul itself and its affections. *Nihil est in intellectu, quod non fuerit in sensu,* excipe: *nisi ipse intellectus.* Now the soul comprises being, substance, unity, identity, cause, perception, reason, and many other notions which the senses cannot give. This view sufficiently agrees with your author of the Essay, who seeks the source of a good part of ideas in the spirit's reflection upon its own nature.

Ph. [I hope, then, that you will agree with this skilful author that all ideas come through sensation or through reflection, that is to say, from observations which we make either upon objects exterior and sensible or upon the inner workings of our soul.

Th. [In order to avoid a discussion upon what has delayed us too long, I declare to you in advance, sir, that when you say that ideas come to us from one or the other of these causes, I understand the statement to mean their actual perception, for I think I have shown that they are in us before they are perceived so far as they have any distinct character.

§ 9. *Ph.* [In the next place let us inquire when we must say that the soul begins to perceive and actually to think of ideas. I well know that there is an opinion which states that the soul always thinks, and that actual thought is as inseparable from the soul as actual extension is from the body. § 10. But I cannot conceive that it is any more necessary for the soul always to think than for the body always to be in motion, perception of ideas being to the soul what movement is to the body. That appears to me very reasonable at least, and I would gladly know your view, sir, thereupon.

Th. You have stated it, sir. Action is no more connected with the soul than with the body, a state without thought in the soul and an absolute repose in the body appearing to me equally contrary to nature, and without example in the world. A substance once in action, will be so always, for all the impressions remain and are merely mingled with other new ones. Striking a body, we arouse therein or determine rather an infinite number of vortices as in a liquid, for at bottom every solid has a degree of liquidity and every liquid a degree of solidity, and there are no means of ever stopping entirely these internal vortices. Now we may believe that if the body is never at rest, the soul, which corresponds to it, will never be without perception either.]

Ph. But it is, perhaps, a privilege of the author and conserver of all things, that being infinite in his perfections, he never slumbers nor sleeps. This is not granted to any finite being, or at least not to such a being as is the soul of man.

Th. [It is certain that we slumber and sleep, and that God is exempt from both. But it does not follow that we have no perception while asleep. Rather just the contrary is found to be the case, if we consider it carefully.]

Ph. There is something in us which has the power to think; [but it does not thereby follow that it is always in action.]

Th. [Real powers are never simple possibilities. They have always tendency and action.

Ph. But this proposition — the soul always thinks — is not self-evident.

Th. I do not say it is. A little attention and reasoning is necessary to discover it; the common people perceive it as little as they do the pressure of the air or the roundness of the earth.]

Ph. I doubt if I thought last night; this is a question of fact, it must be decided by sensible experiences.

Th. [It is decided as it is proved, that there are imperceptible bodies and invisible movements, although certain persons treat them as absurd. There are also numberless perceptions little noticed which are not sufficiently distinguished to be perceived or remembered, but they become known through certain consequences.]

Ph. There was a certain author who raised the objection that we maintain that the soul ceases to exist, because we are not sensible of its existence during our sleep. But this objection can arise only from a strange prepossession, for we do not say that there is no soul in man because we are not sensible of its existence during our sleep, but only that man cannot think without being aware of it.

Th. [I have not read the book which contains this objection, but it would not have been wrong merely to object to you that it does not follow because the thought is not perceived, that it ceases for that reason; for otherwise it could be said for the same reason that there is no soul during the time in which it is not perceived. And to refute this objection it is necessary to point out in particular the thought that it is essential to it that it be perceived.]

§ 11. *Ph.* It is not easy to conceive that a thing can think and not be conscious that it thinks.

Th. There is, doubtless, the knot of the affair and the difficulty which has embarrassed able men. But here are the means of extricating ourselves therefrom. We must consider that we think of many things at a time, but we attend only to the thoughts which are most distinct, and the process cannot go on otherwise, for if we should attend to all, we would have to think attentively of an infinite number of things at the same time, all of which we feel and which make an impression upon our senses. I say even more: there remains something of all our past thoughts, and none can ever be wholly effaced. Now when we sleep without dreaming and when we are stunned by some blow, fall, symptom, or other accident, an infinite number of minute confused sensations take form within us, and death itself can produce no other effect upon the souls of animals, who ought, doubtless, sooner or later, to acquire distinct perceptions, for all goes on in an orderly way in nature. I admit, however, that in this state of confusion, the soul would be without pleasure and without pain, for these are noticeable perceptions.

§ 12. *Ph.* Is it not true that those with whom we have at present to do, [*i.e.* the Cartesians, who believe that the soul always thinks,] grant life to all animals, differing from man, without giving them a soul which knows and thinks; and that these same (Cartesians) find no difficulty in saying that the soul can think independently of a body?

Th. [For myself, I am of another opinion, for although I agree with the Cartesians in their affirmation that the soul thinks always, I am not agreed with them in the two other points. I believe that the beasts have imperishable souls and that human and all other souls are never without some body. I hold also that God alone, as being an *actus purus,* is wholly exempt therefrom.]

Ph. If you had been of the opinion of the Cartesians, I should have inferred therefrom, that the bodies of Castor or Pollux could be sometimes with, sometimes without a soul, though being always alive, and the soul having the ability also to be sometimes in one body and sometimes elsewhere, we might suppose that Castor and Pollux had only a single soul, which was active alternately in the body of these two men sleeping and awake by turns; thus it would be two persons as distinct as Castor and Pollux could be.

Th. I, in my turn, will make you another supposition, which appears more real. Is it not true that we must always admit that after some interval or some great change, one may fall into a state of general forgetfulness? Sleidan [1] (they say), before his death, forgot all he knew; and there are many other examples of this sad event. Suppose that such a man became young again and learned all anew, will he be another man on that account? It is not then memory which, properly speaking, makes the same man. Nevertheless, the fiction of a soul which animates different bodies in turn, without concerning itself in one of these bodies with that which happens to it in the other, is one of those fictions contrary to the nature of things which arise from the imperfect notions of philosophers, as space without body and body without motion, and which disappear when one penetrates a little deeper; for you must know

[1] John Sleidan, original name Philipsohn, c. 1506–1556, the annalist of the Reformation. He was secretary for five years from 1536 to Cardinal du Bellay, minister of Francis I. of France. He was wont to copy all documents bearing upon the Reformation to which he had access, and upon the suggestion of Bucer to Philip of Hesse, after some delay was appointed, with the consent of the heads of the Schmalkaldic League, historian of the Reformation, with a salary and access to all necessary documents. He finished the first volume of his great work in 1545. His work was then interrupted by a diplomatic mission in a French embassy to Henry VIII. of England. While there he improved every opportunity to collect materials for his history. In 1551 he was a member of the Council of Trent for Strassburg. On his return he was made Professor of Law at Strassburg, a position which enabled him to devote his whole attention to his great work. It was finished for the press in 1554, and published at Strassburg in 1555. It is entitled: *Commentariorum de statu religionis et reipublicæ Carolo Quinto, Cæsare, libri XXVI.* The ed. of 1555 contained only 25 books; that of 1559 the 26th and an apology of Sleidan, written by himself. The best edition is that of Francfort, 1785–86, 3 vols., 8vo. The work is "the most valuable contemporary history of the times of the reformation, and contains the largest collection of important documents." It is especially noteworthy for its accuracy, impartiality, and purity of style. There are two English translations, by John Daws, 1560, and G. Bohum, 1689. There are also translations in other languages. *Cf.* H. Baumgarten, *Ueber Sleidanus Leben und Briefwechsel*, 1878; *Sleidans Briefwechsel*, 1881. — TR.

that each soul preserves all its preceding impressions, and cannot divide itself equally in the manner just mentioned; the future in each substance is perfectly united to the past; this is what constitutes the identity of the individual. Memory, furthermore, is not necessary, nor even always possible, because of the multitude of present and past impressions which co-operate in our present thoughts, for I do not believe that there are in man thoughts of which there is not some effect at least confused or some remnant mixed with subsequent thoughts. We can forget many things, but we could also remember them long after if we would recall them as we ought.

§ 13. *Ph.* Those who chance to sleep without dreaming can never be convinced that their thoughts are active.

Th. [One is feebly conscious in sleep, even when it is dreamless. The process of waking up itself shows this, and the easier you are awakened the more you are conscious of what goes on without, although this consciousness is not always strong enough to cause you to awake.]

§ 14. *Ph.* It appears very difficult to conceive that the soul is thinking at this moment in a sleeping man and the next in one awake, without remembering its thoughts.

Th. [Not only is that easy to conceive, but also something like it is observed every day that we are awake; for we always have objects which strike our eyes and ears, and, as a result, the soul is touched also, without our taking notice of it, because our attention is bent upon other objects, until this object becomes strong enough to draw it to itself, by redoubling its action or by some other means; it is like a particular sleep with reference to that object, and this sleep becomes general when our attention ceases to regard all objects together. Division of attention, in order to weaken it, is also a means of putting yourself to sleep.]

Ph. I learned from a man, who in his youth had applied himself to study and had a tolerably felicitous memory, that he never had a dream until he had had the fever, from which he had just recovered at the time he spoke with me, at the age of twenty-five or twenty-six years.

Th. [I have also been told of a student, more advanced in years, who never had a dream. But it is not upon dreams alone that you must base the perpetuity of the soul's perception, since I have shown how, even while asleep, it has some perception of what goes on without.]

§ 15. *Ph.* To think frequently and not to preserve a single moment the memory of your thought, is to think in a useless manner.

Th. [All impressions have their effect, but all the effects are not always perceptible; when I turn to one side rather than to the other, it is very often through a series of minute impressions of which I am not conscious, and which render one movement a little more uncomfortable than the other. All our unpremeditated actions are the results of a concurrence of minute perceptions, and even our customs and passions, which influence so much our deliberations, come therefrom; for these habits grow little by little, and, consequently, without the minute perceptions, we should not arrive at these noticeable dispositions. I have already remarked that he who would deny these effects in the sphere of morals, would imitate the poorly taught class who deny insensible corpuscles in physics; and yet I see that among those who speak of liberty are some who, taking no notice of these unperceived impressions, capable of inclining the balance, imagine an entire indifference in moral actions, like that of the ass of Buridan[1] equally divided between two meadows. Concerning this we shall speak more fully later. I admit, however, that these impressions incline without necessitating.

Ph. Perhaps we might say that in the case of a man awake who thinks, his body counts for something and that memory is preserved by means of marks in the brain, but when he is asleep the soul thinks apart by itself.

[1] John Buridan, a celebrated Nominalist of the 14th century, the date of whose birth and death is unknown. He studied at Paris under William of Occam (died 1347) and was for many years Professor of Philosophy in the University of Paris, and in 1327 its rector. In philosophy his only authority was reason. In the third book, first question, of his *Quæstiones in decem libros ethicorum Aristotelis*, 1489, he discussed in an "independent and interesting manner" the question of the freedom of the will, reaching conclusions similar to those of Locke. In his view the liberty possessed by the soul consists in "a certain power of suspending the deliberative process, and determining the direction of the intellect; otherwise the will is entirely dependent on the view of the mind, the last result of examination." The story of the ass as an illustration of the indeterminism of the will "is not," as Sir William Hamilton says (Reid, 8th ed., Vol. 1, p. 238, note) he has ascertained, "to be found in his writings." On Buridan, *cf.* Ueberweg, *Hist. of Philos.*, English translation, Vol. 1, pp. 465–466; Prantl, *Gesch. d. Logik*, Vol. 4, 14–38; Stöckl, *Gesch. d. Philos. d. Mittelalters*, Vol. 2, 1023–1028. — TR.

Th. I am very far from saying that, since I believe there is always an exact correspondence between the body and the soul, and since I employ the impressions of the body of which we are not conscious, whether awake or asleep, in order to prove that the soul has in itself similar ones. I maintain even that something goes on in the soul which corresponds to the circulation of the blood and to all the internal movements of the viscera, of which we are never conscious however, just as those who live near a water-mill do not perceive the noise it makes. In fact, if there were impressions in the body during sleep or waking hours, by which the soul was not touched or in any wise affected, limits would be given to the union of the soul and of the body, as if corporeal impressions required a certain form and size in order for the soul to perceive them; which is not at all tenable if the soul is incorporeal, for there is no relation between an incorporeal substance and this or that modification of matter. In a word, it is a great source of error to believe that there is no perception in the soul besides those of which it is conscious.

§ 16. *Ph.* The greater part of the dreams which we remember are extravagant and incoherent. We should then say that the soul owes the power of rational thought to the body, or that it retains none of its rational soliloquies.

Th. [The body responds to all the soul's thoughts, rational or not, and dreams have also their marks in the brain as well as the thoughts of those who are awake.

§ 17. *Ph.* Since you are so sure that the soul is always actually thinking, I wish you would tell me what the ideas are which are in the child's soul before it is united to the body, or just at the time of its union, before it has received any idea by means of sensation.

Th. It is easy to satisfy you by our principles. The soul's perceptions correspond always naturally to the constitution of the body, and when there are a multitude of movements confused and little distinguished in the brain, as happens in the case of those who have little experience, the soul's thoughts (following the order of the things) cannot be more distinct. Yet the soul is never deprived of the help of *sensation*, because it always expresses its body, and this body is always impressed by its surroundings[1] in an infinite number of ways, but which often give only a confused impression.

§ 18. *Ph.* But here is still another question which the author of this Essay asks. I very much wish (says he) that those who maintain so confidently that the soul of man or (what is the same thing) man thinks always, would tell me how they know it?

Th. [I do not know but that more confidence is necessary to deny that anything goes on in the soul of which we are not conscious; for that which is perceivable must be composed of parts which are not so, nothing can spring into being at once, thought no more than motion. In short, it is as if some one asked to-day how we know the insensible corpuscles.

§ 19. *Ph.* I do not remember that those who tell us that the soul always thinks ever say that man always thinks.

Th. [I think that is because they understand their statement of the separated soul, and yet they voluntarily admit that man always thinks during the union. For myself, who have reasons for holding that the soul is never separated from the entire body, I believe that we can state absolutely that man always does and will think.]

Ph. To say that the body is extended without having parts, and that a thing thinks without being conscious that it thinks, are two assertions which appear equally unintelligible.

Th. [Pardon me, sir; I am obliged to tell you that when you advance the statement that there is nothing in the soul of which it is not conscious, you beg the question which has already prevailed in all our former discussion, or you have been desirous to use it to destroy innate ideas and truths. If we agree to this principle, in addition to the fact that we believe it contrary to experience and reason, we should surrender without reason to our feeling, which, I believe, I have rendered sufficiently intelligible. But besides the fact that our opponents, skilful as they are, have brought no proof of that which they urge so often and so positively, it is easy to show them the contrary; *i.e.* that it is impossible for us always to think

[1] Gerhardt reads: "frappé par les ambians d'une infinité de manières, mais qui souvent ne donnent qu'une impression confuse." Erdmann and Jacques read: "frappé par les autres, qui l'environnent, d'une infinité de manières, mais qui souvent ne font qu'une impression confuse."—Tr.

expressly upon all our thoughts; otherwise, the spirit would reflect upon each reflection to infinity without ever being able to pass to a new thought. For example, in my consciousness of some present feeling, I should always think that I think, and still think that I think of my thought, and thus to infinity. But it is very necessary that I cease reflecting upon all these reflections, and that there be at length some thought which is allowed to pass without thinking of it; otherwise, we should dwell always upon the same thing.]

Ph. But would there not be as good ground for maintaining that a man is always hungry, by saying that he can be hungry without feeling it?

Th. There is just the difference; hunger has particular reasons which do not always exist. Nevertheless, it is true also that even when you are hungry you do not think of it every moment; but when you do think of it you feel it, for it is a very marked disposition; there is always irritation in the stomach, but it is necessary for it to become very strong to cause hunger. The same distinction ought always to be made between thoughts in general and remarkable thoughts. Thus, what appears to put a ridiculous construction upon our opinion, serves to confirm it.]

§ 23. *Ph.* One can now ask, when man begins to have ideas in his thought? And it seems to me that the reply must be, when he has some sensation.

Th. [I am of the same opinion; but it is by a principle a little peculiar, for I believe that we are never without thoughts, and also never without sensation. I distinguish only between ideas[1] and thoughts; for we always have all pure or distinct ideas independently of the senses; but thoughts always correspond to some sensation.]

§ 25. But the mind is passive only in the perception of simple ideas, which are the rudiments or materials of knowledge, while it is active when it forms complex ideas.

Th. [How can it be that the mind is passive merely with regard to the perception of all simple ideas, since, according to your own admission, there are simple ideas whose per-

[1] Gerhardt reads: "Je distingue seulement entre les idées et les pensées"; Erdmann and Jacques read: "Je distingue seulement entre sensations et pensées." — Tr.

ception comes from reflection, and since the mind[1] gives itself thoughts from reflection, for it is itself which reflects? Whether it can refuse them is another question, and doubtless it cannot (refuse them) without some reason, which turns it aside from them, when there is some occasion for it.]

Ph. [It seems that hitherto we have discussed *ex professo.* Now that we are going to come to the detail of ideas, I hope that we shall be more agreed, and that we shall differ only in some particulars.]

Th. [I shall be delighted to see able men adopting the views which I hold to be true, for they are adapted to improve them and to show them in a good light.]

CHAPTER II

SIMPLE IDEAS

§ 1. *Ph.* I hope then that you will admit that there are simple and complex ideas; thus heat and softness in wax, and cold in ice, furnish simple ideas, for the soul has a uniform conception of them, which is not distinguishable into different ideas.

Th. [I believe that we can affirm that these sense-ideas are simple in appearance, because, being confused, they do not give the mind the means of distinguishing their contents. In like manner distant things appear round, because their angles cannot be discerned, although some confused impression of them is received. It is manifest, for example, that green arises from a mixture of blue and yellow; thus it is possible to believe that the idea of green is also composed of these two ideas. And yet the idea of green appears to us as simple as that of blue or that of warmth. So we are to believe that the ideas of blue and warmth are not as simple as they appear. I readily consent, however, to treat these ideas as simple ideas, because at least our apperception does not divide them, but it

[1] Gerhardt reads: "et que l'esprit se donne"; Erdmann and Jacques read: "et qu'au moins l'esprit se donne," and since the mind at least gives itself. — Tr.

is necessary to proceed to their analysis by means of other experiences and by reason, in proportion as they can be rendered more intelligible.[1] And it is also seen thereby that there are perceptions of which we are not conscious. For the perceptions of ideas simple in appearance are composed of perceptions of the parts of which these ideas are composed, without the mind's being conscious of them, for these confused ideas appear simple to it.]

CHAPTER III

OF IDEAS WHICH COME TO US BY ONE SENSE ONLY

Ph. Now we can arrange simple ideas according to the means by which we perceive them, for that is done, 1, by means of one sense only; 2, by means of more than one sense; 3, by reflection, or 4, by all the ways[2] of sensation as well as by reflection. Thus of those which enter by a single sense which is particularly adapted to receive them, light and colors enter only by the eyes; all kinds of noises, sounds, and tones enter by the ears; the different tastes by the palate; and odors by the nose. These organs or nerves carry them to the brain, and if any one of these organs chance to be disordered, these sensations cannot be admitted by any artificial gate. The most considerable qualities belonging to the touch are cold, heat, and solidity. The others consist either in the configuration of the sensible parts, as smooth and rough, or in their union, as compact, hard, soft, brittle.[3]

Th. [I quite agree, sir, with what you say, although I may remark that, according to the experiment of the late M. Mariotte[4] upon the defect of vision with regard to the optic

[1] Erdmann's and Jacques's texts of chap. 2 end here; Gerhardt's text adds the following: "Et l'on voit encor par là qu'il y a des perceptions dont on ne s'apperçoit point. Car les perceptions des idées simples en apparence sont composées des perceptions des parties dont ces idées sont composées, sans que l'esprit s'en apperçoive, car ces idées confuses luy paroissent simples." — Tr.

[2] Locke's expression. *Philos. Works*, Vol. 1, p. 227, Bohn's ed. — Tr.

[3] Locke uses these forms, instead of the more common abstract forms ending in -ness. Hence I have used them in the translation. — Tr.

[4] Edme Mariotte, a celebrated French physicist, born about 1620, died 1684. He was in some sense the initiator of experimental physics in France. The experiment here referred to, and the resulting discovery of the blind spot at

nerve, it seems to me that the membranes receive the sensation rather than the nerves, and there is an irregular entrance for the hearing and the taste, since the teeth and the *vertex* assist in causing any sound to be heard, and that tastes make themselves known to some extent through the nose, by reason of the connection of these organs. But all that makes no change in the foundation of things as regards the explication of ideas. As for the qualities belonging to touch, you can say that smoothness or roughness, hardness or softness, are only modifications of resistance or solidity.]

CHAPTER IV

OF SOLIDITY

§ 1. *Ph.* You will doubtless agree that the idea of solidity is caused by the resistance we find in a body to the entrance of another body into the place it occupies until it has left it. That which thus hinders the approach of two bodies when they are moved one toward another I call solidity. If any one finds it more to the purpose to call it *impenetrability*, I give my consent. But I believe that the term solidity bears a more positive character. This idea seems most intimately connected with and essential to body, and can be found only in matter.

Th. It is true that we find resistance in touch, when another body reluctantly gives place to our own, and it is also true that bodies dislike to occupy the same place. Many, however, doubt whether this repugnance is invincible, and it is well also to consider that the resistance which is found in matter is derived in more than one way and by means of reasons quite different. A body resists another either when it must leave the place which it has already occupied, or when it fails to enter the place into which it was ready to enter, because the other tries to enter also, in which case it may happen that, the one not yielding to the other, they stop or mutually repel each

the entrance of the optic nerve, was made in 1668. An account of it is given in a short paper in the second volume of his collected works. *Œuvres de Mariotte*, 2 vols., Leyden: 1717, 4to. — Tr.

other. The resistance is seen in the change of that (body) to which resistance is offered, whether it loses its force, changes its direction, or both happen at once. Now you can say in general that this resistance arises from the repugnance which two bodies have to occupy the same place, which may be called impenetrability. Thus when one body makes an effort to enter, it at the same time forces the other to attempt to leave or to prevent its entrance. But that kind of incompatibility which makes one or the other, or both together, yield, being once assumed, there are several reasons besides the one named which make one body resist another which endeavors to compel its departure. They are either in it or in the neighboring bodies. There are two which are in itself; one is passive and constant, the other active and variable. The first is what I call *inertia*,[1] after Kepler[2] and Descartes, which impels matter to resist motion, and which it is necessary to destroy by force in order to move a body, supposing that there were neither gravity nor adhesion. Thus a body which undertakes to drive forward another, experiences for that reason this resistance. The other cause, which is active and variable, consists in the impetuosity of the body itself, which does not yield without resistance at the moment its own impetuosity carries it into a place. The same reasons reappear in the neighboring bodies when the body which resists is unable to yield without causing the others to yield also. But then a new consideration comes in — viz.: *compactness* (*fermeté*) or the adhesion of one body to another. This adhesion[3] makes it impossible to move one body without at the same time moving the other to which it adheres, and this causes a kind of *traction* in reference to this other. This adhesion so acts that, even should we put aside inertia and manifest impetuosity, there would be resistance; for if space is conceived as filled with matter perfectly fluid, and if a single hard body were placed within it, this hard body (supposing there were in the fluid neither inertia nor impetuosity) will be moved therein without finding any resistance; but if space were full of little

[1] Gerhardt reads "incertie"; evidently an error. — TR.

[2] John Kepler, 1571-1630, one of the creators of modern astronomy. His complete works were edited by Dr. Ch. Frisch, *Joannis Kepleri opera omnia*, 8 vols., Frankfort: 1858-1871. — TR.

[3] Erdmann and Jacques add "souvent," often. — TR.

cubes, the resistance which the hard body would find, should it be moved among the cubes, would come from the fact that the little hard cubes, on account of their hardness or because of the adhesion of their parts one to another, would with difficulty be separated as much as would be necessary to make a circle of movement, and to fill up the place of the body moved at the moment it departs. But if two bodies should enter at the same time by the two ends into a tube open on both sides, and should fill it to its capacity, the matter in this tube, however fluid it be, would resist by its impenetrability alone. Thus, in the resistance of which we are here treating, we have to consider the impenetrability of bodies, inertia, impetuosity, and adhesion. It is true that, in my opinion, this adhesion of bodies arises from a more subtile motion of one body toward another; but, as this is a point which may be disputed, it must not be assumed at first. And for the same reason we must only assume at first an original, essential solidity, which makes the place always equal to the body, that is to say that the incompatibility, or, to speak more accurately, the *non-consistence*[1] of bodies in the same place is a perfect impenetrability which receives neither more nor less, since many maintain that *sensible solidity* can arise from a repugnance on the part of bodies to be found in the same place, but which will not prove to be an invincible repugnance. For all the ordinary Peripatetics and many others believe that the same matter can fill more or less space, which phenomenon they call rarefaction or condensation, not in appearance only (as when water is squeezed from a sponge), but rigorously, like the scholastic conception of the air. I am not of this opinion; but I do not think that I ought at first to assume the opposite opinion, the senses, apart from the reasoning faculty, not sufficing to establish this perfect impenetrability, which I hold to be true in the order of nature, but which is not learned by sensation alone. And some one may claim that the resistance of bodies to compression arises from an effort of the parts to spread themselves when they have not their entire liberty. For the rest the eyes aid greatly in proving these qualities, coming to the assistance of

[1] Leibnitz's word is "l'inconsistence," and, as it is apparently technical, I have decided to transfer it, merely changing the form of the negative *in-* to *non-* to avoid ambiguity.—TR.

touch. And at bottom solidity, so long as it presents a distinct idea, is conceived by pure reason, although the senses furnish the reasoning faculty with the proof that it is in nature.

§ 4. *Ph.* We are at least agreed that the *solidity* of a body carries with it the filling of the space it occupies in such a way as absolutely to exclude every other body [if a space can be found in which there was none before], while *hardness* [or the consistence rather which some call compactness (*fermeté*)], is a strong union of certain parts of matter, which make up masses of a sensible size, so that the whole mass does not easily change its form.

Th. [This consistence, as I have already remarked, is precisely what makes it difficult to move one part of a body without the other, so that when one part is pushed, the other, which is not pushed, and which does not fall within the line of tendency, is nevertheless induced to go from that side by a kind of *traction;* and, further, if this last part finds any obstacle which holds or pushes it back, it draws it along, or holds back, also, the first part; and this action is always reciprocal. The same thing sometimes happens in the case of two bodies which do not touch and which do not form a continuous body whose parts are contiguous; and yet, the one pushed compels the other to go without pushing it, so far as the senses can give us knowledge. Of this the animant,[1] electrical attraction,

[1] See Krauth-Fleming, *Vocab. Philos. Sciences*, pp. 28, 29, and 571, edition of 1877, New York: Sheldon & Co., 1883. The *animant* is that which possesses and imparts life. Together with its cognates *animality*, *animalish*, *animalist*, used frequently by Cudworth. See *Intell. Syst.*, 514, "*Ut sit Animans*, that it be Animant, or endued with Life, Sense, and Understanding." *Ibid.*, 198. "But no Atheist ever acknowledged conscious *animality* to be a first principle in the universe; nor that the whole was governed by any *animalist*, sentient, and understanding nature, presiding over it as the head of it." The term being technical, and, with its cognates, more or less current in the seventeenth century, it seemed best to retain it, defining and illustrating as above. Its meaning is, I think, sufficiently evident. It is to be noticed, however, that Erdmann, in his *Errores Typographici*, prefixed to his edition, reads *aimant* instead of *animant*. Jacques's text also has *aimant*. The translation would then be: The *loadstone* or *magnet;* and Schaarschmidt, following this reading, renders it "der Magnet," in his German translation of the *Nouveaux Essais*, in J. H. v. Kirchmann's *Philos. Bibliothek*, Berlin, 1873. As I translate on the basis of Gerhardt's text I retain his reading and its translation, with the note explaining the term, although at the present writing the reading of Erdmann and Jacques seems more congruous with the context, and so more likely to be the true one. — TR.

and that which was formerly ascribed to the fear of a vacuum, furnish examples.]

Ph. It seems that, in general, hard and soft are names which we give to things solely as related to the particular constitution of our bodies.

Th. [But then many philosophers would not ascribe hardness to their atoms. The notion of *hardness* does not depend upon the senses, and its possibility can be conceived by the reason, although we are further convinced by the senses that it is actually found in nature. I should, however, prefer the word *compactness* — *fermeté* (if I were allowed to use the word in this sense) — to that of *hardness,* for there is some compactness even in soft bodies. I seek even a more suitable and general term, like *consistence* or *cohesion.* Thus I would oppose hard to soft, solid to fluid, for wax is soft, but, unless melted by heat, it is not fluid and preserves its bounds; and in fluids even there is ordinarily cohesion, as is shown in drops of water and of mercury. I am also of opinion that all bodies have some degree of *cohesion,* as I also believe that there are none which do not have some *fluidity,* and whose cohesion is not capable of being overcome; so that, in my opinion, the atoms of Epicurus,[1] whose hardness is supposed to be invincible, cannot occur any more than the subtile, perfectly fluid matter of the Cartesians. But this is not the place to justify this opinion or to explain the rationale of cohesion.

Ph. The perfect solidity of bodies seems to be justified by experiment. For example, water incapable of yielding, passed through the pores of a hollow globe of gold, in which it was confined, when this globe was put under pressure in Florence.

Th. [There is something to be said as to the inference which you draw from this experiment, and from what happened in the case of the water. The air as well as the water is a body, which is compressible at least *ad sensum,* and those who would maintain a complete rarefaction and condensation will say that water is already too compressed to yield to our machines, as air very much compressed would resist also a further compression. I admit, however, on the other hand, that if any slight change should be noticed in the volume of the water, it might be ascribed to the air which is enclosed in it. Without enter-

[1] Epicurus, December, 342, or January, 341-270 B.C. — TR.

ing now into the discussion whether pure water is not itself compressible, as it is found that it is dilatable when it evaporates, I am, nevertheless, decidedly of the opinion of those who believe that bodies are perfectly impenetrable, and that there is, save in appearance, neither condensation nor rarefaction. But this kind of experiment is as little capable of proving this as the tube of Torricelli[1] or the machine of Guerike[2] are sufficient to prove a perfect vacuum.[3]

§ 5. *Ph.* If the body were strictly capable of rarefaction and compression, it might change in volume or extension, but that not being so, it will be always equal to the same space; and, moreover, its extension will be always distinct from that of space.

Th. [The body might have its own extension, but it does not thereby follow that it would be always determinate or equal to the same space. Nevertheless, although it may be true that in the conception of body something besides space is conceived of, it does not thereby follow that there are two extensions — that of space and that of body; for it is as when in conceiving several things at once, one conceives something besides the number, viz.: *res numeratœ;* and, moreover, there are not two multitudes, the one abstract — *i.e.*, that of number; the other concrete — *i.e.*, that of the things enumerated. Likewise one can say that it is not necessary to think of two extensions — the one abstract, of space, the other concrete, of body, the con-

[1] Evangelista Torricelli, 1608–1647, a celebrated Italian physicist and mathematician, the inventor of the mercurial barometer, long called the "Torricellian tube." He had a controversy with Roberval (*vid. ante*, p. 107 and note) as to the discovery of the quadrature of the cycloid. Torricelli found the area of the curve, and furnished the demonstration of it, which he published in a tract, *De motu gravium naturaliter accelerato* in his *Opera geometrica*, Florence, 1644. — Tr.

[2] Otto von Guerike, 1602–1686, a German physicist, who devoted himself especially to experimenting upon the vacuum, and who, after many attempts, finally, in 1654, hit upon an air machine, which enabled him to undertake a series of experiments upon the different effects of vacuum. His labors and principal observations have been published under the title, *Experimenta nova, ut vocant, Magdeburgica, de vacuo spatio*, etc., Amsterdam, 1672. — Tr.

[3] Descartes maintained the impossibility of a vacuum. *Cf. Prin. Philos.*, II., § 16; English translation by John Veitch, LL.D., *The Method, Meditations, and Selections from the Principles of Descartes*, etc., 8th ed., p. 241, Edinburgh: William Blackwood & Sons, 1881; also *vid. ante*, p. 16, and the fifth letter to Samuel Clarke, § 34, Gerhardt, Vol. 7, p. 396; Erdmann, p. 766, b; translation, Duncan, *Philos. Works of Leibnitz*, p. 262. — Tr.

crete existing as such only through the abstract. And as bodies pass from one part of space to another — *i.e.*, change order among themselves — things also pass from one part of the order or of a number to the other, when, for example, the first becomes the second and the second the third, etc. In fact, time and space are only kinds of order,[1] and in these orders the vacant place (which in relation to space is called vacuum), if there were any, would show the possibility only of that which is lacking together with its relation to the actual.

Ph. I am nevertheless very glad that you agree with me that matter does not change in volume. But you seem to go too far, sir, in not recognizing two extensions, and you resemble the Cartesians, who do not distinguish space from matter.[2] Now it seems to me that if a class is found who, not having these distinct ideas (of space and of solidity which fills it), blends them and makes of the two one only, we cannot see how these persons can converse with others. They are like a blind man who, when another man speaks to him of scarlet, thinks it resembles the sound of a trumpet.

Th. [But I hold at the same time that the ideas of extension and solidity, like that of scarlet-color, do not consist in an *I know not what.*[3] I distinguish extension and matter, contrary

[1] *Cf.* Letter to Des Bosses, June 16, 1712, Gerhardt, Vol. 2, p. 450; Erdmann, p. 682, b: "Spatium fit ordo coexistentium phænomenorum, ut tempus successivorum," *i.e.* "Space is the order of co-existing, as time of successive phenomena"; also the letters to Clarke, Gerhardt, Vol. 7, pp. 345 *sq.*; Erdmann, pp. 746 *sq.*, translation, Duncan, *Philos. Works of Leibnitz*, pp. 238 *sq.*; Kant, *Kritik d. r. Vernunft*, Erst. Th., Absch. 1 und 2, §§ 2–7, and translations of Max Müller, and Watson in *The Philosophy of Kant, as contained in extracts from his own writings.* New York: Macmillan & Co., 1888. — TR.

[2] *Cf.* Descartes, *Prin. Philos.* II., §§ 8–15; Veitch's translation, pp. 236–240. — TR.

[3] Leibnitz's expression is "un *je ne say quoi.*" Schaarschmidt translates it "ein *undenkbares Etwas.*" It seems to be equivalent to an indefinite somewhat which is the ultimate essence of things, and which is the cause of, and by differentiation becomes, the particular. Leibnitz, then, means to say that the ideas of extension and solidity are distinct. *Cf.* John Dewey, Ph.D., *Leibniz's New Essays concerning the Human Understanding, a Critical Exposition*, p. 134. As applied to personal beings, it seems to be equivalent to the "unconscious presentations" — *i.e.* "the dark side of the soul-life," "the proper basis of Individuality." "Genius, disposition, feeling, are the terms by which a later time has designated what Leibnitz calls the *je ne sais quoi*, whereby every one is preformed by nature to something particular" ("Ganz wie bei dem blossen Monaden ihre individuelle Beschaffenheit in dem Momente der Schranke, der *materia prima*, lag, ganz so werden

to the view of the Cartesians. Still I do not believe that there are two extensions; and since those who dispute over the difference between extension and solidity are agreed on several truths upon this subject and have some distinct notions, they can find therein the means of extricating themselves from their disagreement; thus the assumed difference upon ideas ought not to serve as a pretext for eternal disputes, although I know that certain Cartesians, otherwise very able, are accustomed to intrench themselves in the ideas which they pretend to have. But if they would avail themselves of the means which I have before given for recognizing ideas true and false, and of which we shall speak also in the sequel, they would retire from a position which is not tenable.

CHAPTER V

OF SIMPLE IDEAS WHICH COME BY DIFFERENT SENSES

Ph. The ideas, the perception of which comes to us from more than one sense, are those of space, or extension, or figure, of motion and rest.

Th. [The ideas which are said to come from more than one sense, like those of space, figure, motion, rest, are rather from common-sense, that is to say, from the mind itself, for they are ideas of the pure understanding, but related to externality, and which the senses make us perceive; they are also capable of definition and demonstration.]

hier diese unbewussten Vorstellungen, d. h. wird die dunkle Seite des Seelenlebens, als der eigentliche Grund der Individualität bestimmt. Genius, Gemüth, Gefühl sind die Worte, mit denen eine spätere Zeit das bezeichnet hat, was *Leibnitz* das *je ne sais quoi* nennt, wodurch Jeder von Natur zu etwas Besonderem präformirt ist." Erdmann, *Grundriss d. Gesch. d. Philos.*, 3te Auflage 2te Bd. § 288, 5, s. 161. Berlin, 1878; English translation, Vol. 2, p. 191, London: Swan Sonnenschein & Co., 1889). *Cf.* also Leibnitz, *New Essays*, Preface, *vid. ante*, pp. 47 *sq.*, Book II., chap. 1, § 15, Th., *sq.*, and Erdmann's exposition of the same, *op. cit.*, s. 160, 161. Also Professor Dewey's most excellent work cited above. — TR.

CHAPTER VI

OF SIMPLE IDEAS WHICH COME BY REFLECTION

Ph. The simple ideas which come by reflection are the ideas of the understanding and of the will [for we ourselves perceive them in reflecting upon ourselves.]

Th. [It is doubtful if all these ideas are simple, for it is clear, for example, that the idea of the will includes that of the understanding, and that the idea of motion contains that of figure.

CHAPTER VII

OF IDEAS WHICH COME BY SENSATION AND REFLECTION

§ 1. *Ph.* There are some simple ideas which make themselves perceived in the mind by all the avenues of sensation and by reflection also — viz.: pleasure, pain, power, existence, unity.

Th. [It seems that the senses cannot convince us of *the existence* of sensible things without the aid of the reason. Thus I should think that the idea[1] of existence comes from reflection. That of power also and of unity come from the same source, and are of a wholly different nature from the perceptions of pleasure and pain.]

CHAPTER VIII

OTHER CONSIDERATIONS UPON SIMPLE IDEAS

§ 2. *Ph.* What shall we say of ideas of privative qualities? It seems to me that the ideas of rest, darkness, and cold are as positive as those of motion, light, and heat. Nevertheless, in proposing these privations as the causes of privative ideas I follow the common view; but in the main it will be difficult

[1] The French is "la consideration de l'existence." — TR.

to determine whether there is really any idea which arises from a privative cause until it has been determined whether rest any more than motion is a privation.

Th. [I had not believed that we could have reason to doubt the privative nature of rest. It suffices it that motion in the body be denied, but it does not suffice for motion to deny rest, and it is necessary to add something more to determine the degree of motion, since it receives materially more or less, while all rest is equal. It is another thing when we speak of the cause of rest, which must be positive in the secondary[1] matter or mass. I should furthermore regard the very idea of rest as privative—*i.e.*, that it consists only in negation. It is true that the act of denial is positive.]

§ 9. *Ph.* The *qualities* of things being the faculties they have of producing in us perception of ideas, it is well to distinguish these qualities. They are primary and secondary. Extension, solidity, figure, number, mobility are the original qualities inseparable from body which I call *primary*. § 10. But I call

[1] Leibnitz constantly distinguishes between primary and secondary matter. *Primary matter* is the primitive passive power belonging to each separate being as such, by which it is distinguished from God and in which is grounded the possibility of representing itself as different. It is essential to and inseparable from the entelechy, or principle of activity, which it completes, the two united producing the perfect substance or monad. By itself it is a pure abstraction or potentiality, and not a substance. It is equivalent to confused ideas, thus to an imperfect manifestation or phenomenon of spirit—since all matter is ultimately spirit or has its final reason or source in spirit—but a potentiality of spirit capable sometime of realizing perfectly all its intrinsic, but now latent, activity. *Secondary matter* is a mass resulting from the union of many monads or complete substances, each having its own primary matter and its own entelechy, with their derived forces, activities, receptivities. It is not, however, a substance; and its extension resulting from the union of non-extended simple substances is only phenomenal, though not on that account unreal, being due to our confused perception, and consisting in the impenetrability, resistance, or inertia of the monad on its passive side; an extension which will disappear when the activity of the monad becomes pure and perfect. *Cf.* Letters to Tolomei, Dec. 17, 1705, Gerhardt, Vol. 7, pp. 467–468; Des Bosses, March 11, Oct. 16, 1706, March 16, 1709, Gerhardt, Vol. 2, pp. 304, 324, 368; Erdmann, pp. 435, 440, 456; *De anima brutorum*, 1710, G. 7, 328; E. 463; Letters to Rud. Christ. Wagner, June 4, 1710, G. 7, 528, E. 465; translation, Duncan, *Philos. Works of Leibnitz*, p. 190 *sq.*; Bierling, Aug. 12, 1711, G. 7, 500–502, E. 677–678; Remond, Nov. 4, 1715, G. 3, 656–660; E. 735–737; Feb. 11, 1715, § 4 (reply to Remond's fourth difficulty stated in his letter to Leibnitz, Jan. 9, 1715), G. 3, 636, E. 725; also the writing dated July, 1714, and first published by Gerhardt, 3, 622–624. *Cf.* also Erdmann, *Grund. d. Gesch. d. Philos.*, 3d ed., § 288, 2, 3; Dewey, *Leibnitz*, *New Essays*, chaps. 7 and 8.—TR.

secondary qualities the faculties or powers of bodies to produce certain sensations in us, or certain effects in other bodies, as the fire, for example, produces a certain effect in the wax when melting it.

Th. [I think we can say that when the power is intelligible, and can be distinctly explained, it should be reckoned among *the primary qualities;* but when it is only sensible and gives only a confused idea, it should be put among *the secondary qualities.*]

§ 11. *Ph.* These primary qualities show how bodies act upon one another. Now, bodies act only by impulse, at least so far as we can conceive the process, for it is impossible to understand how bodies can act upon what they do not touch, which is equivalent to imagining that they can act where they are not.

Th. [I am also of the opinion that bodies act only by impulse. Yet, there is some difficulty in the proof of what I have just heard; for attraction sometimes occurs without contact, and we can touch and draw without any visible impulse, as I have shown above [1] in speaking of hardness. In the case of the atoms of Epicurus, the one part pushed would draw the other with it, and would touch it in putting it in motion without impulse. And in the case of attraction between contiguous things we cannot say that the one which draws with itself acts where it is not. This reason would militate only against attractions from a distance, as would be the case in reference to what are called *vires centripetæ* advanced by some scholars.]

§ 13. *Ph.* Now, certain particles, striking our organs in a certain way, cause in us certain sensations of colors or tastes or other secondary qualities which have the power of producing these sensations. And it is no more difficult to conceive that God can attach such ideas (as that of heat) to motions, with which they have no resemblance, than it is difficult to conceive that he has attached the idea of pain to the motion of a piece of iron which divides our flesh; which motion the pain in no manner resembles.

Th. [It is not necessary to suppose that ideas like those of color or of pain are arbitrary and without relation or natural connection with their causes; it is not the custom of God to

[1] *Cf.* Bk. II., Chap. 4, § 4, Th., *ante*, p. 125, *sq.*—TR.

act with so little order and reason. I should rather say that there is a kind of resemblance, not complete and, so to speak, *in terminis*, but expressive, or a kind of orderly relation, as an ellipse, and even a parabola or hyperbola resemble in some sense the circle of which they are a projection upon a plane, since there is a certain exact and natural relation between what is *projected* and the projection which is made, each point of the one corresponding by a certain relation to each point of the other. This the Cartesians do not sufficiently consider, and for once you have deferred to them more than has been customary with you, and without reason for so doing.]

§ 15. *Ph.* I tell you what appears to me, and the appearances are that the ideas of the primary qualities of bodies resemble these qualities, but the ideas produced in us by the secondary qualities resemble them in no way.

Th. [I have just shown how there is resemblance or exact relation in respect to the secondary as well as the primary qualities. It is certainly reasonable that the effect correspond to its cause; and how assert the contrary, since you know distinctly neither the sensation of blue (for example) nor the motions which produce it? It is true that pain does not resemble the motion of a pin, but it may very well resemble the motions which this pin causes in our body, and represent these motions in the soul, as I have no doubt it does. It is also for this reason that we say that the pain is in our body and not that it is in the pin; but we say that the light is in the fire, because there are in the fire motions which are not distinctly sensible apart from it, but whose confusion or conjunction becomes sensible, and is represented to us by the idea of light.

§ 21. *Ph.* But if the relation between the object and the sensation be natural, how can it be, as we notice in fact, that the same water may appear warm to one hand and cold to the other? which shows that the heat is no more in the water than the pain is in the pin.

Th. [This proves all the more that heat is not a sensible quality or power of making itself felt absolutely all at once, but that it is relative to the suitable organs; for a particular motion in the hand may be mixed with it and change its appearance. Light, furthermore, does not make itself evident to badly constituted eyes, and when they are themselves filled with a great light, they are insensible to a less. Even the primary qualities (according to our classification) — for example, unity and number — may not appear as they should; for, as Descartes has already stated, a globe touched by the fingers in a certain way appears double, and mirrors or glasses cut in facets multiply the object. It does not then follow that what does not always appear the same is not a quality of the object, and that its image does not resemble it. And as for the heat, when our hand is very warm, the medium heat of the water does not make itself felt, and modifies rather that of the hand, and consequently the water appears to us cold; as the salt water of the Baltic Sea mixed with the water of the Sea of Portugal[1] would lessen its specific saline quality, although the former be itself salt. Thus, in any case, we can say that the heat belongs to the water of a bath, although it may appear cold to any one, as honey is called absolutely sweet, and silver white, although the one appears bitter, the other yellow to some diseased persons, for the classification is made upon the basis of the most common (conditions); and yet it remains true that, when the organ and the medium are constituted as they should be, the internal motions and the ideas which represent them to the soul resemble the motions of the object which cause color, heat, pain, etc., or, what is here the same thing, express it by means of a relation sufficiently exact, although this relation does not distinctly appear to us, because we cannot disentangle this multitude of small impressions either in our soul or our body or in what is without.

§ 24. *Ph.* We consider the qualities which the sun has of blanching or melting wax or hardening mud only as simple powers, without thinking of anything in the sun corresponding to this blanching, softness, or hardness; but heat and light are commonly regarded as real qualities of the sun. Properly considered, however, these qualities of light and heat which in me are perceptions are not in the sun in any other manner than the changes produced in the wax when it is blanched or melted.

[1] Obsolete name for that part of the Atlantic which washes the coast of Portugal. — TR.

Th. [Some have pushed this doctrine so far that they have desired to persuade us that if any one could touch the sun he would find there no heat. The counterfeit sun which makes itself felt in the focus of a mirror or a burning-glass may disabuse people of this notion. But as to the comparison between the power of heating and that of melting, I dare affirm that if the melted or blanched wax had feeling, it would feel something similar to what we feel when the sun warms us, and would say, if it could, that the sun is warm, not because its whiteness resembles the sun — for when faces are tanned in the sun their brown color should likewise resemble it — but because there are in the wax motions which are related to those in the sun which cause them; its whiteness may come from another cause, but not the motions which it has had in receiving it (whiteness) from the sun.]

CHAPTER IX

OF PERCEPTION

§ 1. *Ph.* Come we now to the ideas of reflection in particular. *Perception* is the first faculty of the soul which is occupied with our ideas. It is also the first and simplest idea which we receive by reflection. *Thought* signifies often the mind's working upon its own ideas, when it acts and considers a thing with a certain degree of voluntary attention: but in what we call *perception* the mind is ordinarily purely passive, not being able to avoid perceiving what it actually perceives.

Th. [We might perhaps add that the animals have perception, and that it is not necessary that they have thought, that is to say, that they have reflection or what may be its object. We ourselves also have minute *perceptions* of which we are not conscious in our present state. It is true that we might very well perceive them ourselves, and reflect upon them, if we were not turned aside by their multitude, which distracts our mind, or if they were not effaced, or rather obscured, by greater ones.

§ 4. *Ph.* I admit that when the mind is strongly occupied

in contemplating certain objects it does not perceive in any way the impression which certain bodies make upon the organ of hearing, although the impression may be quite strong; but no perception arises therefrom if the soul takes no cognizance thereof.

Th. [I should prefer to distinguish between *perception* and *consciousness* (*s'appercevoir*).[1] The perception of light and color, for example, of which we are conscious, is composed of many minute perceptions, of which we are not conscious; and a noise which we perceive, but of which we take no notice, becomes *apperceptible* by a little addition or increase; for if what precedes make no impression upon the soul, this little addition would also make none, and the whole would make no more. I have already touched upon this point (Ch. II,[2] of this book, §§ 11, 12, 15, etc.)].

§ 8. *Ph.* It is proper to remark here that the ideas which arise from sensation are often altered by the mental judgment of grown persons without their perceiving the fact. A flat circle with various light and shade represents the idea of a globe of uniform color. But, as we are accustomed to distinguish the images of bodies and the changes of the reflections of light according to the figures of their surfaces, we put in the place of what appears to us the cause the image itself, and confuse the judgment with the appearance.

Th. Nothing is truer, and this it is which gives to painting the means of deceiving us by the artifice of a very extended perspective. When bodies have flat surfaces, they can be represented without employing shadows by giving only their contours and by simply making pictures after the fashion of the Chinese, but better proportioned than theirs. The same

[1] *Cf.* Leibnitz, *Principes de la nature et de la grace fondés en raison*, § 4. "It is well to make a distinction between the *perception*, which is the internal condition of the monad representing external things, and *apperception*, which is *consciousness* or the reflective knowledge of this internal state: the latter not being given to all souls, nor at all times to the same soul." For the entire piece, which is a brief statement of his philosophical system prepared by Leibnitz himself, with the greatest care, about 1714, *cf.* Gerhardt, Vol. 6, pp. 598–606; Erdmann, pp. 714–718; translation, Duncan, *Philos. Works of Leibnitz*, pp. 209–217, and note 66, p. 387 *op. cit.* Also Hamilton's Reid, 8th ed., Vol. 2, p. 877, note, and Krauth-Fleming, *Vocab. Philos.*, ed. of 1877, articles "Apperception," p. 38, "Consciousness," pp. 109–113, 613, "Perception," pp. 373–374, 807–809, "Perceptions (Obscure)," pp. 374–376. — TR.

[2] This should be chap. 1, I think. — TR.

custom is observed in designing medals, in order that the draughtsman may be less likely to depart from the precise form of the antique. But we cannot distinguish exactly by means of the design the interior of a circle from the interior of a spherical surface bounded by this circle without the aid of shadows, the interior of each having neither points distinguished nor distinguishing features, although there is, however, a great difference which ought to be indicated. Desargues[1] has accordingly given precepts upon the force of tints and shades. When, then, a painting deceives us there is a double error in our judgments; for first we put the cause for the effect, and think we see immediately the cause of the image, in which we resemble a little a dog who barks at a mirror; for, properly speaking, we see only the image, and we are affected only by the rays of light. And since the rays of light require time (however little it be), it is possible for the object to be destroyed in this interval, and for it no longer to exist when the ray reaches the eye, and that which no longer exists cannot be the object present to the sight. In the second place, we further deceive ourselves when we put one cause for another, and think that what comes only from a flat picture is derived from a body, so that in this case there is in our judgments all at once a *metonymy* and a *metaphor;* for even the figures of rhetoric pass into *sophisms* when they impose on us. This confusion of the effect with the cause, whether true or false, often enters into our judgments, moreover, upon other things. Thus we feel our bodies, or what touches them, and we move our arms by means of an immediate physical influence, which we think

[1] Gaspard Desargues, 1593–1662, a French geometer and engineer, a friend of Descartes, Gassendi, Pascal, and Roberval, who wrote on the application of geometry to the arts as well as on geometry itself. These writings have been lost and their titles are known only through the engraver Bosse. Of his *Methode universelle de mettre en perspective des objects donnés réellement, ou en devis, avec leurs proportions, mesures, éloignments, sans employer aucun point qui soit hors du champ de l'ouvrage,* 1630 or 1636, Descartes thus speaks in a letter to Mersenne ("written toward the end of April, 1637," according to Cousin, *Œuvres de Descartes,* Vol. 6, pp. 250–256, Paris: 1824–1826), "Je n'ai reçu que depuis peu de jours le petit livre in folio, qui traite de la perspective: il n'est pas à désapprouver, outre que la curiosité et la netteté du langage de son auteur sont à estimer," I received only a few days ago the little book in folio treating of perspective: it is not to be condemned: further the exactness and perspicuity of the author's language are to be admired. —TR.

constitutes the connection of the soul with the body, while in truth we feel and change in that way only what is in us.

Ph. I will at this time propose to you a *problem* which the learned Mr. Molyneux,[1] who employs so profitably his excellent genius in the promotion of the sciences, communicated to the illustrious Mr. Locke. Here it is nearly in his own terms: Suppose a man blind from birth, now grown up, who has learned to distinguish by touch a cube from a globe of the same metal, and almost of the same size, so that when he touches the one or the other he can tell which is the cube and which the globe. Suppose that the cube and the globe being placed upon the table, this blind man comes to enjoy his sight. The question is, if in seeing them without touching them he could distinguish them, and tell which is the cube and which the globe. I pray you, sir, tell me what is your opinion upon the matter.

Th. I ought to give some time to thought upon this question, which appears to me quite curious: but since you press me for an immediate reply, I would venture to say between ourselves that I think that supposing the blind man knows that these two figures which he sees are those of the cube and the globe, he could distinguish them and say, without touching, This is the globe, this the cube.

Ph. I fear lest it may be necessary to put you in the crowd of those who have failed to answer Mr. Molyneux; for he sent word in the letter which contained this question, that, having proposed it upon the occasion of Mr. Locke's Essay on Understanding to different persons of very penetrating minds, he had found scarcely one among them who at once gave such a reply upon that point as he thinks should be made, although they were convinced of their error after having heard his reasons. The reply of this penetrating and judicious author is negative; for (he adds) while this blind man has learned by experience of some kind the globe and the cube as they affect his touch, he does not, however, yet know that what affects the touch in such or such manner must strike the eyes

[1] William Molyneux, 1656–1698, an eminent mathematician. He founded in Dublin, in January, 1684, a Philosophical Society on the model of the Royal Society at London. His principal work, *Dioptrica Nova*, in two parts, was published at London in 1692–1709, in 4to. — TR.

in such or such manner, nor that the projecting angle of the cube, which presses his hand in an unequal manner, must appear to his eyes as it appears in the cube. The author of the Essay declares himself at once of the same opinion.

Th. Perhaps Mr. Molyneux and the author of the Essay are not so far from my opinion as at first appears, and the reasons for their view, contained apparently in the letter of the former, who has employed them with success in order to convince men of their error, have been purposely suppressed by the latter in order to give more exercise to the minds of his readers. If you will weigh my reply, you will find, sir, that I have placed therein a condition which can be considered as comprised in the question — viz.: that the question is that of distinguishing alone, and that the blind man knows that the two figured bodies, which he should distinguish, are there, and that thus each of the appearances which he sees is that of the cube or that of the globe. In this case it appears to me beyond doubt that the blind man who ceases to be such can distinguish them by the principles of reason, united with that sense-knowledge with which touch has before furnished him. For I do not speak of that which he will do perhaps in fact and immediately, dazzled and confused by the novelty, or from some other cause little accustomed to draw inferences. The basis of my view is that in the globe there are no points distinguished by the side of the globe itself, all there being level and without angles, while in the cube there are eight points distinguished from all the others. If there were not this means of discerning the figures, a blind man could not learn the rudiments of geometry by touch. But we see that those born blind are capable of learning geometry, and have indeed always certain rudiments of a natural geometry, and that most often geometry is learned by sight alone, without the use of touch, as indeed a paralytic or other person to whom touch has been almost denied might and even must do. And these two geometries — that of the blind man and that of the paralytic — must meet and agree, and indeed return to the same ideas, although there are no common images. This again shows how necessary it is to distinguish *images from exact ideas,* which consist in definitions. It would really be very interesting and instructive to make a complete examination of the ideas of a man born blind, to understand the descriptions he makes of figures. For he may come to this, and he may even understand the doctrine of optics, so far as it is dependent upon distinct and mathematical ideas, although he could not attain to a conception of *clair-confus*, that is to say, the image of light and of colors. This is why a certain one born blind, after having attended lessons in optics, which he appeared fully to understand, replied to some one who asked him what he thought light was, that he thought it must be something pleasant like sugar. It would likewise be very important to examine the ideas which a man born deaf and dumb may have of things not figured, whose description we usually have in words, and which he must have in a manner wholly different from, though it may be equivalent to ours, as Chinese writing is in fact equivalent to our alphabet, although it is infinitely different, and might appear to have been invented by a deaf man. I learn, through the favor of a great prince, of one born deaf and dumb in Paris, whose ears have at last attained to the performance of their function, that he has now learned the French language (for it is from the court of France that he was summoned not long since), and that he could say very curious things about the conceptions he had in his former condition and about the change of his ideas when he commenced to exercise the sense of hearing. These persons born deaf and dumb can go farther than we think. There was one in Oldenburg in the time of the last Count who became a good painter, and showed himself very rational in other respects. A very learned man, a Breton by nation, told me that at Blainville, about ten leagues from Nantes, belonging to the Duke of Rohan, there was, about 1690, a poor man, who lived in a hut near the castle outside of the town, who was born deaf and dumb, and who carried letters and other things to the town and found the houses, following some signs which the persons accustomed to employ him made him. Finally the poor man became blind also, but did not give up rendering some service and carrying letters into the town to whatever place they indicated to him by touch. He had a board in his hut which, extending from the door to the place where his feet were, informed him by its motion when any one entered his house. Men are very negligent in not obtaining an exact knowledge of the modes of thought of such persons. If he no longer lives, there is probably some one in the vicinity who could still give some information respecting him, and make us understand how they showed him the things he was to do. But to return to what the man born blind, who begins to see, would think of the globe and the cube, seeing them without touching them, I reply that he will distinguish them, as I have just said, if any one informs him that the one or the other of the appearances or perceptions which he has of them belongs to the cube or to the globe; but, without this previous instruction, I admit that he will not at first venture to think that the kinds of pictures which they make of themselves in the depths of his eyes, and which might come from a flat picture upon the table, represent the bodies, until touch convinces him of the fact, or until, by force of reasoning upon the rays of light according to optics, he understands by the lights and shades that there is a something which arrests these rays of light, and that it must be exactly what remains for him in touch, which result he will finally reach when he sees this globe and this cube revolve, and change the shadows and the appearances in accordance with the motion, or even when, these two bodies remaining at rest, the light which illumines them changes its place, or his eyes change their position. For these are about the means we have of distinguishing from afar a picture or a perspective, which represents a body, from the body itself.

§ 11. *Ph.* [Let us return to perception in general.] It distinguishes animals from inferior beings.

Th. [I am inclined to the belief that there is some perception and appetition also in the plants, because of the great analogy which exists between plants and animals; and if, as is commonly supposed, there is a vegetable soul, it of necessity has perception. Yet I do not cease to attribute to mechanism all that takes places in the bodies of plants and animals, except their first formation. Thus I agree that the movement of the plant called sensitive arises from mechanism, and I do not approve of having recourse to the soul when the question is that of explaining the detail of the phenomena of plants and animals.]

§ 14. *Ph.* It is true that for myself, indeed, I cannot help believing that even in those kinds of animals which are like the oysters and mussels there is some feeble perception; for quick sensations would serve only to discommode an animal which is constrained to live always in the place where chance has put it, where it is watered with water, cold or warm, pure or salt, according as it comes to it.

Th. [Very well, I also believe that we can say almost as much of plants; but in man's case, his perceptions are accompanied with the power of reflection, which passes to the act when there is any occasion. But when he is reduced to a state in which he is as it were in a lethargy and almost without feeling, reflection and consciousness cease, and universal truths are not thought of. But the innate and acquired faculties and dispositions, and even the impressions which are received in this state of confusion, do not cease on that account, and are not effaced, though they are forgotten. They will even have their turn one day in contributing to some notable result, for nothing is useless in nature; all confusion must develop itself; the animals even, having attained to a condition of stupidity, ought some day to return to perceptions more elevated; and, since simple substances always endure, we must not judge of eternity by a few years.]

CHAPTER X

OF RETENTION

§§ 1, 2. *Ph.* The other faculty of the mind, by which it advances farther toward the knowledge of things than by simple *perception*, is that which I call *retention*, which conserves the knowledge received by the senses or by reflection. Retention works in two ways: in actually conserving the present idea, which I call *contemplation;* and in preserving the power to bring them again before the mind, and this is what is called *memory*.

Th. [One retains also and contemplates innate knowledge, and very often one cannot distinguish the innate from the acquired. There is also a perception of images — either those which have already existed for some time, or those which are formed anew in us.]

§ 2. *Ph.* But you believe with us that these images or ideas cease to be anything as soon as they are not actually matters of consciousness; and that to say that there are ideas reserved in the memory means at bottom only that the soul has in some instances the *power* of reviving the perceptions it has already had with a feeling which at the same time convinces it that it has previously had these kinds of perceptions.

Th. [If ideas were only forms or modes of thoughts, they would cease with them; but you yourself have admitted, sir, that they are internal objects, and in this way can subsist. And I am astonished that you can always be satisfied with these naked *powers* or *faculties,* which you would apparently reject in the scholastic philosophers. It would be necessary to explain a little more distinctly in what this faculty consists and how it is exercised; and that would make known that there are dispositions which are the remains of past impressions in the soul as well as in the body, but of which we are conscious only when the memory finds some occasion for them. And if nothing restored past thoughts, as soon as we no longer think of them, it would be impossible to explain how the memory can preserve them; and to recur for this purpose to this naked faculty is to speak nowise intelligibly.

CHAPTER XI

OF DISCERNMENT OR THE FACULTY OF DISTINGUISHING IDEAS

§ 1. *Ph.* Upon the faculty of distinguishing ideas depends the evidence and certainty of several propositions which pass for innate truths.

Th. I admit that to think of these innate truths and to unravel them discernment is necessary; but they do not on that account cease to be innate.]

§ 2. *Ph.* Now, *vivacity* of mind consists in recalling promptly ideas; but *judgment* in representing them clearly and distinguishing them exactly.

Th. [Perhaps each is vivacity of imagination, and judgment consists in the examination of propositions according to reason.]

Ph. [I am not averse to this distinction of mind and judgment. And sometimes there is judgment in not employing it too much. For example: to examine certain witty thoughts by the severe rules of truth and good reasoning is in a certain sense an insult.

Th. [This remark is a good one; witty thoughts must have at least some apparent foundation in reason, but it is not necessary to examine them minutely with too much scrupulousness, as it is not necessary to look at a picture from a position too near it. It is in this, it seems to me, that Father Bouhours fails more than once in his *Art de penser dans les ouvrages d'esprit*[1] as when he despises this sally of Lucan:[2]

Victrix causa diis placuit, sed victa Catoni.

§ 4. *Ph.* Another operation of the mind in respect to its ideas is the *comparison* it makes of one idea with another as regards extension, degrees, time, place, or some other circumstance; it is upon this that the great number of ideas comprised under the term *relation* depends.

Th. [According to my view, relation is more general than comparison, for *relations* are either of *comparison* or of *concurrence.* The first concern the *congruity or incongruity* (I take these terms in a less extended sense) which comprises resemblance, equality, inequality, etc. The second comprise some *connection*, as that of cause and effect, of whole and parts, of position and order, etc.]

§ 6. *Ph.* The *composition* of simple ideas, for the purpose of making complex ideas, is also an operation of our mind. We may refer to this the faculty of *extending ideas* by uniting those of the same kind, as in forming a dozen from several units.

Th. [The one is doubtless as much composition as the

[1] Dominique Bouhours, 1628–1702, one of the ablest masters of the French language in the seventeenth century. The title of his work here given follows Gerhardt's text. The correct title is: *Manière de bien penser dans les ouvrages d'esprit*, Paris, 1687. There were several editions. — Tr.

[2] *Phars.* 1, 128. — Tr.

other; but composition of similar ideas is simpler than that of different ideas.]

§ 7. *Ph.* A dog will nurse young foxes, will play with them, and will have for them the same fondness as for her own puppies, if they can be made to suck her so long as is needful for the milk to spread through their entire body. Moreover it does not appear that animals, who have a large number of young at once, have any knowledge of their *number*.

Th. [The love of animals arises from a pleasure which is increased by habit. But as for the precise number, men even can know the numbers of things only by some skill, as in using numerical names in order to count, or figural arrangements which make them know at once without counting if anything is wanting.]

§ 10. *Ph.* Animals do not form abstract thoughts.

Th. [I agree. They apparently recognize whiteness, and notice it in the chalk or the snow; but this is not yet abstraction, for that demands a consideration of what is common, separated from what is particular, and consequently there enters into it the knowledge of universal truths, which is not given to the animals. It is well said also that the animals which speak do not use words to express general ideas, and that men deprived of the use of speech and of words do not cease to invent other general signs. I am pleased also to see that you here and elsewhere so well observe the advantages of human nature.]

§ 11. *Ph.* If animals have some ideas, and are not pure machines, as some maintain, we cannot deny that they have *reason* in a certain degree, and, for myself, it appears as evident that they reason as that they feel. But it is only upon particular ideas that they reason according as their senses represent these ideas to them.

Th. [Animals pass from one imagination to another by the connection which they have felt here before; for example, when his master takes a stick, the dog fears a whipping. And in many instances children with the rest of mankind proceed nowise differently in their passages from thought to thought. This might be called *consecution* and *reasoning* in a very broad sense. But I prefer to conform to the received usage in consecrating these terms to man and in limiting them to the knowledge of some *reason* of the connection of perceptions, which sensations alone cannot give; their effect being only to cause us naturally to expect at another time this same connection which we have noticed before, although perhaps the reasons are no longer the same, a fact which often deceives those who are governed only by the senses.]

§ 13. *Ph. Idiots* lack vivacity, activity, and movement in the intellectual faculties, whereby they are deprived of the use of reason. *Madmen* seem to be at the opposite extreme, for it does not appear to me that these latter have lost the power to reason, but having wrongly united certain ideas, they take them for truths, and deceive themselves in the same way as those who reason justly upon false principles. Thus you will see a madman who thinks he is king maintaining by a just consequence that he should be served, honored, and obeyed according to his rank.

Th. [*Idiots* do not exercise reason, and they differ from some *stupid persons* who have good judgment, but, not having prompt conception, they are despised and disturbed as he would be who wished to play ombre with persons of distinction and thought too long and too often of the part he must take. I remember a learned man who, having lost his memory by the use of certain drugs, was reduced to this condition, but his judgment always appeared. A man wholly mad lacks judgment on nearly every occasion; but the vivacity of his imagination may make him agreeable. But there are particular madmen who make a false supposition at an important point in their lives, and reason justly thereupon, as you have well said. There is such a man, well known at a certain court, who believes himself destined to redress the affairs of the Protestants and to bring France to reason, for which purpose God caused the greatest personages to pass through his body in order to ennoble it; he desires to marry all the princesses he sees to be marriageable, but after having made them holy, in order to have a holy progeny who are to rule the land; he attributes all the misfortunes of war to the little attention paid to his advice. In speaking with a certain sovereign, he takes every necessary measure not to lower his dignity. When they enter into conversation with him, he maintains himself so well that I have doubted more than once whether his madness is not feigned, for he is not inconvenienced by it. However, those who know him more intimately assure me that his madness is wholly genuine.]

CHAPTER XII

OF COMPLEX IDEAS

Ph. The understanding bears not a little resemblance to a room wholly dark, which has only certain small openings to let in from outside exterior and visible images, so that if these images, coming to be painted in this dark room, could remain there and be placed in order, so that they could be found upon occasion, there would be a great resemblance between this room and the human understanding.

Th. [To make the resemblance greater, you should suppose that in this room there was a canvas to receive the images, not even, but diversified by folds, representing the (kinds of) innate knowledge; further, that this canvas or membrane being stretched would have a kind of elasticity or power of action, and also an action and reaction accommodated as much to the past folds as to the newly arrived kinds of impressions. And this action would consist in certain vibrations or oscillations, such as are seen in a stretched string so touched that it gives forth a kind of musical sound. For not only do we receive images or outlines in the brain; but we form besides new ones, when we look at *complex ideas*. Thus the canvas that represents our brain is necessarily active and elastic. This comparison would explain tolerably well what passes in the brain; but as for the soul, which is a simple substance or *monad*, it represents without extension these same varieties of extended masses and perceives them.[1]]

§ 3. *Ph.* Now complex ideas are either modes or substances or relations.

[1] According to the principle of Pre-established Harmony. *Cf. Systeme noureau de la nature*, etc., 1695, §§ 14, 15; Gerhardt, 4, 484, 485; Erdmann, 127, 128; Jacques, 1, 475, 476; translation, Appendix, p. .—TR.

Th. [This division of the objects of our thought into substances, modes,[1] and relations is sufficiently to my taste. I believe that qualities are only modifications of substances, and that the understanding adds thereto the relations.[2] From this follows more than you think.]

Ph. Modes are either simple (as a dozen, a score, which are composed of simple ideas of the same kind, *i.e.* of units) or mixed (as beauty), into which enter simple ideas of different kinds.

Th. Perhaps *dozen* or *score* are only relations, and are constituted only in connection with the understanding. Units are separate, and the understanding gathers them together however dispersed they be. Yet, although relations are from the understanding, they are not groundless or unreal. For in the first place understanding is the origin of things; and indeed the reality even of all things, simple substances excepted, ultimately consists only of perceptions of the phenomena of simple substances. It is often the same with regard to the mixed modes; *i.e.* it is necessary to refer them rather to the relations.]

§ 6. *Ph.* The ideas of *substances* are certain combinations of simple ideas, which are supposed to represent particular and distinct things, subsisting by themselves, among which ideas the obscure notion of *substance,* which is assumed without knowing what it is in itself, is always considered as the first and chief.

Th. [The idea of substance is not so obscure as you think. You can know what it ought to be, and what it knows of itself in other things; and indeed the knowledge of the concrete always precedes that of the abstract; the hot (thing) rather than the heat.]

§ 7. *Ph.* In regard to substances there are also two kinds of ideas: the one of single substances, like that of a man, or a sheep; the other of several substances joined together, as of an army of men, or a flock of sheep. These collections form also a single idea.

[1] *Cf.* Descartes, *Prin. Philos.*, I., § 56; Veitch's translation, 8th ed., p. 217; Spinoza, *Ethica*, Pt. I., Def. 3; Elwes' translation, Vol. 2, p. 46; Locke, *Essay*, Bk. II., chap. 12, § 4, Vol. 1, p. 280 (Bohn's ed.). — TR.

[2] *Cf.* Leibnitz, *New Essays*, Bk. II., chap. 30, § 4. — TR.

Th. [This unity of the idea of aggregates is very true; but ultimately you must admit that this collective unity is only a congruity or relation, whose ground is in that which is found in each of the single substances separately. Thus these *beings by aggregation* have no other completed unity than the mental; consequently their entity also is in some mental shape or phenomenon, as that of the rainbow.]

CHAPTER XIII

OF SIMPLE MODES, AND FIRST OF THOSE OF SPACE

§ 3. *Ph.* Space considered with respect to the length which separates two bodies is called *distance;* with respect to length, breadth, and depth it may be called *capacity.*

Th. [To speak more distinctly, the *distance* between two fixed things (be they points or extensions) is the length of the shortest possible line that can be drawn from one to the other. This distance may be considered absolutely or in a certain figure which comprises the two distant things. For example, the straight line is absolutely the distance between two points. But these two points, being in the same spherical surface, the distance of these two points in this surface is the length of the shortest great arc of a circle, which may be drawn from one point to the other. It is well also to notice, that distance is not only between bodies, but also between surfaces, lines, points. It may be said that the *capacity* or rather the *interval* between two bodies or two other extensions, or between an extension and a point, is the space constituted by all the shortest lines which may be drawn between the points of each. This interval is filled, except when the two fixed things are in the same surface, when the shortest lines between the points of the fixed things must also fall in this surface or must there be expressly formed.]

§ 4. *Ph.* Besides that which is in nature, men have established in their minds the ideas of certain determinate lengths, as an inch or a foot.

Th. [They cannot do it. For it is impossible to have the

idea of a precisely determined length. You can neither say nor understand by the mind what an inch or a foot is. And you can preserve the meaning of these terms only by real measures, which you suppose unchanging, by means of which you can always recover them. Thus Mr. Greaves,[1] an English mathematician, desired to make use of the pyramids of Egypt, which have endured a long time and will endure apparently some time longer, to conserve our measures, by showing posterity the propositions[2] which have been sketched in definite lengths in one of these pyramids. It is true that a little after it was discovered that pendulums serve to perpetuate measures (*mensuris rerum ad posteros transmittendis*), as Huygens,[3] Mouton,[4] and Buratini, formerly *maistre de monnoye* in Poland, have demonstrated[5] by showing the proportion of our measures of length to that of the pendulum, which beats precisely a second (for example), *i.e.* the 86400th[6] part of a revolution of the fixed stars, or of an astronomical day; and Buratini has composed a treatise expressly thereupon, which

[1] John Greaves, 1602–1652, Savilian Professor of Astronomy at Oxford, 1643–1648. His *Pyramidographia, or a Discourse on the Pyramids in Egypt*, 1646. — TR.

[2] Gerhardt and Erdmann read: "propositions"; Jacques reads: "proportions"; Schaarschmidt translates "Verhältnisse." — TR.

[3] Christian Huygens, 1629–1695, a Dutch physicist, geometer, and astronomer. He discovered the laws of double refraction, and was the first to establish on a sure foundation the wave theory of light, in his *Traité de la lumière*, Leyden, 1690. His researches in physical optics constitute his chief claim to scientific immortality. His application of the pendulum to regulate the movement of clocks, arising from his felt need of an exact measure of time in astronomical observations, dates from 1656. He published his *Description de l'horloge à pendule* in 1657, and presented his first "pendulum-clock" to the States-General June 16, 1657. This *Description* was republished as chap. 1 of his *magnum opus*, the *Horologium oscillatorium, sive de motu pendulorum ad horologia adaptato*, dedicated to Louis XIV., March 25, 1673. In chap. 4 of this work he determined the centre of oscillation of a pendulum, and consequently the length of the simple isochronous pendulum. His works were published in two vols. 4to, *Opera varia*, Leyden, 1724, and two supplementary vols. 4to, *Opera reliqua*, Amsterdam, 1728. — TR.

[4] Gabriel Mouton, 1618–1694, a French mathematician and astronomer, principally known by his *Observationes diametrorum solis et lunæ apparentium*, Lyons, 1670. His principal title to honorable mention in the history of science is the invention of the method of differences for the calculation of tables of every kind, afterwards reduced to a system by Sir Isaac Newton, 1642–1727, and known by us as our method of interpolation. — TR.

[5] Erdmann and Jacques read: "prétendû montrer," *i.e.* claimed to demonstrate. — TR.

[6] Erdmann and Jacques read: "864,000th," evidently an error. — TR.

I have seen in manuscript. But there is, however, this imperfection in this measure of pendulums, which must be limited to certain countries, for pendulums to beat in the same time need to be shorter at the equator. And it is furthermore necessary to assume the constancy of the really fundamental measure, viz.: the length of a day or of a revolution of the globe of the earth around its axis, and also of the cause of gravitation, not to speak of other circumstances.]

§ 5. *Ph.* Observing how extremities are terminated either by straight lines which form distinct angles, or by curved lines in which no angle can be perceived, we form the idea of *figure*.

Th. [A superficial figure is terminated by a line or by lines: but the figure of a body can be limited without determined lines, as for example that of a sphere. A single straight line or plane surface cannot enclose any space or make any figure. But a single line can enclose a superficial figure, for example the circle, the oval, as also a single curved surface can enclose a solid figure, like the sphere and the spheroid. Yet, not only several straight lines or plane surfaces, but also several curved lines or several curved surfaces, can concur together and form even angles between themselves, when the one is not the tangent of the other. It is not easy to give *the definition of figure* in general according to the usage of geometers. To say that it is a limited extension would be too general, for a straight line, for example, although terminated by the two ends, is not a figure and even two straight lines cannot make one. To say that it is an extension limited by an extension is not general enough, for the entire spherical surface is a figure and yet it is not limited by any extension. It may be said, however, that *figure* is a limited extension, in which there are an infinite number of paths from one point to another. This definition comprises limited surfaces without terminating lines which the preceding definition did not comprise, and excludes the lines, because from one point to another in a line there is only one path or a determined number of paths. But it will be still better to say that figure is limited extension, which may admit an extended section, or better which has *breadth*, a term which hitherto had not been further defined.]

§ 6. *Ph.* At the least all figures are only simple modes of space.

Th. [According to your view, the simple modes repeat the same idea, but in figures there is not always the repetition of the same mode. Curves differ much from straight lines and between themselves. So I do not know how the definition of the simple mode will be in place here.]

§ 7. *Ph.* [We need not take our definitions too strictly. But let us pass from figure to *place*.] When we find all the pieces upon the same squares of the chess-board where we left them, we say that they are all in *the same place*, although perhaps the chess-board has been moved. We say also that the chess-board is in the same place, if it remains in the same part of the cabin of the vessel, although the vessel has sailed. The vessel is also said to be in the same place supposing it keeps the same distance with reference to the parts of the neighboring countries, although the earth has perhaps turned round.

Th. [*Place* is either *particular* when considered with regard to certain bodies, or *universal* when it relates to all, and with reference to which all the changes possible in relation to any body are taken into account. And if there were nothing fixed in the universe, the place of each thing could still be determined by reasoning,[1] if there were means of making a record of all the changes, or if the memory of a creature could suffice for them, as they say, the Arabs play chess by memory and on horseback. What we cannot understand, however, is nevertheless determined in the truth of things.]

§ 15. *Ph.* If any man asks me what *space* is, I am ready to tell him when he tells me what extension is.

Th. [I wish I could speak of the nature of fever or any other malady with the same certainty with which I believe the nature of space is expounded. Extension is the abstract of the extended. Now the extended is a continuum whose parts are coexistent, or exist at the same time.]

§ 17. *Ph.* If any one asks whether space without body is

[1] Schaarschmidt says that the statements here made by Leibnitz have since found their confirmation and accomplishment through Gauss' *Theoria motus corporum coelestium*. The work was published at Hamburg, in 1809, and "gave a powerful impulse to the true methods of astronomical observation." The author, Carl Friedrich Gauss, 1777–1855, was an eminent German mathematician. His collected works, edited by E. J. Schering, have been published by the Royal Society of Göttingen, 7 vols., 4to. Göttingen: 1863–1871.—Tr.

substance or accident, I should reply without hesitation that I know nothing about it.

Th. [I fear you may think me vain in wishing to determine what you, sir, admit you do not know. But if it is expedient to judge, (I fear) that you know more about the matter than you state or think you do. Some have believed that God is the place of things.[1] Lessius and Guericke, if I am not mistaken, were of this opinion, but then place contains something more than what we attribute to the space which we deprive of all activity; and in this way it is no more a substance than time, and if it has parts it cannot be God. It is a relation, an order, not only between existences, but also between possibilities as they may exist. But its truth and reality, like all eternal truths, is grounded in God.]

Ph. [I am not far from your view, and you know the passage of St. Paul, who says that we live and move and have our being in God.[2] Thus, according to different ways of considering the matter, it may be said that space is God, and also that it is only an order or a relation.]

Th. [The better statement then will be that space is an order, but that God is its source.]

§ 18. *Ph.* [Yet to know whether space is a substance, it would be needful to know in what the nature of substance in general consists. But in this there is a difficulty. If God, finite spirits, and bodies participate in common in an identical substantial nature, would it not follow that they differ only as different modifications of this substance?]

[1] This doctrine appeared very early. Schaarschmidt refers to the collection of poems of uncertain origin called *Orphica*, where (Fragt. vi., p. 457, ed. Hermann, v. 8 and 9) it is poetically expressed thus: "All that has been and hereafter will be, is formed together in the bosom of Zeus." Again (v. 17–20): "One is the ruling Being, in whom the All moves, fire, water, earth and air, day and night, reason, the first principle and joyful love — all this lies in the great bosom of Zeus," etc. Malebranche represents a phase of the same view in his doctrine that we see all things in God. *Cf.* his *De la Recherche de la Vérité*, III., ii., 6: "We abide thus in the view that God is the intelligible world or the place of spirits, just as the material world is the place of bodies. From His power they receive all their modifications, in His wisdom they find all their ideas, by His love they are moved in all their moral inclinations. But because His power and His love are nothing else than Himself, we will believe with St. Paul, that He is not far from any one of us, and that in Him we live and move and have our being." *Cf.* also James Martineau, *Types of Ethical Theory*, 2d ed., Vol. 1, p. 170 *sq.* New York: Macmillan & Co., 1886. — TR.

[2] Acts 17 : 28. — TR.

Th. [If this result follows, it would follow also, that God, finite spirits, and bodies, participating in common in an identical nature of being, would differ only as different modifications of this being.]

§ 19. *Ph.* Those who first thought of regarding accidents as a kind of real beings, which need something in which to inhere, were constrained to invent the word substance to serve as a support to the accidents.

Th. [Do you then think, sir, that the accidents can subsist apart from the substance? or do you mean that they are not real beings? You seem to multiply difficulties without reason, and I have remarked above that substances or concretes are conceived rather than accidents or abstracts.]

Ph. The words substance and accident are in my view of little use in philosophy.

Th. [I admit that I am of another opinion, and I believe that the consideration of substance[1] is one of the most important and fruitful points of philosophy.]

§ 21. *Ph.* [We have now spoken of substance only by the way, while asking if space is a substance. But it is sufficient for us that it is not a body.] No one will dare to make body infinite like space.

Th. [Descartes and his followers have said, nevertheless, that matter has no limits, in making the world indefinite, so that it is not possible for us to conceive of its extremities. And they have changed the term infinite into indefinite with some reason; for there never is an infinite whole in the world,

[1] *Cf. New Essays*, Bk. II., chap. 23, § 2; *De primæ philosophiæ emendatione et de notione substantiæ*, 1694, Gerhardt, Vol. 4, pp. 468–470; Erdmann, pp. 121–122; A. Jacques, *Œuvres de Leibniz*, Vol. 1, pp. 452–454 (in French); translation, Appendix, pp. ; *Systeme nouveau de la nature et de la communication des substances, aussi bien que de l'union qu'il y a entre l'âme et le corps*, 1695, §§ 2, 3, Gerhardt, Vol. 4, pp. 477 *sq.*; Erdmann, pp. 124–128; Jacques, Vol. 1, pp. 469 *sq.*; translation, Appendix, pp. ; *De ipsa natura, sive de vi insita actionibusque creaturum*, 1698, Gerhardt, Vol. 4, pp. 504–516; Erdmann, pp. 154–160; Jacques, Vol. 1, pp. 455–468 (in French); translation, Appendix, pp. ; *Considérations sur le principe de vie et sur les natures plastiques*, 1705, Gerhardt, Vol. 6, pp. 539–546; Erdmann, pp. 429–432; translation, Duncan, *Philos. Works of Leibnitz*, pp. 163–169; *Principes de la nature et de la grace fondés en raison*, c. 1714, Gerhardt, Vol. 6, pp. 598–606; Erdmann, pp. 714–718; translation, Duncan, *op. cit.*, pp. 209–217; *La Monadologie*, 1714, Gerhardt, Vol. 6, pp. 607–623; Erdmann, pp. 705–712; translation, Duncan, *op. cit.*, pp. 218–232; also F. H. Hedge, in "The Jour. Spec. Philos.," Vol. 1, pp. 129–137. — Tr.

although there are always some wholes greater than others to infinity, and the universe even cannot pass for a whole as I have elsewhere [1] shown.

Ph. Those who take matter and extension as one and the same thing maintain that the inner sides of a hollow vacuous body would touch. But the space which is between two bodies suffices to prevent their mutual contact.

Th. [I am of your opinion, for although I do not admit a vacuum, I distinguish matter from extension, and I admit that if there were a vacuum in a sphere, the opposite poles in the hollow space would not on that account touch. But I believe that this is a case which the divine perfection does not allow.]

§ 23. *Ph.* It seems, however, that motion proves a vacuum. When the least part of the divided body is as large as a grain of mustard-seed, a void space equal to the size of a grain of mustard is requisite in order to make room for the parts of this body to move freely; the same condition will hold good when the parts of the matter are one hundred million times smaller.

Th. [It is true, that if the world were full of hard corpuscles, which could neither yield nor divide, as the atoms are depicted, motion would be impossible. But in truth, there is no original hardness; on the contrary, fluidity is the original condition, and bodies are divided as needful, since there is nothing to prevent it. This takes away all the force in the argument for a vacuum drawn from motion.]

CHAPTER XIV

OF DURATION AND ITS SIMPLE MODES

§ 10. *Ph.* To extension corresponds duration. And a part of duration in which we remark no successions of ideas we call *an instant.*

Th. This definition of *an instant* ought (I believe) to mean the popular notion, like that which the common people have

[1] *Cf. ante*, pp. 16, 17; also *New Essays*, Bk. II., chap. 17, § 1. The proof that the universe is not, strictly speaking, a whole, is given in the letter to Des Bosses, March 11, 1706, Gerhardt, Vol. 2, p. 304 *sq.*, Erdmann, pp. 435–436. — TR.

of a *point*. For strictly the point and the instant are not parts of time or space, neither have they parts. They are extremities only.

§ 16. *Ph.* It is not motion, but a constant succession of ideas which gives us the idea of duration.

Th. [A succession of perceptions awakes in us the idea of duration, but it does not make it. Our perceptions never have a succession sufficiently constant and regular to correspond to that of time, which is a *continuum* uniform and simple, like a straight line. Changing perceptions furnish us the occasion for thinking of time, and we measure it by uniform changes. But were there nothing uniform in nature, time could not be determined, as space likewise could not be determined if there were no fixed or immovable body. So that knowing the rules of different motions, we can always refer them to the uniform intelligible motions, and see beforehand by this means what will happen through the different motions taken together. And in this sense time is the measure of motion, *i.e.* uniform motion is the measure of non-uniform motion.]

§ 21. *Ph.* No two parts of duration can certainly be known to be equal; [and you must admit that observations can attain only approximate equality.] After exact research the discovery has been made that there is really an inequality in the diurnal revolutions of the sun, and we do not know but that the annual revolutions are unequal also.

Th. [The pendulum has made us realize and see the inequality of the days from one noon to another: *Solem dicere falsum audet.* It is true that men knew this already, and that this inequality has its rules. As for the annual revolution, which makes good the inequalities of solar days, it may change in the course of time. The revolution of the earth about its axis which is commonly attributed to the *primum mobile*,[1] is our best measure up to the present time, and clocks and watches serve to divide it for us. Furthermore this same daily revolu-

[1] In Aristotle's philosophy, τὸ πρῶτον κινοῦν, *i.e.* God, who, himself unmoved, is the necessary first and unceasing source of the eternal movement of the universe. *Cf. Metaphys.*, Λ, 6–10, 1071 *sq.*; *Phys.*, VIII., 6, 258ᵇ 10; also Zeller, *Outlines*, § 56, 3, and *Die Philos. d. Griech.*, 3d ed., 1879, Vol. 4, p. 358; Wallace, *Outlines of the Philos. of Aristotle*, 3d ed., § 39; Hegel, *Gesch. d. Philos.*, 2d ed., Vol. 2, p. 289 *sq.*; Benn, *The Greek Philosophers*, Vol. 1, pp. 348–350. — Tr.

tion of the earth may also change in the course of time: and if any pyramid could endure long enough, or if we should build new ones we could perceive it by observing there the length of pendulums a known number of whose beats occurs now during this revolution; we could also know in some way the change by comparing this revolution with others, as with those of Jupiter's satellites, for it is not apparent that, if there is any change in one or the other, it will always be proportional.

Ph. Our measure of time would be more exact if we could preserve a past day in order to compare it with the days to come, as we preserve the measures of space.

Th. [But instead of that we are reduced to preserving and watching bodies which move in nearly equal times. Also we cannot say that a measure of space, as for example, an ell which is preserved in wood or metal remains perfectly the same.]

§ 22. *Ph.* Now since all men manifestly measure time by the motion of the heavenly bodies, it is very strange that one is not permitted to define *time* as the measure of motion.

Th. [I just stated (§ 16) how that should be understood. It is true that Aristotle says[1] that time is the *number* and not the measure of *motion*. And in fact, it may be said that duration is known by the number of periodic equal motions of which one begins when another ends, for example, by so many revolutions of the earth or the stars.]

§ 24. *Ph.* Nevertheless to anticipate these revolutions and say that Abraham was born in the year 2712 of the Julian era, is to speak as unintelligibly, as if you counted from the beginning of the world, although you suppose that the Julian era commenced several hundred years before there were any days, nights, or years marked by any revolution of the sun.

Th. [This vacuum which may be conceived in time, indicates, like that of space, that time and space extend to the possible as well as to the actual. Besides, of all the chronological methods, that of reckoning the years since the beginning of the world is the least convenient, although this would be, without touching upon other reasons, only because of the great difference existing between the Septuagint and the Hebrew text.]

[1] *Phys.*, IV., 11, 219^b 1, 219^b 8; *cf.* Wallace, *Outlines of the Philos. of Aristotle*, 3d ed., § 44. Wallace quotes the Greek of the first passage here referred to. — TR.

§ 26. *Ph.* One may *conceive* the beginning of motion, although he may not *comprehend* that of duration taken in all its extension. One may give limits to the body, but cannot do it with regard to space.

Th. [It is as I just said that time and space indicate the possibilities beyond the supposition of existences. Time and space are of the nature of eternal truths which consider equally the possible and the actual.]

§ 27. *Ph.* In fact the ideas of time and eternity come from the same source, for we can in our thought add certain lengths of duration to one another as often as we please.

Th. [But in order to draw from them the notion of *eternity*, it is necessary to think besides that the same reason always exists for going farther. It is this rational consideration which achieves the notion of the infinite or the indefinite in possible progress. Thus the senses alone cannot suffice to cause the formation of these notions. And ultimately it may be said that *the idea of the absolute*[1] is anterior in the nature of things to *that of the limits* which are added, but we notice the former only as we commence with what is limited and strikes our senses.]

CHAPTER XV

OF DURATION AND EXPANSION CONSIDERED TOGETHER

§ 4. *Ph.* One admits more easily an infinite duration of time than an infinite expansion of space, because we conceive infinite duration in God, and attribute extension only to matter which is finite, and call the space beyond the universe imaginary. But (§ 2) Solomon seems to have other thoughts when, speaking of God, he says: *the heaven and the heaven of heavens cannot contain Thee*;[2] and for myself I believe that he magnifies too highly the capacity of his own understanding who imagines he can extend his thoughts farther than the place where God exists.

[1] *The idea of the absolute* belongs to our reason as such, *cf. New Essays*, Bk. II., chap. 17, § 3, Th., § 16, Th., though we first become aware of it through our consciousness of the particular ideas of the reason as limitations of the idea of the absolute. — TR.

[2] 1 Kings 8:27; 2 Chron. 6:18. — TR.

Th. If God were extended, he would have parts. But duration grants these only to his works. However in relation to space immensity must be attributed to him, which gives also parts and order to the immediate works of God. He is the source of possibilities as of actualities, of the one by his essence, of the other by his will. Thus space like time has its reality only from him, and he can fill the void when it seems to him good. Thus it is that in this respect he is everywhere.[1]]

§ 11. *Ph.* We do not know what relations spirits have with space, nor how they participate therein. But we know that they participate in duration.

Th. [All finite spirits are always united to some organic body, and they represent to themselves other bodies by means of relations to their own. Thus their relation to space is as evident as that of bodies. For the rest, before leaving this subject, I would add a comparison between time and space to those which you have given; viz.: — if there were a vacuum in space (as, for instance, if a sphere were hollow within), you could determine its size; but if there were a vacuum in time, *i.e.* a duration without changes, it would be impossible to determine its length. Whence it comes that you may refute the one who would maintain that two bodies, between which there is a vacuum, touch; for geometry defends the proposition that two opposite poles of a hollow sphere would not touch: but you cannot refute the one who would maintain that two worlds, the one of which succeeds the other, touch as to duration, so that the one necessarily begins when the other ends, without the possibility of an interval. You could not refute it, I say, because this interval is indeterminable. If space were only a line, and if body were immovable, it would no longer be possible to determine the length of the vacuum between two bodies.

[1] God, according to Leibnitz, is *actus purus*, a pure spirit, without body and without extension. All other beings require bodies. His omnipresence is dynamic. *Cf. New Essays*, Bk. II., chap. 1, § 12, Th., *ante*, p. 113; Letter to Des Bosses, Oct. 16, 1706, Gerhardt, Vol. 2, p. 325, Erdmann, p. 440, b.—TR.

CHAPTER XVI

OF NUMBER

§ 4. *Ph.* In numbers ideas are both more precise and more accurately to be distinguished the one from the other than in extension, where you cannot observe or measure each equality and each excess of size as easily as in numbers, because in space we cannot by thought attain a certain definite smallness beyond which we cannot go, like the unit in number.

Th. [That should be understood of the *integer.* For otherwise *number in its extent*, comprising the fraction, the surd, the transcendent, and all that may be assumed between two integers, is proportional to the line, and there is there as little of a *minimum* as in the *continuum.* Thus the definition of number as a multitude of units is in place only among the integers. The precise distinction of ideas in extension does not consist in *size:* for to distinguish size clearly one must have recourse to integers, or to other (measures) known by means of integers; thus from *continuous quantity* it is necessary to recur to *discrete quantity,* in order to have a distinct knowledge of *size.* Thus the modifications of extension, when not joined to numbers, cannot be distinguished by *figure*, taking this term so generally that it means everything which makes two extensions dissimilar the one to the other.]

§ 5. *Ph.* By repeating the idea of a unit and joining it to another unit, we make a *collective* idea, which we call *two.* And whoever can do that and advance always by adding one more to the last collective idea to which he gives a particular name, can *count* so long as he has a set of names and sufficient memory to retain them.

Th. [By this means alone one cannot advance very far. For memory would be *too heavily loaded* if it must retain an entirely new name for each addition of a new unit. That is why a certain order and a certain *repetition* of these names is necessary by recommencing in accordance with a certain progression.]

Ph. The different modes of numbers are capable of no other difference than that of more or less; [this is why there are simple modes like those of extension.]

Th. [That may be said of time and of the straight line, but not of figures, and still less of numbers, which are not only different in size but further unlike. An even number may be divided into two equal numbers, but not an uneven. Three and six are triangular numbers, four and nine are squares, eight is a cube, etc. And this principle has place in numbers still more than in figures, for two unequal figures may be perfectly similar to each other, but never two numbers. But I am not astonished that you are often deceived thereupon, because one does not commonly have a distinct idea of what is *similar* or *dissimilar*. You see then, sir, that your idea or your application of *simple* or *mixed modes* is greatly in need of correction.]

§ 6. *Ph.* [You were right in remarking that it is well to give numbers their own names to be retained.] Thus I believe that it would be convenient in computation to say a *billion* for brevity's sake instead of a million of millions, and instead of a million of millions of millions, or a million of billions, to say a *trillion*, and thus in order to nonillions, for there is little need of going farther in the use of numbers.

Th. These denominations are good enough. Let $x=10$. That posited, a million will be x^6, a billion x^{12}, a trillion x^{18}, etc., and a nonillion x^{54}.

CHAPTER XVII

OF INFINITY

§ 1. *Ph.* One of the most important notions is that of the finite and the infinite, which are regarded as modes of quantity.

Th. [Properly speaking, it is true that there is an infinite number of things, *i.e.* that there are always more of them than can be assigned. But there is no infinite number, neither line nor other infinite quantity, if these are understood as veritable wholes, as it is easy to prove. The schools have meant or have been obliged to say that, in admitting a syncategorematic infinite,[1] as they call it, and not a categorematic infinite. The true infinite exists, strictly speaking, only in *the absolute*, which is anterior to all composition, and is not formed by the additions of parts.[2]]

Ph. When we apply our idea of the infinite to the first Being, we do it primarily in respect to his duration and ubiquity, and, more figuratively, to his power, his wisdom, his goodness, and his other attributes.

Th. [Not more figuratively, but less immediately, because the other attributes make their importance known through relation to those into which enters the consideration of parts.]

§ 2. *Ph.* I thought it was established that the mind regards the finite and the infinite as modifications of extension[3] and duration.

Th. [I do not find that it has been established that the consideration of the finite and the infinite takes place wherever there is bulk and magnitude. And the true infinite is not a *modification*, it is the absolute; on the contrary, when it is modified, it is limited and forms a finite.]

§ 3. *Ph.* We have believed that since the power of the mind to expand without limit its idea of space by new additions is always the same, it is thence that the idea of an infinite space is derived.

Th. [It is well to add that this is because the same ratio is seen always to hold good. Let us take a straight line and prolong it until it is double the length of the first. Now it is clear that the second line, being perfectly similar to the first, may be itself doubled in order to have a third, which is still similar to the preceding; and the same ratio holding good always, it is never possible to stop the process; thus the line may be prolonged to infinity, so that the consideration of the infinite arises from that of similarity or from the same ratio, and its origin is the same with that of universal and necessary truths. This shows us how what gives completion

[1] An incompletely defined infinite, capable of or needing still further definition, but infinite only so far as it cannot really be defined, the *indefinite-infinite* (*infinitum-indefinitum*). — TR.

[2] *Cf. ante*, pp. 16, 17; also *New Essays*, Bk. II., chap. 13, § 21.—TR.

[3] Locke has: "expansion," *Philos. Works*, Vol. 1, p. 331 (Bohn's ed.). — TR.

to the conception of this idea is found in ourselves, and cannot come from the experience of our senses, just as necessary truths cannot be proved by induction nor by the senses. The idea of *the absolute* is in us internally, like that of being; these absolutes are nothing else than the attributes of God, and it may be said that they are not less the source of ideas, because God is himself the principle of beings. The idea of the absolute in relation to space, is only that of the immensity of God, and so of the others. But you deceive yourself in wishing to imagine an absolute space which is an infinite whole composed of parts; there is none such, it is a notion which implies a contradiction, and these infinite wholes, and their opposed infinitesimals, are used only in the calculations of geometers, just like the imaginary roots of algebra.]

§ 6. *Ph.* [We conceive furthermore a magnitude without understanding thereby parts outside of parts.] If to the most perfect idea I have of the whitest whiteness, I add another of an equal or less brilliant whiteness (for I cannot add the idea of a whiter than I have, which I suppose the whitest that I actually conceive), it neither increases nor extends my idea in any way; therefore the different ideas of whiteness are called *degrees.*]

Th. [I do not fully understand the force of this reasoning, for nothing prevents me from receiving the perception of a whiter whiteness than what is actually conceived. The true reason why we are inclined to believe that whiteness cannot be infinitely increased is because it is not an original quality; the senses give us only a confused knowledge of it; and when we have a distinct knowledge of it, we shall see that it arises from the structure, and is limited by that of the organ of vision. But as regards original or distinctly knowable qualities, we see that there are sometimes means of going to infinity, not only in the case of *extension* or, if you prefer, *diffusion* or what the scholastic philosophy calls *partes extra partes*, as in time and place, but also in the case of *intention* or *degrees*, for example, as regards velocity.]

§ 8. *Ph.* We have no idea of infinite space, and nothing is plainer than the absurdity of an actual idea of an infinite number.

Th. [I am of the same opinion. But this is not because we

cannot have the idea of the infinite, but because the infinite cannot be a true whole.]

§ 16. *Ph.* For the same reason we have then no positive idea of an infinite duration or of eternity, any more than of immensity.

Th. [I believe we have a positive idea of both, and this idea is a true one, provided it is not conceived as an infinite whole, but as an absolute or attribute without limits which exists in reference to *eternity*, in the necessity of the existence of God, without depending upon parts and without the notions being formed by an addition of time. We see furthermore in that way, as I have said already, that the origin of the notion of the infinite comes from the same source as that of necessary truths.]

CHAPTER XVIII

OF OTHER SIMPLE MODES

Ph. There are besides many simple modes formed from simple ideas. Such are (§ 2) modes of motion, as sliding, rolling; those of sound (§ 3) which are modified by notes and airs, as colors by degrees, not to speak of tastes and smells (§ 6). These always[1] have neither measures nor distinct names any more than in the case of the complex modes (§ 7), because use regulates them, and we will speak of them more fully when we come to words.

Th. [The majority of modes are not sufficiently simple and can be reckoned with the complex, for example, to explain what sliding and rolling is besides motion, you must consider surface-resistance.]

CHAPTER XIX

OF THE MODES OF THINKING

§ 1. *Ph.* [Let us pass from the modes which come from the senses to those given us by reflection.] *Sensation* is, so to speak, the actual entrance of ideas into the understanding by

[1] Locke: "ordinarily," *Philos. Works*, Vol. 1, p. 346 (Bohn's ed.).—Tr.

means of the senses. When the same idea comes again into the mind, without the action upon our senses, of the external object which at first caused it to spring up, the act of the mind is called *remembrance;* if the mind tries to recall it, and only after considerable effort finds and brings it to view, it is *recollection* (*recueillement*).[1] If the mind looks upon it attentively for a long time it is *contemplation;* when the idea floats about in the mind without any attention on the part of the understanding, it is called *reverie.* When the mind reflects upon ideas, which present themselves, and when it, so to speak, registers them in its memory, it is *attention;* and when the mind fixes itself upon an idea with much application, considers it on all sides, and will not be turned aside notwithstanding other ideas which come in the way, we call it *study* or intenseness of thought. *Sleep* accompanied by no dream is a cessation of all these things; and *dreaming* is having these ideas in the mind while the outer senses are closed, so that they do not receive the impressions of external objects with their usual quickness. It is, I say, having ideas without any suggestion from any external objects or known occasion, and apart from any choice or determination in any way of the understanding. As for that which we call *ecstasy,* I leave others to judge whether it is not dreaming with the eyes open.

Th. [It is well to clear up these notions and I will try to aid in the work. I will say then that it is *sensation* when an external object is perceived; that *remembrance* consists in the repetition without the reappearance of the object; but when we know we have had it, it is *memory. Recollection* (*recueillement*) is commonly understood in a sense different from yours, viz.: as a state in which we disengage ourselves from things in order to apply ourselves to some meditation. But since there is no word known to me corresponding to your notion, sir, one may apply to it that which you employ. We give *attention* to objects which we distinguish and prefer to others. Attention continuing in the mind, whether the external object continues or not, and even whether it is found there or not, is

[1] *Cf.* below, where the French "recueillement," here employed as a translation of the English "recollection," is shown to have a different meaning and use from that of the English word. As "recueillement" is, however, used as an equivalent for the English word, I have translated it in the second paragraph accordingly. — TR.

consideration; which tending to knowledge without reference to action, will be *contemplation.* Attention, whose aim is to learn (*i.e.* the attainment of knowledge for the sake of keeping it), is *study.* To consider in order to form a plan is to *meditate;* but reverie appears to be nothing else than following certain thoughts for the pleasure one takes therein, with no other end; this is why reverie may lead to madness; we forget ourselves, we forget the *dic cur hic,* we approach dreams and chimeras, we build castles in Spain. We can distinguish *dreams* from sensations only because they are not united with them, they are like a world apart. *Sleep* is a cessation of sensations, and in this way *ecstasy* is a very deep sleep from which one finds difficulty in being awakened, a condition which arises from some internal passing cause, which is added in order to exclude this profound sleep, arising from some narcotic or from some continuous injury to the functions, as in lethargy. Ecstasy is sometimes accompanied with *visions;* but there is vision without ecstasy, and *vision* seems to be nothing but a dream which passes for a sensation just as if it acquainted us with the truth of objects. And when visions are divine, there is actually truth in them, which may be known for instance when they contain particular prophecies which the outcome justifies.]

§ 4. *Ph.* From the different degrees of intensity[1] or relaxation of the mind, it follows that thought is the act and not the essence of the soul.

Th. [Doubtless thought is an act and cannot be the essence: but it is an essential act, and all substances are of this character. I have shown above that we always have an infinite number of little perceptions, without being conscious of them. We are never without *perceptions,* but we are necessarily often without *apperceptions,* viz.: when there are no distinct perceptions. It is from not having considered this important point that a relaxed philosophy, as little noble as solid, has prevailed with so many excellent minds, and that we have hitherto almost ignored that which is most beautiful in the soul. This is also the reason why so much probability has been found in that error, which teaches that souls are by nature perishable.]

[1] Locke has: "intention and remission," *Philos. Works* (Bohn's ed.), Vol. 1, p. 349. — TR.

CHAPTER XX

OF MODES OF PLEASURE AND PAIN

§ 1. *Ph.* As the sensations of the body, like the thoughts of the mind, are either indifferent or followed by pleasure or pain, the ideas of them cannot be described any more than all other simple ideas, nor can the words which serve to designate them be defined.

Th. [I believe that there are no perceptions which are wholly indifferent to us, but it is enough that their effect be not notable in order that they may be thus spoken of, for *pleasure* and *pain* appear to consist in a notable aid or impediment. I admit that this definition is not at all nominal and that one may give none at all.]

§ 2. *Ph.* The *good* is that which is fitted to produce and increase pleasure in us, or to diminish and cut short some pain. *Evil* is fitted to produce or increase pain in us, or to diminish some pleasure.

Th. [I am also of this opinion. The good is divided into the virtuous, the agreeable, and the useful, but ultimately I believe that it must be either agreeable itself, or serving something else which may give us an agreeable feeling, that is to say, the good is agreeable or useful, and virtue itself consists in a pleasure of mind.]

§§ 4, 5. *Ph.* From pleasure and pain come the passions. We have *love* for that which can produce pleasure, and the thought of sadness or of pain that a present or absent cause can produce is *hatred.* But *hatred* or *love* which relates to beings capable of happiness or misery is often an uneasiness or delight which we feel to be produced in us by the consideration of their existence or of the happiness which they enjoy.

Th. [I also gave nearly this definition of *love* when I explained the principles of justice, in the preface to my "Codex juris gentium diplomaticus,"[1] viz.: that to *love* is to

[1] The *Codex juris gentium diplomaticus*, 1693, a collection of public acts and treatises, etc. An excerpt from the Preface of this work, entitled *De notionibus juris et justitiæ*, is given by Erdmann, pp. 118–120; translation, Duncan, *Philos. Works of Leibnitz*, note 48, pp. 379–382. — TR.

be inclined to take pleasure in the complete perfection or happiness of the object loved. And for that reason one neither considers nor asks for any other pleasure proper than that indeed which is found in the good or pleasure of the one who is loved; but in this sense we do not, properly speaking, love what is incapable of pleasure or happiness, and we enjoy things of this nature without loving them for that reason, unless by a prosopopoeia, and as if we imagined that they themselves enjoy their perfection. It is not, then, properly love when one says that he loves a beautiful picture for the pleasure which he takes in feeling its perfections. But it is allowable to extend the sense of terms, and their usage varies. Philosophers and theologians even distinguish two kinds of love, viz.: the love which they call the *love of complacency*, which is nothing but the desire or feeling which we have for the one who gives us pleasure, without concerning ourselves whether he receives it; and the *love of benevolence*, which is the feeling that one has for the one who, by his pleasure or happiness, gives us some. The first makes us have in view our pleasure and the second that of another, but as making or rather constituting ours, for if it did not reflect upon us in some way we could not concern ourselves with it since it is impossible, although they affirm it, to be separated from the good proper. And see how it is needful to understand *disinterested* or non-mercenary *love*, in order to reach a favorable conception of nobility and not to fall meanwhile into the chimerical one.]

§ 6. *Ph.* The *uneasiness* (French *inquietude*) which a man feels in himself at the absence of anything which if present would give him pleasure is called *desire*. *Uneasiness* is the principal, not to say the only stimulus which excites human industry and action for whatever good is proposed to man; if the absence of this good is followed by no displeasure or pain, and he who is deprived of it can be content and at his ease without its possession, he does not think of desiring, and less still of making any efforts to enjoy it. He feels for this kind of good only a bare *velleity*,[1] the term used to signify the lowest kind of desire,

[1] Schaarschmidt translates the French "velleité" by the German "Willensneigung," *i.e.* inclination of will. The term is borrowed from the Scholastic "velleitas," and is here equivalent to *imperfect volition* (*imperfecta volitio*) or that condition of the soul in which the will, though not in a state of indiffer-

which approaches nearest to that state in which the soul finds itself with regard to anything which is wholly indifferent to it, when the displeasure which the absence of anything causes is so inconsiderable that it is carried only to feeble longings without being compelled to avail itself of the means of obtaining it. Desire is moreover extinguished or abated by the opinion that the wished for good cannot be obtained in proportion as the soul's uneasiness is cured or allayed by that consideration. [For the rest, I have found what I stated to you about uneasiness in this celebrated English author, whose views I often relate to you. I was a little in difficulty as to the definition of the English word uneasiness. But the French translator[1] whose skill in the fulfilment of this task cannot be called in question, remarks at the foot of the page (chap. 20, § 6,) that by this word the English author understands the state of a man not at his ease, the lack of *ease* and of tranquillity of soul, which in this regard is purely passive, and that it must be translated by the (French) word *inquietude,* which does not express exactly the same idea, but approaches it very nearly. This caution (he adds) is above all needful with regard to the following chapter, "Of Power," in which the author reasons much upon this kind of uneasiness; for if you should not attach to this word the idea which has just been indicated, it would be impossible exactly to understand the matters treated of in this chapter and which are the most important and delicate in the entire work.]

Th. [The translator is right and the reading of his excellent author shows me that this consideration of *uneasiness* is a capital point, in which this author has particularly shown his penetrating and profound mind. For this reason I gave it some attention, and after having well considered the matter, it almost appears to me that the (French) word *inquietude* (*restlessness*), if it does not express quite the meaning of the author, nevertheless sufficiently agrees with the nature of the thing; and that the (English) word uneasiness, if it indicated a displeasure, fretfulness (*chagrin*), inconvenience, in a word some effective pain, would not suit his meaning. For I should pre-

ence, has not as yet sufficient force to pass over into action (*volitio*). *Cf. New Essays*, Bk. II., chap. 21, § 5 *sq.*, also § 30, Th.—TR.

[1] M. Pierre Coste.—TR.

fer to say that in the desire in itself there is rather a disposition and preparation for pain than pain itself. It is true that this perception sometimes differs from that which is in pain only more or less, but it is the degree which is the essence of pain, for it is a notable perception. The same is also seen in the difference between appetite and hunger, for when the stomach's irritation becomes too strong it is uncomfortable, so that we must also apply here our doctrine of perceptions too small to be perceived, for if that which goes on in us when we have appetite and desire, were great enough, it would cause us pain. Hence the infinitely wise author of our being arranged it for our good, when he so arranged it that we should often be in ignorance and among confused perceptions, in order to act more promptly by instinct, and in order not to be disturbed by too distinct sensations of a multitude of objects, which do not recur immediately and the nature of which could not go on to obtain their ends. How many insects we swallow without noticing them, how many persons we see who, having a too penetrating odor, are annoying, and how many disgusting objects we should see if our vision were penetrating enough. It is also for the sake of this skill that nature has given us the stimuli of desire, like the rudiments or elements of pain, or so to speak, of semi-pains, or (if you wish to speak extravagantly in order to express yourself more forcibly) the little imperceptible pains, in order that we might *enjoy the advantage of evil* without its inconvenience; for otherwise if this perception were too distinct, we would always be miserable while awaiting the good, while this continual victory over these semi-pains which are felt in pursuing our desire and satisfying in some way this appetite, or this longing, gives us a quantity of semi-pleasures, whose continuity and mass (as in the continuity of the impulse of a heavy body which falls and acquires impetuosity) becomes at last a complete and genuine pleasure. And finally, without these semi-pains there would be no pleasure at all, nor any means of perceiving that something aids and relieves us while there are some obstacles which prevent us from putting ourselves at ease. It is furthermore in this that we recognize the affinity of pleasure and pain which Socrates in Plato's "Phædo,"[1] noticed when his feet itched. This

[1] *Phædo*, 60 B. — TR.

consideration of little aids or little releases and imperceptible deliverances from the fixed tendency, whose result at last is a notable pleasure, serves also to give a more distinct knowledge of the confused idea which we have, and ought to have, *of pleasure* and *of pain;* just as the sensation of heat and of light results from a quantity of little motions which express those of objects, as I said above (chap. 9, § 13) and differ from them only in appearance and because we ourselves are not conscious of this analysis: while many to-day believe that our ideas of sense-qualities differ *toto genere* from notions and from all that goes on in objects, and are something primitive and inexplicable, and indeed arbitrary, as if God made the soul sensible of whatever seems good to him, instead of what goes on in the body, a view which is far removed from the true analysis of our ideas. But to return to *uneasiness,* that is to say to the little imperceptible solicitations which keep us always in suspense; these are confused determinations, so that often we do not know what we lack, while in the case of the *inclinations and passions* we at least know what we ask for, although confused perceptions enter also into their methods of acting, and the passions themselves also cause this uneasiness or longing. These impulses are like so many little springs which try to release themselves, and which make our machine go. And I have already remarked above that it is in this way that we are never indifferent, when we most appear to be so, for example, in turning to the right rather than to the left at the end of a path. For the side we take arises from these insensible determinations, mixed with the actions of objects and the interior of the body, which makes us find ourselves more at ease in the one or the other manner of bestirring ourselves. The pendulum of a clock is called *Unruhe* in German, *i.e.* uneasiness. We may say that the same condition exists in our body which can never be perfectly at ease; because if it might be so, a new impression of objects, a slight change in the organs, in the vessels and in the viscera would at once alter the balance and cause them to make some slight effort to put themselves again in the best state possible: this produces a perpetual strife, which causes, so to speak, the *uneasiness* of our clock, so that this appellation is quite to my taste.]

§ 6. *Ph.* *Joy* is a pleasure felt by the soul when it considers the possession of a present or future good as assured, and we are *in possession* of a good when it is so in our power that we can enjoy it when we wish.

Th. [Languages lack words sufficiently suitable to distinguish kindred notions. Perhaps the Latin *gaudium* draws nearer this definition of joy than *lætitia,* which is also translated by the word *joy;* but then it appears to me to signify a state in which pleasure predominates in us, for during the profoundest sorrow and in the midst of the most poignant grief one may take some pleasure as in drinking or hearing music, but the unpleasant feeling predominates and so in the midst of the most acute pain the mind can be joyful, as in the case of the martyrs.]

§ 8. *Ph. Sorrow* is an uneasiness of the soul when it thinks of a lost good which it might have enjoyed a longer time, or when it is tormented by an actually present evil.

Th. [Not only the actual presence, but also the fear of coming evil may make one sad, so that I believe the definitions of joy and sorrow which I have just given agree the better with usage. As to *uneasiness,* there is in pain and consequently in sorrow something more: and there is uneasiness even in joy, for it makes a man awake, active, full of hope to go farther. *Joy* has been capable of causing death by excess of emotion, and then there was in it still more than uneasiness.]

§ 9. *Ph. Hope* is the contentment of the soul which thinks of the enjoyment which it is destined probably to have in a thing suited to give it pleasure. § 10. And *fear* is an uneasiness of the soul, at the thought of a future evil that may happen.

Th. [If uneasiness signifies trouble I admit that it always accompanies fear; but taking it as this insensible spur which pushes us on, it may be applied also to hope. The Stoics regarded the passions as thoughts; thus hope was to them the thought of a future good, and fear the thought of a future evil. But I prefer to say that the passions are neither satisfactions nor displeasures, nor thoughts, but tendencies or rather modifications of the tendency, which come from thought or feeling and which are accompanied by pleasure or displeasure.]

§ 11. *Ph. Despair* is the thought one has that a good cannot be obtained, causing sometimes pain and sometimes rest.

Th. [Despair taken as passion is a kind of strong tendency which finds itself suddenly arrested, a condition which causes a violent struggle and much displeasure. But when despair is accompanied with rest and indolence it is rather a thought than a passion.]

§ 12. *Ph.* *Anger* is the uneasiness or discomposure we feel after having received some injury, and which is accompanied with a present desire to avenge ourselves.

Th. [Anger seems to be something simpler and more general, since animals are susceptible to it to whom no injury is done. There is in anger a violent effort tending to annul the evil. The desire for vengeance may remain when one is in cold blood and has hatred rather than anger.]

§ 13. *Ph.* *Envy* is the uneasiness (displeasure) of the soul which arises from the consideration of a good we desire, but which another possesses, who in our opinion should not have had it in preference to ourselves.

Th. [According to this notion envy would be always a praiseworthy passion and always based upon justice, at least in our opinion. But I know not whether men do not often bear envy towards recognized merit, which they would not hesitate to treat ill, if they had the power. They even bear envy towards persons regarding a good which they themselves would not care to have. They would be content to see them deprived of it, without thinking of profiting from their despoilments, and indeed without being able to hope for it. For some good things are like pictures painted *in fresco*, which can be destroyed, but which cannot be taken away.]

§ 17. *Ph.* Most of the passions make in many persons impressions on the body, and cause therein various changes, but these changes are not always sensible; for example, *shame* which is a felt uneasiness of the soul when it comes to consider that it has done something indecent or which may lessen the estimate others have of us, is not always accompanied by blushing.

Th. [If men would study to observe more closely the external movements which accompany the passions, it would be difficult to conceal them. As for shame, it is worthy of consideration that modest persons sometimes feel movements similar to those of shame, when they are witnesses only of an indecent action.]

CHAPTER XXI

OF POWER AND FREEDOM

§ 1. *Ph.* [The mind observing how one thing ceases to be, and how another which was not before comes to exist, and concluding that there will be in the future parallel cases, produced by parallel agents, comes to consider in one thing the possibility that one of its simple ideas may be changed, and in another the possibility of producing that change, and in that way the mind forms the idea of power.]

Th. [If *power* corresponds to the Latin *potentia*, it is opposed to act, and the passage from power to act is *change.* This is what Aristotle understands by the word *motion*, when he says[1] that it is the *act* or perhaps the *actuation* of that which is in power. It may be said then that *power* in general is the possibility of change. Now change or the act of this possibility, being action in one subject and passion in another, there will be two powers, one passive, the other active. The *active* may be called *faculty*, and perhaps the passive might be called *capacity* or *receptivity*. It is true the active power is sometimes taken in a more complete sense, when besides the simple faculty there is a *tendency;* and it is thus that I take it in my *dynamical* considerations.[2] The word *force* might be appropriated to it in particular; and force would be either entelechy or effort; for entelechy (although Aristotle takes it so generally that it comprises also all action and all effort) appears to me more appropriate to *primitive acting forces*, and that of *effort* to the *derivative*. There is even also a kind of *passive power* more particular and more endowed with reality; namely, that which is in matter in which there is not only mobility, which is the

[1] *Cf. Phys.* III., 1, 201^a 10; *Metaphys.* K, 9, 1065^b 16. — TR.

[2] *Cf. De primæ philosophiæ emendatione*, etc., published in the "Acta Eruditorum," 1694, p. 110 *sq.*, Gerhardt, Vol. 4, pp. 468–470; Erdmann, pp. 121–122; Jacques, Vol. 1, pp. 452–454, in French; translation, Duncan, *Philos. Works of Leibnitz*, pp. 68–70; also, *Beilage*, May, 1702, appended by Gerhardt to the letter to Fabri, Gerhardt, *Leibnizens Math. Schriften*, Vol. 6, pp. 98 *sq.*, especially p. 101; *Specimen dynamicum*, published in the "Acta Eruditorum," April, 1695, Gerhardt, *Leibnizens Math. Schriften*, Vol. 6, pp. 234 *sq* — TR.

capacity or receptivity for motion, but also *resistance*, which includes *impenetrability* and *inertia*. Entelechies, *i.e.* primitive or substantial tendencies, when accompanied by perception, are souls.]

§ 3. *Ph.* The idea of power expresses some kind of relation. But what one of our ideas of whatever kind does not include some *relation?* Our ideas of extension, of duration, of number, do they not all contain in themselves a secret relation of parts? The same thing is noticed in a still more visible manner in figure and motion. Sensible qualities, what are they but the powers of different bodies in relation to our perception, and do they not depend in themselves upon bulk, figure, the contexture and motion of the parts? which puts a kind of relation between them. Thus our idea of power may very well be placed in my opinion among the other simple ideas.

Th. [At bottom the ideas which we have just enumerated are composite; those of sensible qualities hold their place among the simple ideas only because of our ignorance, and the others which we know distinctly, keep their place only by an indulgence which it were better they should not have. It is almost the same with regard to the common axioms, which might be and which deservedly should be proved among the theorems, and which are allowed to pass nevertheless as axioms, as if they were primitive truths. This indulgence does more harm than we think. It is true we are not always in a position to do without it.]

§ 4. *Ph.* If we consider the matter carefully, bodies do not furnish us by means of the senses with so clear and so distinct an idea of active power as that which we have from reflection upon the workings of our mind. There are, I believe, but two kinds of actions of which we have an idea, viz.: thinking and motion. Of thought, body gives us no idea, and it is only through reflection that we have it. Neither have we from the body any idea of the beginning of motion.

Th. [These considerations are most excellent, and although here I take *thought* in a manner so general that it includes all perception, I do not wish to dispute the use of terms.]

Ph. When the body is itself in motion, this motion in the body is an action rather than a passion; but when a billiard-ball yields at the stroke of the cue, it is not an action of the ball, but a simple passion.

Th. [There is something to be said upon that point, for the bodies did not receive motion in the impact, according to the laws observed therein, if they already had not motion in themselves. But pass we now this point.]

Ph. The same is true when it pushes another ball which it finds in its way and puts in motion; it only communicates to it the motion it had received, and itself loses just as much.

Th. [I see that this erroneous view, which the Cartesians have brought into fashion, as if bodies lost as much motion as they give to others, which is to-day overthrown by experiments and by reason, and abandoned moreover by the illustrious author of "The Search after Truth,"[1] who has published a brief treatise for the express purpose of retracting it, still gives scholars occasion to be mistaken in constructing trains of reasoning upon so ruinous a foundation.]

Ph. The transfer of motion gives us only a very obscure idea of an active power of motion in the body so long as we see nothing else than that the body transfers motion but does not in any way produce it.

Th. [I do not know whether they here maintain that motion passes from subject to subject, and that the same motion (*idem numero*) is transferred. I know that some, contrary to the view of the entire scholastic philosophy, have gone that far, among others the Jesuit, Father Casati. But I doubt whether this is your view or that of your scholarly friends, ordinarily far removed from such fancies. If, however, the same motion is not transferred, we must admit that a new motion is produced in the body which receives it: thus the one which gives would really act, although it would be passive at the same time while losing its force. For although it is not true that the body loses as much motion as it gives, it is always true that it loses some motion and that it loses as much force as it gives, as I have elsewhere explained, so that it is always necessary to admit in it force or active power. I understand power in the more noble sense which I have explained a little before, in which tendency is united with faculty. Nevertheless,

[1] Malebranche, *De la Recherche de la Vérité*, 1674. The "brief treatise" referred to is entitled: *Traité de la communication du mouvement*, and may be found in Vol. 3 of the German translation of Malebranche's works, Halle, 1777–80. — TR.

I am always agreed with you, that the clearest idea of active power comes to us from the mind. It is also only in things which are analogous to the mind, that is to say, in entelechies, for matter properly speaking shows only passive power.]

§ 5. *Ph.* We find in ourselves the power to begin or not to begin, to continue or to end many actions of our soul and many motions of our body, and this simply by a thought or choice of our mind, which determines and commands, so to speak, that such a particular action be done or not done. This power we call *Will.* The actual use of this power is called *Volition;* the cessation or production of the action which follows such a command of the soul, is called *voluntary,* and all action done without such direction of the soul is called *involuntary.*

Th. [I find all that very good and just. However, to speak more fairly, and to go perhaps a little farther, I will say that *volition* is the effort or tendency (*conatus*) towards what is considered good and against that considered bad, so that this tendency results immediately from the consciousness one has of them. And the corollary of this definition is this celebrated axiom: that will and power united, action follows, since from all tendency action follows when it is not hindered. Thus not only the internal voluntary actions of our minds follow from this *conatus,* but also the external, that is to say, the voluntary movements of our bodies, in virtue of the union of the soul and the body, the reason of which I have elsewhere given. There are besides the efforts resulting from the insensible perceptions, of which we are not conscious, which I prefer to call *appetitions* rather than volitions (although there are also apperceptible appetitions), for those actions alone are called voluntary of which we may be conscious, and upon which our reflection may fall when they follow the consideration of good and evil.]

Ph. The power of perceiving we call *understanding:* it includes the perception of ideas, the perception of the signification of signs, and, finally, the perception of the agreement or disagreement existing between any of our ideas.

Th. [We perceive many things within and without us, which we do not understand, and we *understand* them, when we have distinct ideas of them, together with the power of reflection and of drawing from them necessary truths. Animals therefore have no understanding, at least in this sense, although they have the faculty of perceiving impressions more remarkable and more distinct, as the boar perceives a person who shouts at him, and goes straight for this person, of whom he had had before only a cloudy perception, but confused as of all other objects which fell under his eyes, and whose rays struck his crystalline humor. Thus in my view the *understanding* corresponds to what among the Latins is called *intellectus*, and the exercise of this faculty is called *intellection*, which is a distinct perception united with the faculty of reflection, which is not in animals. Every perception united with this faculty is a thought, which I do not accord to the animals any more than understanding, so that we may say there is intellection when thought is distinct. For the rest, the perception of the signification of signs does not deserve to be distinguished here from the perception of the ideas signified.]

§ 6. *Ph.* It is commonly said that the understanding and the will are two *faculties* of the soul, a term suitable enough if used as we ought to use all words, taking care that they cause no confusion to spring up in the thoughts of men, as I suspect has happened here in the case of the soul. And when we are told that the will is that superior faculty of the soul which rules and orders all things, that it is or is not free, that it determines the lower faculties, that it follows the *dictamen* of the understanding; although these expressions may be understood in a sense clear and distinct, I fear, however, that they have caused to arise in many persons the confused idea of so many distinct *agents* acting distinctly in us.

Th. The question has exercised the scholastics a long time whether there is a real distinction between the soul and its faculties, and whether one faculty is really distinct from another. The Realists have said yes, and the Nominalists, no, and the same question has been agitated as to the reality of many other *abstract entities*, which should meet the same fate. But I do not think we need here decide this question and plunge into these difficulties, although I remember that

Episcopius[1] found it of such importance that he thought he could not maintain the freedom of man if the faculties of the soul were real entities. However, if they were real and distinct entities, they can pass for real *agents* only in extravagant speech. It is not the faculties or qualities which act, but substances by means of the faculties.

§ 8. *Ph.* So long as man has the power to think or to refrain from thinking, to move or not to move according to the preference or choice of his own mind, so long he is *free.*

Th. [The term *freedom* is very ambiguous. There is freedom of right and of fact. As regards that of *right* a slave is not at all free, a subject is not wholly free, but a poor man is as free as a rich man. Freedom of *fact* consists either in the power *to will as one ought*, or in the power to do what one wills. It is of the *freedom to do* of which you speak, and it has its degrees and varieties. *Generally* he who has the most means is the freest to do what he wills: but *in particular* freedom is understood of the use of things which are ordinarily in our power, and above all, of the free use of our body. Thus the prison and the diseases which prevent us from giving to our body and our limbs the motion we wish and which we can ordinarily give them detract from our freedom: thus a prisoner is not at all free, and a paralytic has no free use of his limbs. *Freedom of will* is furthermore understood in two different senses. The first is when it is opposed to the imperfection or the slavery of the spirit, which is a coaction or constraint, but internal like that arising from the passions. The other sense has place when freedom is opposed to necessity. In the first sense the Stoics said that the wise man alone is free; and in fact the spirit is not at all free when it is filled with a great passion, for one cannot then will as he should, that is to say, with the deliberation which is requisite. Thus God alone is perfectly free, and created spirits are so, only to the extent that they are superior to their passions. And this freedom concerns properly our understanding. But the freedom of spirit, opposed to necessity, concerns the naked will, and in so far as it is distinguished from the understanding. This is

[1] Simon Episcopius, 1583–1643. The piece referred to is the *De libero arbitrio*, particularly the second chapter; it is found in his *Opera Theologica*, Vol. 1, p. 198, Div. II., 2d ed. London and Rotterdam, 1665–1678, 2 vols., fol. — TR.

what is called *free-will* (*franc-arbitre*) and it consists in this, that we will that the strongest reasons or impressions which the understanding presents to the will do not prevent the act of the will from being contingent, and do not give it an absolute, and, so to speak, metaphysical necessity. And it is in this sense that I am accustomed to say that the understanding can determine the will, according to the prevalence of perceptions and reasons, in a manner which, even where it is certain and infallible, inclines without compelling.[1]

§ 9. *Ph.* It is well also to consider that no one has yet thought of taking as a *free agent* a ball, whether in motion by the stroke of a racket or at rest. This is because we do not conceive of a ball as thinking or as having any volition, which makes it prefer motion to rest.

Th. [If that were *free* which acts without hindrance, a ball once in motion in a *level horizon* would be a free agent. But Aristotle has already well remarked that to call acts free, we demand not only that they be *spontaneous*, but further that they be *deliberate*.[2]]

Ph. This is why we consider the motion or rest of balls under the idea of a *necessary* thing.

Th. [The appellation *necessary* requires as much circumspection as that of *free*. This conditional truth, viz.: *supposing the ball to be in motion in a level horizon without hindrance, it will continue the same motion*, may pass as in some sort necessary, although at bottom this consequence is not entirely geometrical, being only presumptive, so to speak, and based upon the wisdom of God who changes not his influence without a reason, which it is presumed is not at present to be found. But this absolute proposition: *the ball here is now in motion in this plane*, is only a *contingent truth*, and in this sense the ball is a *contingent, not a free, agent.*]

§ 10. *Ph.* Suppose that a man, while in a profound sleep, is carried into a room, where is a person, whom he much longs to

[1] *Cf. Essais de Théodicée*, Pt. I., §§ 51, 52, Gerhardt, 6, 130–131; Erdmann, 517; also Eduard Dillmann, *Eine neue Darstellung der Leibnizischen Monadenlehre auf Grund der Quellen*, pp. 416 *sq.*; Leipzig: O. R. Reisland, 1891.—Tr.

[2] *Cf. Eth. Nic.*, III., 4, *ad fin.*, 5; 1111 *sq.*; translation by F. H. Peters, M.A., London: C. Kegan Paul & Co., 1881.—Tr.

see and to meet, and that the door is locked upon him; this man wakes up and is delighted to find himself with this person, and lives thus in the room with pleasure. I think no one presumes to doubt that he remains *voluntarily* in that place. Yet he is not at liberty to go out if he wishes. Thus freedom is not an idea belonging to volition.

Th. [I find this example very well chosen to show that in a sense, an act or a state may be *voluntary* without being *free*. Still when philosophers and theologians dispute upon *free will*, they have altogether another sense in view.]

§ 11. *Ph.* Freedom is wanting when paralysis prevents the limbs from obeying the determination of the mind, although, in the case of the paralytic even, to remain sitting still might be voluntary so long as he prefers sitting still to changing his place. *Voluntary* is not then opposed to *necessary*, but to *involuntary*.

Th. [This precision of expression would be agreeable enough to me, but usage is far from it; and those who oppose freedom to necessity, mean to speak not of external acts, but of the act itself of willing.]

§ 12. *Ph.* A man awake is no more at liberty to think or not to think, than he is at liberty to prevent or not to prevent his body from touching any other body. But to transfer his thoughts from one idea to another is often within his determination. And in that case he is as much at liberty as regards his ideas, as he is as regards the bodies upon which he rests, being able to transfer himself from one to the other as the fancy arises. There are, however, ideas, which, like certain (bodily) movements, are so fixed in the mind, that, in certain circumstances, you cannot avoid them whatever effort you make. A man upon the rack is not at liberty to put aside the idea of pain, and sometimes a violent passion acts upon our mind as the most violent wind acts upon our body.

Th. [There is order and connection in ideas, as there is in (bodily) movements, for the one corresponds perfectly to the other, although the determination in the movements be unconscious and free, or with choice in the thinking being whom good and evil only cause to incline without forcing him. For the soul, while representing bodies, preserves its (own) perfections, and although dependent upon the body (in seizing the good) in the voluntary acts, it is independent and makes the body depend upon itself in others. But this *dependence* is only *metaphysical*, and consists in the considerations which God has for the one while ruling the other, or rather for both, according to the original perfections of each; whilst *physical dependence* would consist in an immediate influence, which the one would receive from the other on which it depends. For the rest, there come to us involuntary thoughts, partly from outside by means of objects which strike our senses, and partly from within by reason of the impressions (often insensible) which remain from preceding perceptions whose action continues and which mingle with those which appear for the first time. As regards these we are passive, and even when we wake up, *images* (under which designation I include not only the representations of figures, but also those of sounds and other sensible qualities) come to us, as in dreams, without being called. The German language calls them *fliegende Gedanken*, that is, flying thoughts (*pensées volantes*), which are not within our control, and among which there are sometimes many absurdities which raise scruples in good people, and furnish exercise to casuists and directors of consciences. It is as in the magic lantern, which makes figures appear upon the wall according as something within is turned. But our mind, perceiving some image which recurs to it, may say: stop there, and, so to speak, arrest it. Moreover, the mind enters, as seems good to itself, into certain *trains of thought*, which lead it on to others. But this is true only when internal or external impressions do not at all prevail. It is true that in this thing men differ very much, both according to their temperament and according as they have exercised their control, so that one can master impressions where another lets them go.

§ 13. *Ph. Necessity* takes place wherever thought is wholly wanting. And this necessity, when found, is an agent capable of volition, and when the commencement or continuation of any action is contrary to the preference of his mind, I call it *compulsion;* when the hindering or stopping of an action is contrary to his volition, I may call it *restraint.* Agents which have absolutely neither thought nor volition are in all respects *necessary agents.*

Th. [It seems to me that, properly speaking, although

volitions are contingent, *necessity* should not be opposed to volition, but to *contingency*, as I have already remarked in § 9, and that necessity should not be confounded with determination, for there is no less connection or determination in thoughts than in movements (to be determined being a wholly different thing from being pushed or forced by compulsion). And if we do not always notice the reason which determines us or by which we determine ourselves, it is because we are as little capable ourselves of perceiving the entire play of our mind and its thoughts, very often imperceptible and confused, as we are of recognizing all the machinery which nature causes to play in the body. Thus, if by necessity, you mean the certain determination of man, which a perfect knowledge of all the circumstances within and without could make a perfect mind foresee, it is certain that thoughts being as determined as the motions they represent, every free act would be a necessary act. But necessity must be distinguished from contingency although determined; and not only are contingent truths not at all necessary, but further, their connections are not always of an absolutely necessary character; for it must be admitted that there is some difference in the manner of determining between consequences which take place in necessary matter and those which take place in contingent matter. Geometrical and metaphysical consequences necessitate, but physical and moral incline without necessitating; the physical even having something of the moral and voluntary as related to God, since the laws of movement have no other necessity than that of (the principle, or choice, of — Tr.) the best. Now God chooses freely although he is determined to choose the best; and as bodies themselves do not choose (God having chosen for them), usage has decided that they be called *necessary agents*, to which I am not opposed, provided we do not confound the necessary and the determined, and do not suppose that free beings act in an indeterminate manner, an error which has prevailed in certain minds and which destroys the most important truths, even this fundamental axiom: that *nothing happens without reason*, without which neither the existence of God nor other great truths could be satisfactorily demonstrated. As for *compulsion* it is well to distinguish two kinds, the one physical, as when a man is carried in spite of himself into prison, or thrown down a precipice; the other moral, as, for example, the constraint of a greater evil, and this act,[1] although in a sense forced, does not cease to be voluntary.[2] One may be compelled also, by the consideration of a greater good, as when a man is tempted by proposing to him a too great advantage, although it is not customary to call this constraint.]

§ 14. *Ph.* Let us see now if we cannot put an end to that long agitated, and in my opinion very unreasonable, because unintelligible, question: *Whether man's will is free or no.*

Th. [There is much reason for the exclamation with respect to the strange manner of men who torment themselves by agitating badly conceived questions: *They seek for what they know, and know not for what they seek.*]

Ph. Freedom, which is only a power, belongs only to agents and cannot be an attribute or modification of the will, which is itself nothing else than a power.

Th. [You are right, sir, according to the proper use of words. One can, however, in some measure excuse received usage. Thus it is customary to attribute power to heat or to other qualities, *i.e.* to the body in so far as possessed of that quality: and in like manner the intent here is to ask if man is free in willing.]

§ 15. *Ph.* *Freedom* is the power a man has of doing or not doing any act conformably to his will.

Th. If men understood only that by freedom, when they ask whether the will, or the arbiter is free, their question would be truly absurd. But you will see presently what they ask, and indeed I have already touched upon it. It is true but by another principle, that they (at least many) do not cease to ask for the absurd and the impossible, in desiring a freedom of equilibrium absolutely imaginary and impracticable, and which indeed would not serve them, were it possible for them to have it, *i.e.* to have the freedom of willing against all the impressions which can come from the understanding, which would destroy true freedom together with the reason, and lower us below the beasts.

[1] Gerhardt reads: "et cette action, quoyque forcée en quelque façon"; Erdmann and Jacques: "car l'action, qu'elle fait faire," *i.e.* for the act which it makes you do. — Tr.

[2] *Cf.* Kant, *Kritik d. prakt. Vernunft*, Th. I., Bd. I., Hpst. 1, § 6, Anm.; translation by T. K. Abbott, 4th ed., revised and enlarged. London: Longmans, 1889. — Tr.

§ 17. *Ph.* He who should say that the power of speaking directs the power of singing, and that the power of singing[1] obeys or disobeys the power of speaking, would express himself in as proper and intelligent a manner, as he who says, as has been usual, that the will directs the understanding, and that the understanding obeys or disobeys the will. § 18. Nevertheless this manner of speaking has prevailed, and has caused, if I am not mistaken, much confusion, although the power of thinking operates no more upon the power of choosing and the contrary, than the power of singing upon that of dancing. § 19. I grant that this or that thought may furnish man the occasion of exercising his power of choosing and that the mind's choice may be the cause of its actually thinking on this or that thing, just as actually singing a certain tune may be the occasion of dancing such a dance.

Th. [There is a little more than the furnishing of occasions, since there is some dependence; for you can will only what you find to be good, and according as the faculty of understanding is improved the choice of the will is better, as on the other hand, according as man has *vigor of will* he determines his thoughts according to his choice, instead of being determined and carried away by involuntary perceptions.]

Ph. Powers are relations, not *agents.*

Th. [If the essential faculties are only relations and add nothing whatever to the essence, the qualities and the faculties that are accidental or subject to change are something else, and we may say of these last that the one often depends upon the other in the exercise of their functions.]

§ 21. *Ph.* In my opinion the question should not be, whether the will is free, — that is to speak in a very improper manner, — but whether the *man is free.* That granted, I say that so long as any one can by the direction or choice of his mind prefer the existence of an action to its non-existence, and the contrary, *i.e.* can make it exist or not exist according as he wills, so long he is *free.* And we can scarcely say how we could possibly conceive a being freer than so far as he is able to do what he wills. So that man seems to be as free in refer-

[1] Gerhardt reads: "parler," a MS. or typographical error; *cf.* Locke, *Philos. Works* (Bohn's ed.), Vol. 1, p. 370. Erdmann and Jacques read: "chanter," which the translation follows. — TR.

ence to those actions which depend upon this power he finds in himself, as it is possible for freedom to make him, if I may so express myself.

Th. [When we reason about the freedom of the will or upon free-will (*franc arbitre*), we do not ask if man can do what he wills, but if there is enough independence in his will itself. We do not ask if he has free limbs or elbow-room, but if he has a free spirit, and in what it consists. In this respect one intelligence might be freer than another, and the supreme intelligence will exist in perfect freedom of which creatures are not at all capable.]

§ 22. *Ph.* Men naturally inquisitive, and who love to remove as much as they can from their minds the thought of guilt, although it be by reducing themselves to a state worse than that of a fatal necessity, are not, however, satisfied with this. Unless freedom extends still farther, it is not to their taste, and in their opinion it is a very good proof that man is not at all wholly free, unless he has as well the freedom to will as that of doing what he wills. § 23. Concerning which I believe that man cannot be free in reference to this particular act of willing an action which is in his power, when this action has been once proposed to his mind. The reason therein is wholly manifest, for the action depending upon his will, must unavoidably exist or not exist, and its existence or non-existence following without fail exactly the determination and choice of his will, he cannot avoid willing the existence or non-existence of this action.

Th. [I should think he could suspend his choice, and that this happens very often; above all, when other thoughts interrupt deliberation: thus, although the action deliberated upon necessarily exists or not, it does not at all follow that you must necessarily determine upon its existence or non-existence; for non-existence may happen again for want of resolution. Thus the Areopagites actually released the man whose case they had found too difficult to decide, deferring it to a term far distant, and taking a hundred years to consider it.]

Ph. In making man free in this fashion, I mean in making the act of willing depend upon his will, another will or anterior faculty of volition is necessary in order to determine the acts of this will, and another to determine that, and thus to infinity; for wherever you stop, the actions of the last will could not be free.

Th. [It is true you speak incorrectly when you speak as if we willed to will. We do not will to will, but we will to do, and if we willed to will, we should will to will to will, and this would go on to infinity: meanwhile it is not necessary to conceal that by some voluntary acts we contribute often indirectly to other voluntary acts, and although one cannot will what he will, as he cannot even judge what he will,[1] he can, however, so act in advance that he judges or wills at the time what he would wish to be able to will or judge to-day. Men attach themselves to persons, lectures, and considerations favorable to a certain party, they give no attention to that which comes from the opposite party, and by these addresses and a thousand others which they employ, most frequently without definite design and without thought, they succeed in deceiving themselves or at least in changing and converting or perverting themselves according to what they meet.]

§ 25. *Ph.* Since then it is evident that man is not at liberty to *will to will or not*, the next thing demanded is, *whether man is at liberty to will which of the two he pleases*, for example, *motion or rest?* But this question is in itself so visibly absurd that it may suffice to convince any one who will reflect that freedom in no case concerns the will. For to ask whether a man is free to will what he pleases, motion or rest, speech or silence, is to ask whether a man can will what he wills, or be pleased with that with which he is pleased, a question which, in my opinion, needs no answer.

Th. [It is true, nevertheless, that men find here a difficulty which deserves to be removed. They say that after having known and considered all, it is still within their power to will not only what pleases them the most, but furthermore wholly the contrary, merely to show their freedom. But you must consider that this caprice or obstinacy, or at least this reason which hinders them from following other reasons, also enters into the balance and makes that please them which would otherwise not do so, so that choice is always determined by perception. They do not then will what they would, but what

[1] The French is: "et quoyqu' on ne puisse point vouloir ce qu' on veut, comme on ne peut pas même juger ce qu' on veut." — Tr.

pleases, although the will can contribute indirectly and as it were from afar to make anything pleasurable or otherwise, as I have already remarked. And as men scarcely recognize all these separate considerations, it is not astonishing that the mind is so perplexed in regard to this matter which has so many concealed windings.]

§ 29. *Ph.* When men ask what it is that determines the will, the true reply is, the mind. If this answer is not satisfactory, it is plain that the meaning of the question reduces to this: *What moves the mind on each particular occasion to determine to such particular motion or rest its general power of directing its faculties towards motion or rest?* To this I reply that what leads us to remain in the same state or continue the same action, is solely the present *satisfaction* we find therein. On the other hand, the motive which incites to change is always some *uneasiness.*

Th. [This *uneasiness,* as I have shown (in the preceding chapter), is not always a displeasure, as *ease* when found is not always a satisfaction or pleasure. It is often an insensible perception, which cannot be distinguished or recognized, which makes us lean to one side rather than the other, without our being able to give a reason for so doing.]

§ 30. *Ph. Will* and *desire* should not be confounded: a man desires to be freed from the gout, but understanding that the removal of this pain may cause the transfer of a dangerous humor into some more vital part, his will cannot be determined to any action, which may serve to remove this pain.

Th. [This desire is a kind of an inclination of will (*velleité*)[1] as compared with a complete volition. We should will, for example, if there were no greater evil to be feared, if we obtained what we wish, or if perhaps there were a greater good to be hoped for if we went forward. But we can say that man wills to be delivered from the gout with a certain degree of volition, but which does not always go on to the last effort. This volition is called Velleity when it includes some imperfection or impotency.]

§ 31. *Ph.* It is well to consider, however, that what determines the will to act is not the greater good, as is ordinarily supposed, but rather some actual uneasiness, and ordinarily

[1] *Cf. New Essays,* Book. II., chap. 20, § 6, Ph. and note, *ante,* p. 168. — Tr.

that which is most pressing. We may give it the name of *desire*, which is really an uneasiness of mind, caused by the want of some absent good, over and above the desire of being freed from pain. All absent good does not produce a pain proportionate to the degree of excellence which it has or which we acknowledge it to have; whilst all pain causes a desire equal to itself; because the absence of good is not always an evil, as is the presence of pain. Therefore we can look upon and consider an absent good without pain. But in proportion as there is anywhere desire, so is there uneasiness. § 32. Who is there who has not felt in desire what the wise man says of hope, "that being deferred it makes the heart sick" (Prov. 13:12)? Rachel cries "Give me children, or I die" (Gen. 30:1). § 34. When man is perfectly content with the state he is in, or when he is absolutely free from all uneasiness, what will can remain to him but to continue in that state? Thus the wise Author of our being has put in men the inconvenience of hunger and thirst and other natural desires, in order to arouse and determine their wills to the proper conservation and continuation of their species. "It is better to marry than to burn," says St. Paul (1 Cor. 7 : 9). So true it is that the present sensation of a little burning has more power over us than the attractions of greater pleasures looked at in the distance. § 35. It is true that this maxim, it is the good and the greatest good which determines the will, is so firmly established that I am not at all surprised at having formerly regarded it as beyond doubt. But after strict inquiry I am forced to conclude that the good and the greatest good, although judged and acknowledged such, does not determine the will; unless coming to desire it in a manner proportional to its excellence this desire makes us uneasy at our deprivation of it. Suppose a man convinced of the utility of virtue so far as to see that it is necessary to the man who proposes anything great in this world, or hopes to be happy in the other: but until this man hungers and thirsts after righteousness, his will will never be determined to any action in search for this excellent good, and any other uneasiness coming in the way will drag his will to other things. On the other hand, suppose a man given to wine considers that by leading the life he leads he is ruining his health and wasting his property, that he is coming to be dishonored in the world, to bring upon himself disease and to fall at last into poverty until he no longer has wherewith to satisfy this passion for drink which so strongly possesses him: nevertheless, the returns of uneasiness which he feels in being absent from his companions in debauch, drag him to the tavern at the hours he has been wont to go there, though at the time he has before his eyes the loss of his health and estate, and perhaps even that of the happiness of the other life, happiness which he cannot regard as a good inconsiderable in itself, since he admits that it is much more excellent than the pleasure of drinking or the vain chatter of a company of debauchees. It is not then for want of casting the eyes upon the sovereign good that he persists in this intemperance; for he sees it and acknowledges its excellence, to the extent that during the time that intervenes between his drinking hours, he resolves to apply himself to the search for this sovereign good; but when the uneasiness of being deprived of his accustomed pleasure comes to torment him, this good which he acknowledges more excellent than that of drinking, has no longer power over his mind, and it is this actual uneasiness which determines his will to the action to which it is accustomed, and which thereby making very strong impressions prevails again at the first occasion, although at the same time he binds himself, so to speak, by secret promises no longer to do the same thing, and imagines that this will be the last time that he will act against his highest interest. Thus he finds himself from time to time reduced to saying:

> Video meliora proboque,
> Deteriora sequor.[1]

I see the better way, I approve it, and I take the worse. This sentence which we acknowledge as true, and which is only too well confirmed by a constant experience, is easy to understand in this way, and there is perhaps no other sense in which it can be taken.

Th. [There is something beautiful and solid in these considerations. But I would not have you believe on that account that we must abandon those ancient axioms that the will

[1] Ovid, *Metamorph.* 7:21. — TR.

follows the greatest good, or that it flies from the greatest evil that it perceives. The source of the little application to true goods arises mainly from the fact that in matters and on the occasions where the senses act but little, the greater part of our thoughts are, so to speak, surd[1] (I call them *cogitationes cæcæ* in Latin) *i.e.* void of perception and feeling, and consisting in the wholly empty employment of characters, as happens in the case of those who make algebraic calculations without considering from time to time that the geometrical figures in question and the words ordinarily produce the same effect in this regard as the characters of arithmetic or algebra. One often reasons in words without having quite the same object in mind. Now this knowledge cannot move; something living is necessary in order to arouse us. But thus it is that men most frequently think of God, of virtue, of happiness; they speak and reason without definite ideas. Not that they cannot have them, since they are in their mind. But they do not trouble themselves to press their analysis. Sometimes they have ideas of an absent good or evil, but very feeble. It is then no wonder that they are scarcely affected. Thus if we prefer the bad it is because we perceive the good which it includes without perceiving either the bad therein or the good in the contrary consideration. We assume and believe, or rather we make the statement merely upon another's belief, or at most upon belief in the memory of our past reasonings, that the greatest good is on the better side, or the greatest evil on the other. But when we do not look at these at all, our thoughts and reasonings contrary to the feeling are a kind of *psittacism*[2] which furnishes nothing at present to the mind; and if we take no measures to remedy it, it is idle talk, as I have already remarked above (Bk. I., chap. 2, § 11), and the most beautiful precepts of morality together with the best rules of prudence take effect only in a soul which is *sensible* (either *directly*, or, because that cannot always be, at least *indirectly*, as I shall show presently) and which is no longer sensible to that which is contrary thereto. Cicero well says

[1] The French is: "sourdes." *Cf.* p. 193, near the end of Th. — Tr.

[2] Littré thus defines "psittacisme," quoting this passage and the one further on, § 37, Th., by way of illustration: "État d'esprit dans lequel on ne pense ou ne parle qu'en perroquet," *i.e.* a state of the mind in which one thinks or speaks only as a parrot. — Tr.

somewhere[1] that if our eyes could see the beauty of virtue, we should love it warmly; but that not being at all the case, nor anything equivalent, we must not be astonished if in the struggle between the flesh and the spirit, the spirit so many times yields, since it does not clearly perceive its advantages. The struggle is nothing else than the opposition of different tendencies, which spring from confused and distinct thoughts. Confused thoughts often make themselves clearly felt, but our distinct thoughts are ordinarily clear only potentially; they might be clear, if we would apply ourselves to the penetration of the sense of the words or characters; but not doing so, either through negligence, or because of the shortness of time, we oppose mere words, or at least, too feeble images to living feelings. I knew a man influential in church and state, whose infirmities made him resolve to diet; but he admitted that he had not been able to resist the odor of the viands, which, passing before his apartment, were carried to others. It is doubtless a disgraceful weakness, but it is just what men have done. But if the mind made good use of its advantages, it would triumph grandly. It would be necessary to begin with education, which should be so regulated as to render true good and true evil as sensible as possible, by investing the notions which are formed of them with circumstances more suited to this design; and a full-grown man who lacks this excellent education should commence rather late, than never, to seek pleasures enlightened and reasonable, in order to oppose them to those of the senses, which are confused but impressive. And in fact, divine grace itself is a pleasure[2] which gives light. Thus when a man is in the midst of good impulses, he ought to make laws and regulations for

[1] Perhaps in *De Fin.*, 2, 16, § 52: "Oculorum, inquit Plato, est in nobis sensus acerrimus, quibus sapientiam non cernimus. Quam illa ardentes amores excitaret sui, si videretur," where, however, the discourse is concerned with the particular virtue of wisdom, rather than with virtue in general. The passage of Plato referred to is in the *Phædrus*, 250 D. *Cf.* also, *De Off.*, 2, 37: "Quis non admiretur splendorem pulchritudinemque virtutis"; and *De Off.*, 1, 5: "Formam quidem ipsam, Marce fili, et tanquam faciem honesti vides; quæ si oculis cerneretur, mirabiles amores excitaret sapientiæ." — TR.

[2] *Cf.* Spinoza, *Ethica*, Part V., Props., 32, 33, *sq.*; translation by R. H. M. Elwes, *The Chief Works of Benedict de Spinoza*, Vol. 2, pp. 263 *sq.* (Bohn's Philos. Library), London: George Bell & Sons, 1884. The best edition of Spinoza's Works is that of Van Vloten and Land, The Hague, 1882-1883. — TR.

the future, and execute them rigorously, tearing himself away from those causes able to corrupt him, either brusquely or gradually, according to the nature of the circumstances. A journey expressly undertaken will cure a lover; a retreat will draw us from the companions who support us in some bad inclination. Francis of Borgia, General of the Jesuits, who has at last been canonized, being wont to drink largely when he was a man in high life, reduced himself little by little upon a small scale, when he thought of retiring (from the world) by causing a drop of wax to fall daily into the bottle which he was wont to empty. To dangerous sensibilities we shall oppose some other innocent sensibility, as agriculture, gardening; we shall shun idleness; we shall collect curiosities of nature and art; we shall make experiments and researches; we shall engage in some indispensable occupation, if we have none, or in conversation, or useful and agreeable reading. In a word, we must profit from good impulses as from the voice of God which summons us to make effective resolutions. And as we cannot always analyze the notions of true goods and true evils until we perceive the pleasure and pain they include, we must once for all make this law in order to be moved by them: to attend to and follow henceforth the conclusions of reason once for all understood, although perceived afterward and ordinarily only by *thoughts surd*[1] merely, and destitute of sense attractions; and this in order to put yourselves finally in possession of control over *the passions* as well as of the *insensible inclinations* or uneasinesses, by acquiring this habit of acting according to reason, which makes virtue pleasant, and as it were natural. But it is not our business here to give and teach the precepts of morality, or the spiritual directions and address for the exercise of true piety; it is enough that in considering the procedure of our soul, we see the source of our weaknesses, the knowledge of which gives, at the same time, that of their remedies.]

§ 36. *Ph.* The present uneasiness which presses us, works only upon the will, and naturally determines it in view of that happiness to which we all aim in all our actions; because every one regards pain and *uneasiness* (*i.e.* the restlessness, or rather inconvenience, which prevents us from being at our ease) as

[1] *Cf.* p. 191, near the beginning of Th., and note.—TR.

incompatible with happiness. A little pain suffices to corrupt all the pleasures we enjoy. Consequently that which determines incessantly the choice of our will to the succeeding action will always be the removing of pain, as long as we feel any touch of it; this removal being the first step towards happiness.

Th. If you take your *uneasiness* or *inquietude* as a veritable displeasure, in this sense I do not admit that it is the sole incentive. Most frequently these are the little insensible perceptions which might be called imperceptible pains if the notion of *pain* did not include *apperception.* These little impulsions consist in delivering themselves continually from little obstacles towards which our nature works without thinking of them. This *uneasiness* consists in truth in this, that we feel without knowing it, which fact makes us act in passion as well as when we appear most tranquil; for we are never without some action and motion, which arises only from the fact that nature always labors to put herself more at her ease. And this it is which determines also before all consultation in *the cases which appear to us the most indifferent,* because we are never perfectly in suspense and we cannot be exactly equally divided between two cases. Now if these elements of pain (which degenerate into veritable pain or displeasure sometimes when they overgrow) were true pains, we should always be miserable in pursuing the good that we seek with uneasiness and spirit. But it is wholly the contrary; and as I have already said above (§ 6 of the preceding chapter), the mass of these continual little successes of nature, which puts it more and more at ease in reaching for the good and enjoying its image, or lessening the feeling of pain, is already a considerable pleasure, and often worth more than the enjoyment even of the good; and *very far from being obliged to regard this uneasiness as incompatible with happiness,* I find that uneasiness is essential to the happiness of created beings which never consists in complete possession,[1] — this makes them insensible, and

[1] *Cf.* the famous passage of Lessing, 1729–1781, regarding the 'search after truth, rather than its possession,' in the *Theolog. Streitschriften*, Eine Duplik, 1778, I. *ad fin.*, *Werke*, Bd. 10, s. 19, Stuttgart, 1869: "Nicht die Wahrheit, in deren Besitz irgend ein Mensch ist, oder zu sein vermeint, sondern die aufrichtige Mühe, die er angewandt hat, hinter die Wahrheit zu kommen, macht den Werth des Menschen. Denn nicht durch den Besitz, sondern durch die

as it were stupid, — but in a progress continuous and uninterrupted towards the greatest good, which cannot fail to be accompanied by a desire, or at least, a continual uneasiness, but which, as I have just explained, does not go so far as to inconvenience, but limits itself to those elements or rudiments of pain, partly *unconscious*, which do not cease to be sufficient to serve as an incentive and to arouse the will; as does appetite in a man who is well when it does not go to that inconvenience which makes us impatient and torments us by a too great attachment to the idea of what we lack. These *appetitions*, small or great, are what are called in the schools *motus primo primi*, and are truly the first steps which nature makes us take not so much towards happiness as towards joy, for they relate only to the present; but experience and reason teach us to rule these appetitions and to control them so that they may conduce to happiness. I have already spoken to this effect (Book I., chap. 2, § 3). The appetitions are like the natural tendency of the stone, which goes the most direct, but not always the best path towards the centre of the earth, not being able to see beforehand that it will meet rocks upon which it will break in pieces, whilst it would approach its end more directly if it had mind and the means of turning aside from them. Thus it is that going straight towards present pleasure we sometimes fall over the precipice of misery. Hence, reason opposes thereto images of the greatest good or evil to come, and a firm resolution and habit of thinking before acting, and then of following what shall have been recognized as the best,

Nachforschung der Wahrheit erweitern sich seine Kräfte, worin allein seine immer wachsende Vollkommenheit besteht. Der Besitz macht ruhig, träge, stolz . . ."; *i.e.* "Not the truth, in possession of which at any time a man is, or thinks he is, but the genuine effort he has made to discover the truth, constitutes the worth of the man. For not through possession, but through the search after the truth, are his powers expanded, wherein alone consists his ever growing perfection. Possession makes (him) quiet, lazy, proud . . ."

The real significance of this famous passage in relation to the problem of knowledge is not that knowledge is impossible, *i.e.* Agnosticism, for this is strictly the meaning of the term; but rather that the attainment of truth is possible, and that the human mind, having in its very constitution infinite elements and a capacity for an infinite ideal, can never rest satisfied with any present attainment or form of expression as final, but must continue to strive after the perfect truth as embodied in the infinite. *Cf.* an article by the translator, entitled "Revelation, Inspiration, and Authority," in "The Andover Review," April, 1891. — TR.

even when the sensible reasons of our conclusions are no longer present in the mind, and consist of scarcely more than feeble impressions or even of *surd thoughts,* which give words or signs destitute of an actual explanation, so that all consists in the: *Consider it well,* and in the: *Be mindful;* the first in order to the making of laws, the second for their following, even when you do not think of the reason which has called them into existence. It is, however, well to think of them as much as possible, in order that the soul may be filled with a rational joy and a pleasure accompanied with light.]

§ 37. *Ph.* These precautions are doubtless so much the more necessary as the idea of an absent good can counterbalance the feeling of some uneasiness or displeasure by which we are at present tormented, only so far as this good arouses any desire in us. How many men there are to whose minds the unspeakable joys of paradise are represented by lively pictures which they recognize as possible and probable, who nevertheless would willingly content themselves with the happiness which they enjoy in this world. It is the uneasiness of their present desire getting the better of them and bearing them rapidly towards the pleasures of this life which determines their wills to seek them: and during all this time, they are wholly insensible to the goods of the other life.

Th. [This arises in part from the fact that men very often are but little persuaded; and, although they say they are, a hidden unbelief reigns in the depths of their souls; for they have never understood the excellent reasons which verify this immortality of souls, worthy of the justice of God, which is the foundation of true religion, or rather they no longer remember that they understood them, one or the other of which conditions however is necessary in order to conviction. Few men indeed think that the future life, as true religion and indeed true reason teaches it, is *possible,* and they are still farther from thinking it probable, not to say *certain.* All that they do think about it is but a *psittacism,* or gross and vain images after the Mahometan fashion, in which they themselves see little likelihood. For they are very far from being moved by them, as (according to report) were the soldiers of the Prince of the Assassins, the Old Man of the Mountain,[1] who were carried away when fast asleep into a place full of delights, where, believing themselves in the paradise of Mahomet, they were imbued by the angels or counterfeit saints with such opinions as this prince desired, and whence after having been stupefied anew they were carried to the place whence they had been taken; this emboldened them afterwards to undertake everything, even attempts upon the lives of princes, enemies of their chief. I do not know whether this Lord[2] or Old Man of the Mountain was injured; for not a few great princes may be named whom he had caused to be assassinated, although you may see in the English historians the letter, attributed to him, exonerating King Richard I. of the assassination of a Count or Prince of Palestine,[3] whom this Old Man of the Mountain admitted he had had killed because he had been insulted by him.

[1] The usual translation of "Sheikh-al Jebal," the title of the supreme ruler of the Assassins, a secret society whose distinguishing feature was the employment of secret assassination against all enemies; a practice introduced by Hassan Ben Sabbah, the first chief of the sect. Otherwise the principles of the society were the same as those of the Ismaelites, viz. 1. No fixed rules of religion or morality, all actions indifferent, internal disposition alone of value. 2. Belief that the Immams of Ismael's line were now invisible, hence implicit obedience on part of true believers due to their vicegerents on earth. 3. Allegorical interpretation of the Koran, defending or rejecting any doctrine at pleasure, as occasion required.

The society was made up of seven ranks or orders: 1. The *Sheikh*; 2. the *Daial-Kirbal*, or grand-priors; 3. the *Dais*, or priors; 4. *Refiks*, associates not initiated, as were the former, into all the secret doctrines; 5. the *Fedais*, "devoted ones," a band of youths uninitiated and blindly obedient to the chief; 6. *Lasiks*, or novices; 7. common people, laborers, and mechanics. On these was enjoined the most rigid observance of the Koran. The initiated regarded all positive religion and morality as worthless. The *Fedais* were the assassins proper. Whenever the chief wished for their service he had them intoxicated with *hashish*, or the hemp-plant, and transported into his splendid gardens, where they were surrounded with every sensual pleasure, and by this foretaste of Paradise which the chief alone could grant led to obey his slightest command implicitly, even to the surrender of their own lives. From this circumstance they were called *Hashishin*, or hemp-eaters. This word the Europeans changed into Assassins, and thus it was transplanted into the Western languages with the signification of murderers. See Von Hammer, *Geschichte der Assassinen*, 1818; Michaud, *Histoire des Croisades*, 2, pp. 465–484; F. Walpole, *The Ansayrii*, or Assassins, 3 vols., 1851; Guyard, *Fragments relatifs à la Doctrine des Ismaelis*, 1874; De Sacy, *Memoires de l' Institut*, 4, 1818, discusses the etymology fully.—TR.

[2] Gerhardt reads: "Seigneur ou Senior (Vieux) de la Montagne."—TR.

[3] The Margrave Conrad of Montferrat, one of Saladin's brave adversaries. *Cf.* Gibbon, *Decline and Fall*, Milman's ed., chap. 59, and note 74, also Milman's note; Weil, *Gesch. d. Chalifen*, Vol. 3, p. 423; Wilken, *Gesch. d. Kreuzzüge*, Vol. 4, p. 485 *sq.*—TR.

Although that may be so, it was perhaps because of his great zeal for his religion that this Prince of the Assassins wished to give his people a favorable idea of paradise which should always accompany their thoughts of it and prevent them from being surd; without claiming on that account that they should believe that they had been in paradise itself. But supposing he had made this claim, it would not necessarily be astonishing if these pious frauds had been more efficacious than the truth badly managed. Yet nothing would be stronger than truth if we devoted ourselves to its complete knowledge and cultivation; and we should have in it without doubt the means of strongly influencing men. When I consider how much ambition or avarice can accomplish in all those who once place themselves in this course of life, almost destitute of sensible and present attractions, I despair of nothing, and I hold that virtue would be infinitely more effective accompanied as it is by so many solid goods, if some happy revolution of the human race brought it for a day into demand and made it as it were fashionable. It is very certain that we could accustom the youth to find their greatest pleasure in the practice of virtue. And even grown up men could make themselves laws and a habit of conforming to them, which would influence them as strongly and with as much uneasiness if they were turned aside from them, as a drunken man would feel when he is prevented from going to the ale-house. I am very happy to add these considerations upon the possibility and even upon the ease of the remedies for our evils, in order not to assist in discouraging men from the pursuit of true goods by the mere exposition of our weaknesses.]

§ 39. *Ph.* [Nearly everything consists in making constant the *desire* for true good.] And it rarely happens that any voluntary action is produced in us unless some *desire* accompanies it; this is why *will* and *desire* are so often confounded. But we must not regard the *uneasiness* which makes a part of, or which at least accompanies most of the other passions, as entirely excluded in this case. For hatred, fear, anger, envy, shame, have each their uneasiness, and thereby influence the will. I doubt if any one of these passions exists entirely alone. I believe indeed that it would be difficult to find any passion unaccompanied by *desire.* I am sure, however, that wherever there is uneasiness there is desire. And as our eternity does not depend on the present moment, we look beyond the present, whatever be the pleasures which we actually enjoy, and desire, accompanying these glances anticipative of the future, always impels the will to follow; so that even in the midst of joy that which maintains the action upon which the present pleasure depends, is the desire to continue it, and the fear of being deprived of it, and whenever a greater uneasiness than that takes possession of the mind it immediately determines the mind to a new action and the present pleasure is neglected.

Th. [Many perceptions and inclinations concur in perfect volition, which is the result of their conflict. There are some imperceptible by themselves, whose mass makes an uneasiness which impels us without our seeing the cause; there are many joined together which tend to some object or which remove it, and then it is desire or fear accompanied also by an uneasiness, but which does not always go so far as pleasure or displeasure.[1] Finally, there are impulses really accompanied by pleasure and by pain, and all these perceptions are either new sensations or ideas resting upon some past sensation (accompanied or not by memory), which renewing the attractions these same images had in the preceding sensations, renew also the former impulses in proportion to the vividness of the idea. From all these impulses results at last the *prevailing* effort which makes the will complete. But the desires and tendencies which are perceived are often also called *volitions* though *less complete*, whether they prevail and influence or not. It is thus easy to believe that volition can have but little force without *desire* and without *aversion* (*fuite*); for such I believe we may call the opposite of desire. Uneasiness exists not only in the troublesome passions, as hatred, fear, anger, envy, shame, but further in their opposites, as love, hope, favor, and glory. We may say that whenever there is desire, there will be uneasiness; but the contrary is not always true, because often one is in a state of uneasiness without knowing what he wants, and then there is no full-grown desire.]

§ 40. *Ph.* Ordinarily the most pressing of the uneasinesses

[1] Gerhardt adds: "ou deplaisir." — Tr.

which are judged capable of being removed at that time determines the will to action.

Th. As the result of the balance makes the final determination, I should think it may happen that the most pressing uneasiness does not prevail; for though it might prevail over each of the opposed tendencies taken by themselves, the others united may overcome it. The mind can indeed use skilfully the *dichotomies* in order to cause sometimes the one, sometimes the others, to prevail, as in an assembly we can cause one party to prevail by plurality of votes, according as we shape the order of the question. It is true the mind ought to look far into the future; for in the moment of struggle there is no time to use these artifices. All that then makes an impression, bears hard upon the balance, and helps to form a *compound direction* almost like that in mechanics, and which without some prompt diversion we cannot stop.

Fertur equis auriga nec audit currus habenas.[1]

§ 41. *Ph.* If you ask further *what it is that arouses desire,* I reply, *happiness* and nothing else. *Happiness* and *misery* are the names of two extremes of whose utmost bounds we are ignorant. It is what "eye hath not seen, ear hath not heard, and the heart of man hath never conceived."[2] But both make in us lively impressions by means of different kinds of satisfaction and joy, of torment and sorrow, which for brevity's sake I comprehend under the names of *pleasure* and *pain,* both of which happen to the mind as well as to the body, or, to speak more accurately, pertain only to the mind, although sometimes they originate in the mind upon the occasion of certain thoughts, and sometimes in the body from certain modifications of motion. § 42. Thus happiness, taken in its full extent. is *the utmost pleasure* of which we are capable, as *misery,* taken in the same way, is the greatest pain we can feel. And the lowest degree of what can be called happiness is that state, in which delivered from all pain, we enjoy such measure of present pleasure that we cannot be content with less. We call that a *good* which is adapted to produce in us pleasure, and we call that an *evil* which is adapted to produce in us pain. But it often happens

[1] Verg. *Georg.* 1:514.—TR.

[2] 1 Cor. 2:9.—TR.

that we do not so name it when one or another of these goods or of these evils is found in competition with a greater good or a greater evil.

Th. [I do not know whether the greatest pleasure is possible. I should think rather that it can grow infinitely; for we know not how far our knowledge and our organs may be carried in all that eternity which awaits us. I should think then that *happiness* is a lasting pleasure; which cannot exist without a continual progression to new pleasures. Thus of two, one of whom will advance incomparably more rapidly and by greater pleasures than the other, each will be happy *in himself* although their happiness will be unequal. Happiness is then so to speak a road through pleasures, and pleasure is only a step and an advance towards happiness, the shortest that can be made according to present impressions, but not always the best, as I said towards the end of § 36. One may miss the true road, in desiring to follow the shortest, as the stone going straight may meet too soon obstacles which prevent it from advancing directly towards the centre of the earth. Thus we know that it is the reason and the will which lead us towards happiness, but that feeling and appetite carry us only towards pleasure. Now although pleasure cannot receive a nominal[1] definition, any more than light or color, it can nevertheless receive like them a causal,[1] and I believe that at bottom, pleasure is a feeling of perfection and pain a feeling of imperfection, provided it be marked enough to make us capable of perceiving it: for the little insensible perceptions of a perfection or imperfection, which are like the elements of pleasure and pain, and of which I have spoken so many times, form the inclinations and propensities, but not yet the passions themselves. Thus there are insensible inclinations and these we do not perceive; there are sensible ones whose existence and object we know, but whose formation we do not feel, and there are confused inclinations which we attribute to the body, although there is always something corresponding in the mind; finally, there are distinct inclinations, which reason gives us, whose force and formation we feel; and the pleasures of this kind which are found in the knowledge and production of order and harmony

[1] *Cf. New Essays*, Bk. III., chap. 3, § 18.—Tr.

are the most estimable. You are right in saying that in general all these inclinations, passions, pleasures and pains belong only to the mind or soul; I will add, indeed, that their origin is in the soul itself, taking things in a certain metaphysical strictness, but that, nevertheless, you are right in saying that confused thoughts come from the body, because thereupon the consideration of the body—and not that of the soul—furnishes something distinct and explicable. The good is that which conduces or contributes to pleasure, as the evil is that which contributes to pain. But in collision with a greater good, the good of which we should be deprived would become in truth an evil, in so far as it should contribute to the pain which would spring from it.

§ 47. *Ph.* The soul has the power of suspending the accomplishment of some of these desires, and is consequently at liberty to consider one after another and to compare them. In this consists the freedom of man, and what we call, though in my view improperly, free-will; and it is from the bad use we make of it that all this variety of mistakes, errors, and faults proceeds, into which we rush when we determine our will too promptly or too late.

Th. The execution of our desire is suspended or stopped when this desire is not strong enough to move us and to overcome the trouble or inconvenience there is in satisfying it; and this trouble consists sometimes only in an inactivity or insensible lassitude which discourages without our taking notice of it, and which is greatest in persons reared in indolence or whose temperament is phlegmatic, and in those who are discouraged by age or by poor success. But when desire is strong enough in itself to move, if nothing prevents it, it can be stopped by contrary inclinations; whether they consist in a simple propensity which is as it were the element or beginning of desire, or go as far as desire itself. But as these inclinations, these propensities, and these contrary desires are to be found already in the soul, it does not have them in its power, and consequently it could not resist them in a free and voluntary way in which the reason can share, if it had no other means of diverting the mind elsewhere. But how does it presume to do it in case of need? For there is the point, especially when one is occupied with a very strong passion.

It is then necessary for the mind to be prepared in advance, and to find itself already in process of going from thought to thought, in order not to hesitate too much at a slippery and dangerous step. It is well for that reason to accustom ourselves in general not only to think as it were in passing of certain things in order the better to preserve the freedom of the mind; but it is better to accustom ourselves to proceed methodically, and to fasten ourselves to a train of thoughts whose connection reason and not chance (*i.e.* insensible and casual impressions) makes. And for this purpose it is well from time to time to accustom ourselves to collect our thoughts and to raise ourselves above the present tumult of impressions, to go forth, so to speak, from the place where we are, to say to ourselves: "*Dic cur hic? respice finem,*[1] where are we then? or let us come to the purpose,[2] let us come to the point." Men would very often need some one officially appointed (as Philip, the father of Alexander the Great, had) to interrupt and call them to their duty. But in default of such an officer, it is well for us to be accustomed to render ourselves this service. Now being once in a condition to stop the effect of our desires and passions, *i.e.* to suspend (their) action, we can find means to combat them, whether by contrary desires or inclinations or by diversion, *i.e.* by occupations of another nature. It is by these methods and artifices that we become as it were masters of ourselves, and can make ourselves think and do at the time what we should wish to will and what reason commands. But it is always through determined paths, and never without a reason or by means of the imaginary principle of perfect indifference or equilibrium, in which some would make the essence of freedom to consist; as if one could determine himself without a subject, and even against every subject, and go directly against the entire *prevalence* of impressions and propensities. *Without a reason,* I say, *i.e.* without the opposition of other inclinations, or without being in advance disposed to turn aside the mind, or without any other means equally explicable; (to act) otherwise is to recur to the chimer-

[1] Literally: Why are we here? Consider the end! — Tr.

[2] Erdmann and Jacques omit: "ou venous au propos," found in Gerhardt. — Tr.

ical, as in the empty faculties or occult qualities of the scholastics, in which there is neither rhyme nor reason.]

§ 48. *Ph.* [I am also for this intelligent determination of the will by what is in the perception and the understanding.] To will and do conformably to the final result of a sincere examination is rather a perfection than a defect of our nature. And this so far from being a suppression or an abridgement of freedom, is its greatest perfection and advantage. And the more we are prevented from determining ourselves in this way, the nearer we are to misery and slavery. In fact, if you suppose in the mind a perfect and absolute *indifference* which cannot be determined by the final judgment which it makes of good or evil, you put it in a very imperfect state.

Th. [All this is very much to my taste, and shows that the mind has not entire and direct power always to stop its desires, else it would never be determined, whatever examination it might make, and whatever good reasons or efficacious sentiments it might have, and it would always remain irresolute and fluctuate eternally between fear and hope. It must, then, after all, be determined, and thus it could itself oppose only *indirectly* its desires, by itself preparing in advance the arms which fight them in time of need; as I have just explained.]

Ph. But a man is at liberty to lift his hand to his head or to let it lie quiet. He is perfectly indifferent regarding either of these acts, and it would be an imperfection in him if he lacked that power.

Th. [To speak accurately, one is never indifferent regarding two alternatives,[1] whatever they may propose; for example, turning to the right or the left,[2] putting the right foot forward (as was necessary in the case of Trimalchio) or the left; for we do the one or the other without thinking of it, and this is an indication that a *concurrence* of internal dispositions and external impressions (although insensible) determines us to the side that we take. But the *prevalence* is very

[1] After "partis," Gerhardt reads: "quelsqu'on puisse proposer," which Erdmann and Jacques omit. — TR.

[2] After "gauche," Gerhardt reads: "de mettre le pied droit devant (comme il falloit chez Trimalcion) ou le gauche," which Erdmann and Jacques omit. For the allusion *cf.* Petronius, *Satyricon*, chap. 30. — TR.

small, and in case of need it is as if we were indifferent in this respect, since the least sensible subject which presents itself to us is capable of determining us without difficulty to one rather than to the other; and although there is a little trouble in lifting the arm to raise the hand to the head, it is so small that we overcome it without difficulty; otherwise, I admit it would be a great imperfection if man were less indifferent, and if he were wanting in power to determine easily to raise or not to raise his arm.]

Ph. But it would be as great an imperfection if he had the same indifference on all occasions, as when he would defend his head or his eyes from a blow, by which he saw he was about to be struck. [That is to say, it were as easy for him to stop this movement as others of which we have just spoken, and in which he is almost indifferent; for that would make its influence insufficiently strong and prompt in time of need. Thus determination is useful to us, and, indeed,[1] very often necessary; for if we were less determined on every sort of occasion, and as it were insensible to reasons drawn from the perception of good or evil, we would be without effective choice.] And[2] if we were determined by something else than the final result, which we have formed in our own mind according as we have judged a certain action good or evil, we should not be free.

Th. [Nothing is truer, and those who seek another freedom know not what they ask.]

§ 49. *Ph.* The superior beings who enjoy perfect happiness are determined in the choice of the good more strongly than we, and yet we have no reason to think them less free than ourselves.

Th. [For this reason theologians say that these blessed substances are confirmed in the good and exempt from all danger of falling.]

Ph. I believe indeed that, if it were proper for poor finite creatures like ourselves to judge of what an infinite wisdom and goodness could do, we could say that God himself cannot choose what is not good, and that the freedom of this all

[1] Gerhardt omits "même," which Erdmann and Jacques insert after "et."—TR.

[2] Gerhardt reads: "et"; Erdmann and Jacques, "comme."—TR.

powerful being does not hinder him from being determined by what is best.

Th. [I am so persuaded of this truth that I believe we can boldly assure ourselves of it, wholly poor and finite creatures that we are, and that we should be very wrong in doubting it; for by so doing we should derogate from his wisdom, goodness and other infinite perfections. But choice, however determined the will be, should not be called necessarily and rigorously absolute; the prevalence of perceived good inclines without necessitating, although considered as a whole, this inclination is determinate and never fails to produce its effect.]

§ 50. *Ph.* To be determined by the reason to the best, is to be the freest. Who would wish to be foolish for the reason that a fool is less determined by wise reflections than a man of good sense? If freedom consists in throwing off the yoke of reason, fools and madmen will be the only freemen; but I do not believe that for love of such freedom any one would wish to be a fool, save he who is one already.

Th. [There are people to-day who consider it clever to declaim against reason, and to treat it as an inconvenient pedant. I see little books, discourses about nothing, which make great pretensions, and I sometimes see verses even too beautiful to be employed in such false thoughts. In fact, if those who mock at reason spoke in earnest, it would be a new kind of extravagance unknown to past centuries. To speak against *reason* is to speak against truth; for reason is a concatenation of truths. It is to speak against one's self, against one's good, since the principal point of reason consists in knowing the truth and following the good.]

§ 51. *Ph.* As then the highest perfection of an intelligent being consists in applying himself carefully and constantly to the search for true happiness, so the care we should employ not to take as real happiness that which is only imaginary, is the foundation of our freedom. The more we are bound to the invariable search for *happiness in general which never ceases to be the object of our desires*, the more our will finds itself freed from the necessity of being determined by the desire which bears us towards some particular good, until we have examined whether it agrees with or is opposed to our true happiness.

Th. The true good should always be the object of our desires, but there is room for doubt whether it is so: for often one thinks but little of it, and I have remarked here more than once, that unless appetite is guided by reason it tends to present pleasure and not to happiness, *i.e.* to enduring pleasure, although it tends to protract it; see § 36 and § 41.

§ 53. *Ph.* If some extreme disturbance takes entire possession of our mind, as the pain of a cruel torture, we are not enough masters of our mind. But in order to control our passions as much as possible, we should make our mind relish good and evil really and effectively, and not permit an excellent and considerable good to escape our mind without leaving there some relish, until we have excited in ourselves desires proportioned to its excellence so that its absence renders us *uneasy* as well as the fear of losing it when we enjoy it.

Th. [That sufficiently agrees with the remarks I have just made in §§ 31 and 35, and with what I have said more than once of luminous pleasures, where we understand how they improve us without putting us in danger of some greater imperfection, as do the confused pleasures of sense, against which we must guard ourselves, especially when we have not learned by experience that we shall be able surely to avail ourselves of them.]

Ph. And let no one say here that he cannot master his passions nor hinder them from breaking loose and forcing him to act; for what he can do before a prince or great man, he can do, if he will, when alone or in the presence of God.

Th. [That remark is very good and worthy of frequent reflection.]

§ 54. *Ph.* But the different choices men make in the world, prove that the same thing is not equally good for each of them. And if the interests of men did not extend beyond this life, the reason of this diversity which causes, for example, these to plunge into luxury and debauchery, and those to prefer temperance to pleasure, would arise only from the fact that they placed their happiness in these different things.

Th. [It arises thence even now, although they all have or should have before their eyes this common object of the future life. It is true that the consideration of true happiness, even in this life, should suffice to make those who discard it prefer virtue to pleasure; although the obligation would not then be so strong or so decisive. It is also true that men's *tastes* are different, and it is said that we should not dispute about tastes. But as these are only confused perceptions, we should hold fast to them only in the case of objects found to be indifferent and incapable of harm; otherwise, if one had a relish for poisons which would kill him or render him miserable, it would be ridiculous to say that his taste should not be called in question.]

§ 55. *Ph.* If there is nothing to hope for beyond the grave, the inference is certainly very just: *let us eat and drink*, let us enjoy all that gives us pleasure, *for to-morrow we die.*

Th. [There is something to be said, in my opinion, regarding this inference. Aristotle and the Stoics and many other ancient philosophers held another view, and I believe, indeed, that they were right. If there were nothing beyond this life, the peace of the soul and health of the body would not cease to be preferable to the pleasures which would be contrary thereto. And it is no reason whatever for neglecting a good because it will not endure forever. But I admit that there are cases where there would be no means of demonstrating that the most virtuous course would be the most useful. It is then the thought of God and of immortality only which renders the obligations of virtue and justice absolutely indispensable.]

§ 58. *Ph.* It seems to me that the present judgment we make of good and evil is always right. And as for present happiness or misery, when reflection goes no farther, and all consequences are wholly put aside, man never chooses amiss.

Th. [That is to say, if everything were limited to the present moment, it would not be right to refuse the pleasure which presents itself. In fact, I remarked above that all pleasure is a feeling of perfection. But there are certain perfections which bring with them greater imperfections. If some one devoted himself during his entire life to throwing peas against pins, in order to learn not to fail to make them pierce them, after the example of him to whom Alexander the Great caused to be given as a recompense a bushel of peas, this man would attain a certain perfection, but very slight and unworthy of being compared with so many other very necessary perfections which he would have neglected. Thus the perfection which is found in certain present pleasures should yield especially to the regard for the perfections which are necessary; in order that we be not plunged into misery, which is the state in which we go from imperfection to imperfection, from pain to pain. But if there be only the present, it would be necessary to be contented with the perfection which is present, *i.e.* with present pleasure.]

§ 62. *Ph.* No one would voluntarily render his condition unhappy unless he were led by *false judgments.* I do not speak of mistakes which are the result of invincible error, and which scarcely deserve the name of false judgment, but of that false judgment which every man must confess in himself to be such. § 63. In the first place, then, the soul is mistaken when we compare present pleasure or pain with one to come which we measure by the different distance at which they are found with respect to us; like a spendthrift heir who for the present possession of a little something would renounce a large heritage, which could not fail him. Every one should recognize this false judgment, for the future will become present, and will then have the same advantage of nearness. If at the moment the man takes the glass in his hand, the pleasure of drinking were accompanied with the headache and pains in the stomach, which will follow in a few hours, he would not in the least wish to taste the wine. If a little difference in time causes so much illusion, with much stronger reason a greater distance will produce the same effect.

Th. There is some congruity here between the distance of places and that of times. But there is also this difference, that visible objects diminish their action upon the sight very nearly in proportion to their distance, and it is not at all the same as regards the future objects which act upon the imagination and the mind. Visible rays are straight lines proportionally distant, but there are curved lines which after some distance appear to fall into the straight line and are no longer sensibly divergent: thus are made the asymptotes, whose apparent interval diverges from the straight lines, although in the truth of things they abide eternally separate. We find indeed that at last the appearance of objects does not diminish in proportion to the increase of the distance, for the appearance soon[1] disappears entirely although the distance be not infinite. Thus a short distance of time robs us entirely of the future, as if the object had entirely disappeared. There often remains only the name in the mind and that kind of thoughts of which I have already spoken, which are surd, and incapable of making an impression, unless you have attended to them methodically and habitually.]

Ph. I do not speak here of that kind of false judgment by which what is absent is not only diminished but suddenly annihilated in men's minds, when they enjoy all they can obtain for the present, and then conclude that no evil will happen to them.

Th. [It is another kind of false judgment when the expectation of good or evil to come is annihilated, because the result drawn from the present is denied or made doubtful; but beyond that, the error which annihilates the thought of the future is the same thing as this false judgment of which I have already spoken, which arises from a too feeble representation of the future, which is considered only a little or not at all. For the rest, we might perhaps distinguish here between bad taste and false judgment, for often we do not even question whether the future good should be preferred, and act only upon impression without presuming to come to the examination. But when we think, one of two things happens, either we do not continue sufficiently our thought, and we pass on without pressing the question which has been touched; or we pursue the examination and form a conclusion. And sometimes in each case there remains greater or less self-condemnation: sometimes also there is no *formido oppositi* or scrupulousness at all, whether the mind turns aside at once, or is deceived by its prejudices.]

§ 64.[2] *Ph.* The limited capacity of our mind is the cause of the false judgments we make in comparing good and evil. We cannot well enjoy two pleasures at once, and still less can

[1] Gerhardt reads after "entierement," "bientost," which Erdmann and Jacques omit. — TR.

[2] Gerhardt. So also Locke, *Philos. Works*, Vol. 1, p. 402 (Bohn ed.). Erdmann has § 29: Jacques, § 59. — TR.

we enjoy any pleasure in the time that we are beset by pain. A little bitterness mixed in the cup prevents us from tasting its sweetness. The evil we feel is always the worst; we cry: Ah! any other pain rather than this!

Th. [There is much variety in all this according to men's temperaments, the force of their feelings, and the habits they have contracted. A man who has the gout might be joyful because a large fortune fell to him, and a man who swims in delights, and who might live at his ease upon the earth, is plunged into sadness because of a disgrace at court. The fact is, joy and sadness arise from the result or from the *prevalence* of pleasures or pains, when there is a mixture of them. Leander scorned the inconvenience and danger of swimming over the sea at night, urged on by the attractions of the beautiful Hero.[1] There are people who can neither drink nor eat[2] nor satisfy other appetites without much pain, on account of some weakness or inconvenience; and yet they satisfy these appetites even beyond necessity and just limits. Others are so effeminate or so delicate that they refuse pleasures with which any pain, disgust or any inconvenience is mingled. There are some persons who bravely place themselves beyond pains and pleasures present and ordinary, and act almost alone through fear and hope. Others are so effeminate that they complain of the least inconvenience, or run after the least sensible and present pleasure nearly like children. These are the people to whom the present pain or pleasure always appears the greatest; they are like preachers or panegyrists of little judgment, with whom, according to the proverb: *The idol of the day is always the greatest saint of paradise.*[3] But whatever variety is found among men, it is always true that they act only according to present perceptions, and when the future impresses them, it is always by means of an image they have of it, or by resolution and habit which they have contracted

[1] *Cf.* Vergil, *Georg.* 3, 258; Ovid, *Heroides*, 18, 19 (17, 18, *Ovid. Opera*, ex recog. Rud. Merkelii, Vol. 1, p. 141 *sq.*, Lipsiæ: B. G. Teubner, 1887); and, for "the final form" of "this poem of love and death," the poem of 340 hexameters by Musæus, the grammarian of the fifth century A.D., an extended abstract of which is given in J. A. Symonds' *Studies of the Greek Poets*, Vol. 2, chap. 22, pp. 345–362. New York: Harper & Bros., 1880. — TR.

[2] Gerhardt reads after "manger," "ou qui ne sauroient satisfaire d'autres appetits," which Erdmann and Jacques omit. — TR.

[3] The italics are mine. — TR.

in following even a simple name or other arbitrary character, without having any picture or natural sign, because it would not be without uneasiness, and sometimes without a feeling of chagrin, that they would oppose themselves to a strong resolution already made, and, above all, to a habit.]

§ 65. *Ph.* Men are apt enough to diminish future pleasure, and to conclude in themselves that, when it comes to trial, it may perhaps not correspond to the hope it gives nor to the opinion they generally have of it; having often found by their own experience that not only the pleasures which others have magnified have appeared to them very insipid, but that what has caused themselves much pleasure at one time, has offended and displeased them at another.

Th. [These are mainly the reasonings of voluptuaries, but we ordinarily find that the ambitious and avaricious judge wholly otherwise honors and wealth, although they enjoy only moderately, and often, indeed, very little, these same goods when they possess them, being always occupied in going farther. I find it a beautiful invention of nature's architect to have rendered men so sensible to what appeals so little to their senses; and if they could not become ambitious or avaricious, it would be difficult in the present state of human nature for them to be able to become virtuous and reasonable enough to labor for their perfection in the face of the present pleasures which turn them aside from it.

§ 66. *Ph.* As to things good or bad in their consequences and by their aptness to procure us good or evil, we judge them in different ways; either when we judge them incapable of really doing us as much evil as in fact they do, or when we judge that while the consequence is important it is not so certain that it may not happen otherwise, or at least that it may not be avoided by some means, as by industry, address, change of conduct, repentance.

Th. It seems to me that if by the importance of the consequence we understand that of the consequent, *i.e.* the greatness of the good or evil that may follow, we must fall into the preceding kind of false judgment, in which future good or evil is poorly represented. Thus there remains only the second kind of false judgment, of which we shall presently treat, namely, that in which the consequence is doubtful.]

Ph. It would be easy to show in detail that the subterfuges which I have just alluded to are so many unreasonable judgments; but I shall content myself with remarking in general that it is acting directly contrary to reason to hazard a greater good for a less [or to expose[1] ourselves to misery in order to acquire a little good or to avoid a little evil], and that, too, upon uncertain conjectures and before we have entered upon a due examination.

Th. [As these are two *heterogeneous* considerations (*i.e.* considerations which cannot be compared with each other), that of the greatness of the consequence and that of the greatness of the consequent, moralists in desiring to compare them are much perplexed, as appears in the case of those who have treated of probability. The truth is that here as in other estimates *disparate* and heterogeneous and, so to speak, of more than one dimension, the greatness of that which is discussed is in reason composed of both estimates, and is like a rectangle, in which there are two considerations, viz. that of length and that of breadth; and, as for the greatness of the consequence and the degrees of probability, we still lack *that part of Logic* which is to estimate them,[2] and the most of the

[1] Gerhardt reads: "exposer"; Erdmann and Jacques: "opposer." — TR.

[2] *I.e.* the Calculus of Probabilities, the founder of which was Pascal, 1623–1662, who developed the mathematical theory of probability in his correspondence with Fermat, 1601–1665, concerning certain questions on the equitable division of the stakes in games of chance proposed to Pascal by the Chevalier de Méré. *Cf.* I. Todhunter, *History of the Theory of Probability from the time of Pascal to that of Laplace*, pp. 7–21, 8vo, Cambridge and London, 1865. Contributions were made to the theory by many of the distinguished mathematicians of the period and after, including James Bernoulli, 1654–1705; Huygens (*vid. ante*, p. 150, note 3); Demoivre, 1667–1754, in his *Doctrine of chances, or method of calculating the probabilities of events at play*, 3d ed., London, 1756; Laplace, 1749–1827, in his *Théorie analytique des probabilités* (Vol. 7 of his *Œuvres complètes, publiées sous les auspices de l'Académie des Sciences*, seven vols., 4to Paris, 1878–1886), since which but little advance has been made in the theory; and Poisson, 1781–1840, in his *Recherches sur la probabilité des jugements en matières criminelles*, etc., 4to Paris, 1837. Leibnitz became acquainted with Pascal's labors during his residence in Paris, 1672–1676; *cf.* Guhrauer, *Leibnitz. Leben*, 1, 113 *sq.* He recognized the immense importance of this new "part of Logic," and thought to substitute it for the old and crude casuistry which had so long prevailed. In the letter to Bourguet, March 22, 1714, Gerhardt, 3, 570; Erdmann, 723, Leibnitz glances briefly at the historical rise of the calculus of probabilities. For the philosophical side of the question, *cf.* J. S. Mill, *Logic*, Bk. III., chaps 18, 23, pp. 379 *sq.*, 416 *sq.*, 8th ed., Harper and Bros., New

casuists who have written *on probability* have not even understood its nature, founding it with Aristotle,[1] upon authority, instead of founding it as they ought upon likelihood (*vraisemblance*), authority being only one of the reasons which produce likelihood.]

§ 67. *Ph.* Here are some of the ordinary causes of this false judgment. First, *ignorance*, second, *inattention*, when a man does not reflect upon that of which he is aware. This is an affected and present ignorance which misleads the judgment as well as the will.

Th. [It is always present, but not always affected; for we do not always take it into our heads to think, when it is necessary, of what we know and the memory of which we should recall if we were master of it. *Affected ignorance* is always mixed with some attention at the time it is affected; in the future, it is true, it may ordinarily include somewhat of inattention. *The art of thinking in time of need* of what we know would be one of the most important if it were found; but I do not see that men up to the present time have even thought of forming the elements of it, for the art of memory[2] of which so many authors have written is wholly another thing.]

Ph. If then they bring together in confusion and hastily the reasons from one side and allow through neglect several sums which ought to enter into the *reckoning* to escape, this

York, 1881; F. H. Bradley, *The Principles of Logic*, Bk. I., chap. 7, §§ 32 *sq.*, pp. 201 *sq.*, Kegan Paul, Trench and Co., London, 1883; J. Venn, *The Logic of Chance*, 3d ed., Macmillan and Co., London, 1888; W. S. Jevons, *The Principles of Science*, 3d ed., Macmillan and Co., London, 1889. — TR.

[1] For Aristotle's definition of probability, *cf. Anal. Prior.*, II., 27, 70ª3: "The probable is a generally admitted proposition. For what is known for the most part as thus happening or not happening, or being or not being, this is probable"; *cf.* also Wallace, *Outlines*, § 21, who quotes the Greek of the passage. *Rhet.* I., 2, 1357ª34: "For the probable is that which for the most part happens." Aristotle accordingly rests much more upon experience than upon authority, and Leibnitz has not given his definition accurately. "The probable conclusion," says Schaarschmidt, is for Aristotle, "an incomplete induction, whose problematic character he well understood, but did not determine more closely. Later Greek philosophers of a sceptical creed began to speak of grades of probability, but the moderns have been the first to fall upon the fruitful thoughts of a mathematical estimate of probability." — TR.

[2] Mnemonics, the invention of which was ascribed to the poet Simonides, of Ceos, 556–469 B.C., perhaps because he was famous for the strength of his own memory. *Cf.* Cicero, *De Oratore*, Bk. II., chap. 82. — TR.

haste produces no less false judgments than if it were perfect ignorance.

Th. [In reality many things must be taken into account, as should be the case, when the balance of reasons is discussed; and the process is almost like that in the account-books of merchants. For no sum must be neglected, each must be properly estimated by itself, they must be properly arranged, and finally an exact collection must be made of them. But we neglect many weighty points either by its not occurring to us to think of them or by passing lightly over them; and we do not give each its proper value, like the book-keeper, who was careful properly to calculate the columns of each page, but who calculated very badly the particular sums of each line or posting, before putting them in the columns; this causes the examiners to be deceived, who look principally at what is in the columns. Finally, after having carefully noted all, they may be deceived in the collection of the sums of the columns and even of the final collection, in which is the sum of the sums. Thus we should still need the art of thinking and that of estimating probabilities, and besides the knowledge of the value of goods and evils in order properly to employ the art of consequences; and furthermore, attention and patience would be necessary after all that, in order to push to the conclusion. Finally, a firm and constant resolution to execute the conclusion arrived at is necessary; and address, method, particular laws, and habits entirely formed in order to maintain the course in the future, when the considerations, which have caused it to be taken, are no longer present to the mind. It is true, thank God, that in what is of the greatest importance and which concerns the *summam rerum*, happiness and misery, there is no need of so much knowledge, aid, and address, as it would be necessary to have in order properly to judge in a council of state or of war, in a tribunal of justice, in a medical consultation, in some theological or historical controversy, or in some point of mathematics or mechanics; but as a recompense more firmness and habit is necessary, in what concerns this great point of felicity and virtue, in order always to adopt good resolutions and to follow them. In a word, for true happiness less knowledge suffices with more good will; so that the greatest idiot may attain it as easily as the most learned and most skilful.]

Ph. You see then that without liberty the understanding would be of no use, and that liberty without understanding would signify nothing. If a man could see what may do him good or evil without being able to move a step in advance towards the one or in removal from the other, would he be the better for the sight? He would be indeed more miserable for this reason, for he would uselessly pine after the good and would fear the evil, that he sees is inevitable; and he who is at liberty to run here and there in the midst of perfect darkness, in what respect is he better than if he were tossed about at the pleasure of the wind?

Th. [His caprice would be a little better satisfied, but he would be in no better condition to meet good or to shun evil.]

§ 68. *Ph.* Another source of false judgment. Content with the first pleasure which comes to hand or which custom has rendered agreeable, we do not look farther. This then is also an occasion for men to judge wrongly when they do not regard as essential to their happiness that which really is so.

Th. [It seems to me that this false judgment is comprised under the preceding kind where one is mistaken as to the consequences.]

§ 69. *Ph.* The inquiry remains whether *a man* has the power *to change* the pleasure or displeasure which accompanies any particular action. In many cases he can. Men may, and ought to, correct their palates and make them acquire a taste. They can change also the taste of the soul. A due consideration, practice, application, custom will bring about this result. Thus it is that men accustom themselves to tobacco, which usage or custom at last makes them find agreeable. It is the same as regards virtue. Habits have powerful charms and we cannot depart from them without uneasiness. You will, perhaps, regard it as a paradox that men can make things or actions more or less agreeable to themselves, so much do they neglect this duty.

Th. [I have already made this statement above, § 37, towards the end, and § 47, also towards the end. We can make ourselves will anything and form our taste.]

§ 70. *Ph.* Morality, established upon true foundations, can only determine to virtue: it suffices that infinite happiness and misery after this life are possible. We must admit that a good life, joined with the expectation of possible eternal felicity, is preferable to a bad life, accompanied by the fear of terrible misery, or, at least, of the terrible and uncertain hope of annihilation. All this is in the highest degree self-evident, although virtuous men should have only evil to endure in this world, and the wicked should taste therein perpetual pleasure, which is ordinarily quite otherwise. For rightly considering all things, I believe they have the worst part even in this life.

Th. [Thus were there no life beyond the grave an epicurean life would not be the most reasonable. And I rejoice, sir, that you rectify what you said to the contrary above, § 55.]

Ph. Who could be so foolish, as to resolve (if he had his senses) to expose himself to a possible danger of being infinitely unhappy so that he has nothing to gain therefrom for himself but pure annihilation; instead of putting himself in the condition of the good man who has nothing to fear but annihilation, and who has eternal felicity to hope for? I have forborne to speak of the certainty or probability of the future state, because I have no other design in this place than to show the false judgment of which each should acknowledge himself guilty on his own principles.

Th. [The wicked are very prone to believe that the other life is impossible. But they have no reason for their belief other than that which compels them to limit themselves to what they learn by their senses, and that no one to their knowledge has come back from the other world. There was a time when upon the same principle we could reject the antipodes, when we were unwilling to unite mathematics and the popular notions; and we could do so with as much reason as we can now have in rejecting the other life, when we are unwilling to unite true metaphysics and the notions of the imagination. For there are three degrees of notions or ideas, viz.: popular, mathematical, metaphysical. The first do not suffice to make us believe in the antipodes; the first and the second do not yet suffice to make us believe in the other world. It is true they furnish already favorable conjectures; but if the second established certainly the antipodes before the experience we now have of it (I speak not of the inhabitants, but of the place at least which the knowledge of the roundness of the earth gave them among geographers and astronomers), the last give no less certitude of another life from this time, and before you have gone to see.]

§ 72. *Ph.* Let us now return to power which is properly the subject of this chapter, liberty being only one form of it, but the most important. In order to have more distinct ideas of power, it will be neither beside the purpose nor useless to obtain a more exact knowledge of what is called *action.* I said at the beginning of our discourse on power that there are two kinds of actions, of which we have some idea, viz.: motion and thought.[1]

Th. [I thought you could avail yourself of a more general term than that of *thought,* viz.: that of *perception,* attributing thought only to minds, while perception belongs to all the entelechies. But I do not wish, however, to contest with any one the liberty to take the term thought in the same general way. And for myself indeed I shall perhaps do so some time without being aware of it.]

Ph. Now, although we give to those two things the name of action, we shall find however that it does not always suit them perfectly, and that there are some examples which we shall recognize rather as *passions.* For in these examples substance, in which we find movement or thought, receives purely from without the impression through which action is communicated to it, and acts only by the sole capacity it has of receiving this impression, which is only a *passive power.* Sometimes substance or the agent puts itself in action by its own power, and it is there properly an *active power.*

Th. I have already said that, taking action in metaphysical strictness as that which takes place in substance *spontaneously* and from its own depths, that alone is, properly speaking, a substance which is active,[2] for all arises for it from itself after God; it being impossible for one created substance to have

[1] Locke has: "thinking," *Philos. Works,* Vol. 1, p. 413 (Bohn's ed.).—Tr.

[2] *Cf. De ipsa natura,* etc., 1698, § 9 *ad fin.;* Gerhardt, 4, 509; Erdmann, 157; Jacques, 1, 461 (in French); J. H. v. Kirchmann, *Die klein. philos. wicht. Schrift. v. G. W. Leibniz* (*Philos. Bibliothek,* Bd. 81), p. 121 (in German), Erick Koschny, Leipzig, 1879; also Kuno Fischer, *Gesch. d. neuern Philos.,* Vol. 2 (G. W. Leibniz), p. 334, 3d ed., Heidelberg: C. Winter, 1889.—Tr.

influence upon another. But taking *action* as an exercise of *perception* and *passion* as its contrary, there is *action* in true substance only when their perception (for I grant it to all) is developed and becomes more distinct, as there is *passion* only when it becomes more confused; so that in substances capable of pleasure and of pain, all action is a step towards pleasure and all passion a step towards pain. As for motion, it is only a real phenomenon, because matter and mass to which motion belongs is not properly speaking a substance. But there is an image of action in motion as there is an image of substance in mass; and in this respect we can say that the body *acts* (*agit*) when there is spontaneity in its change and that it *is passive* (*patit*) when it is urged on or hindered by another; as in the veritable action or passion of a veritable substance we may take as its *action*, and attribute to itself, the change by which it tends to its perfection. And in the same manner we can take as *passion* and attribute to a foreign cause the change by which the contrary happens to it; although this cause is not immediate, because, in the first case, the substance itself, and in the second the foreign things serve to explain this change in an intelligible way. I allow bodies only an image of substance and action, because that which is composed of parts cannot pass, to speak accurately, as one substance, any more than a flock; but we can say that there is therein something substantial, of which the unity, that which makes it as it were *one* being, comes from thought.]

Ph. I have thought that the power to receive ideas or thoughts by the operation of some foreign substance was called power of thought, although at bottom it is only a *passive power* or a simple capacity making abstraction from the reflections and internal changes which always accompany the received image, for the expression,[1] which is in the soul is, as it should be, that of a living mirror; but the power which we have of recalling absent ideas at our choice, and of comparing together those that we think to the purpose, is truly an *active power*.

Th. [This also agrees with the notions I have just presented, for there is in this a passage to a more perfect state.

[1] Gerhardt and Erdmann read: "l'expression"; Jacques: "l'impression."—Tr.

But I should suppose that there is also action in sensations so far as they give us more distinct perceptions and consequently the opportunity of making remarks and so to speak of developing ourselves.]

§ 73. *Ph.* Now I think it appears that we can reduce the primitive and original ideas to this small number: *extension, solidity, mobility* (*i.e.* passive power, or rather capacity of being moved), which come to us in the mind by way of reflection, and finally, *existence, duration,* and *number,* which come to us by the two ways of sensation and reflection; for by these ideas we could explain, if I am not mistaken, the nature of colors, sounds, tastes, odors, and all the other ideas we have, if our faculties were subtile enough to *perceive* the different motions of the minute bodies which produce these sensations.

Th. To speak the truth, I believe that these ideas, which you here call original and primitive, are for the most part not wholly so, being susceptible in my view of further resolution; but I do not blame you at all, sir, for having limited yourself and for not having pushed the analysis farther. Moreover,[1] I believe that if their number can be diminished by this means, it can be increased by adding other ideas more original or as much so. As to the question concerning their arrangement, I should consider, following the order of the analysis, existence anterior to the others, number to extension, duration to *motivity* or mobility; although this analytic order is not ordinarily that of the occasions which make us think of them. The senses furnish us the material for reflection and we should not even think of thought, if we did not think of something else, *i.e.* of the particular things which the senses furnish. And I am persuaded that created souls and minds are never without organs and never without sensations, as they cannot reason without characters. Those who have desired to maintain a complete separation and mode of thinking in the separated soul, inexplicable by all that we know, and separated

[1] Gerhardt reads: "D'ailleurs je crois que si le nombre en pourroit estre diminué par ce moyen, il pourroit estre augmenté," *etc.*; Erdmann and Jacques read: "D'ailleurs si c'est vrai, que le nombre en pourroit être diminué par ce moyen, je crois qu'il pourroit être augumenté en y ajoutant d'autres Idées plus originales ou autant." — TR.

not only from our present experiences, but, what is much more, from the general order of things, have given too much influence to so-called strong minds, and have made the finest and the grandest truths objects of suspicion to many people, having indeed deprived themselves thereby of some excellent means of proving them, which this order furnishes us.]

CHAPTER XXII

OF MIXED MODES

§ 1. *Ph.* Pass we on to the *mixed modes.* I distinguish them from the more *simple modes,* which are composed only of *simple ideas* of the same kind. Moreover, the mixed modes are certain combinations of simple ideas which are not regarded as characteristic marks of any real being, which has a fixed existence, but as scattered and independent ideas which the mind joins together; and they are thereby distinguished from the *complex ideas of substances.*

Th. [Properly to understand these we must recall our former divisions. According to you ideas are simple or complex. The complex are either substances, modes, or relations. Modes are either simple (composed of simple ideas of the same kind) or mixed. Thus, in your view, there are simple ideas, ideas of modes, both simple and mixed, ideas of substances and ideas of relations. We could, perhaps, divide the terms or the objects of ideas into abstract and concrete; the abstract into absolute and into those which express relations; the absolute into attributes and into modifications; both into simple and composite; the concrete into substances and into substantial things, made up of or the resultants of true and simple substances.]

§ 2. *Ph.* The mind is purely passive, respecting its simple ideas, which it receives as sensation and reflection present them to it. But it often acts by itself, indeed, in reference to the mixed modes, for it can combine the simple ideas in making complex ideas without considering whether they so exist united in nature. This is why we give to these kinds of ideas the name of *notion.*

Th. [But reflection which makes us think of simple ideas is often voluntary also, and, moreover, the combinations, which nature has not made, can produce themselves in us, as it were in dreams and reveries by means of memory alone, without the mind's acting more than in the simple ideas. As for the term *notion*, many apply it to all sorts of ideas or conceptions, to the original as well as to the derived.]

§ 4. *Ph.* The mark of several ideas combined in one alone is the *name*.

Th. [That means, if they can be combined, in which respect they are often lacking.]

Ph. The crime of killing an old man, not having a name like parricide, is not at first regarded as a complex idea.

Th. [The reason why the murder of an old man has no name is that, the laws not having attached thereto a particular punishment, this name would be useless; but ideas do not depend on names. An ethical author who should invent one for the crime and treat in a special chapter of *Gerontophony*, showing what is due to old men and how it is a barbarous act not to spare them, would not on that account present us with a new idea.]

§ 6. *Ph.* It is always true that the manners and usages of a nation, making combinations familiar to it, cause each language to have particular terms, which cannot always be translated word for word. Thus *ostracism* among the Greeks and *proscriptio* among the Romans were words which other languages cannot express by equivalent words. Therefore, change of customs makes also new words.

Th. [Chance also plays its part, for the French do not use horses as much as other neighboring peoples; but having abandoned their old word, which corresponded to the *cavalcar* of the Italians, they are forced to say by *paraphrase: aller à cheval* — to go on horse-back.]

§ 9. *Ph.* We acquire ideas of mixed modes by observation, as when we see two men wrestling; we acquire them also by invention (or a *voluntary union* of simple ideas), thus, he who invented printing had the idea of it before this art existed. We acquire them finally by explaining terms, affecting actions which we have never seen.

Th. [We can further acquire them while dreaming or in a

state of revery without the combinations being voluntary, for example, when we see in a dream a golden palace without having thought of it before.]

§ 10. *Ph.* The simple ideas which have been most modified are those of thought, motion, and power, whence actions are conceived to flow; for the great business of mankind consists in action; all actions are thoughts or motions. The power or aptitude to do anything which is found in man constitutes the idea which we call *habit,* when this power has been acquired by often doing the same thing; and when we can force it to action upon each occasion that presents itself, we call it *disposition.* Thus, *tenderness* is a disposition to friendship or love.

Th. [By tenderness you understand here, I presume, the tender heart, but elsewhere you seem to me to regard *tenderness* as a quality which one has, as a lover, which renders him very sensible to the good and evil of the object loved. This it is to which it seems to me the chart of affection is moving in the excellent romance *Clelie.*[1] And, as charitable persons love their neighbor with some degree of tenderness, they are sensible to the good and evil of another, and generally those who have the tender heart have some disposition to love with tenderness.]

Ph. *Boldness* is the power to do or say before others what you wish without being put out of countenance, a self-confidence, which, in relation to this last part which concerns discourse, had a particular name among the Greeks.

Th. [It would be well to seek a word for this notion, which is here attributed to that of *boldness,* but which is often employed wholly otherwise, as when we say Charles the Bold. Not to be put out of countenance is a strength of mind, but one which bad men abuse when they have become impudent; as shame is a weakness, but excusable and even praiseworthy in certain circumstances. As for *parrhesia,*[2] which you perhaps understand by the Greek word, it is still attributed to writers who speak the truth without fear, although, then not

[1] *Clélie, Histoire Romaine,* a romance by Mlle. Scudéry, 1607-1701. The scene is laid early in Roman history; the heroine is Cloelia, who escaped from Porsena by swimming the Tiber. — TR.

[2] παρρησία. — TR.

speaking in the presence of people, they are not liable to be discountenanced.]

§ 11. *Ph.* As *power* is the source whence proceed all *actions,* the name of *cause* is given to the substances in which these powers reside, when they reduce *their power* to *act;* and they call *effects* the substances produced by this means, or rather the simple ideas (*i.e.* the objects of simple ideas), which, by the *exercise* of power are introduced into a *subject.* Thus the *efficacy* by which a new substance or idea (quality) is produced, is called *action* in the subject exercising this power and *passion* in the subject in which some simple idea (quality) is altered or produced.

Th. [If *power* is taken as the source of action, it means something more than an aptitude or facility, by which power was explained in the preceding chapter; for it includes, besides, tendency as I have already more than once remarked. This is why in this sense I have been wont to appropriate to it the term *entelechy,* which is either *primitive* and answers to the soul taken as an abstract thing, or *derivative* as it is conceived in conation (*le conatus*) and in vigor and impetuosity. The term *cause* is here understood only as *efficient* cause; but it is also understood as *final* or the motive, not to speak here of matter and form which are also called causes in the schools. I do not know whether we can say that the same being is called action in the agent and passion in the patient, and is thus found in two subjects at once like relation, and, whether it is not better to say that there are two beings, one in the agent, the other in the patient.]

Ph. Many words which seem to express some action signify only the *cause* and the effect; as creation and annihilation contain no idea of action or of the manner, but simply of the cause and the thing which is produced.

Th. [I admit that in thinking of creation, we do not conceive a mode of acting, capable of any detail, which cannot indeed there be expedient; but, since we express something besides God and the world, for we think that God is the cause and the world the effect, or else that God has produced the world, it is manifest that we think still of action.][1]

[1] Leibnitz regards the concept of creation in the sense of the origination of substances as incapable of further explanation because we can form no idea

CHAPTER XXIII

OF OUR COMPLEX IDEAS OF SUBSTANCES

§ 1. *Ph.* The mind notices that a certain number of *simple ideas* constantly go together, which, presumed to belong to one thing only, are called by one name when *thus united in one subject.* Whence it comes that, although this is in truth a mass of many ideas joined together, we are afterwards led by *inadvertence* to speak of them as a single, simple idea.

Th. [I see nothing in the accepted expressions which deserves to be taxed with *inadvertence;* and although we recognize only one subject and one idea, we do not recognize only one simple idea.]

Ph. Not being able to imagine how these simple ideas can subsist by themselves, we are accustomed to assume something which sustains them (*substratum*), in which they subsist or whence they result, to which for this effect we give the name of *substance.*]

Th.[1] [I believe that there is reason in thus thinking, and we have only to accustom ourselves to it or to assume it, since, at first, we conceive several predicates in one and the same subject, and these metaphorical words, *support* (*soutien*) or *substratum* mean only this; so that I do not see why it should cause any difficulty. On the contrary, it is rather the *concretum,* as wise, warm, shining, which arises in our mind, than the *abstractions* or qualities (for these and not the ideas are in the substantial object), as knowledge, heat, light, etc., which are much more difficult to comprehend. We may even doubt whether these accidents are veritable existences, as in fact they are very often only relations. We know also that it is these abstractions which cause the greatest difficulties to spring up when we wish to examine them minutely, as those

of the process. For some other expressions concerning it, *cf. La Monadologie*, § 47, Gerhardt, 6, 614; Erdmann, 708, b.; Letter to Bayle, Gerhardt, 3, 58; Erdmann, 191. Gerhardt, 3, 61, and note, says the original is without date; Erdmann gives it 1702. *Cf.* also Dillmann, *Eine neue Darstg. d. Leibniz. Monadenlehre*, p. 451 *sq.* — Tr.

[1] Erdmann has "Ph.," a typographical error. — Tr.

know who are familiar with the subtilties of the scholastics, the most intricate of which falls at once if we will banish abstract existence and resolve to speak ordinarily only by concretes and admit no other terms in scientific demonstrations but those which represent substantial subjects. Thus it is *nodum quaerere in scirpo*,[1] if I may so speak, and reversing things to take the qualities or other abstract terms as the easier and the concrete as something very difficult.]

§ 2. *Ph.* We have no other notion at all of pure *substance* in general, than of an indescribable subject, which is to us altogether unknown and which is supposed to be the support of qualities. We speak like children to one who has no sooner asked them what a certain thing unknown to them is, than they make this reply very satisfactory to their taste that *it is something*, but, which employed in this way, means that they do not know what it is.

Th. [In distinguishing two things in substance, the attributes or predicates, and the common subject of these predicates, it is no wonder that we can conceive nothing particular in this subject. It must be so, indeed, since we have already separated from it all the attributes in which we could conceive any detail. Thus to demand something more in this pure *subject in general* than what is necessary in order to conceive that it is the same thing (for example, which understands and wills, which imagines and reasons), is to demand the impossible, and to act contrary to our own supposition, which has been made in making abstraction and conceiving separately the subject and its qualities or accidents. We could apply the same pretended difficulty to the notion of *being* and to all that is clearer and more primitive; for we could demand of the philosophers what they conceive when conceiving *pure being in general*; for all detail being excluded by that means there will also be little to say, when we are asked what is *pure substance in general*. Thus I believe that the philosophers do not deserve to be laughed at, as is here done, in comparing them with an Indian philosopher, who, being asked upon what the earth rested, replied, upon a great elephant; and then when asked what sustained the elephant, replied, a great tor-

[1] To seek a knot in a bulrush, to find a difficulty when there is none. *Cf.* Plaut. *Men.* 2, 1, 22; Ter. *And.* 5, 4, 38. — TR.

toise; and, at last, when pressed to say upon what the tortoise rested, was compelled to say *something, I know not what.* But this consideration of substance,[1] entirely slender as it appears, is not so empty and sterile as you think. It gives rise to many consequences of greatest importance in philosophy, and which are capable of giving it a new aspect.]

§ 4. *Ph.* We have no clear idea of substance in general, and § 5, we have as clear an idea of mind as of body; for the idea of corporeal substance in matter is as far from our conceptions as that of spiritual substance. It is almost as the promoter said to this young doctor of law, who cried to him in the solemnity, to say *utriusque:* You are right, sir, for you know as much in the one case as the other.

Th. [As for myself, I believe that this opinion of our ignorance arises from that which demands a kind of knowledge of which the object does not admit. The true mark of a clear and distinct notion of an object is the means we have of knowing therein many truths by *a priori* [2] proofs, as I have shown in a discourse on truths and ideas,[3] published in the "Actes de Leipzig" of the year 1684.

§ 12. *Ph.* If our senses were sufficiently penetrating, the sensible qualities, for example, the yellow color of gold, would disappear, and instead of that we should see a certain admirable contexture of parts. This appears evident by means of microscopes. This present knowledge is suitable to the state in which we find ourselves. A perfect knowledge of things

[1] In Leibnitz's philosophy substance is a unitary, individual, spontaneously active being, as opposed to the "empty and sterile" conception of Aristotelian scholasticism; *cf. ante,* p. 154 and note. Locke's criticism concerns the scholastic conception only. — TR.

[2] *Cf. New Essays,* Bk. IV., chap. 17, § 1, Th.; *Theodicée,* I., § 44, Gerhardt, 6, 127; Erdmann, 515, b. For a brief critical history of the concepts of the *a priori* and the *a posteriori, cf.* Rudolph Eucken, *The Fundamental Concepts of Modern Philosophic Thought,* pp. 81–91, D. Appleton and Co., New York, 1880; and for Leibnitz's use of the terms, *op. cit.,* p. 82, with the note containing references to the places where *a priori* occurs in Erdmann's and Foucher de Careil's editions of his works. — TR.

[3] *Meditationes de Cognitione, Veritate et Ideis,* in the "Acta Eruditorum," Nov., 1684. Gerhardt, 4, 422 *sq.*; Erdmann, 79 *sq.* The passage referred to is found in Gerhardt, 425; Erdmann, 80 b.; translation, Duncan, *Philos. Works of Leibnitz,* 30. The piece has been translated into German, with notes, by J. H. v. Kirchmann in his *Philos. Bibliothek,* Bd. 81, *Die klein. philos. wicht. Schriften v. G. W. Leibniz;* Bd. 82, *Erläuterungen.* — TR.

which surround us, is, perhaps, beyond the capacity of every finite being. Our faculties suffice to make us know the Creator, and to instruct us as to our duties. Should our senses become more acute, such change would be incompatible with our nature.

Th. [All that is true; and I have said something to the same effect above. But the color yellow does not cease to be a reality like the rainbow, and we are apparently destined to a state far beyond the present, and can even go on to the infinite, for there are no elements in the corporeal nature. If there were atoms, as the author appeared to believe in another place, perfect knowledge of the body could not be beyond every finite being. For the rest, if some colors or qualities should disappear from our eyes better armed or become more penetrating, others would apparently spring into being, and it would require a new growth of our perspicacity to make these also disappear, and this could go on to infinity, as the actual division of matter effectively proceeds.]

§ 13. *Ph.* I do not know but that one of the great advantages which some spirits have over us consists in the fact that they can assume to themselves organs of sensation which are precisely suited to their present design.

Th. [We do this indeed in making for ourselves microscopes; but other creatures can go much farther. And, if we could transform our eyes themselves, which we do effectively to some extent according as we wish to see near at hand or at a distance, we should be obliged to have something[1] belonging more exclusively to us than they in order to shape them by its means, for it is necessary, at least, that all be done mechanically, because the mind cannot operate immediately upon the body. For the rest, I am also of the opinion that *genii* perceive things in a manner which is somewhat related to ours, even if they should have the agreeable advantage which the imaginative Cyrano[2] attributes to some animated natures in

[1] *I.e.* the soul to make use of the capacity of the eyes for accommodation. — TR.

[2] Cyrano de Bergerac, c. 1620—1655, in his philosophical romance, *Histoire comique des états et empires du soleil.* He was author also of the *Histoire comique des états et empires de la lune*, or, as the title is sometimes given, *Voyage dans la lune.* — TR.

the sun, composed of an infinite number of little winged creatures, which, by transporting themselves according to the command of the ruling soul, form all kinds of bodies. There is nothing so marvellous that the mechanism of nature cannot produce it; and I believe that the learned fathers of the Church were right in attributing bodies to the angels.[1]]

§ 15. *Ph.* The ideas of thinking and of moving a body, which we find in that of the mind, can be conceived as clearly and distinctly as those of extension, solidity, and mobility, which we find in matter.

Th. [As regards the idea of thought I agree. But I am not of this opinion as regards the idea of moving bodies, for, according to my system of Pre-established Harmony, bodies are so made that being once put in motion, they continue therein, according as the actions of the mind require. This hypothesis is intelligible; the other is not.]

Ph. Each act of sensation gives us an equal view of things corporeal and spiritual; for while sight and hearing give me the knowledge that there is some corporeal being without me, I know in a way still more certain that there is within me a spiritual being which sees and hears.

Th. [It is very well said and very true that the existence of the spirit is *more certain* than that of sensible objects.[2]]

§ 19. *Ph.* Spirits as well as bodies can operate only where they are and in different times and places; thus I can only attribute change of place to all finite spirits.

Th. [I believe that is reasonable, *place* being only an order of coexistences.]

Ph. It is only necessary to reflect upon the separation of the soul and the body by death to be convinced of the movement of the soul.

Th. [The soul might cease to operate in this visible body; and if it could cease thinking all at once, as the author has maintained above, it might be separated from the body without being united to another; thus its separation would be without movement. But for myself, I believe that it thinks

[1] *Cf.* Letters to Des Bosses, Sept. 20, Oct. 4, 1706, Gerhardt, 2, 316, 319; Erdmann, 439. Also Descartes' letters, *passim.* — TR.

[2] *Cf.* Descartes, *Meditations*, especially II. and VI. Veitch's translation, 8th ed., pp. 104 *sq.*, 151 *sq.* — TR.

and feels always, that it is always united to some body, and, indeed, that it never leaves entirely and all at once the body to which it is united.]

§ 21. *Ph.* If anyone says that spirits are not *in loco sed in aliquo ubi* I do not suppose that now we would rely much upon this method of speaking. But if anyone thinks that it can receive a reasonable sense, I pray him to express it in language generally intelligible, and to draw therefrom afterwards a reason showing that spirits are not capable of motion.

Th. [The schools have three kinds of *Ubeity,* or modes of existing somewhere. The first is called *circumscriptive,* which they attribute to bodies in space which are there *punctatim,* in such wise that they are measures according to which we can assign the points of the thing placed corresponding to the points of space. The second is the *definitive,* when we can define, *i.e.* determine, that the situated thing is in such a space, without being able to assign the precise points or the peculiar places exclusive of what is there. Thus it has been considered that the soul is in the body, not supposing it possible to assign a precise point at which the soul or some portion of the soul is, without its being also at some other point. Moreover, many learned men have thus viewed the matter. It is true that Descartes desired to place narrower limits to the soul by locating it properly in the pineal gland.[1] Nevertheless he did not dare to say that it is exclusively at a certain point in this gland; and this not being so he gains nothing, and it is in this respect precisely as if he gave it the entire body as its prison or place. I believe that nearly the same statement as that made regarding souls, must be made in respect to the angels, whom the great doctor, a native of Aquino, believed to be in a place only by operation[2] which in my view is not immediate and reduces itself to pre-established harmony. The third ubeity is the *repletive,* which is attributed to God, who fills all the universe in a still more eminent degree than the disembodied spirits, for he works immediately

[1] *Cf.* Descartes, *Dioptrica,* IV., 1 *sq.; Passiones Animæ,* I., 31 *sq.;* also *Prin. Philos.,* IV., 189, 196, 197, although here the point of contact in the brain of the soul and body is not designated by name. — TR.

[2] *Cf.* Thomas Aquinas, 1225 or 1227–1274, *Summa Theologica,* Pt. I. Quest. 52, Article, 2; also Quest. 53. — TR.

upon all creatures by continually producing them, while finite spirits cannot exercise any immediate influence or operation. I do not know whether this doctrine of the schools deserves to be ridiculed, as it seems some try to do. But we can always attribute a kind of movement to souls at least in relation to the bodies with which they are united, or in relation to their mode of perception.]

§ 23. *Ph.* If any one says he knows not how he thinks, I reply that he knows no more how the solid particles of the body are united to make an extended whole.

Th. [It is difficult enough to explain *cohesion;* but this cohesion of parts does not appear necessary to make an extended whole, since we can say that matter perfectly subtile and fluid constitutes an extension, without the particles being united the one to the other. But, to speak the truth, I believe that perfect fluidity belongs only to the *primary matter,*[1] *i.e.* matter in the abstract, and, as an original quality, just as repose; but not to *secondary matter,* such as is actually found, invested with its derivative qualities; for, I believe that there is no mass, which is of the utmost subtility; and that there is more or less connection everywhere, which arises from movements so far as they are conspirant and would be disturbed by separation, which cannot take place without some violence and resistance. For the rest, the nature of perception and thus of thought furnishes a notion of the most original conditions. I believe, further, that the doctrine of substantial unities or monads will throw much light upon it.]

Ph. As for *cohesion,* many explain it by means of the surfaces by which two bodies touch, which an ambient fluid[2] (for example, the air) presses one against another. It is very true that the pressure § 24 of an ambient fluid can hinder the avulsion of two polished surfaces from one another in a line perpendicular to them; but it cannot hinder them from separating by a movement parallel to these surfaces. This is why, if there were no other cause of the cohesion of bodies, it would be easy to separate all their parts, by making them thus

[1] *Cf. ante,* p. 131 and note. — TR.

[2] Locke's term, *Philos. Works,* Vol. 1, p. 438, § 24 (Bohn's ed.). — TR.

slide laterally, taking therefor any plane you wish which intersects any mass of matter.

Th. [Yes, no doubt if all the smooth particles applied to each other were in one and the same plane or in parallel planes; but that not being so nor capable of so being, it is manifest that in trying to make the one slide, you will act altogether differently upon an infinite number of others, whose plane will make an angle with the first; for you must know that it is difficult to separate two congruent surfaces, not only when the direction of the movement of separation is perpendicular, but further when it is oblique to the surfaces. Thus it may be conceived that there are leaves applied to one another in every direction in the polyhedral bodies that nature forms in ores and elsewhere. But I admit that the pressure of the ambient fluid upon smooth surfaces applied to each other does not suffice to explain the basis of all *cohesion*, for it is tacitly assumed that the tables applied the one against the other already have cohesion.]

§ 27. *Ph.* I have always supposed that the extension of a body was something else than the cohesion of solid particles.

Th. [That does not appear to me to agree with your own preceding explanations. It seems to me that a body in which there are internal movements or whose particles are in the act of detaching themselves one from another (as I believe happens always) cannot be extended. Thus the notion of *extension* appears to me wholly different from that of cohesion.]

§ 28. *Ph.* Another idea we have of body is *the power of communicating motion by impulse;* and another we have of the soul is *the power of producing motion by thought.* Experience clearly furnishes us each day these two ideas; but if we wish to investigate further how this is done, we find ourselves equally in the dark. For, as regards the communication of motion, wherein one body loses as much motion as another receives, which is the most ordinary case, we conceive there nothing else than a motion which passes from one body into another; which is, I think, as obscure and as inconceivable as the manner in which our mind moves or stops our bodies by thought. It is still more difficult to explain the increase of motion by means of impulse, which is observed or believed to happen in certain cases.

Th. [I am not astonished that you find insurmountable difficulties where you seem to assume a thing so inconceivable as the passage of an accident from one subject to another; but I see nothing which compels us to an assumption which is no less strange than that of the scholastics of accidents without a subject, which they have taken care however to attribute only to the miraculous action of the divine omnipotence, while here this passage would be merely an ordinary one. I have already said something about it above (chap. 21, § 4[1]), where I also remarked that it is not true that a body loses as much motion as it gives to another; which they seem to conceive as if motion were a substantial thing and resembled salt dissolved in water, which comparison is actually the one M. Rohaut,[2] if I mistake not, has used. I add here that this is not even *the most usual case,* for I have elsewhere demonstrated that the same quantity of motion is maintained only when the two bodies which come into collision proceed in one and the same direction before the collision and still proceed in one and the same direction after the collision. It is true that the veritable laws of motion are derived from a cause superior to matter. As for *the power of producing motion by thought,* I do not think we have any idea of it, as we have no experience of it. The Cartesians themselves admit that souls cannot give a new force to matter, but they pretend that they give it a new determination or direction of the force it has already. For myself, I maintain that souls change nothing in the force nor in the direction of bodies; that the one would be as inconceivable and unreasonable as the other, and that you must avail yourself of the pre-established harmony in order to explain the union of the soul and the body.]

Ph. It is worth our consideration whether active power is not the proper attribute of spirits and passive power of bodies? Whence we might conjecture that created spirits,

[1] *Cf. ante*, p. 176. — TR.

[2] James Rohaut or Rohault, 1620–1675, a French physicist, a follower of Descartes. His chief work, the *Physics*, was written in French, and translated into Latin, with valuable notes, by Dr. Samuel Clarke, 1675–1729, and into English by his brother Dr. John Clarke. It was a text-book in the University of Cambridge, until supplanted by the treatises of Sir Isaac Newton. The original work first appeared in 1671, and enlarged, in two vols., in 1682. Clarke's Latin version, 8vo., in 1697; the 4th and best edition, *Jacobi Rohaulti Physica*, 8vo., 1718. — TR.

being active and passive, are not totally separate from simply passive matter; and that these other beings, which are active and passive at the same time, partake of both.

Th. [These thoughts greatly please me and entirely express my conviction, provided you explain the word spirit so generally that it comprises all souls, or rather (to speak still more generally) all the entelechies or substantial unities, which are analogous to spirits.]

§ 31. *Ph.* I much wish that you would show me in the notion we have of spirit anything more confused[1] or nearer a contradiction than what the very notion of body includes. I mean infinite divisibility.

Th. [What you here say further in order to make evident that we understand the nature of the spirit as well or better than that of the body is very true; and Fromondus,[2] who has published a book, *De compositione continui*, was right in entitling it *Labyrinth*. But the question arises from a false idea you have of the nature of body as well as of space.]

§ 33. *Ph. The idea of God* indeed comes to us as others do, the complex idea of God we have being composed of the simple ideas which we receive from reflection and which we extend by the idea we have of the infinite.

Th. [Upon that question I refer to what I have already said in several places in order to make evident that all these ideas, and particularly that of God, are in us originally, and that we only make ourselves take notice of them, and that above all, the idea of the infinite is not formed by an extension of finite ideas.[3]]

§ 37. *Ph.* The majority of the simple ideas which compose our complex ideas of substances are, properly considered, only *powers*, whatever our inclination to take them as *positive qualities*.

[1] Locke's word is "perplexed," *Philos. Works*, Vol. 1, p. 443 (Bohn's ed.). — TR.

[2] Libert Froidmont or Fromont — Latin, Fromondus — 1587–1653, a Flemish theologian, Professor of Philosophy and Theology in the University of Louvain. His theological, philological, and scientific knowledge was very extensive. Descartes esteemed highly both his knowledge and his person. *Cf.* Descartes' letters. His book, *Labyrinthus sive de compositione continui*, appeared at Antwerp in 1631. — TR.

[3] *Cf. ante*, pp. 16, 17; *New Essays*, Book II., chap. 14, § 27, Th., and note 1, *ante*, p. 158; chap. 17, § 1, Th., *ante*, p. 162. — TR.

Th. [I think that the *powers*, which are not essential to substance and which include not only an *aptitude*, but also a certain *tendency*, are properly what is or ought to be understood by *real qualities*.]

CHAPTER XXIV

OF COLLECTIVE IDEAS OF SUBSTANCES

§ 1. *Ph.* After simple substances we come to the *aggregates*. Is it not true that the idea of this mass of men composing an army, is as much a single idea as that of one man?

Th. [You are right in saying that this *aggregate* (*ens per aggregationem*, to use the language of the school), makes one single idea, although, properly speaking, this mass of substances does not form in truth one substance. This is a result to which the soul by its perception and its thought gives its last achievement of unity. You may, however, say in a sense that it is something substantial, *i.e.* comprising substances.]

CHAPTER XXV

OF RELATION

§ 1. *Ph.* It remains to consider the ideas of relations which are the poorest in reality. When the mind regards one thing in comparison with another, this is a relation or respect,[1] and the denominations or *relative terms*, which are produced, are like so many marks which serve to lead our thoughts beyond the subject to something distinct from it, and these two are called *subjects of the relation* (*relata*).

Th. [Relations and orders have something of the *essence of reason*, although they have their foundation in things; for we can say that their reality, like that of eternal truths and possibilities, comes from the supreme reason.]

§ 5. *Ph.* There may, however, be a change of relation without any change happening in the subject. Titius, whom to-

[1] Locke's word, *Philos. Works*, Vol. 1, p. 449 (Bohn's ed.).—TR.

day I consider as a father, ceases to be such to-morrow without any change being made in himself, by the sole fact of his son's death.

Th. [That statement may very well be made in view of things which are perceived; although in metaphysical strictness it is true that there is no entirely exterior denomination (*denominatio pure extrinseca*) because of the real connection of all things.]

§ 6. *Ph.* [I think that relation is only between two things.]

Th. [There are, however, examples of relation between several things at once, as that of order or that of a genealogical tree, which expresses the rank and connection of all the terms or members, and even a figure like that of a polygon includes the relation of all the sides.]

§ 8. *Ph.* It is well to consider also that the ideas of relations are often clearer than those of the things which are the subjects of the relation. Thus the relation of father is clearer than that of man.

Th. [That is because this relation is so general that it may also suit other substances. Moreover, as a subject may have clearness and obscurity, the relation might be grounded in the clear. But if the form itself of the relation involved the knowledge of that which is obscure in the subject, it would participate in this obscurity.]

§ 10. *Ph.* The *terms* which *necessarily* lead the mind to other ideas than those which are supposed really to exist in the thing to which the term or word is applied are *relative;* the others are *absolute.*

Th. [You have well added this "*necessarily*" and you might add "*expressly*" or "*at first,*" for you can think of black, for example, without thinking of its cause; but it is by remaining within the limits of a knowledge which presents itself at first and which is confused or very distinct, but incomplete; the one when there is no resolution of the idea, the other when you limit it. Otherwise there is no term so absolute or so loose as not to include relations and the perfect analysis of which does not lead to other things and even to all others; so that you can say that *relative terms* indicate *expressly* the relation they contain. I here oppose the *absolute* to the *relative,* and it is in another sense that I have opposed it above to the *limited.*]

CHAPTER XXVI

OF CAUSE AND EFFECT AND SOME OTHER RELATIONS

§§ 1, 2. *Ph.* *Cause* is that which produces a simple or incomplex idea; *effect* is that which is produced.

Th. [I see, sir, that you often understand by *idea* the objective reality of the idea or the quality which it represents. You define only *efficient cause*, as I have already remarked above. You must admit that, in saying that *efficient cause* is that which produces and *effect* that which is produced, you make use only of synonyms. It is true that I have heard you say a little more distinctly, that *cause* is that which *makes* another thing commence to exist, though this word "*makes*" passes over also the principal difficulty entirely. But that will be explained better elsewhere.]

Ph. In order further to touch some other relations, I remark that there are terms employed to designate time which are ordinarily regarded as signifying only positive ideas, which are nevertheless relative, as *young, old*, etc., for they involve a relation to the ordinary duration of the substance to which you attribute them. Thus a man is called young at the age of twenty years, and very young at the age of seven years. But we call a horse old at twenty years, and a dog at seven. But we do not say that the sun and the stars, a ruby or a diamond, is young or old, because we do not know the ordinary periods of their duration. § 5. The same is true regarding place or extension, as when a thing is said to be *high* or *low, great* or *small.* Thus a horse which will be large according to the idea of a Welshman, appears very small to a Fleming; each thinks of the horses which are raised in his country.

Th. [These remarks are very good. It is true we sometimes swerve a little from this sense, as when we say that a thing is old when comparing it not with those of its kind, but with other kinds. For example, we say that the world or the sun is very old. Some one asked Galileo if he believed that the sun was eternal. He replied: *eterno nò ma ben antico* — eternal, no, but very ancient.

CHAPTER XXVII

WHAT IDENTITY OR DIVERSITY IS

§ 1. *Ph.* A relative idea of the greatest importance is that of *identity* or *diversity.* We never find and we cannot conceive it possible that two things of the same kind exist in the same time in the same place. Therefore when we ask *whether a thing is the same or not,* the question always relates to a thing which at such a time exists in such a place; whence it follows that a thing cannot have two beginnings of existence, nor two things one beginning only in relation to the time and the place.

Th. [It is always necessary that besides the difference of time and place there be an internal *principle of distinction,* and, though there are many things of the same kind, it is nevertheless true that none of them are ever perfectly alike: thus although time and place (*i.e.* external relation) serve us in distinguishing things which we do not easily distinguish by themselves, the things do not cease to be distinguishable in themselves. The essence (*le precis*) of *identity* and *diversity* consists, then, not in time and place, although it is true that the diversity of things is accompanied by that of time or of place, because they bring with them different impressions of the thing; not to say that it is rather by the things that one place or one time must be distinguished from another, for in themselves they are perfectly alike, but they are not, therefore, substances or complete realities. The mode of distinguishing which you seem to propose here, as unique in things of the same kind, is based upon the supposition that penetration is not conformable to nature. This supposition is reasonable, but experience indeed makes it evident that it is not closely applied here, when the question concerns distinction. We see, for example, two shadows or rays of light which interpenetrate, and we might invent for ourselves an imaginary world wherein bodies would act in the same way. But we do not cease to distinguish one ray from another by the very rate of their passage even when they cross each other.]

§ 3. *Ph.* What is called the *principle of individuation* (*principium individuationis*) in the schools, where they torment themselves so much to know what it is, consists in existence itself which determines each being to a particular time and place incommunicable to two beings of the same kind.

Th. The *principle of individuation* [1] reappears in individuals in the principle of distinction of which I just spoke. If two individuals were perfectly alike and equal and (in a word) *indistinguishable* in themselves, there would be no principle of individuation; and I even venture to assert that there would be no individual distinction or different individuals under this condition. This is why the notion of atoms is chimerical, and arises only from the incomplete conceptions of men. For if there were atoms, *i.e.* bodies perfectly hard and perfectly unalterable or incapable of internal change and capable of differing among themselves only in size and shape, it is plain that in the possibility of their being of the same shape and size they would then be indistinguishable in themselves, and could be distinguished only by means of external denominations without an internal basis, which is contrary to the highest principles of reason. But the truth is that every body is alterable, and indeed actually changes so that it differs in itself from every other. I remember that a distinguished princess,[2] who is of a pre-eminently excellent mind, said one

[1] Leibnitz discussed this principle in his disputation for the degree of Bachelor of Philosophy, entitled, *Disputatio metaphysica de principio individui*, which in his sixteenth year he publicly defended at Leipzig, March 30, 1663; *cf.* Guhrauer, *Leibniz. Leben*, 1, 27 *sq.* This piece is found in Gerhardt, 4, 15–26, where the title-page gives the date of the public defence, May 30, 1663; Erdmann, 1–5; it has also been edited, with an extended critical introduction, from a copy found in the Library at Hannover by Dr. G. E. Guhrauer, and published at Berlin in 1837. J. H. von Kirchmann has published a German translation with elaborate and extensive notes in his *Philos. Bibliothek*, Bd. 81, *Die klein. philos. wicht. Schriften G. W. Leibniz*; Bd. 82, *Erläuterungen.* For a recent discussion of the principle of individuality, *cf.* R. Eucken, *The Fundamental Concepts of Mod. Philos. Thought*, pp. 231–248. New York, 1880. — Tr.

[2] Sophie Charlotte, 1668–1705, the first Queen of Prussia, the friend and in a certain sense the pupil of Leibnitz in philosophy. The *Theodicée* originated in his philosophical conversations with her. *Cf.* Gerhardt, 6, 39; Erdmann, 474 b. Leibnitz's correspondence with her is found in O. Klopp, *Die Werke von Leibniz*, Vol. 10, Hannover, 1877; the letters of philosophical importance in Gerhardt, 3, 343 *sq.*; 6, 488 *sq.*; 7, 544; the letter in G. 6, 499 *sq.* is translated in Duncan, *Philos. Works of Leibnitz*, 149 *sq.* *Cf.* also Kuno Fischer, *Gesch. d. n. Philos.*, Vol. 2, p. 261 *sq.*, 3d ed., 1889. — Tr.

day while walking in her garden that she did not believe there were two leaves perfectly alike. A gentleman of distinction, who was walking with her, thought he would easily find some. But although he searched long, he was convinced by his eyes that he could always note the difference. We see by these considerations, hitherto neglected, how far we have wandered in philosophy from the most natural notions, and how far we have departed from the great principles of true metaphysic.]

§ 4. *Ph.* That which constitutes the *unity* (identity) of one and the same plant is the possession of such an organization of parts in a single body, as participates in a common life which endures while the plant subsists, although the parts change.

Th. [The organization or configuration without an existing principle of life, which I call a monad, would not suffice to cause the continuance of *idem numero* or the same individual; for the configuration can abide specifically without abiding[1] individually. When a horseshoe is changed into copper in a mineral spring of Hungary, the *same* figure in kind remains, but not the same as *an individual;* for the iron is dissolved, and the copper, with which the water is impregnated, is precipitated and insensibly takes its place. Now figure is an accident which does not pass from one subject to another (*de subjecto in subjectum*). So we must say that bodies as well organized as others do not remain the same in appearance, and, speaking strictly, not at all. It is almost like a river which always changes its water, or like the ship of Theseus which the Athenians were always repairing.[2] But as regards

[1] Erdmann and Jacques omit "specifiquement, sans demeurer," the reading of Gerhardt. — TR.

[2] *Cf.* Plato, *Phædo.* 58 A; Xenophon, *Memorabilia*, 4, 8, 2. The sacred ship, sent yearly to Delos by the Athenians in consequence of a vow made to Apollo by Theseus when on his way to Crete with the seven youths and seven maidens, the annual tribute of the Athenians to the Minotaur, that if rescued he would send annually to Delos a ship with gifts and sacrifices as a thank-offering for their deliverance, was repaired piece by piece as necessary, so that in form and appearance it remained the same old ship in which Theseus himself sailed, while its substance continually changed. The vessel served the philosophers as an instance in discussions concerning identity and what constitutes it, and as an illustration of a numerical substance continuously the same, though constantly changing by the decay and rejection of old and the growth and acquisition of new parts, as in the case of the living body. — TR.

substances, which are in themselves a true and real substantial unity, to which may belong actions properly called *vital*, and as regards substantial beings, *quæ uno spiritu continentur*, in the words of an ancient jurisconsult,[1] *i.e.* which a certain indivisible spirit animates, you are right in saying that they remain perfectly *the same individual* through this soul or this spirit which constitutes the ego in thinking beings.]

§ 5. *Ph.* The case is not very different in animals and in plants.

Th. [If vegetables and animals have no soul, their identity is only apparent; but if they have, individual identity is in truth strictly speaking there, although their organized bodies do not preserve it.]

§ 6. *Ph.* This also shows wherein the identity of the same man consists, viz. in the fact alone that he enjoys the same life, continued by particles of matter which are in a perpetual flux, but which in this succession are *vitally* united with the same organized body.

Th. [That may be understood in my sense. In fact, the organized body is not the same from one moment to another; it is only equivalent. And if it were not related to the soul, there would no longer be the same life or *vital* union. Thus this identity would be only apparent.]

Ph. Whoever shall connect the *identity of man* with anything else than a well-organized body, in a certain instant, and which thence continues in this *vital organization* by a succession of different particles of matter which are united to it, will have difficulty in making an embryo, a man of years, a fool, and a wise man the same man, unless it follows from this supposition that it is possible for Seth, Ismael, Socrates, Pilate, St. Augustine[2] to be one and the same man, . . . and this would agree still worse with the notions of those philosophers who recognize transmigration and believe that men's souls can be sent for punishment of their irregularities into the bodies of animals; for I do not believe that any one who was assured that the soul of Heliogabalus existed in a hog would mean that this hog was a man, and the same man as Heliogabalus.

[1] Sextus Pomponius, died 138 A.D. The phrase occurs in the Digest, 41, 3, 30, Vol. 2, p. 522, ed. Th. Mommsen, Berlin: Weidmann, 1870.—TR.

[2] Locke has "St. Austin," *Philos. Works*, Vol. 1, p. 463 (Bohn's ed.).—TR.

Th. [There is here a question of name and of thing. As for the thing, the identity of one and the same individual substance can be maintained only by the conservation of the same soul, for the body is in a continual flux, and the soul does not dwell in certain atoms appropriated to itself, nor in a little incorruptible (*indomptable*) bone, such as the *Luz*[1] of the Rabbis. Moreover there is no transmigration by which the soul wholly leaves its body and passes into another. It keeps always, even in death, an organized body, a part of the preceding, although what it keeps is always subject to insensible dissipation and to reparation, and indeed to undergoing in a certain time a great change. Thus instead of a transmigration of the soul there is a transformation, envelopment, or development, and finally a fluxion of the body of this soul. Van Helmont,[2] the son, thought that souls pass from body to body, but always within their kind, so that there will always be the same number of souls of one and the same kind, and consequently the same number of men and of wolves, and that the wolves if diminished or extirpated in England would be proportionally increased elsewhere. Certain meditations pub-

[1] The bone which the Jews regarded as incapable of decay, remaining until the last day and forming the nucleus of the resurrection body. Schaarschmidt says: "According to the opinion of the Rabbis, says Ulrich in his note to this place, the body which we are to receive at the resurrection is already at hand in our backbone. This body or bone, לוז (*Luz*), as it is properly called, they held for this reason to be incorruptible. In the *Jalkut chudasch*, Fol. 142, title *Maschiach*, n. 44, the following account is given of it: This bone decays not, and the holy giving God will make it soft with the dew, and out of it will build the body. The reason why this little bone is not to be exposed to corruption, they place in the fact that it has not enjoyed the pleasures of this world, as the rest of the members. This doctrine is with them no empty speculation. The old Rabbis of blessed memory have not only seen this bone, but have found it actually so strong and hard that their hammer and rock flew in pieces before this little bone was injured in the least. See *Askath Rochel* in the 4th part," etc. — Tr.

[2] François Mercure van Helmont, 1618–1698, a particular friend of the Countess of Connaway, in whose *Opuscula philosophica*, Bk. I., chap. 6, §§ 7, 8, and chap. 7, § 4, London, 1690, this view of his is found in detail. On Leibnitz's relations with Van Helmont, *cf.* Stein, *Leibniz and Spinoza*, pp. 210 *sq.*, and the references in Stein's notes; also *Beilagen*, XV., XVI., *op. cit.* pp. 329–337. Leibnitz composed for him, at the request of his cousin, the Baroness of Merode, a Latin epitaph; *cf.* Burckhard, *Historia Biblioth. Augustæ*, II., p. 326; also Stein. *op. cit.* pp. 336–337. Leibnitz treats of him and his doctrine in his Miscellanies, *cf.* *Otium Hanoveranum*, ed. J. F. Feller, pp. 226–230, Lipsiæ, 1718. — Tr.

lished in France would also seem to tend in that direction. If transmigration is not taken strictly, *i.e.* if any one thought that souls dwelling in the same subtile body change only from a coarser body, it would be possible, even to the passage of the same soul into a body of a different kind after the fashion of the Brahmins and Pythagoreans. But all that is possible is not for that reason conformed to the order of things. But the question whether, in case such a transmigration were true, Cain, Ham, and Ismael, supposing, according to the Rabbis, they were the same soul, would deserve to be called the same man, is only one of name; and I have observed that the celebrated author, whose opinions you have maintained, recognizes and explains it very well (*in the last paragraph of this chapter*). The identity of substance would occur therein, but in case there were no connection of memory between the different persons, as the same soul would make, there would not be sufficient *moral identity* to say that it would be one and the *same person.* And if God willed that the human soul should go into the body of a hog, forgetting the man and performing no rational acts, it would not constitute a man. But if in the body of the animal it had the thoughts of a man, and even of the man whom it animated before the change, like the Golden Ass of Apuleius, one would perhaps have no difficulty in saying that the same Lucius, who had come into Thessaly to see his friends, lived under the ass's hide, where Photis had put him in spite of herself, and wandered from master to master until the roses he ate restored him to his natural form.[1]

[1] *Cf.* Apuleius, *Metamorph.*, Bk. III., Vol. 1, pp. 229 *sq.*; Bk. XI., pp. 770 *sq.*, edition in 6 vols., paging continuous, A. J. Valpy, London, 1825. The *Metamorphoses* is in contents very similar to a work entitled, Λούκιος ἢ ὄνος (*Lucius or Ass*), ascribed to Lucian, a contemporary of Apuleius who flourished about 160 A.D., and is most probably an imitation of it. The incidents and adventures in both are nearly identical, the names only being changed, both writers, however, calling the hero Lucius. In the course of his adventures Lucius became involved in a love-affair with a waiting-woman by the name of Fotis, whose mistress practised the art of magic, and changed at will herself and others into various animals by the use of certain ointments. Lucius, very desirous to learn all about this wonderful art, finally persuaded Fotis, who claimed that she understood her mistress's art, to try it on him. She did so, intending to change him into an owl, into which form her mistress in the sight of them both had just changed herself, but in her haste and confusion using the wrong ointment, she changed him, "in spite of herself," into an ass. The work of Apuleius is much more extended than that of Lucian, and, in

§ 9. *Ph.* I think we can boldly advance the idea that whoever of us saw a creature made and formed like himself, although it had never exhibited more reason than a cat or a parrot, would not cease to call it a man; or if he heard a parrot discoursing rationally and in a philosophical manner would call or think it only a parrot, and would say of the former of these animals that it is an uncultivated man, dull and destitute of reason, and of the latter that it is a parrot full of intelligence and good sense.

Th. [I should be more of the same opinion upon the second point than upon the first, although there is still something to be said thereupon. Few theologians would be venturesome enough to agree at once and absolutely to the baptism of an animal in human form, but without appearance of reason, if he were taken while young in the woods and some priest of the Roman church should perhaps say conditionally, *if you are a man I baptize you;* for they would not know whether he is of the human race and whether a rational soul dwells therein, and this might be an *ourang-outang,* an ape externally very like a man, such as that one whom Tulpius[1] speaks of as having seen, and that one an account of whose anatomy a learned physician has published. It is certain (I admit) that man can become as stupid as an *ourang-outang,* but the interior of a rational soul would abide there in spite of the suspension of the exercise of reason as I have explained above; thus it is a point of which we cannot judge by appearances. As for the second case, nothing prevents there being rational animals of a different kind from ourselves, as those inhabitants of the poetic kingdom of the birds in the sun, where a parrot having come from this world after its death, saved the life of a traveller who had treated him well here below. But if it happened, as it happens in the country of the *fairies* or of *Mother*

spite of its irony, abounds in a mysticism not found in the Λύκιος ἢ ὄνος. A brief sketch of Lucian's work may be found in the *Encyclopædia Britannica,* 9th ed., under the article "Lucius." On Apuleius, and the relation of his work to that of Lucian, *cf.* Teuffel, *Gesch. d. Röm. Lit.,* § 367, 3, 4th ed., Leipzig: B. G. Teubner, 1882; § 367, 1, 5th ed. by Ludwig Schwabe, Leipzig: Teubner, 1890, and from this ed., the English translation in 2 vols., by Geo. C. W. Warr, M.A., Geo. Bell and Sons, London, 1891. — TR.

[1] Nicolas Tulp, 1593–1674, a Dutch physician and magistrate, in Bk. III., chap. 56, of his *Observationum medicarum libri tres,* Amsterdam, 1641, 8th ed., revised with additions, Leyden, 1752. — TR.

Goose, that a parrot was a transformed daughter of a king and became known as such while speaking, doubtless her father and mother would caress her as their daughter whom they thought they possessed though concealed under this strange form. I should not oppose myself, however, to him who should say that in the Golden Ass as the *self* or the individual remained for the sake of the same immaterial spirit, so Lucius or the person remained for the sake of the apperception of this ego, but that this is no longer a man; as in fact it seems necessary to add something of the figure and constitution of the body to the definition of man, when we say that he is a rational animal; otherwise in my view the genii would also be men.]

§ 9. *Ph.* The word *person* carries with it a thinking and intelligent being, capable of reason and reflection, that can consider itself indeed as *the same,* as one and the same thing which thinks at different times and in different places; which it does only by that consciousness [1] which it has of its own acts. And this knowledge always accompanies our sensations and our present perceptions [when they are sufficiently distinguished, as I have more than once before remarked] and it is by this that each one is to himself what he calls *himself.* It is not considered in this case whether the same self is continued in the same or in different substances. For since consciousness [2] always accompanies thought, and is that which makes each one to be what he calls *himself* and by which he is distinguished from every other thinking being; it is also in this alone that personal identity consists, or that which makes a rational being always to be the same; and as far as this *consciousness* can be extended over actions or thoughts already past, so far the identity of this person extends, and the *self* is at present the same as it was then.

Th. [I am also of this opinion that consciousness or the perception of the ego proves a moral or personal identity. And it is by this that I distinguish the *incessability* [3] of the soul of an animal from the *immortality* of the soul of man;

[1] The French is "sentiment."—TR.

[2] The French text is "la conscience (*consciousness* ou consciencciosité)," Gerhardt; "consciosité," Erdmann and Jacques.—TR.

[3] The French is "incessabilité," *i.e.* continuity or perpetuity.—TR.

both preserve *physical and real identity*, but as for man, he is conformed to the rules of divine providence so that the soul preserves also identity moral and apparent to ourselves, in order to constitute the same person, capable consequently of feeling chastisements and rewards. It seems that you, sir, hold that this apparent identity could be preserved, if there were no real identity. I should think that that might perhaps be by the absolute power of God, but according to the order of things, identity apparent to the person himself who perceives the same, supposes real identity to every *proximate transition*, accompanied by reflection or perception of the *ego*, a perception intimate and immediate naturally incapable of deception. If man could be merely a machine and with that have consciousness, it would be necessary to be of your opinion, sir; but I hold that this case is not possible at least naturally. Neither would I say that *personal identity* and even the *self* do not dwell in us and that I am not this *ego* which has been in the cradle, under pretext that I no more remember anything of all that I then did. It is sufficient in order to find moral identity by itself that there be a *middle bond of consciousness* between a state bordering upon or even a little removed from another, although a leap or forgotten interval might be mingled therein. Thus if a disease had caused an interruption of the continuity of the bond of consciousness so that I did not know how I came into the present state, although I remember things more remote, the testimony of others could fill the void in my memory. I could even be punished upon this testimony, if I had just done something bad of deliberate purpose in an interval that I had forgotten a little after on account of this disease. And if I had just forgotten all past things and[1] would be obliged to let myself be taught anew even to my name and even to reading and writing, I could always learn from others my past life in my previous state, as I have kept my rights without its being necessary for me to share them with two persons, and to make me the heir of myself. All this suffices to maintain moral identity, which makes the same person. It is true that if others should conspire to deceive me (as I might indeed be deceived by myself, by some vision, dream, or illness, believing that what I had dreamed had hap-

[1] Gerhardt reads: "et"; Erdmann and Jacques: "que," so that. — TR.

pened to me) the appearance would be false. But there are cases in which we can be morally certain of the truth upon the relation of another, and with God whose social connection with us constitutes the principal point of morality, the error cannot have place. As for *the self*, it will be well to distinguish it from *the phenomenon of self* and from consciousness. *The self* constitutes identity real and physical, and *the phenomenon of self*, accompanied by truth, joins thereto personal identity. Thus not wishing to say that personal identity extends no farther than memory, I would say still less that *the self* or physical identity depends upon it. Real and personal identity is proved with the utmost possible certainty by present and immediate reflection; it is proved sufficiently for ordinary purposes by our memory of the interval or by the conspiring testimony of others. But if God should change in an extraordinary manner real identity, personal identity would remain, provided man preserved the appearances of identity, as well the internal (that is to say, consciousness) as the external, like those which consist in that which appears to others. Thus consciousness is not the sole means for constituting personal identity, and the testimony of another or even other proofs can supply it. But there is some difficulty if contradiction occurs between those diverse appearances. Consciousness may be silent as in forgetfulness; but if it should alter very clearly things which were contrary to the other appearances, we should be embarrassed in the decision and as it were suspended sometimes between two possibilities, that of the error of our memory and that of some deception in external appearances.]

§ 11. *Ph.* [You will say] that the members of the body of every man are a part of himself [and that thus, the body being in a perpetual flux, the man cannot remain the same].

Th. [I should rather prefer to say that *the I* and *the He* are without parts, because it is said, and with reason, that the same substance, or the same physical *ego*, is really preserved. But we cannot say, speaking according to the exact truth of things, that the same whole is preserved when a part is lost. Now whatever has corporeal parts cannot fail to lose some of them at every moment.]

§ 13. *Ph.* The consciousness which one has of his past

actions cannot be transferred from one thinking substance to another [and it would be certain that the same substance abides, because we feel ourselves the same], if this consciousness were a single and indeed an individual act [*i.e.* if the act of reflecting were the same as the act upon which you reflect in perceiving it]. But as it is only an actual representation of a past act it remains to be shown how it is impossible for what has never really been to be represented to the mind as truly having been.

Th. [Memory after an interval may deceive; we have experienced it often, and there are means of conceiving a natural cause of this error. But present or immediate memory, or the memory of what passed immediately before, *i.e.* the consciousness or reflection which accompanies internal action, cannot naturally deceive; otherwise we should not be certain indeed that we think of this or that thing, for this statement is made internally only of the action already past, and not in connection with the action itself. Now if these internal, immediate experiences are not certain, there will be no truth of fact of which we can be assured. And I have already said that there may be intelligible reasons for the error which exposes itself in perceptions mediate and external, but in those immediately internal we cannot find any unless by recurring to the omnipotence of God.]

§ 14. *Ph.* As for the question whether the same immaterial substance remaining there may be two distinct persons, see upon what it is based. It is this: *If the same immaterial being can be deprived of all consciousness* (*sentiment*) *of its past existence*, and lose it wholly, without the power of ever recovering it, so that beginning, so to speak, a new account from a new period, it has a consciousness (*conscience*) which cannot extend beyond this new state. All those who believe in the *pre-existence*[1] *of souls* are evidently of this mind. I have seen

[1] *I.e.* existence before this earthly life. The doctrine was set forth with more or less fulness by the Pythagoreans, Plato, Philo, Origen, and more recently, among others, by Lessing, *Erziehung des Menschengeschlechtes*, § 94 *sq.*; Kant, *Die Religion innerhalb der Grenzen der blossen Vernunft*, Bk. I., 4; Julius Müller, *Die christ. Lehre von der Sünde*, Bk. IV., chap. 4, Vol. 2, pp. 486 *sq.*, Breslau, 1844, and English translation of the same, 2d ed., from the 5th German ed., Halle, 1866, Vol. 2, pp. 357 *sq.*, Edinburgh: T. & T. Clark, 1868. The doctrine has been used chiefly to explain the origin of

a man who was persuaded that his soul had been the soul of Socrates; and I can assure you that in the post he filled and which was not one of little importance he passed for a very rational man, and he appeared by his works which have seen the light to lack neither intelligence nor learning. Now souls being[1] *indifferent to any portion of matter whatever this may be,* as far as we can know it by their nature, this supposition (of the same soul passing into different bodies) involves no apparent absurdity. But he who now has no consciousness of that which Nestor or Socrates ever did or thought, does he or can he conceive himself the same person as Nestor or Socrates? Can he take part in the actions of these two ancient Greeks? Can he attribute them to himself or think them his own actions rather than those of some other man who has already existed? He is no more the same person with one of them than if the soul now present in him had been created when it began to animate the body which it now possesses. This would no more contribute to make him the same person as Nestor, than if some of the particles of matter which once formed part of Nestor were now a part of this man. For the same immaterial substance without the same consciousness no more makes the same person to be united to such or such a body than *the same particles of matter,* united to a body without a common consciousness, can make the same person.

Th. [An immaterial being or a spirit *cannot be stripped* of all perception of its past existence. There remain for it some impressions of all that has formerly happened to it, and it even has some presentiments of all that will happen to it; but these feelings are most often too small to be capable of being distinguished and perceived, although they may perhaps sometime be developed. This continuation and bond of *per-*

evil or sin; but it is an explanation which does not explain, its assumed solution being merely an evasion of the real difficulty by pushing the problem back unsolved into past time. *Cf.* O. Pfleiderer, *Religionsphilosophie auf gesch. Grundlage,* Vol. 2, p. 382, 2d ed., Berlin: G. Reimer, 1884; English translation, Vol. 4, p. 29, London: Williams & Norgate, 1888. For a critique of the theory as held by Julius Müller, *cf.* I. A. Dorner, *System d. christlichen Glaubenslehre,* § 77, 3; § 82, 2, Berlin: Wm. Hertz, 1881; English translation, Edinburgh: T. & T. Clark, 1882. — Tr.

[1] Gerhardt and Jacques read: "les âmes estant" ("étant," J.); Erdmann reads: "tant." — Tr.

ceptions constitutes in reality the same individual, but the *apperceptions* (*i.e.* when past feelings are perceived), prove besides a moral identity and make real identity appear. The pre-existence of souls does not appear to us through our perceptions, but if it were true, it might sometime make itself known. Thus it is not reasonable that the restitution of memory becomes forever impossible, the insensible perceptions (whose use I have set forth on so many important occasions) serving here, moreover, to preserve the seeds. The late Henry More, a theologian of the English church, was convinced of the truth of pre-existence and has written in its defence.[1] The late M. Van Helmont, the son, went much farther, as I just said, and believed in the transmigration of souls, but always into bodies of one and the same species, so that according to him the human soul always animated a man. He believed with some Rabbis in the passage of the soul of Adam into the Messiah as into the new Adam. And I do not know but that he thought he had himself been some ancient, altogether clever man that he was elsewhere. Now if this passage of souls was true, at least in the possible way that I have explained above (but which does not appear probable), *i.e.* that souls, keeping their subtile bodies, pass at once into other coarse bodies, the same individual would always subsist in Nestor, in Socrates, and in any modern, and he could even make his identity known to any one who would penetrate sufficiently into his nature, on account of the impressions or marks which would there remain of all that Nestor or Socrates have done, and which any genius sufficiently penetrating could there read. But if the modern man had no means internal or external of knowing what he had been, it would be as far as the moral is concerned as if he had not been. But it appears that nothing is neglected in the world in relation even to the moral, because God is the monarch thereof whose government is perfect. Souls according to my hypothesis are not *indifferent* regarding any portion of matter whatever, as it seems to you; on the contrary, they originally express those portions to which they are and ought to be united by nature.

[1] *Cf. Opera*, 1, 750–754, London, 1679; following the Kabbala, he thinks all souls were created at the same time as the world, 2, 539; and, like Leibnitz, regards them as always united with some kind of matter, 2, 395, 396.—TR.

Thus, if they pass into a new body coarse or sensible, they would always preserve the expression[1] of all that they had perceived in the old, and it would even be necessary for the new body to manifest it so that the individual continuity will always have its real marks. But whatever our past state may have been, the effect it leaves cannot always be for us *apperceivable.* The clever author of the Essay on Understanding, whose views you had espoused, had remarked (Bk. II., chap. 27. On Identity, § 27) that a part of these suppositions or fictions of the passage of souls, assumed as possible, is founded upon the common view of the mind as not only independent of matter but also as indifferent to every sort of matter. But I hope that what you have said, sir, on this subject here and there will serve to clear up this doubt and to make better known what is naturally possible. We see thereby how the acts of an ancient might belong to a modern who had the same soul, although he did not perceive them. But if he should come to recognize it, still more would personal identity follow. For the rest *a portion of matter* passing from one body into another does not constitute the same human individual, nor what is called the *ego*, but it is the soul which constitutes it.]

§ 16. *Ph.* It is, however, true that I am as much concerned and as justly responsible for an action done a thousand years since, which is now adjudged as mine by this present consciousness (self-consciousness[2]) thereof, as having been done by myself, as I am for what I have just done in the preceding moment.

Th. [This view of having done something may deceive in distant actions. Men have taken as true by force of repetition what they dreamed, or what they invented; this false view may embarrass, but it cannot make them punishable, unless others agree therewith. On the other hand, you can be responsible for what you have done, when you have forgotten it, provided the action be verified elsewhere.]

§ 17. *Ph.* Every one finds every day that while his little

[1] Gerhardt and Erdmann read: "l'expression"; Jacques: "l'impression." —Tr.

[2] Gerhardt's reading; Erdmann and Jacques have, as before (p. 245, note 2), "consciosité ou consciousness."—Tr.

finger is comprehended under this consciousness, it constitutes as much a *part of himself* (of him) as that which is most so.

Th. [I have said (§ 11) why I would not advance the view that my finger is a part of *me;* but it is true that it belongs to me and that it constitutes a part of my body.]

Ph. [Those who hold another view will say that] in the event of this little finger being separated from the rest of the body, if this consciousness accompanies the little finger and leaves the rest of the body, it is evident that the little finger would be the *person*, the *same person*, and that then the *self* would have nothing to do with the rest of the body.

Th. [Nature does not admit these fictions, which are destroyed by the System of Harmony or the perfect correspondence of the soul and the body.]

§ 18. *Ph.* It seems, however, that if the body should continue to live and to have its particular consciousness, in which the little finger had no share, and that meanwhile the soul was in the finger, the finger could not own any of the actions of the rest of the body, and we could no longer impute them to it.[1]

Th. [The soul also which would be in the finger would not belong to this body. I admit that if God caused consciousnesses to be transferred to other souls, it would be necessary to treat them in accordance with moral notions, as if they were the same; but this would disturb the order of things without reason, and make a divorce between the apperceptible and the truth, which is conserved by the insensible perceptions, which would not be reasonable, because the perceptions insensible at present may some day be developed, for there is nothing useless, and eternity gives a large field for changes.]

§ 20. *Ph.* Human laws do not punish the madman for the acts which the sober[2] man does, nor the sober man for what the madman does, thereby making them two persons. Thus they say: he is beside himself.

Th. [The laws threaten to chastise and promise to recompense in order to prevent bad and further good acts. Now a madman may be such that the threats and promises do not operate sufficiently upon him, reason no longer being master;

[1] Locke reads: "him," *Philos. Works*, Vol. 1, p. 475 (Bohn's ed.).—Tr.

[2] Locke's word; *Philos. Works*, Vol. 1, p. 475 (Bohn's ed.).—Tr.

thus in proportion to his weakness the severity of the pain should cease. On the other hand we wish the criminal to feel the effect of the evil he has done in order that he may fear further to commit crimes, but the madman not being sensitive enough, we are well content to wait a good while in order to execute the sentence which punishes him for what he did when sober. Thus what the laws or the judges do in these instances comes not from the conception of two persons.]

§ 22. *Ph.* In fact in the party whose opinions I represent to you, this objection is made, that if a man who is drunk and who is afterwards no longer drunk, is not the same person, he should not be punished for what he did while drunk, since he is no longer conscious of his act. But they reply that he is altogether as much the same person as a man who during his sleep walks and does many other things and who is responsible for all the evil he has happened to do in that state.

Th. [There is much difference between the acts of a drunken man and those of a true and recognized somnambulist. We punish drunkards because they can avoid drunkenness and can even have some memory of pain while drunk. But it is not so much within the power of somnambulists to abstain from their nocturnal walk and from what they do. But if it were true that by giving them a good flogging we could make them stay in bed, we should be right in doing it, and we should not fail either, although this would be rather a remedy than a punishment. In fact it is said that this remedy has restored them.]

Ph. Human laws punish both in accord with a justice conformed to the mode in which men understand things, because in these sorts of cases they cannot certainly distinguish what is real from what is counterfeit; thus ignorance is not received as an excuse for what they have done while drunk or asleep. The deed is proved against the one who has done it, and you cannot prove in his case lack of consciousness.

Th. [The question is not so much about this, as about what must be done when it has been verified, as it may be, that the drunkard or somnambulist were beside themselves. In this case the somnambulist would be considered only as a maniac; but as drunkenness is voluntary, and the disease is not, the one is punished but not the other.]

Ph. But in the great and terrible day of judgment, when the secrets of all hearts shall be uncovered, it is right to think that no one will have to answer for what is wholly unknown to him and that each one will receive what is due him, his own conscience accusing or excusing[1] him.

Th. I do not know whether it will be necessary for the memory of man to be exalted at the day of judgment in order for him to remember all he had forgotten, or whether the knowledge of others and above all of the just judge who cannot be deceived will not suffice. We might devise a fiction little agreeing with the truth, but nevertheless conceivable, to the effect that a man at the day of judgment believed he had been bad and that the same appeared true to all other created spirits, who would be able to judge of it, without its having been true: could we say that the supreme and just judge, who alone knows the contrary, could condemn this person and judge contrary to his knowledge?[2] Yet it seems that that would follow from the notion you gave of moral personality. You will perhaps say that if God judges contrary to appearances he will not be sufficiently glorified and will bring pain upon others; but the reply could be made that he is for himself his unique and supreme law, and that in this case others should consider themselves mistaken.]

§ 23. *Ph.* Could we suppose either *two* distinct and incommunicable *consciousnesses* acting by turns in the same body, the one constantly during the day, the other by night, or that *the same consciousness* acts at intervals in two different bodies; I ask if, in the first case, the day and night man, if I may so express myself, would not be two as distinct persons as Socrates and Plato, and in the second case would he not be a single person in two distinct bodies? It matters not that this same consciousness which affects two different bodies, and these consciousnesses which affect the same body at different times, belong the one to the same immaterial substance, and the two others to two distinct immaterial substances, which introduce these different consciousnesses into these bodies,

1 Erdmann and Jacques omit: "ou excusé." — Tr.

2 Gerhardt reads: "juger contre ce qu'il sait?" Erdmann and Jacques: "juger contre ce qu'ils font?" *i.e.* "pass a judgment contrary to what they do." — Tr.

since personal identity would equally be determined by the consciousness, whether that consciousness were attached to some individual immaterial substance or not. Further, an immaterial thinking thing may sometimes lose sight of its past consciousness, and recall it anew. Now suppose these intervals of memory and forgetfulness return with every day and night, then you have two persons with the same immaterial spirit. Whence it follows that the *self* is not determined by the identity or diversity of substance, which it cannot be sure of, but only by the identity of consciousness.

Th. [I admit that if all the appearances were changed and transferred from our spirit to another, or if God made an exchange between two spirits, giving the visible body and the appearances and consciousnesses of the one to the other, personal identity, instead of being attached to that of substance, would follow the constant appearances which human morality must have in view; but these appearances would not consist in the consciousnesses alone; and it will be necessary for God to make the exchange not only of the apperceptions or consciousnesses of the individuals in question, but also of the appearances which present themselves to others regarding these persons, otherwise there would be a contradiction between the consciousnesses of the one and the testimony of the others, which would disturb the moral order of things. But you must also agree with me that the divorce between the insensible and sensible world, *i.e.* between the insensible perceptions which would remain in the same substances, and the apperceptions which would be changed, would be a miracle, as when you suppose that God makes the vacuum; for I have stated above why that is not in agreement with the natural order. Here is another supposition much more suitable: it may be that in another place in the universe or at another time a globe may be found which does not differ sensibly from this earthly globe, in which we live, and that each of the men who inhabit it does not differ sensibly from each of us who corresponds to him. Thus there are at once more than a hundred million pairs of similar persons, *i.e.* of two persons with the same appearances and consciousnesses; and God might transfer spirits alone or with their bodies from one globe to the other without their perceiving it; but be they transferred or let alone, what will you say of their person or *self* according to your authors? Are they two persons or the same? since the consciousness and the internal and external appearance of the men of these globes cannot make the distinction. It is true that God and the spirits capable of seeing the intervals and external relations of times and places, and even internal constitutions, insensible to the men of the two globes, could distinguish them; but according to your hypotheses consciousness alone discerning the persons without being obliged to trouble itself with the real identity or diversity of the substance, or even of that which would appear to others, how is it prevented from saying that these two persons who are at the same time in these two similar globes, but separated from each other by an inexpressible distance, are only one and the same person; which is, however, a manifest absurdity. For the rest, speaking of what may be in the course of nature, the two similar globes and the two similar souls of the two globes would remain so only for a time. For since there is an individual diversity, this difference must consist at least in the insensible constitutions which must be developed in the course of time.]

§ 26. *Ph.* Suppose a man punished now for what he has done in another life and of which he could cause himself to have absolutely no consciousness; what difference is there between such treatment and that which would be done him in creating him miserable?

Th. [The Platonists, disciples of Origen, some Hebrews and other defenders of the pre-existence of souls believed that the souls of this world were placed in imperfect bodies, in order to suffer for the crimes committed in a preceding world. But it is true, if they neither know nor have ever learned the truth, neither by recall of memory, nor by any traces, nor by the knowledge of another, you cannot call it punishment according to ordinary notions. There is, however, some room for doubt, while speaking of punishments in general, whether it is absolutely necessary that those who suffer should one day learn the reason for their suffering, and whether it would not very often suffice that better informed minds should find therein a motive for glorifying the divine justice. However, it is more likely, at least in general, that the sufferers will know the reason of their suffering.]

§ 29. *Ph.* [Perhaps in the main you can agree with my author who concludes his chapter on identity by saying: that the question whether the same man abides, is a question of name, according as you understand by man either the rational spirit alone or the body alone of this form which is called human, or finally the spirit united to such a body. In the first case the spirit separated (at least from the coarse body) will be still the man; in the second an ourang-outang, perfectly similar to us, reason excepted, would be a man; and if man were deprived of his rational soul and received a soul of an animal, he would continue the same man. In the third case both must remain together with the union itself; the same spirit, and the same body in part, or at least equivalent, as far as the sensible corporeal form is concerned. Thus you could continue the same being physically or morally, *i.e.* the same person without remaining man, in case you consider this figure an essential to man according to this last sense.]

Th. [I admit that in this respect it is a question of name, and in the third sense the same animal is as it were now caterpillar or silk-worm and now butterfly, and some as it were have imagined that the angels of this world were men in a past world. But we have devoted ourselves in this conference to discussions more important than those about the meaning of words. I have shown you the source of true physical identity; I have made it appear that morality contradicts it no more than memory; that they cannot always assign physical identity to the person indeed, whose (identity) is at stake, nor to those who are in connection with him; but that nevertheless they never contradict physical identity and never are completely[1] divorced from it; that there are always some created spirits who know or may know what it is; but that there is room to consider that what is indifferent regarding the persons themselves can be so only for a time.]

[1] Erdmann and Jacques omit: "entier."—Tr.

CHAPTER XXVIII

OF SOME OTHER RELATIONS, AND ESPECIALLY OF MORAL RELATIONS

§ 1. *Ph.* Besides the relations founded upon time, space, and causality, of which we have just been speaking, there are an infinite number of others, some of which I am going to propose for discussion. Every simple idea capable of parts and of degrees, furnishes an occasion for comparing the subjects in which it is found, for example, the idea of more (or less or equally) white. This relation may be called *proportional.*

Th. [There may be, however, excess without proportion; and this is in reference to a *magnitude* which I call *imperfect,* as when we say that the angle which the ray makes with the arc of its circle is less than a right angle, for it is impossible that there be a proportion between these two angles, or between one of them and their difference, which is the angle of contingence.]

§ 2. *Ph.* Another occasion of comparing is furnished by the circumstances of origin which found the relations of father and child, brothers, cousins, countrymen. With us people seldom think of saying this bull is grandfather of such a calf, or these two pigeons are cousins-german; for languages are proportioned to use. But there are countries in which men less curious about their own pedigree than about that of their horses have not only names for each particular horse, but also for their different degrees of relation.

Th. [We can furthermore join the family idea and names to those of relationship. It is true we do not observe under the empire of Charlemagne and for a sufficiently long time before and after family names in Germany, France, and Lombardy. It is moreover not long that there have been families (even noble) in the North who had no name, and in which a man would be recognized in his natal place only by calling his name and that of his father, and besides (in case he transplanted himself) by joining to his own the name of the place whence he came. The Arabs and the Turcomans have also the same custom (I believe), having but few particular family names, and content themselves with naming the father and grandfather, etc., of any one, and they pay the same honor to their valuable horses, which they call by a proper name and the name of the father and even beyond. Thus they spoke of the horses which the Monarch[1] of the Turks sent to the emperor after the peace of Carlowitz;[2] and the late count of Oldenburg, the last of his branch, whose studs were famous, and who lived a very long time, had genealogical trees of his horses so that he could prove their *nobility*, and went so far as to have portraits of their ancestors (*imagines majorum*) which were so much in demand among the Romans. But to return to men, there are among the Arabs and the Tartars names of *tribes*, which are like great families, which are much enlarged in the course of time. And these names are taken either from the progenitor as in the time of Moses, or from the place of abode, or from some other circumstance. Mr. Worsley, an observing[3] traveller, who is informed of the present state of Arabia Deserta, where he has been for some time, affirms that in all the countries between Egypt and Palestine, and where Moses passed, there are to-day only three tribes, who can bring together five thousand men, and that one of these tribes is called *Sali* from the progenitor (as I believe) whose tomb posterity honors as that of a saint, casting upon it dust which the Arabs put upon the heads of themselves and their camels. For the rest *consanguinity* exists when there is a common origin of those whose relation is considered; but we could say there is *alliance* or affinity between two persons, when they may have consanguinity with one and the same person without there being any for that reason between themselves, which happens through the intervention of marriages. But as it is not customary to say that there is affinity between husband and wife, although their marriage may cause affinity in relation to other persons, it would perhaps be better to say that there is *affinity* between those who would have con-

[1] Erdmann and Jacques read: "grand Seigneur." — TR.

[2] Jan. 26, 1699. — TR.

[3] Erdmann and Jacques read: "curieux"; Gerhardt reads: "observatif." — TR.

sanguinity between themselves if husband and wife were taken as one and the same person.

§ 3. *Ph.* The foundation of a *relation* is sometimes a moral right, as the relation of a general of an army or of a citizen. These *relations* depending upon the agreements men have made between themselves are *voluntary* or by *institution*, and may be distinguished from the *natural*. Sometimes the two correlatives have each its name, as patron and client, general and soldier. But it is not so always; as, for example, it is not so in the case of those who are related to the chancellor.

Th. [There are sometimes *natural relations* which men have invested and enriched with certain *moral* relations, as, for example, children have the right to claim the legitimate portion of the estate of their fathers or mothers; young persons are under certain restraints and the aged have certain immunities. But it also happens that some relations are taken as natural which are not so; as when the laws say that the father is he who married the mother within the time which makes it possible for the child to be attributed to him; and this substitution of the *instituted* in the place of the *natural* is sometimes only *presumption*, that is to say, a judgment which causes that to pass as true which perhaps is not so, whilst its falsity is not at all proved. Thus it is that the maxim: *pater est quem nuptiæ demonstrant* is understood in Roman law and among the most of the peoples where it is received. But they tell me that in England it avails nothing in proving his *alibi;* provided he has been in one of the three kingdoms, so that the presumption in that case changes into *fiction* or into what some doctors call *præsumtio juris et de jure.*]

§ 4. *Ph. A moral relation* is the conformity or disagreement which is found between the voluntary acts of men and a rule which makes us judge whether they are *morally good* or bad. § 5. And *moral good* or *moral evil* is the conformity or the opposition which is found between voluntary acts and a certain law which brings upon us good or evil (physical) by the will and power of the lawgiver (or of him who wills to maintain the law) and it is this we call *reward* and *punishment.*

Th. [Authors, as clever as he whose views you, sir, represent, are allowed to adapt their terms as they think proper. But it is also true that according to this notion one and the same act would be morally good and morally bad at the same time under different legislators, entirely as our clever author understood *virtue* above as that which is praised, and consequently the same act would be virtuous or not according to the opinions of men. Now that not being the ordinary sense that is given to morally good and virtuous acts, I prefer for myself, to take as the measure of moral good and of virtue the invariable rule of reason which God is charged with maintaining. We can also be assured that by his mediation all moral good becomes physical,[1] or as the ancients say, every thing virtuous is useful[2]; while in order to express the notion of the author, it would be necessary to say that moral good or evil is an imposed or *instituted good* or *evil*, which he who has the power tries to make us follow or shun by punishments and rewards. The good is that which by the general institution of God is conformed to nature or to reason.]

§ 7. *Ph.* There are three sorts of *laws:* the *divine law*, the *civil law*, and the law of opinion or *reputation*. The first is the rule of *sins* or *duties*, the second of *actions criminal* or *innocent*, the third of *virtues* or *vices*.

Th. [According to the ordinary sense of terms *virtues* and *vices* differ from *duties* and *sins* only as *habits* differ from

[1] What does Leibnitz here mean by "physical"? Possibly "physical" is here equivalent to "real," *i.e.* actual, concrete, objectively realized as distinguished from that which is purely subjective and abstract, and exists in idea only (*cf.* Bk. II., chap. 27, § 9, Th. *prope fin.*, *ante*, p. 247, line 7, where the two terms are united in one phrase "real and physical," and seem to be mutually interpretative and emphatic). Or, possibly, "physical" is here used in the sense of "natural," the meaning of the passage being that moral good is realized by the mediation of God through the natural forces and in accord with the natural laws of the universe, which with Leibnitz have their ultimate source and ground in the nature of God and his choice of "the best and most perfect," as the universal principle of creation. The true view of the world is, according to Leibnitz, both physico-mechanical and moral-teleological, the two finding a higher unity in this principle of "the best and most perfect," the moral-teleological prevailing in case of collision, because of this principle and because the physical is in its last analysis and ground spiritual and possessed of an inner teleological character which is realized by means of mechanism while resting upon the principle of the divine choice of the best. *Cf. Discours de Metaphysique*, § 19 *sq.*, Gerhardt, 4, 444 *sq.;* letter to Bayle, G. 3, 54; Erdmann, 106. — TR.

[2] *Cf.* Cicero, *De Officiis*, Bk. III., chaps. 3 and 7, who shows on the authority of Panætius and others that the virtuous and the useful — *honestum* and *utile* — are identical, a chief point of the Stoic philosophy. *Cf.* also Zeller, *Die Philos. d. Griech.*, III., 1 [Vol. 5], p. 212, 3d ed. 1880. — TR.

actions, and virtue and vice are not understood as something dependent upon opinion.[1] A great sin is called a *crime*, and the *innocent* is not opposed to the *criminal* but to the *blameworthy*. The divine law [2] is of two sorts, natural and positive. Civil law is positive. The law of reputation deserves the name of law only improperly, or is comprised under the natural law, as though I said, the law of health, the law of the family, when actions naturally attract some good or evil, as the approbation of another, health, gain.]

§ 10. *Ph.* The claim is in fact everywhere made that the terms virtue and vice signify actions good and bad in their nature, and so far as they are really applied in this sense, virtue agrees perfectly with the divine (natural) law. But whatever the claims of men, it is evident[3] that these names, considered in their particular applications, are constantly and solely attributed to such or such actions as in each country or in each society are reputed honórable or shameful: otherwise men *would condemn themselves*. Thus the measure of what is called virtue and vice is this approbation or this contempt, this esteem or this blame, which is formed by a secret or tacit consent. For although men united in political societies have resigned into the hands of the public the disposition of all their forces, so that they cannot employ them against their fellow-citizens beyond what the law permits, they nevertheless always retain the power of thinking well or ill, of approval or disapproval.

Th. [If the clever author, who thus explains himself, should declare with you, sir, that it has pleased him to assign this present arbitrary nominal definition to the terms virtue and vice, we could only say that it is allowed him in theory for the

[1] Leibnitz maintains, as against Locke's theory of relativity, the absolute and objective character of Moral Law. It is objective and universal, not subjective and particular; not dependent upon the opinions of men, but grounded in "the general institution of God," and ultimately in his infinitely perfect moral nature, and is thus valid for and binding upon all moral beings as such. This is Moral Law absolute and ideal which changes not; it is progressively and approximately attained or realized in the history of the individual and the race according to men's apprehension of its nature and requirements and their strength of purpose and effort in its pursuit. — TR.

[2] *Cf.* the discussion of Moral Law, in *Principles and Practice of Morality*, pp. 79 *sq.*, by E. G. Robinson, D.D., LL.D., Ex-President of Brown University. Boston: Silver, Burdett & Co., 1888. — TR.

[3] Locke has: "visible," *Philos. Works*, Vol. 1, p. 488 (Bohn's ed.). — TR.

convenience of expression for want perhaps of other terms; but we shall be obliged to add that this meaning is not conformed to usage, nor indeed useful for edification, and that it would sound ill in the ears of many people, if any one should introduce it into practical life and conversation, as this author seems himself to admit in his preface. But it is (for us) to go on farther here, and although you admit that men claim to speak of that which is naturally virtuous or vicious according to immutable laws, you maintain that in fact they mean to speak only of that which depends on opinion. But it seems to me that by the same reasoning you could further maintain that truth and reason and all that could be named as most real, depends upon opinion, because men are mistaken when they judge of it. Is it not better then on all accounts to say, that men understand by virtue as by truth, that which is conformed to nature, but that they are mistaken often in its application; besides *they are mistaken less than they think*, for what they praise ordinarily deserves it in certain respects. The virtue of drinking, *i.e.* of well carrying wine, is an advantage, which served Bonosus, in conciliating the Barbarians and in drawing from them their secrets.[1] The nocturnal powers of Hercules, in which the same Bonosus claimed to resemble him, were no less a perfection. The craft of thieves was praised among the Spartans, and it is not the skill, but the unseasonable use which has been made of it, which is blamable, and those whom we harass in (time of) complete peace may serve sometimes as excellent partisans in time of war. Thus all depends upon the application and the good or bad use of the advantages you possess. It is also very often true and should not be taken as a very strange thing, that men *condemn themselves*, as when they do what they blame in others, and there is often a contradiction between actions and words which scandalizes the public, when what a magistrate or preacher does and defends leaps to the eyes of the whole world.]

§ 11.[2] *Ph.* Everywhere that which passes as virtue is that which is thought worthy of praise. Virtue and praise are often designated by the same name. *Sunt hic etiam sua præmia laudi*, says Vergil (*Aen.* I. 461) and Cicero, *Nihil habet natura*

[1] *Cf.* Vopiscus, *Script. hist. August.*, Vol. 2, pp. 213, 214, ed. Peter. — TR.
[2] Gerhardt and Locke; Erdmann and Jacques have § 12. — TR.

praestantius quam honestatem, quam laudem, quam dignitatem, quam decus.[1] (*Quæst. Tuscul.* Bk. 2. chap. 20) and he adds a little after: *Hisce ego pluribus nominibus unam rem declarari volo.*[1]

Th. [It is true that the ancients have designated *virtue* by the name *honesty* (*l'honneste*), as when they have praised *incoctum generoso pectus honesto.*[2] It is true also that honesty (*l'honneste*) has its name of honor or of praise. But this means not that virtue is that which is praised but that it is that which is worthy of praise and which depends upon truth, and not upon opinion.]

Ph. Many do not think at all seriously of the *law of God*, or hope that they will one day be reconciled with its author, and as regards the *law of the state* they flatter themselves with impunity. But they do not think that he who does anything contrary to the opinions of those with whom he associates, and to whom he wishes to commend himself, can avoid the pain of their censure and of their disdain. No one who retains any consciousness of his own nature can live in society constantly despised; this is the force of the *law of reputation.*

Th. [I have already said that it is not so much the pain of a law, as a natural pain which the act draws upon itself. It is, however, true that many people are but little concerned about it, because ordinarily, if they are despised by some on account of some blameworthy act, they find accomplices or at least partisans, who do not despise them, if they are ever so little commendable in some other respect. They forget even acts the most infamous, and it often suffices to be bold and impudent like that Phormio of Terence in order that all may be overlooked. If *excommunication* produced a truly constant and general contempt, it would have the force of this law of which our author speaks: and it had in fact this force with the first Christians and for them took the place of the right, which they lacked, to punish the guilty; nearly as artisans maintain certain customs among themselves in spite of the laws, through

[1] The quotation is not exact. *Cf. op. cit.*, ed. Klotz, Lipsiæ, B. G. Teubner, 1870, where the text reads thus: "Nihil enim habet præstantius, nihil quod magis expetat quam honestatem, quam laudem, quam dignitatem, quam decus. Hisce ego pluribus nominibus unam rem declarari volo, sed utor, ut quam maxime significem, pluribus." — TR.

[2] Persius. *Sat.* 2, 74. —TR.

the contempt which they show for those who do not observe them. And it is this which has also maintained duels contrary to the ordinances. It would be desirable for the public to agree with itself and with reason in its praise and blame; and that the great above all do not encourage the bad by laughing at their bad actions, in which it oftenest seems that not he who has done them, but he who has suffered them is punished by contempt and ridiculed. We shall see also generally that men despise not so much vice as weakness and misfortune. Thus the law of reputation would need to be greatly reformed, and also to be better observed.]

§ 19. *Ph.* Before leaving the consideration of relations, I would remark that we usually have a notion as clear or clearer of the *relation* than of its *ground.* If I believed that Sempronia took Titus from beneath a cabbage, as they used to tell little children, and that afterwards she had had Caius in the same manner, I should have as clear a notion of the relation of *brother* between Titus and Caius, as if I had all the knowledge of the midwives.

Th. But when they once said to a child, that his little brother, who had just been born, had been drawn from a well (a reply which they make use of in Germany to satisfy the curiosity of children upon this subject) the child replied that he wondered that they did not throw him back again into the same well when he cried so much and disturbed his mother. The fact is this explanation did not make him know any reason for the love his mother showed for the child. We can say then that those who do not know the ground of relations have only concerning them what I call thoughts, surd in part and insufficient, although these thoughts may suffice in certain respects and upon certain occasions.]

CHAPTER XXIX

OF CLEAR AND OBSCURE, DISTINCT AND CONFUSED IDEAS

§ 2. *Ph.* We come now to some differences of ideas. *Our simple ideas* are *clear* when they are such as the objects themselves, from whence they are received, represent or may represent them with all the circumstances requisite to a well-ordered sensation or perception. While the memory retains them in this way, they are in this case clear ideas, and so far as they lack this original exactness or have lost anything so to speak of their first freshness, and are, as it were, tarnished or faded by time, so far are they obscure. *Complex ideas* are *clear*, when the simple ideas which compose them are clear and the number and order of these simple ideas are fixed.

Th. [In a brief discourse on ideas,[1] true or false, clear or obscure, distinct or confused, inserted in the "Leipsic Acts" of the year 1684, I have given a definition of *clear ideas*, common to the simple and complex and which gives the reason of what you say here. I said then that an *idea* is clear when it suffices to recognize and distinguish the thing: as when I have a very clear idea of a color, I shall not take another instead of that which I ask for, and if I have a clear idea of a plant, I shall distinguish it among other neighboring ones; without this *the idea* is *obscure*. I believe that we have but few perfectly clear ideas of sensible things. There are colors which approach each other in such a way that we cannot distinguish them by memory, and yet we will sometimes distinguish them by placing one near the other. And when we think we have fully described a plant, we can bring one from the Indies which will have all we have put into our description and which will not cease making itself known as a different species: thus we can never perfectly determine *species infamæ*, or the lowest species.]

§ 4. *Ph.* As a *clear idea* is that whereof the mind has such a full and evident perception as it receives from an external object operating duly upon a well-disposed organ; so a *distinct* idea is that wherein the mind perceives a difference, which distinguishes it from every other idea; and a confused idea is that which cannot be sufficiently distinguished from another from which it should be different.

Th. [According to this notion which you give of the *distinct* idea, I do not see how you distinguish it from the *clear* idea. This is why I have been wont to follow here the language of Descartes, with whom an idea may be clear and con-

[1] *Meditationes de Cognitione, Veritate et Ideis. Cf. ante*, p. 14, note 2; p. 227, note 3. — TR.

fused at the same time; and such are the ideas of sensible qualities, appropriate to the organs, such as color or heat. They are clear, for they are easily recognized and distinguished the one from the other, but they are not distinct, because they are not distinguished by what they include. Thus we cannot give a definition of them. We make them known only by examples, and for the rest we must say it is an indefinite somewhat, until we can decipher its contexture. Thus although in our view distinct ideas distinguish one object from another; nevertheless, as the ideas clear, but confused in themselves, do so also, we call *distinct* not all those which are very discriminating or which distinguish objects, but those which are well distinguished, *i.e.* which are distinct in themselves and distinguish in the object the marks which make it known, which an analysis or definition of it gives; otherwise we call them *confused*. And in this sense the confusion which reigns in ideas can be exempt from blame, being an imperfection of our nature; for we cannot discern the causes, for example, of odors and tastes, nor the content of these qualities. This confusion can, however, be blameworthy, when it is important and within my power to have distinct ideas, as, for example, if I took adulterated gold as the true, for want of making the necessary assays which contain the marks of good gold.

§ 5. *Ph.* But you will say that there is no idea confused (or rather according to your view, obscure) in itself[1] for it can be only such as it is perceived by the mind, and that distinguishes it sufficiently from all others. § 6. And in order to remove this difficulty it is needful to know that the defect of ideas is related to names, and what renders it faulty is the fact that it can as well be designated by another name as the one which we use to express it.

Th. [It seems to me that we ought not to make this depend upon names. Alexander the Great had seen (they say) in a dream a plant able to cure Lysimachus, which has since been called *Lysimachia*, because it effectually cured this friend of the king. When Alexander had a quantity of plants brought, among which he recognized that which he had seen in his dream, if unfortunately he had not had a sufficient idea of it to recognize it and had needed as Nebuchadnezzar a

[1] Erdmann and Jacques omit: "en elle même." — TR.

Daniel to enable him to recall his dream, it is plain that the idea he would have had of it would have been *obscure* and imperfect (for it is thus I should prefer to call it rather than *confused*), not for want of appositeness in a certain name, for there was none, but for want of application to the thing, *i.e.* to the plant which was to heal. In this case Alexander would be reminded of certain circumstances, but he would have been in doubt about others; and the name serving us to designate anything makes us, when we fail in the application to names, fail ordinarily in regard to the thing which is promised by this name.]

§ 7. *Ph.* As complex ideas are the most subject to this imperfection, it may arise from the fact that the idea is composed of too small a number of simple ideas, as is, for example, the idea of an animal which has the skin spotted, (a term) which is too general, and which does not suffice to distinguish the lynx, the leopard, or the panther, which are besides distinguished by particular names.

Th. [If we were in the condition Adam was in before he had given names to the animals, this defect would not cease to have place. For supposing we knew that among the spotted animals there is one which has extraordinarily penetrating sight, but that we did not know whether it is a tiger or a lynx, or some other species; it is an imperfection not to be able to distinguish it. Thus the question is not so much about the name as about that which may give occasion for it, and which renders the animal worthy of a particular name. It thereby appears also that the idea of a spotted animal is good in itself, and without confusion and obscurity, when it is to serve only the genus; but when joined with some other idea which is not sufficiently remembered it is to designate the species, the complex idea is obscure and imperfect.]

§ 8. *Ph.* There is an opposite defect when the simple ideas which make up the complex idea are sufficient in number, but too confused and involved, like some pictures, which appear so confused that they must be only the representation of the sky covered with clouds, in which case also we could not say that there is confusion any more than if it were another picture made to imitate that one; but when we say that this picture should make us see a portrait, we shall have reason to say that it is confused because we cannot say whether it is that of a man, or of a monkey, or of a fish, but it may be that when we look at it in a cylindrical mirror, the confusion will disappear, and that we shall see that it is a Julius Cæsar. Thus some *mental paintings* (if I may so express myself) cannot be called confused from any way in which the parts are joined together; for whatever these paintings are, they can obviously be distinguished from every other, until they are ranked under some ordinary name, to which we cannot see that they belong any more than to some other name of a different signification.

Th. [This picture whose parts we see distinctly, without noticing the result to which they in a certain way point, resembles the idea of a heap of stones, which is truly confused not only in your sense, but also in mine, so far as we have *distinctly* conceived their number and other properties. If there were thirty-six of them (for example), we would not know, looking at them heaped together without arrangement, that they may produce a triangle or indeed a square, as in fact they can, because thirty-six is a square as well as a triangular number. Thus it is that, in looking at a figure of a thousand sides, we shall have only a confused idea of it, until we know the number of the sides which is the cube of ten. The question, then, is not of names but of the *distinct properties* which are to be found in the idea when we have cleared up its confusion. And it is sometimes difficult to find the key, or the manner of looking at it from a certain point, either by the intervention of a certain mirror or glass in order to see the purpose of him who has caused the thing.]

§ 9. *Ph.* It cannot be denied that there is yet a third defect in ideas, which depends in truth upon the bad use of names; it is when our ideas are uncertain or undetermined. Thus we may see every day men who, making no difficulty of availing themselves of the ordinary words of their mother tongue, before they have learned their precise meaning, change the idea which they attach to them almost as often as they use them in their discourse. § 10. Thus we see how much names contribute to this denomination of ideas distinct and confused, and, without the consideration of distinct names understood as signs of distinct things, it will be very difficult to say what a *confused idea* is.

Th. [I have, however, just explained it without considering the names, whether in the case where *the confusion* is understood with you as what I call *obscurity*, or in that where it is understood in my sense as the defect in the analysis of the notion we have. And I have also shown that every obscure idea is in fact indeterminate or uncertain, as in the example of the spotted animal we have seen, where we know that something further must be added to this general notion, without clearly remembering it; so that the first and third defect which you have specified come to the same thing. It is, however, very true that the abuse of words is a great source of errors, for a kind of error in calculating occurs therefrom, as if in calculating we did not notice carefully the place of the counter, or if we wrote the figures so badly that we could not distinguish a 2 from a 7, or if we omitted or changed them through inadvertence. This abuse of words consists either in not connecting ideas with the whole or in connecting them with an imperfect one, of which a part is empty and abides so to speak in blank; and in these two cases there is a certain void and *surd* in the thought which is filled only by the name. Or, finally, the defect is in attaching to the word different ideas, whether we are uncertain which should be chosen, which makes the idea obscure as well as when a part of it is surd; or whether we select them by turns, and avail ourselves sometimes of one, sometimes of the other as the sense of the same word in one and the same course of reasoning in a way capable of causing error, without considering that the ideas do not agree. Thus the uncertain thought is either void and without idea, or fluctuates between several ideas. This does harm whether[1] we wish to designate some definite thing or whether we wish to give a word a certain sense corresponding either to that of which we have already availed ourselves, or to that which others have used, above all in ordinary language, common to all, or to the artisans. And from this arise an infinite number of vague and vain disputes in conversation, in lecture-rooms, and in books, which we

[1] Erdmann and Jacques omit: "soit qu'on veuille designer quelque chose determinée," the reading of Gerhardt. — TR.

may sometimes avoid by *distinctions*, but which most frequently serve only to confuse the more, by putting in the place of a vague and obscure term other terms still more vague and obscure, as those often are which the philosophers employ in their distinctions, without having good definitions of them.]

§ 12. *Ph.* If there is any other confusion in ideas, than this which has a secret relation to names, this at least casts more disorder than any other into the thoughts and discourse of men.

Th. [I agree, but most frequently some notion of the thing and the purpose which we have in availing ourselves of the name is mixed with it; as, for example, when we speak of *the church*, many have in view a government, while others think of the truth of the doctrine.]

Ph. The way to prevent this confusion is constantly to apply the same name to a certain mass of simple ideas united in a fixed number and into a determined order. But as that suits neither the laziness nor the vanity of men, and as it can be used only in the discovery and the defence of the truth, which is not always the end they propose to themselves, such precision is one of the things that is rather to be wished than hoped for. The vague application of names to ideas indeterminate, variable, and almost wholly empty (in the surd thoughts) is on one side a covering of our ignorance and on the other a confusing and embarrassing of others, which passes as true learning and as a mark of superiority in point of knowledge.

Th. [The affectation of elegance and wit has further contributed much to this intricacy of language; for in order to express thoughts beautifully and agreeably we make no difficulty of giving words in a *tropical* manner a sense different from the ordinary, sometimes more general or more limited, which is called *synecdoche*, sometimes transferred according to the relations of things whose names we change, either by concurrence in *metonymy*, or by comparison in *metaphor*, not to speak of *irony*, which makes use of a term in a sense directly opposite to its real meaning. Thus these changes are named when recognized; but they are recognized only rarely. And in this indeterminateness of language, in which there is lacking a kind of law which regulates the meaning of words, as there is something in the title of the digests of the Roman Law, *De Verborum Significationibus*, persons the most judicious, when they write for ordinary readers, would be deprived of that which gives charm and force to their expression if they should confine themselves rigorously to the fixed meanings of terms. They need only take care that their variation does not cause any error or false reasoning to spring up. The distinction of the ancients between the *exoteric*,[1] *i.e.* popular, and the *acroamatic*[1] mode of writing, which belongs to those who are occupied in the discovery of truth, has place here. And if any one wished to write in mathematical fashion in metaphysics or ethics, nothing would prevent him from so doing with rigor. Some have professed to do this, and we have a promise of mathematical demonstrations outside of mathematics; but it is very rare that they have been successful. This is, I believe, because they are disgusted with the trouble it is necessary to take for a small number of readers where they could ask as in Persius: *Quis leget haec*, and reply: *Vel duo vel nemo.*[2] I believe, however, that if they would undertake it in the proper way they would not be likely to repent it. And I have been tempted to try it.]

§ 13. *Ph.* You will agree with me, however, that complex ideas may be very clear and distinct in one aspect, and very obscure and confused in another.

Th. [There is no reason to doubt it; for example, we have very distinct ideas of a good part of the solid visible parts of the human body, but we have but few of the liquids which enter therein.]

Ph. If a man speaks of a figure of a thousand sides, the

[1] *Cf.* Leibnitz, *De Stilo philos. Nizolii*, Gerhardt, Vol. 4, p. 146; Erdmann, p. 63. "Acroamatic" (*ante*, p. 42), from ἀκρόαμα, anything heard, the verb ἀκροᾶσθαι, the regular word for hearing or attending lectures, the adjective ἀκροαματικός, designed for hearing only, and, when used of the doctrines of philosophers, meaning the *esoteric*, *i.e.* the doctrines in their most rigorous and exact scientific form, their custom being to give these orally to their pupils, while treating them in a more popular, *exoteric* manner in their writings. Such was the method of Plato and of Aristotle, one of whose works is called φυσικὴ ἀκρόασις. Schaarschmidt refers to Bernays, *Die Dialoge d. Aristotles*, p. 30 *sq.* Berlin, 1863, and Madvig, Excursus VII. to his edition of Cicero's *De Finibus*. — Tr.

[2] *Sat.* 1, lines 2, 3. — Tr.

idea of this figure may be very obscure in his mind, although that of the number may be very distinct therein.

Th. [This example is not in point here; a regular polygon of a thousand sides is known as distinctly as the millenary number, because we may discover and demonstrate all kinds of truth.]

Ph. But we do not have a precise idea of a figure of a thousand sides, so that we can distinguish it from another, which has only nine hundred ninety-nine.

Th. [This example shows that you here confound the idea with the image. If any one places before me a regular polygon, sight and imagination cannot make me comprehend the millenary therein; I have only a *confused* idea both of the figure and of its number, until I *distinguish* the number by counting. But having found it, I know very well the nature and the properties of the proposed polygon, as far as they are those of the chiliagon, and consequently I have this idea of it; but I cannot have the image of a chiliagon, and it would be necessary to have senses and imagination more exquisite and better exercised in order to distinguish it thereby from a polygon which had one side less. But the knowledge of figures no more than that of numbers depends upon the imagination, although it is of service therein; and a mathematician can know exactly the nature of a nonagon and a decagon, because he has the means of making and examining them, though he could not discern them at sight. It is true that a workman or an engineer, who does not perhaps know their nature sufficiently, can have this advantage beyond a great geometer that he can discern them by sight only without measuring them, as there are some street-porters[1] (*faquins*) or pedlers, who will state the weight of what they are to carry within a pound, in which respect they will surpass the most skilful statistician in the world. It is true that[2] this empirical knowledge acquired by a long practice may be very useful for prompt action, such as an engineer very often needs to perform because of the danger to which he is exposed in delaying. But this *clear image* or this feeling which we may

[1] Erdmann and Jacques omit: "faquins ou," the reading of Gerhardt. — TR.

[2] Erdmann and Jacques omit: "Il est vray que," the reading of Gerhardt. — TR.

have of a regular decagon or of a weight of ninety-nine pounds consists only in a *confused idea*, since it is of no avail in discovering the nature and properties of this weight or of this regular decagon, which demands a *distinct idea*. And this example conduces to the better understanding of the difference of ideas, or rather that of the idea and the image.]

§ 15.[1] *Ph.* Another example: We are led to believe that we have a positive and complete idea of eternity, which is as much as to say that there is no part of that duration which is not clearly known in our idea; but, however great may be the duration that is represented, as it is a question of an extension without limits, there always remains a part of the idea beyond what is represented which continues obscure and undetermined; and thence it comes that, in discussions and reasonings concerning eternity or any other infinite, we are apt to involve ourselves in manifest absurdities.

Th. [This example does not appear to me to square with your design either; but it is very appropriate to mine, which is to disabuse you of your notions on this point. For the same confusion of the image with the idea reigns here. We have a complete or just idea of eternity, since we have a definition of it, although we have no image of it. But the idea of the infinite is not formed by the composition of parts, and the errors which we meet in reasoning upon the infinite do not arise from the defect of the image.[2]]

§ 16.[3] *Ph.* But is it not true that when we speak of the infinite divisibility of matter, although we have clear ideas of the division, we have only very obscure and very confused ideas of the parts? For I ask whether a man taking the

[1] Erdmann and Jacques have § 25. Gerhardt and Locke, *Philos. Works*, Vol. 1, p. 505 (Bohn's ed.), have § 15. — Tr.

[2] The difficulties and errors in the discussion of the infinite arise not "from the defect of the image" but from the attempt to imagine or picture that which can only be thought. We can think the infinite and absolute, but we cannot form an adequate image or picture of it. The "confusion of the image with the idea," which Leibnitz here speaks of, is one of the causes vitiating much of the "reasoning upon the infinite" in the history of thought, and lying at the basis of all theories, like those of Hamilton, Mansel, and Spencer, which maintain the impossibility on man's part of a knowledge of the infinite. *Cf.* John Caird, *An Introduction to the Philos. of Religion*, p. 36. New York: Macmillan & Co., 1880. — Tr.

[3] So Gerhardt and Locke, *Philos. Works* (Bohn's ed.), Vol. 1, p. 505; Erdmann has § 18; Jacques § 30. — Tr.

smallest atom of dust he ever saw has any distinct idea of the difference between the one hundred thousandth[1] and the millionth part of this atom?

Th. It is the same *qui pro quo* of the *image* for the *idea*, which I am astonished to see so confused. The possession of an image of so great a smallness is not at all the question. It is impossible according to the present constitution of our body, and if we could have it, it would be much the same as that of those things which now appear to us *apperceptible;* but in compensation what is now the object of our imagination would escape us and become too great to be imagined. Size has no images in itself, and those which it has depend only upon comparison with the organs and other objects, and it is useless here to employ imagination. Thus it appears by all that you, sir, have said to me here that you are ingenious in devising difficulties without reason, in demanding more than is necessary.]

CHAPTER XXX

OF REAL AND FANTASTICAL IDEAS

§ 1. *Ph.* Ideas in relation to things are real or fantastical, adequate or inadequate, true or false. By *real ideas* I understand those which have a foundation in nature, and which are conformed to a real being, to the existence of things, or to their archetypes; otherwise they are *fantastic* or chimerical.

Th. [There is a little obscurity in this explication. The idea may have a foundation in nature, without being conformed to this foundation, as when we maintain that the perceptions we have of color and heat do not resemble any original or archetype. An idea is also real when it is possible, although no existing being corresponds thereto. Otherwise if all the individuals of a species were lost, the idea of the species would become chimerical.]

§ 2. *Ph.* Simple ideas are all real, for, although [according to many] whiteness and coldness are no more in snow than is pain, yet their ideas are in us as effects of powers connected

[1] Erdmann and Jacques read: "la 10,000me et la 1000me." — TR.

with external things, and these constant effects serve us in distinguishing things as much as if they were exact images of that which exists in the things themselves.

Th. [I have examined this point above: but it appears thereby that you do not always demand a conformity to an archetype, and, according to the opinion (which, however, I do not approve) of those who think that God has arbitrarily assigned us ideas, destined to mark the qualities of objects without any resemblance or even natural relation, there would be also in that case less conformity between our ideas and the archetypes than there is between the words which we use by institution in language and the ideas, or the things themselves.]

§ 3. *Ph.* The mind is *passive* as regards its simple ideas; but the combinations it makes of them to form complex ideas, where many simple ideas are comprised under one and the same name, have somewhat of the *volitional* element; for one man admits into the complex ideas he has of gold or of justice simple ideas which another does not admit.

Th. [The mind is, however, active in reference to simple ideas when it detaches them one from another to consider them separately, — an act which is voluntary as well as the combination of many ideas; whether it is done to call attention to a complex idea resulting therein, or whether it is the purpose to comprehend them under the name given to the combination. And the mind cannot be deceived therein provided it does not unite incompatible ideas and provided this name is still virginal, so to speak, that is to say, a name to which some notion has not already been attached, which might cause confusion with that which is newly attached thereto, and make arise either impossible notions by joining together what cannot take place, or notions superfluous and containing some *obreption*,[1] by joining ideas, one of which may and ought to be derived from the other by demonstration.]

§ 4. *Ph.* Mixed modes and relations having no other reality than that which they have in *men's minds*, all that is requisite to make these sorts of ideas real is the possibility of existence or of compatibility together.

Th. [*Relations* have a reality dependent upon the mind

[1] *I.e.* Concealment of the truth. — Tr.

like *truths;* but not the mind of men, since there is a supreme intelligence which determines them all for all time. *Mixed modes,* which are distinct from relations, may be real accidents. But be they dependent or not dependent upon the mind, it suffices for the reality of their ideas that these modes be *possible* or, what is the same thing, distinctly intelligible. And for this result it is necessary that their ingredients be *compossible, i.e.* capable of existing together.]

§ 5. *Ph.* But the complex ideas of substances, as they are all formed in relation to things existing outside of us, and as representative of substances such as really exist, are real only so far as they are combinations of simple ideas really both united and coexisting in things coexisting without us. On the contrary those are *chimerical*[1] which are composed of such collections of simple ideas as have never been really united and found together in any substance; like those which form a centaur, a body resembling gold, save in weight, and lighter than water, a body similar in relation to the senses, but endowed with perception, voluntary movement, etc.

Th. [If I take in this manner the terms *real* and *chimerical* otherwise in relation to the ideas of the modes than in relation to those which form a substance, I do not see what common notion in each case you give to real or chimerical ideas; for the modes are real to you when they are possible, and substances have real ideas with you only when they are existent. But in desiring to tally with existence, we can determine but little whether an idea is chimerical or not, because what is possible, although not found in our place or time, may have existed formerly or will perhaps some day exist, or may indeed be found already present in another world, or even in ours without our knowing it, like the idea which Democritus had of the Milky Way[2] which the telescopes have verified: so that it seems better to say that possible ideas only become chimerical when we attach to them without foundation the idea of effective existence, as those do who promise themselves the philosopher's stone or, as those

[1] Locke has: "fantastical," *Philos. Works*, Vol. 1, p. 510 (Bohn's ed.).—TR.

[2] *Cf.* Aristotle, *Meteorologica*, Bk. I., chap. 8, 345ᵃ, 25: "The Milky Way is the light of certain stars." Zeller, *Die Philos. d. Griech.*, 3d ed., Vol. 1, p. 724, note 1; 5th ed., 1892, I. 2 [Vol. 2], p. 897, note 8.—TR.

would do who should believe that there had been a nation of centaurs. Otherwise in not regulating ourselves by existence we shall deviate unnecessarily from the received language, which does not allow us to say that he who speaks in winter of roses or pinks speaks of a chimera, unless he imagines he is able to find them in his garden, as the story is told of Albert the Great[1] or of some other pretended Magician.]

CHAPTER XXXI

OF ADEQUATE[2] AND INADEQUATE IDEAS

§ 1. *Ph.* *Real ideas* are *complete* when they represent perfectly the originals whence the mind supposes them to be taken, which they represent, and to which it refers them. *Incomplete ideas* represent only a part of these originals. § 2. All our simple ideas are complete. The idea of whiteness or of sweetness, which is noticed in sugar, is complete, because it suffices for this,—that it corresponds entirely to the powers that God has put into this body to produce these sensations.

Th. [I see, sir, that you call *complete* or *incomplete* ideas those which your favorite author calls *ideæ adæquatæ aut inadæquatæ;* you might call them *perfect* or *imperfect.* I have sometimes defined *idea adæquata* (a *perfect idea*) as that which is so distinct that all its ingredients are distinct, and such is nearly the idea of a number. But when an idea is distinct and contains the definition or the reciprocal marks of the object, it may be *inadæquata* or *imperfect,* viz.: when

[1] Albertus Magnus, 1193–1280. Schaarschmidt states that "like many other scholars of those dark centuries (Michael Scotus, Roger Bacon, etc.) he was suspected of Magic," and adds that "Trithemius in particular, who, moreover, takes the philosopher into his protection, gives an account thereof in his *Annales Hirsaugienses*, Vol. 2, p. 40. Naudé in his *Apologie des Grands Hommes Soupçonnés de Magie*, chap. 18, Bayle in his *Dictionary*, see under Albert Le Grand, and Brucker, *Hist. Philosophiæ*, 3, 793 *sq.*, have likewise defended him." On his life and philosophy, *cf.* Erdmann, *Grundriss d. Gesch. d. Philos.* §§ 199–202, Vol. 1, pp. 356 *sq.*, and English translation of same; also Stöckl, *Gesch. d. Philos. d. Mittelalters*, Vol. 2, pp. 352 *sq.*, §§ 101–119.—TR.

[2] Locke's title; the French might be rendered "complete and incomplete," as in the text.—TR.

these marks or these ingredients are not also all distinctly known; for example, gold is a metal which resists the cupel and aqua fortis; it is a distinct idea, for it gives the marks or the definition of *gold;* but it is not perfect for the nature of cupellation and the working of aqua fortis is not sufficiently known to us. Whence it comes that, when there is only an imperfect idea, the same subject is susceptible of many definitions independent the one of the other, so that we cannot always derive one from the other nor see beforehand that they must belong to one and the same subject, and then experience alone teaches us that they all belong to it at once. Thus gold may still be defined as the heaviest of our bodies, or the most malleable, without speaking of other definitions which might be invented. But we shall be able to see why it belongs to the heaviest of metals to resist these two tests of the assayers only when men shall have penetrated farther into the nature of things; whilst in geometry, where we have perfect ideas, the case is different, for we can prove that the sections of the cone and of the cylinder, made by a plane, are the same, *viz.* ellipses, and this cannot be unknown to us, if we take notice of it, because the notions we have of them are perfect. With me the division of ideas into perfect and imperfect is only a sub-division of distinct ideas, and it appears to me that only the confused ideas, like that we have of sweetness, of which you, sir, speak, deserve this name; for although they express the power which produces the sensation, they do not express it wholly, or at least we cannot know this, for if we comprehended what is in this idea of sweetness we have we could judge whether it is sufficient as a rational expression of all that experience causes us to notice therein.]

§ 3. *Ph.* From simple ideas let us come to the *complex;* they are either of modes or of substances. Those of *modes* are the voluntary collections of simple ideas which the mind puts together *without regard to certain archetypes* or real and actually existing models; they are complete and cannot be otherwise, because not being copies but archetypes, which the mind forms in order to avail itself of them in ranking things under certain denominations, they can lack nothing, because each includes such a combination of ideas as the mind has *desired* to form, and consequently such perfection as it had planned to give thereto, and we cannot conceive that the understanding of any one can have a more complete or more perfect idea of a triangle than that of a figure of three sides and three angles. He who put together the ideas of danger, of execution, of the trouble that fear produces, of a calm consideration of what it would be reasonable to do, and of an actual application to its execution without being frightened by the danger, formed the idea of *courage*, and had what he desired, viz.: a complete idea conformed to his good pleasure. It is otherwise in our ideas of substances in which we maintain that which really exists.

Th. [The idea of *triangle* or of *courage* has its archetype in the possibility of things as well as the idea of gold. And it is a matter of indifference, so far as the nature of the idea is concerned, whether it was invented in advance of experience, or whether it was retained after the perception of a combination which nature had made. Combination also, which produces the modes, is not wholly *voluntary* or arbitrary, for we can put together what is incompatible, as those do who invent machines for perpetual motion, while others can invent those which are good and practicable which have no other archetypes with us than the idea of the inventor which has as its archetype the possibility of things or the divine idea. Now these machines are substances. We can also invent impossible modes, as when we maintain the parallelism of parabolas, by imagining that we can find two parabolas parallel to each other, like two straight lines or two circles. An idea, then, whether it be that of a mode, or that of a substance, may be complete or incomplete according as we understand well or ill the partial ideas which form the total idea: and it is a mark of a perfect idea when it makes known perfectly the possibility of the object.]

CHAPTER XXXII

OF TRUE AND FALSE IDEAS

§ 1. *Ph.* As truth[1] or falsehood belongs only to propositions,[2] it follows that when ideas are termed true or false there is some tacit proposition or *affirmation;* § 3. or a tacit assumption of their conformity to something, § 5. above all with what others designate by this name (as when they speak of justice) *item* to what really exists (as man exists but not the centaur) *item* to the essence, upon which depend the properties of the thing; and in this sense our ordinary ideas of substances are false when we think of certain substantial forms. Besides, ideas deserve rather to be called accurate or faulty, than true or false.

Th. I believe that true or false ideas might be so understood, but as these different senses do not agree between themselves and cannot be conveniently ranked under a common notion, I prefer to call the *ideas true* or *false* in relation to another tacit *affirmation* which they all include, which is that of possibility. Thus possible ideas are *true*, impossible *false.*]

CHAPTER XXXIII

OF THE ASSOCIATION OF IDEAS

§ 1. *Ph.* We often notice something odd in the reasonings of people, and everybody is subject to this. § 2. It is not alone obstinacy or self-love; for often people who are well disposed are guilty of this fault. It does not indeed suffice to

[1] *Cf. New Essays*, Bk. IV., chap. 5. — Tr.

[2] *Cf.* Aristotle *De Anima*, III. 6,430^a, 27, and E. Wallace, *Aristotle's Psychology in Greek and English, with Introduction and Notes*, pp. 160, 161, Cambridge: University Press, 1882; also *De Interpret.* 1, 16^a, 12, and E. Wallace, *Outlines of the Philos. of Aristotle*, 3d ed., § 11, p. 27. For Leibnitz, the true is the thinkable, *i.e.* that which is free from contradiction in itself and of other truth. Thought-necessity is his criterion of possibility and of truth. — Tr.

attribute it to education and to prejudice. § 4. It is rather a kind of madness, and we should be foolish if we should always act thus. § 5. This fault arises from a non-natural connection of ideas, which has its origin in chance or custom. § 6. Inclination and interest enter into it. Certain tracts of the repeated course of animal spirits become beaten roads; when we know[1] a certain air, we find it as soon as we begin it. § 7. Thence arise the sympathies or antipathies which are not born with us. A child has eaten too much honey and has been surfeited by it, and then having become a full-grown man, he cannot hear the name honey without a rising of the stomach. § 8. Children are very susceptible to these impressions, and it is well to be careful of them. § 9. This irregular association of ideas has a great influence in all our actions and passions natural and moral. § 10. Darkness revives the idea of ghosts in children because of the stories told them about them. § 11. You do not think of a man whom you hate without thinking of the evil he has done or may do. § 12. You shun the room in which you have seen a friend die. § 13. A mother who has lost a very dear child sometimes loses with it all her joy, until time effaces the impression of this idea, which sometimes never[2] happens. § 14. A man perfectly cured of madness by an extremely painful operation acknowledged all his life his obligation to the one who performed this operation; but it was impossible for him to endure the sight of the operator. § 15. Some hate books all their life because of the bad treatment they received in school. Some one having once gotten the upper hand of another upon some occasion keeps it always. § 16. A man was found who had learned to dance finely, but could not execute the dance unless there was in the room a trunk like the one which had been in the room where he had learned. § 17. The same non-natural bond is found in the intellectual habits; you bind matter to being, as if there were nothing immaterial. § 18. The sectarian party in philosophy, religion, and the state is attached to its opinions.

Th. [This remark is important and wholly to my taste, and can be fortified by an infinite number of examples. Descartes

[1] Gerhardt reads: "sait"; Erdmann and Jacques: "suit," follow. — TR.
[2] Gerhardt reads: "jamais"; Erdmann and Jacques: "pas." — TR.

having had in his youth some affection for a squint-eyed person could not prevent himself from having all his life an inclination towards those who had this defect. Hobbes, another great philosopher, could not (they say) remain alone in a dark place, without having his mind frightened by images of ghosts, although he did not believe in them, this impression having remained from the stories told to children. Many persons well informed and sensible, and who are decidedly superior to superstition, cannot bring themselves to be thirteen at a repast without being extremely disconcerted, having sometime been impressed by the fancy that one of them must die during the year. There was a gentleman who, having been injured, perhaps in his infancy, by a badly fastened pin, could not see one in this condition without being ready to fall into a swoon. A prime minister, who bore in the court of his master the name of President, was offended by the title of the book of Ottavio Pisani, called *Lycurgus*, and wrote against this book, because the author, in speaking of the officers of justice whom he thought superfluous, had named also the Presidents, and although this term in the person of this minister meant a totally different thing, he had so attached the word to his person that he was wounded in this word. And this is a case of the most usual of the non-natural associations, capable of misleading, as those of words to things, when indeed there is any ambiguity. In order the better to understand the source of the non-natural bond of ideas, you must consider what I have already said above (Chap. 11, § 11 [1]), in speaking of the reasonings of animals, that man as well as the animal is inclined to put together in his memory and imagination what he has observed united in his perceptions and experience. It is in this that all the reasoning, if so it may be called, of animals consists, and often that of men, so far as they are empirical and govern themselves only by the senses and examples, without examining whether the same reason still has force. And as often the reasons are unknown to us, we must have regard to the examples in proportion to their frequency, for then the expectation or the reminiscence of one perception

[1] *Cf. ante*, p. 145. Gerhardt has § 1; Erdmann and Jacques § 11; the latter reference is the correct one, and has therefore been placed in the text of the translation. — TR.

on the occasion[1] of another perception which is ordinarily connected therewith is reasonable; particularly when the question is about taking precautions. But as the vehemence of a very strong impression often produces as much effect at once as the frequency and repetition of many moderate impressions would be able to make in a long time, it happens that this vehemence engraves upon the fancy an image as profound and as vivid as long experience.[2] Whence it comes that a chance but violent impression unites in our imagination and memory two ideas, at that time together there,[3] altogether as strongly and durably and gives us the same inclination to connect them and to attend to them one after the other, as if a long usage had verified the connection; thus the same result of association is found, although the same reason does not exist. Authority, party,[4] custom, produce also the same effect as experience and reason, and it is not easy to deliver one's self from these inclinations. But it would not be very difficult to keep one's self from being deceived in these judgments, if men would attach themselves seriously enough to the search for truth, or proceed methodically, when they recognize that it is important to them to find it.]

[1] Gerhardt reads: "d'une perception à l'occasion," which Erdmann and Jacques omit. — TR.

[2] Erdmann and Jacques add: "auroit pu le faire," could have done. — TR.

[3] Gerhardt reads: "qui y estoient ensemble alors, tout aussi fortement et durablement; et nous donne," etc. Erdmann and Jacques, "qui déjà y étaient ensemble, et nous donne," etc. — TR.

[4] Erdmann aud Jacques omit: "le parti." — TR.

NEW ESSAYS ON HUMAN UNDERSTANDING

BOOK III. — WORDS

CHAPTER I

OF WORDS OR LANGUAGE IN GENERAL

§ 1. *Ph.* God having made man to be a social being, has not only inspired him with the desire, and placed him under the necessity of living with those of his species, but has given him also the faculty of speech which is to be the great instrument and common bond of this society. Hence it is that *words* arise, which serve to represent and also to explain *ideas.*

Th. [I rejoice to see that you are averse to the view of Hobbes,[1] who did not admit that man was made for society,

[1] Thomas Hobbes, 1588–1679, in his *De Cive*, 1642, and *Leviathan*, 1651, maintained that man, being by nature a selfish and solitary animal, had no natural impulse for society, and that social union sprang simply from fear and from motives of gain, the natural condition being that of universal war. Leibnitz maintains, in agreement with Aristotle and Hugo Grotius, 1583–1645, that Nature herself has destined man for society in order not only that he may the better and more easily realize his highest being, but that he may realize it at all, such realization being impossible in isolation and solitude. *Cf.* Aristotle, *Polit.* I., 2, 1253ª, 2: ὅτι τῶν φύσει ἡ πόλις ἐστί, καὶ ὅτι ἄνθρωπος φύσει πολιτικὸν ζῷον; III., 6, 1278ᵇ, 19: φύσει μέν ἐστιν ἄνθρωπος ζῷον πολιτικόν, διὸ καὶ μηδὲν δεόμενοι τῆς παρ' ἀλλήλων βοηθείας οὐκ ἔλαττον ὀρέγονται τοῦ συζῆν, English translation by B. Jowett, Vol. 1, pp. 4, 78, Oxford: Clarendon Press, 1885; also *Eth. Nic.* IX., 9, 1169ᵇ, 3 *sq.*, espec. 16–19: ἄτοπον δ' ἴσως καὶ τὸ μονώτην ποιεῖν τὸν μακάριον· οὐθεὶς γὰρ ἕλοιτ' ἂν καθ' αὑτὸν τὰ πάντ' ἔχειν ἀγαθά· πολιτικὸν γὰρ ὁ ἄνθρωπος καὶ συζῆν πεφυκός, I., 1, 1094ᵇ, 6 *sq.*, English translation by F. H. Peters, pp. 307 *sq.*, 3; *cf.* also Zeller, *Philos. d. Griech.*, II., 2 [Vol. 4], pp. 680, 662, 3d ed., 1879. Grotius, *De Jure Belli et Pacis*, 1625, Preliminary Discourse, § 6: "Amongst the things peculiar to man, is his desire of society, that is, a certain inclination to live with those of his own kind, not in any manner whatever, but peace-

conceiving that he has been forced into it by necessity and by the wickedness of those of his species. But he did not consider that the best men, free from all wickedness, united themselves the better to obtain their purposes, as the birds flock together the better to travel in company, and the beavers unite in large numbers to make great dams, in which work a small number of these animals could not succeed; and these dams are necessary to them, to provide reservoirs of water or little lakes, in which they build their huts and catch the fish upon which they feed. This then is the foundation of the society of the animals which are adapted to it, and nowise the fear of their kind, which is rarely found among animals.]

Ph. Very true, and it is the better to cultivate this society that man by nature has his *organs* so fashioned that they are adapted to the formation of the articulate sounds which we call *words.*

Th. [As for *organs*, monkeys have them apparently as suitable as ours for the formation of words, but they do not take the least step in this direction.[1] Thus it must be that they lack an invisible something. We must also consider that we

ably, and in a community regulated according to the best of his understanding, which disposition the Stoicks termed οἰκείωσις"; quoted from English translation with "all the large notes of Mr. J. Barbeyrac," etc., London: Printed for W. Innys and R. Manby, and others, 1738. A French translation by Jean Barbeyrac, professor of law at Groningen, "with the author's notes which had not yet appeared in French, and new notes by the translator," 2 vols., 4to, Amsterdam, 1724; a later translation into English by Whewell, 3 vols., 8vo, Cambridge, 1853; a German translation in J. H. v. Kirchmann's *Philos. Bibliothek*, 3 vols., 12mo, Leipzig, 1879.

In the formation of society, language — λόγος, rational speech — plays an important part, serving as a special means of communication between men. *Cf.* Aristotle, *Polit.* I., 2–18, 1253ª; Grotius, *De Jure Belli et Pacis*, Prelim. Disc. § 7: "A man grown up . . . has besides an exquisite desire of society, for the satisfaction of which he alone of all animals has received from nature a peculiar instrument, viz. the use of speech." — TR.

[1] Schaarschmidt states that "this earlier generally diffused view, that the apes had organs of speech — an opinion still at the present day firmly held by the negroes — has already been refuted by Peter Camper," 1722–1789, a distinguished Dutch anatomist and naturalist, in his *Natuurkundige Verhandelingen over den Orang-Outang en eenige andere Aapsoorten; cf.* p. 147 *sq.*, of the German translation by J. F. M. Herbell. Düsseldorf, 1791, 4to. The most important of Camper's works bearing on comparative anatomy, translated into French by H. C. Jansen, were published in *Œuvres de P. Camper qui ont pour objet l'histoire naturelle, la physiologie, et l'anatomie comparée.* Paris, 1803, 3 vols., 8vo. The piece referred to in this note is found in Vol. 1 of this ed. — TR.

could *speak*, *i.e.* make ourselves understood by the sounds of the mouth without forming articulate sounds, if we availed ourselves of musical *tones* for this effect; but more art would be necessary to invent a *language of tones*, whilst that of *words* may have been formed and perfected gradually by persons who found themselves in a state of natural simplicity. There are, however, people like the Chinese, who by means of tones and accents vary their words, of which they have only a small number. Thus it was the opinion of Golius,[1] a celebrated mathematician and great linguist, that their language is artificial, *i.e.* had been invented all at once by some clever man in order to establish verbal intercourse between the large number of different nations inhabiting this great country which we call China, although this language may now be found altered by long use.]

§ 2. *Ph.* [As orang-outangs and other monkeys have organs without forming words, we can say that parrots and some other birds have words without language], for we can train these birds and many others to form sounds quite distinct; but they are nowise capable of language. Man only is in a condition to avail himself of these sounds as signs of internal conceptions, in order that thereby they may be manifested to others.

Th. [I believe in fact that apart from the desire of making ourselves understood we should never have formed language; but being formed, it further serves man in reasoning within himself, both by the means words give him of remembering his abstract thoughts, and the benefit he finds in availing himself in reasoning of characters and surd thoughts; for he would require too much time. if he were obliged to explain everything and always to substitute definitions in the place of terms.]

§ 3. *Ph.* But as the multiplication of words would produce

[1] Jacob Gohl — Latin, Golius — 1596–1667, an eminent Dutch orientalist, who distinguished himself at Leyden University in classics, mathematics, and philosophy, was a pupil of Erpenius in Arabic, and in 1624 succeeded him as professor of Arabic at Leyden. In 1629 he returned from Asia Minor and the East, where he had spent four years, bringing with him a large and valuable collection of Mss. which he placed in the library of the university. His principal work, still to-day esteemed, is the *Lexicon Arabico-Latinum*, 1653, folio. — TR.

confusion in their use, if a distinct term were necessary to designate each particular thing, language has been further perfected by the use of general terms when they signify general ideas.

Th. [*General terms* serve not only for the perfection of languages, but they are necessary even to their essential constitution. For if by *particular things* we mean individual things, it would be impossible to speak if there were only *proper* names and not *appellatives, i.e.* if there were words only for the individuals, since at every moment something now presents itself (to the mind) when individuals, accidents, and particularly acts, which are most frequently designated, are in question. But if by particular things we understand the lowest species (*species infimæ*), besides the fact that it is difficult very often to determine them, it is manifest that they are already universals formed upon similitude. Then as the question is only of a similitude more or less extended, according as we speak of genera or species, it is natural to indicate every sort of similitude or agreement and consequently to employ general terms of all degrees; and indeed the most general being less burdened with relation to the ideas or essences they include, although they are more comprehensive in relation to the individuals to which they apply, were very often the easiest to form and are the most useful. Thus you see that children and those who know only little of the language which they wish to speak, or of the matter of which they speak, avail themselves of general terms as thing, plant, animal, instead of employing the proper terms which they lack. And it is certain that all *proper* or individual names were originally *appellative* or general.[1]]

[1] Leibnitz seems here to be in error in deciding from a logical or metaphysical point of view that language originated in or proceeded from general terms and relations rather than in those which are individual. In the order of experience the individual thing or relation is first, and first receives its name either wholly arbitrarily or by convention, or by this in combination with natural imitation or suggestion; the generalizing process and its result, the general name or term, comes afterwards. Children, it is true, use terms of general import, but with no consciousness that they are general. Everything is for them individual, particular, separate and by itself until continued observation and increasing knowledge enable them to detect similarities and differences and to classify and generalize accordingly. Then only do they, strictly speaking, possess or use general terms. — Tr.

§ 4. *Ph.* There are also words which men employ not to signify an idea, but the lack or absence of a certain idea, as nothing, ignorance, sterility.

Th. [I do not see why we could not say that there are *privative ideas*, as there are negative truths, for the act of denial is positive. I had already touched upon this.]

§ 5. *Ph.* Without disputing about this point, it will be more useful to approach a little nearer the origin of all our notions and knowledge, to observe how the words employed to form actions and notions wholly removed from the senses, derive their *origin* from sensible ideas, whence they are *transferred* to significations more abstruse.

Th. [The fact is our needs have compelled us to leave the natural order of ideas, for this order would be the same for angels, men, and all intelligences in general, and would have to be followed by us, if we had no regard for our interests. It has been necessary to attach thereto what the occasions and accidents to which our species is subject have furnished us; and this order gives not the *origin of the notions*, but so to speak the *history of our discoveries*.[1]]

Ph. [Very true, and it is the analysis of words which may teach us by means of the names themselves this concatenation which that of the notions cannot give by means of the reason, which you have brought forward.] Thus the following words: *imagine, comprehend, to attach, conceive, instil, disgust, trouble, tranquillity*, etc., are all derived from the operations of sensible things and applied to certain modes of thought. The word *spirit* in its primary signification is breath,[2] and *angel* signifies a messenger. Whence we can conjecture what kind of notions

[1] "The natural order of ideas," according to Leibnitz, proceeds from the general to the particular, from the abstract to the concrete, while language shows that "we have advanced from sense-impressions to abstract ideas," and thus "expresses not the *essence* of our knowledge, but only the history of its development. In a still broader sense the history of language is the history of the development of the human spirit in general."—TR.

[2] *Cf.* the Hebrew רוּחַ (Spinoza, *Tract. Theol. Polit.*, chap. 1, *Opera*, ed. Van Vloten and Land, Vol. 1, p. 384; English translation by Elwes, Vol. 1, p. 19); the Greek πνεῦμα from πνεῖν (Cremer, *Bib. Theol. Lexicon of N. T. Greek*, 2d English from 2d German ed., p. 504, Edinburgh: T. and T. Clark, 1878, says that as "*the element of life*" . . . "in a *physiological* sense, we often find it ('πνεῦμα') in profane Greek, especially in the poets and in later Greek: in a *psychological* sense, as the element of human existence and personal life, *never*"); and the Latin *spiritus* from *spirare*.—TR.

they had who spoke these first languages and how nature will suggest unexpectedly to men the origin and the principle of all their knowledge by the terms themselves.

Th. [I have already remarked to you that in the *credo* of the Hottentots they called the Holy Spirit by a term which signifies among them a breath of air benign and sweet.[1] The same is true as regards the majority of other words, and indeed the fact is not always recognized because most frequently the true etymologies are lost. A certain Dutchman, with little regard for religion, abused this truth (that the terms theology, ethics, and metaphysics are taken originally from gross things) in order to ridicule theology and the Christian faith in a little Flemish dictionary, in which he gave to the terms definitions or explications not such as usage demands, but such as the original force of the words seemed to bear, and put upon them a malicious interpretation; and as he elsewhere had given indications of impiety he is said to have been punished in the *Raspel-huys*.[2] It will, however, be well to consider *this analogy of sensible and non-sensible things* which has served as the basis of *tropes:* a matter that you will understand the better by considering a very extended example such as is furnished by the use of *prepositions,* like *to, with, from, before, in, without, by, for, upon, towards* (*à, avec, de, devant, en, hors, par, pour, sur, vers*), which are all derived from place, from distance, and from motion, and afterwards transferred to every sort of change, order, sequence, difference, agreement. *To* (*à*) signifies approach, as in the expression: I go *to* (*à*) Rome. But as in order to attach anything we bring it near that to which we wish to unite it, we say that one thing is attached *to* (*à*) another. And further, as there is, so to speak, an immaterial attachment, when one thing follows the other from moral reasons; we say that what follows the movements and volitions of any one belongs *to* (*à*) that person or adheres to him as if it gave signs to this person to go near it or with it. A

[1] *Cf.* Book I., chap. 3, § 8, Th. The Apostle's Creed, the Ten Commandments, and the Lord's Prayer in the Hottentot language, as sent to Leibnitz by N. Witsen, are given in Dutens, *Leibnit. opera omnia*, Vol. 6, Pt. 2, pp. 204–206. Schaarschmidt remarks that "this observation of both philosophers, that the meaning of words has proceeded and still proceeds from the concrete to the abstract, is the guide to sound etymology and word-explanation." — TR.

[2] Erdmann and Jacques have: "Raspel-huyss." — TR.

body is *with* (*avec*) another when they are in the same place; but they say also that a thing is *with* (*avec*) that which is found in the same time, in the same order, or part of an order, or which concurs in one and the same act. When we come *from* (*de*) any place, the place has been our object through the sensible things it has furnished us, and it is still in our memory, which is entirely filled with it; and thence it comes, that the object is signified by the preposition *of* (*de*) as in the expression, the question is *of* (*de*) that, they speak *of* (*de*) that, *i.e.* as if it arose from it. And as what is included in any place or in any whole is supported by and carried away with it, the accidents are in the same way considered as *in* (*dans*) the subject, *sunt in subjecto, inhærent subjecto.* The particle *upon* (*sur*) is also applied to the object; they say he is *upon* (*sur*) this matter, very much as a workman is *upon* (*sur*) the wood or *upon* (*sur*) the stone, that he cuts or forms; and as these analogies are extremely variable and do not depend on any determinate notions, it thence comes that languages vary much in the use of these *particles* and *cases* which the prepositions govern, or rather in which they are found as things understood and virtually included.]

CHAPTER II

ON THE SIGNIFICATION OF WORDS

§ 1. *Ph.* Now as words are employed by men as signs of their ideas, we may ask in the first place how their words have been determined; and we find that it is not by any natural connection existing between certain articulate sounds and certain ideas (for in this case there would be only one language among men), but by an *arbitrary institution* in virtue of which a given word has been purposely made a sign of a given idea.[1]

[1] For early discussions of the nature and origin of language, and the question whether words were given by nature or convention, *cf.* Plato, *Cratylus*, English translation by B. Jowett, *The Dialogues of Plato*, 2d ed., 1875, Vol. 2, p. 203 *sq.*; 3d ed., 1892, Vol. 1, p. 323 *sq.*, New York: Macmillan & Co.; Aristotle, *De Interpret.*, 2, 16ª, 19 *sq.*; E. Wallace, *Outlines of the Philos. of Aristotle*, 3d ed., § 11, p. 27. For modern discussions, *cf.* W. D. Whitney, *Language*

Th. [I know it has been customary to say in the schools and almost everywhere else that the *meanings* of words are arbitrary (*ex instituto*) and it is true that they are not determined by a natural necessity, but they are nevertheless determined by reasons sometimes natural, in which chance has some share, sometimes moral, where choice enters. There are perhaps some artificial languages which are wholly of choice and entirely arbitrary, as that of China is believed to have been, or as those of George Dalgarno[1] and the late Mr. Wilkins,[1] bishop of Chester. But those which are known to have been coined from languages already known, are from choice mixed with what there is of nature and chance in the languages they suppose. Thus it is in the case of those languages which thieves have coined in order to be understood only by those of their gang, which the Germans call *Rothwelsch*,[2] the

and the Study of Language, Lect. XI., p. 395 *sq.*, 4th ed., New York, 1869; B. Jowett, in his *Introduction* to Plato's *Cratylus*, *op. cit.*, 2d ed., Vol. 2, p. 189 *sq.*; 3d ed., Vol. 1, p. 281 *sq.*; H. Steinthal, *Einleitung in die Psychologie und Sprachwissenschaft*; Herm. Paul, *Principien der Sprachgeschichte*, Halle, 1880; B. Delbrück, *Einleitung in das Sprachstudium*, Leipsic, 1880, 2d ed., 1884. Leibnitz rightly points out that both nature and freedom of choice share in the formation of language. "Nature furnishes to a certain extent the material which the mind in its progressive self-absorption shapes within certain limits arbitrarily; and every human individual in the use of the language already formed is himself still so situated as to be able up to a certain point freely to appropriate and use that which is given." — TR.

[1] George Dalgarno, c. 1626–1687, published at London in 1661, his *Ars signorum, vulgo character universalis et lingua philosophica. Qua poterunt, homines diversissimorum idiomatum, spatio duarum septimanarum, omnia animi sua sensa (in rebus familiaribus) non minus intelligibiliter, sive scribendo, sive loquendo, mutuo communicare, quam linguis propiis vernaculis*, from which Bishop John Wilkins, 1614–1672, derived the idea of his *Essay towards a real character and a philosophical language with an alphabetical dictionary*. London, 1668. For Leibnitz's plan of a General Characteristic (*Characteristica Universalis — Spécieuse générale*) and the extent to which he followed Dalgarno and Wilkins, *cf.* Trendelenburg's paper: *Ueber Leibnizens Entwurf einer allgemeinen Charakteristik*, in his *Historische Beiträge zur Philos.*, Vol. 3, p. 1 *sq.*, Berlin, 1867; *cf.* also Gerhardt, *Die philos. Schrift. v. G. W. Leibniz*, Vol. 7, p. 3 *sq.*; Vol. 3, p. 216; Dutens, *Leibnit. opera omnia*, Vol. 6, p. 262. Dalgarno is credited with the invention of the first manual alphabet. His works were reprinted at Edinburgh, 1834, 4to. — TR.

[2] *Cf.* Avé Lallemant, *Das deutsche Gaunerthum*, 4 vols., Leipzig, 1858–1862, in which, says Schaarschmidt, "the so-called Rothwälsch, the artificial language of thieves in Germany, prominent already in the sixteenth and more so in the seventeenth century, is treated with especial thoroughness of detail. In this work it is shown that the Hebrew especially has contributed to the *Gaunersprache* a strong word-contingent, while its grammar is conformed to

Italians *Lingua Zerga*,[1] the French *Narquois*, but which they usually form upon (the basis of) the languages commonly known to them, either by changing the received significations of the words by means of metaphors, or by making new words by means of a composition or derivation in their own fashion. Languages are also formed through the intercourse of different peoples, either by mingling indifferently neighboring languages, or as most frequently happens, by taking the one as a base which is mutilated and altered, mixed and corrupted by neglecting and changing that which it observes, and even by grafting thereupon new words. The *Lingua Franca*, which is used in the commerce of the Mediterranean, is made from the Italian, and no regard is paid to the rules of grammar. An Armenian Dominican, with whom I conversed at Paris, had himself made, or perhaps learned from his fellows, a kind of *Lingua Franca*, made from Latin, which I found intelligible enough, although it had neither case, nor tense, nor other inflections, and he spoke it with ease, being accustomed to it. Father Labbé,[2] a French Jesuit, very learned, known by many other works, has made a language of which Latin is the base, which is easier and has less constraint than our Latin, but which is more regular than the *Lingua Franca*. He has made a book expressly of it. As for the languages which are found made a long time ago, there are but few which are not greatly

the German. In Italy the *Gaunersprache* bears the name Gergo, which corresponds to the French Argot. To what extent in Leibnitz's time attention was directed to the Rothwälsch the romance literature shows; but especially the *Gesichte Philanders von Sittewald*," a remarkable work, in which, under the name of Philander von Sittenwald, the author, Joh. Mich. Moscherosch, 1600–1669, a German litterateur, whose true name was Kalbkopf, has given a series of satirical pictures of the caprices and the vices of society in his time, and which placed him among the best prose writers of his century. It was published at Strasburg, 1644–1650, 2 vols., 8vo. — TR.

[1] Erdmann and Jacques read: "Gergo." — TR.

[2] Philip Labbé, 1607–1667, a learned French chronologer, a man of vast memory, astonishing erudition, and great mental activity; a voluminous writer, and though gentle in personal character, a fierce and abusive controversialist. Leibnitz mentions him in a letter, July 15, 1709, to Geheimrath von Ilgen; *cf.* Gerhardt, *Leibniz. philos. Schrift.*, 7, 36: "noch des P. Labbé (der die Lateinische mittelst einiger Veränderungen zur allgemeinen Sprach machen wollen)." He was the author of *Concordia chronologica, technica et historica*, 1656; but is chiefly known to-day by his work on Latin pronunciation, *Eruditæ pronuntiationis catholici indices*, enlarged by E. Leeds, and republished in London, 1751. — TR.

altered to-day. This is evident by comparing them with their ancient books and monuments which remain. The old French approached nearer the Provençal and the Italian, and we see the Théotisque[1] with the French or Romance rather (sometimes called *Lingua Romana rustica*) as they were in the ninth century after Jesus Christ in the forms of the oaths of the sons of the Emperor Louis le Débonnaire, which Nithard, their kinsman, has preserved for us.[2] We find little elsewhere of so old French, Italian, or Spanish. But for the Théotisque, or ancient German, there is the gospel of Otfried,[3] a monk of

[1] *Cf.* Grimm, *Deutsches Wörterbuch*, sub "Deutsch." — TR.

[2] For the text of these famous oaths, taken at Strasburg, Feb. 14, 842, *cf.* Nithard, c. 790–c. 858, *Hist.*, written, at the command of Charles the Bald, between 841 and 843, Bk. III., chap. 5, pp. 38, 39, ed. Pertz, and Pertz, *Monumenta Germaniæ Historica*, Vol. 2, pp. 665, 666, where they are preserved in the old Romance — *lingua Romana rustica* — and old German — *lingua Teotisca* — languages. *Cf.* also Dutens, *Leibnitii opera omnia*, Vol. 6, Pt. II., pp. 141–144, where "utramque formulam ('jurarunt *Ludovicus* Romanè, *Carolus* Teutonicè') eodem significatu, conceptis verbis ex *Nithardo* exhibebimus interlineariter colligatam, quia sibi verbotenus respondent, et ipso parallelismo illustrantur." The best edition for the study of the old German part of the oaths is in Karl Müllenhoff u. Wilhelm Scherer, *Denkmäler deutscher Poesie u. Prosa aus VIII–XII Jahrh.*, Denkm. No. 67, 2 Ausg. Berlin, 1873; 3 Aufl. bearbeitet v. E. Steinmeyer. Vol. 2 contains notes summing up the best results of critical study. Explanations of the old German text have also been made by J. Grimm, 1785–1863, in his *Kleinere Schriften*, Vol. 6, pp. 403 *sq.*, see also *Monumenta Germaniæ Historica*, Vol. 2, pp. 465 *sq.*; and by H. F. Massmann, 1797–1874, in his *Die kleinen Sprachdenkmale des VIII bis XII Jahrh.* Quedlinburg u. Leipzig, 1839. Fr. Ch. Diez, 1794–1876, "the real founder of Scientific Romance philology and linguistics," in his *Altromanische Sprachdenkmäler*, Bonn, 1846, has explained the Romance portion of the text, and gives, *op. cit.* pp. 3–5, a good portion of the literature on this interesting linguistic monument. The best textual notes on the Romance or old French part of the oaths are in W. Foerster u. E. Koschwitz, *Altfranzösisches Uebungsbuch*, Heilbronn, 1884; while the best facsimile of the whole fragment, both French and German, is the Album of the Société des anciens textes français (*Les plus anciens monuments de la langue française*), Paris, 1875. The old Romance text, the earliest specimen of French in existence, with a modern French translation, is found in Brachet, *A Historical Grammar of the French Tongue*, 6th English, from 20th French ed., pp. 17, 18, Oxford: Clarendon Press, 1884; while to these a Latin version is added for comparison in the article on the "Latin Language" *prope fin.*, in the *Encyclop. Brit.*, 9th ed., Vol. 14, pp. 340, 341 (American Reprint). — TR.

[3] The gospel of Otfrid, usually called the *Life of Christ*, was written in the South-Frankish dialect of the Old High German in 867 or 868, and dedicated to King Louis the German. Editions of it were published by Matthias Flacius Illyricus, 1520–1575, at Basle in 1571, 8vo, "a book as curious as rare," and by Schilter-Scherz in the *Thesaurus antiquitatum teutonicum*, Vol. 1. Ulmæ, 1727–1728, 3 vols., fol. These have now no critical worth, but merely an historical

Weissenburg of this same time, which Flacius has published and which Schilter[1] wished to edit anew. The Saxons who passed into Great Britain have left us books still more ancient. They have a version or paraphrase of the beginning of Genesis and of some other parts of the Sacred History, made by a Cædmon whom Bede already mentions.[2] But the most ancient book, not only of the Germanic languages, but of all the languages of Europe, except Greek and Latin, is that of the gospel of the Goths of the Pontus Euxinus, known by the name of *Codex Argenteus*,[3] written in characters entirely pecu-

interest and value. *Cf.* H. Paul, *Grundriss d. germ. Philologie*, II, 214, Strasburg, 1889—. It has also been edited by E. Th. Graff, Königsberg, 1831, 4to, an edition good in its day, but now antiquated; and more recently by J. Kelle, with grammar and glossary in 3 vols., Regensburg, 1856–1881; by P. Piper, Paderborn, 1878, containing the fullest critical apparatus; and by Erdmann, Halle, 1882, the most convenient. Piper has also published a student's edition, Freiburg, 1884; and Kelle a translation, *Christi Leben und Lehre besungen von Otfrid*, Prag. 1870. *Cf.* also W. Scherer, *Gesch. d. deutschen Lit.* 6th ed., pp. 48–51. Berlin, 1891; Eng. trans., from 3d Germ. ed., Vol. 1, pp. 44–46, New York, Chas. Scribner's Sons, 1886. To Otfrid is due, for the most part, the introduction into German poetry, in place of the earlier alliterative metre, of the rhymed stanza imitated from that of the Latin Church hymns. — TR.

[1] John Schilter, 1632–1705, a distinguished German jurisconsult and archæologist, Professor of Law at Strasburg, and author of the work referred to in note 3, *Thesaurus antiquitatum teutonicum*, which was edited, after Schilter's death, by Joh. Geor. Scherz, and is filled with documents of great value for the civil and literary history of Germany at the time of the Carlovingians. Schilter was led to linguistic studies through his legal and antiquarian investigations. *Cf.* Dutens, *Leibnit. opera omnia*, 6, Pt. II., p. 222, where Leibnitz remarks: "I am told that Mr. Schilter, of Strasburg, is none too well, and as he is an old man, I fear that his edition of Notger and Otfried will not appear. . . . Mr. Schilter makes use, moreover, of the Gothic Gospels of Ulfilas, of the Anglo-Saxon, and also of the Icelandic, as well as of other old books and glossaries; for we must unite the different dialects of all the Teutonic peoples in order to explain the old books." — TR.

[2] On Cædmon, died 680, *cf.* Bede, *Eccles. Hist.*, Bk. IV., chap. 24, pp. 217–220, 5th ed. (Bohn's Lib.), London: Geo. Bell and Sons, 1884; H. Morley, *English Writers*, Bk. II., chap. 4, Vol. 2, p. 71 *sq.*, London: Cassell and Co., 1888; B. Ten Brink, *Early Eng. Lit.*, trans. by H. M. Kennedy, pp. 39–48 and 371–386, New York: Henry Holt & Co., 1884; S. A. Brooke, *Hist of Early Eng. Lit.*, pp. 275–340, New York: Macmillan & Co., 1892. For the text of the poems ascribed to him, *cf.* Benj. Thorpe, *Cædmon's Metrical Paraphrase of Part of the Holy Scripture in Anglo-Saxon; with an Eng. Trans., Notes, and a Verbal Index*, London: 1832; C. W. M. Grein, *Bibliothek der Angel-Sächsischen Poesie*, 1857, Vol. 1; new ed. by R. Wülker, Vols. 1–3, 1883–1889, still in progress; the vol. containing Cædmon has not yet (1892) appeared; T. W. Hunt, *Cædmon's Exodus and Daniel*, Boston: Ginn & Co., 4th ed., 1889. — TR.

[3] The Codex Argenteus — Silver Codex — so called because written in silver and gold letters upon purple-stained vellum and bound in silver, as was the

liar, which was found in the ancient monastery of the Benedictines of Werden in Westphalia, and has been carried into Sweden, where it is preserved, as with reason it should be, with as much care as the original of the Pandects in Florence, although this version was made by the Eastern Goths and in a dialect far removed from the Scandinavian German; but it is because they believe, with some probability, that the Goths of the Pontus Euxinus came originally from Scandinavia, or at least from the Baltic Sea. Now the language or the dialect of these ancient Goths is very different from the modern German, although it has the same linguistic basis. The ancient Gallic was still more different, to judge by the language most nearly approaching the true Gallic, which is that of the country of Wales, Cornwall, and Basse-Bretagne; but the Irish differs therefrom still more and shows us traces of a Britannic, Gallic, and Germanic language, still more ancient. But all these languages come from one source, and may be

case with costly Mss. in those days, originally consisted of 330 leaves containing the Gospels in the following order: Matt., John, Luke, Mark, translated into the Gothic language, about the middle of the fourth century, by Bishop Ulfilas (Vulfila), 311–383. Only 177 leaves now remain. *Cf.* F. L. Stamm, *Ulfilas*, 1872, new ed. by M. Heyne, Paderborn, 1885, Einleitung, p. ix. The Ms., like all existing Gothic Mss., seems to have been written in Italy during the rule of the East Goths in the first half of the sixth century, and, after many adventures, was at last carried in 1669 to Upsala, where it now is. It is one of the few sources of our knowledge of Gothic, and, as Ulfilas was a fine scholar, and made his translation of the New Testament from the Greek original, with frequent comparison of the Latin versions, it is of some value in New Testament textual criticism. Editions of Ulfilas may be named as follows: The two earlier, by H. C. v. d. Gabelentz and J. Loebe, 3 vols., Altenburg u. Leipzig, 1843–1846, and H. F. Massmann, Stuttgart, 1855–1856, 2 vols. 8vo, rest upon still older single editions with many faults. *Cf.* H. Paul, *Grundriss d. germ. Philologie*, II, 69, Anm. 2. The critical editions of A. Uppström: *Codex Argenteus*, Upsala, 1854–1855; *Decem codicis arg. rediviva folia*, ib. 1857; *Fragmenta gothica selecta*, ib. 1861; *Codices gothici Ambrosiani*, Stockh. u. Leipzig, 1864–1868, in whose work for the first time was laid an entirely secure foundation for Gothic text-criticism, and upon whom the later editions rest. *Cf.* H. Paul, *op. cit.*; and Stamm-Heyne, *Ulfilas*, Einl. p. xi. The larger ed. of E. Bernhardt, *Vulfila, oder die gotische Bibel*, Halle, 1875, is the best for comparison with the Greek; while his smaller ed., *Die gotische Bibel des Vulfila*, Halle, 1884, and that of Stamm-Heyne cited above are the most convenient. The best introduction to Gothic in English is J. Wright, *A Primer of Gothic*, London and New York, Macmillan & Co., 1892. *Cf.* also W. Scherer, *Gesch. d. deutschen Lit.*, 6th ed., pp. 33–36, Eng. trans., Vol. 1, pp. 28–32; Waitz, *Das Leben des Ulfilas*, 1840; Krafft, *Kirchengeschichte d. Deutschen Völker*, Abth. I, 1854, and article "Ulfilas," in Herzog, *Realencyklopädie*, Vol. 16, 1885.—Tr.

taken as modifications of one and the same language, which may be called the *Keltic.* Thus the ancients called both the Germans and the Gauls *Kelts;* and in going back farther in order to understand the origin both of the Keltic and the Latin and the Greek, which have many roots in common with the Germanic or Keltic tongues, we may conjecture that this fact arises from the common origin of all these peoples descended from the *Scythians,* who, having come from the Black Sea, passed the Danube and the Vistula, and of whom one part may have gone into Greece, the other have filled Germany and the Gauls; a consequence of the hypothesis which makes the Europeans come from Asia. The *Sarmatian* (supposing it to be the Sclavonic) has at least half its origin either Germanic or common with the Germanic. The case appears to be somewhat similar, indeed, in the Finnish language, which is that of the most ancient Scandinavians, before the Germanic peoples, *i.e.* the Danes, Swedes, and Norwegians, had taken possession of the land which is the best and nearest the sea; and the language of the Finns or of the northeast of our continent, which is also that of the Lapps, extends from the German or Norwegian Ocean even to the Caspian Sea (although interrupted by the Sclavic peoples which have been thrust in between the two) and has some relation to the Hungarian, having come from the countries which are now in part under the Muscovites. But the Tartar language, which has filled the northeast of Asia, with its variations, appears to have been that of the Huns and Cumans as it is of the Uzbeks or Turkomans, of the Kalmuks and of the Mongols. Now all these languages of Scythia have many roots common among themselves and with ours, and it is found that even the Arabic (under which the Hebrew, the ancient Punic, the Chaldee, the Syriac, the Ethiopic of the Abyssinians are to be comprised) has so great a number of them and an agreement so manifest with ours that it cannot be attributed to chance alone, nor even to commerce alone, but rather to the migrations of the peoples. So that there is nothing in this to combat and not rather to favor the view of the common origin of all nations, and of a primitive root language.[1] If the Hebrew or the Arabic approaches the

[1] Leibnitz was the first who, from the point of view of a presentiment of the kindred connection, first of the European, and then of the remaining lan-

nearest to it, it must be at least much changed, and the German seems to have preserved more completely the natural and (to use the language of Jacob Boehme) the Adamic;[1] for if we had the primitive language in its purity, or sufficiently preserved to be recognizable, the reasons of the connections whether natural or of an arbitrary institution would necessarily appear wise and worthy of the primitive author. But supposing that our languages are derivative as regards their foundation, they nevertheless have something primitive in themselves which has arisen from them in relation to new root words[2] since formed among them by chance but upon natural grounds. Those which signify the sounds of animals or have come from them furnish examples. Such, for example, is the Latin *coaxare* attributed to the frogs, which has some relation to *couaquen* or *quaken* in German. Now it

guages, demanded and himself urged on the comparative study of languages, and in this, as in so many other things, was far in advance of his time. For his linguistic work, *cf.* Dutens, *Leibnit. opera omnia*, Vols. 5 and 6. — Tr.

[1] Jacob Boehme, 1575–1624, a celebrated theosophist, in whom Protestant mysticism reached its highest point. He is called *philosophus teutonicus*, and "in reality through him, for the first time in Germany, did philosophy come forward with a characteristic stamp"; Hegel, *Vorlesung. ü. d. Gesch. d. Philos.*, Vol. 3, p. 270, 2d ed., Berlin, 1833. O. Pfleiderer, *Religionsphilosophie*, Vol. 1, p. 20, 2d ed., Berlin, 1883, says, "The theosophy of Boehme shows itself as the direct forerunner of the metaphysic of Leibnitz, 1646–1716, Schelling, 1775–1854, Baader, 1765–1841, Schopenhauer, 1788–1860, etc." For his philosophy, etc., *cf.* his *Sämmtliche Werke*, hrsg. v. K. W. Schiebler, Leipzig, 1831–47, 2d ed., 1861 *sq.*; also Hegel, *op. cit.*, Vol. 3, pp. 270–297; Stöckl, *Gesch. d. Philos. d. Mittelalters*, Vol. 3, pp. 569–608, §§ 122–128; O. Pfleiderer, *op. cit.*, Vol. 1, pp. 15–23, Eng. trans., Vol. 1, pp. 13–23; B. Pünjer, *Gesch. d. Christ. Religionsphilos.*, 1880–83, Vol. 1, pp. 180–194; Eng. trans., Vol. 1, pp. 243–265, T. and T. Clark, Edinburgh, 1887. Vaughan, *Hours with the Mystics*, Vol. 2, pp. 79–125, 3d ed., London: 1879. According to Boehme, *cf. Das dreyfache Leben*, chap. 8, 2–4; *Princ.*, 10, 8–12; *Myst. Mag.*, chap. 15, 1–9, etc.; also Stöckl, *op. cit.*, §§ 125, 126, Vol. 3, pp. 586 *sq.*; Adam, who stands here in Leibnitz's text "as the symbol and representative of the original unity of the race," and of its language, "was destined to propagate his race in angel-like purity without endangering its integrity." Leibnitz, while acquainted with Boehme's writings, made little use of them in his own thinking, and speaks thus of them in a letter to Fr. S. Loeffler, Jan. 13, 1693, *cf.* Dutens, *op. cit.*, Vol. 5, p. 409: "The controversies over the opinions of Boehme I consider idle, and think that he neither understood himself nor have others understood him." — Tr.

[2] Gerhardt's text reads: "Qui leur est survenu par rapport à des mots radicaux nouveaux, formés depuis chez elles," etc. Erdmann and Jacques read: "qui leur est survenu par rapport à des mots radicaux et nouveaux radicaux formés depuis chez elles," etc.; *i.e.* new root words and new roots since formed among them, etc. — Tr.

seems that the noise of these animals is the primordial root of other words of the German language. For as these animals make much noise, the term is attributed to-day to idle talk and to babblers, who are called *quakeler* in the diminutive form; but apparently this same word *quaken* was formerly understood in a good sense and signified all sorts of sounds made with the mouth not even excepting speech. And as these sounds or noises of animals are an evidence of life, and as we know thereby before we see it that there is life there, *quek* in old German has come to signify life or living, as may be observed in the most ancient books, and there are also traces of the same in the modern language, for *Quecksilber* is quicksilver (*vif-argent*), and *erquicken* is to strengthen, and, as it were, to vivify or recreate after exhaustion or some great labor. Certain weeds are called also in Low German *Quäken*, alive so to speak and running, as they say in German, which spread and propagate themselves easily in the fields to the detriment of the grain; and in English *quickly* means promptly and in a wide-awake manner. Thus we may consider that as regards these words the German language may pass as the primitive, the ancients having no need to borrow elsewhere a sound which is the imitation of that of the frogs. And there are many others in which the same thing appears. For it seems that the ancient Germans, Kelts, and other peoples allied to them have employed by a natural instinct the letter R to signify a violent movement and a noise like that of this letter.[1] It appears in *ῥέω*, *fluo*, *rinnen*, *rüren* (*fluere*), *rutir* (*fluxion*), the *Rhine*, *Rhone*, *Roer* (*Rhenus*, *Rhodanus*, *Eridanus*, *Rura*), *rauben* (*rapere*, *ravir*), *Radt* (*rota*), *radere* (*raser*), *rauschen*, a word difficult to translate into French; it signifies a noise like that which the wind or a passing animal stirs up in the leaves or the trees, or is made by a trailing dress; *reckken* (to stretch with violence), whence it comes that *reichen* is to reach; that *der Rick* signifies a long stick or perch useful for suspending anything, in this kind of Plat-tütsch or Low Saxon which is (spoken) near Brunswick; that *Rige*, *Reihe*,

[1] *Cf.* Plato, *Cratylus*, 434 *sq.*; English Translation by B. Jowett; 2d ed., 1875, Vol. 2, p. 259 *sq.*; 3d ed., 1892, Vol. 1, p. 381 *sq.*, where the author has already made an attempt, similar to that made here and many times before by Leibnitz, to fix the original significance of single letters in the formation of words. — TR.

regula, regere, refer to length or a straight course; and that *Reck* has signified a thing or person very extended and long, and in particular a giant, and then a powerful and rich man, as it appears in the *reich* of the Germans and in the *riche* or *ricco* of the Semi-Latins. In Spanish *ricos hombres* means the nobles or chief men; and this makes it plain at the same time how metaphor, synecdoche, and metonymy have caused words to pass from one signification to another without our being able always to trace them. This noise and violent movement is noticed also in *Riss* (rupture) with which the Latin *rumpo,* the Greek *ῥήγνυμι,* the French *arracher,* the Italian *straccio* are connected. Now as the letter R signifies naturally a violent movement, the letter L designates a gentler one. Thus we see that children and others who find the R too harsh or too difficult to pronounce substitute for it the letter L, saying, for example, *mon lévelend pèle.*[1] This gentle movement appears in *leben* (*vivre* — live), *laben* (*conforter* — comfort, *faire vivre* — make live), *lind, lenis, lentus* (*lent* — slow), *lieben* (*aimer* — love), *lauffen* (*glisser promptement comme l'eau qui coule* — to glide quickly like flowing water), *labi* (*glisser* — to touch lightly, *labitur uncta vadis abies*[2]), *legen* (*mettre doucement* — to place gently), whence comes *liegen* (*coucher* — to lie down), *lage* or *laye* (*un lit, comme un lit de pierres* — a bed, as a bed of rocks), *Lay-stein* (*pierre à couches, ardoise* — slate), *lego, ich lese* (*je remasse ce qu'on a mis* — I collect what has been invested, it is the opposite of *mettre* — to place, and then *je lis* — I read, and finally among the Greeks *je parle* — I speak[3]), *Laub* (*feuille* — leaf), a thing easy to stir, to which are related also *lap, lid,*[4] *lenken, luo, λύω* (*solvo*), *leien*[5] (in Low-Saxon) to dissolve, to melt like the snow, whence the Leine has its name, a river of Hanover, which, rising in the mountainous countries, is greatly enlarged by the melted snows; not to speak of an infinite number of other similar appellations, which prove that there is something natural in the origin of words which indicates a relation between things and the sounds and move-

[1] *I.e.* "Révérend père." — TR.

[2] *Cf.* Vergil, *Æn.* 8, 91. — TR.

[3] Erdmann and Jacques omit: "Et puis je lis et enfin chez les Grecs je parle," the reading of Gerhardt. — TR.

[4] Gerhardt's reading; Erdmann and Jacques have "liel." — TR.

[5] Gerhardt's reading; Erdmann and Jacques have "lien." — TR.

ments of the vocal organs; and it is furthermore for that reason that the letter L joined to other nouns makes their diminutives with the Latins, the Semi-Latins, and the High Germans. But it must not be pretended that this reason can be noticed everywhere, for the lion, the lynx, the wolf, are anything but gentle. But it may be attached to another accident, the speed (*lauf*), which makes them feared or compels flight; as if the one who sees such an animal coming should cry to the others: *lauf* (*fuyez!*—fly!); besides by many accidents and changes the majority of words are very much altered and diverted from their pronunciation and original signification.

Ph. Yet an example would make it better understood.

Th. Here is one plain enough and which comprehends many others. The word *œil* (eye) and its parentage may serve us. To show it I will begin a little further back. *A* (the first letter) followed by a little aspiration makes *Ah*, and as this is an emission of the air which produces a sound clear enough at its beginning and then vanishing, this sound naturally signifies a light breath (*spiritus lenis*) when *A* and *H* are not very strong. Thence it is that ἄω, *aer*, *aura*, *haugh*, *halare*, *haleine*, ἀτμος, *Athem*, *Odem* (in German) have had their origin. But as water is also a fluid and makes a noise, it has come (it seems) that *ah* made rougher by doubling, *i.e.* *aha* or *ahha*, has been taken as water. The Teutons and other Kelts, the better to indicate the motion, have placed their *W* before both. Thence *wehen*, *Wind*, *vent*, indicate the motion of the air, and *waten*, *vadum*, *water*, motion of or in the water. But to return to *aha*, it appears to be (as I have said) a kind of root which means water. The Icelanders, who preserve somewhat of the Scandinavian Teutonic, have lessened the aspiration of some by saying *aa;* others, who say *Aken* (meaning *Aix*, *Aquae grani*[1]), have increased it, as do also the Latins in their *aqua*, and the Germans in certain places, who say *ach* in compositions to indicate water, as when *Schwarzach*[2] means black water, *Biberach* water of the beavers. And instead of *Wiser* or *Weser* they said *Wiseraha* in the old titles, and *Wisurach*[2] among the ancient inhabitants, of which the Latins

[1] *I.e.* Aquis Granum, Aix-la-Chapelle.—TR.

[2] Gerhardt's reading; Erdmann and Jacques read: "Schwartzach," "Wiserach."—TR.

have made *Visurgis*, as from *Iler*, *Ilerach*, they have made *Ilargus*. From *aqua*, *aigues*, *auue* the French have finally made *eau*, which they pronounce *oo*, in which there no longer remains anything of its origin. *Auwe*, *Auge* with the Germans is to-day a place which water often overflows, suitable for pasturage, *locus irriguus*, *pascuus*; but more particularly it signifies an island, as in the name of the monastery of *Reichenau* (*Augia dives*), and many others. And this (process) must have gone on among many of the Teutonic and Keltic peoples, for thence it has come that everything which is, as it were, isolated in a kind of plain has been called *Auge* or *Ouge*, *oculus*. Thus it is they name spots of oil upon water among the Germans; and among the Spaniards *ojo* is a hole. But *Auge*, *Ooge*, *oculus*, *occhio*, etc., have been applied more particularly to the *œil*, as it were, pre-eminently, which makes this isolated brilliant foramen in the countenance; and doubtless the French *œil* comes from it also, but its origin is not at all recognizable, unless by the concatenation I have just given; and the ὄμμα and ὄψις of the Greeks appear to come from the same source. *Oe* or *Oeland* is an island among the inhabitants of the North, and there is some trace of it in the Hebrew, where אי, *Ai*, is an island. Bochart[1] believed that the Phœnicians derived the name which he thinks they gave to the Ægean Sea, full of islands, from the same source. *Augere*, augmentation, comes also from *Auue* or *Auge*, *i.e.* from the effusion of waters, as *ooken*, *auken* in old Saxon was to augment; and *Augustus*, when speaking as Emperor, was translated by *Ooker*. The river of Brunswick, which comes from the Hartz Mountains, and consequently is much subject to sudden accretions, is called *Ocker*, formerly *Ouacra*. And I mention in passing that the names of rivers, having ordinarily

[1] Samuel Bochart, 1599–1667, an eminent French scholar and Protestant theologian, a distinguished orientalist, and a man of profound erudition, thoroughly familiar with all the principal oriental languages, including Hebrew, Chaldaic, Syriac, and Arabic, and so enthusiastic in linguistic studies that even when far advanced in years he desired to learn Ethiopic. His favorite study was Phœnician, and though modest and candid he seeks to derive all languages etymologically "from the Hebrew or Phœnician," a procedure which led him into many fanciful etymologies. *Cf.* Dutens, *Leibnit. opera omnia*, Vol. 6, Pt. II., pp. 223, 226. His complete works were published under the title, *Sam. Bochart, opera omnia*. Leyden, 1675, 2 vols. fol., 1692, 1712, 3 vols. fol. Leibnitz prized and often cited them. — TR.

come from the farthest known antiquity, show best the old language and the ancient inhabitants; hence they deserve particular investigation. And languages in general being the most ancient monuments of peoples, before writing and the arts, show best the origin of cognations and migrations. Hence etymologies much extended would be curious and significant; but it is necessary to unite the languages of many peoples, and not to make too many leaps from one nation to another far distant without having good verifications, in which process it is especially useful to have intervening peoples as guarantees. And in general credence must be given to etymologies only when there is a quantity of concurrent evidence; to do differently is to *goropise*.

Ph. To *goropise?* What does that mean?

Th. It means that the strange and often ridiculous etymologies of Goropius Becanus,[1] a learned physician of the sixteenth century, have passed into a proverb, although otherwise he may not have been excessively wrong in claiming that the German language, which he calls Cimbric, has as many, yes, more, marks of a primitive character than the Hebrew itself. I remember that the late Mr. Clauberg,[2] an excellent philoso-

[1] John Becan, 1518–1572, a Belgian physician and scholar, whose real name was Van Gorp — Latinized as Goropius Becanus. He practised medicine for some years at Antwerp, but finally gave himself wholly to the study of antiquity, belles-lettres, and ancient languages. In a public lecture at Liege, he attempted to demonstrate that the language of Adam was the Flemish or Teutonic, a view which he set forth at length in his *Origines Antwerpianæ sive Cimmeriorum Becceselana*, etc., Antwerp, 1569, fol.; and, as at that time he considered the Netherlands to be the site of Paradise, to derive language in general from the Low-German, which he calls the Cimbric, in his paper *Hermathena*, Bk. II., p. 25 *sq.* *Cf. Joannis Goropii Becani opera hactenus in lucem non edita; nempe, Hermathena*, etc., Antwerp, 1580, fol. — Tr.

[2] John Clauberg, 1622–1665, a German philosopher of the Cartesian school, who, first as a commentator merely and afterwards more independently, introduced and expounded the philosophy of Descartes in the universities at Herborn and Duisburg, where he was professor successively of theology and philosophy. He wrote a commentary on the *Meditations* of Descartes, and in his own speculations anticipated much of the subsequent development of Cartesianism. In his *De conjunctione animæ et corporis humani scriptum*, he maintained that bodily movements are antecedents only and not strictly causes of mental action, a view similar to that of Malebranche. He proposed for metaphysics the name Ontosophy or Ontology, a hint which Christian Wolf, 1679–1754, afterwards followed. *Cf.* Erdmann, *Grund. d. Gesch. d. Philos.*, §§ 268, 4, 290, 4, Vol. 2, pp. 33, 187, 3d ed., Berlin, 1878, and English trans. *ad loc.* His *Ontosophia, de cognitione Dei et nostri* appeared at Muhlberg, 1687,

pher, has published a brief essay upon the sources of the German language which makes one regret the loss of that which he had promised upon this subject. I have myself published some thoughts upon the subject, besides inducing the late Gerard Meier,[1] a theologian of Bremen, to work upon it, which he did till death interrupted him. I hope, however, that the public will yet one day profit from his labors as well as from the similar labors of Mr. Schilter,[2] a celebrated jurisconsult at Strasburg, but who also has just died. It is certain at least that the Teutonic language and antiquities enter into the majority of the researches into European origins, customs, and antiquities. And I wish that learned men would make as much of them in the languages of the Wallachians, Biscayans, Slavonians, Finns, Turks, Persians, Armenians, Georgians, and others, the better to discover the harmony which would particularly be of service, as I have just said, in clearing up the origin of nations.]

§ 2. *Ph.* [This design is important, but at present it is time to leave the *matter of words*, and to return to their *form*, *i.e.* to

1 vol., 12mo; and his *Opera philosophica* at Amsterdam, 1691, 2 vols., 4to. Leibnitz had a high regard for him, both as a philologist and philosopher, and in one expression apparently places him even above Descartes; "Cartesius voluit quædam emendare in physicis, displicet tamen audacia et fastus nimius conjunctus cum stili obscuritate, confusione, maledicentia. Longe magis mihi probatus Claubergius, discipulus ejus, plenus, perspicuus, brevis, methodicus." *Cf. Otium Hanoveranum*, ed. J. F. Feller, p. 181, Lipsiæ, 1718; Dutens, *Leibnit. opera omnia*, Vol. 6, Pt. I., p. 311. Leibnitz frequently mentions him and his works, particularly the *Meditationes et collectanea linguæ Teutonicæ*, Duisburgi, 1663, and the booklet *Ars etymologica Teutonum*; *cf.* Dutens, *op. cit.*, Vols. 5, p. 334; 6, Pt. II., pp. 28, 179, 220. In the *Ars etymol. Teuton.* Clauberg puts it forth as a fundamental proposition that the German must be explained as an original language. *Cf.* L. Neff., *G. W. Leibniz als Sprachforscher und Etymologe*, Pt. I., p. 16 *sq.*, Heidelberg, 1870. — TR.

[1] Gerard or Gerhard Meier or Meyer, who was incited by Leibnitz to the study of German philology, and collected an abundance of select materials for a *Grammatica Germanica* and *Glossarium Saxonicum*, but was prevented from completing the work begun by his early and sudden death; *cf.* Eccard, *Collectanea etymologica*, 2 vols., 8vo, Hannoveræ, 1717, Einleitung, p. 52, and Dutens, *Leibnit. opera omnia*, Vol. 6, Pt II., p. 145, note. Leibnitz states that the *Glossar. Saxon.* was planned and undertaken with his encouragement, and that it will contain much erudition; *cf.* Dutens, *op. cit.*, Vols. 5, p. 115; 6, 114, and note. For the correspondence between Meyer and Leibnitz, which exhibits Meyer's method in his etymological work, *cf.* Dutens, *op. cit.*, Vol. 6, Pt. II., pp. 145–176. Leibnitz says: "His learning and character are esteemed by all" — "Doctrina ejus, et virtus apud omnes in pretio habentur," Dutens, *op. cit.*, Vol. 5, p. 105. — TR.

[2] *Cf. ante*, p. 295, note 1. — TR.

the meaning which is common to the different languages.] Now you will agree with me in the first place, sir, that when one man speaks to another it is of his own ideas that he wishes to give signs; the words cannot be applied by him to things which he does not know. And until a man has ideas of his own he cannot suppose them to correspond to the qualities of things or to the conceptions of another.

Th. [It is true, however, that he intends very often to indicate what others think rather than what he himself thinks, as happens only too much in the case of the laity, whose faith is implicit. But I admit that he always means something general, however hollow and destitute of intelligence the thought may be; and he takes pains at least to arrange his words according to the custom of others, contenting himself with the belief that their sense can be apprehended at need. Thus he is sometimes only the interpreter (*truche-man*) of thoughts, or the bearer of the word of another, just as a letter would be; and indeed this is the case oftener than you think.]

§ 3. *Ph.* [You are right in adding that he always means something general, however idiotic it may be.] A child having noticed in what he hears called gold only a brilliant yellow color, gives the name of gold to this same color which he sees in a peacock's tail; others will add great weight, fusibility, malleability.

Th. [I admit it; but often the idea you have of the object of which you speak, is still more general than that of this child, and I doubt not that a blind person can speak pertinently of colors and make a speech in praise of the light which he does not know, because he has learned its effects and circumstances.]

§ 4. *Ph.* Your remark is quite true. Men often apply their thoughts more to words than to things, and because they have learned most of these words before becoming acquainted with the ideas which they signify, not only children, but also grown-up men often speak like parrots. § 5. But men ordinarily mean to indicate their own thoughts, and further they attribute to words a secret relation to the ideas of another and to things themselves. For if the sounds were attached to another idea by the one with whom we are conversing, it would be necessary to speak two languages. It is true that one does not stop too much to examine what the ideas of others are, and our idea is supposed to be that which the common people and the scholars of the country attach to the same word. § 6. This is particularly the case as regards simple ideas and modes; but as regards substances the belief is more particularly that the words signify also the reality of things.

Th. [Substances and modes are equally represented by ideas; and things, as well as ideas, in both cases are indicated by words; thus I see but little difference, save that ideas of substances and of sensible qualities are more fixed. For the rest, it sometimes happens that our ideas and thoughts are the matter of our discourse and constitute the thing itself which we desire to signify, and that reflective notions enter more than we think into those of things. We speak, indeed, sometimes of words in a material way, without in this case being able to substitute with precision in the place of the word its signification or its relation to the ideas or things.[1]

[1] Leibnitz here points out a source of manifold, far-reaching and influential errors, especially fatal in philosophy, viz. the hypostasizing of concepts, *i.e.* regarding and using universal thought-symbols as substances, a consequence of the excessive use of abstract terms. To these errors thus arising from the imperfection and abuse of words and their influence on the mind, Francis Bacon, 1561–1626, in his *Nov. Org.* Bk. I., Aphor. 43, 59, 60, gives the name of *idola fori*, idols of the market-place, and says they are "omnium molestissima"—"the most troublesome of all." These words are either names merely of non-existent things or of things supposed to exist because of these names, or are names obtained by "vicious and unskilful abstraction"—"mala et imperita abstractione"—from a few objects and indiscriminately applied to all other things having the faintest analogy thereto. The best ed. of Bacon's *Works* is that of Ellis, Spedding, and Heath, 2d ed., 7 vols., London: Longmans, 1870–72. The *Nov. Org.*, in Latin, is in Vol. 1, the Eng. trans. in Vol. 4 of this ed. Editions of the *Nov. Org.* (Latin) have been published with Eng. notes, and an Eng. trans. in a separate vol., by G. W. Kitchin, Oxford: Clarendon Press, 1855; and with Introd., Notes, etc., by Thos. Fowler, Oxford: Clarendon Press, 1878.

For Leibnitz's estimate of Bacon, whose *De Aug. Scient.* he mentions among the writings which happily chanced to come into his hands when a youth, and with others helped to direct his studies in the right path, whom he enumerates among "the founders of modern philosophy," and whose method he applied in his reform of the science of language, *cf.* Gerhardt, *Die philos. Schrift. v. G. W. Leibniz*, Vols. 1 : 196; 3 : 7, 16; 4 : 143, Erdmann, *Leibnit. opera philos.*, p. 61, b; G. 4 : 64, E. 23, a; G. 4 : 105, E. 45, a, also G. 7 : 325, E. 110, b; G. 4 : 337, 343; 7 : 52, 53, E. 91, b, 92; G. 7 : 67; 7 : 495, Dutens. *Leibnit. opera omnia*, 5 : 368; 6 : 303; G. 7 : 518, E. 421, a. *Cf.* also John Nichol, *Bacon*, Vol. 2, pp. 238–239 (Philos. Classics), Edinburgh: Wm. Black-

This occurs not only in speaking as a grammarian, but also in speaking as a lexicographer, in giving the explication of the term.]

CHAPTER III

OF GENERAL TERMS

§ 1. *Ph.* Although particular things alone exist, the largest number of words are *general terms*, because it is impossible, § 2, for each particular thing to have a particular and distinct name; besides the fact that in such case a prodigious memory would be necessary, in comparison with which that of certain generals who could call by name all their soldiers would be nothing. The matter indeed becomes infinite, if every animal, every plant, and even every leaf of a plant, every grain, in short every grain of sand, which might need a name must have its name. [And how name the parts of things sensibly uniform, as water, fire?] § 3. Besides, these particular names would be useless, the principal end of language being to excite in the mind of him who listens to me an idea similar to mine. [Thus the similitude suffices, which is indicated by general terms.] § 4. And particular words alone would not serve to extend our knowledge, [nor to make us judge of the future by the past, or of one individual by another.] § 5. But as it is often necessary to mention certain individuals, particularly of our species, use is made of *proper names;* which are given also to countries, towns, mountains and other distinctions of place. And horse-jockeys give proper names even to their horses, as well as Alexander to his Bucephalus, in order to be able to distinguish this or that particular horse when he is out of their sight.

Th. [These remarks are good, and some of them agree with those I was about to make. But I would add, in accordance with the observation I have already made, that *proper names have been ordinarily appellatives*, that is to say, general

wood & Sons, 1880. For a brief comparison of Leibnitz and Bacon and of their philosophies, *cf.* J. T. Merz, *Leibniz*, pp. 21, 71 (Blackwood's Philos. Classics), Edinburgh: 1884. — TR.

in their origin, as Brutus, Cæsar, Augustus, Capito, Lentulus, Piso, Cicero, Elbe, Rhine, Ruhr, Leine, Ocker, Bucephalus, Alps, Brenner or Pyrenees; for you know that the first Brutus had this name from his apparent stupidity, that Cæsar was the name of a child drawn by incision from the womb of his mother, that Augustus was a name of veneration, that Capito is a large head as also Bucephalus, that Lentulus, Piso, and Cicero were names given in the beginning to those who cultivated in particular certain kinds of vegetables. I have already said what the names of these rivers signify, Rhine, Ruhr, Leine, Ocker. And you know that all rivers are still called Elbe in Scandinavia. Finally *Alps* are mountains, covered with snow (with which agrees *album*, white) and Brenner or Pyrenees signifies a lofty pride, for *bren* was high or chief (as Brennus) in Keltic, as also *brinck* with Low-Saxons is pride, and there is a *Brenner* between Germany and Italy as the Pyrenees are between Gaul and Spain. Thus I would venture to say that nearly all words are originally general terms, because it will only rarely happen that an express name will be invented without reason to indicate one such individual. We can say then that the names of individuals were names of a species which was given *par excellence* or otherwise to some individual, as the name *large head* to that one of the whole city who had the largest or who was the most important of the large heads which were known. Thus it is indeed that we give names of genera to the species, *i.e.* that we shall content ourselves with a term more general or more vague to designate more particular species, when we have no concern for their differences. For example, we are contented with the general name, wormwood, although there are so many species of it that one of the Bauhins[1] has filled a book expressly with them.]

[1] Jean Bauhin, 1541–1613, a Swiss physician and naturalist, who devoted himself chiefly to botany, and with his brother Gaspard, 1560–1624, also a physician and botanist, was born at Basel, whither his father, an eminent French physician, had fled in exile because of his conversion to Protestantism. He studied with the celebrated botanist Fuchs at Tübingen, and after travelling and collecting plants in the Alps, in France, and in Italy, became, in 1570, physician to Duke Ulrich of Würtemberg at Montbeliard, where he remained till his death. The work of his to which Leibnitz here alludes is entitled *De plantis absinthii nomen habentibus.* It appeared at Montbeliard

§ 6. *Ph.* Your reflections upon the origin of *proper names* are very just; but to come to that of *appellative names* or general terms, you will doubtless agree, sir, that words become general when they are signs of general ideas, and ideas become general when separated by abstraction from time, place, or such other circumstances as may *determine* them to this or that particular existence.

Th. [I do not deny this use of abstraction, but it is rather in ascending from species to genera than from individuals to species. For (paradoxical as it may appear) it is impossible for us to have the knowledge of individuals, and to obtain the means of *determining* exactly the individuality of anything, at least of keeping it by itself; for all the circumstances may reappear; the smallest differences are to us insensible; place or time, far from determining themselves, need themselves to be determined by the things they contain. The most important factor in the problem is the fact that *individuality* includes infinity, and only he who is capable of comprehending it can have the knowledge of the principle of individuation of this or that thing. This arises from the influence (understanding it healthfully) of all things in the universe upon each other. It is true that this would be the case, if the atoms of Democritus existed, but in that case also there would be no *difference* between two *different* individuals of the same form and size.]

§ 7. *Ph.* It is, however, wholly evident that the ideas which children frame of persons with whom they converse (to confine ourselves to this example) are similar to the persons themselves, and particular only. The ideas they have of their nurse and their mother are very well traced in their minds, and the names *nurse* and *mamma*, which children use, relate only to these persons. Afterwards when time has shown them that there are many other beings resembling

in 1593. His most important work, composed with the assistance of his fellow-countryman and son-in-law Cherler, and containing descriptions of about 5000 plants with 3577 figures, is the *Historia universalis plantarum nova et absolutissima*, Yverdun, 1650–1651, 3 vols., fol. An abridgment of this great work was published by Chabrée, of Geneva, with the title *Sciagraphia*, 1666, containing in one volume all the figures, together with all of importance on the nomenclature and number of species in the great work. He was one of the founders of modern botany. — TR.

their father or mother, they form an idea in which they find that all these particular beings equally share, and they, as others, give it the name of man. § 8. They acquire in the same way names and notions more general; for example, the new idea of animal is not produced by any addition, but only by removing the figure or the particular properties of man, and retaining a body accompanied by life, feeling, and spontaneous movement.

Th. [Very well; but that shows only what I just said; for as the child advances by abstraction from the observation of the idea of man to that of the idea of animal, he has come from the more specific idea observed in his mother or father and in other persons to that of human nature. For in order to discern that he had not the precise idea of the individual, it is sufficient to consider that an ordinary resemblance would deceive him easily and make him take as his mother another woman. You know the story of the false Martin Guerre,[1] who deceived even the wife of the true, and the near relatives, by resemblance united with skill, and embarrassed for a long time the judges, even when the true Martin had arrived.]

§ 9. *Ph.* Thus this whole mystery of genus and species, which makes so much noise in the schools, but which outside of them is with reason so little regarded, this whole mystery, I say, reduces itself solely to the formation of abstract ideas more or less extended, to which certain names are given.[2]

[1] *Cf. Essais de Théodicée*, Discours préliminaire, § 42, Gerhardt, 6, 74, Erdmann, 491, b, Jacques, 2, 48. In the sixteenth century, Martin Guerre, a gentleman of Gascony, disappeared from home. After a long absence, a man by the name of Arnaud du Thil suddenly appeared, claiming to be Martin Guerre, and was acknowledged by the wife of Guerre as her husband. She had by him two children. Learning, afterwards, that her true husband was in Flanders, she angrily delivered the impostor into the hands of justice. The long trial, one of the most celebrated cases of the century, was brought to an end by the sudden and unexpected arrival of the true Martin Guerre, and Du Thil was sentenced to death. For further details, and the sentence in full, *cf.* P. Larousse, *Grand Dict. Universel de XIXe Siècle*, Vol. 8, p. 1603, b, c. A parallel case in recent times was the Tichborne trial in England. — TR.

[2] The philosophies of Locke and Leibnitz present a sharp contrast on the question of genera and species, and the real existence of the universal. According to Locke, the question is a wholly empty one, an inheritance from the unprofitable discussions of scholasticism. The general term, the universal, is a purely subjective product of the more or less arbitrary activity of man in abstraction, and has nothing whatever to do with reality. Leibnitz maintains that the universal is the inner essence of things, and that the formation of

Th. [The art of classifying things into genera and species is of no little importance and of much use both to the judgment and the memory. You know how important this is in botany, not to speak of animals and other substances, and without mentioning also beings moral and notional,[1] as some call them. Order largely depends upon it, and many good authors so write that their entire discourse can be reduced to divisions and subdivisions, according to a method which has some relation to genera and species, and is of use not only in retaining things, but also in finding them.[2] And they who have arranged all sorts of notions under certain titles or predicaments subdivided have done a very useful thing.]

§ 10. *Ph.* In defining words, we avail ourselves of the genus

general terms is not a mere thought-expedient, but a legitimate and proper apprehension of the true and the real. *Cf.* G. Hartenstein, *Locke's Lehre v. d. menschl. Erkenntniss in Vergleichung m. Leibniz's Kritik derselben*, V., pp. 52 *sq.*, also in his *Histor. Philos. Abhandl.*, Leipzig, 1870, pp. 162 *sq.* — Tr.

[1] Notional or conceptional beings, *begriffliche Wesen, entia rationis*, are those which, as Schaarschmidt says, "serve to indicate that which without being in the ordinary sense of the word substantial (first substance in the language of Aristotle," *cf. Categor.* 5, 2^a, 11; Wallace, *Outlines of the Philos. of Aristotle*, § 10, p. 25; Zeller, *Philos. d. Griech.*, II., 2 [Vol. 4], p. 304 *sq.*, 3d ed., 1879; but *cf.* also, *Metaphys.* VII., 7, 1032^b, 2; Wallace, *op. cit.* § 34, p. 67, Zeller, *op. cit.* II. 2 [Vol. 4], p. 344 *sq.*) "can still lay claim to an ideal reality." For further discussion of the subjects of this and the note next preceding, *cf. New Essays*, Bk. III., chaps. 5, 6, Bk. IV., chaps. 4, 6. — Tr.

[2] *Cf.* Gerhardt, *Leibniz. philos. Schrift.* 7, 67: "Fuere tamen autores non contemnendi, qui methodum rebus junxere ut Theodorus Zwingerus, Joh. Thomas Freigius, Barthol. Kechermannus, et diligentissimus Joh. Henr. Alstedius, cujus Encyclopaedia mihi pro captu illorum temporum laudanda videtur." Alsted, 1588–1638, was Professor of Philosophy and Theology at Herborn in Nassau, but applied himself chiefly to systemizing the several branches of art and science. His *Encyclopædia*, Herbornæ, 1630, 7 vols., fol., reprinted Lugduni, 1649, 4 vols., fol. Leibnitz often mentions it (*cf.* G. 4, 62, 74, E. 22, a, 28, b; Dutens, *Leibnit. opera omnia*, 5, 405, 567), and wrote down some thoughts — *cogitata quædam* — for its enlargement and improvement; *cf.* Dutens, 5, 183–185. The classified contents of the work are given in the article "Encyclopædia," in the *Encyclop. Brit.* 9th ed., Vol. 8, p. 176, b (American Reprint). Schaarschmidt states that the different works of R. Goclen, as well as those of Alsted, are of the kind alluded to in the text. Goclen, 1547–1626, was Professor of Philosophy at Marburg, and published a *Lexicon philosophicum*, Marburg, 1613, 1 vol., 4to, which, though of little value, enjoyed from its novelty considerable celebrity at the time of its appearance. Leibnitz refers to this work in his third letter to Clarke; *cf.* G. 7, 365, E. 752, b, J. 2, 426, D. 2, 122. Goclen was the 'discoverer and signalizer' of the Inverse, Regressive, or Goclenian Sorites, in comprehension; *cf.* Hamilton, *Lects. on Logic*, XIX., p. 273, Amer. ed., and *Goclenii Isagoge in Organum Aristotelis*, p. 255, Francof. 1598. — Tr.

or the next general term; and this is for the purpose of sparing ourselves the trouble of counting the different simple ideas which this genus signifies, or sometimes perhaps for the purpose of sparing ourselves the disgrace of being unable to make this enumeration. But although the shortest way of defining is by means of *genus* and *difference*, as the logicians say, it may be doubted, in my opinion, whether it is the best; at least it is not the only way. In the definition which states that man is a rational animal (a definition which is perhaps not the most exact, but which serves well enough the present purpose), instead of the word animal you might put its definition. And this shows the little necessity of the rule which requires that *a definition must be composed of genus and difference*,[1] and the little advantage there is in its strict observance. Thus languages are not always made according to the rules of logic, so that the meaning of each term may be exactly and clearly expressed by two others. And those who made this rule have done ill in giving us so few definitions conformable to it.

Th. [I agree with your remarks; it would be advantageous, however, for many reasons, if definitions might consist of two terms: it would without doubt greatly shorten them, and all divisions could be reduced to dichotomies which are the best species of divisions, and are particularly useful for invention, judgment, and memory. I do not, however, think logicians always demand that the genus or the difference be expressed in a single word; for example, the term *regular polygon* may pass as the genus of the square, and in the figure of the circle the genus might be a plane curvilinear figure, and the difference might consist in the fact that all points of the circumference are equally distant from a certain point as centre.[2]

[1] *Cf.* Aristotle, *Topica*, VI., 4, 141^b, 26: δεῖ μὲν διὰ τοῦ γένους καὶ τῶν διαφορῶν ὁρίζεσθαι τὸν καλῶς ὁριζόμενον, also I., 8, 103^b, 15: ἐπειδὴ ὁ ὁρισμὸς ἐκ γένους καὶ διαφορῶν ἐστίν, and Wallace, *Outlines*, §§ 14, 15, 25; Zeller, *Philos. d. Griech.*, II., 2 [Vol. 4], p. 255. — Tr.

[2] Leibnitz rightly takes exception to Locke's censure of Aristotle's rule regarding definition, given in the preceding note, viz.: that it must consist of the genus and the species-forming difference, remarking that genus and difference may very often be interchanged, the possibility of this interchange depending upon the principle on which, or the point of view from which, the classification is made, or upon the closeness with which the genus and the species-forming difference approach each other, it being essential to valid interchange that they be actually alike, or so nearly so that the difference is

For the rest, it is also well to remark that very often the *genus* may be changed into a *difference* and the *difference* into a *genus*. For example, the square is a regular quadrilateral, or rather a four-sided figure that is regular, so that the genus or the difference seems to differ only as the substantive and adjective; as if, instead of saying that man is a rational living being (*animal raisonnable*), language allowed the statement that man is a living rational being (*rational animable*), *i.e.* a rational substance endowed with an animal nature; while genii[1] are rational substances whose nature is not animal or common with the animals. And this interchange of genera and differentia depends upon the variation of the order of the sub-divisions.]

§ 11. *Ph.* It follows from what I have just said, that what is called *general* and universal belongs not to the being (*existence*)[2] of things, but that it is a work of the understanding, § 12, and the essences of each species are only abstract ideas.

Th. [I do not quite see this consequence. For generality consists in the resemblance of separate things among themselves, and this resemblance is a reality.]

§ 13. *Ph.* I was going myself to say to you that these species are founded upon resemblances.

Th. [Why, then, not seek therein also the essence of genera and species?]

§ 14. *Ph.* You will be less surprised to hear me say that these essences are the work of the understanding, if you consider that there are at least complex ideas which in the minds of different persons are often different collections of simple ideas, and thus what is *avarice* in the mind of one man is not so in the mind of another.

practically of no account. *Cf. New Essays*, Bk. III., chap. 3, *ante*, p. 308. Such definitions, while not strictly logical or scientific in the full sense of these terms, but tentative rather, and, as it were, popular, are nevertheless useful, and indeed necessary, in ordinary life and in science, where we must classify to a certain extent for the sake of relative clearness, but where strict logical definition is not essential, or is impossible because of the insufficiency of our knowledge. Logically exhaustive definition, save in the realm of pure thought and in such sciences as the pure mathematics, is possible only to an infinite mind who possesses exhaustive knowledge of all principles and facts involved. Exhaustive knowledge of an individual demands an exhaustive knowledge of all other individuals. *Cf. N. E.*, Bk. III., chap. 3, § 6, Th., *ante*, p. 309. — Tr.

[1] *I.e.* angels and archangels. — Tr.

[2] Locke has: "real existence," *Philos. Wks.*, Vol. 2, p. 14 (Bohn's Ed.). — Tr.

Th. [I admit, sir, that there are few cases in which I have less understood the force of your inferences than here, and this troubles me. If men differ in the name, does it change the things or their resemblances? If one applies the name avarice to one resemblance, and another to another, there will be two different species designated by the same name.]

Ph. In that species of substance which is most familiar to us and with which we are most intimately acquainted, it has many times been doubted whether the offspring brought into the world by a woman was a man,[1] even to discussing whether he should be fed and baptized. This could not be if the abstract idea or the essence, to which the name man belongs, were the work of nature, and not a diverse, uncertain collection of simple ideas which the understanding put together, and to which it attached a name, after having made it general by way of abstraction. So that at bottom each distinct idea, formed by abstraction, is a distinct essence.

Th. [Pardon me for telling you, sir, that your language perplexes me, for I do not see its connection. If we cannot always discern by the outside the internal resemblances, are there less of them in nature? When we doubt whether a monster is a man, we doubt whether it has reason. When we know it has, the theologians will order it to be baptized, and the jurisconsults, to be fed. It is true that we may dispute about the lowest species logically considered, which vary by accidents in one and the same physical species, or species by direct descent (*tribu de génération*),[2] but we do not need to determine these; we may, indeed, vary them infinitely, as is seen in the great variety of oranges, lemons, and citrons, which experts know how to name and distinguish. The same thing was seen in tulips and pinks when these flowers were in fashion. For the rest, the fact that men unite these or those ideas, or even that nature actually unites them or not, makes no difference as regards essences, genera, or species, since the question only concerns possibilities, which are independent of our thought.]

[1] *Cf.* Locke, *Philos. Works*, Vol. 2, p. 17, and note (Bohn's Ed.).—TR.

[2] *Cf. New Essays*, Bk. III., chap. 6, § 14, Gerhardt, 5, 288, line 14; Erdmann, 313, a; Jacques, 1, 234. The term "species," in Leibnitz's day, denoted not merely similarity of external form and characteristics, but more essentially the genetic relationship of common descent.—TR.

§ 15. *Ph.* The species of each thing is ordinarily supposed to have a real constitution, and it is beyond doubt that some real constitution must exist upon which every collection of simple ideas or qualities co-existing in this thing must depend. But as it is evident that things are ranked in *sorts* or *species* under certain names only as they agree with certain abstract ideas to which we have attached these names, the *essence* of each genus or species comes thus to be nothing else than the abstract idea signified by the general or specific name, and we shall find this to be the import of the word essence, according to its most ordinary use. It would not be a bad thing, in my opinion, to designate these two kinds of essences by two different names, and to call the one *real*, and the other, *nominal essence.*

Th. [It seems to me that our language makes extreme innovations in the method of expression. We have indeed spoken hitherto of nominal and causal or real definitions, but not within my knowledge of essences other than real, at least by nominal essences have not been understood false and impossible essences, which appear to be essences, but are not; as, for example, would be that of a regular decahedron, *i.e.* of a regular body comprised within ten planes.[1] Essence is at bottom nothing less than the possibility of that which we think. What we assume as possible is expressed by the definition; but this definition is only nominal when it does not express at the same time, possibility; for then we may doubt whether this definition expresses anything real, *i.e.* possible, until experience comes to our aid to make us know this reality *a posteriori*,[2] when the thing is actually found in the world: and this suffices for the defect of the reason, which made us know the reality *a priori*[2] by exposing the cause or the possible generation of the definite thing. It does not then depend on us to unite ideas as seems good to us; at least, this combination is not justified either by reason which shows it as possible, or by experience which shows it as actual, and consequently, also possible. In order the better to distinguish, also, essence and

[1] This figure is impossible, the only possible regular polyhedrons being the tetrahedron, hexahedron, octohedron, dodecahedron, and icosahedron.—TR.

[2] *Cf. ante*, p. 227, note 2.—TR.

definition, you must consider that there is only one essence of the thing, but that there are many definitions which express one and the same essence, as the same structure or the same city may be represented by different scenographies according to the different sides from which it is regarded.]

§ 18.[1] *Ph.* You will, I think, agree with me that the real and the nominal are always the same in simple ideas and in the ideas of the modes; but in the ideas of substances, they are always entirely different. A figure which bounds a space by three lines is the real as well as the nominal essence of the triangle; for it is not only the abstract idea to which the general name is annexed, but the essence or proper being of the thing, or the foundation whence proceed its properties, and to which they are annexed. But it is wholly otherwise as regards gold. The real constitution of its parts, upon which its color, weight, fusibility, firmness, etc., depend, is unknown to us; and, having no idea of it, we have no name that is its sign. Yet these are the qualities which cause the matter to be called gold, and are its nominal essence, *i.e.* which give it a right to the name.

Th. [I should prefer to say, in accord with received usage, that the essence of gold is that which constitutes it and which gives it these sensible qualities, which make it known and which make its *nominal definition*, while we should have the *real and causal definition* if we could explain this contexture or internal constitution. But the nominal definition is here found real also, not by itself (for it does not make known *a priori* the possibility or the genesis of bodies), but by experience, because we have experience of a body in which these qualities are found together: but without this we might doubt whether so much weight would be compatible with so much malleability, as it may be doubted, even at present, whether a glass malleable by cold is possible in nature.[2] I am not, for the rest, of your opinion, sir, that there is here the difference

[1] § 18, in Locke, *Philos. Works*, 2, p. 19 (Bohn's ed.); so Gerhardt: Erdmann, Jacques, and Schaarschmidt in his German translation, have § 19. — Tr.

[2] *Cf.* Pliny the Elder, 23–79, *Histor. Natur.*, Bk. 36, chap. 66; Eng. trans. (Bohn's Class. Lib.), Vol. 6, p. 381, London, 1857. "In the reign of Tiberius, it is said, a combination was devised which produced a flexible glass. . . . This story, however, was, for a long time, more widely spread than well authenticated" — "fama crebrior quam certior." — Tr.

between the ideas of substances and the ideas of predicates, as if the definitions of predicates (*i.e.* of the modes and the objects of simple ideas) were always real and nominal at the same time, and that those of substances were only nominal. I quite agree that it is more difficult to have real definitions of bodies, which are substantial existences because their contexture is less sensible. But it is not the same with all substances; for we have a knowledge of true substances or unities (as God and the soul) as intimate as we have of the most of the modes. Besides, there are some predicates as little known as the contexture of bodies; yellow or bitter, for example, are objects of simple ideas or notions (*phantasies*[1]), and yet we have only a confused knowledge of them.[2] The case is the same in mathematics, where one and the same mode may have a nominal as well as a real definition. Few people have clearly explained in what consists the difference between these two definitions which must distinguish, also, essence and property. In my opinion, this difference is that the real shows the possibility of the thing defined, and the nominal does not.[3]

[1] Schaarschmidt translates: "die Gegenstände einfacher Vorstellungen oder Phantasiebilder." — TR.

[2] *Cf. New Essays*, Preface, *ante*, p. 48, *ad fin*, and Bk. IV., chap. 6, § 7, Th. (2), *infra*, p. 458. According to Leibnitz, sense-knowledge is confused, and needs to be developed into clearness and consistency by the discriminative analysis and unifying power of thought. Phenomena such as colors, sounds, etc., the subjective counterpart or resultant of specific sense-energies, resist all further analysis, and while clear as wholes, are composite, insoluble, and so confused as regards their single elements. Such wholes admit only descriptive, not, strictly speaking, logical definition. *Cf. Med. de Cog., Ver., et Id. ad init.*, Gerhardt, 4. 422, Erdmann, 78, a, trans. Duncan, *Philos. Works of Leibnitz*, 27. — TR.

[3] *Cf. ante*, pp. 17, 201, and *Med. de Cog., Ver., et Id.*, Gerhardt, 4, 424, Erdmann, 80, b, trans. Duncan, *Philos. Works of Leibnitz*, 30; also G. 6, 405, E. 637, a, Dutens, *Leibnit. opera omnia*, 1, 439; 6, 44; G. 7. 194 and note. As the nominal definition explains a thing according to the name, we may have nominal definitions of objectively non-existent or of impossible things, as centaurs, griffins, or any of the creatures of the fancy or the imagination, or the decahedron mentioned in § 15, Th., of this chapter, *ante* p. 315. The real definition explains the thing to be defined by exhibiting its cause or generation, its rise out of its conditions, *i.e.*, its possibility; it is thus identical with the genetic definition, and Leibnitz accordingly calls it the causal definition, *ante* p. 316. *Cf.* also Dewey, *Leibniz's New Essays*, 210; Hamilton, *Logic*, 343; Trendelenburg, *Ueber d. Element d. Definition in Leibniz. Philosophie* in *Histor. Beitr. z. Philos.*, Berlin, 1867, Vol. 3, pp. 48–62. Trendelenburg calls special attention to the fact that Leibnitz, in *definition*, has in mind especially the analytical element, explaining definition as an unfolding of the concept,

The definition of two *parallel straight lines*, which states that they are in one and the same plane and will not meet although continued to infinity, is only nominal, for we could at once doubt whether that is possible. But when we have understood that we can draw a straight line in a plane parallel to a given straight line provided we take care that the point of the style describing the parallel remains always equally distant from the given line, we see at once that the thing is possible, and why they have this property of never meeting, which constitutes their nominal definition, but which is the sign of the parallelism only when the two lines are straight, while if one at least were curved, they might be by nature unable ever to meet, and yet not on that account be parallel.

§ 19. *Ph.* If essence was something else than the abstract idea it would not be ingenerable[1] and incorruptible. A unicorn, a mermaid, a perfect circle, perhaps do not exist in the world.

Th. [I have already told you, sir, that essences are perpetual, because here the question concerns only the possible.]

CHAPTER IV

OF THE NAMES OF SIMPLE IDEAS

§ 2. *Ph.* I confess I have always believed that the formation of the modes was arbitrary; but as regards simple ideas and those of substances, I have been persuaded that, besides possibility, these ideas should signify a real existence.

Th. [I see no necessity for it. God has ideas before creating the objects of these ideas, and nothing prevents Him from being able also to communicate such ideas to intelligent creatures: there is also no exact demonstration proving that the objects of our senses and of the simple ideas which the senses

or its resolution into several concepts equivalent to the one concept — "definire est explicare notionem, resolvere in plures notiones uni aequivalentes;" *cf.* Dutens, *op. cit.*, 4, 68: "definitio nihil aliud, quam accurata nominis explicatio est"; G. 4, 140, E. 60, b: "definitio enim nihil aliud est, quam significatio verbis expressa, sive brevius, significatio significata." — TR.

[1] Locke's word, *Philos. Works*, Vol. 2, p. 20 (Bohn's ed.). — TR.

present to us are outside us.[1] This fact has especial weight in the case of those who believe with the Cartesians and with our distinguished author, that our simple ideas of sensible qualities have no resemblance to that which is outside us in the objects; there would then be nothing requiring these ideas to be grounded in any real existence.[2]]

§§ 4, 5, 6, 7. *Ph.* You will grant me at least this other difference between simple and complex ideas, that the names of *simple ideas* cannot be defined, while those of complex ideas can be. For definitions should contain more than one term, each of which signifies one idea. Thus you see what can or cannot be defined, and why definitions cannot go on to infinity; a remark which no one, so far as I know, has up to this time made.

Th. [I have also made the statement in the brief *Essay upon Ideas*,[3] inserted in the "Actes de Leipzic" about twenty years since, that simple terms cannot have nominal definitions; but I have there added at the same time the statement that terms, when they are simple only as regards us (because we have no means of analyzing them so as to reach the elementary

[1] The demonstrability of the reality of that which lies at the basis of the phenomena of the senses is one of the most difficult problems in the theory of knowledge — *Erkenntnisslehre.* Leibnitz seems nowhere to have discussed the question, at least in this form, nor to have asked himself how, agreeably to his philosophical system, a knowledge of the reality of the external world could be demonstrated or a belief therein justified. So far as his system suggests any answer consistent with itself, that answer is found in his doctrine of pre-established harmony, in the consciousness of which we pass immediately from our inner representative world of ideas to belief in the reality of the external things thus ideally represented. This, however, like Descartes' attempt to bridge the chasm from the subjective to the objective by his doctrine of God's veracity, is mere assumption, not "exact demonstration." The problem belongs to both psychology and metaphysics, and is satisfactorily discussed and solved only when considered in these two aspects. Leibnitz was an idealist in psychology, and a realist in metaphysics, and never really harmonized or united these two points of view. For him, therefore, there could be "no exact demonstration" of the external reality of "the objects of our senses and of the simple ideas which the senses present to us." *Cf. Discours de Metaphysique*, §§ 26 *sq.*, Gerhardt, *Leibniz. philos. Schrift.*, 4. 451 *sq.*, E. Caird, *The Crit. Philos. of Immanuel Kant*, 1, 86–95. New York, Macmillan & Co., 1889. — Tr.

[2] *Cf. New Essays*, Bk. II., chap. 8, §§ 21, 24, *ante*, pp. 133–135; also Bk. IV., chap. 11. The constancy of sense-phenomena is the constraining reason for referring them to something real. *Cf.* Dewey, *Leibniz's New Essays*, 173 *sq.*; Gerhardt, *Leibniz. philos. Schrift.* 7, 319 *sq.* — Tr.

[3] *Cf. ante*, p. 14, note 2; p. 227, note 3. — Tr.

perceptions of which they are composed), as heat, cold, yellow, green, can receive a real definition which would explain their cause. Thus, the real definition of *green* is that of an entity composed of blue and yellow thoroughly mixed,[1] although green is no more susceptible of a nominal definition by which we may recognize it than blue or yellow. Terms on the other hand which are simple in themselves, *i.e.* whose conception is clear and distinct, cannot receive any definition, whether nominal or real. You will find in *this little Essay*, placed in the "Actes de Leipzic," the foundations of a large part of the doctrine concerning the understanding, briefly explained.]

§§ 7, 8. *Ph.* It were well to explain this point and to indicate what can be defined, what not. And I am tempted to believe that often great disputes are raised and much nonsense introduced into men's discourse from a failure to consider this matter. These celebrated trifles about which so much stir is made in the schools have arisen from the fact that no attention has been paid to this difference which is found in ideas. The greatest masters in the art have been constrained to leave the majority of simple ideas without defining them, and when they have undertaken to define them, they have not succeeded. What more superfine nonsense, for example, could the mind of man invent than that which is contained in this definition of Aristotle: *Motion is the realization of that which is possible so far as it is possible?*[2] § 9. And the moderns who define motion as passage from one place into another, merely put one synonymous word in the place of another.

Th. [I have already remarked in one of our past conferences that you consider many ideas as simple which are not so. *Motion* is of this number which I believe to be definable; and the definition which states that it is a change of place is not to be despised. Aristotle's definition is not so absurd as you

[1] This is true of pigments, but not of lights. Blue and yellow lights when mixed produce white light. — TR.

[2] *Cf. New Essays*, Bk. II., chap. 21, § 1, Th. *ante*, p. 174. For Aristotle's definition, *cf. Phys. Acroas.*, III., 1, 201b, 4: ἡ τοῦ δυνατοῦ, ᾗ δυνατόν, ἐντελεχεια φανερὸν ὅτι κίνησίς ἐστιν, 201a, 11: ἡ τῷ δυνάμει ὄντος ἐντελεχεια, ᾗ τοιοῦτον, κίνησίς ἐστιν, *Metaphys.* K, 9, 1065b, 16: τὴν τοῦ δυνάμει ᾗ τοιοῦτόν ἐστιν ἐνέργιαν λέγω κίνησιν, 23: ἡ δὴ τοῦ δυνάμει ὄντος, ὅταν ἐντελεχείᾳ ὂν ἐνεργῇ ἢ αὐτὸ ᾗ ἄλλο ᾗ κινητόν, κίνησίς ἐστιν, also 33; Wallace, *Outlines of the Philos. of Aristotle*, § 42, p. 77; Zeller, *Philos. d. Griec.*, 3d ed., 1879, II., 2 [Vol. 4], p. 350 *sq.*, with the notes. — TR.

think, this supposed absurdity arising from the failure to understand that the Greek *κίνησις* with him did not signify what we call *motion*, but what we would express by the word *change*, whence it comes that he gives it a definition so abstract and metaphysical, while what we call motion is called by him *φορά*, *latio*, and is found among the species of change (*τῆς κινήσεως*[1]).]

§ 10. *Ph.* But you will not apologize, at least, for the same author's definition of *light* as the action of the transparent.[2]

Th. [I find it, as you do, very useless;[3] and he makes too frequent use of his *action*, which does not tell us much. *Diaphanous* is for him a medium across which we can see; and light is, according to him, that which consists in the actual passage. Well and good.]

§ 11. *Ph.* We agree, then, that our simple ideas cannot have nominal definitions, as we cannot know the taste of pineapples by the accounts of travellers, unless able to taste things by the ears, as Sancho Panza had the power to see Dulcinea by hearsay,[4] or as that blind man who, having been heard to speak boldly of the brilliancy of scarlet, thought it must resemble the sound of the trumpet.

Th. [You are right; and all the travellers in the world

[1] *Cf. Phys. Acroas.*, VII. 2, 243ª, 6 *sq.*: ἐπεὶ δὲ τρεῖς εἰσὶ κινήσεις, ἥ τε κατὰ τόπον καὶ κατὰ τὸ ποιὸν καὶ κατὰ τὸ ποσόν, ἀνάγκη καὶ τὰ κινούμενα τρία. ἡ μὲν οὖν κατὰ τόπον φορά, ἡ δὲ κατὰ τὸ ποιὸν ἀλλοίωσις, ἡ δὲ κατὰ τὸ ποσὸν αὔξησις καὶ φθίσις, *Eth. Nic.* X., 3, 1174ª, 30: εἰ γάρ ἐστιν ἡ φορὰ κίνησις πόθεν ποῖ (Alex. Grant, *The Ethics of Aristotle*, Vol. 2, p. 324, line 17, 3d ed., London: Longmans, Green, & Co., 1874); Wallace, *Outlines*, § 42; Zeller, *Philos. d. Griec.*, 3d ed., 1879, II., 2 [Vol. 4], p. 389 *sq.*—Tr.

[2] *Cf. De Anima*, II., 7, 418ᵇ, 9: φῶς δέ ἐστιν ἡ τούτου ἐνέργεια τοῦ διαφανοῦς ᾗ διαφανές, 419ª, 11: ἡ δ' ἐντελέχεια τοῦ διαφανοῦς φῶς ἐστίν. E. Wallace, *Aristotle's Psychology in Greek and English w. Introd. and Notes*, Cambridge: Univ. Press, 1882, pp. 95, 97, translates the two passages: "Light then is the expression of the pellucid *qua* pellucid," "The full play of this pellucid constitutes light," and, in his Introd., p. lxxi., combines them thus: "Light therefore may itself be defined as the actual expression or full play of the pellucid as pellucid." *Cf.* also Zeller, *Philos. d. Griec.*, 3d ed., 1879, II., 2 [Vol. 4], p. 477, note 2.

[3] Schaarschmidt calls attention to "a bad typographical error" in the text of Raspe's edition of the *Nouveaux Essais* at this point. Raspe reads "fort utile," for which Schaarschmidt proposes "futile." Gerhardt, Erdmann, and Jacques all read "fort inutile," which gives the requisite sense, and is accordingly followed in the translation.—Tr.

[4] *Cf.* Cervantes, 1547–1616, *Don Quixote*, Pt. 2, chap. 9, *ad med.*; also, Pt. 1, chap. 31.—Tr.

could not give by their words what we owe to a gentleman of this country who cultivates successfully pine-apples three leagues from Hannover, almost upon the bank of the Weser, and who has found means of multiplying them to such an extent that some day we can perhaps have them of our own growing in as great abundance as the oranges of Portugal, though there would apparently be some loss in the flavor.]

§§ 12, 13. *Ph.* It is wholly otherwise with complex ideas. A blind man can understand what a statue is; and a man who had never seen the rainbow could understand what it is, provided he had seen the colors which compose it. § 15. But though simple ideas are inexplicable, they are the least doubtful. [For experience accomplishes more than definition.]

Th. [There is, however, some difficulty as to the ideas which are only simple as regards us. For example, it would be difficult to indicate precisely the limits of blue and of green, and in general to discriminate colors closely approaching one another, while we can have precise notions of the terms used in arithmetic and geometry.]

§ 16. *Ph.* Simple ideas have further this peculiarity that they have very little subordination in what the logicians call the *line of predication* (*ligne prédicamentale*),[1] from the lowest

[1] Leibnitz here refers to the *Tabula logica*, in which Porphyry, 233–304, and after him the Scholastic logicians, such as Lambert of Auxerre, c. 1250, Petrus Hispanus, c. 1226–1277, Raimund Lulli, 1234–1315, the Pseudo-Thomas, and Johannes Majoris Scotus, 1478–1540, sought, in connection with the five predicables, to arrange in strict logical subordination by the process of dichotomic or bifurcate division, all genera and species from the highest genera to the lowest species, between which is found the scale of subordinate notions which are at the same time both genus and species. This *Tabula logica* was called by the later commentators, who added the diagram illustrating it, not found in Porphyry, the *arbor Porphyriana* or the *arbor praedicamentalis*, and the line of subordination from the highest genus to the lowest species was called the *linea praedicamentalis* or *praedicabilis*, or the *ordo praedieamentalis*. *Cf.* Porphyry, Εἰσαγωγή chap. 2, 1 b. 40 *sq.* (in Aristotle, ed. Berl. Acad., Vol. 4, p. 1); Ἐξήγησις, f. 18 b., Paris, 1543, 4to; Prantl, *Gesch. d. Logik im Abendlande*, Leipzig, 1855–1870, Vol. 1, pp. 627–8, note 41, 633–4, note 67, Vol. 3, pp. 28, note 14: "Praedicamentum autem nihil aliud est, quam ordinatio praedicabilium in linea praedicabile secundum sub et supra et a latere et in linea recta, . . . unde illa tota ordinatio, quae est inter genus generalissimum et speciem specialissimam et genera subalterna et differentias collaterales, vocatur unum praedicamentum, sicut patet in arbore Porphyrii in tractatu Praedicabilium." (Lambert of Auxerre, *Summa logicae*, Paris, MS., *Cod. Sorbonn.* 1797), 46, note 168, 151, note 42, 252, note 315, *cf.* n. 311, Vol. 4, p. 249, note 434; also, Jevons, *Elementary Lessons in Logic*, p. 103 *sq.* — Tr.

species to the highest genus. The reason is that the lowest species being only a simple idea, nothing can be taken from it; for example, nothing can be taken from the ideas of white and red in order to retain the common appearance in which they agree. For this reason, they are included with yellow and others, under the genus or the name, *color*. And when men wish to frame a still more general term, comprising, also, sounds, tastes, and tangible qualities, they avail themselves of the general term, *quality*, in the sense ordinarily given it to distinguish these qualities of extension, number, motion, pleasure, and pain, which act upon the mind and introduce into it their ideas by more than one sense.

Th. [I have something more to say upon this remark. I hope that here and elsewhere you will do me the justice, sir, to believe that this is not from a spirit of contradiction, and that the subject seems to demand it. It is not an advantage that the ideas of sensible qualities have so little subordination and are capable of so few subdivisions; for it arises only from the fact that we know little of them. But the fact itself that all colors have the common property of being seen by the eyes, of all passing into bodies from which one or more of them reappear, and of being reflected from the polished surfaces of bodies which do not allow them to pass, shows us that something can be taken from the ideas we have of them. Colors may indeed be divided with good reason into *extremes* (one of which is *positive*, viz. white; and the other *privative*, viz. black); and into *means*, which are called *colors*,[1] however, in a particular sense, and which spring from light by refraction; which furthermore may be subdivided into those of the convex side, and those of the concave side of the broken ray. And these divisions and subdivisions are of not a little consequence.]

Ph. But how can you find genera in simple ideas?

Th. [As they are simple only in appearance, they are accompanied by circumstances which are bound up with them,

[1] Gerhardt reads: "et en moyens qu'on appelle encor couleurs dans un sens particulier et qui naissent de la lumiere par la refraction; qu'on peut encor," etc.; Erdmann and Jacques read: "et en moyens qu'on appelle encore sous-diviser," etc.; *i.e.* and into means which you are further called upon to subdivide, etc. — TR.

although this bond is not understood by us, and these circumstances furnish somewhat that is explicable and susceptible of analysis, which gives also some hope that hereafter the reasons of these phenomena may be discovered. Thus it happens that there is a kind of *pleonasm* in our perceptions of sensible qualities, as well as sensible masses; and this pleonasm is, that we have more than one notion of the same subject. Gold may be defined nominally in several ways; you may say that it is the heaviest of our bodies, that it is the most malleable, that it is a fusible body which resists the cupel and aqua fortis, etc. Each of these marks is good and is sufficient for the recognition of gold, at least provisionally and in the present state of our bodies, until a heavier body is found, as some chemists maintain is the case in their philosopher's stone, or until that *Luna fixa*[1] is shown, which is a metal said to have the color of silver, and almost all the other qualities of gold, and which Chevalier Boyle[2] seems to say he has produced. Thus you may say that in matters which we know only empirically, all our definitions are merely provisional, as I believe I have already remarked above. It is then true that we do not know demonstratively whether a color may not pos-

[1] *Cf. Fratris Basilii Valentini Benedictiner Ordens Chymische Schrift.*, Hamburg, 1700, Pt. I., p. 272: "Wenn das Gold seiner *Anima* auch verlustig wird / giebt es ein weiss *Corpus* und einen fixen weissen Gold-Leib / der von den suchenden Studenten / und von den Jüngern der Kunst eine *Luna fixa* getaufft und genannt wird;" Pt. II., p. 381, Schluss-Reden Fr. Basilii Valentini, Tract. 1, Sectio iii., De Magneta vulgi, § 3: "Mit dem Magnet und Antimonio wird auch eine *Luna fixa* gemacht / welche alsdann durch das *Oleum Martis & Veneris gradirt* [*sic*], und zu Gold gemacht wird: Jedoch kan mans mit Antimonio und Eisen auch verrichten." Martin Ruland, *Lexicon alchemiæ*, Francofurti, 1612, p. 308: "Luna compacta est argentum fixum vel aurum album: Silber fix oder weiss Gold." Robert Boyle, *Works*, ed. Birch, 5 vols., fol.: London, 1744, Vol. 1, p. 215; 2d ed., 6 vols., 4to: London, 1772, Vol. 1, p. 335, Vol. 3, p. 28.—TR.

[2] Robert Boyle, 1627–1691, a distinguished natural philosopher and chemist, the discoverer of the law of the compressibility of gases, which, confirmed by its independent discovery by Mariotte in 1676, has since been known as "Boyle and Mariotte's Law." He was one of the founders of the Royal Society of London, and by his will established the "Boyle Lectures." Leibnitz often refers to him, *cf. New Essays*, Preface, *ante*, p. 47.—The title of Boyle's work there referred to is, *Of Absolute Rest in Bodies*, *Works*, ed., Birch, 6 vols., 4to, London, 1772, Vol. 1, pp. 443–457, in which he opposes the doctrine with convincing reasons;—Bk. IV., chap. 12, § 13, Th., *infra*, p. 526; Gerhardt, *Leibniz philos. Schrift.*, 7, 342; Dutens, *Leibnit op. om.*, 5, 98; 6, 107; Leibnitz's estimate of his experiments, 6, 318; Eulogy, 6, Pt. II., 217.—TR.

sibly be produced by reflection alone without refraction, and whether the colors we have hitherto noticed in the concavity of the angle of ordinary refraction are not found in the convexity of a kind of refraction hitherto unknown, and *vice versa.* Thus the simple idea of blue would be stripped of the genus which we have assigned it in our experiences. But it is well to stop at the blue we have and at the circumstances attending it. And it is something that they furnish us the means of making genera and species.]

§ 17. *Ph.* But what say you of the remark that has been made that simple ideas, since they are taken from the existence of things, are nowise arbitrary, while those of the mixed modes are wholly so, and those of substances to some extent?

Th. [I believe that the arbitrary quality is found only in the words, and not at all in the ideas. For they express only possibilities. Thus, if there had never been a parricide, and if all the legislators had been as cautious as Solon in speaking of it, parricide would be a possible crime, and its idea would be real. For ideas are in God from all eternity; and indeed they are in us before we actually think of them, as I have shown in our previous conversations.[1] If any one wishes to take them as the actual thoughts of men, it is permitted him to do so, but he will oppose himself without reason to the accepted language.

CHAPTER V

OF THE NAMES OF MIXED MODES AND RELATIONS

§§ 2, 3, *seq.* *Ph.* But does not the mind form mixed ideas by bringing together simple ideas as suits its purpose, without the need of a real model; while simple ideas arise for it

[1] *Cf. New Essays*, Preface, *ante*, p. 42, *sq.*, Bk. I., chap. 1, § 1, *sq.*, *ante*, p. 70, *sq.*, where Leibnitz develops more fully the thought repeated here. Leibnitz assumes that ideas — the pure truths of reason — exist in man, and come into consciousness by the self-development of the spirit. These ideas contain in themselves the potential representation of all possible reality, the realization of which is directly proportional to the measure of man's self-development. In God this realization is complete, since in his thought all real possibility is always actually represented. — TR.

without choice, through the real existence of things? Is not the mixed idea often seen before the existing thing?

Th. If you take the ideas as actual thoughts, you are right. But I do not see that it is necessary to apply your distinction to that which concerns the form itself, or the possibility of these thoughts, and yet this is the question in the ideal world which is distinguished from the existing world. The real existence of beings which are not at all necessary is a matter of fact or of history; but the knowledge of possibilities and necessities (for *necessary* is that the opposite of which is not at all *possible*) constitutes the demonstrative sciences.[1]]

Ph. But is there more connection between the ideas of *killing* and of *man* than between the ideas of killing and of a sheep? Is parricide composed of more connected notions than infanticide? And is it more natural that what the English call *stabbing*, *i.e.*, murder by a thrust, or by striking with the point, which is a greater wrong with them than killing by striking with the edge of the sword, should have deserved a name and an idea which is not accorded, for example, to the act of killing a sheep, or of killing a man by cutting?

Th. [If the question concerns only possibilities, all these ideas are equally natural. Those who have seen sheep killed have had an idea of this act in thought, although they have not deigned to give it their attention.[2] Why, then, limit ourselves to names, when the question concerns ideas themselves, and why occupy ourselves with the worth of the ideas of the mixed modes, when the question concerns these ideas in general?]

§ 8. *Ph.* Men form arbitrarily different kinds of mixed modes, so that words are found in one language for which there are no corresponding words in another. There are no words in other languages corresponding to the word *Versura*[3]

[1] *Cf. New Essays*, Preface, *ante*, p. 43.—TR.

[2] Erdmann reads: "quoiqu'ils ne lui aient point donné de nom et ne l'aient point daigné de leur attention;" Jacques reads, after "daigné," "honorer," otherwise like Erdmann. The rendering then is: although they have not given it a name, nor have they vouchsafed (to honor—Jacques) it (with) their attention.—TR.

[3] "Versura," literally "a turning round," means, in classical usage, "the borrowing of money to pay a debt," a process which resulted simply in changing one's creditor, not in extinguishing the obligation. *Cf.* Cicero, *Epist.*

used among the Romans, nor to *Corban*,[1] used by the Jews. We boldly translate the Latin words *hora*, *pes*, and *libra*, by hour, foot, and pound; but the ideas of the Romans were very different from ours.

Th. I see that many things which we discussed when the question was that of ideas themselves and their kinds, come back now, under cover of the names of these ideas. The statement is true as regards the names and the customs of men, but it changes nothing in the sciences and in the nature of things. It is true that he who would write a universal grammar would do well to pass from the essence of languages to their existence, and compare the grammars of many languages. In like manner, an author who should write a universal jurisprudence drawn from reason, would do well to unite with it the parallel laws and customs of peoples, which would be of service not only in practical life, but also in his reflections, and would give him occasion to consider many points which would otherwise escape him. But in science itself, apart from its history or existence, it is of no consequence whether people are or are not conformed to the dictates of reason.]

§ 9. *Ph.* The doubtful signification of the word *species* makes the statement that the species of mixed modes are made by the understanding offensive to some people. But I leave it to others to consider who fixes the limits of each *sort* or *species*, for these two words are for me wholly synonymous.

ad Atticum, 5, 15, 2; Tacitus, *Ann.*, 6, 16. As a proverb, the word means "to get out of one difficulty by getting into another." *Cf.* Terence, *Phormio*, 5, 2, 15; Lactantius, 2, 8, 24. — TR.

[1] "Corban," Hebrew קָרְבָּן. N.T. *κορβᾶν*, *i.e.* *δῶρον*, originally an offering to God of any kind, particularly in fulfilment of a vow. The original use was in course of time altered by the traditionalists, and the offerer of the gift interdicted from using it for himself, or giving it to others. The "corban" furnished a ready means to any one who wished to relieve himself from any inconvenient obligation, as of assisting his parents in poverty or distress: he simply brought his gift to the temple and offered it to God, saying, "Let it be corban," and departed free, as he said, from any further responsibility in the matter. It was this utter perversion of the spirit of the law, with its resultant positive wrong-doing, that Christ so severely rebuked. *Cf.* Mark 7:11–13; Matt. 15:5, 6; and H. A. W. Meyer, *Krit. Exeg. Kommentar ü. d. N.T.*, 6th ed., Göttingen, 1876 — I., 2 [Vol. 2], p. 104; I., 1 [Vol. 1], p. 333; *Smith's Dict. of the Bible*, ed. Hackett and Abbot, New York, 1877, Vol. 1, p. 491. — TR.

Th. [The nature of things ordinarily fixes the limits of species; for example, of man and beast, of cut and thrust. I admit, however, that there are some notions in which the limit is truly arbitrary; for example, the question of determining a foot, for, the straight line being uniform and indefinite, nature indicates therein no limits. There are also essences, vague and imperfect, into which opinion enters; as when you ask how little hair must be allowed a man in order that he be not bald. This was one of the sophisms of the ancients, when one pressed upon his adversary:

Dum cadat elusus ratione ruentis acervi.[1]

But the true answer is that nature has not determined this notion, and that the opinion has its share therein that there are some persons regarding whom it may be questioned whether they are bald or not, and that there are some doubtful persons who will pass as bald with some and not with others, as you remarked that a horse which will be considered small in Holland, will pass as a large one in the country of the Gauls. There is indeed something of this nature in simple ideas, for I just observed that the final limits of colors are doubtful. There are also *essences* truly *half-nominal*, in which the name enters into the definition of the thing; for example, the degree or quality of doctor, chevalier, ambassador, king, is recognized when a person has acquired the recognized right to avail himself of this name. And a foreign minister, however complete his power and however extended his train, will not pass as an *ambassador* unless his letter of credence gives him the name. But these *essences* and *ideas* are *vague, doubtful, arbitrary, nominal*, in a sense a little different from those which you have mentioned.]

§ 10. *Ph.* But it seems that the name often conserves the essences of the mixed modes which you think are not arbitrary; for example, without the name *triumph*, we should have but little idea of what took place among the Romans upon that occasion.

Th. [I agree that the name serves to call attention to things and to conserve the memory and the actual knowledge of them;

[1] Horace, *Epist.* 2, 1, 47.—TR.

but that accomplishes nothing as regards the point in question, nor does it render the essences nominal; and I do not understand why you gentlemen absolutely require that the essences themselves should depend upon the choice of names. It would have been desirable that your distinguished author, instead of insisting upon that, had preferred to enter into a much more detailed account of ideas and of modes, and to have set them in order and developed the varieties. I would have followed him on this road with pleasure and with profit. For he would doubtless have given us much light.]

§ 12. *Ph.* When we speak of a *horse*, or of *iron*, we regard them as the things which furnish us the original patterns of our ideas; but when we speak of mixed modes or, at least, of the most important of these modes, which are *moral entities*, — for example, *justice, gratitude,* — we consider their original modes as existing in the mind. Therefore we say *the notion* of justice, of temperance; but we do not say the notion of a horse, of a stone.

Th. [The patterns of the ideas of the one are as real as those of the ideas of the other. The qualities of the mind are not less real than those of the body. It is true you do not see justice as you see a horse, but you understand it no less, or rather you understand it better; it is no less in acts than directness or obliqueness is in motions, whether you consider it or not. And to show you that men are of my opinion, and men, indeed, the most capable and most experienced in human affairs, I have only to avail myself of the authority of the Roman jurisconsults, followed by all others, who call these mixed modes or these moral entities, *things*, and in particular, *incorporeal things*. For servitudes,[1] for example (like that of the passage through the ground of one's neighbor), are with them *res incorporales*, in which there is a property which may be acquired by long use, and may be possessed and reclaimed. As for the word *notion*, many clever people have considered it as large as that of idea; Latin usage

[1] *Cf.* Sandars, *Institutes of Justinian*, Lib. II., Tit. III., p. 118, 8th ed., London: Longmans, Green, & Co., 1888; Poste, *Gaius, Elements of Roman Law*, Bk. II., 29, 31, pp. 165–6, 3d ed., Oxford, 1890; Mommsen, Digest, Lib. VIII., 1, Vol. 1, p. 250, Berlin: Weidmann, 1870; Hadley, *Introd. to Roman Law*, pp. 158–161, 180–196, New York, D. Appleton & Co., 1881. — Tr.

is not opposed thereto, nor do I know whether that of the English or the French is contrary to it.[1]]

§ 15. *Ph.* It is further to be remarked that men learn the names before the ideas of the mixed modes; the name showing them that this idea deserves to be observed.

Th. [This remark is a good one, although it is true that now-a-days children, with the aid of nomenclators, ordinarily learn the names not only of the modes, but also of substances, before the things, and indeed rather the names of substances than of the modes; for it is a defect in these same nomenclators that they employ *nouns* only, and not *verbs*; not considering that verbs, although signifying the modes, are more essential in conversation than the majority of nouns, which indicate particular substances.[2]]

CHAPTER VI

OF THE NAMES OF SUBSTANCES

§ 1. *Ph.* The *genera* and *species* of substances, as of other beings, are only *sorts*. For example, suns are a sort of stars, *i.e.* they are fixed stars, for it is not without reason that we think each fixed star would make itself known as a sun to a person placed at a proper distance. § 2. Now that which limits each sort is its essence. It is known either by its interior structure, or by external indications which make us recognize it and call it by a certain name: and thus it is that we may recognize the clock of Strasburg either as the clockmaker who made it, or as a spectator who sees its effects.

Th. [If this is your statement, I have nothing to oppose to it.]

[1] *Cf. New Essays*, Bk. II., chap. 22, § 2, Th. *ante*, p. 222; *Discours de Metaphysique*, 1686, § 29, Gerhardt, 4, 452. For the meaning and use of these terms: in Latin, *idea*, *notio*, *conceptus* or *conceptio*; in French, *idée*, *notion*, *conception*; in German, *Idee*, *Vorstellung*, *Begriff*; in English, *idea*, *notion*, *conception* or *concept*, which varies according to the period in the history of thought in which they are employed, and according to the theory of knowledge implicitly or consciously held by the author using them. *cf.* Krauth-Flemming, *Vocab. of the Philos. Sciences*, ed. of 1877, *sub voc.* — TR.

[2] "For," as Schaarschmidt says, "the activity is first perceived, and by its means the substance recognized and formulated." — TR.

Ph. I express myself in a way suited not at all to renew our discussions. But I add that the essence is related only to *sorts*, and that nothing is essential to *individuals*. An accident or a disease may change my color or shape; a fever or a fall may take away my reason or memory; apoplexy may leave me neither feeling, understanding, nor life. If you ask me if it is essential to me to have reason, I reply: no.

Th. [I think that there is something essential to individuals and more than you suppose. It is essential to substances to act, to created substances to suffer, to minds to think, to bodies to have extension and motion. That is, there are some sorts or species to which an individual cannot (naturally at least) cease to belong, when it has once been of their number, whatever revolutions may happen in nature. But there are some sorts or species, which are accidental (I admit) to the individuals, which may cease to belong to them. Thus you may cease to be healthy, beautiful, wise, and indeed to be visible and palpable, but you cannot cease to have life and organs and perception. I have stated sufficiently above, why it appears to men that life and thought sometimes cease, although they cease not to endure and to have their effects.]

§ 8. *Ph.* Many individuals ranked under a common name, considered as belonging to one species only, have nevertheless very different qualities depending upon their real (particular) constitutions. This is easily observed by all those who examine natural bodies; and chemists often are convinced of it by sad experience, when they vainly seek in one portion of antimony, sulphur, and vitriol for the qualities which they have found in other portions of these minerals.

Th. [No statement has more truth, and I could myself even furnish intelligence concerning it. Books have also been written expressly *de infido experimentorum chymicorum successu*. But the error consists in taking these bodies as *similar* or uniform, while they are more mixed than we suppose; for in *dissimilar* bodies we are not surprised to remark differences between individuals, and physicians do not know how much the temperaments and natural dispositions of human bodies differ. In a word, we shall never find the final logical species, as I have already remarked above, and two real or complete individuals of one and the same species are never perfectly alike.[1]]

Ph. We do not notice all these differences, because we do not know the little parts, nor consequently the interior structure of things. Thus we do not avail ourselves of them in order to determine the sorts or species of things, and if we wished to do so by means of these essences, or by what the schools call substantial forms, we should be like a blind man who desired to arrange bodies according to colors. § 11. We do not indeed know the essences of spirits, we know not how to form distinct specific ideas of angels, although we well know that there must be many kinds of spirits. Thus it seems that in our ideas we put no difference between God and the spirits by any number of simple ideas, save that we attribute infinity to God.

Th. [There is, however, another difference in my system between God and created spirits, viz. that in my view all created spirits must have bodies, just as our soul has one.[2]]

§ 12. *Ph.* I think at least that there is this analogy between bodies and spirits, that as there is no *gap* in the varieties of the corporeal world, so there will be no less variety in intelligent creatures. Commencing from ourselves and proceeding even to the lowest things, a descent is made by *very small*

[1] *Cf. New Essays*, Preface, *ante*, p. 51, Bk. II., chap. 27, *ante*, p. 238 *sq.*; *De ipsa natura*, § 13, Gerhardt, 4, 512, Erdmann, 158, b, Jacques, 1, 464 (in French), trans. Duncan, *Philos. Works of Leibnitz*, 122, 123; *Monadologie*, § 9, G. 6, 608, E. 705, J. 2, 392, trans. D. 219, F. H. Hedge, "Jour. Spec. Philos.," 1, 129; 4th letter to Clarke, §§ 4 *sq.*, G. 7, 372, E. 755, b, J. 2, 432, trans. D. 247, 5th letter to Clarke, § 21, G. 7, 393, E. 765, J. 2, 449, trans. D. 258. This is the principle of the identity of indiscernibles, *principium identitatis indiscernibilium* — *i.e.* that "things qualitatively undistinguishable are absolutely identical." According to Leibnitz, there are no such things, there being in the universe no two objects perfectly alike; though abstractly possible, they are inconsistent with the order of things, and with the divine wisdom, which admits nothing therein without reason. *Cf.* also Kant's development and criticism of Leibnitz's principles in his *Dilucidatio nova*, 1755. *Werke*, ed. Rosenkranz & Schubert, Leipzig, 1838–42, Vol. 1, p. 1; ed. Hartenstein, Leipzig, 1867–68, Vol. 1, p. 365, *Krit. d. r. Vernunft*, *V. d. Amphibolie d. Reflexionsbegriffe*, ed. R. & S. 2, 214, ed. H. 3, 225, 4th ed., J. H. v. Kirchmann, Leipzig, 1877, p. 268 *sq.*, E. Caird, *The Crit. Philos. of Immanuel Kant*, 1, 106 *sq.*, 445 *sq.*, 500 *sq.*, New York, Macmillan & Co., 1889; Ueberweg, *Hist. of Philos.*, 2, 144, 173, Ueberweg-Heinze, *Gesch. d. Philos.*, 7th ed., 3, 215, 259. — Tr.

[2] *Cf. New Essays*, Preface, *ante*, p. 52, Bk. II., chap. 1, § 12, Th. *ante*, p. 113, chap. 15, § 4, Th. *ante*, p. 159, and note. — Tr.

degrees, and by a continued series of things, which in each remove differ very little one from the other. There are fishes that have wings, and to whom the air is not strange, and there are birds inhabiting the water whose blood is cold like that of the fishes, and whose flesh so strongly resembles theirs in taste that the scrupulous are allowed to eat them on fish-days. There are animals so closely approaching the species of birds and of beasts that they hold the middle ground between them. The amphibia contain both terrestrial and aquatic animals. Seals live upon the land and in the sea; and porpoises (whose name signifies sea-hog) have the warm blood and the entrails of a hog. Not to speak of that which is reported of sea-men,[1] there are *some animals* who seem to have as much knowledge and reason as some that are called men; and there is so close a relation between animals and vegetables, that if you take the most imperfect of the one and the most perfect of the other, you will scarcely perceive any considerable difference between them. Thus, until we reach *the lowest and least organized parts of matter*, we shall find everywhere species bound together, and differing only by degrees almost imperceptible. And when we consider the wisdom and infinite power of the Author of all things, we have reason to think that it is conformed to the magnificent *harmony of the universe* and to the great design as well as to the infinite goodness of this sovereign architect, that the different species of creatures ascend, also, little by little from us towards his infinite perfection. Thus we have reason to be persuaded that there are many more species of creatures above us than below us, because we are much more distant in degrees of perfection from the infinite being of God than from that which approaches nearest to nothing. Yet we have no clear and distinct idea of all these different species.

Th. [I had intended in another place to say something not unlike what you, sir, have just set forth; but I am glad to have been anticipated when I see that you state things better than I could hope to have done. Clever philosophers[2] have

[1] *I.e.* mermaids; so Locke, "mermaids or sea-men," *Philos. Works*, Vol. 2, p. 49 (Bohn's ed.). — Tr.

[2] *Cf. Théodicée*, Pt. I., § 14, Gerhardt, 6, 110, Erdmann, 507, b, Jacques, 2, 80, Dutens, 1, 131 (in Latin); Reply to Bayle, *ad fin.*, G. 4, 570, E. 190, b,

discussed this question: *utrum detur vacuum formarum, i.e.* whether there are possible species, which, however, do not exist, and which nature may seem to have forgotten. I have reason to believe that all possible species are not compossible in the universe, great as it is, and that, too, not only in relation to things which exist contemporaneously, but also in relation to the whole series of things. That is to say, I believe that there are of necessity species which have never existed and never will exist, not being compatible with this series of creatures which God has chosen. But I believe that all things, which the perfect harmony of the universe can receive, exist therein. That there may be intermediate creatures between those which are far apart is in conformity with this same harmony, although this is not always in one and the same globe or system, and that which is between two species is sometimes so in relation to certain circumstances and not in relation to others. Birds, so different from man in other things, approach him in speech; but if monkeys could speak like parrots, they would go farther. *The law of continuity*[1] declares that nature leaves no gap in the order she follows; but every form or species is not the whole order. As for spirits or genii, as I hold that all created intelligences have organized bodies, whose perfection corresponds to that of the intelligence, or the mind, which is in this body in virtue of the pre-established harmony, I hold that in order to gain any conception of the perfections of spirits above us, it will be of great service to imagine these perfections also in bodily organs which surpass our own. It is a case in which the liveliest

D. 2, 93: "Il se peut cependant, que ce Chevalier ait encor eu quelque bon enthousiasme, qui l'ait transporté *dans ce monde invisible, et dans cette étendue infinie*, dont il parle, et que je crois estre celle des idées ou des formes, dont ont parlé encor quelques Scholastiques en mettant en question, *utrum detur vacuum formarum.*" — Tr.

[1] *Cf. New Essays*, Preface, *ante*, p. 50, Bk. IV., chap. 16, § 12, Tb., *infra*, p. 552; *Théodicée*, III., § 348, Gerhardt, 6, 321, Erdmann, 605, b, Jacques, 2, 270; Letter to Bayle, in the "Nouvelles de la République des Lettres," July, 1687, G. 3, 52, E. 104, trans. Duncan, *Philos. Works of Leibnitz*, 33; Letter to Arnauld, 1690, G. 2, 136, E. 107, b, J. 1, 444, trans. D. 38. *Animadversiones in partem generalem Principiorum Cartesianorum*, Pt. II., ad Art. 45, G. 4, 375, Duncan, 61; Guhrauer, *G. W. Freiherr v. Leibniz, eine Biographie*, 1, 264, and notes, pp. 31–33, a letter to an unknown person, Oct. 16, 1707, containing a very clear statement of the principle or law of continuity; translation, Appendix, pp. 712–714. — Tr.

and richest imagination, and, to avail myself of an Italian term which I cannot well express otherwise, the *invenzione la più vaga,* will be most timely in raising us above ourselves. And what I have said in justification of my system of harmony, which exalts the divine perfections beyond what we had dared to think, will assist us also in having ideas of creatures incomparably grander than we have had hitherto.

§ 14.[1] *Ph.* To return for a little to the reality of species even in substances, I ask you if water and ice are different species?

Th. [I, in my turn, ask you if gold melted in the crucible and gold cooled in bullion are of one and the same species?]

Ph. He does not reply to the question, who proposes another,

Qui litem lite resolvit.[2]

But you thereby admit that the reduction of things to species relates solely to the ideas we have of them, which suffice to distinguish them by names; but if we suppose that this distinction is founded upon their real and internal constitution, and that nature distinguishes existing things into so many species by their real essences, in the same manner as we ourselves distinguish them into species by these or those names, we shall be liable to great mistakes.

Th. There is some ambiguity in the term *species*, or *a being of a different species,* which causes all this confusion; and when we have removed it, there will no longer be discussion save perhaps as regards the name. We may take species mathematically and physically. In mathematical strictness the least difference making two things in any respect dissimilar, makes them *different in species.* Thus, in geometry, all circles are of one and the same species, for they are all perfectly alike, and for the same reason all parabolas are also of the same species; but it is not the same with ellipses and hyperbolas, for of these there is an infinite number of sorts or species, as well as an infinite number of each species. All the numberless

[1] Locke has § 13, *Philos. Works*, Vol. 2, p. 50. The numbering § 14 in the French text of all the editions is an error, as will be seen upon comparing the numbering of the next §, also 14, with Locke's text. Here also the texts coincide with Locke's. — TR.

[2] *Cf.* Horace, *Satires*, 2, 3, 103. — TR.

ellipses, in which the distance of the foci has the same ratio to the distance of the apices, are of one and the same species; but as the ratios of these distances vary only in size, it follows that all these infinite *species* of ellipses make only one *genus*, and that there are no subdivisions. On the other hand, an oval of three foci would have indeed an infinite number of such *genera*, and would have an infinitely infinite number of *species*, each genus having a number of them simply infinite. In this sense two physical individuals will never be perfectly similar, and what is more, the same individual will pass from species to species, for it is never wholly similar to itself even for more than a moment. But the men who establish physical species do not adhere to this strictness, and it depends upon them to say that a mass which they can make return to themselves under its first form continues to be one and the same *species* in their view. Thus we say that water, gold, quicksilver, common salt, continue the same, and are only disguised in ordinary changes; but in organized bodies, or in species of plants and of animals, we define species by generation, so that this similarity, which comes or may have come from one and the same origin or seed, would be of one and the same species.[1] In man, besides human generation, we fasten upon the attribute rational animal; and, although there are men who live like beasts all their lives, we presume that it is not for want of faculty or principle, but that it is through impediments which stand in the way of this faculty. But it is not yet determined as regards all the external conditions which we wish to regard as sufficient to give this presumption. But whatever regulations men make for their denominations and for the rights attached to names, provided that their regulation is followed or made fast and intelligible, it will be founded in reality, and they will not be able to imagine species which nature, which includes even possibilities, has not produced or distinguished before them. As for the interior, although there is no external appearance which is not based upon the internal constitution, it is nevertheless true that one and the same appearance may sometimes result from two different constitutions. But in

[1] *Cf. New Essays*, Bk. III., chap. 3, § 14, Th. (2), *ante*, p. 314; Dewey, *Leibniz's New Essays*, p. 215 *sq.*—Tr.

that case there will be something in common, and this is what we philosophers call the *proximate formal cause.* But although this should not be, as if according to Mariotte[1] the blue of the rainbow had an entirely different origin from the blue of the turquoise, unless there were a common formal cause (in which opinion I do not at all agree with him), and although we should agree that certain apparent natures which make us give names have nothing internal in common, our definitions would not cease to be grounded in real species; for the phenomena themselves are realities. We can say, then, that all which we truthfully distinguish or compare, nature distinguishes or makes agree also, although she has distinctions and comparisons which we do not know and which may perhaps be better than ours. Thus much care and experience is yet necessary in order to assign genera and species in a manner sufficiently like nature. Modern botanists think that the distinctions taken from the forms of flowers most resemble the natural order.[2] But they find therein, however, still much difficulty, and it would be advantageous to make comparisons and arrangements not only upon a single character, like that of which I have just spoken, which is taken from flowers, and is perhaps the most suitable up to this time for a possible system and convenient for learners, but also upon characters taken from other parts and relationships of plants: each basis of comparison deserving tables of its own;[3] without which we shall allow many subaltern genera, and many comparisons, distinctions, and useful observations to escape. But the more thoroughly we examine the generation of species, and the more we follow in the classifications the conditions which are there requisite, the closer we shall approach the natural order. Therefore, if the conjecture of some intelligent persons were found true, that there is in the plant besides the

[1] *Cf. ante*, p. 121, note 4. — TR.

[2] *Cf.* Dutens, *Leibnit. opera omnia*, Vol. 2, Pt. II., p. 169 *sq.*, *Epistola G. G. Leibnitii ad A. C. Gackenholtzium, M. D. De Methodo Botanica*, April 23, 1701. — TR.

[3] *Cf.* Mor. Wilh. Drobisch, *Neue Darstg. d. Logik*, 3d ed., Leipzig, 1863, p. 141 *sq.*, where the so-called Collateral Distributions or Co-divisions, which Leibnitz here calls to mind, and "which are of especial importance in Statistics," are discussed. Drobisch's work is considered "one of the most perfect presentations of the subject-matter from the point of view of formal logic." — TR.

seed (*la graine*) or the recognized seed (*la semence*) corresponding to the egg of the animal, another seed which would deserve the name masculine, *i.e.* a powder (*pollen*, visible very often, though sometimes, perhaps, invisible, as the seed (*la graine*) itself is in certain plants) which the wind or other ordinary accidents scatter in order to unite it with the seed which comes sometimes from one and the same plant, and sometimes, also (as in the hemp), from another neighboring plant of the same species, which plant consequently will be analogous to the male, though perhaps the female is never wholly destitute of this same *pollen;* if this conjecture, I say, were found true, and if the mode of generation of plants became better known, I do not doubt that the varieties which would be noticed would furnish a basis for very natural divisions. And if we had the penetration of some superior geniuses and knew enough about things, perhaps we should find therein fixed attributes for each species, common to all the individuals and always subsisting in the same living organism, whatever alterations or transformations may happen to it, as in the best known of the physical species, the human, reason is such a fixed attribute, granted to each individual, and never to be lost, although it cannot always be perceived. But in default of this knowledge we avail ourselves of the attributes which appear to us most convenient for distinguishing and comparing things, and in a word, for recognizing in them species or sorts; and these attributes have always their real grounds.]

§ 14. *Ph.* In order to distinguish substantial beings according to the usual supposition, that there are certain essences or precise forms of things, whereby all existing individuals are naturally distinguished into species, it would be necessary to be assured, § 15. *first,* that nature always proposes, in the production of things, to make them participate in certain regular and established essences, as models; and, § 16. *secondly,* that nature always attains this end. But monsters give us reason to doubt both. § 17. It would be necessary to determine, *in the third place,* whether these monsters are really a distinct and new species, for we find that some of these monsters have few or none of those qualities which are supposed to result from the essence of that species whence they derive their origin, and to which they seem to belong in virtue of their birth.

Th. When it is a question of determining whether monsters belong to a certain species, we are often reduced to conjecture. This shows us that we are not, then, limited to external considerations, since we should divine whether the *internal nature* (as, for example, reason in man) common to the individuals of such a species, still suits (as birth makes us conjecture) these individuals, in whom a portion of the *external characteristics*, ordinarily found in this species, is lacking. But our incertitude nowise affects the nature of things, and if there is such a common internal nature, it will or will not be found in the monster, whether we know it or not. And if the internal nature of any species is not found therein, the monster will be of its own species. But if there were no such internal nature in the species under discussion, and if the question was not decided by birth either, then the external marks alone would determine the species, and monsters would not belong to that species from which they deviate, unless taken in a manner a little vague and with some latitude; and in this case, also, our trouble in desiring to divine the species would be in vain. This is perhaps what you mean by all the objections you make to species taken as real internal essences. You ought then to prove, sir, that no common internal specific mark exists, since the external is wholly missing. But the contrary is found in the human species in which sometimes children who have some monstrosity reach an age in which they exhibit reason. Why, then, could there not be something similar in other species? It is true that for want of knowledge of them we cannot avail ourselves of it to define them, but the exterior takes its place, although we recognize the fact that it is insufficient for an exact *definition*, and that the *nominal definitions* themselves in these instances are only conjectural; and I have already stated above how sometimes they are only *provisional*. For example, we might find a way to counterfeit gold so that it might satisfy all the tests which we have up to the present time; but we might also then discover a new method of testing which would give the means of distinguishing natural gold from this *which is artificially made*. The old journals attribute both (discoveries) to Augustus, Elector of Saxony;[1]

[1] Augustus I., the brother of Maurice, was Elector 1553–1586, and, according to Schaarschmidt, "shared with his wife, Anna of Denmark, the love for alchemy." —Tr.

but I am not the man to guarantee this fact. But if it were true, we could have a *more perfect definition* of gold than we have at present, and if *artificial gold* could be made in quantity and cheap, as the alchemists claim, this *new proof* would be important; for by its means we could preserve for the human race the advantage which *natural gold* gives us in commerce by its rarity, while furnishing ourselves with a substance which is durable, uniform, easy to divide and to recognize, and precious in small volume. I wish to avail myself of this occasion to remove a difficulty (see § 50 of the chapter, "On the Names of Substances," in the author of the *Essay on Understanding*). The objection is made that in saying: All gold is fixed, if we understand by the idea of gold the mass of certain qualities in which fixedness is comprised, we make only an identical and useless proposition, as if we said: Fixedness is fixedness; but if we understand thereby a substance given a certain internal essence, of which fixedness is a result, we shall not speak intelligibly, for this real essence is wholly unknown. I reply that the body given this internal constitution is designated by other external marks in which fixedness is not comprised, as if any one said: the heaviest of all bodies is also one of the most fixed. But all that is only provisional, for we might some day find a volatile body, as a new mercury, which would be heavier than gold, and upon which gold would float, as lead floats upon our mercury.

§ 19. *Ph.* It is true that in this way we can never know precisely the number of properties depending on the real essence of gold unless we know the essence of gold itself. § 21. [But if we limit ourselves precisely to certain properties, that will be sufficient to enable us to have exact nominal definitions which will serve us for the present, reserving to ourselves the privilege of changing the signification of names, if any new useful distinction is discovered.] But it is necessary at least that this definition correspond to the use of the name, and be capable of being put in its place. This serves to refute those who maintain that extension constitutes the essence of body, for when it is said that one body gives an impulse to another, the absurdity would be manifest, if substituting extension (for body) we should say that one extension puts in motion another extension by means of an impulse, for in addition solidity is necessary. In like manner no one will say that reason, or that which makes man rational, makes conversation; for reason does not constitute the entire essence of man; there are rational animals who converse with each other.

Th. I think you are right: for the objects of abstract and incomplete ideas are not sufficient to give the subjects of all the actions of things. But I think that *conversation* agrees with all minds who can interchange their thoughts. The scholastics are greatly troubled regarding the *angelic* method of communication; but if they would accord the angels subtile bodies, as I do, following the ancients, they would experience no further difficulty in that regard.[1]

§ 22. *Ph.* There are some creatures in the world which have forms similar to ours, but are hairy and use neither language nor reason. There are imbeciles[2] among us who have exactly the same form as ourselves, but who are destitute of reason, and some of them make no use of language. There are some creatures, as it is said, which, with the use of language and of reason and a form similar in every other respect to ours, have hairy tails; at least, it is not impossible that there are such creatures.[3] There are others, where the males have no beard, and others, where the females have. If you ask whether all these creatures are men or not, whether they

[1] *Cf. New Essays*, Preface, *ante*, p. 52, Bk. III., chap. 6, *ante*, p. 332, note 2; also letters to Des Bosses, Sept. 20, Oct. 4, 1706, Gerhardt, 2, 316, 319, Erdmann, 439, 440. — Tr.

[2] Locke has: "naturals," *Philos. Works*, Vol. 2, p. 53 (Bohn's ed.). — Tr.

[3] The myth of men with tails, here mentioned and accepted as credible by Locke, arose either from the superficial observation of African travellers, or from their uncritical acceptance and rehearsal of the stories of such Negroes as claimed to have seen such beings, assumed by them to be endowed with reason, although covered with hair and furnished with tails — stories which seem to rest upon a confusion of men with man-like apes, a confusion the more naturally suggested as many tribes of negroes regard the apes as rational but uncivilized human beings. The myth has been exploded in our day by the knowledge furnished by scientific explorers into the interior of Africa (the assumed abode of these beings), such as Dr. Georg August Schweinfurth, who states that among the tribes of Central Africa the Dyoor, the Niam-niam, and the Bongo, fasten upon themselves behind, as a part of their dress, the tails of animals, as, for example, that of "the quereza monkey (*Colobus*)," or tails "composed of the bast of the Sanseviera." Cf. his *Im Herzen von Afrika*, English trans. by Ellen E. Frewer, 2 vols., New York: Harper & Bros., 1874, Vol. 1, pp. 201, 294–6, Vol. 2, pp. 2, 6, 11, 137. — Tr.

belong to the human species, it is plain that the question refers only to the nominal definition, or to the complex idea we have made for ourselves in order to indicate it by this name; for the internal essence is absolutely unknown to us, although we have reason to think that where the faculties, or rather the external figure, are so different, the internal constitution is not the same.

Th. I think we have in the case of man a definition at once real and nominal. For nothing can be more internal to man than reason, and ordinarily it makes itself well known. Therefore the beard and the tail will not be considered in comparison with it. A man of the forest, though hairy, will make himself recognized; and it is not the hair of a magot[1] which excludes him. Imbeciles lack the use of reason; but as we know by experience that reason is often bound and cannot appear, and as this happens in the case of men who have exhibited and will exhibit reason, we make, probably, the same judgment regarding these imbeciles upon other indications, *i.e.* upon their bodily figure. It is only by these signs, united with their birth, that we presume that infants are men, and will manifest reason; and we are seldom deceived. But if there were rational animals with an external form a little different from ours, we should be embarrassed. This shows that our definitions, when dependent upon the exterior of bodies, are imperfect and provisional. If any one called himself an angel, and knew, or knew how to do, things much above us, he might be believed. If some one else, like Gonzales,[2] came from the moon by means of some extraordinary machine, and told us credible things about his native country, he would pass

[1] The Barbary ape. — Tr.

[2] Cf. *L'Homme dans la lune, ou le voyage chimérique fait au monde de la lune, nouvellement découvert par Dominique Gonzales, avanturier Espagnol, autrement dit le courier volant, mis en nostre langue par J. B. D.* (Jean Baudoin), Paris, 1648, 8vo, pp. 176; reprinted Paris, 1666, with illustrations, and also Paris, 1731, 12mo. Brunet states that this is the French translation of Franc. Godwin, *The Man in the Moon, or a discourse of a voyage thither by Domingo Gonsales*, London, 1638, also 1657, etc., 12mo; that it had some success, and that it is supposed that Swift borrowed some passages from it for his *Gulliver's Travels.* Cf. E. A. Poe, *Works*, New York, 1867, Vol. 1, p. 49, who gives, in a note at the end of the story of "The unparalleled adventure of one Hans Pfaall," the full title of the French book, together with some account of its contents, including the machine of Gonzales. — Tr.

as a lunar being, and yet we might accord him indigineity and the rights of citizenship, with the title of man, entire stranger as he would be to our globe; but if he asked for baptism and wished to be received as a proselyte of our law, I think that we should see great discussions arise among the theologians. And if communication were opened with these planetary men, sufficiently approaching ourselves according to Huygens,[1] the question would require a universal council in order to know whether we ought to extend the care of the propagation of the faith even beyond our globe. Many would doubtless maintain that the rational animals of these countries, not being of the race of Adam, have no part in the redemption of Jesus Christ; but others would perhaps say that we have not sufficient knowledge either of the place where Adam has always been, or of what has been done with all his posterity, since there have been theologians, indeed, who believed that the moon was the place of paradise; and perhaps that with the plurality we should conclude for the surest thing, viz., to baptize these men upon condition that they be susceptible of baptism; but I doubt whether we should ever wish to make them priests in the Roman Church, because their consecration would always be doubtful, and we should expose the people to the danger of a material idolatry, according to the hypothesis of this church. Happily the nature of things exempts us from all these embarrassments; but these bizarre fictions are useful in speculation, in order rightly to know the nature of our ideas.

§ 23. *Ph.* Not only in theological questions, but also on other occasions some would perhaps wish to regulate themselves by the race, and to say that in animals propagation by the copulation of the male and the female, and in plants by means of the seeds, keeps *the supposed real species* distinct and entire. But this would serve only to fix the species of animals and vegetables. What must be done about the rest? And even as regards these it is not sufficient, for if history is to be believed, women have been gotten with children by magots. And here is a new question: Of what species must such a production be? You often see mules and jumarts (see Diction-

[1] *Cf. ante*, p. 150, note 3. *Leibnizens u. Huyghen's Briefwechseln, v. E. Gerland*, Berlin, 1881. — Tr.

naire Étymologique de M. Ménage[1]), the first begotten by an ass and a mare, the last by a bull and a mare. I have seen an animal begotten of a cat and a rat, which had visible marks of these two animals.[2] Whoever will add thereto the monstrous productions, will find that it is very hard to determine species by generation; and if it can only be done by that means, must I go to the Indies to see the father and mother of a tiger, and the seed of the tea-plant, and could I not otherwise decide whether the individuals which come to us are of these species?

Th. Generation or race gives at least a strong presumption (*i. e.* a provisional proof) and I have already said that very often our signs are only conjectural. The race has sometimes been contradicted by the figure, as when the child is unlike the father and mother, and the mixture of figures is not always the sign of the mixture of races; for it may happen that a female gives birth to an animal which seems to belong to another species and that the mother's imagination alone has caused this irregularity: to say nothing of what is called *mola*.[3] But as meanwhile we judge provisionally the species by the race, we also judge the race by the species. For when a forest child,[4] taken from among the bears, who had many of their ways, but who made himself known at last as a rational animal, was presented to John Casimir,[5] king of Poland, he did not scruple to believe him of the race of Adam, and to baptize him under the name of Joseph, although perhaps upon the condition, *si baptizatus non es*, according to the usage of the Roman church, because he might have been carried off by a bear after baptism. We have not as yet sufficient knowledge

[1] *Cf.* Dutens, *Leibnit. op. om.*, 5, 350, 543; 6, Pt. II., 21, Gerhardt, 2, 530, 539. Gilles Ménage, 1613–1692. The first ed. was entitled *Origines de la langue françoise*, Paris, 1650, 4to. A new ed. appeared at Paris, 1694, fol., under the name, *Dictionnaire Étymologique de la langue françoise*, etc.; and this was afterwards enlarged and edited by A. F. Jault, Paris, 1750, 2 vols., fol. — TR.

[2] An instance of superficial observation and hasty inference, like that of the men with tails above mentioned, *ante*, p. 341, note 3. — TR.

[3] An amorphous fleshy mass in the uterus. — TR.

[4] Schaarschmidt states that J. H. F. Ulrich, in his German trans., with additions and notes, Halle, 1778–80, of Raspe's *Œuvres philosoph. latines et françaises de feu Mr. Leibniz*, "gives in a note, p. 139–140, information concerning the child of the bears found in the forest, without, however, quoting the source of his communications." — TR.

[5] John II., Casimir V., 1609–1672. He was elected king of Poland in 1614, and abdicated in 1688. — TR.

of the effects of the intermixture of animals: and often monsters are destroyed, instead of being brought up, whilst they are seldom long lived. The belief is that mixed animals do not multiply; but Strabo[1] attributes propagation to the mules of Cappadocia, and letters from China tell me that in neighboring Tartary there are race-mules. We see also that the mixtures of plants are capable of preserving their new species.[2] We do not always indeed know in the case of animals whether it is the male or the female, or both, or neither, which determines the species. The doctrine concerning the eggs of females which the late Mr. Kerkring[3] made famous, seemed to reduce the males to the condition of moist air as related to plants, which furnishes seeds with the means of pushing and raising themselves from the earth; following the verses of Vergil which the Priscillianists[4] were wont to repeat:

[1] *Cf. Geographica*, p. 212, ed. Casaubon, 1620; Bk. V., chap. 1, § 4, ed. by Gustav Kramer, Berlin, 1844–52, 3 vols., 8vo; English trans. Vol. 1, p. 316 (Bohn's Class. Lib.), London, 1887. — Tr.

[2] *Cf.* C. Darwin, 1809–1882, *Origin of Species*, and the new inquiries and investigations consequent upon it. — Tr.

[3] Theodore Kerkkrinck, 1640–1693, a Dutch physician, born at Amsterdam, died at Hamburg, a fellow-pupil with Spinoza, 1632–1677, of a physician, Francis Van der Ende, and author of works on medicine, anatomy, and chemistry, among which was the one here referred to by Leibnitz: *Anthropogeniæ ichnographia sive conformatio fœtus ab ovo usque ad ossificationis principia, in supplementum osteogeniæ fœtuum*, 4to, Amstelodami, 1671. His *Opera omnia anatomica*, 2d ed., 4to, Lugd. Bat., 1717. *Cf.* Dutens, *Leibnit. op. om.*, 5, 173, 199; F. Pollock, *Spinoza: His Life and Philosophy*, p. 13. — Tr.

[4] The Priscillianists were an heretical sect which appeared in Spain toward the close of the fourth century, and continued till about the middle of the sixth. Their speculative doctrines are a combination of Christianity with Gnosticism and Manichæism. Their moral system was rigidly ascetic, and celibacy was required. The charges of immorality and licentiousness so frequently brought against them by their adversaries, "are, to say the least, not sufficiently well authenticated." The information that they made use of these verses of Vergil, to which they attached a religious dogma, as a foundation for their heresy and alleged sexual license comes from a letter of Jerome, c. 346–420, to Ctesiphon, *Epist.* 133 *ad Ctesiphontem*, *Opera*, ed. Vallarsi, Veronæ, 1734–42, Vol. 1, p. 1029, a; 2d ed., Venetiis, 1766–72; J. P. Migne, *Patrol. s. Lat.*, Vol. 22, p. 1150–51, Paris, 1845, latest ed., Paris, 1864–66. *Cf.* also Sulpicius Severus, 363–406, or 410, *Histor. Sacra*, or *Chronica*, Bk. II., chaps. 46–51, and *Dialog.*, III., 11–13, ed. C. Halm, Vienna, 1866 (Vol. 1 of the *Corpus Script. Eccles. Latinorum*), and J. Bernays, *Die Chronik des Sulp. Severus*, Berlin, 1861; A. Neander, *Hist. of the Christ. Relig. and Church*, 2, 771–779, Boston, Houghton, Mifflin & Co.; Gibbon, *Decline and Fall*, Milman's ed., chap. 27; Smith and Wace, *Dict. of Christ. Biog.*, 4, 470–478, London, John Murray, 1887. — Tr.

Cum pater omnipotens fœcundis imbribus æther
Conjugis in lætæ gremium descendit et omnes
Magnus alit magno commistus corpore fœtus.[1]

In a word according to this hypothesis the male would no longer be more than the rain. But Leeuwenhoek[2] has rehabilitated the masculine genus, and the other sex is in its turn degraded, as if it performed only the earth's function as regards seeds, by furnishing them place and nourishment; a view which might obtain even if we still maintained the theory of the eggs. But this does not prevent the imagination of the female from having a great influence upon the form of the fœtus, even if we supposed that the animal has already come from the male. For this is a condition destined ordinarily to a great change, and much more susceptible also to extraordinary changes. It is asserted that the imagination of a woman in this condition, who was shocked by the sight of a cripple, caused the separation of the hand of the fœtus very near its term, and that this hand was subsequently found in the after-birth; a statement, however, which requires confir-

[1] *Georg.*, 2, 325–327. — TR.

[2] Antoon van Leeuwenhoek, 1632–1723, a distinguished Dutch naturalist, "the father of scientific microscopy," who shares with Malpighi, 1628–1694, the discovery of the capillary circulation of the blood, thus completing the doctrine of Harvey, 1598–1657, and with his own pupil, Ludwig Hamm, the discovery of the active moving constituents of the seminal fluid, which he called "animalcula spermatica," or "spermatozoa." Leeuwenhoek communicated his discovery, 1677, of the spermatozoa in a letter to Sir Christopher Wren, 1631–1723, President of the Royal Society, 1681, "De ovario, et imaginovis ejus ovis; homo ex animalculo oritur." The letter is found in Leeuwenhoek's *Arcana naturæ detecta sive epistolæ ad societatem Regiam Angliam scriptæ*, Delft, 1695, 4to, p. 28 *sq.* Leeuwenhoek strenuously opposed the doctrine of "spontaneous generation," and did more than any other naturalist to overthrow it. *Cf.* Dutens, *Leibnit. op. om.*, 5, 173, 174, 319, 337; 6, Pt. I., 211, 213, 218, Gerhardt, *Leibniz. philos. Schrift.*, 3, 562, 565, 571, 579, 580, Dutens, 2, Pt. I., 329, 330; Pt. II., 214, *Protogæa*, § 17; *Système nouveau*, § 6, Gerhardt, 4, 480, Erdmann, 125, b, Jacques, 1, 471, trans. Duncan, *Philos. Wks. of Leibnitz*, 73; *Principes de la Nature et de la Grace*, § 6, G., 6, 601, E., 715, b, trans. D., 212; G., 7, 568. He published the greater part of his discussions and investigations in 112 papers in the *Philos. Transactions* of the Royal Society, and in 26 papers in the *Memoirs of the Paris Academy of Sciences*, of both of which bodies he was a member. The most complete collection of his works is the *Opera omnia seu arcanæ naturæ ope microscopiorum detecta*, Leyden, 1719–22, 4 vols., 4to; from this, *Select Works*, trans. by Samuel Hoole, London, 1800–1807, 2 vols, 4to, does not contain the letter to Wren. There is a Life in Dutch by Haaxman, Leyden, 1875. — TR.

mation. Perhaps some one will arise who will maintain that, although the soul can come only from one sex, both sexes furnish something of the organism, and that from the two bodies one is made, just as we see that the silk-worm is as it were a double animal, and encloses a flying insect under the form of the caterpillar: in such darkness are we still upon so important a point. Some day perhaps the analogy of plants will give us some light, but at present we have but little information regarding the generation of plants themselves, the surmise concerning the pollen which has been remarked, as that which might correspond to the masculine semen, not yet being very clear. Besides a slip of a plant is very often capable of giving a new and complete plant, to which no analogy is as yet seen in animals; also we cannot say that the foot of an animal is an animal, as each branch of the tree seems to be a plant capable of fruit-bearing by itself. Furthermore the intermixture of species, and even the changes in one and the same species often go on with much success in plants. Perhaps at some time or place in the universe the species of animals are, or were, or will be more subject to change than they are at present with us, and many animals who have somewhat of the cat, as the lion, the tiger, and the lynx, might have been of one and the same race and may now be as it were new subdivisions of the ancient species of cats. Thus I always return to what I have more than once said that our determinations of physical species are provisional and proportional to our knowledge.[1]

§ 24. *Ph.* Men at least in making their divisions of species have never thought of substantial forms, save those who, in this single corner of the world where we are, have learned the language of our schools.

Th. It seems that lately the term *substantial forms* has come into disrepute with certain classes and that they are ashamed to speak of them. Meanwhile there is perhaps in that circumstance more of fashion than of reason. The scholastics employed inaptly a general notion, when they used it to explain particular phenomena; but this abuse does not destroy the thing. The soul of man is a little disconcerting to

[1] Leibnitz here touches upon the theory of evolution, or development, but keeps himself within very moderate limits in the statement of his views. — TR.

the dogmatism of some of our moderns. There are some who admit that it is the form of man; but they also affirm that it is the only substantial form of known nature. Descartes thus speaks of it, and he censures Regius[1] because he contested this quality of a substantial form of the soul and denied that man was a *unum per se*, a being endowed with a veritable unity.[2] Some think that this excellent man did this as a matter of policy. I doubt this a little because I think he had reason for so doing. But this privilege is not given to man only, as if nature were made of broken sticks. There is room for the judgment that there is an infinite number of souls, or, to speak more generally, of primitive entelechies, which have something analogous to perception and appetite, and which are all, and remain always, substantial forms of bodies. It is true that species apparently exist which are not truly a *unum per se* (*i.e.* bodies endowed with a veritable unity, or with an invisible essence which makes their entire active principle), any more than a mill or watch might be. The salts, the minerals, and the metals may be of this nature, *i.e.* simple contextures or masses in which there is a certain regularity. But the bodies of both, *i.e.* animate bodies as well as the contextures without life will be specified by their internal structure, since in those indeed which are animate, the soul and the machine,[3] each by

[1] Pierre Sylvain Régis — Latin, Regius — 1632–1707, a celebrated Cartesian, at first destined for the church, but who, on going to Paris to study theology at the Sorbonne, heard Rohault (*cf. ante*, p. 233, note 2) on Cartesianism, became a zealous adherent of the doctrine, renounced the priesthood, and gave himself up to teaching the new philosophy. His enormous success aroused the opposition of Harlay, the Archbishop of Paris, who forbade his teaching. He therefore turned to composition, expounding his philosophical ideas in his *Cours entier de philosophie*, or *Système général selon les principes de Descartes*, 4 vols., 4to, Paris, 1690, 2d ed., 3 vols., Amsterdam, 1691. He interpreted Descartes in the sense of empiricism, and thus drew upon himself the philosopher's censure, *cf.* Descartes, Remarks on the Programme of Regius, *Works*, ed. Cousin, Paris, 1824–26, Vol. 10, pp. 70–111; see also Veitch, *The Method, Meditations and Selections from the Principles of Descartes*, 8th ed., Edinburgh, 1881, pp. 278, 287. His doctrines were a reaction against the ultra idealism of Malebranche. Other works of his are *Response à la censura philosophiæ cartesianæ*, 12mo, Paris, 1691; *L'Usage de la Raison et de la Foi*, 4to, Paris, 1704. — TR.

[2] *Cf.* Descartes, 1596–1650, *Epist.*, I., 89, pp. 292–293, ed. of 1668, p. 261, ed. of 1692, Cousin's ed., Vol. 8, pp. 579–583; Gerhardt, *Leibniz. philos. Schrift.*, 6, 547, 550 *sq.* — TR.

[3] *I.e.* body, according to the linguistic usage of the Cartesians. — TR.

itself, suffice for the determination; for they agree perfectly, and although having no immediate influence the one upon the other, they are mutually expressive, the one having concentrated into a perfect unity all that the other has dispersed in the manifold. Thus, when the arrangement of species is the question, it is useless to dispute about the substantial forms, although it may be well for other reasons to know if there are any and what their nature is; for without this one would be a stranger in the intellectual world. For the rest the Greeks and the Arabians have spoken of these forms as well as the Europeans, and if the common people do not speak of them, no more do they speak of algebra or of surds.[1]

§ 25. *Ph.* Languages were formed before the sciences, and ignorant and unlettered people reduced things to certain species.

[1] The doctrine of the *substantial forms*, of which the Mediæval schoolmen made so much use, finds its origin and point of departure in the εἶδος and οὐσία of Plato and Aristotle. Aristotle used οὐσία in two senses; in its primary and proper signification, as a concrete and individual substance, a compound (σύνολον) of matter (ὕλη) and the determining principle, form (εἶδος), in which sense individual things were called "first substances" (πρῶται οὐσίαι); secondly, as applied to the genus, in which sense species were called "second substances" (δεύτεραι οὐσίαι). According as they were nominalists or realists, the Schoolmen, in their interpretation of Aristotle, regarded the substantial forms as mere concepts of genus and species, the product of the abstraction-power of the mind, which might correspond to, though they did not constitute, the reality of things; or, as real universals existing in concrete things, constituting their inmost essence and determining its nature. Locke adopts the nominalistic view of these forms as purely subjective having no corresponding reality in nature. Leibnitz maintains them in the realistic sense as expressions of the reality of the "first substances," and in direct connection with them develops his doctrine of monads. *Cf. Discours de Metaphys.*, 1686, § 10 *sq.*, Gerhardt, 4, 443; *Système nouveau*, 1695, §§ 3, 4, 11, G. 4, 478 *sq.* (also *ibid.* first draft, G. 4, 473), Erdmann, 124, Jacques, 1, 470, trans. Duncan, *Philos. Wks. of Leibnitz*, 72; *De ipsa natura*, 1698, §§ 11, 12, G. 4, 510, E. 157, J. 1, 462, D. 120; also G. Hartenstein, *Ueber Leibniz's Lehre v. d. Verhältniss d. Monaden z. Körperwelt*, in his *Histor. philos. Abhandl.*, Leipzig, 1870, 469 *sq.*, Stein, *Leibniz u. Spinoza*, Berlin, 1890, 158 *sq.*, Dillmann, *Eine n. Darstg. d. Leibniz. Monadenlehre*, Leipzig, 1891, 225 *sq.* For Leibnitz's theological use of Aristotle's forms — εἴδη — *cf. Théodicée*, Pt. III., §§ 335–6, and J. H. v. Kirchmann's note 246 thereto, Band 80, p. 133, and note 62 f., Bd. 82, p. 87, of his *Philos. Bibliothek*. Leipzig, 1879. On the εἶδος and οὐσία of Plato and Aristotle, *cf.* Wallace, *Outlines of the Philos. of Aristotle*, §§ 10, 31, 32, 34, 37, and Zeller, *Philos. d. Griech.*, II., 1 [Vol. 3], 658 *sq.*, 4th ed. 1889, II. 2 [Vol. 4], 304 *sq.*, 3d ed., 1879. For the Scholastic doctrine, *cf.* B. Hauréau, *Histoire de la philos. scholastique*, 2d ed., Paris, 1872–80; A. Stöckl, *Gesch. d. Philos. d. Mittelalters*, Mainz, 1862–66; C. Prantl, *Gesch. d. Logik im Abendlande*, Leipzig, 1855–1870, *passim*. *Cf.* also G. 1, 16, 22 *sq.*, 4, 208. — Tr.

Th. True, but persons who study these matters rectify the popular notions. Assayers have found exact means of discerning and separating the metals; botanists have enriched wonderfully the doctrine of plants, and the experiments made upon insects have opened for us a new path in the knowledge of animals, but we are still very far distant from the half of our course.

§ 26. *Ph.* If species were a work of nature they could not be conceived so differently by different persons. Man appears to one person an animal without feathers, with two feet and with large nails, and another after a more profound examination adds to these reason. Many people, however, determine the species of animals by their *external form* rather than by their *birth*, since the question has been put more than once whether certain human *fœtuses* should be admitted to baptism or not, for the sole reason that their external configuration differed from the ordinary form of infants, without knowing whether they were not as capable of reason as infants cast in another mould, some of whom are found, who, although of an approved form, are never able to exhibit during their entire life as much reason as appears in an ape or elephant, and who never give any indication of being governed by a rational soul. Whence it appears evident that the external form which alone has found mention, and not the faculty of reasoning which no one could know would be wanting in its time, has been regarded essential to the human species. And in these circumstances theologians and jurisconsults the most learned have been compelled to renounce their sacred definition of rational animal, and to put in its place some other essence of the human species. "Mr. Ménage," (Menagiana Tom. I. p. 278, of the Dutch edition of 1694,)[1] "furnishes us the example of a certain abbot of St. Martin, which deserves to be related. When this abbot of St. Martin, he says, came into the world, he had so little the figure of a man, that he resembled rather a monster. For some time they deliberated whether he should be baptized. He was baptized however, and declared a man provisionally, *i.e.* till time should show what he was. He

[1] *Menagiana sive excerpta ex ore Ægidii Menagii*, 1st ed., 1 vol., 12mo, Paris, 1693, 3d ed., enlarged and corrected by La Monnoye, Paris, 1715. Erdmann, Jacques, and Schaarschmidt in his German trans. erroneously read 1649. —Tr.

was so disfigured by nature, that they called him all his life the Abbot Malotru. He was of Caen." There was a child who came very near being excluded from the human species simply because of his shape. He narrowly escaped as it was, and it is certain that a figure a little more deformed would have deprived him of it for ever and have caused him to perish as a being who ought not to pass for a man. Yet no reason can be given why a rational soul could not have been lodged in him, if the lineaments of his face had been a little more altered; why a visage a little longer, or a flatter nose, or a wider mouth could not have subsisted as well as the rest of the irregular figure with a soul and with qualities which made him capable, wholly disfigured as he was, of being clothed with dignity in the church.

Th. Up to the present time, no rational animal has been found with an external figure very different from ours, therefore, when the question arose of baptizing a child, race and figure have always been considered only as marks by which to judge whether it was a rational animal or not. Thus theologians and jurisconsults have never needed to renounce for that reason their sacred definition.

§ 27. *Ph.* But if that monster, of which Licetus,[1] Bk. I., chap. 3, speaks, with a man's head and a hog's body, or other monsters, with the heads of dogs and of horses, etc., upon the bodies of men had lived and could have spoken, the difficulty would be much greater.

[1] Fortunio Liceti, 1577–1657, a celebrated Italian physician and scholar, who taught logic at Pisa, 1600–1609; philosophy at Padua till 1631; then philosophy at Bologna; and finally, theoretic medicine at Padua from 1645 till his death. He was a great admirer of Aristotle, and wished to admit nothing beyond his doctrines, and thus contributed to render both philosophy and medicine stationary. For the matter to which Leibnitz here refers, *cf.* Licetus, *De spontaneo viventium ortu, lib. quat.*, fol., Vicentiæ, 1618, Bk. I., chap. 28, pp. 34–36, Sexta confirmatio spontanei ortus hominum petita ex humanis figuris in belluis, ac lapidibus enodatur aperiendo talium figurarum caussas, in which chapter Licetus treats of various monsters, referring to his *De monstrorum* mentioned below, and to his father's, Giuseppe Liceti, an Italian physician, died 1599, *Dialogus de genitalium usu et dignitate*, or *Il Cera, dell' ouvero eccellenza ed uso de' genitali*, 1598, *De monstrorum caussis, natura, et differentiis lib. duo*, 2d ed., 4to, Petavii, 1634, pp. 13, 183, 194: "De monstrorum humanorum reale existentiæ"; the same, with additions by Gerard Blasius, 4to, Amstelodami, 1665, pp. 13, 183, 194; the same, in the French trans., *Traité des monstres*, by Jean Palfyn, 1650–1730, in his *Description anatomique des parties de la femme qui servent à la génération*, etc., 4to, Leyden, 1708, pp. 13, 197, 208. — Tr.

Th. I admit it, and if that occurred and if any one had done, as a certain writer, a monk of the olden time, named Hans Kalb (Jean le veau — John the calf) who[1] painted himself with a calf's head, the pen in his hand, in a book he had written, which procedure caused some foolishly to think that this writer had in reality a calf's head, — if, I say, that happened, we should be more cautious hereafter in getting rid of monsters. For there is some probability that reason would maintain it with theologians and with jurisconsults in spite of the figure and even in spite of the differences which the anatomy would furnish to the physicians, which would as little injure the quality of man as the reversal of the viscera in that man whose anatomy some persons of my acquaintance have seen at Paris, which has made some stir, in which nature

> "Peu sage et sans doute en débauche
> Plaça le foye au costé gauche
> Et de même vice versa
> Le cœur à la droite plaça,"

i.e. "unwise and doubtless in debauch placed the liver upon the left side and likewise *vice versa* the heart upon the right," if I rightly remember some of the verses which the late Mr. Alliot[2] the father (a famous physician because he passed as skilful in the treatment of cancers) showed me of his own making upon this prodigy. It is a matter of course, provided the variety of conformation does not go too far in the case of rational animals and that no return is made to the times when animals spoke, for then we should lose our especially peculiar advantage of reason[3] and should henceforth be more attentive to birth and the external in order to be able to dis-

[1] Erdmann and Jacques add "qui" after "le veau." — TR.

[2] Pierre Alliot, a French physician of the seventeenth century, born at Bar-le-Duc, reputed to have great skill in the treatment of cancer and other malignant ulcers. His most distinguished patient was Anne of Austria, the mother of Louis XIV., whom he treated unsuccessfully in Paris in 1665. Notwithstanding his failure, he was appointed physician to the king. His published works include *Theses medicæ de motu sanguinis circulato et de morbis ex ære*, Pont-à-Mousson, 1663, 8vo; *Epistola de cancro apparente*, and *Nuntius profligati sine ferro et igne carcinomatis*, both Bar-le-Duc, 1664, 12mo. His son, Jean Baptiste Alliot, was physician to Louis XIV., and published *Traité du cancer où l'on explique sa nature et où l'on propose les moyens les plus sûrs pour le guerir methodiquement*, Paris, 1698, 12mo. — TR.

[3] The French text is: "nostre privilege de la raison en preciput," etc. — TR.

cern those of Adam's race from those who may descend from a king or patriarch of some canton of apes in Africa; and our learned author was right in his remark (§ 29) that if Balaam's ass had all her life discoursed as rationally as she did once with her master (supposing it was a prophetic vision), she would always have had difficulty in obtaining rank and a seat among women.

Ph. You laugh, I see, and perhaps the author laughed also; but, to speak seriously, you see that you cannot always assign fixed limits to species.

Th. I have already agreed to this; for when the question concerns fictions and the possibility of things, the passage from species to species may be insensible, and to discern them would sometimes be about as impossible as to decide how much hair a man must be allowed that he may not be bald. This indeterminateness would be true even when we knew perfectly the internal nature of the creatures under discussion. But I do not see that it can prevent things from having real essences independent of the understanding, and us from knowing them. It is true that the names and limits of species would sometimes be like the names of measures and weights, where choice is necessary in order to have fixed limits. But ordinarily there is nothing of the kind to fear, species too much alike seldom occurring together.

§ 28. *Ph.* It seems we agree here at bottom, although we differ somewhat in terms. I also admit that there is less arbitrariness in the denomination of *substances* than in the names of the *mixed modes.* For few venture to unite the bleating of a sheep with the figure of a horse, or the color of lead with the weight and fixedness of gold, and we prefer to draw copies after nature.[1]

Th. This is not so much because in substances regard is had only to that which exists effectively, as because there is no certainty in the case of physical ideas (which are not very thoroughly understood) that their union is possible and useful, if there is no actual existence to guarantee it. But this also takes place in the modes, not only when their obscurity is impenetrable by us, as sometimes happens in physics, but also

[1] That is, to follow experience in the formation of our ideas, and to conform our inner world in general to that furnished by nature. — TR.

when it is difficult of penetration, enough examples of which occur in geometry. For in both of these sciences it is not within our power to make combinations according to our fancy, otherwise we should be right in speaking of *regular decahedrons*, and should seek in the semicircle[1] a *centre of magnitude*, as there is in it *a centre of gravity*. For it is in fact surprising that the first is there, and that the second cannot be. Now while in the modes the combinations are not always arbitrary, we find on the other hand that in substances they sometimes are so; and it often depends on ourselves to make combinations of qualities in order further to define substantial beings in advance of experience, when we understand enough of these qualities to judge of the possibility of the combination. Thus it is that expert gardeners in the orangery can rationally and successfully propose to produce some new species and give it a name in advance.

§ 29. *Ph.* You will always agree with me that when the question arises of defining species, the number of ideas combined depends upon the different application, industry, or fancy of the one forming this combination, as it is the figure which regulates most frequently the determination of the species of vegetables or animals, and likewise as regards the majority of natural bodies which are not produced by seeds, it is the color which is most strongly adhered to. § 30. In truth these are often only confused conceptions, gross and inexact, and it is very essential that men agree as to the precise number of simple ideas or qualities which belong to a given species or a given name, for pains, skill, and time are needed to find simple ideas which are constantly united. However a few of the qualities composing these inexact definitions are ordinarily sufficient in conversation; but in spite of the stir about genera and species, the forms, of which so much has been said in the schools, are only chimeras which avail us nothing in furnishing an entrance into the knowledge of specific natures.

Th. Whoever makes a possible combination, is not at all mistaken therein, nor in giving it a name; but he is mistaken

[1] Such combinations of essentially self-contradictory ideas may easily be united in a complex term, and be apparently clear and possible, until analyzed and compared with reality, when their confusion and impossibility is at once made evident. — TR.

if he thinks that his conception is altogether that which others more expert have conceived under the same name or in the same body. He perhaps conceives a genus too common instead of another more specific. There is nothing in all this contrary to the schools, and I do not see why you return here to the charge against genera, species, and forms, since it is necessary for you to recognize indeed the genera, species, and even the internal essences or forms, which we do not pretend to employ in order to know the specific nature of the thing, although we admit we are still ignorant of them.

§ 30. *Ph.* It is at least evident that the limits we assign to species are not *exactly conformed* to those established by nature. For in our need of general names for present use, we do not put ourselves to the trouble of discovering the qualities which would give us superior knowledge of their most essential differences and agreements, but we ourselves distinguish them into species in virtue of certain appearances which are manifest to everybody, that we may more easily communicate with others.

Th. If we combine compatible ideas, the limits we assign to species are always *exactly conformed* to nature; and if we are careful to combine ideas actually found together, our notions are also conformed to experience; and if we consider them as provisional only for actual bodies, without excluding experiment made or to be made for further discovery therein, and if we have recourse to experts, when a definite question arises with reference to what is openly understood by the name, we shall not err in the matter. Thus nature may furnish ideas the most perfect and most convenient, but she will not give the lie to those we have which are good and natural, although not perhaps the best and most natural.

§ 32. *Ph. Our generic ideas* of substances, as that of metal, for example, do not follow exactly *the models* set them by nature, since you cannot find any body including simply malleability and fusibility without other qualities.

Th. No one asks for such models and it would not be reasonable to ask for them; furthermore they do not occur in the most distinct notions. We never find a number in which there is nothing to notice but multitude in general, an extension in which there is only extension, a body in which there is only solidity, and no other qualities; and when the specific differences are positive and contrary it is very essential that the genus share in them.

Ph. If, then, any one thinks that a man, a horse, an animal, a plant, etc., are distinguished by *real essences* made by nature, he must think that nature is *very liberal with these real essences,* if she produces one of them for the body, another for the animal, and still another for the horse, and that she bestows freely all these essences upon Bucephalus; whilst genera and species are only signs more or less comprehensive.

Th. If you take real essences as these substantial models, which exist as a body and nothing more, an animal and nothing more specific, a horse without individual qualities, you are right in treating them as chimeras. And no one has maintained, I think, not even the greatest *Realists* of former times, that there are as many substances confining themselves to the generic as there are genera. But it does not follow that if general essences are not this, they are merely signs; for I have many times remarked to you that there are *possibilities in the resemblances.* In like manner from the fact that colors are not always substances or extracted dyes, it does not follow that they are imaginary. For the rest you cannot think nature too *liberal;* she is so beyond all that we can invent, and all advantageous compatible possibilities are found realized upon the grand theatre of her representations. There were formerly two axioms among philosophers: that of the *Realists* seemed to make nature prodigal, and that of the *Nominalists* seemed to declare her stingy. The one says that nature suffers no vacuum, and the other that she does nothing in vain. These two axioms are good provided you understand them; for nature is like a good economist, who saves where it is necessary in order to be grand at times and places. She is grand in effects, and sparing in the causes she employs.

§ 34. *Ph.* Without amusing ourselves longer with this discussion upon real essences, it is enough that we obtain the purpose of language and the usage of words which is to indicate our thoughts in an abridged form. If I wish to speak to any one of a species of birds three or four feet in height, whose skin is covered with something between feathers and hair, of a dark brown color, without wings, but in their place two or three small branches, like those of the broom, which descend to the lower part of the body, with long and large legs, the feet armed only with three claws and without a tail; I am compelled to make this description whereby I can make myself understood by others. But when I am told that the name of this animal is *Cassowary*, I can then use this name to designate in discourse this entire complex idea.

Th. Perhaps a very exact idea of the covering of the skin or of some other part would suffice by itself alone to distinguish this animal from every other known, as Hercules was known by his gait, and as the lion was recognized by his claw according to the Latin proverb. But the more circumstances you heap up, the less provisional is your definition.

§ 35. *Ph.* We may curtail the idea in this case without prejudice to the thing; but when nature curtails it, it is a question whether the species remains. For example: if a body existed having all the qualities of gold except malleability, would it be gold? it depends upon men to decide. They are then the ones who determine the species of things.

Th. Not at all; they would determine only the name. But this experience would teach us that malleability has no necessary connection with the other qualities of gold taken together. It would teach us then a new possibility and consequently a new species. As for gold which is eager[1] or brittle, this comes only from additions, and is not consistent with the other tests of gold; for the cupel and antimony remove this eagerness from it.

§ 36. *Ph.* A portion of our doctrine follows that will appear very strange. Each abstract idea having a certain name forms a distinct species. But what of that, if nature so wills it? I should be glad to know why a *lap-dog* and a *greyhound* are not as distinct species as a *spaniel* and an *elephant.*

Th. I have distinguished above the different senses of the word *species.* Taking it logically, or mathematically rather, the least dissimilitude may suffice. Thus each different idea will give another species, and it makes no difference whether it has a name or not. But, physically speaking, we do not attend to all the varieties, and we speak either distinctly when the question concerns only appearances, or conjecturally when the

[1] *Cf.* Locke, *Philos. Works*, Vol. 2, p. 65 (Bohn's ed.). — Tr.

question concerns the inner truth of things, presuming therein some essential and immutable nature, like reason in man. We presume then, that whatever differs only by accidental changes, like water and ice, quicksilver in the liquid form and as sublimate, is of the same species: and in organic bodies the provisional mark of the same species is usually placed in the generation or race, as in those most alike it is placed in reproduction. It is true we cannot judge with precision, for lack of knowledge of the inner nature of things; but, as I have said more than once, we judge provisionally and often conjecturally. But when we wish to speak only from the external, for fear of saying nothing certain, there is some latitude; and to dispute then whether a difference is specific or not is to dispute about the name; and in this sense there is so great a difference between dogs, that we may very well say that the house-dogs of England and the dogs of Boulogne belong to different species. It is not impossible, however, that they belong to a remote identical or similar race, which we should find if we could go back very far, and that their ancestors were alike or identical, but that after great changes, some of the posterity have become very large and others very small. We may indeed believe also without offending reason that they have in common an inner nature, constant, specific, which is no longer subdivided thus, or which is not found here in several other such natures, and consequently is no longer varied save by accidents; although there is also nothing to make us judge that this must necessarily be so in all that which we call the lowest species (*species infima*). But there is no likelihood that a spaniel and an elephant are of the same race, and that they have such a specific common nature. Thus in the different sorts of dogs, speaking of appearances, we may distinguish species, and speaking of the inner essence we may be in suspense: but comparing the dog and the elephant there is no reason for attributing to them externally or internally that which would make us think them of one and the same species. So there is in this case no occasion for suspense in the face of the presumption. In man we can also distinguish species logically speaking, and if we stopped with the external we should find also, speaking physically, differences which could pass as specific. Thus a traveller was found who thought that the Negroes, Chinese, and finally the Americans were not of one and the same race among themselves nor with the peoples resembling us. But as we know the essential inner nature of man, *i.e.* the reason, which dwells in the man himself and is found in all men, and as we notice nothing fixed and internal among us which forms a subdivision, we have no reason to judge that there is in men, according to the truth of the inner nature, an essential specific difference, while such difference is found between man and beast, supposing that the beasts are only empirical, according as I have explained above, as in fact experience gives us no reason for forming any other judgment.

§ 39. *Ph.* Let us take the example of an artificial thing whose internal structure is known to us. A time-piece that only indicates the hours, and one that strikes, are of one species only for those who have only one name by which to designate them; but for him who designates the first by the name *watch*, and second *clock*, they are *in relation to him* different species. It is the name and not the inner disposition which makes a new species, otherwise there would be too many species. There are watches with four wheels, and others with five; some have strings and fusees,[1] and some not; some have a free balance, and others are regulated by a spiral spring and others by hog's bristles. Does any one of these things suffice to make a specific difference? I say no, so long as these time-pieces agree in name.

Th. And I for my part say yes, for without stopping at names, I should consider the varieties of contrivance and especially the differences of the balance; for since a spring has been applied which governs the vibrations according to its own and consequently renders them more equal, pocket-watches have changed their character, and have become incomparably more accurate. I have indeed mentioned before another principle of equality which might be applied to watches.

Ph. If any one wishes to make divisions based upon the differences which he knows in the internal configuration he may do so; but they would not be distinct species with relation to the people who are ignorant of this construction.

[1] Locke has "physics," *Philos. Works*, Vol. 2, p. 67 (Bohn's ed.). — Tr.

Th. I do not know why those with you always wish to make virtues, truths, and species depend upon our opinion or knowledge. They exist in nature, whether we know it and approve or not. To speak otherwise is to change the names of things and received language without any reason. Men up to the present time have believed that there are many kinds of clocks or watches, without informing themselves in what they consist or how they may name them.

Ph. You have however recognized not long since that when men wish to distinguish physical species by appearances, they limit them in an arbitrary way, where they find it to the purpose, *i.e.* according as they find the difference more or less considerable and according to the end they have. And you yourself have made use of the comparison of weights and measures, which are regulated and given their names according to the good pleasure of man.

Th. It is since then that I have begun to understand you. Between *specific differences* purely *logical*, for which the least variation of assignable definition suffices, however accidental it be, and between *specific differences* purely *physical*, based upon the essential or immutable, we may place a mean, which cannot be precisely determined; it is regulated by the most important appearances, which are not altogether immutable, but which do not change easily, the one approaching the essential more than the other. And as a connoisseur too may go farther than another, the thing appears arbitrary and has some relation to men, and it appears convenient to regulate names also according to these principal differences. We can then speak thus, that there are *specific civil differences* and *nominal species* which must not be confounded with what I have called above *nominal definitions*, and which have place in differences specifically logical as well as physical. For the rest, besides common usage, the laws themselves may give authority to the significations of words, and then *the species* would become *legal*, as in the contracts which are called *nominati, i.e.*, designated by a particular name. For example as the Roman Law made the age of puberty commence at the end of the fourteenth year. This entire consideration is not to be despised, but I do not see that it is of very much use here, for besides the fact that you have appeared to me to apply it sometimes where it did not apply, we shall accomplish nearly the same result if we consider that it rests with men to proceed in subdivisions as far as they find them to the purpose, and to abstract ulterior differences without the necessity of denying them; and that it also rests with them to choose the certain, notwithstanding the uncertain, in order to fix some notions and measures by giving them names.

Ph. I am much pleased that we are here no longer so far apart as we appeared. § 41. You agree then, sir, I see, that artificial as well as natural things are species contrary to the view of some philosophers. § 42. But before leaving the names of substances, I would add that of all the diverse ideas we have, they alone are ideas of substances which have proper or individual names; for it rarely happens that men need to make frequent mention of any individual quality or other individual accident. Besides individual acts perish at once and the combination of circumstances which thereby comes about only subsists as in the substances.

Th. There are, however, cases where it has been necessary to remember an individual accident and to give it a name; thus your rule is ordinarily good, but there are exceptions to it. Religion furnishes us with them; for example we celebrate each year the memory of the birth of Jesus Christ. The Greeks call this event Theogeny, and that of the adoration of the Magi, Epiphany. And the Hebrews call the *Passah par excellence* the passage of the angel who caused the death of the eldest sons of the Egyptians without touching those of the Hebrews; and this is why they were to celebrate its memory every year. As for the *species of artificial things*, the scholastic philosophers found difficulty in admitting them into their *predicaments;* but there was little necessity for their hesitation since these predicamental tables were destined for use in making a general review of our ideas. It is well however to recognize the difference existing between perfect substances and between the assemblages of substances (*aggregata*) which are substantial entities composed either by nature or by the art of man. For nature has also such aggregates, as the bodies whose mixture is imperfect (*imperfecte mixta*) to use the language of our philosophers, which constitute no *unum per se* and do not possess in themselves a perfect unity. I believe however that the four bodies which they call elements, and think simple, and the salts, metals, and other bodies which they think are perfectly mixed, and to which they attribute their temperaments,[1] are not *unum per se* either; so much the more as we must judge that they are uniform and homogeneous only in appearance, and even a homogeneous body would not cease to be a mass. In a word, the perfect unity must be reserved to bodies animated, or endowed with primitive entelechies; for these entelechies are analogous to souls and are as individual and imperishable as they; and I have elsewhere affirmed that their organic bodies are practically machines, but which surpass the artificial machines of our invention as much as the inventor of the natural machines surpasses us. For these natural machines are as imperishable as the souls themselves, and the animal with the soul subsists always: it is (the better to explain myself by something pleasing, wholly laughable as it is,) as if a harlequin wished to strip himself in the theatre, but could not succeed because he had an indefinite number of garments one upon another; although these infinite replications of organic bodies, which exist in an animal, are not so similar nor so applied the one to the other, as the garments, nature's art being of a wholly different subtility. All this shows that the philosophers have not been wholly in the wrong in putting so great distance between artificial things and between natural bodies endowed with a real unity. But it belonged only to our time to develop this mystery and make understood its importance and consequences in order thoroughly to establish natural theology and what is called Pneumatics,[2] in a manner

[1] Leibnitz here alludes to the four elements of Empedocles, c. 492–c. 432, B. C., *viz.*, fire, air, earth, water, adopted by Plato and Aristotle and called by the Peripatetics warmth, cold, dryness, humidity, a mixture of which in varying proportions constituted all bodies. *Cf.* Zeller, *Philos. d. Griec.*, I. 2 [Vol. 2], 758 *sq.*, 5th ed., 1892, II. 1 [Vol. 3], 796 *sq.*, 4th ed., 1889, II, 2 [Vol. 4], 431, *sq.*, 832 *sq.*, 3d ed., 1879. The state of a body resulting from the proportional disposition of these primary constituent elements or qualities was called its temperament, the character of the temperament varying according to the predominance of one or more of the elements. The scholastics discussed the question whether the temperament comprised these four primary qualities, or whether it did not consist in a fifth simple quality, the outcome of the reciprocal action of the four primary qualities, which resulted in their entire destruction. *Cf.* also Gerhardt, *Leibniz. philos. Schrift.*, 4, 207. — TR.

[2] *Cf. ante*, p. 50, note 2. Schaarschmidt states that Pneumatics — *Pneumatik* — with the meaning — Doctrine of the Spirit, *Lehre vom Geiste* — Psychology

truly natural and in agreement with our experiments and understanding, and requiring the loss of none of the important considerations they are destined to furnish, or rather enhancing their value, as does the system of pre-established harmony.[1] And I believe that we can best conclude this long discussion of the names of substances only by that means.

— occurs in Alsted's *Encyclopædie*, Herborniæ, 1630, *cf. ante*, p. 311, note 2, and that Stephen Chauvin in his *Lexicon philosophicum*, Leovardiæ, 1713, adopted it and explained it by Pneumatology and Pneumatosophy. The term is now confined to physical science, and denotes that department of hydrodynamics which treats of the properties of gases as distinguished from liquids. *Cf.* Krauth-Flemming, *Vocab. of the Philos. Sciences*, p. 388, New York, Sheldon & Co., 1883. — TR.

[1] *Cf. New Essays*, Bk. IV., chap. 10, §§ 7 and 9, *infra*, pp. 505, 507; *Système nouveau*, §§ 14–16, Gerhardt, 4, 484–86, Erdmann, 127, a–128, Jacques, 1, 475–77, trans. Duncan, *Philos. Wks. of Leibnitz*, 77–79; *Considerations sur les principes de vie*, etc., G. 6, 541, E. 430, trans. D. 165; *Principes de la nature et de la grace*, §§ 7–13, G. 6, 602–604, E. 716, trans. D. 212–215; *Animadversiones in partem generalem Principiorum Cartesianorum*, Pt. I. ad Art. 14, G. 4, 358, trans. D. 50; *Leibniz gegen Descartes und den Cartesianismus*, G. 4, 292–294, 401–403, 405–406, E. 176, trans. D. 132–138, and his note 49, p. 382; *Med. de Cog. Ver. et Ideis*, G. 4, 424, E. 80, a, trans. D. 30. According to Leibnitz, his doctrine of monads requires as its necessary complement the existence of God, since the single monads, expressing in their own experience all that is beyond them, yet without influence on other monads, cannot furnish a sufficient ground or reason for the harmony and connection of things in a universal world-order. This harmonious world-order existing, its sufficient ground or reason must be found in the absolute being, God, who has given to each monad the nature which makes it capable of developing itself in its extreme individuality in accord and correspondence with every other. The pre-established harmony is thus an actual proof, in accord with experience, of the existence of God, and the suggestion of reason in the ontological argument as improved by Leibnitz, is confirmed by the comparative and comprehensive study of the phenomena of nature. For expositions and criticisms of Leibnitz's doctrine, *cf.* Dewey, *Leibniz's New Essays*, chaps. 11, 12; E. Zeller, *Gesch. d. deutschen Philos. seit Leibniz*, 2d ed., München, 1875, pp. 88–98, 124–127; F. A. Lange, *Gesch. d. Materialismus*, 3d ed., Leipzig u. Gerlohn, 1875 *sq.*, Bk. I., Sect. IV., chap. 4, Eng. trans. by E. C. Thomas, 3 vols., Boston, Vol. 2, pp. 124 *sq.*; Kuno Fischer, *Gesch. d. n. Philos.*, Bd. II., Leibniz, 3d ed., Heidelberg, 1889, pp. 455 *sq.*, 539 *sq.* — TR.

CHAPTER VII

OF PARTICLES

§ 1. *Ph.* Besides the words which are used to *name* ideas, we need those which signify the *connection* of ideas or propositions. *This is, this is not,* are general signs of *affirmation* or *negation.* But besides the parts of propositions the mind also binds together sentences and entire propositions, § 2. availing itself of words expressing this union of different affirmations and negations and which are called *particles;* in whose proper use the art of speaking well principally consists. It is in order that reasoning be consecutive and methodical that terms showing the *connection, restriction, distinction, opposition, emphasis,* etc., are needed. And when they are despised the hearer is embarrassed.

Th. I admit that particles are very useful; but I am not aware that the art of speaking well consists principally in their proper use. If any one presents only aphorisms or detached theses, as they often do in the universities, or as in the case of that which they call among the jurisconsults an *articulate* libel, or as in the *articles* which are offered to the witnesses, then provided we arrange these propositions well we shall accomplish very nearly the same result in making them understood as if we had put in the connective and the particles; for the reader supplies them. But I admit there would be trouble if you put in the particles badly, and much more than if you omitted them. Particles seem to me also to unite not only the parts of discourse composed of propositions and the parts of the proposition composed of ideas, but also the parts of the idea, composed in many ways by the combination of other ideas. And it is this last connection which is indicated by the *prepositions,* while the *adverbs* modify the affirmation or negation in the verb; and the *conjunctions* modify the connection of different affirmations or negations. But I doubt not that you have noticed all this yourself, although your words seem to state otherwise.

§ 3. *Ph.* The part of grammar which treats of particles has been cultivated less than that which represents in order the *cases, genders, modes, tenses, gerundives,* and *supines.* It is true that in some languages they have also arranged the particles under some titles by distinct subdivisions with great appearance of exactness. But it is not sufficient to run through these catalogues. One must reflect upon his own thoughts in order to observe the forms which the mind takes in discoursing, for the particles are so many indications of the action of the mind.

Th. It is very true that the doctrine of the particles is important, and I wish we might enter into much greater detail thereupon. For nothing would be more suited to make known the different forms of the understanding. *Genders* are of no account in philosophical grammar, but the cases correspond to the *prepositions,* and often the preposition is enveloped in the noun and as it were absorbed, and other particles are concealed in the inflections of the verbs.

§ 4. *Ph.* In order properly to explain particles it is not sufficient to render them (as is usual in a dictionary) by the words of another language which approach most nearly their meaning, because it is as difficult to comprehend their precise meaning in one language as in another; besides the significations of related words in two languages are not always exactly the same and indeed they vary in one and the same language. I remember that in the Hebrew language there is one particle of a single letter[1] of which there are reckoned up more than fifty significations.

Th. Scholars have attempted to make special treatises upon the particles of the Latin, Greek, and Hebrew; and Strauchius,[2] a celebrated jurisconsult, has published a book upon the use of particles in jurisprudence, where their signification is of no small consequence. We ordinarily find, however, that it is rather by means of examples and synonymes that they attempt to explain them, than by distinct notions. Further we can

[1] *I.e.* the adverb ל. — TR.

[2] Johann Strauch, 1612–1680, the maternal uncle of Leibnitz, a distinguished jurisconsult, Professor at Leipzig, Jena, and Giessen, and Syndicus in Braunschweig; *cf.* Guhrauer, *G. W. Freiherr v. Leibnitz,* Pt. I., Bk. I., pp. 6, 35 *sq.*, and *Anmerkungen z. erst. Buche,* pp. 6, 7. The book here referred to by Leibnitz is entitled: *Lexicon particularum juris s. de usu et efficacia quorundam syncategorematum et particularum indeclinabilium.* — TR.

not always find a general or formal signification for them, as the late Bohlius[1] called it, which can satisfy all the examples; but notwithstanding this we can always reduce all the uses of a word to a definite number of significations. And this is what should be done.

§ 5. *Ph.* In fact the number of significations greatly exceeds that of the particles. In English the particle *but* has very different significations: (1) when I say: *but to say no more,* (*mais* pour ne rien dire de plus) as if this particle indicated that the mind stops in its course before it has reached the end. But saying: (2) *I saw but two planets* (je vis *seulement* deux planetes), the mind restricts the sense of what it means to that which has been expressed by the exclusion of everything else. And when I say (3): *you pray, but it is not that God would bring you to the true religion, but that he would confirm you in your own* (vous priez Dieu *mais* ce n'est pas qu'il veuille vous amener à la connaissance de la vraye Religion, *mais* qu'il vous confirme dans la vostre), the first *but* (or *mais*) designates a supposition in the mind which is otherwise than it should be, and the second shows that the mind puts a direct opposition between what precedes and what follows. (4) *All animals have sense, but a dog is an animal* (tous les animaux ont du sentiment, *mais* le chien est un animal). Here the particle signifies the connection of the second proposition with the first.

Th. The French *mais* (but) may be substituted in all these instances except the second; but the German *allein,* taken as a particle, which signifies a kind of mixture of *mais* (but) and *seulement* (only), may doubtless be substituted instead of *but* in all these examples except the last, where its use may be a little doubtful. *Mais* (but) is also rendered in German sometimes by *aber,* sometimes by *sondern,* which indicates a separation or segregation and approaches the particle *allein.* For a proper explanation of the particles, it is not sufficient to make an abstract explication as we have just made here; but we must proceed to a paraphrase which may be substituted in

[1] Samuel Bohl, 1611–1689, Professor at Rostock, who devoted himself to the furtherance of the study of Hebrew in Germany, and whom Leibnitz mentions because of his works on the doctrine of the Hebrew Vowel- and Accent-Signs; *cf.* Dutens, *Leibniz. op. om.*, 5, 190. He published a large number of works, among which were *Scrutin. S. s. ex accentibus*, 1636, and *Dissertat. pro formali Signif. S. S. eruenda*, Rostock, 1637.—TR.

its place, as the definition may be put in the place of the thing defined. When we have striven to seek and to determine these *suitable paraphrases*, in all the particles so far as they are susceptible of them, we shall have regulated their significations. Let us try to attain this result in our four examples. In the first we mean: Thus far only speak we of this, and no farther (*non più*); in the second: I see only two planets, and no more; in the third: You pray God, and for this only, viz. to be confirmed in your religion, and no more, etc.; in the fourth, it is as if we said: all animals have sense; it is sufficient to consider that only, and no more is needed. The dog is an animal, he then has sense. Thus all these examples indicate limits, and a *non plus ultra*, whether in things, or in discourse. Thus *but* is an end, a limit of the course, as if we said: stop, we are there, we have reached our *But*. *But*, *Bute*, is an old Teutonic word, signifying something fixed, an abode. *Beuten* (an obsolete word found still in some church songs) is to abide. *Mais* originates from *magis*, as if any one wished to say: *as for the surplus we must leave it*, which is the same as saying: No more is needed, it is enough, let us come to something else, or this is something else. But as the use of languages varies in a strange manner, it would be necessary to enter much farther into the detail of examples in order sufficiently to regulate the significations of particles. In French we avoid the double *mais* by a *cependant* (however), and we should say: Vous priez, *cependant* ce n'est pas pour obtenir la verité, mais pour estre confirmé dans vostre opinion (You pray, not however (*cependant*) to obtain the truth but (*mais*) to be confirmed in your opinion). The *sed* of the Latins was often expressed formerly by *ains*, which is the *anzi* of the Italians, and the French in modifying it have deprived their language of an advantageous expression. For example: There was no certainty about it, yet (*cependant*) we were persuaded of what I have informed you, because we like to believe what we wish; but it has been found that it was not so; but (*ains*) rather, etc. (Il n'y avoit rien de seur, *cependant* on estoit persuadé de ce que je vous ay mandé, parce qu'on aime à croire ce qu'on souhaite; mais il s'est trouvé que ce n'estoit pas cela; ains plustost, etc.).

§ 6. *Ph.* My purpose has been to touch this matter only

very slightly. I would add that particles often include either constantly or in certain constructions the sense of an entire proposition.

Th. But when it is *a complete sentiment*, I think that it is only by means of a kind of ellipsis; otherwise it is the *interjections* alone which in my opinion can subsist by themselves and say all in a word, as *ah! (hoi me!)*. For when we say *mais*, adding nothing more, it is an ellipsis for: *but let us wait for the confirmation of intelligence* and not flatter ourselves unduly. There is something approximating to this in the *nisi* of the Latins: *si nisi non esset*, if there were not but (*mais*). For the rest I should not be displeased, sir, had you entered a little farther into the detail of the turns of the mind which appear marvellous in the use of the particles. But since we have reason for hastening to conclude this investigation of words and to return to things, I do not wish to delay you longer, although I truly think that languages are the best mirrors of the human mind, and that an exact analysis of the signification of words would show us better than anything else the workings of the understanding.

CHAPTER VIII

OF ABSTRACT AND CONCRETE TERMS

§ 1. *Ph.* It is further to be remarked that terms are abstract or concrete. Each abstract idea is distinct, so that of two the one can never be the other. The mind must perceive by its intuitive knowledge the difference between them, and *consequently* two of these ideas can never be affirmed one of another. Every one sees at once the falsehood of these propositions: *humanity is animality or rationality:* this is as evident as any of the generally received maxims.

Th. There is still something to be said thereupon. We admit that justice is a virtue, a habit (*habitus*), a quality, an accident, etc. Thus two abstract terms may be stated one of another. I am furthermore wont to distinguish two kinds of abstracts. There are abstract *logical* terms, and there are also abstract *real* terms. The *abstract real* terms, or conceived at least as real, are either essences or parts of the essence, or accidents, *i.e.* beings added to substance. The *abstract logical* terms are the predications reduced to terms, as if I said: to be a man, to be an animal; and in this sense the one can be stated of the other, by saying: *to be a man is to be an animal.* But in the realities this has no place. For we cannot say that humanity or man-ness[1] (*l'hommëité*) — (if you please), which is the essence of the whole man, is animality, which is only a part of this essence; yet these abstract and incomplete beings signified by the abstract real terms have also their genera and species which are not less expressed by the abstract real terms: thus there is predication between them, as I have shown by the example of justice and virtue.

§ 2. *Ph.* One may always say that substances have only few abstract names; they have scarcely spoken in the schools of humanity, animality, corporality; and they have never been authorized in the world.

Th. The reason is that but few of these terms were necessary to serve as examples and to throw light upon the general notion, which was the reason why they were not wholly neglected. If the ancients did not use the word *humanity* in the sense of the schools, they said *human nature,* which is the same thing. It is certain also that they said divinity, or rather divine nature; and theologians having found it needful to speak of these two natures and of real accidents, they were attached to these abstract entities in the schools of philosophy and theology, and perhaps to a greater extent than was proper.

CHAPTER IX

OF THE IMPERFECTIONS OF WORDS

§ 1. *Ph.* We have already spoken of the *double use of words.* The one is to register our own thoughts in order to aid our memory which makes us talk to ourselves; the other is to communicate our thoughts to others by means of speech.

[1] I have taken the liberty to coin the word as an equivalent of the French, which I think is also coined by Leibnitz to express the abstraction of the scholastics. — Tr.

These two uses show the perfection or imperfection of words. § 2. When we speak only to ourselves, it is a matter of indifference what words we employ, provided we remember their meaning and do not change it. But § 3. *the use of communication* is also of two kinds, civil and philosophic. The *civil* consists in the conversation and use of the civil life. The *philosophic use* is that made of words for the purpose of giving precise notions and to express in general propositions certain truths.

Th. Very good: words are not less *marks* (*notæ*) for us (as the characters of arithmetic or algebra may be) than signs for others; and the use of words as of signs is as much in place when the question concerns the application of general precepts to the usage of life, as when it concerns the discovery or verification of these precepts. The first *use of signs* is *civil*, and the second *philosophic.*

§ 5. *Ph.* Now it is difficult, chiefly in the following cases, to learn and retain the idea which each word signifies, (1) when these ideas are very complex; (2) when the ideas composing a new one have no natural bond between them, so that there is in nature no fixed measure nor any model to rectify and regulate them; (3) when the model is not easy to be known; (4) when the meaning of the word and the real essence are not exactly the same. The names of the modes are most liable to be doubtful and imperfect for the two first reasons, and those of substances for the two second. § 6. When the idea of the modes is very complex, as that of the majority of the terms of ethics, they rarely have precisely the same signification in the minds of two different persons. § 7. The defect also of the models renders these words equivocal. He who first invented the word *brusquer* (to be abrupt with) understood thereby what he found to the purpose, without informing those who have used it as he of his precise meaning, and without having shown them any constant model. § 8. Common use regulates sufficiently the sense of words for ordinary conversation, but it has no precision; and the signification most conformed to the peculiar nature of the language is every day disputed. Many speak of *glory*, but few have the same understanding of it. § 9. They are only simple sounds in the mouths of many, or at least their meanings are very indefinite. And in a discourse or conversation in which mention is made of *honor, faith, grace, religion, the church,* and above all in discussion, you will notice at once that men have different notions which they apply to the same terms. And if it is difficult to understand the meaning of the terms of the people of our time, it is much more difficult to understand *ancient books.* Fortunate is it that we may pass them by save when they contain what we should believe and do.

Th. These remarks are good: but in regard to ancient books, as we need to understand Holy Scripture above all, and as Roman laws are still of great use in a good part of Europe, we are indeed compelled to consult a great many other ancient books; the Rabbis, the Church Fathers, even the profane historians. Besides the ancient physicians also deserve to be understood. The practice of medicine by the Greeks came through the Arabs to us; the water from the fountain has been made turbid in the streams of the Arabs, and purified in many respects since we have begun to have recourse to the original Greeks. But these Arabs do not cease to be of use and we are assured that Ebenbitar,[1] for example, who in his books on Simples has copied Dioscorides, often serves to throw light upon him. I find also that, next to religion and history, it is chiefly in medicine, as far as it is empirical, that the tradition of the ancients preserved in writing, and in general the observations of another

[1] Ibn-al-Baitar, c. 1197–1248, a distinguished Arabian botanist, — according to Pouchet the most learned that the Arabian School has produced, — who wrote a general history of simples, or of plants alphabetically arranged, a *materia medica*, based upon and said to contain for the most part the work of the Greek physician Dioscorides, c. 100 A.D., Περὶ Ὕλης Ἰατρικῆς, as well as a variety of facts from other sources, including descriptions of plants not mentioned by either Dioscorides or Pliny the Elder, 23–79. Most of Baitar's works still remain in MSS. in the libraries of Paris and the Escurial. Fr. R. Dietz published a small fragment of the work on Simples in his *Analecta medica ex libris MSS.*, Lipsiæ, 1833, 8vo. There are also *Grosse Zusammenstellung ü. d. Kräfte d. bekannt. einfachen Heil-und-Nahrungsmittel v. . . . Ebn Baithar. Aus d. Arabischen übersetzt v. Dr. Joseph v. Sontheimer*, 2 vols., Stuttgart, 1840–42, and *Traité des simples*, trans. by L. Leclerc, in Inst. de France, Notices et extraits des MSS. de la Bibl. Nationale, vol. 23, Pt. I., Paris, 1877, 4to. For some account of Baitar, *cf.* Leclerc in *Gazette hebdom. de médicine et de chirurgie*, xxii., 97, 129, Paris, 1875; F. A. Pouchet, *Histoire des sciences naturelles au moyen âge*, Paris, 1853, 8vo. Schaarschmidt says that Leibnitz may have been led to the remark which he here makes upon Baitar by the *Exercitationes de homonymis hyles iatricæ*, appended to Claud. Salmasius, 1588–1653, *Plinianæ exercitationes*, P. 104. a. B. 110. a. A., Trajecti-ad-Rhenum, 1689, 2 vols., fol., where different accounts of Dioscorides are amended from Ebnbitar. TR.

may be of service. I have therefore always held in high esteem physicians much versed in the knowledge of antiquity; and I was very sorry that Reinesius,[1] excellent in both departments (of knowledge), had turned aside to explain the rites and history of the ancients, rather than to recover a part of the knowledge they had of nature, in which it has been shown that he would have been able furthermore marvellously to succeed. When the Latins, Greeks, Hebrews and Arabs shall some day be exhausted, the Chinese, supplied also with ancient books, will enter the lists and furnish matter for the curiosity of our critics. Not to speak of some old books of the Persians, Armenians, Copts and Brahmins, which will be unearthed in time so as not to neglect any light antiquity may give on doctrines by tradition and on facts by history. And if there were no longer an ancient book to examine, languages would take the place of books and they are the most ancient monuments of mankind. In time all the languages of the world will be recorded and placed in the dictionaries and grammars, and compared together; this will be of very great use both for the knowledge of things, since names often correspond to their properties (as is seen by the names of plants among different peoples), and for the knowledge of our mind and the wonderful variety of its operations. Not to speak of the origin of nations, which is known by means of solid etymologies which the comparison of languages will best furnish. But of this I have already spoken. And all this shows the use and extent of *criticism*, little considered by some otherwise very clever philosophers who take the liberty to speak with contempt of *Rabbinage*[2] and in general of *philology*. We see also that critics will find for a long time yet matter for fruitful exercise,

[1] Thomas Reinesius, 1587–1667, a physician who wrote on natural history and medicine, and afterwards devoted himself to philological and antiquarian studies. Among his works were, *Schola jureconsultorum medica relationum libris aliquot comprehensa, quibus principia medicinæ in jus transmuta ex professo examinantur*, Lipsiæ, 1679, 12mo; *Syntazma inscriptionem antiquarum cum primis Romæ veteris, quarum omissa est recensio in Gruteii opere, cum comment*, Lipsiæ, 1682, fol. *Cf.* B. Schuchardt, *Lebensbeschreibungen berühmter Ærzte und Naturforscher, welche aus Thüringen stammen. Correspondenz-Blätter des allgemeinen ärztlichen Vereins von Thüringen*, Weimar, 1888, xvii., 556, 601. — TR.

[2] A term of disparagement, meaning the study made of the books of the rabbis. — TR.

and they will do well not to amuse themselves too much with minutiæ, since they have so many objects more pleasing for treatment; though I well know that minutiæ also are often very necessary with the critics for the discovery of more important knowledge. And as criticism turns in large measure upon the meaning of words and the interpretation of authors, especially the ancients, this discussion about words joined with the mention you made of the ancients, makes me touch upon this important point. But to return to your four defects of nomination, I tell you, sir, that we can remedy them all, especially since writing has been invented and they subsist only through our negligence. For it depends upon us to fix their meanings, at least in any scholarly language, and to agree to destroy this tower of Babel. But there are two defects where the remedy is more difficult, consisting the one in the doubt which exists whether the ideas are compatible, when experience does not furnish them all combined in one and the same subject; the other in the necessity for making provisional definitions of sensible things, when our experience with them is insufficient for more complete definitions: but I have spoken more than once of both these defects.[1]

Ph. [I am going to tell you some things which will serve further to clear up to some extent the defects you have just remarked, and the third of those which I have indicated makes it seem that these definitions are provisional; viz.: — when we have no sufficient knowledge of our sensible models, *i.e.* the substantial beings of corporeal nature. This defect also makes us ignorant as to whether we may combine the sensible qualities which nature has not combined, because at bottom we do not understand them.] Now if the signification of the words which serve for the mixed modes is uncertain, for lack of models which show the same composition, that of the names of the substantial beings is uncertain for a wholly contrary reason, because they must signify what is supposed to be conformed to the reality of things, and to be related to the models formed by nature.

Th. I have already more than once remarked in our previous conversations that this is not essential to the ideas of

[1] *Cf. New Essays*, Bk. III., chap. 6. — TR.

substances; but I admit that ideas made after nature are the surest and most useful.

§ 12. *Ph.* When then we follow the models wholly made by nature, unless the imagination finds it necessary to retain their representations, the names of substances have in ordinary use *a double relation,* as I have already shown. The *first* is that they signify the internal and real constitution of things, but this model cannot be known and consequently cannot serve to regulate the significations.

Th. That is not the question here, since we are speaking of ideas of which we have models; the internal essence is in the thing, but we agree that it cannot serve as a pattern.

§ 13. *Ph.* The *second relation* is then that which the names of substances immediately have to the simple ideas, which exist at the same time in the substance. But as the number of these ideas united in one and the same subject is great, men speak of this same subject, forming very different ideas of it, both by the different combination of the simple ideas they make and because the greater part of the qualities of bodies are the powers which they have of producing changes in other bodies and receiving them; witness the changes one of the basest metals is capable of undergoing through the operation of fire, and it receives many more yet at the hands of a chemist, through the application of other bodies. Further, one is contented with weight and color as criteria for a knowledge of gold; another includes ductility, fixedness; and the third desires to make us take into consideration its solubility in aqua regia. § 14. As things likewise often resemble each other, it is sometimes difficult to designate their precise differences.

Th. As bodies are really liable to be altered, disguised, falsified, counterfeited, it is a great point to be able to distinguish and recognize them. Gold is disguised in solution, but it may be drawn off, either by precipitating it or distilling the water; and counterfeit or adulterated gold is recognized or purified by the art of the assayers, which not being known to everybody, it is not strange that men do not all have the same idea of gold. And ordinarily it is only the experts who have sufficiently just ideas of these matters.

§ 15. *Ph.* This variety does not, however, cause so much confusion in civil intercourse as in philosophic researches.

Th. It would be more tolerable if it had no influence in practical life where it is often important not to receive a *Qui pro quo,* and consequently to know the characteristics of things or to have at hand the class who know them. And it is especially important as regards drugs and materials which are costly, and of which you may have need on important occasions. The philosophical confusion will manifest itself rather in the use of more general terms.

§ 18. *Ph.* The names of *simple ideas* are less liable to equivocation, and we are rarely mistaken as regards the terms white, bitter, etc.

Th. It is, however, true that these terms are not wholly exempt from uncertainty; and I have already noticed the example of neighboring colors which are within the confines of two species and whose species is *doubtful.*

§ 19. *Ph.* After the names of simple ideas, those of the *simple modes* are least doubtful, as for example, those of figures and numbers. But, § 20. the mixed modes and substances cause all the trouble. § 21. Men will say that instead of imputing these imperfections to the words, we should rather put them to the account of our understanding; but I reply that words interpose themselves to such an extent between our mind and the truth of things, that we may compare them with the medium, across which pass the rays from visible objects, and which often spreads a mist before our eyes; and I have tried to think that, if the imperfections of language were more thoroughly examined, the majority of the disputes would cease of themselves, and the way to knowledge and perhaps to peace would be more open to men.

Th. I think we could succeed from this time in written discussions, if men would agree upon certain rules and execute them with care. But in order to proceed exactly *viva voce* and at once, some change in the language would be necessary. I have elsewhere[1] entered upon this enquiry.

[1] In his writings in furtherance of his plan for the establishment of a General Characteristic or Philosophical Language, *Spécieuse générale*, a project which Leibnitz had very much at heart, as appears from his frequent allusion to the subject, and upon which throughout his entire life he spent much labor, chiefly

§ 22. *Ph.* While waiting for this reform which will not be ready very soon, this uncertainty regarding words should teach us to be moderate, especially when it is a question of imposing upon others the sense attributed by us to the ancient authors, since in the Greek authors it is found that nearly every one speaks a different language.

Th. I have been rather surprised to see that Greek authors so distant from one another in time and place, as Homer, Herodotus, Strabo, Plutarch, Lucian, Eusebius, Procopius, Photius, approach so closely, while the Latins have changed so much, and the Germans, English, and French much more. But the fact is, the Greeks since Homer's time, and still more when Athens was in a flourishing condition, had good authors which posterity has taken as models, at least in writing. For no doubt the common language of the Greeks must have been much changed already under the rule of the Romans. And this same reason accounts for the fact that the Italian has not suffered so great a change as the French, because the Italians, having had earlier writers of durable reputation, imitated and moreover esteemed Dante, Petrarch, Boccaccio, and other authors at a time when those of the French were no longer appreciated.

CHAPTER X

OF THE ABUSE OF WORDS

§ 1. *Ph.* Besides the natural imperfections of language, there are some that are voluntary and arise from negligence, and it is an *abuse* of words to use them so badly. The first and most palpable abuse is, § 2. that we attach no clear idea to them. Of these words there are two classes: the first have never had any definite idea, either in their origin or ordinary use. For the most part philosophical and religious sects have introduced

preparatory, and with little positive results in accomplishing his plan. *Cf. New Essays*, Bk. IV. chap. 6, § 2, Th., chap. 17, § 13, Th.; Gerhardt, *Leibniz. philos. Schrift.*, 3, 216; 4, 27 *sq.*, Erdmann, 6 *sq.*; G. 7, 3 *sq.*, E. 82 *sq.*, 669 *sq.*; Trendelenburg, *Ueber Leibniz. Entwurf einer allgemeinen Characteristik*, in his *Histor. Beiträge z. Philos.*, vol. 3, pp. 1 *sq.*, Berlin, 1867; L. Neff, *G. W. Leibniz als Sprachforscher und Etymologe*, Pt. II., pp. 13 *sq.*, Heidelberg, 1870-1.— Tr.

them in order to support some strange opinion, or to conceal some weak place in their system. They are, however, distinguishing characters in the mouth of members of the party. § 3. There are other words, which in their first and common use have some clear idea, but which have since been appropriated to very important matters without attaching to them any certain idea. In this way the words *wisdom*, *glory*, *grace*, are often in the mouths of men.

Th. I believe that insignificant words are less in number than you think, and that with a little care and good will you can fill up their void or fix their indefiniteness. *Wisdom* appears to be nothing else than the science of happiness. *Grace* is a favor done to those who do not deserve it and who find themselves in a state where they need it. And *glory* is the fame of the excellence of some one.

§ 4. *Ph.* I do not wish now to examine whether there is anything to be said in regard to these definitions, but rather to notice the causes of the abuse of words. *In the first place*, we learn the words before we learn the ideas belonging to them, and children accustomed thereto from the cradle use them in like manner during their whole life: the more as they do not cease to make themselves understood in conversation, without ever having fixed their idea, by using different expressions in order to make others understand their meaning. This, however, often fills their discourses with a quantity of vain sounds, especially in matters concerning morals. Men take the words they find in use among their neighbors, and in order not to appear ignorant of their meaning employ them confidently without giving them a certain sense: and, as in this kind of discourse they are rarely in the right, they are also rarely convinced that they are wrong; and to wish to draw them from their error is to wish to dispossess a vagabond.

Th. Men in fact take so rarely the necessary trouble to understand terms or words that I have more than once been astonished that children can learn languages so soon, and that men furthermore speak them so accurately; a view to which we attach so little in instructing children in their mother tongue and which others think of so little in acquiring clear definitions; the more so as those we learn in the schools do not ordinarily concern the words in public use. For the rest, I admit that men frequently happen to be wrong when indeed they discuss seriously and speak in accord with their feeling; but I have also remarked often enough that in their speculative discussions upon matters within the province of their mind, they have every reason for two sides, except in the oppositions they make to each other where they misconstrue another's view. This arises from the bad use of terms and sometimes also from a spirit of contradiction and affectation of superiority.

§ 5. *Ph.* In the *second place* the use of words is sometimes *inconstant,* a practice only too general *among scholars.* It is nevertheless a plain cheat, and if voluntary, is folly or malice. If any one so conducted himself in his accounts (as to take an X for a V), who, I pray, would have anything to do with him?

Th. This abuse being so common not only among scholars but also in the world at large, I believe that it is due rather to bad custom and inadvertence than to malice. Usually the different significations of the same word have some affinity; this makes one pass for another and does not give time to consider what is said with all the precision that is desirable. We are accustomed to tropes and figures, and some elegance or brilliant falsehood easily imposes upon us. For we oftener seek pleasure, amusement, and appearance, than truth; besides, vanity mixes itself therein.

§ 6. *Ph. The third abuse* is an affected *obscurity,* either by giving terms in use *unusual meanings,* or by introducing *new terms* without explaining them. The ancient Sophists, whom Lucian ridicules so properly, pretending to speak of everything, covered their ignorance under the veil of the obscurity of words. Among the sects of philosophers the Peripatetic has shown itself remarkable by this defect; but the other sects, even among the moderns, are not wholly exempt from it. For example, the people who abuse the term *extension,* and find it necessary to confuse it with that of *body.* § 7. Logic or the art of discussion, which is held in such high esteem, has helped to maintain this obscurity. § 8. Those who have given themselves up to it have been useless or rather detrimental to the state; § 9. while mechanics, though despised by the learned, have been serviceable to human life.

But these obscure doctors have been admired by the ignorant; and they have been thought invincible because provided with briers and thorns, into which it was no pleasure to thrust one's self, their obscurity alone serving as a defence of their absurdity. § 12. The evil is that this art of obscuring words has confused the great rules of men's action, religion and justice.

Th. Your complaint is largely just: it is nevertheless true that there are, though rarely, pardonable and even praiseworthy obscurities, as when we profess to be enigmatical, and the *enigma* is timely. Pythagoras[1] so used it, and it is frequently the manner of the Orientals. The alchemists, who are called adepts, declare that they wish to be understood only by the *sons of the art.* And that would be well, if these pretended sons of the art had the key to the cipher. A certain obscurity may be allowed; but something must be concealed which is worth divining, and the enigma must be decipherable. But *religion* and *justice* demand clear ideas. It seems that the little order brought into their teaching has made the confusion in their doctrine; and the indeterminateness of the terms is perhaps more harmful than their obscurity. Now as *logic* is the art which teaches the order and connection of thoughts, I do not see any reason for blaming it. On the contrary it is for want of logic that men deceive themselves.[2]

§ 14. *Ph.* The *fourth abuse* is when we take words for things, *i.e.* believe that the terms correspond to the real essence of the

[1] Pythagoras, c. 580–570–c. 500 B.C. The reference is to his so-called Symbols, or sayings preserved in a symbolic form, in order that their meaning might be concealed from the uninitiated, and the characteristic of which is the union of an ethical prescript with an external action relatively indifferent. *Cf.* Diogenes Laërtius, *De vitis, dogmatibus, et apophthegmatis clarorum philosophorum*, VIII, 17 *sq.*, who gives some of these symbols with interpretations of a part of them; Zeller, *Philos. d. Griec.*, 5th ed., 1892, Vol. 1, p. 324, note 2, 462. Mullach, *Fragmt. Philos. Græc.*, Vol. 1, p. 504 *sq.*, gives a collection of these sayings. Examples are: "Carry not the image of God in the finger-ring," "Stir not the fire with the sword," "Sacrifice and pray with bare feet." Göttling, *Gesammlt. Abhandl.*, Vol. 1, p. 278 *sq.*, 2, 280 *sq.*, has given them a "penetrating investigation," on which see the note of Zeller above cited. Leibnitz on Pythagoras, *cf.* Gerhardt, *Leibniz. philos. Schrift.*, 7, 147. — TR.

[2] Leibnitz, while rejecting the over-refinements of the scholastic logic, nevertheless rightly values formal logic as an aid to clear thinking and correct reasoning. *Cf.* the letter to Gabriel Wagner, 1696, Gerhardt, *Leibniz. philos. Schrift.*, 7, 512 *sq.*, Erdmann, 418 *sq.*, Guhrauer, *Leibniz. deutsche Schrift.*, 1, 374 *sq.*, Berlin, 1838. — TR.

substances. Who is there brought up in the Peripatetic philosophy who does not think that the ten names which represent the *predicaments* are exactly conformed to the nature of things; that the *substantial forms, vegetative souls, abhorrence of a vacuum, intentional species*, etc., are something real? The Platonists have their *soul of the world*, and the Epicureans the *tendency* of their atoms *towards movement* at the time when they are at rest. If the *aërial or ethereal vehicles*[1] of Dr. More had prevailed in any corner of the world they would have been thought no less real.

Th. Properly speaking this is not to take words for things, but to believe that true which is not so, an error too common with all men, depending not alone upon the abuse of words, but consisting in something entirely different. The design of the *predicaments* is a very useful one, and we ought to think of rectifying rather than of rejecting them. Substances, quantities, qualities, actions or passions, and relations, *i.e.* five general names of things may, together with those formed by their composition, suffice, and have not you yourself, in marshalling ideas, been willing to grant them as the predicaments? I have spoken above of *substantial forms.*[2] And I know not whether we have sufficient reason for rejecting the *vegetative souls,*[3] since persons of much experience and judgment recog-

[1] The *aërial or ethereal vehicles* are the aërial or celestial bodies of the spirits, which, according to More, the souls of men after sufficient purification attain, either at death, in the case of a very few of the noblest and most heroic, or at some period after death. *Cf.* H. More, *Opera omnia*, Londini, 1679, 2 vols., fol.; *Tract. de immortalitate animæ*, Bk. III. chap. 1, *Axioma*, 27, §§ 3, 28 *sq.*, Vol. 2, p. 396 *sq.*, chap. 11, § 2, p. 427; *Antidotus adversus Atheismum*, Bk. III. chap. 3, § 9, Vol. 2, p. 99. — Tr.

[2] *Cf. ante*, p. 349 and note. — Tr.

[3] The scholastic philosophy recognized three forms or kinds of souls, corresponding to the three orders of life, plants, animals, and men, viz.: the *vegetative, sensitive*, and *intellective* (*anima vegetabilis* or *nutritiva*, *sensibilis* or *sensitiva*, *intellectiva* or *rationalis*). Of these the vegetative is the lowest, the sensitive the next higher, the intellective the highest; and the higher form includes potentially in itself the lower and subordinate form and its functions. The functions of the vegetative soul are nutrition, growth, reproduction; of the sensitive soul, sensation, feeling, perceptional, appetitive and emotional activity; of the intellective, those of the reason and the will. In man, these several functions are all united in the intellective or rational soul, which he alone possesses, and which comprises within itself the sensitive and vegetative souls. *Cf.* Stöckl, *Gesch. d. Philos. d. Mittelalters*, II. 2 [Vol. 3], 592 *sq.*, 618 *sq.*, 633 *sq.* — Tr.

nize a great analogy between plants and animals, and you, sir, have appeared to admit animal souls. *Abhorrence of a vacuum* may be soundly understood; *i.e.* supposing nature has once filled space, and that bodies are impenetrable and non-condensable, she could not admit any vacuum; and I consider these three suppositions well grounded. But the *intentional species*,[1] which are to make the connection between the soul and the body, are not so, though we may excuse the *sensible species*,[1]

[1] *Cf.* 5th letter of Leibnitz to Clarke, § 84, Gerhardt, 7, 410, Erdmann, 773, b, Jacques, 2, 465, Dutens, 2, Pt. I, 161, trans. Duncan, 275.

The doctrine of the *intentional species* (*species intentionales*) to which were opposed the *real species* (*species reales*) or the actual forms of things, arose in the attempts of the Mediæval Schoolmen to explain the process and philosophy of sense-perception and cognition. Two views have in general been held concerning their nature: 1. That they were the forms, similitudes, or images (*formæ, similitudines, simulacra*) of external objects, different both from the mind and from these objects, the intermediate and vicarious representatives of these objects in perception and thought, the media through which the mind infers and comes to know these external objects — a form of the doctrine of mediate perception. 2. That they were modifications of the mind itself, occasioned by the action upon the mind of the external object and the mind's responsive reaction thereto, by which the mind is likened or conformed to the given object and so determined immediately to cognize it. The latter view is maintained by the Roman Catholic psychologists, as being the doctrine of the greatest of the schoolmen, such as Albertus Magnus, Thomas Aquinas, Duns Scotus, and as giving the real meaning of the terms they use. It is the more correct interpretation.

The intentional species, according as they affected or were modifications of the sense or the intellect, were divided into *sensible species* (*species sensibiles*) and *intelligible or intellectual species* (*species intelligibiles vel intellectuales*). Both the *sensible* and the *intelligible species* were further distinguished as *impressed species* (*species impressa*) and *expressed species* (*species expressa*). According to the representative theory of the *intentional species*, the *species impressa* was the vicarious existence emitted by the object, impressed on the particular faculty, and concurring with it in its operation; while the *species expressa* was the actual operation elicited by the faculty and the impressed species conjointly, *i.e.* the sensations and intellections. The direct or immediate theory regarded the genesis of *species*, whether as *sensible* or *intelligible*, as exhibiting two stages: 1. In sensuous cognition, (a) the *species sensibilis impressa*, or "the modification of the sensuous faculty viewed as an impression wrought in the mind by the action of the object," and (b) the *species sensibilis expressa*, or "the reaction of the mind as an act of cognitive consciousness." 2. In intellectual cognition, (a) the *species intelligibilis impressa*, or the "modification effected in the recipient capacity" of the *intellectus patiens vel possibilis* (the *passive* intellect — Aristotle's νοῦς παθητικός), and (b) the *species intelligibilis expressa*, or the "mental modification reflecting the essence of the object, and by means of which the object is apprehended," a modification due to the act of the *intellectus agens* (the *active* intellect — Aristotle's νοῦς ποιητικός).

which proceed from the object to the distant organ, meaning thereby the propagation of motion. I admit that there is no Platonic *soul of the world,* for God is beyond the world, *extramundana intelligentia,* or rather *supramundana.*[1] I know not whether by *the tendency to movement* of the Epicurean atoms you understand the weight attributed to them, no doubt with reason, since they maintain that bodies all move of themselves in one and the same direction. The late Henry More, a theologian of the English Church, wholly clever as he was, showed himself a little too ready to invent hypotheses which were neither intelligible nor apparent; witness his *Hylarchic principle*[2] of matter, a cause of weight, elasticity, and other wonders which are met with. I have nothing to say of these ethereal vehicles, having never examined their nature.

§ 15. *Ph.* An example touching the word matter will assist you the better to enter into my thought. Matter is taken as

The doctrine of the *intentional species* was held by the Realists, Aquinas, Duns Scotus, and others. The Nominalists, especially Durandus, Biel, and Occam, rejected it, and the doctrine was exploded in the seventeenth century, largely by the arguments of Gassendi, Hobbes, and Descartes. On the whole subject, *cf.* Hamilton's *Reid*, 8th ed., Edinburgh, 1880, Vol. 1, p. 267 *sq.*, and Note M., Vol. 2, p. 951 *sq.; Lects. on Metaphys.*, Boston, 1875, p. 291 *sq.*, and notes; Stöckl, *Gesch. d. Philos. d. Mittelalters*, II. 1 [Vol. 2] 463 *sq.*, II. 2 [Vol. 3] 808, 965, 978, 991 *sq.*, III. [Vol. 4] 634 *sq.*; Hauréau, *Histoire de la philos. scolastique*, II. 1 [Vol. 2] 417 *sq.*, II. 2 [Vol. 3] 247 *sq.*, 378 *sq.*; Prantl, *Gesch. d. Logik im Abendlande*, Vol. 3, pp. 113, 210 *sq.*, 294, 335 *sq.*; Maher, S. J., *Psychology* (Manuals of Catholic Philosophy — Stonyhurst Series), pp. 49–53, 290–297, London: Longmans, Green & Co., 1890; Zigliara, *Summa Philosophica*, 3d ed., Lugduni, 1880, Vol. 2, pp. 243–4, 260 *sq.*; Suarez, *De Anima*, Lib. III. cc. 2, 3; Kleutgen, *Philos. d. Vorzeit*, §§ 18–52; Sanseverino, *Dynamilogia*, Neapoli, 1862–66, Vol. 1, pp. 373–403 (of which pp. 390–400 contain "an effective refutation of the charge of representationism against St. Thomas and the leading scholastics, based on the doctrine of *species*"), Vol. 2, pp. 586 *sq.* — Tr.

[1] *Cf. Théodicée*, Pt. II. § 217, Gerhardt, 6, 248, Erdmann, 571, a, Jacques, 2, 205. — Tr.

[2] *Cf.* Gerhardt, *Leibniz. philos. Schrift.*, 7, 339; letter to Placcius, Sept. 8, 1690, Dutens, *Leibnit. op. om.*, 6, 48; to T. Burnett, Aug. 24 (v.s.) 1697, G. 3, 217, D. 6, 263. More rejected the mechanical explanation of physical nature, and adopted the *principium hylarchicum*, or *spiritus naturæ* as he designates it, the immaterial force in all nature, the principle of the movement and sympathy of beings, similar to the *anima mundi* of the Platonists and the *archæus* (*cf. ante*, p. 67, note 3) of the Alchemists. *Cf.* H. More, *Opera omnia*, Londini, 1679, *Enchiridion metaphys.*, especially in the Scholia, to chap. 13, § 4, Vol. 1, p. 222 *sq.*; also *Tract. de immortalitate animæ*, Bk. III. chap. 12, Vol. 2, p. 430. — Tr.

an entity really existing in nature, distinct from the body; which indeed is thoroughly self-evident; otherwise these two ideas might be put indifferently the one in the place of the other. For we may say that *one single matter composes all bodies,* but not that a single body composes all matter. Neither will we say, I think, that one matter is greater than another. Matter expresses the substance and solidity of body; thus we no more conceive different matters than different solidities. But since matter has been taken as a name of something existing under this determination, this thought has produced unintelligible discourse and confused discussion upon *materia prima.*

Th. This example appears to me to serve rather to excuse than to blame the Peripatetic philosophy. If all silver were figured, or rather because all silver is figured by nature or art, is it less allowable to say that silver is an entity really existing in nature, distinct (taking it in its *precision*) from the plate or the money? You will not on that account say that silver is nothing else than certain qualities of money. Thus it is not so useless as you suppose to reason in general physics about *materia prima* and to determine its nature in order to know whether it is always uniform, whether it has some other property besides impenetrability (as I in fact have shown [1] after Kepler that it also has what may be called *inertia*), etc., although it is never found wholly pure; as it would be allowable to reason about pure silver, although we had none with us nor the means of purifying it. I do not at all disapprove what Aristotle has said about *materia prima;* [2] but one cannot

[1] *Cf. De ipsa natura,* 1698, § 11, Gerhardt, *Leibniz. philos. Schrift.,* 4, 510, Erdmann, 157, a, Jacques, 1, 462 (in French), Dutens, 2, Pt. II., 54, trans. Duncan, 119; *Théodicée,* Pt. I., § 30, G. 6, 119, E. 512, a, J. 2, 89, Dutens, 1, 141 (in Latin); *Specimen dynamicum,* 1695, Pt. I., Gerhardt, *Leibniz. math. Schrift.,* 6, 234 *sq.,* Dutens, 3, 315 *sq.,* trans. Appendix, 670 *sq.;* G. *Leibniz. philos. Schrift.,* 4, 464–7, Dutens, 2, Pt. I., 234–7, two letters to the editor of the "Journal des Savans," in the numbers for June 18th, 1691, January, 1693, the first originally a fragment from a letter to Antonio Alberti, G. 7, 447–9; 5th letter to Clarke, § 102, G. 7, 414, E. 775, b, J. 2, 470, Dutens, 2, 165, trans. Duncan, 280. In the letter to Jac. Thomasius, April 20–30, 1669 (*cf.* G. 1, 17, 18, 24), Leibnitz affirmed that matter consisted of extension and inpenetrability only. — TR.

[2] *Cf.* Zeller, *Philos. d. Griech.,* 3d ed., 1879, II. 2 [Vol. 4], p. 320, note 2; and Bonitz, *Ind. Arist. sub voc.* ὕλη, in vol. 5 of Berlin Academy, ed. of Aristotle. *Cf.* also Gerhardt, *Leibniz. philos. Schrift.,* 7, 259. — TR.

help blaming those who have stopped too soon and have conjured up chimeras out of the ill-understood words of this philosopher, who perhaps also has given too much occasion sometimes for this misconception and nonsense. But we should not exaggerate so much the defects of this celebrated author, because we know that many of his works were not completed or published by himself.

§ 17. *Ph.* The *fifth abuse* is the putting of words in the place of things which they do not and cannot in any way signify. It occurs when by the names of substances we mean to say something more than this: what I call gold is malleable (although at bottom then gold signifies nothing else than what is malleable), intending to have it understood that malleability depends upon the real essence of gold. Thus we say that it is right to define man with Aristotle as a reasonable animal; and that it is not right to define him with Plato as a two-legged animal without feathers and with broad nails. § 18. There is scarcely any one who does not suppose that these words signify a thing having a real essence upon which these properties depend; but it is a plain abuse when the complex idea signified by this word does not include this thing.

Th. For myself I should rather think that we are plainly wrong in censuring this common usage, since it is very true that in the complex idea of gold is included the thought that it is a thing having a real essence, whose constitution is unknown to us in detail otherwise than that upon it depend such qualities as malleability. But in order to express its malleability without identity and without the defect of *coccysm* or repetition (see chap. 8, § 18),[1] we must recognize this thing by other qualities, as color and weight. And it is as if we said that a certain fusible body, yellow and very heavy, called gold, has a nature which gives it besides the quality of being very soft to the hammer and capable of being made very thin. As for the *definition of man* attributed to Plato, which he appears to have made only for practice, and which you would not, I think, compare seriously with that which is received, it is manifestly a little too external and provisional; for if this *Cassowary*, of which you recently spoke (chap. 6, § 34), had

[1] The reference is incorrect. Perhaps chap. 6, § 18, is meant, or chap. 10, § 18. — TR.

been found to have wide nails, it would be man; for it would not have been necessary to strip it of its feathers, as in the case of the cock which Diogenes, as they say, wished to make a Platonic man.[1]

§ 19. *Ph.* In the mixed modes, as soon as an idea entering therein is changed, you at once recognize it as another thing, as plainly appears in the words, *murder*, which signifies in English (as *Mordt* in German), homicide premeditated with design; *manslaughter* (a word corresponding in origin to homicide), a voluntary but not premeditated homicide; *chance-medley* (a chance melée, according to the force of the word), homicide committed without design; for what is expressed by the names and what I think to be in the thing (which I called before *nominal essence* and *real essence*) is the same. But it is not so in the names of substances; for if one puts into the idea of gold what another leaves out, for example fixedness and solubility in aqua regia, men do not think for that reason that its species has been changed, but only that the one has a more perfect idea than the other of what constitutes the real concealed essence to which the name of gold is given, although this secret relation is useless and serves only to involve us in difficulties.

Th. I think I have already made this statement; but I am going also to show you clearly here, that what you, sir, have just said, is found in the modes, as in the substances, and that we have no ground for censuring the internal essence for this relation. Here is an example: we may define a parabola, in the sense of the geometers, as a figure in which all the lines parallel to a certain straight line are united by thought in a certain point or *focus*. But it is rather the *exterior* and the *effect* which is expressed by this idea or definition, than the *internal essence* of this figure or what can at once make known its *origin*. We may at the beginning even doubt if such a figure as we wish and which ought to produce this effect is a *possible* thing; and it is this which with me shows whether a

[1] *Cf.* Diogenes Laërtius, c. 230–250, *De vitis, dogmatibus et apophthegmatis clarorum philosophorum lib. decem*, VI. 40: Πλάτωνος ὁρισαμένου, Ἄνθρωπος ἐστὶ ζῶον δίπουν, ἄπτερον, καὶ εὐδοκιμοῦντος, τίλας [Διογένης ὁ κύων] ἀλεκτρυόνα εἰσήνεγκεν εἰς τὴν σχολὴν αὐτοῦ, καί φησιν, Οὗτός ἐστιν ὁ Πλάτωνος ἄνθρωπος. ὅθεν τῷ ὅρῳ προσετέθη Τὸ πλατυώνυχον. The *definitions* ascribed to Plato, and found in some editions of his works, are beyond doubt spurious. — TR.

definition is only nominal and taken from the properties, or whether it is also *real.* But he who mentions the parabola and knows it only by the definition I have just spoken of, ceases not, when speaking of it, to understand a figure which has a certain construction and constitution unknown to him, but which he wishes to learn in order to be able to draw it. Another who has examined it more thoroughly will add some other property, and will discover, for example, that in the figure asked for, the portion of the axis intercepted between the ordinate and the perpendicular drawn to the same point of the curve is always constant, and equal to the distance from the *vertex* to the focus. He will thus have a more perfect idea than the former, and will come more easily to the drawing of the figure, although he is not yet there. And, moreover, we shall agree that it is the same figure, the constitution of which is still concealed. You see then, sir, that all that you have found and partly censured in the use of words signifying substances is also found and found plainly justified in the words signifying the mixed modes. But what has made you think that there was some difference between the substances and the modes,[1] is merely the fact that you have not consulted here the intellectual modes difficult of discussion, which are found to resemble in all this bodies which are still more difficult to know.

§ 20. *Ph.* Thus I fear I must suppress what I wished to say to you, sir, of the cause of what I have thought an abuse, as if it were because we falsely think that nature always acts with regularity and fixes limits to each species by this specific essence or internal constitution which we there understand and which always follows the same specific name.

Th. You see clearly then, sir, by the example of the geometrical modes, that we are not wrong in referring them to internal and specific essences, although there is great difference between sensible things, whether substances, or modes, of which we have only nominal provisional definitions, and of which we do not readily hope for real ones, and between the intellectual modes, difficult of discussion since we can at last reach the internal constitution of the geometrical figures.

[1] Jacques reads: "c'est que vous n'avez point consulté," etc. Gerhardt and Erdmann read: "n'est que vous," etc. — TR.

§ 21. *Ph.* [I see at last that I should have been wrong in laying the blame of this relation upon the essences and internal constitutions, under the pretext that this would render our words signs of nothing or of an unknown something. For what is unknown in certain respects may make itself known in another way, and the inner nature may partly reveal itself by the phenomena which spring from it. And as for the question: whether a *monstrous fœtus* is a man or not? I see that, if it cannot be decided at once, this fact does not prevent the species from being well fixed in itself, our ignorance nowise changing anything in the nature of things.]

Th. In fact, some very clever geometers have chanced to possess insufficient knowledge as to what the figures were, many qualities of which seemingly exhaustive of the subject they knew. For example, there were some lines called *pearls*,[1] of which there were given indeed the quadratures and the measure of their surfaces and of the solids made by their revolution, before it was known that they were only a composition of certain cubic paraboloids. Thus in considering beforehand these pearls as a particular species, they had only provisional knowledge of them. If this may happen in geometry, do you wonder that it is difficult to determine the species of corporeal nature which are incomparably more complex?

§ 22. *Ph.* Let us pass to the *sixth abuse* in order to continue the enumeration begun, although I see clearly that some of the points must be struck from the list. This general but little noticed abuse is this: men having by long use attached certain ideas to certain words, imagine that this connection is manifest and that everybody agrees to it. Whence it comes that they feel very strange, when asked the meaning of the words they employ, when indeed the question is an absolutely necessary one. There are few people who do not take it as an

[1] *Cf. New Essays*, Bk. IV., chap. 7, § 4, Th. *infra*, p. 465. René François Walter de Sluse, 1622–1685, a Flemish geometer, canon of Liege cathedral, and author of the method for the construction of the roots of equations of the 3d and 4th degree, "which consists in reducing the resolution of the proposed equation to that of the system of two equations representing two conics, by introducing an unknown auxiliary whose elimination reproduces the primitive equation." He developed this method in his *Mesolabium et problemata solida*, etc., 4to, Leodii Eburonum, 1668. Leibnitz mentions this work in a letter to Hobbes, 13–22 July, 1670, Gerhardt, *Leibniz. philos. Schrift.*, 7, 573. — Tr.

affront if asked what they mean when speaking of *life*. But the vague idea they may have of it is insufficient when the question arises as to the knowledge whether a plant, already formed in the seed, or a pullet in the egg not yet in process of incubation, or a man in a swoon without sense or motion, has life. And although men do not wish to appear so little *intelligent* or so *obtrusive* as to find it necessary to ask for an explanation of the terms used, nor *critics* so disagreeable as to censure others unceasingly for the use they make of words, nevertheless when it is a question of exact research, such explication is necessary. Often scholars of different parties in the reasonings they display the one against the other merely speak different languages and think the same thing, although perhaps their interests are different.

Th. I think I have explained sufficiently my views upon the *notion of life*, which must always be accompanied by perception in the soul; otherwise it would be only an appearance, as the life which the American savages attributed to watches or clocks, or which those magistrates attributed to the marionettes, who believed them animated by demons, when they desired to punish as a sorcerer the one who had first presented this spectacle in their city.

§ 23. *Ph.* In conclusion, words serve (1) to make our thoughts understood, (2) to do this easily, and (3) to furnish entrance into the knowledge of things. Words fail at the first point, when they have no definite and constant idea either received or understood by others. § 23. They fail in facility, when they have very complex ideas, without distinct names; this is often the fault of the languages themselves which have no names; often also of the man who is ignorant of them; in that case extensive paraphrases are necessary. § 24. But when the ideas signified by the words do not agree with what is real, they fail in the third point. § 26. (1) He who has terms without ideas is like a man who has only a catalogue of books. § 27. (2) He who has very complex ideas is like a man who has a quantity of books in loose sheets without titles, and who could not give the book save by giving the sheets in succession. § 28. (3) He who is not constant in the use of signs is like a merchant who sells different goods under the same name. § 29. (4) He who attaches particular ideas to received words cannot enlighten others by the light he may have. § 30. (5) He who has in his head ideas of substances which never had existence, cannot advance in real knowledge. § 33. The first will speak in vain of the tarantula or of charity. The second will see new animals without being able easily to show them to others. The third will take body sometimes as a solid, sometimes as a mere extension; and by frugality he will designate sometimes the virtue, sometimes the kindred vice. The fourth will call a mule by the name horse, and what everybody calls prodigal will be to him generous; and the fifth will seek in Tartary on the authority of Herodotus[1] a nation composed of men having only one eye. I remark that the first four defects are common to the names of substances and modes, but that the last is peculiar to substances.

Th. Your remarks are very instructive. I will only add that you seem to have something chimerical still in your ideas of the accidents or forms of being; and so the fifth defect is also common to substances and to accidents. The *extravagant shepherd* was not so, only because he believed there were nymphs concealed in the trees, but also because he always expected romantic adventures.

§ 34. *Ph.* I had thought to conclude, but I remember the *seventh and last abuse*, which is that of figurative terms or allusions. But there will be difficulty in thinking it an abuse, because what is called wit and imagination is better received than truth wholly dry. It goes well in discourse where you only seek to please; but at bottom, order and clearness excepted, all the art of rhetoric, all these artificial and figurative applications of words, serve only to insinuate false ideas, to excite the passions and seduce the judgment, so that they are nothing but pure frauds. Nevertheless this fallacious art is given the first rank and rewards. It is evident that men care but little for truth and much prefer to deceive and to be deceived. This is so true that I doubt not that what I have just said against this art is regarded as the result of an extreme audacity. For eloquence, like the fair sex, has charms too powerful to allow itself to be opposed.

[1] Book III., chap. 116; IV., chaps. 13, 27; *cf.* also Æschylus, *Prometheus*, 823 (804, Dindorf), 3d ed., F. A. Paley, London, 1870; Pausanias, 1, 24, 6. — Tr.

Th. Very far from censuring your zeal for the truth, I find it just. And would that it might be effective. I do not wholly despair of it, because you seem to me, sir, to combat eloquence with its own weapons, and to have an eloquence of another species superior to this deceptive kind, as there was a Venus Urania, mother of divine love, before whom this other bastard Venus, mother of a blind love, dared not appear with her child with eyes blinded.[1] But that indeed proves that your thesis needs some moderation, and that certain adornments of eloquence are like the Egyptian vases which you could use in the worship of the true God. It is as in painting and music, which are abused, one of which often represents grotesque and even hurtful imaginations, and the other softens the heart, and the two amuse in vain; but they can be usefully employed, the one to render the truth clear, the other to make it effective, and this last result must be also that of poetry which contains rhetoric and music.

CHAPTER XI

OF THE REMEDIES WHICH MAY BE APPLIED TO THE IMPERFECTIONS AND ABUSES JUST SPOKEN OF

§ 1. *Ph.* This is not the place to plunge into this discussion upon the use of a true eloquence, and still less to reply to your obliging compliment, since we ought to think of bringing this matter of *words* to an end, by seeking the remedies for the imperfections we have noticed therein. § 2. It would be ridiculous to attempt to reform the languages, and to desire to compel men to speak only according to the measure of their knowledge. § 3. But it is not too much to desire that philosophers speak exactly, when the question concerns a serious search for the truth: without this all will be full of error, opiniativeness, and vain disputes. § 8. The *first remedy* is to use no word

[1] For the myth here referred to by Leibnitz, *cf.* Plato, *Symposium*, 180, D, Jowett's trans. Vol. 2, p. 32, 2d ed., 1875, Vol. 1, p. 550, 3d ed., 1892: Pausanias, 9, 16, 3; also Harrison-Verrall, *Mythology and Monuments of Ancient Athens*, 212 *sq.*, London, Macmillan & Co., 1890; Preller, *Griech. Mythol.*, 2d ed., 1860, Vol. 1, p. 265. — TR.

without attaching thereto an idea, instead of frequently employing words like instinct, sympathy, antipathy, without attaching any sense to them.

Th. The rule is good; but I know not whether the examples are pertinent. Everybody seems to understand by *instinct* an inclination of an animal to what is proper for it, without on that account apprehending its reason; and men indeed ought less to neglect these instincts, which they discover moreover in themselves, although their artificial method of living has for the most part nearly effaced them; the physician of his own accord, indeed, has carefully observed it. *Sympathy* or *antipathy* signifies that which in bodies destitute of feeling corresponds to the instinct for union or separation found in animals. And although we have no such knowledge of the cause of these inclinations or tendencies, as is to be desired, we nevertheless have a notion of them sufficient to discourse of them intelligibly.

§ 9. *Ph.* The *second remedy* is that the ideas of the names of the modes at least be determined and, § 10. that the ideas of the names of substances be more conformed to what exists. If any one says that *justice* is conduct conformed to the law relating to the good of another, this idea is not sufficiently determined, so long as we have no distinct idea of that which is called *law.*

Th. We might say here that the *law* is a precept of wisdom or of the science of happiness.

§ 11. *Ph.* The *third remedy* is to employ terms so far as possible in conformity with received usage. § 12. The *fourth* is to declare in what sense we take the words, whether we coin new ones or employ the old in a new sense, (or) whether we find that use has not sufficiently fixed their meaning. § 13. But there is some difference. § 14. The words for simple ideas which cannot be defined, are explained by synonymous words, when they are better known, or by showing the thing. It is by these means that we can make a peasant understand what the color *feuille morte* is, by telling him that it is that of dry leaves which fall in the autumn. § 15. The names of the mixed modes should be explained by definition, for that is possible. § 16. It is upon this ground that ethics is susceptible of demonstration. We shall take man as a corporeal rational being without troubling ourselves about his external figure, § 17. for it is by means of definitions that the matters of morality may be clearly treated. We shall rather define justice according to the idea we have in our mind than seek a model therefor outside of us, as Aristides, and form it thereupon. § 18. And as the majority of the mixed modes nowhere exist together, we can fix them in defining them only by the enumeration of that which is scattered. § 19. In substances there are ordinarily some *directing* or *characteristic qualities* which we consider as the most distinctive idea of the species, to which we suppose the other ideas forming the complex idea of the species are attached. It is form in vegetables and animals, and color in animate bodies, and in some color and form together. This is why, § 20. the definition of man given by Plato is more characteristic than that of Aristotle; or why we should not cause the death of monstrous productions, § 21. and often sight avails as much as any other test; for persons accustomed to test gold often distinguish by sight the true from the false, the pure from that which has been adulterated.

Th. Everything doubtless returns to the definitions which may extend even to primitive ideas. One and the same subject may have several definitions, but the knowledge that they agree with themselves, must be learned by reason, by demonstrating one definition by another, or by experience, by proving that they constantly go together. As for morality, one part is wholly grounded in reason; but there is another depending upon experience and related to the disposition. For a knowledge of substances, form and color, *i.e.* the visible, gives us the first ideas, because it is by these that we know things at a distance; but they are ordinarily too provisional, and in things of importance to us we try to know substance more closely. I am astonished, moreover, that you return again to the definition of *man*, attributed to Plato, since you have just yourself stated, § 16. that in morals man must be taken as a corporeal rational being without troubling ourselves about the external form. For the rest it is true that a large practice does much for discerning at sight what another may scarcely know through arduous experiments. And physicians of large experience, with very good sight and memory, often know at the first appearance the disease which another will draw out for himself with difficulty by force of questioning and trying the pulse. But it is well to unite all the indications we may have.

§ 22. *Ph.* I admit that he to whom a good assayer makes known all the qualities of gold, will have a better knowledge of them than sight could give. But if we could learn its internal constitution, the meaning of the word *gold* would be as *easily* determined as that of the triangle.

Th. It would be wholly as determined, and it would have in it no *provisional* element; but it would not be so easily determined. For I think a distinction a little prolix would be necessary in order to explain the contexture of gold, as is the case indeed in geometry with figures whose definition is long.

§ 23. *Ph.* Spirits separated from bodies have doubtless knowledge more perfect than ours, although we have no notion of the manner in which they may acquire it. But they may have as clear ideas of the radical constitution of bodies, as we have of a triangle.

Th. I have already remarked, sir, that I have reasons for thinking that no created spirits exist entirely separate from bodies; but there are no doubt some whose organs and understanding are incomparably more perfect than ours, and which surpass us in every kind of conception, as much and more than Mr. Frenicle,[1] or that Swedish boy of whom I have spoken to you, surpassed the common run of men in the calculation of numbers, made by imagination.

§ 24. *Ph.* We have already noticed that the definitions of substances which may serve in explaining names are imperfect in relation to the knowledge of things. For usually we put

[1] *Cf.* Gerhardt, *Leibniz. philos. Schrift.*, 4, 319. Bernard Frénicle de Bessy, c. 1605–1675, brother of the poet Nicolas Frénicle, 1600–1661, "conseiller à la cour des monnaies," member of the Paris Academy of Sciences, who acquired the reputation of being the first arithmetician of his age by the rapidity with which he solved the most complicated numerical problems, and by his ingenious researches upon the solution in whole numbers of indeterminate equations. His method, known as the *method of exclusions*, appears to have been an ingenious groping, but based on some general propositions which greatly restricted this groping, and which have since been rigorously demonstrated by Léonard Euler, 1707–1783 and Jos. Louis Lagrange, 1736–1813. Pierre de Fermat, 1601–1665, and Descartes, 1596–1650, greatly admired his work, astonished that he could go so far without the aid of algebra and that his arithmetic could conduct him where analysis finds so much difficulty in going. His principal work was, *Traité des triangles, rectangles en nombre*, Paris, 1676. — Tr.

the name in the place of the thing; then the name says more than the definitions; thus to give a good definition of substances, we must study natural history.

Th. You see then, sir, that the name gold, for example, signifies not only that which he who pronounces it knows of it, — for example, something yellow, very heavy, — but also what he does not know, and which another may know, *i.e.* a body endowed with an internal constitution from which proceed color and weight, and from which spring still other properties admitted to be better known by experts.

§ 25. *Ph.* It were now to be wished that those practised in physical researches would set down the simple ideas in which they observe that the individuals of each species constantly agree. But the composition of a dictionary of this kind which would contain, so to speak, a natural history, would require too many persons, too much time, trouble, and sagacity for such a work ever to be hoped for. It would be well, however, to accompany words with small copper-plate engravings of things known by their external form. Such a dictionary would be of much service to posterity and would spare future critics much trouble. Small figures as of the celery-plant (*apium*), of a *Bouquetin* (*ibex*, a kind of wild goat), would be more valuable than long descriptions of this plant or of this animal. And in order to know what the Latins called *strigiles* and *sistrum, tunica* and *pallium,* figures in the margin would be incomparably more valuable than the pretended synonymes, currycomb, cymbal, dress, cloak, mantle, which show but little of them. For the rest I shall not stop upon the seventh remedy of the abuse of words which is to employ constantly the same term in the same sense, or to give notice when you change it. For we have spoken sufficiently of this subject.

Th. Rev. Father Grimaldi,[1] President of the Mathematical

[1] Claudius Philip Grimaldi, with whom Leibnitz became acquainted during his stay in Rome in 1689, and with whom he corresponded, receiving from him after his return to Pekin much interesting information. *Cf.* Guhrauer, *G. W. Freiherr v. Leibniz,* 2, 95 *sq.*; Kuno Fischer, *Gesch. d. n. Philos.*, Vol. 2, p. 201, 3d ed., Heidelberg, 1889; Dutens, *Leibniz. op. om.*, 4, Pt. I. 81, 83 *sq.*, 88; 6, 106, 128, 227, Gerhardt, *Leibniz. philos. Schrift.* 3, 166, 174. Schaarschmidt states that such dictionaries as Leibnitz here mentions on the authority of Grimaldi exist in fact among the Chinese, and have been brought to Europe, that the Bonn University library possesses a couple of parts of one such dictionary, and that it must be regarded as an alphabetically arranged *orbis pictus.* — Tr.

Society at Pekin, tells me that the Chinese have illustrated dictionaries. There is a small nomenclator printed at Nuremberg in which there are such figures for each word which are good enough. Such an illustrated *universal dictionary* were to be desired, and would not be very difficult to make. As for the *description of species*, it is properly natural history, and we are working at it by degrees. Were it not for the wars (which have troubled Europe since the first foundation of the Societies or Royal Academies) it would be farther advanced, and already in a condition to profit from our labors; but the great for the most part do not recognize its importance, nor what good they deprive themselves of by neglecting the advancement of solid knowledge; and besides they are ordinarily too much indisposed by the pleasures of peace or by the cares of war to weigh things which do not strike them at once.

ESSAY ON UNDERSTANDING

Book IV. — Of Knowledge

CHAPTER I

OF KNOWLEDGE IN GENERAL

§ 1. *Ph.* Hitherto we have spoken of *ideas* and of *words* which represent them; let us come now to the *knowledge*, which the ideas furnish, for it rests only upon our ideas. § 2. *Knowledge* is simply the perception of the connection and agreement, or of the opposition and disagreement, which we find between *two of our ideas.* Whether we imagine, conjecture, or believe, it is always that. We perceive, for example, by this means, that white is not black, and that the angles of a triangle and their equality to two right angles have a necessary connection.

Th. Knowledge has a still more general signification, so that we find it also in ideas or terms, before we reach propositions or truths. And it may be said that he who has attentively looked at more pictures of plants and animals, more diagrams of machines, more descriptions or representations of houses or fortresses, who has read more ingenious romances, heard more curious narratives, this one, I say, will have more knowledge than another, even though there should not be a word of truth in all that which was portrayed or related to him; for the custom he has of representing in his mind many express and actual conceptions or ideas, renders him more fit to conceive what is placed before him; and it is certain that he will be better instructed and more capable than another who has neither seen nor read nor heard anything, provided that in these stories and representations he takes nothing as true which is not so and that these impressions do not prevent him elsewhere from distinguishing the real from the imaginary, or the existent from the possible. This is why certain logicians of the period of the Reformation who were in some measure of the party of the Ramists,[1] were not wrong in saying that the *topics* or orders of invention (*argumenta*, as they call them) serve as much for the explication or very detailed description of an *incomplex theme, i.e.* of a thing or idea, as for the proof of a *complex theme, i.e.* of a thesis, proposition, or truth. And indeed a thesis may be explained, in order that its sense and force may be well known, without raising the question of its truth or proof, as is seen in sermons and homilies explaining certain passages of Holy Scripture, or in instruction or lectures upon certain texts of civil or canon law whose truth is presupposed. We can even say that there are some themes which are means between an idea and a proposition. These are the *questions*, some of which demand only yes or no; and they are the nearest to propositions. But there are some also which demand the how, the circumstances, etc., where there is more to be supplied in order to make propositions. It is true, it may be said, that in descriptions[2] (even of things purely ideal) there is a tacit affirmation of possibility. But it is also true that, as we may undertake the explanation and proof of a falsehood, a method which sometimes serves as its best refutation, the art of description may fall upon the impossible also. Something like this is found in the *novelle* of the Count of Scandiano followed by Ariosto,[3] and in the

[1] The Ramists were disciples of Peter Ramus (*cf. infra* p. 408, note 1). Schaarschmidt states that Leibnitz probably has in mind chiefly J. H. Alsted, whom he has previously (*cf. ante*, pp. 311, note 2, 362) cited, and whom he greatly prized and studied, in whose *Systema logicæ harmonicum*, Herborniae, 1614, p. 69, the *argumentum* is divided into *argumentum simplex* (which Leibnitz calls *thème incomplexe*) and into *argumentum complexum*. The former, according to Alsted, is a "terminus extra omnem dispositionem dirigens materiam" (Leibnitz says: "une chose ou idée"), the latter is a "definitio et distributio" (Leibnitz says: "une thèse, proposition ou vérité"). *Cf.* Alsted, p. 261. — Tr.

[2] *I.e.* in the sense of nominal definitions, which allow the really impossible. *Cf. ante*, p. 317, note 3. — Tr.

[3] Leibnitz here refers to Matteo Maria Boiardo, c. 1434–1494, Count of Scandiano, and the author of *Orlando Innamorato*, which a recent writer calls "the most chivalrous poem of the Renaissance," and "a masterpiece of

"Amadis of Gaul"[1] or other old romances, in the fairy-stories which were again in fashion some years since, in the "True History"[2] of Lucian and in the "Voyages" of Cyrano de Bergerac;[3] to say nothing of the grotesque figures of the painters. So we know stories with the rhetoricians belong in the number of *progymnasmata* or preliminary exercises. But taking *knowledge* in a narrower sense, *i.e.* as knowledge of

inventive genius," and which furnished Ludovico Ariosto, 1474–1533, with the theme of his *Orlando Furioso*. For an account of the two writers and their works, *cf.* J. A. Symonds, *Renaissance in Italy*, Pt. IV., *Italian Literature*, Vol. 1, pp. 456 *sq.*, Vol. 2, pp. 1 *sq.* New York, H. Holt & Co., 1885.

Through a misunderstanding of Leibnitz's reference to the Count of Scandiano, Schaarschmidt, in his note to the passage, has wrongly identified him with Tito Giovanni Ganzarini, 1518–1582, Professor of Literature at Modena, called il Scandianese, from his birthplace, Scandiano. Ariosto published his *Orlando Furioso* in 1516, two years before Ganzarini was born, and could scarcely be said to have "followed" an author who was only fifteen years old when the poet himself died. — TR.

[1] The *Amadis de Gaula*, the best of all the old romances of chivalry, was originally written, it is supposed, about 1390, by Vasco de Lobeira, a Portuguese knight attached to the court of John I. of Portugal, and who died in 1403. The oldest text now extant is in Spanish prose, a version from the Portuguese original, now lost, made by Garcia Ordoñez de Montalvo, between 1492 and 1504. Editions of the Spanish version are numerous, the earliest accessible being that of 1519; and there are translations in English, French, German, Italian, and other languages. The best and at present the only readable edition in English is the abridged translation (with a Preface giving an account, not, however, without error, of the work), made from the Spanish, by Robert Southey, London, 1803, 4 vols., 12mo, new ed., London, 1872, 3 vols., 16mo. *Cf.* also, V. de Lobeira, *Amadis de Gaula*, Barcelona, 1847–8, 4 vols., 16mo; George Ticknor, *Hist. of Spanish Lit.*, 3d ed., Boston, 1863, Vol. 1, pp. 198–207; L. Braunfels, *Kritischer Versuch über Amadis*, Leipzig, 1876. It may be added that the writer of the article, "Amadis of Gaul," in the *Encyclop. Brit.*, 9th ed., argues for the Anglo-Norman origin of the romance, on the ground that all its ideas and materials, its design and machinery, belong to the Anglo-Norman romance-cycle in vogue before Lobeira was born. — TR.

[2] The Ἀληθοῦς ἱστορίας λόγος (*Veræ Historiæ*) of Lucian is one of the witty satirist's cleverest works, written in easy and elegant Greek, and exhibiting great fertility of invention. It was purposely composed, says Lucian, as a satire on the poets and logographers who have written so many marvellous tales, and contains things which neither he nor any one else has ever seen, which not only do not, but cannot, exist, and descriptions of experiences and adventures which are absurd and impossible, chief among which is a voyage to the moon. Lucian himself says that the only true statement in his History is that it contains nothing but lies from beginning to end. It has without doubt supplied hints to, or served as a model for, writers like Rabelais, Swift, and Cyrano de Bergerac. — TR.

[3] *Cf. ante*, p. 228, note 2. Amid many imaginative extravagances, these *Voyages* contain a pretty exact knowledge of the philosophy of Descartes. — TR.

truth, as you, sir, do here, I say it is quite true that truth is always grounded in the agreement or disagreement of ideas, but it is not true in general that our knowledge of truth is a perception of this agreement or disagreement. For when we know truth only empirically, from having experienced it, without knowing the connection of things and the reason there is in what we have experienced, we have no perception of this agreement or disagreement, unless we mean that we feel it in a confused way without being conscious of it. But your examples, it seems, show that you always demand a knowledge in which one is conscious of connection or opposition, and this is what cannot be granted you. Further, we can treat a complex theme not alone by seeking the proofs of its truth, but also in explicating and otherwise illustrating it, according to the topical order, as I have already observed. Finally, I have a further remark to make upon our definition: viz. that it appears only suited to categorical truths, in which there are *two ideas*, the subject and the predicate; but there is besides a knowledge of hypothetical truths or what may be reduced thereto (as disjunctives and others) in which there is connection between the antecedent and the consequent proposition; thus more than two ideas may enter therein.

§ 3. *Ph.* [Let us limit ourselves here to the knowledge of truth and then apply what will be said of the connection of ideas to the connection of propositions, in order to include in one whole the categorical and hypothetical truths.] Now I believe that this agreement or disagreement may be reduced to four kinds: (1) Identity or diversity, (2) Relation, (3) Coexistence or necessary connection, (4) Real existence. § 4. For the mind perceives immediately that one idea is not another, that white is not black; § 5. then it perceives their relation by comparing them with each other; for example, that two triangles whose bases are equal and which are found between two parallels are equal. § 6. Next there is coexistence (or rather connection), as fixedness always accompanies the other ideas of gold. § 7. Finally there is real existence beyond the mind, as when it is said: God is.

Th. I believe it may be said that the connection is nothing else than the *agreement* or the relation taken generally. And I have remarked above that every relation is either of *com-*

parison or *concurrence*. That of *comparison* gives diversity and identity, either complete or partial; whereby are constituted the concepts of the same or the diverse, the like or unlike. *Concurrence* contains what you call coexistence, *i.e.* connection of existence. But when we say that a thing exists or that it has real existence, this existence itself is the predicate, *i.e.* it has a notion joined with the idea in question, and there is connection between these two notions. The *existence* of the object of an idea may also be conceived, as the concurrence of this object with the Ego. Thus I believe it may be said that there is only comparison or concurrence; but that the comparison which marks identity or diversity, and the concurrence of the thing with the Ego, are the relations which deserve to be distinguished among others.[1] More exact and more profound researches might perhaps be made; but I content myself here with making remarks.

§ 8. *Ph.* There is *actual knowledge*, which is the present perception of the relation of ideas; and there is *habitual knowledge*, when the mind has so evidently perceived the agreement or disagreement of ideas, and so placed it in its memory, that every time it comes to reflect upon the proposition, it is at once certain of the truth it contains without the least doubt. For being capable of thinking clearly and distinctly of but one thing at once, men would all be very ignorant if they knew only the actual object of their thoughts; and he who knew most would know but one truth.

Th. It is true that our science, the most demonstrative indeed, being very often obliged to acquire its existence by a long chain of inferences, must involve the memory of a past demonstration which is no longer distinctly in view, when the conclusion is made; otherwise it would always be repeating this demonstration. And even while it lasts it cannot be understood as a complete whole at once; for all its parts cannot be present in the mind at the same time; thus always recalling the preceding part to mind, we should never advance to the last which achieves the conclusion. This is the reason also

[1] Leibnitz reduces Locke's four kinds of agreement or disagreement to two, and thus generalizes the relation and considers the existence as the concurrence of the object with the Ego. This concurrence Leibnitz explains by his doctrine of pre-established harmony.—TR.

that without writing it would be difficult properly to establish the sciences, the memory not being sufficiently reliable. But having put in writing a long demonstration, like, for example, those of Apollonius,[1] and having gone over again all its parts, as if they were examining a chain, link by link, men can assure themselves regarding their reasonings; for which purpose proofs are also of use, and the result at last justifies the whole. But we see by this that as all belief consists in the memory of past life, of proofs or reasons, it is not within our power or choice to believe or disbelieve, since memory is not a thing depending on our will.

§ 9. *Ph.* It is true that our habitual knowledge is of two sorts or degrees. Sometimes, truths laid up as it were in the memory no sooner present themselves to the mind, than it sees the relation between the ideas entering therein; but, sometimes, the mind contents itself with the memory of the conviction, without retaining the proofs, and often, indeed, without the power to recall them if it wished. It may be thought that this is rather to believe one's memory than really to know the truth in question, and this formerly appeared to me to be a mean between opinion and knowledge, a kind of assurance superior to simple belief based upon the testimony of another. But upon due reflection I find that this knowledge contains perfect certainty. I remember, *i.e.* I know (memory being only the reviving of something past), that I was once certain of the truth of this proposition, that the three angles of a triangle are equal to two right angles. Now, the immutability of the same relations between the same immutable things is at present *the mediate idea* which shows me that, if they were once equal, they will be so still. It is upon this ground that in mathematics *particular demonstrations* furnish general knowledge; otherwise a geometer's knowledge would not extend beyond this particular figure which he had drawn while demonstrating it.

Th. The mediate idea of which you, sir, speak, presupposes the fidelity of our memory; but it sometimes happens that our memory deceives us, and that we have not made every necessary effort, although we now believe we have. This is clearly seen in the examination of accounts. Sometimes there are

[1] *Cf. ante*, p. 108, note 1.—TR.

examiners officially appointed, as at our mines in the Harz, and to make the receivers of the particular mines more attentive, they have imposed a money penalty upon every error in calculation; nevertheless they find them in spite of this penalty. But the more care we employ, the more reliance we can place upon past reasonings. I have devised a method of keeping accounts, by which he who collects the sums of the columns leaves upon the paper traces of the progress of his reasoning, so that he does not reason in vain. He can always revise and correct the last errors without affecting the first: the examination, also, which another desires to make costs, in this way, almost no trouble, because he can examine the very same traces at a glance. There are, besides, means of verifying the accounts of each article, by a very convenient kind of proof, without increasing to any considerable extent the labor of the computation. And all this easily shows that men may have rigorous demonstrations on paper, and have an infinite number of them. But unless we remember that we have been absolutely accurate, we cannot have this certainty in the mind. And this accuracy consists in an orderly procedure, the observance of which in each part is an assurance as regards the whole; as in the examination of a chain by links, in which inspecting each to see if it is strong, and measuring with the hand so as not to skip any, assurance is obtained of the good quality of the chain. And by this means we have all the certitude of which human things are capable. But I do not agree that in mathematics *particular demonstrations* upon the figure which is drawn furnish this general certitude, as you seem to take it. For you must know that it is not the figures which furnish the proof with geometers, although the style of the exposition may make you think so. The force of the demonstration is independent of the figure drawn, which is drawn only to facilitate the knowledge of our meaning, and to fix the attention; it is the universal propositions, *i.e.* the definitions, axioms, and theorems already demonstrated, which make the reasoning, and which would sustain it though the figure were not there. Hence it is that a learned geometer, like Scheubelius,[1] has given Euclid's figures without the letters which might

[1] Johann Scheybl — Latin, Scheubelius — 1494–1570, was, according to Jöcher, *Allgemeines Gelehrten-Lexicon*, Leipzig, 1750–51, Vol. 4, p. 257, a professor

bind them to the demonstration he has put with them; and another, like Herlinus,[1] has reduced the same demonstrations to syllogisms and prosyllogisms.

CHAPTER II

OF THE DEGREES OF OUR KNOWLEDGE

§ 1. *Ph.* *Knowledge* is then *intuitive* when the mind perceives the agreement of two ideas immediately by themselves without the intervention of any other. In this case, the mind takes no pains to prove or examine the truth. As the eye sees the light, the mind sees that white is not black, that a circle is not a triangle, that three is two and one. This knowledge is the clearest and most certain of which human weakness is capable; it acts in an irresistible manner without allowing the mind to hesitate. It is knowledge that the idea is in the mind as perceived. Whoever asks for greater certitude, knows not what he asks.

Th. *Primitive* truths, which are known by *intuition*, are of two kinds, like the *derivative.* They are truths of *reason* or truths of *fact.* Truths of reason are necessary, and those of fact are contingent. The primitive truths of reason are those which I call by the general name of *identical,* because they seem only to repeat the same thing without giving us any information. They are affirmative or negative. The *affirmative* are such as the following: *Each thing is what it is,* and in

of mathematics in the University at Tübingen. His *Euclidis sex libri primi de geometricis principiis gr. et lat. cum commentario* appeared at Basle, 1590. —Tr.

[1] Christian Herlinus, whom Leibnitz also mentions toward the end of his *Meditationes de Cog., Verit., et Ideis,* as co-editor with Conrad Dasypodius (1532–1600, professor of mathematics in Strassburg University, and Canon of St. Thomas' Church) of Euclid, appears to be otherwise unknown. Their joint work, of which Herlinus did the first and fifth books, and Dasypodius the other four, appeared under the title *Analysis geometriæ sex librorum Euclidis,* etc., Strassburg, 1566, fol. It is, says Michaud, *Biog. Universelle,* Vol. 10, p. 560, a pedantic work in which the demonstrations of the Greek geometer are reduced to syllogistic form, so that a proposition of fifteen or twenty lines is spun out into several pages, and is often more involved or at least more difficult to follow. — Tr.

as many examples as you please, A is A, B is B. I shall be what I shall be. I have written what I have written. And *nothing* in verse as in prose, *is to be nothing* or a trifle. *The equilateral rectangle is a rectangle.*[1] *The rational animal* is always *an animal.* And in the hypothetical: *If the regular figure of four sides is an equilateral rectangle, this figure is a rectangle.* Copulatives, disjunctives, and other propositions are also susceptible of this identicism, and I reckon indeed among the affirmatives: non-A is non-A. And this hypothetical: if A is non-B, it follows that A is non-B. Again, if non-A is BC, it follows that non-A is BC. *If a figure having no obtuse angle may be a regular triangle, a figure having no obtuse angle may be regular.* I come now to the identical *negatives* which belong either to the *principle of contradiction* or to the *disparates.* The principle of contradiction is in general: *a proposition is either true or false:* this contains two true statements, one that the true and the false are not compatible in one and the same proposition, or *that a proposition cannot be true and false at once;* the other that the opposition or the negation of the true and the false are not compatible, or that there is no mean between the true and the false, or rather: *it is impossible for a proposition to be neither true nor false.* Now all this is also true in all imaginable propositions in particular, as *what is A cannot be non-A.* Again,[2] AB cannot be non-A. An equilateral rectangle cannot be non-rectangle. Again, *it is true that* every man is an animal, then it is false that *any man is found who is not an animal.* We may vary these statements in many ways, and apply them to copulatives, disjunctives, and others. As for the *disparates,* they are the propositions which state that the object of one idea is not the object of another idea; as, *that heat is not the same thing as color;* again, *man and animal are not the same,* although every man is an animal. All this may be asserted independently of all proof or of reduction to opposition, or to the principle of contradiction,

[1] Erdmann and Jacques omit: "Est un rectangle. L'animal raisonnable est toujours un animal. Et dans les hypothetiques: Si la figure reguliere de quatre costés est un rectangle equilateral." — TR.

[2] Erdmann and Jacques omit: "Item AB ne sauroit estre non-A. Un rectangle equilateral ne sauroit estre non-rectangle. Item il est vray que tout homme est un animal, donc il est faux," and instead of the last four words, read: "Item il est vray," etc. — TR.

when these ideas are sufficiently understood not to require here analysis; otherwise they are liable to be misunderstood: for in saying, *the triangle and the trilateral are not the same,* we should be mistaken, since upon proper consideration we find that three sides and three angles always go together. In saying, *the quadrilateral rectangle and the rectangle are not the same,* we should also be mistaken. For it is found that the four-sided figure alone can have all the angles right angles. But we may also say in the abstract that *the triangle is not the trilateral,* or that *the formal causes* of the triangle and of the trilateral are not the same, as the philosophers express it. They are different relations of one and the same thing.

Some one after having heard with patience what we have just said up to this point, will lose it after all and will say that we are amusing ourselves with frivolous statements, and that all identical truths are useless. But he will make this judgment for want of having thought sufficiently upon these matters. The deductions of logic, for example, are demonstrated by identical principles; and geometers require the principle of contradiction in their demonstrations which reduce to the impossible.[1] Let us be content here to show the use of identicals in the demonstrations of rational deduction. I say, then, that the principle of contradiction alone suffices to demonstrate the second and the third figures of the syllogism by means of the first. For example, we may conclude in the first figure, in *Barbara:*

All B is C,
All A is B,
Then All A is C.

Suppose that the conclusion is false (or that it is true that some A is not C), then one or the other of the premises will be false also. Suppose that the second is true, the first must then be false, which maintains that all B is C. Then its contradictory will be true, *i.e.* some B will not be C. And this will be the conclusion of a new argument, drawn from the

[1] *I.e.* the so-called indirect proof, which provisionally assumes the truth of the contradictory opposite of the proposition to be proved, and then, having discovered the impossibility of this assumption, concludes, by the aid of the principle of contradiction, that the original proposition is correct.—TR.

falsity of the conclusion and the truth of one of the premises of the preceding argument. Here is this new argument:

Some A is not C.

This is opposed to the preceding conclusion supposed false.

All A is B.

This is the preceding premise supposed true.

Then some B is not C.

This is the present true conclusion, opposed to the preceding false premise.

This argument is in the mode *Disamis* of the third figure, which is thus plainly demonstrated and at once from the mode *Barbara* of the first figure by employing simply the principle of contradiction. And I noticed in my youth, when I examined minutely these things, that all the modes of the second and third figure may be drawn from the first by this method alone, by supposing that the mode of the first is valid, and consequently that the conclusion being false, or its contradictory being taken as true, and one of the premises being taken as true also, the contradictory of the other premise is true. It is true that in the schools of logic they prefer to make use of conversions to draw the *less principal figures* from the first which is the *principal*, because this method appears better suited to the scholars. But for those who seek demonstrative reasons, in which the least possible suppositions must be employed, we shall not demonstrate by the supposition of conversion what may be demonstrated by the primitive principle alone, which is that of contradiction and which assumes nothing. I have also made this apparently remarkable observation, that only the *less principal figures* which are called *direct*, viz. the second and the third, can be demonstrated by the principle of contradiction by itself: but the *less original indirect figure*, the *fourth*, whose invention the Arabs attribute to *Galen*,[1] although we found nothing concerning it in the

[1] Claudius Galenus, c. 130–c. 201, a very celebrated physician and medical writer, who also wrote a large number of philosophical and logical works, the greater part of which are now lost. His medical and scientific treatises contain considerable philosophical and logical discussion, and his *De usu partium*

works of his remaining to us, nor in the other Greek authors, the fourth, I say, has this disadvantage, that it cannot be derived from the first or principal figure by this method alone, and it is necessary besides to employ another supposition, viz. conversions, so that it is farther removed by one degree than the second and the third, which are on a level and equally removed from the first; while the fourth needs also the second and the third for its demonstration. For it is found very opportunely that the conversions required are demonstrated by the second or third figure, demonstrable independently of the conversions, as I have just shown. It is Peter Ramus[1] who already made this remark concerning the demonstrability of conversion by these figures; and (if I am not mistaken) he reproached the logicians, who make use of conversion to demonstrate these figures, with arguing in a circle, although it was not so much the circle that he found it necessary to reproach them with (for they did not use these

corp. hum. is, says Janet, "an apology for and a continual application of the principle of final causes." The most complete ed. of his works containing the Greek text and a Latin version is the *Opera Omnia*, cur. C. G. Kühn, Leipzig, 1821–33, 20 vols., 8vo. For his philosophical views, *cf.* K. Sprengel, *Beitr. z. Gesch. d. Medicin*, 1, 117–195, Halle, 1794–6; on his logic, *cf.* Prantl, *Gesch. d. Logik*, 1, 559–577. A brief account of his philosophy is given by Zeller, *Philos. d. Griech.*, III., 1 [Vol. 5], 823 *sq.*, 3d ed., Leipzig, 1880.

The invention of the fourth syllogistic figure was ascribed to Galen by Averroes, 1105–1198, but without adequate foundation. Galen was led through the additions to the first figure already made by Theophrastus, c. 373–c. 288 B.C., to transpose the premises in the same, and only by this means indirectly to the fourth arrangement of the middle term. *Cf.* Prantl, *Gesch. d. Logik im Abendlande*, 1, 570–574; also Sir W. Hamilton, *Lects. on Logic*, Boston, 1873, Lect. XX., ¶ LXXIII., pp. 285–6; Lect. XXI., ¶ LXXIV., p. 302–3, and notes. — TR.

[1] Petrus Ramus — Pierre de la Ramée — 1515–1572, murdered during St. Bartholomew's Night, was a determined opponent of Aristotelian scholasticism, and especially of its logic or dialectic, in the place of which he attempted to set up a new, simpler, and better grounded dialectic. For this purpose he wrote and published his two works, *Animadversiones Aristotelicæ*, Paris, 1534, etc., and *Institutiones dialecticæ*, Paris, 1543. Following Cicero and Quintilian, his scheme was a blending of logic and rhetoric. For a long time after him, logicians were divided into Ramists and Anti-Ramists, while the Semi-Ramists, among whom were Alsted and Goclen (*cf. ante*, p. 311, note 2), sought to mediate between the Aristotelic dialectic, as set forth by Melanchthon, and that of Ramus. The remarks to which Leibnitz here refers are found, according to Schaarschmidt, in *Animad. Aristotel.*, Lutetiæ, 1548, pp. 388 *sq.* For a good account of Ramus, *cf.* Stöckl, *Gesch. d. Philos. d. Mittelalters*, III. [Vol. 4], pp. 296 *sq.*; also Ueberweg-Heinze, *Gesch. d. Philos.*, 7th ed., 3, 24, 26. — TR.

figures in their turn to justify the conversions) as the *hysteron proteron* or the reversal (*le rebours*); because conversions need rather to be demonstrated by these figures, than these figures by the conversions. But as this demonstration of conversions shows also the use of the *identical affirmatives*, which many take as altogether frivolous, it will be so much more to the purpose to introduce them here. I wish to speak only of conversions without contraposition, which suffice me here, and which are simple or *per accidens*, as they are called. Simple conversions are of two kinds: that of the universal negative, as: *no square is obtuse-angled,* then *no obtuse-angled figure is a square;* and that of the particular affirmative, as: *some triangles are obtuse-angled,* then some *obtuse-angled figures are triangles.* But *conversion per accidens,* as it is called, concerns the universal affirmative, as: *every square is a rectangle,* then *some rectangles are squares.* A *rectangle* is here always understood to be a figure all of whose angles are right angles, and by the *square* is understood a regular quadrilateral. Now the question is to demonstrate these three kinds of conversion, which are:

(1) No A is B, then no B is A.
(2) Some A is B, then some B is A.
(3) All A is B, then some B is A.

Demonstration of the first conversion in *Cesare,* which belongs to the second figure.

No A is B.
All B is B.
Then no B is A.

Demonstration of the second conversion in *Datisi,* which belongs to the third figure.

All A is A.
Some A is B.
Then some B is A.

Demonstration of the third conversion in *Darapti,* which belongs to the third figure.

All A is A.
All A is B.
Then some B is A.

This shows that the purest and apparently most useless identical propositions are of considerable use in the abstract and general; and that may teach us that we should not despise any truth. As for this proposition, that *three is as much as two and one,* which you, sir, still adduce as an example of intuitive knowledge, I have to say that it is only the definition of the term *three,* for the simplest definitions of numbers are formed in this way: *Two* is one plus one, *three* is two plus one, *four* is three plus one, etc. It is true that there is therein a concealed statement, which I have already spoken of, viz. that these ideas are possible: and this is here known *intuitively,* so that it may be said, that an intuitive knowledge is comprised in definitions when their possibility appears at once. And in this way all *adequate* definitions contain primitive truths of reason and consequently intuitive knowledge. In short, you can say in general that all primitive truths of reason are immediate with respect to an *immediateness of ideas.*

As for the *primitive truths of fact,* they are the immediate internal experiences of an *immediateness of feeling.* And here it is that the first truth of the Cartesians or of St. Augustine: *I think, therefore I am,* i.e. *I am a thing which thinks,* holds good.[1] But we must know, that as the identicals are general or particular, and as one is as clear as the other (since the statement that A *is* A is as clear as the statement that *a thing is what it is*), so is it also with the first truths of fact. For not only is it immediately clear to me that *I think,* but it is wholly as clear to me that *I have different thoughts,* that sometimes *I think* of A, and sometimes of B, etc. Thus the Cartesian principle is valid, but it is not the only one of its kind. You see by this that all *primitive truths* of reason or of fact have this in common, that they cannot be proved by anything more certain.

§ 2. *Ph.* I am very glad, sir, that you have carried forward

[1] *Cf.* Augustine, *Solil.* II., 1: "Tu qui scis te nosse, scis te esse? Scio! Unde scis? Nescio! Simplicem te sentis an multiplicem? Nescio! Cogitare te scis? Scio!" in *Opera,* Vol. 1, p. 369, Benedictine ed., Paris, Franciscus Muguet, 1679; Vol. 1, p. 885, ed. Migne, Paris, 1841. Augustine, 354–430, thus anticipated the principle of Descartes, 1596–1650, "Cogito ergo sum," a fact unknown however to Descartes, who was not one of the class of reading philosophers, until brought to his knowledge by Arnauld, 1612–1694, and Mersenne, 1588–1648, in their criticism of his philosophy. — TR.

farther than I had done that which relates to *intuitive* knowledge. Now *demonstrative knowledge* is only a concatenation of intuitive knowledge in all the connections of mediate ideas. For often the mind cannot unite, compare, or apply immediately the ideas one to the other, and this compels it to make use of other ideas (one or more) as means to the discovery of the agreement or disagreement it seeks, and this is what we call *reasoning*. As in demonstrating the three angles of a triangle to be equal to two right angles, it finds some other angles which are seen to be equal both to the three angles of the triangle and to two right angles. § 3. These intervening ideas are called *proofs*, and the disposition of the mind to discover them is called *sagacity*. § 4. And even when found, this knowledge cannot be acquired without pains and attention and by more than a single passing view; for the mind must enter upon a progression of ideas, made gradually and by degrees, § 5. and there is doubt before the demonstration. § 6. It is not so clear as the intuitive knowledge, as the image reflected by several mirrors from one to another grows more and more faint with each reflection, and is no longer at once so recognizable especially by weak eyes. It is the same with knowledge produced by a long train of proof. § 7. And although each step taken by reason in the demonstration is intuitive knowledge or simple sight, nevertheless as in this long train of proofs the memory does not so exactly preserve this connection of ideas, men often take fallacies for demonstrations.

Th. Besides natural sagacity or that acquired by exercise, there is an art of finding mediate ideas (the *medium*), and this art is *analysis*. Now it is well to consider here, that the question is sometimes to find the truth or falsehood of a given proposition, which is nothing else than an answer to the question *An? i.e.* whether it is or is not. Sometimes it concerns an answer to a more difficult (*cæteris paribus*) question, where it is asked for example *by whom and how?* and where there is more to be supplied. And it is these questions alone, which leave a part of the proposition blank, which the mathematicians call *problems*. As, when we are asked to find a mirror which collects all the rays of the sun in one point, we are asked for its form, or how it is made. As for the first questions in which the point at stake is only truth and falsehood and where there is nothing to be supplied in the subject or predicate, there is less *invention*, yet there is some, and the judgment alone is not sufficient. It is true that a man of judgment, *i.e.* one who is capable of attention and reserve, and who has the leisure, the patience, and the necessary freedom of mind, may understand the most difficult demonstration if properly set before him. But the most judicious man in the world, without other aid, will not always be capable of discovering this demonstration. Thus there is still some invention therein; and with geometers there was more of it formerly than now. For when analysis was less cultivated, more sagacity was necessary to attain it, and it is on this account that some geometers still of the old school,[1] or others who have not yet sufficient aptness in the new methods, think they have done something wonderful when they discover the demonstration of some theorem that others have invented. But those who are versed in the art of invention know when this is estimable or not; for example, if some one sets forth the *quadrature* of a space comprised within a curved and a straight line, which is successful in all its segments and which I call general, it is always within our power according to our methods to discover its demonstration, provided we are willing to take the trouble. But there are some particular quadratures of certain portions, where the thing may be so involved, that it will not always be possible (*in potestate*) thus far to develop it. It happens also that induction presents us with truths in numbers and in figures whose general reason is not yet discovered. For much is needed in order to attain perfection of analysis in geometry and in numbers, as many are becoming conceited upon the basis of the boasts of some men otherwise excellent, but a little too hasty or too ambitious.

But it is much more difficult to discover important truths, and still more to discover means of producing what is sought, when it is justly sought, than to discover the demonstration of truths which another has discovered. Beautiful truths are often attained by *synthesis*, by passing from the simple to the complex; but when it is a question of discovering exactly the means of producing what is proposed, synthesis is ordinarily

[1] Gerhardt reads: "roche"; Erdmann and Jacques: "race." — TR.

not sufficient, and often to be willing to make all the requisite combinations would be an endless task, although one might often be aided therein by the *method of exclusion*,[1] which cuts off a good portion of useless combinations, and often nature does not admit any other method. But the means are not always at hand for the proper pursuit of this method. Analysis then must give us a thread in this labyrinth, when it is possible, for there are cases where the nature itself of the question demands that we grope about, short cuts not being always possible.

§ 8. *Ph.* Now as in demonstration intuitive knowledge is always supposed, it has, I think, given occasion for this maxim: *that all reasoning springs from things already known and agreed to* (*ex præcognitis et præconcessis*).[2] But we shall have occasion to speak of the falsity of this axiom when we speak of the maxims which are improperly taken as the foundation of our reasoning.

Th. I am curious to learn what falsehood you can find in an axiom apparently so reasonable. If it were always necessary to reduce everything to intuitive knowledge, demonstration would often be insufferably prolix. This is why mathematicians have had the cleverness to divide the difficulties and to demonstrate separately the intervening propositions. And there is art also in this; for as the mediate truths (which are called *lemmas*, since they appear to be a digression) may be assigned in many ways, it is well, in order to aid the understanding and the memory, to choose those of them which greatly shorten the process, and appear memorable and worthy in themselves of being demonstrated. But there is another

[1] The "method of exclusion" or elimination, says Schaarschmidt, proceeds from a disjunctive judgment, the predicate of which embraces in the sum of its divisional members all possible determinations of the subject. After it has been shown that individual divisional members cannot be united with the subject in a categorical judgment, that one alone of the divisional members which cannot be separated from the subject remains as the actual predicate for the valid determination of the subject. For example: A is B, or C, or D, or E. In this formula, B, C, D, E must include all thinkable predicate-determinations of A. In the question: Is A, B, or C, or D, or E, it is then proved that A is not C, D, E, in which case A must be B; or that A is not B, D, E, in which case A must be C, and so on. — Tr.

[2] *Cf.* Aristotle, *Analyt. Post.*, I., 1, p. 71ᵃ, 1: πᾶσα διδασκαλία καὶ πᾶσα μάθησις διανοητικὴ ἐκ προϋπαρχούσης γίνεται γνώσεως. — Tr.

obstacle, viz.: that it is not easy to demonstrate all the axioms, and to reduce demonstration wholly to intuitive knowledge. And if we had chosen to wait for that, perhaps we should not yet have the science of geometry. But we have already spoken of this in our former conversations, and we shall have occasion to speak of it again.

§ 9. *Ph.* We shall come to that presently; now I shall remark again what I have already touched upon more than once, that it is a common opinion that only the mathematical sciences are capable of a demonstrative certainty; but as the agreement and disagreement which may be known intuitively is not a privilege belonging only to the ideas of numbers and figures, it is perhaps for want of application on our part that mathematics alone have attained to demonstrations. § 10. Many reasons conspired to this end. The mathematical sciences are very generally useful; the least difference therein is very easily recognized. § 11.[1] These other simple ideas, which are appearances or situations produced in us, have no exact measure of their different degrees. § 12.[2] But when the difference of these visible qualities, for example, is sufficiently great to excite in the mind clearly distinct ideas, as those of blue or red, they are as capable of demonstration as those of number and extension.

Th. There are notable examples enough of demonstration outside of mathematics, and it may be said that Aristotle has already given some in his "Prior Analytics." In fact logic is as susceptible of demonstrations as geometry, and it may be said that the logic of the geometers, or the methods of argumentation explained and established by Euclid in reasoning upon propositions, are a particular extension or promotion of general logic. Archimedes[3] is the first, whose works we have, who has practised the art of demonstration upon an occasion where he is treating of physics, as he has done in his book on

[1] § 11, as also § 12, is § 17 in the texts of Erdmann and Jacques.—TR.

[2] § 12 is § 13 in Locke, *Philos. Works*, Vol. 2, p. 140 (Bohn's ed.).—TR.

[3] Archimedes, 287–212 B.C., the greatest mathematician among the Greeks, distinguished also for his discoveries in hydrostatics and hydraulics, and for his ingenious inventions. He first placed the science of engineering upon a sound mathematical basis. The most complete and magnificent edition of his extant works is that edited by Torelli and published at Oxford, at the Clarendon Press, 1792, fol.—TR.

Equilibrium. Furthermore, jurists may be said to have many good demonstrations; especially the ancient Roman jurists, whose fragments have been preserved to us in the Pandects. I am wholly of the opinion of Laurentius Valla,[1] who cannot enough admire these authors among others, because they all speak in a manner so just and so clear and in fact reason in a way closely approaching the demonstrative, and often it is wholly demonstrative.[2] Indeed, I do not know any science outside that of law and that of arms, in which the Romans have made any considerable addition to what they received from the Greeks.

> Tu regere imperio populos Romane memento:
> Hæ tibi erunt artes pacique imponere morem,
> Parcere subjectis, et debellare superbos.[3]

This precise manner of expressing themselves is the reason that all the jurists of the Pandects, though sometimes quite

[1] Laurentius Valla — Lorenzo della Valle — c. 1407–1457, a humanist and philologian of the earlier Italian Renaissance, was an earnest opponent of the scholastic dialectic, a determined foe of tradition and authority, and the initiator and champion of a bold and unbiassed criticism which he applied to language, historical documents, and ethical opinions. He was eminent as a Latinist, and his treatise *Elegantiæ latinæ linguæ*, c. 1431, in six books, — the Preface to the third book of which Schaarschmidt thinks Leibnitz probably had in mind in referring to Valla's admiration for the style of the Roman jurists, therein very highly praised, — subjected the forms of Latin grammar and rhetoric to critical investigation and analysis, and established upon a scientific foundation the principles of Latin style. His *De falso credita et ementita Constantini Donatione*, 1440, destroyed the claims of the Papacy to temporal power based upon this alleged "Donation," by proving its documentary foundations to be forgeries. His principal philosophical writings are: *De voluptate et vero bono*, 1431, in which he boldly defended the Epicurean doctrine of pleasure as the true and only good; *De libero arbitrio*; and the *Dialecticæ disputationes contra Aristotelicos*, 1499, of which Prantl, *Gesch. d. Logik im Abendlande*, 4, 161–167, gives some account with citations. Valla's *Opera Omnia*, Basiliæ, 1465 and 1540–1543. Leibnitz refers to him and his *De lib. arbit.* and *De voluptate* in the *Théodicée*, Pt. III., §§ 405 *sq.* For accounts of his life and works, *cf.* G. Tiraboschi, *Storia della Letteratura Italiana*, Vol. 6, Pt. II., pp. 339–340, Rome, 1784; Symonds, *Renaissance in Italy*, Pt. II., *The Revival of Learning*, p. 258 *sq.*, New York, H. Holt & Co., 1881. For his philosophy, *cf.* Stöckl, *Gesch. d. Philos. d. Mittelalters*, III. [Vol. 4], 279–283. Mancini published at Florence, 1891, a brilliant and exhaustive monograph investigating and settling disputed points in Valla's life. — TR.

[2] *Cf.* Leibnitz's letter to Kestner, No. 15, in Ch. Kortholt, *Leibnit. epist. ad diversos*, Lipsiæ, 1734–1742, Vol. 3, p. 256, Dutens, *Leibnit. opera omnia*, Vol. 4, Pt. III., p. 267, where he expresses himself similarly as here. Also, Guhrauer, *Leibniz, eine Biographie*, Pt. I., pp. 36, 37. — TR.

[3] Verg. *Æn.* 6, 851–853. — TR.

distant from one another in time, seem to be a single author, and there would be much difficulty in distinguishing them, if the names of the writers were not at the beginning of the extracts; as it would be difficult to distinguish Euclid,[1] Archimedes and Apollonius[2] in reading their demonstrations upon matters which the one as well as the other has touched upon. It must be admitted that the Greeks have reasoned with all possible accuracy in mathematics, and that they have left the human race models in the art of demonstration: for if the Babylonians and the Egyptians had anything more than an empirical geometry, nothing of it at least remains; but it is astonishing that these same Greeks lost it to such an extent[3] at once as soon as they turned aside ever so little from numbers and figures in order to proceed to philosophy. For it is strange that we do not see a shadow of demonstration in Plato and in Aristotle (his "Prior Analytics" excepted) and in all the other ancient philosophers. Proclus[4] was an excellent geometer, but he seems another man when he speaks on philosophy. What has made it easier to reason demonstrably in mathematics is largely the fact that experience can there guarantee the reasoning at every moment, as is also the case in the syllogistic figures. But in metaphysics and ethics this parallelism of reason and experience is no longer found; and in

[1] *Cf. ante*, p. 93, note 1. — TR. [2] *Cf. ante*, p. 108, note 1. — TR.

[3] A strange remark for Leibnitz to make, who had so thoroughly studied Aristotle in his youth, and in later years Plato, whose works contain demonstrations inferior in no respect certainly to the precision of the Pandects. The only explanations that seem to touch the case are that Leibnitz had in mind the stringency and completeness of mathematical demonstration, which in *form*, and sometimes in *content* also, is apparently, and sometimes really, superior, though not necessarily so merely because mathematical, to the demonstrations of philosophy; or, as he seems to suggest in the immediately following context, that metaphysics being a matter of pure thought and ethics largely an ideal not as yet realized in the actual, their demonstrations cannot, like those of mathematics, be experimentally verified, and must thus be regarded as, in a sense, lacking in completeness as demonstrations. — TR.

[4] *Cf. ante*, p. 108, note 2. Leibnitz's remark concerning Proclus has its justification in the fact that his philosophical system, while embracing the entire philosophy and theology of his predecessors methodically elaborated with great dialectic art and skill, is yet purely formal in its completeness, its thought exhibiting little freedom or creative power, and wholly lacking in any real scientific basis and character. Though presenting here and there evidence of deep speculative ability on the part of its author, his philosophy is nevertheless wholly wanting in such demonstration as is found in his mathematical work. — TR.

physics experiments demand labor and expense. Now men at once relaxed their attention, and as a consequence were led astray when they were destitute of this faithful guide, experience, who aided and sustained them in their walk, as that little revolving machine does, which prevents children from falling when walking. There was a *succedaneum*,[1] but it is something that has not been and is not yet sufficiently considered. And I shall speak of it in its place. For the rest, blue and red are scarcely capable of furnishing matter for demonstration by means of the ideas we have of them, because these ideas are confused. And these colors do not supply matter for reasoning so long as in experience they are found accompanied by some distinct ideas, but in which the connection with their own ideas does not appear.]

§ 14. *Ph.* Besides *intuition* and *demonstration*, which are the two degrees of our knowledge, all the rest is *faith* or *opinion*, and not knowledge, at least as regards all *general truths.* But the mind has also another perception, regarding the particular existence of finite beings outside of us, and this is *sensitive knowledge.*[2]

Th. [*Opinion,* based on probability, deserves perhaps the name knowledge also ; otherwise nearly all historic knowledge and many other kinds will fall. But without disputing about terms, I hold that the *investigation of the degrees of probability* is very important, that we are still lacking in it, and that this lack is a great defect of our logics.[3] For if the question cannot always be decided absolutely, the degree of resemblance *ex datis* can always be determined, and consequently one can reasonably judge what view is the most likely. And when

[1] *I.e.*, a substitute. The expression was much used by the later Roman jurists. — TR.

[2] Locke's word is "sensitive," *Philos. Wks.* (Bohn's ed.), Vol. 2, p. 141, *ad fin.* His three degrees of knowledge are intuitive, demonstrative, and sensitive, *cf. infra*, p. 420. — TR.

[3] *Cf.* Leibnitz's letter to Kestner, No. 11, Jan. 30, 1711, § 3 (Dutens, *Leibnit. op. om.* 4, Pt. III., 264, and Kortholt, *Leibnit. epist. ad diversos*, 3, 251) : "Ea vero pars Logicæ, qua sc. gradus verisimilitudinum et argumentorum pondera constituerentur, nuspiam hactenus reperitur traditur. Ego juvenis aliquando aggressus sum, sed per varia dissipatus, fere intra voluntatem steti. Topica Aristotelis scopo meo non respondet. Congerit regulas, quæ occasionem aliquam præbere possunt de argumentis cogitandi, sed quæ non possunt docere, quantum cuique argumento aut judicio ponderis insit." — TR.

our moralists (I mean the wisest of them, such as the present (*moderne*) General of the Jesuits)[1] unite the safest and the most probable, and prefer even the safe to the probable,[2] they are not far in fact from the most probable; for the question of *safety* is here that of the little probability of an evil to be feared. The fault of the moralists lax upon this article[3] has largely been, that they have had a too limited and too inadequate notion of the *probable*, which they have confounded with the *Endoxon*[4] or *the probable* (*opinable*) of Aristotle; for Aristotle in his "Topics" did not mean to accommodate himself to the opinion of others, as did the orators and sophists. *Endoxon* is with him what has been received from the greatest number or the most authoritative: he is wrong in having restricted his "Topics" to this, and this view caused him to adhere only to received maxims, for the most part vague, as if he wished

[1] Leibnitz probably refers to Tirso Gonzalez, General of the Jesuits from 1687–1705, and author of a work on probabilism, opposing the doctrine and maintaining that the Jesuits did not originate it, entitled *Fundamentum theologiæ moralis, id est tractatus theologicus de recto usu opinionum probabilium*, 4to, Dillingen, 1689, Naples, 1694. An abridgment with the title *Synopsis tract. theol. de recto usu opinionum probabilium, concinnata a theologo quodam Soc. Jesu: cui accessit logistica probabilitatum*, 3d ed., appeared at Venice, 1696, 8vo. *Cf.* Michaud, *Biog. Univ.* 18, 111–112, Du Pin, *Biblioth. des aut. eccles. du XVII. siécle*, and, for the *De recto usu opin. prob.*, Migne, *Theol. cur. compl.* Vol. 11, p. 1397. — TR.

[2] The theory of moral probabilism is, perhaps the most celebrated question discussed in Moral Theology, and formed one of the chief subjects of controversy between the Jansenists and the Jesuits of the seventeenth century. The aim of moral probabilism is to find some rule by which action may be determined in that portion of the moral realm in which certainty is impossible, and probability only can be attained. The *probable* opinion being that which has a certain number of arguments in its favor, either *intrinsic*, i.e., grounded in reason, judgment in regard to which was restricted to men of considerable education and especially to those versed in moral theology, or *extrinsic*, *i.e.*, resting on some external authority, such as that of some theologian of repute; and the *safe* opinion, that which conforms to the moral law, casuists distinguish the following doctrines: 1. *Probabilism*, which permits action in accord with the opinion which is least probable and least safe; 2. *Probabilorism*, or the preference of the most probable opinion, regardless of its relative safety; 3. *Tutiorism*, or the choice of the safest opinion, without regard to its relative probability. On the whole subject, *cf.* the dissertation of Pierre Nicole annexed to his Latin trans. of Pascal's *Lettres provinciales*, and Janet, *La Morale*, Bk. III., Chap. 3, Paris, 1874, Eng. trans., *The Theory of Morals*, pp. 292–308, New York, Chas. Scribner's Sons, 1883. — TR.

[3] According to Janet, the casuists refuted by Pascal. — TR.

[4] *Cf. Topics*, I., 1, 100^b 21: ἔνδοξα δὲ τὰ δοκοῦντα πᾶσιν ἢ τοῖς πλείστοις ἢ τοῖς σοφοῖς, καὶ τούτοις ἢ πᾶσιν ἢ τοῖς πλείστοις ἢ τοῖς μάλιστα γνωρίμοις καὶ ἐνδόξοις. — TR.

to reason only by means of quodlibets[1] or proverbs. But the probable or the likely is more extended: it must be drawn from the nature of things; and the opinion of persons whose authority has weight is one of the things which may contribute to render an opinion probable, but not what completes the entire verisimilitude. At the time when Copernicus[2] was almost alone in his opinion, it was still incomparably more *probable* than that of all the rest of the human race. Now I do not know but that the establishment of *the art of estimating probabilities*[3] would be more useful than a majority of our demonstrative sciences, and I have thought of this more than once.]

Ph. Sensitive knowledge, or that which establishes the existence of particular beings without us, goes beyond bare probability; but it has not all the certainty of the two degrees of knowledge of which we have just spoken. Nothing is more certain than that the idea we receive of an external object is in our mind, and this is intuitive knowledge: but the knowledge whether from this we can certainly infer the existence of anything without us corresponding to this idea, this it is which certain persons think may be questioned, because men may have such ideas in their minds, when no such thing actually exists. For myself I believe, however, that there is a degree of evidence which elevates us beyond doubt. One is unalterably convinced that there is a great difference between the perceptions which he has when by day he looks at the sun, and when by night he thinks about it; and the idea which is

[1] The Mediæval Latin "quodlibetum" was a very elaborate and subtle scholastic argumentation upon a question chosen at pleasure — "quod libet" — but almost always of a theological or philosophical character. Such questions were called "quodlibetariæ quæstiones"; they were proposed chiefly for the exercise of students, and their discussion was carried on to satisfy curiosity or for entertainment, and, for the most part, served rather to exhibit the skill and dexterity of the dialectician than to establish truth. The French word "quolibet," starting from the scholastic use of the term in the sense of an argumentative subtlety, came by a debasing extension of this meaning to signify a witty, but not always appropriate commonplace, a bad joke, a pun, an epigram; and it is in this sense that Leibnitz, coupling the word with "proverbs," uses the term. — TR.

[2] Nicolas Copernicus, 1473–1543, published his theory of the planetary system in his *De orbium cœlestium revolutionibus lit. VI.*, Nuremberg, 1543, 2d ed., Basle, 1566, both fol. 3d ed., with notes by Nicolas Muler in his *Astronomia Instaurata*, Amsterdam, 1617 and 1640, 4to. — TR.

[3] *Cf. ante*, p. 213, note 2, p. 214, note 1; also Erdmann, *Leibnit. opera philos.*, 84. — TR.

renewed by recourse to the memory is very different from that which actually comes to us by means of the senses. Some one will say that a *dream* may produce the same effect. I reply in the first place *that it matters little that I remove this doubt,* because if all is but a dream, reasoning is useless, truth and knowledge nothing at all. In the second place, he will acknowledge, in my opinion, the difference between dreaming of being in a fire, and being actually in it. And if he persists in appearing sceptical, I shall tell him that it is enough that we certainly find pleasure or pain following the application to ourselves of certain objects, true or dreamt of, and that this certitude is as great as our happiness or misery; two things beyond which we have no interest. Thus I think we may count three sorts of knowledge: *intuitive, demonstrative* and *sensitive.*

Th. [I think you are right, sir, and I also think that to these species of *certitude* or *certain knowledge* you can add the *knowledge of the probable;* thus there will be two sorts of *knowledge*, as there are two sorts of *proofs*, the first of which produce *certitude*, and the second end only in *probability.* But let us come to this dispute of the Sceptics and the Dogmatists upon the existence of things without us. We have already touched upon it, but we must return to it here. I formerly discussed the subject a great deal *viva voce* and in writing with the late Abbé Foucher,[1] Canon of Dijon, a learned and

[1] Simon Foucher, 1644–1696, a devoted student of the Platonic philosophy, in consequence of which he was called "the restorer of the philosophy of the Academy." His *Critique de la Recherche de la Vérité*, here mentioned by Leibnitz, appeared at Paris, 1675. It was based upon the sceptical principles of the Middle Academy, and was subjected to a very sharp criticism by Malebranche in the Preface to the next edition of the *Recherche de la Vérité*. Foucher also wrote *Dissertation sur la recherche de la vérité ou sur la philosophie des académiciens*, Paris, 1673, said to be his best work, and *De la Sagesse des anciens*, Paris, 1683. For Foucher's "objections" (published in the "Journal des Savans" of Sept. 12, 1695) to Leibnitz's doctrine of pre-established harmony as set forth in the *Système nouveau* ("Jour. des Savans," June 27, 1695), *cf.* Gerhardt, 1, 424, and 4, 487, Erdmann, 129, Dutens, 2, Pt. I., 102, trans. Duncan, 81; and for Leibnitz's reply ("Jour. des Savans," April 2 and 9, 1696), *cf.* G. 4, 493, E. 131, Dutens, 2, Pt. I., 67, trans. Duncan, 85. The correspondence of Foucher with Leibnitz was first published by Foucher de Careil in his *Lettres et opuscules inédits de Leibniz*, Paris, 1854, pp. 27–131 (*cf.* Introd. pp. 22–41, where the controversy over Malebranche is thoroughly considered), and more recently, 1875, after a new comparison with the originals in the Royal Library at Hannover, by Gerhardt, *Leibniz. philos. Schrift.*, 1, 363 *sq.*—Tr.

subtile man, but a little too prepossessed in favor of his Academicians, which sect he was very desirous of reviving, as Gassendi[1] had brought upon the stage that of Epicurus.[2] His critique upon "The Search after Truth,"[3] and the other minor treatises which he afterwards published, have made their author quite well known. He published also in the "Journal des Savans" some objections to my System of Pre-established Harmony, when I gave it to the public after having digested it for many years; but death prevented him from replying to my answer. He always preached the necessity of guarding against prejudice and of using great accuracy, but besides the fact that he himself did not make it his duty to carry out his counsel to others, in which he was perhaps excusable, it seems to me that he was not careful whether another did it, anticipating doubtless that no one would ever do it. Now I showed him that the truth of sensible things consisted only in the connection of phenomena, which must have its reason and is that which distinguishes them from dreams; but that the

[1] *Cf. ante*, pp. 64, note 2, 65, n. 3. Gassendi published on the life and philosophy of Epicurus: *De vita, moribus et doctrina Epicuri*, Lugd. Bat., 1647; *Animadversiones in libr. X. Diog. Laert. de Epicuro*, Lugd. Bat. 1649; *Syntagma philos. Epicuri*, The Hague, 1655. For his philosophy, *cf.* his *Syntagma philosophicum*, Vols. 1 and 2 of his *Opera omnia;* also Stöckl, *Gesch. d. Philos. d. Mittelalters*, III. [Vol. 4], 316–327; Lange, *Gesch. d. Materialismus*, Vol. 1, Eng. trans. Vol. 1, pp. 253–269; R. Adamson, article "Gassendi," in *Encyclop. Brit.*, 9th ed. — TR.

[2] *Cf. ante*, p. 126, note 1. On his life and philosophy, *cf.* Zeller, *Philos. d. Griech.*, III., 1 [Vol. 5], 363 *sq.*, 3d ed., Leipzig, 1880; Lange, *Gesch. d. Materialismus*, Vol. 1, Eng. trans., Vol. 1, pp. 98 *sq.*; Benn, *The Greek Philosophers*, Vol. 2, pp. 53 *sq.;* Wm. Wallace, *Epicureanism*, in the series of "Chief Ancient Philosophies," pub. by the Society for promoting Christian Knowledge, London, 1880. — TR.

[3] The *De la Recherche de la Vérité*, the principal work of Malebranche, 1638–1715, appeared in 1674–1679. The most recent edition is that of F. Bouillier, with an introduction and notes, 2 vols., Paris, 1880. On Malebranche's philosophy, *cf.* Bouillier, *Histoire de la Philos. Cartesienne*, Paris, 1854; Ollé-Laprune, *La Philos. de Malebranche*, 2 vols., Paris, 1870–1872; Kuno Fischer, *Gesch. d. n. Philos.*, 3d ed., I., 1, Eng. trans. by J. P. Gordy, New York, Scribners, 1887; Martineau, *Types of Ethical Theory*, 2d ed., Vol. 1, p. 159 *sq.* For a critical account of Malebranche's place in the history of philosophy, *cf.* Edward Caird, article "Cartesianism," in *Encyclop. Brit.*, 9th ed. For Leibnitz's correspondence with Malebranche, *cf.* Gerhardt, *Leibniz. philos. Schrift.*, 1, 315-361; for his discussion of Malebranche's philosophy, *cf.* Gerhardt, 3, 656–660, Erdmann, 735–737, Dutens, 2, Pt. I., 213, trans. Duncan, 233–237; G. 6, 579–594 (*cf.* also 481–483), E. 690–697, D. 2, Pt. I., 201; G. 6, 574–578 (*cf.* also 480–483; Locke's examination of Malebranche is in his *Philos. Works*, Vol. 2, 413–458, Bohn's ed.), E. 450–452, trans. Duncan, 185–189. — TR.

truth of our existence and the cause of phenomena is of a different nature, because it establishes substances, and that the Sceptics spoiled what they rightly say by carrying it too far, and by wishing indeed to extend their doubts even to immediate experience, and to the geometrical truths, a thing which Foucher did not do however, and to the other truths of reason, which he did a little too much. But to return to you, sir, you are right in saying that there is ordinarily some difference between feelings and imaginations; but the Sceptics will say that the more or less does not alter the species. Besides, although feelings are wont to be more vivid than imaginations, it is nevertheless a fact that there are cases where imaginative persons are impressed as much or perhaps more by their imaginations than another is by the truth of things; so that I think the true *criterion* concerning the objects of the senses is the connection of the phenomena, *i.e.* the connection of that which takes place in different places and times, and in the experience of different men who are themselves, each to the others, very important phenomena in this respect. And the connection of the phenomena which guarantees the *truths of fact* in respect to sensible things outside of us, is verified by means of the *truths of reason;* as the phenomena of optics are explained by geometry. It must, however, be admitted that none of this certitude is of the highest degree, as you have well recognized. For it is not impossible, metaphysically speaking, that there may be a dream continuous and lasting like the life of a man; but it is a thing as contrary to reason as would be the fiction of a book which should be formed by chance by throwing together the type pell-mell. For the rest, it is also true that, provided the phenomena are connected, it does not matter whether they are called dreams or not, since experience shows that we are not deceived in the measures we take concerning phenomena when they are understood according to the truths of reason.[1]]

[1] *Cf. New Essays*, Bk. III., chap. 4, § 2, Th., *ante*, pp. 318, 319, notes 1 and 2, and Bk. IV., chap. 11, § 10, Th., *infra*, p. 512. The principle of the "connection of the phenomena," their constant occurrence in the same order and relations, giving them a certain measure of objectivity in our consciousness and enabling us to predict the appearance of other members of the series when one member presents itself, is for Leibnitz the guarantee of the truth of our sense-knowledge and the ground of our greatest possible certainty therein;

§ 15. *Ph.* For the rest, knowledge is not always clear, though ideas may be. A man who has as clear ideas as any mathematician in the world of the angles of a triangle and of equality to two right angles, may yet have a very obscure perception of their agreement.

Th. [Ordinarily when ideas are thoroughly understood their agreements and disagreements appear. I admit, however, that at times some of them are so complex, that much care is needed to develop what they conceal; and in this respect certain agreements or disagreements may still remain obscure. As to your example, I remark that if we have in the imagination the angles of a triangle we do not on that account have clear ideas of them. The imagination cannot furnish us an image common to acute-angled and obtuse-angled triangles, and yet the idea of triangle is common to them: thus this idea does not consist in images and it is not as easy as you may think thoroughly to understand the angles of a triangle.]

CHAPTER III

OF THE EXTENT OF HUMAN KNOWLEDGE

§ 1. *Ph.* Our knowledge does not extend beyond our ideas, § 2. nor beyond the perception of their agreement or disagreement. § 3. It cannot always be intuitive, because we cannot always compare things immediately, for example, the size of two triangles upon one and the same base, equal, but very different. § 4. Our knowledge, also, cannot always be demonstrative, for we cannot always find mediate ideas. § 5. Finally, our sensitive knowledge regards only the existence of things which actually strike our senses. § 6. Thus not only our ideas are limited, but also our knowledge is more limited than our ideas. I do not doubt however that human knowledge can be carried much farther if men will devote them-

but he holds that this guarantee is "verified," and the consecutions of experience supplemented, "by means of the truths of reason," and particularly by the use of the principles of logic. The position here taken is also that of the modern scientist, who keeps strictly within the scientific realm and does not pass on to consider the ultimate metaphysical nature and ground of the phenomena he investigates.—TR.

selves sincerely to discovering the means of perfecting truth, with entire freedom of mind and with all the application and industry they employ in coloring or maintaining falsehood, in defending a system in favor of which they have declared themselves, or else a certain party and certain interests, with which they find themselves united. But after all our knowledge can never embrace all we may wish to know concerning the ideas we have. For example, we shall never perhaps be able to find a circle equal to a square, and know certainly that *it is so.*

Th. [There are confused ideas in which we cannot promise ourselves a complete knowledge, like those of certain sensible qualities. But when they are distinct, there is room to hope for all. As for the square equal to the circle, Archimedes has already shown that there is one. For it is the one whose side is the mean proportional between the semi-diameter and the semi-circumference. He has also determined a straight line equal to the circumference of the circle by means of a straight line tangent to the spiral, as others by the tangent to the quadratrix; a method of quadrature with which Clavius[1] was wholly content; not to speak of a thread applied to the circumference and then stretched out, or of the circumference which revolves to describe the cycloid and is changed to a straight line. Some demand that the construction be made by employing only the ruler and the compasses; but the majority of geometrical problems cannot be constructed by this means. The question then is rather that of finding the proportion between the square and the circle. But this proportion not being capable of expression in finite rational numbers, it has been necessary, in order to employ only rational numbers, to express this same proportion in an infinite series[2]

[1] Christopher Clavius, 1537–1612, a Jesuit and distinguished mathematician, Professor of Mathematics at Rome, and called "the Euclid of the sixteenth century," was employed by Pope Gregory XIII. in the reformation of the calendar, for which he made the principal calculations. Among his works are: *Euclidis elementorum*, Rome, 1574; *Sinus lineæ tangentes*, etc., Rome, 1586, 4to; *Romani Calendarii a Gregorio XIII. P.M. restituti Explicatio*, Rome, 1603. His *Opera mathematica*, containing these and several other works, appeared at Mayence, 1612, 5 vols., fol. — Tr.

[2] Leibnitz's infinite series, which, according to Schaarschmidt, he had discovered before he became acquainted with Huygens, and also before his discovery of the infinitesimal calculus, is $\frac{\pi}{4} = 1 - \frac{1}{3} + \frac{1}{5} - \frac{1}{7} + \frac{1}{9} - \frac{1}{11} + \frac{1}{13} \cdots$, and

of these numbers, which I have assigned in a manner quite simple. Now we should like to know whether there is not some finite quantity, although it be irrational only, or more than irrational, which can express this infinite series, that is to say, whether we can find exactly an abbreviated expression for this series. But finite, especially irrational, expressions, if we proceed to the most irrational of all, may vary in too many ways for us to be able to make an enumeration of them or to determine easily all that they are capable of. There might be perhaps a means of doing it if this irrationality should be explained by an ordinary, or even more, an extraordinary equa-

as related to unity it expresses the proportion obtaining between the circle and the circumscribed square. *Cf. De vera proportione circuli ad quadratum circumscriptum in numeris rationalibus*, "Acta Erud. Lips.," February, 1682, p. 41 *sq.*, Gerhardt, *Leibniz. math. Schrift.*, II., 1 [Vol. 5], 118, Dutens, *Leibnit. op. om.*, 3, 140 *sq.*; *Quadratura arithmetica*, "Acta Erud. Lip.," April, 1691, p. 180, Gerhardt, *Leibniz. math. Schrift.*, II., 1 [Vol. 5], 130, Dutens, 3, 242; also letter to Conring, Jan. 3, 1678, Gerhardt, *Leibniz. philos. Schrift.*, 1, 187.

The problem of which Leibnitz here speaks is the modern form of the problems of the rectification and quadrature of the circle or the calculation and construction of π and of a square mathematically exactly equal in area to a given circle. In referring to it he distinguishes between an "ordinary," or algebraic, and an "extraordinary," or, as it is now termed, transcendental equation. The problem is to prove that π cannot be the root of any equation having whole numbers for coefficients, or that π is not algebraical. The quadrature of the circle has long been known to be an unsolvable problem, — Leibnitz knew this, — but the impossibility of its solution has only recently been demonstrated. Not until mathematicians possessed the methods furnished by the theory of definite integrals and the departments of higher algebra developed in the last few decades was this demonstration possible. With the aid of these methods Prof. Lindemann of Königsberg succeeded, in June, 1882, in demonstrating with exactness the non-algebraic character of π, and thus proved for the first time that the rectification and the squaring of the circle with ruler and compasses is impossible. For his proof, *cf. Über die Ludolph'sche Zahl*, in the "Sitzungsberichte d. köngl. Pr. Akad. d. Wiss., zu Berlin," June 22, 1882, pp. 679–682; the "Comptes Rendus" of the French Academy, Vol. 115, pp. 72–74, "Math. Annalen," Vol. 20, pp. 213–225.

For an historical sketch of the problem of circle-quadrature, *cf.* Holtzendorff and Virchow, *Sammlung gemeinverständlicher wissenschaftlicher Vorträge*, Heft 67; an article from this by H. Schubert, in "The Monist," January, 1891, Vol. 1, No. 2, pp. 197–228, reprinted in Smithsonian Report, 1890, pp. 97–120; and the article "Squaring of the Circle," in the *Encyclop. Brit.*, 9th ed., Vol. 22, pp. 450–454 (American Reprint). On Leibnitz's relation to the problem, *cf.* Kummer, *Festrede am Leibniztage*, in the "Monatsberichte d. Pr. Akad. d. Wiss.," July, 1867, p. 387 *sq.*, an article which, while not directly taking into consideration the present interesting passage for the history of mathematics, is admirable in its understanding of the peculiarities of Leibnitz's method of thought. — TR.

tion, which would introduce the irrational or even the unknown quantity into the exponent,[1] for which, however, an extended calculation would be required, and in which the difficulty will not easily be solved unless we some day find a short method for its solution. But to exclude all the finite expressions is impossible, as I myself know, and to determine exactly the best is an immense task. And all this shows us that the human mind proposes questions so strange, especially when the infinite enters therein, that we must not be astonished if there is some difficulty in making them out, so much the more as all depends often on a short method in these geometrical matters, which cannot always be determined on, just as fractions cannot always be reduced to the lowest terms or the divisors of a number be found. It is true that we may always have these divisors if they are possible, because their number is finite; but when what we have to examine is infinitely variable and ascends by degrees, we are not its master though we wish to be, and it is too laborious to do all that is necessary in order to attempt methodically to reach the short method or the rule of progression exempting us from going farther. And as its usefulness does not correspond to the labor, its success is left to posterity, which will be able to enjoy it when this labor or prolixity is diminished by the new preparations and means which time may furnish. Unless the persons who devote themselves from time to time to these studies determine to do properly what is necessary in order to further progress, we cannot hope to advance much in a short time. And we must not think that all is done, since indeed in ordinary geometry, we still have no method for determining the *best constructions* when the problems are a little complex. A certain progression of synthesis should be mixed with our analysis in order the better to succeed. And I remember to have heard it said that the Pensionary De Witt[2] had some thoughts on this subject.]

[1] *Cf.* Letter to Arnauld, Gerhardt, *Leibniz. philos. Schrift.*, 2, 61, 62, Janet, *Œuvres philos. de Leibniz*, 1, 622.—TR.

[2] John De Witt, 1625–1672, an illustrious Dutch statesman, was a steadfast opponent of the House of Orange, whose re-elevation to power in the United Provinces he labored earnestly and for many years successfully to prevent. His plans for his country were finally defeated by the diplomacy of Louis XIV., the opposition of the Calvinist clergy, and the change in the popular

Ph. There is, indeed, another difficulty, to know *whether a purely material being thinks or not,*[1] and perhaps we shall never be capable of knowing this, although we have ideas of *matter* and of *thought,* for the reason that it is impossible for us to discover by contemplation of our own ideas without revelation, whether God has not *given* to some masses of matter, fitly disposed, the *power* to perceive and to think, or whether he has not united and joined to matter so disposed an immaterial substance that thinks. For as regards our notions, it is no more difficult for us to conceive that God, if he pleases, can add to our idea of matter the faculty of thinking, than to understand that he joins to it another substance with the faculty of thinking, since we know not *wherein thinking consists,* nor to what kind of substance this all powerful Being has been pleased *to give* that *power,* which cannot exist in any created being save by virtue of the *good pleasure* and the bounty of the Creator.

Th. [This question is without doubt incomparably more important than the preceding; but I venture to say to you, sir, that I wish it were as easy to touch souls in order to influence them for their good, and to heal bodies of their diseases, as I think it is in our power to determine this question. I hope you will admit at least that I can advance *without offending against modesty* and *without speaking as a master* in default of good reasons; for besides speaking only according to received and common opinion, I think I have brought thereto an attention not common. In the first place, I grant you, sir, that when we have only confused ideas of *thought* and of *matter,* as is ordinarily the case, we must not be astonished if we do not see the means of solving such questions. As I remarked a little before, one who has only the ideas of the angles of a triangle commonly held will never think of finding

feeling towards the Prince of Orange, occasioned by the recollection of their country's obligations to his ancestors. He was massacred, with his brother Cornelius, in the revolution which put the Prince William (afterwards William III. of England) at the head of the United Provinces. He published *Elementa linearum curvarum,* Leyden, 1650; The Hague, 1709. — TR.

[1] *Cf. ante,* p. 56 *sq.,* where Leibnitz shows that Locke afterwards gave up the opinion which he once advanced as possible that matter can think. For Leibnitz, who regards matter as a mere phenomenon and not a reality, the question does not exist. — TR.

them always equal to two right angles. We must consider that *matter* taken as a *complete being* (*i.e. secondary matter* in distinction from the *primary*, which is something purely passive and consequently incomplete) is only a mass, or that which results therefrom, and that every *real mass* supposes *simple substances* or *real unities*, and when we further consider what belongs to the nature of these real unities, *i.e. perception* and its consequences, we are transferred so to speak into another world, that is to say into the *intelligible world of substances* while before we have been only among the *phenomena of the senses*. And this knowledge of the interior of matter shows us sufficiently its natural capability, and that whenever God shall give it organs suitable for rational expression, the immaterial substance which reasons will not fail to be given it also, in virtue of that harmony which is also a natural consequence of substances. Matter cannot subsist without immaterial substances, *i.e.* without the unities; after which the question should no longer be asked whether God is free to give them to it or not; and if these substances had not in themselves this correspondence or harmony of which I have just spoken, God would not act in accordance with the natural order. To speak in an entirely simple manner of *giving* or *according* powers is to return to the *naked faculties* of the schoolmen and to imagine minute self-subsisting entities, which may go in and out like pigeons from a pigeon-house. It is making substances of them without being aware of it. The *primitive powers* constitute substances themselves, and the *derivative* powers, or, if you prefer, the faculties, are only *modes of being*, which must be derived from substances, and are not derived from matter so long as it is only a machine, *i.e.* so long as it is abstractly considered only as the *incomplete essence* of primary matter, or passivity pure and simple. As to which I think you will agree, sir, that it is not within the power of mere mechanism to produce perception, sensation, reason. They must then spring from some other substantial thing. To desire God to act otherwise and to give to things accidents which are not *modes of being* or modifications derived from substances, is to have recourse to miracles and to what the schoolmen called the *obediential power*, by a kind of supernatural exaltation, as when certain theologians claim that the fire of hell burns up sepa rated souls. In which case it may indeed be doubted whether it was the fire that acted or whether God did not himself produce the effect, acting in place of the fire.]

Ph. You surprise me somewhat by your elucidations, and you anticipate me in many of the things I was going to say to you upon the limits of our knowledge. I should have said to you that we are not in a *state of vision*, as the theologians call it, that faith and probability must suffice us as regards many things, and particularly as regards the *immateriality of the soul;* that all the great ends of morality and religion are established upon sufficiently good foundations without the aid of the proofs of this immateriality drawn from philosophy; and that it is evident that he who has begun to make us subsist here as sensible and intelligent beings, and who has preserved us many years in this state, can and will make us enjoy also a similar state of sensibility in the other life, and make us capable of receiving there the retribution he has designed for men according as they shall have conducted themselves in this life; in fine that we may judge by this that the necessity to determine for or against the immateriality of the soul is not so great as some people too zealous for their own views have wished to persuade us. [I was going to say all this to you, and more besides to the same effect, but I see now how different is the statement that we are sensible, thinking, immortal beings by nature and the statement that we are so only by miracle. It is a miracle, in fact, which I know I must admit if the soul is not immaterial; but this view of miracle, besides being without foundation, will not produce a sufficiently good effect in the minds of most people. I see clearly also from the way you understand the matter, that we can decide rationally as regards the present question, without finding it needful to depart to the enjoyment of the *state of vision* and to find ourselves in the company of those superior spirits who penetrate very deeply into the internal constitution of things and whose living and penetrating sight and vast field of knowledge may make us imagine by conjecture what happiness they must enjoy.] I had supposed it entirely beyond our knowledge *to combine sensation with extended matter, and existence with a thing which has absolutely no extension.* I had therefore become convinced that those who took sides here followed the unreasonable method of certain persons, who, seeing that things considered from a certain side are incomprehensible, throw themselves headlong upon the opposite side, although it is no less unintelligible; a procedure which arose in my opinion from the fact that some having their mind too deeply buried so to speak in matter, could not accord any existence to that which is not material; and others not finding that thought is included in the natural faculties of matter, concluded that God himself could not give life and perception to a solid substance without putting therein an immaterial substance; while I now see that if He had done so it would be by a miracle, and that this incomprehensibility of the union of the soul and the body or of the *union of sensation with matter* seems to cease through your *hypothesis of pre-established harmony* between different substances.]

Th. [In fact there is nothing unintelligible in this new hypothesis, since it attributes to the soul and to bodies only the modifications which we experience in ourselves and in them; and only makes them appear more regular and more connected than has been thought hitherto. The difficulty which remains exists only as regards those who wish to *imagine* what is only *intelligible,*[1] as if they wished to see sounds or hear colors, and these are they who *refuse existence to everything which is not extended,* a view which will compel them to refuse it to God himself, *i.e.* to renounce the causes and reasons of changes and of such changes: these reasons being incapable of arising from extension and from natures purely passive, and not indeed wholly from particular and inferior active natures without the pure and universal act of the supreme substance.]

Ph. One objection remains for me with reference to things whose matter is naturally susceptible of feeling. The body so far as we can conceive it, is capable only of striking and effecting a body, and motion can produce nothing but motion: so that when we agree that the body produces pleasure or pain or the idea of a color or sound, we seem compelled to abandon our reason, to go beyond our own ideas, and to attribute this production solely to the *good pleasure* of our Creator. What reason have we then to conclude that it is not the same with perception in matter? I almost see what

[1] *Cf. ante,* p. 274, note 2. — TR.

reply you can make, and although you have already said something regarding it more than once, I understand you better now, sir, than I have done. But I shall be very glad to hear further what reply you will make regarding it upon this important occasion.

Th. [You rightly judge, sir, that I shall say that matter cannot produce pleasure, pain, or thought in us. It is the soul itself which produces them in conformity to what takes place in matter. And some clever people among the moderns begin to declare that they understand occasional causes only as I. Now this being posited, there occurs nothing unintelligible, except that we cannot distinguish all that enters into our confused perceptions, which contain even the infinite, and which are the detailed expression of what occurs in bodies. As for the *good pleasure* of the Creator, it must be said that he is ruled by the natures of things, so that he produces and conserves therein only what suits them and can be explained, at least in general, by their natures; for the detail often surpasses us as much as the care and power of arranging the grains of a mountain of sand according to the order of the figures, although there is here nothing difficult to understand but the multitude. Otherwise if this knowledge were in itself beyond us, and if we could not indeed conceive the reason of the relations of the soul and body in general, in fine, if God gave to things *accidental powers detached from their natures,* and consequently removed from reason in general, there would be a back door for calling back the *too occult qualities* which no mind can understand, and these little goblins of *faculties* incapable of reason,

Et quidquid Schola finxit otiosa:

helpful goblins who proceed to appear like the gods of the theatre, or like the fairies of the Amadis, and who will do at need all that a philosopher wishes, without ceremony and without tools. But to attribute the origin of these powers to the good pleasure of God appears to me a thing not quite congruous with him who is the supreme reason, with whom everything is regular, everything consistent. This good pleasure would not indeed be *good,* nor *pleasure,* if there were not a perpetual parallelism between the power and the wisdom of God.]

§ 8. *Ph.* Our knowledge of *identity* and *diversity* goes as far as our ideas, but that of the connection of our ideas, §§ 9, 10. as regards their *coexistence* in one and the same subject is very imperfect and almost nothing § 11. especially as regards secondary qualities as colors, sounds, and tastes § 12. because we do not know their connection with the primary qualities, *i.e.* § 13. how they depend upon size, figure, or motion. § 15. We know a little more of the incompatibility of the secondary qualities; for a subject cannot have, for example, two colors at the same time, and when they seem to be seen in an opal or in an infusion of *lignum nephriticum*, it is in different parts of the object. § 16. It is the same with the active and passive powers of bodies. Our researches in this direction must depend on experience.

Th. [The ideas of sensible qualities are confused, and the powers which should produce them furnish in consequence only ideas into which some confusion enters: thus the connections of these ideas can be known otherwise than by experience only as they are reduced to the distinct ideas which accompany them, as has been done (for example) in regard to the colors of the rainbow and of prisms. And this method presents a beginning in analysis which is of great use in physics; and by following it I doubt not that medicine in time will find itself considerably more advanced, especially if the public is a little better interested than hitherto.]

§ 18. *Ph.* As for the knowledge of relations it is the largest field of our knowledge and it is difficult to determine how far it may extend. Progress depends on our sagacity in finding intermediate ideas. Those who are ignorant of *algebra* cannot imagine the wonderful things that may be done in this field by means of this science. And I do not see that it is easy to determine what new means of perfecting other parts of our knowledge may yet be found out by a penetrating mind. At least the ideas regarding quantity are not the only ones capable of demonstration; there are others, perhaps *the most important part of our contemplation*, from which we might deduce certain knowledge, if vices, passions, and domineering did not directly oppose the execution of such enterprise.

Th. [Nothing is truer than what you, sir, here say. What is there more important, supposing it is true, than what I believe we have determined upon the nature of substance, upon unity and multiplicity, upon identity and diversity, upon the constitution of individuals, upon the impossibilities of void and atoms, upon the origin of cohesion, upon the law of continuity, and the other laws of nature; but chiefly upon the harmony of things, the immateriality of souls, the union of the soul and the body, the conservation of souls, and even of the animal after death. And there is nothing in all this which I do not think demonstrated or demonstrable.]

Ph. [It is true that *your hypothesis* appears extremely consistent and of great simplicity: a clever man in France who desired to refute it, admits publicly that he was impressed by it. And it is a simplicity very different from that which I see. It will be well to show this doctrine more and more in its true light. But in speaking of things *which are of most importance to us,* I thought of morality to which I admit your metaphysic gives wonderful foundations: but without digging so deep, it has sufficiently firm foundations, although perhaps they do not extend as far (as I remember that you remarked) when a natural theology like yours is not their base. Yet the consideration of the goods of this life alone already serves to establish important consequences for regulating human society. We can estimate justice and injustice as incontestably as in mathematics; for example this proposition: *There cannot be injustice where there is no property,* is as certain as any demonstration which is in Euclid; *property* being the right to a certain thing, and *injustice* the violation of a right. It is the same with this proposition: *No government allows absolute liberty.* For *government* is the establishment of certain laws, whose execution it demands, and *absolute liberty* is the power each one has of doing whatever he pleases.

Th. [You use the word *property* a little differently from its ordinary use, for you mean by it the right of one person to a thing to the exclusion of the right of another. Thus if there were no property, as if all were common, there nevertheless might be injustice. By *thing* in the definition of property you must also further understand action; for otherwise, if there were therein no right to things, it would be always an injustice to prevent men from acting where they find it needful. But according to this explanation it is impossible that there be no property. As for the proposition concerning the incompatibility of government with absolute liberty, it belongs to the number of the corollaries, *i.e.* the propositions, which it is sufficient to point out. There are some in jurisprudence which are more complex, as for example, those concerning what is called *jus accrescendi*,[1] concerning the conditions and many other matters; and I indicated them when I published in my youth some theses upon the *conditions*, in which I demonstrated some of them. And if I had leisure, I would retouch them.[2]]

Ph. [That would afford pleasure to the curious, and serve to anticipate any one who might reprint them without revision.]

Th. [That is what happened to my "Ars Combinatoria,"[3] as I have already complained. It was a fruit of my early youth, and yet it was reprinted a long time after without consulting me and without indicating even that it was a second edition, and this made some think to my prejudice that I was capable

[1] *Cf.* Poste, *Gaius, Elements of Roman Law*, Bk. II., 199 (p. 262, 3d ed., Oxford, 1890): "Illud constat si duobus pluribusve per vindicationem eadem res legata sit, sive conjunctim, sive disjunctim, si omnes veniant ad legatum, partes ad singulos pertinere, et deficientis portionem collegatario adcrescere." Also Sandars, *Inst. of Justinian*, Lib. II., Tit. XX., 8 (p. 226, 8th ed., London, 1888): "Si eadem res duobus legata sit, sive conjunctim sive disjunctim: si ambo perveniant ad legatum, scinditur inter eos legatum; si alter deficiat, quia aut spreverit legatum, aut vivo testatore decesserit, vel alio quolibet modo defecerit, totum ad collegatarium pertinet."

In reference to the *jus accrescendi*—the law of increase—Sandars says, p. 198: "If any one instituted heir died before the testator, or refused to take his share of the inheritance, his share was, in fact, undisposed of. But as the testator was always supposed to have disposed of his whole estate, if he disposed of any part, this share was divided among all those who entered on the inheritance *in proportions* corresponding to the share given them by the will. Their claim was called the '*jus accrescendi.*'"—Tr.

[2] Leibnitz here refers to his thesis *De conditionibus*, which he defended under the presidency of Prof. Leonhard Schwendendörfer, at Leipzig, in 1665. Guhrauer states (*cf. Leibniz, eine Biographie*, Pt. I., pp. 36-37) that we do not know the treatise in its original form, but in the revision and rearrangement of its material made by Leibnitz in 1672, in a collection of his juristic treatises under the title *Specimina juris*, and which is found in Dutens, *Leibnit. op. om.*, 4, Pt. III., 92 *sq.*—Tr.

[3] The *Dissertatio de Arte Combinatoria*, *cf.* Gerhardt, 4, 27 *sq.*, Erdmann, 6 *sq.*, Dutens, 2, Pt. I., 341 *sq.*, appeared at Leipzig in 1666. The pirated edition here referred to by Leibnitz was published at Frankfort, 1690, and reviewed by him in the "Acta Erud.," February, 1691. *Cf.* Guhrauer, *Leibniz. eine Biog.*, Pt. I., pp. 37-38, and *Anmerkungen z. erst. Buche*, pp. 7, 8; Dutens, 6, 295.—Tr.

of publishing such a piece in my mature years; for although it contains thoughts of some consequence, which I still approve, it also contains some which could become only a young student.]

§ 19. *Ph.* I find that diagrams are a great remedy for the uncertainty of words, but they cannot have place in moral ideas. Most moral ideas are more complex than the diagrams ordinarily considered in mathematics; thus the mind finds it difficult to retain the precise combinations of what enters into moral ideas, in a manner as perfect as is necessary in long deductions. And if in arithmetic the different stages are not designated by marks whose precise meaning is known, and which last and remain in sight, it is well-nigh impossible to make extended computations. § 20. Definitions furnish some remedy provided they are constantly employed in ethics. And for the rest, it is not easy to foresee what methods may be suggested by *algebra* or by some other means of this nature to remove other difficulties.

Th. [The late Erhard Weigel,[1] a mathematician of Jena in Thuringia, ingeniously invented diagrams to represent moral things; and when the late Samuel Puffendorf,[2] his disciple, pub-

[1] Erhard Weigel, 1625–1699, a distinguished German mathematician and astronomer, was professor of mathematics in Jena from 1653 on, where he was Leibnitz's first teacher in the subject, when he studied there in 1663, *cf.* Guhrauer *Leibniz. eine Biographie*, Pt. I., pp. 26, 32. The Diet of Ratisbon appointed him to organize a commission for the correction of the calendar. He also labored earnestly for the reform of the school system in Germany, travelling through the country in 1696 for this purpose, *cf.* Guhrauer, *op. cit.*, Pt. II., pp. 211–214, and the correspondence of Leibnitz and Placcius, from Feb. 12, 1696 on, Dutens, *Leibnit. op. om.*, 6, 61 *sq.*

Weigel, who was a philosopher, moralist, and an original investigator of the law of nature (*Naturrecht*) as well as a mathematician, published many works, among them the *Exposé arithmétique de la morale*, or, as the German title runs, *Arithmetische Beschreibung der Moralweisheit von Personen und Sachen, woraus das gemeine Wesen besteht, nach der pythagorischen Kreutzzahl in lauter tetraktische Glieder eingetheilt*, Jena, 1674, 4to, in which he attempted a mathematical exposition of moral philosophy, based upon the Pythagorean principle that the essence of things consists in numbers. Leibnitz thus speaks of this book in the *Miscellanea*, No. CLIII., Dutens, 6, 325: "M. *Weigelius* a fait un excellent livre en Allemand sur la morale éclairée par les nombres, et je ne crois pas que les Pythagoriciens ayent rien dit de plus beau sur ce chapitre." For further remarks of Leibnitz on Weigel, *cf.* Guhrauer, *Leibnitz's deutsche Schriften*, 2, 473 *sq.* — TR.

[2] Samuel Pufendorf, 1632–1694, was one of the greatest German publicists and historians, and one of the founders of the science of public law. He studied at Jena under Weigel, with whom he formed an intimate friendship,

lished his "Elements of universal Jurisprudence" sufficiently conformed to the thoughts of Weigel, there was added thereto in the Jena edition the "*Moral Sphere*" of this mathematician. But these diagrams are a kind of allegory nearly like the table of Cebes,[1] but less popular and serving the memory in the retention and arrangement of its ideas rather than the judgment in the acquisition of demonstrative knowledge. They do not cease to have their use in arousing the mind. Geometrical diagrams appear simpler than moral things; but they are not so, because continuity includes the infinite from which it must be chosen. For example, to cut a triangle into four equal parts by two straight lines perpendicular to each other is a question apparently simple but really quite difficult. It is not the same in questions of morality since they are determinable

and to whose teaching and influence he largely owes the orderly method and mathematical precision and dryness which characterize his style, and that independence of character which never yielded to the "ipsedixitism" of other writers, however high their position and authority. Among his works are: *Elementa jurisprudentiæ universalis, cum appendice de Sphæra morali* (of Weigel), Hag. Com., 1660, 12mo — also Jena, 1660, "bei Meyer"; the ed. here meant by Leibnitz, according to Schaarschmidt, who states that in the 2d Jena ed., 1669, the *Sphæra moralis* occurs, p. 313 *sq.*, — the book which obtained for him from the elector Charles Louis, to whom it was dedicated, the newly created chair of the law of nature and of nations at Heidelberg; *De statu imperii germanici*, Geneva, 1667, — the book which first called forth Leibnitz's aversion and criticism, — small in bulk, but great in significance, in which he criticised the political organization of the empire, suggested a remedy for the evils therein, and revealed himself as a consummate statesman, subsequent events proving the justness of his conclusions; and the work on which his fame chiefly rests, *De jure naturæ et gentium*, 1672, trans. into French, with notes, by Barbeyrac, Amsterdam, 1712, and into English by Basil Kennett, London, 1729, and résumé of the same, *De officio hominis et civis*, 1675.

For Leibnitz's criticism of Pufendorf and his work, — the severest, perhaps, he ever made on any one, and through which he is, to a considerable extent, responsible for the failure of posterity justly to estimate and acknowledge its debt to him, — *cf.* letter to Kestner, No. 7, § 2, Dutens, 4, Pt. III., 261; *Monita quædam ad S. Puffendorfii principia, ibid.*, 275–283; letter to S. Kortholt, No. 3, Dutens, 5, 305; letters to Bierling, Gerhardt, *Leibniz. philos. Schrift.*, 7, 487, 488, 490, 499, 506, 511, Dutens, 5, 355, 358, 361, 371, 386, 390 — Dutens gives Bierling's letters to Leibnitz also; letter to Bourguet, G. 3, 590, Erdmann, 734, b., Dutens, 2, Pt. I., 334. For a comparison of the views of Leibnitz and Pufendorf on the ultimate foundations of natural and public law, *cf. Monita quædam* above cited, and Guhrauer, *Leibniz. eine Biog.*, Pt. I., 223 *sq.* — TR.

[1] Cebes of Thebes, a disciple of Socrates, distinguished for his virtue and love of truth; *cf.* Plato, *Phædo*, 59 C, 60 C *sq.*, 63 A. His Πίναξ, *Tabula*, or 'picture,' is, according to Zeller, *Philos. d. Griech.*, II., 1 [Vol. 3], 242, 4th ed., 1889, "certainly spurious." — TR.

by reason alone. For the rest it is not the place here to speak *de proferendis scientiae demonstrandi pomoeriis*, and to propose true means of extending the art of demonstration beyond its ancient boundaries which have been nearly the same up to the present time as those of mathematics. If God gives me the time necessary for it, I hope some day to publish an essay upon this subject, putting these means into effective use without limiting myself to precepts.][1]

Ph. [If you carry out this plan, sir, and as it should be, you will infinitely oblige the *Philalethes* like myself, *i.e.* the class who sincerely desire to know the truth.] For truth is naturally agreeable to the mind, and there is nothing so deformed and so incompatible with the understanding as a lie. But men must not be expected to apply themselves much to these discoveries, so long as the desire and the esteem of riches or of power shall lead them to espouse opinions authorized by fashion, and to seek in consequence arguments either to make them pass as good or to varnish over and cover their deformity. And while the different parties make all men whom they can get into their power receive their opinions without examining whether they are true or false, what new light can be hoped for in the sciences belonging to morals? This part of the human race which is under the yoke, ought to expect in most places in the world instead of that light, darkness as thick as that of Egypt, were not the candle of the Lord itself found present in the mind of men,[2] a sacred light which all human power cannot wholly extinguish.

Th. [I do not despair that at some time and in a more tranquil country men will betake themselves more to reason than they have done. For in fact we must despair of nothing; and

[1] Leibnitz's plan to extend and perfect the science of demonstration, or that part of logic which is concerned with the methods of proof, and which in his view was conceived up to his own time too narrowly as virtually identical with the method of mathematics, is closely connected, but not identical, with his Universal Characteristic; *cf. ante*, pp. 292, note 1, 375, note 1. Leibnitz, however, never carried his plan into execution, but left some preliminary essays or sketches which serve to indicate what he thought desirable in this direction, and what he purposed himself some day to provide. *Cf. Préceptes pour avancer les sciences*, Erdmann, *Leibnit. op. philos.* 165–171, published in a more complete form in Gerhardt, *Leibniz. philos. Schrift.*, 7, 157 *sq.;* and the fragment without title treating of the means of philosophical demonstration, G., 7, 280–301. — Tr.

[2] *Cf.* Proverbs 20:27. — Tr.

I believe that great changes for evil and for good are reserved for the human race, but in the end more for good than for evil. Suppose we see some day a great prince, who, like the ancient kings of Assyria or of Egypt or like another Solomon, reigns a long time in a profound peace, and that this prince, loving virtue and truth and endowed with a great and solid mind, takes it into his head to make men happier and more accommodating among themselves and more powerful over nature; what wonders will he not do in a few years? For it is certain that in this case more would be done in ten years than in a hundred or perhaps a thousand while letting things follow their ordinary course. Moreover, if the path were opened once for all, many people would enter therein as the geometers do, though this would be only for their pleasure and to acquire fame. The public better civilized will some day turn more than it has hitherto done to the advancement of medicine; natural histories of all countries will be published like almanacs or like the *Mercures galans;*[1] no valuable observation will be left without being registered; those who will apply themselves thereto will be aided; the art of making such observations will be perfected, and further that of employing them to establish aphorisms. The time will come when the number of good physicians having become greater and the number of people of certain professions of which there will then be less need having become proportionally less, the public will be in a condition to give more encouragement to natural research, and above all to the advance of medicine, and then this important science will be carried far beyond its present condition and will grow apace. I believe indeed that this business of the police should be the object of the greatest care of those who govern, after that of virtue, and that one of the greatest fruits of good morals or politics will be to produce a better (science of) medicine,

[1] "Mercure galant," the title of different periodicals treating of politics, literature, and containing announcements, and news of various kinds; in particular, the title of a journal founded by De Visé in 1672, and continued, with several short periods of suspension, under various names and editors, till 1853. Leibnitz, in a letter to Sebastian Kortholt, Jan. 9, 1711, inquires whether a complete set can be obtained, and at what price: "Discere etiam velim, an totus *Mercurius Gallant*, ut sic dicam, vulgo *Mercure Galant* a *Devisæo* nuper extincto a multis annis compositus, tolerabili pretio haberi possit, et quanti?" (*cf.* Dutens, *Leibnit. op. om.* 5, 315). — TR.

when men shall begin to be wiser than they are and the nobility shall learn the better to employ their wealth and their power for their own welfare.]

§ 21. *Ph.* As for the knowledge of *real existence* (which is the fourth kind of *knowledge*) it must be said that we have an *intuitive* knowledge *of our existence*, a *demonstrative* knowledge *of that of God*, and a *sensitive* knowledge *of other things.* We shall speak of these fully in what follows.

Th. [You could say nothing more justly.]

§ 22. *Ph.* Having now spoken of *knowledge*, it appears appropriate the better to discover the present condition of our mind that we should consider a little the dark side and take knowledge of *our ignorance:* for it is infinitely greater than our knowledge. The *causes* of this ignorance are as follows: (1) Want of ideas; (2) Inability to discover the connection between the ideas we have; (3) Neglect to trace and examine them with exactness. § 23. As for the *want of ideas*, we have as simple ideas only those coming to us from the senses [internal or external]. Thus as regards an infinite number of the creatures of the universe and their qualities we are like the blind as regards colors not indeed possessing the faculties necessary in order to their knowledge; and according to all appearances man holds the lowest rank among intellectual beings.

Th. [I do not know but that there are also some below us. Why should we degrade ourselves unnecessarily? Perhaps we hold a sufficiently honorable rank among rational animals; for superior genii may have bodies of another kind so that the name animal cannot agree with them. We cannot say whether our sun among the great number of other suns has more above than below it, and we are well placed in his system: for the earth occupies the middle course between the planets, and its distance appears well chosen for a contemplative animal who should inhabit it. Besides we have incomparably more reason to praise than to complain of our lot, the majority of our evils rightly being imputed to our fault. Above all we should be very wrong to complain of the defects of our knowledge, since we avail ourselves so little of that which charitable nature presents to us.]

§ 24. *Ph.* It is, however, true that the extreme distance of nearly all parts of the world which are exposed to our sight conceals them from our knowledge, and apparently the visible world is only a small part of this immense universe. We are confined in a small corner of space, *i.e.* in the system of our sun, and yet we do not know even what takes place in the other planets which as well as our ball revolve about it. § 25. This knowledge escapes us by reason of size and distance; but other bodies are concealed from us because of their minuteness; and these are the ones which it would most concern us to know; for from their contexture we could infer the use and operation of those which are visible, and know why rhubarb purges, hemlock kills, and opium produces sleep. Thus § 26. whatever distance human industry may advance experimental philosophy upon physical things, I am compelled to believe that we can attain upon these matters a *scientific knowledge.*

Th. [I fully believe that we shall never advance so far as will be desirable; but it seems to me that some considerable progress will be made in time in the explication of certain phenomena, because the large number of experiments which we are led to make may furnish us *data* more than sufficient, so that only the art of employing them will be lacking, (an art) the small beginnings of which I do not despair of seeing pushed forward, since the *infinitesimal analysis*[1] has given us the means of uniting geometry with physics, and *dynamics* has furnished us with the general laws of nature.]

§ 27. *Ph.* Spirits are still further removed from our knowledge; we cannot form any idea of their different orders, and yet the *intellectual world* is certainly grander and more beautiful than the material world.

Th. [These worlds are always perfectly parallel as regards efficient causes, but not as regards final. For in proportion as spirits rule in matter they produce therein wonderful arrangements. This appears in the changes men have made, in order to embellish the earth, as little gods imitating the great architect of the universe, though only by employing bodies and

[1] Sir Isaac Newton, 1642–1727, in his *Principia*, was the first to apply in a systematic way the infinitesimal calculus to physics, after that Galileo, 1564–1642, had paved the way for a theory of universal gravitation by his determination of the law of acceleration in falling bodies. — TR.

their laws. What may not be conjectured concerning this immense multitude of spirits which surpass us? And as spirits form all together a kind of state under God, whose government is perfect, we are far removed from comprehending the system of this intelligible world and from conceiving the punishments and rewards prepared for those who deserve them according to the most exact standard, and from imagining what eye has not seen, nor ear heard, nor has ever entered into the heart of man. But all this shows that we have all the distinct ideas necessary for knowing bodies and spirits, but not sufficient detail of facts, nor senses penetrating enough to distinguish confused ideas or sufficiently extended to perceive them all.]

§ 28. *Ph.* As for the connection, the knowledge of which is wanting to us in the ideas which we have, I was going to say to you that the mechanical affections of bodies have no connection with the ideas of colors, sounds, smells, tastes, pleasure, and pain; and that their connection depends only upon the good pleasure and the arbitrary will of God. But I remember that you think there is a perfect *correspondence,* although this is not always an entire *resemblance.* But you recognize that the too great detail of small things entering therein hinders us from discerning that which is concealed, though you hope still that we shall make much advance therein; and that thus you do not wish to say with my illustrious author (§ 29), that *it is labor lost to engage in such a search,* from fear that this belief would injure the growth of science. I should have spoken also of the difficulty which has hitherto been found in explaining the connection between the soul and the body, since a thought cannot be conceived as producing a motion in the body, nor a motion as producing a thought in the mind. [But since I comprehend your hypothesis of pre-established harmony, this difficulty of which they despaired appears to me removed at once, and as it were, by magic.] § 30. There remains then the third cause of our ignorance, viz. that we do not follow the ideas we have or may have, and do not apply ourselves to finding intermediate ideas. Thus it is that we are ignorant of mathematical truths, although there is no imperfection in our faculties, nor any incertitude in the things themselves. The bad use of words has contributed the most to prevent us from finding the agreement or disagreement of ideas; and the mathematicians who form their thoughts independently of names and accustom themselves to present to their minds *the ideas themselves* instead of their sounds, have thereby escaped a great deal of embarrassment. If men had acted in their discoveries in the material world as they have been wont to do in regard to those having reference to the intellectual world, and if they had been wholly lost in a chaos of terms of an uncertain meaning, they would have disputed endlessly about the zones, the tides, the building of vessels, and the routes; they would never have gone beyond the line, and the antipodes would still be as unknown as they were when to maintain them was declared a heresy.

Th. [This third cause of our ignorance is the only blamable one; and you see, sir, that the despair of further advance is therein contained. This discouragement does much injury; and persons of ability and importance have hindered the progress of medicine by the false persuasion that it is labor lost to work therein. When you see the Aristotelian philosophers of past time speak of meteors, as the rainbow, for example, you will find that they believed they should not think alone of explaining distinctly this phenomenon; and the attempts of Maurolycus,[1] and afterwards of Marc Antony de Dominis[2] appeared to them like the flight of Icarus. But the

[1] Francesco Maurolico, 1494–1575, a celebrated Italian mathematician, whose father, a Greek, came originally from Constantinople, taught mathematics at Palermo, Naples, Rome, and Messina. In his *Treatise on Conics* he sought for the first time to deduce the properties of these curves from the corresponding curves in the circle of which they are the perspective. He first introduced secants into trigonometrical calculations, constructing and publishing a table of them in his *Theodosii sphæricorum*, Messina, 1558, fol. He also investigated the structure of the eye, seeking therein the explanation of the phenomena of vision. He described exactly the course of the rays of light across the cornea and the crystalline lens, but stopped in utter astonishment when he discovered that his theory led him to admit that the images of objects upon the retina are found inverted. The work of Maurolico, here referred to by Leibnitz, is his *Problemata ad perspectivam et iridem pertinentia*, appended to his *Photismi* [or *Theoremata*] *de lumine et umbra ad perspectivam radiorum incidentium*, Venice, 1575, 4to, new ed., with notes of Clavius, Lyons, 1613.—Tr.

[2] M. Ant. de Dominis, 1566–1624, a native of Dalmatia, was professor of eloquence, philosophy, and natural sciences at the University of Padua. Though archbishop of Spalatro, he was republican in his views of the constitution and administration of the church and strongly opposed to the doctrine

sequel has disabused the world of this. It is true that the bad use of terms has caused a good part of the confusion found in our knowledge, not only in ethics and metaphysics, or in what is called the intellectual world, but also in medicine where this abuse of terms increases more and more. We cannot always aid ourselves with figures as in geometry: but algebra shows us that great discoveries may be made without recurring always to the ideas themselves of things. In reference to the pretended heresy about the antipodes I will say in passing that it is true that Boniface,[1] Archbishop of Mayence, accused Virgil of Salzburg,[2] in a letter, which he wrote

of papal supremacy. While in England he published his views in his *De republica ecclesiastica*, London, 1617–1620, reprinted Frankfort, 1658, both eds., 3 vols., fol. For some specimen quotations from this book, *cf.* Larousse, *Grande Dict. Univ. de XIXe Siècle*, Vol. 6, p. 1068, a. Returning to Italy, he and his book were condemned as heretical, in spite of his retraction of his errors, and he was imprisoned, and probably poisoned, in the Castle of St. Angelo, and his body exhumed and burned with great ceremony in the Campo de' Fiori in Rome in January, 1625.

In his *De radiis visus et lucis in vitris perspectivis et iride*, Venice, 1611, 4to, cited with high praise by Newton in his *Optics*, he presented to the world the first attempt at a theory of the rainbow. He successfully reflected rays of light through the interior of raindrops before making them come out again, but could not account for the angle at which the observer sees the ray of the bow. On his theory, *cf.* Venturi, *Commentarii sopra la storia e le teorie dell' ottica*, Bologna, 1814, Vol. 1, p. 149. Of the *De radiis visus et lucis*, chap. 9 and chap. 13, "*Vera iridis tota generatio explicatur*," are printed in Libri, *Histoire des Sciences math. en Italie depuis la Renaissance jusqu'à la fin du XVIIe siècle*, 1838–1841, 4 vols., 8vo, Vol. 4, p. 436 *sq.* Leibnitz thus speaks of him in the *Miscellanea Leibnitiana*, ed. Feller, No. CXV., p. 198 (*cf.* also Dutens, *Leibnit. op. om.*, 6, 319): "Elegantissime materiam tractavit demonstrationibusque mathematicis confirmavit. Iridis etiam et nonnullorum aliorum ejusmodi meteorum causam ab Aristotele assignatam recte expendit." — TR.

[1] Boniface (Winfrid, the Anglo-Saxon Benedictine monk, named *Bonifacius* by Pope Gregory II.), 680–755, the apostle to the Germans, became archbishop of Mayence (Mainz) in 748. On his life and labors, *cf.* Neander, *Hist. of the Christ. Relig. and Church*, 3, 46 *sq.;* Smith and Wace, *Dict. of Christ. Biog.*, Vol. 1, p. 324. His *Opera quæ extant omnia*, ed. J. A. Giles, Londini, 1844, 2 vols., 8vo; also in Migne, *Patrol. s. Lat.*, Vol. 89, Paris, 1863. His letters were edited, with notes, by the Jesuit Nic. Serarius, 1555–1609, Mayence, 1605 and 1629, 4to; and by Würdtwein, Moguntiæ, 1789, fol. — TR.

[2] St. Fergil, best known by the Latinized form of his name, — Virgilius, — was an Irish priest from Aghavoe, Queen's Co., who came to Bavaria, became at first abbot of St. Peter's monastery in Salzburg, and finally, on the martyrdom of Boniface, 755, and the death of John, bishop of Salzburg, was appointed and consecrated bishop, June 13, 766 or 767. One of his last acts as bishop was to visit his entire diocese and to pay a long deferred visit to Carinthia. He died Nov. 27, 789.

to the Pope against him on this subject, and that the Pope replied thereto in a way which showed that he employed the term quite in the sense of Boniface; but it does not appear that this accusation has had any results. Virgil has always held his own. The two antagonists pass for saints, and the savants of Bavaria who regard Virgil as an apostle of Carinthia and the neighboring countries, have justified their memory of him.]

CHAPTER IV

OF THE REALITY OF OUR KNOWLEDGE

§ 1. *Ph.* Some one who has not understood the importance of having good ideas, and of understanding their agreement or disagreement, will think that in reasoning upon them so carefully we have been building castles in the air, and that there will be in our entire system only the ideal and imaginary. An extravagant man, whose imagination is heated, will have the advantage of possessing ideas more vivid and in greater number, thus he would also have more knowledge. There will be as much certitude in the visions of an enthusiast as in the

Virgil was involved in two controversies with Boniface. First, in regard to the validity of an informally administered baptism in which the officiating and ignorant priest had mutilated the Latin formula. Boniface said the baptism was invalid, and must be repeated; Virgil maintained its validity, and on his appeal to Pope Zachary (741–752), was sustained. Second, in regard to the "antipodes" here mentioned. Virgil published a philosophical treatise maintaining the rotundity of the earth and the antipodes, which Boniface regarded as heretical because the view advanced was thought to imply the existence of two races of men, one of which did not spring from Adam, was therefore free from original sin, and had no need for or share in the work of the Redeemer. Pope Zachary, in the letter to Boniface here referred to (*cf.* letters of Boniface, No. 140, in *Bibl. Max. Vet. Patr.*, 27 vols., fol. Lugd., 1677, Vol. 13, p. 131–133), characterized as perverse and heretical the doctrine of another world and other men under the earth, — "De perversa doctrina, quam contra Dominum et animam suam locutus est (quod scilicet alius mundus, et alii homines sub terra sint aliusque sol et luna)," etc.; but Virgil showed that his speculations were purely scientific and did not touch the theological doctrines of original sin or the unity of the human race. He was accordingly acquitted of the charge of heresy, and canonized by Gregory IX. in 1233. *Cf.* Smith and Wace, *Dict. of Christian Biog.*, Vol. 4, pp. 1160, 1211, London, 1887; Neander, *Hist. of the Christ. Relig. and Church*, 3, 63; also Bayle, *Dict. histor. et crit.*, 2d ed., 1702 (which was, perhaps, Leibnitz's source of information on the subject), Eng. Trans., London, 1738, Vol. 5, p. 493; and for a justification of Virgil, *cf.* "Mémoires de Trévoux," Jan. 1708. — TR.

reasonings of a sober man, provided this enthusiast speaks consistently; and it will be as true to say that a harpy is not a centaur as to say a square is not a circle. § 2. I reply that our ideas agree with things. § 3. But the *criterion* will be demanded. § 4. I reply further *in the first place* that this agreement is manifest as regards the simple ideas of our mind, for being unable to form them itself, it must be that they are produced by things acting upon the mind; and *in the second place*, § 5. all our complex ideas (those of substances excepted) being archetypes which the mind itself has made, not intended to be copies of anything nor referred to the existence of anything as to their originals, they cannot fail to be completely conformed to the things necessary to real knowledge.

Th. Our certitude would be small, or rather nothing, if it had no other basis of simple ideas than that which comes from the senses. Have you forgotten, sir, how I have shown that ideas are originally in our mind, and that indeed our thoughts come to us from the depths of our own nature, other creatures being unable to have an immediate influence upon the soul. Besides the ground of our certitude in regard to universal and eternal truths is in the ideas themselves, independently of the senses, just as ideas pure and intelligible do not depend on the senses, for example, that of being, unity, identity, etc. But the ideas of sensible qualities, as color, savor, etc. (which in reality are only phantoms),[1] come to us from the senses, *i.e.* from our confused perceptions. And the basis of the truth of contingent and singular things is in the succession which causes these phenomena of the senses to be rightly united as the intelligible truths demand.[2] That is the difference which

[1] *Cf. ante*, p. 317 (where the term "phantasies," in line 12, rendered by the word "notions," would have been better rendered, perhaps, by "phantasms" or "phantoms"), notes 1 and 2, and *infra*, p. 459. Schaarschmidt translates: "Phantasie-Erscheinungen." The term "phantom," or, as it might perhaps have been translated, "phantasm,"—the Greek φάντασμα, and the Scholastic "phantasma," — signifies here a mental modification given or produced through the agency of the senses, but having no corresponding external object, *i.e.* an entirely subjective phenomenon, real as such, but which, since it corresponds to no objective external reality, has, to a certain extent, the character of a mere appearance. — Tr.

[2] *Cf. New Essays*, Bk. IV., chap. 2, § 14, Th. (2), *ante*, p. 422, note 1. Leibnitz felt, says Schaarschmidt, that we could not be satisfied from a philosophical point of view with the old definition of truth as consisting in the agreement of thought with reality. — Tr.

should be made, while that which you here make between simple and complex ideas, and ideas complex belonging to substances and to accidents, does not appear to me well founded, since all intelligible ideas have their archetypes in the eternal possibility of things.]

§ 5. *Ph.* It is true that our complex ideas need archetypes outside the mind only when the question concerns an existing substance which must effectively unite outside us these complex ideas, and the simple ideas of which they are composed. The knowledge of mathematical truths is real, although it revolves only upon our ideas, and finds nowhere exact circles. But we are assured that existing things will agree with our archetypes according as what we suppose therein is found existing. § 7. This serves to justify the reality of moral things. § 8. Nor are Cicero's "Offices" less conformed to truth, because no one in the world rules his life exactly according to the pattern of a virtuous man such as Cicero has painted for us. § 9. But (it will be said) if moral ideas be of our invention, what a strange notion shall we have of justice and temperance?

§ 10. I reply that the uncertainty will be only in the language, because what is said is not always understood, or always understood in the same way.

Th. [You might reply also, sir, and much better in my opinion, that the ideas of justice and temperance are not of our invention, any more than those of the circle or the square. I think I have sufficiently shown this.]

§ 11. *Ph.* As for the ideas of substances existing outside us, our knowledge is real so long as it is conformed to these archetypes; and in this respect the mind must not combine ideas arbitrarily, so much the more as there are very few simple ideas of which we can be certain that they can or cannot exist together in nature beyond what appears by sensible observations.

Th. It is, as I have more than once said, because these ideas, when reason cannot judge of their compatibility or connection, are confused, like those of the particular qualities of the senses.

§ 13. *Ph.* It is well also as regards existing substances not to limit ourselves to names or to species supposed to be established by names. This makes me return to discussions we have often enough had regarding the definition of man. For speaking of an *innocent*[1] who has lived forty years without giving the least sign of reason, could we not say that he holds the middle place between man and beast? It would possibly be thought a very bold paradox, or even a falsehood with very dangerous consequences. But it seemed to me formerly and it seems still to some of my friends whom I cannot disabuse as yet (of the idea) that it is only in virtue of a prejudice based upon this false supposition that these two names *man* and *beast* signify distinct species, so well marked by real essences in nature that no other species can intervene between them, as if all things were thrown into the mould according to the precise number of these essences. § 14. When these friends are asked what species of animals these *innocents* are, if they are neither men nor beasts, they reply they are *innocents*, and that is sufficient. If asked further what they will become in the next world, our friends reply they are not concerned to know or inquire. *Let them fall or stand to their own master* (Rom. 14:4), who is good and faithful and disposes of his creatures not according to the narrow limits of our particular thoughts or opinions, nor does he distinguish them conformably to the names and species *it has pleased us to invent;* let it suffice us that those who are capable of instruction will be called to render an account of their conduct and will receive their reward *according to the deeds done in their bodies* (2 Cor. 5:10). § 15. I shall exhibit to you the rest of their reasonings. The question (say they) *whether imbeciles must be deprived of a future state* rests upon two equally false *suppositions: first* that every being having the form and external appearance of man is destined to an immortal state after this life; and *second* that everything having a human birth must enjoy this privilege. Remove these imaginative ideas, and you will see that such questions are ridiculous and groundless. In fact I think we shall disallow the first supposition and shall not have the mind so buried in matter as to believe that eternal life is due to any form of material mass, so that the mass must have feeling eternally because moulded upon such a figure. § 16. But the

[1] Locke's word is "changeling," *Philos. Works* (Bohn's ed.), Vol. 2, p. 176 *sq.*, and note. — TR.

second supposition comes to the rescue. We shall say that this *innocent* comes from rational parents and that consequently it must have a rational soul. I know not by what rule of logic we can establish such a consequence, nor how after that we should dare to *destroy* these ill-formed and disfigured productions. Oh, they are *monsters,* it will be said. Very well, so be it. But what will this always intractable innocent be? Shall a defect in the body make a monster, and not a defect in the mind? This is to return to *the first supposition,* already refuted, that the external suffices. A well-formed innocent is a man, as we believe; he has a rational soul, although it does not appear; but make the ears a little longer and more pointed, and the nose a little flatter than usual, then you begin to hesitate. Make the face narrower, flatter, and longer; there you are all at once decided. And if the head is perfectly that of any animal, it is no doubt a monster; and this is for you a demonstration that it has no rational soul and that it should be *destroyed.* I ask you now where to find the just measure and the final limits bearing with them a rational soul. There are human *fœtuses,* half beast, half man, others three parts of which belong to the one, and one part to the other. How determine precisely the lineaments which indicate reason? Further, will not this *monster* be a species midway between man and beast? And such is the *innocent* in question.

Th. [I am astonished that you return to this question sufficiently examined by us, and that more than once, and that you have not better catechized your friends. If we distinguish the man from the beast by the faculty of reason, there is no middle ground, the animal in question must have it or not have it; but as this faculty sometimes does not appear, we judge of it by indices which are not demonstrative of the truth till this reason manifests itself: for we know by the experience of those who have lost it and who at last have recovered its exercise, that its function may be suspended. Birth and form furnish presumptions of that which is concealed. But the presumption of birth is effaced (*eliditur*) by a figure very different from the human, such as that of the animal was, born of a woman of Zealand according to Levinus Lemnius[1]

[1] Livin Lemmens — Latin, Levinus Lemnius — 1505–1568, a Dutch physician, who was very successful in practice, and had in his time a very great reputa-

(Book I., Chap. 8), which had a hooked beak, a long and round neck, flashing eyes, a pointed tail, and great agility at first in running about the room. But you will say that there are some monsters or *brothers of the Lombards* (as the physicians formerly called them because it was said that the women of Lombardy were subject to this kind of childbirth) who approach more and more the human figure. Very well; so be it. How then (say you) can the proper limits of the figure which is to pass as human be determined? I reply that in a conjectural matter there is no precision. And there the affair ends. You object that the innocent does not exhibit reason, and yet passes as a man, but if it had a monstrous figure, it would not be man, and thus you have more regard for figure than for reason. But, does this monster exhibit reason? Certainly not. You see, then, that it lacks more than the innocent. The defect of the exercise of reason is often temporal, but it does not cease in those in whom it is accompanied by a dog's head. For the rest, if this animal with a human figure is not a man, there is no great harm in guarding it during the uncertainty as to its fate. And whether it has a rational soul or not, God will not have made it for nothing, and we may say of the souls of men who live in a state always similar to that of early infancy that their fate may be the same as that of the souls of those infants who die in the cradle.

CHAPTER V

OF TRUTH IN GENERAL

§ 1. *Ph.* For many centuries the question has been asked, What is truth? § 2. Our friends think it is the joining or separating of signs according as the things themselves agree or disagree among themselves. By the joining or separating of signs must be understood what is otherwise called a *proposition.*

tion. Lemnius relates this marvellous occurrence, which he states was reported to him by the woman herself, as soon as she had barely recovered, but in which there must have been some deception, in his *De miraculis occultis naturæ*, Bk. I., chap. 8, p. 37, Francofurti, 1628, Eng. trans., p. 24, London, 1658. — Tr.

Th. But an *epithet* does not make a proposition; for example, *the wise man.* But there is a union of two terms. Negation also is different from separation; for saying *man*, and after an interval saying *wise*, is not a denial. *Agreement* also, or *disagreement* is not properly speaking what is expressed by the proposition. Two eggs have agreement and two enemies have disagreement. The question here concerns an entirely particular mode of agreement or disagreement. Thus I think this definition fails wholly to explain the point in question. But what I find least to my taste in your definition of truth is that you seek truth in words. Thus the same sense expressed in Latin, German, English, French, will not be the same truth, and it will be necessary to say with Hobbes,[1] that

[1] *Cf.* Leibnitz, *De stilo philos. Nizolii*, § 28, *ad fin.*, Gerhardt, 4, 158, Erdmann, 69 b, Dutens, 4, Pt. I., 60, where, after expressing his belief that "Occam himself was not more of a Nominalist than Thomas Hobbes now is, who, in truth, seems to me more than a Nominalist," Leibnitz continues: "Non contentus enim cum Nominalibus universalia ad nomina reducere, ipsam rerum veritatem ait in nominalibus consistere, ac, quod majus est, pendere ab arbitrio humano, quia veritas pendeat a definitionibus terminorum, definitiones autem terminorum ab arbitrio humano." Hobbes in his *Leviathan* (Morley's Universal Library, No. 21), 3d ed., London: Geo. Routledge & Sons, 1887, Pt. 1., chap. 4, p. 24, after speaking of "the imposing of 'names,' and the 'connection of them,'" says: "When two names are joined together into a consequence, or affirmation, as thus, 'a man is a living creature' . . . if the latter name 'living creature,' signify all that the former name 'man' signifieth, then the affirmation, or consequence, is 'true'; otherwise 'false.' For 'true' and 'false' are attributes of speech, and not of things. . . ." And in the next paragraph: "Seeing then that truth consisteth in the right ordering of names in our affirmations, a man that seeketh precise truth had need to remember what every name he uses stands for, and to place it accordingly." Leibnitz, probably, had this or some similar passage in mind, in his references to Hobbes' doctrine, and his statement is a possible and seemingly fair interpretation of many passages in Hobbes' writings, which passages, however, might be offset by others of a different character. Hobbes, nevertheless, seems never to have gone beyond his nominalistic position, never, at least, so far as consciously to connect his doctrine of truth with the facts of experience and the reality of things; while Leibnitz's doctrine of truth has to a certain extent at least an objective reference in affirming an actual or at least possible existence of the objects of ideas, *cf. ante*, pp. 422, note 1, 445, note 2, *infra*, p. 452, note 1.

For further exposition of Hobbes' doctrine, *cf.* G. Croom Robertson, *Hobbes*, pp. 83–90, espec. p. 87 (Philos. Classics), Edinburgh: Wm. Blackwood & Sons, 1886. On the relation of Leibnitz to Hobbes, *cf.* F. Tönnies, *Leibniz und Hobbes*, in the "Philos. Monatshefte," vol. 23, 1887, 557–573; see also, "Mind," No. 50, April, 1888, pp. 312–314. For two letters of Leibnitz to Hobbes, *cf.* Gerhardt, *Leibniz. philos. Schrift.*, 1, 82–87, also, 7, 572–574, where the first letter is given with an amended text. Leibnitz appended to his *Théodicée* a short piece entitled *Reflexions sur l'ouvrage que M. Hobbes a publié en*

truth depends on the good pleasure of men; which is to speak in a very strange manner. You attribute, indeed, truth to God, who, you will agree with me (I think), has no need of signs. Finally, I have been astonished already more than once at the disposition of your friends who are pleased to make essences, species, and truths *nominal*.

Ph. Do not advance too fast. Under signs they include ideas. Thus, truths will be either *mental* or *nominal*, according to the species of signs.

Th. [We shall then have also *literal* truths, which may be distinguished as truths upon paper or parchment, of ordinary black ink or of printer's ink, if truths must be distinguished by signs. It were then better to place truths in the relation between the objects of ideas which causes the one to be or not to be included in the other. That does not depend upon languages, and is common to us with God and the angels; and when God manifests a truth to us we shall acquire that which is in his understanding, for although there is an infinite difference between his ideas and ours, as regards perfection and extent, it is always true that they agree in the same relation. It is, then, in this relation that truth must be placed, and we can distinguish between the *truths* which are independent of our good pleasure, and between the *expressions* which we invent as seems good to us.]

§ 3. *Ph.* It is only too true that men, even in their minds, put words in the place of things, especially when the ideas are complex and indeterminate. But it is also true as you have observed, that then the mind contents itself with the indication only of the truth, without for the present understanding it, in the persuasion that it depends upon itself to understand it when it will. For the rest, the act which takes place in *affirming* or *denying* is more easily conceived by reflecting upon what goes on in us, than explained in words. Therefore, you do not take it ill that in default of something better we have spoken of *joining together* or of *separating*. § 8. You will also agree that propositions at least may be called verbal, and that, when they are true, they are

Anglois, de la liberté, de la necessité et du hasard, cf. Gerhardt, 6, 388–399, Erdmann, 629–634, Janet, *Œuvres philos. de Leibniz*, 2, 424–437, Dutens, 1, 415–429 (in Latin).—Tr.

both verbal and also real, for, § 9. *falsehood* consists in joining names otherwise than as their ideas agree or disagree. § 10. Words are at least great *vehicles* of truth. § 11. There is also a *moral truth*, which consists in speaking of things according to the persuasion of our mind; there is finally *metaphysical* truth which is the real existence of things in conformity to the ideas we have of them.

Th. [Moral truth is by some called *veracity*, and *metaphysical truth* is commonly taken by the metaphysicians as an attribute of being, but it is an attribute very useless and almost void of meaning. Let us content ourselves with seeking truth in the correspondence of the propositions in the mind with the things in question. It is true that I have also attributed truth to ideas in saying that ideas are true or false; but then I mean, in reality, the truth of propositions affirming the possibility of the object of the idea. In the same sense we can say also that a *being is true*, that is to say, the proposition affirming its actual, or at least, possible existence.] [1]

CHAPTER VI

OF UNIVERSAL PROPOSITIONS, THEIR TRUTH AND CERTITUDE.

§ 2. *Ph.* All our knowledge is of general or particular truths. We can never make the former, which are the most important, well understood, and can ourselves, indeed, very rarely comprehend them save as they are conceived and expressed by words.

Th. [I think that other marks also can produce this effect; we see it in the characters of the Chinese. A *universal char-*

[1] *Cf. New Essays*, Bk. II., chap. 32, *ante*, p. 281, and notes; also Bk. III., chap. 3, *ante*, p. 317, note 3; and Bk. IV., chap. 1, *ante*, pp. 397–8. Locke in the first of these passages agrees with the view of Aristotle, *De Interpret.*, 1, 16ª, 12, that truth or falsity is predicable not of single ideas, but only of their union in judgments or propositions; and Leibnitz in the present passage maintains essentially the same doctrine in saying that by the truth he attributes to ideas he means the truth of the propositions affirming the possibility of the objects of the ideas. Such "true" or "false" ideas must, then, be regarded simply as abbreviated propositions, or as tacitly involving propositions. The idea of the decahedron (*cf. ante*, p. 315, and note 1) is false, although we have its nominal definition, because the figure is impossible.—TR.

acteristic[1] very popular and better than theirs might be introduced if small figures were employed in the place of words, which would represent visible things by their lines, and the invisible by the visible which accompany them, adding thereto certain additional marks suitable to make understood the flexions and the particles. This would be of service at first for easy communication with distant nations; but if introduced also among us without, however, renouncing ordinary writing, the employment of this mode of writing would be very useful in enriching the imagination, and in giving thoughts less surd and verbal than we now have. It is true that the art of drawing not being known by all, it follows that, excepting the books printed in this way (which everybody would soon learn to read), everybody could not avail themselves of it otherwise than by a method of printing, *i.e.* having the figures all engraved ready for printing upon paper, and adding thereto afterwards with the pen the marks of the flexions or particles. But in time everybody would learn the plan in youth, so as not to be deprived of the convenience of this *figured character*, which *would speak* in truth *to the eyes*, and would be very agreeable to the people, just as in fact the peasants already have certain almanacs, telling them without words much that they ask; and I remember to have seen some satirical impressions in copper-plate which possessed a somewhat enigmatical character in which there were *figures significant of themselves*, mingled with words,[2] while our letters and the Chinese characters are significant only by the will of men (*ex instituto*).

§ 3. *Ph.* [I think your thoughts will some day be carried out, so agreeable and natural appears to me this *writing*, and it seems to be of no little consequence for increasing the perfection of our mind, and rendering our conceptions more real.] But to return to general knowledge and its certainty, it will be proper to remark that there is a *certainty of truth* and also a *certainty of knowledge*. When words are so joined in propositions that they express exactly the agreement or disagree-

[1] *Cf. ante*, p. 375, note 1.

[2] Probably something similar to what is now known by the term "Rebus." For a brief statement of the development of writing from the picture stage, its earliest form, to the alphabetic as we now have it, *cf.* E. Benj. Andrews, *Institutes of Gen. Hist.*, chap. 2, § 13, p. 49, 2d ed. Boston: Silver, Burdett & Co., 1888.—TR.

ment as it really is, it is a *certainty of truth;* and the *certainty of knowledge* consists in perceiving the agreement or disagreement of ideas so far as it is expressed in propositions. This is what we ordinarily call being *certain* of a proposition.

Th. [In fact this last kind of *certainty* will also suffice without the use of words, and is nothing else than a perfect knowledge of the truth; while the first kind of certainty appears to be nothing else than the truth itself.]

§ 4. *Ph.* Now as we cannot be assured of the truth of any *general proposition,* unless we know the precise limits of the signification of the terms of which it is composed, it will be necessary for us to know the essence of each species, which is not difficult as regards the *simple ideas* and the *modes.* But in substances wherein a real essence distinct from the nominal is supposed to determine the species, the extent of the general term is very uncertain, because we do not know this real essence; and consequently *in this sense we cannot be assured* of any *general proposition* made upon the basis of these substances. But when we suppose the species of substances to be nothing else than the reduction of substantial individuals into certain sorts, arranged under different general names according as they agree with the different abstract ideas which we designate by these names, we cannot doubt whether a proposition, well known as it should be, is true or not.

Th. [I do not know why you, sir, return again to a point sufficiently discussed by us, and which I believe an empty one. But, after all, I am very glad of it, because you give me an opportunity very suitable (it seems to me) to disabuse you anew. I say then to you that we can be assured, for example, of a thousand truths regarding gold, or that body whose internal essence makes itself known by the greatest weight known here below, or by the greatest ductility, or by other marks. For we say that the body of the greatest known ductility is also the heaviest of all known bodies. It is true that it is not impossible that all which has hitherto been noticed in gold will some day be found in two bodies distinguishable by other new qualities, and that thus gold would no longer be the lowest species, as it has hitherto been regarded provisionally. We might also, if the one kind remained rare, and the other became common, think it proper to reserve the name of true gold to the single rare species, in order to retain it in use as money by means of new assays which would be suited to it. After which we shall not doubt, also, that the internal essence of these two species is different; and if indeed the definition of an actually existing substance should not be fully determined in all respects (as in fact, that of men is not as regards the external figure), we should not cease to have an infinite number of general propositions upon its subject, which would follow from reason and the other qualities which we recognize in it. All that we can say regarding these general propositions is, that in case man is taken as the lowest species and restricted to the race of Adam, we shall have no properties of man such as are named *in quarto modo*,[1] or may

[1] The term *in quarto modo*, here used by Leibnitz, refers to a classification of *propria* — ἴδια, properties — existent in the time of Porphyry, 233–304, though not accepted by him, — *cf.* Εἰσαγωγή, chap. 4, 4ª, 14 (in Aristotle, ed. Berl. Acad., Vol. 4, p. 4): τὸ δὲ ἴδιον διαιροῦσι τετραχῶς . . . (18.) τέταρτον δὲ ἐφ' οὗ συνδεδράμηκε τὸ μόνῳ καὶ παντὶ καὶ ἀεὶ, ὡς τῷ ἀνθρώπῳ τὸ γελαστικόν . . . (22.) ταῦτα δὲ καὶ κυρίως ἴδιά φησιν, ὅτι καὶ ἀντιστρέφει — and due, perhaps, to some one of the old Peripatetics, and prevalent in different forms in the Middle Age, according to which classification as given by Porphyry there were four classes: 1. Propria belonging to one species only, but not to every individual thereof, as *grammatical* to man; 2. Propria belonging to every individual of the species, but not to this species alone, as *biped* to man; 3. Propria belonging to one species only and to every individual thereof, but not always, as *hoary* to man; 4. Propria belonging to one species only, to every individual thereof, always, as *risibility* or *risible* to man.

The *propria* of this fourth class — *quartus modus* — are, each, of equal breadth with its subject, and, though no part of the essence of the species of which they are predicated, — man, for example, without the proprium *risible*, still being man, — as a matter of fact belong to every individual of the species on all occasions, and to no individual of any other species. Propositions predicating such *propria* are judgments in A, according to Archbishop Thomson's terminology, of the type "Common Salt is Chloride of Sodium," and are of course convertible.

Propria of this fourth class alone, *i.e. propria* each of which would be coincident with its subject so as to be enouncible in a judgment in A — reciprocal — constitute the fourth predicable, and answer to the ἴδιον of Aristotle and Porphyry, and the *proprium* of Appuleius, Marcianus Capella and Boethius. These writers, with the exception of Aristotle, to whom probably the four-fold division of *propria* was unknown, regard the other three classes, which were *propria* according to the Middle Age schoolmen, as *accidents*, — *accidentia*, συμβεβηκότα, — a fact which explains the somewhat peculiar language of Leibnitz: "We shall have no properties of man *such as* (*of the sort that*) are named *in quarto modo*," etc. Leibnitz's thought is this: "In the case of 'man'" taken as the lowest species — *species infima* — and "limited to Adam's race, there is, except provisionally, no such *proprium*. 'Sole-rational-animal' would be, provisionally, such a *proprium*, because up till now we know no men whom it

be enounced concerning him by a reciprocal or simply convertible proposition, unless provisionally, as in saying: *man is the only rational animal.* Taking man as those of our race, the *provisional* consists in the assumption that he is the only rational animal of those known to us; for we might some day find other animals who would have in common with the posterity of men of the present time all that which we have hitherto observed in them, but who would have another origin. It is as if the so-called Australians should overrun our countries: in all likelihood we should then discover some means of distinguishing them from ourselves. But in case this should not happen, and supposing that God had forbidden this mixture of these races, and that Jesus Christ had redeemed ours only, it would be necessary to try to make some artificial marks in order to distinguish between them. There would doubtless be an internal difference, but as it would not make itself recognizable, we should be reduced to the *extrinsic denomination* of birth alone which we should try to accompany with a durable artificial mark that would give an *intrinsic denomination,* and a constant means of distinguishing our race from the others. These are all fictions, for we have no need to recur to these distinctions, being the only rational animals of this globe. Yet these fictions are useful in knowing the natures of ideas, substances, and truths general in their character. But if man were not taken as *the lowest species* nor as that of the rational animals of the race of Adam, and if, instead of that, he signified a genus common to several species, which belonged now to a single known race, but which might belong also to others distinguishable either by birth or even by their natural marks, as, for example, in the case of the supposed Australians; then, I say, this genus would have *reciprocal propositions,* and the present definition of *man* would not be provisional. It is

would not fit, and know of no other species any of whose individuals it would fit. Only provisionally, however, for future discoveries may show, in either of these respects, that 'sole-rational-animal,' and 'man' are not exactly coincident concepts." On the whole subject, *cf.* Prantl, *Gesch. d. Logik,* Vol. 1, pp. 343, 395, 425, 581, 584, 630, 674, 676, 696, Vol. 2, pp. 342–343, Vol. 3, p. 102, Vol. 4, p. 241, note 383; Aldrich, *Artis Logicæ Rudimenta,* ed. Mansel, Oxford, 1856, pp. 32–34.

I would add that for much of the material as well as of the language of the above note, I am indebted to the kindness of Pres. E. B. Andrews of Brown University. — TR.

the same with *gold;* for suppose that some day there were two kinds of it distinguishable, the one rare and hitherto unknown, the other common and perhaps artificial, discovered in the course of time; then suppose that the name gold should continue for the present species, *i.e.* for the natural and rare gold, in order to preserve by its means the commodity of gold money, based upon the rarity of this substance, its definition known hitherto by intrinsic denominations would have been provisional only, and should be augmented by new marks which will be discovered, to distinguish the rare gold or the ancient species from the new artificial gold. But if the name gold should then remain common to the two species, *i.e.* if by gold you mean a genus of which up to the present time we know no subdivision, and which we now take as the lowest species (but only provisionally until the subdivision is known) and if some day a new species were found, *i.e.* an artificial gold, easy to make, and which might become common; I say that in this sense the definition of this genus should not be judged provisional, but perpetual. And indeed, without troubling ourselves with the names man or gold, whatever name is given to the genus or to the lowest known species, and even if none should be given them, what has just been said would be always true of ideas, genera or species, and species will be defined provisionally only by the definitions of genera. But it will always be allowable and reasonable to assume, by means of a reciprocal proposition, that there is a real internal essence belonging either to the genus or the species, which makes itself known ordinarily by external marks. I have assumed hitherto that the race does not degenerate or change; but if the same race passed into another species, we should be so much the more obliged to recur to other marks and denominations intrinsic or extrinsic, without confining ourselves to the race.

§ 7. *Ph.* Complex ideas, which the names we give to the species of substances justify, are collections of ideas of certain qualities which we have observed *coexisting* in an unknown *substratum* which we call substance. But we cannot know certainly what other qualities coexist necessarily with such combinations, unless we can discover their dependence as regards their primary qualities.

Th. I have already remarked before that the same (difficulty) is found in the ideas of *accidents*, whose nature is a little abstruse, as, for example, are the figures in geometry; for when the question concerns, for example, the figure of a mirror which collects all the parallel rays into one point as a focus, many properties of this mirror may be found before its construction is known, but we shall be uncertain about many other relations it may have, until we find in it that which corresponds to the internal constitution of substances, *i.e.* the construction of this figure of the mirror, which will constitute as it were the key to ulterior knowledge.]

Ph. But if we had known the internal constitution of this body, we should have found therein only the dependence which the primary, or what you call manifest, qualities may have, *i.e.* you would know what size, figure, and moving force depend thereupon; but we should never know the connection which they may have with the *secondary* or confused *qualities*, *i.e.* with the sensible qualities, as colors, tastes, etc.

Th. The fact is, you still assume that these sensible qualities, or rather the ideas we have of them, do not depend upon figure and movement in a natural way, but only upon the good pleasure of God, who gives us these ideas. You appear to have forgotten, sir, the remonstrance I have more than once made to you against this opinion, in order to make you think rather that these *sensitive ideas* depend in detail upon the figures and movements, and express them exactly, although we cannot distinguish therein this detail in the confusion of too great a multitude and minuteness of mechanical actions which strike our senses. But if we had reached the internal constitution of some bodies, we should see also how they must have these qualities, which would themselves be reduced to their intelligible reasons; although it would never be in our power to recognize them sensibly in these sensitive ideas which are a confused resultant of the actions of bodies upon us, as, now that we have the perfect analysis of *green* into blue and yellow,[1] and have scarcely anything more to ask in regard to it save as related to these ingredients, we are, however, incapable of analyzing the ideas of blue and yellow in our

[1] *Cf. ante*, p. 320, note 1; also Leibnitz's letter to Th. Burnett, without date, but written, according to Gerhardt, in 1699, G., *Leibniz. philos. Schrift.*, 3, 256. — TR.

sensitive idea of green, for the very reason that it is a confused idea. It is much the same as we cannot analyze the idea of the teeth of the wheel, *i.e.* of the cause, in the perception of an *artificial transparency,* which I have noticed among the clock-makers, made by the rapid rotation of a cog-wheel, which makes the teeth disappear, and an imaginary continuous transparency appear in their place, composed of the successive appearances of the teeth and their intervals, but in which the succession is so rapid that our phantasy cannot distinguish it. We find then, indeed, these teeth in the distinct notion of this transparency, but not in this confused sensitive perception, whose nature is to be and to remain confused; otherwise if the confusion ceased (as if the motion were so slow that we could observe its parts and their succession) this notion, *i.e.* this phantasm[1] of a transparency would no longer exist. And as there is no need of imagining that God for his good pleasure gives us this phantasm, and that it is independent of the movement of the teeth of the wheel and their intervals, and as, on the contrary, we conceive it to be only a confused expression of what takes place in this movement, an expression, I say, that consists in the fact that these successive things are confounded in an apparent simultaneity: it is thus easy to think that it will be the same as regards other *sensitive phantasms,* of which we have not as yet so perfect an analysis, as of colors, tastes, etc. For, to speak the truth, they deserve this name phantasms rather than that of *qualities* or even of *ideas.* And it would suffice us in all respects to understand them as well as this artificial transparency, without its being reasonable or possible to claim a further knowledge of them; for to desire these confused phantasms to abide, and yet to distinguish therein their ingredients by the phantasy itself, is a contradiction, is a desire to have the pleasure of being deceived by an agreeable perspective, and to desire that at the same time the eye see the deception, which would destroy it. It is a case, in short, where —

nihilo plus agas
Quam si des operam, ut cum ratione insanias.[2]

[1] *Cf. ante,* p. 445, note 1. Schaarschmidt here translates: "Phantasie-Erscheinung"; in line 17 of this page, "Phantasievorstellung"; in lines 24, 26, 31, "Erscheinungen." — TR.

[2] Terence, *Eun.*, 1. 1. 17, 18. — TR.

But it often happens that men seek *nodum in scirpo* [1] and make difficulties where there are none, by demanding the impossible, and afterwards complaining of their impotence and of the limits of their light.

§ 8. *Ph.* *All gold is fixed* is a proposition, the truth of which we cannot certainly know. For if *gold* signifies a species of things, distinguished by a real essence, which nature has given it, we are ignorant what particular substances are of this species. Thus, although this may be gold, we cannot affirm it with certainty. If we take gold as a body endowed with a certain yellow color, malleable, fusible, heavier than any known body, it is not difficult to know what is or is not *gold;* but with all that, *no other quality* can be affirmed or denied with certainty of gold, than that which has a connection with this idea, according to a connection or incompatibility which may be discovered.[2] Now fixity having no known connection with color, weight, and the other simple ideas which I have supposed to constitute the complex idea we have of gold, it is impossible that we can know with certainty the truth of this proposition, that all gold is fixed.

Th. We know almost as certainly that the heaviest of all bodies known here below is fixed, as we know certainly that it will be light to-morrow. This is because we have tried it a hundred thousand times; it is an experimental certainty, and of fact, although we do not know the bond which unites the fixity with the other qualities of this body. Moreover, it is unnecessary to oppose two things which agree and amount to the same thing. When I think of a body, which is at the same time yellow, fusible, and which resists the cupel, I think of a body whose specific essence, although unknown in its interior, makes these qualities emanate from its depths, and makes itself known confusedly at least by means of them. I see nothing wrong in that, nor anything which requires you to return so often to the charge in order to attack it.

§ 10. *Ph.* It is enough for me now that this knowledge of the fixity of the heaviest of bodies is not known to us by the

[1] *Cf. ante*, p. 226, note 1.—TR.

[2] According to the texts of Gerhardt and Erdmann. Jacques and Janet read: "Que ce qui a avec cette idée une connexion ou une incompatibilité qu'on peut découvrir"; *i.e.* than that which has a discoverable connection or incompatibility with this idea.—TR.

agreement or disagreement of ideas. And I for myself think that among the secondary qualities of bodies and the powers relating to them there cannot any two be named whose necessary coexistence or incompatibility can be known with certainty, except the qualities which belong to the same sense and necessarily exclude one another, as when you can say that what is white is not black.

Th. I believe, however, that you might perhaps find them; for example, every palpable body (or that which may be felt by touch) is visible. Every hard body makes a noise when struck in the air. The tones of strings or wires are semi-proportional to the weights which cause their tension. It is true that what you ask succeeds only as far as you conceive distinct ideas united with confused sensitive ideas.

§ 11. *Ph.* It is not always necessary to think that bodies have their qualities by themselves independently of anything else. A piece of gold, separated from the impression and influence of every other body, would immediately lose its yellow color and weight; perhaps, also, it would become friable and lose its malleability. You know how vegetables and animals depend upon the earth, air, and sun; how do you know whether the very distant fixed stars have not also an influence upon us?

Th. This is a very excellent remark; and if the contexture of certain bodies were known to us, we could not judge wholly of their effects without knowing the interior of those which touch and traverse them.

§ 13. *Ph.* Our judgment, however, may go further than our knowledge. For people sedulous in making observations can penetrate farther, and by means of certain probabilities resulting from an exact observation and by certain hints purposely put together, often make just conjectures regarding that which experience has not yet discovered to them; but it is always only conjecture.

Th. But if experience justifies these consequences in a constant manner, do you not find that you can acquire certain propositions by this means? Certain, I say, at least as those which assert, for example, that the heaviest of our bodies is fixed and that the one which is after it the heaviest is volatile, for it seems to me that the *certainty* (understanding it as *moral* or *physical*), but not the *necessity* (or *metaphysical* certainty) of these propositions which are learned by experience alone and not by analysis and the bond of ideas, is established among us and with reason.[1]

CHAPTER VII

OF PROPOSITIONS CALLED MAXIMS OR AXIOMS

§ 1. *Ph.* There is one species of propositions which under the name of *maxims* or *axioms* pass as *principles* of science, and because they are *self-evident*, we have been contented to call them *innate*, although no one *that I know of* has ever tried to show the reason and ground of their extreme clearness, which forces us, so to speak, to give them our consent. It is not, however, useless to enter into this investigation and to see whether this great evidence is peculiar to these propositions alone, as also to examine how far they contribute to our knowledge.

Th. This investigation is very useful and very important. But you must not suppose, sir, that it has been entirely neglected. You will find in a hundred places that the Scholastics have said that these propositions are evident *ex terminis*, as soon as the terms are understood, so that they were persuaded that the force of conviction was grounded in the knowledge of the terms, *i.e.* in the connection of their ideas. But geometers have done very much more: that is

[1] Metaphysical and moral or physical certainty differ as the certainty of the truths of reason and the truths of fact. The truths of reason ground themselves in the necessities of thought, and their certainty is accordingly absolute. The truths of fact, in Leibnitz's view, rest upon the divine choice of the best, and have an evidence merely relative and established with the aid of experience; their necessity is accordingly only hypothetical. *Cf. New Essays*, Bk. II., chap. 21, § 8, Th., *ante*, pp. 179–180, and § 13, Th., *ante*, p. 183. The principle upon which the whole matter depends is the famous distinction of the mediæval scholastics between the understanding and the will of God, a principle to which Leibnitz very often recurs, especially in order to maintain the contingency of the world, and to escape from the universal fatalism of Spinoza. According to this principle, the understanding of God is the source of the necessary truths, and the will of God the source of the contingent truths. The distinction, however, does not solve the problem either of the contingency of the physical universe or of the moral freedom of man. — Tr.

they have undertaken very often to demonstrate them.[1] Proclus already attributes to Thales of Miletus, one of the oldest known geometers, the wish to demonstrate the propositions which Euclid has since assumed as evident.[2] It is said that Apollonius has demonstrated other axioms, and Proclus has also done so. The late Mr. Roberval, already eighty years old or thereabouts, intended to publish the new elements of geometry of which I think I have already spoken to you.[3] Perhaps the "New Elements" of Arnauld, which at that time made some stir, had contributed thereto.[4] He exhibited specimens of them in the Royal Academy of Sciences, and some found fault that assuming this axiom, *if equal mag-*

[1] Leibnitz frequently refers, both in the *New Essays* and elsewhere, to the demonstrability of the axioms, and the thought was evidently a favorite one with him. It is a weighty thought, too; for all real advance in speculative and truly and lastingly constructive thinking rests upon just this "working-over of the notions," as Herbart expresses it, this deeper penetration into their real meaning and content, and its exposition in the simplest possible intelligible forms. — TR.

[2] Proclus cites Thales of Miletus in prop. XV., theor. VIII., of his *In primum Euclidis Elementorum lib. Commentarii*, ex recog. G. Friedlein, p. 299. Thales, c. 624–c. 550 B.C., was the founder of the Greek geometry, astronomy, and philosophy. For his geometry, *cf.* G. J. Allman, *Greek Geometry from Thales to Euclid*, Dublin, 1889; for his philosophy, *cf.* Zeller, *Philos. d. Griech.*, I., 1 [Vol. 1], 180–196, 5th ed., Leipzig, 1892. — TR.

[3] *Cf. ante*, p. 107, note 1. — TR.

[4] The work of Antoine Arnauld, 1612–1694, here referred to is the *Nouveaux Elemens de Géométrie*, Paris, 1661, mentioned among the most prominent books of that time by Ch. Wolf in his *Kurzer Unterricht v. d. vornehmsten math. Schrift.*, Wien, 1763. Arnauld was an excellent mathematician, an able philosopher and theologian, a celebrated controversialist, and the indefatigable champion and mouthpiece of the Jansenists against the Jesuits. A zealous Catholic, he repeatedly tried to convert Leibnitz to that faith. Leibnitz's correspondence with him contains important matter regarding his own philosophy. It was originally edited and published by C. L. Grotefend, *Briefwechsel z. Leibniz, Arnauld u. d. Landgrafen Ernst v. Hessen-Rheinfels aus d. Handschriften der Königl. Bibliothek z. Hannover*, Hanover, 1846, and was reprinted conformably to Grotefend's text by Janet, *Œuvres philos. de Leibniz*, Vol. 1, pp. 577–691, and, with a new comparison of the original Mss., by Gerhardt, *Leibniz. philos. Schrift.*, Vol. 2, pp. 11–138; *cf.* also his Einleitung, *ib.* p. 5 *sq.*, and Vol. 1, p. 65, and for Leibnitz's first letter, unanswered, to Arnauld, *ib.* 68–82 (Grotefend, *op. cit.* 137 *sq.*).

Arnauld's *Œuvres complètes*, with a life by Larrière, appeared at Paris and Lausanne, 1775–1783, 45 vols., Vols. 38–40 containing the philosophical works. Of these the most important are: *Des vraies et des fausses idées*, 1683, directed against Malebranche, in which Arnauld develops his doctrine of perception and attacks the theory of representative ideas, on which *cf.* Hamilton's Reid, 8th ed., Vol. 1, pp. 295–298, Vol. 2, pp. 823 b, 963; *Reflexions philos. et théolog. sur le nouveau systême de la nature et de la grace du P. Malebranche*, 1685–

nitudes are added to equals, equals arise therefrom, he demonstrated this other which is considered equally evident: *if equals are taken from equal magnitudes, equals remain.* It was said he should have assumed both or demonstrated both. But I was not of that opinion, and I believed that it was always so much gained to have diminished the number of the axioms. Addition is no doubt anterior to subtraction and more simple, because the two terms are employed in addition in the same way, which is not the case in subtraction. Arnauld did the opposite of Roberval. He assumed still more than Euclid. As for the *maxims,* they are sometimes taken as established propositions whether evident or not. That may be well for beginners whom scrupulousness holds back; but when the establishment of science is the question, it is a different matter. Thus it is that they are often taken in ethics and even among the logicians in their topics, in some of which there is a good supply, but a part of which contain enough of them vague and obscure. For the rest, I said a long time since publicly and privately that it is important to demonstrate all our secondary axioms, which we ordinarily use, by reducing them to the *primitive* or immediate and indemonstrable *axioms,* which I recently and elsewhere called the *identicals.*

§ 2. *Ph.* Knowledge is *self-evident* when the agreement or disagreement of ideas is immediately perceived. § 3. But there are truths, not recognized as axioms, which are none the less self-evident. Let us see if the four species of agreement of which we spoke not long since (chap. 1, § 3, and chap. 3, § 7), viz.: identity, connection, relation, and real existence, furnish us with them. § 4. As for *identity or diversity,* we have as many evident propositions, as we have distinct ideas, for we can deny both, as in saying *man is not a horse, red is not blue.* Further the statement *what is, is,* is as evident as the statement *a man is a man.*

Th. It is true, and I have already remarked that it is as evident to say *ectheticalIy* in particular A is A, as to say in

1686; *Objections contre Descartes;* and *La Logique ou l'Art de Penser,* or the celebrated Port Royal Logic, 1662, written in conjunction with Nicole (*cf. infra,* p. 530, note 1), the best specimen of the logic of the Cartesian school. It has been translated into English most admirably by Prof. Thos. Spencer Baynes. — TR.

general: *it is what it is.* But to deny the subjects of different ideas one of another is not always certain, as I have already remarked; as if any one wished to say, *the trilateral* (or that which has three sides) *is not a triangle,* because, in fact, trilaterality is not triangularity; again, if any one had said: *the pearls of Slusius*[1] (of which I spoke to you not long since) *are not the lines of the cubic parabola,* he would have been mistaken, and yet that would have appeared evident to many people. The late Mr. Hardy,[2] Conseiller au Châtelet de Paris, an excellent geometer and orientalist and well versed in the ancient geometers, who has published the commentary of Marinus on the Data of Euclid, was so prepossessed with the fact that the oblique section of the cone called an ellipse is different from the oblique section of the cylinder, that the demonstration of Serenus[3] appeared to him paralogistic, and I could gain nothing against him by my remonstrances: as he was nearly as old as Roberval, when I saw him, and I was a very young man, a difference which could give me very little persuasive power as regards him, although in other respects I was on very good terms with him. This example may show in passing what prepossession may do even in the case of clever people, for he was truly prepossessed, and Hardy is spoken of

[1] *Cf. ante*, p. 387, note 1.—TR.

[2] Claude Hardy, born near the close of the sixteenth century, died in 1678, was a barrister by profession, and became in 1626 "Conseiller au Châtelet de Paris." He was acquainted with not less than thirty-six ancient and modern languages, and made a profound study of mathematics. Descartes chose him as one of his judges in his controversy with Fermat, in 1698, over Fermat's *De maximis et minimis.* Hardy published the *Data Euclidis*, Greek text, with Latin trans., together with the commentary of Marinus, the Neo-Platonist (*cf.* Zeller, *Philos. d. Griech.*, III., 2 [Vol. 6], 833, 3d ed., 1881), who lived in the fifth century, and was a disciple and the successor of Proclus (*cf. ante*, p. 108, note 2), at Paris, 1625, 4to. Leibnitz speaks of Hardy as an "homme de mérite, grand géomètre, et grand orientaliste," *cf.* Dutens, 5, 610.—TR.

[3] Serenus of Antissa, in the island of Lesbos, a Greek geometer, who lived in the fourth century, was the author of two treatises, *De Sectione Cylindri et Coni, libri duo*, which, according to Brunet, appeared, together with the *Conics* of Apollonius of Perga, the *Lemmas* of Pappus of Alexandria, and the commentaries of Eutocius of Ascalonita, at Bonn, 1566, fol., reprinted at Pistoja, 1696, fol., and afterwards edited and published by Halley, Oxford, 1710, fol. Hardy could not have seen either of the last two editions, since he died in 1678, but possibly he may have been acquainted with that of 1566; and, if not, then, as Schaarschmidt says, he must refer to Mersenne's Synopsis, Paris, 1644, which contains, pp. 276–312, an abridgment of Apollonius and Serenus.—TR.

with esteem in the letters of Descartes.[1] But I brought him forward only to show how we may be mistaken in denying one idea of another, if we have not thoroughly enough examined them where it is necessary.

§ 5. *Ph.* As regards *connection* or *coexistence*, we have very few self-evident propositions; there are, however, some, and it appears to me that this is a self-evident proposition: *two bodies cannot be in the same place.*

Th. Many Christians contest the point with you, as I have already remarked, and even Aristotle and those who after him admit real and exact condensations, reducing one and the same entire body into a smaller place than it before filled, and those who, as the late Mr. Comenius[2] has done in a little book written expressly for the purpose, claim to overthrow[3] modern natural philosophy by the experiment of the air-gun, cannot be expected to agree therewith. If you take the body as the impenetrable mass, your statement will be true, because it will be identical or nearly so; but that the real body is such will be denied you. At least it will be said that God could

[1] Schaarschmidt thinks that Leibnitz here confounded Hardy with Roberval, whom he had mentioned just before. Descartes frequently mentions Hardy in his letters, *cf.*, for example, Pt. I., epist. 111, Pt. II., epist. 61, 98, 101, 108, Pt. III., epist. 34, 60, 63, etc.; he also corresponded with him, and doubtless valued him highly, as witness his choice of him as arbiter in his controversy with Fermat, but he nowhere in his letters appears expressly to praise him; while he speaks thus of Roberval in Lib. III., epist. 56, ad Fermatium: "qui procul dubio inter primarios seculi nostri geometras censeri debet." — Tr.

[2] John Amos Comenius, 1592–1671, the last bishop of the old Moravian and Bohemian Brethren, devoted himself chiefly to the reform and regulation of public education and instruction, and wrote many works on pedagogy, which he collected and published under the title *Opera didactica omnia*, Amsterdam, 1657, 4 vols., fol. He also did some work in physical science, publishing his *Disquisitio de caloris et frigoris natura*, Amsterdam, 1659, 12mo, which the writer in Michaud, *Biog. Univ.*, 9, 345, says is the only one of his physical works deserving to be in demand, and his *Physicæ ad lumen divinum reformatæ synopsis*, Leipsig, 1633, and Amsterdam, 1643, Eng. trans., London, 1651, which is, perhaps, the book to which Leibnitz here refers. For Leibnitz's estimate of a portion of the writings of Comenius, *cf.* Dutens, 5, 181. For an account of his life and work, *cf.* S. S. Laurie, *Comenius. His Life and Educational Works*, 4th ed. (Pitt Press Series), Cambridge, Univ. Press, 1893; also a reprint of the same, with five portraits, a somewhat extended and annotated bibliography, and photographic reproductions of pages from early editions of Comenius' works, published by C. W. Bardeen, Syracuse, N. Y., 1893. — Tr.

[3] Gerhardt reads "reserver," probably a Ms. or typographical error; Erdmann, Jacques, and Janet read "renverser," which, as the context requires, the translation follows. — Tr.

make it otherwise, so that this impenetrability will be admitted only as conformed to the natural order of things which God has established and of which experiment assures us, although elsewhere it would be necessary to admit that it is also very conformable to reason.

§ 6. *Ph.* As for the *relations* of the modes, mathematicians have formed many axioms upon the one relation of equality, like that of which you have just spoken, that if equals be taken from equals the remainders are equal. But it is not less evident, I think, that *one and one are equal to two,* and that if from the five fingers of one hand you take away two and then two others from the five fingers of the other hand, the number of the fingers remaining will be equal.

Th. That one and one make two, is not properly a truth, but it is the definition of *two;* although it is true and evident that it is the definition of a possible thing. As for the axiom of Euclid applied to the fingers of the hand, I willingly admit that it is as easy to conceive what you say of the fingers as to see it in the case of A and B; but in order not to do often the same thing, you observe it generally, and afterwards it is sufficient to make subsumptions. Otherwise, it is as if you preferred calculation by particular numbers to universal rules, which would be obtaining less than is possible. For it is of more account to solve the general problem: to find two numbers whose sum makes a given number, and whose difference also makes a given number, than merely to seek two numbers whose sum makes ten, and whose difference makes six. For if I proceed in this second problem according to the method of numerical algebra, mixed with the literal (*specieuse*), the calculation will be as follows: $a + b = 10$, and $a - b = 6$; of which by adding together the right side to the right, and the left side to the left, I produce the result, $a + b + a - b = 10 + 6$, *i.e.* (since $+ b$ and $- b$ cancel each other) $2a = 16$ or $a = 8$. Subtracting the right side from the right, and the left from the left (since to take away $a - b$ is to add $- a + b$) I produce the result $a + b - a + b = 10 - 6$, *i.e.* $2b = 4$ or $b = 2$. Thus, I shall in truth have the a and b I ask for, which are 8 and 2, which satisfy the problem, *i.e.* whose sum is 10 and whose difference is 6; but I have not thereby the general method for any other numbers, which we might wish or be able to put in the place of 10 or 6, a method which I could, however, find with the same facility as these two numbers 8 and 2, by putting x and v in the place of the numbers 10 and 6. For proceeding the same as before we shall have $a + b + a - b = x + v$, i.e. $2a = x + v$ or $a = \frac{1}{2}x + v$, and we shall also have $a + b - a + b = x - v$, i.e. $2b = x - v$ or $b = \frac{1}{2}x - v$. This calculation gives this theorem or general *canon*, that when two numbers are required whose sum and difference are given, you have only to take as the greater of the required numbers, half of the sum made from the given sum and difference; and for the less of the required numbers, half of the difference between the given sum and difference. You see also that I might have dispensed with the letters, if I had treated the numbers as letters, *i.e.* if instead of putting $2a = 16$ and $2b = 4$, I had written $2a = 10 + 6$ and $2b = 10 - 6$, which would have given me $a = \frac{1}{2}(10 + 6)$ and $b = \frac{1}{2}(10 - 6)$. Thus, in the particular calculation itself I should have had the general calculation, taking these symbols 10 and 6 as general numbers, as if they were the letters x and v; in order to have a truth or method more general, and taking these same characters 10 and 6 also for the numbers they ordinarily signify, I shall have a sensible example which may serve, indeed, as a proof. And as Vieta[1] has substituted letters for numbers for the sake of greater generality, I have desired to reintroduce the numerical characters, since they are more serviceable in algebra (*specieuse*) even than the letters. I have found this of much use in large calculations for avoiding errors and even

[1] François Viète, 1540–1603, better known by the Latin form of his name, Vieta, was a distinguished French mathematician, who is often regarded as the founder of modern algebra, because of his introduction of the general use of letters as symbols of undetermined, and therefore general, quantities, thus opening up the way for the higher mathematical analysis, afterwards carried on by Descartes and others. To him is also due the invention of the different simple transformations now used in the solution of equations, such as adding to or subtracting from the members of an equation the same quantity, or multiplying or dividing them by the same quantity. He first enounced the *principle of homogeneity* or the principle that all the quantities in an equation should be of one kind,—lines, surfaces, solids, or supersolids,—a principle which, after three centuries of controversy, has now been adopted generally by mathematicians. His various mathematical writings, which, being a man of wealth, he printed at his own expense and distributed among the scholars of Europe, were collected and edited by F. van Schooten, Professor of Mathematics at Leyden, aided by J. Golius and Mersenne, and published under the title of *Opera mathematica*, Leyden, 1646, 1 vol., fol. — TR.

in the application of proofs, such as the casting away of the nines in the midst of the computation without waiting for the result, when there are only numbers instead of letters; which may often be when you employ skill in the positions, so that the suppositions are found true in the particular case, besides the use there is of seeing the connections and orders which the letters alone cannot always make the mind discern so well, as I have elsewhere shown, after I found that the good *characteristic* is one of the greatest aids of the human mind.

§ 7. *Ph.* As for *real existence* which I had counted as the fourth species of existence which may be noticed in ideas, it can furnish us no axiom, for we have not indeed a demonstrative knowledge of beings outside us, God alone excepted.

Th. We can always say that this proposition *I exist,* is of the highest evidence, being a proposition which cannot be proved by any other, or rather an *immediate truth.* And to say *I think, therefore I am,* is not properly to prove existence by thought, since to think and to be thinking is the same thing; and to say, I am thinking, is already to say, *I am.* You can, however, exclude this proposition from the number of the axioms with some reason, for it is a proposition of fact, based upon an immediate experience, and it is not a necessary proposition, whose necessity is seen in the immediate agreement of ideas. On the contrary, it is only God who sees how these two terms, *I* and *existence* are united, *i.e.* why I exist. But if the axiom is taken more generally as an immediate or *non-provable* truth, we may say that this proposition, *I am,* is an axiom, and in every case we may be assured that it is a *primitive truth,* or rather *unum ex primis cognitis inter terminos complexos, i.e.* that it is one of the first known statements which is understood in the natural order of our knowledge, for it may be that a man has never thought expressly of forming this proposition, which, however, is innate to him.

§ 8. *Ph.* [I have always believed that the axioms have little influence upon the other parts of our knowledge. But you have disabused me, since you have indeed shown an important use of identical propositions. Suffer me, however, sir, to set before you still what I have in mind upon this article, for your explanations may also serve to make others return from their error.] § 8. It is a celebrated rule in the schools that all reasoning comes from things already known and admitted, *ex praecognitis et praeconcessis*. This rule seems to cause these maxims to be regarded as truths known to the mind before the others, and the other parts of our knowledge as truths dependent upon the axioms. § 9. [I think I have shown (Book I., chap. 1) that these axioms are not the first known, the child knowing much sooner that the rod which I show him is not the sugar he has tasted, than all the axioms you please. But you have distinguished between particular knowledge or experiences of facts and the principles of a universal and necessary knowledge (and herein I admit that it is necessary to recur to axioms) as also between the natural and accidental order].

Th. I have also added that in the natural order the statement, that a thing is what it is, is prior to the statement that it is not another; for the question here does not concern the history of our discoveries, which is different in different men, but the connection and natural order of truths, which is always the same.[1] But your remark, viz.: that what the child sees is only a fact, deserves still more reflection; for the experiences of the senses do not give truths absolutely certain (as you have often yourself, sir, observed not long since), nor are they exempt from all danger of illusion. For if it is allowable to make fictions metaphysically possible, sugar might imperceptibly be changed into a rod, in order to punish the child who has been naughty, as water is changed into wine with us on Christmas eve, if it has been well prepared (*morigené*).[2] But in all cases the pain (you will say) that the rod inflicts will never be the pleasure the sugar gives. I reply that the child will take it into his head as late to make an express proposition about this, as to notice this axiom, that you can-

[1] Leibnitz here calls attention to a very important distinction, viz.: the distinction between the historical and the natural or logical order of our knowledge. The genesis of our knowledge, its gradual rise in the course of our lives, is always a matter of individual experience, the experience of no two individuals being precisely alike; while the natural or logical order and connection of truths, being grounded in reason, is always the same for all. Leibnitz's remark further suggests that the origin of a principle or truth is not its justification, a common fallacy in much of the investigation of the present day, and that the ultimate criteria of truth are philosophical, not historical. *Cf.* Bowne, *Metaphysics*, pp. 13 *sq.*, New York: Harper and Bros., 1882. — TR.

[2] Duncan, *Philos. Wks. of Leibnitz*, p. 354, translates: "rectified." — TR.

not truly say that what is is not at the same time, although he can very well perceive the difference of the pleasure and the pain, as well as the difference between perceiving and not perceiving.

§ 10. *Ph.* There are, however, a number of other truths as self-evident as these maxims. For example, *that one and two are equal to three,* is as evident a proposition as that axiom which states: *that the whole is equal to the sum of all its parts.*

Th. You appear to have forgotten, sir, that I have shown you more than once that the statement *one and two is three* is only the definition of the term *three,* so that to say that one and two is *equal to three,* is to say that a thing is equal to itself. As for this axiom, that *the whole is equal to the sum of all its parts,* Euclid makes no express use of it. This axiom also needs limitation, for it must be added that these parts must not themselves have a common part, for seven and eight are parts of twelve, but they make more than twelve. The bust and the trunk taken together are more than the man, in that the thorax is common to them both. But Euclid says, that *the whole is greater than its part,* a statement which is wholly trustworthy. And the statement that the body is greater than the trunk, differs from the axiom of Euclid only in this, that this axiom is limited to what is exactly necessary: but in exemplifying it and clothing the body you make the intelligible become also sensible, for the statement that a *given* whole is larger than a *given* part, is in fact the proposition that a whole is larger than its part, but the features of which are embellished with some coloring or addition: it is as if he who says A B says A. Thus it is not necessary here to oppose the axiom and the example as different truths in this regard, but to consider the axiom as embodied in the example and rendering it true. It is a different matter, if the evidence is not observed in the example itself, and when the affirmation of the example is a consequence, and not merely a *subsumption* of the universal proposition, as may occur indeed in the case of the axioms.

Ph. Our clever author says here: I should like to ask these gentlemen who maintain that all other knowledge (not of fact) depends upon general principles innate and self-evident, what principle they need to prove that *two and two are four?* for we know (according to him) the truth of this kind of propositions without recourse to any proof. What do you say about it, sir?

Th. I say that I was awaiting you there well prepared. That two and two are four is not a truth at once immediate, supposing that *four* signifies three and one. We can then demonstrate it, and in this way: —

Definitions. — (1) *Two* is one and one.
(2) *Three* is two and one.
(3) *Four* is three and one.

Axiom. — Putting equal things in their place, the equality remains.

Demonstration. — 2 and 2 is 2 and 1 and 1 (by def. 1).......$2 + \overbrace{2}$

2 and 1 and 1 is 3 and 1 (by def. 2).....$\underbrace{2 + 1} + 1$

3 and 1 is 4 (by def. 3)..................$\underbrace{3 + 1}_{4}$

Then (by the axiom) 2 and 2 is 4. Which was to be demonstrated.

I might, instead of saying that 2 and 2 is 2 and 1 and 1, say that 2 and 2 is equal to 2 and 1 and 1, and thus with the others. But it may be understood throughout in order to shorten the process; and that, in virtue of another axiom which states that a thing is equal to itself, or that what is the same, is equal.

Ph. [This demonstration, as little necessary as it is in relation to its too well known conclusion, serves to show how truths depend on definitions and axioms. Thus I foresee what reply you will make to many objections that are made against the use of axioms. You object that there will be an innumerable multitude of principles; but this is when you reckon among the principles the corollaries which follow from the definitions by the aid of some axiom. And since the definitions or ideas are innumerable, so also will the principles be in this sense, supposing also with you that the undemonstrable principles are the identical axioms. They become innumerable also by exemplification, but at bottom you can reckon A is A and B is B as one and the same principle differently clothed.

Th. Further, this difference of degrees in the evidence makes me disagree with your distinguished author that all these truths called *principles* and which pass as self-evident, because they are so near the indemonstrable primitive axioms, are entirely independent and incapable of receiving the one from the other any light or proof. For they may always be reduced either to axioms, themselves, or to other truths nearer the axioms, as this truth, that two and two make four, has shown you. And I just told you how Roberval diminished the number of Euclid's axioms, by sometimes reducing one to another.

§ 11. *Ph.* This judicious writer, who has furnished an occasion for our conferences, agrees that maxims have their use, but he believes that it is rather that of closing the mouth of the obstinate, than of establishing the sciences. I should be very glad, said he, if you would show me some one of these sciences built upon these general axioms which cannot be shown to be sustained as well without axioms.

Th. Geometry is, without doubt, one of these sciences. Euclid expressly employs axioms in demonstration, and this axiom: *that two homogeneous magnitudes are equal when one is neither larger nor smaller than the other*, is the basis of the demonstrations of Euclid and Archimedes respecting the size of curvilinears. Archimedes employed axioms of which Euclid had no need; for example, of two lines, each of which is concave always on the same side, that which encloses the other is the greater. We cannot also dispense with the *identical* axioms in geometry, as, for example, the principle of contradiction, or the demonstrations which lead to the impossible. And as for the other axioms, which are demonstrable, we may dispense with them, absolutely speaking, and draw conclusions immediately from the identicals and from the definitions; but the prolixity of the demonstrations, and the endless repetitions into which you would then fall, would cause a horrible confusion, if it were always necessary to begin *ab ovo;* while by assuming the mean propositions, already proved, we easily pass much farther. This assumption of truths already known is useful, especially as regards the axioms, for they recur so often that geometers are compelled to make use of them constantly without citing them; so that we should be mistaken in thinking that they are not there, because we do not perhaps always see them quoted in the margin.

Ph. But he objects to the example from theology. For the knowledge of this holy religion came to us from revelation (says our author), and without this aid the maxims would never have been able to make us know it. The light comes to us then from the things themselves, or immediately from the infallible *veracity* of God.

Th. It is as if I said, medicine is based upon experience, reason then is of no use therein. Christian theology, which is the true medicine for souls, is based upon revelation which corresponds to experience; but to make of it a perfect body, we must unite therewith natural theology, which is drawn from the axioms of eternal reason. Is not this principle indeed that *veracity is an attribute of God*, upon which you acknowledge that the certainty of revelation is based, a maxim taken from natural theology?[1]

Ph. Our author wishes to distinguish between the means of acquiring knowledge and of teaching it, or rather between teaching and communicating. After schools had been erected and professors established to teach the sciences that others had found out, these professors availed themselves of these maxims in order to impress the sciences upon the minds of their scholars, and to convince them by means of the axioms of certain particular truths; while the particular truths have served the first discoverers in finding the truth without the general maxims.

Th. I wish that this pretended procedure had been justified for us by examples of some particular truths. But rightly considering things, we shall not find it practised in the establishment of the sciences. And if the discoverer finds only a particular truth, he is only half a discoverer. If Pythagoras[2]

[1] Locke, without discussing its possibility or its method, assumes a special source of religion in an immediate revelation of God to the soul of man, and rests the truth of this revelation upon the "unerring veracity" of God. *Cf. Philos. Wks.*, Vol. 2, p. 209, Bohn's ed. Leibnitz, who elsewhere discusses to a certain extent both the possibility and the method of revelation, and admits its possibility, and also its actuality, especially as regards those things which are beyond the limits of our finite experience, emphasizes the rational element in theology by calling attention to the fact that revelation presupposes a natural idea of God, philosophically derived and including the attribute of veracity, to which it may appeal and by which its character and claims to authority must be judged. — TR.

[2] *Cf. ante*, p. 379, note 1. On his life and philosophy, *cf.* Zeller, *Philos. d. Griech.*, 5th ed., Vol. 1, pp. 296 *sq.* For his mathematical work, *cf.* G. J.

had only observed that the triangle whose sides are 3, 4, 5, has the property of the equality of the square on the hypothenuse with those on the sides (*i.e.* that $9 + 16 = 25$), would he on that account have been the discoverer of this great truth which includes all right-angled triangles, and which has passed into a maxim with the geometers? It is true that often an example, seen by chance, serves as the occasion which suggests to a clever man the search for general truth, but it is still very often no easy matter to find it; besides, this path of discovery is not the best nor the most employed by those who proceed in an orderly and methodical way, and they make use of it only upon the occasions when better methods fall short. In the same way, some have thought that Archimedes found the quadrature of the parabola by weighing a piece of wood cut parabolically, and that this particular experiment caused him to discover the general truth; but those who know the penetration of this great man see clearly that he had no need of such an aid. Moreover, if this empirical way of particular truths had been the occasion of all the discoveries, it would not have been sufficient to give them; and the discoverers themselves have been delighted with observing the maxims and the general truths if they have been able to attain them, otherwise their discoveries would have been very imperfect. All that may then be attributed to the schools and to the professors, is that they have collected and arranged the maxims and other general truths: and would God they had done so still more and with more care and choice, the sciences would not be found so scattered and so confused. For the rest I admit, that there is often some difference between the method we use in teaching the sciences and that which has produced their discovery: but this is not the point in question. Sometimes, as I have already observed, chance has given occasion for discovery. If we had noticed these occasions, and had preserved the memory of them for posterity (which would have been very useful), this detail would have been a very considerable part of the history of the arts, but it would not have

Allman, *Greek Geometry from Thales to Euclid*, Dublin, 1889, and, by the same author, *Pythagorean Geometry*, being the mathematical part of the article "Pythagoras" in the *Encyclop. Brit.*, 9th ed., Vol. 20, pp. 146–149 (Amer. ed.). — TR.

been proper to make systems of them. Sometimes also discoverers have proceeded rationally to the truth, but by extended circuits. I find that in matters of importance authors would have rendered service to the public, if they had been willing sincerely to indicate in their writings the traces of their experiments; but if the system of science should be built upon that foundation, it would be as if in a finished house you wished to preserve all the apparatus which[1] the architect required in building it. Good methods of teaching are all such that by their means science could certainly have been discovered; and then if they are not empirical, *i.e.* if the truths are taught by reasons or by proofs drawn from ideas, it will always be by axioms, theorems, canons, and such other general propositions. The case is different when the truths are *aphorisms* like those of Hippocrates,[2] *i.e.* truths of fact either general, or

[1] Gerhardt reads "donc," manifestly a manuscript or a typographical error. Erdmann, Jacques, and Janet read "dont," which the translation follows. — Tr.

[2] Hippocrates of Cos, 460–375 B.C., the "Father of Medicine," was the first to base the practice of medicine on the observation of nature and the principles of an inductive philosophy. Though descended from a family of priest-physicians, he put aside all its traditions and prejudices, gave himself up to the study of the natural history of disease in the living subject, and treated it always as subject to natural laws. He placed especial emphasis on symptomology and dieteties. The two chief modern critical editions of his writings, or those ascribed to him, are E. Littré, *Œuvres complètes d'Hippocrate*, 10 vols., Paris, 1839–61, and F. Z. Ermerins, *Hippocratis et aliorum medicorum veterum reliquiæ*, 3 vols., Utrecht, 1859–64. The 'Αφορισμοί — Aphorisms — are accepted as absolutely genuine by Littré, but rejected as spurious by Ermerins. The Greek text with French trans. is found in Littré, *op. cit.*, Vol. 4, pp. 396 *sq.*; with Latin trans., in Ermerins, *op. cit.*, Vol. 1, pp. 397 *sq.* For an English translation, *cf.* F. Adams, *Genuine Wks. of Hippocrates* (Sydenham Soc.), 2 vols., London, 1849, Vol. 2, p. 685.

In this connection I may add that Professor Schaarschmidt of Bonn University has kindly informed me that the phrase σύμπνοια πάντα cited by Leibnitz from Hippocrates, *cf. ante*, p. 48 (*ad fin.*) is to be found in the Περὶ τροφῆς, § 23, Littré, *Œuvres d'Hippocrate*, Vol. 9, p. 106, where it runs thus: Ξύρροια μία, ξύμπνοια μία, ξυμπαθέα πάντα· κ.τ.λ. Professor Schaarschmidt thinks that Leibnitz probably read: ξύμπνοια πάντα, — *conspirantia omnia*, — omitting μία and ξυμπαθέα, and took ξύμπνοια for an adjective, while it is in the text a substantive meaning concordance, — *conspiratio*, — a usage which sometimes occurs, *cf.* Stephanus, *Thesau. Ling. Græc.*, Vol. 3, p. 416, C; or that he quoted from memory, as he often does. Σύμπνους — *conspirans* — as an epithet of the universe occurs in Plutarch, *De fato*, 2, 574, E: τὸ φύσει διοικεῖσθαι τόνδε τὸν κόσμον, σύμπνουν, καὶ συμπαθῆ, αὐτὸν αὑτῷ ὄντα, *i.e.* "that the world is governed by Nature, and that it conspires, consents, and is compatible with itself." *Plutarch's Morals*, Eng. trans., by several hands, corrected and revised by W. W. Goodwin, Ph.D., Vol. 5, p. 308, Boston: Little, Brown & Co., 1870. — Tr.

at least true most frequently, learned by observation or based on experience, and for which there are no reasons immediately convincing. But the question here is not about this, for these truths are not known by the connection of ideas.

Ph. Here is the manner in which our ingenious author conceives that the need of maxims has been introduced. The schools having established *disputation* as the touchstone of the ability of people, they adjudged the victory to the one who holds the field of battle and speaks the last word. But in order to furnish means of convincing the obstinate, it was necessary to establish maxims.

Th. The schools of philosophy had done better, no doubt, to unite practice with theory, as do the schools of medicine, chemistry, and mathematics; and to give the prize to the one who had done the best, especially in ethics, rather than to the one who had spoken the best. Yet as there are matters in which discourse itself is an effect and sometimes the sole effect and masterpiece which can make known the ability of a man, as in metaphysical matters, we have had reason on some occasions to judge of the ability of people by their success in the conferences. We know, indeed, that at the beginning of the *Reformation* the Protestants challenged their adversaries to come to colloquies and discussions, and sometimes upon the success of these discussions the public concluded for the reform. We know, also, how much the art of speaking and of giving birth and force to reasons, and, if it may be so called, the art of discussion, can accomplish in a council of state and of war, a court of justice, a medical consultation, and even in a conversation. And we are obliged to recur to this means and to content ourselves with words instead of acts on those occasions, for this very reason that the question then concerns an event or future fact where it would be too late to learn the truth by the effect. Thus the art of discussion or of contending by reasons (whereby I here understand the quotation of authorities and examples) is very great and very important; but unfortunately it is very badly managed, and for this reason also often reaches no conclusion or a bad one. It is for this reason that I have more than once intended to remark upon the colloquies of theologians, accounts of whom we have, in order to show the defects which may be noticed in them and the remedies that might be employed therefor. In consultations upon business, if those who have the most power have not a very solid mind, authority or eloquence prevail ordinarily, although they are banded against the truth. In a word, the art of conferring and discussing would need to be entirely remodelled. As for the advantage of the one who has the last word, it is almost wholly in free conversations; for in councils suffrages or votes go by order, whether they begin or finish with the last in rank. It is true that it ordinarily belongs to the president to begin and end, *i.e.* to propose and decide; but he decides according to the plurality of the votes. In academic discussions it is the *respondent* or maintainant (of the thesis) who speaks last, and the field of battle abides with him, almost always by an established custom. It is a question of testing him, not of confounding him; otherwise it would be treating him as an enemy. In reality, there is almost no question of truth on these occasions: indeed, opposite theses are maintained at different times in the same chair. The hall of the Sorbonne was shown to Casaubon,[1] and they said to him: this is the place where they have disputed for so many centuries; he replied, to what conclusion have they come?

Ph. The wish was, however, to prevent the dispute from going on to infinity, and to furnish means of deciding between two equally expert combatants, in order that the dispute enter not upon an *infinite series* of syllogisms. This means was the introduction of certain general propositions, the larger part self-evident, and which being of such a nature as to be received by all men with entire consent, were to be regarded as general measures of truth, and to hold the place of *principles* (when the disputants had posited no others), beyond which none could go, and to which both sides were obliged to hold. Thus these maxims having received the name of principles which could be denied in the dispute, and which ended the question, they were taken *erroneously* (according to my author) as the sources of knowledge and the foundations of the sciences.

[1] Isaac Casaubon, 1559–1614, a great classical scholar and editor, who had the reputation of being, next to Scaliger, the most learned man of his age. Leibnitz also relates this anecdote in his letter to Thomas Burnett, Feb. 1–11, 1697, Gerhardt, 3, 192, Dutens, 6, 245. — Tr.

Th. Would to God we had made use of them in this way in the discussions, there would be nothing to say in reply, for we should decide something. And what better thing could we do than to reduce controversy, *i.e.* contested truths to truths evident and incontestable? would not that be to establish them in a demonstrative fashion? And who can doubt that these principles, which would end disputes by establishing truth, would not be at the same time sources of knowledge? For, provided the reasoning is good, it matters not whether it is carried on silently in one's study, or exposed for sale publicly in a professor's chair. And even if these principles were assumptions rather than axioms, taking the assumptions not as Euclid, but as Aristotle, *i.e.* as suppositions which must be admitted while waiting opportunity to prove them, these principles would always have this use, that by means of them all the other questions would be reduced to a small number of propositions. Thus I am the most surprised of anybody to see a praiseworthy thing blamed by I know not what prepossession, to which we clearly see by the example of your author the most clever men are susceptible through want of attention. Unfortunately they do an entirely different thing in academic disputes. Instead of establishing general axioms, they do all they can to weaken them by vain and little understood distinctions, and it pleases them to employ certain philosophical rules, of which there are large books completely full, but which are little certain and little determined and which they have the pleasure of eluding while distinguishing them. This is not the way to end the disputes, but to render them infinite, and finally to wear out the adversary. It is as if we put him in a dark place, where we strike at random and no one can judge the blows. This invention is admirable for the maintainants (*Respondentes*) who are engaged in maintaining certain theses. It is a buckler of Vulcan which renders them invulnerable; it is *Orci galea*, Pluto's helmet, which renders them invisible. They must be very unskilful or very unfortunate if they can be caught with that. It is true there are some *rules* which have *exceptions*, especially in questions into which many circumstances enter, as in jurisprudence. But to render their use sure these exceptions must be determined in number and sense so far as possible; and then it may be that the exception itself has its *sub-exceptions, i.e.* its *replications,* and that the replication has its *duplications,* etc., but at the end of the reckoning, all these exceptions and sub-exceptions, clearly determined, and joined with the rule, must achieve universality. Of this jurisprudence furnishes very remarkable examples. But if these kinds of rules, loaded with exceptions and sub-exceptions, should enter into academic disputes, it would always be necessary to dispute pen in hand, holding as a *protocol* what is said by both sides. And this would be more necessary elsewhere, in disputing constantly *pro forma* by means of many syllogisms, mixed from time to time with distinctions, which the best memory in the world must confound. But we are not kept from giving ourselves this trouble, from pushing sufficiently the *formal syllogisms* and from registering them, in order to discover the truth when it is without recompense, and we should not indeed succeed therein, if we wished, unless the distinctions are excluded or better regulated.

Ph. It is, however, true, as our author observes, that the scholastic method having been introduced also into conversations outside the schools, in order to shut the mouths of cavillers, has produced a bad effect. For, provided we have mediate ideas, we may have the connection without the aid of the maxims and before they have been produced, and that would be sufficient for sincere and tractable people. But the method of the schools having authorized and encouraged men in opposing and resisting evident truths until they are reduced to contradict themselves or to fight established principles, it is no wonder that in ordinary conversation they are not ashamed to do what in the schools is a subject of glory and counted a virtue. The author adds that reasonable people, among the rest of the world, who are not yet corrupted by education, will find it very difficult to believe that such a method has ever been followed by persons who make a profession of loving truth, and who pass their lives in studying religion or nature. I shall not inquire here (says he) how this method of instructing is fitted to turn away the minds of young people from the love of and sincere search for the truth, or rather to make them doubt if there really is any truth in the world, or at least any which deserves their adherence. But what I strongly think (he adds) is this, that excepting those places which have admitted the Peripatetic philosophy into their schools, where it has reigned many centuries without teaching the world anything but the art of disputation, these maxims are nowhere regarded as the foundations of the sciences nor as important aids to advancement in the knowledge of things.

Th. Your clever author will have it that the schools alone have been led to form maxims; but it is the general and very rational instinct of the human race. You can infer this from the proverbs which are in use among all nations, and which are usually only maxims which the public acknowledge. But when persons of judgment make a statement which appears to us contrary to the truth, we must do them the justice to suspect that there is a greater defect in their expressions than in their sentiments: a procedure confirmed here in our author, of whose motive animating him against the maxims, I begin to catch a glimpse. Cavilling, as well as the desire to be convinced in order to yield, exists as really in ordinary discourse, where there is no question of exercise, as in the schools; elsewhere most frequently they have the better grace to suppress the majors which are understood, and to be contented with enthymemes, and indeed without forming premises it is sufficient often to use the simple *medius terminus* or mediate idea, the mind understanding sufficiently its connection without expressing it.[1] And this is satisfactory when this bond is incontestable; but you, sir, will also agree with me that often we go too fast in assumption, and that paralogisms arise so that it would very often be better to have regard for certainty, in expressing ourselves, than to prefer thereto brevity and elegance. But the prejudice of your author against maxims

[1] Ordinarily in argumentation we omit one of the premises, usually the major, as easily understood and too clearly manifest to require statement. Sometimes, but less commonly, we omit the minor premise, and occasionally the conclusion, as in epigrams and other forms of wit, the whole point of which very often consists in making apparent the unexpressed truth. Leibnitz emphasizes the sufficiency of the middle term — *medius terminus* — or mediate idea, because through it, the common term in the premises expressing the particular reason in the given case, the conclusion is reached, whence the middle term is sometimes called *the argument*. The mind having grasped the particular reason expressed in this term, can easily supply the rest of the argument, and, if necessary, state it in due syllogistic form. — TR.

made him reject altogether their utility for the establishment of the truth, and goes as far as to make them accomplices with disorders in conversation. It is true that young people accustomed to academic exercises in which they are occupied a little too much with exercise and not enough in drawing from the exercise the greatest fruit it should have, viz.: knowledge, have some difficulty in emancipating themselves therefrom in the world. And one of their cavillings is not to wish to yield themselves to the truth save when it has been rendered entirely palpable to them, though *sincerity* and indeed *civility* should compel them not to wait for these extremes, which make them disagreeable and give a bad opinion of them. It must also be admitted that it is a vice with which men of letters are often found infected. But the fault is not in wishing to reduce truths to maxims, but in wishing to do it unseasonably and needlessly, for the human mind sees much at a glance, and it is to restrain it that we wish to compel it to stop at every step it takes and to express all that it thinks. It is precisely as if when making his account with a merchant or host one should compel him to reckon the whole with the fingers in order to be more certain of it. And to make that demand he must be either stupid or capricious. In fact, sometimes we find that Petronius had reason for saying *adolescentes in scholis stultissimos fieri*,[1] that young people sometimes become stupid and even harebrained in places, which ought to be schools of wisdom; *corruptio optimi pessima*.[2] But still oftener they become vain, blundering, and confused, whimsical, troublesome, and that often depends on the disposition of their masters. For the rest, I find that there are far greater faults in conversation than that of demanding too much clearness. For usually we fall into the opposite vice and neither give nor ask for enough of it. If the one is troublesome, the other is hurtful and dangerous.

[1] Petronius, *Satyricon*, chap. 1: "Et ideo ego adolescentulos existimo in scholis stultissimos fieri, quia nihil ex iis, quæ in usu habemus, aut audiunt, aut vident," etc. — TR.

[2] The phrase is not found in any classical author. It was perhaps suggested by Aristotle, *Politics*, Δ, 2, 1289[a], 39: ἀνάγκη γὰρ τὴν μὲν τῆς πρώτης καὶ θειοτάτης [πολιτείας] παρέκβασιν εἶναι χειρίστην, thus translated by Jowett, *The Politics of Aristotle*, Vol. 1, p. 109, Oxford: Clarendon Press, 1885: "That which is the perversion of the first and most divine [government] is necessarily the worst." — TR.

§ 12. *Ph.* The use of maxims is sometimes also, when attached to false notions, vague and uncertain; for then the maxims serve to confirm us in our errors, and even to prove contradictions. For example, he who with Descartes[1] forms an idea of what he calls *body*, as of a thing which is nothing but extension, may demonstrate easily by this maxim *what is, is*, that there is no vacuum, *i.e.* space without body. For he knows his own idea, he knows that it is what it is and not another idea; thus extension, body, and space being with him three words signifying one and the same thing, it is also as true for him to say, that space is body, as to say that body is body. § 13. But another for whom body signifies a solid extension, will conclude in the same way that to say: that space is not a body is as certain as any proposition we can prove by this maxim: *it is impossible for a thing to be and not to be at the same time.*

Th. The bad use of maxims should not cause their general use to be censured; all truths are liable to this disadvantage, that, by uniting them with falsehoods, false or even contradictory conclusions may be drawn. And in this example there is but little need of these identical axioms to which is imputed the cause of the error and contradiction. This would be seen if the argument of those who concluded from their definitions, that space is body, or that space is not body, were reduced to form. There is, indeed, something excessive in this inference: body is extended and solid, then extension, *i.e.* the extended is not body, and extension is not a corporeal thing; for I have already remarked that there are *superfluous expressions* of ideas, or those which do not multiply things, as if some one said, by *triquetrum* I mean a trilateral triangle, and concluded therefrom that every trilateral is not a triangle. Thus a Cartesian might say that the idea of a solid extension is of this same nature, *i.e.* that it is superfluous; as in reality, taking extension as something substantial, every extension will be solid, or rather every extension will be corporeal. As for the *vacuum*, a Cartesian will be right in concluding from his idea or *form of idea* that there is none, supposing his idea to be valid; but another will not be

[1] *Cf. Princip. Philos.*, II., §§ 1, 4, 11, Veitch's trans., pp. 232, 237, 8th ed., Edinburgh, 1881.—Tr.

right in concluding at once from his form that there may be a vacuum, as in reality, although I am not for the Cartesian view, I nevertheless think there is no vacuum,[1] and I find that in this example a worse use is made of *ideas* than of *maxims*.

§ 15. *Ph.* It seems at least that from such use as you would make of maxims in verbal propositions they cannot give us the least knowledge of substances existing outside us.

Th. I am altogether of another opinion. For example, this maxim that nature proceeds by the shortest paths, or at least by the most definite, suffices alone to give a reason for nearly the whole of optics, catoptric and dioptric, *i.e.* of what takes place outside us in the action of light, as I have formerly shown[2] and Molyneux has strongly approved in his Dioptric, which is a very excellent book.[3]

Ph. It is maintained, however, that when use is made of identical principles to prove propositions in which there are words signifying complex ideas as *man* or *virtue*, their use is extremely dangerous, and invites men to regard or receive falsehood as manifest truth. And this is because men think that when the same terms are retained the propositions revolve about the same things, although the ideas which these terms signify are different; so that men taking the words for the things, as they usually do, these maxims commonly serve to prove contradictory propositions.

Th. How unjust to blame the poor maxims for that which should be imputed to the bad use of terms and to their equivocations. By the same reasoning you will blame the syllogisms because they conclude badly when the terms are equivocal. But the syllogism is innocent, because in reality there are then four terms contrary to the rules of the syllogism. By the same reasoning you would also blame the calculations of arithmeticians, or of algebraists, because by putting *X* for *V* or by taking *a* for *b* by inadvertence, they draw therefrom false and contradictory conclusions.

[1] *Cf. ante*, p. 16, and *New Essays*, Bk. II., chap. 4, *ante*, pp. 125–127; also Descartes, *Princip. Philos.*, II., §§ 16 *sq.*, Veitch's trans., pp. 241 *sq.* — Tr.

[2] Leibnitz probably refers to his article *Unicum opticæ catoptricæ et dioptricæ principium*, published in the "Acta Erud. Lips.," June, 1682, pp. 185–190, and found in Dutens, 3, 145–150. — Tr.

[3] *Cf. ante*, p. 138, note 1. Molyneux's *Dioptrica nova* was for a long time the chief work on Optics. — Tr.

§ 19. *Ph.* I should think at least that maxims are of little use when we have clear and distinct ideas; and others will have it indeed that then they are absolutely of no use, and maintain that any one who in these instances cannot discern truth and falsehood without these kinds of maxims, will not be able to do so by their agency; and our author (§§ 16, 17) shows indeed that they are of no use in deciding whether such a one is a man or not.

Th. If the truths are very simple and evident, and closely approaching the identicals and the definitions, there is but little need of expressly employing maxims to draw from them these truths, for the mind virtually employs them and makes its conclusion all at once without intermediate ideas. But without axioms and theorems already known, mathematicians would have much trouble in advancing; for in long processes of reasoning (*consequences*), it is well to stop from time to time, and to set up, as it were, military columns in the midst of the road, which will serve furthermore to indicate it to others. Otherwise these long roads will be too inconvenient, and will appear even confused and obscure, while we are unable to discern anything, or to point out what place we are in. It is like going to sea without a compass in a dark night, seeing neither bottom, shore, nor stars; it is like travelling in vast moors in which there are neither trees nor hills nor streams; it is like a linked chain destined for the measurement of lengths, in which there are some hundreds of links, perfectly alike, without a distinction of a bead, or of coarser grains or of larger links or other divisions which might indicate the feet, fathoms, perches, etc. The mind which loves unity in multiplicity then joins together some of the consequences to form from them mediate conclusions, and this is the use of maxims and theorems. By this means there is more pleasure, more light, more memory, more application and less repetition. If some analyst in calculating should choose not to assume these two geometrical maxims, that the square on the hypothenuse is equal to the two squares of the sides about the right angle, and that the corresponding sides of similar triangles are proportional, thinking that, because we have the demonstration of these two theorems by the connection of the ideas they contain, he can pass them by easily by putting the ideas themselves in their place, he will find himself far removed from his reckoning. But that you may not think, sir, that the proper use of these maxims is confined to the limits of the mathematical sciences alone, you will find that its use is not less in jurisprudence, and one of the principal means of rendering it easier, and of looking at its vast ocean as upon a geographical map, is to reduce a multitude of particular decisions to more general principles. For example, you will find that a multitude of laws, of Digests, of actions or exceptions, of those which are called *in factum*,[1] depend on this maxim, *ne quis alterius damno fiat locupletior*,[2] let no one profit by the injury which might happen to another, a principle which should, however, be expressed with a little more precision. It is true that there is a great distinction to be made between the rules of law. I speak of good ones, and not of certain brocards (*brocardica*)[3] introduced by the doctors which are vague and obscure; although these rules also might often become good and useful, if reformed, while with their infinite distinctions (*cum suis fallentiis*) they serve only to confuse. Now good rules are either aphorisms or maxims, and under maxims I include both axioms and theorems. If these are *aphorisms* which are formed by induction and observation, and not by reason *a priori* and which clever people have made after a review of established law, this text of the jurisconsult Paulus in the title of the Digests, which speaks of the rules of law, has place: *non ex regula jus sumi*,

[1] *Cf. Digest.*, Lib. XLIV., Tit. VII., 25, Ulpianus, lib. singul. Regularum: "§ 1.—*In factum* actio dicitur, qualis est (exempli gratia) actio quæ datur patrono adversus libertum, a quo contra edictum prætoris in jus vocatus est."—Tr.

[2] For a similar expression, *cf. Digest.*, Lib. L., Tit. XVII., 206, Pomponius, lib. 9, ex variis Lectionibus: "Jure naturæ æquum est, neminem cum alterius detrimento et injuria fieri locupletiorem"; *Digest.*, Lib. XII., Tit. VI., 14; also Lib. XXIII., Tit. III., 6, Pomponius, lib. 14 ad Sabinum, § 2: ". . . quia bono et æquo non conveniat, aut lucrari aliquem cum damno alterius, aut damnum sentire per alterius lucrum"; Lib. XIV., Tit. III., 17, § 4, ad fin.—Tr.

[3] *Cf.* Letter 11, to Kestner, Jan. 30, 1711, § 2 (Dutens, 4, Pt. III., 264, also Kortholt, *Leibnit. epist. ad diversos*, Lips. 1734–1742, 3, 251): "Brocardica quæ vocant, vel sunt ipsa solida juris principia, vel regulæ, quædam topicæ: priora necessaria sunt: posteriores utiles forent, si satis examinatæ, explicatæque haberentur: pertinent enim fere ad facti quæstionem, artemque conjiciendi, ad quam refero etiam interpretandi artificium." *Cf.* also Leibnitz's *Nova methodus discendæ docendæque jurisprudentiæ*, Pt. II., § 25, Dutens, 4, Pt. III., 188–189.—Tr.

sed ex jure quod est regulam fieri,[1] *i.e.* we draw rules from a law already known, in order the better to remember them, but we do not establish the law upon these rules. But there are *fundamental maxims* constituting the law itself and forming actions, exceptions, replications, etc., which, when they are taught by pure reason, and do not arise from the arbitrary power of the state, constitute natural law; and such is the rule of which I have just spoken, which forbids tortious profit. There are also rules whose exceptions are rare, and which consequently pass as universal. Such is the rule of the Institutes of the Emperor Justinian in § 2 of the title Actions, which declares that when the question concerns corporeal things, the actor does not possess, except in a single case which the emperor states is indicated in the Digests; but he leaves us to search for it. It is true that some read instead of *sane uno casu, sane non uno;*[2] and from one case you can sometimes make many. Among the physicians the late Mr. Barner,[3] who, in giving us his *Prodromus,* made us hope for a new Sennertus,[4] or system of medicine accommodated

[1] *Cf. Digest.*, Lib. L., Tit. XVII., 1. Paulus [lib. 16 ad Plautium]: "Regula est, quæ rem, quæ est, breviter enarrat. Non ut ex regula jus sumatur, sed ex jure, quod est, regula fiat." Gerhardt's text omits the name Paulus, and his footnote states that there is a gap in the Ms. — TR.

[2] *Cf.* Sandars, *Inst. of Justinian*, Lib. IV., Tit. VI., *De actionibus*, § 2, *ad fin.* (p. 431, 8th ed., London, 1888): "Quod genus actionis in controversiis rerum corporalium proditum non est, nam in his is agit qui non possidet: ei vero qui possidet, non est actio prodita per quam neget rem actoris esse. Sane uno casu, qui possidet, nihilominus actoris partes obtinet, sicut in latioribus Digestorum libris opportunius apparebit." The reading "sane uno casu" is adopted and followed by the modern editors. The references to the Digests are, according to Sandars, Lib. VIII., 5, 2, Lib. XXXIX., 1, 15, ed. Mommsen, Berlin: Weidmann, 1870, pp. 267, 378. — TR.

[3] Jacob Barner, 1641–1686, a German physician, was professor of chemistry at Padua, and of philosophy and medicine at Leipzig, and the author or compiler of a large number of works which give a sufficiently faithful account of the medicine and especially the chemistry of his time, wholly occupied as it was in the chimerical search for the philosopher's stone. His *Prodromus Sennerti novi*, Augustæ Vindelicorum, 1674, 4to, was published as the prospectus of a proposed, but never completed, work, which, like that of Sennert, should cover the history of medicine from the earliest times to his own day. — TR.

[4] Daniel Sennert, 1572–1637, a celebrated German physician, was professor of medicine in the University of Wittemberg from 1602–1637, and introduced into its curriculum the teaching of chemistry, in spite of strong and continued opposition from those who thought it useless. He disputed the doctrine of the soul held by the Schoolmen, and by maintaining the immateriality of the souls of animals raised against himself many adversaries, among whom was Honora-

to the new discoveries or views, advances the opinion that the method which physicians ordinarily observe in their systems of practice is to explain the art of healing by treating of one disease after another following the order of the parts of the body human or other, without having given universal precepts of practice common to many diseases and symptoms, and that this involves them in an infinite number of repetitions; so that we might suppress, in his view, three-quarters of Sennertus, and abridge the science infinitely by universal propositions, and especially by those with which agrees the καθόλου πρῶτον of Aristotle,[1] *i.e.* which are reciprocal, or approach thereto. I think there is reason in advising this method, especially as regards the precepts wherein *medicine is ratiocinative;* but in proportion as it is *empirical,* it is not so easy nor so certain to form universal propositions. Further, there are usually complications in particular diseases, which form, as it were, an imitation of substances, so that a disease is like a plant or an animal, which demands a history by itself, *i.e.* they are *modes* or forms of being with which agrees what we have said of bodies or substantial things, a quartan[2] fever being as difficult to examine thoroughly as gold or quicksilver. Thus it is well, without detriment to the universal precepts, to seek in the

tus Fabri, who accused him of blasphemy and impiety, because he had not seen the bearing of his reasonings. Sennert protested that he had never maintained the immortality of the souls of animals, but it was a strict consequence of his principle.

In his *Institutiones medicæ et de origine animarum in brutis*, Wittemberg, 1611, 4to, Sennert endeavored to unite for the first time the principles of Galen (*cf. ante*, p. 407, note 1) with those of Paracelsus, 1493–1541. His *Opera omnia*, ed. novissima, Lugduni, 1676, 6 vols., fol. Sprengel says he was "the most celebrated of all the conciliators of the seventeenth century," "a man who united to immense erudition and to a perfect knowledge of the ancients great credulity, a taste little refined, and a weak judgment." — Tr.

[1] Aristotle limited scientific consideration to that which is universally or for the most part valid. His καθόλου πρῶτον is the universal in its original and proper sense, as the essential attribute of individual things in which alone it has any realization, and whose essence consists in just this realization of the universal in them. This universal is conceived of as the cause, and as such becomes the middle term in the syllogism, and constitutes the absolutely essential element in logical demonstration, in the absence of which the reasoning has no validity. *Cf.* Wallace, *Outlines of the Philos. of Aristotle*, 3d ed., §§ 23, 32–34, pp. 47, 64; Zeller, *Philos. d. Griech.* II. 2 [Vol. 4], 304 *sq.*, 3d ed.; Prantl, *Gesch. d. Logik*, 1, 104 *sq.*, 119 *sq.*; Windelband, *A Hist. of Philos.*, trans. by J. H. Tufts, Ph.D., 133–143. New York: Macmillan & Co., 1893. — Tr.

[2] *I.e.* a fever running in periods of four days. — Tr.

different kinds of diseases methods of healing, and remedies which satisfy many symptoms and complications of causes, and especially to gather together those which experience has approved. This Sennertus has not sufficiently done, for competent judges have remarked that the compositions of the receipts he proposes are often made more *ex ingenio* by estimate than authorized by experience, as would be necessary if one would be more certain of his case. I think then that the better course would be to unite these two ways, and not to complain of repetitions in a matter so delicate and so important as is medicine, wherein I find that we lack what we have in too large measure in my view in jurisprudence, *i.e.* books of particular cases, and repertories of observations already made. For I think that a thousandth part of the books of the jurisconsults would suffice us, but that we would have none too many in the matter of medicine, if we had thousands more of well-detailed observations. The fact is, jurisprudence is wholly based upon reasons in regard to which nothing is expressly indicated by laws or by customs. For we can always derive it either from law or, in default of this, from natural right by means of the reason. The laws of each country are finished and determined, or may become so; while in medicine, the principles of experience, *i.e.* the observations, cannot be too greatly multiplied in order to give more opportunity to the reason to decipher what nature only half allows us to know. For the rest, I do not know any one who employs the axioms in the way that the clever author of whom you speak does (§§ 16, 17), as if any one, in order to demonstrate to a child that a negro is a man, availed himself of the principle what is, is, by saying: a negro has a rational soul; now the rational soul and man is the same thing, and consequently if having a rational soul he were not a man, it would be false that what is, is, or rather one and the same thing would be or would not be at the same time. For without employing these maxims, which are not in season here, and do not enter directly into the reasoning, as they also do not advance it in any respect, everybody will be content to reason thus: a negro has a rational soul, whoever has a rational soul is a man, therefore the negro is a man. And if any one assuming that there is no rational soul if it does not appear to us, concluded that infants just born and imbeciles do not belong to the human species (as, in fact, the author states that he has conversed with very reasonable persons who made this denial), I do not think that the bad use of the maxim, that it is impossible for a thing to be and not to be, would delude them, nor that they think of it even in drawing this conclusion. The source of their error would be an extension of the principle of our author, which denies that there is anything in the soul of which it is not conscious, while these gentlemen would proceed as far as to deny the soul itself, when others did not perceive it.

CHAPTER VIII

OF TRIFLING PROPOSITIONS

Ph. I believe, indeed, that reasonable persons have not been disinclined to employ *identical* axioms in the way of which we have just spoken. § 2. It also seems that these purely identical maxims are only *trifling propositions* or *nugatoriæ*, as the schools indeed call them. I should not be content to say that they seem thus, did not your surprising example of *the demonstration of conversion* by the agency of the identicals[1] make me proceed, bridle in hand, thenceforth, when contempt for anything is the question. But I shall tell you that what you allege in their favor proclaims them wholly trifling; viz.: (§ 3) you recognize at first sight that they contain no instruction unless to show a man sometimes the absurdity in which he is involved.

Th. Do you count that as nothing, sir, and do you not recognize that to reduce a proposition to absurdity is to demonstrate its contradictory? I indeed believe that you will instruct no man by telling him that he must not deny and affirm the same thing at the same time, but you instruct him by showing him by the force of the consequence, that he does this without thinking of it. It is difficult, in my opinion, always to pass

[1] *Cf. New Essays*, Bk. IV., chap. 2, *ante*, p. 409.—TR.

from these *apagogical demonstrations, i.e.* demonstrations which reduce to absurdity, and to prove everything by *the ostensives,*[1] as they are called; and geometers, who are very curious on this point, have tried it sufficiently. Proclus speaks of it from time to time, when he sees that certain ancient geometers, coming after Euclid, have found a demonstration more direct (as they think) than his. But the silence of this ancient commentator sufficiently shows that they did not always accomplish it.

§ 3. *Ph.* You will at least admit, sir, that a million propositions may be formed at little expense, but also of very little use; for is it not trifling to remark, for example, that the oyster is the oyster, and that it is false to deny it, or to say that the oyster is not the oyster? As to which our author agreeably says that a man who would make this oyster sometimes the subject, sometimes the attribute, or the *predicatum,* would justly be like a monkey who should amuse himself by throwing one oyster from one hand to the other, which proceeding could altogether as well satisfy the hunger of the monkey as these propositions are capable of satisfying the understanding of man.

Th. I find that this author, as full of intelligence as gifted with judgment, has every reason in the world for speaking against those who would so use them. But you certainly see how the identicals must be employed to render them useful; viz.: by showing by force of consequences and definitions that other truths which you wish to establish reduce to them.

§ 4. *Ph.* I know it and I see clearly that they may be applied with much stronger reason to propositions which appear trifling and on many occasions are so, wherein a part of the complex idea is affirmed of the object of this idea, as in the statement: *lead is a metal.* In the mind of a man who is acquainted with the meaning of these terms and who knows that lead signifies a very heavy fusible and malleable body, there is this use alone, that in saying metal, you indicate to him at once many simple ideas instead of enumerating them one by one. § 5. The same is true when part of the defini-

[1] *I.e.* direct demonstrations, a term used as the opposite of the indirect or *apagogical* demonstrations, which show the truth of a thing by proving the absurdity of denying it. — TR.

tion is affirmed of the thing defined; as in the statement: *all gold is fusible*, supposing you have defined gold as a yellow, heavy, fusible, and malleable body. Again, to say that the triangle has three sides, that man is an animal, that a palfrey (*palefroy*, an old French word) is an animal which neighs, serves to define the words, but not to teach anything besides the definition. But we learn something from the statement that man has a notion of God and that opium plunges him into sleep.

Th. Besides what I have said of the identicals which are wholly so, we shall find that these semi-identicals have also a particular use. For example, *a wise man is always a man;* that gives us the knowledge that he is not infallible, that he is mortal, etc. Some one in danger needs a pistol-ball, and lacks the lead to found it in the form he has; a friend says to him: remember that the *silver* you have in your purse is *fusible;* this friend will not teach him a quality of the silver, but will make him think of a use he may make of it, in order to have pistol-balls in this pressing need. A large part of *moral truths* and of the most beautiful *sentences* of authors is of this nature: they very often teach us nothing, but they make us think at the right time of what we know. That iambic senarius of the Latin tragedy,—

Cuivis potest accidere, quod cuiquam potest,[1]

which might be expressed thus, although less prettily: that which may happen to one, may happen to everybody, only makes us remember the human condition, *quod nihil humani a nobis alienum putare debemus.*[2] This rule of the jurisconsults: *qui jure suo utitur, nemini facit injuriam*[3] (he who uses his

[1] Publilius Syrus, in Seneca, *De Tranquillitate*, chap. 11. — Tr.

[2] *Cf.* Terence, *Heauton.* 1. 1. 23–25: "Homo sum; humani nihil a me alienum puto." — Tr.

[3] Schaarschmidt states that this rule of the jurisconsults comes from the "*Regulæ et præcepta juris*," which were customarily appended to the older editions of the *Institutiones*. The exact phrase does not occur in the *Corpus Juris Civilis;* but *cf.* Digest, Lib. XXXIX., Tit. II., 24, *ad fin.*, where Trebatius says: "non teneri me damni infecti: neque enim existimari, operis mei vitio damnum tibi dari in ea re, in qua jure meo usus sum"; *ib.* 26: "Proculus ait, cum quis jure quid in suo faceret," etc.; Digest, Lib. L., Tit. XVII., 55, where Gaius says: "Nullus videtur dolo facere, qui suo jure utitur"; *ib.* 129, where Paulus says: "Nihil dolo creditor facit, qui suum recipit." — Tr.

own right, injures no one) appears trifling. But it is very useful on certain occasions and makes one justly think of what is necessary. If, for instance, any one raised his house as far as he is allowed by the statutes and usages, and by so doing deprived his neighbor of some view, he would pay this neighbor at once, according to this rule of law, if he ventured to complain. For the rest, propositions of fact, or experiences, like that which states that opium is a narcotic, carry us farther than the truths of pure reason, which can never make us go beyond that which is in our distinct ideas.[1] As for this proposition, that every man has a notion of God, it is from the reason, since notion signifies idea. For the idea of God, according to my view, is innate in all men: but if this notion signifies an idea in which you actually think it, it is a proposition of fact which depends on the history of the human race. § 7. Finally, to say that a triangle has three sides is not so identical as it seems, for a little attention is required to see that a polygon must have as many angles as sides; it would also have an additional side, if the polygon were not supposed to be closed.

§ 9. *Ph.* It seems that the general propositions concerning substances are for the most part trifling, if they are certain. He who knows the meanings of the words: substance, man, animal, form, soul, vegetative, sensitive, rational, will form from them many indubitable but useless propositions, particularly about the soul, of which we often speak without knowing what it really is. Every one may see an infinite number of propositions, reasonings, and conclusions of this nature in the books of metaphysics, scholastic theology, and a certain kind of physics, the reading of which will teach him nothing more of God, spirits, and bodies than he knew before having run through these books.

Th. It is true, that abstracts of metaphysics and such other books of this character as are commonly seen, teach only words. To say, for example, that metaphysics is the *science* of being in general, which explains the principles and affections emanating from it; that the principles of being are

[1] Truths of fact furnish occasion for inductive conclusions which enlarge our knowledge; while truths of reason can only be explicated, or made clearer as to their already existing content. — TR.

essence and existence; that the affections are either primitive, viz.: unity, truth, the good, or derivative, viz.: identity, diversity, simplicity, complexity, etc., and, in speaking of each of these terms, to give only vague notions and verbal distinctions is indeed to abuse the name of *science*. But we must render this justice to the more profound Scholastics, like Suarez[1] (whom Grotius valued so highly) and admit that there is sometimes in them discussions of value, as upon the continuum, the infinite, the contingent, the reality of abstracts, the principles of individuation, the *origo et vacuum formarum*, the soul and its faculties, the concurrence of God with his creatures, etc., and even in ethics, upon the nature of the will and the principles of justice; in a word, we must admit that there is still some gold in these scoriæ, but it is only enlightened persons who can profit from it; and to load the youth with the rubbish of inutilities, because there is something of value here and there, would be badly to dispose of the most precious of all things, time. For the rest, we are not wholly destitute of general propositions regarding substances which are certain, and deserve to be known; there are grand and beautiful truths concerning God and the soul which

[1] Francisco Suarez, 1548–1617, a famous Jesuit and a distinguished philosopher, theologian, and philosophical jurist, was "the last great Scholastic." In philosophy he was a moderate Thomist. As a theologian, he advocated the system known as "congruism." In his *Tractatus de legibus ac Deo legislatore*, reprinted, London, 1679, wherein he was to a certain extent the forerunner of Grotius and Pufendorf, he maintained the theory of conditional obedience to authority. For an account of his views on natural law and sovereignty, *cf.* Larousse, *Grande Dict. Univ. de XIXe Siècle*, Vol. 14, pp. 1164 c–1165 a; for his "congruism," *ibid.*, Vol. 4, p. 934 a. His *Opera omnia*, 23 vols., fol., appeared at Mainz and Lyons, 1630 *sq.*, Venice, 1640, new revised ed., 26 vols., 8vo, Besançon and Paris, 1856–62. The most important of his works are, perhaps, the *Disputationes metaphysicæ*, 1605, and the *Tract. de leg.*, cited above. For an account of his philosophy, *cf.* Stöckl, *Gesch. de Philos. d. Mittelalters*, III. [Vol. 4], 634 *sq.*, and K. Werner, *Suarez u. d. Scholastik d. letzten Jahrhunderte*, Regensburg, 1861.

Huig van Groot — Latin, Hugo Grotius — *cf. ante*, p. 285, note 1, one of the founders of the philosophy of law, in his theological writings occasionally cites Suarez as an authority; *cf.*, for example, *Opera omnia theologica*, Amsterdam, 1679, Vol. 4, pp. 206, a, 50, 621, a, 54; and in his *Epistolæ ad Gallos*, epist. 154 ad Joa. Cordesium, p. 335, ed. Leipzig, 1674, and new ed. 1684, also *Epistolæ quotquot reperiri potuerunt*, epist. 329, p. 118, Amsterdam, 1687, praises him thus: "Quorsum tantus Suarezii contemtus? hominis, si quid recte judico, in philosophia cui hoc tempore connexa est scholastica, tantæ subtilitatis, ut vix quemquam habeat parem?" — Tr.

our clever author has taught either in his own right or in part after others. We have perhaps added something also thereto. And as for general knowledge concerning bodies, considerable additions are being made to what Aristotle left, and it should be said that physics, even general physics, has become much more real than it was heretofore. As for real metaphysics, we are beginning, as it were, to establish it, and we find important truths grounded in reason and confirmed by experience, which belong to substances in general. I hope, also, that I have advanced a little the general knowledge of the soul and of spirits. Such a metaphysic was the demand of Aristotle, it is the science which he called Ζητουμένη, the desired (*la desirée*) or that which he sought, which must be as regards the other theoretic sciences what the science of happiness is to the arts which it needs, and what the architect is to the workmen. This is why Aristotle said that the other sciences depend upon metaphysics as the most general science and must derive from it their principles, demonstrated by it.[1] You must know also that true ethics is to metaphysics what practice is to theory, because upon the doctrine of substances in common depends the knowledge of spirits and particularly of God and the soul which gives a proper meaning to justice and virtue. For as I have elsewhere[2] remarked, if there were neither providence nor a future life, the wise man would be more limited in the practice of virtue, for he would refer everything merely to his present satisfaction, and even this satisfaction, which appears already in Socrates, in the emperor Marcus Aurelius, in Epictetus and other ancients,[3]

[1] *Cf.* Aristotle, *Metaphys.*, A, 2, 982ª–983ª, the object of which is to prove the dependence of the other sciences upon metaphysics, and in which the term ζητεῖν frequently occurs in this specific sense; *cf.* especially 982ᵇ, 7, 8: ἐξ ἁπάντων οὖν τῶν εἰρημένων ἐπὶ τὴν αὐτὴν ἐπιστήμην πίπτει τὸ ζητούμενον ὄνομα. For the comparison to the architect, *cf.* 1, 981ª, 30. — TR.

[2] Leibnitz refers perhaps to what he said in *New Essays*, Bk. I., chap. 2, § 2, Th. (2), *ante*, pp. 86–87; or in the Preface to his *Codex juris gentium diplomaticus*, § 13 (Dutens, 4, Pt. III., 296): "Ut vero universali demonstratione conficiatur, omne honestum esse utile, et omne turpe damnosum, assumenda est immortalitas animæ, et rector universi Deus," etc. — TR.

[3] Marcus Aurelius Antoninus, 121–180, the noblest of the Roman Emperors, whose *Meditations* or *Thoughts* exhibit the Stoic philosophy at its best on the moral and religious side, and present a morality nearer to that of the New Testament than that of any other pagan writer. Eds. of the Greek Text τὰ εἰς αὑτον by J. M. Schultz, Leipzig, 1802, reprinted by Tauchnitz, 1821, and

would not be so well grounded always without these beautiful and grand views which the order and harmony of the universe open for us even in a future without limits; otherwise the tranquillity of the soul would be only what is called a forced patience, so that we may say that *natural theology*, comprising two parts, theoretical and practical, contains altogether real metaphysics and the most perfect ethics.[1]

§ 12. *Ph.* There is doubtless knowledge which is far re-

by J. Stich, Leipzig, 1882. Eng. trans., *The Thoughts of the Emperor M. Aurelius Antoninus*, by Geo. Long, revised ed. in Bohn's Class. Library; also Boston: Ticknor and Fields, 1864. On his life and philosophy, *cf.* Zeller, *Philos. d. Griech.*, III., 1 [Vol. 5], 754–763, 3d ed., 1880; Capes, *Stoicism* (in series of "Chief Anct. Philosophies," pub. by the Soc. for promoting Christian Knowledge), chap. 13, pp. 200–239, London, 1880; F. W. Farrar, *Seekers after God*, pp. 257–317, London, Macmillan & Co., 1877.

Epictetus, the date of whose birth and death is unknown, lived in Rome under Nero, 54–68, and his successors, and, when Domitian in 94 banished all philosophers from the Imperial City, went to Nicopolis in Epirus, and there taught till his death, which appears to have occurred in the reign of Trajan, 98–117, or shortly after. At first a slave, but afterwards a freedman, he represented Stoicism in the cottage, while in Aurelius we see it on the throne. He left no writings, but his discourses, Διατριβαί, were carefully taken down as far as possible in his own words as he uttered them, by his pupil and admirer Arrian. The best ed. is that by Schweighäuser, 6 vols., 8vo, Leipzig, 1799–1800. Eng. trans., *The Discourses of Epictetus, with the Encheiridion and Fragments*, by Geo. Long, in Bohn's Class. Library; also by T. W. Higginson, Boston: Little, Brown & Co., 1865. On his life and philosophy, *cf.* Zeller, *Philos. d. Griech.*, III., 1 [Vol. 5], 738–754, 3d ed., 1880; Capes, *Stoicism*, chap. 12, pp. 180–199; Farrar, *Seekers after God*, pp. 186–256, London, 1877. — TR.

[1] The old scholasticism made natural theology a part of metaphysics, which included besides natural theology, ontology, cosmology, and psychology. *Cf.* Thos. Aquinas, *Summa Theol.*, Pt. I., Quest. 1, Art. 1, *ad fin.*: "Unde theologia, quæ ad sacram doctrinam pertinet, differt secundum genus ab illa theologia quæ pars philosophiæ ponitur." Leibnitz, in a writing without place or date, which Gerhardt (*Leibniz. philos. Schrift.*, 4, 268, note **) thinks was undoubtedly addressed to the Duchess Sophie, says (G. *op. cit.*, 4, 292, and Foucher de Careil, *Nouvelles lettres et opuscules de Leibniz inédits*, Paris, 1857, p. 25): "En effect la metaphysique est la théologie naturelle, et le même Dieu qui est la source de tous les biens, est aussi le principe de toutes les connoissances." *Cf.* also *Discours de metaphys.*, § 28, G. 4, 453.

Leibnitz finds the source of ethical truths in natural theology, because God, the idea of whom is the subject of natural theology, is also the object of man's highest moral aspiration and effort, so far as he seeks lovingly to comprehend him, a point of view from which Leibnitz sought to develop the ethical conceptions published under the title of *Definitiones ethicæ*, G. 7, 73 *sq.*, Erdmann, 670, trans. Duncan, *Philos. Wks. of Leibnitz*, 130, and which controls the thought-development in the Preface to the *Codex juris gentium diplomaticus*, *cf.* § 13, Dutens, 4, Pt. III., 296, in the *Théodicée*, Preface, G. 6, 26–28, E. 469, Jacques, 2, 3–4, Janet, 2, 3–4, and in the *Discours de metaphys.*, §§ 2–4, 35–37, G. 4, 427–430, 460–463. — TR.

moved from being trifling or purely verbal. But this last seems to be that in which two abstracts are affirmed the one of the other; for example, that *parsimony is frugality*, that *gratitude is justice;* and however specious these and other propositions sometimes appear at first sight, yet when we press their force, we find that it all amounts to nothing else than the signification of the terms.

Th. But the significations of terms, *i.e.* definitions united with identical axioms, express the principles of all demonstrations: and as these definitions can make known at the same time the ideas and their possibility, it is plain that what depends on them is not always purely verbal. As for the example that *gratitude is justice*, or rather a part of justice, it is not to be despised, for it shows that what is called *actio ingrati*,[1] or the complaint which can be made against the ungrateful, should be less neglected in the tribunals. The Romans received this action against the Liberti,[2] or freedmen, and still to-day it should have place as regards the revocation of gifts. For the rest, I have already said elsewhere[3] that abstract ideas also may be attributed to one another, the genus to the species, as in the statements: *duration is a continuity, virtue is a habit;* but universal justice is not only a virtue, but it is indeed the complete ethical virtue.

CHAPTER IX

OF OUR KNOWLEDGE OF OUR EXISTENCE[4]

§ 1. *Ph.* We have hitherto considered only the essences of things, and as our mind knows them only by *abstraction*, by detaching them from every particular existence, other than that which is in our understanding, they give us absolutely no knowledge of any real existence. And the universal prop-

[1] *Cf. Cod. Justin.*, 8, 56, 1, 8, and 10.—TR.

[2] Gerhardt, Erdmann, and Janet read "les libertes"; Jacques reads "les libérés."—TR.

[3] *Cf.* Bk. III., chap. 3, § 10, Th., *ante*, p. 313.—TR.

[4] Locke's title is, "Of our knowledge of existence," *Philos. Works*, Vol. 2, p. 228, Bohn's ed.—TR.

ositions of which we may have a certain knowledge, do not relate to existence. Further, every time we attribute anything to an individual of a genus or a species by a proposition, which would not be certain if the same were attributed to the genus or species in general, the proposition belongs only to the existence and makes known only an accidental union in the things existing in particular, as when we say, such a man is learned.

Th. Very well, and it is in this sense that the philosophers also, distinguishing so often between what is *essence* and what *existence,* refer to existence everything which is *accidental* or *contingent.* Very often we do not even know whether the universal propositions, which we know only by experience, are not perhaps accidental also, because our experience is limited; as in the countries where water is not frozen, this proposition which will be formed about it, that water is always in a fluid state, is not essential, and we know it by coming into colder countries. But we may take *the accidental* in a more limited sense, so that there will be, as it were, a mean between it and *the essential;* and this mean is *the natural* (*le naturel*), *i.e.* that which does not belong to the thing necessarily, but which, nevertheless, agrees with it of itself if nothing prevents. Thus, some one might maintain that it is not indeed essential, but that it is at least natural, for water to remain fluid. We might maintain this, I say, but it is not, however, a demonstrated fact, and perhaps the inhabitants of the moon, if there are any, would have reason to believe the statement no less grounded that it is natural for water to be frozen. There are other cases, however, where the natural is less doubtful; for example, a ray of light always continues straight in the same medium unless it accidentally meets some surface which reflects it. For the rest, Aristotle was accustomed to refer to matter the source of *accidental* things;[1] but then we must understand thereby secondary matter, *i.e.* the heap or mass of bodies.

§ 2. *Ph.* I have already[2] remarked, following the excellent English author who wrote the Essay concerning Understanding, that we know *our existence* by intuition, that *of God* by

[1] *Cf. Metaphys.*, E, 2, 1027[a], 14: ὥστε ἡ ὕλη ἔσται αἰτία ἡ ἐνδεχομένη παρὰ τὸ ὡς ἐπὶ τὸ πολὺ ἄλλως τοῦ συμβεβηκότος. — TR.

[2] *Cf.* Bk. IV., chap. 3, § 21, *ante*, p. 439. — TR.

demonstration, and that *of other things* by sensation. § 3. Now this intuition which makes known our existence to ourselves, makes it known to us with an evidence complete, incapable of being proved and having no need of proof; so that even when I attempt to doubt all things, this doubt itself does not allow me to doubt my own existence. In fine, we have on this point the highest degree of certainty that can be imagined.

Th. I am entirely agreed as to all this. And I add that the immediate apperception of our existence and of our thoughts furnishes us the first truths *a posteriori*, or of fact, *i.e.* the *first experiences*, as the identical propositions contain the first truths *a priori*, or of reason, *i.e. the first lights* (*les premières lumières*).[1] Both are incapable of proof, and may be called *immediate;* the former, because they are immediate between the understanding and its object; the latter, because they are intermediate between the subject and the predicate.

CHAPTER X

OF OUR KNOWLEDGE OF THE EXISTENCE OF GOD

§ 1. *Ph.* God having given to our soul the faculties with which it is adorned, has not left himself without a witness; for the senses, perception, and the reason furnish us manifest proofs of his existence.

Th. God has not only given the soul faculties suitable for knowing him, but he has also impressed upon it characters which indicate him, although the soul needs faculties to perceive these characters. But I do not wish to repeat the discussions we have already had upon ideas and innate truths, among which I reckon the idea of God and the truth of his existence. Let us come rather to the fact.

Ph. Now, although the existence of God is the truth most easily proved by the reason, and its evidence equals, if I am not mistaken, that of mathematical demonstrations, it yet demands attention. It needs at once only reflection upon

[1] Schaarschmidt translates: "die ersten Erleuchtungen aus dem Innern," *i.e.* the first illuminations from within. — TR.

ourselves and our own indubitable existence. § 2. Thus I suppose that *every one knows that something actually exists*, and that thus there is a real being. If there is any one who can doubt his own existence, I declare that I do not speak to him. § 3. We know also by an intuitive knowledge that *bare nothing cannot produce a real being*. Whence it follows, with mathematical evidence, that *something has existed from all eternity*, since everything which has a beginning must have been produced by something else. § 4. Now every being which draws its existence from another, draws also from it all it has, and all its faculties. The eternal source of all beings is then also the principle of all their powers, so that *this eternal being must be also all-powerful*. § 5. Further, man finds in himself knowledge. *There is*, then, *an intelligent being*. Now it is impossible for a thing absolutely destitute of knowledge and perception to produce an intelligent being, and it is contrary to the idea of matter, deprived of thought, to produce it of itself. The source of things is then intelligent, and *there has been an intelligent being from all eternity*. § 6. An eternal, very powerful, and very intelligent being is what we call *God*. If, however, any one were found so unreasonable as to suppose that man is the only being having knowledge and wisdom, but that, nevertheless, he has been formed by pure chance, and that it is this same principle, blind and without knowledge, which carries on all the rest of the universe, I shall advise him to examine at his leisure the wholly solid and emphatic censure of Cicero ("De Legibus," lib. 2). Certainly, he says, no one could be so foolishly arrogant as to think that he has within himself an understanding and reason, and yet that there is no intelligence governing the heavens and all this vast universe.[1] From what I have just said it clearly follows that we have a more certain knowledge of God than of anything else outside us.

Th. I assure you, sir, with perfect sincerity, that I am extremely sorry to be obliged to say something against this demonstration; but I do it solely in order to give you an opportunity to fill up the void. It is principally in the part

[1] Cicero, *De Leg.*, Bk. II., chap. 7: "Quid est enim verius, quam neminem esse oportere tam stulte arrogantem, ut in se rationem et mentem putet inesse, in cœlo mundoque non putet? Aut ut ea quæ vix summa ingenii ratione comprehendat, nulla ratione moveri putet?" — TR.

where you conclude (§ 3) that something has existed from all eternity. I find therein some ambiguity, if that means *that there never has been any time in which nothing existed.* I admit it, and it follows truly from the preceding propositions by an inference wholly mathematical. For if there had always been nothing, there would always have been nothing, nothing being unable to produce a being; then we ourselves should not be, which is contrary to the first truth of experience. But the consequence appears at once, that by the statement that something has existed from all eternity, you mean an eternal thing. But it does not at all follow in virtue of what you have hitherto advanced, that if there has always been something, there has always been a certain thing, *i.e.* an eternal being. For certain opponents will say that I have been produced by other things, and these things by others. Further, if some admit eternal beings (as the Epicureans their atoms) they will not think themselves compelled for that reason to admit an eternal being who is the only source of all the others. For if they should admit that this which gives existence, gives also the other qualities and powers of the thing, they will deny that a single thing gives existence to the others, and they will say also that in each thing many others must concur. Thus we shall not reach by this alone a source of all the powers. Yet it is very reasonable to judge that there is one, and also that the universe is governed with wisdom. But when we believe matter susceptible of thought, we may be disposed to believe that it is not impossible that it may produce something. At least it will be difficult to bring forward a proof which does not show at the same time that it is wholly incapable of it; and, assuming that our thought comes from a thinking being, may we take it as admitted, without prejudice to the demonstration, that this must be God?

§ 7. *Ph.* I do not doubt that the excellent man from whom I have borrowed this demonstration is capable of perfecting it; and I shall try to influence him to do so, since he could scarcely render a greater service to the public. You also desire it. This makes me think that you do not consider it necessary, in order to shut the mouths of atheists, to make everything revolve upon the existence of the idea of God in us, as some do, who attach themselves too strongly to this favorite discovery even to rejecting all other demonstrations of the existence of God,[1] or at least attempting to weaken them and forbidding to employ them as if they were weak or false; although at bottom they are proofs which show us so clearly and in a manner so convincing the existence of this sovereign being by the consideration of our own existence, and of the sensible parts of the universe, that I think no wise man ought to resist them.

Th. Although I am for innate ideas, and in particular for that of God, I do not think that the demonstrations of the Cartesians drawn from the idea of God are perfect. I have shown fully elsewhere[2] (in the "Actes de Leipsic," and in the "Memoires de Trevoux") that what Descartes has borrowed from Anselm,[3] Archbishop of Canterbury, is very beau-

[1] Descartes relied mainly, and Spinoza exclusively, on the ontological or *a priori* argument for the proof of God's existence. Spinoza's system, in fact, did not admit the possibility of any other argument, since God is the only substance and all other things are merely modes, accidents, or expressions of that substance. *Cf.* Descartes, *Meditations*, III. and V., Veitch's trans., pp. 115 *sq.*, 143 *sq.*, *Princip. Philos.*, Pt. I., §§ 13 *sq.*, Veitch, pp. 198 *sq.*, *Discours de la Methode*, Pt. IV., Veitch, pp. 34 *sq.*; Spinoza, *Ethica*, Pt. I., ed. Van Vloten and Land, Vol. 1, pp. 39 *sq.*, trans. Elwes, Vol. 2, pp. 45 *sq.*; letter to De Vries, V. V. & L., 2, 34, trans. E. 2, 315. Also on Descartes, Windelband, *Hist. of Philos.*, trans. by Tufts, 392–3, 405; on Spinoza, *ibid.*, 401, 407–10. Leibnitz, while seeking to correct and complete the ontological argument, makes the teleological form of the *a posteriori* argument, in his doctrine of monads and their preestablished harmony, one of the constituent principles of his system. *Cf. Confessio naturæ contra atheistas*, 1668, Gerhardt, 4, 105–109, Erdmann, 45–47, Dutens, 1, 5–8; *Principes de la nature et de la grâce*, §§ 11 *sq.*, G. 6, 603, E. 716, trans. Duncan, 214, *Monadologie*, §§ 38 *sq.*, G. 6, 613, E. 708, trans. D., 223. Leibnitz's doctrine of monads demands the existence of God as its necessary ground and complement. *Cf. ante*, p. 363, note 1. He regarded all the arguments for God's existence as valuable and urged men to perfect them. *Cf. infra*, p. 505, note 2. On his doctrine, *cf.* Windelband, *op. cit.*, 420–425. — TR.

[2] Leibnitz means the *Med. de Cog., Ver. et Id.*, published in the "Acta Erud. Lips.," Nov., 1684, and found in Gerhardt, 4, 422, Erdmann, 79, Dutens, 2, Pt. I., 14, Janet, 2, 514 (in French), trans. Duncan, 27; and the *De la démonstration Cartesienne*, etc., published in the "Mémoires de Trévoux," 1701, G. 4, 405, E. 177, Dutens, 2, Pt. I., 254, Janet, 2, 568, trans. Duncan, 136.—TR.

[3] Anselm, 1033–1109, archbishop of Canterbury from 1093 till his death, and the real founder of the Christian Scholasticism of the Middle Age, was a distinguished philosopher and theologian, whose fame rests chiefly upon his ontological or *a priori* argument for the existence of God, and his theory of the incarnation and atonement. His *Opera* are found in Migne, *Patrol. Cur. Compl.*, Vol. 155. The most important for philosophy are the *Cur Deus Homo?*, the *Monologium*, and the *Proslogium*. The two latter, with Gaunilo's

tiful and really very ingenious, but that there is still a gap therein to be filled. This celebrated archbishop, who was without doubt one of the most able men of his time, congratulates himself, not without reason, for having discovered a means of proving the existence of God *a priori*, by means of its own notion, without recurring to its effects. And this is very nearly the force of his argument: God is the greatest, or (as Descartes says) the most perfect of beings, or rather a being of supreme grandeur and perfection, including all degrees thereof. That is the notion of God. See now how existence follows from this notion. To exist is something more than not to exist, or rather, existence adds a degree to grandeur and perfection, and as Descartes states it, existence is itself a perfection. Therefore this degree of grandeur and perfection, or rather this perfection which consists in existence, is in this supreme all-great, all-perfect being: for otherwise some degree would be wanting to it, contrary to its definition. Consequently this supreme being exists. The Scholastics, not excepting even their Doctor Angelicus,[1] have misunder-

refutation of the *Proslogium*, entitled *Liber pro insipiente*, and Anselm's reply, *Liber apologeticus*, were edited by C. Haas, Tübingen, 1863. There is a French trans., with notes, of the *Monologium* and *Proslogium* by Bouchitté, *Le Rationalisme Chrétien*, Paris, 1842; and an English trans. of the *Proslogium* and *Lib. apologet.* in the "Bibliotheca Sacra," Vol. 8 [1851], pp. 529 *sq.*, 704 *sq.*, and of the *Cur Deus Homo?*, *ibid.*, Vol. 11 [1854], pp. 729 *sq.*, 12 [1855], 52 *sq.* His ontological argument is found in the *Proslogium* and the *Liber apologeticus.* An excellent account of it is given in Ueberweg-Heinze, *Gesch. d. Philos.*, 7th ed., Berlin, 1888, Vol. 2, p. 152 *sq.*, Eng. trans. from 4th German ed., New York, 1871, Vol. 1, pp. 383–86. *Cf.* also Windelband, *Hist. of Philos.*, trans. by Tufts, pp. 291–294; Mulford, *The Republic of God*, pp. 4, 5, 4th ed., Boston, 1882. For further account of Anselm's life and philosophy, *cf.* Hasse, *Anselm von Canterbury*, 2 vols., Leipzig, 1843, 1852 (ontolog. argt. in Vol. 2, pp. 233–286); Stöckl, *Gesch. d. Philos. d. Mittelalters*, 1, 151–208; Hauréau, *Histoire de la Philos. Scholastique*, Paris, 1872–80, 1, 265–87.

For expositions and criticisms of the ontological argument, *cf.* Kant, *Krit. d. r. Vernunft.*, ed. Rosenkranz and Schubert, 2, 462–470, ed. Hartenstein, 1838, 2, 456–464, 1867, 3, 405–411, ed. Kirchman, Leipzig, 1877, 1, 476–483, trans. Müller, 1 vol. ed., 509–518; E. Caird, *The Philos. of Kant*, Glasgow, 1877, 630, 642, *The Crit. Philos. of Kant*, New York, 1889, 2, 110, 120; Hegel, *Vorlesungen ü. d. Beweise vom Dasein Gottes*, in his *Philos. d. Relig.*, Anhang, 2, 357 *sq.*, 2d ed., Berlin, 1840; Dorner, *Christ. Glaubenslehre*, 1, 201 *sq.*, Eng. trans., 1, 214 *sq.*; Pfleiderer, *Philos. d. Relig.*, 2, 271 *sq.*, 2d ed., Berlin, 1884, Eng. trans., 3, 271 *sq.* — TR.

[1] *I.e.* Thomas Aquinas, 1225 or 1227–1274. For his critique of the ontological argument, *cf.* *Summa theologiæ*, Pt. I., Quest. 2, Article 1; *Contra gentiles*, Bk. I., chap. 11; and Stöckl, *Gesch. d. Philos. d. Mittelalters*, II., 1 [Vol.

stood this argument, and have taken it as a paralogism; in which respect they were altogether wrong, and Descartes, who studied quite a long time the scholastic philosophy at the Jesuit College of La Fleche, had great reason for re-establishing it. It is not a paralogism, but it is an imperfect[1] demonstration, which assumes something that must still be proved in order to render it mathematically evident; that is, it is tacitly assumed that this idea of the all-great or all-perfect being is possible, and implies no contradiction. And it is already something that by this remark it is proved that, *assuming that God is possible, he exists,* which is the privilege of divinity alone. We have the right to presume the possibility of every being, and especially that of God, until some one proves the contrary. So that this metaphysical argument already gives a morally demonstrative conclusion, which declares that according to the present state of our knowledge we must judge that God exists, and act in conformity thereto. But it is to be desired, nevertheless, that clever men achieve the demonstration with the strictness of a mathematical proof, and I think I have elsewhere[2] said something that may serve this end. The other argument of Descartes, which undertakes to prove the existence of God because the idea of him is in our soul, and must have come from the original, is still less conclusive. For in the first place this argument has this defect, in common with the preceding, that it assumes that there is in us such an idea, *i.e.* that God is possible. For what Descartes alleges, that in speaking of God we know what we

2], 498. Spinoza also censures Aquinas for his rejection of the ontological argument; *cf. Korte Verhandeling van God*, in Spinoza, *Opera*, ed. Van Vloten and Land, Vol. 2, p. 265, and Schaarschmidt's German trans. of the same (Vol. 18 of J. H. v. Kirchmann's *Philos. Bibliothek*), p. 6, 2d ed., Berlin, 1874. — TR.

[1] Gerhardt reads "parfaite"; Erdmann, Jacques, and Janet "imparfaite." The reading of G. is evidently a Ms. or typographical error, as the sense requires that of E., J., and J. — TR.

[2] Leibnitz here probably refers to the *De la démonstration Cartesienne*, etc., 1701, Gerhardt, 4, 405, Erdmann, 177, Dutens, 2, Pt. I., 254, trans. Duncan, 136. But *cf.* also G. 4, 292–294, 401–403, trans. Duncan, 132–136; *Animadversiones in partem generalem Principiorum Cartesianorum*, 1692, Pt. I., ad art. 14, 18, 20, G. 4, 358–60, trans. Duncan, 50–51, and Letters to Jacquelot, Nov., 1702, G. 3, 442 *sq.*, Letter to Conring, Jan. 3, 1678, G. 1, 188, E. 78; correspondence with Eckhard, G. 1, 212 *sq.*; and Stein, *Leibniz u. Spinoza*, Beilage VII., p. 306: *Probatio existentiæ Dei ex ejus essentia.* — TR.

are saying, and that consequently we have an idea, is a deceptive indication, since in speaking of perpetual mechanical movement, for example, we know what we are saying, and yet this movement is an impossible thing, of which, consequently, we can have only an apparent idea. Secondly, this same argument does not sufficiently prove that the idea of God, if we have it, must come from the original. But I do not wish to delay here at present. You will say, sir, to me, that recognizing in us the innate idea of God, I ought not to say that we may question whether there is one. But I permit this doubt only in relation to a strict demonstration based upon the idea alone. For we are otherwise sufficiently assured of the idea and of the existence of God. And you will remember that I have shown how ideas are in us, not always in such wise that we are conscious of them, but always in such wise that we may draw them from our own depths and make them perceivable. And this is also my belief concerning the idea of God, the possibility and existence of which I hold to be demonstrated in more than one way. And the *pre-established harmony* itself furnishes a new and incontestable means of so doing.[1] I believe also that nearly all the means which have been employed to prove the existence of God are good and might be of service, if we would perfect them, and I am not at all of the opinion that we should neglect that drawn from the order of things.[2]

§ 9. *Ph.* It will perhaps be proper to insist a little upon this question, whether a thinking being can come from a non-thinking being deprived of all sensation and knowledge such as matter may be. § 10. It is indeed quite evident that a part of matter is incapable of producing anything of itself, and of giving itself motion; its motion must then either be eternal or be impressed upon it by a more powerful being. If this motion were eternal, it would always be incapable of producing knowledge. Divide matter into as many little parts as you please, in order, as it were, to spiritualize it, give it all

[1] *Cf. ante*, p. 363, note 1. — TR.

[2] Leibnitz's idea is that all right thought, if thorough-going and deep enough, must at last lead back to God, its original source. None of the proofs of God's existence are therefore to be cast aside, but the essential significance of each is to be sought out and ascertained and its form perfected, and all are to be united into one organic whole. — TR.

figures and motions you wish, make it a globe, a cube, a prism, a cylinder, etc., whose diameters are only the one-millionth part of a gry, which is one-tenth of a line, which is one-tenth of an inch, which is one-tenth of a philosophical foot, which is one-third of a pendulum, each vibration of which in the latitude of forty-five degrees is equal to one second of time. This particle of matter, small as it is, will act upon other bodies of a size proportional to itself no differently than bodies of an inch or a foot in diameter act among themselves. And we may hope as rationally to produce feeling, thought, and knowledge, by putting together gross parts of matter in a certain figure and motion, as by means of the smallest parts of matter in the world. These last knock, push, and resist each other just as the great ones do, and this is all they can do. But if matter could draw from its bosom feeling, perception, and knowledge, immediately and without machinery, or without the aid of figures and motions, then their possession must be an inseparable property of matter and of all its parts. To which one could add that, though the general and specific idea we have of matter leads us to speak of it as if it were a thing single in number, yet all matter is not properly one individual thing, which exists in a material being or a single body that we know or can conceive. So that if matter were the first eternal thinking being, there would not be one eternal infinite and thinking being, but an infinite number of eternal infinite[1] thinking beings, independent of one another, whose forces would be limited and thoughts distinct, and who consequently could never produce this order, harmony, and beauty which is seen in nature. Whence it necessarily follows that the eternal first being cannot be matter. I hope that you, sir, will be more content with this reasoning taken from the celebrated author of the preceding demonstration than you have appeared to be with his demonstration.

Th. I find the present reasoning the most solid in the world, and not only exact, but further profound and worthy of its author. I am perfectly of his opinion that no combination and modification of the parts of matter, however small they

[1] Locke has "finite" here, *Philos. Works*, Vol. 2, p. 237, Bohn's ed. Gerhardt, Erdmann, Jacques, and Janet all read "infinis." — TR.

may be, can produce perception; forasmuch as the gross particles could not give it (as is manifestly admitted) and as all is proportional in the small parts to what may take place in the great. It is furthermore an important remark regarding matter which the author makes here, that it must not be taken as a thing single in number, or (as I have been wont to state it) as a true and perfect *monad* or *unity*, since it is only a *mass* of an infinite number of beings. Here this excellent author needed but a step to arrive at my system. For in fact I give perception to all these infinite beings, each one of which is like an animal endowed with a soul (or some active analogous principle which makes its true unity), together with what is necessary to this being in order to be passive and endowed with an organic body. Now these beings have received their nature, active as well as passive (*i.e.* what they have of immaterial and material), from a general and supreme cause, because otherwise, as the author very well says, being independent of one another, they could never produce this *order*, *harmony*, and *beauty* which is seen in nature. But this argument, which appears to possess only a moral certainty, is pushed to a necessity wholly metaphysical by the *new kind of harmony* I have introduced, which is the *pre-established harmony*. For each one of these souls expressing in its way what takes place outside it and being unable to have any influence on other particular beings, or rather, being obliged to draw this expression from the depths of its own nature, each one must necessarily have received this nature (or this internal reason of the expression of that which is outside) from a universal cause upon which all these beings depend and which makes one perfectly in accord and correspondent with another; a thing impossible without an infinite knowledge and power and with an artifice great as regards especially the spontaneous agreement of the mechanism with the acts of the rational soul. The illustrious author[1] who made objections against it

[1] Leibnitz here refers to Pierre Bayle, 1647–1706, a celebrated critic, philosopher, and controversialist, who published in his *Dictionnaire historique et critique*, Rotterdam, 1695–97, 2 vols., 2d ed., revised and enlarged, 1702, article "Rorarius," a criticism of Leibnitz's *Système nouveau de la nature*, etc., published in the "Jour. des Savants," June, 1695, pp. 449 *sq.* Leibnitz sought to repel his criticisms in a writing, July, 1698, addressed to Basnage de Beauval, editor of the "Histoire des ouvrages des Sçavans," and published therein,

in his wonderful Dictionary doubted, as it were, whether this condition of things did not surpass all possible wisdom, saying that the wisdom of God did not appear to him too great for such an effect, and recognized at least that never had the feeble conceptions we may have of the divine perfection been so set in relief.

§ 12. *Ph.* How delighted I am at this agreement of your thoughts with those of my author! I hope you will not be displeased, sir, if I give you an account also of the rest of his reasoning upon this article. First he examines whether the thinking being, upon whom all the other intelligent beings depend (and with much stronger reason all other beings) is material or not. § 13. It is objected that a thinking being might be material. But he replies that if that were so, it is enough that this be an eternal being which has an infinite knowledge and power. Further, if thought and matter can be separated, the eternal existence of matter will not follow from the eternal existence of a thinking being. § 14. It will further be asked of those who make God material whether they imagine that every part of matter thinks. In that case it will follow that there would be as many Gods as particles of matter. But if each part of matter does not think, then there is a thinking being composed of non-thinking parts, which has already been disproved. § 15. To say that any single atom of matter thinks, and that the other parts,

July, 1698, p. 329 *sq.*, *cf.* Gerhardt, *Leibniz. philos. Schrift.*, 4, 517–24, Erdmann, 150–154, Jacques, 1, 481–87, Dutens, 2, Pt. I., 74–80. In the 2d ed. of his *Dictionnaire*, p. 2599 *sq.*, Eng. trans. from 2d ed., carefully collated with the several eds. of the original, 5 vols., London, 1738, 4, 900–916, Bayle again discussed Leibnitz's views, and to this discussion Leibnitz made a thorough and searching reply, first published by Gerhardt, 4, 524–54, with the title: *Extract du Dictionnaire de M. Bayle, article Rorarius*, p. 2599 *sqq. de l'Edition de l'an* 1702 *avec mes remarques.* Leibnitz pub. a revision of this detailed refutation, in 1712, in the "Histoire critique de la République des Lettres," Vol. 2, p. 78 *sq.* Gerhardt has published it, 4, 544–71, with many additions by Leibnitz. *Cf.* also Erdmann, 183–191, Dutens, 2, Pt. I., 80–93, Janet, 2, 579–94. Leibnitz elsewhere frequently refers to Bayle, especially in the *Théodicée*, in the preliminary essay entitled, *Discours preliminaire sur conformité de la foi avec la raison*, in which Bayle's objections are carefully examined, and in Pts. II. and III., where he is cited on nearly every page, and which presents a continuous polemic against him. The composition of the *Théodicée* was occasioned by the discussions held by Leibnitz with Queen Sophie Charlotte of Prussia on philosophical and theological topics suggested by the reading of Bayle's Dictionary. For the correspondence of Leibnitz and Bayle, *cf.* Gerhardt, 3, 21 *sq.* — Tr.

though equally eternal, do not think, is to make the *gratuitous* statement that one part of matter is infinitely above another and produces thinking beings not eternal.[1] § 16. If we will have it that the thinking eternal and material being is a certain particular mass of matter whose parts are non-thinking, we fall back upon the view which has been disproved; for the parts of matter are united in vain, they can acquire only a new local relation, which cannot give them knowledge. § 17. It matters not whether this mass is at rest or in motion. If at rest, it is only an inactive mass which has no privilege above one atom; if in motion, since this motion, which distinguishes it from other parts, is destined to produce thought, all these thoughts will be accidental and limited, each part by itself being without thought, and having nothing which regulates its movements. Thus there will be neither freedom, nor choice, nor wisdom, any more than in simple brute matter. § 18. Some believe that matter is at least coeternal with God. But they do not say why: the production of a thinking being, which they admit, is much more difficult than that of matter which is less perfect. And perhaps (says the author) if we would withdraw ourselves a little from common ideas, give wings to our mind, and engage in the profoundest examination we could make of the nature of things, *we might be able to attain a conception, though in an imperfect manner, how matter may at first have been made, and how it commenced to exist by the power of this eternal first being.* But we should see at the same time that to give being to a spirit is an effect of this eternal and infinite power much more difficult to comprehend. But because this would perhaps lead me too far (he adds) *from the notions upon which the philosophy now in the world is based*, it would not be excusable in me to deviate so far from them or to inquire, so far as grammar would permit, whether at bottom the commonly established opinion is contrary to this particular view; it would be wrong, I say, for me to engage in this discussion, especially *in this corner of the world*, where the received doctrine is good enough for my purpose, since it posits as an indubitable thing that if the creation or beginning of any *substance* whatever from nothing be once

[1] Leibnitz anticipates this argument of Locke by his law of continuity. — Tr.

admitted, the creation of every other substance, except the Creator himself, may with the same facility be assumed.

Th. You have given me genuine pleasure, sir, by giving me some account of a profound thought of your clever author, which his too scrupulous prudence has prevented him from producing in its entirety. It would be a great wrong, if he should suppress it and leave us there, after having made our mouths water. I assure you, sir, that I believe there is something beautiful and important concealed behind this enigmatical manner.[1] The *substance* in large letters might make one suspicious that he conceives the production of matter in the same way as that of the accidents, which we find no difficulty in drawing from nothing: and in distinguishing his particular thought *from the philosophy now prevalent in the world or in that corner of the earth*, I do not know but that he had in mind the Platonists, who take matter as something fleeting and transitory, after the manner of the accidents, and had an altogether different idea of spirits and souls.

§ 19. *Ph.* Finally, if some deny *creation*, by which things are made from nothing, because they cannot conceive it, our author, writing before he knew your discovery on the reason of the union of the soul and the body, holds against them, that they do not understand how voluntary movements are produced in bodies by the will of the soul, and they cease not to believe the fact, being convinced by experience; and he replies with reason to those who answer that the soul being unable to produce a new motion, produces only a new determination of the animal spirits, he replies to them, I say, that the one is as inconceivable as the other. And nothing can be better said than what he adds on this occasion, that to wish to limit what God can do to what we can comprehend, is to give an infinite extent to our comprehension, or to make God himself finite.

Th. Although now the difficulty regarding the union of the soul and the body has in my view been removed, there remain difficulties elsewhere. I have shown *a posteriori* by the pre-

[1] With regard to this riddle or enigma, Professor Schaarschmidt informs me that Raspe, in his ed. of the *Nouveaux Essais*, 1765, says, p. 409: "Mr. Coste l'a expliqué d'après le Chevalier Newton dans la remarque (2) au § 18, de ce chapitre. Edition de Locke d'Amsterdam, de 1755, p. 523." — TR.

established harmony, that all the monads have received their origin from God and depend upon him. But we cannot comprehend the how in detail; and at bottom their conservation is nothing else than a continual creation,[1] as the Scholastics have very clearly recognized.

CHAPTER XI

OF OUR KNOWLEDGE OF THE EXISTENCE OF OTHER THINGS

§ 1. *Ph.* As, then, the existence of God only has a necessary connection with ours, the ideas we may have of anything no more prove the existence of this thing than the portrait of a man proves his existence in the world. § 2. The certainty, however, I have of black and white upon this paper by means of *sensation* is as great as that of the motion of my hand, which is second only to the knowledge of our own existence, and of that of God. § 3. This certainly deserves the name of knowledge. For I do not believe that any one can seriously be so sceptical as to be uncertain of the existence of things which he sees and feels. At least, he who can carry his doubts so far will never have any controversy with me, since he can never be certain that I say anything contrary to his opinion. The perceptions of sensible things § 4. are produced by external causes which affect our senses, for we do not acquire these perceptions without the organs, and if the organs sufficed, they would always produce them. § 5. Further, I sometimes experience the fact that I cannot prevent these ideas from being formed in my mind, as, for example, the light, when I have my eyes open in a place into which the light may enter: while I can lay aside the ideas which are in my memory. There must be, then, some external cause of this living impression whose efficacy I cannot overcome. § 6. Some of these

[1] *Cf. Observatio ad Recensionem libri de Fidei et Rationis consensu a Domino Jaqueloto editi, mense Octobri proxime præcedenti factam*, pub. in the "Acta Erud. Lips.," Dec. 1705, p. 553, *ad fin.*, Gerhardt, 6, 556–8, Erdmann, 433–4, Dutens, 2, Pt. I., 256–8; *Théodicée*, Pt. III., §§ 382, 385, 391–3, G. 6, 342, E. 614, Jacques, 2, 290, Janet, 2, 388, Dutens, 1, 387; Pichler, *Die Theologie des Leibniz*, 1, 252, München, 1869; *Monadologie*, § 47, G. 6, 614, E. 708, Jacques, 2, 397, Janet, 2, 601, trans. Duncan, 225; Nolen, *Leibniz, La Monadologie*, 3d ed., Paris, 1893, pp. 148, 211. — Tr.

impressions are produced in us with pain, although afterwards we remember it without feeling the least inconvenience. And although mathematical demonstrations do not depend on the senses, yet the examination made of them by means of diagrams is of much use in proving the evidence of our sight, and seems to give to it a certainty approaching that of demonstration itself. § 7. Our senses also in many cases bear witness to each other. He who sees the fire may feel it if in doubt of it. And in writing this, I see that I can change the appearance of the paper, and say beforehand what new idea it is going to present to the mind; but, when these characters are traced, I can no longer avoid seeing them as they are, in addition to the fact that the sight of these characters will make another man utter the same sounds. § 8. If any one thinks that all this is but a long dream, he may dream, if he pleases, that I make this response to him, that our certainty based upon the testimony of our senses is as perfect as our nature allows, and our condition demands. He who sees a candle burning, and tries the heat of the flame, which hurts him if he does not withdraw his finger, will not ask for a greater certainty in order to govern his actions, and if this *dreamer* did not so do (*i.e.* withdraw his finger) he would find himself awakened. Such an assurance then suffices us, which is also as certain as pleasure or pain, two things beyond which we have no interest in knowledge or the existence of things. § 9. But beyond our actual sensation, there is no knowledge, and it is only *probability*, as when I believe that there are men in the world; of which fact there is a high degree of probability, although at present, alone in my chamber, I see none of them. § 10. It is also folly to expect a demonstration of everything and to act not in accord with clear and *evident* truths though they are not demonstrable. A man who should so use them could be assured of nothing but of dying in a very short time.

Th. I have already remarked in our preceding conferences that the truth of sensible things is justified by their connection,[1] which depends upon the intellectual truths grounded in reason and upon constant observations in the sensible things

[1] *Cf. New Essays*, Bk. IV., chap. 2, § 14, Th. (2), *ante*, p. 422, note 1. From the idealistic point of view, the only possible criterion of the truth of the phe-

themselves even when the reasons do not appear. And as these reasons and observations give us the means of judging the future as related to our interest, and as success corresponds with our rational judgment, we could not demand, nor have indeed, a greater certainty regarding these objects. We can also give a reason for dreams themselves, and for their slight connection with other phenomena. Nevertheless, I believe that we might extend the appellation of knowledge and of certainty beyond actual sensations, since clearness and manifestness go beyond, which I consider as a species of certainty; and it would undoubtedly be folly seriously to doubt whether there are men in the world when we do not see any. *To doubt seriously* is to doubt in relation to the practical, and we might take *certainty* as a knowledge of truth which we cannot doubt in relation to the practical without madness; and sometimes we take it still more generally, and apply it to cases where we could not doubt without deserving to be severely blamed. But *evidence* would be a luminous certainty, *i.e.* where we do not doubt because of the connection we see between ideas. According to this definition of certainty, we are certain that Constantinople is in the world, that Constantine, Alexander the Great, and Julius Cæsar lived. It is true that some peasant of Ardennes might justly doubt about these, for lack of information; but a man of letters and of the world could not do so without great derangement of mind.

§ 11. *Ph.* We are assured in truth by our memory of many things which are past, but we shall not be able to judge easily whether they exist still. I saw yesterday water, and a certain number of beautiful colors upon bubbles formed upon this water. Now I am certain that those bubbles as well as that water existed, but I do not know with any more certainty the present existence of the water than that of the bubbles, although the former is infinitely more probable because the water has been observed to be lasting and the bubbles to disappear. § 12. Finally, outside of ourselves and God we know other spirits only by *revelation*, and we have concerning them only the certainty of *faith.*

nomena of the senses is the constancy and regularity in their connection or consecution. *Cf.* also *De modo distinguendi phænomena realia ab imaginariis*, Gerhardt, *Leibniz. philos. Schrift.*, 7, 319 *sq.*; Erdmann, 443–445. — TR.

Th. It has already been remarked that our memory sometimes deceives us. And we put confidence in it or not, according as it is more or less vivid, and more or less connected with the things we know. And even when we are assured of the principal fact we may often question the circumstances. I remember to have known a certain man, for I feel that his image as well as his voice is not new to me; and this double indication is a better guarantee to me than one of the two, but I cannot remember where I have seen him. It happens, however, though rarely, that a person is seen in a dream before he is seen in flesh and blood. And I am assured that a lady of a well-known court saw in a dream and described to her friends the person she afterwards married, and the hall in which the betrothal was celebrated, and she did this before she had seen or known either the man or the place. They attributed the circumstance to some indefinite secret presentiment; but chance may produce this effect, since it is quite rare that it happens, besides, dream-images being somewhat obscure, there is more liberty in connecting them afterwards with certain others.

§ 13. *Ph.* Let us conclude that there are two kinds of propositions, the one particular and concerning existence, as, for example, that an elephant exists; the other general, concerning the dependence of ideas, as, for example, that men should obey God. § 14. The majority of these general and certain propositions bear the name of *eternal truths*, and, in fact, they all are such. This is not because these are propositions actually formed somewhere from all eternity, or because they are graven upon the mind after some model, which always existed, but because we are assured that when a creature enriched with faculties and means therefor, applies his thoughts to the consideration of his ideas, he will discover the truth of these propositions.

Th. Your division appears to return to mine of *propositions of fact* and *propositions of reason*. Propositions of fact also may become general in a way, but it is by induction or observation, so that it is only a multitude of similar facts, as when it is observed that all quicksilver is evaporated by the force of fire; and this is not a perfect generality, because we do not see its necessity. General propositions of reason are necessary, although the reason also furnishes some which are not absolutely general, and are only probable, as, for example, when we presume an idea to be possible until its contrary is discovered by a more exact research. There are finally *mixed propositions*, drawn from premises, some of which come from facts and observations, and others are necessary propositions; and such are a number of geographical and astronomical conclusions regarding the globe of the earth and the course of the stars, which spring from the combination of the observations of travellers and astronomers with the theorems of geometry and arithmetic. But as, according to the usage of logicians, *the conclusion follows the weakest of the premises*[1] and cannot have more certainty than they, these mixed propositions have only the certainty and generality which belong to the observations. As for the *eternal truths*, it must be observed that at bottom they are all conditional and say in effect: such a thing posited, such another thing is. For example, in saying: *every figure which has three sides will also have three angles*, I say nothing else than that, supposing there is a figure with three sides, *this same* figure will have three angles. I say *this same*, and it is in this respect that the categorical propositions which may be stated unconditionally, although at bottom conditional, differ from those called *hypothetical*, as this proposition would be: *if a figure has three sides, its angles are equal to two right angles*, in which we see that the *antecedent* proposition (viz.: the figure of three sides) and the *consequent* (viz.: the angles of the figure of three sides are equal to two right angles) have not the same subject as they have in the preceding case, in which the antecedent was: *this figure has*

[1] The variously phrased formula: *conclusio sequitur partem debiliorem* or *deteriorem; sectetur partem conclusio deteriorem; pejorem sequitur semper conclusio partem*, is the Scholastic expression of the fundamental principle of the categorical syllogism, according to which the conclusion cannot contain more than is contained in the premises, or, as given by Hamilton (*Lects. on Logic*, p. 219, Boston, 1873), in his third rule of the syllogism, "The conclusion must correspond in quantity with the subsumption [minor premise], and in quality with the sumption [major premise]." Logicians regarded negative and particular propositions as weaker or worse as related to universal and affirmative propositions, the negative being weaker in quality and the particular in quantity, so that in the syllogism if one of the premises is particular the conclusion will be particular, and if one of the premises is negative the conclusion will be negative. For the history of the subject, *cf.* Prantl, *Gesch. d. Logik*, 1, 371, 587; 2, 275; 3, 48. — TR.

three sides, and the consequent: *the said figure has three angles.* Although, again, the hypothetical may often be transformed into the categorical, merely by changing a little the terms, as if instead of the preceding hypothetical, I said: *the angles of every figure with three sides are equal to two right angles.* The Scholastics have hotly disputed *de constantia subjecti,* as they called it, *i.e.* how the proposition made upon a subject can have a real truth, if this subject does not exist. The fact is that the truth is only conditional, and says, that in case the subject ever exists, it will be found such. But it will be further demanded, in what is this connection founded, since there is in it some reality which does not deceive. The reply will be, that it is in the connection of ideas. But it will be asked in reply, where would these ideas be if no mind existed, and what then would become of the real ground of this certainty of the eternal truths? This leads us finally to the ultimate ground of truths, viz.: to that Supreme and Universal Mind, which cannot fail to exist, whose understanding, to speak truly, is the region of eternal truths, as St. Augustine has recognized and expresses in a sufficiently vivid way.[1] And in order not to think that it is unnecessary to recur to this, we must consider that these necessary truths contain the determining reason and the regulating principle of existences themselves, and, in a word, the laws of the universe. Thus these necessary truths being anterior to the existence of contingent beings, must be grounded in the existence of a

[1] Aurelius Augustinus, 354–430, grounded his philosophy in the principle of the absolute and immediate certainty of consciousness or inner experience. *Cf. De Beata Vita,* chap. 7; *Solil.* II., 1 (*ante,* p. 410, note 1); *De Vera Relig.,* 39, 72 *sq.*; *De Trin.,* X., 14, XIV., 7. In this certainty of the individual consciousness, *i.e.* in thought itself, is immediately involved the idea of God in whom exist the universal truths as the ideas or norms of all reality. *Cf. De Ideis,* 2: "Sunt namque ideæ principales formæ quædam, vel rationes rerum stabiles et incommutabiles, quæ ipsæ formatæ non sunt atque per hoc æternæ ac semper eodem modo se habentes, quæ in divina intelligentia continentur, et quum ipsæ neque oriantur neque intereant, secundum eas tamen formari dicitur omne, quod interire potest et omne, quod oritur et interit."

For a good account of Augustine's philosophy, *cf.* Ueberweg-Heinze, 7th ed., Berlin, 1888, 2, 97–115, especially 106–7, Eng. trans. from 4th Germ. ed., New York, 1871, 1, 333 *sq.*, especially 339–40; Windelband, *Hist. of Philos.*, trans. by Tufts, 276 *sq.* Augustine's works form Vols. 32–47 of the Latin Fathers in Migne, *Patrol. cur. compl.*, Paris, 1835 *sq.*; Eng. trans. by Dods, 15 vols., Edinburgh, 1871–77, and in Schaff's lib. *Nicene and Post-Nicene Fathers,* Vols. 1–8, Buffalo, 1886–88. — TR.

necessary substance. Here it is that I find the original of the ideas and truths which are graven in our souls, not in the form of propositions, but as the sources out of which application and occasion will cause actual judgments to arise.[1]

CHAPTER XII

OF THE IMPROVEMENT OF OUR KNOWLEDGE

§ 1. *Ph.* We have spoken of the kinds of knowledge we have. Now let us come to the means of improving the knowledge or of finding the truth. It is the received opinion among scholars, that the maxims are the bases of all knowledge, and that each particular science is based upon certain things already known (*præcognita*). § 2. I admit that mathematics seem to favor this method by their good success, and you have given considerable support to this view. But it is still doubtful whether it is not rather the ideas which were of service therein through their connection than two or three general maxims which were posited at the beginning. A young lad knows that his body is greater than his little finger, but not by virtue of this axiom, that the whole is greater than its part. Knowledge commenced by particular propositions; but afterwards it was desired to relieve the *memory* by means of general notions from a cumbersome *load of particular ideas.* If language were so imperfect that there were no relative terms, *whole* and *part,* could he not know that his body is larger than his little finger? I at least give you the reasons of my author, although I think I foresee what you will say thereto in conformity with what you have already said.

Th. I know not why you bear the maxims such ill will as to attack them yet again; if they serve to relieve the memory *of a multitude of particular ideas,* as you admit, they must be very useful, although they had no other use. But I add that

[1] For Leibnitz God is the source of all truths as well as of all beings. The idea of God contains in itself potentially all truth, and is the regulative (but not in the Kantian sense of the term), or better, the constitutive, principle of all thought, just as his actuality contains potentially within itself all existences, and is the regulative, *i.e.*, constitutive, principle of all being. *Cf.* also, *ante*, p. 496, note 1. — TR.

they do not spring from particular ideas, for they are not found by induction from examples. He who knows that ten is more than nine, that the body is larger than the finger, and that the house is too large to be able to run away with the door, knows each one of these particular propositions, by one and the same general reason which is, as it were, incorporated therein and illuminated, just as we see designs adorned with colors in which the proportion and configuration consists properly in the outlines, whatever the color may be. Now this common reason is the axiom itself which is known, so to speak, implicitly, although it does not exist at first in an abstract and separate manner. The examples derive their truth from the incorporated axiom, and the axiom has not its ground in the examples. And as this common reason of these particular truths exists in the minds of all men, you see clearly that it is not necessary that the words *whole* and *part* be found in the language of him who is imbued therewith.

§ 4. *Ph.* But is it not dangerous to authorize assumptions under the pretext of axioms? One will assume, with some of the ancients, that all is matter; another, with Polemo,[1] that the world is God; a third will assert that the sun is the principal divinity. Judge what a religion we should have, if that were allowed. So true is it that it is dangerous to receive principles without questioning them, especially if they concern morality. For some one will expect another life, like that of Aristippus,[2] who placed happiness in the pleasures of the body, rather than like that of Antisthenes,[3] who main-

[1] Polemo, the successor of Xenocrates, 396–314 B.C., as scholarch, or head, 314–270 B.C., of the school of the Old Academy, and the third in that office from Plato (Speusippus holding it from Plato's death in 347 to 339, and Xenocrates from 339–314), devoted himself chiefly to ethics. The statement that he declared the universe to be God — Πολέμον τὸν κόσμον θεὸν ἀπεφήνατο — rests on the authority of Stobæus, *Eclogæ phys.*, Bk. I., chap. 2, 5, § 62, p. 15, ed. A. Meineke, Leipzig, 1855–64. For his philosophy, *cf.* Zeller, *Philos. d. Griech.*, II., 1 [Vol. 3], 993–4, 1045–6, 4th ed., Leipzig, 1889. — TR.

[2] Aristippus, c. 435–c. 366 B.C., the founder of the Cyrenaic school, made pleasure, which, according to Diog. Laertius, II., 85, 86, he defined as the feeling of a gentle motion — τέλος δ' ἀπέφαινε τὴν λείαν κίνησιν εἰς αἴσθησιν ἀναδιδομένην . . . τὴν μὲν λείαν κίνησιν τὴν ἡδονὴν — the end of life, the wise man aiming to enjoy pleasure without being controlled by it. For his writings, *cf.* Mullach, *Fragt. philos. Gr.*, II., 397 *sq.* On his life and philosophy, *cf.* Zeller, *Philos. d. Griech.*, II., 1 [Vol. 3], 336 *sq.*, ethical doctrine, 352 *sq.* — TR.

[3] Antisthenes, c. 440–c. 369 B.C., a pupil of Gorgias and Socrates, was the founder of the Cynic school, and taught, according to Diog. Laertius, VI., 11,

tained that virtue suffices to produce happiness. And Archelaus,[1] who will lay it down as a principle that justice and injustice, honesty and dishonesty, are defined only by the laws and not by nature, will no doubt have other measures of moral good and evil than those who admit obligations anterior to human constitutions. § 5. It must be, then, that principles are certain. § 6. But this certainty comes only from the comparison of ideas: thus we have no need of other principles, and according to this rule alone we shall advance much farther than by putting our minds at the disposal of another.

Th. I am astonished, sir, that you turn against maxims, *i.e.* against evident principles, that which can and must be said against principles assumed *gratis*. When one demands *præcognita* in the sciences, or anterior knowledge, which serves to ground science, he demands *known principles* and not arbitrary positions, whose truth is not known; and even Aristotle understands that the inferior and subaltern borrow their principles from other superior sciences in which they have been demonstrated, except the first of the sciences, which we call metaphysics, which, according to him, asks nothing from the others, and furnishes them the principles they need; and when he says: *δεῖ πιστεύειν τὸν μανθάνοντα*,[2] the apprentice must

that virtue only is a good, and that it is sufficient for happiness — αὐτάρκη γὰρ τὴν ἀρετὴν εἶναι πρὸς εὐδαιμονίαν. For his writings, *cf.* Mullach, *Fragt. philos. Gr.*, II., 261 *sq.* On his life and philosophy, *cf.* Zeller, *Philos. d. Griech.*, II., 1 [Vol. 3], 281 *sq.*, ethical doctrine, 303 *sq.* — Tr.

[1] Archelaus, the dates of whose birth and death are unknown, was a physicist, and the disciple of Anaxagoras, c. 500–428 B.C., whose physical doctrine he seems to have modified in the direction of the Ionic school as represented by Anaximines, c. 588–c. 524 B.C., and Diogenes of Apollonia. Zeller says that the statement, as given by Diog. Laertius, II., 16, that he derived the distinction of good and bad from custom rather than nature — τὸ δίκαιον εἶναι καὶ τὸ αἰσχρὸν οὐ φύσει ἀλλὰ νόμῳ — appears to be due to a mistake in interpreting his language, and that he merely said that men at the beginning were without custom and law, and first attained thereto in the course of time. On his philosophy, *cf.* Zeller, *Philos. d. Griech.*, I., 2 [Vol. 2], 1031–1038, 5th ed., Leipzig, 1892. — Tr.

[2] *Cf.* Aristotle, *Sophist. Elench.*, chap. 2, 161, b, 1–3: διδασκαλικοὶ μὲν οἱ ἐκ τῶν οἰκείων ἀρχῶν ἑκάστου μαθήματος καὶ οὐκ ἐκ τῶν τοῦ ἀποκρινομένου δοξῶν συλλογιζόμενοι (δεῖ γὰρ πιστεύειν τὸν μανθάνοντα), *i.e.* discussions for the purpose of teaching proceed from the special principles of each science, and do not draw their conclusions from the opinions of the participating pupil; Aristotle's thought being that the pupil will receive a confirmation of the mere faith in the principles demanded of him at the outset, in the course of the explanation and demonstration of these principles in his presence, and in the agreement of the scientific results with the facts and his further knowledge. Leibnitz here

believe his master, his thought is that he must do it only while waiting, while he is not yet instructed in the higher sciences, so that it is only provisionally. Thus we are very far from receiving *gratuitous principles.* To this it must be added that even principles whose certainty is not complete may have their use if we build upon them only by demonstration; for although all the conclusions in this case are conditional only, and are valid only upon the supposition that this principle is true, nevertheless this connection itself and these conditional enunciations would at least be demonstrated; so that it were much to be desired that we had many books written in this way, where there would be no danger of error, the reader or disciple being warned of the condition. And practice will be regulated by these conclusions only as the supposition shall be found verified elsewhere. This method also serves very often itself to verify suppositions or hypotheses, when many conclusions arise from them, the truth of which is otherwise known, and sometimes this gives a perfect proof (*retour*) sufficient to demonstrate the truth of the hypothesis. Mr. Conring,[1] a physician by profession, but a clever man in every kind of learning, except perhaps mathematics, wrote a letter to a friend engaged in reprinting at Helmstädt the book of Viottus,[2] an esteemed Peripatetic philosopher who tried to

expresses a similar thought, in premising the *provisional character* of that faith which the beginner should have in his teacher. — Tr.

[1] Hermann Conring, 1606–1681, one of the most learned men of his age, possessed of vast erudition, and thoroughly informed on medicine, law, theology, history, physics, philology, etc., taught at Helmstädt, and wrote an immense number of works, which have been united in part and published under the title of *Opera omnia*, Brunswick, 1730, 7 vols., fol. For an account of him, *cf.* Michaud, *Biog. Univ.*, Vol. 9, pp. 447–452. For his correspondence with Leibnitz, *cf.* Gerhardt, *Leibniz. philos. Schrift.*, 1, 153–206. — Tr.

[2] Bartolommeo Viotto, or Viotti, surnamed a Clivolo, son of a distinguished surgeon, Tommaso Viotto, who was the first in the University of Turin to receive the laurel crown in surgery from the Decurions of Trino, was a philosopher and physician of Turin, and, in the five years preceding 1552, public professor of logic in that city. He died in 1568. He was author of *De balneorum naturalium viribus lib. IV.*, Lugduni, 1552, reprinted in *De balneis omnia quæ extant apud Græcos, Latinos, et Arabas*, fol. Venetiis, 1553, pp. 247–71; and of the work here and elsewhere referred to by Leibnitz, *Demonstrationum in methodum medendi lib. V.*, 8vo, Parisiis, 1560, and under the editorship of A. Frolingius, Helmstädt, 1661, Braunschweig, 1684. *Cf.* Correspondence of Leibnitz and Conring, Gerhardt, *Leibniz. philos. Schrift.*, 1, 184, 187; of Leibnitz and Placcius, Dutens, *Leibnit. op. om.*, 6, 45.

Conring, *Introd. in univ. art. med.*, Halæ et Lipsiæ, 1726, p. 23, says of

explain the demonstration and "Posterior Analytics" of Aristotle. This letter was appended to the book, and in it Conring criticised Pappus when he said that *analysis* proposes to discover the unknown by assuming it, and by reaching therefrom, by inference, known truths;[1] a method which is contrary to logic (he said) which teaches that from falsehood we cannot infer truths. But I made known to him afterwards that analysis makes use of definitions and other reciprocal propositions which furnish means of making the proof (*retour*), and of discovering synthetic demonstrations.[2] And even when this proof is not demonstrative, as in physics, it is nevertheless sometimes highly probable, when the hypothesis explains easily many phenomena, difficult without it and very independent of one another. I hold to the truth, sir, that the principle of principles is in a way the good use of ideas and of experience; but by examining it thoroughly we shall find that, as regards ideas, it is nothing else than the union of definitions by means of identical axioms. Nevertheless, it is not always an easy thing to come to this ultimate analysis, and whatever desire the geometers, at least the ancient geometers, have shown to succeed therein, they have not yet been able to do so. The celebrated author

him: "Certe qui necessitatem ejus in medicina simul et ipsam artem demonstrandi post Galenum ostenderit, hactenus nemo inventus est, si excipias unum Bartholomæum Viottum hominem longe doctissimum; cujus de demonstratione præclarum opus ante centum annos prodiit." *Cf.*, also, G. Pasch, *De novis inventis*, 2d ed., 4to, Lipsiæ, 1700, p. 26; J. A. van der Linden, *De scriptis medicis*, 8vo, Amstelredami, 1637, p. 82, *Linden. renovat.*, 4to, Norimbergæ, 1686, pp. 114, 119; Kestner, *Medicinisches-Gelehrten-Lexicon*, 4to, Jena, 1740, p. 897; G. G. Bonino, *Biografia medica piemontese*, 8vo, Torino, 1824, Vol. 1, pp. 199–201. — TR.

[1] Pappus of Alexandria was a Greek geometer "of a very high order," who flourished, according to the best recent opinion, in the reign of Diocletian, 284–305, and whose Συναγωγή, or *Collection*, is of very great value in the history of mathematics. From Bk. VII. of this work is derived a large part of our knowledge of Greek geometry. The best ed. of the whole work is F. Hultsch, *Pappi Alexandrini Collectionis quæ supersunt*, 3 vols., Berlin, 1876–78.

Pappus' explanation of the nature of analysis and synthesis, which Conring erroneously criticised, is found in the preface of Bk. VII. of the Συναγωγή, *cf.* Hultsch, *op. cit.*, Vol. 2, pp. 634–6; C. I. Gerhardt, *Der Sammlung des Pappus von Alexandrien, siebentes u. achtes Buch*, Halle, 1871, pp. 2–4. According to Schaarschmidt, this explanation is perhaps the clearest and best concise statement that has been made of the nature of the analytic and synthetic method. — TR.

[2] *Cf.* Correspondence of Leibnitz and Conring, Letter of Jan. 3d, 1678, Gerhardt, *Leibniz. philos. Schrift.*, 1, 187–8; also, *ibid.*, 185, 190, 193 *sq.* — TR.

of "The Essay on Human Understanding," would give them much pleasure if he would complete this investigation, a little more difficult than we think. Euclid, for example, has put among the axioms one which amounts to saying: that two straight lines can meet only once. The image derived from the experience of the senses, does not permit us to picture to ourselves more than one meeting of the two lines; but it is not upon this that science must be founded. And if any one believes that this image gives the connection of distinct ideas, he is not sufficiently instructed concerning the source of truths, and a multitude of propositions, demonstrable by others anterior, would pass with him as immediate. Many of those who have criticised Euclid, have not sufficiently considered this: these kinds of images are only confused ideas, and he who knows the straight lines only by this means will not be capable of demonstrating anything. Euclid, therefore, for want of a distinctly expressed idea, *i.e.* a definition of a straight line (for that which he gives meanwhile is obscure and of no use to him in his demonstrations), was obliged to return to two axioms which for him took the place of definitions and which he employed in his demonstrations: the one that two straight lines have no common part, the other that they enclose no space. Archimedes has given a kind of definition of the *straight line*, in saying that it is the shortest line between two points. But he tacitly assumes (by employing in his demonstrations elements like those of Euclid, based upon the two axioms I have just mentioned) that the properties (*affections*) of which these axioms speak, accord with the line which he defines.[1] Thus if you believe, with your friends, under the pretext of the agreement or disagreement of ideas, that what these images tell us was allowed and is still to be received in geometry, without seeking that strictness of demonstration by means of definitions and axioms which the ancients demanded in this science (as I believe many people will believe for lack of information), I will admit, sir, that you may be contented as regards those who trouble themselves only about practical geometry such as it is, but not as regards those who desire to have the science which serves indeed to perfect the practical. And if the ancients had been of this opinion and had relaxed their efforts

[1] Gerhardt and Erdmann read "définit"; Jacques "décrit." — TR.

on this point, I think they would have made but little advance, and would have left us only an empirical geometry such as that of the Egyptians apparently was, and such as that of the Chinese seems still to be; this would have deprived us of the most worthful physical and mechanical knowledge which geometry has caused us to discover, and which is unknown wherever our geometry is unknown. It is also apparent that in following the senses and their images we should fall into errors; much the same as we see that all those who are not instructed in exact geometry receive as an indubitable truth upon trust in their imagination, that two lines continually approaching each other, must finally meet; while geometers give contrary instances in the case of certain lines called asymptotes. But besides this we should be deprived of what I value most highly in geometry as related to reflection, viz.: permitting us to catch a glimpse of the true source of eternal truths and of the means of making us comprehend their necessity, a matter which the confused ideas of the sense-images could not show us distinctly. You will say to me that Euclid was obliged, however, to confine himself to certain axioms whose evidence is seen only confusedly by means of the images. I agree with you that he has limited himself to these axioms, but it was better for him to limit himself to a small number of truths of this nature which appeared to him the simplest and to deduce from them the others which another less exact would also have taken as certain without demonstration, than to leave many of them undemonstrated, and what is worse, to allow people the liberty of extending their laxity according to their fancy. You see then, sir, that what you and your friends have said regarding the connection of ideas as the true source of truths needs explication. If you are willing to content yourself with the confused sight of this connection, you weaken the exactness of demonstrations, and Euclid has done incomparably better in reducing all to definitions and to a small number of axioms. Yet if you wish this connection of ideas to be distinctly seen and expressed, you will be obliged to recur to definitions and identical axioms, as I claim; and sometimes you will be obliged to content yourself with some axioms less primitive, as Euclid and Archimedes have done, when you find difficulty in attaining a perfect analysis, and you will do better in that way than to neglect or defer some fortunate discoveries which you can already make by their means: as in fact I have already said to you at another time, sir, that I believe we should not have a geometry (I mean a demonstrative science), if the ancients had not been willing to advance until they had demonstrated the axioms they were obliged to employ.

§ 7. *Ph.* I begin to understand what a distinctly known connection of ideas is, and I see clearly that in this sense axioms are necessary. I see clearly also how necessary it is that the method we follow in our researches, when the question is that of the examination of ideas, be regulated by the example of the mathematicians who from certain very clear and easy beginnings (which are nothing else than the axioms and definitions) proceed by small degrees and a continual chain of reasoning to the discovery and demonstration of truths that appear at first beyond human capacity. The art of finding proofs, and these admirable methods they have invented for separating and putting in order mediate ideas is what has produced such wonderful and unexpected discoveries. But whether with time a similar method may not be found out useful in respect to other ideas as well as those belonging to magnitude is a question I will not determine. At least, if other ideas were examined according to the ordinary method of the mathematicians, they would lead our thoughts farther than we are perhaps led to imagine. § 8. And this might be done particularly in the case of morality, as I have more than once said.

Th. I believe you are right, sir, and I have been disposed for a long time to make it my business to accomplish your predictions.

§ 9. *Ph.* In regard to the knowledge of bodies we are compelled to take a directly contrary path; for having no ideas of their real essences, we are obliged to recur to experience. § 10. But I do not deny that a man accustomed to making rational and regular experiments is capable of forming juster conjectures regarding their still unknown properties than another not so accustomed, but it is judgment and opinion, not knowledge and certainty. This makes me think that physics is incapable of becoming a science in our hands. But experiments and historical observations may be of use to us as regards the health of our bodies and the conveniences of life.

Th. I admit that physics as a whole will never be a perfect science among us, but we shall not cease to be able to have some physical science, and indeed we have already some specimens of it. For example, magnetology may pass for such a science, for, making a few suppositions based upon experience, we can demonstrate from them by a certain inference a number of phenomena which really occur as we see that reason declares. We ought not to hope to give a reason for all experiments, as indeed the geometers have not yet proved all their axioms; but just as they are satisfied to deduce a large number of theorems from a small number of principles of the reason, so is it sufficient that the physicists by means of certain principles of experience give a reason for a multitude of phenomena and can indeed prove them in practice.

§ 11. *Ph.* Since then our faculties are not fitted to make us discern the internal fabric of bodies, we must consider that it is enough that they discover to us the existence of God, and a sufficiently extended knowledge of ourselves to instruct us in our duties and in our greatest interests, particularly as related to eternity. And I think I am right in inferring therefrom that *morality is the proper science and the important business of mankind in general, as, on the other hand, the different arts which are conversant about different parts of nature are the lot of particular men.* It may be said, for example, that ignorance of the use of iron is a reason in the countries of America, where nature has spread abroad abundantly all kinds of goods, for the lack of the greatest part of the conveniences of life. Thus very far from despising the science of nature, § 12. I hold, that if this study is directed, as it ought to be, it may be of greater use to the human race than all that has been done up to this time; and he who invented printing, who discovered the use of the compass, and who made known the virtue of quinquina, has contributed more to the propagation of knowledge and to the advancement of the useful conveniences of life, and has saved more people from the grave, than the founders of colleges and hospitals and other monuments of the most exemplary charity, which have been built at great expense.

Th. You could say nothing, sir, more to my liking. True morality or piety, very far from favoring the inactivity of certain idle quietists, must impel us to cultivate the arts. And as I said not long since, a better police would be able to bring us some day a much better medical science than that we have at present. We cannot preach this doctrine enough, next to the care for virtue.

§ 13. *Ph.* Although I recommend experiments, I do not despise probable hypotheses. They may lead us to new discoveries, and are, at least, a great aid to the memory. But our mind has a great tendency to go too fast and to be satisfied with certain superficial appearances, for lack of taking the necessary time and trouble to apply them to a multitude of phenomena.

Th. The art of discovering the causes of phenomena, or true hypotheses, is like the art of deciphering, in which an ingenious conjecture often greatly shortens the road. Lord Bacon began to put the art of experimenting into precepts, and Chevalier Boyle[1] had a great talent for practising it. But if the art of employing experiments and of drawing consequences therefrom is not joined with it, we shall never with the utmost cost attain to what a man of great penetration might discover at first sight. Descartes, assuredly such a man, has made a similar remark in one of his letters[2] regarding the method of the Chancellor of England; and Spinoza (whom I do not hesitate to quote when he says a good thing) in one of his letters[3] to the late Mr. Oldenburg, Secretary of the Royal Society of England, printed among the posthumous works of this subtle Jew, makes a similar reflection upon a work of Boyle, who, to speak the truth, stops a little too much to draw from a great number of fine experiments no other con-

[1] *Cf. ante*, p. 324, note 2. — Tr.

[2] The remark here referred to by Leibnitz as occurring in one of Descartes' letters has not as yet been found in any of those now extant; and, as mention is made of Bacon in Spinoza's remark cited immediately after, it is possible that Leibnitz confounded the two authors, a thing which might readily happen, especially as Leibnitz was often out of the reach of books when composing his works, as probably in this case, *cf. ante*, p. 8, note 1. — Tr.

[3] *Cf.* Spinoza, *Opera*, ed. Van Vloten and Land, 2, 19: "Sed interim nescio, cur clarissimus vir hoc" (*i.e.* universal mechanism) "adeo sollicite conetur colligere ex hoc suo experimento; cum jam hoc a Verulamio, et postea a Cartesio satis superque demonstratum sit." — Tr.

clusion than this which he might take as a principle, viz.: that everything in nature takes place mechanically, a principle which can be rendered certain by reason alone, and never by experiments, whatever their number.

§ 14. *Ph.* After having established clear and distinct ideas with fixed names, the great means of extending our knowledge is the art of finding mediate ideas which can show us the connection or incompatibility of the extreme ideas. The maxims at least are of no avail in furnishing them. Suppose a man has not an exact idea of a right angle, he will vainly torment himself in demonstrating something about the right-angled triangle: and whatever maxims he employs, he will have difficulty in attaining by their aid the proof that the first squares of the sides enclosing the right angle are equal to the square on the hypothenuse. A man might ruminate upon these axioms a long time without ever seeing more clearly into mathematics.

Th. It is of no avail to ruminate upon the axioms without having something to which to apply them. Axioms often serve to connect ideas, as, for example, this maxim, that similar extensions of the second and third dimensions are in reason double and triple the corresponding extensions of the first dimension, is of very great use; and the quadrature, for example, of the lune of Hippocrates[1] springs from it at once in the case of the circles by uniting therewith the application of these two figures the one to the other, when their given position furnishes the opportunity for so doing, as their known comparison promises light thereupon.

[1] Hippocrates of Chios, c. 440 B.C., a contemporary of Hippocrates of Cos, the physician (*cf. ante*, p. 476, note 2), was a celebrated Greek geometer, whose most noted achievement was the discovery of the quadrature of the lune, or the crescent-shaped plane figure produced by drawing two perpendicular radii in a circle and describing upon the line joining their extremities a semicircle. This lune is famous as the first curvilinear space whose area was exactly determined, and its area is exactly equal to that of the triangle formed by the two radii and the line joining their extremities. For the demonstration of this, *cf.* Larousse, *Grande Dict. Univ. de XIXe Siecle*, Vol. 10, p. 791, a, b. On Hippocrates and his services to mathematics, *cf.* Allman, *Greek Geom. from Thales to Euclid*, 64 *sq.*; Gow, *A Short Hist. of Greek Math.*, 164 *sq.*; H. Suter, *Gesch. d. math. Wissenschaften*, 2d ed., Vol. 1, pp. 33-36, Zürich, 1873.—TR.

CHAPTER XIII

OTHER CONSIDERATIONS CONCERNING OUR KNOWLEDGE

§ 1. *Ph.* It will be perhaps further appropriate to add, that our *knowledge* has a close relation to our sight in this, as well as in other things, that it is neither wholly *necessary* nor wholly *voluntary*. We cannot fail to see when our eyes are open to the light, but we can turn them towards certain objects, § 2. and consider them with more or less application. Thus when the faculty is once applied, it does not depend upon the will to determine the knowledge; no more than a man can prevent himself from seeing what he sees. But he must employ his faculties, as it is necessary in order to inform himself.

Th. We have spoken before of this point, and established the fact that it does not depend upon man to have this or that opinion in the present state, but it depends upon him to prepare himself to have it or not to have it eventually, and that thus opinions are voluntary only in an indirect manner.

CHAPTER XIV

OF JUDGMENT

§ 1. *Ph.* Man would be found without direction in the greater part of the arts of his life, if he had nothing to conduct him from the point where certain knowledge fails him. § 2. He must often be contented with a simple *twilight of probability*. § 3. The faculty of using this is *judgment*. One is contented with it often of necessity, but often through want of diligence, patience, and skill. § 4. It is called *assent* or *dissent*, and is employed when anything is *presumed*, *i.e.* when it is *taken* as true *before* it is proved. When this is done conformably to the reality of things, it is a *right judgment*.

Th. Others call *judgment* the act which is performed every time a statement is made after some knowledge of a cause; and there will be some also who will distinguish judgment from opinion, as not of necessity being so uncertain. But I do not wish to criticise any one regarding the use of words, and it is allowed you, sir, to take judgment as a probable opinion. As for *presumption*, which is a term of the jurisconsults, good use with them distinguishes it from *conjecture*. It is something more, something which must pass for truth provisionally until there is proof of the contrary, while a *sign*, a *conjecture*, must often be weighed against another conjecture. Thus it is that he who admits having borrowed money from another, is *presumed* to pay the debt, unless he shows that he had done so already, or that the debt ceases by some other principle. *Presumption* is not then in this sense *taking before* proof, which is not allowed, but *taking in advance* but with foundation, while awaiting a contrary proof.

CHAPTER XV

OF PROBABILITY

§ 1. *Ph.* If *demonstration* shows the connection of ideas, *probability* is nothing else than the appearance of this connection based upon proofs in which immutable connection is not seen. § 2. There are several degrees of assent from *assurance* down to *conjecture, doubt, distrust.* § 3. When there is *certainty,* there is intuition in all parts of the reasoning which show its connection; but what makes me *believe* is something *extraneous.* § 4. Now probability is grounded in its conformity with what we know, or in the testimony of those who know.

Th. I prefer to maintain that it is always grounded in likelihood (*vraisemblance*) or in conformity with the truth; and the testimony of another is also a thing which the truth has been wont to have for itself as regards the facts that are within reach. It may be said then that the similarity of the probable and the truth is taken either from the thing itself, or from some extraneous thing. The rhetoricians employ two kinds of *arguments:* the *artificial,* drawn from things by reasoning, and the *non-artificial,* based only upon the express testimony either of man or perhaps also of the thing itself.

But there are *mixed* arguments also, for testimony may itself furnish a fact which serves to form an artificial argument.

§ 5. *Ph.* It is for lack of similarity to truth that we do not readily believe that which has nothing like that which we know. Thus when an ambassador told the king of Siam that with us the water was so hardened in winter that an elephant might walk thereon without breaking through, the king said to him: Hitherto I have believed you as a man of good faith; now I see that you lie. § 6. But if the *testimony* of others can render a fact probable, the *opinion* of others should not pass of itself as a true ground of probability. For there is more error than knowledge among men, and if the belief of those whom we know and esteem is a legitimate ground of assent, men have reason to be Heathen in Japan, Mahometans in Turkey, Papists in Spain, Calvinists in Holland, and Lutherans in Sweden.

Th. The testimony of men is no doubt of more weight than their opinion, and in reason it is also the result of more reflection. But you know that the judge sometimes makes them take the oath *de credulitate,* as it is called; that in the *examinations,* we often ask witnesses not only what they have seen but also what they think, demanding of them at the same time the reasons of their judgment, and whether they have reflected thereupon to such an extent as behooves them. Judges also defer much to the views and opinions of experts in each profession; private individuals, in proportion as it is inconvenient for them to present themselves at the appropriate examination, are not less compelled to do this. Thus a child, or other human being whose condition is but little better in this respect, is obliged, whenever he finds himself in a certain situation, to follow the religion of the country, so long as he sees nothing bad therein, and so long as he is not in a condition to find out whether there is a better. A tutor of pages, whatever his sect, will compel them each to go to the church where those who profess the same belief as this young man go. The discussions between Nicole[1] and others on *the argument from the great number* in a matter of

[1] Pierre Nicole, 1625–1695, one of the most distinguished of the Port-Royalists, and, with the exception of Arnauld (*cf. ante*, p. 463, note 4) and Pascal, the most accomplished member of the school, was author with Arnauld of the fa-

faith may be consulted, in which sometimes one defers to it too much and another does not consider it enough. There are other similar *prejudgments* by which men would very easily exempt themselves from discussion. These are what Tertullian, in a special treatise, calls *Prescriptiones*,[1] availing himself of a term which the ancient jurisconsults (whose language was not unknown to him) intended for many kinds of exceptions or foreign and predisposing allegations, but which now means merely the temporal prescription when it is intended to repel the demand of another because not made within the time fixed by law. Thus there was reason for making known the *legitimate prejudgments* both on the side of the Roman Church and on that of the Protestants. It has been found that there are means of opposing novelty, for example, on the part of both in certain respects; as, for example, when the Protestants for the most part abandoned the ancient form of ordination of clergymen, and the Romanists changed the ancient canon of the Old Testament books of Holy Scripture, as I have clearly enough shown in a discussion I had in writing, and from time to time, with the bishop of Meaux, whom we have just lost, according to the news which came some days since.[2] Thus these censures being mutual, the novelty, although it presents a suspicion of error in these matters, is not a certain proof thereof.

mous *L'Art de Penser* or the Port Royal Logic. His most important work is his *Essais de Morale*, Paris, 1671–74. It was about his *De l'unité de l'église ou réfutation du nouveau système de Jurien*, Paris, 1687, that the theological controversies here alluded to by Leibnitz centred, and "in which the question was considered, whether Roman Catholicism allows itself to engage in the — undoubtedly questionable — argument of the 'majority of professors.'" An account of Nicole's *De l'unité de l'église* will be found in Bayle's Dict., Eng. transl., Vol. 4, p. 363, London, 1737. — Tr.

[1] Tertullian, 150–160 — 220–240, sought in his *De Præscriptione Hæreticorum* to produce a formal general argument against all heresies — "adversus hæreses omnes" — his object being to prevent heretics, in accordance with certain just and necessary rules (*præscriptiones*), from appealing to Scripture in support of their views. For an account of the work, *cf.* Smith and Wace, *Dict. of Christ. Biog.*, Vol. 4, p. 837 a, *sq.* — Tr.

[2] Leibnitz here refers to his correspondence with Jacques Bénigne Bossuet, 1627–1704, Bishop of Meaux from 1681 till his death. This correspondence was irenic in character, and extended, with some interruptions, over a period of about 25 years, but was without result, because Leibnitz would not suffer the freedom of scientific inquiry to be taken away, while Bossuet desired subjection to the infallible authority of the church. The entire correspondence has been published by Foucher de Careil, *Œuvres de Leibniz*, Vols. 1, 2,

CHAPTER XVI

OF THE DEGREES OF ASSENT

§ 1. *Ph.* As for the *degrees of assent*, we must take care that the grounds of probability we have do not operate beyond the degree of *likelihood* found therein or which has been found therein when they are examined. For we must admit that assent cannot always be based upon an actual view of the reasons which have prevailed with the mind, and it would be very difficult even for those[1] who have an admirable memory

Paris, 1859–60. A portion of the same is found in Dutens, *Leibnit. op. om.*, 1, 507 *sq*. The letters especially referred to are (1) of Leibnitz: Dec. 11, 1699, (Foucher de Careil, *Œuvres de Leibniz*, 2, 274–277; Dutens, *Leibnit. op. om.*, 1, 594–596), May 14 and 24, 1700 (F. 2, 314–369; D. 1, 612–642); (2) of Bossuet: Jan. 9 and 30, 1700 (F. 2, 278–306; D. 1, 596–611), Aug. 17, 1701 (F. 2, 396–426; D. 1, 657–673). For an account of the controversy, *cf.* Pichler, *Die Theologie des Leibniz*, Vol. 2, pp. 206–215.

The present passage is important, as it enables us to determine the date of the composition of the *New Essays*, or at least of this portion of them. Bossuet died April 12, 1704. This passage must then have been written in the second half of April, 1704; and from other data (for which *cf.* Guhrauer, *Leibniz. Eine Biographie*, Bk. II., p. 282 and Anmerkungen z. zweiten Buche, pp. 38–39; and Gerhardt's Introduction to the *New Essays*, *ante*, pp. 8, 9, and notes) it is evident that the entire work was substantially completed in 1704, though the revision of the French style, and possibly some minor additions or alterations, occupied Leibnitz to a certain extent after this date.

In this connection it is to be noted that the date given, *ante*, p. 9, line 15, 1709, should be 1704 (*cf.* Gerhardt, *Leibniz. philos. Schrift.*, 3, 297, note *), and that Gerhardt's remark, *ante*, p. 9: "On the other hand, he remarks, well-nigh it seems in the opposite sense," etc., as well as that by the Translator, *ante*, p. 101, note 1, *prope. fin.*: "As Leibnitz was occupied . . . with the composition and revision of his *New Essays*, from 1700 . . . to 1709 and perhaps later . . . possibly even as late as 1714 or 1716," should be modified accordingly. — Tr.

[1] Gerhardt's text reads: "Sur une veue actuelle des raisons, *qui ont prevalu sur l'esprit, et il seroit très difficile, même à ceux*, qui ont une memoire admirable," etc. The words italicised above are not found in the texts of Raspe, Erdmann, Jacques and Janet; and Janet restores the sense of "this incorrect phrase" thus: " . . . Sur une vue actuelle des raisons, *comme il arrive* chez ceux qui ont une mémoire admirable, *capable* de toujours retenir. . . . " Gerhardt's reading agrees with Locke's text, *cf. Philos. Wks.*, Vol. 2, p. 271, Bohn's ed., and is therefore to be preferred. — Tr.

always to retain all the proofs which have compelled them to a certain assent, and which sometimes might fill a volume on a single question. It suffices that they have once examined the matter minutely with sincerity and with care, and that they have, so to speak, *cast up the account*. § 2. Without this men must be very sceptical, or change their view at every moment, in order to yield themselves to every man who, having examined the question of late, offers them arguments which they cannot at once wholly answer, for lack of memory or of application at leisure. § 3. It must be admitted that this often makes men *obstinate* in error: but the fault is, not that they rely upon their memory, but that they have badly judged before. For often the remark that they have never thought otherwise takes the place of an examination and of reason with men. But ordinarily those who have least examined their opinions hold them most tenaciously. Holding to what one has *seen* is praiseworthy, but not always to what one has *believed*, because some consideration may have been left behind capable of overturning all. There is perhaps no one in the world who has the leisure, patience, and means of assembling all the proofs on both sides of the question upon which he has his opinions in order to compare these proofs and safely to conclude that nothing more remains for him to know for his more ample instruction. But the care of our life and of our more important interests cannot bear the delay, and it is absolutely necessary that our judgment be determined upon the points when we are incapable of attaining to a certain knowledge.

Th. There is nothing but what is good and solid in what you, sir, have just said. It would be desirable, however, for men to have at certain junctures *written abstracts* (in form of memoranda) *of the reasons* which have led them to an important opinion, which they are obliged often to justify afterwards to themselves or others. Besides, although in a matter of justice it is not usually allowable to retract the judgments which have been passed, and to revise the verdicts agreed upon (otherwise there would necessarily be perpetual unrest, which would be so much the more intolerable as the accounts of things past cannot always be preserved), yet one is sometimes allowed upon new light to sue for justice, and also to obtain what is called *restitutio in integrum*[1] contrary to the decision that has been given. And likewise in our own affairs, especially in matters very important, where it is still allowable to embark or to put back, and where it is not prejudicial to suspend their execution and to proceed bridle in hand, the decisions of our minds based upon probabilities should never so pass *in rem judicatam*,[2] as the jurisconsults call it, *i.e.* to a settlement, that we may not be disposed to the *revision* of the reasoning when new counter reasons of weight present themselves. But when there is no more time for deliberation, we must follow the judgment we made with as much firmness as if it were infallible, but not always with so much strictness.[3]

§ 4. *Ph.* Since, then, men cannot avoid exposing themselves to error in judgment and having different opinions, since they cannot look at things from the same points of view, they must maintain peace between themselves and the duties of humanity amid this diversity of opinions without claiming that another should promptly change a rooted opinion upon our objections, especially if there is room for supposing that his adversary acts from interest or ambition or from some other private motive. Most frequently those who would impose upon others the necessity of yielding to their opinions have examined things with but little thoroughness. For those who have entered beforehand sufficiently into the discussion to extricate themselves from doubt are so few in number, and find so little reason to condemn others, that nothing violent is to be expected on their part.

Th. Really that which one has the most right to censure in men is not their opinion, but their rash judgment in censuring

[1] *Cf.* Paulus, *Sententiarum*, Lib. I., Tit. VII. 1.: "Integri restitutio est redintegrandæ rei vel causæ actio. 2. Integri restitutionem prætor tribuit ex his causis, quæ per metum, dolum et status permutationem, et justum errorem, et absentiam necessariam, et infirmitatem aetatis gesta esse dicuntur;" also *Digest*, Lib. XLII., Tit. I. 33.

[2] *Cf. Digest*, Lib. XLII., Tit. I. 1: "*Res judicata* dicitur, quæ finem controversiam pronunciatione judicis accipit: quod vel condemnatione vel absolutione contingit." — TR.

[3] Janet cites as a parallel passage Descartes, *Discours de la Méthode*, Pt. III.: "Ma seconde maxime était d'être le plus ferme et le plus résolu en mes actions que je pourrais, et de ne suivre pas moins constamment les opinions les plus douteuses lorsque je m'y serais une fois déterminé que si elles eussent éte très-assurées." — TR.

that of others, as if it were necessary to be stupid or wicked to judge differently from themselves; a condition of things which, in the authors of these passions and hatreds who spread them among the public, is the effect of a mind haughty and unfair, which loves to rule and cannot suffer contradiction. Not that there is not, in truth, reason very often for censuring the opinions of others, but it must be done in a spirit of fairness, and sympathy with human weakness. It is true that we are right in taking precautions against bad doctrines, which are influential upon manners and upon practical piety: but we must not attribute them to people to their prejudice without having good proofs of the same. If fairness wishes to spare persons, piety demands the representation, where it is fitting, of the bad effects of their dogmas when they are injurious, as those are which are contrary to the providence of a perfectly wise, good, and just God, and contrary to that immortality of souls which renders them susceptible of the effects of his justice, not to speak of other opinions dangerous as regards morality and the police. I know that excellent and well-meaning men maintain that these theoretic opinions have less influence upon practice than is thought, and I also know that there are persons of an excellent disposition whom these opinions will never make do anything unworthy of themselves: as also those who have reached these errors by speculation, are by nature wont to be farther removed from the vices to which men in general are susceptible, besides the fact that they are careful of the dignity of the sect in which they are, as it were, chiefs; and it may be said that Epicurus and Spinoza, for example, have led a life wholly exemplary. But these reasons cease most frequently in their disciples or imitators, who, believing themselves released from the troublesome fear of an overseeing Providence and of a menacing future, give loose reins to their brutish passions, and turn their mind to the seduction and corruption of others; and if they are ambitious and of a disposition somewhat harsh, they will be capable, for their pleasure or advancement, of setting on fire the four corners of the earth, as I have known from the character of some whom death has swept away. I find also that similar opinions insinuating themselves little by little into the minds of men of high life who rule others and upon whom affairs depend, and slipping into the books in fashion, dispose all things to the general revolution with which Europe is threatened, and accomplish the destruction of what still remains in the world of the generous sentiments of the ancient Greeks and Romans, who preferred love of country and of the public good, and regard for posterity to fortune, and even to life. These *public spirits,* as the English call them, are fast diminishing, and are no longer in fashion; and they will diminish still faster when they are no longer sustained by the good morality and true religion which even natural reason teaches us. The best of the opposite character who are beginning to rule have no other *principle* than that they call *honor.* But the mark of the honest man and of the man of honor with them is only to do no baseness as they understand it. And if for the sake of power or through caprice anyone poured forth a deluge of blood, if he turned every sense upside down, that would be counted as nothing, and a Herostratus [1] of the ancients or a Don Juan in the "Festin de Pierre" [2] would pass for a hero. Boldly they scoff at the love of country, they ridicule those who care for the public, and when any well-meaning man speaks of what will become of posterity, they reply: we shall see when the time comes. But these persons will possibly experience themselves the evils they think reserved for others. If, however, this disease of an epidemic mind whose bad effects begin to be visible is corrected, these evils will perhaps be prevented; but if it goes on increasing, Providence will correct men by the revolution itself which must spring therefrom: for whatever may happen, everything will always turn out for the better in general at the end of the account, although that ought not and cannot happen without the punishment of those who have contributed even to the good by their bad acts. But I return from a digression into which the consideration of truthful opinions and of the right of censuring them has led me.

[1] Herostratus, an Ephesian, who, for the sake of making his name famous, as he himself confessed on being put to torture, set fire to the temple of Artemis at Ephesus, on the night in which Alexander the Great was born, 356 B.C. — TR.

[2] The *Don Juan ou le Festin de Pierre*, 1665, a comedy of Molière, 1622–1673, the principal character of which is Don Juan. The play, written in prose, was versified in 1677, at the request of Molière's widow, by Thomas Corneille, 1625–1709. — TR.

Now as in theology *censures* go very much farther than elsewhere, and as those who lay great stress upon their orthodoxy, often condemn their adversaries, to whom those in the same party who are called *syncretists* by their adversaries are opposed, this opinion has caused civil wars to spring up between the rigid and condescending in one and the same party. But, as to refuse eternal salvation to those who are of another opinion is to encroach upon the rights of God, the wisest of those who condemn, only indicate the peril in which they think they see erring souls, and leave to the peculiar mercy of God those whose wickedness does not render them incapable of profiting therefrom, and on their part believe themselves obliged to make all imaginable efforts to withdraw them from a condition so dangerous. If these persons who thus judge of the perils of others have come to this opinion after a suitable examination and there are no means of disabusing them of it, their conduct cannot be censured so long as they use only fair means. But as soon as they go farther, they violate the laws of equity. For they should consider that others persuaded like themselves have an equal right to maintain their views, and even to spread them if they think them important. Opinions must be excepted which teach crimes that should not be allowed, and which it is right to suppress by stringent means, if it should be true, indeed, that he who maintains them cannot be rid of them;[1] as it is right to destroy even a poisonous animal, wholly innocent as it is. But I speak of suppressing the sect and not men, since we can prevent them from doing harm and dogmatising.

§ 5. *Ph.* To return to the ground and degrees of assent, it is proper to remark that propositions are of two kinds. Some are of fact, and, depending upon observation, may be based upon human testimony; others are speculative, and, regarding things which our senses could not discover, are incapable of similar testimony. § 6. When a particular fact is in conformity with our constant observations, and with the uniform report of others, we rest upon it as firmly as if it were certain knowl-

[1] Gerhardt reads: "ne peut point s'en defaire." Erdmann, Jacques and Janet read: "ne peut point s'en faire," and Janet in his note says: "supply 'd'autres.'" With this reading the meaning is: "cannot procure for himself others." —TR.

edge, and where it is in conformity with the testimony of all men, in all ages, so far as can be known, it is the *first* and highest degree of probability; for example, that fire warms, that iron sinks to the bottom of the water. Our *belief* built *upon* such foundations rises to *assurance*. § 7. In the second place, all historians relate that such an one has preferred his individual interest to that of the public, and as it has always been observed that this is the custom of the majority of men, the assent I give to these histories is *confidence*. § 8. Thirdly, when there is nothing either for or against it in the nature of things, a fact, vouched for by the testimony of unsuspected people, for example, that Julius Cæsar lived, is received with a *firm belief*. § 9. But when the testimony is found contrary to the ordinary course of nature or the witnesses vary among themselves, the degrees of probability may vary infinitely, whence arise these degrees which we call *belief, conjecture, doubt, uncertainty, distrust;* and there it is that exactness is necessary to form a right judgment and to proportion our assent to the degrees of probability.

Th. Jurisconsults in treating of proofs, presumptions, conjectures, and indices, have said a number of good things on this subject, and have gone into some considerable detail. They begin with *notoriety*, in which there is no need of proof. Afterwards they come to *complete proofs*, or those which pass as such, upon which they pronounce sentence, at least, in a civil process, but upon which in some places they are more reserved in a criminal process; and they are not wrong in demanding in such case *proofs more than complete*, and especially as regards what is called *corpus delicti*, according to the nature of the act. There are then *proofs more than complete*, and there are also ordinary *complete proofs*. Then there are *presumptions*, which pass provisionally as complete proofs, *i.e.* so long as the contrary is not proved. There are *proofs more than half complete* (to speak precisely), in which the one who relies upon them is allowed to swear to make them good (the *juramentum suppletorium*) ; there are others *less than half complete*, where wholly to the contrary the oath is administered to him who denies the act, to purge himself (the *juramentum purgationis*). Beyond this there are many degrees of *conjectures* and *indices*. Particularly in a criminal process there are indices (*ad torturam*) to proceed to the torture, which itself has its degrees indicated by the formulas of arrest; there are indices (*ad terrendum*) sufficient to show the instruments of torture and to prepare things as if they intended to come to it. There are some (*ad capturam*) to make sure of a suspected man; and (*ad inquirendum*) to make inquiries secretly and without noise. And these differences may be of use also on other similar occasions. The entire *form of judicial procedure* is nothing else in fact than a species of *logic* applied to questions of law. Physicians also have a number of degrees and differences in their *signs* and *indications* which may be seen among them. The mathematicians of our times have begun to calculate chances upon the occasion of games. Chevalier de Méré,[1] whose "Agrémens" and other works have been printed, a man of penetrating mind who was both a player and a philosopher, gave them an opportunity by forming questions regarding the profits in order to know how much the game would be worth, if interrupted at such or such a stage. In this way he induced Pascal, his friend, to examine these things a little. The question made a stir and gave Huygens the opportunity to produce his treatise "de Alea."[2]

[1] *Cf. ante*, p. 213, note 2; also *Response* (*Réplique*) *aux reflexions contenues dans la seconde Edition du Dictionnaire Critique de M. Bayle*, Gerhardt, 4, 570, Erdmann, 190, Janet, 2, 593, Dutens, 2, Pt. I., 92. Antoine Gombault, chevalier de Méré, c. 1610–1684, was erroneously confounded with a Georges Brossin, chevalier de Méré, belonging to another family, by all biographers since Moreri, until the special researches of M. de Brémont d'Ars proved the error and assigned him his right name. He had an inordinately exalted idea of his own importance and attainments, especially in mathematics. His *Agréments, discours de M. le chevalier de Méré à Mme ***, appeared in 1677, 12mo, and in the collected edition of all his works, entitled *Œuvres du chevalier de Méré*, Amsterdam, 1692, 2 vols., 12mo. A volume of *Œuvres posthumes*, 12mo, appeared at Paris, 1700, and again at The Hague, 1701. For further account of him, *cf.* Larousse, *Grande Dict. Univ. de XIXme Siècle*, Vol. 11, p. 72. — TR.

[2] *Cf. ante*, p. 150, note 3. Huygens' *De ratiociniis in aleæ ludo*, dated The Hague, 1657, is found in F. van Schooten, *Exercitat. math. lib. V.*, pp. 514–539, Lugd. Bat. 1657, 4to. It was written by Huygens in Dutch and translated into Latin by Schooten. There are two English translations, one attributed to Motte, but probably by Arbuthnot; the other by W. Brown. *Cf.* I. Todhunter, *Hist. of the Math. Theory of Probability*, pp. 22–23, Cambridge and London, Macmillan & Co., 1865. Leibnitz, *Miscellan. Leibnit.*, No. CXIII., *cf.* Dutens, 6, Pt. I., 318, says of it: "Christiani Hugenii ratiocinia *de lusu aleæ*, Franc. Schotenii scriptis mathematicis adjecta, sunt elegans specimen ratiocinationis de gradibus probabilitatis."

Spinoza also discussed the calculation of probabilities in games of chance,

Other learned men entered into the subject. Some principles were established of which the Pensioner De Witt also availed himself in a brief discourse printed in Dutch on annuities.[1] The foundation on which they have built goes back to the *prosthaphæresis*,[2] *i.e.* the taking of an *arithmetical* mean between several equally receivable suppositions. Our peasants also have made use of it for a long time according to their *natural mathematics.* For example, when some inheritance or land is to be sold, they form three bodies of appraisers; these bodies are called *Schurzen* in Low Saxon, and each body makes an estimate of the property in question. Suppose, then, that the first estimates its value to be 1000 crowns, the second 1400, the third 1500; the sum of these three estimates is taken, viz. 3900, and because there were three bodies, the third, *i.e.* 1300, is taken as the mean value asked for; or rather, they take the sum of the third part of each estimate which is the same thing. This is the axiom: *æqualibus æqualia*, equal suppositions must have equal consideration. But when the suppositions are unequal they compare them with each other. Suppose, for example, that with two dice, the one ought to win if it makes 7 points, the other if it makes 9, the question is asked what proportion obtains between their probabilities of winning? I reply that the probability of the last is worth only two-thirds of the

in a letter to Jan van der Meer. *Cf.* Epistola No. 38 (formerly 43), Spinoza, *Opera*, ed. Van Vloten and Land, 2, 145–149 (in Latin and Dutch): *Spinoza's Briefwechsel*, in J. H. v. Kirchmann's *Philos. Bibliothek*, Vol. 46, pp. 145–147. — TR.

[1] *Cf. ante*, p. 426, note 2. John De Witt appears to have been "the first to apply scientific principles to the calculations connected with annuities, which are analogous to those connected with assurances." His report on this subject was presented to the States General, July 30, 1671. It was entitled *De vardye van de lif-renten na proportie van de los-renten*, and appeared at La Haye, 1671. An abstract of it, showing exactly how De Witt reasoned on the subject, will be found in M. Nicolas Struyck, *Inleiding tot het algemeine geography*, etc., p. 345, Amsterdam, 1740, 4to, and an English translation of the tract is printed in *Contributions to the Hist. of Insurance* by Frederick Hendriks in the "Assurance Magazine," Vol. 2 (1852), p. 231. For some remarks on De Witt's hypothesis as to the rate of mortality, *cf.* the same vol., p. 393. — TR.

[2] Prosthaphæresis — προσθαφαίρεσις — = a previous subtraction. The term here signifies "the fundamental principle for the ascertainment of the degree of probability which requires us to take the arithmetical mean of the existing suppositions estimated according to their relative value." — TR.

probability of the first, for the first can make 7 in three ways with two dice, viz.: by 1 and 6, or 2 and 5, or 3 and 4; and the other can make 9 in two ways only, by throwing 3 and 6, or 4 and 5; and all these methods are equally possible. Then the probabilities, which are as the numbers of equal possibilities, will be as 3 to 2, or as 1 to $\frac{2}{3}$. I have more than once said that a *new kind of logic* would be required which would treat of the degrees of probability, since Aristotle in his "Topics" has done nothing less than this, and has contented himself with putting in a certain order certain popular rules distributed according to the common topics, which may be of use on some occasion where the question concerns the amplification of the discourse and the giving to it probability without putting it to the trouble of furnishing us a necessary balance for weighing probabilities and forming thereupon a solid judgment.[1] It would be well for him who should treat of this matter to pursue the examination of *games of chance;* and in general I wish that some skilful mathematician would produce an ample work with full details and thoroughly reasoned upon all sorts of games, which would be very useful in perfecting the art of invention, the human mind appearing to better advantage in games than in the most serious matters.

§ 10. *Ph.* The law of England observes this rule, that the copy of an act received as authentic by witnesses is a good proof, but *the copy of a copy,* however attested, and by witnesses the most credible, is never admitted as a proof in a trial. I have never yet heard any one censure this wise precaution. This observation at least may be drawn from it, that testimony has less force in proportion as it is farther removed from the *original truth* which is in the thing itself; while among certain peoples use is made of it in a directly contrary manner, opinions acquiring force as they grow older, and what would not at all have appeared probable a thousand years ago to a reasonable man a contemporary of the one who first certified it, passes at present as certain because many have related it upon his testimony.

Th. Historical critics have great regard for contemporary witnesses of things: but a contemporary even merits belief chiefly as regards public events only; but when he speaks of

[1] *Cf. ante*, p. 417, note 3.—TR.

motives, secrets, hidden forces, and things which may be disputed, as, for example, poisonings, assassinations, we acquaint ourselves with what many have believed. Procopius is very credible when he speaks of the war of Belisarius against the Vandals and the Goths, but when he retails horrible scandals against the Empress Theodora in his "Anecdotes," he may believe them who will.[1] Generally, we should be very reserved in believing satires; we see some published in our times which, although wholly improbable, have nevertheless been greedily swallowed by the ignorant. And some day perhaps it will be said: Is it possible that one would have dared to publish these things at that time, if there had been any apparent foundation for them? But if this statement is some day made, the judgment will be a very erroneous one. The world, however, is inclined to indulge in satire; and, to quote but one example, the late Mr. Maurier, the son,[2] having published, from some caprice, in his memoirs printed some years since, certain things wholly without foundation against the incomparable Hugo Grotius, ambassador from Sweden to France, stirred apparently by some unknown circumstance against the memory of this illustrious friend of his father, I have noticed that many authors have repeated them from envy, although the negotiations and letters of this great man sufficiently make known the contrary. We have emancipated ourselves indeed from writing romances in history, and he who produced the last life of Cromwell thought that in order to enliven the subject he was allowed, in speaking of the life, still private, of this clever usurper, to make him travel in France, where he follows him into the public houses of Paris as if he had

[1] For critical discussion of the authorship of the Τὰ Ἀνέκδοτα — *Anecdota* or *Historia Arcana* — of Procopius, and of the credibility of its contents, *cf.* J. H. Reinkens, *Anecdota sintne scripta a Procopio Cæsariensi inquiritur*, Breslau, 1858, who denies, and F. Dahn, *Prokopius von Cäsarea*, Berlin, 1865, who affirms, that Procopius is the author. Prof. James Bryce gives a brief account and estimate of the work in his article on "Procopius," in the *Encyclop. Brit.* 9th ed. *Cf.* also M. Debidour, *Thesis*, 1877, who tries to make out the best case he can for Theodora, and Prof. Bryce in the "Contemporary Review," Feb. 1885. — TR.

[2] Louis Aubery du Maurier, the historian, died 1687, was the son of Benjamin Aubery, an ambassador from France to Holland, and published *Mémoires pour servir à l'Histoire de Hollande*, 1680, *Mémoires de Hamburg, de Lubeck, de Holstein*, etc. Leibnitz refers to him in his letter to Bierling, Oct. 24, 1709, Gerhardt, 7, 487. — TR.

been his master.[1] But it appears by the history of Cromwell written by Carrington, a well-informed man, and dedicated to his son Richard when he acted the part of the Protector, that Cromwell never went out of the British Isles. Detail especially is uncertain. There are almost no good accounts of battles; the majority of those of Titus Livius appear to be imaginary, as well as those of Quintus Curtius. It would be necessary to have on both sides the accounts of exact and capable men, who indeed would draw up plans of them like those which the Count of Dahlberg, who had already served with distinction under the King of Sweden, Charles Gustavus, and who, being Governor-General of Livonia, recently defended Riga, has had engraved touching the actions and battles of this prince. We must not, however, at once decry a good historian at a word from some prince or minister who has exclaimed against him on some occasion, or in regard to some subject not to his taste or wherein there really is perhaps some fault. The story is told that Charles the Fifth, wishing to have something of Sleidan[2] read, said: "Bring me my story-teller (*menteur*)," and that Carlowitz, a Saxon gentleman, of good repute at that time, said that the history of Sleidan destroyed in his mind all the good opinion he had had of the ancient histories. That statement, I say, will have no force in the minds of well-informed persons in overthrowing the authority of the history of Sleidan, the best part of which is a series of the public acts of the Diets and Assemblies, and of the writings authorized by the princes. And if there remained the least scruple regarding it, it has just been removed by the excellent history of my distinguished friend, the late Mr. Von Seckendorf[3] (in which I cannot, however, refrain

[1] Leibnitz here refers, according to Schaarschmidt, to Jas. Heath's *Flagellum; or the Life and Death, Birth and Burial of Oliver, the late Usurper*, London, 1663, 8vo. In this book the Protector is generously slandered and abused. S. Carrington's *The Hist. of the Life and Death of Oliver Cromwell*, London, 1659, 8vo, is a panegyric, in which Cromwell is compared, among others, with Alexander the Great. An abridgment of Heath's book may be found in the "Harleian Miscellany," I, 279, ed. Park. It may be added that "the earliest lives of Cromwell were either brief chronicles of the chief events of his life or were panegyrics." — TR.

[2] *Cf. ante*, p. 114, note 1. — TR.

[3] Veit Ludwig von Seckendorf, 1626–1692, a distinguished German scholar and statesman, whose *Commentarius historicus et apologeticus de Lutheran-*

from disapproving the term "Lutheranism" on the title-page, which a bad custom has authorized in Saxony), wherein the majority of the statements are justified by extracts from an immense number of pieces, drawn from the Saxon archives which he had at his disposal, although the Bishop of Meaux, who contested their validity, and to whom I sent it, merely replied to me that this book is horribly prolix; but I could wish that it were twice as large on the same scale. The more ample it is, the more hold it must give, since one has only to choose his passages; besides, there are some esteemed historical works which are much greater. For the rest, we do not always despise authors posterior to times of which they speak when what they relate is apparently otherwise. Sometimes, also, it happens that they preserve some most ancient pieces. For example, there has been doubt as to what family Suibert, Bishop of Bamberg, since Pope under the name of Clement II., belonged. An anonymous author of the history of Brunswick, who lived in the fourteenth century, named his family, and some persons learned in our history desired to pay no regard whatever to it; but I have had a chronicle much more ancient, not yet printed, in which the same statement is made with more details, from which it appears that he belonged to the family of the ancient allodial seigniors of Hornbourg (not far from Wolfenbuttel), the territory of which was given by the last owner to the cathedral church of Halberstadt.

§ 11. *Ph.* I do not wish you to think that I desired to lessen the authority and use of history by my remark. It is from this source that we receive with a convincing evidence a large

ismo sive de Reformatione, Leipzig, 1692, 3 vols., fol., occasioned by and directed against the *L'Histoire du Luthéranisme*, Paris, 1680, of the Jesuit Maimbourg, is his most important work, and a rich storehouse of authentic materials for the history of the reformation from 1517–1547, drawn from documents contained in the Saxon archives, the writings of the reformers and their contemporaries, accompanied by a polemical and historical commentary. It is the work of an able, philosophic mind, with scarcely a trace of the sectarian spirit. Leibnitz gives a brief account and estimate of the book in his letters to Bossuet, Jan. 8–18, and April 8–18, 1692 (*cf.* Foucher de Careil, *Œuvres de Leibniz*, 1, 228, 275, Dutens, *Leibnit. op. om.*, 1. 523–4, 530–531). It is also referred to in Bossuet's letters to Leibnitz, Jan. 10, 1692 (F. 1, 226, D. 1, 522), March 26 or May 26, 1692 (F. 1. 253), and Leibnitz to Bossuet, without dates (F. 1, 223, 254–255). For further remarks of Leibnitz concerning it, *cf.* Dutens, 5, 90, 93, 566. — TR.

part of our useful truths. I see nothing more valuable than the records of antiquity remaining to us, and I wish we had more of them, and less corrupted. But it is always true that no copy raises itself higher than the certainty of its first original.

Th. It is certain, that when we have a single ancient author as the authority for a fact, all those who have copied him add no weight thereto, or rather should be reckoned as nothing. It should be wholly as if what they said belonged to the number, τῶν ἅπαξ λεγομένων, of things which have been said only once, a collection of which Menage[1] wished to make. Moreover, to-day, if a hundred thousand petty writers should repeat the slanders of Bolsec[2] (for example), a man of judgment would value it no more than the noise of goslings. Jurisconsults have written *de fide historica;* but the subject merits a more exact research, and some of these gentlemen have been too indulgent. As for that which is of great antiquity, some of the most noted facts are doubtful. Clever people have doubted, with reason, whether Romulus was the first founder of the city of Rome. There is dispute about the death of Cyrus, and besides, the discrepancy between Herodotus and Ctesias has spread doubt upon the history of the Assyrians, Babylonians, and Persians. That of Nebuchadnezzar, of Judith, and even of the Ahasuerus of Esther suffer from great difficulties. The Romans, when speaking of the gold of Toulouse, contradict the story of the defeat of the Gauls by Camillus. Above all, the particular and private history of peoples is without credit, unless it is taken from very ancient originals, and is sufficiently in conformity with public history. This is why the

[1] *Cf. ante*, p. 350, note 1.—TR.

[2] Jérôme Hermès Bolsec, born at Paris, died 1685, at Lyons, was a Carmelite of Paris, who forsook his order, became a Protestant, fled to Italy and thence to Geneva, where he set up as a physician, but not meeting with the success he desired, gave himself up to theology, discoursed publicly on the doctrine of Predestination, advocating the views of Pelagius, and thus incurring the censure of Calvin, was imprisoned and then banished by the Senate of Geneva, Dec. 29, 1551. He went thence to Bern, whither Calvin pursued him. These persecutions developed in him a violent hatred towards Calvin, which, after his return to the Catholic faith, he vented in his *L'Histoire de la vie, mœurs, actes, doctrine et mort de Jean Calvin*, Paris, 1577, 8vo. He also published a similar work, *L'Histoire de la vie, mœurs, doctrine et déportements de Théodore de Bèze*, Paris, 1580, 8vo. Both works are merely pamphlets, with no historical authority.—TR.

stories told us of the ancient German, Gallic, British, Scotch, Polish, and other kings pass with reason as fabulous and made up. Trebeta, son of Ninus, founder of Treves, Brutus, ancestor of the Britons, or Britains, are as real as the Amadis. The tales taken from certain story-tellers, which Trithemius,[1] Aventin,[2] and even Albinus[3] and Sifrid Petri[4] have taken the liberty to tell of the ancient princes of the Franks, Boii, Saxons, Frisians; and what Saxo Gramaticus and the Edda tell us of the remote antiquities of the north, cannot have more authority than what Kadlubko,[5] the first Polish historian, says of one of their kings, a son-in-law of Julius Cæsar. But when the histories of different peoples agree in instances where there is no appearance that one has copied another, it is a great sign of their truth. Such is the

[1] Johann Trithemius, 1462–1516, abbot of Spanheim, whose *Compendium, sive breviarium primi voluminis annalium, sive historiarum, de origine rerum et gentis Francorum* appeared at Mainz, 1515, reprinted, Paris, 1539. Leibnitz speaks of him in his *Introd. in collectionem Scriptorum Histor. Brunsvicensi inservientium*, Dutens, 4, Pt. II., 4, 5. For an account of him, *cf.* Michaud, *Biog. Univ.* Vol. 46, pp. 551–559. — Tr.

[2] Johann Thurmayr Aventinus, 1466–1534, author of *Annales Boiorum*. His history, the materials of which were drawn from authentic sources, was finished in 1528, and published "with some important omissions" of passages adverse to the Roman Catholics by Zeigler in 1554. The omitted passages were afterwards restored by Nicolas Cisner in the Basle ed., 1580. Leibnitz mentions him in his *Introd. in col. Script. Histor. Brunsvic.*, Dutens, 4, Pt. II., 4. — Tr.

[3] Alcuin, — Latin, Alcuinus or Albinus Flaccus, — c. 735–804, the instructor of Charlemagne, whose collected works, containing among other things some historical treatises, were first published by And. Duchesne, Paris, 1617, 1 vol., fol., and afterwards by Froben, *Alcuini opera, post editionem ab And. Quercetano curatam, de novo collata, emendata, aucta et illustrata*, 2 vols., fol., Ratisbon, 1777. Migne, *Patrol.*, Vols. 100, 101, is a reprint of this ed. — Tr.

[4] Sifrid or Suffrid Petri, 1527–1597, a Dutch philologist of great learning, but deficient in critical ability and taste, was Professor of Latin and Greek in the University of Erfurt, 1557, of Law at Cologne, 1577, and of Canon Law at Louvain and Cologne, 1585. He was the historiographer of the States of Friesland, and published *De Frisiorum antiquitate et origine lib. III.*, Cologne, 1590; *De Scriptoribus Frisiæ decades XVI. et semis*, Cologne, 1593. His *Historia veterum episcoporum Ultrajectinæ sedis et comitum Hollandiæ*, appeared at Franeker, 1612. — Tr.

[5] Vincent Kadlubek or Kodlubko, 1161–1223, bishop of Cracow, a Latin chronicler of the early history of Poland, whose *Historia Polonica*, Dobromiel, 1612, 12mo, written with spirit, but in a barbarous style, throws much light on the events of his own time, but must be received with caution, as regards the early period, since he treated the early legendary stories, many of which closely resemble the Scandinavian sagas, as genuine history. The work is in four books and extends to the year 1202, and is true and faithful in relating events in Poland in the 11th and 12th centuries. — Tr.

accord of Herodotus with the history of the Old Testament in many things, for example, when he speaks[1] of the battle of Megiddo between the king of Egypt, and the Syrians of Palestine, *i.e.* the Jews, in which, according to the testimony of the sacred history we have of the Hebrews, King Josias was mortally wounded. The consent of the Arabic, Persian, and Turkish historians with the Greeks, Romans, and other occidentals gives pleasure to those who seek for facts; as also the testimony which the medals and superscriptions, remaining from antiquity, render to the books which have come down from the ancients to us and which are, in reality, copies of copies. We must wait for what we shall yet learn of the history of China, until we are in a better condition to judge of it, and until it shall bear its credibility with itself. The use of history consists principally in the pleasure there is in knowing origins, in the justice rendered to the men who have deserved well of other men, in the establishment of historical criticism, and especially of sacred history, which supports the foundations of revelation, and (putting also aside the genealogies and laws of princes and powers) in the useful teachings which the examples furnish us. I do not despise the thorough examination of antiquities, even to the smallest trifles; for sometimes the knowledge which the critics draw from them may be of use in more important matters. I consent, for example, to the writing even of the entire history of clothing and of the tailor's art, from the garments of the Hebrew priests, or, if you please,-from the peltries which God gave to the first bride and bridegroom at their departure from Paradise, to the top-knots and furbelows of our time, and to the union therewith of all that can be drawn from ancient sculptures and from paintings also made some centuries after. I will furnish indeed, if any one desires it, the memoirs of a man of Augsburg of the past century, who is described with all the clothes which he wore from his infancy up to the age of 63 years. I do not know who told me that the late Duke of Aumont,[2] a

[1] *Cf.* Herodotus II. 159, and notes of Bähr and Rawlinson on the passage. —TR.

[2] Louis-Marie-Victor d'Aumont, 1632–1704, a French scholar, numismatist, and "brigadier du roi" under Louis XIV. in the Low Countries, contributed much to the progress of the knowledge of medals, and was a member of the "Académie des inscriptions et Belles-Lettres." —TR.

great connoisseur of fine antiquities, had a similar curiosity. This may perhaps be of use in distinguishing the legitimate monuments from those which are not so, not to speak of other uses. And since men are allowed to play, they will still further be allowed to divert themselves with these kinds of work, if their essential duties do not suffer thereby. But I wish there might be some persons who would devote themselves preferably to drawing from history that which is more useful, as the extraordinary examples of virtue, remarks upon the conveniences of life, stratagems of politics and of war. And I wish that a kind of universal history were written which should indicate only such things, and some few others of more consequence; for sometimes one reads an extensive historical work, learned, well-written, suited also to the end of the author, and excellent of its kind, but which contains little useful instruction, by which I do not mean here simple morality, with which the "Theatrum vitæ humanæ"[1] and other such *florileges* are filled, but skill and knowledge of which everybody would not think in case of need. I wish also that an infinite number of things of this nature, by which we might profit, might be drawn from books of travel, and be arranged according to the order of the subjects. But it is astonishing that while so many useful things remain to be done, men amuse themselves almost always with what is already done, or with purely useless things, or at least with what is the least important, and I see little remedy therefor until the public is more concerned about them in more tranquil times.

§ 12. *Ph.* Your digressions give pleasure and profit. But from the probabilities of facts, let us come to those of opinions concerning things which do not fall under the senses. Such things are incapable of any testimony, for example, the existence and[2] nature of spirits, angels, demons, etc., the material substances which are in the planets and other mansions[3] of

[1] Theodore Zwinger, 1533–1588, a celebrated Swiss physician, whose *Theatrum vitæ humanæ*, "a vast compilation of historical facts and anecdotes, and of curious and piquant observations," in preparing which he availed himself of the materials which his father-in-law, Lycosthenes [Conrad Wolffhart], 1518–1561, had collected and asked him to set in order, appeared at Basle, 1565–1604, 5 vols., fol. — TR.

[2] Gerhardt reads: "de," a Ms. or typographical error; Erdmann, Jacques, and Janet have "et." — TR.

[3] Locke's word, *Philos. Works*, Vol. 2, p. 279 (Bohn's ed.). — TR.

this vast universe; finally, upon the mode of operation of the majority of the works of nature, and of all these things we can have merely conjectures, wherein *analogy*[1] is the great rule of probability. For being incapable of attestation, they can appear probable only so far as they agree more or less with established truths. As violent friction of two bodies produces heat and even fire, as the refractions of transparent bodies produce the appearance of colors, we think that *fire* consists in a violent agitation of the imperceptible parts, and that *colors* also, whose origin we do not see, come from a similar refraction; and finding that there is a *gradual connection* in all the parts of the creation that may be subject to human observation, without any considerable gap between any two, we have every reason to think that things rise also towards perfection gradually and by insensible degrees.[2] It is difficult to say where the sensible and the rational begin, and what is the lowest degree of living things; it is like the increase or diminution of quantity in a regular cone. The difference is exceeding great between certain men and certain animals; but if we wish to compare the understanding and capacity of certain men and certain brutes, we shall find so little difference, that it will be very difficult to assert that the understanding of these men is clearer or more extended than that of these brutes. When, therefore, we observe such an insensible gradation between the parts of creation from man to the lowest parts beneath him, the rule of analogy makes us regard it as probable that there is a parallel gradation in the things above us and beyond the sphere of our observation, and this kind of probability is the broad foundation of rational hypotheses.[3]

[1] In the case of natural phenomena beyond the reach of the senses, analogy is the great rule of probability, the reasoning in general being hypothetical only, and the force and certainty of the conclusion therefrom being directly proportional to the reality and degree of the resemblance or similarity of the phenomena. Since Locke's and Leibnitz's day, great advance has been made in our knowledge of the nature of the materials existing in the various heavenly bodies, chiefly through the aid of the spectroscope and spectral analysis, not only strengthening and increasing the measure of probability in the application of the conclusion from analogy to the conjectured conditions of other worlds, but in some cases and to a certain extent giving us well accredited positive knowledge in regard to their constitution. — TR.

[2] *Cf.* A. C. Fraser, *Locke's Essay Concerning Human Understanding*, Vol. 2, p. 380, note 2. Oxford, Clarendon Press, 1894. — TR.

[3] The probable conclusion from analogy is a rational hypothesis, whose

Th. It is upon the ground of this *analogy* that Huygens, in his "Cosmotheoros,"[1] judges that the condition of the other principal planets is quite similar to ours, excepting the difference which their different distance from the sun must cause: and Fontenelle,[2] who had already before published his conversations full of wit and knowledge on the plurality of worlds,

hypothetical character consists in the fact that it is not a completely exhaustive induction or a mathematical demonstration from the given data, therefore still problematical, and whose rationality consists in the fact that no known reason exists against the assumed instance, but on the contrary the analogy itself directly furnishes occasion for a provisional consideration of, if not a belief in, the hypothesis. — TR.

[1] *Cf. ante*, p. 150, note 3. Huygen's *Cosmotheoros, sive de terris cœlestibus earumque ornatu conjecturæ* — a speculation concerning the inhabitants of the planets, and the last work of the great physicist and mathematician — appeared posthumously, at the Hague, 1698, and in a German trans., Leipzig, 1703, just before Leibnitz wrote Bk. IV. of the *New Essays*, and in an English trans., entitled, *The Celestial World discovered; or Conjectures concerning the Inhabitants, Plants, and Productions of the Worlds in the Planets*, London, 1699, 8vo; *Conjectures concerning the Planetary Worlds*, Glasgow, 1727, 12mo. The work is found in Huygens, *Opera Omnia*, Leyden, 1824, 2 vols., Vol. 1, pp. 641–722. — TR.

[2] Bernard le Bovier de Fontenelle, 1657–1757, a litterateur rather than a philosopher, who, nevertheless, according to Janet, "belongs to the history of philosophy, through the spirit of inquiry and criticism which animates his works," attempted, and successfully, in his *Entretiens sur la pluralité des mondes*, Paris, 1686, 12mo (a sixth *Entretien* was added in the Paris ed. of 1687, according to Brunet) to popularize the astronomical theories and doctrines of Copernicus and Descartes. The work is a fine illustration of the possibility of making science, without ceasing to be scientific, intelligible and interesting to the men of the world. Fontenelle became a member of the "Académie Française" in 1691, and, on the revival of the "Académie des Sciences de Paris" in 1699, was nominated its perpetual secretary, and continued in that office for fifty-eight years, publishing each year a volume of the *Histoire* of this *Académie*, containing clear and orderly arranged extracts from or analyses of the papers read before the *Académie*, often accompanied with new and profound views of his own, together with *Éloges* of the members dying in each year, among which is the *Éloge de Leibniz*, "a masterpiece," found in *L'Histoire de l'Académie Royale des Sciences de Paris, année* 1716; in Vol. 3, 1722, of the collection of these *Éloges*, 69 in number, entitled *Histoire du renouvellement de l'Académie Royale des Sciences en 1699, et Éloges historiques des Académiciens morts depuis ce temps-là*, 3 vols., Paris, 1708–1722; in *Œuvres de Fontenelle*, 3 vols., La Haye, 1728–29, Vol. 3, pp. 232–259; new ed., 11 vols., Paris, 1766, Vol. 5, pp. 447–506; and in F. Bouillier, *Éloges de Fontenelle avec une Introd. et des Notes*, Paris, 1883, pp. 103–134; *cf.* also Jacques, *Œuvres de Leibniz*, Vol. 2, pp. i–xxiv, Dutens, *Leibnit. op. om.*, Vol. 1, pp. xix–liii.

The *Entretiens sur la pluralité des mondes* is found in *Œuvres de Fontenelle*, La Haye, 1728–1729, Vol. 1, pp. 149–234; new ed., Paris, 1766, Vol. 2, pp. 1–190; there is a German trans. by Gottsched, 1751, Eng. trans. by Glanvill, London, 1688, 1768, by A. Behn and others, London, 1801, and from the

has said some pretty things thereupon, and has discovered the art of enlivening a difficult[1] subject. He would say, as it were, that a harlequin in the empire of the moon is altogether what it is here. It is true that we judge in a wholly different way of moons (which are satellites merely) than of the principal planets. Kepler[2] has left a little book which contains an ingenious story upon the condition of the moon, and an Englishman,[3] an *homme d'esprit*, has published the humorous description of a Spaniard (of his own invention) whom some birds of passage transported to the moon, not to mention Cyrano,[4] who since went to find this Spaniard. Some clever men, wishing to present a beautiful picture of the other life, conduct very happy souls from world to world; and our imagination finds therein a part of the agreeable occupations which may be ascribed to genii. But however it may strive, I doubt if it can attain its object, because of the great interval between us and these genii, and the great variety found therein. And until we find telescopes like those Descartes made us hope for in order to discern parts of the moon's sphere no larger than our houses, we cannot determine what there is in a globe different from ours. Our conjectures will be more useful and

"last and best" ed., with notes and a critical account of the author's writing by the astronomer Jerome de la Lande, Paris, 1800, by Miss E. Gunning, 1803.

Fontenelle was author also of *Dialogues des morts*, Paris, 1683; *L'Histoire des Oracles*, Paris, 1687; *Doutes sur le système physique des causes occasionelles*, against Malebranche, Paris, 1686. — TR.

1 Jacques reads: "fort difficile." — TR.

2 *Cf. ante*, p. 123, note 2. The book of Kepler here referred to by Leibnitz is his *Somnium seu de astronomia lunari*, Francofurti, 1634, 4to, published after his death by his son, and found in Frisch, *J. Kepleri opera omnia*, Vol. 8, Pt. I., pp. 21-39. The concluding paragraphs, pp. 38-39, are of a zoölogical and ethnological character. Michaud (*Biog. Univ.* 22, 313) says it is a philosophical and allegorical romance, in which the author exposes the astronomical phenomena as they would appear to the inhabitants of the moon, who like ourselves think that they are at the centre of the universe, but who are not so well situated as we to raise themselves to the "idea" of the true system. Schaarschmidt states that Kepler had occupied himself with Plutarch's *De facie in orbe lunæ* (Eng. trans. in *Plutarch's Morals*, ed. Goodwin, 5, 234-292 — the Moon-Dæmons, 289) and from the tales about the moon-dæmons therein contained related by Sylla, had derived his idea of a lunar geography. — TR.

3 Franc. Godwin. *Cf. ante*, p. 342, note 2. — TR.

4 *Cf. ante*, pp. 228, note 2; 309, note 3. The reference is to his *Voyage dans la lune*. *Cf. Théodicée*, Pt. III., § 343; Gerhardt, 6, 318; Erdmann, 603 b; Jacques, 2, 268; Janet, 2, 359, 360; Dutens, 1, 364. — TR.

more true upon the internal parts of our bodies. I hope that we shall go beyond conjecture on many occasions, and I already now believe that at least the violent agitation of the parts of the fire of which you just spoke should not be reckoned among the things which are only probable. It is a pity that the hypothesis of Descartes regarding the constitution (*contexture*) of the parts of the visible universe has been so little confirmed by the researches and discoveries since made, or that Descartes did not live fifty years later to give us an hypothesis upon the basis of present knowledge as ingenious as the one he gave upon the basis of the knowledge of his time.[1] As for the gradual connection of species, we have said something concerning it in a preceding conference, in which I remarked that philosophers had already reasoned *upon the vacuum in the forms* or species.[2] Everything goes by degrees in nature, and nothing by leaps, and this rule regarding changes is a part of my law of continuity.[3] But the beauty of nature, which desires distinct perceptions, demands the appearance of leaps, and so to speak musical cadences in phenomena, and takes pleasure in mixing the species. Thus although there may be in some other world mediate species between man and beast (according as we understand these words), and although there may be somewhere rational animals surpassing us, nature has found it good to keep them away from us, in order to give us without contradiction the superiority we have in our globe. I speak of mediate species, and I should not wish to regulate myself here by human individuals, who approach the brutes, because apparently this is not a defect of faculty, but a hindrance to its exercise; so that I think that the most stupid of men (who is not in a condition contrary to nature by reason of some disease or some other permanent defect taking the place of the disease) is incomparably more rational and more docile than the most spiritual of all

[1] Leibnitz here refers to Descartes' theory of vortices, which he elaborated in his *Principia Philosophiæ*, Pts. III. and IV. A brief account of it will be found in the *Encyclop. Brit.*, 9th ed., article "Descartes," Vol. 7, pp. 107–108 (American Reprint). *Cf.* also J. H. v. Kirchmann's German translation, with notes, of the *Prin. Philos.* (Vol. 26, Pt. I., of his *Philos. Bibliothek.*), 2d ed. Heidelberg, 1887. For other references of Leibnitz to the theory, *cf.* Gerhardt, *Leibniz. philos. Schrift.*, 4, 283, 288–289, 340 (Dutens, *Leibnit. op. om.*, 3, 252–253), 348. — Tr.

[2] *Cf. ante*, p. 333–334. — Tr.

[3] *Cf. ante*, p. 334, note 1. — Tr.

the beasts, although the contrary is sometimes said by way of a witticism. For the rest, I strongly approve the search for analogies: plants, insects, and the comparative anatomy of animals will furnish them more and more, especially if we continue to avail ourselves of the microscope still more than we have done. And in matters more general you will find that my views concerning the Monads diffused everywhere, their unending duration, the conservation of the animal with the soul, the perceptions undistinguished in a certain condition, such as the death of simple animals, the bodies which it is rational to attribute to genii, the harmony of souls and bodies, which causes each to follow perfectly its own laws without being disturbed by the other and without the necessity of distinguishing therein the voluntary or the involuntary: you will find, I say, that all these views are entirely conformed to the analogy of the things which we observe and which I merely extend beyond our observations, without limiting them to certain portions of matter or to certain kinds of actions, and that the only difference therein is from the great to the small, from the sensible to the insensible.

§ 13. *Ph.* Yet there is one case where we defer less to the analogy of natural things which experience has made known to us, than to the contrary testimony of a strange fact which is far from it. For when supernatural events are conformed to the ends of him who has the power to change the course of nature, we have no reason for refusing to believe them when well attested, and this is the case of *miracles* which find not only belief for themselves, but give it also to other truths which need such confirmation.[1] § 14. Finally, there is a testi-

[1] Leibnitz here takes no notice of this remark of Locke concerning miracles, but expresses himself briefly on the subject in the *New Essays*, Preface, *ante*, p. 55, and Bk. IV., chaps. 17 *ad fin.*, *infra*, p. 582, 19 *ad fin.*, *infra*, p. 606; and more fully in the *Théodicée*, Discours préliminaire, etc., § 3, Gerhardt, 6, 50, Erdmann, 480, Jacques, 2, 26, Janet, 2, 34, Dutens, 1, 65, Pt. I., § 54, Pt. II., §§ 207, 208, Pt. III., § 249; *Discours de metaphysique*, 1686, §§ 7, 16, G. 4, 432, 441; *Remarques sur la lettre de M. Arnaud*, May 13, 1686, G. 2, 40; Letters to Clarke, G. 7, 352 *sq.*, E. 746 *sq.*, Js. 2, 414 *sq.*, Jt. 2, 617 *sq.*, D. 2, Pt. I., 110 *sq.*, trans. Duncan, 238 *sq.*, No. 1, § 4, No. 2, § 12, No. 3, §§ 13–17, No. 4, §§ 33, 40, 42–45, No. 5, §§ 107, 109–113, 115–118; *Response aux Objections contre le Système de l'harmonie préétablie qui se trouvent dans le livre* [du P. François Lami] *de la Connoissance de soy-même*, 1709, G. 4, 594, E. 460, D. 2, Pt. I., 100, and the Essay, first printed by Gerhardt, 4, 577–590, referring to the same book, and dated Berlin, Nov. 30, 1702, G. 4, 587; Letter to Tentzel, 1693, Dutens, 5, 401;

mony which outweighs all other assent, viz. *revelation, i.e.* the testimony of God, who can neither deceive nor be deceived; and the assent we give to it is called faith, which excludes all doubt as perfectly as the most certain knowledge. But the point is, to be assured that the revelation is divine, and to know that we understand its real sense; otherwise, we are exposed to fanaticism and the errors of a false interpretation. And when the existence and the sense of revelation is only probable, the assent cannot have a greater probability than that found in the proofs. But we shall speak of this still farther.

Th. Theologians distinguish between the *motives of credibility* (as they call them), together with the natural assent which must spring from them and which cannot have more probability than these motives, and the *supernatural assent*, which is an effect of the divine grace. Books have been

Annotatiunculæ subitaneæ ad Tolandi librum, De Christianismo mysteriis carente, written Aug. 8, 1701, Dutens, 5, 146, 148; Letters to Hartsoeker, Feb. 6, 1711, G. 3, 517–518, D. 2, Pt. II., 61, Dec. 7, 1711, G. 3, 529; *Systema theologicum*, written probably c. 1686, ed. C. Haas, Tübingen, 1860, p. 139. *Cf.* also the discussions by Pichler, *Theol. d. Leibniz*, 1, 226–237; K. Fischer, *Gesch. d. n. Philos.*, Bd. II., Leibniz, 3d ed., pp. 573–576; O. Pfleiderer, *Religionsphilosophie*, 2d ed., Berlin, 1883, Vol. 1, pp. 90–94, Eng. trans., Vol. 1, pp. 91–93.

Leibnitz — whether consistently or not with his philosophical system is fairly open to question — certainly admits the possibility, and upon sufficient and proper evidence the actuality, of miracles in the sense of personal acts of God in his universe, should a sufficient and proper reason therefor exist in God's mind. Such acts were not violations of law, but consisted simply in the substitution of a higher law for a lower, and the introduction of a new force in accord therewith. Leibnitz justifies his view thus: (1) The laws or order of nature are not metaphysical necessities, but positive truths, resting on the divine choice of the best as governed by the divine wisdom, and therefore amenable to the requirements of that wisdom, the physical always being subject to the moral order and purpose — "Cum natura rerum nihil aliud sit quam consuetudo Dei, ordinarie aut extraordinarie agere æque facile ipsi est, prout sapientia ejus exigit" (*Syst. theol.* p. 139, ed. Hass, Tüb. 1860); (2) All these acts were foreseen as *possible*, and as such included in the original ideal world-plan by the divine intelligence, and therefore involve no change or inconsistency in that plan; *cf. Discours de metaphys.*, § 7, G. 4, 432: "Or puisque rien ne se peut faire, qui ne soit dans l'ordre, on peut dire que les miracles sont aussi bien dans l'ordre que les operations naturelles, qu'on appelle ainsi parce qu'elles sont conformés à certaines maximes subalternes que nous appellons la nature des choses." And he continues in language which would be quoted more appropriately as a parallel passage to that just cited from the *Syst. theol.*: "Car on peut dire que cette nature n'est qu'une coustume de Dieu, dont il se peut dispenser à cause d'une raison plus forte, que celle qui l'a mû à se servir de ces maximes." — TR.

written expressly on the *Analysis of Faith* which do not altogether agree among themselves, but since we shall speak of this in the sequel, I do not wish to anticipate here what we shall have to say in its place.

CHAPTER XVII

OF REASON

§ 1. *Ph.* Before speaking distinctly of faith, we shall treat of *reason.* It signifies sometimes clear and true principles, sometimes conclusions deduced from these principles, and sometimes the cause, and particularly the final cause. Here we consider it as a faculty by which man is supposed to be distinguished from the beasts and in which it is evident that he much surpasses them. § 2. We need it both to extend our *knowledge*[1] and to regulate our *opinion,* and it constitutes, properly understood, two faculties, *sagacity,* for the discovery of mediate ideas, and the faculty of drawing conclusions, or *inference.* § 3. We may consider in reason these four degrees: (1) the discovery of proofs; (2) their orderly arrangement showing their connection; (3) the perception of the connection in each part of the deduction; (4) the drawing of the conclusion. We may observe these degrees in mathematical demonstrations.

Th. The *reason* is the known truth whose connection with another less known makes us give our assent to the latter. But in particular and pre-eminently we call it reason, if it is the cause not only of our judgment, but also of the truth itself,

[1] Locke, and in agreement with him here Leibnitz, uses "reason," as Schaarschmidt says, not in the sense of the νοῦς of Plato and Aristotle, as the faculty of ideas and first principles, but in the sense of the Greek λόγος, as the power or faculty of drawing conclusions, thus serving to extend our knowledge, a process which may be synthetic and deductive as well as analytic and inductive. The function of logic in regulating opinion as opposed to its function in extending knowledge is the production of the logical arrangement of knowledge and the classification of concepts, both of which greatly influence the reasoning process and its result, and thereby effect both the extension of knowledge and the regulation of opinion. For a fuller exposition of Locke's view, *cf.* J. H. v. Kirchmann, *Erläuterungen zu J. Locke's Versuch ü. d. menschl. Verstand,* No. 432, Vol. 52, Pt. II., pp. 105–108, of his *Philos. Bibliothek,* Berlin, 1874. — Tr.

which we also call *reason a priori,* and the *cause* in things corresponds to the *reason* in truths. This is why cause indeed is often called reason, and particularly final cause. Finally, the faculty which perceives this connection of truths, or the faculty of reasoning, is also called *reason,* and this is the sense you employ here. Now this faculty is really affected by man alone here below, and does not appear in other animals here below; for I have already shown above that the shadow of reason seen in the beasts is only the expectation of a similar event in a case apparently similar to the past, without knowing whether the same reason holds good. Men themselves act no differently in the cases where they are only *empirical.* But they raise themselves above the beasts, in so far as they see the connections of truths, the connections, I say, which themselves indeed constitute the necessary and universal truths. These connections are indeed necessary although they produce only an opinion, when after an exact research the prevalence of probability, so far as may be judged, may be demonstrated, so that then there is *demonstration,* not of the truth of the thing, but of the side prudence requires us to take. In dividing this faculty of reason, I think we do no wrong in recognizing two parts, according to a sufficiently received opinion which distinguishes *invention* and *judgment.* As for the four degrees which you remark in mathematical demonstrations, I find that usually the first, viz.: the discovery of proofs, does not appear therein, as is to be desired. There are syntheses, found sometimes without analysis, and sometimes the analysis has been suppressed. Geometers in their demonstrations put first the *proposition* which is to be proved, and in order to come to the demonstration they set forth by some figure what is given. This is called *ecthesis.* After this they come to the *preparation* and draw new lines which they need in the reasoning; and often the greatest art consists in finding this preparation. This done, they construct the *reasoning* itself, by drawing inferences from what was given in the ecthesis and from what has been added thereto by the preparation; and employing for this purpose truths already known or demonstrated, they reach the *conclusion.* But there are cases where they dispense with the ecthesis and the preparation.

§ 4. *Ph.* It is generally believed that the *syllogism* is the great instrument of reason and the best means of making use of this faculty. For myself I doubt it, for it serves only to show the connection of proofs *in one single example* and no more; but the mind sees the connection as easily and perhaps better without it. Those who know how to use the figures and the moods most frequently take their use for granted by an implicit faith in their masters without understanding their reason. If the syllogism is necessary, no one knew anything whatever by reason before its invention, and it will be necessary to say that God having made man a two-legged creature, left it to Aristotle to make him a rational animal; I mean from that small number of men that he could induce to examine the grounds of syllogisms, where among more than sixty ways of forming the three propositions there are only *about fourteen of them valid*. But God has been much kinder to men; he has given them a mind capable of reasoning. I do not say this to lower Aristotle, whom I regard as one of the greatest men of antiquity, whom few have equalled in extent, subtility, penetration of mind, and strength of judgment, and who by the very fact that he has invented this brief system of the forms of argumentation has rendered a great service to savants against those who are not ashamed to deny everything. But yet these forms are not the only nor the best means of reasoning; and Aristotle did not find them by means of the forms themselves, but by the original way of the manifest agreement of ideas; and the knowledge acquired of them in the natural order in mathematical demonstrations appears better without the aid of any syllogism. To *infer* is to draw a proposition as true from another already advanced as true, by supposing a certain connection of mediate ideas; for example, from the proposition that men will be punished in another world, we infer that they can determine themselves here. Here is the connection: *Men will be punished and God is the one who punishes;* therefore *punishment is just;* therefore *the punished is guilty;* therefore *he could have done otherwise;* therefore *he is free;* therefore finally *he has the power of self-determination.* The connection is seen better here than if there were five or six involved syllogisms, in which the ideas would be transposed, repeated, and enshrined in artificial forms. The question is to know what connectiou a mediate idea has with the extremes in a syllogism; but *this is what no syllogism can show.* It is the mind which can perceive these ideas so placed by a kind of *juxtaposition,* and that too by its own view. Of what use then is the syllogism? It is of use *in the schools* where *men are not ashamed* to deny the agreement of ideas which plainly agree. Whence it comes that men never make syllogisms in their own inquiries after truth or in their teaching of those who sincerely desire to know it. It is quite plain, also, that this order is the more natural: —

man — animal — alive;

i.e. man is an animal, an animal is alive, therefore man is alive, than that of the syllogism: —

animal — alive, man — animal, man — alive;

i.e. the animal is alive, man is an animal, therefore man is alive. It is true that syllogisms may be of use in discovering a fallacy concealed under the brilliant splendor of an ornament borrowed from rhetoric, and I had sometimes thought that the syllogism was necessary, at least to guard against sophisms disguised under florid discourse; but after a more severe examination, I have found that we have only to distinguish the ideas upon which the conclusion depends from those which are superfluous, and to arrange them in a natural order to show their incoherence. I knew a man to whom the rules of the syllogism were wholly unknown, who perceived at once the weakness and false reasoning of a long artificial and plausible discourse with which others better skilled in all the finesse of logic suffered themselves to be entrapped; and I believe that there will be few of my readers who do not know such persons. If that were not so, princes in matters relating to their crown and dignity would not fail to introduce syllogisms into the most important discussions, where, however, everybody believes it would be a ridiculous thing to make use of them. In Asia, Africa, and America, among peoples independent of the Europeans, scarcely any one has ever been heard to speak of them. Finally, it is found after all that these scholastic forms are not less liable to error; people also are rarely reduced to silence by this scholastic method and still more rarely convinced and won. They will recognize at most that their adversary is more adroit, but they do not cease to be persuaded of the justice of their cause. And if fallacies may be involved in the syllogism, the fallacy must be discovered by some other means than that of the syllogism. Yet I am not of the opinion that syllogisms are to be rejected or that we are to deprive ourselves of any means capable of aiding the understanding. There are eyes which need spectacles; but those who use them should not say that no one can see well without spectacles. This would be lowering nature in favor of an art, to which they are perhaps debtors. Unless it may have happened to them wholly contrary to the experience of persons who have availed themselves too much or too soon of spectacles, so that they have so thoroughly obscured their sight by means of them that they are no longer able to see without their aid.

Th. Your reasoning on the little use of syllogisms is full of a number of solid and fine remarks, and it must be admitted that the scholastic form of syllogisms is little employed in the world and that it would be too long and perplexing if one desired to employ it seriously. And yet, would you believe it, I consider the invention of the form of syllogisms one of the most beautiful, and also one of the most important, made by the human mind.[1] It is a species of *universal mathematics* whose importance is not sufficiently known; and it may be said that an *infallible art* is therein contained, provided we know and can use it, which is not always allowed. Now you must know that by *arguments in form,* I mean not merely this scholastic mode of argument used in colleges, but all reasoning which concludes by the force of the form, and in which there is no need of supplying anything, so that a *sorites,* another syllogistic series which avoids repetition, even an account well drawn up, and algebraic calculation, an infinitesimal analysis, will be for me almost arguments in form, because their form of reasoning has been predemonstrated, so that we are certain not to be deceived thereby. The demonstrations of Euclid most frequently come near being arguments in form; for when he apparently produces *enthymemes,* the proposition suppressed and seemingly lacking is supplied by the citation on the margin where is given the means of finding it already demonstrated;

[1] *Cf. ante*, p. 379, note 2. The letter to G. Wagner is Leibnitz's most complete expression of his estimate of the worth of formal logic. — TR.

this gives a great abstract without taking anything from its force. These inversions, compositions, and divisions of reasons which he makes use of are only the species of forms of argumentation peculiar and characteristic of the mathematicians and to the matter they treat; and they demonstrate these forms with the aid of the universal forms of logic. Further, you must know that there are *good asyllogistic conclusions* which also cannot be rigorously demonstrated by any syllogism without changing somewhat its terms; and this change itself of terms makes the conclusion asyllogistic. There are several of these, as among others, *a recto ad obliquum;* for example, Jesus Christ is God; therefore the mother of Jesus Christ is the mother of God. Again, that which clever logicians have called *inversion of relation,* as, for example, this conclusion: if David is the father of Solomon, without doubt Solomon is the son of David. These conclusions do not cease to be demonstrable by the truths on which the common syllogisms themselves depend. Syllogisms also are not merely categorical, but also hypothetical, in which are comprised the disjunctives. And we may say that the categorical are simple or complex. The simple categoricals are those which are usually reckoned, *i.e.* according to the moods of the figures; and I have found that the four figures have each six moods, so that there are twenty-four moods in all. The four common moods of the first figure are only the result of the meaning of the signs, All, No, Some. And the two which I add to them in order to omit nothing are only the subalterns of the universal propositions. For of these two ordinary moods, All B is C, and all A is B, therefore all A is C; again, No B is C, All A is B, then no A is C, we make these two *additional moods,* All B is C, All A is B, then some A is C; again, No B is C, All A is B, then some A is not C. For it is not necessary to demonstrate the *subaltern* and to prove its conclusions: All A is C, then some A is C; again, No A is C, then some A is not C, although we may, however, demonstrate it by the identicals joined with the moods already received of the first figure, in this way: All A is C, Some A is A, then some A is C; again, No A is C, Some A is A, then some A is not C. So that the two additional moods of the first figure are demonstrated by the first two ordinary moods of the said figure with the intervention of the subaltern, itself demonstrable by the other two moods of the same figure.[1] In the same way the second figure receives also two new ones. Thus the first and the second have six; the third has had six always; the fourth was given five, but it is found to have six also by the same principle of addition. But we must know that logical form does not bind us to this order of propositions which we commonly use, and I am of your opinion, sir, that this other arrangement is superior in value: All A is B, All B is C, therefore all A is C, which would be particularly by the sorites, which are a *chain* of such syllogisms. For if there were one more of them: All A is C, All C is D, therefore all A is D, we may make a chain of these two syllogisms, which avoids the repetition by saying: All A is B, All B is C, All C is D, therefore all A is D, wherein we see that the useless proposition All A is C is neglected, and the useless repetition of this same proposition which the two syllogisms would demand is avoided; for this proposition is henceforth useless, and the chain is an argument perfect and in good form without this same proposition when the force of the chain of reasoning has once for all been demonstrated by means of these two syllogisms. There is an infinite number of other chains of reasoning more complex, not only because a greater number of simple syllogisms enter therein, but also because the *ingredient* syllogisms exhibit greater differences among themselves, for there may be made to enter into them not only simple categoricals, but also copulatives, and not only categoricals, but also hypotheticals; and not only complete syllogisms, but also enthymemes, wherein the propositions believed evident are suppressed. And all this joined with the asyllogistic conclusions, and with the transpositions of the propositions, and with a multitude of turns and thoughts which conceal these propositions through the natural inclination of the mind to abridge, and by the properties of language appearing in part in the employment of the particles, will make a *chain* of reasoning which will represent the entire argumentation indeed of an orator, but emaciated

[1] *Cf. Difficultates quædam logicæ*, Gerhardt, 7, 211–217, Erdmann, 101–104; also Leibnitz's letter to Bourguet, March 22, 1714, G. 3, 569–70, E. 723 b. The youthful demonstration referred to in this letter is found in the *Dissertatio de Arte Combinatoria*, 1666, Problem II., § VI., G. 4, 46 *sq.*, E. 13 b. *sq.*, Dutens, 2, Pt. I., 352 *sq.*, and is Leibnitz's most thorough and elaborate treatment of the moods and figures of the syllogism. — Tr.

and stripped of its ornaments and reduced to *logical form*, not scholastically, but always sufficiently to recognize its force, according to the laws of logic, which are none else than those *of good sense*, placed in order and in writing, and which differ no more than the custom of a province differs from what it had been when from unwritten as it was, it has become written, except that being put in writing and being capable of being better seen at once, it furnishes more light to enable it to be pushed and applied; for natural good sense without the aid of art, making the analysis of certain reasoning, will sometimes be a little in trouble regarding the force of conclusions, finding some, for example, which include some mood, valid for truth but less ordinarily used. But a logician who wished us not to make use of such series, or wished not to make use of them himself, claiming that we must always reduce all the complex arguments to the simple syllogisms on which in fact they depend, would be, according to what I have already said to you, like a man who wished to compel the merchants of whom he buys something to count for him the numbers one by one, as we count on the fingers, or as we count the hours of the town-clock; a procedure which would indicate his stupidity, if he could not count otherwise, or if he could discover only at his fingers' ends that five and three make eight, or rather it would indicate a caprice if he knew these short methods and did not wish to use them or to allow us to use them. He would be also like a man who wished us not to employ axioms and theorems already demonstrated, claiming that we must always reduce all reasoning to first principles in which is seen the immediate connection of the ideas upon which in reality these mediate theorems depend.

After having explained the use of the forms of logic in the way in which I think it should be understood, I come to your considerations; and I do not see, as you wish, sir, that the syllogism serves merely to exhibit the connection of proofs *in a single example.* To say that the mind always sees easily the conclusions, is a statement which will not be found true; for we sometimes see some (at least in the reasonings of another) where there is room for doubt at first so long as their demonstration is not seen. Ordinarily, we use examples to justify conclusions, but this method is not always sufficiently sure, although there is an art of choosing examples which would not be found true if the conclusions were not valid. I do not believe it would be permitted in well-governed schools *to deny without any shame* the manifest agreement of ideas, and it does not appear to me that we employ the syllogism to show them. At least this is not its unique and principal use. You will find oftener than you think (in examining the paralogisms of authors) that they have sinned against the rules of logic, and I have myself found by experience sometimes in discussion, even by writing, with persons of good faith, that we began to be understood only when we argued in form in order to disentangle a chaos of reasonings. It would without doubt be ridiculous to wish to argue after the scholastic fashion in important deliberations, because of the importunate and embarrassing prolixities of this form of reasoning, and because it is like counting on the fingers. But yet it is only too true that in the most important deliberations regarding life, the state, salvation, men allow themselves to be dazzled often by the weight of authority, by the gleam of eloquence, by examples badly applied, by enthymemes falsely supposing the evidence of that which they suppress, and even by faulty conclusions; so that a severe logic, but of another turn than that of the School, would be only too necessary for them, among other things, to determine upon which side is the greatest probability. For the rest, the fact that the common herd of men ignore artificial logic, and that they do not cease thereby to reason well and sometimes better than the class practised in logic, this fact proves not its inutility any more than it would prove the inutility of artificial arithmetic, because we see that some persons count well on ordinary occasions without having learned to read or write and without knowing how to handle the pen or the tokens as far as to rectify the errors of another who has learned to calculate, but who may be neglectful or confused in the characters and signs. It is true that syllogisms also may become sophistical, but their own laws serve to recognize them; and syllogisms do not convert or indeed conquer always; but this is because the abuse of distinctions and of badly understood terms renders their use prolix until it becomes insupportable, if it must be driven to extremities.

It remains for me here only to consider and to supplement

your argument, employed as an example of clear reasoning without the form of the logicians: *God punishes man* (an assumed fact); *God punishes justly the one he punishes* (a truth of reason which may be regarded as demonstrated); therefore *God punishes man justly* (a syllogistic conclusion extended asyllogistically *a recto ad obliquum*); therefore *man is justly punished* (an inversion of relation, but which is set aside because of its evidence); therefore *man is guilty* (an enthymeme, in which is suppressed this proposition which in reality is only a definition: he who is punished justly is *guilty*); therefore *man could have done differently* (a suppression of this proposition: he who is guilty could have done differently); therefore *man was free* (a further suppression: he who could have done differently was free); therefore (by the definition of *freedom*) *he had the power of self-determination;* which was to be proved. Regarding which I remark further that this *therefore* itself includes in reality both the unexpressed proposition (that he who is *free* has the power of self-determination) and is useful in avoiding the repetition of terms. And in this sense nothing would be omitted, and the argument in this view might pass as complete. You see that this reasoning is a *series of syllogisms* entirely in accord with logic; for I do not now wish to consider the matter of this reasoning, wherein there might perhaps be some remarks to make or some explanations to demand. For example, when a man cannot do differently, there are some cases in which he might be guilty before God, as if he were very glad to be unable to aid his neighbor in order to have an excuse. To conclude, I admit that the scholastic form of arguing is ordinarily inconvenient, insufficient, badly managed, but I say at the same time that nothing would be more important than the art of arguing in form according to true logic, *i.e.* fully as to matter and clearly as to the order and force of the conclusions, whether self-evident or predemonstrated.

§ 5. *Ph.* I thought that the syllogism would be still less useful, or rather of absolutely no use in probabilities, because it pushes only a single *topical* argument.[1] But I see now that

[1] Aristotle, *Topics*, I., 1, 100^a 27 *sq.*, designates the "topical argument" as ὁ διαλεκτικὸς συλλογισμός, or ὁ ἐξ ἐνδόξων συλλογιζόμενος, *i.e.* the dialectic syllogism, or the syllogism which reasons from the probable in distinction from ἀπόδειξις, or the proof resting upon and leading back to first and necessary

it must always furnish solid proof of what is certain in the topical argument itself, *i.e.* the probability therein found, and that the force of the conclusion consists in the form. § 6. But if syllogisms serve only in judging, I doubt whether they are capable of use in invention, *i.e.* in finding proofs and making new discoveries. For example, I do not think that the discovery of the 47th proposition of the first book of Euclid is due to the rules of ordinary logic, for we first know it and then are able to prove it in syllogistic form.

Th. Comprising under syllogisms also the series of syllogisms and everything which I call formal argumentation, we may say that knowledge, not self-evident, is acquired by inferences which are valid only when they have their due form. In the demonstration of the said proposition which makes the square of the hypothenuse equal to the squares of the two sides, we divide the large square into parts and likewise the two small ones, and we find that the parts of the two small squares may all be found in the large one and neither more nor less. This is the proof of equality in form, and the equality of the parts is also proved by arguments in valid form. The analysis of the ancients was, according to Pappus, to take what is asked and to draw therefrom conclusions until they come to something given or known. I have remarked that for this result the proposition must be reciprocal in order that the synthetic demonstration may return in the contrary direction by the paths of analysis, but it is always a drawing of conclusions. It is well, however, to remark here that in astronomical or physical hypotheses the return does not take place; but in like manner success does not demonstrate the truth of the hypothesis. It is true it renders it probable, but as this probability appears to violate the rule of logic which teaches that the true may be drawn from the false, it will be said that logical rules will not have entire sway in probable questions. I reply that it is possible for the true to be concluded from the

truths. *Cf.* also *Topics*, VIII., 11, 162[a] 15, where he calls the συλλογισμὸς διαλεκτικός an ἐπιχείρημα or attempted proof, and the συλλογισμὸς ἀποδεικτικός a φιλοσόφημα or demonstration. On the whole subject, *cf.* Zeller, *Philos. d. Griech.*, II., 2 [Vol. 4], 242 *sq.*, 3d ed., 1879; Prantl, *Gesch. d. Logik*, 1, 95 *sq.*; Wallace, *Outlines of the Philos. of Aristotle*, § 23, pp. 47–48. *Cf.* also, *New Essays*, Bk. II., chap. 21, § 66, Th. (2), *ante*, p. 214, note 1; Bk. IV., chap. 2, § 14, Th., *ante*, p. 418, note 4. —TR.

false, but it is not always probable, especially when a simple hypothesis gives a reason for many truths, a thing which is rare and difficult to find. We might say with Cardan,[1] that the logic of the probable has other consequences than the logic of the necessary truths. But the probability itself of these conclusions must be demonstrated by the conclusions of the logic of the necessary truths.

§ 7. *Ph.* You appear to apologize for common logic, but I see clearly that what you bring forward belongs to a more sublime logic, to which the common is only what the alphabet is to scholarship: a fact which makes me remember a passage of the judicious Hooker, who in his book entitled "Ecclesiastical Polity," Book I., § 6, thinks that if we could furnish *the true helps of knowledge and of the art of reasoning,* which in this age passing as enlightened are not much known and for which people put themselves to very little trouble, there would be as much difference as regards maturity of judgment between men who would make use of them and what men now are, as between the men of the present and imbeciles.[2] I wish that our conference may give occasion to some to make a discovery of these *true helps of the art* of which this great man who had so penetrating a mind speaks. They will not be the imitators who like the cattle follow the beaten track (*imitatorum servum pecus*).[3]

[1] Girolamo Cardano, 1501–1576, an Italian physician, mathematician, and philosopher, whose complete works appeared at Lyons, 1663, 10 vols., fol., and an account of whose philosophy will be found in Stöckl, *Gesch. d. Philos. d. Mittelalters*, III. [Vol. 4], 452–458. — Tr.

[2] Richard Hooker, 1553–1600, attempted, in his *Laws of Ecclesiastical Polity*, to defend the Episcopal form of government of the Church of England, as established by the Protestant sovereign and Parliaments, against the attacks of the Presbyterians. To this end he gives in the two first books of his work an exposition of the fundamental principles by which the disputed question should be decided, especially of the nature of law in general, as a philosophical basis for the rest of his discussion. It is this portion of his work that gives it its permanent place and value in English literature and philosophy.

The passage here referred to by Locke and Leibnitz runs thus, *Eccles. Pol.*, Bk. I., chap. 6, § 3, *Works*, ed. Isaac Walton, Oxford, Univ. Press, 1841, 2 vols., 8vo, Vol. 1, p. 164 : "Wherefore if afterwards there might be added the right helps of true art and learning (which helps, I must plainly confess, this age of the world, carrying the name of a learned age, doth neither much know nor greatly regard), there would undoubtedly be almost as great difference in maturity of judgment between men therewith inured, and that which men now are, as between men that are now and innocents." — Tr.

[3] *Cf.* Horace, *Epist.*, 1, 19, 19. — Tr.

Yet I dare say there are in this age some persons of such strength of judgment and of such large extent of mind, that they could discover new paths for the advance of knowledge, if they would take the trouble to turn their thoughts in that direction.

Th. You have well remarked, sir, with the late Mr. Hooker, that the world troubles itself but little about this; otherwise I think there are and have been persons capable of succeeding therein. We must admit, however, that now we have great helps both on the side of mathematics and of philosophy, in which the Essay concerning Human Understanding of your excellent friend is not the least. We shall see if we may not be able to profit therefrom.

§ 8. *Ph.* I must further tell you, sir, that I have believed that there was a visible mistake in the rules of the syllogism; but since we have conferred together you have made me hesitate. I will, however, set before you my difficulty. It is stated that *no syllogistic reasoning can be conclusive unless it contains at least one universal proposition.*[1] But it seems that there are in the syllogism only particular things, which are the immediate object of our reasonings and knowledge; they revolve only about the agreement or disagreement of ideas, each of which has only a particular existence and represents only an individual thing.

Th. As far as you conceive the similarity of things you conceive something more, and the universality consists only in that. Yet you will never propose to me any one of our arguments without therein employing the universal truths. It is, however, well to remark that (as far as form is concerned) the particular propositions are comprised within the universals. For although it is true that there is only a single St. Peter the

[1] Locke's sensistic realism appears in sharp outlines in the present passage and its immediate context; *cf.* further, Locke, *Philos. Wks.*, Vol. 2, pp. 295–296. He maintains the existence, and consequently the knowledge, of the particular and individual only, and that our reasoning, which relates to the agreement or disagreement of things, must accordingly, in order to hit the mark, confine itself to the particular. Leibnitz argues, on the other hand, that our knowledge of things, while beginning with the particular in the sense-act, does not rest there, but through thought, especially through the medium of the linguistic form of our mental creation, gives to the individual and particular at once the character of universality. With Locke the element of universality is accidental; with Leibnitz it is essential. — TR.

apostle, we may nevertheless say that whoever was St. Peter the apostle denied his master. Thus this syllogism: St. Peter denied his master, St. Peter was a disciple, therefore some disciple denied his master (although it has only particular propositions), is considered to have them as universal affirmatives, and the mood will be *Darapti* of the third figure.[1]

Ph. I wished also to say to you that it appeared to me better to transpose the premises of the syllogisms and to say: All A is B, All B is C, therefore All A is C, than to say: All B is C, All A is B, therefore All A is C. But it seems from what you have said that they do not differ, and that both are counted as one and the same mood. It is always true, as you have remarked, that the disposition different from the common is better adapted to making a chain of several syllogisms.

Th. I am wholly of your opinion. It seems, however, that the belief has been that it was more didactic to begin with universal propositions like the majors in the first and second figures; and there are indeed orators who have this custom. But the connection appears better as you propose. I have before remarked that Aristotle may have had a particular reason for the common disposition. For instead of saying A is B, he was wont to say B is in A. And with this method of statement, the connection itself which you demand will arise for him in the received disposition. For, instead of saying B is C, A is B, therefore A is C, he will state it thus: C is in B, B is in A, therefore C is in A. For example, instead of saying: *The rectangle is isogon* (or has equal angles), *the square is a rectangle,* therefore *the square is isogon,* Aristotle, without transposing the propositions, will preserve the middle place to the middle term by this method of stating the propositions, which reverses the terms, and will say: *The isogon is in the rectangle, the rectangle is in the square,* therefore *the isogon is in the square.* And this mode of statement is not to be despised, for in reality

[1] Peter being the middle term, and disciple the subject of the conclusion, the minor premise must be converted, by which process the universal affirmative, "St. Peter was a disciple," becomes the particular affirmative, "Some disciple was St. Peter," from which the particular conclusion, "Some disciple denied his master," immediately follows. The mood Darapti of the third figure thus becomes the mood Darii of the first. The universality of the premises consists in the fact that Peter constitutes the entire class to which he belongs. *Cf.* Hamilton, *Logic*, Boston, 1873, pp. 314–315. — TR.

the predicate is in the subject, or rather the idea of the predicate is included in the idea of the subject. For example, the isogon is in the rectangle, for the *rectangle* is the figure all of whose right angles are equal to each other, therefore in the idea of the rectangle is the idea of a figure all of whose angles are equals, which is the idea of the isogon. The common mode of statement regards rather individuals, but that of Aristotle ideas or universals. For in saying, *every man is an animal*, I mean to say that all men are included in all animals; but I mean at the same time that the idea of animal is included in the idea of man. Animal includes more individuals than man, but man includes more ideas or more formalities;[1] the one has more examples, the other more degrees of reality; the one more extension, the other more intension. It may also be truly said that the entire syllogistic doctrine may be demonstrated by that *de continente et contento*, the containing and the contained, which is different from that of the whole and the part; for the whole always exceeds the part, but the containing and the contained are sometimes equal, as is the case in reciprocal propositions.[2]

§ 9. *Ph.* I begin to form for myself a wholly different idea of logic from that I formerly had. I regarded it as a scholar's diversion, but I now see that, in the way you understand it, it is like a universal mathematics. Would to God that it might push on to something more than it yet is, in order that we

[1] *I.e.* essences. "The *formality* of the vow lies in the promise made to God." — Stillingfleet. — TR.

[2] Leibnitz's thought, as Schaarschmidt says, is that sometimes the principle, what is predicable of the whole is predicable of the parts — *ab universali ad particulare consequentia valet* — is not applicable, as in cases where the concepts found in the conclusion are coördinate rather than subordinate, *i.e.* coincident or identical in extension. In such cases the coördination or coincidence of the concepts — *principium identitatis* — might be adduced as a fundamental logical principle. To avoid this, Leibnitz proposes the principle *De continente et contento*, in which in a certain sense is given the higher unity of subordination and identity, *i.e.* the subject may always be thought of as contained in the predicate, although coincident with it in extension. The principle, however, necessarily considers "the containing" as more extended than the "contained." Cases such as Leibnitz here refers to, in which the coördination or agreement of terms is such as to make them identical — "important cases" "for the most part strangely overlooked" by logicians (Jevons, *Lessons in Logic*, p. 124, new ed., 1880) — are discussed by Jevons in his little work entitled *The Substitution of Similars*, London, Macmillan & Co., 1869. — TR.

might be able to find thereby *these true helps of reason* of which Hooker spoke, which would raise men far above their present condition. Reason is a faculty which so much the more needs it, as its *extent* is quite limited and as it fails us in many instances. (1) Because often ideas themselves fail us. § 10. Then (2) they are often obscure and imperfect; whilst where they are clear (and distinct), as in *numbers*, we find no insurmountable difficulties, and fall into no contradiction. § 11. (3) Often also the difficulty comes from the fact that mediate ideas are wanting. You know that before *algebra*, that great instrument and noteworthy proof of human sagacity, was discovered, men regarded with amazement many demonstrations of the ancient mathematicians. § 12. It also happens (4) that the mind builds upon false principles, which may entangle it in difficulties where the reason is more involved and very far from clearing them up. § 13. Finally (5), terms whose meaning is uncertain embarrass the reason.

Th. I do not know whether we so much lack *ideas* as you think, that is to say, *distinct ideas*. As for *confused ideas*, or rather *images*, or, if you prefer, *impressions*, as colors, tastes, etc., which are a resultant of many little ideas distinct in themselves, but of which we are not distinctly conscious, we lack an infinite number of them suitable to other creatures rather than to ourselves. But these impressions also serve rather to give rise to the *instincts* and to establish the observations of experience than to furnish matter to the reason, except so far as they are accompanied by distinct perceptions. It is then principally the defect of the knowledge we have of these distinct ideas, concealed within the confused, that stops us, and even when all is distinctly exposed to our senses or to our mind, the multitude of things that must be considered sometimes perplexes us. For example, when there is a pile of one thousand cannon-balls before our eyes, it is plain that in order properly to conceive the number and properties of this multitude, it is very useful to arrange them in figures as is done in the magazines in order to have distinct ideas of them and to fix them, indeed, so that we may be spared the trouble of counting them more than once. It is the multitude of considerations also which causes some very great difficulties in the science of numbers themselves; for short methods are sought and sometimes we do not know whether nature has them within its folds for the case in question. For example, what is apparently simpler than the notion of the *prime number?* *i.e.* a whole number indivisible by every other except unity and itself. Yet we seek also a positive and easy sign in order to recognize them certainly without trying all the prime divisors less than the square root of the given prime. There are a number of signs which make known without much calculation that a given number is not prime, but we ask for one which is easy and which makes known certainly that it is prime when it is so. This it is which also makes algebra as yet so imperfect, although nothing is better known than the ideas of which it makes use, since they signify only numbers in general; for the public has not yet the means of extracting the irrational roots of any equation beyond the fourth degree[1] (excepting in a very limited case), and the methods which Diophant,[2] Scipio Ferreus,[3]

[1] In Leibnitz's day, as the text states, equations of the 2d, 3d, and 4th degrees were reduced to pure equations, but the reduction of equations of higher degrees than the 4th remained an unsolved problem, on which mathematicians spent much labor, until Niels Henrik Abel, 1802–1829, a Norwegian mathematician of great ability and acuteness, demonstrated (1824) that the quintic equation and *a fortiori* the general equation of any order higher than five, is incapable of solution by radicals. *Cf.* Abel, *Démonstration de l'impossibilité de la résolution algébrique des équations générales qui passent le quatrième degré*, in *Œuvres complètes*, ed. by Holmboe, 2 vols., Christiania, 1839, Vol. 1, pp. 5–24, and in Crelle, "Journ. f. Math.," 1826, Vol. 1, pp. 65–84. — TR.

[2] Diophantus, c. 325–c. 409, a celebrated Greek mathematician of the Alexandrian school, gave, in his *Arithmeticorum lib. VI.*, a method for the solution of equations of the 1st and 2d degrees. The Ms. of his *Arithmetic* was discovered in 1460 in the Vatican Library by the astronomer Regiomontanus, 1436–1476, and was published in a Latin trans., without the original, by Xylander, in 1575. The Greek text, with a more complete trans., and a commentary by Bachet de Merzeriac, whose skill in indeterminate analysis especially fitted him for the task, appeared in 1621. The best ed., based upon that of Bachet, including the Greek text with Latin trans., is that by Pierre Fermat, 1601–1665, the celebrated French mathematician, who supplemented the commentary of Bachet by valuable notes of his own. It is found in Vol. 1, pp. 65–341 of Fermat, *Opera Mathematica*, 2 vols., fol., Tolosæ, 1670, 1679. — TR.

[3] Scipione del Ferro or Ferri, c. 1465–1525, an Italian mathematician, taught arithmetic and geometry at Bologna from 1496 till his death. About 1505 he discovered the solution of a particular case of cubic equations, which he did not publish, but communicated to his favorite pupil Antonio del Fiore, who in 1635 challenged Tartaglia to a trial of skill in resolving algebraical problems requiring a knowledge of this rule. Tartaglia in 1630 had already solved two cases of cubic equations, and before the time for the contest came solved two

and Lewis Ferrari[1] used respectively for the second, third, and fourth degrees in order to reduce them to the first, or in order to reduce an affected equation to a pure, are wholly different from each other, *i.e.* that which is used for one degree differs a degree from that used for another. For the second degree, or the quadratic equation, is reduced to the first by merely eliminating the second term. The third degree, or the cubic equation, has been solved, because in separating the unknown quantity into parts there happily arises from these an equation of the second degree. And in the fourth degree, or the biquadratics, something is added to the two sides of the equation to render it capable of extraction on both sides, and then it is happily found that to obtain this result an equation of the third degree only is needed. But all this is only a mixture of good luck or chance with art or method. And in trying it on these last two degrees we knew not whether it would be successful. Further still, another artifice is necessary to success in the fifth or sixth degree, which are the sursolids or bicubes. And although Descartes believed that the method he used in the fourth, conceiving the equation as produced by two other quadratic equations (but which cannot at bottom give more than that of Lewis Ferrari), would succeed also in the sixth, it is not found to be so. This difficulty shows that even the clearest and most distinct ideas do not always give us all we ask for and all that may be drawn from them. And this makes us also judge that algebra is very far from being the art

more. He thus easily won the victory, as his problems could be solved only by one or the other of his own three rules which were unknown to Fiore, and not by the remaining rule which was the only one known to Fiore. Tartaglia's discoveries were improved and published by Cardan in connection with his own in 1545, as a supplement to a treatise on arithmetic and algebra published in 1539. *Cf.* Cardan, *Opera omnia*, Vol. 4, pp. 249–264. On Ferro, *cf.* Libri, *Hist. des Sciences Math. en Italie*, Vol. 3, pp. 148–151; Montucla, *Hist. des Math.*, Vol. 1, p. 479, ed. 1758, Vol. 1, p. 591, ed. 1799–1802. — Tr.

[1] Ludovico or Luigi Ferrari, 1522–1562, or 1565, an Italian mathematician, a pupil of Cardano (*cf. ante*, p. 566, note 1), and Professor of Mathematics at Milan and at the University of Bologna, discovered the demonstration of the formula for the resolution of equations of the 3d degree, sent by Tartaglia, c. 1500–1557, to Cardan under the form of an enigma, and shortly after this discovery solved equations of the 4th degree. For an account of his demonstration, *cf.* Cardan, *Ars magna*, 1545, chap. 15. De cubo et quadratis æqualibus numero, § 3, *Opera omnia*, 10 vols., Lugduni, 1663, Vol. 4, p. 254. On Ferrari, *cf.* Libri, *Hist. des Sciences Math. en Italie*, Vol. 3, pp. 180, 181; Montucla, *Hist. des Math.*, Vol. 1, pp. 484, 485, ed. 1758, Vol. 1, pp. 596, 597, ed. 1799–1802. — Tr.

of invention, since it needs a more general art; and we may say, indeed, that the art of signs (*Specieuse*) in general, *i.e.* the art of characters, is a marvellous means of assistance, since it aids the imagination. It will not be doubted in view of the arithmetic of Diophant and the geometrical books of Apollonius and Pappus that the ancients possessed it to a certain extent. Vieta[1] has given it more extension by expressing not only what is asked for, but also the given numbers, by general characters, doing in calculating what Euclid already did in reasoning, and Descartes has extended the application of this calculus to geometry, indicating lines by equations. Nevertheless, even after the discovery of our modern algebra, Bouillaud[2] (Ismael Bullialdus), no doubt an excellent geometer, whom, moreover, I knew in Paris, regarded only with wonder the demonstrations of Archimedes upon the spiral, and could not understand how this great man had thought of employing the tangent of this line as the dimension of the circle. Father Gregory of St. Vincent[3] appears to have divined it, thinking that it was attained by the parallelism of the spiral and the parabola. But this method is only a particular one, whilst the new calculus of infinitesimals[4] which proceeds by the method of the differences which I have thought of and successfully shared with the public, gives a general one, wherein this discovery concerning

[1] *Cf. ante*, p. 468, note 1. — TR.

[2] Ismael Boulliau, 1605–1694, a French mathematician and astronomer, who was the first to give, in his *Ad astronomos monita duo*, 1657, a plausible explanation of the change in the light of some stars by attributing to them an axial revolution which shows successively their obscure and luminous parts. He was the author of several works, among which is the *De lineis spiralibus demonstrationes*, 1657, which Leibnitz, perhaps, had in mind here. — TR.

[3] Grégoire de Saint-Vincent, 1584–1667, a Flemish geometer who was much occupied with the problem of the quadrature of the circle, and whose principal work is the *Opus geometricum quadraturæ circuli et sectionum coni*, 1647. — TR.

[4] For Leibnitz's account of his discovery of the "calculus of infinitesimals," *cf.* his *Historia et origo calculi differentialis*, Gerhardt, *Leibniz. math. Schrift.*, II., 1 [Vol. 5], 392–410; also his letter, April 18, 1716, to the Countess Kielmannsegge, Dutens, *Leibnit. op. om.*, 3, 456–461. For Leibnitz's various writings on the subject, *cf.* Gerhardt, *op. cit.*, II., 1 [Vol. 5], 141–418; Dutens, *op. cit.*, Vol. 3, passim. Dutens, Vol. 3, contains also much material concerning the controversy between Leibnitz and Newton regarding the discovery of the calculus. Further accounts are given in Guhrauer, *Leibnitz, Eine Biographie*, 1, 286–320, Jaucourt, *Historia vitæ Leibnitii*, and Montucla, *Hist. d. Math.*, Vol. 2 (both in Dutens, *op. cit.* Vol. 3, pp. xii–xl, xli–lv), and in *Encyclop. Brit.*, 9th ed., Vol. 13, Article, "Infinitesimal Calculus." — TR.

the spiral is mere play and a sample of the easiest, like nearly all we have before discovered in the matter of the dimensions of curves. The reason of the advantage of this new calculus is, moreover, that it relieves the imagination in the problems, which Descartes excluded from his geometry under the pretext that they most frequently lead to mechanics, but at bottom because they did not agree with his calculus. As for errors arising from ambiguous terms, it is our business to avoid them.

Ph. There is also a case in which reasoning cannot be applied, but in which also there is no need of it and in which sight is worth more than reasoning. It is in *intuitive knowledge,* where the connection of ideas and truths is immediately seen. Such is the knowledge of indubitable maxims, and I am tempted to believe that this is the degree of evidence which the angels have at present, and which the spirits of just men made perfect will have in a *future state* regarding a thousand things which now escape our knowledge. § 15. But demonstration, based upon mediate ideas, gives a *reasoned knowledge.* This is because the connection of the mediate idea with the extremes is necessary and is seen by a *juxtaposition* of evidence, similar to that of a yard-stick applied now to one cloth and now to another to show that they are equal. § 16. But if the connection is only probable, the judgment gives only an *opinion.*

Th. God alone has the advantage of having only intuitive knowledge. But very happy souls, however detached they are from these material bodies, and the genii themselves, however exalted they are, although they have a knowledge without comparison more intuitive than ours, and often see at a glance what we discover only by the force of consequences after having employed time and labor, must likewise find difficulties in their path without which they would not have the pleasure of making discoveries, which pleasure is one of the greatest. And we must always admit that there will be an infinite number of truths concealed from them either wholly or for a time, whereto they must attain by force of consequences and by demonstration or even frequently by conjecture.

Ph. [These genii then are only animals more perfect than we; it is just as if you said with the emperor of the moon: *it is all as here.*]

Th. I will say so, not entirely, but in regard *to the ground* of things, for the modes and degrees of perfection vary infinitely. Meanwhile the ground is everywhere the same, a *maxim* which is *fundamental* with me and reigns in all my philosophy. I conceive things unknown or confusedly known only after the manner of those which are distinctly known to us; a procedure which makes philosophy very easy, and I believe indeed that it must do so. But if this philosophy is simplest in its ground, it is also the richest in its modes, because nature may vary them infinitely, as indeed she has done with as much abundance, order, and ornateness as it is possible to imagine. This is the reason why I believe there is no genius however sublime who has not an infinite number of them above him. Yet although we are very inferior to so many intelligent beings, we have the advantage of not being visibly controlled upon this globe where we hold indisputably the first rank; and with all the ignorance in which we are immersed we have always the pleasure of seeing nothing which surpasses us. And if we were vain we might judge as Cæsar, who preferred to be first in a country town rather than second in Rome. For the rest, I speak here only of the natural knowledge of these spirits and not of the *beatific vision*,[1] or of the supernatural light that God is pleased to give them.

[1] The term "beatific vision" (*visio beatifica*) denotes in theological and religious thought the direct and immediate or intuitive vision of God enjoyed by the saints and angels in heaven and supposed to constitute their essential bliss. The philosophical significance of the idea as historically developed, with respect both to its speculative and practical uses, lies in the fact that the *visio beatifica* was regarded as the sole means of obtaining absolute truth and of realizing absolute blessedness. The idea thus involved more or less explicitly a species of knowledge supernaturally mediated in some unknown and unexplained way, but considered, because of the method of its mediation, as far superior in certainty and completeness to any knowledge that finite beings could attain through the unaided action of their own intellectual powers—in brief, as the very perfection of knowledge attainable by such beings.

The idea originated in Plato's conception of an immediate intuition, going beyond rational thought, of the pure forms of reality or the Ideas. Transformed by Philo and Plotinus into their ecstatic intuition, or that identification of the human with the Divine in which all consciousness of individual personality is lost; combined by Clement and Origen, in view of certain expressions in the Pauline epistles, with the thought of a personality in union with whom the self-consciousness of the individual is preserved; and still further developed by Augustine, as the principle of the absolute and immediate certainty of inner experience or consciousness involving within itself the idea of God as the absolute personality and the sum and essence of all

§ 19. *Ph.* As each one makes use of reasoning either with regard to himself or with reference to another, it will not be useless to make some reflections upon *four sorts of arguments* which men are wont to use in order to draw others to their opinions or at least so to keep them in awe as to prevent them from contradicting. The first argument may be called *argumentum ad vercundiam,* when we cite the opinion of those who have acquired authority by their knowledge, rank, power, or otherwise; for when another does not yield to it promptly, he is liable to be censured as full of vanity and even to be charged with insolence. § 20. There is also 2) *argumentum ad ignorantiam, i. e.* to demand that the opponent admit the proof or assign a better. § 21. There is 3) *argumentum ad hominem,* when we press a man by what he has himself said. § 22. Finally, there is 4) *argumentum ad judicium,* which consists in employing proofs drawn from some one of the sources of knowledge or probability. This is the only one of all which advances and instructs us; for if from respect I dare not contradict, or if I have nothing better to say, or if I contradict myself, it does not follow that you are right. I may be modest, ignorant, deceived, and you prove yourself to be mistaken also.

Th. It is doubtless necessary to make a difference between what is proper to be said and what is truly to be believed. Yet as the majority of truths may be boldly maintained, there is some prejudice against an opinion that it is necessary to conceal. The argument *ad ignorantiam* is valid in cases of presumption where it is reasonable to hold to an opinion till the contrary is proved. The argument *ad hominem* has this effect, that it shows that one or the other assertion is false and that

truth, this conception passed into the philosophical and religious thinking and life of the Christian Church, and became especially prominent in the teachings of the Mediæval Mystics. On this historical development *cf.* Windelband, *Hist. of Philos.*, trans. by Tufts, pp. 119 *sq.*, 227 *sq.*, 249 *sq.*, 276 *sq.*; Zeller, *Philos. d. Griech.*, III., 2 [Vol. 6], 413 *sq.*, 611 *sq.*, 854, note 4, 3d ed., 1881; Benn, *Greek Philosophers*, 2, 311 *sq.*

In a modified form this intuition of divine things became what the Church fathers and the theological and philosophical writers of the Middle Age termed the *lumen gratiæ*, "the light of grace," the supernatural light given through divine inspiration, in opposition to the *lumen naturale* or "natural light," the rational knowledge given by nature to all men as such. *Cf. New Essays*, Bk. I., chap. 1, § 21, Th., *ante*, p. 71; Gerhardt, *Leibniz. philos. Schrift.*, 6, 494 *sq.*, 503 *sq.*; Hamilton's Reid, Note A, § V., IV., 1, note †, Vol. 2, p. 763, § VI., 20–22, 25–26, pp. 776–778, 54, p. 785, 8th ed., 1880. — Tr.

the opponent is deceived whatever way he takes it. We might bring yet other arguments which are used, for example the one we might call *ad vertiginem,* when we reason thus: if this proof is not received we have no means of attaining certainty upon the point in question, which we take as an absurdity. This argument is valid in certain cases, as if any one wished to deny primitive and immediate truths, for example, that anything can be and not be at the same time, or that we ourselves exist, for if he were right there would be no means of knowing anything whatever. But when certain principles are produced and we wish to maintain them because otherwise the entire system of some received doctrine would fall, the argument is not decisive; for we must distinguish between what is necessary to maintain our knowledge and between what serves as a foundation for our received doctrines or practices. Use was sometimes made among jurisconsults of probable reasoning in order to justify the condemnation or torture of pretended sorcerers upon the deposition of others accused of the same crime, for it was said: if this argument falls, how shall we convict them? And sometimes in a criminal case certain authors maintain that in the facts where conviction is more difficult, more slender proofs may pass as sufficient. But this is not a reason. It proves only that we must employ more care, and not that we must believe more thoughtlessly, except in the case of extremely dangerous crimes, as, for example, in the matter of high treason, where this consideration has weight, not to condemn a man, but to prevent him from doing harm; so that there may be a mean, not between *guilty and not guilty,* but between *condemnation* and *banishment* in the judgments, where law and custom admit it. Use has been made of a similar argument in Germany for some time in order to give color to the coining of bad money; for (they say) if we must keep to the prescribed rules, we cannot coin it without loss. We must be allowed then to debase its alloy. But besides the fact that we must diminish the weight only and not the alloy or superscription the better to obviate frauds, we suppose a practice necessary which is not so; for no command of heaven nor any human law exists obliging those who have no mine nor occasion to have silver in bars to coin money; and to make money out of money is a bad practice which naturally carries deterioration with it. But how (they say) shall we exercise our *regale* in coining it? The reply is easy. Content yourselves with coining a little from good silver, even at a small loss, if you think its coinage a matter of importance to yourselves, since you have no need nor right to flood the world with debased small coin.

§ 23. *Ph.* After having said a word concerning the relation of our reason to other men, let us add something about its relation to God, which makes us distinguish between what is *contrary to reason* and what is *above reason.* Of the first class is everything which is incompatible with our clear and distinct ideas; of the second is every thought whose truth or probability evidently cannot be deduced from sensation or reflection by the aid of reason.[1] Thus the existence of more than one God is *contrary* to reason, and the resurrection of the dead is *above* reason.

Th. I find something to say regarding your definition of that which is *above reason,* at least if you connect it with the received use of this phrase; for it seems to me that from the manner in which this definition is couched, it goes too far in one direction and not far enough in the other; and if we follow it, all that of which we are ignorant and which in our present condition we are unable to know, would be above reason, for example, that a given fixed star is greater or less than the sun; again, that Vesuvius will send out fire in such a year; these are facts the knowledge of which is beyond us, not because they are above reason, but because they are beyond our senses; for we could very well judge of them, if we had more perfect organs or more information about the circumstances. There are also difficulties which are beyond our present faculty, but not beyond reason as a whole; for example, there is no astronomer here below who can calculate the detail of an eclipse in the space of a *pater* and without taking the pen in hand, yet there are perhaps genii to whom that would be mere play. Thus all things might be made known or practicable by the aid of reason, by supposing more information concerning the facts, more perfect organs, and a more elevated mind.

[1] *Cf.* Locke, *Exam. of Malebranche,* § 53, *Philos. Wks.,* Vol. 2, p. 455 (Bohn's ed.). — TR.

Ph. This objection ceases if I understand my definition not only of our sensation or reflection, but also of that of every other possible created spirit.

Th. If you take it so, you are right. But the other difficulty remains, viz.: that there will be nothing above reason according to our definition, because God will always be able to give the means of apprehending by sensation and reflection any truth whatever; as in reality the greatest mysteries become known to us by the testimony of God which we recognize by the *motives of credibility,* upon which our religion is based. And these motives undoubtedly depend upon sensation and reflection. The question then seems to be not whether the existence of a fact or the truth of a proposition can be deduced from the principles which reason uses, *i.e.* from sensation and reflection, or rather the external and internal sense, but whether a created spirit is capable of knowing the how of this fact, or the *a priori reason* of this truth; so that we may say that what is *beyond reason* may indeed be *apprehended,* but it cannot be *comprehended* by the means and forces of created reason, however great and exalted it be. It is reserved to God alone to understand it, as it belongs to him alone to assert it.[1]

Ph. This consideration appears to me a good one, and it is

[1] *Cf. Théodicée,* Discours prélim., especially §§ 2, 5, 23, 56; *New Essays,* Preface, *ante,* pp. 55, 60; *Annotatiunculæ subitanæ ad Tolandi librum, De christianismo mysteriis carente,* 1701, Dutens, *Leibnit. op. om.,* 5, 142, 143; Pichler, *Theol. d. Leibniz,* 1, 208–225; K. Fischer, *Gesch. d. n. Philos.,* Bd. II., Leibniz, 3d ed., pp. 541–547.

According to Leibnitz, reason and faith are not absolutely opposed. Reason must be capable of *apprehending* the supernatural as fact, even though in its present stage of development — and perhaps in all its development — it may never be able to *comprehend* it exhaustively. The supernatural, while it may be outside of and beyond any present or future possible finite experience, is not then contrary to reason. In fact, to be apprehended or accepted as fact at all, it must present such intrinsic rationality as is sufficient to induce belief, *i.e.* it must show itself to be intrinsically possible and not contrary to any well-established knowledge. In this sense it is not wholly above reason, — if it were, it would not at all concern us, — and may therefore become a part of the sum-total of our knowledge. The contention of both Leibnitz and Locke is, in fact, that the opposition is not between reason and faith, but rather between reason and unfounded authority. Leibnitz rejects entirely both belief based on blind submission to mere authority, and that ultra-rationalism which refuses to admit the existence of anything not coming entirely within the range of experience, particularly that experience which is sensuous and individual and excludes that which is spiritual and universal. — Tr.

thus that I wish my definition to be understood. This same consideration confirms me also in my present opinion that the manner of speaking which opposes reason to faith, although it has weighty authority, is improper; for it is by reason that we verify what we must believe.[1] Faith is a firm assent, and assent, regulated as it should be, can only be given upon good reasons. Thus he who believes without any reason for believing may be in love with his fancies, but it is not true that he seeks the truth, nor that he renders lawful obedience to his divine Master, who would have him make use of the faculties with which he has enriched him in order to preserve him from error. Otherwise if he is in the good way, it is by chance; and if in the bad, it is by his fault, for which he is accountable to God.

Th. I commend you strongly, sir, when you wish faith to be grounded in reason: without this why should we prefer the Bible to the Koran or to the ancient books of the Brahmins? Our theologians also and other learned men have clearly recognized it, and it is this which has caused us to have such fine works concerning the truth of the Christian religion, and so many excellent proofs as have been put forward against the heathen and other unbelievers, ancient and modern. Wise persons also have always regarded as suspicious those who have maintained that it was not necessary to trouble themselves about reasons and proofs when it was a question of belief; an impossibility in fact unless *to believe* signifies to recite or repeat or to let pass without troubling themselves, as many people do, and as indeed is the character of some nations more than others. This is the reason why, when some Aristotelian philosophers of the fifteenth or sixteenth century, whose remains were still extant a long time after (as we may judge by the letters of the late Mr. Naudé[2] and the *Naudeana*),

[1] Gerhardt reads: "car c'est par la raison que nous verifions ce que nous devons croire." Erdmann, Jacques, and Janet read: "car c'est par la raison que nous devons croire." — Tr.

[2] Gabriel Naudé, 1600–1653, a celebrated French scholar, bibliographer and librarian, who at first studied medicine and was physician to Louis XIII, but who afterwards devoted himself entirely to literary and library work. He was the creator of the celebrated *Bibliothèque Mazarine*. His *Naudeana*, a collection of anecdotes drawn from his conversations, appeared at Paris, 1701. — Tr.

desired to maintain two opposite truths, one philosophical, the other theological, the last Lateran Council under Leo X was right in opposing them, as I think I have already remarked.[1] And a dispute wholly similar was raised at Helmstädt in former times between Daniel Hofmann, a theologian, and Corneille Martin, a philosopher, but with this difference, that the philosopher reconciled philosophy to revelation and the theologian wished to decline its use. But the Duke Julius,

[1] *Cf. Théodicée*, Discours prélim., §§ 7, 8, 11. The "Aristotelian philosophers" here referred to, were divided into two schools, the Alexandrists and the Averroists, according as they followed the interpretation of Aristotle given by Alexander of Aphrodisias, c. 200, or Averroes, 1126–1198. Both schools denied the immortality of the individual soul; the Averroists grounding their denial on, and finding a compensation for such immortality in, the unity of the intellect — the rationally active part of the soul (νοῦς) — in all men; while the Alexandrists regarded individual souls, including this rational part, as naturally mortal.

Both schools were opposed and condemned by the Church, and the theory of "the double truth" (philosophical truth having its source in natural reason, theological in a supernatural revelation), held by both schools as a shield to protect them, in the exposition and dissemination of their views, from the interference and persecution of the Church, was adjudged heretical in the decree "Apostolici Regiminis" of the fifth Lateran Council of December 19, 1512, under Leo X. This theory in the case of many of its advocates was, no doubt, the natural and "honest expression of the inner discord" resulting from the opposition of the two then prevalent authorities, Greek philosophy and religious tradition.

Chief among those who advocated this theory of "the twofold truth" was Pietro Pomponazzi, 1462–1525, an Italian physician and philosopher, in his time one of the most sagacious and subtle interpreters of Aristotle of the Alexandrian school. He maintained, in his *Tractatus de immortalitate animi*, Bologna, 1516, 8vo, that none of the reasons assigned for the dogma of immortality were categorically demonstrative, and that therefore the doctrine must depend upon revelation. When accused of heresy, he stoutly asserted his innocence, saying that he taught nothing contrary to the belief of the Church, but simply expounded Aristotle, and adding that he denied as a Christian what he affirmed as a philosopher. He attempted to discover a deeper foundation for the theory of "the twofold truth," through the recognition of the twofold nature of reason, the speculative and the practical, the former furnishing the basis of philosophy, the latter that of theology and ethics.

On the whole subject, *cf.* M. Maywald, *Die Lehre v. d. zweifachen Wahrheit*, Berlin, 1871; Windelband, *Hist. of Philos.*, trans. by Tufts, pp. 318 *sq.*, 339 *sq.*, 359; Pünjer, *Gesch. d. christ. Religionsphilos.*, 1, 28–29, 37, Eng. trans., 1, 39 *sq.*, 50–52; Stöckl, *Gesch. d. Philos. d. Mittelalters*, III [Vol. 4], 202–207, and for an account of Pomponazzi and his philosophy, *ibid.* 213–244; *cf.* also L. Ferri, *La Psicologia di P. Pomponazzi*, Rome, 1877. For the decree "Apostolici Regiminis," *cf. Acta Concil. Reg.*, Vol. 34, p. 333, Paris, 1644, 37 vols., fol.; Labbé, *Concil.*, tom. 19, col. 842; Stöckl, *op. cit.*, III [Vol. 4], 206, n. 1. — TR.

founder of the university, decided for the philosopher.[1] It is true that in our time a person of the most exalted position said that in a matter of faith he must put out his eyes in order to see clearly, and Tertullian says somewhere: this is true, because it is impossible:[2] it must be believed, for it is an absurdity. But if the intention of those who explain themselves in this way is good, these expressions are always exaggerated and may do harm. St. Paul speaks more justly when he says that the wisdom of God is foolishness with men; because men judge of things only according to their experience, which is extremely limited, and everything not agreeing therewith appears to them an absurdity. But this judgment is very rash, for there is indeed an infinite number of natural things which would pass with us as absurd, if they were told us, as the ice which was said to cover our rivers appeared to the king of Siam. But the order of nature itself not being of any metaphysical necessity, is grounded only in the good pleasure of God, so that he may deviate therefrom by the superior reasons of grace,[3] although he must proceed therein only upon good proofs which can come only from the testimony of God himself, to which we must defer absolutely when it is duly verified.

[1] *Cf. Théodicée*, Discours prélim. § 13. On the controversy itself, extending from 1598–1601, *cf.* Pünjer, *Gesch. d. christ. Religionsphilosophie*, 1, 132–141, Eng. trans., 1, 178–190. For the fullest accounts, *cf.* G. Thomasius, *De Controversia Hofmanniana*, Erlangen, 1844, and E. Schlee (who gives the external history with complete references to the literature), *Der Streit d. Dan. Hofmann ü. d. Verhältniss d. Philos. z. Theol.*, Marburg, 1862. Schaarschmidt refers to E. L. Th. Henke, *Georg Calixtus u. seine Zeit*, Einleitung, p. 73 *sq.*, and says that Duke Julius [Henry Julius, son of the founder of the University, and the successor of his father in the government in 1589], who had examined the documents in the controversy and reached a decision, did rightly in protecting the philosopher against his opponents, who spread abroad the most horrible calumnies concerning him, and treated him in general very harshly. — Tr.

[2] *Cf.* Tertullian, *De Carne Christi*, chap. 5: "Mortuus est dei filius; prorsus credibile est, quia ineptum est. Et sepultus resurrexit; certum est, quia impossibile est." Leibnitz also refers to this passage in the *Théodicée*, Discours prélim. § 50. — Tr.

[3] *Cf. ante*, p. 462, note 1. — Tr.

CHAPTER XVIII

OF FAITH AND REASON AND THEIR DISTINCT LIMITS

§ 1. *Ph.* Let us accommodate ourselves meanwhile to the received mode of speech, and suffer faith to be distinguished in a certain sense from reason. It is proper that this sense be very accurately explained and the limits existing between these two things be established; for uncertainty regarding these limits has certainly produced in the world great disputes and perhaps caused even great disorders. It is at least manifest that, until these have been determined, it is in vain for us to discuss, since we must employ reason in discussing faith. § 2. I find that each sect uses reason with pleasure so long as it believes it can derive therefrom any aid: but as soon as reason fails, they cry out: it is an article of faith, which is above reason. But the opponent could make use of the same evasion if any one took it upon himself to argue against him, unless we indicate why that would not be permitted him in a case seemingly parallel. I suppose that reason is here the discovery of the certitude or probability of propositions drawn from knowledge which we have acquired by the use of our natural faculties, that is to say by sensation and by reflection; and that faith is the assent given to a proposition based upon *revelation*, that is to say upon an extraordinary communication from God which has made it known to man. § 3. But a man inspired of God cannot communicate to others any new simple idea, because he uses only words or other signs which awake in us the simple ideas that custom has attached to them or their combination; and whatever new ideas St. Paul received when he was carried up to the third heaven, all that he could say was: *they are things eye hath not seen, ear hath not heard, and which have never entered into the heart of man.*[1] Suppose there were creatures in the planet Jupiter provided with six senses and that God in a supernatural way gave to a man among us the ideas of this sixth sense, he could not by means of words make them

[1] 1 Cor. 2, 9. — Tr.

spring up in the minds of other men.[1] We must then distinguish between *original* and *traditional revelation.* The first is an impression which God makes immediately upon the mind, and to this we can fix no limits; the other comes only by the ordinary means of communication and cannot give new simple ideas. § 4. It is true, however, that the truths which may be discovered by reason can be communicated to us by a traditional revelation, as if God had desired to communicate to men geometrical theorems, but this would never amount to so great a certainty as if we had their demonstration drawn from the connection of ideas. It is also as if Noah had a more certain knowledge of the deluge than that which we have acquired from the book of Moses and as if the assurance of one who has seen that Moses actually wrote it and that he did the miracles which justify his inspiration was greater than ours. § 5. This it is which makes it impossible for revelation to go against the clear evidence of reason, because whenever the revelation is immediate and original we must know with certainty that we are not deceived in attributing it to God and that we comprehend its meaning; and this evidence can never be greater than that of our intuitive knowledge; and consequently no proposition can be received as divine revelation when it is contradictorily opposed to this immediate knowledge. Otherwise there would no longer remain any difference in the world between truth and falsehood, any measure of the credible and incredible. And it is inconceivable that a thing comes from God, this beneficent author of our being, which received as true must overturn the foundations of our knowledge and render all our faculties useless. § 6. Those who have revelation only mediately, or by tradition from mouth to mouth or by writing, have again more need of reason to assure themselves of it. § 7. Meanwhile it is always true that the things which are beyond what our faculties can discover are the proper matters of faith,

[1] *Cf.* Lessing's amplification of a similar thought, perhaps suggested by this passage of Leibnitz, in his Fragment: *Dass mehr als fünf Sinne für den Menschen sein können*, *Sämmt. Schrift*, ed. Lachmann-Maltzahn, Leipzig, 1853–1857, Vol. 11, Pt. 2, p. 458. On the relation of Lessing to Leibnitz, *cf.* Zimmermann, *Leibniz und Lessing, Eine Studie*, Wien, 1855; Pünjer, *Gesch. d. christ. Religionsphilosophie*, 1, 421–425, Eng. trans., 1, 566–570; Pfleiderer, *Religionsphilosophie*, 1, 143, Eng. trans., 1, 145–146; K. Fischer, *Gesch. d. n. Philos.*, Bd. II., Leibniz, 3d ed., pp. 617–619. — TR.

as the fall of the rebellious angels, the resurrection of the dead. § 9. Here we must listen solely to revelation. And even as regards probable propositions an evident revelation will determine us against the probability.

Th. If you take faith as that which is grounded in *the motives of credibility* (as they are called) and detach it from the internal grace which immediately determines the mind, all that you say, sir, is beyond dispute. It must be admitted that there are many judgments more evident than those depending upon these motives. Some are urged on by them farther than others, and there are indeed many persons who have never known them and still less considered them and who consequently have not even that which might pass as a *motive of probability*. But the internal grace of the Holy Spirit immediately supplies it in a supernatural way, and this it is which produces what the theologians properly call a divine faith. It is true that God never gives it except when the belief it produces is founded in reason; otherwise he would destroy the means of knowing the truth and open the door to enthusiasm; but it is not necessary for all who have this divine faith to know these reasons and still less to have them always before their eyes. Otherwise simple-minded people and idiots, to-day at least, would never have the true faith, and the most enlightened would not have it when they were most in need of it, for they cannot always remember the reasons for their belief. The question of the use of reason in theology has been one of the questions most discussed, both between the Socinians and those who may be called Catholics in a general sense, and between the Reformers and the Evangelicals, as those are named by way of preference in Germany whom many inaptly call Lutherans. I remember to have read once a Metaphysic of one Stegmann,[1] a Socinian (a different man from Joshua Stegmann,[2] who himself wrote against them), which so

[1] *Cf. Théodicée*, Discours prélim., § 16, where Leibnitz refers to him as Christopher Stegmann, a Socinian. He was the youngest brother of Joachim Stegmann, also a Socinian and author of many works on mathematics and theology, who died in exile at Clausenburg in Siebenbürgen in 1632. Christopher wrote a work entitled *Dyas philosophica*, which is, perhaps, the "Metaphysic" of which Leibnitz here speaks. For further account of him, *cf.* Jöcher, *Allgemeines Gelehrten-Lexicon*, Pt. IV., 794, Leipzig, 1750. — TR.

[2] Joshua Stegmann, 1588–1632, a Lutheran divine, was Professor at Leipzig, Wittenberg, and Rinteln, and the author of many theological works, and of

far as I know has not yet been printed; on the other hand, one Kessler,[1] a theologian of Saxony, has written a Logic and some other philosophical treatises expressly opposed to the Socinians. We may say in general, that the Socinians are too quick to reject everything which is not conformed to the order of nature, even when they cannot prove absolutely its impossibility. But their opponents also sometimes go too far and push mystery to the verge of contradiction; in which they injure the truth they try to defend. I was surprised to see once in the "Summa Theologiæ" of Father Honoré Fabry,[2] who otherwise was one of the most clever of his order, which he denied in divine things (as do also some other theologians), this great principle which states *that things which are identical with a third thing are identical with each other.* This is to give

the famous German hymn, "Ach, bleib' mit deiner Gnade" (Eng. trans. in *Lyra Germanica*, 2, 120, "Abide among us with thy grace, Lord Jesus, evermore"). He was opposed to the Socinians or Photinians, and wrote against them his *Photinianismus, h. e. Succincta Refutatio Errorum Photinianorum, quinquaginta sex disputationibus breviter comprehensa*, Rinteln, 1623, 8vo; Frankfort, 1643. Leibnitz mentions him again in the *Théodicée*, Discours prélim., § 62. For further account of him, *cf.* Winer, *Handbuch d. theolog. Lit.*, 1, 354; 2, 748; Jöcher, *Allgemeines Gelehrten-Lexicon*, Pt. IV., 794, Leipzig, 1750. — TR.

[1] Andreas Kessler, 1595–1643, a Lutheran divine, studied at Jena and Wittenberg, and was pastor at Eisfeld, Eisenach, and Coburg, where he died in consequence of a stroke of apoplexy received while preaching. He wrote against the Socinians or Photinians his *Physicæ Photinianæ examen*, Eisfeld, 1628, Wittenberg, 1656, 8vo; *Metaphysicæ Photinianæ examen*, 3d ed., Wittenberg, 1648, 8vo; *Logicæ Photinianæ examen*, 2d ed., Wittenberg, 1624, 4to, new ed. 1642, 8vo. His writings exhibit a good deal of method and exactness. Leibnitz also refers to him in the *Théodicée*, Discours prélim., § 16. For further account of him, *cf.* Jöcher, *Allgemeines Gelehrten-Lexicon*, Pt. II., 2072, Leipzig, 1750. — TR.

[2] Honoré Fabri, 1607–1688, a French mathematician and philosopher, and a Jesuit, who taught philosophy and mathematics in the college of his order at Lyons, and later became Grand-Penitentiary at the holy office in Rome. Among his writings are, *Synopsis geometrica*, Lugd., 1669; *Physica seu scientia rerum corporearum in decem tractatus distributa*, Lugd., 1669; *Summula Theologiæ*, Lyons, 1669. Leibnitz regarded him as one of the most distinguished men of his time, and frequently mentioned him with praise. *Cf. Théodicée*, Pt. III., § 348; *Hypoth. phys. nova*, §§ 56, 59, Gerhardt, *Leibniz. philos. Schrift.*, 4, 208, 214, 216; *Theoria motus abstracti, prope fin.*, *ibid.*, 240, and Appendix thereto, containing a letter of Fabri to Leibnitz, *ibid.*, 241–244, and of Leibnitz to Fabri, *ibid.*, 244–261 (also Gerhardt, *Leibniz. math. Schrift.*, II., 2 [Vol. 6], 81–98). For another Appendix to a letter of Leibnitz to Fabri, *cf.* Gerhardt, *Leibniz. math. Schrift.*, II., 2 [Vol. 6], 98–106, trans. *infra*, Appendix, pp. 699 *sq.* — TR.

a gained case to the opponent without thinking and to deprive all reasoning of certainty. We must say rather that this principle is badly applied. The same author rejects in his philosophy the virtual distinctions, which the Scotists put into created things, because they reversed, he says, the principle of contradiction: and when the objection is made to him that these distinctions must be admitted in God, he replies that faith orders it. But how can faith order that, whatever it be, which reverses a principle without which all belief, affirmation, or negation would be vain? Two propositions true at the same time must therefore necessarily not be wholly contradictory; and if A and C are not the same thing, it is clearly necessary that B which is identical with A be taken otherwise than B which is identical with C. Nicolaus Vedelius,[1] a professor at Geneva and afterward at Deventer, once published a book entitled "Rationale Theologicum," to which Jean Musæus,[2] a professor at Jena (which is an Evan-

[1] *Cf. Théodicée*, Discours prélim., §§ 20, 67. Nicolas Vedel, a German Reformed (Calvinistic) divine, was Professor of Philosophy and minister at Geneva, of Theology and Hebrew at Deventer, 1630–1638, and of Theology at Franeker from 1638 till his death in 1642. He was a great adversary of the Arminians, and wrote against them his *De Arcanis Arminianismi*, Leyden, 1632–1634. His *Rationale theologicum, seu de necessitate et vero usu principiorum rationis ac philosophiæ in controversiis theologicis, lib. tres*, Geneva, 1628, was attacked by Barth. Nihus, 1584–1657, in his *Morosophus seu Vedelius in suo rationali prorsus irrationalis*, Cologne, 1646, as well as by Musæus. On the controversy between Vedelius and Musæus, *cf.* Pünjer, *Gesch. d. christ. Religionsphilosophie*, 1, 118–124, Eng. trans., 159–167. For further account of Vedel, *cf.* Winer, *Handbuch d. theol. Lit.*, 1, 353, 375, 565; J. P. Niceron, *Mém. d'hommes*, Vol. 33, 1736. — Tr.

[2] *Cf. Théodicée*, Discours prélim., §§ 20, 67. Johannes Musæus, 1613–1681, a Lutheran divine, was Professor of History, 1642–1646, and of Theology, 1646 till his death, at Jena. He was the greatest Lutheran divine of his century after J. Gerhard, 1582–1637, and Geo. Calixtus, 1586–1656. He distinguished between theology and the confessions and favored liberty of scientific and theological researches. He was everywhere acknowledged as a very learned man, and his writings are distinguished by philosophical acumen so that he was accused of "magis philosophari quam quod loquatur eloquia Dei." He wrote in defence of Christianity against Herbert of Cherbury, 1581–1648, a work entitled *De luminis naturæ et ei innixæ theologiæ naturalis insufficientia ad salutem*, Jena, 1667; against Spinoza, his *Tractatus theolog.-polit.*, etc., Jena, 1674 (on Musæus and Spinoza, *cf.* Pünjer, *Gesch. d. christ. Religions-philos.*, 1, 322–323, Eng. trans., 1, 435). His *De usu principiorum rationis et philosophiæ in controversiis theologicis lib. tres Nic. Vedelii Rationali Theologico potissimum oppositi* appeared at Jena, 1644; 2d ed., 1665. For further account of Musæus, *cf.* Herzog, *Realencyklopädie*, 2d ed., 10, 376–380. — Tr.

gelical university in Thuringia), wrote another book in opposition upon the same subject, *i.e.* upon "The Use of Reason in Theology." I remember to have considered these formerly, and to have remarked that the principal controversy was obscured by incidental questions, as when it is asked, what a theological conclusion is, and whether it is necessary to judge of it by the terms which compose it, or by the means which prove it, and consequently whether Occam [1] was right or not in saying that the knowledge of one and the same conclusion is the same whatever [2] the means employed to prove it; and he delays upon a multitude of other minutiæ of still less importance, which concern only terms. Meanwhile Musæus agreed with him that the principles of reason necessary by a logical necessity, *i.e.* the opposite of which implies a contradiction, must and may be employed safely in theology; but he had reason to deny that what is only necessary by a physical necessity (*i.e.* founded upon induction from that which is customary in nature, or upon natural laws which, so to speak, are of divine institution) is sufficient to refute the belief in a mystery or miracle, since it depends upon God to change the ordinary course of things. Thus it is according to the order of nature that we may be certain that one and the same person cannot be at the same time a mother and a virgin, or that a human body cannot fail to be obvious to the senses, although the contrary of both may be possible to God. Vedelius also appears to agree to this distinction. But we sometimes dis-

[1] William of Occam, the date of whose birth is unknown, and who died at Munich in 1347, renewed and developed Nominalism in the form of *Terminism*, the *Termini* (concepts) being subjective signs of really existing things, and not mere names—*flatus vocis*—as so frequently regarded. The relations of his philosophy to subsequent thinking are well set forth by Windelband-Tufts, *Hist. of Philos.*, pp. 312, 315, 325 *sq.*, 342 *sq.* For Leibnitz's view of his Nominalism, *cf. De stilo philos. Nizolii*, § 28, Erdmann, 68 b–69 b; Gerhardt, 4, 157–158. On his life and philosophy, *cf.* Stöckl, *Gesch. d. Philos. d. Mittelalters*, II., 2 [Vol. 3], 986–1021; Hauréau, *Hist. d. la Philos. scolastique*, II., 2 [Vol. 3], 356–430; Prantl, *Gesch. d. Logik*, 3, 327–420.—TR.

[2] Gerhardt reads: "quel moyen qu'on employe," etc.; Erdmann, Jacques, and Janet read: "que le moyen qu'on emploie," etc., *i.e.* "as the means employed," etc. Schaarschmidt, in his translation, follows the reading of Erdmann, Jacques, and Janet, and says in his note to the passage: "Dass wir mit andern Worten bei unserm Schlussverfahren uns nothwendig im Cirkel bewegten," *i.e.* "That we, in other words, in our reasoning, necessarily moved in a circle." The correct reading can be determined only by the exact language of Occam, which thus far I have been unable to find.—TR.

pute about certain principles, whether they are logically necessary, or only physically so. Such is the dispute with the Socinians, whether substance can be multiplied when the individual essence does not exist; and the dispute with the Zwinglians, whether a body can be only in one place. Now we must admit that every time that logical necessity is not demonstrated, we can presume in a proposition only physical necessity. But it seems to me that a question remains, which the authors of whom I have just spoken have not sufficiently examined, namely this: Suppose that on one side we find the literal sense of a text of Holy Scripture, and on the other a great appearance of logical impossibility, or at least an admitted *physical impossibility,* is it more reasonable to deny the literal sense or the philosophical principle? It is certain that there are passages where to abandon the letter occasions no difficulty, as when Scripture gives hands to God and attributes to him anger, penitence, and other human affections; otherwise it would be necessary to array ourselves on the side of the anthropomorphists, or of certain English fanatics who believe that Herod was really changed into a fox when Jesus Christ called him by that name. It is here that the rules of interpretation are in place, and if they furnish nothing which combats the literal sense in order to favor the philosophic maxim, and if in addition the literal sense has nothing which attributes to God any imperfection, or entails any danger in the practice of piety, it is safer and indeed more reasonable to follow it. These two authors whom I have just named dispute further upon the undertaking of Keckermann,[1]

[1] Bartholemew Keckermann, 1573–1609, a Semi-Ramist, was Professor of Hebrew at Heidelberg, and, from 1601, of Philosophy at the Gymnasium at Dantzic. He was the author of many compilations, made for the use of his pupils in the gymnasium, in which he presented all the sciences in a methodical and systematic form. His *Opera omnia* appeared at Geneva, 1614, 2 vols., fol. Leibnitz refers to him in the same connection in the *Théodicée*, Discours prélim., § 59. For further account of him, *cf.* W. Gass, *Gesch. d. protestantischen Dogmatik in ihrem Zusammenhange mit d. Theologie*, Vol. 1, pp. 408 *sq.* Pünjer, *Gesch. d. christ. Religionsphilos.*, 1, 118, 127, 128, Eng. trans., 1, 158, 170, 172, briefly refers to him.

According to Schaarschmidt, Keckermann's proof of the Trinity from reason, which is quite closely connected with that of Lully, as Lully's with the thoughts of Augustine, is found in his *Systema ss. theologiæ* (1st ed., 1602; 2d ed., Hanoviæ, 1607), chap. 3, pp. 20 *sq.*, 3d ed., Hanoviæ, 1615. In the introduction Keckermann expresses himself very decidedly. "Fateor

who wished to demonstrate the Trinity by reason, as Raymond Lully[1] had also tried to do formerly. But Musæus acknowledged with sufficient fairness that if the demonstration of the Reformed author had been valid and just, he would have had nothing to say on the subject; that he would have been right in maintaining as regards this article that the light of the Holy Spirit might be illumined by philosophy. They have also discussed the famous question, whether those who, without any knowledge of the revelation of the Old or New Testament, died in the opinions of a natural piety, could have been saved by this means and obtained the remission of their sins? We

equidem ultro, circa mysterium de ss. Triade, ad id esse omnem intellectum humanum, quod est oculus vespertilionis ad solem," etc. Keckermann's demonstration was refuted by Musæus in the "Dissertatio altera," appended to his *De usu princip. rationis et philos. in controversiis theologicis*, 2d ed., Jenæ, 1665. — TR.

[1] Raymond Lully, 1234 or 1235–1315, best known as the inventor of the "Great Art," attempted to demonstrate against the assertions of the Averroists, the inherent rationality of the doctrines of Christianity. His *Opera omnia*, 10 vols. (Vols. 7 and 8 probably never printed), fol., appeared at Mainz, 1721–1742. For an account of his life and philosophy, *cf.* Stöckl, *Gesch. d. Philos. d. Mittelalters*, II., 2 [Vol. 3], 924–952; Erdmann, *Grund. d. Gesch. d. Philos.*, § 206, Vol. 1, pp. 375–393, Eng. trans., 1, 447–468; Neander, *Hist. of the Christ. Relig. and Church*, 4, 65–71, 426, 435 *sq.*; for his Logic, *cf.* Prantl, *Gesch. d. Logik im Abendlande*, 3, 145–177. *Cf.* also an article by Delecluse in the "Revue de Deux Mondes," 1840.

Lully occupied himself much with the proof of the Trinity, discussing it, according to Schaarschmidt, in his *Quæstiones* [*Disputatio Erimitæ et Raymundi* — Erdmann] *super lib. Sententiarum*, Lib. I., quæst. 6; *Disputatio fidelis (catholici) et infidelis*, pp. 2, 3; and especially in the *Disputatio fidei et intellectus*, Pt. I., where the question of the demonstrability of the Trinity is considered in detail, and Pt. II., where the proof is attempted. Schaarschmidt thinks that Leibnitz probably has in mind this last work. All three works are found in *Opera*, Vol. 4, ed. Mainz, 1729. Stöckl, *op. cit.*, II., 2 [Vol 3], 942–944, gives an account of Lully's argument on the Trinity, based chiefly on the *Articuli fidei sacrosanctæ*, found in the collection of Lully's works entitled *Opera ea quæ ad inventam a Lullo artem universalem pertinent*, Argentorati, 1598, 1607, and 1617, and also in *Opera*, Vol. 2, ed. Mainz, 1722. In his list of Lully's works, Stöckl cites the following which discuss the Trinity: *Liber contradictionis inter Raymundum et Averroistam de centum syllogismis circa mysterium Trinitatis; Liber de substantia et accidente in quo probatur Trinitas.* *Cf.* also Neander, *op. cit.*, 4, 465.

For Leibnitz's own views on the Trinity, *cf.* his *Defensio Trinitatis per nova reperta logica, contra Epistolam Ariani*, Dutens, *Leibnit. op. om.*, 1, 10–16; *Duæ Epist. ad Læflerum de Trinitate et Definitionibus Mathematicis circa Deum, Spiritus*, etc., Dutens, *op. cit.*, 1, 17–23; *Remarques sur le livre d'un Antitrinitaire Anglois*, etc., Dutens, *op. cit.*, 1, 24–27, and Feller, *Leibnit. Miscellanea*, No. IV., pp. 8–15; *Théodicée*, Discours prélim., § 22; Letter to M. B., 1696, Feller, *op. cit.*, No. VIII., pp. 26 *sq.* — TR.

know that Clement of Alexandria, Justin Martyr, and St. Chrysostom to a certain extent were inclined thereto,[1] and indeed I once showed Pelisson[2] that a number of excellent doctors of the Roman church, far from condemning non-opinionative Protestants, even desired to save the heathen and to maintain that the persons of whom I have just spoken could have been saved by an act of *contrition, i.e.* penitence grounded in *the love of benevolence,* in virtue of which we love God above everything, because his perfections render him supremely lovable. This brings it about that afterwards we are led with all our hearts to conform to His will and to imitate His perfection in order the better to unite ourselves with Him, since it appears right for God not to refuse his grace to those who hold such views. Not to speak of Erasmus and of Ludovicus Vives,[3]

[1] Clement of Alexandria, born c. 150–160, date and place of death unknown. *Cf. Stromata* (or *Miscellanies*), Bk. VI., chaps. 5 and 6.—Justin Martyr, c. 114–c. 163. *Cf. First Apology,* chap. 46; *Second Apology,* chaps. 8 and 13.—John Chrysostom, c. 347–407. Clement and Justin entered the Christian church as thinkers trained in Greek philosophy, which they regarded as the gift of God in preparation for the fuller light and life of Christianity—Justin in particular through his view of the "spermatic logos," "the seed of reason implanted in every race of men"; while Chrysostom, trained in Greek rhetoric and oratory, took a similar view of Greek culture as from God and not from the evil one. All three would naturally look upon those who lived up to the light they had as likely to receive more in due time, and to accept it and live in it when it came.—TR.

[2] Paul Fontanier-Pellisson, 1624–1693, born and educated a Protestant, followed at first the profession of the law, but afterwards abandoned it for that of literature. He held several public offices, among others that of historiographer to Louis XIV. To obtain this position he was obliged to become a Catholic. He published a large number of works, among which was a Latin paraphrase of the first book of the Institutes of Justinian, 1645; *Histoire de l'Académie française jusqu'en 1652,* 1653, 8vo; *Traité de l'Eucharistie,* 1694, 12mo, and other religious works. He corresponded extensively with Leibnitz on religious and theological subjects. The correspondence is contained in his *Réflexions sur les différends en matière de religion,* 1686, and following years, 4 vols., 12mo. Portions of the same in Dutens, *Leibnitz op. om.*, 1, 678 *sq.;* most complete in Foucher de Careil, *Œuvres de Leibniz,* Vol. 1. For the letter here referred to by Leibnitz, *cf.* Dutens, *op. cit.*, 1, 681–684, Foucher de Careil, *op. cit.* 1, 55–66; for Pellisson's replies, *cf.* Dutens, *op. cit.*, 1, 697, 700–702, Foucher de Careil, *op. cit.*, 1, 90–92, 96–100. For account of the controversy, *cf.* Guhrauer, *Leibnitz, Eine Biog.*, Pt. II., 35 *sq.*—TR.

[3] Juan Luis Vives, 1492–1540, a Spanish scholar and philosopher, a younger contemporary and friend of Erasmus, 1467–1536, and for a time the instructor of the Princess Mary, daughter of Henry VIII., was a persistent and successful opponent of scholastic Aristotelianism, and, as an advocate of the direct study of Nature by the way of experiment, the precursor of Descartes and Bacon. His *Opera omnia* appeared at Basle, 1555, 2 vols., fol., and at Valencia,

I bring forward the view of Jaques Payva Andradius,[1] a Portuguese doctor very celebrated in his time, who was one of the theologians of the Council of Trent, and who said indeed that those who did not agree with this view made God supremely cruel (*neque enim, inquit, immanitas deterior ulla esse potest*). Pelisson found difficulty in finding this book in Paris, an indication that authors esteemed in their time are often neglected afterwards. This is what made Bayle think that many cite Andradius only upon the testimony of Chemnitius,[2] his antagonist. This may indeed be so, but for myself I had read him before quoting him; and his disputes with Chemnitius made him celebrated in Germany, for he had written in behalf of the Jesuits against this author, and we find in his book some par-

1782–1790, 8 vols., fol. On his life and philosophy, *cf.* Stöckl, *Gesch. d. Philos. d. Mittelalters*, III. [Vol. 4], 285–287; Ueberweg-Heinze, *Gesch. d. Philos.*, 7th ed., 1888, Vol. 3, pp. 24, 25; Lange, *Gesch. d. Materialismus*, Vol. 1, p. 106, Iserlohn, 1866, Eng. trans., 1, 228, 2d ed., Boston, 1879; and Lange's article on "Vives," in *Encykl. d. ges. Erzieh.- u. Unterrichtswesen*, Vol. 9, pp. 737–814. — Tr.

[1] Diego Payva d'Andrada, 1528–1575, a celebrated theologian of one of the most noble Portuguese families, who, after completing his studies chiefly in the Scriptures and the Fathers, devoted himself with zeal to missions for instructing the ignorant, and was sent at the age of thirty-three by King Sebastian of Portugal to the Council of Trent to assist as a theologian. There he composed his *Orthodoxarum explicationum de religionis Christianæ capitibus lib. X. adversus hæreticos, contra Chemnicium*, Venetiis, 1564, 8vo; and his *Defensio Tridentinæ fidei catholicae et integerrimæ V. lib. comprehensa adversus hæreticorum detestabiles calumnias et praesertim Martini Chemnicii Germani*, Olyssipone, 1578, 4to, Ingolstadt, 1580, 8vo. In the latter book he maintained the opinions of Zwingli and Erasmus on the salvation of the heathen, in consequence of which the book was much quoted by Protestants. Leibnitz refers to him in this same connection in the *Théodicée*, Pt. I., § 96; in an excerpt from a letter to a friend written Nov. 1697, *cf.* Dutens, *Leibnit. op. om.*, 1, 33; in his letters to Pellisson, Dutens, *op. cit.*, 1, 683, Foucher de Careil, *Œuvres de Leibniz*, 1, 65–66; and in his letters to Ant. Magliabechius, No. 28, 26 Nov., 6 — Dec., 1697, Dutens, *op. cit.*, 5, 121, and to Joh. Fabricius, Prof. at Helmstadt, No. 16, Sept. 20, 1698, Dutens, *op. cit.*, 5, 235. — Tr.

[2] Martin Chemnitz, 1522–1586, a German Lutheran theologian, a disciple of Melancthon, 1497–1560, and said to be the ablest theologian of the period immediately succeeding Luther, was Professor of Theology at Wittemberg, 1551–1554, and then for thirty years pastor at Brunswick. To him more than to any other the Lutheran church owes its purity of doctrine and compact organization. His *Loci Theologici*, Frankfort, 1591, is one of the best expositions of Lutheran theology as modified by Melancthon. His greatest work, the *Examen Concilii Tridentini*, appeared at Frankfort in four parts, 1565–1573, again in 1585, 4 vols., fol., and in later eds. For further account of Chemnitz, *cf.* Schenkel's article in Herzog, *Realencyclop.*, 2d ed., Leipzig, 1878, Vol. 3, pp. 184–192. Leibnitz refers to him also in the *Théodicée*, Discours prélim. § 67. — Tr.

ticulars touching the origin of this famous society. I have remarked that some Protestants called those *Andradians*, who were of his opinion upon the subject of which I have just spoken. There have been authors who have written expressly upon the salvation of Aristotle upon the basis of these same principles with the approbation of the Censors. The books also of Collius[1] in Latin and La Mothe le Vayer[2] in French on the salvation of the heathen are well known. But a certain Franciscus Puccius[3]

[1] Francesco Collio — Latin, Collius ("Collins" being a misprint for "Collius" in all the editions of Leibnitz's text) — was an Italian theologian of great learning, a doctor of the Ambrosian College at Milan, and Grand Penitentiary of the diocese of Milan from 1631 till his death in 1640. In his *De animabus paganorum*, 2 vols., 4to, Mediol. 1622–1623, 2d ed., 1738–1740, he discussed the question of the eternal salvation of the pagans, deciding as to the fate of individuals on the ground of their knowledge of divine things, their moral life, sentiments and writings, and the testimony regarding them given by ecclesiastical and profane writers. He considers Aristotle as unsaved. Dupin, *Bibl. des Aut. ecclés.*, 1711, tom. 17, pp. 109–116 *sq.*, gives a long abstract from this work, and an estimate of its character and value. *Cf.* also Tiraboschi, *Storia della Letteratura Italiana*, Vol. 14 [Tomo VIII, Parte Prima, ed. Rome, 1782–1784], pp. 167–168, Milan, 1824. — TR.

[2] François de La Mothe le Vayer, 1588–1672, a French writer and philosopher, was from 1652–1660 the instructor of Louis XIV. of France, for whom he composed many elementary treatises on various subjects of study. The book here referred to by Leibnitz is his *De la vertu des païens*, Paris, 1642, 4to., 3d ed., 1647. The subject is treated in the conclusion of Pt. I., *cf. Œuvres*, Vol. 1, p. 582, Paris, A. Courbe, 1662. The best ed. is that published at Dresden, 1756–1759, 7 vols. in 14, 8vo. The *De la vertu des païens* — avec les preuves des citations mises sous le texte — is found in Vol. 5, pp. 1 *sq.* of this ed. Le Vayer goes back to the Church Fathers and later ecclesiastical writers, and gives much literature. — TR.

[3] Francesco Pucci, an Italian theologian (died 1660), was led to devote himself to theology by his participation in religious controversies at Lyons, whither he had gone to learn commerce. Adopting mostly Protestant ideas, he went to England, where he received an Oxford M.A. in 1574. Opposing, in his *De fide in Deum, quæ et qualis sit*, the Calvinism then ruling at Oxford, he went to Basle and joined himself to F. Socinus, but soon returned to England in consequence of persecution on account of his views on universal grace, put forth in theses entitled *Universum genus humanum in ipso matris utero efficaciter particeps esse beneficiorum Christi et vitæ immortalis et beatæ*, etc. He finally became a Catholic, 1588, and secretary of Cardinal Pompei. In his *De immortalitate naturali primi hominis ante peccatum* he combatted certain ideas of Socinus, and in his *De Christi Salvationis efficacitate omnibus et singulis hominibus quatenus homines sunt assertio catholica*, Gouda, 1592, 8vo, he maintained the view that all men could be saved through the natural power of reason, or through the natural belief in the Creator. He proposed to prove by Scripture and the Fathers that Christ by his death made satisfaction for all men, so that all having a natural knowledge of God will be saved, although having no knowledge of Jesus Christ. — TR.

went too far. St. Augustine, wholly clever and penetrating as he was, threw himself into another extreme view, even condemning infants dying without baptism,[1] and the Scholastics appear to have been right in abandoning it; although persons otherwise clever and some of great merit, but of a disposition a little misanthropic in this respect, desired to revive this doctrine of this Father and have perhaps exaggerated it. This spirit also may have had some influence in the dispute between several excessively vehement doctors and the Jesuit missionaries in China, who had insinuated that the ancient Chinese had had the true religion of their time and the true saints, and that the doctrine of Confucius was in no respect idolatrous or atheistic. It seems that there was more reason in Rome in being unwilling to condemn one of the greatest nations without understanding it. It is well for us that God is more philanthropic than men. I know some persons who, thinking to show their zeal by severe opinions, fancy that we cannot believe in original sin without being of their opinion, but in this they are mistaken. And it does not follow that those who justify the heathen, or others who lack ordinary aid, must attribute it to the forces of nature only (although perhaps some Fathers were of this opinion), since we may maintain that God in giving them the grace exciting an act of contrition gives them also, either explicitly or virtually, but always in a supernatural way, before they die, even if

[1] On this and the immediate context, *cf. Théodicée*, Pt. I., §§ 92–95, Pt. III., § 283. Augustine's view is found in his works *passim*. *Cf.*, among others, *Enchir. ad Laurent.*, chap. 43; *De nuptiis et concupiscentia*, Bk. I., chap. 22, with which *cf. Contra Julianum Pelagianum*, Bk. III., chap. 12 (infants under the power of the devil on account of original sin — the "potestas diaboli" is "peccatum originale"), and Bk. V., chap. 44; *Contra duas epist. Pelag.*, Bk. IV., chap. 4; *De peccatorum meritis et Remissione et de Baptismo Parvulorum*, Bk. I., chap. 25, Bk. III., chap. 7; *De peccato originale*, chap. 36; *De civitate Dei*, Bk. XIII., chap. 14. *Cf.* also Shedd, *Hist. of Christ. Doct.*, 2, 76, note 2, 77, note 1; Hagenbach, *Hist. of Doct.*, ed. H. B. Smith, 1, 360, and trans. from later German ed. T. & T. Clark, 1880, 3 vols., Vol. 2, pp. 73 *sq.* Augustine believed that infants because of hereditary depravity — original sin — belonged to the "massa perditionis," and, unless relieved from the penalty therein inhering by the sacrament of baptism, which was thus a means of salvation to the infant, must incur the penalty and be lost. Their condemnation, however, since they were guilty of no personal sin, would be the lightest of all — "in damnatione omnium levissima" (*C. Jul. Pelag.*, V. 44).

For a brief, but most excellent and satisfactory, discussion of the Salvation of Infants, *cf.* E. G. Robinson, *Christian Theology*, § 28, pp. 164–169, Rochester, N.Y., Press of E. R. Andrews, 1894. — TR.

only at the last moment, all the light of faith and all the warmth of love necessary to their salvation. Thus it is that the Reformers explain with Vedelius the view of Zwingli,[1] who had also expressed the same view upon this point of the salvation of the virtuous men of Paganism, as the doctors of the Roman church have done. This doctrine also has nothing in common for that reason with the particular doctrine of the Pelagians or Semi-Pelagians, from which we know that Zwingli was far removed. And since we teach against the Pelagians a supernatural grace in all those who possess faith (in which the three received religions agree, excepting perhaps the disciples of Pajon)[2] and as they allow also either faith or at least similar movements to infants who receive baptism, it is not very extraordinary to allow as much at least in the article of death to persons of good will who have not had the good fortune to be instructed as usual in Christianity.[3] But the part of the wisest is to determine nothing upon points so little known, and to content himself with the general judgment that God can do nothing which is not full of goodness and justice: *melius est dubitare de occultis quam litigare de incertis* (Augustine, lib. 8, Genes. ad lit. c. 5).

[1] Ulrich Zwingli, 1484–1531, introduced the Reformation into Switzerland about the same time that Luther, 1483–1546, introduced it into Germany. His view on the salvation of the heathen, a consequence of his milder view of original sin or innate depravity, is found in his *Christ. Fidei brevis et clara expositio*, *Werke*, ed., Schuler u. Schulthess, Zürich, 1828–1842, 8 vols., Vol. 4, pp. 42–78. In his treatise *De Providentia* (*ibid.*, Vol. 4, pp. 79–144) he advanced the principle that pagans who have acknowledged the true God and have led a good life, such as Socrates and Seneca, are capable of being saved without faith; and he extended this principle to all who have no knowledge of the gospel. — Tr.

[2] Claude Pajon, 1626–1685, a French Protestant theologian, Professor of Theology at Saumer, 1666, and later pastor at Orleans. Pajon taught that in conversion the Holy Spirit did not act immediately or irresistibly upon the heart, but that the soul was itself active in the work of salvation, allowing itself to be convinced by the efficacious word of truth found in Scripture with which the Spirit's influence was intimately united. His views were opposed by both Lutherans and Reformed. For further account of him, *cf.* Alex. Schweizer, *Central-Dogmen d. Reform. Kirche*, 2 vols., 1854–1856, Vol. 2, pp. 564–663, and in Herzog, *Realencyclop.* 2d ed., Leipzig, 1883, Vol. 11, pp. 161–163; W. Gass, *Gesch. d. prot. Dogmatik*, 2, 359 *sq.* — Tr.

[3] *Cf.* Feller, *Otium Hanoveranum*, No. LXXXVIII., pp. 181–183 (Dutens, 6, 311, 312). — Tr.

CHAPTER XIX

OF ENTHUSIASM

§ 1. *Ph.* [Would to God that all theologians and St. Augustine himself had always practised the maxim expressed in this passage.] But men think that the dogmatic spirit is an indication of their zeal for the truth, while it is wholly the contrary. We love the truth in reality only in proportion as we love to examine the proofs which make it what it is. And when we judge hastily we are always pressed by less sincere motives. § 2. The spirit of authority is not one of the less common motives, and a certain satisfaction it has in its own reveries is another motive which causes *enthusiasm* to spring up. § 3. This is the name which is given to the failing of those who believe an immediate revelation when it is not grounded in reason. § 4. And as we may say that *reason* is a natural revelation of which God is the author, just as he is the author of nature, we may also say that *revelation* is a supernatural reason, *i.e.* a reason extended upon the basis of new discoveries emanating directly from God. But these discoveries suppose that we have the means of discerning them, which is reason itself; and to desire to proscribe reason in order to make way for revelation would be to pluck out the eyes the better to see the satellites of Jupiter through a telescope. § 5. The source of enthusiasm is that an immediate revelation is more convenient and shorter than the long and difficult process of reasoning which is not always followed by a happy result. Men have been seen in all ages whose melancholy mingled with devotion, united with the good opinion they have had of themselves, has made them believe that they had an altogether different intercourse with God from other men. They suppose he has promised it to them and believe themselves his people preferably to others. § 6. Their fancy becomes an illumination and a divine authority, and their plans are an infallible direction from heaven, which they are obliged to follow. § 7. This view has produced great results and caused great evils, for a man acts more vigorously when he follows his own impulses and when the opinion of a divine authority is sustained by his inclinations. § 8. It is difficult to draw him therefrom, because this pretended certainty without proof flatters his vanity and love for that which is extraordinary. Fanatics compare their opinions to sight and feeling. They see the divine light as we see that of the sun at noon without needing the twilight of their reason to show it to them. § 9. They are certain because they are certain, and their persuasion is right because it is strong, for this is the result to which their figurative language reduces itself. § 10. But as there are two perceptions, that of the proposition and that of the revelation, we may ask them where is clearness. If it is in the sight of the proposition, what good is revelation? It must then be in the feeling of revelation. But how can they see that it is God who reveals and not a will-of-the-wisp which leads them around this circle: this is a revelation because I believe it strongly, and I believe it because it is a revelation. § 11. Is there anything more suited to throw one into error than to take the imagination for a guide? § 12. St. Paul had great zeal when he persecuted the Christians and did not allow himself to be mistaken. We know that the devil has had martyrs, and if it is sufficient to be well persuaded we shall not be able to distinguish the delusions of Satan from the inspirations of the Holy Spirit. § 14. It is then the reason which makes known the truth of revelation. § 15. And if our belief proved it, it would be the circle of which I just spoke. The holy men who received the revelations of God had *external signs* which persuaded them of the truth of the inner light. Moses saw a bush which burned without being consumed, and heard a voice from the midst of the bush, and God, in order to give him more assurance concerning his mission when he sent him to Egypt to deliver his brethren, made use of the miracle of the rod changed into a serpent. Gideon was sent by an angel to deliver the people of Israel from the yoke of the Midianites; yet he demanded a sign in order to be convinced that this commission was given him on the part of God. § 16. I do not, however, deny that God sometimes illumines the minds of men, in order to make them understand certain important truths or to lead them to good acts, by the immediate influence and assistance of the Holy Spirit without any extraordinary sign accompanying this influence. But in these cases also we have reason and Scripture, two infallible rules for judging of these illuminations; for if they agree with these rules we run at least no risk in regarding them as inspired of God, although it is not perhaps an immediate revelation.

Th. Enthusiasm was at the beginning a good term. And as the sophism properly indicates an exercise of wisdom, enthusiasm signifies that there is a divinity in us. *Est Deus in nobis.*[1] Socrates maintained that a god or dæmon[2] gave him internal warnings, so that *enthusiasm* would be a divine instinct. But men having consecrated their passions, fancies, dreams, and even their anger as something divine, enthusiasm began to signify a mental disturbance attributed to the influence of some divinity, which is supposed to be in those who are smitten therewith; for the soothsayers, male and female, showed a mental derangement, when their god seized them, as the Cumæan Sibyl in Vergil.[3] Since then we attribute it to those who believe without foundation that their movements come from God. Nisus in the same poet thinking himself pressed by I know not what impulse to a dangerous enterprise, in which he perished with his friend, proposed it to him in these terms full of a reasonable doubt:—

Di ne hunc ardorem mentibus addunt,
Euryale, an sua cuique Deus fit dira cupido?[4]

[1] Ovid, *Fasti*, 6, 5: "Est Deus in nobis, agitante calescimus illo."—Tr.

[2] On the dæmon of Socrates, *cf.* Zeller, *Philos. d. Griech.*, II., 1 [Vol. 3], 73–91, 4th ed., Leipzig, 1889; J. S. Blackie, *Four Phases of Morals*, pp. 125–127, New York. 1872: H. Jackson, "On the δαιμόνιον of Socrates" in the "Journal of Philology." V., and article "Socrates," *Encyclop. Brit.*, 9th ed., Vol. 22, p. 246 (Amer. reprint).—Tr.

[3] *Cf.* Vergil. *Æneid*, 6, 49: "Et rabie fera corda tument." The view here mentioned by Leibnitz, that persons gifted with inspiration or enthusiasm were also affected with some derangement or disturbance of the ordinary mental processes, was current in one form or another throughout all antiquity, and had its influence, through the contact of Greek thought with Christianity, in shaping the Christian doctrine of inspiration. *Cf.* Plato, *Phædrus*, 244, Jowett's trans., 2d ed., 1875, 2, 121, 3d ed., 1892, 1, 449–450; *Ion*, 533–534, Jowett, 2d ed., 1, 247–248, 3d ed., 1, 501–503; *Timæus*, 71–72, Jowett. 2d ed., 3, 654–656, 3d ed., 3, 492–494; the Stoic view, Zeller, *Philos. d. Griech.*, III., 1 [Vol. 5], 336 *sq.*, Plutarch, *ibid.*, III., 2 [Vol. 6], 193 *sq.*, Philo, 414 *sq.*, Plotinus, 611 *sq.*; Pfleiderer, *Religionsphilosophie*, 2d ed., 1884, 2, 339 *sq.*, Eng. trans., 4, 46 *sq.*—Tr.

[4] Verg. *Aen.* 9, 184–185.—Tr.

He ceased not to follow this instinct although he knew not whether it came from God or from an unfortunate desire to distinguish himself. But if he had been successful, he would not have failed to acquire authority in another case and to think himself impelled by some divine power. The enthusiasts of the present think that they receive also from God the dogmas which they observe. The Quakers belong to this persuasion, and Barclay, their first systematic author, maintains that they find in themselves a certain light which is made known by itself.[1] But why call that *light* which reveals nothing? I know that there are some persons of this disposition of mind who see sparks and even something more luminous, but this image of material light excited when their minds are aroused gives no light to the mind. Some idiots with a restless imagination form conceptions which they had not before; they are in a condition to say fine or at least very animated things in their opinion; they admire themselves and make others admire this fertility which passes for inspiration. This advantage comes to them largely from a vivid imagination which passion rouses and from an excellent memory which has well retained the methods of speech of the prophetic books which the reading or discourse of others has rendered familiar to them. Antoinette de Bourignon made use of the facility she had in speaking and writing as a proof of her divine mission.[2] I know a visionary who based his divine mission upon the tal-

[1] *Cf.* Leibnitz's letter to Thos. Burnett, July 17–27, 1696; Gerhardt, *Leibniz. philos. Schrift.*, 3, 184. On the doctrine of the "inner light," the immediate revelation of the Spirit of God in each individual soul, "the light that lighteneth every man,"—the most characteristic doctrine of the Quakers,—*cf.* Robert Barclay, 1648–1690, *An Apology for the True Christian Divinity*, Prop. II., Of Immediate Revelation; and the excellent account of Bancroft, *Hist. of the U. S.*, chap. 23, Vol. 2, pp. 78 *sq.*, Centenary ed., Boston, 1876.—Tr.

[2] Antoinette Bourignon, 1616–1680, an enthusiast whose religious doctrines made considerable stir in her lifetime and for a short time after in Holland and Scotland, but have long ceased to have any influence and are now almost wholly forgotten. Her complete works in French appeared at Amsterdam, 1686, 19 vols., 8vo; 1717, 21 vols., 8vo, with a life of the author by Pierre Poiret, 1646–1719, a Calvinistic minister and famous mystic, who became her disciple, edited her works, and attempted to reduce to system her vague reveries in his *Œconomie de la nature*, Amsterdam, 1686, 21 vols., 8vo. Her prophetic views were expounded in her *Traité de l'aveuglement des hommes* (*Œuvres*, ed. 1686, Vol. 15), her *La lumière du monde* (*ibid.*, Vol. 7), and her *De la lumière née en ténèbres* (*ibid.*, Vol. 4), the last work being "a collection of letters, with a large explanation of Matt. 24 and 25"; Eng. trans. *The Light of the*

ents he had in speaking and praying aloud almost an entire day without ceasing and without becoming exhausted. There are some persons who, after having practised austerities or after a state of sadness, taste a peace and consolation in the soul which enraptures them, and they find therein so much delight that they believe it to be an effect of the Holy Spirit. It is true that the contentment they find in considering the greatness and goodness of God, in the accomplishment of his will, in the practice of the virtues, is a grace of God and one of the greatest; but it is not always a grace which needs a new supernatural aid, as many of these good people maintain. Not long since there was a young lady very wise in everything else, who believed from her youth that she spoke with Jesus Christ and was his wife in a wholly peculiar manner. Her mother, to whom this was related, was a little given to enthusiasm, but the daughter having commenced early had gone very much farther. Her satisfaction and joy was unspeakable, her wisdom appeared in her conduct, and her intelligence in her discourse. The thing went, however, so far that she received letters addressed to our Lord and she sent them back sealed as she received them with a reply which sometimes appeared appropriate and always reasonable. But finally she ceased to receive them from fear of making too much disturbance. In Spain she would have been another St. Theresa. But all persons who have similar visions do not conduct themselves in the same way. There are some who seek to form a sect, and even to make trouble: and England furnishes a strange proof of this.[1] When these persons act in good faith it is difficult to

World, London, 1696; *The Light risen in Darkness*, London, 1703. Leibnitz refers to her in a fragment, *Sur l'esprit Sectaire*, 1697, *cf.* Dutens, 1, 740. For further account, *cf.* J. C. Adelung, *Gesch. d. mensch. Narrheit*, Leipzig, 1785–1789, 7 vols., 16mo, Vol. 5, pp. 245–391; Gottfried Arnold, *Kirchen u. Ketzerhistorie*, Frankfort-on-the-Main, 1729, Theil. III., Cap. XVI., Vol. 2, pp. 153–176, Th. IV., Sect. III., Num. XVII., Vol. 2, pp. 1065–1089; Wetzer u. Welte, *Kirchenlexicon*, Vol. 2, pp. 1167–1170, ed. 1883. — Tr.

[1] Leibnitz here refers to the Independents, who, arising in obscurity in England in the reign of Elizabeth and gradually gaining in numbers and influence as a result of the persecution to which they were subject at the hands of the established Church and the State, and of their success in founding the New England States, came to the front in the time of the Revolution and changed at length the political as well as the religious life of England, and became a powerful and controlling force in the life and institutions of the American people. In their fundamental principle that religion is a matter of the indi-

reform them: sometimes the overthrow of all their plans corrects them, but often it is too late. There was a visionary who lately died who believed himself immortal because he was very old and very well, and without having read the book of an Englishman lately published (who wished to make us believe that Jesus Christ came to exempt true believers from bodily death) was almost of the same opinion for some years past; but when he perceived that he was dying he went so far as to doubt all religion because it did not correspond to his chimera. Quirin Kulman [*sic*],[1] a Silesian, a man of knowledge and judgment, but who had since indulged in two kinds of visions, equally dangerous, the one of the enthusiasts, the other of the alchemists, and who made some stir in England, Holland, and even in Constantinople, being at last advised to go into Russia and there to mix himself up in certain intrigues against the minister, at the time when the Princess Sophia governed it, was condemned to be burned, and did not die like a man per-

vidual reason and conscience, wholly free from State or other control, they bore in a general way a somewhat close resemblance to the Quakers and other enthusiasts of their time.

In this connection Schaarschmidt ventures the conjecture that Leibnitz may have had his attention called to the persons and circumstances mentioned in this chapter by a large work, appearing not long before, entitled, *Anabaptisticum et enthusiasticum Pantheon,* und Geistliches Rüsthauss wider die Alten Quäcker und Neuen Frey-Geister, u. s. w., Cothen, W. A. Meyer, 1702, since his allegations strikingly call to mind this work. But may not Bayle's *Dictionnaire* as well have been the source of his information, inasmuch as it contains considerably extended articles on the persons mentioned, and was a work with which Leibnitz was thoroughly familiar?—TR.

[1] Quirin Kuhlmann, 1651-1689, in consequence of a disordered brain resulting from a severe illness at the age of 18, became subject to hallucinations, lost his previous taste for study, claimed to possess a method by which he might know everything independent of the usual processes of acquisition, and that the Holy Ghost was his only teacher, and on these grounds considered himself a saint. At Leyden, falling in with the works of Boehme, he immediately became an enthusiastic disciple. It is said that he wished to marry Antoinette Bourignon, but that her "inviolable chastity" caused her to refuse him. Leaving Holland in 1675 he travelled, it is believed, in England, France, and Turkey. At Constantinople he addressed a letter, Aug. 1, 1678, to the Sultan Mahomet IV., in which he predicted the conversion of the Turks, and sought to win the Sultan to his views. Failing to attain his desired end, he went to Russia to set up the true kingdom of God, was opposed by Peter the Great, and after a brief trial condemned by the Greek Patriarch—it is said at the suggestion of a Lutheran clergyman—to be burned alive as a heretic in 1689. For further account, *cf.* Adelung, *Gesch. d. mensch. Narrheit,* Vol. 5, pp. 3-90 (allusion to his alchemistic impostures, *ibid.*, pp. 52, 53, 65, 81); Wetzer und Welte, *Kirchenlexicon,* 7, 1237.—TR.

suaded of that which he had preached. The dissensions of these people among themselves ought further to convince them that their pretended *internal witness* is not divine; and that other signs are necessary to justify it. The Labadists,[1] for example, do not agree with Mademoiselle Antoinette, and although William Penn appears to have had the design in his travels in Germany, of which he has published an account, of establishing a kind of understanding between those who rely upon this witness, he does not appear to have succeeded.[2] It is desirable for the truth's sake that good people be intelligent and act in concert: nothing would be more capable of rendering the human race better and happier, but it would be necessary for them to be truly of the number of the good people, *i.e.* of the beneficent, and, further, docile and reasonable; instead

[1] The Labadists were a mystic sect or community of the Reformed Church founded by Jean de Labadie, 1610–1674, a noted Pietist or Mystic, who, originally a Roman Catholic, had become a Protestant, joined the Reformed Church, and afterwards at the head of his separatist congregation at Middleburg developed his scheme for the reformation of that ecclesiastical body. His doctrine was in many points similar to that of the Anabaptists. Labadie and his disciples wished to settle with A. Bourignon at Noordstrandt, but she would not consent, saying: "I perceive and know that we can never agree together. Their opinions and the spirit that governs them are altogether contrary to my light and the spirit that governs me." Leibnitz refers to Labadie in the *Théodicée*, Discours prélim., § 14; in a letter to Theophilus Spizel, April 7, 1671, Dutens, 5, 351–352; *cf.* also, Guhrauer, *Leibnitz's deutsche Schrift.*, 2, 498–499. For further account, *cf.* the writings of two of his most enthusiastic disciples, Pierre Yvon, *Abrégé précis de la vie et de la conduite et des vrais sentiments de feu M. de Labadie;* Anna Maria v. Schürman, *Eucleria* (said to be, perhaps, the best exposition of his views), Altona, 1673, 1678; also Arnold, *Kirchen und Ketzerhistorie*, Theil. II., Buch. XVII., Cap. XXI., Vol. 1, pp. 1186–1200; Vol. 2, pp. 1302–1350; H. van Berkum, *De Labadie en de Labadisten*, Sneek, 1851; Goebel, *Gesch. d. christ. Lebens in d. rheinisch-westphälischen Kirche*, Vol. 2, Coblentz, 1852; Heppe, *Gesch. d. Pietismus*, Leyden, 1879; Ritsche, *Gesch. d. Pietismus*, Vol. 1, Bonn, 1880. — TR.

[2] William Penn, 1644–1718, made a missionary journey through Holland and Germany in 1671–1672, in the course of which he founded a Quaker society at Embden and became an intimate friend of the Princess Elizabeth of the Palatinate, to whom Descartes dedicated his *Princip. Philos.* His letters written during this journey contain a full account of the doctrine of the "inward light." In 1677 he made another missionary journey to the Continent, and published in 1694 a full account of the same, entitled *Journal of my Travels in Holland and Germany. Cf. A Collection of the Works of Wm. Penn*, London, 2 vols., fol., 1726, Vol. 1, pp. 50–116; *Select Works*, 3d ed., London, 1782, 5 vols., 8vo, Vol. 3, pp. 373 *sq.* For short selections therefrom, *cf.* Janney, *Life of Wm. Penn*, chap. 9, pp. 125–137, 4th ed. revised, Phila., 1878; for more extended extracts, *cf. Passages from the Life and Writings of Wm. Penn*, Phila., 1882, VIII., pp. 141–199. — TR.

of which only too many of those who are called devout to-day are accused of being severe, imperious, obstinate. Their dissensions make it appear at least that their internal witness needs an external verification in order to be believed, and miracles would be necessary in order for them to have the right to pass as prophets and inspired men. There might, however, be a case where these inspirations would carry their proofs with them. This would be if they really enlightened the mind by important discoveries of some extraordinary knowledge, which without any external aid would be beyond the powers of the person who should have acquired them. If Jacob Boehme,[1] a famous shoemaker of Lusace, whose writings have been translated from German into other languages under the name of the Teutonic Philosopher, and in reality possess something of grandeur and beauty for a man in this condition, had known how to make gold, as some are persuaded he did, or as St. John the evangelist did, if we believe what is said in a hymn[2] composed in his honor: —

> Inexhaustum fert thesaurum
> Qui de virgis fecit aurum,
> Gemmas de lapidibus,

there would have been some reason for giving more credence to this extraordinary shoemaker. And if Mademoiselle Antoinette Bourignon had furnished to Bertrand la Coste, a French engineer at Hamburg, the light in the sciences which he believed he had received from her, as he indicated in dedicating to her his book on the Quadrature of the Circle (in which, making allusion to Antoinette and Bertrand, he called her the A in theology, as he said he himself was the B in mathematics), we should not have known what to say.[3] But we do not see exam-

[1] *Cf. ante*, p. 298, note 1. — Tr.

[2] *Cf.* L. Gautier, *Œuvres Poétiques d'Adam de S.-Victor*, Paris, 1858, 2 vols., 12mo, Vol. 1, p. 229, and the editor's learned note; D. S. Wrangham, *The Liturgical Poetry of Adam of St. Victor, from the text of Gautier, with trans. into English in the original metres*, etc., 3 vols., London, Kegan Paul, 1881, Vol. 1, p. 190. Leibnitz probably knew the hymn in Clichtoveus, *Elucidatorium Ecclesiasticum*, Pt. IV., of which there were several editions from 1515–1556, at Paris, Basel, Geneva. — Tr.

[3] Bertrand de Lacoste, a French engineer, born early in the 17th century, who, after some service as colonel of artillery in the army of the Duke of Brandenburg, obtained his discharge in 1663 and retired to Hamburg, where he devoted himself to the study of mathematics in general, and in particular

ples of a considerable success of this nature, nor well-detailed predictions which have succeeded in the case of such persons. The prophecies of Poniatovia,[1] of Drabitius and others, which the good man Comenius[2] published in his "Lux in Tenebris," and which contributed to the disturbances in the hereditary lands of the emperor, were found false, and those who believed them were unfortunate. Ragozky, Prince of Transylvania, was impelled by Drabitius[3] to the attack upon Poland in which he

to the problem of the quadrature of the circle. On this subject he published two works: *Scheda de inventa quadratura circuli*, 1663, and, in reply to a refutation of the same by Prof. Müller, *Démonstration de la quadrature du cercle*, Hamburg, 1666, 4to, 1677, 8vo. A Flemish translation appeared in 1677, with the title *Klarer Bewys von't Quadrat des Cirkels*, dedicated to Antoinette Bourignon, whose person and teachings he for a time greatly admired; but failing to interest her equally in his mathematical studies, he finally opposed her and her doctrines as strongly as he had before advocated them, exciting the populace of Hamburg against her and forcing her to leave the city. He wrote against her his *Scheda contra Ant. Bourignoniam*. —TR.

[1] Christine Poniatowa, 1610–1644, a famous enthusiast, the daughter of a Polish noble and unfrocked monk, claimed in 1627–1628 that she had visions regarding the persecutions of the Evangelical Church which were soon to end in its triumph. Jan. 27, 1629, she fell into a lethargy so profound that they thought her dead; but at length awaking, she declared that her visions were ended, her mission complete. Chagrin at seeing her predictions denied at last caused her death. She wrote out her revelations in the order in which she said she had received them from heaven. Comenius (*cf. ante*, p. 466, note 2) translated them into Latin, and published them, together with those of Drabitius, Kotter, 1585–1647, and other enthusiasts, in his very rare *Lux in Tenebris*, 1650, 1657, 4to, 1659, with title *Historia revelationum Ch. Kotteri, Chr. Poniatoviæ, Nic. Drabitii, etc.* (the only ed. known to Bayle, and the least rare and complete), 1665, 2 vols., 4to, also several other eds., more or less incomplete. The rarity of the work is due to the fact that Comenius, fearing on the one hand to disobey a divine command if he refused to translate these prophecies out of the Bohemian or Czech language in which they had first appeared, and on the other of covering himself with ridicule if the event not far distant did not verify them, allowed but few copies to be printed. For further account of Poniatowa, *cf.* Adelung, *Gesch. d. mensch. Narrheit*, Vol. 6, pp. 231-267. — TR.

[2] *Cf. ante*, p. 466, note 2. The *Lux in Tenebris* appeared in 1650. — TR.

[3] Nicolas Drabitius or Drabicius, c. 1587–1671, a Bohemian-Moravian minister at Drakatutz, who was compelled by the severity of the imperial edicts against the Protestants to retire to Lednitz in Hungary, turned to secular pursuits, became very dissipated, and was suspended from the ministry. In 1638 he claimed to be inspired and to have divine revelations, the chief of which predicted the fall of the House of Austria in 1657, and the success of the expedition, which he urged upon Prince George II. Rakoczy of Transylvania, against Poland in the same year. Both predictions failed. Prince George was totally defeated July 16, 1657, and compelled to fight the Turks, roused to hostility by his attack on Poland, till his death, June 26, 1660. The House

lost his army, a result which finally cost him the loss of his estates together with his life; and the poor Drabitius a long time after, at the age of eighty years, at last had his head cut off by the order of the emperor. Yet I do not doubt that there are people now who cause these predictions to be revived inaptly in the present conjuncture of disorders in Hungary, not considering that these pretended prophets spoke of the events of their time; in which respect they did almost as he who, after the bombardment of Brussels, published a loose sheet, in which there was a passage taken from a book of Mademoiselle Antoinette, who did not wish to come into this city because (if I remember rightly) she had dreamed that she saw it on fire; but this bombardment happened a long time after her death. I knew a man who went to France during the war which was terminated by the Peace of Nimwegen to importune M. de Montausier[1] and M. de Pomponne[2] upon the trustworthiness of the prophecies published by Comenius; and he would himself have believed himself inspired (I think), if he had happened to make his propositions in a time parallel to ours. This shows not only the little foundation, but also the danger of these waywardnesses. Histories are full of the bad effect of false or misunderstood prophecies, as may be seen in a learned and judicious dissertation, "De officio viri boni circa futura contingentia," which the late Jacobus Thomasius, a celebrated professor at Leipzig, formerly gave the public.[3] It is true, however, that

of Austria, resolving to rid itself of the pretended prophet, arrested him as a state criminal, tried and condemned him to death. His head and right hand were cut off and burned with a copy of his books, and the ashes thrown into the Danube, July 17, 1671. For further account, *cf.* Adelung, *Gesch. d. mensch. Narrheit*, Vol. 2, pp. 27–62. — TR.

[1] Charles de Sainte-Maure, Marquis and then Duke de Montausier, 1610–1690, to whom Louis XIV., in 1668, entrusted the education of the Dauphin, then seven years of age, for whose instruction he edited the Delphine Classics and a *Recueil de maximes morales et politiques*. — TR.

[2] Simon Arnauld, Marquis de Pomponne or Pompone, 1618–1699, was ambassador to Sweden under Louis XIV., and concluded the Peace of Nimwegen, 1678–1679. His *Mémoires de Marquis de Pomponne* appeared at Paris, 1861–1863, 2 vols., 8vo. — TR.

[3] Jacob Thomasen, — Latin Thomasius, — 1622–1684, was for many years Professor of Philosophy and Eloquence in the University of Leipzig, the founder of the scientific study of the history of philosophy in Germany, and the first to recommend disputed questions in this subject as themes for dissertations. He was Leibnitz's first teacher in philosophy, early discerned the eminent abilities and promise of his subsequently very distinguished

these persuasions sometimes produce a good effect and render great service, for God can make use of error to establish or maintain truth. But I do not believe that it is easily permitted us to make use of pious frauds for a good end; and as for the dogmas of religion, we have no need of new revelations; it is enough that we propose to ourselves salutary rules in order that we may be obliged to follow them, although the one proposing them performs no miracle. And although Jesus Christ was provided with miracles, he did not cease to refuse sometimes to perform them in order to please that perverse race who demanded signs, when he preached only virtue and what had already been taught by natural reason and the prophets.[1]

pupil, taught him to take a broad and, for that time, critical view of the history of philosophy, and introduced him early into the polemic against empiricism. The pupil regarded his teacher with reverent gratitude (*cf.* Leibnitz's letters to Thomasius, April 20–30, 1669, Gerhardt, *Leibniz. Philos. Schrift.*, 1, 15, 26–27; to J. Christ. Wolf, Dec. 11, 1711, Dutens, 5, 447, Kortholt, *Leibnit. Epist.*, 1, 270; *Leibnit. Vita a Jac. Bruckero scripta*, § 3, Dutens, 1, LVIII.–LXI., and Brucker, *Philos. Historia*, 5, 336–340, Lipsiæ, 1742–1767), and each prized the esteem and friendship of the other. Leibnitz sent Thomasius his own early works for criticism ("Neque vero laudem, sed examen peto," letter of April 20–30, 1669, G. 1, 27); Thomasius presided when Leibnitz defended his *De princ. indiv.* for the degree of Bachelor of Philosophy (*cf. ante*, p. 239, note 1), and when it was published wrote the Preface (for which *cf.* Dutens, 2, Pt. I., 11–14). For their correspondence, the preservation of Leibnitz's part of which we owe to the care of Thomasius, *cf.* Gerhardt, *op. cit.*, 1, 1–39. Most important for the philosophy of Leibnitz, especially as regards the beginning of his independent speculations, and as a statement of principles from which he never departed but simply worked out into clearer and completer forms, is the letter of April 20–30, 1669, *cf.* G. 1, 15–27, Erdmann, 48–54, Dutens, 4, 7–19, also Guhrauer, *Leibniz' Dissert. de princ. indiv.*, p. 33. Leibnitz refers frequently to Thomasius; *cf.* for example, *Théodicée*, Pt. II., §§ 184, 220.

The essay of Thomasius here referred to by Leibnitz is also cited, according to Schaarschmidt, under the title *De officio hominis circa notitiam futurorum contingentium*, and, in his opinion, is probably the same as the one which Christian Thomasius, after his father's death, had printed in his *Dissertationes LXIII. magnam partem ad historiam philosophicam et ecclesiasticam pertinentes*, Halle, 1693, 8vo, as Programma XXXVI., p. 396, under the title, *De provisione circa futura contingentia*. Thomasius was the author of a great number of dissertations, full of research and written with purity and elegance. One of them, *Origines historiæ philosophicæ et ecclesiasticæ*, Leipzig, 1665, 4to, ed. by Ch. Thomasius, Halle, 1699, 8vo, was for a long time the most accurate history of ancient philosophy. Brucker was greatly indebted to it. — TR.

[1] *Cf. ante*, pp. 553, note 1, 582. Leibnitz, while admitting the possibility and on sufficient and proper evidence the actuality of miracles, nevertheless regards them from the philosophic point of view as exceptional and relatively

CHAPTER XX

OF ERROR

§ 1. *Ph.* After having spoken of all the means which make us know or divine the truth, let us also say something about our errors and bad judgments. Men must often be mistaken since there are so many dissensions among them. The reasons of this may be reduced to these four: (1) the lack of proofs; (2) little skill in using them; (3) lack of will to make use of them; (4) false rules of probability. § 2. When I speak of the lack of proofs, I understand also those which we might find if we had the means and the opportunity, but this it is which we most frequently lack. Such is the condition of men whose life is passed in seeking their subsistence: they are as little informed of what goes on in the world, as a draught horse who always goes by the same road may become skilled in the map of the country. They would require languages, reading, conversation, observations of nature and the experiments of art. § 3. Now, all this not agreeing with their condition, shall we say then that the bulk of men are led to happiness or misery only by blind chance? Must they abandon themselves to the current opinions and authorized guides in the country, even as regards eternal happiness or misery? Or will they be eternally unhappy to have been born rather in one country than in another? We must admit, however, that no one is so completely occupied with the care of providing for his subsistence as to have no time left to think of his soul and to be instructed in that which concerns religion, if he were to apply himself thereto as he does to less important things.

Th. Suppose that men are not always in a condition to instruct themselves, and that not being able to give up with

unimportant, and emphasizes, as here, the view that the essence of Christianity consists in its ethical content, a content intrinsically rational and accordant with nature. In addition to the authors referred to, *ante*, p. 553, note 1, *cf.* Pünjer, *Gesch. d. christ. Religionsphilos.*, 1, 359–360, 372–375, Eng. trans., 480–515, espec. 485–486, 501–504; and for an acute and able discussion of Miracles, their idea, office, etc., *cf.* E. G. Robinson, *Christian Theology*, § 20, pp. 103–109, Rochester, N. Y., Press of E. R. Andrews, 1894. — Tr.

prudence the care of the subsistence of their family in order to investigate difficult truths, they are obliged to follow the opinions authorized among them, it will always be necessary to judge that in the case of those who have the true religion without having its proofs, internal grace will supply the lack of the motives of credibility, and charity makes us also judge, as I have already indicated to you, that God does for persons of good will, brought up among the thick darkness of the most dangerous errors, all that his goodness and justice demand, although perhaps in a way which is unknown to us. We have histories commended in the Roman church of persons who have been expressly raised up in order that salutary aid be not wanting. But God can assist souls by the internal operation of the Holy Spirit, without the need of so great a miracle; and because it is good and consoling for the human race to put itself in the condition of the grace of God, only the good but sincere and serious will is needed. I admit that we have not indeed this good will without the grace of God, forasmuch as all natural or supernatural good comes from him; but it is always enough that we must only have the will, and that it is impossible that God can demand a condition easier and more reasonable.

§ 4. *Ph.* There are those who are *sufficiently at their ease* to have all the opportunities suited to illumine their doubts; but they are deterred from this by obstacles full of craftiness, which it is easy enough to see, while it is not necessary to display them in this place. § 5. I prefer to speak of those who lack the skill to avail themselves of the proofs which they have, so to speak, under their hand, and who cannot retain a long course of argument nor weigh all the circumstances. There are some people of a single syllogism, and there are some of two only. This is not the place to determine whether this imperfection arises from a natural difference of the souls themselves or of the organs, or whether it depends upon the lack of exercise which polishes the natural faculties. It is sufficient for us here that it is visible, and that we have only to go from the palace or from the exchange to the hospitals and small houses to perceive it.

Th. It is not the poor alone who are needy; certain rich people lack more than they, because these rich people demand too much and put themselves voluntarily in a kind of poverty which hinders them from applying themselves to important considerations. Example does much here. One tries to conform to that of his equals, so that he is compelled to practise without showing a spirit of perverseness, and that makes it easy for him to become like them. It is very difficult to satisfy at the same time reason and custom. As for those who lack capacity, they are fewer perhaps in number than you think; I think that good sense with application can suffice for everything which does not demand promptness. I presuppose good sense, because I do not think you would demand the search for truth from the dwellers in small houses. It is true that there are not many who could not learn something of it, if we knew the means of so doing and what original difference exists between our souls (as I believe does in reality exist); it is always certain that one soul might go as far as another (but not perhaps so rapidly) if it were led as it should be.

§ 6. *Ph.* There is another sort of people who lack only will. A strong attachment to pleasure, a constant application to what concerns their fortune, a general idleness or negligence, a particular aversion to study and meditation, prevents them from thinking seriously of the truth. There are even some who fear that a research free from all partiality would not be favorable to the opinions which most suit their prejudices and plans. We know persons who will not read a letter which they suppose brings bad news, and many people avoid agreeing upon their accounts or informing themselves of the state of their property, for fear of learning what they would desire always to be ignorant of. There are some who have large revenues and employ them all in provisions for the body without dreaming of the means of perfecting the understanding. They take great care always to appear in a suitable and brilliant equipage, and they suffer without difficulty their soul to be covered with the wretched rags of prejudice and error, and its nakedness, *i.e.* its ignorance to appear as an eccentricity. Not to speak of the interest they ought to take in a future state, they do not in the least neglect what they are interested to know in the life they lead in this world. And it is strange that very often those who regard power and authority as an appanage of their birth or their fortune, carelessly abandon it to people of a condition inferior to theirs, but who surpass them in knowledge. For it is very necessary that the blind be led by those who see, lest they fall into the ditch, and there is no worse slavery than that of the understanding.

Th. There is no more evident proof of the negligence of men as regards their true interests, than the little care they take to know and practise what agrees with their health, which is one of our greatest blessings; and although the great feel as much and more than others the bad effects of this negligence, they do not alter their course. As far as faith is concerned, many regard the thought which would lead to its discussion as a temptation of the devil, which they think they can the better surmount only by turning their minds to an entirely different thing. Men who only love pleasure, or who are attached to some occupation, are wont to neglect other matters. A player, a hunter, a drinker, a debauchee, and even a man curious about trifles, will lose his fortune and his property for lack of giving himself the trouble to institute a process or to speak to the men in a guard-house. There are some like the Emperor Honorius, who, when the news of the destruction of Rome was brought to him, thought it was his hen who bore this name, and this offended him more than the truth.[1] It is desirable that men who have power have knowledge in proportion; but if the details of the sciences, of the arts, of history and languages, should not be theirs, a solid and practised judgment and a knowledge of things equally great and general, in a word, *summa rerum*, might suffice. And as the Emperor Augustus had an abstract of the forces and needs of the State which he called *Breviarium Imperii*, he might have an abstract of human interests which would deserve to be called *Enchiridion Sapientiæ*, if men would care for that which is of most importance to them.

§ 7. *Ph.* Finally, the majority of our errors arise from the *false measures of probability* which we take, whether by sus-

[1] The anecdote here mentioned by Leibnitz is thus given by Giovanni Battista Egnazio, 1473–1553, in his *De Romanis principibus*, Lib. III., Venice, 1516, near the end of Book I. (*cf.* Haurisius, *Scriptores historiæ Romanæ Latini veteres, quæ extant omnes*, Heidelberg, 1743–1745, 3 vols., fol., Vol. 3, p. 625): "Quum nuntiatum Honorio esset Ravennæ *Romam perditam*, credidit ille de pugnaci Gallo, cui nomen erat Romæ, significatum esse: admiratumque vehementer tam subito periisse eum quo cum paullo ante festivissime luserat." — Tr.

pending our judgment in spite of manifest reasons, or in giving it notwithstanding contrary probabilities. These false measures consist (1) in doubtful propositions taken as principles, (2) in the accepted hypotheses, (3) in the dominant passions or inclinations, (4) in authority. § 8. We ordinarily judge of truth by its conformity with what we regard as indisputable principles, and this makes us despise the testimony of others and indeed of our own senses when they appear contrary thereto: but before relying upon these with so much assurance, we should examine them with the utmost exactness. § 9. Children receive the propositions taught them by their father and mother, nurses, teachers and others who are about them, and these propositions having taken root, are regarded as sacred as a *Urim* and *Thummim* which God might himself have put in the soul. § 10. We have some difficulty in admitting that which clashes with these *internal oracles*, while we believe the greatest absurdities which agree with them. This appears in the extreme obstinacy which we notice in different men who believe strongly opinions as directly opposed as the articles of faith, although they are very often equally absurd. Take a man of good sense, but persuaded of this maxim *that he must believe what they of his communion believe*, as they teach at Wittenberg or in Sweden, what disposition has he not to receive without difficulty the doctrine of *consubstantiation*, and to believe that one and the same thing is flesh and bread at the same time.

Th. It is very apparent, sir, that you have not been sufficiently instructed in the views of the Evangelicals,[1] who admit the real presence of the body of our Lord in the Eucharist. They have explained a thousand times that they do not mean the consubstantiation of bread and wine with the flesh and blood of Jesus Christ, and still less that one and the same thing is flesh and bread at the same time. They teach only that, in receiving the visible symbols, we receive in an invisible and supernatural manner the body of our Saviour, without its being enclosed in the bread; and the presence which they mean is not local or spatial, so to speak, *i.e.* determined by the dimensions of the present body, so that all that the senses can oppose

[1] *I.e.* Lutherans. For the views and controversies regarding the Eucharist, and the Confessions alluded to in the remainder of this section, *cf.* the various Church Histories and Histories of Doctrine.—TR.

to it does not concern them. And in order to show that the inconveniences which may be derived from reason no longer affect them, they declare that what they mean by the substance of the body does not consist in extension or dimension; and they make no difficulty in admitting that the glorious body of Jesus Christ preserves a certain ordinary and local presence, but congruous with his position in the exalted place where he is found, altogether different from this sacramental presence herein questioned, or from his miraculous presence by which he governs the church, which causes him to be not everywhere like God, but there where he prefers to be. This is the view of the more moderate, so that, in order to show the absurdity of their doctrine, it would be necessary to show that the entire essence of the body consists only in extension, and in that which is solely measured thereby, which no one, so far as I know, has yet done. This whole difficulty also concerns not less the Reformers who follow the Gallican and Belgian confessions, the declaration of the Council of Sendomir, composed of people of the two confessions, Augustan and Swiss, conformed to the Saxon confession, destined for the Council of Trent; the profession of faith of the Reformers who came to the Conference of Thorn, convoked under the authority of Vladislas, King of Poland, and the constant doctrine of Calvin and of Beza, who have declared the most distinctly and the most strongly of everybody that the symbols really furnish what they represent, and that we become participants in the body and blood of Jesus Christ. Calvin, after having refuted those who content themselves with a metaphorical participation of thought or of seal and with a union of faith, adds that we can say nothing sufficiently strong to establish its reality, that he is not ready to subscribe to, provided we avoid everything which looks to the circumscription of place or the diffusion of dimension; so that it appears that at bottom his doctrine was that of Melanchthon and even of Luther (as Calvin himself conjectured in one of his letters), except that in addition to the condition of the perception of the symbols with which Luther contents himself, he demands also the condition of faith, in order to exclude the participation of the unworthy. I have found Calvin so positive upon this real communion in a hundred places in his works, and even in his familiar letters, where there was no need of being so, that I do not see any reason to suspect artifice.

§ 11. *Ph.* [I ask your pardon if I have spoken of these gentlemen according to the common opinion. I remember now having remarked that some very clever theologians of the Anglican church have been for this real participation. But from established principles let us pass to the *accepted hypotheses.* Those who admit that they are only hypotheses often cease not to maintain them with warmth, almost as if assured principles, and to despise contrary probabilities. It would be unendurable to a learned professor to see his authority overturned in an instant by a new comer who should reject his hypotheses; his authority, I say, which has been in vogue for thirty or forty years, acquired by much labor at night, sustained by much Greek and Latin, confirmed by a general tradition and by a venerable beard. All the arguments which we can employ to convince him of the falsity of his hypothesis will be as little capable of prevailing upon his mind as the efforts Boreas made to compel the traveller to leave his cloak, which he held so much the more firmly as the wind blew with more violence.

Th. In reality the Copernicans have experienced in the case of their adversaries that hypotheses recognized as such ceased not to be maintained with an ardent zeal; and the Cartesians are not less positive regarding their grooved particles and little balls of the second element [1] than if they were the theorems of Euclid; and it seems that zeal for our hypotheses is merely a result of the passion we have of making ourselves respected. It is true that those who condemned Galileo believed that the rest of the earth was more than an hypothesis, for they judged it in conformity with Scripture and reason. But since then it has been perceived that reason at least sustained it no longer; and as for Scripture, Father Fabry, Penitentiary of St. Peter, an excellent theologian and philosopher, publishing in Rome itself an Apology for the Observations of Eustachio Divini,[2]

[1] *Cf. New Essays*, Preface, *ante*, p. 51, line 11; Descartes, *Princip. Philos.*, Pt. III., §§ 52, 90. The "grooved particles" and "little balls of the second element" are a part of the vortices-theory (*cf. ante*, p. 552, note 1). For the "matter of the first and second element" and the genesis of the "perfect globes" or "balls of the second element," *cf. Princip. Philos.*, Pt. III., § 48 *sq.* The notes of J. H. von Kirchmann in his German trans. of this work of Descartes (*Philos. Bibliothek.*, Vol. 26, 2d ed., Heidelberg, 1887) are a valuable aid in the study of the theory. — TR.

[2] Eustachio Divini, c. 1620 — c. 1666, an Italian mechanician, optician, and astronomer, noted for his skill in making optical instruments, especially tel-

a famous optician, hesitated not to declare that it was only provisionally that they understood in the sacred text a true movement of the sun, and that if the view of Copernicus were found true, there would be no difficulty in explaining it in like manner as this passage of Vergil:

terræque urbesque recedunt.[1]

However, they did not cease to continue in Italy and in Spain and even in the hereditary states of the emperor to suppress the doctrine of Copernicus, to the great detriment of these nations whose scholars might have raised themselves to more beautiful discoveries had they enjoyed a reasonable and philosophic liberty.

§ 12. *Ph.* The dominant passions appear to be in reality, as you say, the source of the love we have for hypotheses: but they also extend very much farther. The greatest probability in the world will avail nothing in showing his injustice to an avaricious and ambitious man; and a lover will have every facility in the world for allowing himself to be duped by his mistress, so long as it is true that we easily believe whatever we wish, and according to the remark of Vergil,

qui amant ipsi sibi somnia fingunt.[2]

This is what makes them make use of two *means of escaping* the most apparent *probabilities* when they attack our passions and our prejudices. § 13. The first is to think that there may be some sophistry concealed in the argument which they oppose to us. § 14. The second in supposing that we might put beforehand wholly as good or even better arguments in order to beat the adversary, if we had the opportunity, or skill, or aid, which

escopes, was the reputed author of a little work entitled *Brevis annotatio in Systema Saturnium Christiani Hugenii* [Hag. Com., 1659, 4to], Rome, 1660, 8vo, in which an attempt was made to refute Huygens' theory of the planet Saturn. Divini, however, was no Latinist, and probably had little share in the book, contributing merely "his pretended observation of the three separate bodies"; the real author was most likely the Jesuit, Honoré Fabri (*cf. ante*, p. 586, note 2). Huygens reprinted the work together with his reply, *Brevis assertio systematis Saturnii sui*, Hag. Com., 1660; and Divini published his rejoinder, *Septempedanus pro sua annotatione in syst. Saturn. Ch. Hugenii, adversum ejus assertionem*, Rome, 1661. On the whole subject, *cf.* Huygens, *Œuvres complètes*, La Haye, 1888–1893, 5 vols., *passim*. — Tr.

[1] *Æn.* 3, 72. — Tr.

[2] *Eclog.* 8, 108. — Tr.

we must have to discover them. § 15. These means of shielding themselves from conviction are sometimes good, but they are also sophisms when the matter is sufficiently explained and everything has been taken into account; for after that there are means of knowing with regard to all upon what side the probability is found. Thus there is no room for doubting that the animals have been formed by the movements of an intelligent agent, rather than by a fortuitous concourse of atoms; as there is no one who doubts in the least whether the characters of printing which form an intelligent discourse have been brought together by an attentive man, or by a confused medley. I should think then that it does not depend upon us to suspend our assent in these instances; but we can give it when the probability is less evident, and we can even content ourselves with more feeble proofs which better agree with our inclination. § 16. It appears to me impracticable for the truth for a man to lean to the side upon which he sees the less probability; perception, knowledge and assent are not arbitrary, as it does not depend upon me to see or not to see the agreement of two ideas, when my spirit is turned toward them. We can however voluntarily arrest the progress of our researches; without this ignorance or error could not in any case be a sin. It is in this that we exercise our liberty. It is true that in the instances where we have no interests, we embrace the common opinion, or the view of the first comer; but in the points where our happiness or misery is concerned, the mind applies itself more seriously to weighing the probabilities, and I think that in this case, that is, when we are attentive, we have no choice in determining ourselves for the side we prefer, if between the two sides there are differences at once visible, and that it will be the greatest probability that will determine our assent.

Th. I am of your opinion at bottom, and we have given sufficient explanation upon this matter in our preceding conferences when we spoke of liberty. I showed then that we never believe what we wish, but rather what we see is the most apparent; and that nevertheless we can make ourselves believe indirectly what we wish by turning away the attention from a disagreeable object in order to apply ourselves to another which pleases us. This makes us in regarding more the reasons of a favorite side believe at last the more probable. As for the opinions in which we take little interest and which we receive upon slight reasons, we do this because, noticing scarcely anything which opposes them, we find that the opinion which makes us regard them favorably surpasses as much or more the opposite opinion, which has nothing in its behalf in our perception, as if it had had many reasons on both sides, for the difference between 0 and 1, or between 2 and 3, is as great as between 9 and 10, and we perceive this advantage, without thinking of the examination which would still be necessary in order to judge, but to which nothing impels us.

§ 17. *Ph.* The last false measure of probability that I intended to notice is *improperly understood authority*, which keeps more people in ignorance and error than all the others together. How many people we see who have no other basis for their views than the opinions received among our friends or among the members of our profession or of our party, or of our country! Such a doctrine has been approved by venerable antiquity; it comes to me under the passport of preceding centuries; other men yield to it; this is why I am shielded from error in receiving it. We have as much authority for tossing up in order to take these opinions, as to take them upon the basis of such rules. And besides the fact that all men are liable to error, I believe that if we could see the secret motives which actuate the scholars and chief men of a sect, we should find often something wholly different from the pure love of the truth. It is certain at least that there is no opinion so absurd that it cannot be embraced upon this basis, since there is scarcely an error which has not had its partisans.

Th. It must, however, be admitted that in many instances we cannot avoid yielding to authority. St. Augustine has produced quite a remarkable book "De utilitate credendi,"[1] which deserves to be read on this subject, and as for the received opinions, they have for themselves something approaching to that which gives what is called *presumption* with the jurisconsults: and although we are not obliged to follow them always without proofs, we are no more authorized to destroy them in the mind of another without having contrary proofs. This it is which does not allow us to change anything without reason.

[1] *Cf. Opera*, Benedictine ed., Vol. 8, pp. 45–70, Paris, 1688; Migne, *Patrol. s. Lat.*, Vol. 42 [Vol. 8 of Augustine], pp. 65–92. — Tr.

The argument drawn from the great number of the approvers of an opinion has been much disputed since the late M. Nicole published his book on the church;[1] but all that may be drawn from this argument, when the question is of approving a reason and not of attesting a fact, may be reduced merely to what I have just said. And as one hundred horses do not run faster than one horse, though they can draw more, so it is with one hundred men as compared with one single man; they cannot go more justly, but they will work more effectively; they cannot judge better, but they will be capable of furnishing more matter upon which the judgment may be exercised. This is the meaning of the proverb: *plus vident oculi quam oculus.* We notice it in the councils, where really a multitude of considerations are put upon the carpet which would perhaps escape one or two, but they run a risk often of not taking the better side in concluding upon all these considerations, when there are no skilful persons charged with directing and weighing them. Hence some judicious theologians of the Roman party, seeing that the authority of the church, *i.e.* that of the most exalted in dignity and the most supported by the multitude, could not be certain in a matter of reasoning, have reduced it to the mere attestation of the facts under the name of tradition. This was the opinion of Henry Holden,[2] an Englishman, doctor of the Sorbonne, author of a book entitled "Analysis of the Faith," in which, following the principles of the "Commonitorium" of Vincent de Lerins,[3] he maintained that we cannot make new

[1] *Cf. ante*, p. 530, note 1. — TR.

[2] Henry Holden, 1596–1662, was an English Roman Catholic divine, who graduated at the Sorbonne, and was appointed Professor of Theology there. In 1647 he petitioned the House of Commons for toleration of the Catholics, provided they would take the oath of allegiance. His *Divinæ Fidei Analysis*, a concise exposition of the Catholic articles of faith as distinguished from matters of opinion, appeared at Paris, 1652, with an appendix consisting of a short treatise on Schism. It was reprinted at Paris, 1685, 1767, at Cologne, 1655, 1782, Eng. trans., by "W. G.," 1658. Dupin, who gives a full abstract of the book in his *Bibl. des Aut. ecclés.*, 1711, tom. 17, pp. 194–203, considers him one of the ablest controversialists of his time. In 1656 he was engaged in a controversy with Antoine Arnauld, the Jansenist (*cf. ante*, p. 463, note 4), and his letters to Arnauld were printed in later editions of the *Analysis*. — TR.

[3] St. Vincent of Lerins, of Gallic origin, who died about 450. His *Adversus profanas omnium novitates Hæreticorum Commonitorium*, written in 434, three years after the Council of Ephesus, energetically affirms the authority of tradition against all religious and doctrinal innovations. In chap. 2 of this short treatise occurs the famous threefold test of orthodoxy: "Quod semper,

decisions in the church, and that all the bishops assembled in council can do is to attest the fact of the doctrine received in their dioceses. The principle is specious so long as we continue in generalities; but when we come to the fact, it is found that in different countries different opinions have been received for a long time; and in the same countries also they have gone from one extreme to another, notwithstanding the arguments of Arnauld against insensible changes; besides often without confining themselves to attest them, they have taken it upon themselves to judge. It is also at bottom the opinion of Gretser,[1] a learned Jesuit of Bavaria, author of another Analysis of Faith, approved by the theologians of his order, that the church may judge controversies by making new articles of faith, since the assistance of the Holy Spirit is promised it, although most frequently they try to disguise this view, especially in France, as if the church were only to explain doctrines already established. But the explanation is a statement already received, or a new one which they believe may be drawn from the received doctrine. Practice is most frequently opposed to the first sense, and in the second, what can the new statement which is established be but a new article? I am not, however, of the opinion that we despise antiquity in the matter of religion; and I also believe that we may say that God has preserved the truly ecumenical councils hitherto from all error contrary to wholesome doctrine. For the rest, sectarian prejudice is a strange thing. I have seen people embrace with ardor an opinion for the sole reason that it is received in their order, or even solely because it is contrary to that of a man of a religion or of a nation which they do not like, although the

quod ubique, quod ab omnibus creditum est." The work has been edited by Baluze, Paris, 1663, 1669, 1684, Klüpfel, Vienna, 1809, Pusey, Oxford, 1838, Herzog, Breslau, 1839, and others; Eng. trans. by Flower. London. 1866. See also Migne, *Patrol. Theol. cur. compl.*, Vol. 1, p. 911, Paris, 1846. A full account of it is given in Smith-Wace, *Dict. of Christ. Biog.*, 4, 1154-1158. — TR.

[1] Jac. Gretser, 1561-1625, a learned Jesuit, was Professor of Philosophy and various parts of Theology at Ingolstadt for twenty-four years. A man of immense erudition, and a voluminous author, he was lacking in taste and critical power, and was very harsh and bitter in discussion. It is said of him that, when asked by the magistrates of Marckdorf in Swabia, his birthplace, for his portrait to be placed in the town hall, he refused it, saying they had no place therein for the head of an ass. His complete works appeared at Ratisbonne, 1739 *sq.*, 17 vols., fol. — TR.

question had almost no connection with the religion or the interests of the people. They did not know perhaps what was in reality the source of their zeal; but I knew that, upon the first news that such an one had written this or that thing, they would ransack the libraries and puzzle their brains to find something to refute it. This it is which is practised so often by those who maintain theses in the universities and who seek to distinguish themselves against their adversaries. But what shall we say of the doctrines prescribed in the Symbolic books of the sect, even among[1] the Protestants, which we are often obliged to embrace with an oath? which some think signifies with us only the obligation to profess what these books or formularies contain of Holy Scripture; in which they are contradicted by others. And in the religious orders of the Roman party, without contenting themselves with the doctrines established in their church, they prescribe narrower limits to those who teach them; witness the propositions the teaching of which in their schools the General of the Jesuits, Claudio Acquaviva[2] (if I am not mistaken), defends. It would be well (to mention it in passing) to make a systematic collection of the propositions determined and censured by councils, popes, bishops, superiors, faculties, which would be of use in ecclesiastical history. We may distinguish between teaching and embracing an opinion. There is no oath in the world nor prohibition which can force a man to abide in the same opinion, for opinions are involuntary in themselves: but he may and should abstain from teaching a doctrine which is regarded as dangerous, unless he finds himself compelled thereto by his conscience. In this case he must declare himself sincerely and leave his post when he has been charged with teaching; supposing, however, that he can do so without exposing himself to an extreme danger which might force him to leave without

[1] Gerhardt, Erdmann, and Jacques read: "parmi"; Janet reads: "par," *i.e.* "by."—TR.

[2] Claudius Aquaviva, 1543–1615, General of the Jesuits, 1581–1615. For a brief account of his *Ratio Studiorum*, 1599, *cf.* Hughes, *Loyola and the Educational System of the Jesuits*, pp. 141 *sq.* (in The Great Educators Series, ed. by Nicolas Murray Butler), New York: Chas. Scribner's Sons, 1892. For the text of the *Ratio*, and a full account of its growth from its preliminary to its final form, with the letters of Aquaviva and other documents, *cf. Monumenta Germaniæ Pædagogica*, Berlin, A. Hofmann & Co., 1886 *sq.*, Bd. V., Tom. II. —TR.

fame. We see but little other means of reconciling the rights of the public and of the individual; the one being under obligation to prevent what it judges bad, and the other not being able to dispense with the duties demanded by his conscience.

§ 18. *Ph.* This opposition between the public and the individual and even between the public opinions of different sects is an inevitable evil. But often these very oppositions are only apparent and consist only in the formulas. I am obliged also to say, in order to be just to the human race, that there are not so many people involved in error as is ordinarily supposed. Not that I think that they embrace the truth, but because in reality upon the doctrines upon which they make so much stir, they have absolutely no positive opinion, and because without having examined anything and without having in the mind the most superficial ideas upon the matter in question, they are resolved to hold themselves fast to their party, as soldiers who do not examine the cause they defend: and if the life of a man shows that he has no sincere regard for religion, it is sufficient for him to have the hand and tongue ready to maintain the common opinion, in order to commend himself to those who can procure him support.

Th. This justice which you render to the human race does not redound to its praise; and men would be more excusable in following their opinions than in disguising them for the sake of their interests. Perhaps, however, there is more sincerity in their deeds than you seem to give any one to understand. For without any knowledge of a reason, they can perhaps attain to an *implicit faith* by submitting themselves in general and sometimes blindly, but often in good faith, to the judgment of others whose authority they have once recognized. It is true that the interest they find therein contributes to this submission, but this does not prevent them at last from forming an opinion. They are contented in the Roman church with this almost implicit faith, not perhaps having any article thereupon, due to the revelation which is judged absolutely *fundamental* thereto and which is considered as necessary *necessitate medii, i.e.* the belief of which is a condition absolutely necessary to salvation. And they are all *necessitate præcepti*, by the necessity therein taught of obeying the church, as they call it, and of giving all attention to that which is proposed therein, all under pain of mortal sin. But this necessity demands only a reasonable docility and does not compel absolute assent, according to the most learned doctors of this church. Cardinal Bellarmine himself believed, however, that nothing was better than this faith of a child who submits himself to an established authority, and he relates with approval the statement of a dying man, who escaped the devil by this circle, which they heard him often repeat:

I believe all that the church believes,
The church believes what I believe.

CHAPTER XXI

OF THE DIVISION OF THE SCIENCES

§ 1. *Ph.* Here we are at the end of our course, and all the operations of the understanding are explained. Our purpose is not to enter into the detail indeed of our knowledge, yet it will perhaps be proper here, before we conclude, to make a general review by considering the division of the sciences. All that can enter into the sphere of human understanding is either the nature of things in themselves, or in the second place, man in the character of an agent, tending towards his end and in particular towards his happiness, or in the third place the means of acquiring and communicating knowledge. *Science* then is divided into three kinds. § 2. The first is *Physics* or Natural Philosophy, which comprises not only bodies and their properties, as number, figure, but also spirits, God himself and the angels. § 3. The second is *Practical Philosophy* or *Ethics*, which teaches the means of obtaining good and useful things, and proposes to itself not only the knowledge of the truth, but also the practice of that which is right. § 4. Finally, the third is *Logic* or the knowledge of signs, for λόγος signifies word. We need *signs* of our ideas to enable us to communicate our thoughts to one another, as well as to register them for our own use. Perhaps if we should consider distinctly and with all possible care that this last kind of science revolves about ideas and words, we should have a logic and criticism [1] different from that which has

[1] Locke has: "critic," *Philos. Wks.*, Vol. 2, p. 338, Bohn's ed.; Fraser, *Locke's Essay concerning Human Understanding*, Vol. 2, p. 462. — TR.

hitherto been seen. And these three kinds, Physics, Ethics, and Logic, are like three great provinces in the intellectual world, entirely separate and distinct the one from the other.

Th. This division has already been a celebrated one among the ancients; for under *Logic* they comprised, as you do, all that relates to words and to the explication of our thoughts: *Artes dicendi.* Nevertheless, there is some difficulty therein; for the science of reasoning, of judgment, of invention appears very different from the knowledge of the etymologies of words and the use of languages, which is something indefinite and arbitrary. Farther, in explaining words, we are obliged to make an incursion into the sciences themselves, as appears by the dictionaries; and on the other hand, we cannot treat of science without giving at the same time definitions of the terms. But the principal difficulty found in this division of the sciences is that each part appears to absorb the whole; in the first place, Ethics and Logic will fall into Physics, taken as generally as you have just stated; for in speaking of spirits, *i.e.* of substances having understanding and will, and in explaining this understanding to the bottom, you will make it include all logic: and in explaining in the doctrine of spirits what belongs to the will, it would be necessary to speak of good and evil, of happiness and misery, and it will only depend upon you to push this doctrine far enough to make it include all practical philosophy. In return, all might be included in practical philosophy as serving for our happiness. You know that Theology is rightly considered as a practical science, and Jurisprudence as well as Medicine are not less so; so that the doctrine of human happiness or of our good and ill will absorb all these branches of knowledge, should we desire to explain sufficiently all the means serving the end which reason proposes to itself. Thus it is that Zwinger has included all in his "Magnum theatrum vitæ humani," which Beyerling has disturbed by arranging in alphabetical order.[1] And in treating all matters in dictionaries fol-

[1] Laurent Beyerlinck, or Beierlynck, 1578–1627, a Flemish scholar, Professor of Poetry and Rhetoric at Vaulx, and Canon of the Antwerp Cathedral, published, with additions and corrections, the *Theatrum vitæ humanæ* of Zwinger (*cf. ante*, p. 548, note 1), with the title *Magnum theatrum vitæ humanæ*, Cologne, 1631, 8 vols., fol. Schaarschmidt states that this new edition in alphabetical order is, in fact, worth less than the old redaction of the book, which handled the materials systematically in their essential aspects. — Tr.

lowing the order of the alphabet, the doctrine of languages (which you with the ancients put in *Logic*), *i.e.* in discursive logic, takes possession in its turn of the territory of the two others. Here, then, your three great provinces of encyclopedia are in continual war, since one is always encroaching upon the rights of the others. The Nominalists believed that there were as many particular sciences as truths,[1] which they composed after the wholes according as they arranged them; and others compare the entire body of our knowledge to an ocean, which is all of a piece and which is divided into Caledonian, Atlantic, Ethiopic, Indian only by arbitrary lines. It is usually found that one and the same truth may be put in different places, according to the terms it contains, and also according to the mediate terms or causes upon which it depends, and according to the inferences and results it may have. A simple categoric proposition has only two terms; but a hypothetic proposition may have four, not to speak of complex statements. A remarkable history may perhaps be placed in the annals of universal history and in the history of the country where it happened, and in the history of the life of a man who was interested therein. And suppose the question therein concerns some fine precept of morals, some stratagem of war, some invention useful in the arts which serve the conveniences of life or the health of men, this same history will be related to some purpose in the science or art it concerns, and indeed it can be mentioned in two parts of this science, viz., — in the history of the discipline in order to recount its efficient growth, and also in the precepts to confirm them or illuminate them by examples. For example, what is very properly told in the life of Cardinal Ximenes, that a Moorish woman cured him by rubbings only of a hectic almost desperate, deserves also place in a system of medicine, as well in the chapter on hectic fever, as when the question concerns a

[1] The phrase "as many sciences as truths" — "tot esse scientias quot veritates" — is, as Schaarschmidt says, "the sharpest expression of nominalistic individualism." "According to Nominalism, we have a knowledge of particulars only, all universals being merely *figmenta mentis*, products of abstraction. Hence true and genuine science always relates to particulars only, and thus there are as many sciences as (particular) truths."

On Leibnitz's studies of Nominalism, *cf.* Guhrauer, *Leibnit. Dissertatio de princ. individ.*, pp. 39 *sq.*, Leibnitz, *De stilo philos. Nizolii*, § 28, Gerhardt, 4, 157–158, Erdmann, 68–69. — TR.

medicinal diet comprising these exercises; and this observation will serve also the better to discover the causes of this disease. But we might further speak of this in medicinal logic, where the question is about the art of discovering remedies, and in the history of medicine, in order to show how remedies have come to the knowledge of men, and that it is often by the aid of simple empirics and even charlatans. Beverovicius,[1] in a remarkable book on ancient medicine, drawn wholly from authors not physicians, would have rendered his work still more useful, if he had passed down to modern authors. We see by this that one and the same truth may have many places according to the different relations it can have. Those who arrange a library very often do not know where to place certain books, being in suspense between two or three places equally suitable. But let us now speak only of general doctrines and put aside particular facts, history and languages. I find two principal dispositions of all doctrinal truths, each of which should have its deserts and which it would be well to unite. The one would be *synthetic* and *theoretic*, ranking truths according to the order of proofs, as the mathematicians do, so that each proposition would come after those on which it depends. The other disposition would be *analytic* and *practical*, commencing with the end of men, *i.e.* with the goods whose consummation is happiness, and seeking in order the means available for acquiring these goods or avoiding the contrary evils. These two methods have place in general encyclopedia, while some have practised them in particular sciences; for geometry itself, treated synthetically by Euclid as a science, has been treated by some others as an art, and might nevertheless be treated demonstratively under this form, which would show indeed some invention; as if some

[1] Jan van Beverwyck, — Latin Beverovicius, — 1594–1647, a noted Dutch physician, who studied at Leyden, Caen, Paris, Montpelier and Padua, where he received his M.D., and on his return became Professor of Medicine at Dordrecht and physician to the city, in which also he held several civil offices, among them that of burgomaster. He labored to simplify the methods of prescribing for disease. He published a number of books distinguished for purity of style and relation of facts, and which, adorned with copper-plates and with the verses of Jakob Cats, 1577–1660, one of the oldest and most popular Dutch poets, "made in his time much sensation and met with much approbation." Among them was the *Idea medicinæ veterum*, Lugd. Bat., 1637, 12mo, here mentioned by Leibnitz. His entire works were published at Amsterdam, 1651, etc. — TR.

one proposed to measure all kinds of plane figures, and beginning with rectilinears, reflected that they may be divided into triangles and that each triangle is half of a parallelogram, and that parallelograms can be reduced to rectangles whose measure is easy. But in writing the encyclopedia, following both these two dispositions together, we might take measures for references in order to avoid repetitions. To these two dispositions *the third according to the terms* should be joined, which in reality would be only a kind of *index*, either systematic, arranging the terms according to certain predicaments which would be common to all the notions, or alphabetical according to the languages received among scholars. Now this index would be necessary in order to find together all the propositions into which the term enters in a sufficiently remarkable manner; for according to the two preceding ways, where the truths are arranged according to their origin or use, truths concerning one and the same term cannot be found together. For example, it was not permitted Euclid, when he was teaching how to find the half of an angle, to add the means of finding its third, because he would have been obliged to speak of the conic sections, knowledge of which he could not yet assume in this place. But the index may and should indicate the places where are found the important propositions which concern one and the same subject. And we still lack such an *index* in geometry, which would be of great use in facilitating indeed invention and in pushing the science, for it would relieve the memory and often spare us the trouble of seeking again that which has already been found. And these indices would further be of use for a much stronger reason in the other sciences, where the art of reasoning has less power, and would be above all extremely necessary in Medicine. But the art of making such indices would be no slight one. Now considering these three dispositions, I find it remarkable that they correspond to the ancient division, which you have renewed, which divides science or philosophy into theoretic, practical and discursive, or rather into Physics, Ethics, and Logic. For the synthetic disposition corresponds to the theoretic, the analytical to the practical, and that of the index according to the terms to logic: so that this ancient division does very well, provided we understand these dispositions as I have just explained, *i.e.* not as distinct sciences, but as different arrangements of the same truths as far as we judge it advisable to repeat them. There is also a *civil division* of the sciences according to the faculties and professions. We make use of it in the universities, and in the arrangements of libraries;[1] and Draudius,[2] with his continuer Lipenius,[3] who have left us the amplest, but not the best catalogue of books, instead of following the method of the Pandects of Gesner,[4] which is wholly systematic, have contented themselves with the use of the great division of the materials (much

[1] For Leibnitz's sketch of a library classification and catalogue, *cf.* his *Idea Leibnitiana Bibliothecæ Publicæ secundum classes scientiarum ordinandæ*, Dutens, 5, 209–214. *Cf.* also his *Representation à S. A. S. le Duc de Wolfenbuttel, pour l'encourager à l'entretien de sa Bibliothèque, ibid.*, 5, 207–208; the same, in German, Guhrauer, *Leibnitz's Deutsche Schrift.*, 2, 470–472. — Tr.

[2] Georg Draud, 1573–1630 or 1635, a student at Marburg University and afterwards a proof-reader at Frankfort, Basle, and at the famous typography at Feyerabend, and minister of the gospel at Gros-Carben, Ortenberg and Dauernheim, was the first to attempt an extended systematic bibliography. His *Bibliotheca classica sive catalogus officinalis, in quo singuli singularum facultatum ac professionum libri — secundum artes et ordine alphabetico recensentur*, Frankfort, 1611, was the most complete bibliography of printed books that had then appeared. A 2d ed., increased by all the books printed from 1611–1625 of which the editor had knowledge, appeared in 1625. — Tr.

[3] Martin Lipenius, 1630–1692, a learned German bibliographer, who studied at Wittemberg, and was co-rector of the gymnasium at Halle, and of the academy at Lubeck, and rector and professor in the gymnasium at Stettin. He published *Bibliotheca realis juridica*, 1679, the most valuable of his series, edited with additions by F. W. Struve, in 1720, by G. A. Jenichen, 1709–1759, a jurist, philologian and historian, with corrections in 1736, and a supplement in two parts, 1742; also several subsequent editions with corrections and additions; *Bibliotheca realis medica*, 1679, *philosophica*, 1682, *theologica*, 1685. They were called *realis* because the books were listed in the alphabetical order of subjects and not under the names of their authors. — Tr.

[4] Conrad Gesner, 1516–1565, called the "German Pliny," because of his vast erudition, was Professor of Greek, 1537, at Lausanne, and of Physics and Natural History, 1541, at Zürich. He made "the first comprehensive attempt at a general encyclopedia of literature, constructed in the form of a catalogue" in his *Bibliotheca universalis*. The work contained the titles of all then known books, existent or lost, published or announced, in Hebrew, Greek and Latin, giving under each important name a vast amount of bibliographical information and criticism, original and selected, and often some specimens of their style. The first vol., Zürich, 1545, is arranged alphabetically according to the authors' names; the second, entitled *Pandectæ sive partitionum universalium, lib. XXI., — totius philosophiæ et omnium bonarum artium atque studiorum locos communes et ordines universales simul et particulares*, — Zürich, 1548, is arranged according to subjects and divided into 19 books, book 21, a theological encyclopedia, not being published till 1549, and book 20, the medical writings, never appearing because in the author's view too imperfect for publication. It was reprinted and greatly enlarged by Simler in 1574, and by J. J. Fries, Zürich, 1583. — Tr.

the same as the libraries) following the four faculties (as they are called) of theology, jurisprudence, medicine and philosophy, and have afterwards arranged the titles of each faculty according to the alphabetical order of the principal terms entering into the inscription of the books: this lightened the task of these authors, because they had no need to see the book or to understand the matter which the book treats, but it does not sufficiently serve others, at least it does not make references in the titles to others of parallel signification; for not to speak of a number of mistakes they have made, we see that often one and the same thing is called by different names, as, for example, *observationes juris, miscellanea, conjectanea, electa, semestria, probabilia, benedicta,* and a multitude of similar inscriptions; such books of the jurisconsults signify only the miscellanies of the Roman Law. This is why the systematic disposition of the materials is without doubt the best, and we may join with it alphabetical indices very full according to the terms and the authors. The civil and received division, according to the four faculties, is not to be despised. *Theology* treats of eternal felicity and all that relates thereto, so far as it depends on the soul and the conscience; it is like a jurisprudence which regards what is said to exist *de foro interno* and employs invisible substances and intelligences: *Jurisprudence* has for its object government and the laws, whose end is the happiness of men so far as the external and sensible can contribute thereto; but it regards principally only that which depends upon the nature of the spirit, and does not enter much farther into the detail of material things whose nature it assumes in order to employ them as means. Thus is it relieved at once of an important point which concerns the health, strength and perfection of the human body, the care of which is given to the faculty of *Medicine.* Some have believed with some reason that we might add to the others the *Economic Faculty,* which would contain the Mathematical and Mechanical Arts, and all that concerns the detail of the subsistence of men and of the conveniences of life, in which *Agriculture* and *Architecture* would be included. But we abandon to the faculty of *Philosophy* all which is not included in the three faculties which we call superior. We do this quite badly, for we do it without giving means to those who are of this fourth faculty for perfecting themselves by practice as those can do who teach the other faculties. Thus the mathematics perhaps excepted, we consider the faculty of philosophy only as an introduction to the others.[1] This is why we wish the youth to learn history, and the arts of speaking and some rudiments of theology and natural jurisprudence, independent of divine and human laws, under the title of metaphysics or psychology, ethics and politics with a little of physics also, in order to serve as young physicians. This, then, is the civil division of the sciences following the bodies and professions of the scholars who teach them, without speaking of the profession of those who work for the public otherwise than by their discourses and who ought to be directed by true scholars, if the limits of knowledge were well understood. And even in the more noble manual arts, knowledge has been very much bound up with performance, and might be more so. As in fact they are joined together in medicine, not only formerly among the ancients (where physicians were also surgeons and apothecaries), but also to-day especially among the chemists. This alliance also of practice and theory finds itself at variance both among those who teach what are called exercises, as also among the painters, or sculptors and musicians, and among some other kinds of *virtuosi*. And if the principles of all these professions and arts, and even of the trades, were taught practically among the philosophers, or in some other faculty of scholars as they might be, these scholars would be truly the teachers of the human race.[2] But it would be necessary to change much of

[1] *I.e.* in the broader sense of the term in which it is equivalent to the Humanities, — *artes liberales*, — the liberal education, disciplinary, stimulative and cultural of the student's entire powers, which was considered until very recently, and is regarded even now by many of the deepest and farthest-sighted thinkers on education, as an essential precedent and preparation for all later special professional study. The custom of regarding the Faculty of Arts or Philosophy as introductory to that of Theology, Medicine and Jurisprudence, goes back to the university curricula of the Middle Age, the Trivium and the Quadrivium, with their respective degrees of A.B. and A.M., which in their essential character and principles, with the necessary changes incident to an advancing civilization, have been, till within a short time at least, the controlling influence in shaping the curricula and methods of all modern collegiate and university education. — TR.

[2] On this, as on every subject he touched, Leibnitz utters a suggestive and stimulating thought, which has in recent times brought forth much fruit in the establishment and maintenance of technical and art schools of every kind. — TR.

the present state of things in literature and the education of the youth, and consequently of the government. And when I consider how much men have advanced in knowledge in the last century or two, and how easy it would be for them to go incomparably farther in order to render themselves happier, I do not despair that a considerable improvement will come in a more tranquil period under some great prince whom God will be able to raise up for the good of the human race.[1]

[1] Leibnitz constantly labored to secure the sympathy and active co-operation of the "great princes" in the initiation and furtherance of learning, science, and the higher ideal interests of mankind in general, a conspicuous example of his success being that of the great reformatory genius of his time, Peter the Great of Russia. Their correspondence is found in Foucher de Careil, *Œuvres de Leibniz*, 7, 395–598. *Cf.* also W. Guerrier, *Leibniz in seinen Beziehungen zu Russland und Peter dem Grossen*, St. Petersburg and Leipzig, 1873; Foucher de Careil, *Leibniz et Pierre le Grand*, Paris, 1873. For a general account of his various efforts in this direction, *cf.* Fischer, *Gesch. d. n. Philos.*, Vol. 2, Leibniz, 3d ed., 1889, pp. 211-249; and for a brief account, Merz, *Leibniz* (Blackwood's Philos. Class.), pp. 74-83. — Tr.

APPENDIX

I

LEIBNITZ TO JACOB THOMASIUS[1]

April 20-30, 1669

[*From the Latin*]

How much that γεῦμα of philosophical history of yours has made the mouths of all water cannot be told; for it is apparent how much difference there is between mere enumerations of names and those profound views concerning the connections of opinions. And certainly all acquainted with the subject that I hear speak of your essay (you know that I never flatter), unanimously affirm that from no one man can a complete body of philosophical history preferably be expected. Very many skilled in antiquity rather than in art have given us lives rather than opinions. You will give the history not of philosophers but of philosophy. They say in England that Joseph Glanvill's History of the growth of the sciences since Aristotle is in press.[2] But I think he will pursue for the most part the mathematical, mechanical, and physical periods of this inquiry only, so I think

[1] Gerhardt, *Leibniz. philos. Schrift.* 1, 15–27; Erdmann, 48–54; Dutens, 4, Pt. I. 7–19; Kortholt, *Leibnit. epist. ad diversos*, Lipsiæ, 1734–42, 2, 121–142. Kortholt's text gives the piece as printed by Leibnitz in his edition of Nizolius, and differs considerably from that given by Gerhardt, which is the text followed in this translation. *Cf.* also, Gerhardt, *Leibniz. philos. Schrift.*, 4, 162–174. In this "impression," says Gerhardt, Einleitung, *ibid.*, p. 9, note **, "the copy of the Royal Library at Hanover has been used, in which are found *MS.* notes of Leibnitz." — Tr.

[2] Joseph Glanvill, 1636–1680, Court Chaplain to Charles II., published his defence of the Royal Society of London, entitled *Plus Ultra, or the Progress and Advancement of Knowledge since the days of Aristotle*, in 1668. In his idea of causation Glanvill was a predecessor of Hume. His *Scepsis scientifica*, or *Vanity of Dogmatising*, London, 1665, edited by John Owen, 1885, and his *De incrementis scientiarum*, London, 1670, attacked the Aristotelian and Cartesian dogmatism. Though a thorough-going sceptic in the direction of the scholastic philosophy, he was opposed to the materialism of Hobbes. Some account of Glanvill's views will be found in Lecky, *Rationalism in Europe*, 1, 129 *sq.* D. Appleton & Co., New York, 1876. — Tr.

he has forestalled you in nothing. But I wish that you would produce a style and form for this more modern age and admonish our inconsiderate youth that neither everything nor nothing is to be attributed to the restorers. Bagheminus[1] is not the only critic to whom you are indebted; there are the Patricii, Telesii, Campanellæ, Bodini, Nizolii, Fracastorii, Cardanii, Galilæi, Verulamii, Gassendi, Hobbii, Cartesii, Bassones, Digbæi, Sennerti, Sperlingii, Derodones, Deusingii, and many other names among whom the cloak of philosophy is divided.[2] To remind the world of these will be a diversion for you, a profit to the public.

Who does not assent to your estimate of Bagheminus? There is no skilful adjustment in hypotheses,[3] no logical sequence of reasons, but in a word strange notions; certainly unless he has something to observe useful in special physics, he will better be silent. But Scaliger, Sennert, and Sperling, — for he acknowledged himself a pupil of this one also, — seem to me to be the parents of the opinion of that one concerning God, the primary matter of things, who think that forms are produced not from the passive power of matter, but from the active power of the efficient one. Wherefore the conclusion is that they believe that God produces creatures rather from his own active power, than from nothing by objective and as it were passive power. God therefore in their opinion produces things out of himself, and so will be the primary matter of things. But as to this you will more properly judge.

As to Descartes and Clauberg, I think in brief with you that the disciple is clearer than the master. Nevertheless, I should venture again to affirm that hardly any one of the Cartesians have added anything to the discoveries of the master. Certainly Clauberg, Ræus,[4]

[1] *Cf.* the letter of Jacob Thomasius to Leibnitz, October 2, 1668, Gerhardt, *Leibniz. philos. Schrift.*, 1, 14; Kortholt, *Leibnit. Epistolæ ad diversos*, 3, 35: "Bagheminus ille, cujus negotium geritur, Scabinus est Stetinensis, et a nostra tum theologica, tum philosophica facultate petiit philosophiæ suæ novæ censuram. Theologi responderunt. A nobis nihil aliud repositum illi est, quam disputatio mea, quæ si in manus hominis pervenit, facile judicabit, quo in hanc novitatem animo simus." — Tr.

[2] For some account of the lives and philosophy of the persons whose names are here mentioned, *cf.* Lasswitz, *Gesch. d. Atomistik*; Stöckl, *Gesch. d. Philos. d. Mittelalters*, III. [Vol. 4]. — Anton Deusing, 1612–1666 (not referred to in the works cited), was a German physician and Professor of Medicine at Groningen. He had an extended knowledge of philosophy, mathematics, and oriental languages, and published many works, among them, *De vero systemate mundi, dissertatio mathematica, qua Copernici systema mundi reformatur*, etc., Amsterdam, Elzevir, 1643, 4to. — Tr.

[3] Erdmann reads: "hypothesibus ejus," *i.e.* his hypotheses. — Tr.

[4] Jean de Raey, date of birth unknown, died 1702, was Professor of Philosophy in the University of Leyden 1652–1668, and entered upon his Professorship at Amsterdam in January, 1669, with an *Oratio de sapientia veterum*. In his

Spinoza,[1] Clerselier,[2] Heerbord,[3] Tobias Andreæ,[4] Henry Regius,[5] have published nothing but paraphrases of their master. But I call those Cartesians only who follow the principles of Descartes, from which number those great men Bacon, Gassendi, Hobbes, Digby, Cornelius of Hogheland,[6] etc., whom the common people confound with the

Claris philosophiæ naturalis seu introductio ad naturæ contemplationem Aristotelico-Cartesianam, 1654, 2d ed., 1677, he sought to improve and complete the doctrine of Aristotle through that of Descartes. He explained *Erkenntnisslehre* wholly after the manner of Aristotle; but contested his assumption of the eternity of the world or the divine nature of the stars. He discussed mainly the nature of matter and the origin of motion, wholly on a Cartesian basis. — Tr.

[1] In the impression of this letter given by Gerhardt, *Leibniz. philos. Schrift.*, 4, 162 *sq.*, Leibnitz has erased the names of Spinoza and Cornelius van Hooghelande, and added after Bacon that of Galileo. This impression omits also the names of Ræus and Clerselier. For the other textual changes, *cf.* the impression itself. — Tr.

[2] Claude Clerselier, 1614–1684, the father-in-law of Rohault (*cf. ante*, p. 233, n. 2), was a zealous disciple of Descartes and edited some of his works: *Le monde, ou traité de la lumière*, Paris, 1677; *Traité de l'homme*, Paris, 1664; *Les lettres de René Descartes*, 3 vols., Paris, 1657–1667. — Tr.

[3] Adrian Heereboord, 1614–1659, Professor of Philosophy in the University of Leyden, was one of the first and most zealous advocates of the new tendency of thought introduced by the philosophy of Descartes. He united to a certain extent Cartesianism with the traditional authority of Aristotle, evidence of which appears in his *Parallelismus Aristotelicæ et Cartesianæ philosophiæ naturalis*, 1643. Other writings of Heereboord are: *Meletemata philosophica*, 1654; *Philosophia rationalis, moralis, et naturalis*, 1654, 2d ed., 1660; *Philosophia pneumatica*, 1659. — Tr.

[4] Tobias Andreæ, 1604–1674, Professor of History and Greek Language at Groningen, successfully cultivated philosophy and became known as a zealous partisan of the philosophy of Descartes. He wrote, in 1653, against Jacob Revius, *Assertio methodi Cartesianæ*, and was also author of *Brevis explicatio, brevi explicatione mentis humanæ Henr. Regii reposita.* — Tr.

[5] Hendrik van Roy, 1598–1679, usually called Regius, was a Dutch physician, who in 1638 became Professor of Botany and Theoretical Medicine at Utrecht. He was a zealous disciple and advocate of the ideas of Descartes, until the Voët-Schoock-Descartes controversy and Descartes' rejection of him as a true representative of his views resulted in their falling out. Regius regarded the soul as a mode of the bodily substance, and in physics, while resting throughout on Cartesian principles, differed from Descartes in his conception of motion and rest. On this doctrine of Regius, significant for the problem of body, *cf.* Lasswitz, *Gesch. d. Atomistik*, 2, 405–408. Regius published, among other works, *Fundamenta physicæ*, Leyden, 1646; *Philosophia naturalis*, Amsterdam, 1661. Dr. James Martineau, *A Study of Spinoza*, London, Macmillan & Co., 1882, page 75, line 7, and foot-note 1, in translating "Regis" instead of "Regius" has misunderstood Leibnitz's reference and wrongly attributed to him a "*lapsus memoriæ.*" — Tr.

[6] Cornelius Van Hooghelande, a Catholic nobleman who lived at Leyden, was a friend and disciple of Descartes. In his *Cogitationes*, 1646, Hooghelande "so developed the fundamental doctrines of Descartes that the only Cartesian-

Cartesians, must in a word be left out, since however they were either the equals or even the superiors of Descartes in age and natural capacities; I acknowledge that I am anything but a Cartesian. That rule I hold common to all these renovators of philosophy, that nothing is to be explained in bodies except by magnitude, figure, and motion. In respect to Descartes I hold the argument only of his method, for when we come to the present matter, he relaxed utterly from that severity, and descended abruptly to certain extraordinary hypotheses, a course which in his case Vossius rightly indeed reprehended in his book on Light.

Wherefore I do not hesitate to say that I approve more things in the books of Aristotle περὶ φυσικῆς ἀκροάσεως, than in the Meditations of Descartes; so far am I from being a Cartesian. Nay more, I would venture to add that all those eight books can be received without violation of the reformed philosophy. By which very method those difficulties will *ipso facto* be met which you, most distinguished man, are investigating in regard to the irreconcilable Aristotle. For the conclusions of Aristotle concerning matter, form, privation, nature, place, infinity, time, motion, are for the most part certain and demonstrated, this one thing generally excepted, what he asserted about the impossibility of a vacuum and motion in a vacuum. For to me neither vacuum nor plenum is necessary, and the nature of things seems capable of explanation by either method. In behalf of the vacuum contend Gilbert, Gassendi, Gericke; for the plenum, Descartes, Digby, Thomas Anglus,[1] Clerk[2] in his book "De plenitudine mundi." For the possibility of each, Thomas Hobbes and Robert Boyle. And I confess that, with difficulty indeed, yet without a vacuum, the rarefactions of things can be explained. I saw recently the book of John Baptist du Hamel,[3] a French scholar, on the

ism of his work was the dedication." Descartes regarded him, says Kuno Fischer, *Descartes and his School*, translated by Gordy, p. 503, "as a well-disposed man without a calling to philosophy, and without understanding his doctrine." Cousin, *Œuvres de Descartes*, 6, 279–281, gives a letter, with a foot-note of an unknown editor stating his belief that Descartes wrote this letter to Van Hooghelande in March, 1636, at Amsterdam. — Tr.

[1] Thomas White, 1582–1676, called Anglus, Albius, Candidus, etc., published his *Institutionum Peripateticarum ad mentem summi clarissimique Philosophi Kenelmi Equitis Digbæi* at Lyons, 1646. Leibnitz refers to him briefly in the *Theoria motus concreti*, § 55 (Gerhardt, *Leibniz. philos. Schrift.*, 4, 207; *Math. Schrift.*, II., 2 [Vol. 6], 47), and in the *Theoria motus abstracti* (*ibid.*, 4, 228; II., 2 [Vol. 6], 67), as "subtilissimus" and "acutissimus." — Tr.

[2] Gilbert Clerke, 1626–1697 ?, a mathematician and theological writer, in his first work, *De Plenitudine Mundi*, etc., 1660, reviewed Descartes and attacked Bacon and Hobbes, and published in 1662 his *Tractatus de Restitutione Corporum*, results of studies following Torricelli and Boyle. — Tr.

[3] Jean Baptiste du Hamel, 1624–1706, was a French experimental philosopher and astronomer, who lectured on physics and experimented so far as his

harmony of ancient and modern philosophy, published not long since at Paris, in which he elegantly expounds and often acutely estimates the hypotheses of some of the most celebrated ancients and moderns. He also has not a few words concerning the conflicting views about the vacuum. As to the rest, scarcely any sane man will call in question all the remaining things discussed by Aristotle in Bk. VIII. Phys. and the entire Metaphysics, Logic, and Ethics. Who does not admit the substantial form also; namely, that by which the substance of one body differs from the substance of another body? Nothing is truer than primary matter. This one thing is in question, whether the abstract discussions of Aristotle concerning matter, form, and change, are to be explained by magnitude, figure, and motion. The Scholastics deny, the Reformers affirm, it. The opinion of the Reformers seems to me not only the truer, but the more in harmony with that of Aristotle; I will speak briefly of each.

And first of Aristotle. For that the Scholastics strangely preverted his meaning, to whom is it better known than to you, most distinguished man, who have been the first to bring forth into the light a good many of this class of errors? Since with you in metaphysics Soner[1] and Dreier,[2] in logic Viottus, Zabarella,[3]

position and the instruments then existing allowed. He published, among other works, *Astronomia physica*, and *De meteoribus et fossilibus*, Paris, 1660; *De consensu veteris et novæ philosophiæ*, Paris, 1663 and later editions, the work here referred to by Leibnitz; *De corporum affectionibus*, 1670; his *Opera*, Norimberga, 1681. *Cf.* Lasswitz, *Gesch. d. Atomistik*, 2, 493, 494. — TR.

[1] Ernst Soner, 1572-1612, was Professor of Philosophy and Medicine at Altdorf, and in philosophy an Aristotelian. He was the author of many *Disputationes*, the greater part of which appeared in Felwinger's *Philosophia Altdorfiana*, Norimberga, 1644; also of Commentaries on Aristotle's Metaphysics and Physics, 1607; he also wrote against eternal punishment in his *Demonstrationes quid æterna impiorum supplicia non arguant Dei justitiam sed injustitiam*, and some medical works. *Cf.* Magn. Dan. Omeisius, *Gloria Academiæ Altdorfianæ*, etc., Altdorf, 1683. Leibnitz in his *Preliminary Dissertation* to his edition of Nizolius (Gerhardt, 4, 155: Erdmann, 68 a; Dutens, 4, Pt. I., 57) speaks of his contribution, together with that of Dreier, to the understanding of Aristotle's Metaphysics; and in the *Théodicée*, Pt. III., § 266, of his argument against eternal punishment. — TR.

[2] Christian, or Peter, Dreier, 1610-1688, was Professor of Theology at Königsberg, and published his *Sapientia seu Philosophia prima, ex Aristotele ejusque optimis commentatoribus, conscripta*, Königsberg, 1644, 4to. Leibnitz refers to him in his *Preliminary Dissertation* to Nizolius (Gerhardt, 4, 155; Erdmann, 68 a; Dutens, 4, Pt. I. 57) and also in the *Théodicée*, Pt. II., § 184: "M. Dreier de Königsberg a bien remarqué que la vraie métaphysique qu'Aristote cherchait, et qu'il appelait τὴν ζητουμένην, son *desideratum*, était la théologie." — TR.

[3] Jacopo Zabarella, 1533-1589, was a teacher of Logic at Padua. His *De rebus naturalibus, lib. XXX.*, appeared at Col., 1590, fol.; his *Opera logica*, Col., 1597, fol.; both also in several later editions. An account of Zabarella will be found in Stöckl, *Gesch. d. Philos. d. Mittelalters*, III. [Vol. 4], 263-272. — TR.

Jung,[1] in civics Jason Denores,[2] Piccart,[3] Couring, Felden,[4] Durrius,[5] and many others, acknowledge this, why, I pray, shall we not suspect the same or worse in physics, aids in the knowledge of which must be sought from sense and experiment, of which means the Scholastics confined for the most part in closed monasteries were absolutely deprived? It is probable enough, therefore, that in physics they were deceived; how if I shall show more than this, that it is altogether certain? In which thing I may be engaged again in a twofold way. For either it is shown that the Reformed Philosophy can be reconciled with the Aristotelian and is not contrary to it, or further, it is shown that the one not only can, but also must, be explained by the other; nay, rather, that the very things which are discussed with so much pomp by the moderns flow from the Aristotelian principles. By the former way the possibility, by the latter the necessity, of the reconciliation is accomplished, although in this very instance if a possible reconciliation is shown, the thing is accomplished. For

[1] Joachim Jung, 1587-1657, an eminent mathematician and physicist, and an earnest advocate of the corpuscular theory, published *Logica Hamburgensis*, Hamburg, 1638, 8vo; *et recensente Joh. Vegetio*, 1681, 8vo; and various disputations. Leibnitz refers to his *Geometria empirica*, Hamburg, 1681, 8vo, in the *Théodicée*, Pt. II., § 214. For an account of him and his corpuscular theory, *cf.* Lasswitz, *Gesch. d. Atomistik*, 2, 245-261; E. Wohlwill, *J. Jungius und die Erneurung atomistischer Lehren im 17 Jahrhundert*, Hamburg, 1887; G. E. Guhrauer, *J. Jung und sein Zeitalter*, Stuttgart u. Tübingen, 1859. — Tr.

[2] Jason Denores, died 1590, was well acquainted with the peripatetic philosophy, and published *Dell' ottima republica*, Venice, 1578, 4to; and *De constitutione philos. Aristotelis*, Patavii, 1584, 4to. — Tr.

[3] Michael Piccart, 1574-1620, Professor of Philosophy and Poetry at Altdorf, was one of the most learned men of his times, and especially distinguished as an interpreter of Aristotle. Among his works were *Isagoge in lectionem Aristotelis*, Nuremberg, 1605, 8vo, reprinted with the notes of J. C. Durrius, Altdorf, 1660, 1666, 8vo; *Organum Aristotelicum in quæst. et respons. redactum*, Leipzig, 1613, 8vo; *In politicos libros Aristotelis*, Leipzig, 1615, 8vo, Jena, 1659, 8vo, a highly esteemed work, which was reprinted with the title: *Argumenta librorum politicorum Aristotelis, cum præfatione de nævis istius operis Aristotelici*, Helmstadt, 1715, 4to. *Cf.* Morhof, *Polyhistoria*, 2, 63. — Tr.

[4] Johannes Felden, a jurisconsult, lived during the seventeenth century. Leibnitz refers to him in his *Prelim. Dissert.* to Nizolius (Gerhardt, 4, 155-156; Erdmann, 67 b, 68 a; Dutens, 4, Pt. I., 57, 58), as the author of *eruditissimæ . . . meditationes* on the *Topics* and *Analytics* of Aristotle, "not yet published," of notes on Grotius, of *Elementa Juris universalis*, and *Analysis Politicorum Aristotelis*. *Cf.*, also, Morhof, *Polyhistoria*, 2, 559. — Tr.

[5] Johann Conrad Durrius, 1625-1677, was Professor of Theology and Moral Philosophy at Altdorf. Among his writings were *Compendium theologiæ moralis*, in several editions, one of the best being that of 1698, 4to; *Oratio adversus Spinozam*, Jena, 1672; *Notæ in Isagogen Piccarti*, perhaps the work Leibnitz here had in mind in referring to Durrius. Morhof, *Polyhistoria*, 2, 63, gives some account of an edition of Piccart's *Isagoge in lectionem Aristotelis*, by Durrius, which appeared at Altdorf, 1665, 8vo. — Tr.

although each explanation, both of the Scholastics and of the moderns, were possible, nevertheless from two possible hypotheses must always be chosen the clearer and more intelligible, such as indisputably is the hypothesis of the moderns, which makes for itself no incorporeal entities in the midst of bodies, but besides magnitude, figure, and motion assumes nothing. What possibility there is of reconciliation I cannot better show than by asking that some principle of Aristotle be given me which cannot be explained by magnitude, figure, and motion.

Primary matter is the mass itself, in which there is nothing else than extension and ἀντιτυπία or impenetrability; it has extension from the space which it fills; the nature itself of matter consists in this, that it is something crass and impenetrable, and consequently movable when another meets it (while the second must yield). Now this continuous mass filling the world, while all its parts are at rest, is primary matter, from which all things are produced through motion, and into which they are resolved through rest. For there is in it no diversity, mere homogeneity, except through motion. Hence already all the difficulties of the Scholastics are solved. First, they inquire concerning its entitative character previous to all form. And the reply must be that it is an entity previous to all form, since it has its own existence. For all that exists, which is in any space, a fact which cannot be denied of that entire mass although without motion and discontinuity. But the essence of matter or the form itself of corporeity consists in ἀντιτυπία or impenetrability; matter also has quantity, but interminate, as the Averroists say, or indefinite; for while it is continuous, it is not cut into parts, and therefore no termini are actually given in it: yet extension or quantity is given. All things not concerning the extrinsic termini of the world, or the entire mass, but concerning the intrinsic termini of the parts, harmonize in a wonderful manner.

From matter let us pass to form through the dispositions. Here again, if we assume form to be nothing else than figure, all things wonderfully accord. For since figure is the terminus of body, to introduce figures into matter there will be need of a terminus. In order, therefore, that various termini may arise in matter, there is need of a discontinuity of parts. For while for this very reason the parts are discontinuous, any one you please has separate termini (for Aristotle defines continua ὧν τὰ ἔσχατα ἕν); but discontinuity can be induced in that mass before continuous in two ways; in one way so that at the same time contiguity is destroyed, which happens when they are so violently separated from one another that a vacuum is left, or so that contiguity remains, which happens when those which are immediate to themselves remain, yet are moved in different directions; for example, two spheres, one of which includes the other, can be moved in different directions, and yet remain contiguous, although they cease to be continuous. From these considerations it is evident that, if indeed from the beginning a mass discontinuous or broken up by vacuities was created, some forms of matter are at once concrete; but if, indeed, it is continuous from the beginning, forms must of necessity arise through motion (for concerning the annihilation of certain parts in order to obtain vacuities in matter, because it is beyond nature I do not speak, because from motion division, from division termini of parts, from termini of parts their figures, from figure forms, therefore from motion forms arise). From which it is evident that all disposition to form is motion, evident also the solution of the vexed question concerning the origin of forms. Which question the distinguished man Herm. Conring could satisfactorily answer by his special dissertation only by asserting that forms arise from nothing.[1] We shall say they arise from the power of matter, not by producing anything new, but only by destroying the old, and causing termini by division of the parts, as he who makes a column does nothing else than [2] remove the useless parts, the residuum after the other parts are removed by this very means receiving that figure which we call a column; that is to say, all the figures or forms which are contained in the mass itself need only determination and actual separation from the others adhering to them. If this explication is admitted, whatever arguments are produced against the origin of forms from the power of matter are mere trifles.

It now remains for us to come to changes. Changes are enumerated commonly and rightly: generation, corruption, increase, diminution, alteration, and local change or motion. The moderns think all these can be explained through local motion alone. And first, From increase and diminution the thing is manifest; for a change of quantity in the whole takes place when a part changes its place, and either approaches or departs. It remains for us to explain generation and corruption and alteration through motion, and I note beforehand that the same numerical change is a generation and alteration of different things, for example, since it is evident that putrefaction consists in those worms imperceptible to

[1] Gerhardt reads: "Conringius peculiari dissertatione non aliter satisfacere potuit, quam formas ex nihilo oriri." Erdmann reads: "Conringius peculiari dissertatione non aliter occurrit, quam concedendo formas ex nihilo oriri, sed meditationes istae compendiosiorem viam monstrant, ut illuc confugere necesse non sit. Discimus enim formas oriri," etc.; *i.e.*, Conring met in his special dissertation not otherwise than by admitting that forms spring from nothing, but these very meditations show a more advantageous way, so that it is not necessary to flee thither. For we say that forms arise, etc.

[2] Erdmann and Dutens read: " quam quod inutilia tollit," *i.e.*, than that which removes the useless parts. — TR.

the naked eye, any putrid infection will be an alteration of the man, a generation of the worm. In a similar way Hooke [1] shows in his "Micrographia," that rust in iron is a minute little forest (*sylvulam*) which has sprung up; to rust therefore will be an alteration of the iron, a generation of little shrubs. But both generation and corruption, as well as alteration, can be explained by a minute motion of parts; for example, since white is that which reflects the most light, black that which reflects little, those things will be white whose surface contains the largest number of little *specula;* this is the reason why foaming water is white, because it consists of innumerable little bubbles; moreover as many bubbles, so many *specula*, since before well-nigh the entire water was nothing but one *speculum*, as in a broken glass mirror (*speculum*), so many parts become so many mirrors (*specula*): which, indeed, is the reason why ground glass is whiter than that which is whole. In a similar manner, therefore, when water is broken by bubbles into separate *specula*, whiteness arises, which is the reason also why snow is whiter than ice, and ice than water. For it is false that snow is condensed water, since it is rarefied rather, whence also it is lighter than water and occupies more space. By which reasoning the sophism of Anaxagoras concerning black snow is explained (*diluitur*). From these considerations it is evident that colors arise from change alone of figure and position in the surface; the same explanation as regards light, heat, and all qualities, if occasion should allow, could easily be given. But now, if qualities are changed through motion alone, by the same process also substance will be changed: for if all, nay even if some, of the necessary qualities are changed, the thing itself is destroyed; for example, if you destroy either the light or heat, you will destroy the fire. And if the motion is set in operation (*inhibito*), you will produce each. And this is the reason why a closed fire dies for want of the nourishing air, so that I may pass over in silence the fact that the essence differs

[1] Robert Hooke, 1635–1703, Professor of Geometry in Gresham College, Oxford, and Secretary of the Royal Society, published his *Micrographia, or some Physiological Descriptions of Minute Bodies* in 1665. This book "contained the earliest investigation of the 'fantastical colours of' thin plates, with a quasi-explanation by interference, the first notice of the 'black spot' in soap-bubbles, and a theory of light, as 'a very short vibrative motion' transverse to straight lines of propagation through a 'homogeneous medium.' Heat was defined as 'a property of a body arising from the motion or agitation of its parts.'" From his paper (May, 1666) on curvilinear motion, illustrated with the aid of the "circular pendulum," showing experimentally that the centre of gravity of the earth and moon is the point describing an ellipse around the sun, dates "the clear statement of the planetary movements as a problem in mechanics." For an account of his Vibration-theory, *cf.* Lasswitz, *Gesch. d. Atomistik*, 2, 329–338. An abridgment of his *Micrographia* appeared at London, 1780. — Tr.

from its own qualities only in relation to the sense. For as the same city presents another aspect of itself, if you look down from a tower in the midst of the city (*in Grund gelegt*), which is just the same as if you beheld its essence; it appears otherwise if you approach from without, which is just the same as if you perceive the qualities of the body; and as the external aspect of the city varies, according as you depart from the eastern or the western side, so in a similar way the qualities vary in proportion to the variety of the organs. From these considerations now it is easily manifest that all changes can be explained through motion. It is no objection that generation takes place in an instant, that motion is successive, for generation is not motion but the end of motion; therefore the end of motion is in an instant, for some figure is produced or generated by the very last instant of motion, as the circle is produced by the very last moment of the circumgyration. From these considerations it is evident why the substantial form consists in the indivisible, and does not receive more or less. For figure also does not receive more or less. For although one circle may be greater than another, yet the one circle is not more a circle than the other, for the essence of the circle consists in the equality of the lines drawn from the centre to the circumference; now equality consists in the indivisible and does not receive more or less. Nor, indeed, must the figure or the magnitude of the object be accidents, nor in fact are they always accidents; for although, for example, flowing is an accident of lead, for it flows not unless in the fire, it is nevertheless of the essence of mercury. Now the cause of flowing is without doubt the free curvilineity of the parts, whether it consists of globes or cylinders or ovals or other spheroids: the curvilineity therefore of the subtile parts is an accident of the lead, but essential to the mercury. The reason is, because all metals arise from fixed mercury by means of the salts, and the nature of the salts consists in rectilinear figures fitted for rest; hence, if we allow salts dissolved in water to crystallize freely, some forms known to the chemists as tetraedric, others as hexaedric, octaedric, etc., but none round or curvilinear, appear. Hence salts are the cause of fixity; therefore those acid salts mixed with the mercury in the bowels of the earth, as it were, through the smallest parts impede the freedom of the curvilinear parts by their interposition and constitute the metal. But in the fire the metal returns to the nature of mercury, for the fire interposing itself in the subtile parts, frees the curvilinear hydrargyrate parts from the plane-sided salts; hence the flowing in the fire. Thus it is evident that there is scarcely anything in the Aristotelian physics which cannot be properly explained and illustrated by the reformed.

These examples, indeed, have occurred to me spontaneously (*de meo*), while writing; very many more are collected by others through all natural philosophy. Nor do I fear that in what I have hitherto said, you will think that I have followed too much the descriptions of Ræus or his authority. I was acquainted with such things some time before I even heard of Ræus. I read Ræus, to be sure, but in such a way that I now scarcely remember what subjects he discussed. Nor, indeed, was Ræus the first and only one of those promoting a union between Aristotle and the moderns. Scaliger seems to me to have been the first to pave the way; in our times Kenelm Digby and his follower, Thomas Anglus, the latter in his book on the immortality of the soul, the former in his "Peripatetic Institutions," treated *ex professo* the same subject long before Ræus. Nor do both Abdias Trew[1] and especially Erhard Weigel differ from them. Hitherto we have shown the possibility only of reconciliation; it remains for us to show the necessity also. Of what else, namely, does Aristotle in the eight books of the "Phys. Auditus" treat than figure, magnitude, motion, place, time? If therefore the nature of body in general is completed (*absolvitur*) by these, the nature of body in particular will be completed by a given figure, a given magnitude, etc. And, indeed, he himself says, Book 3, chapter (*text.*) 24, Phys., that all natural science is concerned with magnitude (with which figure is connected), motion, and time. Aristotle often says the same, that movable being is the subject of physics, that natural science treats of matter and motion; he himself also makes heaven the cause of all things which take place in the sublunary worlds. Now heaven, he says, does not act upon the bodies below it except through motion. But motion does not produce anything but motion or termini of motion, namely magnitude and figure, and from these the resulting position, distance, number, etc. From these, therefore, everything in nature must be explained. The same Aristotle likewise often says (as Book I. of the "Phys. Aud.," chap. 69) that the relation of the brass to the figure of the statue is the same as that of the matter to the form. But I might prove that the figure is the substance, or rather that the

[1] Abdias Trew, 1597–1669, was Professor of Physics and Astronomy in the University of Altdorf, where he erected, 1657, the first observatory seen in that part of the world. He made discoveries in the theory of music, especially as regards the most accurate temperament, which he set forth in his *Janitor lycæi musici*, Rothenburg, o. T., 1635. His chief work was in astronomy and meteorology, and he carefully observed all the comets appearing during his lifetime. As a chronologer he contributed to the adoption of the Gregorian calendar by the Protestant states. He published, among other works, *Directorium mathematicum*, Nuremberg, 1657; *Lehrbuch d. sphärischen Astronomie*, Nuremberg, 1637; *Gründliche Calendarkunst*, Lüneberg, 1666. — Tr.

space is the substance, that the figure is something substantial, because all science is concerned with substance; further it cannot be denied that geometry is a science. You replied that you could produce the place in which Aristotle had denied that geometry was a science sooner than I would produce that in which he affirmed it. I do not indeed doubt, illustrious sir, that there are some places of Aristotle which can be drawn or twisted to this purpose, but yet I think that these are overthrown by a very large number of his other expressions. For what is more frequent in all the books of the "Analytics" than examples of geometers, so that he seems to have wished geometrical demonstrations to be, as it were, the measure of the rest. Now the more ignoble is absurdly constituted the measure of the more noble. And so meanly, indeed, did the Scholastics think of mathematics at first, that they made every effort to exclude mathematics from the number of the perfect sciences, principally by means of this argument, because it does not always demonstrate from causes. But if we consider the matter more accurately, it will appear that it does demonstrate from causes. For it demonstrates figures from motion: from the motion of the point is produced the line, from the motion of the line the surface, from the motion of the surface the body. From the motion of the right line upon right lines arises the rectangle. From the motion of a right line about an immovable point arises the circle, etc. The constructions of figures, therefore, are motions; now from constructions relations (*affectiones*) concerning the figures are demonstrated. Therefore from motion, and consequently *a priori*, and from cause. Geometry, therefore, is a true science. Therefore with Aristotle's consent its subject, namely space, will be a substance. Nor is it so very absurd that geometry treats of the substantial form of bodies. For behold the passage of Aristotle, 13 "Met." chap. 3, in which he expressly says that geometry abstracts from matter, from the final and the efficient cause; in accordance with which supposition it follows that he treats either of the substantial or accidental form. But he does not treat of the accidental, because the accidental form in its own real definition involves the subject or matter in which it is, although Aristotle nevertheless says that geometry abstracts from matter. Therefore geometry treats of the substantial form. Hence there immediately arises in my mind as I write these things a certain beautiful harmony of the sciences, the matter, of course, having been accurately considered: theology or metaphysics treats of the efficient cause of things, namely mind; moral philosophy (whether practical or civil, for, as I learned from you, it is one and the same science) treats of the final cause of things, namely the good; mathematics (I mean the pure, for the rest is a part of physics) treats of the form or idea of things, namely figure; physics treats of the matter of things, and of the single affection resulting from its combination with other causes, namely motion. For the mind in order to obtain for itself a good and pleasing figure and position of things, supplies motion to matter. For matter by itself is devoid of motion. For the origin of all motion is mind, as Aristotle also rightly saw.

For to come to this point, Aristotle seems nowhere to have pictured to himself any such substantial forms, which are in themselves the cause of motion in bodies, as the Scholastics conceive; he indeed defines nature as the origin of motion and rest, and form and matter he calls nature, but form in a higher degree than matter, but from this what the Scholastics mean (*volunt*) does not follow, that form is a certain immaterial entity, irrational nevertheless in bodies, which itself spontaneously without the impact of an external thing gives motion downwards to a body, for example, to a stone. For the form, indeed, is a cause and source of motion, but not at first. For a body is not moved, except from the outside, as Aristotle rightly not only says, but also demonstrates; for example, a globe may be in a plane, if it is once at rest it will not move of itself forever, unless in consequence of an added external impulsor, for example, another body. If this now approaches, the second body is the source of the impressed motion, but the figure, namely globosity, is the source of the motion taken up, for if globosity were absent, having been produced by chance according to circumstances, the body would not yield to the second body so easily. From this it is evident that the scholastic concept does not follow from the definition of the Aristotelian form. Form, therefore, is the source of motion in its own body, and body itself is the source of motion in another body, I confess; but the primary source of motion is the primary and in reality from matter abstracted form (which at the same time is efficient), namely mind. Hence liberty and spontaneity occur in minds alone. Therefore it is not absurd that of the substantial forms mind only is called the primary source of motion, the others having their motion from mind. And by this argument he[1] ascends to the first mover. To this objection you give a twofold reply; first, this argument can avail nothing with Epicurus, who bestows upon his atoms *per se* downward motion. I admit that this argument can avail nothing with him, unless it be previously demonstrated to him that this itself is absurd and impossible, namely, that a body has motion from its own self, a thing which Cicero also if I am not mistaken already at that time did in his books "De natura Deorum," gracefully laughing at Epicurus because he introduced in this way something without cause and reason in his hypotheses. For in the nature of things nothing is down save as regards us,

[1] Aristotie. — *Gerhardt's Note.* — Tr.

and so there is no reason why any body should move in this rather than in that direction (*plagam*). Therefore we shall easily answer Epicurus, denying that whatever is moved is moved by another outside itself, and shall vindicate the laboring certainty of the existence of God. Second, you object that Aristotle seems to have reasoned not so much from this axiom that the source of all motion is outside the moved body, as from the other that progress into infinity is not granted. But in truth, most noble sir, consider carefully whether or not either connection of ideas is needed. For unless it is admitted that what is moved extraneously is moved, plainly we shall arrive at no progress, still less at infinity; for the opponent will resist steadfastly from the beginning and any given body will reply that it is itself sufficient to produce its own motion through its own substantial form, and needs therefore no mover, much less the first. Therefore that ladder will tumble down as soon as the first step, and as it were the foundation, is taken away. Then also Epicurus was wont to admit progress into infinity; therefore we must consider not so much what Epicurus admits or does not admit, as what can certainly be demonstrated. The Aristotelian philosophy, the inevitable result of the reformed philosophy itself, must be briefly touched upon.[1] It is plain that what must be discussed by the theologians must be discussed by the philosophers also. The holy fathers illustrated the Holy Scripture by the best interpretations: soon the monks obscured them by superstitions. The light of souls having arisen, the reformed theology is threefold: the one heretical, which rejects the scriptures themselves, as of the fanatics; the second schismatical, which harmonizes the ancient fathers, the doctors of the church, with the sacred scripture and the primitive church, as of the Evangelicals.[2] In like manner the Greek interpreters[3] illustrated Aristotle, the Scholastics obscured

[1] The Latin text reads: "Aristotelicam philosophiam reformatæ ipsius philosophiæ inevitabilis eventus breviter attingenda est." Gerhardt's note reads: "In diesem Satze fehlt etwas," *i.e.* In this sentence something is wanting. Erdmann gives the following: "*Observ. Thomasii.* Sic scriptum erat a librario, sed hiat alias haec periodus: nec lectionem ejus constituo," *i.e.* Note of Thomasius. Thus it was written by the copyist, but this sentence is otherwise lacking: I do not determine its reading. — Tr.

[2] Gerhardt's note reads: "Auch hier scheint etwas zu fehlen," *i.e.* Here also something appears to be wanting. Erdmann gives the following: "*Observ. Thomasii.* Etiam hic aliquid deest; datur enim pro triplici theologia tantum duplex. Scripsisse puto: alia schismatica, alia vera, quæ priscos Patres, etc. Confer sequentem," *i.e.* Note of Thomasius. Here also something is wanting; for, instead of the threefold theology, only a twofold is given. I think he wrote: the second schismatic, the third true, which the ancient Fathers, etc. *Cf.* the following. — Tr.

[3] Gerhardt reads, "interpretes"; Erdmann, "Patres." — Tr.

him with trifles. The light having arisen, the reformed philosophy is threefold: the first stupid, like that of Paracelsus,[1] Helmont,[2] and of the others who utterly reject Aristotle; the second bold, which with small regard for the ancients, nay with open contempt for them, render(s)[3] (their) its own meditations even when good suspected, such as that of Descartes; the third true, by whom Aristotle is recognized as a great man and in most things right.

The reformed philosophy having just been reconciled with Aristotle, it now remains to show its truth *per se*, precisely as the Christian religion can be proved both from reason and history and from the sacred Scripture. But it must be proved that no entities are given in the world besides mind, space, matter, motion. Mind I call thinking being. Space is a primarily extended entity or mathematical body, which manifestly contains nothing else than three dimensions, and is also that universal place of all things. Matter is a secondarily extended entity, or that which besides extension or mathematical body has also physical body, that is, resistance, ἀντιτυπίαν, density, the power of filling (*repletivitatem*) space, impenetrability, which consists in this, that it is compelled by the approach of another such being to move or to stop the other; from which nature of impenetrability therefore motion flows. Matter therefore is an entity which is in space or an entity coextensive with space. Motion is a change of space. But figure, magnitude, position, number, etc., are not entities really distinct from space, matter, and motion, but only conditions (*habitudines*) amid space, matter, motion, and their parts made by the supervenient mind. I define figure further as the terminus of extension, magnitude as the number of parts in the extension. I define number as one, and one, and one, etc., or unities. Position is reduced to figure, for it is a formation (*configuratio*) of many (figures). Time is nothing else than magnitude of motion. And since every magnitude is a number of parts, what wonder Aristotle defined time as the number of motion? But thus far termini only have been explained, and the sense in which we use them set forth, but nothing as yet proved. Now let us show that there is no need of any other things in order to explain the phenomena of the

[1] Theophrastus Paracelsus, 1473–1541. On his philosophy, *cf.* Stöckl, *Gesch. d. Philos. d. Mittelalters*, III. [Vol. 4], 430–452; Lasswitz, *Gesch. d. Atomistik*, 1, 298–306. — Tr.

[2] Joh. Bapt. Van Helmont, 1577–1644. On his philosophy, *cf.* Stöckl, *Gesch. d. Philos. d. Mittelalters*, III. [Vol. 4], 458–472; Lasswitz, *Gesch. d. Atomistik*, 1, 343–351. — Tr.

[3] The Latin text reads, "suas suspectas reddunt," as though the writer had in mind those holding the view rather than the view itself with which the sentence began, and in consistency with which beginning the verb should have been "reddit." — Tr.

world and to assign their causes, nay, also that there can be no other things, although if we show that there is no need of other things besides mind, matter, space, and motion, by this very thing it will be shown that the hypotheses of the moderns who employ these things alone in the assignment of phenomena are the better. For it is a defect in an hypothesis to assume unnecessary things. Now that all things in the entire world can indeed be explained from these alone, the reading of the modern philosophers sufficiently teaches, and it is evident from the considerations which I put down a little before when I was showing the possibility of an Aristotelic harmony. Then it must also be noted that these hypotheses are the better which are the clearer. Now, indeed, the human mind can imagine nothing else than mind (when, namely, it thinks of itself), space, matter, motion, and what results from these when united with each other; whatever else you add are words only, which can be named and variously combined with each other, but cannot be explained and understood. For who can imagine to himself a being which partakes of neither extension nor thought? What need therefore to posit souls of animals and plants, the incorporeal forms of the elements, the substantial forms of the metals, devoid of extension? More correctly therefore Campanella[1] in his book "De Sensu rerum et Magia," and Marcus Marci,[2] "De Ideis operatricibus," falsely indeed, yet in agreement nevertheless with their hypotheses, attributed to these substantial forms of inanimate things, deprived of extension, sense, knowledge, imagination, will. Nor is the occult philosophy of Agrippa,[3] who adds an Angel as it were an obstetrician to everything, unlike it, nor the discussions of Scaliger περὶ δυνάμεως πλαστικῆς and its intelligence. Thus it returns to as many little gods (*deunculos*) as substantial forms, and to a race almost πολυθεϊσμόν. For hence is attributed to them appetite, and the natural instinct from which also follows natural cognition, hence these axioms: Nature does nothing in vain, everything shuns its own destruction, like takes pleasure in like, matter desires a nobler form, and others of this description, since nevertheless there is, in truth, in nature no wisdom, no appetite, but a beautiful Order springs out of it, because it is the clock of God. From these considerations it is evident that the hypotheses of the reformed philosophy are superior to the scholastic hypotheses for this

[1] Tommaso Campanella, 1568–1639. Brief account of his views is given in Lasswitz, *Gesch. d. Atomistik*, 1, 340–343. *Cf.*, also, Stöckl, *Gesch. d. Philos. d. Mittelalters*, III. [Vol. 4], 343–366.—Tr.

[2] *Cf. infra*, p. 676, n. 2.—Tr.

[3] Heinrich Cornelius Agrippa von Nettesheim, 1486–1535. His *Opera omnia*, Lugduni, 1600; the *De occulta philosophia* in Vol. 1. For an account of his views, *cf.* Stöckl, *Gesch. d. Philos. d. Mittelalters*, III. [Vol. 4], 412–426; Lasswitz, *Gesch. d. Atomistik*, 1, 290–293.—Tr.

reason, because they are not superfluous, while, on the other hand, they are clear.

It remains for us to prove by more subtle reasoning that other entities than those I have mentioned cannot indeed be assumed in explaining the nature of bodies. It will be done thus: All call that body which is endowed with some sensible quality, then out of the sensible qualities many can be taken away, provided nevertheless that the body remains. For although a body is deprived of all color, odor, taste, yet it is called a body. For you will grant that air, for example, is a body, although it is transparent, and so not colored, besides it is devoid of taste, and for the most part also of both odor and sound. Therefore the qualities visible, audible, and those of taste and smell, may be cast aside as least constitutive of the nature of body. To tactile qualities, therefore, everything returns. And indeed these primary qualities — heat, moisture, dryness, cold — can each be absent; heat can be absent from water, moisture from the earth, dryness from the air, cold from the fire, and yet any of these is a body. The other tactile qualities — for example, smoothness, lightness, tenacity, etc., are acknowledged even by you not to belong to the constitutive nature of a body, for this very reason, because they are called secondary, and so have arisen from others, and further because there is no one of them which cannot be absent from a body. There remains, therefore, to be sought for some sensible quality which is competent to all and single bodies and from which as it were by a sign men may distinguish body from non-body. This without doubt is density (*crassities*), or *ἀντιτυπία*, taken with extension. Whatever men certainly think extension is (although in truth it always is body and has *ἀντιτυπία*, although insensible to us, yet perceptible by the intellect), they do not at once call that body, for they sometimes think that it is a mere appearance and *φάνтασμα*. But whatever they not only see but also touch, that is, in which they find *ἀντιτυπία*, that they call body; but whatever lacks *ἀντιτυπία*, that they deny to be body. In the two, therefore, men both educated and uneducated place the nature of body, in extension and *ἀντιτυπία* taken together; they take that from sight, this from touch; whence also from the union of both senses we are wont to be certified concerning things that they are not phantasmata. But extension is nothing else than existence in space; *ἀντιτυπία* is the inability to exist with another in the same space, but the one or the other (*alterutrum*) must be moved or keep quiet. From these considerations it is evident that the nature of body is constituted by extension and antitypy, and since there is nothing in things without cause, nothing even must be assumed in bodies, the cause of which cannot be made to appear from their primary constitutive principles. Now the cause cannot be made to appear from these except through their definitions. Nothing, therefore, is to be assumed in bodies which does not flow from the definition of extension and antitypy. But there flow from this definition only magnitude, figure, position, number, mobility, etc. Motion itself does not flow from these. Whence, properly speaking, motion is not given in bodies as a real entity in them, but I have demonstrated that whatever moves is continually created, that bodies at any instant in assignable motion are something, at any intervening time between the instants in assignable motion are nothing, a thing which was unheard of till now, but which is plainly necessary and will shut the mouth of the atheists. From these considerations it is evident that the explanation of all qualities and changes must be taken from magnitude, figure, motion, etc., and that heat, color, etc., are nothing but subtile motions and figures. As to what remains, I dare affirm that atheists, socinians, naturalists, sceptics, would never have been truly met unless by this established philosophy; which I indeed believe a gift of God given to the old age of the world as an unique plank by which pious and prudent men are about to save themselves in the shipwreck of the now overhanging atheism. However small my knowledge of learned men after a little time, I nevertheless tremble as often as I think how many men at the same time intellectual and absolutely atheistic I have met. And there is flying through the hands of men an unknown book of Bodin[1] (and would, as I wish in the case of Naudæus, it was never to be published), powerful certainly, which he calls, "Arcana sublimium," in which he is the professed enemy of the Christian religion. The dialogues of Vaninus[2] are child's play when compared with it. I have read it carefully, and I thank God from my heart, because he furnished me with those defences of

[1] Jean Bodin, 1530–1596 or 1597, the eminent writer on Political Science, and advocate of tolerance in religion, published his greatest work,—"the first elaborate attempt in modern times to construct a system of political science," —*Les six Livres de la République*, at Paris, 1576. His *Universæ naturæ theatrum* appeared at Hanover, 1605, the Preface dated February 25, 1596. For some account of its doctrine, *cf.* Lasswitz, *Gesch. d. Atomistik*, 1, 326–327, 411–413. G. E. Guhrauer published an Abstract, in German, with a partial translation of the Latin text, of his very famous MS., here referred to by Leibnitz, the *Colloquium heptaplomeres de abditis rerum sublimium arcanis*, Berlin, 1841, and the complete original text, from a MS. in the Giessen Library, was edited and published by L. Noack, Schwerin, 1857. The work is "a conversation between seven learned men,—a Jew, a Mahometan, a Lutheran, a Zwinglian, a Roman Catholic, an Epicurean, and a Theist"; and "the conclusion to which they are represented as coming is, that they will live together in charity and toleration and cease from further disputations as to religion."—Tr.

[2] Lucilio Vanini, 1585–1619, who called himself by the name, among others, of Julius Cæsar, was a disciple of Pomponatius (*cf. ante*, p. 581, n. 1). He denied the immortality of the soul, and advocated a doctrine of pantheistic

philosophy (in which I should be ungrateful, if I should deny that I owed much to you), by which I repelled his weapons with no difficulty. The labor of the distinguished Spizel is to be praised, which he now again expends in eradicating atheism. His letter on this subject, recently published (in these nine days), I think you have seen. Hear what happened to me in connection with him. I had written some time when at leisure, a leisure nevertheless disturbed in the inn, about two sheets, in which I was discussing the demonstration more accurately than usual of the immortality of the soul and the existence of God. These I had sent to my friend. Through him they came into the hands of the Most Reverend Spener,[1] pastor at Frankfort, a neglected yet deserving author. Spener sent them to Spizel;[2] Spizel placed them at the end of that recent letter of his to Ant. Reiser[3] on the eradication of atheism, under the title "Confessio naturæ contra atheistas." I do not blame him, but I am grieved, because that σχέδιον was so very incorrectly printed; that sorites, especially, by which I tried to demonstrate the immortality of the soul, was thrown into strange confusion by the misplacing of its opening lines. Spizel acknowledged that he was ignorant of the author. I desire a judgment

naturalism. He published *De admirandis naturæ reginæ deæque mortalium arcanis, lib. quat.*, Paris, 1616. His philosophical works, translated into French by Rousselot, appeared at Paris, 1841. Leibnitz, in a letter to Sebastian Kortholt, March 15, 1713, says: "Apologiam Vannini nondum vidi, nec magnopere dignam legi puto. Scripta ejus parvi momenti sunt, sed homo ineptus, imo stultus comburi non merebatur, claudi jure poterat, ne alios inficeret" (Dutens, 5, 321). — Tr.

[1] Philip Jacob Spener, 1635–1705, was chief pastor of the Lutheran church at Frankfort-on-the-Main, from 1666–1686, first Court-chaplain at Dresden, 1686–1691, and rector of St. Nicolas, in Berlin, with the title of "Consistorialrath," from 1691. He directed the foundation of the University of Halle in 1691. Though, according to Ritschl, *Gesch. d. Pietismus*, 2, 163, Bonn, 1884, "himself not a Pietist," Spener has justly been called "the father of Pietism." He was a voluminous author. Two letters of Leibnitz to Spener are given by Dutens, 5, 467–468. — Tr.

[2] Theophil Gottlieb Spitzel, or Spizel, 1639–1691, a German pastor and polyhistorian, was deacon of St. James's church, Augsburg, in 1662 and pastor from 1682 to 1690. "As a theologian, in spite of his many-sided and universal scientific interests, he remained well-nigh unfruitful." Leibnitz refers to the matter here alluded to again in his letter to Spizel, December 12–22, 1669; *cf.* Dutens, 5, 343. The *Confessio Naturæ contra Atheistas* first appeared as a *Postscriptum in Theo. Spizelii de Atheismo eradicando ad Virum præstantissimum Dr. Antonium Reiserum Augustanum, etc., Epistola. . . .* August. Vindel. 1669. — Tr.

[3] Anton Reiser, 1628–1686, a learned and distinguished Lutheran theologian, was an earnest defender of evangelical truth. He published *De origine, progressu et incremento antitheismi seu Atheismi*, Augsburg, 1669, 8vo; *Index MSS. bibliothecæ Augustanæ*, Augsburg, 1675, 4to. — Tr.

concerning the reasoning itself of the demonstration. Nor do I seek praise, but criticism, since it is important to religion that it be not perfunctorily defended. Although meanwhile I seem to myself to have penetrated far more deeply into both. For neither the thoughts which I have thrown out since that time concerning perpetual creation in motion, nor the inmost nature of thinking being or mind, are brought together therein. I wrote you at one time about the society which certain Germans are starting. It will show its existence by a German paper published by the bookseller Goezius with the title "Collegium Philadelphicum." But to me it seems a pleasant dream, like the society of the Red Cross. It is wonderful how great a dissension in Parnassus that Schurzfleisch[1] who is with you excited. I very much wish to know what the great men with you by whom he hopes he will be advanced, think of this specimen. Boecler[2] threatens that one from the court. The author of the "Itinerarium politicum" which is now appearing is without doubt Burgoldensis,[3] that commentator on the "Instrumentum pacis." I am astounded at the audacity of the man.

As for the rest, most illustrious sir, I have discoursed the more

[1] Konrad Samuel Schurtzfleisch, 1641–1708, was Professor of History at Wittenberg, and because of his great learning was given the nickname of a living library and a walking museum. While at Wittenberg he published, under the name of Eubulus Theosdatus Sarckmasius, a pamphlet, *Judicia de novissimis prudentiæ civilis Scriptoribus*, Leipzig, 1669, in which he freely expressed his opinion of the most celebrated German jurisconsults, and which aroused against him many adversaries. He continued the history of Sleidan (*cf. ante*, p. 114, n. 1). — Tr.

[2] Johann Heinrich Boecler, 1611–1692, Professor of Eloquence at Strassburg and Upsala, and afterwards of History at Strassburg, was author of many commentaries on classical authors and of works of history, politics, criticism, morals, etc. Among them were: *De jure Galliæ in Lotharingiam*, Strassburg, 1663; *Ad Grotium de jure belli et pacis dissert.*, *V.*, 1665. The Elector of Mayence appointed him "conseiller" in 1662, and the next year the Emperor Ferdinand III. bestowed on him the same title and made him Count Palatine. — Tr.

[3] Philippus Andrea Oldenburgerus, the anagram of which is Burgoldensis, a pupil of H. Conring, was Professor of Law and History at Geneva, where he died in 1678. He published a large number of valuable works, some of them under assumed names, among which are: *Itinerarium Germaniæ Politicum, modernam præcipuarum Aularum Imperii faciem repræsentans*, Cosmopoli (Geneva), 1668, 12mo; *Limnæus enucleatus*, an abstract of Limné, *De jure imperii Romano-germanici*, Geneva, 1670, fol.; *Notitia Imperii, sive Discursus in Instrumentum Pacis Osnabrugo-Monasteriensis* (this work under the name of Burgoldensis), Freistadt, 1669, 4to. Of the *Itinerarium Germaniæ Politicum*, Morhof, *Polyhistoria*, 2, 497, says: "in quo multa est rerum ineptissimarum farrago, quibus nonnunquam immiscentur aliqua notatu non indigna, sed lectore prudente opus est, qui cum judicio illa legere posit." The freedom with which the author spoke of the political interests and vices of the German courts led to the interdiction of his book. It was, nevertheless,

at length of this whole matter to you for this reason, because I had no more learned and equitable judge of these things. Since you have examined all the recesses of the ancients and do not despise the discoveries of the moderns when deserving, you alone of all can best examine this and also illustrate them. For you rightly judge, that although new opinions are brought forth and their truth most evidently shown, yet from the views publicly received we must scarcely ever depart, a thing which we should not strive for if the Scholastics had done it. Farewell, ornament of our country, and do not bring to an end (*absolve*) your noble thoughts (for many are both begun and at the same time perfected with rare felicity of mind), but produce them.

II

FRAGMENT[1]

[*From the Latin*]

The primary matter[2] of Aristotle is identical with the subtile matter of Descartes. Each is divisible to infinity. Each is *per se* lacking in form and motion, and each receives forms through motion. Each receives motion from mind. Each is formed into certain rings (*gyros*), and there is no more solidity in the vortices of Aristotle than of Descartes. Each has solidity from motion, because nothing drives it asunder, although Descartes himself has not assigned this cause of solidity. Each ring (*gyrus*) extends (*propagat*) the action impressed through motion on account of the continuity of matter into another ring. For Aristotle also, no less than Descartes or Hobbes, derives all particulars from the motion alone of universal rings. Whence Aristotle adds intelligences only to the principal rings, because from the impacts of these rings the actions of the others follow. In this Aristotle erred, because he made the earth the centre of the universe and of all gyrations. But he should be par-

several times reprinted. In Pt. IV. of his *Thesaurus rerum publicarum totius orbis*, Geneva, 1675, 4 vols., 8vo, he repudiated the errors and condemned the reprehensible expressions which he had employed in the earlier work. Of the *Discursus in Instrumentum Pacis*, Lenglet du Fresnoy remarks: "a bold and learned piece." — TR.

[1] Gerhardt, *Leibniz.philos. Schrift.*, 7, 259-60. In his *Einleitung*, *ibid.*, 251, G. says: "The fragment, n. I., which was written, perhaps, at the time of the composition of the *Hypothesis physica* (1671), contains a comparison of the metaphysics of Aristotle and Descartes, what Leibnitz borrowed from both, and what he has added of his own." — TR.

[2] Upon a bit of paper without date and superscription, proceeding according to the handwriting from the earliest period. — *Gerhardt's Note.* — TR.

doned for this, because philosophy was not yet sufficiently instructed by observations.

To these I now add, that *primary matter if at rest is nothing.* This also is a statement which certain Scholastics have obscurely made, that primary matter also has existence from form. Of this fact there is demonstration. Because whatever does not think, is nothing. But that in which there is no variety also does not think. In like manner: If primary matter moves in one direction, that is, in *parallel lines, it is at rest,* and consequently is nothing. *All things are full,* because primary matter and space is the same thing. Therefore *every motion is circular,* either composed of circulars or at least returning into itself. Many circulations mutually hinder each other, or mutually lead into each other. *Many circulations try to unite in one* or all bodies tend to rest, that is, annihilation. *If bodies are without mind, it is impossible for motion to have been eternal.*[1] *From universal conflicting circulations are produced particular bodies. Matter is actually divided into infinite parts. There are infinite creatures in any given body whatever. All bodies cohere among themselves. All are indeed forcibly separated* (*distrahuntur*) *from all, but not without resistance. There are no atoms,* or bodies whose parts are never forcibly separated. There are two principles by which motion is changed: compositions of efforts (*conatuum*), and compositions . . . [a word and two lines are in consequence of the destruction of the paper illegible. — Gerhardt].

III

DEMONSTRATION AGAINST ATOMS TAKEN FROM THE CONTACT OF ATOMS[2]

October 23, 1690

[*From the Latin*]

Definition I. A thing is distinguished from other things in two ways, either through itself, or extrinsically. *Through itself a thing is distinguished from another,* when a method of distinguishing through the consideration alone of the thing is used, no operation or change being made in the thing. *Extrinsically,* when by external application something new is produced in the thing, which does not appear in

[1] Over the words, "motum fuisse æternum," Leibnitz has written, "potest diminui sine fine," *i.e.* can be diminished without end. — *Gerhardt's Note.* — Tr.

[2] Gerhardt, *Leibniz. philos. Schrift.*, 7, 284–288; Stein, *Leibniz. u. Spinoza,* Beilage XIV., pp. 325–328. — Tr.

another. Thus the sphere and the cube can be distinguished both by consideration and also by operation; by consideration, because in the sphere no angles are found, of which there are eight in the cube; by operation, as, if both are placed upon an inclined plane, the sphere will descend the plane by rolling, the cube by sliding.

Axiom. Whatever is distinguishable extrinsically from another, is also distinguishable through itself.[1]

For example, let there be two coins from the same stamp (*typo*), one of true gold, the other of false, which may be easily distinguished extrinsically by the blow of the hammer. I say even before the blow, by an attentive consideration, differences in the composition itself of each would be detected by the naked or equipped eye, and although the keenness of vision could not reach thither, yet differences exist within and can be detected by some more acute creature (for example, by an angel).[2]

Observation. Certain bodies are mutually separated violently from each other.

Conceded Hypothesis. Matter is uniform, or, motion and figure excepted, everywhere like itself.

Definition II. An *Atom* is a body which cannot be broken.

Postulate. If there are atoms, we may assume them of any figure and size whatever and in any position whatever.

THEOREM.

It is impossible for all bodies to consist of atoms.

Let us assume (by the postul.) three atoms, *A*, *B*, *C*, of which *A* is cubical, but *B* and *C* are triangular prisms, composing the cube *D*, similar and equal to the former *A*. The cube *D* cannot (by the conceded hypothesis) be distinguished from the cube *A*. Therefore they cannot be distinguished extrinsically (by Axiom I.). If therefore other bodies strike against the cube *D*, they will be able either to separate the atoms *B* and *C*, or they will not be able. If able to separate them, then the same bodies striking in the same way against

[1] On the margin of the Ms., Leibnitz has remarked: "Whatever is distinguishable in itself, is also distinguishable extrinsically. If two bodies are similar through a third similar body, they cannot be distinguished. If two bodies are *similar*, but mutually *unequal per se*, they can be distinguished, no third body even being assumed. Similar and equal bodies cannot be distinguished extrinsically, nay, rather, in any way, and so are one and the same." — *Gerhardt's Note.* — Tr.

[2] Stein here inserts in his text the following marginal gloss, wanting in Gerhardt's text: "Hic ostenditur ex hypothesi Atomistica sequi, quod novæ Atomi nasci possint, nec tamen iterum dissolvi contra naturæ morem," *i.e.* Here it is shown to follow from the Atomistic hypothesis, that new atoms can be produced, but nevertheless cannot again be dissolved contrary to the law of nature. — Tr.

the cube *A* will be able violently to separate the same into parts, for otherwise *A* and *B* might be distinguished extrinsically (by Defin. I.), the contrary of which has been shown. But if the cube *A* is violently separated into parts, it certainly (by Defin. II.) will not be an atom, as was supposed. But if other bodies cannot again separate the cube *D* into component parts, it follows that the atom was not

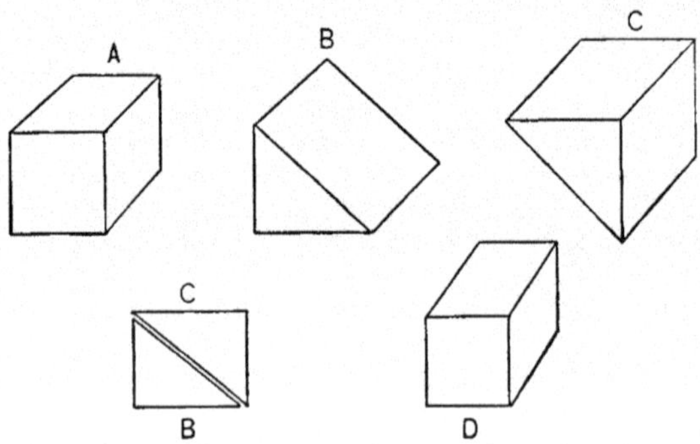

FIG. 1.

produced from non-atoms through contact. And the same principle will hold, whatever figure the atoms be assigned. Whence it follows that atoms which have once touched each other cannot again be violently separated. Now if all bodies are composed of atoms, bodies do not touch each other except through the atoms. Therefore they cannot be violently separated after contact, unless the atom of the one is violently separated from the atom of the other, which we have shown cannot be done. But bodies not be violently separated. . . .[1] And so it is not true that all bodies are composed of atoms. Q. E. D.

SCHOLIUM TO THE DEMONSTRATION AGAINST ATOMS TAKEN FROM THE CONTACT OF ATOMS.

October 24, 1690.

I do not see what reply can be made to this demonstration unless by a denial of the postulate. For we postulated that it be conceded us: If there are atoms, they can be assumed of any figure and size and in any position whatever. This alone seems possible to be said with any reason, atoms cannot be granted, the parts of which are connected only by a point or line. And so there cannot (for example) be an

[1] More words illegible. — *Gerhardt's Note.* Stein omits this incomplete sentence. — TR.

atom similar to one composed from two spheres touching each other. But if then atoms spherical or terminated by any other curved surfaces whatever are granted, they never touch each other save in a point, and so never compose a body similar to an atom. Here in some way I think a reply can be made, in the first place if the contact in the surface is the cause of stability, it follows that stability is greater when the surface is greater. Whence the atoms would not be equally stable. And so there would be a certain determinate force of violent separation by which stabilities could be measured. I do not see where we can find this force, if it is not in the motion of bodies, unless we advocate certain spiritual powers whose method of acting in bodies nevertheless cannot be known. But if the stability of all atoms is equal, it does not matter how great the contact is; even contact in a line, nay in a point, would suffice.

A second reply which can be made is this: it has at least been demonstrated by us that bodies cannot be composed of atoms terminated by plane sides. But besides the fact which can be doubted, whether indeed curvilinears properly called are granted, this exception does not seem in agreement with the reasons of things, that if composition from atoms is possible it must necessarily take place through bodies destitute of a plane surface.

The third reply is this: not only the atoms of plane surfaces but also of concave must be assumed (*tollendas*) from nature. Otherwise we shall be permitted to make atoms from the non-atom, as often as the concave surface of one atom happens to be applied to the convex surface of another, and that will happen until all the atoms of the concave surfaces shall be filled as far as can be done by the convex existing in nature. But this restriction also does not seem in harmony with the reasons of things. And in general, if any one denies that there are other atoms than the perfectly spherical, in order to escape the force of the demonstration, these things are devised which indeed are accommodated to the latter, but do not accord with the primal reasons and amplitude of nature. In brief: from the hypothesis of atoms I can deduce absurdity, provided I am allowed to assign to the atoms size, figure, and motion as I will.[1]

[1] On the margin of the Ms., Leibnitz has remarked: "Another argument could be set up, namely: If atoms could be granted, bodies similar and equal, and nevertheless different from each other, as would be two equal spheres, could be granted. If atoms were granted, no cause of reflection, which in fact must be taken from an elastic body (*Elaterio*), could be perceived, nor would the atoms striking each other leap apart, in turn, from each other. Further superficial contact is the cause of cohesion, two atoms coming together in sides or surfaces would not leap apart; thus, if the velocity of each approach is equal, the whole force would perish." — *Gerhardt's Note.* Stein has put this marginal gloss into the text, with a note stating that it is a marginal gloss. — Tr.

Appendix to the Demonstration against Atoms taken from the Contact of Atoms.

If any one denies that there can be atoms, the parts of which touch each other in a point only or line, and so requires contact in the surface for cohesion, that he may avoid the force of our demonstration, that one will entangle himself in other new difficulties.

For if cohesion arises from superficial contact, a case can be seen in which an atom is unable to graze (*radere*) an atom; for where a part of the side of the atom B coincides with a part of the side of the atom $_3A$, they are not only unable to leap apart and also to separate violently, but even the one will not be able to slide upon the other, for they touch each other in the surface. Nay, rather, what is more wonderful, the atom A coming by its own motion from the place $_1A$ into the place $_2A$ so situated, that it is unable to proceed farther, because it grazes the atom B, is there arrested without any obstacle as if it were an enchanted object. Nor does it suffice to say that no such atoms are given, and that no others exist unless spherical or at least bounded by convex surfaces. For it suffices that atoms bounded by plain or concave sides are possible, if those bounded by convex sides are possible; and from the supposed possibility of these that which is absurd follows, whence it follows that convex atoms are not to be admitted.

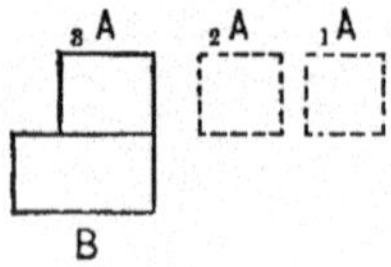

Fig. 2.

But if any one because of these considerations now requires no longer superficial contact only, but also the rest of bodies tangent to each other for cohesion, lest forsooth one atom be kept from sliding upon another, that one is unable to bring forth proof of his opinion, nor does it appear why the nature and the force of the present state which is contact must depend upon a past state, so that forsooth the present contact causes cohesion, if it has remained for some considerable time in the same place, as if there were need of a certain habitude, whence indeed it would follow that stability is increased by duration and that atoms newly produced are the more stable the longer they cohere, a fact which no one will surely easily affirm. But neither can the moment be assigned in which the cohesion of two atoms begins, because it is entirely perfect at once. And if it does not begin unless it has continued for some time, it will never begin, for it would itself be prior to itself. Moreover, all rest can be understood as composed of two motions, so that if a body is moved at the same time by two moving bodies and so remains quiet accidentally, shall it then be understood also to adhere to the sides of another body which it grazes? And so whithersoever we are turned, we fall into ἄπορα, which is not strange, because we assumed an hypothesis lacking in reason, namely, that the highest stability is without an intelligible cause.

But if any one thinks that atoms can be produced at least by the decree of God, we confess to him that God can make atoms, but a perpetual miracle would be needed to resist a forcible separation, since in a body itself a principle of perfect stability cannot be perceived. God can perform whatever is possible, but it is not always possible to transfer his power to creatures, and to bring it to pass that they themselves can do *per se* what they accomplish through his own power alone.

IV

ESSAY ON DYNAMICS ON THE LAWS OF MOTION, IN WHICH IT IS SHOWN THAT NOT THE SAME QUANTITY OF MOTION IS PRESERVED, BUT THE SAME ABSOLUTE FORCE, OR RATHER THE SAME QUANTITY OF MOVING ACTION (*L'ACTION MOTRICE*)[1]

[*From the French*]

The opinion that the same quantity of motion is preserved and abides in the concourse of bodies has reigned a long time, and passed as an incontestable axiom among modern philosophers. We understand by the *quantity of motion* the product of the mass by the velocity, so that the mass of the body being as 2 and the velocity as 3, the quantity of motion of the body will be as 6. Thus if there were two concurrent bodies, multiplying the mass of each by its velocity and taking the sum of the products, it is maintained that this sum must be the same before and after the concourse.

We begin now to be disabused of this opinion, especially since it has been abandoned by some of its most ancient, most skilful, and most eminent defenders, and above all by the author himself of the "Search after Truth."[2] But in this case an inconvenience has arisen, namely, that we have been thrown too far into the other extreme, and do not recognize the conservation of anything absolute which might hold the place of the quantity of motion. But our mind looks for this, and it is for this reason that I remark that philosophers who do

[1] Gerhardt, *Leibniz. math. Schrift.*, II. 2 [Vol. 6], pp. 215–231. Published from the Ms. in the Royal Library at Hanover. Written, according to Gerhardt, probably about 1691, *cf. op. cit.*, *Einleitung*, p. 14. — Tr.

[2] *Cf. ante*, p. 176, note 1. — Tr.

not enter into the profound discussions of mathematicians have difficulty in abandoning an axiom such as this of the quantity of conserved motion without giving themselves another to which they may hold.

It is true that the mathematicians who a long time since established the rules of motion based on experiments have remarked that the same relative velocity is preserved between the concurrent bodies. For example, if one of the two is at rest, or if both are in motion, and proceed the one against the other, or in the same direction, there is a relative velocity, with which they approach or depart the one from the other; and we find that this relative velocity remains the same, so that the bodies depart after the impact with the velocity with which they were approaching before the impact. But this relative velocity can remain the same although the true velocities and absolute forces of the bodies change in an infinite number of ways, so that this conservation does not concern that which is absolute in bodies.

I remark also another conservation, namely, that of the quantity of progress, but neither is this the conservation of that which is absolute. I call *progress* the quantity of motion with which a body proceeds in a certain direction, so that if the body went in a contrary direction, this progress would be a negative quantity. Now if two or more bodies are concurrent, we take the progress from the direction whence proceeds their common centre of gravity, and if all these bodies proceed from the same direction, then we must take the sum of the progress of each for the total progress; and it is plain that in this case the total progress and the total quantity of motion of the bodies are the same thing. But if one of the bodies proceeded from a contrary direction, its progress in the direction in question would be negative and consequently must be subtracted from the others in order to have the total progress. Thus if there are only two bodies, one of which proceeds in the direction of the common centre, and the other in a contrary direction, from the quantity of motion of the first must be subtracted that of the second, and the remainder will be the total progress. Now it will be found that the total progress is conserved, or that there is as much progress in the same direction before or after the impact. But it is also plain that this conservation does not correspond to that which is demanded of something absolute. For it may happen that the velocity, quantity of motion, and force of bodies being very considerable, their progress is null. This occurs when the two opposed bodies have their quantities of motion equal. In such case, according to the sense we have just given, there is no total progress at all.

Long since I corrected and rectified this doctrine of the conservation of the Quantity of Motion, and put in its place the conservation of some other absolute thing; but as regards the precise form in which this doctrine should be conceived,[1] that is to say, the conservation of absolute force, it is true that commonly they do not appear to have entered sufficiently into my reasons nor to have apprehended the beauty of that which I have observed, as I remark in all that has been published in France or elsewhere on the laws of motion and mechanics, even after what I have written on Dynamics. But as some of the most profound mathematicians after many discussions have yielded to my opinion, I promise myself with time general approval. To return then to what I said of the conservation of absolute force, we must know that the origin of the error concerning the quantity of motion arises from that which has taken it as force. We have been led, I think, naturally to believe that the same quantity of the total force abides before or after the impact of the bodies, and I have found this very true. Now the quantity of motion and force being taken as one and the same thing, we have concluded that the quantity of motion is conserved. What has contributed the most to confound force with quantity of motion is the abuse of the static doctrine. For we find in statics that two bodies are in equilibrium when in virtue of their position their velocities are reciprocal to their masses or weights, or when they have the same quantity of motion.

But we must know that this equality of force in this case arises from another principle, for generally *absolute force* must be estimated by the violent effect which it can produce. I call *the effect violent* which consumes the force of the agent, as, for example, to give such a velocity to a given body, to raise a given body to such a height, etc. And we can conveniently estimate the force of a heavy body by the product of the mass or of the weight multiplied by the height to which the body might rise by virtue of its motion. Now two bodies being in equilibrium, their heights to which they might rise or from which they might descend are reciprocal to their weights, or rather the products of the heights by the weights are equal. And it happens only in the case of equilibrium or of dead force, that the heights are as the velocities, and that thus the products of the weights by the velocities are as the products of the weights by the heights.[2] This, I say, happens only in the case of *dead force*, or of the infinitely small motion which I am accustomed to call *solicitation*, which takes place

[1] The French is: "Mais justement de cette chose qu'il fallait." — Tr.

[2] On the margin of the manuscript Leibnitz has remarked: "Thus it is astonishing that Descartes has avoided so well the rock of velocity taken for force, in his little treatise on Statics or dead force, where there was some danger, having reduced all to weights and heights, when it was indifferent, and that he has abandoned the heights for the velocities in the case where he should have done wholly the contrary; that is to say, when he discusses percussions or living forces which must be measured by weights and heights." — *Gerhardt's Note.* — Tr.

when a heavy body tries to commence movement, and has not yet conceived any impetuosity; and this happens precisely when bodies are in equilibrium, and, trying to descend, are mutually hindered. But when a heavy body has made some progress in descending freely, and has conceived some impetuosity or *living force*, then the heights to which this body might attain are not proportional to the velocities, but to the squares of the velocities. And it is for this reason that in case of living force the forces are not as the quantities of motion or as the products of the masses by the velocities.

Nevertheless it is noticeable, and has contributed to the error,[1] that two bodies unequal in absolute living force, — for it is of this I speak, — but whose quantity of motion is equal, can stop each other, which fact has made men believe them absolutely equal in force; as, for example two bodies *A* of mass 3 velocity 2, and *B* of mass 2 velocity 3. For although *A* is absolutely weaker than *B*, *A* being able to raise a pound only 12 feet, if *B* can raise a pound 18 feet; nevertheless in the concourse they can stop each other, the reason of which is that bodies are hindered only according to the laws of dead or static force. For being elastic as we suppose, they act between themselves only by dead forces or according to the equilibrium in the concourse, that is to say, by inassignable changes, because in pressing, resisting, and continually weakening each other more and more until they come to rest, they destroy one another at each moment only by the infinitely small motion, or dead force, equal on both sides; now the quantity of dead force is estimated according to the laws of equilibrium by the quantity of motion, infinitely small in truth, but whose continual repetition exhausts at last the whole quantity of motion of the two bodies, which being supposed equal in both bodies, each quantity of motion is exhausted in the same time, and consequently the two bodies are reduced to rest in the same time by the pressures of their elasticities, which, restoring themselves afterwards, reproduce the motion. It is (in) this continual diminution of the quantity of motion according to the equilibrium in the concourse of the two elasticities that the cause of this paradox consists, that two absolute unequal forces, but which have the quantities of motion equal, must stop each other because this happens in a relative action where the contest takes place only according to the quantities of motion infinitely small continually repeated.

Now it is found by reason and by experiment, that it is *living absolute force*, or that which is estimated by the violent effect it can produce, which is preserved, and nowise the quantity of motion. For if this living force could ever be augmented, the effect would be more

[1] The French text reads: "Cependant il est remarquable et à contribuer à l'erreur," etc. The reading should be: "et a contribué," etc. — Tr.

powerful than the cause, or rather the perpetual mechanical motion, that is to say, which could reproduce its cause and something more, which is absurd. But if the force could be diminished, it would perish at last entirely; for never being able to increase, and being able nevertheless to diminish, it would always go more and more into decay, which is without doubt contrary to the order of things. Experiment confirms it also, and we shall find always that if bodies should convert their horizontal into ascending motions, they could always raise on the whole the same weight to the same height before or after the impact, supposing that no force has been absorbed in the impact by the parts of the bodies, when these bodies are not perfectly elastic, without speaking of that which the medium, the base, and other circumstances absorb. But as this is a thing which I have sufficiently explained before, I will not repeat it here.

Now I am very happy to give still another turn to the matter and to show further the conservation of something approaching more the quantity of motion, namely, *the conservation of moving action (l'action motrice)*. Here then is the general rule that I establish. Whatever changes may take place between concurrent bodies, of whatever number, *there must always be in the concurring bodies between themselves alone the same quantity of moving action in one and the same interval of time.* For example, there must be during this hour as much moving action in the universe or in the given bodies, acting between themselves alone, as there will be during any other hour whatever.

To understand this rule, it is necessary to explain the estimate of moving action (*l'action motrice*), wholly different from the quantity of motion, in the manner that the quantity of motion has been wont to be understood as has been explained above. Now in order that the moving action may be estimated, we must first estimate the *formal effect* of motion. This formal or essential effect of motion consists in that which is changed by the motion, namely, in the quantity of the mass which is transferred, and in the space or in the length through which this mass is transferred. There is the essential effect of motion, or that which finds itself changed: for this body was there, now it is here: the body is so much and the distance is so much. I conceive in order to greater facility that the body is moved so that each point describes a straight line equal and parallel to that of every other point of the same body. I mean also a motion uniform and continuous. This assumed, the *formal effect of motion* is the product of the mass which is transferred multiplied by the length of the removal, or rather the formal effects are in reason composed of the masses and the lengths of the removal, so that a body, as 2, being transported the length of 3 feet, and another body, as 3, being transported the length of 2 feet, the formal effects are equal. It is necessary carefully to distinguish what I here call the *formal effect*, or that essential to motion, from that which I called above the *violent effect*. For the violent effect consumes the force and is exercised upon something without; but the formal effect consists in the body in motion, taken in itself, and does not consume the force, and even conserves it rather, since the same translation of the same mass must always be continued, if nothing from without prevents; it is for this reason that the absolute forces are as the violent effects which consume them, but nowise as the formal effects.

Now it will be easier to understand what moving action (*l'action motrice*) is: it must then be estimated not only by the formal effect which it produces, but also by the vigor or velocity with which it produces it. We wish to transport 100 pounds to a distant place; that is the formal effect which is demanded. One desires to do it in one hour, another in two hours; I say that the action of the first is double that of the second, being doubly quick with reference to an equal effect. I suppose always continual and uniform motion. We may say also that a body, as 3, being transported the length of 5 feet, in 15 minutes, is the same action as if a body, as 1, were transported the length of one foot in one minute.

This definition of moving action (*l'action motrice*) is justified sufficiently *a priori* because it is manifest that in a purely formal action taken by itself, as is here that of a moving body considered by itself, there are two points to examine,—the formal effect or that which is changed, and the promptness of the change; for it is very manifest that that which produces the same formal effect in less time is the more active. But if any one is obstinately bent upon disputing with me this definition of moving action, it would suffice me to say that I am free to call moving action what I just explained, provided that nature justifies afterwards the reality of this nominal definition, which will be when I shall show that it is precisely this whose quantity nature conserves.

Now since moving action is that which comes by multiplying the formal effect by the velocity, I wish to give more distinctly the estimate of velocity. We know that when two movable bodies run over uniformly the same space in unequal times, the velocity of that one which runs over it in less time will be the greater, in proportion as the time is shorter. Thus the spaces gone over being equal, the velocities are reciprocally proportional to the times. But if the times were equal, the velocities would be as the spaces gone over. For one body in motion having gone over a foot in one minute, and the other two feet, it is manifest that the velocity of the second is double. Thus the velocities are in reason composed of the direct of the spaces gone over and of the reciprocal of the times employed. Or what is the same thing, to estimate the velocity, we must take the space and divide it by the time. For example, *A* accomplishes 4 feet in 3 seconds and B 2 feet in 1 second; the velocity of A will be as 4 divided by 3, namely as $\frac{4}{3}$, and the velocity of B will be as 2 divided by 1, namely as 2, so that the velocity of A will be to that of B as $\frac{4}{3}$ to 2, that is to say, as 2 to 3.

Now the question is to verify the conservation of the moving action (*l'action motrice*). I can give its general demonstration in a few words, because I have already proved elsewhere that the same force is conserved, and because at bottom the exercise of force or the force taken at the time is action, the abstract nature of force consisting only in that. Thus since the same force is conserved, and since action is the product of the force by the time, the same action will be conserved in equal times. But I wish to verify it by the detail of the laws of motion established by experiment and commonly received. I shall content myself with one example; but we shall find it the same in every other example we might choose. And indeed we could see at once the general reason of it, by making the calculation *in abstracto*, or in general and by letters, without employing any particular numbers. But to suit the intelligence of everybody I prefer to give an example in numbers.

Let there be a right angle LMN (Fig. 3), whose sides LM, MN may

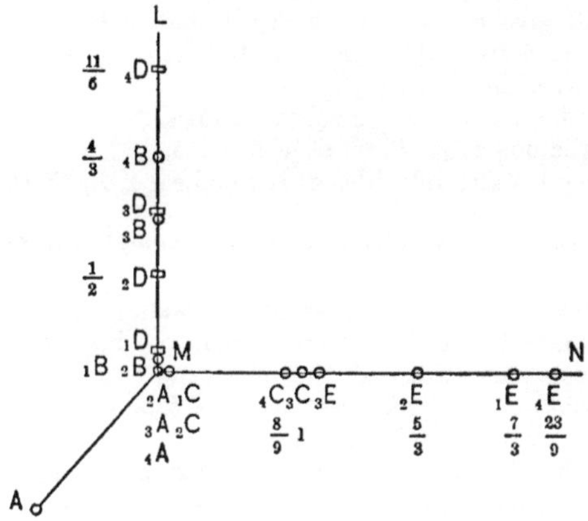

FIG. 3.

be prolonged at discretion. Let a straight line AM be taken, so that prolonged beyond the point M it would cut the angle LMN into two equal parts. We might consider $_1AM$ as the hypotenuse of a square whose side may be called 1. This being so, I suppose that the body, A,[1]

[1] We take no account here of the thickness of the bodies, which we suppose inconsiderable.—*Leibnitz's Note.*

being in the place ${}_1A$ at the moment 1, A goes from the point ${}_1A$ to the point M, during the time 1, 2, and there meets at the moment 2 the two bodies B and C, which had been in repose during the 1, 2, which is known in the figure in that their place is designated by ${}_1B$ and by ${}_2B$, as also by ${}_1C$ and by ${}_2C$. Now the body A meeting the two bodies in M at the moment 2, being in M or ${}_2A$, will drive them forward and come to rest in M, a point which will also be ${}_3A$ and ${}_4A$, because A will remain there during the times 2, 3 and 3, 4, as I suppose the two mutually equal, and to the times 1, 2. But B will go towards L from the moment 2 during the time 2, 3 with a velocity as 1, and will meet at the moment 3 the body D, which had before gone in front of it during the times 1, 2, from the place ${}_1D$ to the place ${}_2D$, and during the times 2, 3, from the place ${}_2D$ to the place ${}_3D$, with a velocity as $\frac{1}{2}$. Now B, meeting D at the moment 3, will give it the velocity ${}_3D_4D$; that is to say, in the times 3, 4, ${}_1D$ will reach ${}_4D$, and during that time, B will go from ${}_3B$ to ${}_4B$ with the velocity ${}_3B_4B$. It will be the same on the other side, where C, pushed by A in the moment 2, will go towards N with the velocity 1, and will meet, at the moment 3, the body E, which goes against it, having gone before, during the times 1, 2, from the place ${}_1E$ to the place ${}_2E$, and during the times 2, 3 from the place ${}_2E$ to the place ${}_3E$, with a velocity as $\frac{2}{3}$. Now C, meeting E at the moment 3, will give it the velocity ${}_3E_4E$; that is to say, that in the times 3, 4, it comes from ${}_3E$ to ${}_4E$. And during this time, C will go from ${}_3C$ to ${}_4C$ with the velocity ${}_3C_4C$.

The register of the masses and velocities follows.

The masses of the bodies A, B, C, D, E are 1, 1, 1, 2, $\frac{1}{2}$.

During the times 1, 2 the velocities of the bodies A, B, C, D, E are $\sqrt{2}$, 0, 0, $\frac{1}{2}$, $\frac{2}{3}$.

During the times 2, 3 the velocities of the bodies A, B, C, D, E are 0, 1, 1, $\frac{1}{2}$, $\frac{2}{3}$.

During the times 3, 4 the velocities of the bodies A, B, C, D, E are 0, $\frac{1}{3}$, $\frac{1}{9}$, $\frac{5}{6}$, $\frac{14}{9}$, where it is to be remarked that the body C, instead of advancing, reflects backward with the velocity $\frac{1}{9}$.

The justification of these numbers will be found in the rules or equations which we shall assign farther on.

Let us now make the calculation of the moving actions (*actions motrices*) during the times equal between them — 1, 2; 2, 3; 3, 4.

During the times 1, 2.

A is in mass 1, the length of the transfer ${}_1A_2A$ is $\sqrt{2}$. Then multiplying one by the other, the formal effect is $\sqrt{2}$. The velocity comes from dividing the length $\sqrt{2}$ by the time 1, which makes $\sqrt{2}$. And multiplying the effect by the velocity, the moving action is 2.

B and C are at rest during this time in ${}_1B$, ${}_2B$, or ${}_1C$, ${}_2C$, consequently their moving action is 0.

D is in mass 2, the length of the transfer $\frac{1}{2}$, the formal effect 2 by $\frac{1}{2}$ or 1. The length $\frac{1}{2}$ being divided by the time 1, the velocity $\frac{1}{2}$ arises, and the effect multiplied by the velocity is 1 by $\frac{1}{2}$, or $\frac{1}{2}$, which is the action of D.

E is in mass $\frac{1}{2}$, the length of the transfer $\frac{2}{3}$, consequently the effect $\frac{1}{3}$. Now the length $\frac{2}{3}$ divided by 1 gives the velocity $\frac{2}{3}$, which, multiplied by the effect, furnishes $\frac{2}{9}$ the action of E.

And the sum of all the moving actions of the bodies A, B, C, D, E, during the times 1, 2, is $2+0+0+\frac{1}{2}+\frac{2}{9}=\frac{49}{18}$.

During the times 2, 3.

A is at rest, and its action is 0.

B is in mass 1, the length of the transfer 1 (namely, ${}_2B_3B$), the formal effect 1; the length 1 divided by the time 1 gives the velocity 1, which, being multiplied by the effect 1, 1 arises, which is the action of B.

C; the calculation is the same in regard to C and there arises the same action 1.

D has the same action as in the preceding time; namely, $\frac{1}{2}$.

E likewise has the same action as in the preceding time; namely, $\frac{2}{9}$.

And the sum of all the moving actions of the bodies A, B, C, D, E, during the times 2, 3, is $0+1+1+\frac{1}{2}+\frac{2}{9}=\frac{49}{18}$, as before.

Finally, during the time 3, 4.

A is at rest, and its action is 0.

B is in mass 1, the length of the transfer, namely, ${}_3B_4B$, is $\frac{1}{3}$, consequently the effect is $\frac{1}{3}$. The same length, $\frac{1}{3}$, divided by the time 1, gives $\frac{1}{3}$ for the velocity, which multiplied by the effect, $\frac{1}{9}$ arises, the action of B.

C is in mass 1, the length of the transfer ${}_3C_4C$ is $\frac{1}{9}$, consequently the formal effect is $\frac{1}{9}$. For it matters not here when we seek absolute things, whether C advances by ${}_3C_4C$, or reflects backward, as it does in fact. The same length, $\frac{1}{9}$, divided by the time 1 gives the velocity $\frac{1}{9}$, which, multiplied by the effect, there arises $\frac{1}{81}$ as the action of C.

D is in mass 2, the length of the transfer ${}_3D_4D$ is $\frac{5}{6}$, consequently the effect is $\frac{5}{3}$. The same length divided by the time 1 is $\frac{5}{6}$, or the velocity, which multiplied by the effect, there arises $\frac{25}{18}$, which is the action of D.

E is in mass $\frac{1}{2}$, the length of the transfer is $\frac{14}{9}$, the effect $\frac{7}{9}$. The same length divided by the time 1 is $\frac{14}{9}$, that is to say, the velocity, which, multiplied by the effect, produces $\frac{98}{81}$ for the action of E.

And the sum of all the moving actions of the bodies A, B, C, D, E, during the time 3, 4, is

$$0+\frac{1}{9}+\frac{1}{81}+\frac{25}{18}+\frac{98}{81}=\frac{18+2+225+196}{162}=\frac{441}{162}=\frac{49}{18},$$

as in each one of the preceding times.

I have followed in this calculation the general method, for as the moving actions are not only equal in equal times, but proportional to the times in unequal times, I have divided the space by the time, in order to have the velocity; but when the time is always the same, as here, and thus we can take it as unity, the division by the time changes nothing, and consequently for the velocity we can take the number of the length of the transfer, the velocities being as the spaces: whence it is manifest that the effect being the product of the mass and the space, and the velocity being as the space, the action is as the product of the mass by the square of the space of the transfer (we mean a horizontal transfer in falling bodies), or as the product of the mass by the square of the velocity. Now, I shall prove, further on, in the 3d equation, that the sum of these products of the masses by the squares of the velocities is conserved in the concourse of the bodies. Consequently, it is proved that the moving action is conserved, without speaking of other proofs by which I have shown elsewhere that the forces are conserved, and that the forces are as the products of the masses by the squares of the velocities, while the actions are as the products of the forces by the times, so that if we did not know elsewhere this estimate and conservation of force, we might learn it here, in finding by the calculation in detail, or even in general, by the 3d equation, further on, that the moving action is conserved; now it is clear that the moving actions are in reason composed of the forces and the times, and the times being the same, the moving actions are as the powers or forces.

But shall we be astonished whence comes this success, which will never fail, however intricate may be the example which we may choose? It may be proved *a priori*, independently of the rules of motion received; and this is what I have shown many times in different ways. But here I shall show that it is proved by these very rules of percussion which experience has justified, and whose *rationale* we may give by the method of a boat, as Huygens has done, and in many other ways, although we are always obliged to assume something non-mathematical, which has its source higher. But I shall reduce the whole to three equations very simple and beautiful, and which contain all which concerns the central concourse of two bodies in one and the same straight line.

Conspiring velocities			
of the body	a before the impact	v after	x.
	b	y	z.

I call these *conspiring velocities*, because I suppose they all tend from the side whence proceeds the centre of gravity common to the two bodies. But if perchance any velocity proceeds really in the contrary direction, then the letter which expresses the conspiring velocity signifies a negative quantity. But we shall always take the body a as a body whose velocity is really conspiring, or proceeds from the side of the centre of gravity before the impact, and also in such a manner that the body a follows and does not precede the common centre of gravity. Thus the signs do not vary in v, but they may vary in y, z, x. Here, now, are our three equations:—

I. *Lineal equation*, which expresses the conservation of the cause of the impact, or of the relative velocity

$$v - y = z - x,$$

and $v - y$ signifies the relative velocity between the bodies before the impact with which they approach, and $z - x$ signifies the relative velocity with which they depart after the impact. And this relative velocity is always the same in quantity before or after the impact, supposing that the bodies are very elastic, which this equation states. It is necessary only to remark that while the signs vary in the explication of the detail, this general rule will embrace all the particular cases. This also occurs in the following equation:—

II. *Plane equation*, which expresses the conservation of the common or total progress of the two bodies

$$av + by = ax + bz.$$

I call *progress* here the quantity of motion which proceeds from the side of the centre of gravity, so that if the body b, for example, should proceed in the contrary direction before the impact, and thus its conspiring velocity y be negative or be expressed by $-(y)$, understanding by (y) mass (*molem*), or that which is positive in y, then the progress of a will be av, the progress of b will be $-b(y)$. And the total progress will be $av - b(y)$, which is the difference of the quantities of motion of the two bodies. If the bodies a and b proceed from one and the same side before and after the impact, these letters, v, y, x, z, signify only conspiring velocities real or affirmative, and consequently in this case it appears by this equation that the same quantity of motion will be conserved after and before the impact. But if the bodies a and b should proceed in a contrary direction before the impact and in the same direction after the impact, the difference of the quantity of motion before the impact would be equal to the sum of the quantity of motion after the impact. And there will be other similar variations according to the variation of the signs of the letters y, x, z.

III. *Solid equation*, which expresses the conservation of the total absolute force or of the moving action

$$avv + byy = axx + bzz.$$

This equation has this excellence, that all the variations of the signs which can arise only from the diverse direction of the velocities y, x, z, y cease, by the fact that all the letters which express these velocities mount here to the square. Now $-y$ and $+y$ have the same square $+yy$, so that all these different directions of y produce nothing more. And it is also for that reason that this equation gives something absolute, independent of the relative velocities, or of the progressions from a certain side. The question here concerns only the estimating of masses and velocities, without troubling ourselves from what side these velocities arise. And this it is which satisfies at the same time the rigor of the mathematicians and the wish of the philosophers, — the experiments and reasons drawn from different principles.

Although I put together these three equations for the sake of beauty and harmony, nevertheless two of them might suffice for our needs. For, taking any two of these equations, we can infer from them the remaining one. Thus, the first and the second give the third in the following manner. By the first, we shall have $v + x = y + z$; by the second, we shall have $a, v - x = b, z - y$; and, multiplying one equation by the other, according to the corresponding sides, we shall have $a, v - x, v + x = b, z - y, z + y$, which makes $avv - axx = bzz - byy$, or the third equation. In the same way, the first and the third give the second; for $a, vv - xx = b, zz - yy$, which is the third, divided by the first $v + x = z + y$, side by side, we shall have $a, vv - xx, :, v + x = b, zz - yy, :, z + y$, which makes $a, v - x = b, z - y$, that is, the second equation. Finally, the second and the third equation give the first. For the third $a, vv - xx = b, zz - yy$ divided by the second, namely, by $a, v - x = b, z - y$, gives

$$\frac{a, vv - xx}{a, v - x} = \frac{b, zz - yy}{b, z - y},$$

which makes $v + x = z + y$, according to the first equation.

I would add only one remark, which is that many distinguish between hard and soft bodies, and the hard themselves as elastic or not, and build thereupon different rules. But we may take bodies naturally as hard-elastic, without however denying that the elasticity must always come from a fluid more subtile and penetrating, whose motion is disturbed by the tension or by the change of the elasticity. And as this fluid must be composed itself in its turn of little solid bodies, elastic between themselves, we see well that this replication of solids and of fluids continues to infinity. Now this elasticity of bodies is necessary to nature, in order to obtain the execution of the grand and beautiful laws which its infinitely wise author has proposed, among which not the least are these two laws of nature which I first made known, *the first* of which is *the law of the conservation of absolute force* or of moving action in the universe, with some other absolutely new conservations which depend upon it and which I will explain some day, and *the second* is *the law of continuity*, in virtue of which, among other effects, every change must take place through inassignable passages and never by a leap. This also is the reason why nature suffers no hard non-elastic bodies. In order to show this, let us pretend that a hard non-elastic globe proceeds to strike against a similar globe at rest: after the impact it is necessary that the two globes rest, in which case the law of the conservation of force is violated, or that there be some motion and that the globe which was at rest receive it, being unable to be taken as immovable, although even if it should feign to be such, the striking body (in order to preserve the force) would necessarily be reflected suddenly backward. This is a forbidden (*defendu*) change, since it would be by a leap, a body which proceeds from a certain side being obliged to abate its motion, even to rest, before beginning to proceed gradually further and further backward. But the globe which is struck being obliged to receive motion, there will also be a change by a leap, the struck globe which was at rest being obliged to receive a certain degree of velocity suddenly, not being pliable so as to receive it gradually and by degrees. It being also manifest, as is necessary, either that the globe striking passes suddenly to rest, which would be already a change by a leap, or that if this striking globe retains a certain velocity, the struck globe which was at rest receives suddenly an amount which is not less than that of the striking globe, since the globe struck must either stop the striking globe, or go before it. Thus the striking globe passes suddenly from velocity to rest, or at least the struck globe passes suddenly from rest to a certain degree of velocity, without passing through the intermediate degrees, which is contrary to the law of continuity, which admits no change by a leap in nature. I have also many other reasons all of which concur in banishing hard non-elastic bodies, but this is not the place to enlarge upon them.

But it is necessary to admit, that although bodies must be thus naturally elastic in the sense which I have just explained, nevertheless the elasticity often appears insufficient in the masses or bodies which we employ, even if these masses should be composed of elastic parts and should resemble a sack full of hard balls which would yield to a moderate impact, without leaving the sack, as we see in the case of soft bodies or those which yield without recovering themselves sufficiently. The reason is that the parts are not sufficiently united therein to transfer their change to the whole. Whence it comes that in the impact of such bodies a part of the force is absorbed by the small parts which compose the mass, without this force being given to the whole; and this must always happen when the pressed mass does not recover perfectly; although it also happens that a mass shows itself more or less elastic according to the different manner of the impact, witness the water itself which yields to a moderate impression, and makes a cannon-ball rebound.

Now when the parts of the bodies absorb the force of the impact, as a whole, as when two pieces of rich earth or of clay come into collision, or in part, as when two wooden balls meet, which are much less elastic than two globes of jasper or tempered steel; when, I say, some force is absorbed by the parts, it is as good as lost for the absolute force, and for the respective velocity, that is to say, for the third and the first equation, which do not succeed, since that which remains after the impact has become less than what it was before the impact, by reason of a part of the force being turned elsewhere. But the quantity of progress, or rather the second equation, is not concerned therein. And even the motion of this total progress remains alone, when the two bodies proceed together after the impact with the velocity of their common centre, as do two balls of rich earth or clay. But in the semi-elastics, as two wooden balls, it happens still further that the bodies mutually depart after the impact, although with a weakening of the first equation, following this force of the impact which has not been absorbed. And in consequence of certain experiments touching the degree of the elasticity of this wood, we might predict what should happen to the balls which should be made of it in every kind of collision or impact. But this loss of the total force, or this failure of the third equation, does not detract from the inviolable truth of the law of the conservation of the same force in the world. For that which is absorbed by the minute parts is not absolutely lost for the universe, although it is lost for the total force of the concurrent bodies.

V

ESSAY ON DYNAMICS IN DEFENCE OF THE WONDERFUL LAWS OF NATURE IN RESPECT TO THE FORCES OF BODIES, DISCLOSING THEIR MUTUAL ACTIONS AND REFERRING THEM TO THEIR CAUSES[1]

[*From the Latin*]

Part I

From the time we made mention of the founding of a New Science of Dynamics, many distinguished men in various places have asked for a fuller explication of this doctrine. Since, therefore, we have not

[1] Gerhardt, *Leibniz. math. Schrift.*, II., 2 [Vol. 6], pp. 234–246. Dutens, *Leibnit. op. om.*, 3, 315–324. First published in the "Acta Eruditor. Lips.," in April, 1695.—Tr.

yet leisure to compose the book,[1] we will give in this place those things which may kindle some light, which perhaps will return to us with interest, if, indeed, we shall elicit the opinions of those who unite energy of thought with elegance of speech, whose judgments also we openly confess will be acceptable to us, and we hope useful in the setting forward of the work. We have elsewhere suggested that there is in corporeal things something besides extension, nay, prior to extension, namely, the force itself of nature everywhere implanted by its Author, which consists, not in the simple faculty with which the schools seem to have been content, but, besides, is provided with a tendency (*conatu*) or effort (*nisu*) which will have its full effect unless impeded by a contrary tendency (*conatu*). This effort often appears to the senses, and in my judgment is known everywhere in matter by the reason, even when it does not appear to the sense. But if now this force must not be assigned to God through a miracle, it is certainly necessary that this force in bodies themselves be produced from the body itself, nay, that it constitute the inmost nature of bodies, since to act is a mark of substances, and extension means nothing else than the continuation or diffusion of the already presupposed struggling and withstanding, that is, resisting substance, so far is it from being itself able to produce substance. Nor is it necessary, because every corporeal action arises (*est*) from motion, and motion itself does not exist unless from motion, either in the body already before existing or impressed from something external to it (*aliunde*). For motion (just as time) never exists, if you reduce the thing to ἀκρίβειαν, because a whole never exists, when it has not coexisting parts. And nothing is so real in itself, as that momentary increment (*momentaneum*) which must be constituted in a force striving for change. To this, therefore, returns whatever there is in corporeal nature besides the object of geometry or extension. And by this method, in fact, regard is had at the same time for both the truth and the doctrine of the ancients. And as our age has freed from contempt the atoms of Democritus, the ideas of Plato, and the tranquillity of the Stoics in the best nexus of things, so now the traditions of the Peripatetics concerning forms or entelechies (which deservedly seemed enigmatical and scarcely rightly perceived by the authors themselves) will be referred to intelligible notions, so that we think it necessary rather to explain the philosophy thus received by so many ages, so that it may be consistent (where this is permitted) and to illustrate and then increase it with new truths, than to destroy it.

And this kind of studies seems to me especially suited both to the intelligence (*prudentiæ*) of the teacher and to the profit of the learners,

[1] For the work referred to, *cf.* Gerhardt, *Leibniz. math. Schrift.*, II., 2 [Vol. 6], pp. 281 *sq.* — Tr.

so that we may not seem more desirous of destroying than of building, nor be tossed between perpetual changes of doctrine, daily uncertain because of the pride of audacious geniuses, but at length the human race, the lust of sects being curbed (which the inane glory of change [*novandi*] stimulates), the certain dogmas established, without stumbling, not less in philosophy than in mathematics, will make further advance, since in the writings of distinguished men, ancient and modern (if you take away entirely those things in which they speak too severely against others), there is wont to be very much that is true and good, which deserves to be rescued and to be distributed into the public treasury. And would that men preferred to do this rather than spend their time in censures by which they only appease their own vanity. But somehow very many even hostile views do not displease us certainly, whom fortune has so favored in certain new views of ours, that friends often bade us think of these only, and each view is considered according to its own value, although diverse; the reason of which perhaps is that in discussing many things we have learned to despise nothing. But now let us return to our subject.

Active force (which with some you call not ill *power — virtus*) is twofold, namely *primitive*, which exists in every corporeal substance *per se* (since I think a wholly quiescent body abhorrent to the nature of things), or *derivative*, which by a limitation as it were of the primitive, resulting through the conflicts of bodies with each other, is variously exercised. And the primitive force indeed (which is nothing else than ἐντελέχεια ἡ πρώτη) corresponds to *the substantial soul or form*, but indeed for this reason pertains only to general causes, which cannot suffice for the explanation of phenomena. And so we agree with those who deny that forms must be employed in handing down the particular and special causes of sensible things: to point out which is worth while, lest, while we lead them as it were back again to the open fountains of things, at the same time we seem to desire to return to the 'vain repetitions' (*battologias*) of the vulgar school. Meanwhile a knowledge of them is necessary to correct philosophizing, nor may any one think he is master of the nature of body, unless he has turned his mind to such things and understood that that crass notion of corporeal substance is imperfect, not to say false, and depends upon the imagination alone and was introduced inconsiderately some years since by an abuse of the corpuscular philosophy (in itself excellent and most true), as indeed is evident by this argument which does not entirely exclude cessation and rest from matter, and cannot bring forward reasons for the laws controlling the derivative force of nature. In like manner passive force also is twofold, either primitive or derivative. And indeed *the primitive force of enduring or resisting* constitutes that very thing which is called *primary matter*, if you rightly interpret it, in the schools, by which it happens that body is not penetrated by body, but forms an obstacle to it, and it is endowed at the same time with a certain laziness, so to speak, that is, repugnance to motion, and does not indeed suffer itself to be set in motion unless by the somewhat broken force of the active body. Whence afterwards *the derivative force of enduring* variously exhibits itself in *secondary matter*. But it is our part now to proceed farther, having removed those general and primitive forces and substituted those by which we are taught that because of form every body always acts and because of matter every body always endures and resists, and in this doctrine *of derivative forces and resistances* to investigate how far bodies prevail by various efforts or again variously resist; for the laws of actions, which are known not only by reason, but are confirmed also by sense itself through phenomena, are adapted to these.

Derivative force therefore, by which bodies in action act mutually on each other or mutually suffer from each other, we understand in this place as no other than that which is connected with motion (*i.e.* local), and in turn tends to produce further local motion. For we admit that through local motion other material phenomena can be explained. Motion is a continual change of place, and thus requires time. Yet the movable element (*mobile*) existing in motion, as it has motion in time, so in any moment whatever has *velocity*, which is so much the greater as more space is run over and less time is expended. Velocity taken in connection with direction is called *conatus;* but *impetus* is the product of the mass of the body into the velocity, and its quantity is so much that the Cartesians are wont to call it the quantity of motion, namely, the momentary increment (*momentaneum*), although, speaking more accurately, the quantity of motion itself, existing forsooth in time, arises from the aggregate of the impetuses (equal or unequal) existing in the movable element in the given time multiplied in order into the time. We, nevertheless, in discussing with these have followed their fashion of speaking. Nay even as (not inconveniently for the doctrinal use of speaking) we can distinguish the accession which now is made from the accession already made or to be made, as an increment of accession or element; or as we may distinguish the present descent from the descent already made, which it increases; so we can discern and call Motion the momentary or instantaneous element of motion diffused by the motion itself through a period of time; and so that which is commonly ascribed to motion is called *the quantity of motion*. And although in the use of terms we are compliant (*faciles*) in accord with an accepted interpretation, nevertheless it especially behooves us to be careful in their use lest we be caught by their ambiguity.

Moreover, as the estimate of motion through a period of time is made from infinite impulses, so in turn the impulse itself (although a momentary thing) is made from infinite degrees successively impressed upon that same movable body (*mobile*), and has a certain element from which, unfolded, nothing but infinity can arise.

Conceive a tube AC (Fig. 4) to revolve with a certain fixed uniform velocity in the horizontal plane of this page about an immovable centre C, and a ball B, existing in the cavity of the tube, to be freed from its chain or impediment, and to begin to be moved by the centrifugal force; it is manifest that the attempt in the beginning to depart from the centre by which, namely, the ball in the tube tends towards its extremity A, is infinitely small in respect to the impulse which it already has from the rotation, or by which with the tube itself, the ball B tends from the place D towards (D), its distance from the centre being retained. But with the continuance for some time of the centrifugal impression proceeding from the rotation, from its own progress there must arise in the ball a certain complete centrifugal impulse $(D)(B)$, comparable with the impulse of rotation $D(D)$. Hence it is evident that the *effort* is twofold, elementary to be sure, or infinitely small, which I call, also, *solicitation*, and formed by the continuation or repetition of elementary efforts; that is, the impulse (*impetum*) itself, although I do not, for that reason, mean that these mathematical entities are really so found in nature, but only that they are useful in making accurate estimates by mental abstraction.

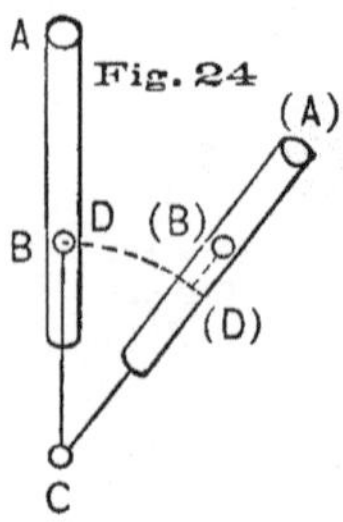

FIG. 4.

Hence *force* also is twofold: the one elementary, which I call also *dead*, because motion (*motus*) does not yet exist in it, but only a solicitation to motion (*solicitatio ad motum*), such as that of the ball in the tube, or of the stone in the sling, even while it is held still by the chain; the other, however, is ordinary force, united with actual motion, which I call *living*. And an example of dead force indeed is the centrifugal force itself, and likewise the force of gravity or centripetal force, the force also by which the tense elastic body (*elastrum*) begins to restore itself. But in percussion, which arises from a heavy body falling already for some time, or from a bow restoring itself for some time, or from a similar cause, the force is living force, which has arisen from an infinite number of continued impressions of dead force. And this is what Galileo meant, when in his enigmatical manner of speaking he spoke of the infinite force of percussion, namely if compared with the simple effort of gravity. But although the impulse (*impetus*) is always united with living force, yet we shall show below that these two are different.

Living force in any aggregate of bodies again can be known as twofold, namely *total,* or *partial;* and *partial* again is either respective or directive, that is, either proper or common to the parts. *Respective* (*respectiva*) or *proper* (*propria*) force is that by which the bodies comprised in the aggregate can act among themselves mutually; *directive* or *common* force is that by which, besides, this aggregate can act outside itself. But I call it direct, because the total force of direction is preserved intact in this partial force. But this alone would remain, if suddenly the aggregate were imagined to congeal by the intercepted motion of its parts among themselves. Whence from respective and directive taken together *total absolute force* is composed. But these things will be better understood from the rules to be propounded below.

The ancients, as far as known, had a science of dead force alone, and this it is which is commonly called Mechanics, treating of the lever, block, inclined plane (where belongs the wedge and the spiral), the equilibrium of liquids, and similar things, in which they treat in turn only of the first tendency (*conatu*) of the bodies among themselves, before they received an impulse by acting. And although the laws of dead force can in some fashion be transferred to living force, yet there is need of great caution, as even they may have been deceived, for this reason, who confounded force in general with the quantity produced by the multiplication of the mass into the velocity, because they understood that force is dead in the regular theory of these. For this thing happens there for a special reason, as we already long ago suggested, since (for example), in different descending weights, in the very beginning of motion at least the descents themselves or the quantities of the spaces gone through in the descent, certainly infinitely small or elementary hitherto, are proportional to the velocities or to the efforts to descend. But the progress being made and living force having arisen, the acquired velocities are no longer proportional to the spaces already run over in the descent, by which, nevertheless, we have shown formerly and shall further show, that the force must be estimated, but only to the elements of these velocities. Galileo began to discuss concerning living force (although under another name, nay, I should rather say, concept) and was the first to explain how by the acceleration of descending weights motion arises. Descartes rightly distinguished velocity from direction, and saw even in the conflict of bodies that follow by which the former conditions are least changed. But he did not rightly estimate the least change, while he changes the direction alone or the velocity alone, since the change moderated by mixing would be obtained from both: but how this must come about escaped him, because to him, intent at that time upon modal manifestations rather than upon realities, phenomena so heterogeneous did not seem capable of being compared and modified by union, so that we shall say no more of his other errors in this doctrine.

Honoratus Fabri,[1] Marcus Marci,[2] Joh. Alph. Borellus,[3] Ignatius Baptista Pardies,[4] and Claudius de Chales,[5] and other men very acute in learning have published things not to be despised on motion, but nevertheless have not shunned these capital errors. Huygens,[6] the first that I know who has adorned our age with splendid discoveries, seems to me in this argument also to have reached the pure and unadulterated truth and to have freed this doctrine from paralogisms,

[1] *Cf. ante*, p. 586, note 2.—Tr.

[2] Johannes Marcus Marci von Kronland, 1595–1667, a German physician, mathematician, and physicist, published his *De proportione motus, seu regula sphygmica ad celeritatem et tarditatem pulsuum, ex illius motu ponderibus geometricis librato, absque errore metiendam*, Pragæ, 1639, a remarkable work on the theory of impact, preceding by thirty years the researches of Wallis, Wren, and Huygens. This is probably the work to which Leibnitz here refers.—Tr.

[3] Giovanni Alfonso Borelli, 1608–1679, a distinguished Italian physician and mathematician, the founder of the iatromathematical theory of medicine, was Professor of Mathematics at Pisa and Naples. He was the author of several medical and mathematical works, among which were *Theorica mediceorum planetarum ex causis physicis deducta*, Florent., 1666; *De motu animalium*, Rome, 1680–1681; *De vi percussionis*, Lugd. Bat., 1686; and *De Motionibus naturalibus, a gravitate pendentibus*, Lugd. Bat., 1686. The two latter works are probably the ones referred to by Leibnitz. For an account of his views, *cf.* Lasswitz, *Gesch. d. Atomistik*, Hamburg u. Leipzig, 1890, Vol. 2, pp. 300–328.—Tr.

[4] Ignace Gaston Pardies, 1636–1673, a French Jesuit and geometer, was Professor of Philosophy, and afterwards of Mathematics, at Paris. In his correspondence with Newton, he sought to explain the dispersion of light as a diffraction by aid of the assumption that the transmission of light depends upon a wave-movement. He intended to write a great work on Mechanics, of which only Pts. 1 and 2, *Discours du mouvement local*, Paris, 1670, and *La statique ou la science des forces mouvantes*, Paris, 1673, appeared. His *Œuvres de mathématiques*, etc., 4th ed., appeared à La Haye, 1710. *Cf.* Lasswitz, *Gesch. d. Atomistik*, 2, 340. Leibnitz refers to Pardies in a communication to H. Fabri, *cf.* Gerhardt, *Leibniz. math. Schrift.*, II., 2 [Vol. 6], 81, 84; Gerhardt, *Leibniz. philos. Schrift.*, 4, 244, 247.—Tr.

[5] Claude François Milliet Deschales, 1621–1678, a French Jesuit and distinguished mathematician and physicist, published his *Cursus seu mundus mathematicus*, 3 tomi, 1st ed., Lugduni, 1674, 2d ed., 1690. Leibnitz refers to him briefly in a communication to H. Fabri, Gerhardt, *Leibniz. philos. Schrift.*, 4, 245; *Leibniz. math. Schrift.*, II., 2 [Vol. 6], 81. Brief account of his views is given in Lasswitz, *Gesch. d. Atomistik*, 2, 487–490.—Tr.

[6] *Cf. ante*, p. 150, note 3. The doctrine of Huygens, here referred to, is found in his *De motu corporum ex percussione* (1669), which was first published in 1703; *Opera reliqua*, Amstel., 1728, Vol. 2; *Œuvres complètes*, La Haye, 1888 *sq.* His correspondence with Leibnitz is found in Gerhardt, *Leibniz. math. Schrift.*, I., 2 [Vol. 2], 1–208. References to the doctrine of motion occur on pp. 140, 184. An account of Huygens' physical and mechanical views is given in Lasswitz, *Gesch. d. Atomistik*, 2, 341–397.—Tr.

by certain rules formerly published. Wren [1] also, Wallis [2] and Mariotte,[3] men excellent in these studies though diverse in method, demonstrated nearly these same rules. But concerning the causes, nevertheless, opinion is not the same; whence men distinguished in these studies do not always admit the same conclusions. And indeed the true sources of this science have not yet, as is evident, been disclosed. Nor indeed is what seems certain to me admitted by all: that rebounding or reflection springs only from elastic force, that is, from internal resistance to motion. Nor has any one before us explained the notion itself of forces, which thing hitherto has disturbed the Cartesians and others, who, even for this reason, could not comprehend that the sum of the motion or impulse (which they regard as the quantity of the forces) can appear different after the encounter from before, because for this very reason they believed the quantity of the forces to be changed.

From me, still a youth, and at that time constituting the nature of body, with Democritus and his adherents in this matter, Gassendi and Descartes, in inert mass alone, there escaped a little book "Hypothesis Physica" [4] by title, in which I set forth a theory of motion, at the same time abstract (*abstractam*) from the system and concrete (*concretam*) for the system,[5] which beyond the merit of its

[1] Sir Christopher Wren, 1631-1723, best known as the architect of St. Paul's, London, was distinguished at Oxford for his knowledge of geometry and applied mathematics. In 1660 he was elected Savilian Professor of Astronomy at Oxford. Newton, in his *Principia*, ed. 1713, p. 19, speaks highly of his work as a geometrician. Leibnitz refers to him in the *Hypoth. phys.*, *cf.* Gerhardt, *Leibniz. math. Schrift.*, II., 2 [Vol. 6], 26, 29, 30, 75; *Philos. Schrift.*, 4, 187, 190, 191, 236. — Tr.

[2] John Wallis, 1616-1703, an eminent English mathematician, appointed Savilian Professor of Geometry, at Oxford, 1649, published his *Mechanica, sive de Motu Tractatus Geometricus*, 3 parts, 1669-1671. His complete works were published, Oxford, 1695-1699, 3 vols., fol. The correspondence between Leibnitz and Wallis is found in Vol. 3 of this ed., and also in Gerhardt, *Leibniz. math. Schrift.*, I., 4 [Vol. 4], 1-82. — Tr.

[3] *Cf. ante*, p. 121, note 4. An elaborate treatise on the percussion of bodies, *De la percussion ou choc des corps*, probably the one to which Leibnitz here refers, is found in first volume of his *Œuvres*, Leyden, 1717. — Tr.

[4] *Cf.* Gerhardt, *Leibniz. math. Schrift.*, II., 2 [Vol. 6], 17-80; Gerhardt, *Leibniz. philos. Schrift.*, 4, 177-240; Dutens, *Leibnit. op. om.*, 2, Pt. II., 1-48. — Tr.

[5] The compressed and somewhat obscure text is explained by the titles of two essays forming the *Hypothesis Physica nova*. The title of the first essay is: *Theoria motus concreti seu Hypothesis de rationibus phænomenorum nostri Orbis*; that of the second is: *Theoria motus abstracti seu Rationes motuum universales a sensu et phænomenis independentes*. *Cf.* Gerhardt's Einleitung, *Leibniz. philos. Schrift.*, 4, 9-12, and especially the portion, there quoted, of a letter to Foucher, found also in *op. cit.*, 1, 415; Erdmann, *Leibnit. op. philos.*, 117; F. de Careil, *Lettres et Opuscules inédits de Leibniz*, Paris, 1854, 119-120; Dutens, *Leibnit. op. om.*, 2, Pt. I., 242; transl. Duncan, *Philos. Wks. of Leibnitz*, 64-65. — Tr.

mediocrity I see has pleased many distinguished men. I there established, having assumed such a conception of body, the fact that every striking body gives its impulse (*conatum*) to the receiving or directly opposing body as such. For since, in the moment of attack, the receiving body undertakes to go forward and thus run away with itself, and that impulse (on account of the indifference then believed by me of the body to motion or rest) must have its effect wholly in the receiving body, unless hindered by a contrary impulse, nay, even if hindered by it, since it is so necessary that these different impulses should be adjusted among themselves; it was manifest that no cause could be given why the striking body should not attain the effect towards which it tends, or why the receiving body should not receive the entire impulse of the striking body, and so the motion of the receiving body was composed of its own pristine impulse, and of the newly received or foreign impulse. From which then I was showing that if mathematical notions alone, — magnitude, figure, place, — and the change of these, or in the moment itself of impact (*concursus*) the impulses to change were perceived in the body, no theory of metaphysical notions being held, namely, of power active (*actricis*) in form and of inactivity (*ignaviæ*), or of resistance to motion in matter, and so if it were necessary for the concourse of events to be determined by the geometrical composition of impulses alone, as we have explained: then it must follow that the impulse of the striking body, even the least, is impressed upon the entire receiving body, although the greatest, and so the greatest body at rest is dragged away by the striking body, however small, without any retardation of this body, since indeed no repugnance, but rather indifference of it to motion, is contained in such a notion of matter. Whence it would not be any more difficult to impel a large quiescent body than a small one, and thus there would be action without reaction, and there could be no estimate of power, since anything whatever could be proved by anything whatever. And since these things, and many others of the same kind, are opposed to the order of things and conflict with the principles of a true metaphysic, I thought at that time therefore (and indeed truly) that the most wise Author of things in the construction of the system shunned those things which would follow of themselves from the mere laws of motion derived from pure geometry.

But afterwards, having examined things more deeply, I saw in what the systematic explanation of things consisted, and regarded that former hypothesis of the notion of the body as incomplete, and both by other arguments and also by this itself it was proved that in body there must be placed something besides magnitude and impenetrability, whence the consideration of forces arises, by adding the metaphysical laws of which to the laws of extension those very rules of motion are produced which I called systematic; namely, that every change takes place gradually, and every action is accompanied with reaction, and new force is not produced without loss of the former, and so the one dragging always is retarded by the one dragged, and neither more nor less power is contained in the effect than in the cause. And since this law is not derived from the notion of mass, it must necessarily follow from another thing, which is in bodies, namely, from the force itself, which certainly always preserves its own quantity the same, although it is employed by different bodies. Hence therefore, besides considerations purely mathematical, and subject to the imagination, I have concluded that certain considerations metaphysical, and perceptible by the mind alone, must be admitted, and a certain principle superior to the material mass, and, so to speak, a formal addition, since indeed all the truths of corporeal things cannot be concluded from logical and geometrical axioms alone, namely, from great and small, whole and part, figure and position, but some others must be added from cause and effect, and action and passion, by which the reasons of the order of things are saved. Whether we call that principle form, or ἐντελέχεια, or force, does not matter, provided we remember that it is intelligibly exhibited through the notion of forces alone.

But although to-day certain distinguished men, seeing this very thing, that the common notion indeed of matter is not sufficient, fetch in God ἀπὸ μηχανῆς, and take away all force of acting from things, a kind of Mosaic philosophy as it were (as Fludd once called it), I cannot assent. For although I admit that it has been very clearly perceived by them that there is no proper influx of one created substance into another, if the thing is driven to metaphysical strictness, and I confess even freely that all things always proceed from a continuous creation by God; yet I think there is no natural truth in things, the reason of which is to be sought immediately in the divine action or will, but that always in the things themselves something has been placed by God, whence all their predicates are explained. It is certainly evident that God has created not only bodies, but also souls, to which correspond the primitive entelechies. But these things will be demonstrated elsewhere by their own proper reasons more profoundly drawn out.

Meanwhile, although I admit an active principle superior to material notions and, so to speak, vital everywhere in bodies, yet I do not therefore here agree with Henry More and other men, distinguished for piety and genius, who so make use of a certain Archæus[1] or hylarchic principle even for the management of phenomena (*ad phænomena procuranda*), as if forsooth all things cannot be explained mechanically in nature, and as if those who undertake this seem to make way

[1] *Cf. New Essays, ante*, p. 67, note 3. — Tr.

with incorporeal things, not without suspicion of impiety; or as if with Aristotle it is necessary to imagine intelligences in the revolving orbs, or the elements must be said to be driven up or down by their own form, by a short (*compendiosa*) but useless method of teaching: with these, I say, I do not agree, nor has that philosophy pleased me any more than that theology of certain ones, who so believed that Jupiter thundered or snowed that they even branded the searchers after proper causes with the crime of atheism. In my opinion the temperament is the best which satisfies both piety and science, so that we admit that all corporeal phenomena indeed can be sought from efficient mechanical causes, but we know that the mechanical laws in the universe are derived from higher reasons, and so we make use of a higher efficient cause only in establishing general and remote things. But these once established, as often as afterwards we treat of the near and special efficient causes of natural things, we give no place to souls or entelechies, no more than to the idle faculties or inexplicable sympathies, since the primal and most universal efficient cause itself, must not intervene unless as far as the ends are regarded, which the divine wisdom had in so ordering things, that we neglect no occasion of singing his praise and the most beautiful hymns.

And in truth final causes (as I have shown by a wholly remarkable example of an optical principle, with the strong approval of the very celebrated Molyneux in his "Dioptrics") are repeatedly employed with large result even in special physics, not only that we may admire the more the most beautiful works of the supreme Author, but also that we may sometimes in this way divine what through the way of efficient causes not equally or only hypothetically are manifest. Thus far perhaps philosophers have not yet sufficiently observed this use. And it must be maintained in general, that everything in things can be explained in two ways: through *the kingdom of power* or *efficient causes*, and through *the kingdom of wisdom* or through *final causes*; God regulating bodies as machines after the manner of an architect according to *the laws of magnitude or mathematical laws*, and indeed for the use of souls; but souls, capable of wisdom, as his own fellow-citizens and sharers of a certain society with himself, after the manner of a leader, nay of a father rather according to *the laws of goodness or moral laws* for his own glory, both kingdoms everywhere interpenetrating, yet unconfused and undisturbed the laws of each, so that at the same time both in the kingdom of power the greatest and in the kingdom of wisdom the best is obtained. But we propose in this place to establish the general rules of productive forces, which we can then use in the explanation of special efficient causes.

Next I came to the true, and indeed precisely the same, estimate of forces, by the most different ways: one indeed *a priori*, from the simplest consideration of space, time, and action (which I elsewhere will explain), the other *a posteriori*, namely, by estimating the force by the effect which it produces in consuming itself. For I understand here not any *effect*, but that for which force must be expended or in which it must be consumed, which you can call, for that reason, *violent*, such as that effect is not, which a heavy body employs in running through a perfectly horizontal plane, because in such an effect however produced it always retains the same force, although also in this very *effect* rightly treated, so to speak, as *harmless*, we have followed this our method of estimating, but now it is laid aside by us. Further I chose that effect of the violent effects which is especially capable of homogeneity or division into similar and equal parts, such as exists in the ascent of a body possessed of weight: for the elevation of a heavy body two or three feet is precisely double or triple the elevation of the same heavy body one foot; and the elevation of a doubly heavy body one foot is precisely double the elevation of a single heavy body to the height of one foot; whence the elevation of a doubly heavy body three feet is precisely six times the elevation of a simple heavy body one foot, supposing namely (at least for the sake of teaching, although perhaps in truth the matter is otherwise constituted, but the error here nevertheless is imperceptible), that the heavy bodies gravitate equally in the greater or less distance from the horizon. For in an elastic body homogeneity has not with equal ease a place. When therefore I wished to compare bodies different or endowed with different velocities, I easily saw that, if the body *A* is single and the body *B* is double, but the velocity of each equal, the force of that one is simple, of this double, since, in short, whatever is placed in that once is placed in this twice. For in *B* there is a body twice the equal and equivalent of *A* itself, and nothing besides. But if the bodies *A* and *C* are equal, but the velocity in *A* is simple and in *C* double, I saw that, not in short what is in *A*, is doubled in *C*, since the velocity indeed is doubled, yet not also the body. And I saw that here an error has been made by those who believed that the force itself is doubled by that reduplication of modality (*modalitatis*) alone; as already I once observed and suggested, and that the true and not hitherto (although after so many *Elements of universal Mathematics* have been written) handed-down *art of estimating* consists in this, that finally it attains to something homogeneous; that is, a reduplication accurate and of all kinds, not only of modes, but also of things. Of which method no other better or more remarkable specimen could be given than that which is exhibited in this argument itself.

In order, therefore, to obtain these results, I considered whether these very two bodies *A* and *C*, equal in magnitude but different in velocity, could produce some effects equal to their causes and homogeneous among themselves. For thus those things which by themselves could not easily be compared, by their effects at least might be compared accurately. I assumed, moreover, that the effect must be equal to its cause if it is produced by the expenditure or consumption of the entire force: in which case it matters not in how much time it is produced. Let us suppose, therefore, the bodies *A* and *C* (Fig. 5) to be heavy, and to convert their force into an ascent, which will happen, if at the moment in which they have their said velocities, *A* simple, *B* double, are known to exist at the extremities of the vertical pendulums *PA*, *EC*. But it is evident from the demonstrations of Galileo and others that, the body *A* with a velocity as 1 at the highest ascending above the horizon *HR* to the height of one foot $_2AH$, the body *C* with a velocity as 2 can surely ascend (at the highest) to the height $_2CR$ of four feet. Whence it already follows that a heavy body having a velocity as 2 is in power four times as much as the one having a degree of velocity as 1, since by the expenditure of all its force it can accomplish, in short, four times as much. For raising a pound (that is, itself — *id est se ipsum*) four feet, in short raises four times one pound one foot. And in the same manner it is inferred generally that the forces of equal bodies are as the squares of the velocities, and thence the forces of bodies in general are in reason composed of the simple of the bodies and the doubles of the velocities.

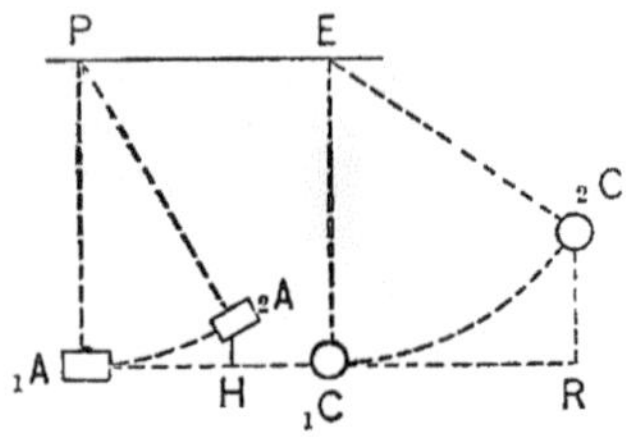

FIG. 5.

I have confirmed the same things to absurdity (namely, to perpetual motion) by bringing back the contrary opinion, generally received, especially among the Cartesians, according to which forces are believed to be in reason composed of bodies and velocities: which method, indeed, I used repeatedly to define *a posteriori two states unequal in force*, and to distinguish the greater at the same time from the less by a certain mark. And since in substituting the one for the other, perpetual mechanical motion or an effect more powerful than the cause does not arise, those states are not in the least equivalent to themselves, but that which was substituted for the other was more powerful because it has caused something greater to be performed. But I assume as certain that nature never substitutes things unequal to the forces themselves, but the complete effect is always equal to the full cause; and, in turn, those things which are equal to the forces, with safe reckoning can be substituted by us for them with the freest supposition, as if we made that substitution in act, and thus with no fear[1] of perpetual mechanical motion. But if, therefore, it were true, as men generally persuade themselves, that a heavy body A as 2 (for so now we assume it) endowed with a velocity as 1, and a heavy body C as 1 endowed with a velocity as 2, are equivalent to each other, we ought to be able to substitute with impunity the one for the other. But this is not true. For let us assume that A as 2 has acquired a velocity as 1 in the descent ${}_2A\,{}_1A$ from the height ${}_2AH$ less than a foot; and now in ${}_1A$ itself or in the existing horizon, let us substitute instead of it the equivalent (as they wish) weight (*pondus*) C as 1 with a velocity as 2, which ascends as far as to C, or to the height of four feet. And so by the descent alone of the weight A of two pounds from the height of one foot ${}_2AH$, and having substituted its equivalent, we have accomplished the ascent of one pound four feet, which is double the former. Therefore we have gained just as much force, or we have produced perpetual mechanical motion, which is certainly absurd. And it does not matter whether by the laws of motions we can actually accomplish this substitution; for between equivalents indeed substitution can safely be made. Although, indeed, we have thought out various plans by which it will be accomplished actually so nearly as we wish, that the entire force of the body A will be transferred to the body C, before at rest, but which now (A itself being brought to rest) is alone put in motion. Whence it will happen, that, instead of a weight of two pounds of a velocity as 1, would succeed one pound of a velocity as 2, if these were equivalent; whence we have shown that an absurdity arises. For these things are not indeed worthless, nor do they consist in logomachies, but are of the greatest use in comparing machines and motions. For if any one has force from water or animals or from other cause, by which a heavy body of a hundred pounds is kept in constant motion, so that within a fourth part of a minute of time it can complete a horizontal circle of a diameter of thirty feet; but another maintains that a double weight in its place, in the same time, uniformly accomplishes only half the circle with less expenditure, and reckons that to you as if it were a gain; be it known that you are deceived and caught by half of the forces. But now having put to flight errors, let us set forth a little more distinctly in the second part of this hastily thrown-off production (*Schediasmatis*) the true and truly to be admired laws of nature.[2]

[1] Gerhardt reads, "motu," evidently a typographical error. Dutens, *Leibnit. op. om.*, 3, 324, reads, "metu," which the translation follows. — Tr.

[2] Dutens (*Leibnit. op. om.*, 3, 324) adds: "proponemus, mense Maio exhibenda," *i.e.* to be presented in the month of May. The article, however, never appeared in print, but remained in Ms. among Leibnitz's papers, and was first printed by Gerhardt, in his edition of Leibnitz's mathematical writings. A translation of the article is herewith given. — Tr.

ESSAY ON DYNAMICS IN DEFENCE OF THE WONDERFUL LAWS OF NATURE IN RESPECT TO THE FORCES OF BODIES, DISCLOSING THEIR MUTUAL ACTIONS AND REFERRING THEM TO THEIR CAUSES[1]

[*From the Latin*]

PART II

The nature of body, nay, of substance in general, not being sufficiently known, had brought it about (a fact we have already touched upon) that certain distinguished philosophers of our time, since they placed the notion of body in extension alone, were compelled to have recourse to God in order to explain the union between the soul and the body, nay, also, the communication of bodies with each other. For it must be confessed that it is impossible for a mere extension, involving only geometrical notions, to be capable of action and passion: and so this alone seemed to be left to them, that, when man thinks and undertakes to move his arm, God, as it were, by a primeval compact, moves his arm instead of he himself; and on the other hand, when the motion exists in the blood and spirits,[2] God excites perception in the mind. But these very things, since they are foreign to a correct method of philosophizing, ought to admonish the authors that they are resting upon a false principle, and that they have not assigned rightly the notion of body, from which such things followed. We have shown, therefore, that there is in every substance a force of action and, if it is created, of passion also, that the notion of extension is in itself not complete, but that a relation to something which is extended, whose diffusion or continued replication it makes known, and so the substance of a body is presupposed, which involves a power of acting and resisting, and everywhere exists as a corporeal mass, and the diffusion of this is involved in extension. Whence one day we shall kindle a new light, also, for the explanation of the union of the soul and the body. But now we must show how from thence follow wonderful and extremely useful practical theorems, pertaining to Dynamics, that is, the science which teaches the rules especially of corporeal forces.

It must be known before all things that force, indeed, is something truly real, even in created substances; but space, time, and motion have something of a rational entity, and are true and real,

[1] Gerhardt, *Leibniz. math. Schrift.*, II., 2 [Vol. 6], pp. 246–254; aus d. Manuscript. der Königl. Biblioth. zu Hannover.

[2] *Cf.* Bacon's theory of the *Spiritus*, a brief account of which is given by Lasswitz, *Gesch. d. Atomistik*, 1, 431–432. — TR.

not of themselves, but since they involve divine attributes, — immensity, eternity, operation, or the force of created substances. Hence it already follows that there is no vacuum in space or time; that motion, moreover, separated from force, or where in it only the geometrical notions, — magnitude, figure, — and the variation of these are considered, is in truth nothing else than a change of position, and so *motion, as far as (quoad) phenomena are concerned, consists in a mere relation,* which also Descartes acknowledged, when he defined translation from the neighborhood of one body into the neighborhood of another. But in deducing his consequences he forgot his definition, and determined the rules of motions as if motion was something real and absolute. So, therefore, we must consider, if an indefinite number of bodies are in motion, that from the phenomena it cannot be deduced in which of them absolute determinate motion or rest exists, but to any one you please taken from these can be attributed rest, provided that the same phenomena come forth. Hence it follows (a result which Descartes did not notice) that *the uniformity of the hypotheses is changed neither by the encounters (concursus) of bodies with each other;* and besides, that such rules of motions must be assigned that the respective nature of motion may remain intact, nor from the event after the encounter can it be divined through the phenomena where before the encounter there had been rest or determinate absolute motion. Whence the rule of Descartes does not at all accord with the facts, by which he asserts that a body at rest can in no way be driven from its place by another smaller body, and other things of this sort. Than which nothing is more remote from the truth. It follows, also, from the relative nature of motion, that *the action of bodies against each other by turns or percussion is the same, provided they approach each other with the same velocity;* that is, the same appearance remaining in the given phenomena, whatever at length be the true hypothesis, or to whichever at length we rightly ascribe motion or rest, the same event appears in the phenomena sought or resulting, even in respect to the action of bodies among themselves. And this also is what we find by experience (*experimur*), that we shall feel the same pain, whether our hand runs against a stone at rest, suspended, if you please, from a thread, or the stone with the same velocity runs against our hand at rest. Meanwhile, we speak thus, according as the thing demands, for a more suitable and simpler explanation of the phenomena, precisely as in spherics we employ the motion of the *primum mobile,* and in the theory of the planets we must use the Copernican hypothesis, so that already these disputes, urged on with so much effort (in which even theologians were implicated), straightway disappear. For although force is something real and absolute, nevertheless motion pertains to the class of relative phenomena, and truth is looked for not so much in phenomena as in causes.

From our notions also of body and forces this principle arises, *that what happens in substance can be known to happen spontaneously and in an orderly manner.* With this is connected the principle that *no change takes place by a leap.* This posited, it follows also that *atoms cannot be allowed.* That we may seize the force of this conclusion, let us assume that the bodies A and B (Fig. 6) meet together and that ${}_1A$ comes to ${}_2A$, and again ${}_1B$ to ${}_2B$, and thus meeting in ${}_2A_2B$ are reflected from ${}_2A$ to ${}_3A$ and from ${}_2B$ to ${}_3B$. But supposing that atoms exist, that is, bodies extremely hard and thus inflexible, it is evident that the change takes place by a leap or momentary increment (*momentaneam*), for direct motion in the moment (*momento*) itself of the encounter becomes retrograde unless we can assume that immediately after the encounter the bodies rest, that is, lose their force, which thing, besides the fact that it would otherwise be absurd, would continue again the change by a leap, a momentary increment (*momentaneam*), namely, from motion to rest, and not however a transition by intermediate steps. And so we must know, if the bodies A and B (Fig. 7) meet and come from ${}_1A_1B$ into the place of concourse ${}_2A_2B$, that there they are gradually compressed like two inflated balls, and more and more approach each other in turn by the continually increased pressure; that, moreover, by this thing the motion itself is weakened, the force itself of the effort being carried over into the elasticities (*elastra*) of the bodies, until at length they are reduced to rest; but then at length the elasticity of the bodies restoring them, they themselves rebound from each other in turn with a retrograde motion begun again from rest and continually increasing; at length with the same velocity with which they approached each other, regained but turned in the opposite direction, they recede in turn from each other and return into the positions ${}_3A_3B$ which coincide with the positions ${}_1A_1B$, if the bodies are supposed equal and of equal velocity. Thence it is already evident how no change takes place by a leap, but the progress being gradually diminished and at length reduced to rest, then at length a regress arises. So that as from one figure another is not made (as from a circle an oval) unless through innumerable intermediate figures, nor is there any passing over from a place to a place or from a time to a time unless through all intermediate places and times, so not from motion is rest produced, and much less an opposite motion, unless through all the intermediate degrees of motions. And since this principle

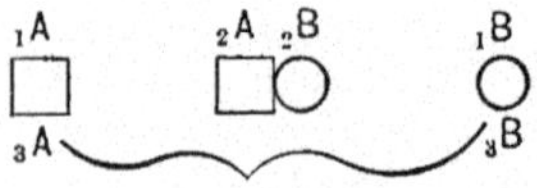

FIG. 6.

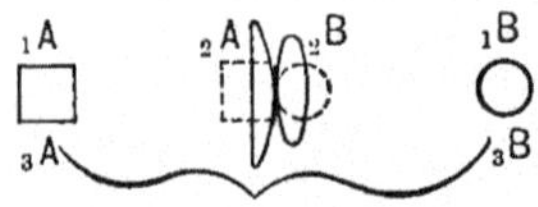

FIG. 7.

is of so great consequence in nature, I wonder it is so little thought of. From these considerations follows what Descartes had attacked in his letters, and now also certain great men are unwilling to admit, that *all reflection arises from elasticity*, and a reason is given of many remarkable experiments which indicate that *a body bends before it is propelled*, as Mariotte has very beautifully illustrated. Finally, that especially wonderful principle follows from these considerations, that no body is so poor but that it has elasticity, and so is pervaded by a fluid still more subtile; and then that *there are no elements of bodies*, and that neither the most fluid matter nor certain solid globules of the second element, exact and durable, are to be granted, but that analysis proceeds to infinity.

It is consistent with this *law of continuity*, excluding leap from change, that a case of rest can be considered as a special case of motion, namely, as an evanescent or very small motion, and a case of equality can be considered as a case of evanescent inequality. Whence the consequence is, that such laws of motions must be assigned that there be no need for peculiar rules for bodies equal and at rest, but these rules spring from the rules of bodies unequal and moving of themselves, or, if we wish to enounce peculiar rules for rest and equality, we must be careful lest we assign such as do not agree with the hypothesis which considers rest as the last motion or equality as the last inequality, otherwise we shall violate the harmony of things and our rules will not agree among themselves. This new system of testing our own or others' rules, I published first in the "Nouvelles de la République des Lettres," July, 1687, article 8,[1] and called it a general principle of order (*principium ordinis generale*), springing from the notion of the infinite and the continuum, adding to it the axiom, that from orderly data the results also are orderly (*datis ordinatis etiam quæsita sunt ordinata*). I expressed the principle universally thus: *If a case approaches a case continually in the data and at length disappears in itself, the results of the cases must also approach each other continually in the things sought for, and at length cease in turn in themselves.* (*Si casus ad casum continue accedat in datis tandemque in ipsum evanescat, necesse est ut etiam eventus casuum sibi continue accedant in quæsitis tandemque in se invicem desinant.*) Precisely as in geometry the case of the ellipse approaches continually the case of the parabola, in proportion as one focus remaining another more and more remote is regarded as assumed, until in the case of another focus infinitely removed the ellipse passes into the parabola. Whence all the rules of the ellipse must be verified in the parabola (taken as an ellipse whose other focus is infinitely distant). Whence the radii falling parallel into a parabola can be conceived as coming from

[1] *Cf.* Gerhardt, *Leibniz. philos. Schrift.*, 3, 51-55; Erdmann, 104-106.—Tr.

another focus or tending towards it. Since, therefore, in the same way a case in which the body A runs against B in motion can be varied continually, so that the motion of A itself remaining, the motion of B itself is regarded as less and less, until at length it is regarded as disappearing in rest and thence again grows in the contrary direction; I say the result of the attack, but rebounding into what whether in A itself or in B itself, continually approaches by both motions the result of the attack which exists in the case of B at rest, and in it finally ceases; and thus the case of rest both in the data (*in datis*) and in the result or that which is sought (*quæsitis*) is the limit of the cases of motion in a straight line, or the common limit of direct and continuous motion, and thus as it were a special example of either. With regard to this touchstone (*lydium lapidem*), brought over by me from geometry to physics, when I examined the Cartesian rules of motions, it happened, wonderful to say, that a certain hiatus or leap showed itself utterly abhorrent to the nature of things, for in expressing quantities by lines, and taking for abscissas (*pro abscissis*) the motions of B itself before the encounter, the data, and for ordinates (*pro ordinatim applicatis*) the motion of the same after the encounter, the results sought for, and by drawing the line through the extremities of the ordinates (*ordinatarum*), according to the precept of the rules of Descartes, this line was not a continuum, but something wonderfully gaping and leaping in a certain absurd and unthinkable manner. And when on that occasion I observed also that the rules of Rev. Father Malebranche did not bear this examination in all things, the distinguished man having considered the matter again according to his candor, declared publicly that from this an occasion had arisen for him to change his rules, for which reason, also, he published a brief pamphlet. Although it must be confessed, that because he had not yet directed his attention sufficiently to the use of this new system, he has left something now also not yet sufficiently in all things complete (*quadrant*).

From what has been said, this wonderful principle also follows, *that the passion of every body is spontaneous, or arises from internal force, although upon external occasion.* I understand here, however, passion proper, which arises from percussion, or which remains the same, whatever hypothesis at length is assigned, or to whatever at length we ascribe absolute rest or motion. For since the percussion is the same, to whatever at length true motion corresponds, it follows that the result of the percussion is distributed equally between both, and thus *both act equally in the encounter*, and thus half the result arises from the action of the one, the other half from the action of the other; and since half, also, of the result or passion is in one, half in the other, it is sufficient that we derive the passion which is in one from the action also which is in itself, and we need no influence of the one upon the other, although by the action of one an occasion is furnished the other for producing a change in itself. Certainly, while *A* and *B* meet, the resistance of the bodies, united with their elasticity, causes them to be compressed because of the percussion, and the compression is equal in each and according to whatever hypothesis, as the experiments show also, if any one conceives two inflated balls to meet, whether both are in motion, or each is at rest, even if the one at rest be suspended from some thread, in order that it may most easily recede; for, always provided the velocity of approach or the respective velocity be the same, the compression, or the intensity of the elasticity, will be the same and equal in both. Then the balls *A* and *B*, restoring themselves by the force of their own violent, namely, compressed and confined, elasticity, mutually repel each other by turns, and spread out, as it were, in an arc, and, with a force equal on both sides, each is driven back by the other, and so, not by the force of the other, but by its own force, it recedes from that one. But what is to be understood in the case of inflated balls is to be understood in the case of every body so far as it is passive in percussion, namely, that the rebounding and leaping apart arises from the elasticity in itself, that is, from the motion of the permeating etherial fluid matter, and thus from force internal, or proceeding from within. I understand, however, as I have said, that the *proper motion* of bodies is separated from the *common*, which can be ascribed to the centre of gravity; whence their proper motion is so to be conceived (to be conceived, I say, by the way of hypothesis) as if they were produced on board a ship, which would have the motion of their common centre of gravity, but they themselves on board ship were so moved that from the composite common motion of the ship or centre, and their own proper motion, the phenomena are preserved. From what has been said, also, it is understood that *the action of bodies is never without reaction, and both are equal to each other, and directly contrary.*

Since, then, only force, and thence nascent effort exists in any moment (for motion never truly exists, as we have explained above), and every effort tends in a straight line, it follows that *all motion is rectilinear, or composed of rectilinears.* Hence, already it not only follows that *those bodies which move in a curved line, try always to proceed in the straight line tangent to it,* but also, what any one least expects, hence arises *the true notion of stability* (*firmitatis*). For, if we suppose that some one of those bodies which we call stable (although in truth nothing is absolutely stable or fluid, but everything has a certain degree of stability or fluidity, by us, however, it is named from a predominant regard for our senses) circulates about its own centre, the parts will attempt to fly away by the tangent, nay, they will really begin to fly away; but since this separation of themselves from each other in turn disturbs the motion of the encircling body, hence they are repelled, or

2 Y

again crowded together towards themselves in turn, as if there were in the centre, a magnetic force of attraction, or as if there were in the parts themselves a centripetal force, and therefore the revolution will arise from the composition of the effort (*nisu*) to recede from the rectilinear by the tangent and the centripetal effort (*conatu*). And thus it remains that all curvilinear motion arises from the composition among themselves of rectilinear efforts, and at the same time it is understood that this crowding together by the encircling body is the cause of all stability. Otherwise it could not be that all curvilinear motion was composed of nothing but rectilinear motions. Whence, also, again, we have a new and not less than before unexpected argument against atoms. Moreover, nothing could be devised more inconsistent with things than that stability be sought from rest, for *true rest never exists in bodies*, nor from rest can anything arise but rest; but although *A* and *B* are mutually at rest with themselves, if not in fact, at least relatively (although this never occurs exactly, for *no body preserves exactly the same distance from another, however small the time*), and although whatever is once at rest will always be at rest unless a new cause is added, nevertheless it does not follow, for this reason, that because *B* resists the impelling body, it resists, also, the one separating it from another, so that certainly, as the resistance of *B* itself is overcome, or *B* itself driven forward, at the same time *A* follows. But were the *attraction*, which is not given in nature, but from the primitive stability (*firmitate*), explained through rest or something similar, it would assuredly follow. And so stability, also, should not be explained unless by the crowding together produced by the encircling body. For pressure alone does not sufficiently explain the matter, as if the separation of *B* itself from *A* itself only is impeded, but it is to be understood that in fact they separate from each other in turn, that moreover one is again impelled to the other by the encircling body, and thus, from the composition of the two motions, this conservation of the conjunction is produced. And so those who conceive in bodies certain tablets or insensible layers (for example, of two polished marbles, which are exactly applied to each other), whose separation is made difficult on account of the resistance of the ambient body, and hence explain the stability of two sensible bodies, although very often they speak truly, yet when they suppose some stability in the layers again, they do not give the last reason for stability. From these considerations, also, it can be understood why I cannot in this thing continue (*stare*) in certain philosophic opinions of certain great mathematicians, who, besides the fact that they admit vacant space, and seem not to shrink back from attraction, consider motion, also, as an absolute thing, and hasten to prove it from the revolution and the centrifugal force which has thence arisen. But since the revolution also arises only from the composition of rectilinear motions, it follows, if the equivalent of the hypotheses is sound in rectilinear motions, however assumed, that it will be sound in the curvilinears.

From what has been said it can also be understood that *the common motion in many bodies does not change their actions among themselves*, since the velocity with which they approach each other in turn, and thus the force of the encounter by which they act on each other in turn, is not changed. Whence the remarkable experiments follow which Gassendi mentions in his letters on motion impressed by a transferred motor, that he might satisfy those who seemed to themselves to be able to infer the rest of the earth's sphere from the motion of projectiles. Nevertheless, it is certain that, if any [persons] are borne in a large ship (closed, if agreeable, or certainly so constituted that the external phenomena cannot be observed by the travellers), and if the ship is moved, although with great velocity, yet quietly or uniformly, they themselves will have no principle by which to distinguish (from those things, namely, which take place on shipboard) whether the ship is at rest or moves, even if by chance they play ball on the ship, or practice other movements. And this fact must be noted in favor of those whose belief accords with the not rightly understood notion of the Copernicans, that according to these, things projected from the earth into the air are carried off (*abripi*) by the air with the gyrating earth, and thus the motion of the bottom follows, and fall back upon the earth just as if this were at rest; a view which is properly judged insufficient, since the very learned men who make use of the Copernican hypothesis conceive, rather, that something on the surface of the earth is moved with the earth, and, just as if discharged from a bow or hurling machine (*tormento*), carries with itself the impetus made by the gyration of the earth, together with the impetus made by the projection. Thence, when their double motion is the one common with the earth, the other peculiar to the projection, it is no wonder that the common motion changes nothing. Meanwhile, it is not to be disguised that, if the projectiles could be driven so far, or if the ship were conceived so large, and borne with such velocity, that before the descent the heavy earth or ship described an arc perceptibly different from a straight line; a distinction would be discovered, because then, indeed, the motion of the earth or ship (because circular) does not remain common to the motion which was impressed upon the missile by the gyration of the ship or earth (because rectilinear). And in the effort of heavy bodies towards the centre, external action is added, which can no less produce a diversity of phenomena, than if the compass were kept closed on the ship, which would certainly indicate a variation of the ship. As often, however, as the question concerns the equivalence of hypotheses, all things must be united which concur in the phenomena. From these considerations, also, it is understood that any composition of motions or resolution, whatever, of one motion into two or more can safely be employed, concerning which, nevertheless, a certain very clever man in the works of Wallis had hesitated, not without reason. For the matter certainly deserves proof, and cannot (as is done by many) be assumed as in itself known.

VI

ON THE RADICAL ORIGIN OF THINGS[1]

November 23, 1697

[*From the Latin*]

Besides the world or the aggregate of finite things, there is a Unique Being who rules, not only as the mind in me, or rather as I in my body rule myself, but also in a much higher manner. For this unique sovereign of the universe not only rules the world, but also frames or fashions it, and is superior to the world and, so to speak, outside the world (*extramundanum*), and thus is the ultimate reason of things. For the sufficient reason of existence can be found neither in any single thing, nor in the entire aggregate and series of things. Let us suppose that there was an eternal book of the Elements of Geometry, one copy always made from another, it is evident that, although we can account for the present book by the past, whence it has been copied, nevertheless we never, by assuming in the past as many books as we please, come to the complete reason, for we may always wonder why, from all time, such books have existed; that is to say, why these books were written, and why so written. What is true of books is likewise true of the different states of the world, for the following state has in a measure been copied from the preceding (although according to certain laws of change), and so to whatever extent you go back into anterior states, you will never find in these states the full reason; that is to say, why any world exists rather than none, and why such an one.

Therefore, although you imagine the world to be eternal, since, nevertheless, you assume only a succession of states, and do not find in any one of these whatever the sufficient reason, nay more, since by assuming any number you please you do not advance even the least towards accounting for them, it is evident that the reason must be sought elsewhere. For in eternal things we must understand that,

[1] Gerhardt, *Leibniz. philos. Schrift.*, 7, 302-308; Erdmann, 147-150; Janet, 2, 546-553 (in French). — Tr.

even if there were no cause, yet there is a reason, which in persisting things is the necessity itself or the essence; but in a series of changing things, if we suppose that this series proceeds from a prior series eternally, the reason would be the prevalence of inclinations, as we shall soon see, in which, that is to say, the reasons do not necessitate (with an absolute or metaphysical necessity so as to imply the contrary), but incline. From these considerations it is evident that we cannot escape the ultimate extramundane reason of things or God by assuming the eternity of the world.

The reasons therefore of the world lie concealed in something outside the world, different from the chain of circumstances or series of things, whose aggregate constitutes the world. We must then come from physical or hypothetical necessity, which determines the posterior states of the world from the prior states, to something which is of absolute or metaphysical necessity, the reason for which cannot be given. For the present world is physically or hypothetically but not absolutely or metaphysically necessary. In fact, having assumed that it is what it is, it follows that henceforth things must be what they are. Since, therefore, the ultimate root must be in something which is metaphysically necessary, and since there is no reason of the existing unless from the existing, it is therefore necessary that a unique being exist of metaphysical necessity, or whose essence is existence, and that thus something exists different from the plurality of beings or the world, which we have admitted and shown not to be of metaphysical necessity.

But that we may explain a little more distinctly how temporal, contingent or physical truths originate in eternal, or essential or metaphysical truths, we must first know, that, by the very fact itself that something rather than nothing exists, there is some demand for existence in possible things or in possibility itself or essence, or (so to speak) a stretching forth to existence, and, to sum it up in a word, that essence *per se* tends to existence. Whence it hereafter follows, that all possible things, or those expressing essence or possible reality, with equal right tend to essence (*essentiam*[1]) in proportion to the quantity of essence or reality, or in proportion to the degree of perfection which they involve; for perfection is nothing else than quantity of essence.

But from this we see most clearly that from the infinite combinations of possible things and possible series there stands forth one through which the greatest quantity of essence or possibility is brought through to existence. There is always, in fact, in things a

[1] The reading according to both Gerhardt and Erdmann. Janet's French version reads: "l'existence." The argument would seem to require the reading "existentiam."—TR.

principle of determination which is to be sought from the maximum or minimum, so that beyond question the greatest effect is manifested with, so to speak, the least expense. And here time, place, or, in a word, the receptivity or capacity of the world can be considered as the expense or ground upon which, as conveniently as possible, it must be built, while the varieties of the forms correspond to the proportion of the building and the number and elegance of the rooms. And it is as in certain games when all the places at a table must be filled according to certain laws, where, unless you employ a certain skill, hindered finally by the unfavorable places, you will be compelled to leave vacant more places than you were able or desired to do. There is, however, a certain method by which the greatest possible space is most easily filled. If therefore, for instance, we assume that it has been decreed that there be a triangle, though with no other accidentally determining condition, the result is an equilateral triangle; and if it is assumed that we must proceed from point to point, though nothing determines the road beyond, the easiest and the shortest way will be chosen; thus having once assumed that being prevails over non-being, or that there is a reason why something rather than nothing existed, or that from possibility a transition must be made to act, it follows hence, in the absence of any further determination, that the quantity of existence is as great as possible in proportion to the capacity of the time and place (or the order of possible existence), just as tiles are so laid that in the proposed area as many as possible may be contained.

From these considerations we understand already in a wonderful way how, in the very original formation of things, a certain Divine Mathematics or Metaphysical Mechanics is employed, and the determination of the greatest amount of existence has place. Thus the right angle is the determinate of all the angles in Geometry, and liquids placed in different media arrange themselves in the most capacious form, namely, the spherical; but especially in general Mechanics itself, when many heavy bodies struggle with each other, such a motion at length arises, through which the greatest descent on the whole is accomplished. For if all possibilities with equal right tend to existence according to the measure of reality, so all weights by equal right tend to descend in proportion to the measure of gravity, and as here the motion appears, in which is contained the greatest possible descent of the heavy bodies, so there the world appears, through which is realized the greatest possible production of possibilities.

And so also we already have physical necessity from metaphysical: for although the world is not metaphysically necessary, so that the contrary implies contradiction or logical absurdity, it is nevertheless physically necessary or determined so that the contrary implies imperfection or moral absurdity. And as possibility is the source of essence, so perfection or the degree of essence (through which the greatest number of things are compossible) is the source of existence. Whence it is at the same time evident how freedom exists in the Author of the world, although he does all things determinately because he acts from the principle of wisdom or perfection. Indifference certainly arises from ignorance, and the greater one's wisdom the more he is determined to the most perfect.

But (you will say) this comparison of a certain determining metaphysical mechanism with the physical one of heavy bodies, although it seems elegant, nevertheless is wanting in this because the struggling heavy bodies truly exist, but the possibilities or essences before or besides existence are imaginary or fictitious, therefore no reason of existence can be sought in them. I reply that neither these essences nor the eternal truths which they call from them are fictitious, but exist in a certain so to speak region of ideas, namely in God himself, the source of every essence and of the existence of the rest. That we do not seem to have spoken gratuitously, the existence itself of an actual series of things indicates. For since reason is not found in this series, as we showed above, but must be sought in metaphysical necessities or eternal truths; moreover, since existences cannot exist unless from existences, as already we maintained above, eternal truths must have existence in a certain absolute or metaphysically necessary subject, that is in God, through whom these things, which otherwise would be imaginary, are (to speak barbarously but significantly) realized.

And in truth actually in the world we observe that all things take place according to the laws of the eternal verities not only geometrical but also metaphysical, that is, not only according to material necessities, but also according to formal reasons; and that is true not only generally in that reason of the existing rather than non-existing, and the so rather than otherwise existing world which we have now explained (which certainly is to be sought from the tendency of possibilities to existence), but also by descending to specials we see, by a wonderful plan in all nature, the metaphysical laws of cause, power, action, have place, and these prevail over the purely geometrical laws themselves of matter, as in giving the reasons of the laws of motion I have observed to such an extent that I was finally compelled to abandon, as elsewhere I have more at length explained, the law of the geometrical composition of impulses (*conatuum*), defended formerly by me, a youth, when I was more materialistic.

Thus, therefore, we have the ultimate reason of reality both of essences and of existences in one, which assuredly greater, above and before the world itself is necessarily existent, since through itself not only existences, which the world embraces, but also possibilities, have reality. But this can be sought only in one source on account of the connection of all things with each other. It is evident, moreover, that from this source existing things continually spring forth (*promanare*) and are produced and the products exist, since it is not apparent why one state of the world rather than another, yesterday rather than to-day, flows from itself. It is also evident how God acts not only physically but also freely, and is in himself not only the efficient but also the final cause of things, and how an account is taken by him, not only of grandeur and power in the mechanism of the universe already constituted, but also of goodness and wisdom in that to be constituted.

And lest any one may think that moral perfection or goodness is here confounded with metaphysical perfection or magnitude, and the latter being granted may deny the former, it is to be understood that it follows from what has been said, not only that the world is the most perfect physically, or, if you prefer, metaphysically, or that that series of things has been produced in which the greatest possible reality is actually manifest, but also that it is the most perfect morally, because in reality moral perfection in souls themselves is physical. Whence the world is not only an especially admirable mechanism, but also, as far as it is composed of souls, is the best Republic, through which there is brought to souls the greatest possible felicity or joy in which their physical perfection consists.

But, you will say, we experience the contrary in the world, for the best very often fare the worst, the innocent, not only beasts, but also men, are struck down, and even killed with torture; finally, the world, especially if the government of the human race be regarded, seems rather a certain confused chaos than a thing arranged by a certain supreme wisdom. So at first view I confess it seems, but the contrary must be established by a more thorough inspection; *a priori*, it is evident from these very considerations which have been brought forward, that the highest possible perfection, namely, of all things, and so also of mind, is obtained.

And in truth it is unjust to judge, unless after an investigation of the whole law, as the jurisconsults say. We know a small part of the eternity extending into immensity; for how little is the memory of a few thousands of years which history recounts for us. And yet, from so small experience we judge rashly concerning the immense and the eternal, as men in a prison, or, if you prefer, born and educated in the subterranean salt-pits of the Sarmatians, thought that there is no other light in the world but that dim lamp light scarcely sufficient to direct their steps. We look at a very beautiful picture, we cover this entirely, reserving a small portion; what else in this will appear, even if you look very attentively, nay, how much more will you observe from near by than a certain confused congeries of colors without choice, without art; and nevertheless, when the whole covering is removed, and you shall see the whole picture in the proper position, you will know that that which seemed thoughtlessly spread upon the canvas has been done with the highest art by the author of the work. What the eyes observe in pictures, the ears perceive in music. Eminent composers very often mix discords with concords in order to arouse, and, as it were, sting the hearer, and as more solicitous concerning the outcome, all having soon been restored to order, that he may rejoice so much the more, in short, that we may take pleasure in petty dangers or experiences of evils by the sense itself, or by the display of either our power or happiness; or, as we delight in the spectacle of the rope-dancers, or in the sword-dance (*saltatione inter gladios — sauts perilleux*, Leibnitz), things that themselves excite terror, and we, our very selves, half let down the children in sport, as it were, now almost about to throw them before us, just as the ape bore Christian, king of Denmark, when an infant, and wrapped in swaddling clothes, to the roof of the house, and while all were anxious, like one in sport bore him safe back again into his cradle. In accord with the same principle, it is insipid always to eat sweet things; sharp, sour, nay more, bitter things which excite the taste, are to be mixed with them. He who has not tasted the bitter, has not deserved, nay more, will not appreciate the sweet. This itself is the law of joy, that pleasure does not proceed uninterruptedly; for this produces disgust, and makes us inert, not joyful.

But what we have said of this part which can be disturbed while the harmony on the whole is preserved is not so to be interpreted as if no account is taken of the parts, or as if it would suffice that the whole world be complete in its own parts, although it can happen that the human race is wretched, and that there is no care for justice in the universe, or account taken of us, as some think, who judge not rightly enough concerning the totality of things. For we must know that, as in the best constituted republic, care is taken that it be as well as possible with individuals, so the universe would not be sufficiently perfect unless, while the harmony of the universe is preserved, as much regard is had for particular interests. Of which thing no better measure could be constituted than the law itself of justice, saying that each should take part in the perfection of the universe, and in happiness proper in proportion to the measure of his own virtue and of that will which is a disposition of mind (*affectus*) toward[1] the common good, by which that itself is completed which we call the affection and love of God, in which alone the force and also the power of the Christian religion consists, in the judgment even of the wise theologians. Nor should it seem wonderful that so much is conferred

[1] Gerhardt reads, incorrectly, "ergo"; Erdmann, correctly, "erga" — TR.

upon souls in the universe, since they very closely reproduce the image[1] of the supreme author, and are related to him not only as machines to the maker (like the rest), but also as citizens to the prince, and will continue in existence equally with the universe itself, and express and concentrate in a measure the whole in themselves, so that it can be said that souls are the entire parts.

But as regards the sufferings especially of good men, it must certainly be maintained that they result in their greater good, and that is true not only theologically, but also physically, as the grain cast into the earth suffers before it bears fruit. And on the whole, it can be said that sufferings, temporarily evil, are in effect good, since they are the short roads to greater perfection. So, in physics, those liquors which ferment slowly are improved more slowly, but those in which the fermentation is stronger are improved more readily, the parts being thrown off with greater force. And this is, as you would say, to go back, in order, by a greater effort, to leap forwards (*qu'on recule pour mieux sauter*, — you go back to take a better leap). These views, therefore, must be maintained to be not only pleasing and comforting, but also most true. And in general, I think there is nothing, both truer than happiness, and more propitious and more delightful than truth.

Respecting the increase also of the beauty and general perfection of the divine works, a certain perpetual and very free progress of the whole universe is to be recognized, so that it proceeds to ever greater culture. As for instance, a great part of our earth receives culture and will receive more and more. And although it is true that sometimes some parts grow wild again or are destroyed and depreciated, yet this must so be understood, as a little before we interpreted suffering, namely, that this destruction and depreciation itself is useful in the attainment of something greater, so that in some measure we gain by the very loss.

And as to the objection which might be made that thus the world should long ago have been made a paradise, the reply is at hand: although already many substances have attained great perfection, nevertheless, on account of the divisibility of the continuum to infinity, there always remain in the abyss of things parts hitherto asleep, to be aroused and carried forwards to something greater and better, and, in a word, to a better culture. And accordingly, progress never comes to an end.

[1] Both Gerhardt and Erdmann read, "imagine"; manifestly a typographical error for "imaginem." — Tr.

VII

APPENDIX[1]

May, 1702

[*From the Latin*]

Up to the present time, I have published no book, indeed, against the Cartesian philosophy, but often in the "Acta Eruditorum Lipsiensium" and the "Journaux" of France and Holland hastily-thrown-off productions (*Schediasmata*) will be found inserted by me, in which I have borne witness to my dissent from it. But first (not to speak now of the others), about the nature of the body and what motive forces are in the body; in all others my opinion was the same. The Cartesians, it is true, place the essence of body in extension alone, but I, although with Aristotle and Descartes against Democritus and Gassendi I admit no vacuum, and against Aristotle with Democritus and Descartes think there is nothing but an apparent rarefaction and condensation, yet I think with Democritus and Aristotle against Descartes, that there is something passive in body besides extension, that, namely, by which body resists penetration; but besides this, I also recognize with Plato and Aristotle against Democritus and Descartes an active force or **ἐντελέχεια**, so that I think Aristotle so far rightly defined nature as the source (*principium*) of motion and rest, not because I think any body, unless already in motion, can be moved by itself or be put in motion by any quality such as gravity, but because I think every body always has implanted in it motive force (*motricem*), nay, rather motion actually intrinsic (*motum intrinscum actualem*), from the very beginning of things. Moreover, I agree with Democritus and Descartes against the multitude of the Scholastics, that the exercise of the motive (*motricis*) power and the phenomena of bodies can always be explained mechanically, the causes themselves of the laws of motion being withdrawn which spring from a higher source, namely, from the entelechy, which cannot be derived from the passive mass alone and its modifications.

But in order that my opinion may be better understood and its reasons also may be somewhat apparent, I think, in the first place, that the nature of body does not consist in extension alone, because in evolving the notion of extension we must notice that it is relative to something that is extended and signifies a diffusion or repetition

[1] Gerhardt, *Leibniz. math. Schrift.*, II, 2 [Vol. 6], 98–106; Gerhardt, *Leibniz. philos. Schrift.*, 4, 393–400; *cf.* G.'s *Einleitung*, *ibid.*, 271–272. The letter to Honoratus Fabri, and this Appendix, were printed by Gerhardt from the Ms. in the Royal Library at Hanover.

of a certain nature. For every repetition (or multitude of the same things) is either discrete, as in numbers where aggregate parts are discerned; or is continuous, where the parts are indeterminate and can be assumed in infinite ways. *Continua*, however, are of two kinds; the one successive, as time and motion, the other simultaneous or consisting of coexisting parts, as space and body. And as in time we conceive nothing else than the disposition or series itself of variations, which can occur in itself, so in space we perceive nothing else than the possible disposition of bodies. And so when space is said to be extended, we accept the statement in the same sense as when time is said to endure or number to be numbered; for, in truth, time adds nothing to duration nor space to extension, but as successive variations are in time, in body those things are diverse which can be diffused. For, because extension is a simultaneous continuous repetition as duration is a successive one, as often as the same nature is diffused at the same time through many things, as ductility or specific gravity or the yellow-color in gold or the white-color in milk, extension is said to have place generally in body as resistance or impenetrability, although it must be confessed that that diffusion continuous in color, weight, ductility, and things similar in kind but homogeneous, is only apparent and has no place in parts however small, and so the extension of resistance alone which is diffused through matter preserves this name with the strict investigator. But it is evident from these considerations, that extension is not an absolute predicate, but relative to that which is extended or diffused, and from the nature of which, diffusion can just as little be separated as number from the thing numbered. And hence those who assumed extension as an absolute primitive attribute, indefinable and ἄρρητον, erred by defect of analysis and took refuge in the occult qualities which for the rest they so despised, as if extension were something that cannot be explained.

The question now is asked, What is that nature whose diffusion constitutes body? We have already said that matter is constituted by the diffusion of resistance; but since in our opinion there is something else in body besides matter, the question is asked in what its nature consists. We say, therefore, it can consist in nothing else than ἐν τῷ δυναμικῷ or the indwelling principle of change and persistence. Whence also it uses the physical doctrine of the two mathematical sciences to whose principles it was subordinated, geometry and dynamics, the elements of which latter science not yet sufficiently propounded, I have elsewhere promised. Moreover, geometry itself, or the science of extension, again is subordinated to arithmetic, because in extension, as I said above, there is repetition or multitude, and dynamics is subordinated to metaphysic which treats of cause and effect.

Again, τὸ δυναμικόν or power in body is twofold, — passive and active. Passive power properly constitutes matter or mass, active ἐντελέχεια or form. Passive power is the resistance itself by which body resists not only penetration but also motion, and by which it happens that another body cannot enter into its place unless itself yields, but itself does not yield unless by retarding somewhat the motion of the impelling body, and so it attempts to continue steadfastly in its former state, not merely that it may not depart thence voluntarily, but also that it may resist change. And so there are therein two resistances or masses: the first antitypy, as they call it, or impenetrability; the second resistance, or what Kepler calls the natural inertia of bodies, which Descartes also somewhere in his letters acknowledged, from the fact that bodies certainly receive no new motion unless by force, and so resist the impression and break its force. This would not happen if there were not in the body, besides extension, τὸ δυναμικόν or the principle of the laws of motion, by which it happens that the quantity of forces cannot be increased, nor can a body even be impelled by another unless its own force is broken. This passive force in the body, moreover, is everywhere the same and proportional to its magnitude. For although some bodies appear more dense than others, this nevertheless happens because their pores are more filled with matter pertaining to the body, while, on the contrary, the rarer bodies have the nature of a sponge, so that another more subtile matter glides through their pores which is not reckoned with the body nor its motion followed or looked for.

Active force, which also absolutely is customarily called force, is not to be conceived as a simple common power of the schools, or as a receptivity of action, but involves a conatus or tendency to action, so that, unless something else hinders, action follows. And in this properly consists ἐντελέχεια, too little understood by the schools; for such a power involves act (*actum*), and does not persist in a naked faculty, although it does not always proceed wholly to the action (*actionem*) to which it tends, as often, namely, as an impediment is thrown in its way. Again active force is twofold, — primitive and derivative; that is, either substantial or accidental. Primitive active force, which is called by Aristotle ἐντελέχεια ἡ πρώτη, generally the form of substance (*forma substantiæ*), is another natural principle which with material or passive power completes the corporeal substance, which is, forsooth, *a unum per se*, not a mere aggregate of many substances; for there is much difference, for example, between an animal and a flock. And so this entelechy or soul, or something analogous to the soul, exists, and always naturally actuates some organic body, which itself separately assumed (*quod ipsum separatim sumtum*), when the soul is separated forsooth or removed, is not one substance, but an aggregate of many; in a word, a natural machine.

This natural machine, moreover, has this highest prerogative as compared with an artificial, that exhibiting a proof of a divine author, it consists of infinite organs wrapped up in itself, and so can never be utterly destroyed, just as it cannot be absolutely produced, but can be diminished only and increased, and be involved and evolved, this being to a certain extent itself a substance, and in it (however transformed) a certain degree of vitality, or, if you prefer, of primitive activity being always preserved. For what is said of animate things must also be said proportionally of those which are not properly animals. Meanwhile, it must be maintained that intelligences, or the more noble souls which are also called spirits, are ruled by God not only as machines, but also as subjects, and are not liable to those changes to which other living beings are exposed.

Derivative force is that which some call impetus, a conatus evidently or tendency, so to speak, to a certain determinate motion, by which accordingly primitive force or the principle of action is modified. I have shown that this is not preserved the same in the same body, but yet, however distributed in many, it remains the same in the amount and differs from motion itself, whose quantity is not preserved. And this itself also is the impression which a body receives by impulse, by whose aid projectiles continue their motion and do not need any new impulse, which Gassendi also has illustrated by elegant experiments made on shipboard. Thus also some incorrectly think that projectiles have their motion continued by the air. Further, derivative force differs from action only as the instantaneous from the successive; for there is already force in the first instant, but action requires a period of time, and so is brought to pass by the prolongation of forces in time, which is perceived in any part of the body whatever. And so action is in reason composed of body, time, and force (*vis*) or energy (*virtutis*), since by the Cartesians the quantity of motion is estimated by the calculation of velocity in the body, and forces are considered far otherwise than as velocities, as will soon be stated.

To place active force in bodies moreover, many things compel us, and especially the experience itself, which shows that motions are in matter, although these motions must be attributed originally to the general cause of things,— God; immediately, however, and specifically, they must be attributed to the force placed in things by God. For to say that God in creation has given to bodies a law of action, is nothing unless he has given at the same time something by which the law is observed; otherwise he himself will be obliged always to procure in an extraordinary manner the observance of the law. Yea, rather his law is efficacious, and makes bodies efficient; *i.e.* he gave to them natural (*insitam*) force. Further, we must consider that derived force and action is a certain mode (*modale*), since it admits change. But every mode is constituted by some modification of something persisting or more absolute. And just as figure is a certain limitation or modification of passive force or extended mass, so derivative force and moving action (*actio motrix*) is a certain modification not certainly of a thing merely passive (otherwise a modificatiou or limit would involve more reality than the thing itself which is limited), but of something active, that is, of the primitive entelechy. Therefore, derivative and accidental or changeable force will be a certain modification of the primitive energy (*virtutis*) essential to and abiding in every corporeal substance. Whence the Cartesians, since they acknowledge no active principle substantial and capable of modification in the body, are compelled themselves to reject (*abjudicare*) all action, and to transfer it to God alone, a far-fetched mechanical view (*accersitum ex Machina*), which is not philosophical.

But primitive force is changed by derivative in the impacts of bodies, according as the exercise of primitive force is turned within or without. For in truth, every body has an internal motion, nor can it ever be brought to rest. This internal force, again, turns itself without, when it performs the duty of elastic force, when, namely, internal motion is impeded in its accustomed course, whence every body is essentially elastic, water not even excepted, and how violently this rebounds, even the cannon balls (*pilæ tormentariæ*) show. And unless every body were elastic, the laws of motions could not be proved true and binding. Meanwhile this force does not always render itself conspicuous in the sensible parts themselves of bodies, since these manifestly do not sufficiently cohere. But the harder a body is, the more elastic it is and the more strongly it rebounds. Indeed in impact, when bodies mutually rebound from each other, this occurs through elastic force, whence indeed bodies always have their own special motion from impact by their own special force, to which a foreign impulse furnishes only an occasion of acting, and, so to speak, a determination.

Hence, moreover, we understand that, although that primitive force or form of substance (which, it is true, determines even the forms in matter, while it produces motion) is admitted, yet in explaining elastic force and other phenomena we must always proceed mechanically, certainly by the forms which are modifications of matter and by impulses which are modifications of form. And it is useless, when distinct and specific reasons should be given, to have recourse immediately and in general (*generice*) to form or primitive force in a thing, as it is useless in explaining the phenomena of created things to recur to the first substance or God, unless his means or ends are at the same time specifically explained, and the proximate efficient or even the special final causes are rightly assigned, so that his power and wisdom appear. For in general (whatever Descartes may have said), not only efficient, but also final causes, belong to physical discussion (*tractationis*); precisely as a house is badly exhibited, if any of its parts betrays its structure only, not its use. I have further already pointed out above that, since we affirm that all things in nature are explained mechanically, the reasons themselves of the laws of motion or the principles of mechanics must be excepted, which should be deduced not from mathematics alone and the imagination of the subject, but from a metaphysical source, namely, from the equality of cause and effect, and from other laws of this kind which are essential to entelechies. Certainly, as has already been said, physics is subordinate through geometry to arithmetic, through dynamics to metaphysics.

But the Cartesians, not sufficiently understanding the nature of forces, confounding motive force with motion, have seriously erred in determining the laws of motions. For although Descartes knew that the same force must be preserved in nature, and that a body, although he attributed a part of its force (namely, the derivative) to another, so retains a part that the sum of the forces remains the same, (yet), deceived by the example of equilibrium or dead force as I call it (which here does not enter into the reckoning, and of living force or of that which is now in question, it is only an infinitesimal part), (he) believed that force exists in a composite system (*ratione composita*) of masses and velocities, or that it is the same as that which he calls quantity of motion, by which term he understands the product of the mass into the velocity (*ex ductu massæ in celeritatem*), when, nevertheless, it has elsewhere been demonstrated by me *a priori* that forces exist in a composite system of simple masses and double velocities. I know that lately certain learned men, when at length they were compelled to admit against the Cartesians that the same quantity of motion is not preserved in nature, and considered this too alone as absolute force, concluded that this force also does not abide, and took refuge in the conservation alone of relative (*respectivæ*) force, but we have discovered that not in the conservation of absolute force even has nature been mindful of her own constancy and perfection. And the opinion of the Cartesians indeed, in which the quantity of motion is preserved, contradicts all the phenomena, (while) ours is wonderfully confirmed by experiments.

The Cartesians err, also, in this, because they think that changes occur by a leap (*per saltum*); as if, for example, a body at rest can in a moment pass over into a state of determined motion, or as if a body placed in motion can suddenly be brought back to rest, not by passing through the intermediate grades of velocity, because they have plainly not understood the use of elastic force in the concourse of bodies. Which, if it were absent, I confess that neither the law which I call the law of continuity would be observed in things, through which leaps are avoided, nor the law of equivalence by which absolute forces are conserved, nor other excellent inventions of nature's architect have place, by which the necessity of matter and the beauty of form are united. Moreover, the elastic force itself implanted in every body shows that there is in every body, also, internal motion and infinite (so to speak) primitive force, although in the impact itself, when circumstances demand, it is determined by derivative force. [For, as in an arch, any part whatever sustains the entire weight, or in a tense cord the traction, and any portion whatever of compressed air, has as much force as the weight of the air pressing upon it, so any corpuscle whatever, of the entire ambient (*ambientis*) mass is solicited to action by the conspiring force, and awaits nothing but an occasion for exercising its power, as is shown by the example of gunpowder (*pulveris pyrii*)].

There are many other things in which I have been obliged to depart from Descartes, but those which I have now brought forth relate chiefly to the principles themselves of corporeal substances, and, if you interpret them rightly, are capable of vindicating the ancient philosophy of a healthier school, which I see deserted by many of the more recent scholars, even those well disposed towards it, where there was no need. The philosophy of Rev. Father Ptolemæus,[1] a man very versed in the principles of the ancients and the moderns, whose remarkable teaching I examined myself, at Rome (from which philosophy I promise myself very much), has not yet reached us.

In a note, Leibnitz has added: In addition, I am pleased to state, that although very many Cartesians boldly reject forms and forces in bodies, Descartes nevertheless spoke more moderately, and professed this only, that he found no reason for using them. I indeed admit that they should be rejected if of no use; but in this very thing I have shown that Descartes has erred. For not only in entelechies, or τῷ δυναμικῷ, are placed the principles of mechanism, by which all things are regulated in bodies, but I have also shown in the "Acta Eruditorum,"[2] when I was replying to the very celebrated man, John Christopher Sturm,[3] who attacked, in his "Physica Eclectica," my in-

[1] Giovanni Battista Tolomei, 1653–1726, was acquainted with all the European languages and had a very extensive knowledge of all the sciences of his time, and was reputed a profound theologian and skilful critic. Among his works was *Philosophia mentis et sensuum*, Romæ, 1696, fol., Augustæ Vindelicorum, 1698, fol. — Tr.

[2] Sept. 1698. The piece is the *De ipsa natura*, *cf.* Gerhardt, *Leibniz. philos. Schrift.*, 4, 504–516; Erdmann, 154–160; Jacques (in French), 1, 455–468; Janet (in French), 2, 553–567; transl., Duncan, 112–126. *Cf.* also Gerhardt's *Einleitung*, *op. cit.*, 4, 417. — Tr.

[3] Johann Christoph Sturm, 1635–1703, was, from 1669, Professor of Mathematics and Physics at the University of Altdorf. His *Physica Eclectica* appeared at Nuremburg, 1697, 4to. While not celebrated for physical dis-

sufficiently understood doctrine, with irrefragable demonstration that, completeness being assumed, if there were nothing in matter but mass itself and arrangement of its parts, it would be impossible for any perceptible variation whatever to occur, since equivalences are substituted for limits, and by banishing conatus, or the force of tendency, to the future (the entelechies, that is, being removed), the state of things present at one moment cannot be distinguished from the state at any other moment. And I think Aristotle perceived this when he saw that, besides local motion, change is necessary in order to satisfy the phenomena. But changes, although in appearance manifold, just as qualities, are reduced in the last analysis to variation alone of forces. For all the qualities of bodies, that is, all their real stable accidents, except forms (that is, those which do not exist in transition, as motion, but are known as present, although referred to the future), are at length, when analysis is set up, reduced to forces. Further, when forces are removed, nothing real remains in motion itself, for from variation alone of arrangement it cannot be determined where the true motion or the cause of variation is.

VIII

LETTER OF LEIBNITZ TO BASNAGE DE BEAUVAL, EDITOR OF THE "HISTOIRE DES OUVRAGES DES SAVANTS," PRINTED IN THAT JOURNAL, JULY, 1698, pp. 329 *sq.*[1]

Explanation of the difficulties which M. Bayle has found in the New System of the Union of the Soul and the Body

[*From the French*]

I take the liberty, Sir, to send you this explanation of the difficulties which M. Bayle has found in the hypothesis which I have proposed in order to explain the union of the soul and the body. Nothing is kinder than the manner which he has used towards me, and I consider myself honored by the objections he has placed in his excellent Dictionary, in the article Rorarius. Moreover, a mind as great and as profound as his cannot make them without instructing, and I shall try to profit by the light which he has shed upon

coveries, he emphasized the method of experiment, and spread abroad a taste for experimenting. Germany is said to owe to him the introduction of the teaching of mathematics into the gymnasia and the common schools. — Tr.

[1] *Cf.* Gerhardt, *Leibniz. philos. Schrift.*, 4, 517–524, *cf.* G.'s *Einleitung*, *ibid.*, 419; Erdmann, *Leibnit. op. philos.*, 150–154; Jacques, *Œuvres de Leibniz*, 1, 481–487; Dutens, *Leibnit. op. om.*, 2, Pt. I., 74–79.

these matters in this part as well as in many other parts of his work. He does not reject what I had said of the conservation of the soul and also of the animal, but he does not yet appear satisfied with the manner in which I have claimed to explain the union and the intercourse of the soul and the body in the "Journal des Savants" of June 27 and of July 4, 1695, and in the "Histoire des ouvrages des savants," February, 1696, pp. 274, 275.

Here are his words, which seem to indicate wherein he has found difficulty: "I cannot understand," he says, "the series of actions, internal and spontaneous, which would cause the soul of a dog to feel pain immediately after having felt joy, although it were alone in the universe." I reply that when I said that the soul, although only God and it should exist in the world, would feel all that it now feels, I only employed a fiction in supposing that which cannot happen naturally, in order to show that the feelings of the soul are only a consequence of that which is already in it. I know not whether the proof of incomprehensibility which M. Bayle finds in this series must be sought alone in that which he calls lower, or whether he wished to introduce it from this time by the example of the spontaneous passage from joy to pain; perhaps, by wishing to throw out a hint that this passage is contrary to the axiom which teaches us that a thing always continues in the state in which it is once if nothing occurs which obliges it to change, and that thus the animal having once joy will always have it if it is alone or if nothing external makes it pass to pain; in every case I agree with the axiom, and, further, I maintain that it is in my favor, as in fact it is one of my grounds. Is it not true that from this axiom we conclude, not only that a body at rest will always be at rest, but also that a body which is in motion will always preserve this motion or change, that is to say, the same volocity and the same direction, if nothing occurs to hinder it? Thus a thing does not remain only so long as it depends upon itself (*d'elle*) in the state in which it is; but also when this is a state of change, it continues to change, following always one and the same law. Now it is, according to my view, the nature of created substance to change continually according to a certain order which conducts it *spontaneously* (if I may avail myself of this word) through all the states which will happen to it, so that he who sees all, sees in its present state all its past and future states. And this law of order, which constitutes the individuality of each particular substance, has an exact relation to that which happens in every substance and in the entire universe. Perhaps I do not make too bold a statement if I say that I can demonstrate all this, but at present the question is only of maintaining it as a possible hypothesis suitable for explaining the phenomena. Now in this way the law of the change of the substance of the animal bears it from joy to pain at the moment that a continuous solution is made in its body, because the law of the indivisible substance of this animal is to represent what is done in its body in the way that we experience it, and also to represent in some fashion and in relation to this body all that is done in the world; the unities of substance being nothing else than different concentrations of the universe represented according to the different points of view which distinguish them.

M. Bayle continues: "I understand why a dog passes immediately from pleasure to pain when, being very hungry, and eating bread, we give him a blow with a stick." I do not know whether we understand it sufficiently. No one knows better than M. Bayle himself, that it is in this that the great difficulty consists of explaining why that which passes in the body produces a change in the soul, and that it is this which has forced the defenders of occasional causes to recur to the care which God must take to represent continually to the soul the changes which take place in the body; whilst I believe that it is the nature itself which God has given it to represent in virtue of its own laws what passes in the organs. He continues:

"But that his soul is constructed in such a way that at the moment he is struck he would feel the pain, although we should not strike him, although he should continue to eat the bread undisturbed and unhindered, this is what I cannot understand." I do not remember, also, to have said it, and we could say it only by a metaphysical fiction, as when we suppose that God annihilates a body in order to produce a vacuum, both being equally contrary to the order of things. For since the nature of the soul was made at first in a manner suited to represent successively the changes of matter, the case we suppose cannot happen in the natural order. God could give to each substance its phenomena independent of those of others; but in this way he would have made, so to speak, as many worlds without connection as there are substances; almost, as we say, that when we dream we are in a world apart, and that we enter into the common world when we awake. It is not that the dreams are unrelated to the organs and the rest of the body, but that they are related in a manner less distinct. Let us continue with M. Bayle:

"I find, also," says he, "the spontaneity of this soul very incompatible with the feelings of pain, and, in general, with all the perceptions which are displeasing to it." This incomprehensibility would be certain, if spontaneous and voluntary were the same thing. Everything voluntary is spontaneous; but there are spontaneous actions which are without choice, and consequently are not voluntary. It does not depend upon the soul, always, to procure feelings which please it, since the feelings it will have depend upon those which it has had. M. Bayle proceeds:

"Moreover, the reason why this clever man does not approve the

Cartesian system appears to me to be a false supposition : for it cannot be said that the system of occasional causes makes the action of God intervene by a miracle (*Deum ex machina*) in the reciprocal dependence of the body and soul; for, as God intervenes only according to general laws, he does not act there in an extraordinary way." It is not for this reason alone that I do not approve of the Cartesian system; and if you consider mine a little, you see clearly that I find in itself that which leads me to embrace it. Moreover, if the hypothesis of occasional causes should not need miracle, it seems that mine would not cease to have other advantages. I have said that we may imagine three systems to explain the intercourse we find between the soul and the body; namely, first, the system of the influence of the one upon the other, which is that of the schools taken in the common sense, which I believe impossible, after the Cartesians; second, that of a perpetual overseer, who represents in the one that which takes place in the other, very much as if a man were charged with making two bad clocks always to agree, which of themselves would not be capable of agreeing, and this is the system of occasional causes; and third, that of the natural agreement of two substances such as would exist between two very accurate clocks; and I find this as possible as the system of the overseer, and more worthy of the author of these substances, clocks or automata. But let us see whether the system of occasional causes does not in reality suppose a perpetual miracle. They say here, no, because God would act according to this system only through general laws. I agree, but, in my opinion, that is not sufficient in order to remove the miracles: if God did it continually, they would not cease to be miracles, taking this word not popularly, as a thing rare and wonderful, but philosophically, as that which exceeds the forces of created beings. It is not sufficient to say that God has made a general law; for, besides the decree, there must also be a natural means of executing it; that is to say, what takes place must be capable of being explained by the nature which God gives to things. The laws of nature are not so arbitrary or so indifferent as many think. If God decreed, for example, that all bodies should have a tendency toward a circular line, and that the radii of the circles should be proportional to the size of the bodies, it would be necessary to say that there is a means of executing this decree by more simple laws, or rather, it would be necessary to admit that God will execute it miraculously, or at least by angels expressly charged with this care, very nearly like those who were sometimes given to the celestial spheres. It would be the same if some one said that God has given to the bodies natural and primitive gravities by which each should tend to the centre of its globe, without being pushed by other bodies; for in my opinion this system would need a perpetual miracle, or at least the assistance of the angels.

"Does the internal and active property communicated to the forms of bodies know the series of actions it is to produce? Not at all; for we know by experience that we are ignorant that we have in an hour such or such perceptions." I reply that this property, or rather this soul or form, does not know them distinctly, but that it feels them confusedly. There is in each substance traces of all which has happened to it and of all which will happen to it. But this infinite multitude of perceptions hinders us in distinguishing them; as when I hear a great confused noise of a whole people, I do not distinguish one voice from another.

"It would be necessary, then, that the forms be directed by some external principle in the production of their acts; would not this be the *Deus ex machina*, just the same as in the system of occasional causes?" The preceding reply puts a stop to this inference. On the contrary, the present state of each substance is a natural result of its preceding state; but there is only one infinite intelligence therein which can see this result, for it envelops the universe in souls as well as in each portion of matter.

M. Bayle concludes with these words: "Finally, as he supposes with much reason that all souls are simple and indivisible, we cannot understand how they can be compared to a pendulum, that is to say, that by their original constitution they can diversify their operations, by availing themselves of the spontaneous activity which they would receive from their Creator. We conceive clearly that a simple being will always act uniformly, if no foreign cause turns it aside. If it were composed of many pieces, as a machine, it would act diversely, because the particular activity of each piece might change at every moment the course of that of the others; but in a single substance, where will you find the cause of the change of operation?" I find that this objection is worthy of M. Bayle, and that it belongs to those which most deserve to be cleared up. But I also think that if I had not provided for it at first, my system would not deserve to be examined. I have compared the soul to a pendulum only in regard to the regulated precision of its changes, which is indeed but imperfect in the best clocks, but which is perfect in the works of God; and we may say that the soul is an immaterial automaton of the most accurate kind. When it is said that a simple being will always act uniformly, there is a distinction to be made, if *to act uniformly* is to follow perpetually one and the same law of order or of continuity, as in a certain rank or series of numbers, I admit that every simple being itself, and indeed every complex being acts uniformly; but if *uniformly* means likewise, I do not agree. To explain the difference of this sense by an example, a movement in a parabolic line is uniform in the first sense; but it is not so in the second, the portions of the parabolic line not being similar among themselves like those of the straight lines. It is true, to mention it in passing, that a simple body left to itself describes only straight lines, if we speak only of the centre which represents the motion of this entire body; but when a simple and rigid body, having once received a turbination or circulation around its centre, retains it in the same sense and with the same velocity, it follows that a body left to itself may describe circular lines by its points distant from the centre, when the centre is at rest, and even *certain quadratrices*, when this centre is in motion, which have the ordinate composed of the straight line running through the centre, and of the right sine whose versed sine is the abscissa, the area being to the circumference as this straight line is to a given straight line. We must consider also that the soul, wholly simple as it is, has always a feeling composed of many perceptions at once, which fact effects as much for our purpose as if it were composed of pieces like a machine. For each preceding perception influences the following, conformably to a law of order which exists in perceptions as in movements. Thus the majority of philosophers, for many centuries, who allow thoughts to souls and to angels, which they believe destitute of all body, to say nothing of the intelligences of Aristotle, admit a spontaneous change in a simple being. I add that since the perceptions which are found together in one and the same soul, at the same time, involve a multitude veritably infinite of minute indistinguishable feelings as the sequel must develop, we must not be astonished at the infinite variety of that which must result therefrom in time. All this is only a consequence of the representative nature of the soul, which must express what passes and indeed what will pass in its body, and in some fashion in all others, through the connection or correspondence of all parts of the world. It would perhaps suffice to say that God, having made atoms corporeal, might also well have made them immaterial to represent the first; but we have thought it would be well to dwell upon it a little more.

For the rest, I have read with pleasure what M. Bayle says in the article Zeno. It might, perhaps, be perceived that what can be drawn therefrom agrees better with my system than with every other, for what there is of reality in extension and motion consists only in the ground of the order and the regulated series of phenomena and perceptions. In like manner, as many academicians and sceptics as those who wish to reply to them, seem to be embarrassed principally only because they sought a greater reality in sensible things outside of us than that of the regulated phenomena. We conceive *extension* in conceiving an order in coexistences, but we must not conceive it any more than space, after the fashion of a substance. It is like *time*, which presents to the mind only an order in changes. And as for *motion*, what is real therein is the *force* or the power; that is to say, what there is in the present state which carries with itself a change for the future. The rest is only phenomena and relations. The consideration of this system shows also that, when we enter into the heart of things, we find more reason than we thought in the majority of the philosophic sects. The little substantial reality of the sensible things of the Sceptics; the reduction of all to harmonies or numbers, ideas, and perceptions of the Pythagoreans and Platonists; the one and also the all of Parmenides and of Plotinus without any Spinozism; the Stoic connection, compatible with the spontaneity of the others; the vital philosophy of the Kabbalists and Hermetics who put feeling above everything; the forms and entelechies of Aristotle and the Scholastics, and even the mechanical explanation of all particular phenomena, according to Democritus and the moderns, and so forth, find themselves reunited as in a centre of perspective, whence the object, obscured in regarding it from an entirely different point, shows its regularity and the agreement of its parts; we have failed through a sectarian spirit in limiting ourselves by the rejection of others. The formalist philosophers blame the material or corpusculary ones, and *vice versa.* We wrongly give limits to the division and subtilty as well as to the richness and beauty of nature when we posit atoms and the vacuum, when we imagine certain primary elements, such as the Cartesians, instead of veritable unities, and when we do not recognize the infinite in everything, and the exact expression of the greatest in the smallest, united to the tendency of each to develop itself in a perfect order, which is the most admirable and the most beautiful result of the sovereign principle, whose wisdom would leave nothing better to be desired by those who could understand its economy.

IX

FRAGMENT OF A LETTER TO AN UNKNOWN PERSON

October 16, 1707 [1]

[*From the French*]

I think, then, I have good reasons for believing that all the different classes of beings whose union forms the universe, exist in the ideas of God only as so many ordinates of the same curve, the union of which does not allow the placing of others between them, because that would indicate disorder and imperfection. Men are connected

[1] Guhrauer, *Leibnitz, Eine Biographie,* Anmerkungen z. zw. Buche, pp. 31–33. Guhrauer says in the note which contains the Fragment here translated: "The Principle of Continuity, with which Leibnitz accomplishes so much in

with the animals, these with the plants, and these again with the fossils, which will be united in their turn with bodies which the senses and the imagination represent to us as perfectly dead and shapeless. Now since the law of continuity demands that *when the essential determinations of a being approach those of another so that likewise accordingly all the properties of the first must gradually approach those of the last*, it is necessary that all the orders of natural beings form only one chain, in which the different classes, like so many links, connect so closely the one to the other, that it is impossible for the senses and the imagination to fix the precise point where any one begins or ends: all the species which border on or which occupy, so to speak, the regions of inflection and retrogression being obliged to be equivocal and endowed with characters which can refer to the neighboring species equally. Thus the existence of Zoophytes for example, or, as Buddeus[1] calls them, *Plant-Animals*, is nowise monstrous, but it is indeed agreeable to the order of Nature that there are some. And such is the force of the principle of continuity with me that, not only should I not be astonished to learn that beings had been found which as regards many properties, for example, those of maintaining and multiplying themselves, might pass for vegetables with as good right as for animals, and which would reverse the ordinary rules, based upon the supposition of a perfect and absolute separation of the different orders of simultaneous beings which fill the universe; I should be so little astonished, I say, that I am indeed convinced that there must be such, that Natural History will perhaps some day succeed in knowing them, when it shall have studied more this infinite number of living beings, whose minuteness hides them from ordinary observation and which are found concealed in the

Psychology, led him to surprising glimpses in his views of animate nature. Nowhere has Leibnitz expressed himself so clearly upon this subject, as in the letter to an unknown person, of Oct. 16, 1707, of which a fragment occasioned the notorious controversy between Maupertuis and König, 1752. It stands with many others in König's *Appel au Public du jugement de l'académie royale de Berlin*, etc. See p. 45. [Then follows the letter]. . . . This is the same letter which the Berlin Academy, under the inspiration of Maupertuis, declared a forgery, and struck off the list of the Academicians Professor König as an impostor. — There are perhaps few pieces of Leibnitz, whose genuineness are so certified to the connoisseur, as this letter (which Dutens and Erdmann have overlooked). Voltaire also (in his letter to König) recognized its genuineness at once, although only from motives which he drew from the style. The Academy was right only in the fact that the letter could not have been addressed to Hermann. *Cf. Leibn. opp.* [ed. Dutens], 3, 531." — Tr.

[1] Leibnitz probably refers to Johann Franz Buddeus, 1667–1729, assistant in the philosophical faculty at Wittenberg, Professor of Greek and Latin at Coburg Gymnasium, of Philosophy at Halle, and of Theology at Jena. He published *Elementa philosophiæ practicæ instrumentalis et theoreticæ*, Halæ, 1703. — Tr.

bowels of the earth and the depths of the waters. We remarked only since yesterday what grounds have we for denying to reason what we have not yet had occasion to see? The principle of continuity is then beyond doubt with me, and might aid in establishing many important truths in the true philosophy, which, raising itself above the senses and the imagination, seeks the origin of phenomena in the regions of the intellect. I flatter myself that I have some ideas concerning them, but this age is not qualified to receive them.

X

THAT THE MOST PERFECT BEING EXISTS[1]

[*From the Latin*]

I call every simple quality which is positive and absolute, or expresses whatever it expresses without any limits, a *perfection.*

But a quality of this sort, because it is simple, is therefore irresolvable or indefinable, for otherwise, either it will not be a simple quality but an aggregate of many, or, if it is one, it will be circumscribed by limits and so be known through negations of further progress[2] contrary to the hypothesis, for a purely positive quality was assumed.

From these considerations it is not difficult to show that *all perfections are compatible with each other* or can exist in the same subject.

For let the proposition be of this kind:

A and *B* are incompatible

(for understanding by *A* and *B* two simple forms of this kind or perfections, and it is the same if more are assumed like them[3]), it is evident that it cannot be demonstrated without the resolution of the terms *A* and *B*, of each or both; for otherwise their nature would not enter into the ratiocination and the incompatibility could be demonstrated as well from any others as from themselves. But now (by hypothesis) they are irresolvable. Therefore this proposition cannot be demonstrated from these forms.

But it might certainly be demonstrated by these if it were true, because[4] it is not true *per se*, for all propositions necessarily true are

[1] Gerhardt, *Leibniz. philos. Schrift.*, 7, 261–262. *Cf.* Gerhardt's *Einleitung*, *ibid.*, 251. — Tr.

[2] Leibnitz had first written: "atque ita ope negationum," *i.e.* and thus also by means of negations. — *Gerhardt.* — Tr.

[3] The words, "idemque est . . .," were added later. — *Gerhardt.* — Tr.

[4] For the following, up to the words: "aut per se notæ," Leibnitz at first wrote: "(esset enim necessaria, neque tamen per se nota)" *i.e.* for it would be necessary, and yet not known *per se.* — *Gerhardt.* — Tr.

either demonstrable or known *per se*. Therefore, this proposition is not necessarily true. Or[1] if it is not necessary that *A* and *B* exist in the same subject, they cannot therefore exist in the same subject, and since the reasoning is the same as regards any other assumed qualities of this kind, therefore all perfections are compatible.

It is granted, therefore, that either a subject of all perfections or the most perfect being can be known.

Whence it is evident that it also exists, since existence is contained in the number of the perfections.[2]

Gerhardt says: "In the foregoing is found what Leibnitz brought before Spinoza. The following he appears later to have added:"

[The same can be shown also as regards the forms composed from the absolute forms, provided they are granted.]

I showed this reasoning to D. Spinoza when I was in The Hague,[3] who thought it solid; for when at first he opposed it, I put it in writing and read this paper before him.

Schol.

The reasoning of Descartes concerning the existence of the most perfect being assumed that the most perfect being can be known, or is possible. For this being assumed because a notion of this kind is granted, it immediately follows that that being exists, since we framed the notion in such a way that it immediately contains existence. But the question is asked whether it is within our power to conceive such a being, or whether such a notion exists on the side of the thing, and can be clearly and distinctly known without contradiction. For the opponents will say that such a notion of the most perfect being or of a being existing through his essence is a chimera. Nor is it sufficient for Descartes to appeal to experience and to allege that he perceives the same in such a manner in himself clearly and distinctly, for this is to break off, not to complete the demonstration, unless he shows the method through which others also can attain the same experience; for as often as we bring experiences into the midst of the demonstration, we ought to show others also the method of producing the same experience, unless we wish to convince them by our authority alone.

[1] This sentence up to "omnes perfectiones," was added later. — *Gerhardt*. — Tr.

[2] At first: "inter perfectiones." — *Gerhardt*. — Tr.

[3] November, 1676; *cf.* Guhrauer, *Leibnitz, Eine Biographie*, Pt. I., 184. — Tr.

XI

WHAT IS IDEA[1]

[*From the Latin*]

First of all (however), by the term *Idea* we mean *something which is in our mind;* marks (*vestigia*) therefore impressed upon the brain are not ideas, for I assume as certain that the mind is something else than the brain, or a more subtile part of the brain substance.

But there are many things in our mind — for example, thoughts, perceptions, affections — which we know well are not ideas, although without ideas they would not be produced. For idea for us *consists not in a certain act of thought, but in a power* (*facultate*), and we say we have an idea of a thing, although we do not think of it, provided we can on a given occasion think of it.

There is nevertheless also in this a certain difficulty, for we have a remote power of thinking about all things, even of those of which we have not perchance ideas, because we have the power of recovering them; idea, therefore, demands a *certain power near at hand of thinking about a thing or facility.*

But not even this suffices, for he who has a method which if he follows he can attain the thing, does not, therefore, have an idea of it. As, if I should enumerate in order the sections of a cone, it is certain that I would come into the knowledge of opposite hyperbolas, although I have not yet an idea of them. There must necessarily, therefore, be something in me, *which not only leads to the thing, but also expresses it.*

That is said to *express* anything in which are contained conditions corresponding to the conditions of the thing to be expressed. But these expressions are varied; for example, the model of the machine expresses the machine itself, a perspective drawing of a thing in a plane expresses a solid, an oration expresses thoughts and truths, letters express numbers, an algebraic equation expresses a circle or other figure; and because these expressions have something common, from the contemplation of the conditions of the expressing thing, we can come into the knowledge of the corresponding properties of the thing to be expressed. Whence it is evident that it is not necessary that that which expresses be similar to the thing expressed, provided a certain analogy of conditions is preserved.

It is also evident that some expressions have a basis in nature, but others at least are partly based in will (*arbitrio*), as are the expressions which are produced by sounds or characters. Those things which

[1] Gerhardt, *Leibniz. philos. Schrift.*, 7, 263–264. *Cf.* Gerhardt's *Einleitung*, *ibid.*, 251–252. — Tr.

are based upon nature demand either some similitude, such as exists between a great circle and a little one, or between a region and a map of the region; or at least a connection such as exists between a circle and an ellipse which represents it in perspective (*optice*), for any point whatever of an ellipse corresponds, according to a certain fixed law, to some point of a circle. Nay, rather, the circle, by any other similar figure in such a case, would be badly represented. In like manner, every complete effect represents a complete cause; for I can always, from the knowledge of such effect, come to the knowledge of its cause. Thus the deeds of each one represent his mind, and the world itself in a measure represents God. It can also happen that those things which arise from the same cause express themselves by turns; for example, gesture and discourse. So certain deaf persons understand those who speak, not by the sound, but by the motion of the mouth.

And so the idea of things existing in us is nothing else than the fact that God, the author alike of things and the mind, has impressed this power of thought upon the mind, so that out of its own workings it can draw those things which perfectly correspond to those which follow from things. And so, although the idea of a circle is not like the circle, yet from it truths can be drawn which in the true circle experience would no doubt confirm.

XII

ON THE METHOD OF DISTINGUISHING REAL FROM IMAGINARY PHENOMENA[1]

[*From the Latin*]

Being is that the concept of which involves something positive, or that which can by us be conceived, provided that which we conceive is possible, and does not involve a contradiction, which we know, both if the concept is perfectly explained, and involves no confusion; and briefly, if the thing actually exists, for that which exists is certainly a being or a possible thing.

But as far as Being is explained by a distinct concept, so is Existence by a distinct perception; and that we may the better understand this, we must see in what ways existence is proved. And in the first place, without proof, I affirm existence, from the simple perception or experience of which I am conscious within myself; that is, in the first place, *myself*, thinking the various things, then the various *phenomena*

[1] Gerhardt, *Leibniz. philos. Schrift.*, 7, 319–322; Erdmann, *Leibnit. opera philos.*, 443–445. — Tr.

themselves, or the appearances which exist in my mind. For these two, since they are immediately perceived by the mind with the intervention of no other, can be wholly proved, and it is equally certain that there exists in my mind the species of a mountain of gold or of a centaur, when I dream of these, as it is certain that I exist who dream; for each is contained in this one thing, that it is certain that the centaur appears to me.

Let us now see by what signs we may know what phenomena are real. We determine this now, both from the phenomenon itself, and from the antecedent and consequent phenomena. From the phenomenon itself, whether it be vivid, multiplex, congruous. It will be vivid, if the qualities, as light, color, heat, appear sufficiently intense; it will be multiplex if they are varied, and adapted to many tests and to the institution of new observations; for example, if we experience in the phenomenon not only colors but also sounds, odors, flavors, tactile qualities, and those things both in the whole and in its various parts, which again we can discuss in various relations (*variis causis tractare*). Which things, indeed, a long series of observations, instituted especially with design and with choice, is wont to meet neither in dreams nor in those images which the memory or the phantasy presents, in which the image is very often weak and also disappears (*disparet*) in the course of the discussion. The phenomenon will be congruous when it consists of many phenomena, the reason of which can be given from themselves in turn, or from some common hypothesis sufficiently simple; then it will be congruous if it preserves the usage of other phenomena which have frequently presented themselves to us so that the parts of the phenomenon have that position, order, result, which similar phenomena have had. Otherwise, they will be suspected; for if we should see men moved in the air, sitting upon the hippogryphs of Ariosto, we should doubt, I think, whether we were dreaming or awake. But this proof can be referred to another head of considerations assumed from the preceding phenomena. With which phenomena the present phenomenon must be congruous, if, namely, they preserve the same usage, that is, if the reason of this can be given from the preceding, or all agree with the same hypothesis as a common reason. But, undoubtedly, the strongest proof is the agreement with the whole course of life, especially if very many others affirm that the same agrees with their own phenomena also; for, that other substances similar to us exist, is not only probable, but indeed. certain, as I shall soon say. But the most powerful proof of the reality of phenomena, which, indeed, alone suffices, is the success in predicting future phenomena from the past and present, whether that prediction is founded in reason, or in the hypothesis thus far succeeding, or in the usage thus far observed. Nay, although this entire life were said to be nothing but a dream, and the visible world nothing but a phantasm, I should call this dream or phantasm real enough, if, using reason well, we were never deceived by it; but just as we know from these what phenomena must be regarded as real, so, on the other hand, whatever phenomena conflict with these which we judge real, also those whose fallacy we can explain from their own causes, these only we think apparent.

But it must be confessed that the proofs of real phenomena which thus far have been brought forward, howsoever united, are not demonstrative; for, although they have the greatest probability, or, as is commonly said, produce a moral certainty, they, nevertheless, do not create a metaphysical certainty, so that the assertion of the contrary implies a contradiction. And thus, by no argument can it be absolutely demonstrated that there are bodies, nor anything keep certain well-ordered dreams from being objects to our mind, which are considered by us as true, and on account of the agreement among themselves with respect to use are equivalent to truths. Nor is the argument of great weight, as they commonly allege, that thus God would be a deceiver; certainly, every one sees how far this is from a demonstration of metaphysical certainty, for we are deceived by our own judgment, not by God, when we assert anything without accurate proof. And although there is present great probability, nevertheless God is not therefore a deceiver who presents this to us. For what, if our nature were not perchance capable of real phenomena; surely God would be not so much to be blamed as to be thanked, for, by causing these phenomena, since they could not be real, to be at least accordant, he showed us that which in the entire usage of life would equal in worth real phenomena; what, indeed, if this whole short life were nothing but a certain long dream, and we should awake only in death? a conception such as the Platonists seemed to have; for since we are destined for eternity, and this whole life, although it should continue many thousands of years, has in respect of eternity the value of a point, how small will be the interposition of such a little dream in the full truth, the ratio of which is much less than that of the dream to life; and yet no sane person will say that God is a deceiver, if by chance he should happen to observe any short but distinct and congruous dream in his mind.

Hitherto I have spoken of those things which appear; now we must see about those which do not appear, which, nevertheless, can be inferred from those which do appear. And indeed it is certain that every phenomenon has some cause. Now if any one says that the cause of the phenomena is in the nature of our mind, in which the phenomena are, he will affirm nothing indeed false, but nevertheless he will not express the whole truth. For, in the first place, there is necessarily a reason why we ourselves exist rather than not exist, and although we should assume that we existed from eternity, yet the reason of the eternal existence must be sought, which reason must be found either in the essence of our mind or outside it. And, indeed, there is nothing to prevent the existence of innumerable other minds as well as ours; but all possible minds do not exist, which I prove from this, because all existing things have intercourse with each other. Further, minds can be known of another nature than ours and having intercourse with this of ours. Moreover, that all existing things have intercourse with each other is demonstrated both from this, that otherwise we cannot say whether anything in respect to these things happens now or not, and so the truth or falsity of such a proposition is not given, which is absurd, and because many extrinsic denominations are given; nor does any one become a widower in India by the death of his wife in Europe, without a real change happening in him. For every predicate is truly contained in the nature of the subject. If now some possible minds exist, we ask why not all; then because it is necessary that all existing things have intercourse, it is necessary that there be a cause of this intercourse, nay, it is necessary that all express the same nature, but in a different way; but the Cause through which it happens, that all minds have intercourse or express the same thing and so exist, is that which perfectly expresses the universe, namely God. The same cause has no cause and is unique. Hence it is at once evident that many minds exist besides ours, and since it is easy to think that men who are conversant with us can have just as much reason to doubt concerning us as we concerning them, and no greater reason wages war in our behalf, they also exist and will have minds. Hence already, sacred and profane history, and whatever things pertain to the state of minds or rational substances, are considered as confirmed.

With respect to bodies, I can demonstrate that not only light, heat, color, and similar qualities are apparent, but also motion and figure and extension. And if anything is real, that alone is the power of acting and enduring, and so in this (as it were matter and form), consists the substance of the body; but those bodies which have no substantial form, those only are phenomena, or at least aggregates of the true.

Substances have metaphysical matter or passive power as far as they express anything confusedly, active, as far as they express it distinctly.

ADDITIONS AND CORRECTIONS

The following Additions and Corrections are made in the interest of the greater accuracy and completeness of the book. The material incorporated therein has been obtained chiefly since the earlier portion of the book was in type. As it could not be introduced in its proper place, it is deemed best to insert it here rather than to omit it altogether. It will be noticed that it pertains chiefly to the earlier portion of the *New Essays*, the annotation of which, not a part of the Translator's plan at the outset, began with the printing and has grown with the progress of the work. — Tr.

Page 3, note 2, add: Erdmann, 677–678. The letter, after speaking of the nature, processes, and extent of our knowledge of physics, proceeds thus: "You enquire concerning the things of spirits or rather concerning incorporeal things; and you say that we see the mechanical disposition of the parts, but that we do not see the principles of the mechanism. Very well, but when we see motion also, then we know the cause of the motion or force. The source of the mechanism is primitive force (*vis primitiva*), but the laws of motion, according to which impulses (*impetus*) or derivative forces arise out of this primitive force, proceed from the perception of good and evil, or from that which is most fitting. Thus it happens that efficient causes depend upon final causes, and spiritual things are by nature prior to material things, as indeed to us they are prior in knowledge, because we perceive more immediately (*interius*) the mind (nearest — *intimam* — to us) than the body, as indeed Plato and Descartes have observed. This force, you say, is known by its effects, not as it is in itself. I reply that so it would be if we had no mind, and did not know. The mind has in itself perceptions and appetites, and in these its nature consists. And as in the body we know *ἀντιτυπίαν*, and form in general, although we do not know what the forms of the insensible bodies are, so in the mind we know perception and appetite, although we do not know distinctly the insensible ingredients of the confused perceptions, by which the insensible things of bodies are expressed. Spiritual things are perceived, you say, just as the air, the wind, the light, yet not on that account sufficiently known; but to me the air, the wind, the light seem to be no more spiritual than running water, nor do they differ from this save in subtility. Spirits, minds, and simple substances or monads in the universe cannot be comprehended by the senses and the imagination, because lacking in parts. Do you ask whether I believe that there are bodies which do not fall within the range of vision? Why may I not believe? nay, rather, concerning them I think I cannot doubt. In microscopes we see animalcula otherwise imperceptible, and the nerves of these animalcula and other animalcula by chance swimming in their own fluids cannot be seen. The subtility of nature proceeds into infinity. Finally you seek for definitions of matter, body, spirit. *Matter* is that which consists in antitypia, or that which resists penetration, and so naked matter is merely passive. *Body*, moreover, has besides matter also active force. *Body*, moreover, is either a corporeal substance or a mass collected from corporeal substances. *Corporeal substance* I call that which consists in a simple substance or monad (*i.e.* in the mind or somewhat analogous to the mind) and in an organic body united to it. But *mass* is an aggregate of corporeal substances, as a cheese sometimes consists of a conflux of worms. Then a *monad* or a substance simple in kind contains perception and appetite, and is either primitive or *God*, in which is the ultimate reason of things, or derivative, that is a created monad, and this is either endowed with reason, *Mind* (*mens*), or endowed with sense, that is *Soul* (*anima*), or endowed with a certain lower grade of perception and appetite, or *analogous with soul* (*animæ analoga*), which is content with the naked name of monad, since we do not know its various grades. Every monad, furthermore, is inextinguishable; for simple substances can neither begin nor end, except by creation or annihilation, that is, miraculously. And, moreover, every created monad is endowed with a certain organic body, by means of which it perceives and appetizes, although it is variously (e)volved through births and deaths, involved, transformed, and exists in a perpetual flux. Monads, then, contain in themselves the Entelechy, or the primitive force (*vis primitiva*), and without them matter would be passive merely; and any mass whatever contains innumerable monads, for although each organic body of nature has its own corresponding monads, yet it contains in the parts other monads endowed in like manner with their own organic bodies serving the primary body; and all nature is nothing else, for all aggregates must necessarily result from simple substances, as it were from true elements. But atoms or extended bodies, and yet infrangible, are a fiction, which cannot be explained except by a miracle, and are without reason; nor may we from them assign the causes of the forces and motions. And although they might be admitted, they would not be truly simple, for this very reason, because they are extended and endowed with parts. Thus I have replied to your questions, and set forth my views, as far as may be in a few words and by letter."

PAGE 9, line 15. For "1709," read "1704," and *cf. infra*, p. 101, note 1, line 3 from bottom, and *infra*, p. 531, note 2, ¶¶ 2, 3, where this portion of note 1, p. 101, is corrected.

PAGE 13, note 1. Add: translation also in Duncan, *Philos. Wks. of Leibnitz*, 94–99; German translation in J. H. v. Kirchmann, *Die klein. philos. wichtig. Schrift. v. Leibniz*, 86–92 (*Philos. Bibliothek*, Bd. 81; *Erläuterungen*, Bd. 82), Leipzig, 1879.

PAGE 15, note 2. After "translation," instead of "Appendix," etc., read "Duncan, *Philos. Wks. of Leibnitz*, pp. 71–80; German translation in J. H. v. Kirchmann, *Die klein. philos. wichtig. Schrift. v. Leibniz*, 55–67."

PAGE 16, line 22, "Huygens." *Cf. infra*, p. 150, note 3. On Huygens' physical views, *cf.* Lasswitz, *Gesch. d. Atomistik*, 2, 341–397. New ed. Huygens, *Œuvres complètes*, La Haye, 1888–1893, 5 vols., still in progress. These 5 volumes contain correspondence only.

PAGE 16, line 30, "pliable." "Leibnitz means," says J. H. v. Kirchmann, *Erläuterungen zu Leibniz. d. klein. philos. wichtig. Schrift.*, Leipzig, 1879, p. 109, "that, although bodies contain no vacuum, yet from the fact that they can become greater or lesser in extent, the other substances which fill out the gaps of the body proper are by pressure removed from it, or conversely with the cessation of the pressure penetrate into its vacuum. An actual extension or cohesion of a definite homogeneous body, which contains no gaps, Leibnitz does not assume, although the Scholastics affirmed it for a long time." On the development of Leibnitz's views from the atomism to which he was at first inclined, but almost immediately rejected, to the dynamic idealism of his monad doctrine, *cf.* D. Selver, *Der Entwicklungsgang d. Leibniz. Monadenlehre bis 1695*, Leipzig, William Englemann, 1885; Lasswitz, *Gesch. d. Atomistik*, 2, 446 *sq.*

PAGE 17, line 11, "De Scriebus infinitis." *Cf. infra*, p. 424, note 2.

PAGE 21, line 12, "Fabritius." *Cf. infra*, p. 102, note 2. The letter of Fabritius to Spinoza here mentioned is found in Spinoza, *Opera*, ed. Van Vloten and Land, 2, 181–182; *Philos. Wks.* Elwes' translation, 2, 374.

PAGE 26, line 4, "Clerc." Jean Le Clerc, 1657–1736, Professor of Philosophy, Belles-Lettres, and Hebrew in the Remonstrant Seminary at Amsterdam, 1684–1712, and thereafter of Church History, exercised considerable influence in the direction of scientific Biblical criticism, and wrote several philosophical works; but his greatest literary influence was exercised through the serials or reviews of which he was the editor, among which were the "Bibliothèque universelle et historique," here mentioned; the "Bibliothèque choisie," Amsterdam, 1703–1713; and the "Bibliothèque ancienne et moderne," 1714–1726.

PAGE 28, line 6, "Understanding." *Cf.*, also, *infra*, p. 41. The term is used in the sense of the Greek νοῦς, Latin *intellectus*, to indicate the totality of the human intellectual powers, the Reason in the larger sense of that term, in the language of Kant and his school, *Vernunft.*

PAGE 42, line 10, "Plato." Schaarschmidt says: "This comparison is to be considered as provisional only, in order to illustrate the opposition between the author's and Locke's point of view by a familiar example. Strictly taken the parallel does not hold good, as may be seen from the addition Leibnitz makes. Aristotle, that is to say, — to call to mind only the chief antitheses of the respective theories of knowledge, — assumes before all things principles which are peculiar to the spirit as such, while Locke denies the same; Plato, again, recognizes experience by means of sense-perception in a wholly different, more real, sense than Leibnitz and affirms in no wise, as Leibnitz, an absolute spontaneity of the presentative power."

PAGE 42, line 13, "Acroamatic." *Cf. infra*, p. 272, note 1.

PAGE 42, line 5 from bottom, "Aristotle." Schaarschmidt says: "Aristotle has certainly compared the mind (or the Reason — in his language *νοῦς*), though not the soul in general, with an unwritten tablet." *Cf.* Περὶ Ψυχῆς, Bk. III., chap. 4, § 11, Berlin Academy ed., 439 b 31; ed. E. Wallace, Cambridge, 1882, p. 159: *δεῖ δ' οὕτως ὥσπερ ἐν γραμματείῳ ᾧ μηθὲν ὑπάρχει ἐντελεχείᾳ γεγραμμένον· ὅπερ συμβαίνει ἐπὶ τοῦ νοῦ.* "This meanwhile is by no means to be understood in the sense that thought is merely something taken up from without, the spirit a merely receptive faculty. According to Aristotle, the thinking spirit is rather partly receptive or passive, partly productive or active, as is clear from this same Bk. III. of the Περὶ Ψυχῆς." *Cf.*, also, Zeller, *Philos. d. Griech.*, 3d ed., II., 2 [Vol. 4], 566 *sq.*

PAGE 43, line 1, "Schoolmen." The Scholastic philosophy, to which Leibnitz frequently refers in this and other works, "assumed," says Schaarschmidt, "a three-fold source of knowledge: 1. *Experientia*, experience through the senses; 2. *Ratio*, the logical faculty of drawing conclusions; 3. *Intellectus*, the faculty of ideas, which is precisely the understanding (or spirit) of Aristotle, active for itself from within, not creative out of sense-experience."

PAGE 43, line 4, "Prolepses." The Stoics derived general ideas or conceptions, — *κοιναὶ ἔννοιαι* or *προλήψεις*, *communes notiones*, — like all knowledge, from sensuous perception, explaining them by the persistence and combination of the sense-impressions. They are not to be understood, therefore, in the later sense as innate ideas, independent of experience and peculiar to the spirit as such. The Stoic theory was more like Locke's than like Aristotle's; and according to Plutarch, *Placita philosophorum*, IV., 11, considered the soul as originally a blank tablet (*tabula rasa*), upon which the outer world made its impressions. Through Boethius [470–524] the Stoic theory of knowledge became the source of mediæval nominalism. On the Stoic doctrine of knowledge, *cf.* Zeller, *Philos. d. Griech.*, 3d ed., Leipzig, 1880, III., 1 [Vol. 5], 70–86; Benn, *Greek Philosophers*, 2, 15; Windelband-Tufts, *Hist. of Philos.*, 202 *sq.*

PAGE 43, line 14, "Necessary truths." "Leibnitz," says Schaarschmidt, "here hints at his later more closely grounded division of truths into necessary and factual (contingent). The former are, according to

Leibnitz, the 'eternal truths of reason,' partly logical laws, partly general notions which belong to the mind as such, and are developed out of itself in order to come into consciousness. The latter, the factual truths, are formed by us through abstraction from experience, and therefore real. To this antithesis, further developed in the second book, Kant joins on that of the so-called *a priori* and *a posteriori* thought, in that he assigned to the former the character of necessity and universality, to the latter that of contingency and actuality (particularity)."

PAGE 44, line 13, "Innate." Leibnitz, in here maintaining that experience can never furnish anything absolutely and universally valid, and is therefore incapable of serving as the foundation of the sciences dealing with and requiring absolutely universal fundamental truths, such as Logic, Metaphysics, and Ethics, indicates in the sharpest and clearest manner his opposition to Locke's theory of knowledge.

As regards the nature of these pure truths of reason and the method by which they arise in consciousness, Leibnitz assumes and maintains that they are developed by the mind out of itself, and thus come into consciousness. Of this self-development, "this transition from potentiality to actuality (*a potentia ad actum*)," sense-experience furnishes the occasion, but is not the sufficient reason. Leibnitz to this extent, therefore, maintains against Locke the "Innateness of Ideas." But "he oversteps this idealistic principle in so far as he assumes an absolute spontaneity of the understanding, while at the same time that the understanding itself in its development is plainly shown in *reciprocal action* with experience, which forms the expression of *real* relation to other beings. In Leibnitz's theory the 'eternal' and 'necessary' truths of reason are in substance the principles of all knowledge, and furnish accordingly not only the ground-principles of the formal sciences, like Logic and Mathematics, but also of Metaphysics and Ethics" (Schaarschmidt).

PAGE 44, line 9 from bottom, "The same reasons hold good." *Cf.* H. S. Reimarus, 1694–1768, *Allgemeine Betrachtungen über die Kunsttriebe der Thiere*, 1760, 4th ed. 1798, chap. 2, who, says Schaarschmidt, has treated the antithesis between the knowledge of man and brute, the investigation of which in our times has led to interesting controversies, better than most of the later writers. Leibnitz assumes a specific difference between the souls of brute and man, and does not at all agree with Descartes' view that animals are living but soulless automata. On animal intelligence, *cf.* Romanes, *Animal Intelligence* [International Scientific Series, Vol. 44, D. Appleton & Co., New York, 1st ed. 1883, 2d ed. 1886]; *Mental Evolution in Animals*, New York, 1884, D. Appleton & Co.; Wm. Wundt, *Lectures on Human and Animal Psychology*, translated from the 2d German edition, by J. E. Creighton and E. B. Titchener, London and New York, 1894, Lectures 23, 24, pp. 340–366. Wundt's Lectures include some criticism of Romanes, as somewhat wanting in critical attitude and exhibiting too much sympathetic imagination.

PAGE 45, line 6 from bottom, "Intellectual ideas." Intellectual, *i.e.* as opposed to "sensuous" (*i.e.* belonging to, or arising from, the senses). Leibnitz means to say, says Schaarschmidt, either we fasten our attention upon sense-pictures, whose source is sense-perception, or upon intellectual, *verstandesmässigen* (formulated, *sprachgeformten*), ideas, thought-pictures, for whose rise those general ideas, which Kant called Kategories or original notions of the understanding, are requisite; general ideas which do not arise from experience through the senses, but must belong to our understanding as such and therefore be considered as "innate" or "implanted."

PAGE 46, line 18, "Virtual." *I.e.* Potential, or, as opposed to "actual," the real-possible. "It is here," says Schaarschmidt, "the faculty through which a substance (the soul) out of its own supreme power goes over into a new condition as for it a new realization. Our soul contains an unending number of possible ideas, as capacities, seeds or traces left behind and remains of former activity, which upon definite occasion it realizes, *i.e.* calls into consciousness. This Leibnitzian application of the — originally wider — Aristotelian concept of power to the soul has become for modern philosophy in the highest degree weighty and fruitful."

PAGE 46, line 7 from bottom, "Reminiscence." On the Platonic doctrine of "reminiscence" or "recollection" (ἀνάμνησις), an essential part of his *doctrine of Ideas*, *cf.* Windelband-Tufts, *Hist. of Philos.* pp. 118, 119; Zeller, *Philos. d. Griech.*, 4th ed. 1889, II., 1 [Vol. 3], 823, 824, 835, 836.

In Plato's philosophy the ideas which are the objects of our rational thought were intuited by the soul in its pre-existent and exalted state when it dwelt in the presence of the archetypal forms (παραδείγματα), which Plato called *ideas* (εἴδη or ἰδέαι). The soul in its earthly life is but dimly, if at all, conscious of these archetypal forms, till the perception of their imperfect copies in corporeal things arouses the slumbering recollection and stimulates the soul to reproduce them in consciousness and with the aid of dialectic again to attain the knowledge of true and ideal reality. *Cf.*, also, *New Essays*, Book I., chap. 1, § 5, Th. (3), *infra*, p. 79

PAGE 47, line 8, "Reflection." "Provided," as Schaarschmidt says, "that Reflection, which with Locke has to do only with the activities of the inner nature as such, receives that further content which embraces the 'eternal' and 'necessary' ground-truths, and to which we are in fact led if we keep in mind the presuppositions and modalities under which those activities proceed."

PAGE 47, lines 18, 19, "The book of Boyle against absolute rest." *Cf. infra*, p. 324, note 2. The treatise is also found in Vol. 1 of the Latin version of his works, *Opera varia*, Geneva, 1680, and later, with the title *Dissertatio de intestinis motibus particularum solidorum quiescentium, in qua absoluta corporum quies in disquisitionem vocatur.* On Boyle, *cf.*

Lasswitz, *Gesch. d. Atomistik*, 2, 261–293; Lange, *Gesch. d. Materialismus*, 2d ed. Iserlohn, 1873. 1, 255; English translation, Boston, 2d ed. 1879, 1, 299–306.

Page 47, line 21, "Doing away with atoms." Leibnitz rejects atoms in favor of his own monads, because the monads contain in themselves the principle of motion as active force, while the atoms are assumed in consequence of a force in movement foreign to them. On Leibnitz's view and its development, *cf.* Lasswitz, *Gesch. d. Atomistik*, 2, 470 *sq.*

Page 48, line 7 from bottom, "Confused in the parts." *Cf. infra*, pp. 120, 317, note 2, 319, 320, 458, 459. Leibnitz's doctrine of "minute perceptions" or, in the philosophical language of to-day, "unconscious mental states," is of the greatest significance in psychology and epistemology, and never more so than at the present time. For an excellent exposition of it, *cf.* Windelband-Tufts, *Hist. of Philos.*, pp. 423 *sq.*, 462 *sq.*

Page 48, last line, "Hippocrates." *Cf. infra*, p. 476, note 2.

Page 49, line 15, "Sufficiently distinguished." That is, to reach consciousness. The perceptions are not sufficiently strong to call forth a conscious activity of the soul.

Page 49, line 12 from bottom, "Author of the most excellent of dictionaries." The reference is to Bayle. *Cf. infra*, p. 507, note 1.

Page 49, note 1. The note should read: *Cf.* Vergil, *Georg.* IV., 393. Gerhardt's reading: "que" is evidently a typographical error. Erdmann and Janet read: "*quæ* mox futura," etc.; Jacques, correctly: *quæ* mox *ventura* trahantur."

Page 50, line 15, "Pneumatology." *Cf. infra*, p. 362, note 2.

Page 50, line 20, "*Law of Continuity*." *Cf. infra*, p. 334, note 1; p. 552.

Page 50, note 3. Add: The correspondence of Leibnitz and Basnage is found in Gerhardt, *Leibniz. philos. Schrift.*, 3, 73 *sq.*

Page 51, line 7, "*Numero*." *Cf.*, also, *infra*, p. 332, note 1.

Page 51, lines 11–13, "Perfect globes of the second element, born of cubes perfect and original." The reference is to Descartes, *Principiæ Philosophiæ*, Pt. III., §§ 48 *sq.* *Cf.*, also, *New Essays*, *infra*, p. 552, note 1. Mahaffy, *Descartes*, Blackwood's Philosophical Classics, Edinburgh, 1881, p. 159, says Descartes' theory of general physics was elaborated as regards minerals. This fact perhaps accounts for Schaarschmidt's translation: "des sichtbaren Metalls" and his reference to *Prin. Philos.*, Pt. IV., §§ 70, 75, in his note, *Erläuterung*, 400, p. 101, to the passage, *New Essays*, Bk. IV., chap. 16, § 12, Th., p. 532 of his German translation. Descartes, says Mahaffy, *ibid.*, p. 159, gave special explanation of the growth of the human body, but that of plants and the lower animals was wanting when he died. On Descartes' theory, *cf.* Lasswitz, *Gesch. d. Atomistik*, 2, 89.

PAGE 51, lines 19, 20, "Present considerations." While the process of abstraction allows us, in order to their better apprehension, to concentrate our attention for the time on certain properties or attributes of a subject to the exclusion of others, yet we must remember that in so doing we are departing from reality and only partially representing it in consciousness.

PAGE 51, line 20. Instead of the rendering: "If it were very well understood," read, after Schaarschmidt, "If we take it as pure and simple gospel," etc.

PAGE 51, line 29, "Some exception." Nature gives us no perfect circles, perfect spheres, etc. Perfect mathematical regularity of form exists only in thought.

PAGE 52, line 7 from bottom, "Strong-minded." That is, the "Freethinkers," as Leibnitz at other times called them, who thought they might deny immortality itself after the pretended proofs for it given by Scholasticism had been disproved.

PAGE 53, line 8 from bottom, "Averroists and some bad Quietists." *Cf. infra*, p. 581, note 1. The Mystics and Quietists approached very nearly this Averroistic doctrine of a denial of personal immortality. In Leibnitz's time the Mystics and Quietists were especially the followers of Madame Guyon, who was ready "to burst from an overplus of divine grace," and of Ant. Bourignon, on whom *cf. infra*, p. 599, note 2; also, according to Schaarschmidt, Leibnitz's letter CXLIV., Feder, *Commercii epistolici Leibnitiani*, Hanover, 1805, p. 459.

PAGE 54, note 1. Add: Leibnitz was much interested in the Locke-Stillingfleet controversy, as his correspondence with Thomas Burnett shows. *Cf.* Gerhardt, *Leibniz. philos. Schrift.*, 3, 149–329, *passim*, and especially pp. 205, 216, and the two essays, pp. 223–242; also Foucher de Careil, *Lettres et opuscules inédits de Leibniz*, Paris, 1854, Introduction, pp. lxii *sq.*, and Leibnitz's *Remarques sur le Sentiment de M. de Worcester et de M. Locke*, *ibid.*, pp. 1–26. The latter piece is identical with that published — not therefore for the first time — by Gerhardt, *op. cit.*, 3, 229–242. The controversy, like that of Leibnitz and Arnauld, served to bring Locke to the further explication and limitation of his views.

PAGE 55, lines 16, 17, "French version." That is, by Pierre Coste, with the co-operation of Locke. It appeared in 1700, then in 1729, and again in 1742. *Cf. ante*, p. 4, note 1. For the correspondence of Leibnitz and Coste, *cf.* Gerhardt, *Leibniz. philos. Schrift.*, 3, 377–436. Before Locke published, in 1690, his Essay, he published an abstract, translated into French by Le Clerc in Le Clerc's "Bibliothèque universelle," January, 1688. *Cf. ante*, p. 4, note 1, and Fraser's *Locke's Essay*, 1, 15, note 2. The abstract or "Epitome" is found in Lord King's *Life and Correspondence of Locke*, new ed., London, 1830, 2, 231–293; Bohn's ed., 1858, 1 vol., pp. 365–399.

Page 55, last line, "Intentional species." *Cf. infra*, p. 381, note 1.

Page 56, line 3. For the Latin verse, *cf.* Ovid, *Tristia*, I., 8, 7.

Page 59, line 4 from bottom, "Inexplicable qualities." That is, the *qualitates occultæ* of the mediæval philosophers.

Page 60, line 6 from bottom, "Instructive." Leibnitz, as Schaarschmidt says, "avails himself of Stillingfleet's polemic against Locke, which is of particular interest because it shows Locke's uncertainty in regard to the weighty question of the substantiality of the soul, to add thereto the statement that the soul must be immaterial. Locke himself, so he argues, has admitted that thought is not conceivable as a modification of matter, or that, in other words, a thinking being cannot be a mere mechanism; thus the soul is to be considered as something immaterial, since the thought, that God may through a miracle have bestowed thought upon matter, is an unpermissible subterfuge." For further discussion of the point, *cf. New Essays*, Bk. IV.

Page 62, line 10 from bottom, "Miracle pure and simple." *Cf. infra*, p. 428. The doctrine of a purifying fire through which souls have to pass after death goes back to the early period of the church, but became more prominent and was more generally adopted from the time of Gregory the Great (c. 540–604). *Cf.* Hagenbach, *Hist. of Doctrines*, ed. H. B. Smith, § 141, Vol. 1, p. 373; § 206, Vol. 2, p. 126. Clement of Alexandria, *Stromateis*, vii., 6, says: φαμὲν δ' ἡμεῖς ἁγιάζειν τὸ πῦρ, οὐ τὰ κρέα, ἀλλὰ τὰς ἁμαρτωλοὺς ψυχάς· πῦρ οὐ τὸ πάμφαγον καὶ βάναυσον, ἀλλὰ τὸ φρόνιμον λέγοντες, τὸ διϊκνούμενον διὰ ψυχῆς τῆς διερχομένης τὸ πῦρ, *i.e.* "We say that fire sanctifies not flesh, but sinful souls, speaking of that fire which is not all-devouring, such as is used by artisans, but of that which is discriminative, pervading the soul which passes through the fire" (the phrase "discriminative" (φρόνιμον), or as Bigg, *The Christian Platonists of Alexandria* [Bampton Lectures for 1886], p. 113, translates it, "wise fire," "comes," says Bigg, "from Heraclitus and the Stoics.") *Cf.* Bigg, *op. cit.*, 295; Hagenbach, *op. cit.*, § 77, 1, 222. And Augustine, *De Civit. Dei*, Bk. XXI., chap. 10, Benedictine ed., Paris, 1685, Vol. 7, p. 631, says: "Cur enim non dicamus, quamvis miris, tamen veris modis etiam spiritus incorporeos posse pœna corporalis ignis affligi, si spiritus hominum, etiam ipsi profecto incorporei, et nunc potuerunt includi corporalibus membris, et tunc poterunt corporum suorum vinculis insolubiliter alligari?" *i.e.* "For why may we not assert that even immaterial spirits may, in some extraordinary way, yet really be pained by the punishment of material fire, if the spirits of men, which also are certainly immaterial, are both now contained in material members of the body, and in the world to come shall be indissolubly united to their own bodies?" (*The City of God*, 2, 435, translated by Rev. Marcus Dods, M.A., T. & T. Clark, Edinburgh, 1871). In chapter 7, after having in previous chapters cited many real or supposed facts from the natural world in support of the possibility at least of the view, he admits that it is miraculous and beyond our knowledge, and maintains the omnipotence of God as the ultimate reason for belief in miracles. Thos. Aquinas, *Summa Theol.*, Quæst. 70, Art. 3, Concl., says: "Respondeo: Dicendum quod ignis inferni [*i.e.* purgatorial fire, according to the context] non sit metaphorice dictus, nec ignis imaginarius, sed verus ignis corporeus," etc. Only those requiring purgatory go there, according to St. Thomas, *cf.* Quæst. 69, Art. 2. Bellamin, 1542–1621, in his *De Purgatorio*, chaps. 10–12, investigates the method of the purgatorial fire and follows Augustine in teaching that it is material and miraculous in its action upon the soul.

PAGE 63, line 10 from bottom, "Demons or goblins." "Leibnitz is perhaps here thinking," says Schaarschmidt, "of the so-called Spirits of the Elements (*Elementargeister*), of which the 'philosophers and physicians of the past,' especially Theoph. Paracelsus [*cf. infra*, p. 645, note 1], had treated, both in his *Philosophia sagax.* and in a special book, *De nymphis, sylphis, pygmæis et salamandris*, or even of the '*spiritus familiaris*' of others, as of the Italian philosopher and physician Hieronymus Cardanus [*cf. infra*, p. 566, note 1], who in his interesting autobiography [*De vita propria*], chap. 47, discusses the subject and at the same time narrates marvellous experiences of his own past life."

PAGE 63, note 3. Add: In the *Philos. Mosaica*, and also in his *Utriusque Cosmi — Metaphysica, physica atque technica Historia*, Oppenheimii, 1617 fol., "God appears," says Schaarschmidt, "as the animating and moving principle of things, in that all power streams forth in a miraculous way from him into matter, in order afterwards to turn back again from the thereby occurring differentiation to unity." On Fludd, *cf.* Lasswitz, *Gesch. d. Atomistik*, 1, 329; Stöckl, *Gesch. d. Philos. d. Mittelalters*, III. [Vol. 4], 472–476.

PAGE 64, note 1. Add: Prof. A. C. Fraser, in his edition of Locke's *Essay concerning Human Understanding*, Oxford, 1894, follows Coste's French version in separating the introductory chapter from the First Book, and making, with Leibnitz here, but three chapters in Bk. I.

PAGE 64, note 2, line 2. After "1674," add: new ed. with notes by Bouillier, Paris, 1880, 2 vols.; line 4, after "Bernier," add: On Gassendi, *cf.* Stöckl, *Gesch. d. Philos. d. Mittelalters*, III. [Vol. 4] 316–327; Lange, *Gesch. d. Materialismus*, 2d ed., Gerlohn, 1873, 1, 223–234, Eng. trans. 2d ed. 1, 253–269; Lasswitz, *Gesch. d. Atomistik*, 2, 126–188. On Bernier's later divergence from Gassendi, *cf. ibid.* 2, 504.

PAGE 65, line 13. Instead of "Doctors," read: "scholars."

PAGE 65, note 1. Add: Lady Masham, 1659–1708, was one of Locke's most intimate and truest friends, kept him by her at her country seat at Oates and nursed him in his last illness. *Cf.* Gerhardt, *Leibniz. philos. Schrift.* 3, 365. Lady Masham presented Leibnitz with a copy of her father's *Intellectual System*, as appears by his letter of March 29, 1704, *cf.* Gerhardt, 3, 338.

PAGE 65, note 3. Add: The objections referred to in the text are the *objectiones quintæ* against Descartes' *Meditationes de prima philosophia*, "which indeed," as Schaarschmidt says, "contain a series of very acute objections and gave Descartes much trouble." The *Cinquièmes Objections* of "Gassendy," with the *Réponses* of Descartes thereto, are found in Cousin, *Œuvres de Descartes*, 2, 89 *sq.*, 241 *sq.*

PAGE 66, line 6, "Inclined towards ethics." Leibnitz, who to a certain extent may be considered as giving utterance to his own views in the person of Theophilus, here throws out a hint to be well taken to heart as regards his own course of development. As a natural consequence of his early studies in jurisprudence; Leibnitz was led to a deeper study of ethical conceptions, and in like manner his study of Descartes made him acquainted with the problems of mathematics and physics, which he thoroughly examined only later after his sojourn in Paris.

PAGE 66, lines 13, 14, "No longer a Cartesian." *Cf.* the entire context, pp. 66–69, also Leibnitz's letter to Remond de Montmort, January 10, 1714, Gerhardt, *Leibniz. philos. Schrift.* 3, 606–607, Erdmann, 701–702, in which Leibnitz gives a brief account of his own philosophical studies and development, including, Plato, Aristotle, and the Scholastics and thence passing to the moderns, rejecting the "substantial forms" for the mechanism of the Cartesian system, and then developing his own doctrine of Pre-established Harmony. The difficulties and controversies within the Cartesian School and against it led Leibnitz to his own doctrine, and he remarks in his *Considérations sur le Principe de Vie*, 1705, Gerhardt, 6, 540, Erdmann, 430, as also in the letter here cited, that if Descartes had known that Nature conserves not only the same force, but also the same total direction in the laws of motion, he would himself have come to the system of pre-established harmony. *Cf.* W. Sigwart, *Die Leibniz'sche Lehre v. d. prästabilirten Harmonie.* Tübingen, 1822, pp. 110-112, 117, 118, 121, 132, etc. For Leibnitz against Descartes and Cartesianism, *cf.* Gerhardt, 4, 265–406; also, Stein, *Leibniz u. Spinoza*, 60 *sq.*

PAGE 66, line 17, "New System." That is, The System of Pre-established Harmony, in explanation and defence of which Leibnitz published in the journals mentioned many essays, most, if not all, of which are mentioned later in either the text of the *New Essays* or notes thereto. "Leibnitz," as Schaarschmidt well says, "can truly boast that he has turned to account for his own system moments of all the doctrines named in the text," it being "a characteristic feature of Leibnitz's thought to ascribe a relative truth to each philosophic system and accordingly to wish to extract from it a good side in order, by harmonizing these different elements, to bring to pass the possibly best view of the world." *Cf.* Leibnitz's letter to Remond de Montmort, January 10, 1714, Gerhardt, *Leibniz. philos. Schrift.* 3, 606, Erdmann, 701: "Outre que j'ay eu soin de tout diriger à l'édification, j'ay taché de déterrer et de réunir la vérité ensevelie et dissipée sous les opinions des differentes Sectes des Philosophes, et je crois y avoir adjouté quelque chose du mien pour faire quelques pas en avant."

PAGE 66, note 1. Add: Geronimo Rorario, 1485–1566, an Italian littérateur, Nuncio of Clement VII. at the Court of Ferdinand, King of Hungary, maintained, against the Cartesians and the followers of Aristotle, that the beasts have reason and make better use of it than man. His book, *Quod animalia bruta sæpe ratione utantur melius homine*, appeared first in 1648, then 1654 at Amsterdam.

PAGE 67, lines 3, 4, "Life and perception in all things." The doctrine of the universal soulhood (*Allbeseeltheit*) goes back to the world-soul of Plato, as developed especially by Plotinus (*cf.* Windelband-Tufts, *Hist. of Philos.*, 245 *sq.*), and is connected in part therewith, and partly with the pantheistic tendencies represented, for example, by the Averroists (*cf. New Essays*, *infra*, p. 581, note 1). Leibnitz rejects both errors by his Monadology, which conceives the universal soulhood of substances in an individual and not in a pantheistic way. In modern times the doctrine appears in Giordano Bruno, 1548–1600 (*cf. Della Causa*, Vol. II., pp. 239–241, ed. A. Wagner, Leipzig, 1829, new ed. by P. de Lagarde, 2 vols., Göttingen, 1888, German trans. by Lasson, Berlin, 1872, in J. H. v. Kirchmann's *Philos. Bibliothek*, Vol. 53), and in Jacob Boehme (*cf. infra*, p. 298, note 1). On the doctrine as found in Bruno and Boehme, *cf.* Windelband-Tufts, *op. cit.*, 367 *sq.*, 373 *sq.* Spinoza, *Ethica*, Pt. II., Prop. XIII., Scholium, ed. Van Vloten and Land, 1, 86–88; Elwes' trans., 2, 92, also gives expression to the same thought.

PAGE 67, line 5, "Countess of Connaway." Anne — Viscountess Conway — died Feb. 23, 1678–9, was a metaphysician and an earnest student of Plato, Plotinus, Philo Judæus and the "Kabbala Denudata." In spite of never-ceasing sufferings from a severe headache lasting till her death, she pursued her metaphysical studies with extraordinary devotion and assiduity. Her physician, Francis Mercury van Helmont (*cf. infra*, 242, note 2), encouraged her in this course. She was very friendly with H. More and corresponded with him on philosophical and theological topics. She wrote many works of which only one has been printed: *Opuscula philosophica quibus continentur principia philosophiæ antiquissimæ et recentissimæ*, Amsterdam, 1690. It was the first in a collection of philosophical treatises appearing in Latin in that year at Amsterdam, translated as "a work by a certain English countess, 'learned beyond her sex,'" and ascribed by Leibnitz in a German literary journal, on the authority of Van Helmont, to the Countess of Conway. The treatise was re-translated into English and published with the title *The Principles of the Most Ancient and Modern Philosophy*, etc., London, 1692, 8vo.

PAGE 67, note 1. Add: On Campanella, *cf.* Stöckl, *Gesch. d. Philos. d. Mittelalters*, III. [Vol. 4.], 343–366; Lasswitz, *Gesch. d. Atomistik*, 1, 340–342.

PAGE 67, note 2. Add: On Van Helmont, *cf. infra*, p. 242, note 2; on H. More, *cf. infra*, pp. 380, note 1; 382, note 2, and addition thereto, *infra* p. 768.

PAGE 67, note 3. Add: Further references to Archæus in Leibnitz's writings are: *Specimen Dynamicum*, Gerhardt, *Leibniz. math. Schrift.*, II., 2 [Vol. 6], 242, also *infra*, Appendix, p. 679; *Hypothesis phys. nova, Theoria motus concreti*, § 60, Gerhardt, *Leibniz. philos. Schrift.* 4, 217; *math. Schrift.*, II., 2 [Vol. 6], 57; Dutens, *Leibnit. op. om.*, 2, Pt. II., 33; *Leibnit. Animadversiones circa Assertiones aliquas Theoriæ Medicæ veræ Clar. Stahlii*, Dutens, *op. cit.*, 2, Pt. II., 136. *Cf.*, also, Windelband-Tufts, *Hist. of Philos.* 371 *sq.*

PAGE 68, line 10, "*Morte carent animæ.*" *Cf.* Ovid, *Metamorphoses*, 15, 158.

PAGE 68, line 20, "Spontaneity." Leibnitz ascribes absolute spontaneity to the soul, to which the activity of the body perfectly corresponds through the Pre-established Harmony, and therefore neither influences nor disturbs it.

PAGE 68, line 7 from bottom, "Epitome." That is in the Monad, each monad representing in itself and to itself the entire universe. Leibnitz constantly recurs to this thought, which is one of the chief points of his system. *Cf. Système nouveau de la nature*, § 16; *Monadologie*, § 65, etc.

PAGE 69, note 1. Add: also G. Croom Robertson, *Philos. Remains*, Williams & Norgate, 1894, pp. 334–342.

PAGE 70, line 5 from bottom, "Copernicans." Kant, later in the Preface to the 2d ed. of his *Kritik d. reinen Vernunft*, makes use of the same comparison of Copernicus.

PAGE 71, line 24, "Confused perceptions." *Cf. ante*, p. 48 and note to line 7 from bottom, *ante*, p. 727. "While Leibnitz," says Schaarschmidt, "often returns to this antithesis of truths of reason and of fact, he has unfortunately nowhere given accurate definitions of the former, nor any wholly satisfactory criterion of a truth of reason. Kant first undertook this task, in that he certainly on the one side significantly restricted the service of the truths of reason, on the other, that against Leibnitz he recognized that for the reason as such complete (*fertige*) concepts are to arise out of the truths of reason."

PAGE 72, note 1. Add: "The Later Arminians," says Schaarschmidt, "are here referred to, as the leaders of this religious sect, such as Episcopius, Limborch, J. Clericus, like Descartes and Leibnitz himself, assume a knowledge of God derived from natural reason."

PAGE 74, line 8 from bottom, "Natural light." *Cf. infra*, pp. 575–576, note 1.

PAGE 74, lines 4, 3, from bottom, "Verification." *Cf. ante*, p. 71, note to line 24, above, and also *New Essays*, Bk. IV., chaps. 9, 11. Leibnitz here presents as the criterion or test of innate ideas their immediacy in consciousness. Spinoza before him (*Ethica*, Pt. II., Prop. 43, Scholium, *ad fin.*, ed. Van Vloten and Land, 1, 111; Elwes' trans., 2, 115; *cf.*, also, F. Pollock, *Spinoza, his Life and Philosophy*, 129 *sq.*), said: "Sane sicut lux seipsam et tenebras manifestat, sic veritas norma sui et falsi est." *Cf.*, also, Descartes, *Prin. Philos.*, Bk. I., § 45; ed. Cousin, 3, 90; Veitch's trans., 212, where he sets forth the doctrine of "clear and distinct" knowledge and of intuition through which we become immediately conscious of the truth as such. *Cf.*, also, Descartes, *Regulæ ad directionem ingenii* (*Règles pour la direction de l'esprit*), *Opuscula posthuma Cartesii*, Amsterdam, 1701, III., p. 6; IV., p. 9; VI., p. 14; ed. Cousin, 11, 209, 215, 226.

PAGE 75, note 1. *Dele* note. The Ludolph here referred to by Leibnitz is Ludolph van Ceulen, or Keulen, 1539–1610, Professor of Military Architecture in the University of Leyden since 1600, and previously teacher of mathematics in Breda, Amsterdam, and Leyden. He published his *Van de Circkel, daarin geleert wird te finden de næste proportie des Circkels-diameter tegen synen Omloop*, Delft, 1596; Latin trans. by Snellius, entitled *De circulo et adscriptis*, 1615. His *De arithmetische en geometrische fondamenten*, etc., Leyden, 1616. *Fundamenta arithmetica et geometrica* and *Zetemata* (*seu Problemata*) *geometrica*, both trans. from the Dutch by Snellius, Lugd. Bat., 1615. He computed the ratio of the diameter to the circumference of the circle to 35 places of decimals. The ratio is commonly known in Germany by the name "Ludolphische Zahl." Leibnitz refers to him in his mathematical writings, *cf.* Gerhardt, *Leibniz. math. Schrift.* II., 1 [Vol. 5], 95, 119. For Leibnitz's discussions of the subject, *cf. infra*, p. 424, note 2.

PAGE 77, line 6 from bottom, "*Subvenire*." Schaarschmidt translates "Beikommen," and in his note to the passage states that "the French *souvenir* (to remember) made from *subvenire*, originally means: to come to the aid of. The expression of help introduced by the Herbartian philosophy could, unfortunately, not be used, since the word-play would be wholly lost."

Leibnitz's thought is that *reminiscence*, the active and voluntary factor in the reproduction of the past and in bringing the now unconscious knowledge again into consciousness, requires and receives the aid of *remembrance* or memory, the conservative factor in the process, which in some unknown and mysterious way, and out of consciousness, preserves as in a store-house the knowledge previously acquired or possessed. *Cf.* Hamilton, *Metaphys.*, Lect. 20, pp. 274–275, American ed., Boston, 1875.

PAGE 78, line 16 from bottom. The sentence should read thus: "For through an admirable arrangement of nature we cannot have abstract thoughts which do not require something sensuous, although this should consist only of such characters as are the forms of the letters and the sounds."

PAGE 79, line 8 from bottom, "Opinion of the Platonists." *Cf. ante*, p. 46, and note to line 7 from bottom, *ante*, p. 726.

PAGE 80, note 1. Add: Janet also reads: "ou." Schaarschmidt translates "wo," *cf.* his translation, p. 45, line 13 from bottom. The context seems to require here the reading "où," where. The reading "ou" is probably a MS. or typographical error.

Page 83, note 1. Add: For an account of his views, *cf.* Lasswitz, *Gesch. d. Atomistik*, 2, 188–207. Digby's doctrine on the subject mentioned in Leibnitz's text is found in his *Demonstratio immortalitatis animæ rationalis*, Tract. I., cap. 3, p. 26 *sq.*, ed. Francofurti, 1664, full title of which Lasswitz gives, *op. cit.*, 2, 188, note 3; and in his *Institutiones peripateticæ*, published as an Appendix to the *Demonstratio*, ed. of 1664. Schaarschmidt gives 1st ed. of *Demonstratio*, Paris, 1655. *A treatise of the nature of bodies*, Paris, 1644.

Page 86, line 8, "Sadness is." Says Schaarschmidt: "We are immediately conscious of the theoretical ground-truths as such. With the practical, the case is different. Joy and sorrow we certainly feel immediately as such, but to find out their real nature requires subsequent reflection."

Page 87, note 2. After "Erdmann," add: Janet; and after "Bohn's edition," add: Fraser's *Locke's Essay*, I, 67, line 18.

Page 88, line 13 from bottom, "*Instinct.*" "Leibnitz understands here by instinct," says Schaarschmidt, "a definite inclination to a certain manner of action, which arises out of need and serves to satisfy the same. 'Truths of instinct' thus refer themselves back to our nature and are accordingly, in conformity with Leibnitz's general view, innate truths."

Page 89, note 2. Add: A German translation, by G. E. Böttger, appeared at Nordhausen, Gross, 1787.

Page 89, note 3. Add: According to Schaarschmidt, the story is found in Bk. II., chap. 1, p. 73, of Baumgarten's, "very interesting but rare," *Perigrinatis in Ægyptum, Arabiam, Palæstinam et Syriam*, Noribergæ ex off. Gerlachiana, p. P. Kaufmannum, 1694, 4to.

Page 91, line 5, "*esse.*" *Cf.* Digest or Pandects, Bk. I., Tit. 1, § 3, where Florentinus says: "Ut vim atque injuriam propulsemus. Nam jure hoc evenit, ut quod quisque ob tutelam corporis sui fecerit, jure fecisse existimetur, et, cum inter nos cognationem quandam natura constituit, consequens est hominem homini insidiari nefas esse." *Corpus Juris Civilis Academicum Parisiense*, p. 229, 7th ed., Lutetiæ Parisiorum 1862; *Corpus Juris Civilis* (*Digesta* recog. T. Mommsen, and paged separately), Berlin, Weidmann, 1893, Vol. 1, p. 1.

Page 91, line 8 from bottom, "Complete certitude to morals." Schaarschmidt here compares Hume, "the most acute (*scharfsinnigste*) of the English philosophers," who "reached a similar result, wholly independent of Leibnitz," in his *An Inquiry concerning the Principles of Morals*, Section I., *cf. The Philos. Wks. of David Hume*, 4 vols., Little, Brown, & Co., Boston, 4, 233: "The final sentence, it is probable, which pronounces characters and actions amiable or odious, praiseworthy or blamable;

that which stamps on them the mark of honor or infamy, approbation or censure; that which renders morality an active principle, and constitutes virtue our happiness, and vice our misery; it is probable, I say, that this final sentence *depends on some internal sense or feeling, which nature has made universal in the whole species.* . . . But in order to pave the way for such a sentiment, and give a proper discernment of its object, it is often necessary, we find, that much reasoning should precede, that nice distinctions be made, just conclusions drawn, distant comparisons formed, complicated relations examined, and general facts fixed and ascertained." *Cf.*, also, Hume, *A Treatise of Human Nature*, Bk. III. *Of Morals*, Pt. I., Sect. II., ed. Green and Grose, 2, 247.

PAGE 91, line 3 from bottom, "Boutan." That is, Bhután, a district in the Eastern Himalayas, north of Assam.

PAGE 92, line 6, "Often confused." "Feeling here means," as Schaarschmidt says, "not the sensuous-psychical sensation, but the confused complex of presentations (*Vorstellungen*) — a frequently used signification of the term — which occupies the soul and therefore often drives it to action. Feelings of this kind may by self-reflection be resolved into more or less clear and distinct ideas (*Vorstellungen*), a process necessary for testing and correctly estimating their content. Leibnitz at this time appears to regard all feelings without exception as such undeveloped ideas and judgments."

PAGE 93, line 20, "Joseph Scaliger." *Cf. infra*, p. 106, note 2.

PAGE 95, note 1. Add: The five principles here referred to are found in the *De Veritate*, and in the *De Religione Laici*, annexed to the 3d ed., London, 1645, of the *De Verit.* *Cf.* Fraser's *Locke's Essay*, 1, 80, note 2; 81, note 1.

PAGE 96, note 1. After "*ad init.*," add: 15, Berlin Academy ed., 1106b 36: ἔστιν, ἄρα ἡ ἀρετὴ ἕξις προαιρετικὴ ἐν μεσότητι οὖσα τῇ πρὸς ἡμᾶς ὡρισμένῃ λόγῳ καὶ ὡς ἂν ὁ φρόνιμος ὁρίσειεν· μεσότης δὲ δύο κακιῶν, τῆς μὲν καθ' ὑπερβολὴν τῆς δε κατ' ἔλλειψιν . . . διὸ κατὰ μὲν τὴν οὐσίαν καὶ τὸν λόγον τὸν τί ἦν εἶναι λέγοντα μεσότης ἐστὶν ἡ ἀρετή, κατὰ δὲ τὸ ἄριστον καὶ τὸ εὖ ἀκρότης.

PAGE 97, note 1. Add: A long time after this note was in type, I came across the following in Guhrauer, *Leibnitz's Deutsche Schriften*, 2, 509, among some *Vermischte Bemerkungen und Urtheile . . . Aus dem Monatlichen Auszuge*: "(October, 1701). Herr *Boileau Despreaux*, ein französischer Academicus und berühmter Satyricus, hat eine neue und vermehrte Edition seiner Satyren machen lassen, und denselben seinen Namen vorgesetzt, und dabey zu verstehen gegeben, dass er diese und keine andere Edition vor die *seine* erkenne." Possibly the edition here referred to contained the lines as Leibnitz gives them, the author changing them in later editions.

PAGE 99, lines 7–9. *Cf. ante*, p. 66, and note to line 17, *ante*, p. 731.

Page 99, note 1. Add: The *Chronicon*, 379–468, is also found in M. Bouquet, *Rec. hist. Gaules*, new ed., Paris, 1869–1880, 19 vols., fol., Vol. 1, p. 612; A. Duchesne, *Hist. Franc. Script.*, 1, 183; Migne, *Patrol. s. Lat.*, 74, 675.

Page 100, lines 16, 17. "The knowledge of being is wrapped up in that knowledge which we have of ourselves." *Cf. New Essays*, Bk. II., chap. 27, § 9, Th., *infra*, pp. 245 *sq.*, and note to p. 247, lines 7–9, *infra*, p. 760. Also Kant's doctrine of the categories, to which Leibnitz's thought at this point is very closely related. Our self-consciousness gives us an immediate knowledge of being, *i.e.* of our own particular being, but not yet the concept of being or substance in general nor any "eternal truth." What is given is an internal experience, whose essential and necessary content, implications and full significance are reached only after profound and protracted thought.

Page 101, note 1. The following changes or corrections are to be made in this note: In line 23, instead of "Appendix," read: Duncan, 37–40; in line 25, after "*Math. Schrift.*, 6, 234 *sq.*," insert: trans., Appendix, *infra*, pp. 670–692; in line 27, instead of "Appendix," read: Duncan, 71–80; in line 28, instead of "Appendix," read: Duncan, 112–126; in line 30, *dele* "trans., Appendix"; line 5 from bottom, "As Leibnitz was occupied," etc., *cf. infra*, p. 531, note 2, ¶¶ 2, 3. The statement made in these two notes would probably more nearly represent the truth in the matter if made thus: "As Leibnitz was occupied with the composition of his 'New Essays' from 1700–1704, and with their revision until the end of 1707, and perhaps later (*cf.* Gerhardt's Introduction to the 'New Essays,' *ante*, pp. 8, 9, and Leibnitz's Correspondence with Coste, Gerhardt, *Leibniz. philos. Schrift.*, 3, 377 *sq.*, especially 391–400) the relative date," etc.

Page 103, line 7, "Witsen." Nicolas Witsen, c. 1640–1717, Dutch ambassador at the Russian Court, alderman and burgomaster at Amsterdam, published *Architectonica nautica nov-antiqua*, Amstelod., 1671; *Noord-en Oost-Tartarye, met Landkaerten, beschreven, getekent*, etc., 2 vols., fol., *ib.*, 1692 and 1705. For Witsen's correspondence with Leibnitz, *cf.* Dutens, 6, Pt. II., 199–203; Foucher de Careil, *Œuvres de Leibniz*, 7, 450, 453–459, 464.

Page 103, line 8, "Barantola." The old name for Lhasa, the capital of Thibet. *Cf.* Dutens, 6, Pt. II., p. 201.

Page 103, note 2. Add: Chap. 3 in Fraser's *Locke's Essay.*

Page 103, note 3. Add: Fraser's *Locke's Essay*, 1, 99.

Page 105, note 1. Add: *Cf.* Fraser's *Locke's Essay*, 1, 109. Fraser numbers 21, and states in his note that the section was added in the second edition

Page 108, note 2, line 5 from bottom. Instead of "Vol. 3," read: III., 2 [Vol. 6].

PAGE 109, note 2. *Cf. ante*, p. 733, note to p. 68, line 7 from bottom. Leibnitz regards each monad, and especially the human soul, as a mirror of the universe. So far as the ideas are clear and distinct, the soul expresses the picture of the ideal universe existing in the mind of God as the "best world" and realized out of his goodness; so far as they are confused, the soul is like the phenomenal world in space and time.

PAGE 110, lines 18, 19, "*Intrinsic connotations.*" The intrinsic, inner activity of every "substantial thing" determines its external activity and relations to each and all other things. In Leibnitz's view, this activity consists in representation or is conceived as analogous to representation. That is, all external change is apparent merely, depending upon that internal change in the condition of substances which we call representation and which is the real occurrence.

PAGE 112, line 11 from bottom, "Certain author." Locke, Bk. II., chap. 1, § 10 (in Coste's translation, which, it will be remembered, was the one used by Leibnitz as the basis of his critique, 4th ed., Amsterdam, 1742, p. 65, 4 vol. ed., Amsterdam, 1774, 1, 152), says: "Car il s'est trouvé un Auteur qui ayant lû la première Edition de cet Ouvrage, et n'étant pas satisfait de ce que je viens d'avancer contre l'opinion de ceux qui soûtiennent que l'*Ame pense toujours*, me fait dire, qu'*une chose cesse d'exister parceque nous ne sentons pas qu'elle existe pendent notre sommeil*," etc.; but he does not name the author referred to. In the English editions of the Essay, for example, Bohn's, Vol. 1, p. 212; Fraser's, Vol. 1, p. 129, Locke makes the reference general: "How could any one make it an inference of mine," etc. Philalethes rightly takes exception to the opinion thus falsely imputed to the partisans of Locke.

PAGE 118, line 10 from bottom, "Beg the question." Schaarschmidt has put the argument in logical form thus: "That of which we are not conscious is not in the soul; We are often conscious of no ideas; therefore, We are often without ideas (or, therefore, often we do not think). And he goes on to say that, the circle, of which Leibnitz speaks, consists in the fact that he who so concludes has already put the conclusion in the major premise in assuming that to have no consciousness of ideas is the same as to be without ideas (*Nichtvorstellen*) or not to think (*Nichtdenken*). The latter statement is false. One can have ideas, and actually does have them, without being directly conscious of his ideas (*Vorstellens*). Thus the major premise of that argument is false, and therefore the conclusion likewise, while the minor is true. According to Leibnitz, substance is always active — is indeed action itself — thus also the soul, since for him it is a substance, and since the proper activity of the soul is to have ideas (*das Vorstellen*), therefore the soul is always having ideas (*vorstellend*)."

PAGE 118, note 1, line 2. After "Erdmann," add: Janet.

PAGE 119, line 8 from bottom, "Independently of the senses." *Cf. ante*, p. 723, note to p. 42, line 10, *ad fin.*; p. 725, note to p. 44, line 13;

p. 733, note to p. 68, line 20. In accord with Leibnitz's principle of the absolute spontaneity of substances, all activity, that of the soul as well, springs out of the depths of its own being.

Page 119, note 1, line 2. After "Erdmann," add: Janet.

Page 120, line 6, "*Ex professo*." Schaarschmidt says the term *Ex professo* is a technical expression occurring in classical literature (for example, Seneca and Quintilian), which signifies: in a positive, precise way, in a pronounced or aforementioned manner. Leibnitz means to say, hitherto have we each set forth and justified his own speculative point of view (*erkenntniss-theoretischen Standpunkt*); now we come to the consideration of some classes of ideas in which we shall more than hitherto agree with each other.

Page 120, note 1. After "Erdmann," add: Janet.

Page 121, note 1. After "Erdmann's," add: Janet's.

Page 122, lines 1, 2. "The membranes receive the sensation," etc. *Cf.* Leibnitz's letter to Arnauld, April, 1687 (Gerhardt, *Leibniz. philos. Schrift.*, 2, 90, 91): "Les nerfs et les membranes sont des parties plus sensibles pour nous que les autres, et ce n'est peutestre que par elles que nous nous appercevons des autres, ce qui arrive apparemment, parceque les mouvemens des nerfs ou des liqueurs y appartenantes imitent mieux les impressions et les confondent moins, or les expressions plus distinctes de l'ame repondent aux impressions plus distinctes du corps. Ce n'est pas que les nerfs agissent sur l'ame, à parler metaphysiquement, mais c'est que l'un represente l'estat de l'autre *spontanea relatione*," *i.e.* "The nerves and the membranes are the parts more sensitive for us than the others, and it is perhaps only by them that we perceive the others, which happens apparently, because the movements of the nerves or of the fluids belonging thereto imitate better the impressions and confuse them less, now the more distinct impressions of the soul correspond to the more distinct impressions of the body. Not that the nerves act upon the soul, to speak metaphysically, but that the one represents the state of the other by reason of a *spontaneous relation*." Modern psychological investigation and experiment prove that the end-organs rather than the nerves "receive the sensation," or, in modern phrase, 'are acted upon directly by the stimulus,' the character of the sensation depending upon the peculiar structure of these different end-organs, and not upon the nerves. The formerly held doctrine of the "specific energy of the nerves" as being the cause of specific sensations, or as 'accounting for the quality of the sensation' — a doctrine which, according to Schaarschmidt in his note to the passage (*Erläuterungen z. d. Neuen Abhandlungen ü. d. menschlich. Verstand v. G. W. Leibniz*, Berlin, 1874, J. H. v. Kirchmann's *Philos. Bibliothek*, Bd. 56, Erläuterung. 92, p. 27) contradicts Leibnitz's statement in the text, — is now given up. Leibnitz's statement, while partly true, is nevertheless incomplete. He is right in stating "that tastes make themselves known to some extent through the nose, by reason of the connection of these organs," — modern experiments having proved taste and smell to be interdependent in their action in sensation, — but wrong as to the assistance of the teeth in the transmission of sound, the teeth not being ordinarily concerned in the process. If by "membranes" Leibnitz meant "end-organs," his statement, with the exception of the part regarding the hearing, would be correct, and his theory exhibit a remarkable degree of insight and foresight and of approximation to the modern view of the subject. But this interpretation of his language seems on the whole inadmissible, "membranes" with him signifying probably the skin and the muscles, so that, while we may not justly regard him as having attained the fulness and completeness of the modern understanding of the sensation-process, we may yet justly attribute to him a measure of insight into, and foresight of, what through subsequent investigation and experiment has been proved to be its true nature.

PAGE 122, Chap. IV., § 1, line 5, "Solidity." On Locke's idea of solidity, *cf.* Lasswitz, *Gesch. d. Atomistik*, 2, 505–508.

PAGE 123, note 3. After "Erdmann," add: Janet.

PAGE 124, lines 9, 10 from bottom, "The scholastic conception of the air." *Cf. New Essays*, Bk. I., chap. 1, § 18, Th., *ante*, p. 83, lines 11, 12. On "rarefaction and condensation," line 12 from bottom, *cf.* Lasswitz, *Gesch. d. Atomistik*, Vol. 1, *passim*.

PAGE 125, last line of text and note 1, "Animant." Some time after the text and note were in type, I came upon Leibnitz's letter to Leuwenhoek, "Sur l'Aimant," *cf.* Dutens, *Leibnit. op. om.*, 2, Pt. II., 92–94. In the correspondence, in Latin, of Leibnitz with Des Bosses there is considerable allusion to the Magnet, *cf.* Gerhardt, *Leibniz. philos. Schrift.*, 2, 437 (Postscript to Letter of Leibnitz to Des Bosses, February 5, 1712), 492–495, 497–498 (Leibnitz to Hartsoeker, April 29, 1715, in French), 505, 513 (Response de Mr. Hartsoeker, in French). As from this correspondence it is evident that Leibnitz was occupied more or less with the study of the Magnet, it seems as if the reading of the text should be "aimant," and the translation accordingly "magnet," and thus the view expressed in the last sentence of note 1, *ante*, p. 125, is confirmed. Janet also reads "aimant." *Cf.*, also, a rough draft of letter of Leibnitz to Peter the Great, January 16, 1712, Foucher de Careil, *Œuvres de Leibniz*, 7, 507, and a rough draft of a memorial of Leibnitz concerning the study of languages and the observation of the variation of the magnetic needle in the Russian Empire, *ibid.*, 519, 531 *sq.*; also, *Observations über die Magnet-Nadel*, *ibid.*, 562 *sq.*

PAGE 126, line 1, "Vacuum." That is, the effort of all bodies, particularly air and water, to fill up empty space. The doctrine of the universal attraction of all bodies has put an end to this false notion of "the fear of a vacuum" — *horror vacui*. On the vacuum, *cf.* Lasswitz, *Gesch. d. Atomistik*, *passim*.

PAGE 127, note 2. Add: Leibnitz's correspondence with Guerike, *cf.* Gerhardt, *Leibniz. philos. Schrift.*, 1, 89–112.

PAGE 129, line 1, "The view of the Cartesians." Janet, *Œuvres philos. de Leibniz*, 1, 95, note 1, refers to Descartes, *Prin. Philos.*, II., § 4. *Cf.* Veitch's trans., pp. 233–234.

PAGE 129, line 6, "Disagreement." Schaarschmidt remarks on this chapter as follows: "In this chapter on Solidity the antithesis of the Lockian and Leibnitzian view comes out with great acuteness. Locke, starting out from Sensualism, affirms that solidity is the most real property of bodies, a statement which, if logically developed, must lead to the assumption of hard impenetrable atoms. On the other hand, Leibnitz rightly maintains that all the properties of the body which Locke derives from solidity may be won without the assumption of a space-filling and impenetrable first being, and that 'solidity . . . is conceivable by pure reason, although the senses furnish the reason with the means of proof thereto.'" He also compares, on the atoms, Leibnitz's *Nouveau système de la nature*, § 11 *sq.*

PAGE 129, last line, "Demonstration." This view of Leibnitz, as developed by Christian Wolf, became the seed from which sprang the Kantian doctrine of the categories.

PAGE 130, line 13 [Chap. 7, line 6], "Idea of existence." Schaarschmidt says: "The validity of this protest is clear, although Sensualism until the present time has not allowed itself to be brought back from the Lockian view. The concept of existence springs from the source of self-consciousness, not from the sensitivity. Sense-perception is as such first possible, after we have won the concept of existence from self-consciousness, and now after the analogy of our own being have placed it under the sense-phenomena for their explanation."

PAGE 130, note 1. Add: Schaarschmidt translates: "Inbetrachtnahme des Daseins."

PAGE 136, note 1. Add: Dr. E. G. Robinson, President of Brown University, and Professor of Philosophy, 1872–1889, gave in his MS. Lectures to his classes on Psychology the following account of *Consciousness:*

CONSCIOUSNESS

"As this is the one controlling source of all our knowledge of mind, it is indispensable that we determine as precisely as we can just what we understand by it.

"It is manifest at the outset that consciousness is the invariable accompaniment and necessary condition of all actual knowledge and of every cognitive act. It is itself never an act but always a state of mind without which mental acts are impossible and which itself is possible only through cognitive acts, and this is true whatever the acts of cognition may be, whether relating to objects in the external world, to the bodily organism, or to strictly subjective thought and feeling.

"It is evident, therefore, that we cannot with Reid regard consciousness as a faculty. A faculty can be called into exercise, consciousness cannot be, but always exists as a condition of the exercise of a faculty. Neither can we regard it as an intuitive idea, a regulative notion. An intuitive idea can exist only in consciousness. If consciousness be an intuitive idea, it must itself exist as the condition of its own existence. Neither can we regard it as identical with feeling, as sundry sensationalists do, since feeling can exist only in consciousness. Nor yet again can we with Sir William Hamilton regard consciousness as the genus of which cognitive acts are the species, as the complement of the cognitive faculties.[1] A genus can exist only as made up of species. The distinction between consciousness and cognition is, according to their definition when analyzed, only verbal and not real. Consciousness can be neither a special faculty, nor an intuitive idea, nor a distinct species of knowledge, nor the complement of the cognitive faculties, but is that within which all ideas must exist, any species of knowledge be acquired, and every faculty be exercised.

"It cannot, accordingly, be correct to define consciousness as the soul's knowing that it knows,[1] or 'the power by which the soul knows its own acts and states,'[2] or the power to know that it is itself that knows.[3] But consciousness is rather *the soul's actual knowing with itself that it knows*, that is, is that relation to itself into which the ego is brought by cognition of any object other than itself, is the ego as subject communing with itself as object through the mediation of some object distinct from itself. It is not a power of the soul but is a state,[4] a condition, a function of the soul which always necessarily accompanies any normal or voluntary exercise of the soul's powers. Speaking figuratively and popularly, it is the mind's illumination of itself by its own action.

"That the foregoing is a correct account of consciousness seems evident:

"1. From the difference between cognition and consciousness and the relation of the one to the other. Cognition is a voluntary act of the ego, and consciousness is an involuntary state or condition of the ego which always accompanies its cognitions, and neither one can by any possibility exist without the other. Simple cognition is only a given correlation of subject and object; whereas in consciousness, which must always accom-

[1] Sir William Hamilton, *Metaph.*, 133 *sq.*, 143 *sq.*, Amer. ed.; *Discussions*, p. 54, Amer. ed.

[2] President Noah Porter, *Hum. Intellect*, p. 83.

[3] President Mark Hopkins, *Outline Study of Man*, p. 107.

[4] In the oral exposition of this passage, Dr. Robinson remarked in substance as follows: "A 'state' is usually considered as something inert, stable, inactive; but not so with Consciousness. Consciousness is an *active* state. 'State' is preferable to 'act,' as the latter implies volition. Consciousness is an involuntary state or condition of the ego."

pany cognition, the knowing subject is in and by the cognitive act brought into correlation to itself as coexistent or conjunctive object.

"2. The very word *consciousness*, which all are agreed in using, implies in its composition a partnership and an intercommunication between self as knowing subject and self as known object, an intercommunication which occurs momentarily and continuously in every cognitive act. Whatever may have been the origin of the word, whether with philosophers or the unlettered, it etymologically vindicates the view of consciousness here given.

"3. It is admitted on all hands that knowledge is impossible without consciousness. But if consciousness itself be a distinct kind of knowledge, whether generic or specific, then since all knowledge is possible only in consciousness, consciousness itself must have its conditioning consciousness and so on *ad infinitum*. But not only does the consciousness of every individual being have an absolute beginning, but every given instant of consciousness is as distinct and separate from the preceding as is every act of cognition from its preceding, and every given instant of consciousness is dependent on some given act of cognition. Consciousness, therefore, is not an act of cognition, nor a power to cognize, but is the simple reflex action of the ego upon itself in its own acts of cognition ; and it cannot be the mind's power to know itself or to know that it is itself that knows, since it is a state or a relation of the ego to itself which is always dependent on the exercise of the power to know.

"If what has been said be true, then it is evident that consciousness, although always inseparable from bodily sensation, is predicable only of mind as active intelligence or intellect. It is by the mind alone as the perceiving, thinking power of the soul that any of the soul's energies, cognitive, cogitative, emotive, volitional, can be brought into exercise or continued in action, and since it is only by the exercise of these energies that consciousness exists, it is of the mind alone, the perceiving and thinking power of the soul, that consciousness is predicable. Again, it also follows that there can be but one kind of consciousness, that it is always spontaneous, the invariable and necessary accompaniment of cognition, that is, it always accompanies cognition whether the cognition be of objects external or internal. It may vary in degree according to degrees of attention in acts of cognition, but it never changes from itself into consciousness of another kind.

"The so-called self-consciousness or the reflective, acquired, philosophical consciousness, is nothing else than that act of mind by which the ego itself, its acts or states or its consciousness are made objects of attention. This does not differ from any other act of cognition and knowledge. It furthermore, like every other act of knowledge, is always accompanied by a consciousness of the act, and the consciousness of our consciousness, when it is made an object of attention and knowledge, is just as clear as the consciousness we have when we perceive an external object or when we make a percept, a concept, or an inward emotion an object of attention and scrutiny."

THE COMPONENTS OF CONSCIOUSNESS AND THEIR REALITY

"When we make consciousness an object of attention and analyze it into its component parts, we find it always to consist of three distinguishable elements, namely: the ego cognizing, the object cognized, and the communion of the ego with itself in the cognitive act; that is, we find the soul communing with itself in the act of knowing something which is not itself. But these three elements, when themselves analyzed, reveal the existence of but two distinct quantities or entities, the ego and the object of its knowledge. Out of these two factors, subject and object, carefully analyzed, come directly or indirectly the entire materials of mental philosophy.

"As to the real existence of these factors of consciousness, the subject and its objects, we may begin with the objects. If there be any doubt as to the reality of the mind's objects, the so-called subject-objects, whether they be sensations, feelings, perceptions, ideas, volitions, or whatever else simple or complex, there is still stronger reason for doubting the existence of an external world from which as cause or occasion these subject-objects have sprung, and reasons stronger still for doubting the existence of our doubt. If mental objects be unreal, doubt has no existence. The truth is, if there be any reality anywhere it is in the mind's own acts of subjective cognition.

"In like manner, if the object in consciousness has a real existence, still more indubitably real is the existence of the personal ego that knows the object in consciousness. This is evident in three ways:

"First. We are conscious only while one of our mental faculties or powers is in exercise. In the act of its exercise the ego immediately intuits itself as exercising its own energy. Self immediately cognizes self as active in every successive moment of consciousness.

"Second. It is plain that the objects cognized on which the existence of consciousness is always dependent, even the most subjective and subtle of them, are clearly distinguishable from the ego that cognizes the object. In fact, no object in consciousness is ever cognized unless the cognizing self clearly distinguishes between itself and the object. Such discrimination cannot take place unless the ego that makes it has an indubitably real existence.

"Third. The existence of memory proves the real existence of the personal ego. Consciousness is a succession of instants each of which is distinct from the preceding and following and each of which changes with the ever-changing objects of cognition and thought, and yet these vanishing instants so leave their traces on the personal ego that it can at will recall long series of them. Thus memory not only proves the existence but the persistent identity of the ego that has an object of thought with its accompanying consciousness to-day which it can reproduce to-morrow, the next day, and with indefinite frequency thereafter.

"Finally. The real existence of object and subject being indubitably established, it necessarily follows that the existence of consciousness, within which both subject and object are found, and consequently its trustworthiness as a source of knowledge in Psychology, must be unhesitatingly admitted." (*Lects. on Psychol.*, MS., §§ 12, 13, as given to the class of 1884.)

Requisites and Difficulties in Consulting Consciousness

"That is, in practising the so-called self-consciousness.

"First. Requisites: It is necessary that there be close and concentrated attention, patience and persistence in observation, frequent and varied observations, careful discrimination between different classes as well as between different species of the same class of mental phenomena; that each particular phenomenon be analyzed and traced to its cause or causes; that there be a distribution of phenomena according to their nature and causes so far as these can be ascertained.

"But with the utmost care, attention, and discrimination in the analysis and classification of the phenomena given in consciousness, there is a constant liability to error. The nature, relations, and causes of the phenomena to be observed are many of them so subtle and obscure that diversity and even conflict of view may be inevitable, but the disagreements, it must be remembered, turn chiefly on the theories respecting the origin of the phenomena and their relation to realities and not on the reality of the existence of the mental phenomena themselves.

"Second. Difficulties: The observation and examination of the phenomena of consciousness, however, as compared with the observation and examination of phenomena in the external world, is attended with various, and to inexperienced minds with serious, difficulties. Thus:

"(*a*) So large a portion of early life is spent among and in the observation of the phenomena of the outer world that it is difficult for many persons to acquire the habit of accurate observation of the subjective phenomena of mind. This difficulty is heightened:

"(*b*) By the necessity the conscious subject is under of becoming the object of its own observation, the necessity of compelling himself to act and to observe himself at the same instant. Upon the phenomena of the outer world the mind can concentrate an undivided attention, but when the mind makes its own action an object of attention there is requisite the double effort to produce mental movement and to observe oneself in the process, the result being at best but constrained and halting action of which from divided attention we can catch only hasty and imperfect views.

"(*c*) Subjective acts and states occurring in rapid succession can be observed only instantaneously, while most objects of sense remaining comparatively permanent in form can generally be examined repeatedly and at leisure. The most evanescent of physical phenomena give ample time for observation in comparison with the most enduring phenomena of mind.

"(*d*) Every individual consciousness is isolated from that of every other, and the report of no one's consciousness, notwithstanding the unanimity in the deliverance of all consciousnesses, can be accepted or even understood by another without a personal scrutiny of his own; whereas in the natural sciences there may be many or few observers, and their reports can be understood and received without personal experiment.

"(*e*) The objects of consciousness are many of them complex in themselves and their causes and subtle in their relations to one another; they therefore are much more difficult of observation and require much more careful discrimination in observing them than objects in the external world, the mechanical and chemical origin of which are at once and palpably discernible." (*Lects. on Psychol.*, § 14, ed. of 1884.)

To the above, as presenting more completely Dr. Robinson's view of Consciousness, — a subject which "he regarded as fundamental to all order and rectitude of thought" in Psychology, and on which "he expended much time and thought" in perfecting his conception and its statement, — may be added what he dictated to his classes on the question:

"CAN THERE BE AN UNCONSCIOUS MODIFICATION OF MIND?

"That is, can there be mental processes and the mind itself unaware of them? The answer must manifestly depend on the meaning attached to the word *mind*. If by mind be meant the thinking personal essence, or if it denotes the co-ordinated psychical forces which constitute personal being, there can be no good ground for doubting that there may be unconscious modifications of both its states and its powers. There are depths in the potentialities of the personal being which consciousness never reaches. Consciousness knows nothing of the inner sources of energy whence thoughts, feelings, desires, and volitions emanate, but only of thoughts, feelings, desires, and volitions after they have taken form in the mind. It is upon the existence of these that consciousness depends, and of their existence alone can consciousness inform us. There may therefore be modifications of states of soul, increments and diminutions of intellectual and moral power, and losses of intellectual possessions of which we may be unconscious and of which we may remain unconscious till we learn them from unwonted phenomena.

"So also thoughts and accompanying states of consciousness often spring from instinct and hereditary bias which have long lain latent and have existed and operated below consciousness. Instances of knowledge lost under some given condition of the brain and restored under other cerebral conditions are examples of the same kind of unconscious changes. Every species of mental action is more or less dependent on the state of the brain, but to ascribe these changes to unconscious cerebration is to assume that thought is the equivalent of physical force, is both the quantitative and qualitative product of the brain alone, rather than the product of an active agent which uses the brain, and it is an assumption for which there is no sufficient ground.

"But if by mind be meant the soul's acquisitive and cogitative powers, the intellect, the intelligence, the question whether it may not be unconsciously modified is equivalent to the query whether there may not be an unconscious mental act or (which is the same thing) an unconscious state of consciousness, a contradiction of terms. Every modification of mind, in the sense of the word *mind* here under consideration, must be by some mental act. But any mental act in order to be such must be a conscious mental act. Cognition and consciousness always coexist. An unconscious modification of mind would necessitate a mental act of which one was unconscious.

"The facts often cited in proof of an unconscious modification of mind do not seem to warrant the conclusions drawn from them; for instance, acts performed in obedience to any established habits, single but synthetic visions of complex objects, sudden and apparently unaccountable thoughts, sudden and mysterious recollection of long-forgotten persons and events, the apparently simultaneous carrying forward of several trains of thought. All these may be instances, not of unconscious cerebration or of unconscious modification of the mind, but of mental movements, the successive steps of which are too occult or too rapid and minute for the mind in the study of itself to follow. In compound and complex mental processes it is possible that simple steps may be so inadvertently taken as to be apparently taken unconsciously; but an analysis of the process will show that while the degrees of consciousness may be indefinitely numerous, running down to the lowest stages of latent or sub-consciousness, yet unconsciousness is so far removed from ever so low a degree of consciousness as to be separated from it by an impassable chasm. As there are many degrees in life but none in death, so there are degrees in consciousness but none in unconsciousness." (*Lects. on Psychol.*, § 20, ed. of 1884.)

PAGE 138, note 1. Add: For the letter of Molyneux here referred to, dated March 2, 1693, *cf.* Locke's correspondence with Molyneux, in Locke's *Works*, 9, 34, 12th ed., London, 1824, 9 vols. 8vo. Berkeley, *An Essay toward a New Theory of Vision*, §§ 132, 133, Fraser's ed., Vol. 1, pp. 96, 97, refers to it; also Locke, *Philos. Wks.*, Bohn's ed., 1, 257–258, note †. On the relations of Locke and Molyneux, *cf.* Fraser, *Locke*, Blackwood's Philos. Classics, Edinburgh and Philadelphia, 1890, p. 234 *sq.*, the letter referred to, p. 238. Molyneux died as a result of a journey, undertaken when ill, to see Locke.

PAGE 139, lines 17–20, "In this case . . . united with that sense-knowledge with which touch has before furnished him." *Cf.* "The Mentor," a monthly, published by the Alumni Association of the Perkins Institution for the Blind, Boston, Mass., U.S.A., Vol. 2, No. 3, March 1892, pp. 81–86. "Sculpture by the sense of Touch," giving an account of a blind sculptor. Johnson M. Mundy, whose sight began to fail in his youth and slowly but surely grew less, until it practically vanished entirely. He learned the sculptor's art between the ages of 22 and 29, and practised it for twenty years till the loss of sight compelled him to give it up. Unable, however, long to endure "the monotony of an idle and useless existence" and "with unabated aspiration and fondness for his art," he resumed his work, performing the actual work of sculpture by the sense of touch. His last work up to the date of the article here referred to was a heroic statue of Washington Irving.

PAGE 144, note 1. Add: *Cf.* Gerhardt, *Leibniz. philos. Schrift.*, 6, 522–528, letter 5 to Sophie Charlotte ("hitherto not published," Gerhardt, *op. cit.*, 6, 477, note * — he should have said 'published entire,' as Foucher de Careil, *Lettres et opuscules inédits de Leibniz*, Paris, 1854, pp. 252–254, published a fragment of the same), in which Leibnitz subjects Bouhours' book to a sharp critique. Leibnitz also refers to Bouhours in his letter to Sebastian Kortholt, Sept. 30, 1708, Kortholt, *Leibnit. Epistolæ*, 1, 282; Dutens, *Leibnit. op. om.*, 5, 306–307; to Fried. Wilhelm Bierling, Oct. 24, 1709, Kortholt, *op. cit.*, 4, 8; Dutens, *op. cit.*, 5, 355; Gerhardt, *Leibniz. philos. Schrift.*, 7, 487: "Bouhursius mihi contemtu vindicandus, nec verbis a Germanis, sed rebus refellendus videbatur." *Cf.*, also, Dutens, *op. cit.*, 5, 190: "Mediocris vir fuit Bouhursius, qui neglecto religionis suæ, cui se addixerat, habitu. Damaretum quendam effingere, et fœmineam elegantiam exprimere satagebat."

PAGE 147, line 2 from bottom, "Modes." *Cf.* Descartes, *Prin. Philos.*, Bk. I., § 56, ed. Cousin, 3, 98; Veitch's English trans., 217; German trans. by J. H. v. Kirchmann, 2d ed., Heidelberg, 1887 (Bd. 26 of his *Philos. Bibliothek*), p. 28: "Lorsque je dis ici façon ou mode, je n'entends rien que ce que je nomme ailleurs attribut ou qualité. Mais lorsque je considère que la substance en est autrement disposée ou diversifiée, je me sers particulièrement du nom de mode ou façon; et lorsque, de cette disposition ou changement, elle peut être appelée telle, je nomme qualités les diverses façons qui font qu'elle est ainsi nommée; enfin, lorsque je pense plus généralment que ces modes ou qualités sont en la substance, dans les considérer autrement que comme les dépendances de cette substance, je les nomme attributs. Et, parceque je ne dois concevoir en Dieu aucune variété ni changement, je ne dis pas qu'il y ait en lui des modes ou des qualités, mais plutôt des attributs; et même dans les choses créées, ce qui se trouve en elles toujours de même sorte, comme l'existence et la durée en la chose qui existe et qui dure, je le nomme attribut, et non pas mode ou qualité." *Cf.*, also, *New Essays*, Bk. II., chap. 30, § 4, *infra*, p. 276, and note to p. 277, line 8, *infra*, p. 763.

PAGE 147, note 1. *Dele* "Appendix, p. ——." and substitute "Duncan, 71–80." *Cf.*, also, *New Essays*, Bk. IV., chap. 10, § 7, Th., *ad fin.*, *infra*, p. 505, § 9, Th., p. 507.

PAGE 149, line 15 from bottom, "The shortest great-arc of a circle." The French text is: "La longueur du plus petit grand-arc de cercle," etc.

PAGE 150, line 13, "Buratini." *Cf.* Dutens, *Leibnit. op. om.*, 6, Pt. I., 319: "*Gravius*, Anglus, in descriptione Ægypti apud *Thevenot*, Vol. 1, p. 14, mentionem facit, *Titi Livii Buratini*, jeune homme Venitien fort spirituel, qui étoit dans la compagnie. *Thevenot* in margine annotat: Buratini est maintenant maître de la monnoye du Roi de Pologne, et c'est de lui que l'on vit il y a dix ou douze ans un modelle d'une *machine pour voler.*"

PAGE 153, line 7, "Lessius." Léonard Lessius, 1554–1623, a Flemish Jesuit, was Professor of Philosophy at Douay, and of Theology, 1583–1623, at Louvain. He opposed the doctrine of grace of Thos. Aquinas, and was charged with favoring Semi-Pelagianism. He was well acquainted with theology, law, mathematics, medicine, and history. For two of his *Opera*, *cf.* Migne, *Theol. cur. compl.*, 3, 787; 15, 445. Janet, *Œuvres philos. de Leibniz*, 1, 120, note 1, states that he was a celebrated casuist, often cited in Pascal's *Provinciales*, and adds that of his ethical works the chief is the *De justitia et jure* (Migne, *op. cit.*, 15, 445); and that of the theological works we have *De perfectionibus moribusque divinis; De libertate arbitrii et præscientia Dei; De summo bono; De Providentia numinis.*

PAGE 154, line 13, "Accidents or abstracts." The strong contrast between Locke's and Leibnitz's philosophies comes here again to the front. Locke regards substance as a mere creation of thought, a subjective expedient of the understanding which "invents" it as a unitary support to, or bearer of, the accidents. Leibnitz looks upon the "substance-concept as the suitable expression of the idea of the actual, to which we refer back the accidents. Every phenomenon as such, in his view, presupposes an actual being, since through such an actual being the phenomenon is first possible. Substance, accordingly, is in the case of all phenomena that which is constantly to be presupposed, the non-irrational (*Nicht-nichtzudenkende*), but in no sense a mere auxiliary concept of only subjective validity."—Schaarschmidt. Leibnitz is in the direct line of Hegel in his emphasis of the concrete rather than the abstract.

PAGE 154, line 4 from bottom, "Indefinite." *Cf.* Descartes, *Prin. Philos.*, Pt. II., § 21, ed. Cousin, Vol. 3, p. 138: "Nous saurons aussi que ce monde, ou la matière étendue qui compose l'univers, n'a point de bornes, parceque, quelque part où nous en voulions feindre, nous pouvons encore imaginer au-delà des espaces indéfiniment étendus, que nous n'imaginons pas seulement, mais que nous concevons être tels en effet que nous les imaginons; de sorte qu'ils contiennent un corps indéfinement étendu," *i.e.* We know that this world, or the extended matter which composes the universe, has no limits because, should we wish anywhere to feign such limits, we can still imagine beyond spaces indefinitely extended, which we do not imagine only, but which we conceive to be in fact such as we imagine them, so that they contain an indefinitely extended body.

PAGE 154, note 1, line 4. Instead of "Appendix," read: Duncan, pp. 68–70; line 7, ditto, pp. 71–80; line 10, ditto, pp. 112–126.

PAGE 155, line 26, "Motion." *Cf.* Leibnitz's 4th letter to Clarke, *ad fin.*, Gerhardt, 7, 377; Erdmann, 758; Jacques, 2, 437; Janet, 2, 640;

trans. Duncan, 253; 5th letter to Clarke, § 22, Gerhardt, 7, 394; Erdmann, 765; Jacques, 2, 450; Janet, 2, 654; Duncan, 259.

PAGE 156, note 1. *Phys.*, VIII. [or H], 6, 258^{b} 10: *ἐπεὶ δὲ δεῖ κίνησιν ἀεὶ εἶναι καὶ μὴ διαλείπειν, ἀνάγκη εἶναί τι ὃ πρῶτον κινεῖ, εἴτε ἓν εἴτε πλείω, καὶ τὸ πρῶτον κινοῦν ἀκίνητον.*

PAGE 157, note 1. Add: Φυσικῆς Ἀκροάσεως, Δ, 11, 219^{b} 1: *τοῦτο γάρ ἐστιν ὁ χρόνος, ἀριθμὸς κινήσεως κατὰ τὸ πρότερον καὶ ὕστερον. οὐκ ἄρα κίνησις ὁ χρόνος ἀλλ' ᾗ ἀριθμὸν ἔχει ἡ κίνησις.* Φυσικῆς Ἀκροάσεως, Δ, 11, 219^{b} 8: *ὁ δὲ χρόνος ἐστὶ τὸ ἀριθμούμενον καὶ οὐχ ᾧ ἀριθμοῦμεν.* *Cf.* Zeller, *Philos. d. Griech.*, 3d ed., 1879, II., 2 [Vol. 4], 402.

PAGE 158, note 1. Add: Spinoza regards all determination as a negation — *Omnis determinatio est negatio* — of this originally posited or necessarily presupposed absolute. Hegel likewise in his *Logik* maintains essentially the same position as Leibnitz, so that Leibnitz may rightly be said to be in the direct line of the philosophical development culminating in Hegel. *Cf.* Wallace, *The Logic of Hegel*, 1st ed., 1874; 2d ed., revised and augmented, Oxford, Clarendon Press, 1892–1894, *passim*.

PAGE 160, line 9, "Transcendent." Janet, *Œuvres philos. de Leibniz*, 1, 128, in his note to this passage, says: "Expressions of the scholastic mathematical language, rarely employed to-day. The *surd* (*le sourd*) is the incommensurable, for example, $\sqrt{2}$; *le rompu* — the broken — is the fraction, as $\frac{1}{2}$; the transcendent is that which cannot be calculated by a limited number of arithmetical operations, for example, log 3. These three terms are comprised between two whole numbers."

PAGE 162, note 1. Add: *Locke's Essay*, ed. Fraser, 1, 295, line 9 from bottom.

PAGE 162, note 2. Add: *Cf.* the note of Foucher de Careil, *Sur les trois sens du mot infini dans la philosophie de Leibniz*, *Nouvelles Lettres et Opuscules inédits de Leibniz*, Paris, 1857, pp. 404–407; also A. Penjon, *De infinito apud Leibnitium*, Paris, 1878.

PAGE 162, note 3. Add: *Locke's Essay*, ed. Fraser, 1, 277, line 14.

PAGE 166, note 1. Add: *Locke's Essay*, ed. Fraser, 1, 300, line 10.

PAGE 167, note 1. Add: The definition referred to runs as follows: "*Amare* autem sive *diligere* est felicitate alterius delectari, vel quod eodem redit, felicitatem alienam adsciscere [Erdmann — asciscere] in suam. Unde difficilis nodus solvitur, magni etiam in Theologia momenti, quomodo amor non mercenarius detur, qui sit a spe metuque et omni utilitatis respectu separatus: scilicet quorum utilitas [Erdmann — felicitas] delectat, eorum felicitas nostram ingreditur, nam quæ delectant per se expetuntur." *Cf.* Dutens, *Leibnit. op. om.*, 4, Pt. IV., 295; Erdmann, 118, b. The entire preface to the *Codex juris* is given in Dutens, *op. cit.*, 4, Pt. III., 287–328.

PAGE 168, note 1, *ad fin.* Add: *Infra*, pp. 177 *sq.*, 188. Also, *Théodicée*, III., § 404, Gerhardt, 6, 357; Erdmann, 620; Jacques, 2, 300; Janet, 2, 402. *Cf.*, also, J. H. v. Kirchmann, *Erläuterungen zur Théodicée von Leibniz* (Bd. 80, of his *Philos. Bibliothek*, Leipzig, 1879), Erläuterung, 264, pp. 145–147.

PAGE 172, line 4 from bottom, "Displeasure." Schaarschmidt says that neither Locke nor Leibnitz have yet reached the distinction between emotion and passion, as appears from the language of both; and that Kant first grasped the distinction and attempted to determine it more accurately.

PAGE 174, note 1. Add: *Phys.*, Γ, 201ª 10: *ἡ τοῦ δυνάμει ὄντος ἐντελέχεια, ᾗ τοιοῦτον, κίνησίς ἐστιν, οἷον τοῦ μὲν ἀλλοιωτοῦ, ᾗ ἀλλοιωτόν, ἀλλοίωσις, τοῦ δὲ αὐξητοῦ καὶ τοῦ ἀντικειμένου φθιτοῦ (οὐδὲν γὰρ ὄνομα κοινὸν ἐπ' ἀμφοῖν) αὔξησις καὶ φθίσις τοῦ δὲ γενητοῦ καὶ φθαρτοῦ γένεσις καὶ φθορά, τοῦ δὲ φορητοῦ φορά.* *Metaphys.*, K, 1065ᵇ 16: *τὴν τοῦ δυνάμει ᾗ τοιοῦτόν ἐστιν ἐνέργειαν λέγω κίνησιν.* *Cf.* Zeller, *Philos. d. Griech.*, II., 2 [Vol. 4], 351 *sq.*, 389 *sq.*; Wallace, *Outlines of the Philos. of Aristotle*, § 42, p. 77, 3d ed., 1883.

PAGE 174, note 2. Add: Translations of the two pieces last referred to will be found in the Appendix, *infra*, the *Beilage* to the letter to Fabri, pp. 699 *sq.*; the *Specimen Dynamicum*, pp. 670 *sq.*

PAGE 175, line 5, "Idea of power." Leibnitz carefully distinguishes between mere power and force ("Macht" and "Kraft"). *Cf. De primæ philos. emendatione*, etc., Gerhardt, 4, 469; Erdmann, 122; Jacques, 1, 453 [in French]; Janet, 2, 525 [in French]; Duncan, *Philos. Wks. of Leibnitz*, 69.

PAGE 175, line 18, "Because of our ignorance." That is, we are thus far incapable of resolving our sense-impressions, *i.e.* the simple sense-qualities, into anything more simple, and are therefore compelled to regard them as simple presentations, although in themselves possibly composite and in fact in many cases in indirect ways shown to be so. *Cf.*, also, *New Essays*, Bk. III., chap. 3, § 18, Th., *infra*, p. 317, and note 2.

PAGE 175, line 24, "Primitive truths." *Cf. New Essays*, Bk. I., chap. 1, and Bk. IV., chap. 2, *infra*, pp. 404 *sq.*

PAGE 176, line 13 from bottom, "Casati." Paolo Casati, 1617–1707, a learned Italian Jesuit, who taught mathematics and theology at Rome, and was said to have converted Queen Christiana, of Sweden, to the Catholic faith. On his return from Sweden he became Director of the University of Parma. Among his works are *Vacuum proscriptum*, Genoa, 1649; *De terra machinio mota*, Rome, 1668; *Mechanicorum lib. VIII.*, Lyons, 1684; *De igne dissertationes physicæ*, Venice, 1686, 1695; *Hydrostaticæ dissert.*, 1695; *Opticæ dissert.*, 1705. Lasswitz, *Gesch. d. Atomistik*, 2, 490, says: "Im Einzelnen ebenfalls durchaus korpuskular sind die physikalischen Erklärungen des Jesuiten Paolo Casati . . . Aber seine allgemeine Auffassung der Natur ist dabei vollständig scholastisch."

PAGE 176, note 1. Add: *Cf.* Lasswitz, *Gesch. d. Atomistik*, 2, 421–428, especially 423–424. Malebranche changed his views under the influence of Huygens and Leibnitz. The *Loix générales de la communication des mouvements*, Lasswitz says, was added as an Appendix to the later editions of the *Recherche de la vérité*.

PAGE 180, note 1. Add: *Cf.* § 13 of this chapter, *infra*, pp. 182–184, *New Essays*, Bk. IV., chap. 6, *ad fin.*, *infra*, p. 462, note 1; also, Gerhardt, 7, 108–111; Erdmann, 669; also the fragment entitled *De Libertate*, published by Foucher de Careil, *Nouvelles Lettres et Opuscules inédits de Leibniz*, Paris, 1857, pp. 178–185. "Apart from the freedom of fact and of right," says Schaarschmidt, "Leibnitz distinguishes between ethical freedom and free-will (*Willkür*). The former, ethical freedom, is the power to follow the ethical insight in spite of opposing internal hindrances, such as the passions. This concept also is clear and simple. The difficulty proper lies hidden in the conception of free-will (*der Willkür*), the *liberum arbitrium*, by which, as Leibnitz expresses himself, is meant, 'that the strongest reasons or impressions which the understanding presents to the will do not prevent the act of the will from being contingent, and do not give it an absolute and, so to speak, metaphysical necessity.'" Leibnitz regards the action of the will as a motive which *inclines*, but does not compel, — but at the same time he assumes, *Théodicée*, Pt. I., § 52, a self-determination of the will over against which the expression *incline* appears as a mere evasion. *Cf. infra*, p. 462, note 1. On Leibnitz's doctrine of the Will and Freedom, *cf.* G. Class, *Die metaphys. Voraussetzungen d. Leibnitzisch Determinismus*, Tübingen, 1874, pp. 9, 78 *sq.*; F. Kirchner, *Leibniz's Psychologie*, Cöthen, 1875, pp. 82 *sq.*; M. Penzler, *Die Monadenlehre u. ihre Beziehung z. griech. Philos.*, Minden, 1878, p. 23; L. Braeutigam, *Leibniz und Herbart über die Freiheit des menschl. Willens*, Heidelberg, 1882, pp. 3–17, 28–39; M. Nourrisson, *La Philosophie de Leibniz*, Paris, 1860, pp. 268–286; Kuno Fischer, *Gesch. d. n. Philos.*, Vol. 2 [Leibniz] pp. 512–533, 3d ed. Heidelberg, 1889. For a clear analysis and able, though brief, discussion of the various senses in which the "freedom of will" is used, and of "determinism," *cf.* Robinson, *Principles and Practice of Morality*, pp. 122–137.

PAGE 180, note 2. After "1881," add: pp. 68 *sq.* The Greek text of the passages referred to reads thus: Ἠθικὰ Νικομάχεια, Γ, 4, 1112ª 15: ἡ γὰρ προαίρεσις μετὰ λόγου καὶ διανοίας. 5, 1112ª 30: βουλευόμεθα δὲ περὶ τῶν ἐφ' ἡμῖν πρακτῶν. *Cf.*, also, Sir Alexander Grant, *The Ethics of Aristotle*, 3d ed., London, 1874, Vol. 2, pp. 17, 19, Ἠθ. Νικ., III., chap. 2, § 17; chap. 3, § 7. Peter's translation follows the chapter and section numbering of Grant's text. *Cf.*, also, the following pasages from the so-called Ἠθικὰ Μεγάλα — *Magna Moralia* — "which," Schaarschmidt says, "at least for Leibnitz, was a genuine work of Aristotle," — though now regarded, according to Zeller, as "a sketch compiled from both" the Nicomachean and Eudemian ethics, "but more especially from the Eudemian" (*Philos. d. Griech.*, II., 2 [Vol. 4], 102, note 1; *Outlines of the Hist. of Greek Philos.*, New York, 1886, p. 175): A, 16, 1188ᵇ 25: *ἐπεὶ δὲ τὸ ἑκούσιον ἐν οὐδεμιᾷ ὁρμῇ ἐστίν, λοιπὸν ἂν εἰή τὸ ἐκ διανοίας γιγνόμενον.* 1188ᵇ 31: *ὡς τοῦ ἑκουσίου ὄντος ἐν τῷ διανοηθῆναι.* 1188ᵇ 37: *ἐνταῦθα ἄρα τὸ ἑκούσιον πίπτει εἰς τὸ μετὰ διανοίας.* A, 17, 1189ᵃ 31: *εἰ τοίνυν ἡ προαίρεσις ὄρεξίς τις βουλευτικὴ μετὰ διανοίας, οὐκ ἔστι τὸ ἑκούσιον προαιρετόν. ἑκόντες γὰρ πολλὰ πράττομεν πρὸ τοῦ διανοηθῆναι καὶ βουλεύσασθαι, οἷον καθίζομεν καὶ ἀνιστάμεθα καὶ ἄλλα πολλὰ τοιαῦτα ἑκόντες μὲν ἄνευ δὲ τοῦ διανοηθῆναι, τὸ δὲ κατὰ προαίρεσιν πᾶν ἦν μετὰ διανοίας. οὐκ ἄρα τὸ ἑκούσιον προαιρετόν, ἀλλὰ τὸ προαιρετὸν ἑκούσιον· ἄν τι γὰρ προαιρώμεθα πράττειν βουλευσάμενοι, ἑκόντες πράττομεν.* With this last passage, *cf.* 'Ηθ. Νικ., Γ, 4, 1111ᵇ 6: *ἡ προαίρεσις δὴ ἑκούσιον μὲν φαίνεται, οὐ ταὐτὸν δέ, ἀλλ' ἐπὶ πλέον τὸ ἑκούσιον.* 1112ᵃ 14: *ἑκούσιον μὲν δὴ φαίνεται [ἡ προαίρεσις], τὸ δ' ἑκούσιον οὐ πᾶν προαιρετόν.* 1113ᵃ 9: *ὄντος δὲ τοῦ προαιρετοῦ βουλευτοῦ ὀρεκτοῦ τῶν ἐφ' ἡμῖν, καὶ ἡ προαίρεσις ἂν εἴη βουλευτικὴ ὄρεξις τῶν ἐφ' ἡμῖν.* The 'Ηθ. Νικ., Γ, 3, 1111ᵃ 22, defines *τὸ ἑκούσιον*, the voluntary, — *das Freiwillige*, — thus: *τὸ ἑκούσιον δόξειεν ἂν εἶναι οὗ ἡ ἀρχὴ ἐν αὐτῷ εἰδότι τὰ καθ' ἕκαστα ἐν οἷς ἡ πρᾶξις.* 'Ηθ. Εὐδήμια, B, 8, 1224ᵃ 6: *λείπεται ἐν τῷ διανοούμενόν πως πράττειν εἶναι τὸ ἑκούσιον.* B, 9, 1225ᵃ 36: *ἐπεὶ δὲ τοῦτ' ἔχει τέλος, καὶ οὔτε τῇ ὀρέξει οὔτε τῇ προαιρέσει τὸ ἑκούσιον ὥρισται, λοιπὸν δὴ ὁρίσασθαι τὰ κατὰ διάνοιαν.* B, 10, 1226ᵇ 6: *ἡ γὰρ προαίρεσις αἵρεσις μὲν ἐστιν, οὐχ ἁπλῶς δέ, ἀλλ' ἑτέρου πρὸ ἑτέρου· τοῦτο δὲ οὐχ οἷόν τε ἄνευ σκέψεως καὶ βουλῆς. διὸ ἐκ δόξης βουλευτικῆς ἐστὶν ἡ προαίρεσις.* *Cf.*, also, Zeller, *Philos. d. Griech.*, 3d ed., II., 2 [Vol. 4], 587 *sq.*

On Aristotle's doctrine of the Will and Freedom, *cf.* 'Ηθ. Νικ., Γ. 1–8, 1109–1115; Grant, *Ethics of Aristotle*, 2, 5–32, and notes; also his Plan of Book III., *ibid.*, iii., iv., and Essay V., 1, 284 *sq.*; Essay VII., 1, 376 *sq.*; J. A. Stewart, *Notes on the Nicomachean Ethics of Aristotle*, Oxford, Clarendon Press, 1892, Vol. 1, pp. 224–230, 232–236, 240, 243–245, 250, 279; Vol. 2, pp. 16, 17, 379, 380; Trendelenburg, *Histor. Beiträge z. Philos.*, 2, 149 *sq.*; Windelband-Tufts, *Hist. of Philos.*, § 16, 2, pp. 191, 192.

On Leibnitz's relations and indebtedness to Aristotle, *cf.* D. Jacoby, *De Leibnitii Studiis Aristotelicis*, Berlin, 1867; D. Nolen, *Quid Leibnizius Aristoteli debuerit*, Paris, 1875: M. Penzler, *Die Monadenlehre u. ihre Beziehung z. griech. Philosophie*, Minden, 1878, p. 29.

PAGE 183, line 13 from bottom, "The best." *Cf. New Essays*, Bk. IV., chap. 6, *ad fin.*, *infra*, p. 462, note 1.

PAGE 184, lines 7, 6 from bottom, "A freedom of equilibrium absolutely imaginary and impracticable." Leibnitz argues against indeterminism and equilibrium of will, *cf.* Gerhardt, 7, 109: "*Libertas indifferentiæ est impossibilis.* Adeo ut ne in Deum quidem cadat, nam determinatus ille est ad optimum efficiendum. Et creaturæ semper ex rationibus internis externisque determinantur" (*ib.*, 110, in French); Erdmann, 669 (in Latin). *Cf.* Robinson, *Principles and Practice of Morality*, p. 126.

PAGE 185, line 20, "*Vigor of Will.*" *Cf.* Robinson, *Principles and Practice of Morality*, p. 138, where Virtue is defined as "the soul's or the will's persistency of compliance, — its *energy* in complying with the moral law," — a definition perhaps suggested by that of Kant, quoted in the foot-note: "the strength of the human will in the performance of duty."

PAGE 185, note 1. After "Erdmann," add: Janet.

PAGE 192, line 8, "Clearly felt." Schaarschmidt says: "Our feelings can be very lively, while the ideas causing them may be obscure, confused, nay even senseless (let one think, for example, of religious fanaticism, of drunkenness, the aberrations of revenge, etc.); on the other hand, our thoughts can be distinctly, *i.e.* from one another, indeed be distinguishable, without being clearly, *i.e.* in their own content, conceived."

PAGE 192, note 2. Add: The passage from the *Ethica* referred to in this note is found in Vol. 1, pp. 270 *sq.* of this edition. *Cf.* also the *Short Essay on God*, etc., *Korte Verhandeling van God*, etc., Bk. II., chaps. 5 and 19, ed. Van Vloten and Land, 2, 310, 338; Schaarschmidt's German trans., pp. 54, 84 *sq.*, in J. H. v. Kirchmann's *Philos. Bibliothek*, Bd. 18, 2d ed., Berlin, 1874.

PAGE 193, line 6, "Francisco Borgia." General of the Jesuits, 1565–1572.

PAGE 199, note 1. Add: The texts of Erdmann, Jacques, and Janet, and the translation of Schaarschmidt end at "pleasure."

PAGE 203, note 2. The note should read as follows: Gerhardt reads: "Ou venons au propos;" the phrase is wanting in the texts of Erdmann, Jacques, Janet, and in Schaarschmidt's translation.

PAGE 204, note 1. After "proposer," the note should read: wanting in the texts of Erdmann, Jacques, Janet, and in Schaarschmidt's translation.

PAGE 204, note 2. After "gauche," the note should read: wanting in the texts of Erdmann, Jacques, Janet, and in Schaarschmidt's translation. For the allusion, etc.

PAGE 205, note 1. After "Erdmann," add: Janet.

PAGE 205, note 2. After "Erdmann," add: Janet.

PAGE 206, line 12 from bottom, "Following the good." Leibnitz is a forerunner of Kant in the expression here used that the chief end of reason is practical. "In Kant's view," says Schaarschmidt, "theoretical reason has only the negative significance of raising us above the contemplation of nature and the sphere of experience to that position where beyond the sensuous the practical principles, by means of a legislation derived from freedom, unconditionally determine the will." *Cf.* also Leibnitz's definition in the same sense of "wisdom as the science of happiness," Gerhardt, *Leibniz. philos. Schrift.*, 7, 86; Erdmann, 671: "Weisheit ist nichts anders als die Wissenschaft der Glückseeligkeit, so uns nehmlich zur Glückseeligkeit zu gelangen lehret."

PAGE 208, line 21, "Endure forever." *Cf.* Spinoza, *Korte Verhandeling van God*, Bk. II., chap. 26, ed. Vloten and Land, 2, 359; Schaarschmidt's trans. 105: "Zo konnen wy 't met reden voor een groote ongerijmtheid achten, 't geene veele, en die men anders voor groote god-geleerde acht, zeggen; namelijk, byaldien op de liefde Gods geen eeuwig leeven en kwam te volgen, zy als dan haar zelfs best zouden zoeken; even als of zy iets dat beter was, als God, zouden uytvinden. Dit is alzo onnozel als of een vis wonde zeggen (voor welke doch buyten het water geen leven is): by aldien my op dit leven in het water geen eeuwig leven en zoude komen te volgen, zo wil ik uyt het water na het land toe; ja maar wat konnen ons die God niet en kennen dog anders zeggen?" *i.e.* "Thus we can rightly pronounce exceedingly absurd the statement which many, whom we otherwise deem great theologians, make; namely, that if eternal life did not follow from the love of God, then man should seek his own best good, as though man thereby could find something better than God. This were just as foolish as if a fish [for whom out of the water there is no life] should say, if for me after this life in the water no eternal life follows, I will go out of the water on to the land. What else, however, can they who do not know God say to us?" Schaarschmidt thinks that Leibnitz's accord with Spinoza was perhaps mediated by the Stoic doctrine.

PAGE 208, line 25, "Absolutely indispensable." *Cf. infra*, p. 261, note 2. Leibnitz, while admitting the truth of the Aristotelian and Stoic view, nevertheless contests that in this life we cannot always demonstrate the identity of the virtuous and useful, and supports the life of duty and overcomes the dualism between duty and pleasure through the "thought of God and immortality." Kant grounded rational belief in immortality upon this very dualism.

PAGE 210, note 1. After "Erdmann" add: Janet.

PAGE 210, note 2. Add: Fraser, *Locke's Essay*, 1, 358, reads: § 66. His edition gives full account of all the various readings and changes in the various editions of Locke's Essay, including those in the translation of Coste. It is in all respects the best edition of the Essay yet issued, and the thanks of all students of philosophy are most heartily rendered to Prof. Fraser for his splendid work.

PAGE 211, note 1. Add: 3d ed., enlarged, 2 vols., 8vo, A. & C. Black, Edinburgh, 1893.

PAGE 212, line 25, "Turn them aside from it." *Cf. New Essays*, Bk. II., chap. 27, § 36, Th.; *ante*, pp. 194 *sq.*, § 53, Th., 207. Perfectibility is Leibnitz's ethical norm, and the "luminous pleasures" are those which assist us in our efforts to attain this perfection, because they spring out of the need of, and therefore also out of the idea, though obscure, of the true good.

PAGE 213, line 12, "Greatness of the consequent." Janet, *Œuvres philos. de Leibniz*, 1, 185, note 1, says: "*The greatness of the consequence*, *i.e.* the greater or less probability that the foreseen good or evil will occur; *the greatness of the consequent*, *i.e.* the greater or less good or evil which the outcome must bring."

PAGE 213, note 1. After "Erdmann," add: Janet.

PAGE 214, note 1, line 1. After "70ª 3," add: τὸ μὲν εἰκός ἐστι πρότασις ἔνδοξος· ὃ γὰρ ὡς ἐπὶ τὸ πολὺ ἴσασιν οὕτω γινόμενον ἢ μὴ γινόμενον ἢ ὂν ἢ μὴ ὄν, τοῦτ' ἐστιν εἰκός, *i.e.* "The probable," etc. And in line 5, after "1357ª 34," add: τὸ μὲν γὰρ εἰκός ἐστιν ὡς ἐπὶ τὸ πολὺ γινόμενον, *i.e.* "For the probable," etc.

PAGE 217, line 2 from bottom, "World." "Because," as Schaarschmidt says, "mathematics as the science of magnitude is applicable only to sensible things."

PAGE 218, lines 18, 19, "The term thought in the same general way." "We exercise an inner activity," says Schaarschmidt, "either so that we produce perception-(phantasie-) images or (formulated — *sprachgeformte*) thought-images. The lower situated entelechies do the former, of the latter minds only are capable. We can, continues Leibnitz, in case of necessity designate both of these activities as thought. To-day we [the Germans] use 'Vorstellen' as the most general expression to indicate the inner activity."

PAGE 218, note 1. Add: Fraser's *Locke's Essay*, 1, 371, line 3.

PAGE 219, line 26, "Comes from thought.]" Schaarschmidt says in his note to this passage: "These weighty expressions are the pure result of the fundamental thought, that every substance acts from an inner spontaneity. Passion thus has for the spirit only the significance of a confused and therefore imperfect activity, whose most pregnant expression for the subject is pain; for bodies, however, passion means an imparted or mediated activity, in connection with which it is to be considered that, since bodies are mere phenomena, their changes are also only phenomenal, whose grounds must always be sought in the spontaneous forces of simple substances (out of whose joint-existence — *Zusammensein* — our confused thought forms the corporeal mass)." *Cf. New Essays*, Bk. II., chap. 8, *ante*, p. 131, note 1. Schaarschmidt adds: "Activity in the absolute sense, however, is the transition to greater perfection and thence also accompanied with pleasure."

PAGE 219, note 1. After "Jacques," add: and Janet.

PAGE 220, line 2 from bottom, "Complete separation." Schaarschmidt says in his note to the text at this point, "Separation arises from the Aristotelian concept χωρισμός. Χωρίζειν is the separation or loosing of the purely spiritual from the material. After Descartes had again renewed the ancient Platonic-Aristotelian Dualism in another way, Spinoza and Leibnitz, each in his own way, again set up a monism, which the realistic tendency of Locke in another way and towards another goal also endeavored to attain."

PAGE 220, note 1, line 2. After "Erdmann," add: Janet.

PAGE 222, line 10 from bottom, "Old word." That is "chevauchier," "chevalchier," "chevaucher," "chevalcher," "cevancier," all these different forms occurring in the old writers. For examples, *cf.* Littré, who gives the Provençal "cavalcar," "cavalguar," Italian "cavalcare," all derived from the Low-Latin "caballicare." "Chevaucher," says Littré, is reserved for elevated style and especially for narrations regarding the Middle Age; "aller à cheval" is the common and daily form of speech.

PAGE 222, line 2 from bottom, "Seen." Schaarschmidt says: "That Locke here makes the formation of the mixed or compound modes proceed from wider experience, to which he certainly adds 'invention'—from a purpose—Leibnitz not only allows in a noteworthy fashion, but he also adds thereto as a further source the activity of the fancy. Locke undoubtedly understands by mixed modes something wholly different from that which is formed by means of dreams and fancies; namely, abstractions from given compound relations, which, according to the measure of our interest, or at least of our attention, are formed and linguistically fixed."

PAGE 223, note 1. Add: For Leibnitz on Mademoiselle de Scudery, in the "Monatlicher Auszug aus allerhand neu herausgegeben, nützlichen und artigen Büchern," Dec., 1700, pp. 909, 910, and Dec., 1701, IV., *cf.* Guhrauer, *Leibnitz's Deutsche Schriften*, 2, 414–420. *Cf.*, also, Foucher de Careil, *Lettres et opuscules inédits de Leibniz*, Paris, 1854, pp. 254–260; F. de Careil, *Œuvres de Leibniz*, 2d ed., Paris, 1869, 2, 515–517.

PAGE 224, line 23, "Called causes in the schools." *Cf.* Appendix, *infra*, pp. 637, 672 *sq.*, 699 *sq.*, for Leibnitz's further exposition of the doctrine here set forth. In this place, "without allowing himself to enter upon a critique of Locke's exposition of the term *primal cause*, Leibnitz," says Schaarschmidt, "contents himself with ascribing to it a double signification, one of which goes back to the Aristotelian terminology; the other indicates the end. At the same time, however, he mentions the fact that the primal cause may also be understood as the material ground of a thing. Critical investigation of this important conception first begins with Hume."

PAGE 227, line 11, "Promoter." Chéruel, *Dictionnaire des Institutions Françaises*. sub voc., says: "Promoteur": "Ecclésiastique chargé du ministère public dans les officialités (voy. ce mot) [in that article it is explained that officialité = the court of a bishop or archbishop], dans les assemblées du clergé, dans les chambres supérieurs ecclésiastiques, en un mot dans tous les tribunaux ecclésiastiques. Les fonctions des promoteurs consistaient surtout à maintenir les droits, libertés et immunités de l'Église ; à veiller à l'observation de la discipline ecclésiastique et à poursuivre les crimes et délits qui étaient de la compétence des juges de l'Église. Il y avait quelquefois dans les officialités un vice-promoteur ; il était, comme le promoteur, nommé par l'évêque."

In short, the promoteur was a sort of ecclesiastical district attorney, and he is here on the opposite side of the case from the young lawyer. When he calls the lawyer "doctor juris," the latter objects that he ought to call him "doctor juris utriusque," *i.e.*, doctor of both civil and canon law, or in our phrase, doctor of laws, LL.D. To which the promoteur replies sarcastically.

PAGE 227, note 2, line 3. After "Eucken," insert: *Gesch. und Kritik der Grundbegriffe der Gegenwart*, Leipzig, 1878, pp. 69–78 (Leibnitz, p. 70); *Die Grundbegriffe der Gegenwart historisch und kritisch entwickelt*, 2te, völlig umgearbeitete Auflage, Leipzig, 1893, pp. 98–102 (Leibnitz, p. 98), but not so fully as in the 1st ed., the author stating in the Preface, that "the historical statements are strictly limited to that which appears immediately requisite to the understanding of the present time." Eng. trans. of 1st ed., *The Fundamental Concepts*, etc. At end of note, add: Schaarschmidt states Leibnitz's view thus: "Knowledge *a priori* means with Leibnitz, who with his predecessors in this matter attached himself to the Aristotelian conception of the *πρότερον τῇ φύσει*, knowledge from the cause, and, accordingly, knowledge *a posteriori* means with him knowledge from the working or result, and therefore from external experience resting upon the phenomenon of things." Kant's usage differs from that of Leibnitz. *A priori* knowledge is for Kant that which proceeds from pure reason and *not* from experience; while *a posteriori* knowledge comes only from external experience, not "from result and working in general." *Cf.*, also, J. H. von Kirchmann's Erläuterung, No. 25, to the *Théodicée*, Bk. I., § 44; p. 34 of his *Erläuterungen zur Théodicée v. Leibniz*, Leipzig, 1879.

PAGE 228, note 2. *Cf. infra*, pp. 399, note 3, 551, note 4.

PAGE 229, note 2, line 1. After "II. and VI.," add: ed. Cousin, 1, 246 *sq.*, 322 *sq.*

PAGE 230, note 1. After "*Dioptrica*, IV., 1 *sq.*," add: ed. Cousin, 5, 34 *sq.*; after "*Passiones Animæ*, I., 31 *sq.*," add: ed. Cousin, 4, 63 *sq.*; after "*Prin. Philos.*, IV., 189, 196, 197," add: ed. Cousin, 3, 500, 507, 509.

PAGE 230, note 1. Add: *Cf.*, also, Cousin, *Œuvres de Descartes*, 8, 200, where Descartes, in a letter (dated by the annotator 1640 — the letter in Bk. II., No. 36, in ed. of 1666) to Meissonier, "médecin de Lyon," says: "Mon opinion est que cette glande" ["la petite glande nommée *conarion*"] "est le principal siége de l'âme, et le lieu où se font toutes nos pensées. La raison qui me donne cette créance est que je ne trouve aucune partie en tout le cerveau, excepté celle-là seule, qui ne soit double," etc. In a letter to Mersenne, dated by the annotator April 1, 1640, Cousin, *Œuvres de Descartes*, 8, 215 *sq.* [ed. of 1666, Bk. II., Letter No. 38], Descartes makes substantially the same statement and gives the same reasons therefor, and adds: "Mais je crois que c'est toute le reste du cerveau qui sert le plus à la mémoire," etc.

PAGE 233, line 4 from bottom, "The union of the soul and the body." Leibnitz was undoubtedly satisfied that his Pre-established Harmony satisfactorily explained the "union of the soul and the body," and for those who accept his philosophy it does. But those who look for another explanation, for example, in a real reciprocal action between the soul and certain substances of the body, find in Leibnitz's semi-spiritualistic interpretation of matter a clue or suggestion thereto.

PAGE 235, end of chap. 24, "Comprising substances." Leibnitz, according to Schaarschmidt, means to say that, strictly understood, the collective ideas are not signs of substances, rather, indeed, are the single objects themselves substances, as, for example, the army, the herd, consist of substances. Yet the collective ideas serve to a certain extent indirectly to indicate substances. Leibnitz adds this concession here because in his system of monads he departs very widely from the customary conception of substance, and yet may not lose all touch with the linguistic usage.

PAGE 235, line 6, 5 from bottom, "*Essence of reason.*" That is, *ens rationis*, which actuality reaches only so far as it is a thought-image.

PAGE 235, line 3 from bottom, "Comes from the supreme reason." "Relations, so Leibnitz will have us understand the matter," says Schaarschmidt, "are in the first place products of our thought, for they are neither the expression of substances, nor of the determinations (*Attribute, Modi*) inhering in them, but the expression of our subjective conception of the relation of things to one another. But this human conception, although also subjective, is yet again grounded in the nature of things, in particular in the nature of the mind, and to this extent springs out of its own constitution, like the eternal truths. And the constitution of the mind, as the 'mirror of the universe,' corresponds again to reality in virtue of the pre-established harmony. The thoroughgoing parallelism of the inner with the outer occurrence gives consequently to the relations, according to Leibnitz, a certain real meaning."

PAGE 239, note 1, line 4. Instead of "*Leben*," read: *Eine Biographie.*

PAGE 241, note 1. Add: *Corpus Juris Civilis*, 6th stereotyped ed., Vol. 1, p. 659, a; *Digesta*, ed. Mommsen, Berlin, Weidmann, 1893. Schaarschmidt says it is "a definition springing from Stoicism," and compares Göppert. *Ueber einheitliche, zusammengesetzte und Gesammtsachen nach röm. Recht*, pp. 7 *sq.*, 20 *sq.*, Halle, 1871.

PAGE 242, line 4, "Soul." Leibnitz is right in placing the identity of man in the soul and its conservation, instead of in the "well-organized body," as Locke does. The relative unity of the bodily organism results from the absolute unity of the soul.

PAGE 245, note 1. *Cf.* Fraser, *Locke's Essay*, 1, 448, note 3. This section is numbered § 11 in Fraser's ed.

PAGE 245, note 2. After "Erdmann," add: Janet.

PAGE 246, note 1. After "Erdmann," add: Janet.

PAGE 247, lines 7–9. "*The self* constitutes identity real and physical," etc. This sentence contains the gist of the whole discussion. "*The self*" or *the ego* which "constitutes identity real and physical" is "the presupposition of that consciousness of the subject of itself to which the conviction of its own reality attaches." Consciousness itself is an active though involuntary modification or state of this self or ego. "*The phenomenon of self*" is the ego's actual consciousness of itself, as the subject of all its inner experience, and as the constant accompaniment of the same. The self is accordingly by Leibnitz regarded as a real entity, a substance, constituting in itself "real and physical identity" which is recognized as "personal" in consciousness. But it must be remembered that for Leibnitz substance is dynamic, its essence is action, and its real identity consists in the continuity and connection of its activity. When this activity becomes distinctly conscious or is brought into distinct consciousness, it constitutes moral and personal identity.

PAGE 249, note 1. Add: Janet reads: "étant."

PAGE 250, note 1. Add: *Cf.*, also, *The Immortality of the Soul*, Bk. II., chaps. 13, 14; *Philos. Writings*, ed. in 1 vol., London, 1662, pp. 116–121 (each treatise paged separately in this ed.).

PAGE 251, lines 12, 13, "Indifferent to every sort of matter." Janet, *Œuvres philos. de Leibniz*, 1, 224, in his note to this passage, says: "Aristotle believed also that the soul is not indifferent to every kind of matter, and avails himself of the fact to combat the doctrine of metempsychosis." *Cf.* Περὶ Ψυχῆς, Bk. I., chap. 5, Berlin Academy ed., 409^a 31–411^b 30; ed. E. Wallace, Cambridge, 1882, pp. 44–57.

PAGE 251, note 1. After "Gerhardt," add: Janet.

PAGE 251, note 2. After "Erdmann," add: Janet.

PAGE 252, line 6 from bottom, "Two persons." On double and alternate personality, *cf.* James, *Psychology*, 1, 379–392.

PAGE 252, note 1. Add: Fraser's *Locke's Essay*, 1, 460, line 8.

PAGE 252, note 2. Add: Fraser's *Locke's Essay*, 1, 461, line 6. "Sober" = "sane."

PAGE 254, note 1. After "Erdmann," add: Janet.

PAGE 254, note 2. After "Erdmann," add: Janet.

PAGE 256, lines 17–20. "For since there is an individual diversity," etc. *Cf. New Essays*, Bk. II., chap. 27, § 3, Th., *ante*, p. 239, and note 1; Bk. III., chap. 6, § 8, Th., *infra*, pp. 331, and 332, note 1. All true or actual difference is individual difference, consisting in some internal differentiating principle specifying the existence in this or that definite way, even though it first reveals itself only in "the course of time." With this thought is closely connected that of identity, on which *cf. ante*, p. 247, and note to lines 7–9, *ante*, p. 760.

PAGE 257, note 1. After "Erdmann," add: Janet.

PAGE 258, line 10, "*Magnitude* which I call *imperfect*." An imperfect magnitude is one which, because of its infinite minuteness, admits of no measurement.

PAGE 259, note 1. After "Erdmann," add: Janet.

PAGE 259, note 3. After "Erdmann," add: Janet.

PAGE 261, note 1. Add: Pünjer, *Gesch. d. christlich. Religionsphilosophie*, Braunschweig, 1880, 1, 123, Eng. trans., Edinburgh, 1887, 1, 165, in his account of the controversy of Vedelius and Joh. Musæus (*cf. ante*, p. 587, notes 1, 2), gives, from Musæus, another use of the term. Pünjer says: "Ist aber die philosophische Prämisse allgemein, die theologische partikular, dann muss sorgfältig untersucht werden, ob die betreffenden philosophischen Principien nothwendig und allgemein gelten (absolute et simpliciter necessaria) oder nur für ein besonderes Gebiet, *bedingungsweise* (secundum quid et *physice*)"; *i.e.* "But if the philosophical premiss is universal and the theological premiss is particular, then it must be carefully examined whether the philosophical principle in question is necessarily and universally valid (absolute et simpliciter necessaria), or applies only to a particular sphere and *conditionally* (secundum quid et *physice*)." [Italics are mine. — TR.]

PAGE 261, note 2. Add: *Cf. New Essays*, Bk. II., chap. 21, § 55, *ante*, p. 208, and note to p. 208, line 25, *ante*, p. 755.

PAGE 262, note 1. Add: Leibnitz, *Observationes de Principio Juris*, § 13 (Dutens, *Leibnit. op. om.*, 4, Pt. III., 273), says: "Deum esse omnis naturalis juris auctorem (quod ait § 41) verissimum est, at non voluntate, sed ipsa essentia sua, qua ratione etiam auctor est veritatis," etc.

PAGE 262, note 2. Add: *Cf.*, also, Dr. Robinson's Lecture, "Moral Law in its relations to Physical Science and to Popular Religion," in Boston Monday Lectures — *Christ and Modern Thought* — 1880–1881, pp. 31–59.

PAGE 263, note 1. Add: Teubner, Leipzig, 1865. Vopiscus says of Bonosus: "Bibit, quantum hominum nemo. De hoc Aurelianus saepe dicebat: 'Non ut vivat natus est, sed ut bibat,' quem quidem diu in honore habuit causa militiæ. Nam siquando legati barbarorum undecumque gentium venissent ipsi propinabantur, ut eos inebriaret atque ab his per vinum cuncta cognosceret. Ipse quantumlibet bibisset, semper securus et sobrius et, ut Onesimus dicit, scriptor vitæ Probi, adhuc in vino prudentior."

The reference in the next line, also taken from Vopiscus, *ibid.*, is to Proculus, and not Bonosus, and the text should be corrected accordingly.

PAGE 264, line 10, "Depends upon truth." *I.e.*, as Schaarschmidt says, "upon the ever-equal reality of the ethical world-order."

PAGE 267, note 1. After "Erdmann," add: Janet.

PAGE 270, note 1. After "Erdmann," add: Janet.

PAGE 273, note 1. After "Erdmann," add: Janet.

PAGE 273, note 2. After "Erdmann," add: Janet.

PAGE 274, note 1. After "Erdmann," add: Janet. After "§ 15," add: So also Fraser's *Locke's Essay*, 1, 493.

PAGE 274, note 3. Add: Fraser's *Locke's Essay*, 1, 494, reads § 16.

PAGE 275, note 1. After "Erdmann," add: Janet. Fraser's *Locke's Essay*, 1, 494, reads: "betwixt the 100,000th and the 1,000,000th part of it."

PAGE 276, note 1. Add: *Cf.* Gerhardt, *Leibniz. philos. Schrift.*, 3, 225, where Leibnitz says: "Il est encor à propos de considerer qu'il y a deux abus considerables dans les definitions, qu'on peut commettre en voulant former des idées: l'un est ce que l'excellent Jungius (*cf.* Appendix, *infra*, p. 636, note 1), appelloit obreption, l'autre est ce que j'appelle chimerisme, par exemple si quelqu'un raisonnoit ainsi: il m'est permis de combiner les idées, et de donner un nom à ce qui en resulte; prenons donc l'idée d'une substance où il n'y ait rien que de l'etendue et appellons cela corps, donc les corps qui sont dans la nature n'ont rien que de l'etendue, il y auroit à la fois ces deux fautes dans ce raisonnement. *L'obreption* y seroit en ce qu'ayant donné au mot: corps, la definition qui bon me semble (ce qui est en quelque façon arbitraire), je veux par après l'appliquer à ce que d'autres hommes appellent corps. C'est comme si dans la Geometrie quelqu'un donnoit à ce mot: ovale, la definition que d'autres Geometres donnent à l'Ellipse, et vouloit prouver par après que les ovales de M. des Cartes sont des sections du cone. *Le chimerisme* est icy d'avoir fait une combinaison impossible, car on n'accorde point qu'il est possible qu'il y ait une substance qui n'ait que de l'etendue. Je sçais que ces Messieurs veulent se justifier de l'obreption, en disant qu'on ne sçauroit concevoir autre chose dans les corps qui sont dans la nature, que ce qu'ils ont mis dans leur definition; mais en cela ils commettent une fausse supposition, ou bien ils confondent concevoir et imaginer; car il est bien vray qu'on ne sçauroit imaginer que ce qui est étendu, mais ils reconnoissent eux mêmes ailleurs qu'on conçoit des choses qui ne sont pas imaginables. Ouy, diront ils, mais ce n'est que la pensée qu'on ne peut point imaginer. Je reponds, qu'en cela ils font encor une autre fausse supposition, en pretendant que rien ne sçauroit estre conçu que pensée et étendue, oublians qu'ils parlent souvent eux mêmes de la force qui n'est pourtant ny l'un ny l'autre, outre qu'ils n'ont point prouvé qu'il n'y a rien de possible que ce que nous concevons."

PAGE 277, line 8, "Capable of existing together." Leibnitz, in arguing against Locke's view of the passivity of the mind in relation to its "simple ideas" and its activity in their combination into "complex ideas," affirms that the mind "is active in reference to simple ideas," that the relations are objectively significant and valid through the determination of the "supreme intelligence," that the mixed modes "may be real accidents," which do not become merely subjective from the fact that we perceive them by thought. According to Leibnitz, everything really possible is in a certain sense an actual object of intelligence: to the divine intelligence an actual, to the human intelligence a universally possible object. The external existence of this thought-object really adds nothing to the being of this object, and alters nothing in the relation of the thought to it. *Cf.*, also, *New Essays*, Bk. II., chap. 12, § 3, Ph., *ante*, p. 147, and note to line 2 from bottom, "modes," *ante*, p. 748.

PAGE 277, note 1. Add: Fraser's *Locke's Essay*, 1, 500. In § 1, Locke has "*Fantastical* or *chimerical*," Fraser's ed., 1, 497; Bohn's ed., 1, 508.

PAGE 277, note 2, line 1. After "345ª 25," add: οἱ δὲ περὶ Ἀναξαγόραν καὶ Δημόκριτον φῶς εἶναι τὸ γάλα λέγουσιν ἄστρων τινῶν· τὸν γὰρ ἥλιον ὑπὸ τὴν γῆν φερόμενον οὐχ ὁρᾶν ἔνια τῶν ἄστρων.

PAGE 281, note 2. Add: The Greek text of the passages referred to in the note is as follows: Περὶ Ψυχῆς Γ, 6, 430ª 26–30: ἡ μὲν οὖν τῶν ἀδιαιρέτων νόησις ἐν τούτοις, περὶ ἃ οὐκ ἔστι τὸ ψεῦδος· ἐν οἷς δὲ καὶ τὸ ψεῦδος καὶ τὸ ἀληθές, συνθεσίς τις ἤδη νοημάτων ὥσπερ ἓν ὄντων, καθάπερ Ἐμπεδοκλῆς ἔφη "ᾗ πολλῶν μὲν κόρσαι ἀναύχενες ἐβλάστησαν," ἔπειτα συντίθεσθαι τῇ φιλίᾳ. Περὶ Ἑρμηνείας I., 16ª 12: σημεῖον δ' ἐστὶ τοῦδε· καὶ γὰρ ὁ τραγέλαφος σημαίνει μέν τι, οὔπω δὲ ἀληθὲς ἢ ψεῦδος, ἐὰν μὴ τὸ εἶναι ἢ μὴ εἶναι προστεθῇ, ἢ ἁπλῶς ἢ κατὰ χρόνον. *Cf.*, also, *New Essays*, Bk. III., chap. 3, *infra*, pp. 310–318, and the notes, especially pp. 310, note 2, 317, note 3.

PAGE 281, line 17, "Possibility." Schaarschmidt states that Christian Wolf placed this definition of truth here given by Leibnitz at the head of his collected science. According to Wolf, *Log. Disc. prœlectt.*, philosophy is the science of the possible so far as it can be. Ueberweg, *Hist. of Philos.*, Eng. trans. by Morris, New York, 1871, Vol. 1, p. 4, gives it, *Philos. Rationalis. Disc. Prœlim.*, § 29: "philosophia est scientia possibilium, quatenus esse possunt."

PAGE 281, note 1. After "Essays," add: Bk. III., chap. 3, § 15, Th., *infra*, pp. 315 *sq.*, especially p. 317, note 3; after "chap. 5," add: *ad fin.*, *infra*, p. 452, and note 1.

PAGE 282, note 1. After "Erdmann," add: Janet.

PAGE 282, note 2. After "Erdmann," add: Janet.

PAGE 283, line 17, "Ottavio Pisani." An Italian jurist, who published in Italian his *Lycurgus seu leges promptam justitiam promoventes*; translated into German, and published, Sulzbach, 1666, 12mo. Leibnitz mentions him in his *Bedenken welchergestalt den Mängeln des Justiz-Wesens* IN THEORIA *abzuhelfen*, *cf.* Guhrauer, *Leibnitz's deutsche Schrift.*, 1, 257, also Beilagen, *ibid.*, 42; Dutens, *Leibnit. op. om.*, 4, Pt. 3, 230-234 (Latin trans. of the same, regarding which, *cf.* Guhrauer, *op. cit.*, 1, 41 *sq.*—On p. 41, *op. cit.*, line 9 from bottom, "220-24" should read: 230-234, as above cited, the present reading being a typographical error).

PAGE 283, note 1. After "Erdmann," add: Janet.

PAGE 284, line 17, "Inclinations." Schaarschmidt says that "in these remarks lies the germ of the recognition of the law of association, which" Johann Gebhard Ehrenreich Christian Maass, 1766-1823, Professor of Philosophy at Halle University, "further elaborated in his *Versuch über die Einbildungskraft*, Halle and Leipzig, 1797; afterwards J. F. Fries, 1773-1843, in his *Neue Kritik der Vernunft*, 2d ed., 1828-1831, p. 148 *sq.*, and which finally J. F. Herbart, 1776-1841, and his school have attempted more closely to investigate and establish." F. H. Bradley, *The Principles of Logic*, pp. 279, 297, 312, 313, refers to a portion of Maass' discussion. *Cf.*, also, Hamilton's *Reid*, Notes D** and D***, 2, 882-917, especially 890, 899, 913 *sq.* Maass followed Wolff's *Psych. Emp.*, Frankfort and Leipzig, 1732, *ed. Nova*, 1738; but he may also have been influenced somewhat by Leibnitz, as the *New Essays* were published in 1765 by Raspe, and therefore accessible for nearly thirty years before his own work appeared.

PAGE 284, note 1. After "Erdmann," add: Janet.

PAGE 284, note 2. After "Erdmann," add: Janet.

PAGE 284, note 3. After "Erdmann," add: Janet.

PAGE 284, note 4. After "Erdmann," add: Janet.

PAGE 286, note 1. Add: Recently Mr. R. L. Garner has been investigating the language of monkeys, with the aid of the phonograph, and published an account of his investigations in an interesting book entitled *The Speech of Monkeys*, New York, Chas. L. Webster & Co., 1892. An unfavorable notice of the book appeared in "The Nation," October 6, 1892, p. 267 b, the gist of which appears in the following sentence: "As a scientific record of original discoveries, it has little value."

PAGE 288, note 1. Add: *Cf. New Essays*, Bk. III., chap. 3, § 5, Th., *infra*, pp. 307, 308. Also, Hamilton, *Metaphysics*, Lect. XXXVI., pp. 492 *sq.*, Boston, 1875.

PAGE 297, line 11, "Hypothesis," etc. Leibnitz's hypothesis has been wholly verified by modern philology.

PAGE 297, note 1. Add: For an interesting account of Leibnitz's services to comparative philology, *cf.* Max Müller, *Lects. on the Science of Language*, 2d ed., London, 1862, Lect. 4, pp. 131-135; New York, Chas. Scribner, 1862, pp. 135-139. *Cf.*, also, Guhrauer, *Leibnitz, Eine Biographie*, 2, 126 *sq.;* Foucher de Careil, *Œuvres de Leibniz*, 7, 519 *sq.*, a rough draft of a memorial of Leibnitz concerning the study of languages . . . in the Russian Empire.

PAGE 298, note 1, line 3 from end. After "p. 409," insert: "Lites de Boehmianis sententiis inanes esse censeo, et *Boehmium* nec sibi, nedum aliis intellectum," *i.e.* etc.

PAGE 300, note 3. After "Erdmann," add: Janet.

PAGE 300, note 4. After "Erdmann," add: Janet.

PAGE 300, note 5. After "Erdmann," add: Janet.

PAGE 304, note 1, line 8. After "Dutens, *op. cit.*, Vols.," add: 4, Pt. II., p. 56: Ab insigni apud Bremenses Theologo Gerhardo Meiero, qui (ut hoc obiter dicam) hortatu meo præclarum opus aggressus est *Glossarii Saxonici* titulo, in quo origines Germanicarum vocum multas eruet illustrabitque, nec pauca non pervulgata proferet in lucem." At end of note, add: Janet, *Œuvres philos. de Leibniz*, 1, 274, note 3, gives the dates of Meier's birth and death, 1646-1680, and titles of his "principal philosophical works": *Compendium logicæ divinæ; Aranearum telas divinæ existentiæ testes; De dubitatione sceptica et cartesiana.*

PAGE 304, note 2. Add: The date of Schilter's death being 1705, and the mention of the same in the text as having "just" occurred, is evidence that Leibnitz at least briefly touched up this part of the *New Essays* as late as 1705.

PAGE 308, line 10 from bottom. Read: *Greathead*, instead of "*large head;*" and line 8 from bottom, read: great, instead of "large."

PAGE 308, line 3 from bottom. After "wormwood," insert: (*absinthium*).

PAGE 313, line 8, "Living rational being." *Cf.* Trendelenburg, *Histor. Beitr. z. Philos.*, 3, 53, 54.

PAGE 316, note 1. After "(Bohn's ed.)," add: Fraser's *Locke's Essay*, 2, 28.

PAGE 317, note 1. Add: *cf. New Essays*, Bk. IV., chap. 4, § 5, Th., *infra*, p. 445, note 1.

PAGE 317, note 2. Add: *Cf.*, also, *New Essays*, Bk. II., chap. 21, § 3, Th., *ante*, p. 175, and note to p. 175, line 18, *ante*, p. 751.

PAGE 317, note 3. Add: *Cf.*, also, Prantl, *Gesch. d. Logik*, Bd. 1, p. 516, note 33, where he refers to Cicero, *Off.*, I., 2, 7; *Fin.*, II., 2, 5; *D. orat.*, I., 42, 189: "est enim definitio earum rerum, quæ sunt eius rei propriæ quam definire volumus, brevis et circumscripta quædam explicatio"; II., 39, 164; III., 29, 113; *Orat.*, 33, 166; Top. 5, 26; Quint., *Inst.*, VII., 3, 15.

PAGE 318, note 1. Add: Fraser's *Locke's Essay*, 2, 29.

PAGE 319, note 2. Add: Erdmann, 443–445.

PAGE 321, note 4. After "chap. 9, *ad med.*," add: "'How can that be?' cried Don Quixote; 'didst thou not tell me that thou *sawest* her winnowing wheat?' 'Take no heed of that, sir,' replied the squire; 'for the fact is, her message, and the sight of her too, were both by *hearsay*, and I can no more tell who the lady Dulcinea is than I can buffet the moon.'"

PAGE 322, note 1. Add: Aldrich, *Artis logicæ rudimenta*, ed. H. L. Mansel, 3d ed., Oxford, 1856, pp. 30, 31 (diagram on p. 31).

PAGE 323, note 1, line 3. After "Erdmann," add: Janet.

PAGE 324, note 2. Add: *Hypoth. phys. nova*, § 57; Gerhardt, 4, 208. *Cf.*, also, *New Essays*, note to p. 47, lines 18, 19, *ante*, p. 726.

PAGE 326, note 1. Add: *Cf.* note to p. 43, line 14, *ante*, p. 724. "Leibnitz," says Schaarschmidt, "makes here a weighty remark. All demonstration appeals only to the (real) possible and to that which in a logical way inferred from the same is so far thought-wise necessary; reality or the actual, on the other hand, can be known only historically or empirically, not, however, philosophically."

PAGE 326, note 2. Add: Janet, *Œuvres philos. de Leibniz*, 1, 293, agrees with the reading of Jacques.

PAGE 329, note 1, line 2. After "1888," add: Paris Academy ed., by C. M. Galisset, 7th ed., 1862, p. 140; *Corpus Juris Civilis*, Berlin, Weidmann, 1893 (*Inst. of Justinian*, ed. by Paul Krueger), Vol. 1, p. 13 b; line 3, after "1890," add: *Collectio Librorum Juris Antejustiniani*, ed. Krueger, Mommsen, and Studemund, Vol. 1, pp. 50, 51, 3d ed., Berlin, Weidmann, 1891; line 4, after "1870," add: *Corpus Juris Civilis* (*Digest*, ed. by Mommsen, and paged separately), Vol. 1, p. 112. At end of note, add: Rudolph Sohm, *Institutes of Roman Law*, trans. from 4th German ed., by Jas. Cranford Ledlie, Oxford, Clarendon Press, 1892, pp. 258–268.

PAGE 332, note 1. Add: For Hegel's interpretation of Leibnitz's principle of individuation,—*principium individuationis*,—(*cf. New Essays*, *ante*, p. 239, note 1) *cf.* Wallace, *The Logic of Hegel*, 2d ed., Oxford, Clarendon Press, 1892, pp. 217, 218.

PAGE 333, note 1. Add: Fraser's *Locke's Essay*, 2, 68.

PAGE 334, note 1. Add: On the natural order in the vegetable kingdom, Schaarschmidt cites J. H. Burckhardi, *Epist. ad Leibnitium*, Wolffenbüttel, 1703. *Cf.*, also, *Epist. G. G. Leibnitii ad A. C. Gackenholtzium, M.D., de methodo Botanica*, § 10; Dutens, *Leibnit. op. om.*, 2, Pt. II., 173.

PAGE 335, note 1, line 1. After "50," add: Fraser's *Locke's Essay*, 2, 69. So also Coste's translation, p. 360, ed. Amsterdam, 1742, Vol. 3, p. 129, ed. in 4 vols., Amsterdam, 1774.

PAGE 337, note 3. Add: A 5th ed., Hamburg, 1887.

PAGE 343, note 1. Add: Also Gerhardt, *Leibniz. math. Schrift.*, I., 2 [Vol. 2], 1–208, *Briefwechsel zwischen Leibniz und Hugens van Zulichem.* Also an earlier ed. in Pt. II. of *Christ. Hugenii aliorumque seculi XVII. virorum celebrium exercitationes mathematicæ et philosophicæ. Ex manuscriptis in bibliotheca Lugduno-Batavæ servatis edidit.* P. I. Uylenbroek, Hagæ Comitum, 1833. On the relation of Gerhardt's ed. to that of Uylenbroek, *cf.* Gerhardt, *op. cit.*, II., 2 [Vol. 2], 9, 10. Gerhardt says, p. 10: "Es hätte mithin in jedem Falle auf die Sammlung Uylenbroek's Rücksicht genommen werden müssen, der die Leibnizischen Originale vor sich hatte." *Cf.*, also, *New Essays*, note to p. 16, line 22, *ante*, p. 723.

PAGE 344, note 4. Add: Professor Schaarschmidt having kindly sent me Ulrich's note, and Ulrich's translation being rare and generally inaccessible, it is here given: "Dieser Knabe ward 1661 in einem Alter von neun Jahren in einem Walde von Litthauen von den Jaegern unter den Bären gefunden. Es war noch ein anderer Knabe bei ihm, der aber den Jaegern entwischte. Dieser wehrte sich als man ihn fangen wollte anfänglich mit seinen Nägeln und Zähnen ungemein tapfer, musste aber zuletzt der Gewalt nachgeben. Er war übrigens wohl proportionirt, weiss, hatte blonde Haare und eine angenehme Gesichtsbildung; man konnte ihn aber durch nichts bändigen, vielweniger zu Kleidung und menschlicher Nahrung gewöhnen. Er erhielt in der Taufe den Namen Joseph Ursinus."

The story is of course fabulous, it being impossible during the winter to live in Poland without clothes, even were it anywise probable that bears would live with children without eating them."

PAGE 349, note 1, line 3 from bottom. Dele "2d ed."—since, according to the author's "Avertissement," the work "is not a 2d ed." of his earlier work, entitled *De la philosophie scholastique*, 2 vols., Paris, 1850, but an entirely new and independent work.

PAGE 353, line 5, "Prophetic vision." Leibnitz wrote a critical essay on the Story of Balaam, which is found in Dutens, *Leibnit. op. om.*, 4, Pt. II., 275–278. Wilhelm Brambach has published a monograph, entitled *Gottfried Wilhelm Leibniz Verfasser der Histoire de Bileam*, Leipzig, 1887, in which he gives an account of the various arguments for and against its Leibnitzian authorship, maintains that Leibnitz was the author, and gives Leibnitz's approved text of the piece.

PAGE 357, note 1. Add: Fraser's *Locke's Essay*, 2, 86.

PAGE 359, note 1. Add: Fraser's *Locke's Essay*, 2, 88.

PAGE 380, note 1. Add: On More, *cf.* Tulloch, *Rational Theology and Christian Philosophy in England in the 17th Century*, Edinburgh,

Wm. Blackwood & Sons, 1872, 2, 303–409, the "ethereal vehicles," 396, the "spirit of nature," 397.

PAGE 382, note 1. Add: *Cf. New Essays*, Bk. I., chap. 1, *ante*, p. 67, and note to p. 67, lines 3, 4, *ante*, p. 732.

PAGE 382, note 2. Add: *Cf.* also, Dutens, *Leibnit. op. om.*, 6, Pt. I., 315, Leibnitiana, No. C., where Leibnitz says: "Henricus Morus statuit præexistentiam *animarum*, sive quod animæ creatæ fuerint cum mundo, quam sententiam Plato, Origines, aliique jampridem foverunt. Mea opinio est, omnia, ut sic dicam, plena esse animarum vel analogarum naturarum, et ne brutorum quidem animas interire."

PAGE 386, note 1. Instead of "Jacques reads," read: Jacques and Janet read, etc.

PAGE 387, note 1. Add: In the "Bulletin des Sciences Mathématiques, 2d Series, Vol. 16, 1892, Pt. I., p. 18, in a review of C. Huygens, *Œuvres complètes*, La Haye, 1888 *sq.*, the following statement occurs: "La courbe $a^2y = x^2(a - x)$ rentre dans la catégorie générale des courbes $a^{p+q-r}y^r = x^p(a-x)^q$, qu'on appelle les *perles* de de Sluse. Elle est une cubique à centre (au point d'inflexion $x = \frac{2}{3}a, y = o$)." *Cf.*, also, the letters in this ed. of Huygens, Nos. 401, 403, 408, 419, 434, 436, referred to in this review. In letter 461, the review goes on to say: "il est question d'un rapport remarquable entre les deux perles $a^2y^2 = x^3(a - x)$ et $y^4 = x^3(a - x)$." *Cf.*, also, letter 435.

PAGE 388, lines 23, 27, 32, "§§ 23, 23, 24." These sections are numbered, respectively, §§ 23, 24, 25, in Fraser's *Locke's Essay*, 2, 142–143; also in Locke, *Philos. Works*, Bohn's ed. 2, 108–109; and in Coste's French trans., Amsterdam, 1742, pp. 409, 410, 4 vols. ed., Amsterdam, 1774, 3, 248, 249.

PAGE 392, lines 6, 7. "The majority of the mixed modes nowhere exist together." The French text of all the editions is: "La pluspart des modes composés n'existent nulle part ensemble." The grammatical confusion of a singular subject and plural verb is probably occasioned by the too condensed summary of Locke's statement, *i.e.* "Another reason that makes the defining of mixed modes so necessary, especially of moral words, is what I mentioned a little before, viz. that it is the only way whereby the signification of the most of them can be known with certainty. For the ideas they stand for, being for the most part such whose component parts nowhere exist together," etc. (Fraser's *Locke's Essay*, 2, 158; Locke, *Philos. Works*, Bohn's ed., 2, 122); in Coste's trans., ed. 1742, p. 421, ed. 4 vols., 1774, 3, 276: "Une autre raison qui rend la définition des *Modes mixtes* si nécessaire, et sur-tout celle des mots qui appartiennent à la Morale, c'est ce que je viens de dire en passant, que c'est *la seule voie par où l'on puisse avoir certainement la signification de la plupart de ces mots.* Car la plus grande partie des idées qu'ils signifient, étant de telle nature qu'elles n'existent nulle part ensemble," etc.

PAGE 404, note 1. Add: For a specimen of Euclid reduced to syllogisms, extracted from the very curious and rare *Analyses Geometricæ* of Herlinus and Dasypodius, *cf.* Aldrich, *Artis Logicæ Rudimenta*, ed. Mansel, Oxford, 1856, 3d ed., Appendix, note L, *ad fin.*, pp. 264–266. Sir William Hamilton calls Herlinus and Dasypodius "zealous but thick-headed logicians," Aldrich, *op. cit.*, p. 248, note r (Mansel). The 5th proposition of the 1st Bk. is also analyzed by Mill, *Logic*, Bk. II., chap. 4, pp. 162, 163, 8th ed., New York, Harper and Bros., 1881.

PAGE 405, note 1. After "Erdmann," add: Janet.

PAGE 405, note 2. After "Erdmann," add: Janet.

PAGE 408, note 1. Add: For a brief account of the Ramist-Aristotelian controversy, *cf.* Pünjer, *Gesch. d. Christlich. Religionsphilos.*, 1, 89–92; Eng. trans., *Hist. of the Christian Philos. of Religion*, 1, 118–123.

PAGE 412, note 1. After "Erdmann," add: Janet.

PAGE 414, note 1. After "Erdmann," add: Janet.

PAGE 414, note 2. Add: Fraser, *Locke's Essay*, 2, 185.

PAGE 425. At end of first paragraph of note continued from p. 424, after "1, 187," add: letter to Conring, March 19, 1678, *ibid.*, 1, 199; also the writing with "neither superscription nor place nor date," *ibid.*, 4, 274 *sq.*, especially 277, 278.

PAGES 428, 429. "Certain theologians claim that the fire of hell burns up separated souls." *Cf. New Essays*, Preface, *ante*, p. 62, and note to line 10 from bottom, *ante*, p. 729, 730.

PAGE 431, line 10 from bottom. "Et quidquid Schola finxit otiosa." I have not been able to find the author or source of the Latin line.

PAGE 432, line 11, "*Lignum nephriticum.*" A term used by the old pharmacologists, signifying a wood, supposed to be that of the horse-radish tree, which has been used in decoction for affections of the kidneys,— *Nephritic wood*, from the Greek *νεφρός*, a kidney.

PAGE 434, note 1. Line 2, after "1890)," add: *Collectio Librorum Juris Antejustiniani*, ed. Krueger, Mommsen and Studemund, Berlin, Weidmann, 1891, 1, 86; and line 6, after "1888)," add: *Corpus Juris Civilis*, Berlin, Weidmann, 1893, 1, 23 b.

PAGE 445, note 1. Add: On the history and significance of the terms *φαντασία*, *φάντασμα*, "phantasma," *cf.* Siebeck, *Gesch. d. Psychologie*, Gotha, 1880, 1884, *passim.* Leibnitz in his letter to Thomasius, Feb. 16, 1666, Gerhardt, *Leibniz. philos. Schrift.*, 1, 8, says: "Omnis color est impressio in sensorium, non qualitas quædam in rebus, sed extrinseca denominatio, seu ut Th. Hobbes appellat, phantasma." On Hobbes' use of the term, *cf.* his *Works*, and Lange, *Hist. of Materialism*, 2d ed., 1, 288–289. For Thomas Aquinas' use of the term, *cf.* Ueberweg, *Hist. of Philos.*, New York, 1875, 1, 449.

PAGE 447, note 1. Add: Fraser, *Locke's Essay*, 2, 237–239, and *cf. ibid.*, 2, 73, note 3: "An idiot, 'Such men do chaungelings call, so chaunged by faries' theft.' Spenser, *Faerie Queen*, Bk. I., canto X.; also Shakespeare, *Midsummer Night's Dream*, ii., 1., 21."

PAGE 450, note 1, line 4 from bottom. After "pp. 312–314," add: also, G. Croom Robertson, *Philos. Remains*, Williams & Norgate, 1894, pp. 274-278.

PAGE 462, note 1. Add: *Cf.* "Leibnitz and Protestant Theology," by Professor John Watson, of Queen's University, Kingston, Canada, in "The New World," March, 1896, Vol. 5, pp. 112–122. *Cf.*, also, *New Essays*, Bk. IV., chap. 7, § 11, Th. (2), *infra*, p. 474, and note 1; chap. 17, § 23, Th. (2), *infra*, p. 579, and note 1.

PAGE 464, line 6, "The number of the axioms." Mansel, in the Appendix to his ed. of Aldrich, *Artis Logicæ Rudimenta*, 3d ed., Oxford, 1856, p. 258, says: "The numerous attempts of Geometers to diminish or get rid of their axioms have been steps in a wrong direction. The number of axioms, instead of being diminished, should be very considerably increased; and the errors that have hitherto prevailed on the nature and foundation of Geometrical reasoning have been mainly owing to the manner in which many indispensable assumptions have been either omitted altogether, or concealed among the definitions."

PAGE 465, note 1. Add: *Cf.* also addition to this note, *ante*, p. 768.

PAGE 474, note 1. Add: *Cf. New Essays*, Bk. IV., chap. 6, *ad fin.*, *ante*, p. 462, note 1, and addition thereto above; chap. 17, § 23, Th. (2), *infra*, p. 579, and note 1, and addition thereto, *infra*, p. 773. Dieckhoff, *Leibnitz Stellung zur Offenbarung*, Rostock, 1888.

PAGE 481, note 1. Add: For Aristotle on the "middle term," *cf.* Wallace, *Outlines of the Philos. of Aristotle*, 3d ed., 1883, §§ 23, 24, especially the latter, and the passage of Aristotle there quoted. For the history of the term, *cf.* Prantl, *Gesch. d. Logik.*

PAGE 482, lines 1–3. The text should read: "Made him reject altogether their use in the establishment of the truth, and goes as far as to make them a party to confusion [of ideas] in conversation."

PAGE 483, note 1. After "*Princip. Philos.*, II., §§ 1, 4, 11," add: ed. Cousin, 3, 120, 123, 129.

PAGE 484, note 1, line 2. After "§§ 16 *sq.*," add: ed. Cousin, 3, 133 *sq.*

PAGE 486, note 1. Add: *Corpus Juris Civilis* (*Digest* ed. Mommsen, and paged separately), Berlin, 1893, 1, 718 b.

Page 486, note 2. Line 3, after "locupletiorem," add: *Corpus Juris Civilis*, Berlin, 1893, 1, 873 b; after "Tit. VI., 14," add: *ibid.*, 1, 169 b; line 6, after "lucrum," add: *ibid.*, 1, 300 a; after "§ 4, ad fin.," add: 1, 190 a.

PAGE 487, note 1. After "Tit. XVII., 1," add: *Corpus Juris Civilis*, Berlin, 1893, 1, 868 a.

PAGE 487, note 2. Line 2, after "1888)," add: *Collectio Librorum Juris Antejustiniani*, Berlin, Weidmann, 1893 (*Inst.* ed. Krueger), 1, 47 b; at end of note, add: ed. 1893, 1, 120 a, 593 a.

PAGE 487, note 4. At end, add: On Sennert, *cf.* Lasswitz, *Gesch. d. Atomistik*, 1, 436–454.

PAGE 492, note 3. Line 4, after "24, *ad fin.*," add: ed. Mommsen, 1893, 599 b; line 6, after "*ib.*, 26," add: *ib.*, 599 b; line 7, after "55," add: *ib.*, 869 b; line 8, after "*ib.*, 129," add: *ib.*, 871 b.

PAGE 495, note 1. Add: *Cf.*, also, the quotation from the *Théodicée*, P. II., § 184, *infra*, p. 635, note 2, *ad fin.*

PAGE 495, note 2. Add: *Cf.*, also, Leibnitz's letter to Conring (without place or date; probably written at the beginning of 1670 — Gerhardt's note), Gerhardt, *Leibniz. philos. Schrift.*, 1, 160: Ego suppono cum Carneade (et Hobbius consentit) Justitiam sine utilitate propria (sive præsente sive futura) summam esse stultitiam longe enim absunt ab humana natura Stoicorum et Sadducæorum de virtute propter se colenda superbæ jactationes. Ergo omne justum debet esse privatim utile, sed cum Justitiæ forma consistat in publica utilitate, sequitur quod non possit accurate demonstrari hæc propositio: *homo prudens debit semper agere quod justum est*, nisi demonstretur esse quendam perpetuum vindicem publicæ utilitatis (nam aliorum oculi metusque non ultra ligabunt prudentem, quam quousque juvare aut nocere possunt) id est Deum, cumque sensu manifestum sit, eum non esse semper vindicem in hac vita, superesse aliam, id est *esse aliquem Deum, et humanam animam esse immortalem.*"

PAGE 496, line 7 of note continued from p. 495. After "1877," add: J. L. Lincoln, "Marcus Aurelius Antoninus," in *In Memoriam John Larkin Lincoln, 1817–1891*, pp. 484–502, Boston, Houghton, Mifflin & Co., 1894.

PAGE 506, note 1. After "Bohn's ed.," add: Fraser, *Locke's Essay*, 2, 315. Coste's translation of Locke's Essay, ed. 1742, p. 519, 4 vol. ed., 1774, 4, 131, reads: "finis."

PAGE 510, note 1. Add: The note here referred to (*cf.*, also, Coste's translation of Locke's Essay, ed. 1742, p. 523, note 2, 4 vol. ed. 1774, 4, 141, note 2; translation of a part of the note, Fraser *Locke's Essay*, 2, 321, note 2), reads thus: "Ici M. Locke excite notre curiosité, sans vouloir la satisfaire. Bien des gens s'étant imaginés qu'il m'avoit communiqué cette manière d'expliquer la création de la matière, me priérent peu de tems après que ma traduction eut vu le jour, de leur en faire part; mais je fus obligé de leur avouer que M. Locke m'en avoit fait un secret à moi-même. Enfin long-tems après sa mort, M. le Chevalier *Newton*, à qui je parlai par hazard de cet endroit du livre de M. Locke, me découvrit tout le mystère. Souriant, il me dit d'abord que c'étoit lui-même qui avoit imaginé cette manière d'expliquer la création de la matière, que la pensée lui en étoit venue dans l'esprit un jour qu'il vint à tomber sur cette question avec M. Locke et un seigneur Anglois [Le feu Comte de *Pembroke*, mort au mois de Février de la présente année, 1738]. Et voici comment il leur expliqua sa pensée. 'On pourroit,' dit il, 'se former en quelque manière une idée de la création de la matière en supposant que Dieu eût empêché par sa puissance que rien ne pût entrer dans une certaine portion de l'espace pur, qui de sa nature est pénétrable, éternel, nécessaire, infini; car dès-là cette portion d'espace auroit l'impénétrabilité, l'une des qualités essentielles à la matière: et comme l'espace pur est absolument uniforme, on n'a qu'à supposer que Dieu auroit communiqué cette espece d'impénétrabilité à une autre pareille portion de l'espace, et cela nous donneroit, en quelque sorte, une idée de la mobilité de la matière, autre qualité qui lui est aussi très-essentielle.' Nous voilà maintenant délivrés de l'embarras de chercher ce que M. Locke avoit trouvé bon de cacher à ses lecteurs: car c'est là tout ce qui lui a donné occasion de nous dire, 'Que si nous voulions donner l'effort à notre esprit, nous pourrions concevoir, quoique d'une manière imparfaite, comment la matière pourroit d'abord avoir été produite,' etc. Pour moi, s'il m'est permis de dire librement ma pensée, je ne vois pas comment ces deux suppositions peuvent contribuer à nous faire concevoir la création de la matière. A mon sens, elles n'y contribuent non plus qu'un pont contribue à rendre l'eau qui coule immédiatement dessous, impénétrable à un boulet de canon, qui venant à tomber perpendiculairement d'une hauteur de vingt ou trente toises sur ce pont y est arrêté sans pouvoir passer à travers pour entrer dans l'eau qui coule directement dessous. Car dans ce cas-là, l'eau reste liquide et pénétrable à ce boulet, quoique la solidité du pont empêche que le boulet ne tombe dans l'eau. De même, la puissance de Dieu peut empêcher que rien n'entre dans une certaine portion d'espace, mais elle ne change point par-là la nature de cette portion d'espace, qui restant toujours pénétrable, comme toute autre portion d'espace, n'acquiert point en conséquence de cet obstacle, le moindre degré de l'impénétrabilité qui est essentielle à la matière," etc.

Fraser, *Locke's Essay*, 2, 321, 322, note 2, above referred to, states that "the idea of the creation of matter which Locke had in view in this curious passage has occasioned various conjectures," and he refers to that of Leibnitz in this passage, to Reid's in *Intell. Powers*, Essay II., 10 [ed. Hamilton, 8th ed., 1880, 1, 287 a], and to Dugald Stewart, *Essay* II., chap. 1, p. 63. Reid thinks Locke agrees with Berkeley; Stewart is almost tempted to think that Locke's idea of matter is "somewhat analogous to that of Boscovich." Fraser says that "this 'dim conception,' if it means that the material world may be resolved into a constant manifestation of God's power to man's senses, conditioned by space, so far coincides with Berkeley's account of it; he emphasises the sensuous manifestation of divine power in selected spaces, as well as the ultimate dependence of space on sense. Newton, it seems, suggested that 'creation of matter' means, God causing in sentient beings the sense-perception of resistance, in an otherwise pure space, — a theory akin to Berkeleyism in its recognition of the Supreme Power, and to Boscovich in its conception of the effect."

PAGE 513. At end of note, add: translation, Appendix, *infra*, p. 717 *sq*.

PAGE 522, note 1. After "Gerhardt," add: Janet.

PAGE 534, note 1. Line 1, after "Tit. VII., 1," add: *Collectio Librorum Juris Antejustiniani*, ed. Krueger, Mommsen and Studemund, Berlin, Weidmann, 1878, 2, 52; line 5, after "Tit. I., 33," add: *Corpus Juris Civilis* (*Digest*, ed. Mommsen), Berlin, 1893, 1, 667 b.

PAGE 534, note 2. Add: ed. Mommsen, 1893, 1, 665 a.

PAGE 534, note 3. Add: ed. Cousin, 1, 148.

PAGE 545, note 2. Add: New ed. of Bolsec, *Vie de Calvin*, by P. L. Chastel, Lyons, 1875.

PAGE 548, note 3. Add: Fraser, *Locke's Essay*, 2, 379.

PAGE 552, note 1. Add: *Cf.*, also, note to *New Essays*, Preface, *ante*, p. 51, lines 11–13, *infra*, p. 727; also, *New Essays*, Bk. IV., chap. 20, § 11, Th., *infra*, p. 613, and note 1.

PAGE 567, note 1, line 3. After "296," add: Bohn's ed.; Fraser, *Locke's Essay*, 2, 403–405.

PAGES 575, 576, note 1. Add: The doctrine set forth in the note is closely allied to the *inner light* of the Quaker theology. *Cf. New Essays*, Bk. IV., chap. 19, *infra*, p. 599, and note 1; also, Bancroft, *Hist. of the United States*, Centenary ed., 1876, Vol. 2, pp. 87–92.

PAGE 579, note 1. Add: *Cf. New Essays*, Bk. IV., chap. 6, *ad fin.*, *ante*, p. 462, note 1; 7, § 11, Th. (2), *ante*, p. 474, note 1; also, on the general philosophical question, "The Roots of Agnosticism," by Professor James Seth, in "The New World," September, 1884, Vol. 3, pp. 458–471; and on the special problem here under discussion, "Leibnitz and Protestant Theology," by Professor John Watson, in "The New World," March, 1896, Vol. 5, pp. 102–122. Professor Watson's statement and criticism of Leibnitz's doctrine is admirable. He holds that Leibnitz's distinction of two kinds of truth, truths of reason and truths of fact, cannot be maintained, that "for a Being of infinite knowledge the possible and the actual are coincident," that "the only possible reality is that which is capable of being actualized," that there can be no choice between hypothetical worlds, and that the existing world is the only possible one, and is "necessary just because it is the expression of an absolute reason."

PAGE 581, note 1. At end, add: Further references on the whole subject: Lange, *Gesch. d. Materialismus*, 2d ed., 1, 182 *sq*; Eng. trans., 1, 218 *sq.;* E. Renan, *Averroès et l'Averroisme*, Paris, 1852; 3d ed., Paris, 1869.

PAGE 585, line 6, "Motives of credibility." *Cf. New Essays*, Bk. IV., chaps. 16, § 14, Th., *ante*, p. 554; 17, § 23, Th. (2), *ante*, p. 579, and note 1. *Cf.*, also, Dutens, *Leibnit. op. om.*, 1, 680, where Leibnitz says: "Motifs de croyance ou de crédibilité (comme ils les appellent) c'est-à-dire, outre les raisons explicables de nôtre Foi, qui ne sont qu'un amas d'argumens de différens degrés de force, et qui ne peuvent fonder tous ensemble qu'une foi humaine, ils demandent une lumière de la grace du Ciel, qui fasse une entière conviction, et forme ce qu'on appelle la Foi divine," *i.e.* "Motives of belief or of credibility (as they call them), that is to say, besides the explicable reasons of our faith, which are only a mass of arguments of different degrees of force, and which all together can establish only a human faith, they demand a light of the grace of heaven, which produces a complete conviction, and forms what is called the divine faith."

PAGE 588, lines 16–19. "What is only necessary by a physical necessity (*i.e.* founded upon induction from that which is customary in nature, or upon natural laws which, so to speak, are of divine institution)," etc. *Cf. ante*, p. 261, note 1, and addition thereto, *ante*, p. 761.

PAGE 606, note concluded from p. 605. Line 10, after "April 20–30, 1669, G. 1, 27," add: Appendix, *infra*, 650; line 20, after "p. 33," add: translation, Appendix, *infra*, 631–651.

PAGE 613, note 1. Line 1, after "p. 51, line 11," add: and note thereto, *infra*, p. 727; line 2, after "§§ 52, 90," add: ed. Cousin, 3, 217, 256; line 5, after "§ 48 *sq.*," add: *ibid.*, 3, 214 *sq.*

PAGE 634, line 24, "Gilbert." William Gilbert, 1540–1603, private physician to Queen Elizabeth, was "the first real physicist and positively methodical experimenter known in the History of Physics before Kepler and Galileo." By the experiments and discoveries published in his *De magnete magneticisque corporibus et de magno magnete tellure, Physiologia nova*, London, 1600, later editions, Sedan, 1628, 1633, Frankfort, 1629, 1638, he became "the founder of the doctrine of magnetism and electricity." He called the latter *vis electrica.* For an account of his philosophy, *cf.* Lasswitz, *Gesch. d. Atomistik*, 1, 315–321; for his view of vacuum, *ibid*, 319.

PAGE 634, line 24, "Gassendi." For Gassendi on the vacuum, *cf.* Lasswitz, *Gesch. d. Atomistik*, 2, 136 *sq.*, 168–169.

PAGE 634, line 24, "Gericke." *Cf. ante*, p. 127, note 2. An account of his views is given by Lasswitz, *Gesch. d. Atomistik*, 2, 293–300.

PAGE 634, line 25, "Digby." *Cf. ante*, p. 83, note 1. On Digby's philosophy, *cf.* Lasswitz, *Gesch. d. Atomistik*, 2, 188–207; on his view of the vacuum, *ibid*, 199.

PAGE 641, line 11, "Anglus." *Cf. ante*, p. 634, note 1. A peculiar notion of White's concerning the state of the soul separated from the body, involved him in a controversy with the Bishop of Chalcedon. White wrote two tracts on the subject: *De Medio Animarum Statu*, Paris, 1653, 8vo, Agr. 1659, 8vo; *Responsio ad duos Theologos Parisienses Hen. Holdenum, et alium de Medio Animarum Statu*, 1662, 8vo. The former, together with Hobbes' *Leviathan*, was censured by the House of Commons in 1666. Archbishop Francis Blackburne, 1705–1787, gives an extended account of both tracts in his own *Historical View of the Controversy concerning an Intermediate State*, 1st ed., 1765, 2d, much enlarged, 1772; in Vol. 3 of his *Works, Theolog. and Miscellaneous*, 7 vols., 1804. Hobbes and White frequently engaged in disputations, in which White commonly proved himself the abler dialectician.

PAGE 657, note 1. Add: On Leibnitz's dynamical views, *cf.* P. Harzer, "Leibniz' dynamische Anschauungen, mit besonderer Rüchs. auf d. Reform des Kräftemaasses u. d. Entwickelung des Princ. der Erhaltung der Energie," in "Vierteljahrsschr. f. wissenschaftl. Philos.," 1881, Vol. 3, pp. 265–295; D. Selver, *Der Entwicklungsgang der Leibniz'schen Monadenlehre bis 1695*, Leipzig, 1885; M. Zwerger, *Die lebendige Kraft und ihr Mass*, München, 1885; M. Planck, *Das Princip der Erhaltung der Energie*, Leipzig, 1887, p. 6 *sq.*

PAGE 679, note 1. Add: and additions thereto, *infra*, p. 733.

PAGE 692, note 1. Add: Translated also by Duncan, *Philos. Wks. of Leibnitz*, with the title "On the Ultimate Origin of Things."

PAGE 705, line 10 from bottom (of text). The Latin text reads: "Prӕterquam finiam, adjicere placet," etc., of the first phrase of which I have not been able to find any better rendering than that given in the text.

PAGE 712, note 1, at the end (p. 713). Add: *Cf.*, also, Foucher de Careil, *Nouvelles Lettres et Opuscules inédits de Leibniz*, Paris, 1857, pp. 412–437, — *Note sur la loi de continuité*, by the editor. The passage referring to the letter here translated occurs p. 433. The note itself is a very complete and valuable account of Leibnitz's principle. *Cf.*, also, Nourrisson, *La Philosophie de Leibniz*, Paris, 1860, pp. 221–238.

INDEX A

TO THE CRITIQUE OF LOCKE

INDEX B.

TO THE APPENDIX

INDEX C

TO THE NOTES, ADDITIONS, AND CORRECTIONS

Lightning Source UK Ltd.
Milton Keynes UK
UKHW010951060223
416537UK00007B/1554

9 789354 040009